NEW TESTAMENT EPISTLES

2 CORINTHIANS GALATIANS

A CRITICAL AND EXEGETICAL COMMENTARY

by

GARETH L. REESE

HEAD OF NEW TESTAMENT DEPARTMENT
CENTRAL CHRISTIAN COLLEGE OF THE BIBLE
MOBERLY, MISSOURI

Scripture Exposition Books, LLC
803 McKINSEY PLACE
MOBERLY, MISSOURI
65270

ACKNOWLEDGMENT

The Scripture quotations contained herein, unless otherwise noted, are from the New American Standard Bible, copyrighted 1960, 1962, 1963, 1971, 1972, 1975, 1977, 1995 by the Lockman Foundation. Used by permission.

SUGGESTED CATALOGING INFORMATION

Reese, Gareth L., 1932-
    New Testament Epistles: 2 Corinthians and Galatians. A critical and exegetical commentary by Gareth L. Reese.

    xxviii, 384; lii, 296 p., maps.
    Spine title: 2 Corinthians and Galatians.
    Includes bibliographical references and index.
    ISBN: 097-176-5278

  1. Bible. NT. 2 Corinthians – Commentaries.   2. Bible. NT. Galatians – Commentaries.

DEDICATION

Thank you to the friends and supporters of Central Christian College of the Bible. For over half a century, you have made it possible for me to teach and write.

TABLE OF CONTENTS

Commentary On

2 Corinthians

PREFACE

One value of studying 2 Corinthians results from interacting with the letter's emphasis on the apostolic message and apostolic authority. Apostles of Jesus are mouthpieces for God, delivering an inspired message from God to men. Early in this 21st century, this is an emphasis that sorely needs to be heard and heeded. In contrast to earlier commentaries on 2 Corinthians which tended to treat it as a manual to guide modern preachers in their ministry, this commentary emphasizes a return to an appreciation for apostolic authority.

The new covenant promised by Jeremiah (Jeremiah 31:31-34) has been inaugurated and ratified by Christ's death on Calvary. The new covenant gospel message which reflects the truths Jesus taught during His earthly ministry is what is now to be preached, and the new covenant Scriptures are to be treated as our rule of faith and practice.

The early threat to New Testament Christianity posed by the Judaizers is better understood with the information learned from 2 Corinthians included in our sources of information. As this 21st century begins, there are those who seek evidence that in the early decades after Jesus' resurrection there were competing Christianities, with the strand that survived being that which is represented in our New Testament Scriptures. Once it is recognized that the Judaizers were not Christians but false brethren (Galatians 2:4) and false apostles (2 Corinthians 11:13), the Judaizers' message cannot be appealed to by those who would try to make a case for competing 1st century Christianities. Such views are a false presentation of what Christianity as preached by Jesus' apostles was like. Instead of preaching competing messages, the apostles of Christ were in agreement with each other on matters of doctrine and practice, and there was one faith (not many faiths) which they once and for all delivered to the saints (Jude 3).

As Paul wrote 2 Corinthians he pointed the way to reconciliation between human beings and reconciliation between God and man. This, too, is a needed message in our day.

2 CORINTHIANS

TABLE OF CONTENTS

Introductory Studies

Commentary

2 Corinthians

INTRODUCTORY STUDIES

A. HISTORICAL ALLUSIONS

As we study these historical allusions, we are looking for anything that will help us answer questions about the author, date, destination, and purpose of the letter.

1. Historical Allusions from the beginning of the letter.   1:1-2:13

1:1 - Paul signs this letter.[2]   Timothy is with Paul when this letter is written.   He was not with Paul when 1 Corinthians was written.   Before the writing of that letter (1 Corinthians 4:17), Timothy had been sent to Macedonia with Erastus to organize the collection (Acts 19:22).   According to 1 Corinthians 16:10,11, Timothy was expected to finally arrive at Corinth.   That trip has been completed, Timothy has returned to Paul, and is again with the apostle when 2 Corinthians is written.

The destination of the letter is given.   "To the church of God which is at Corinth with all the saints that are throughout Achaia."   What do we know about Christians in Achaia other than those at Corinth?   There were several at Athens (Acts 17:34).   We also know about a church at Cenchrea (Romans 16:1).   We know of none elsewhere from the extant New Testament records.   Acts just does not record any missionary activities in the outlying regions of the province, but we must remember Paul's oft-used method of evangelism was to himself work in the metropolitan centers, while his helpers evangelized the villages and communities for miles around.

We have our first help on the date of this letter.   It cannot be before there was a church in Corinth.   The church there was begun during Paul's second missionary journey, AD 51-54 (Acts 18:1-18).

---

[1] The "second group" of Paul's epistles includes 1 & 2 Corinthians, Galatians and Romans. While some emphasize the technical distinction between "epistle" and "letter," this commentator uses the terms interchangeably.

[2] As has often been noted, there were three elements in the customary beginning of a letter in the 1st centuries BC and AD.   (1) The signature was put first;   (2) The destination was given next;   and (3) A word of greeting followed.

1:2 - The usual Pauline greeting. Paul does not use the conventional greeting regularly found in letters in the Hellenistic and Roman worlds, which was simply "Greetings" *(charein)*. Paul instead combines both the Hebrew and Greek form of greeting *(shalom* and *charein)*. This is done, it appears, for two reasons: 1) People of both Greek and Hebrew descent were to be found in the churches. 2) These terms "grace and peace" have a new meaning now, a Christian meaning, and are most appropriate. Grace – i.e., unmerited favor to you – is a prayer for their continuing salvation. Peace to you – i.e., peace with God and peace with man – is a prayer that the result of salvation will be experienced by the readers to an ever fuller extent.

1:3-5 - Paul's usual thanksgiving. It is Paul's custom, after the opening greeting, to write words of thanksgiving to God for the people to whom he is writing. There is a thanksgiving in every letter but Galatians (where he was so stirred up by the apostasy that he leaves out the thanksgiving). Usually, in the thanksgiving, there are intimations of what the rest of the letter is about. The keynote of this thanksgiving is "comfort." See how often the word "comfort" appears in the next few verses.

1:8-11 - Something recently happened to Paul in Asia that left him in mortal danger. It is doubtful that the riot of Demetrius and the silversmiths at Ephesus (Acts 19:23-41) is the event alluded to. Verse 9 speaks of a "sentence of death." The apostle, in his own mind, was convinced that his days were numbered.

1:15,16 - Paul here explains a recent change in his travel plans. Originally, his planned itinerary was to go to Corinth from Ephesus, then to Macedonia, and from thence back to Corinth, and then to go on to Jerusalem with the offering. Apparently, Paul's plans were changed for him by some unforeseen circumstances in the church at Corinth. Because of the change in plans, some people at Corinth charged Paul with vacillation (1:17) and perhaps with being afraid to come again to Corinth.

1:19 - Paul and Timothy and Silas had preached among the readers. This occurred during Paul's first trip to Corinth (Acts 18:1-5), when the church was first planted there.

1:23 - "To spare you I came no more to Corinth." Most commentators put this verse with verses 15,16 and understand it to be an explanation as to why Paul changed his travel plans.

2:1 - Paul says he determined not to come to Corinth again in sorrow. This could mean sorrow which he would feel, or sorrow which he would cause. It sounds as though there has been a very recent "sorrowful" visit made by Paul to Corinth.

2:3,4 - "This very thing I wrote you ...." The Greek verb *egrapsa* is an aorist tense. It may be an historical aorist (i.e., referring to some letter before the one now being written),[3] or it may be an epistolary aorist (i.e., referring to the letter now being written). Paul seems to be saying that he is writing this very letter to the Corinthians so that when he comes he will not have sorrow from them.

2:6-8 - Some individual in the Corinthian church has been disciplined and the discipline has led that person to repent. Who was the man? Was he the incestuous man of 1 Corinthians 5?[4] These verses also point to a difference of opinion among the Corinthians as to exactly what to do with the offender. The "majority" inflicted the discipline. What was the position of the minority? Were they opposed to any discipline being practiced in this case? Did the minority believe the social ostracism involved in the discipline had not yet been of sufficient duration? Whichever it may have been, the disciplined member had repented, and Paul here urges that the penitent be publicly restored to fellowship.

2:9 - Again, a decision must be made concerning "I wrote." Is it historical or epistolary? Paul seems to be saying that he is writing this very letter to the Corinthians to put them to the test, to see if they would obey him in all things. His apostolic authority is being tested.

2:12-13 - Shortly before writing this letter, Paul has been to Troas. He came to do evangelistic work because there was an open door of opportunity. At the same time, he also expected to meet Titus (who had been sent to Corinth on a trouble-shooting mission) at Troas and hear a report from him. But Titus did not come as soon as Paul expected. Paul was so intensely anxious about Titus' mission to Corinth that he could not carry on the work at Troas. He instead departed to Macedonia in order that he might the sooner meet Titus and hear of the progress of affairs in Corinth. (Some of these details we ascertain from what Paul writes in 2 Corinthians 7:5-7.)

2:14 - 7:4 contain a long presentation of Paul's apostolic credentials.

2. Historical allusions in the closing chapters of the letter. 11:1-13:14

11:1ff - Paul is still calling for recognition of his apostleship. In 11:5 and in 12:11,

---

[3] When the verb is treated as an historical aorist, Bible students begin to offer conjectures concerning the identification of the letter. Is it the one we now call 1 Corinthians? Is it a hypothetical severe letter, perhaps now lost, or perhaps embedded somewhere in one of our canonical letters? A multitude of imaginary reconstructions of the background to 2 Corinthians rests on these conjectures, concerning which, see below.

[4] Or, instead of being the incestuous man of 1 Corinthians 5, is this man none other than the leader of the Judaizers who have come to Corinth and attempted to destroy Paul's apostolic reputation among the Corinthian Christians?

Paul insists he is not inferior to "the most eminent apostles." If we may let Galatians 2 guide us, "most eminent apostles" reflects the exalted view (held by the Judaizers) of Jesus' original apostles over against Paul. The "most eminent apostles" should not be identified with the "false apostles" (the Judaizers) of 11:13.

11:23-27- Note all that has happened to Paul before this letter was written. Very few of these things are mentioned by Luke in Acts 13-19.

11:32,33 - Chronologically, the danger at Damascus preceded most of the hardships just catalogued in verses 23-27. The attempt by certain Jews to capture and kill Paul at Damascus occurred after his call to be an apostle (Acts 26:16-18) and his three-year stay in Arabia.[5] Does Paul put this attempt on his life at the end of the list of his hardships because it is an example of how Jewish religious leaders, all along, have been trying to get rid of Paul, the apostle of Christ?

12:2-4 - Paul was caught up to Paradise fourteen years before the writing of this epistle. As indicated below, we will date the writing of 2 Corinthians in the Fall of AD 57. Fourteen full years before the writing of 2 Corinthians would bring us to the Fall of AD 43, a few months before the first missionary journey began.[6] If this dating is accurate, the vision of Paradise concerning which Paul here speaks is nowhere else recorded.[7]

12:14 - This is the third time Paul is "ready to come" to Corinth. Have there been two other trips to Corinth before 2 Corinthians is written? Or does this verse speak only of Paul's plans and intentions which could not be carried out to completion? Acts does not record two other trips antecedent to the one from which 2 Corinthians was written. Do we get help later in 2 Corinthians (e.g., 13:1-2)? Has Paul been to Corinth more than once before 2 Corinthians was written?

12:18 - Titus and "the brother" have previously been sent by Paul to Corinth. When was this trip? 12:17 indicates this trip is already in the past as 2 Corinthians is being written, so it cannot be the same as the up-coming trip made by Titus and two brothers to implement the collection of the offering at Corinth (2 Corinthians 8:16-23). Who is "the brother"? When was the trip here-indicated made?

---

[5] See "New Testament Chronology" in Gareth L. Reese, *New Testament History: Acts* (Moberly, MO: Scripture Exposition Books, 2002).

[6] The first missionary journey began after Passover in AD 44, according to Acts 12 and 13.

[7] If the fourteen years include twelve full years and parts of two others, then the timing might correspond to Paul's being stoned at Lystra, during his first missionary journey. It may be that Paul was actually dead (Acts 14:19), and, after being a few moments in Paradise, was raised from the dead by God. (Paul says his experience may have been "out of the body," i.e., while he was dead.)

12:19 - "We have been speaking all for your upbuilding, beloved." This verse has implications concerning the tone of the whole letter. Paul says it is "all" for their upbuilding.

12:20 - Paul is afraid he may yet find trouble when he arrives at Corinth. He was anxious that before he next arrives in town the church correct all the evils mentioned in his correspondence with them. Two issues were paramount: the disharmony in the life of the congregation resulting from the divisive work of the Judaizers (12:20) and continuing immorality by some in the church (12:21).[8]

12:21 - Paul is anxious, lest he be humiliated (humbled) when he next comes into their presence. Does this not sound a bit like he had been humiliated once before this letter is written?

13:1,2 - This is "the third time" that Paul was coming to Corinth. He has already been present there "the second time." 12:14 therefore must mean more than that other trips were just planned but never carried out. He had been there twice before this proposed trip. On the second trip he had warned those who persisted in their old sins. Now he says that when he arrives on this third visit, should he find some still continuing to practice their sins, he will not spare them. There will be discipline administered by an apostle of Christ.

13:5 - "Test yourselves to see if you are in the faith; examine yourselves!" Something has happened (Judaizers) that leaves the Corinthians vulnerable. They may very well be departing the faith once-for-all delivered to the saints. May we see in this call for spiritual examination one of Paul's purposes for writing this letter?

13:10 - "I am writing these things ... in order that when present I may not use severity." This sounds as though it might be another part of his purpose for writing.

13:11 - "Finally, brethren, rejoice, be made complete, be comforted, be like-minded, live in peace" seems to sum up all Paul has written in this letter.

Subscription (KJV) - "The second epistle to the Corinthians was written from Philippi, a city of Macedonia, by Titus and Lucas." Is this uninspired ascription accurate? It is supported by various older manuscripts, including B², Syr.P., Syr.H., and Copt.

---

[8] Other than taking action in the case of the offender, it seems that the Corinthian church perhaps never did solve all their problems. I Clement 47.1 (written to Corinth in AD 96) pleads that the Corinthian church cease their divisions and bickerings.

3. Other historical allusions in the book

7:5-7 - Paul came to Macedonia from Troas still troubled in heart. Then Titus came with news that the Corinthians were sorry for their actions and wanted to see Paul. A tremendous relief came over Paul at hearing this news.

7:8-10 - Paul had made them sorry with a letter he had written, but their sorrow had led them to repentance. Was this letter that made them sorry a "severe letter" (as some conjecture), or was the letter that made them sorry the letter we call 1 Corinthians? It seems to us that 1 Corinthians is severe enough to cause Paul some worrying about how it would be received, and to cause some godly sorrow on the part of the Corinthians who took Paul's words to heart. (For more on this question, see below.)

7:12 - "I wrote" is still making reference to the letter introduced in 7:8. Just as he explained why he is writing this second letter to Corinth (2:3,4,9), he here explains why he wrote the letter we call 1 Corinthians, namely, to give the Corinthians opportunity to show whether or not they would be loyal to an apostle of Jesus such as he was.

7:14-16 - The Corinthians (with fear and trembling) obeyed Titus when he came to Corinth at the beginning of the visit just recently ended. As far as the context is concerned, the obedience has to do with the repentance of the Corinthian Christians.[9]

8:1-4 - The Macedonian churches are in the midst of taking up a generous offering for the poor Christians at Jerusalem. When they heard about the offering, the Macedonians came to Paul and begged to be allowed to participate in the offering.

8:6-9 - Titus, on an earlier occasion, had begun the collection of the offering at Corinth. Now, Paul has urged him to return to Corinth to continue the mechanics of collecting it. He appeals to the Corinthians to respond with the same kind of loving generosity that characterized the Macedonians and that characterized their Lord.

8:10 - A year previous to the writing of 2 Corinthians, the Corinthian church desired to take up an offering for the Jerusalem Christians. The Corinthian church was the first to even want to take up an offering, and the first to do anything about taking up one. So with all their faults there were still many good points about the church – and there is no wonder Paul loved them deeply. He offers his opinion that it would be well for them to finish what they had started.

---

[9] Chapter 7 is filled with nouns that tell of their response to Titus's recent visit (and also, belatedly in a sense, to 1 Corinthians): their "longing, mourning, and zeal" for Paul (7:7); their "repentance" (7:9); "earnestness" (7:11); "vindication of yourselves" (7:11); "indignation" (7:11); "fear, longing, zeal, what avenging of wrong" (7:11); they are now "innocent in the matter" (7:11).

8:16-22 - Titus is going to come to Corinth with two helpers to keep the fund raising campaign moving. The three were being sent by Paul (2 Corinthians 9:3).[10]

9:2-4 - Paul is in Macedonia when he writes. He has been telling them about how the Corinthians were eager to be involved in the offering. Paul hopes his boast will not be disappointed. Is it implied that the trouble caused by the Judaizers has temporarily caused a suspension of the raising of the offering among the Corinthians?

10:1 - Paul signs his name again.

10:2 - When he arrives at Corinth this third time, Paul is going to deal with "some", i.e., those who falsely accuse him. (Those false accusers will be identified as Judaizers later in these introductory studies.)

10:9,10 - "Letters" (plural). Has Paul written more than one letter to Corinth? If not, what is the meaning of this plural? Is this evidence that Paul's already-written letters are in circulation among the churches?

B. A REMINDER OF THE HISTORY AS GIVEN IN ACTS

1. Paul first came to Corinth during his second missionary journey, about AD 51. He stayed with Aquila and Priscilla (Acts 18), and planted a church in Corinth (1 Corinthians 3:10). Departing from Corinth after 18 months (AD 54), and leaving Aquila and Priscilla at Ephesus, he went on to Caesarea, Jerusalem, and Antioch of Syria. This concluded his second missionary journey.

2. The third missionary tour began with an overland journey from Antioch of Syria, through south Galatia, and on to Ephesus (Acts 18:23-19:1). His great Ephesian ministry lasted three years (Acts 20:31).

3. According to Acts 19:22, near the end of those three years, Timothy and Erastus were sent to Macedonia. Paul himself stayed on in Asia. Perhaps after their departure, around Passover time, AD 57, Paul wrote 1 Corinthians and sent it off to Corinth.[11] In it, he indicated his plans to remain at Ephesus until Pentecost (1 Corinthians 16:8). 1 Corinthians 4:17 alludes to Timothy's trip.

---

[10] "We have sent" (verses 18,22) are epistolary aorists. They are being sent at the same time this letter is being written and sent.

[11] In the author's commentary *New Testament Epistles: 1 Corinthians* (Moberly, MO: Scripture Exposition Books, 2004) in comments on 1 Corinthians 5:9, the notion that Paul wrote a "previous letter" to Corinth was rejected.

4. Acts 19:23-41 relates the riot in Ephesus by Demetrius and the silversmiths. The yearly festival in honor of Artemis was celebrated by the idolaters about the same time on the calendar (May or June) that Pentecost was celebrated by the Jews. Perhaps the riot caused Paul to leave Ephesus earlier than he originally expected to, perhaps not.

    If we read 2 Corinthians 1:8-11 aright, between the writing of 1 Corinthians and his departure from Asia, Paul found himself in the midst of mortal peril.[12] Were Judaizers, like those recently come to Corinth, behind that peril? Was this the occasion when Aquila and Priscilla risked their lives to rescue Paul (Romans 16:3,4)?

5. Acts 20:1 indicates that after the riot of Demetrius, Paul departed from Ephesus for Macedonia.

6. Per Acts 20:2, Paul went through Macedonia giving exhortation, then came to Greece.

7. Per Acts 20:3, three months were spent in Greece (the winter of AD 58), and then Paul departed for Jerusalem with the offering. He originally had intended to sail; but a plot by unbelieving Jews against him was discovered, and so Paul went overland and escaped the danger from the Jews.

    The book of Acts records two visits to Corinth made by Paul, one on the second missionary journey, and one at the close of the third journey, on the eve of the departure for Jerusalem with the offering. (Acts 20:4 likely names some of the delegates of the churches who carried the offering.)

C. AUTHORSHIP AND ATTESTATION

1. Internal evidence as to authorship

    Paul twice signs the letter, 1:1 and 10:1. While some have questioned the unity of 2 Corinthians, there has been near-unanimous agreement concerning the Pauline authorship of 2 Corinthians. When one studies the internal evidences, "the elusive (from the standpoint of the modern reader) references to movements, people, and events are just what one would expect from an authentic letter. No forger would write of these matters so artlessly."[13] Internal evidence points to genuineness.[14]

---

[12] We doubt 2 Corinthians 1:8 = Acts 19:30. The riot of Demetrius, where Paul wanted to go into the midst of the theater at Ephesus but his friends and certain of the Asiarchs hindered him, does not look sufficiently life-threatening to satisfy 2 Corinthians 1:8.

[13] Fred Fisher, *Commentary on 1 & 2 Corinthians* (Waco, TX: Word Books, 1975), p.279.

2. External evidence as to the authorship of 2 Corinthians

There are allusions and annotated quotations in the Early Christian writers which abundantly attest to this letter.

1) Allusions[15]

    a) Polycarp (AD 115) in his *Epistle to the Philippians* at 11:3 has an allusion to 2 Corinthians 3:2; at 2:4 is an allusion to 2 Corinthians 4:14; at 6:2 is an allusion to 2 Corinthians 6:7; at 6:2 is an allusion to 2 Corinthians 5:10; and perhaps at 4:1 is an allusion to 2 Corinthians 6:7.

    b) In the *Epistle to Diognetus*, (chapter 5:8) there are certain expressions which remind one of 2 Corinthians 6:8-10 and 10:3.

    c) Theophilus of Antioch (AD 115-188) alludes in *ad Autol.* iii.30 to "pledge," perhaps an allusion to 2 Corinthians 1:22. Allusions to 2 Corinthians 7:1 and 11:19 have been seen in *ad Autol.* i.2 and iii.4.

2) Annotated Quotations[16]

a) Irenaeus (AD 180)

> "Paul has plainly said in the second to the Corinthians, 'in whom the god of this world has blinded the minds of the unbelievers'" (2 Corinthians 4:4). *Adv. Haeres.* 3.7.1

> "For the apostle does also say in the second [Epistle] to the Corinthians: 'For we are unto God a sweet savour of Christ, in them which are saved, and in them which perish ...'" (2 Corinthians 2:15,16). *Adv. Haeres.* 4.28.3.

> "The apostle Paul ... says in the second [Epistle] to the Corinthians: 'And lest I should be lifted up by the sublimity of the revelations, there was given unto me a thorn in the flesh, the messenger of Satan to buffet me ...'" (2 Corinthians 12:7-9). *Adv. Haeres.* 5.3.1.

b) Athenagoras (c. AD 180)

---

[14] A book is said to be "genuine" if it was written by the author named in it, or when written by the author to whom it is attributed.   2 Corinthians is genuine only if Paul wrote it.

[15] An allusion is a reference that shows the passage or book being quoted was known to exist. Ideas from the book are quoted, or paraphrased, without citing the author or the sources.

[16] In annotated quotations, we find the author and or the source definitely named.

"It is manifest therefore, that according to the apostle this corruptible and dissipated must put on incorruption; that the dead being raised up to life ..." (2 Corinthians 5:10). *De Resurrect. Mort.* 18.

c) Clement of Alexandria (AD 190)

"The apostle calls the common doctrine of the faith a taste of knowledge in the second to the Corinthians (2 Corinthians 2:14), for until this day the same veil remains (2 Corinthians 3:14)." *Stromata* IV.16.

"Hence also Paul ... 'ye have these promises,' says he, 'dearly beloved; let us cleanse our hearts from all filthiness of the flesh and spirit, perfecting holiness in the fear of God" (2 Corinthians 7:1). *Stromata* III.14.

d) Tertullian (AD 200)

"For indeed they suppose that the Apostle Paul, in the second to the Corinthians, forgave the same fornicator whom in the first he had declared out to be delivered to Satan for the destruction of the flesh." (2 Corinthians 2:10). *De Pudicitia*, c.XIII.

e) Firmilian, in his epistle to Cyprian (lxxiv.14) quotes 2 Corinthians 11:2, attributing the words to "the apostle."   (ANF, V.5, p.393)

f) Cyprian (c. AD 250)

"Likewise the blessed apostle Paul, full of the inspiration of the Lord, 'Now he that ministereth,' says he, 'seed to the sower, will both minister bread ...'" (2 Corinthians 9:10,11). *De Opp. et Eleemos.*

g) Novatius (c. AD 250)

"Lastly, the apostle Paul, 'Having,' says he, 'the same spirit, as it is written, I believed, therefore have I spoken; we also believe, and therefore speak'." (2 Corinthians 4:13). (Cap XXIX).

3) Canonical Listings

Marcion's *Apostolicon* (AD 140) had 2 Corinthians in it.

The Muratorian Canon (AD 170) includes 2 Corinthians.

3. Summary:

The internal evidence and the external evidence as to the genuineness of 2 Corinthians is so strong many writers do not even spend time on the subject, merely taking it for granted. In fact, while scholars may differ as to the continuity and integrity of the text, there is no serious divergence among them in the opinion that all the parts of the epistle are genuine writings of the apostle Paul.

D. OCCASION OF WRITING

At the time of the writing of 1 Corinthians, and in the days shortly after that letter was dispatched, Paul was dealing with a very serious crisis in the church at Corinth. He had made a hasty, unplanned trip to Corinth, where he was rejected, and as a result left town very sorrowful at heart. His apostolic authority had been opposed, questioned, and by some (outsiders who infiltrated the church) scornfully denied.

From Ephesus, Paul had sent Titus to Corinth to deal with their failure to practice church discipline on a flagrant offender (2 Corinthians 2:13; 7:6,7,13-15). Titus was apparently instructed to report back to Paul as soon as possible concerning the response of the Corinthians to his mission. As time passed, and Titus did not come, Paul became more and more intensely anxious to hear news from Corinth.

Paul left Ephesus for Troas (though not forced to leave by the riot of Demetrius, perhaps the riot made further work there extra difficult), hoping that Titus would return from Corinth and meet him there. In Troas, he found an opening for missionary work (2:12). Weeks passed, Titus did not arrive, and Paul became anxious (2:13). "The suspense at last became so intolerable that he threw up his work in Troas and crossed over into Macedonia, in order to meet Titus the sooner."[17]

According to 2 Corinthians 7:5-7, the occasion of this second letter to the Corinthians is the return of Titus from Corinth and his report to Paul.

In the report Titus brought about the progress of the gospel in Corinth, there was much good news, and some bad. Titus reported his mission had had good results: the church had cut off from membership the brother who had committed the grave offense (2:6); the Corinthian Christians had repented sincerely for the painful lowering of the ethical standards of their church (7:11); they had displayed deep sorrow for causing Paul to write such a letter as he did to them (7:3.9); and they had shown sincere affection for Paul (7:7), and submission to Titus as Paul's representative. Paul, in a fervor of thanksgiving, affection, and comfort, is thus prompted to write this letter.

---

[17] Alfred Plummer, *A Critical and Exegetical Commentary on the Second Epistle of St. Paul to the Corinthians* in the International Critical Commentary series (Edinburgh: T&T Clark, 1915), p.xiv.

If this had been the only information which Titus had brought from Corinth, 2 Corinthians would have been an expression of unalloyed thanksgiving and joy. But unfortunately such was not the case. Titus also brought news that some false teachers had come to town and were seriously attacking Paul's apostolic authority and message. If the Christian faith of the Corinthians is not to be seriously undermined, this attack will have to be answered. That is precisely what Paul does in this letter.

E. PURPOSE OF WRITING

In a sentence, Paul's purpose in writing 2 Corinthians was to restore his apostolic reputation in the minds of the Corinthian Christians. 2 Corinthians is the most sustained and extended presentation of his apostolic credentials found in any of his letters. Servants of Satan (2 Corinthians 11:14,15) had come to Corinth and attacked his legitimacy as an apostle of Christ, and a significant minority of the church has been persuaded he might not be an apostle of Jesus. In passage after passage, as he writes 2 Corinthians, Paul reflects the nasty insinuations made against him by the Judaizers, and in each case he sets the record straight.[18] Reconciliation between Paul and the Corinthians will be possible and be complete only if the Corinthians continue to recognize who he is and Who sent him to Corinth.

Some of the subordinate ideas behind the main purpose for writing can be learned by listening to Paul's own words. (1) He explains the reason for his change of travel plans (1:15-16); it was not that he was vacillating (1:17), but, rather, it was to spare them (1:23-2:1) and to spare himself (2:3) another painful visit. Several times he returns to this theme (10:2,6) and explains he is writing these things so that, hopefully, he will not have to use apostolic severity when he next comes to their town (13:10). If they will take advantage of the interlude before his next visit to repent, severity can be avoided. (2) There is a call for the Corinthians to repudiate the Judaizers (6:14-7:1) who had brought strife to the congregation (2 Corinthians 12:20). Such a repudiation of the false apostles (2 Corinthians 11:13) will be an acid test of their recognition of Paul's apostolic authority. (3) For over a year prior to writing 2 Corinthians, an offering for the poor Christians at Jerusalem has been Paul's passion. If the Corinthians will again get involved in that (2 Corinthians 8-9), it will show they and Paul are on the same wavelength. (4) Everything he has written has been intended for their spiritual upbuilding (12;19). (5) His appeal near the end of the letter for them to test and examine themselves to see if they are in the faith (13:5) tells us what was on Paul's heart as he wrote. (6) 13:11 neatly summarizes what Paul hoped to accomplish by this letter he has written to Corinth.

---

[18] The Corinthians should have been proud of Paul (1:14) and defended him when the Judaizers came to town. He gives them some ammunition to do that. He answers the specific charges and slanders the Judaizers have raised as they tried to destroy Paul's reputation among the Corinthians.

F. TIME AND PLACE OF WRITING

1. Place

The place is Macedonia (2 Corinthians 2:13, 7:5, 9:2-4). The Subscription says "Philippi." This is one subscription that may be right, as far as the place of writing is concerned, but we cannot be sure. Some early Christian writers suggested Berea or Thessalonica as the place of writing. Lipscomb argues for Thessalonica as the place of writing from the fact that all the churches of Macedonia are said to be giving generously to the offering for Jerusalem, and it is (in his opinion) not likely that Paul would have made such a statement unless he had already visited most of the Macedonian churches.[19] Philippi would be the first of the Macedonian churches to be visited by a man traveling from Troas. If it is true that Paul must have visited several of the Macedonian churches before writing 2 Corinthians 8:1, then obviously the letter could not have been written from Philippi.

2. Time

The allusions that point to the time of writing are these: (1) A mortal danger at Ephesus is past (2 Corinthians 1:8-10). (2) The offering for the saints at Jerusalem, delivered at the end of the third missionary journey (AD 54-58), is still being collected. (3) The letter was written some time before Paul's three month stay at Corinth (Acts 20:2,3 v. 2 Corinthians 8,9). (4) The time of writing fits best at Acts 20:2, where Paul is said to have gone through those districts of Macedonia.

So we conclude that 2 Corinthians was written *in the fall of AD 57, about six months after the writing of 1 Corinthians*.[20]

G. THE TRAVELS OF PAUL AND HIS COMPANIONS

1. **Paul's visits to Corinth** and a summary of his activities in this period of his life:

How many trips did Paul make to Corinth? Acts records two trips: one at the founding of the church (Acts 18), and one near the end of the third missionary journey, when the collection for the Jerusalem poor was being put together (Acts 20). The Corinthian correspondence records three trips (2 Corinthians 12:14,21; 13:1,2;

---

[19] David Lipscomb, "Second Corinthians and Galatians," in *A Commentary on the New Testament Epistles* (Nashville, TN: Gospel Advocate, 1960), Vol.3, p.12.

[20] There is no serious objection to assigning both Corinthian epistles to the same year, even if we believe that between the two letters Paul made a brief visit to Corinth.

2:1).   The third trip of Corinthians is the same as the second trip of the Acts record.

How do we reconcile the two accounts?   Did Paul make only two trips to Corinth, as Acts records?   Or, did Paul make a trip to Corinth which is not related by Luke in Acts?   If Paul made but two visits to Corinth, then it was the visit on which the church was planted that is being described as a sorrowful visit (2 Corinthians 2:1). This conclusion is hard to believe.   Nor is it acceptable to suppose Paul's second missionary tour visit to Corinth was divided into two parts – that he started work in Corinth, made an excursion to neighboring parts of Achaia, and then returned to Corinth to finish the 18-month stay there – which would allow him to call his visit on the third missionary tour his third visit to Corinth.   There is precious little evidence of a two-part visit to Corinth on his second missionary tour.   And again, it will not do to count a letter to Corinth as a visit.   2 Corinthians 13:2 indicates actual visits are intended.   Taking what is written in 2 Corinthians at face value, the only conclusion possible is that Paul has made a trip to Corinth that is not recorded in Acts.[21]

When was the trip (the one unrecorded in Acts) made by Paul to Corinth?   Two answers to this question have been advanced by students of Paul's writings to Corinth: (1) The trip was made before 1 Corinthians was written, or (2) The trip was made in the interval between the writing of 1 Corinthians and 2 Corinthians.   Either way, since this "unrecorded trip" falls between the two trips recorded in Acts, it is often called "the intermediate trip."   While the first option has been defended (often including many pages of arguments discussing whether this intermediate trip either preceded or followed an alleged "previous letter" to Corinth), in this commentator's judgment there are several points that militate against this hypothesis.   The second visit to Corinth left Paul with some unpleasant memories (2 Corinthians 2:1).   If it occurred before 1 Corinthians was written, why do we read nothing about it in 1 Corinthians?   Why revive memories of this painful visit in 2 Corinthians after ignoring them in 1 Corinthians?   The better way of reconstructing Paul's travels at this time in his life is to have the intermediate trip between the writing of 1 and 2 Corinthians.   Against this hypothesis, it has been objected that there is not enough time between the writing of 1 Corinthians in the spring of AD 57 and the writing of 2 Corinthians in the fall of AD 57 for such a trip to be made.   However, there was a trade route across the Aegean Sea between Ephesus and Corinth.   Paul could have gone by ship to Corinth from Ephesus and then back to Ephesus in three weeks or less.

We are now ready for a summary of Paul's activities at this period of his minis-

---

[21] In the historical allusions, attention was called to the fragmentary character of Luke's history in Acts.   The majority of the hardships related in 2 Corinthians 11:23-28 are not recorded in Acts. If, therefore, Paul made some journeys not recorded in Acts, we would not be surprised.   It is not recorded in Acts that Paul wrote letters to the churches.   It is not recorded in Acts that Titus was one of Paul's closest companions and fellow-workers.

try per the information given in Acts and in the Corinthian correspondence:

(a) Paul, at Ephesus, writes 1 Corinthians in the spring of 57 AD. In this letter, he announces a change in his travel plans (1 Corinthians 16:5-8). Paul's directions concerning needed discipline (1 Corinthians 5:1-8) for the immoral man are ignored by the church at Corinth. Timothy arrives at Corinth (1 Corinthians 4:17), but is unable to deal with the crisis. Timothy returns to Paul with adverse news of the continued disorder at Corinth.[22]

(b) Because conditions in the church have deteriorated since he wrote 1 Corinthians, Paul makes a brief and hurried trip to Corinth, the purpose of which was to encourage the church to practice church discipline in the case of the incestuous man. The results of this "intermediate trip" were so disappointing to Paul that he spoke of it being a sorrowful trip. It would appear that, just as they had earlier, a vocal minority continued to object to the exercise of any discipline against the incestuous offender (2 Corinthians 2:6). One immediate consequence of the minority's behavior was to raise a serious question about Paul's apostolic authority. Apparently, during this visit, Paul rebuked others in the church who were guilty of immorality (2 Corinthians 12:21), but did not on this occasion immediately discipline. The guilty were given time to repent. And another factor may have contributed to Paul's humiliation: have the Judaizers already arrived, and when they begin to attack his apostleship, did the Corinthians fail to champion his cause against the Judaizers?

(c) From Corinth, Paul returned to Ephesus.[23] Shortly after his return to Ephesus, Titus is sent to attempt to deal with the problem at Corinth. (This trip by Titus is alluded to in 2 Corinthians 2:13 and 7:6,13.)

(d) Sometime after the riot of the silversmiths (Acts 19:23-41), Paul leaves Ephesus. We may conjecture the riot occurred after a poorly attended Artemision in June of AD 57 had resulted in meager profits for the craftsmen. In any case, Paul had planned to stay in Ephesus until Pentecost of that year (1 Corinthians 16:8).

(e) Having departed from Ephesus, Paul came to Troas. Here he awaited Titus, who does not come as expected. Paul either arrived there earlier than expected, or Titus was delayed longer than expected.

(f) Having departed from Troas, Paul went across the sea to Macedonia. Here, Titus meets him with news from Corinth. Titus reports there has been a change

---

[22] For details, see below, the journeys of Timothy.

[23] Those who allege that Paul wrote a "severe letter" to Corinth place it here, after Paul's unsuccessful trip to Corinth. See more on this matter in notes below.

of attitude. The majority had disciplined the incestuous man. The discipline had produced its intended results; the man repented. By this positive response, Paul is comforted. The majority have returned to being supporters of Paul. However, Titus also has some sad news. Judaizers have begun to deceive the church, and not a few Corinthians are entertaining serious doubts about Paul's apostolic authority. So, in the fall of AD 57, Paul pens his second letter to Corinth. Titus is sent to Corinth to revive their participation in the offering for Jerusalem, and we may also presume Titus carries this recently penned second letter from Paul to Corinth.[24]

(g) Departing from Macedonia, Paul went to Corinth, just as he announced in his changed travel plans that he would (2 Corinthians 1:15,16), where he stayed three months, the winter of AD 58.

(h) In the spring, when weather allows travel on the Mediterranean to resume, Paul then begins the trip to Jerusalem with the offering. The men named in Acts 20:4 are likely the messengers chosen by each of the churches to carry their respective portions of the total offering.

2.   **The journeys of Timothy** as indicated by the Corinthian correspondence:

The verses which deal with this subject are: (a) 1 Corinthians 4:17 and 16:10. Timothy's trip started before 1 Corinthians was written. He was going through Macedonia; the possibility was good that he would, at length, arrive in Corinth. The purpose of this trip was to encourage the churches of Macedonia and Achaia to participate in the offering for the poor at Jerusalem.   (b) 2 Corinthians 1:1. Timothy is with Paul in Macedonia when 2 Corinthians is written.

There are three suggestions given concerning Timothy's ministry.   (a) Suggestion #1 is he never got to Corinth. The theory is that he met Paul when the apostle finally arrived in Macedonia, and thus Timothy never got to Corinth. But if Timothy had never arrived in Corinth, or had been recalled by Paul (so that he did not go to Corinth), we would expect some explanation in 2 Corinthians. Certainly, if Paul had recalled a messenger whose coming had been expected and so distinctly announced we should suppose he would have felt called upon to justify such a proceeding against the objections of his opponents. We therefore conclude that Timothy actually did get to Corinth. (b) Suggestion #2 is that Timothy did get to Corinth but that nothing noteworthy happened during his visit there. No mention is made in 2 Corinthians of Timothy's visit to Corinth, or of its results, or of his reception and treatment there, it is said. Why is this? Some assert that the most natural solu-

---

[24] For details, see below, the journeys of Titus.

tion is that the 1 Corinthian letter was not well-received; and when Timothy saw that the church declined to comply with its injunctions, he immediately came to Paul to report his ill-success. Whereupon, Paul took other steps, such as Titus being sent, as is mentioned in 2 Corinthians. But there seems to be a better answer than this. (c) Suggestion #3 is that Timothy did get to Corinth, but that his visit was unsuccessful. This conjecture differs from #2 above in that this one suggests Timothy worked hard trying to right the wrongs but was unsuccessful, and therefore returned to Paul in accordance with the instructions of 1 Corinthians 16:10. If he reached Corinth and was contemptuously treated, he probably returned as quickly as possible to Paul at Ephesus; and his report of the grave condition of things at Corinth would account for the apostle's decision to hurry across to Corinth himself.

3. The journeys and work of Titus, as indicated in 2 Corinthians:

Titus seems to have made three trips to Corinth.

(a) 2 Corinthians 8:6 tells of the first of these trips. Titus started the collection for the Jerusalem poor at Corinth. This seems to have been before 1 Corinthians was written. 1 Corinthians 16:1 implies the Corinthian Christians already had information concerning the collection before Paul wrote the 1 Corinthian letter. Those who think Paul wrote a "previous letter" put it in here, and have it carried by Titus. It is most probable that Titus was sent out at the same time Timothy and Erastus were sent to Macedonia (Acts 19:22).

(b) 2 Corinthians 2:13 and 7:6,13 speak of the second journey by Titus. After the failed intermediate visit made by Paul, Titus was apparently sent to correct the situation at Corinth. Timothy, we believe, was unsuccessful in his attempts to right the problems, and so returned to Paul without the problems being settled. Paul himself made a quick trip to Corinth over the trade route, but was not successful in handling the problems. Titus, therefore, is sent to set things in order. Those who believe there was a "severe letter" put it here, with Titus carrying it. Under Titus' guidance, the Corinthians took proper action, especially in the case of the offender (7:14-16). Titus then returned to Paul, meeting him in Macedonia (7:5-7), which meeting was the occasion for the writing of 2 Corinthians.

(c) 2 Corinthians 8:6,17,18,22 tell of a third trip. Titus and two helpers are being sent to finish the job of the collection. Who are the two helpers? Verse 18 speaks of "the brother whose fame in the things of the gospel ...." The most common opinion is that this was Luke.[25] Others suggested are Barnabas, Mark, Silas, Trophimus, or Timothy. Verse 22 identifies "another brother." This companion has been

---

[25] So say Ignatius, Origen, Jerome, Ambrose, and the subscription of 2 Corinthians.

variously identified as Apollos, Silas, Sosthenes, Zenas. In other words, we just do not know for sure who these companions of Titus were. Titus and his two helpers are being sent back to Corinth by Paul, sent from Macedonia, and probably are the ones who carried this second Corinthian letter (8:23, 9:3,5) to Corinth.

H. OTHER CRITICAL MATTERS (necessarily raised in the interprettation of 2 Corinthians)

1. Paul's Corinthian correspondence

2 Corinthians 10:9,10 speak of "letters" (plural). Is this an indication that Paul has written more than one letter to Corinth before our 2 Corinthian epistle? Does the use of the plural word "letters" mean the Corinthians had received several letters from Paul?[26] Might the plural "letters" mean that the Corinthians have in their possession some of Paul's epistles to other churches. Both Thessalonian letters were written from Corinth, and the Corinthians would be aware of them and of their contents.[27] Or, again, might Paul have been including this letter which he was then writing, by way of anticipation? Or, the possibility exists the plural word is used in the same way we use the word "correspondence." Remember, Clement of Rome knew of only one letter written to Corinth, so we must be careful in saying that there were several written, some of which may now be lost. The plural in 2 Corinthians 10:9,10 does not necessarily indicate more letters written to Corinth than the two we now possess.

2. The Integrity of 2 Corinthians[28]

Based wholly on internal evidence, and in some cases on dubious interpretation of certain verses, doubts have been raised about the integrity of several parts of 2 Cor-

---

[26] See "Communications of Paul with Corinth" in the Introductory Studies in the author's *New Testament Epistles: 1 Corinthians* (Moberly, MO: Scripture Exposition Books, 2004). Arguments are there presented that Paul wrote two letters to Corinth, the ones we have in our Bibles called 1 and 2 Corinthians.

[27] It may very well be that a copy of each of the Thessalonian letters was kept at Corinth when the letters were sent. In the *Shepherd of Hermas*, an angel standing next to the Shepherd said, "Make a copy for Grati, (who will take it to the widows) and a copy to be taken to the churches (i.e., a foreign copy) and a copy for yourself." This apocryphal letter shows a custom of making three copies of an important document.

[28] Integrity is a technical term dealing with the wholesome preservation of the text in substantially the form we now have it. 2 Corinthians would enjoy integrity if Paul wrote and sent all 13 chapters on one scroll at the same time.

inthians.[29]   The following chapters (or portions of chapters) have been treated as not enjoying integrity:

(a) 2 Corinthians 2:14-7:4 (minus 6:14-7:1)

Based on the fact that 7:5 continues the thought begun in 2:13, this long section has been treated either as part of a separate letter of defense written to Corinth by Paul, or it has been called the "great digression."   It is the judgment of this present commentator that such a treatment of this section misses the very point why Paul included it where he does in 2 Corinthians.   The fact that Paul was an apostle of Christ and ministering under the new covenant were the heart and soul of his attempt to restore his apostolic reputation among the Corinthians.   It is incorrect to speak of this as a great digression.

(b) 2 Corinthians 6:14-7:1

Over a century ago, James Denney expressed his opinion that, after reading 2:4-6:13, this paragraph "jolts the mind as a stone on the road does a carriage wheel."[30]   While Denney went on to defend the integrity of this paragraph, the same cannot be said for many who have written commentaries on 2 Corinthians.   During the past century, arguments marshaled to disprove integrity were worded this way: (1) The paragraph is a self-contained unit unrelated to the rest of the book.   (2) In these few verses there are four Greek words not found elsewhere in the Greek Bible, and two more words which are found only in the New Testament.[31]   (3) When these verses are removed, 6:11-13 flow right into 7:2 (the topic is an "open heart").   (4) The citations from the Old Testament (6:16-18) are introduced by a non-Pauline cita-

---

[29] Two influential attempts to dissect 2 Corinthians have been those by J.S. Semler (1767) and Gunther Bornkamm (1971).   Since then, one or the other, or a modification thereof, has tended to be repeated as one of the assured conclusions of higher critical studies of the Corinthian correspondence.   Semler believed he had located parts of four letters: (1) 2 Corinthians 1-8 (plus Romans 16) plus 2 Corinthians 13:11-13 constituted one epistle;   (2) 2 Corinthians 10:1-10 was the last chapter of another letter, he supposed;   (3) 10:11-13:10 constituted another letter;   (4) Then chapter 9 was said to be a small circular epistle, addressed not to the Corinthians, but to the Christians of Achaia.   A contemporary scholar, Gunther Bornkamm has found parts of five letters in 2 Corinthians: (1) Letter C (letter of defense):   2:14-6:13 plus 7:2-4;   (2) Letter D (letter of tears): 10:1-13:10;   (3) Letter E (letter of reconciliation):   1:1-2:13 plus 7:5-16;   (4) Letter F (letter of commendation for Titus and two brothers): 8:1-24;   and (5) Letter G (letter concerning arrangements for the collection):   9:1-15.   Cited in Murray J. Harris, *The Second Epistle to the Corinthians: A Commentary on the Greek Text* in the New International Greek Testament Commentary series (Grand Rapids: Eerdmans, 2005), p. 9.

[30] James Denney, *The Second Epistle to the Corinthians*, in the Expositor's Bible (London: Hodder, 1894), p.775.

[31] Using the NASB translation of these words, they are: "bound together" and "partnership" (v. 14), "harmony" and "Belial" (v.15), and "agreement" (v.16).   Based on these words, the allegation is made that this paragraph is non-Pauline material which someone else inserted at this place.

tion formula.   (5) Pauline terms (righteousness [6:14], flesh and spirit [7:1]) are used in a non-Pauline sense.[32]

Thankfully, recent studies have not been so radical, due in no small part to the fact that there is no external manuscript evidence to support the idea that this passage was not part of the original form of the epistle, or that the passage was originally located elsewhere in this epistle.   All the available manuscript evidence has this paragraph precisely where it appears in our Bibles.   And it is in this place because Paul put it here; it exactly suits the argument Paul is making.   He is identifying the ones who have been the cause of the recent strained relations between the Corinthians and himself.   Get rid of the Judaizers and one of the major causes of the strained relations will also be gone.

(c) 2 Corinthians 8

The proposals to separate chapter 8 from chapters 1-7, and to separate chapter 9 from chapter 8, have met with very little approval.   The restoration of Paul's apostolic reputation is still the theme underneath the appeal concerning a revival of their interest in the offering for Jerusalem.   9:1 begins with "for" showing that the subject in the closing verses of chapter 8 is being continued.   "For it is superfluous for me to write to you about this ministry to the saints" is not the way a new topic would be begun; it is not a proof that chapter 8 and chapter 9 do not go together.   The verb tense is present; Paul says it is "superfluous to go on writing."   As he comes toward the conclusion of this topic of the offering, there are two more things he wants to say: (1) he gives his reasons for sending the brethren instead of coming himself (9:1-5), and (2) he calls attention to the blessings of Christian giving (9:6-15).

(d) 2 Corinthians 11:32,33

The case here is somewhat similar to 6:14-7:1.   There is said to be a violent transition in the vein of thought; and if we omit the verses which produce this abrupt change, we are told that we have a good sequence of thought.   But there is no agreement among those who propose to excise the sentences as to how much ought to be cut out in order to make a good junction.   It is by no means incredible that Paul dictated just what has come down to us.   Could not Paul be closing the list of hardships he has suffered at the hands of the unbelieving Jews by recalling one of the very first instances of such persecution, namely that at Damascus.   The implication

---

[32] About the time the Dead Sea Scrolls were published, Joseph Fitzmyer treated this paragraph as a non-Pauline interpolation reflecting "Christianized" Essene theology.   Joseph A. Fitzmyer, "Qumran and the Interpolated Paragraph in 2 Cor 6,14-7,1," CBQ 23 (1961), p.271-280.   It can be shown there is a reason for the striking affinities between 6:14-7:1 and Qumran terminology and theology.   First-century Judaism, whether of the Pharisaic or Essene type, had their man-made religious rules known as "works of the Law."   If the Pharisees were in error (Matthew 15:3-9), so were the other Jewish sects who had similar man-made rules.

is that the Judaizers caused the problems at Damascus, just like they are causing the problems at Corinth.

(e) 2 Corinthians 10 to 13

Hypotheses concerning the separation of these four chapters from the remainder of 2 Corinthians rest on a common conviction that there is a drastic change of tone (from relief and unbridled joy to biting irony and sarcasm) at 2 Corinthians 10:1 that signals the last four chapters cannot be a part of the same letter as chapters 1-9.[33] Those who have challenged the integrity of these chapters have tended to adopt one of two alternatives: (1) One follows the lead of A. Hausrath (1870) who proposed the hypothesis that chapters 10-13 were part of a "severe letter" written earlier than the letter that contained chapters 1-9.[34] (2) The other follows the lead of J.S. Semler whose hypothesis was that chapters 10-13 were part of a letter written later than the one containing chapters 1-9.[35] Proponents of each proposal put forward arguments to prove theirs is correct and the other is wrong. The result is that the arguments cancel each other out, leaving the integrity of 2 Corinthians intact.

By far the strongest argument in favor of recognizing the integrity of the epistle in exactly the form it has come down to us is that the proposals to make 1-9 or 10-13 parts of two different epistles *rest entirely upon internal evidence alone*; none of the alternative proposals receives any support whatsoever from manuscripts,

---

[33] In comments beginning at 10:1, this commentator questions the commonly stated "drastic change of tone" posited for these final four chapters. If we hear an apostle of Jesus speaking in the tone of the gentleness and meekness of Christ, and if we treat the verses usually pointed to as being harsh as being a reflection of Judaizers' attacks on Paul, all of a sudden there is no harsh tone. What we have, instead, is an apostle of Christ speaking the truth in love as he attempts to restore his apostolic reputation among the Corinthian Christians who are his readers. Much could be said that the claim for a change of tone is part and parcel of higher criticism's reading of the epistle. It is instructive that few commentators who wrote in pre-higher critical times spoke about this change of tone. This commentator does not find Clarke or Jameson, Fausset, and Brown so charging Paul with stern, menacing commands, defiance, and the language of sarcasm and irony. That causes us to wonder whether it is folk who are not certain we have a sure word from the Lord in our Bibles who propose to find this language harsh, and the tone [allegedly] sarcastic. Have modern Bible students read so often in recent works on 2 Corinthians the charge about a change of tone here that we have just accepted it without thinking? Then, having accepted the assertion of a change of tone, we find ourselves having a hard time defending the integrity of 2 Corinthians, or answering the conjectures about these chapters being part of a severe letter to Corinth that somehow became connected to a joyous 2 Corinthians 1-9. This commentator is persuaded that the assured claims of higher criticism should be abandoned.

[34] Plummer (*op. cit.*, p.xxvii-xxxvi) gives the most extended and cogent arguments for believing chapters 10-13 were once part of a painful letter written before chapters 1-9. G. Bornkamm, "The History of the Origin of the so-called Second Letter to the Corinthians" in *New Testament Studies*, Vol.8 [1962], p.258-264) agrees with Plummer.

[35] Margaret Thrall, *The Second Epistle to the Corinthians I: Introduction and Commentary on 2 Corinthians I-VIII* (Edinburgh: T & T Clark, 1994); *idem., II: Commentary on II Corinthians VIII-XIII* (Edinburgh: T&T Clark, 2000), is the most classic recent defense of Semler's view.

versions, or quotations. It takes too many assumptions to say chapters 10-13 form part of another letter. It must be assumed, first, that the ending of chapters 1-9 was somehow lost. It must be assumed, second, that the beginning of chapters 10-13 was somehow lost. And third, it must be assumed that some unknown person put what was left of 1-9 and 10-13 together. This is too much assumption for this commentator!

We are thus pleased to defend the integrity of the epistle; i.e., that it was delivered to the Corinthian church in substantially the same form as we now have it. A strong case can be made for the integrity of 2 Corinthians, and its being dispatched as a single composition.[36]

3.   The identity of the offender of 2 Corinthians 2:5-10

The traditional identification is that the offender of 2 Corinthians 2:5-10 is the incestuous man of 1 Corinthians 5:1-8. So Tertullian wrote (*De Puciditia* XIII). If the references to a sorrowful letter in 2 Corinthians speak of 1 Corinthians, then the offender undoubtedly is the incestuous man.

Once higher critical studies resulted in a denial of the integrity of 2 Corinthians, it was not long until new hypotheses were advanced concerning the identity of the offender. The hypothesis that has gotten the most traction is the one which proposes that the offender is the leader of the Judaizers, those opponents of Paul who recently have invaded Corinth. By their vicious attacks they have offended Paul, the theory goes; 2 Corinthians 2:10 is then interpreted to mean that Paul forgives this man. However, in the light of 7:12,13 where Paul distinguishes between the "offended" and himself, it is hard to accept this suggestion that the offender is the leader of the opposition party, and that Paul is the offended one. Paul's forgiveness of the incestuous man (2 Corinthians 2:10) is done in harmony with an apostle's authority to forgive sins or retain sins on earth since they are simply reflecting what has already taken place in Heaven (John 20:23).

4. The identity of the unbelievers who tried to destroy Paul's apostolic reputation.

Since the 17th century, scholars have offered three basic theories concerning the

---

[36] Authors who have defended the integrity of 2 Corinthians include: W.H. Bates, "The Integrity of 2 Corinthians," *New Testament Studies* 12 (1965-66), p.56-69; P.E. Hughes, *Paul's Second Epistle to the Corinthians* (Grand Rapids: Eerdmans, 1962); Donald Guthrie, *New Testament Introduction* (Downers Grove, IL: InterVarsity, 1971); A.M.G. Stephenson, "A Defense of the Integrity of 2 Corinthians," in *The Authorship and Integrity of the New Testament* (London: SPCK, 1965), p.82-97.

identity of Paul's detractors at Corinth: (1) They were Gnostics.[37] (2) They were Judaizers.[38] (3) They were a mixture of the two, such as found in the group known as Essenes.[39]

The general consensus of opinion is that these were Judaizers. According to 11:22,23, the opponents were men who boasted about their relation to Abraham, the Law, and the traditions of Israel. They were ethnically Jewish. The comparison between the ministries of the old and new covenants in 2 Corinthians 3:6-18 is indirectly aimed at the Judaizing party (11:22,23). Shortly after he wrote this second letter to Corinth, Paul wrote the letter to the Galatian churches, to deal with the Judaizers who recently had come among those churches. A few months after the writing of 2 Corinthians and Galatians, Paul wrote his letter to the Romans, and he warns them to beware of the Judaizers (Romans 16:17-19). These letters form Group Two of Paul's writings. Coming from the same period of time in his ministry, it is reasonable to believe the errorists attacked in 2 Corinthians were Judaizers.[40]

Everything we read in 2 Corinthians points in this direction. The Judaizers who troubled the churches in Galatia were not even Christians, but merely pretended to be Christians in order to enter and control the churches (Galatians 2:4). Likewise, the Judaizers at Corinth were leading their followers astray from the simplicity and purity of devotion to Christ (11:3). In language that reminds us of Galatians 2:6-8, Paul affirms they preached a different Jesus (11:4). What they taught was not the gospel (11:4) but, raising up speculations against the knowledge of God, their teaching was contrary to any real knowledge of God (10:5). They offered an alien spirit (11:4, a "spirit of bondage"). They diluted or adulterated the word of God (4:2). They led people astray from the simplicity that is in Christ Jesus (11:3).

---

[37] R. Bultmann (*The Second Letter to the Corinthians* [Minneapolis: Augsburg, 1985]) and W. Schmithals (*Gnosticism in Corinth*, 1971) defend this hypothesis. In this present commentator's Introductory Studies to Colossians, Timothy and Titus, and the Johannine literature, it is explained that the Gnostic heresy that will trouble the church after the apostolic age ended actually began as a heresy among the Jews, from whence it was imported into the church. Its beginning stages in the church can be seen in the Colossian heresy, and in the communities to which the Johannine literature was sent, as well as the communities to whom 2 Peter and Jude were sent.

[38] C.K. Barrett, *The Second Epistle to the Corinthians* (New York: Harper & Row, 1973) defends this hypothesis. *idem.*, "Paul's Opponents in II Corinthians" in *New Testament Studies*, XVII (3, 1971), pp.233-254.

[39] Dieter Georgi (*The Opponents of Paul in Second Corinthians* [Philadelphia: Fortress, 1986] is a proponent of this view. So is J.J. Gunther, *St. Paul's Opponents and their Background* (Leiden: Brill, 1973).

[40] The author's commentary on Galatians is bound together with this commentary on 2 Corinthians. From the details given in Galatians, a Judaizer was likely a Pharisee (Acts 15:5 compared with Galatians 2:4) who tried to impose Jewish "works of the Law" upon Gentiles as conditions either for salvation or for the enjoyment of table fellowship. Both Galatians and 2 Corinthians identify the Judaizers as not being Christians, but rather "unbelievers."

A reading of Paul's replies to their crafty and insidious defamation of his apostleship leads us to see certain glimpses of who they were and what they did. They had arrived in Corinth carrying "letters of commendation" (3:1), perhaps from churches they had already infiltrated and deceived. They are characterized as false apostles (11:13), suggesting they were traveling missionaries who, upon arriving in Corinth, claimed to be apostles of Christ.[41] Unlike the apostles of Jesus, they were still emphasizing the old covenant (3:6). They were greedy and avaricious (11:20). They were lawless (6:14). They were deceitful workers (11:13). They were servants of Satan (11:15). They commended themselves and measured themselves by themselves (10:12). They intruded into and appropriated other men's labors rather than starting works themselves (10:16). They took financial advantage of the Corinthians (12:17). They were peddlers of the word of God (2:17). Their influence was destructive to the peace and harmony of the church (12:20). They boasted they had received visions and revelations from the Lord (12:1). They pretended to be "servants of righteousness" (11:15).[42]

Some of the things the Judaizers said as they tried to destroy Paul's apostolic influence by ridicule, innuendo, and misrepresentation, included:

- He carried no letters of commendation (3:1; 10:13,14), but he was a braggart who was always commending himself (4:2,5; 5:12; 6:4; 10:12,19; 12:11).
- His personal appearance was unimpressive (10:10) and he was unskilled in speech (10:10, 11:6).
- He was a man of mere human motives (10:2).
- He never gave any thought to whether or not he could deliver on what he promised (1:17).
- He always was trying to say "Yes" and "No" in the same breath (1:17,18).
- He talked about his authority like a tyrant (1:24; 10:8), and, like many tyrants, he was actually a coward. For example, he said that he would come to Corinth, and yet did not dare show himself there (1:23; 13:2).
- When he came to Corinth, the Judaizers said, he had gone outside the limits of the area he was assigned to evangelize (10:13,14).
- They said his refusal to accept financial support was proof he didn't love the Cor-

---

[41] When had they come to Corinth? It might be affirmed that they arrived before 1 Corinthians was written if it could be shown that one or more of the parties alluded to in 1 Corinthians 1-4 had been influenced by them, or if the matter of foods offered to idols (1 Corinthians 8-10) was a topic the Judaizers would have been particularly interested in. Had they arrived in Corinth before Paul made his sorrowful intermediate trip to that town? Was their negative influence part of the reason Paul's attempt to help correct the problem at Corinth ended in failure? Titus was sent to Corinth to attempt to get the Corinthians to repent. Perhaps the Judaizers arrived after Paul's intermediate trip but before Titus' came. When Titus reported back to Paul, did he bring word not only about the lapse in the offering, but also about Judaizers? Any of these options might be correct; we just do not have enough information to decide.

[42] Perhaps this has reference to their insistence on keeping the "works of the Law," whereas Paul ignored those man-made rules (the traditions of the elders) and he also declared the Law itself it to be obsolete and superseded by the new covenant.

inthians (11:7-11) and that he knew he was inferior to the original twelve apostles chosen by Jesus (11:5; 12:11; 13:3).

- More than that, he was getting money from them by false pretenses, either by having his helpers get money for him (12:17), or he was going to misappropriate some of the money being collected for the poor at Jerusalem (8:20,21 and 12:16-13).

Their aim was to undermine and destroy Paul's apostolic authority in order to bring about his downfall at Corinth and to establish their own credentials. Because of this masterful defense of his apostolic authority, the effort of the Judaizers to thwart the advance of Christianity came to failure.

I. SUGGESTED TOPICS FOR FURTHER STUDY

As 2 Corinthians is read, ideas are introduced which seem to ask for deeper reflection and study. Included in this list are some that have caught the imagination of the writer of this commentary:

1. How to share the comfort one receives from Christ with others who are hurting. (1:3-11)

2. How discouragement and anxiety can hinder a ministry. (2:12,13; 7:5)

3. Can sin in one place (Corinth) have a negative effect on people becoming Christians in another (Troas)?

4. What it means to acknowledge the authority of an apostle of Christ.

5. What happens on the day of our Lord Jesus? (1:14; 4:14; 5:10)

6. The doctrine local autonomy. The power of the local church in cases of discipline (2:3-8). The extent of an apostle's authority when it comes to discipline.

7. The need to reaffirm love for an erring member who has repented. (2:5-10)

8. The importance of not being outwitted by Satan (2:11). What does the devil do to hinder folk from becoming believers in Jesus? (4:3,4)

9. The contrast between the two covenants, the Mosaic and the New. (3:3-18)

10. What is the "inner man" (4:16)?   What is it to be renewed day by day?

11. A reflection on the nature of physical death for the Christian, going home to be with Jesus; plus a contemplation of the nature of the resurrection body. (5:1-8)

12. The reasons for which Christ died. (5:14-21; 8:9)

13. The need of being ambassadors for Christ, and the imperative of evangelism. (5:11-21)

14. How is 6:14-7:1 applied in the 21st century?

15. The nature of godly sorrow and repentance. (7:8-11)

16. What can be learned about charitable contributions in chapters 8 & 9?

17. Identify some characteristics of genuine Christian stewardship (8,9).[43]

18. The signs of a genuine apostle of Christ. (12:12)

19. The famous benediction (Son – Father – Spirit) at 13:14.

20. The value of a helper like Titus.

21. What Old Testament records does Paul treat as being actual history?

22. What does 2 Corinthians say about "grace"?

23. How can congregations show in a tangible way their harmony and brotherly affection? (13:12,13)

---

[43] M.J. Harris (op. cit., p.124) has suggested these emphases: genuine Christian stewardship is voluntary, not enforced (8:3, 9:5,7); it is generous, not parsimonious (8:2, 9:6,13); it is enthusiastic, not grudging (8:4,11-12, 9:7); it is deliberate, not haphazard (9:7); and it is sensible, not reckless (8:11-15).

J. OUTLINE

COMMENTARY ON
2 CORINTHIANS

INTRODUCTION. 1:1-11

A. Apostolic Salutation. 1:1,2

1:1 – *Paul, an apostle of Christ Jesus by the will of God, and Timothy* our *brother, to the church of God which is at Corinth with all the saints who are throughout Achaia*

Paul - Ancient letters began with an epistolary opening that gave the name of the writer, the address to which the letter was being sent, and a word of greeting. Paul regularly follows this ancient letter-writing custom. As he signs this letter, Paul uses the name by which he was known since the first missionary journey (Acts 13:9). Before the beginning of that first missionary journey, he was known as "Saul." "Paul" was a Roman name; "Saul" was a Hebrew name. Perhaps Paul's father, strict Pharisee that he was, gave his son two names: "Saul," after the one king that his tribe of Benjamin produced for Israel, and being a Roman citizen of Tarsus (Acts 22:28), we suppose the father gave the boy a Roman name, also.[1] When Paul's mission work among the Gentiles began in earnest, when working among Greeks, and when his Roman citizenship became a valuable asset to him, the sensible thing for him to do was to confine himself to the use of his Roman name, which he did.

An apostle of Christ Jesus - The word "apostle" means a commissioned messenger, an official envoy. Such messengers were dispatched to deliver a specific message from the sender. They had no authority of their own, but had delegated power from the one who sent them. Christ Jesus is identified as the one who sent Paul.[2] Paul here sounds a key note of this epistle. Paul's apostolic authority and mission is a major topic in 2 Corinthians, because Judaizers who had infiltrated the church there had disparaged Paul's apostleship. He asserts his apostolic authority at the very outset of the letter.[3] It is instructive to see how Paul words his commission in Gala-

---

[1] The idea that Paul took this name from Sergius Paulus (Acts 13:9) is probably incorrect.

[2] There are two kinds of apostles in the New Testament: apostles of Jesus (such as Paul here designates himself), and apostles of churches (2 Corinthians 8:23), being so designated because some local congregation had commissioned them to do a certain task in behalf of that congregation. During His earthly ministry, there were twelve men chosen by Jesus to be apostles (Matthew 10:1-4). When Judas disqualified himself, Matthias was chosen to be an apostle of Jesus (Acts 1:24-26). Later Barnabas (Acts 14:14) and James, the brother of the Lord (Galatians 1:19), and perhaps Andronicus and Junias (Romans 16:7), were chosen to be apostles. To this number we add Paul (Acts 26:16-18).

[3] In letters to churches where his apostolic authority has been challenged, Paul does not hesitate to assert it. In letters like Philippians and Philemon there was no need to call attention to his credentials.

tians 1:1, a letter that deals with Judaizers just as 2 Corinthians does.   In the church, the apostles of Jesus were first in rank, first in time, and first in dignity.   The apostles had administrative functions in the whole church.   They had authority over the whole church.   They were not limited to any one congregation, as were the elders and deacons.   We have apostles in the church today, not in the flesh, but in the sense that we have their writings.[4]   "Christ" is a transliteration of *christos*, which means "anointed"; this Greek word is the usual one used to translate the Hebrew word "Messiah" (John 1:41).   The name "Jesus" is the transliteration of the Greek *Iēsous*, which in turn is parallel to the Hebrew "Joshua" ("Jehovah saves" or "salvation of Jehovah").   Jesus is His name.   Christ is His title.

By the will of God - In the Corinthian church, certain evil workers had been opposing Paul, deprecating his apostolic authority.[5]   Because of their influence, Paul lays great stress on his credentials.   He affirms that his call to be an apostle was because God willed it.   To the Galatians, troubled by Judaizers, Paul put emphasis on the fact he was chosen by God before he was born (Galatians 1:15).

And Timothy *our* brother - Like here, Timothy is named by Paul in Philippians, Colossians, 1 and 2 Thessalonians, and Philemon.   The Corinthians already were acquainted with Timothy.   Timothy had come to Corinth while Paul was in town the first time planting the church (Acts 18:5).   He had visited the church about the time 1 Corinthians was written (1 Corinthians 4:17; 16:10).   Why Paul includes him in the signature part of the letter is not known for certain.   It may mean no more than Timothy has been traveling with Paul and is present when the letter is written.   It more likely means that Timothy served as Paul's amanuensis as Paul dictated this letter.   That Timothy is a "brother" sounds another key note in the letter.[6]   There is a brotherhood that exists between Paul, Timothy, and the Corinthians that is in danger of being ruptured.

To the church of God which is at Corinth - The words assembly, congregation, or community catch the idea in the Greek word *ekklēsia* (literally, "called out") transla-

---

[4] There can be no apostles in the flesh today, for to be an apostle, in the sense the twelve and Paul were, one had to be an eyewitness of the death, burial, and resurrection of Christ (Acts 1:21,22.)

[5] The Judaizers could call attention to the fact that Paul was not one of the original twelve apostles.   They might affirm that it was the church at Antioch, not Jesus, which sent him out (Acts 13:1-3).   They could claim something faulty about Paul's commission and message if the mother church at Jerusalem had not sent him (as the Judaizers falsely claimed for themselves), but, instead, the inferior Gentile church at Antioch had sent him (a church which had altered the gospel [they alleged] by removing the requirements to observe the "works of the Law" in order to attract the Gentiles).

[6] When folk are immersed believers in Jesus, they become adopted into the family of God (Romans 8:15; Galatians 3:26,27).   That is why believers can be called brothers and sisters in Christ.

ted "church."[7]   The term *ekklēsia* is used in Scripture both of a local congregation (as here) and also in a universal sense (as in Acts 9:31 where all the congregations in Judea, Samaria, and Galilee are called the "church").   In its local sense, the term "church" embraces all the people in a community who have been called out, separated from the world by the gospel, and who are bound together by a common faith in Jesus Christ.   That the church is God's is something the Corinthians needed to be reminded of.   If the church is His, then members of the congregation are "not free to make whatever decisions they think best; they were required to submit their decisions to His will."[8]   In an effort to call Bible things by Bible names, which in this commentator's judgment is a wise thing to do, it is needful to search out the Scriptural terms for the body of Christ.[9]   Biblical names for local congregations include "church of God" (Acts 20:28), which pictures a community made up of all of God's faithful people from both Old and New Testament times; "church of the firstborn [ones]" (Hebrews 12:23), which describes those who make up the congregation; church of Christ (Romans 16:16), which speaks of Christ's ownership.   In the early church, geographical divisions (such as "at Corinth") are the only divisions in the church recognized in the New Testament.   The church in one place, or city, is always spoken of as a unit.   Though consisting of one or more distinct congregations, it is regarded as an organic whole.   The local congregation is the only divine organizational expression of the Kingdom of God on earth.   These local churches were bodies distinct and separate, without any organic connection with one another.   Each was a distinct body within itself.   The members of these local assemblies, under the direction of the Holy Spirit, chose their own overseers and workers.

With all the saints who are throughout Achaia - In the New Testament, the words "saint, sanctify, sanctification, hallow, holy, and holiness" are all translations of the same Greek root, *hagi*.   A saint is a person who is set apart to the service of God, something that occurs when that person becomes a Christian.   Before the name "Christian" had come into general use (after Acts 11:26), "saints" (Acts 9:13) and "brethren" (Acts 1:15) were common designations of those who were the followers of Christ.[10]   Since the Roman province was created in 146 BC, "Achaia" included all of the Peloponnesus south of Macedonia.   Before the Romans changed the boundaries, "Achaia" included only the maritime regions of the western part of the Peloponnesus.

---

[7] The English word "church" comes from the Scottish "Kirk," a word originally used to distinguish the Church (Kirk) of Scotland from the Church of England.   Kirk was an attempt to render into English the Greek word *kuriakon* (the Lord's house).

[8] Fred Fisher, *Commentary on 1 & 2 Corinthians* (Waco, TX: Word Books, 1975), p.280.

[9] It is a shame that we have been forced by division in the religious world to go looking for an appropriate Biblical name to attach above the door of the building in which we worship.

[10] Contrary to the doctrine of the Roman Catholic church, where a saint is someone now dead and who has been canonized, the saints in Achaia were very much alive, and the ones in Corinth (1 Corinthians 1:2) were hardly sinless perfect.

The term "Achaia" in the New Testament generally refers to the Roman Province (see Acts 18:12 where Gallio is proconsul of Achaia, yet is located in Corinth).[11] Saints "throughout Achaia" indicates there were congregations in other towns besides Corinth; we know of one at Cenchrea (Romans 16:1) and perhaps one at Athens (Acts 17:34). Paul intends this letter to be circulated and read in more congregations than just the one at Corinth.[12] "With" (*sun*), which joins the saints in Achaia with the church at Corinth, indicates there are things in this letter that pertain to all the Christians in the province of Achaia. If Judaizers have not come to their towns, the possibility is good they will. To be forewarned is to be forearmed.

1:2 – *Grace to you and peace from God our Father and the Lord Jesus Christ.*

Grace to you and peace - This prayer for grace and peace is Paul's greeting in all his epistles (except the pastoral epistles, in which he beautifully adds the word "mercy"). It is a remarkable blending of Greek and Jewish salutations. The Greeks, when greeting someone, said *charein* ("hail!" a word almost synonymous with our "good day to you"). Paul modifies this usual Greek greeting only slightly, writing *charis,* "grace" to you. Scripturally, "grace" speaks of unmerited favor, loving kindness. It would include all the blessings bestowed on man by God. Paul prays that God will give his readers an abundance of His undeserved gifts. The Hebrew greeting "Peace be to you" is a prayer for the one being greeted that refers to his entire welfare, both spiritual and physical. Peace is not only the absence of strife, but the presence of positive blessings. It speaks of tranquility for the soul. And of course, peace can come to a person only after grace. The Greek word is *eirēnē*, from the verb *eirō* which means "to join." When things are disjointed, there is lack of harmony and well-being. So, this Greek and Hebrew prayer for blessing is especially significant in this letter to a town where the Judaizers have come, preaching a doctrine that causes splits and hard feelings between Christians. Our Lord has bound together the believing sinner and God, thus making peace.

---

[11] The expression "saints in Achaia"(KJV) has led to the supposition that there is a contradiction between the household of Stephanas being the firstfruits of Achaia (1 Corinthians 16:15), and Romans 16:5 where the KJV has Epaenetus as the firstfruits of Achaia. However, the better manuscripts at Romans 16:5 read "Asia." This answers this alleged contradiction. Others have supposed there is a contradiction between Acts 17:34 which speaks of converts at Athens and 1 Corinthians 16:15 which has the household of Stephanas being the firstfruits of Achaia. This alleged contradiction may be solved if it be seen that Acts 17:34 speaks of individuals, whereas 1 Corinthians 16:15 speaks of a household. Paul himself baptized Stephanas (1 Corinthians 1:16). Others offer the solution that in 1 Corinthians 16:15 Paul is using "Achaia" in a limited sense, whereas his "throughout Achaia" (Greek, "all") shows he is speaking of the whole Roman province.

[12] The probability is to be considered that addressing this letter to numerous audiences led to the beginning of making collections of New Testament writings. The congregations were in the practice of sharing with others the apostolic writings they possessed (see Colossians 4:16; 2 Peter 3:16). The inspired writings that were thus circulated, copied, and collected became the books in our New Testament.

From God our Father and the Lord Jesus Christ - God and Jesus are linked equally as the sources of grace and peace.   A single preposition "from" unites God and Jesus. One of the members of the Godhead is described as "our Father," a distinctive Christian designation for God learned from Jesus Himself.[13]   The other member of the Godhead is described as "Lord."   The distinction is in respect of relation to believers.   To the receivers of grace and peace, God is in the relation of *Father*.   To the same subjects, Christ is in the relation of *Lord*.   In Old Testament times, the Hebrews were reluctant to pronounce the ineffable name YHWH ("Jehovah") lest they take the name in vain.   So, for YHWH they substituted the term "Lord" (*adonai*, Hebrew).   When the LXX translators came to *adonai*, they wrote *kurios* ("Lord") in the Greek.   If Jesus is called "Lord," it is because He, like the Father, is equally a "self-existent one" ("Jehovah").[14]   This emphasis, too, is important in this letter, for the Judaizers apparently denied the deity of Jesus (2 Corinthians 11:4).

B. Preamble of Thanksgiving and Hope. 1:3-11

1.   Paul's prayer of thanks for the comfort of God.   1:3-7

*1:3 – **Blessed** be **the God and Father of our Lord Jesus Christ, the Father of mercies and God of all comfort;***

Blessed *be* - After an epistolary opening, ancient letters regularly included a word of thanksgiving.   Following this custom, Paul's letters frequently have a thanksgiving for something the readers are doing well, and sometimes he gives thanks to God for what He is doing for the readers.   Here he thanks God for what He has done recently for Paul.   Perhaps there is no word of thanksgiving to the church because there is so much in the congregation that needs to be changed, topics which this letter addresses. There are two Greek words translated "blessed" in the New Testament: *makarios* which means "happy, spiritually prosperous," and *eulogētos*, used here, which is made up of *legō*, "to speak," and *eu*, "well," and thus Paul is saying (the verb "be" must be supplied) let God be spoken well of, or let Him be praised.   The word expresses gratitude and adoration.   This verse introduces an expression of gratitude to God for the relief to his anxious mind that the report of Titus, recently returned from Corinth, has brought.

---

[13] See His prayer in John 17:1,24; His prayer in Gethsemane (Mark 14:36); and His reply to Joseph and Mary at the age of twelve, "I had to be in My Father's house" (Luke 2:49).

[14] For a more thorough explanation of Jesus' deity, and at the same time, while He was incarnate, His subordination to the Father, see the author's comments at 1 Corinthians 1:3 in his *New Testament Epistles: 1 Corinthians* (Moberly, MO: Scripture Exposition Books, 2004), p.8,9.

The God and Father of our Lord Jesus Christ - Translators are faced with two options for translating the Greek: (1) Blessed be He who is both God and Father of our Lord Jesus Christ; and (2) Blessed be God, who also is Father of our Lord ..., the Father of mercies, and the God of all comfort (i.e., God is described by three phrases). Since there is only one article ("the") in the Greek, the first option is likely the correct one.   If we take this first option, this verse must not be interpreted as detracting from the deity of Jesus.   On the cross Jesus addressed the Father in these words, "My God, My God, why?"   Members of the Godhead recognize each other as co-equal, and address each other as God (see Hebrews 1:8).   That God is called the "Father of our Lord Jesus Christ" brings into view the incarnation.   We hear the language of sonship most often while Jesus was in the flesh.   It must be remembered that when Jesus called God His Father, he was claiming to be equal with God (John 5:18).   At the same time, to speak of the Father as being Jesus' God is an affirmation of the temporary subordination of the Son to the Father as He became incarnate.   This lofty title for Jesus ("Our Lord Jesus Christ") was full of meaning in the apostolic age.   It is a succinct capsule of Christian doctrine about who God is.   The God Christians worshiped revealed Himself in the incarnation of Jesus, the One who has been powerfully demonstrated to be both "Lord" and "Christ" (Acts 2:36).   Jesus, one day, asked "Why do you call me Lord, and do not do what I say?" (Luke 6:46).   This emphasis on Jesus being Lord might be just what the Corinthians needed to hear since the Judaizers have come to town and spoke slightingly of Jesus.

The Father of mercies - The Hebrews often used the word "father of" to denote the author, or source, of anything; so the likely meaning of this phrase is that "mercies" come from God.   He is the source of "mercies" (plural); that is, each and every special mercy needed comes from Him.   Or, since it is "the mercies" in the Greek, the plural might be equivalent to our word "compassion," the tender feeling of pity for those in distress.   The Old Testament attributes both mercy (Exodus 33:19) and compassion (Psalm 103:13) to God.

The God of all comfort - The Greek word *parakalēsis* translated "comfort" is a compound word made up of "to call" and "alongside," i.e., to call someone alongside to give us courage, hope, or confidence.   In modern English, "comfort" has come to denote ease, so we may need a different word to translate the Greek.   Perhaps "encouragement" is best.   The kind of comfort or consolation or encouragement that Paul here has in mind has its source in God (Isaiah 51:3).   In the introduction and thanksgivings of his letters, Paul frequently gives us hints of what will be discussed in the letter.   This word "comfort" is one of the emphases of this epistle, for the word occurs, either in noun or verb form, 29 times.   In noun or verb form, it occurs ten times in verses 3-7.   Early in the letter there are two things that have brought Paul comfort or encouragement: the good report concerning the Corinthian church brought to Paul by Titus (7:6,7), and Paul's recent deliverance from a life-threatening affliction (1:8-11).

1:4 - *Who comforts us in all our afflictions so that we may be able to comfort those who are in any affliction with the comfort with which we ourselves are comforted by God.*

Who comforts us in all our affliction - Paul can write about "the God of all comfort" based on his own personal experience.[15] "Comforts" (a cognate of the word used at the close of verse 3) is a present tense verb; this is something God does continually. *Thlipsis* ("affliction") literally means pressing or pressure[16] and then metaphorically it means oppression, affliction, tribulation, or distress brought about by outward circumstances.[17] "All our affliction" is an apt rendering of the Greek which has an article between *pasē* ("all") and *thlipsis* ("affliction"); the construction regards all of one's afflictions as a whole. Paul has experienced many afflictions for Christ. There has been the recent anxiety over the rebelliousness of the Corinthians toward his ministry. In verse 8 Paul refers to another specific affliction. In 12:10 he identifies some other "weaknesses, insults, distresses, persecutions, difficulties" all for Christ's sake. See also 11:23.

So that we may be able to comfort those who are in any affliction - The New English Bible reads, "So that we in turn may be able to comfort others in any trouble of theirs." God, who is the source of all comfort, works through people He has comforted (such as Paul) to bring comfort to others. "Any affliction" is an apt translation,[18] for God's comfort is not limited to one particular type of affliction. God's "comfort" does not always mean deliverance from the cause of the suffering and pressure, but from the anxiety which the suffering has caused. When Paul writes "those who are in any affliction" he may have in mind the Corinthians who recently have been experiencing remorse as the result of the recent visit of Titus which led them to repentance. However, the truth which Paul here writes, concerning being comforted so as to be able to comfort others, is not limited to the immediate past relations with Corinth. Paul, having been comforted by God, can assure other sufferers they are in the hands of a loving Father.

With the comfort with which we ourselves have been comforted - Again, the New English Bible reads, "And share with them the consolation we ourselves receive from

---

[15] Paul often uses the first person (sometimes plural, sometimes singular) when referring to himself. He uses "you" when speaking of his readers.

[16] The verb form of *thlipsis* ("affliction") was the word used of the pressing and crushing of grapes to extract the juice (Genesis 40:11). What an instructive way to look at afflictions suffered for Christ.

[17] William F. Arndt and F. Wilbur Gingrich, *A Greek Lexicon of the New Testament And Other Early Christian Literature* (Chicago: University of Chicago Press, 1957), p. 362)

[18] There is a slight change in the word order in the Greek. In the previous clause ("all our affliction") the Greek is *epi pasē tē thlipsei*. In this clause Paul wrote *en pasē thlipsei* ("in any affliction").

God."   "God had given comfort to Paul so that he would be able to comfort others who were in need of comfort, in the same way God had comforted him."[19]   "The encouragement to be dispensed comes from God.   The Christian is not a psychologist pointing to human solutions of man's problems, but a witness pointing to divine solutions."[20]

1:5 - *For just as the sufferings of Christ are ours in abundance, so also our comfort is abundant through Christ.*

For just as the sufferings of Christ are ours in abundance - "For" explains the particular afflictions Paul had in mind in the previous verse.   "The sufferings of Christ" are the sufferings which He suffered in the days of his flesh, at the hands of those who opposed His message and ministry (Hebrews 12:4, "Consider Him who has endured such hostility by sinners against Himself").   Just like the Messiah suffered at the hands of the unbelieving Jews, so Paul's opponents have regularly been unbelieving Jews.[21]   That is certainly the case now, in Corinth, where the Judaizers have caused serious trouble for the church and for Paul.   Christ promised his apostles that in this world they would have persecutions (Mark 10:30; John 15:20).   Paul certainly did, and "in abundance," that is, he suffered more than most of the other servants of Christ did.[22]

So also our comfort is abundant through Christ - "Our comfort" speaks of comfort Paul receives.   The Messiah, the very one the Judaizers failed to recognize, is the one who comforts Paul.   The comfort and encouragement which Paul receives from Christ exceed ("is abundant") the sufferings.   Comfort comes when the servant of Christ "realizes that his suffering is not meaningless."[23]

1:6 - *But if we are afflicted, it is for your comfort and salvation; or if we are comforted, it is for your comfort, which is effective in the patient enduring of the same sufferings which we also suffer.*

---

[19] David Lipscomb, *A Commentary on the New Testament Epistles* (Nashville, TN: Gospel Advocate Co., 1960), Vol. III, p.22,23.

[20] Fisher, *op. cit.*, p.282.

[21] This expression has been given several interpretations by the commentators: (1) It means the sufferings which the Christian endures because of his identification with Christ (cf. 1 Peter 4:13).   (2) It means the sufferings which the glorified Christ suffers when Christians suffer (Acts 9:4).   (3) It means the sufferings of the Messiah on the cross, and they abound to us in the sense that we share in the benefits of the cross" (Fisher, *ibid.*).   While each of these ideas express a Biblical truth, in this commentator's judgment they all fail to meet the needs of the context here in 2 Corinthians 1.

[22] "Abundance" does not mean that Paul is suffering more than Christ did.

[23] James Thompson, *The Second Letter of Paul to the Corinthians* (Austin, TX: R.B. Sweet Co., 1970), p.23.

But if we are afflicted, it is for your comfort and salvation - Verse 6 relates Paul's afflictions and sufferings at the hands of enemies of Christ to the spiritual welfare of the Corinthians. The way the if-clause is worded in the Greek, it implies the truth of the statement. Paul in fact was afflicted abundantly (verse 5). "Afflicted" is a passive voice verb in the present tense; the enemies of the gospel were the ones who continually afflicted Paul. "For your comfort and salvation" says Paul has endured affliction at the hands of the enemies of Christ so that he might bring the gospel to the Corinthians, a gospel which will result in their salvation and comfort.[24] "Your comfort" may reflect the fact that the Corinthians have recently been alienated from Paul, at least since before his intermediate trip to visit their church, and that Paul is still trying to work out reconciliation. "Salvation" has to do with their eternal salvation, a thing which has been put in jeopardy by their willingness to listen to the Judaizers who were false teachers (2 Corinthians 11:13). "All the hardships endured by the apostle were for the sake of the eternal salvation of his converts. This is the motivation which even yet supplies the energy for many faithful ministries of the gospel."[25]

Or if we are comforted, it is for your comfort - Again, the Greek wording shows this if-clause assumes the truth of the statement. Paul had been comforted by Christ (verse 5). He had been comforted by Christ so that he could bring comfort to them.

Which is effective in the patient enduring of the same sufferings which we also suffer - The Greek says it is the comfort he can give them that is being effective[26] in producing "patient enduring" of the same kind of sufferings that Paul himself experiences. The way the Greek participle ("is effective") is spelled means it can be either middle (the subject acts for its own benefit) or passive (the subject is acted upon) in voice. If we treat the participle as middle, it says that it is as the comfort makes itself felt that it helps produce "patient enduring." If we treat it as passive, it says the comfort does not work by itself; the One who is the source of all comfort must make it work. Perhaps we should treat it as passive. "Endurance" is *hupomonē,* a word which does not denote passive acceptance of trouble and trial, but a positive attitude that anticipates something will be done to turn the trials into blessings for someone else. In Romans 5:3, Paul writes that "tribulation (*thlipsis*) produces endurance (*hupomonē*)." "The same sufferings which we also suffer" seems to say the Corinthians recently have been on the receiving end of the same hatred and opposition from unconverted Jews which Paul has experienced during his

---

[24] He did not mean that his afflictions had the same redemptive quality that Christ's sufferings did.

[25] James B. Coffman, *Commentary on 1 and 2 Corinthians* (Austin, TX: Firm Foundation Publishing House, 1977), p.308.

[26] The noun *paraklēseōs* ("comfort") in the previous clause is in the genitive singular. The articular participle *tēs energoumenēs* ("which is effective") is also in the genitive singular, which shows the participle agrees with "comfort."

whole ministry.   The ones who instigated the suffering and affliction in Corinth were actually servants of Satan (2 Corinthians 11:14,15).   The Christian answer to opposition from the devil is endurance; take what he does and turn it into something good.   In this letter Paul will show how the Corinthians can do that very thing.   Paul seems to be anticipating the attempts he will make in this letter to bring about their reconciliation toward himself and to influence their attitudes toward the Judaizers by recalling their common experience of suffering.   Calling their attention to their common experience is a way to enlist their sympathy for what he is writing.

1:7 - *And our hope for you is firmly grounded, knowing that as you are sharers of our sufferings, so also you are* **sharers** *of our comfort*

And our hope for you is firmly grounded - This is Paul's way of saying he had a firm and unshaken[27] hope in the Corinthian Christians.[28]   If we assume that as a result of Titus' recent visit to the church the majority of the members are reconciled to Paul and to the gospel he preached, Paul can express this hope for them that they will be sharers of the kind of comfort he has received from the Lord.

Knowing that as you are sharers of our sufferings - Here, Paul gives the reason for his hope.[29]   "Sharers" (*koinōnoi*) means to participate together or share something in common.   "Sharers of our sufferings," as "same sufferings which we also suffer" meant in verse 6, makes it evident the Corinthian Christians have been subjected to the same kind of hostile behavior from unbelieving Jews that Paul had been subjected to.[30]

So also you are *sharers* **of our comfort** - Paul does not claim all the credit for comforting them.   Rather this clause says that just as God through Christ had comforted (encouraged) Paul when he was afflicted by the devil's helpers, so Paul is confident God will through Christ comfort (encourage) the Corinthian Christians.   Nor should we think that this is something that may happen out in the distant future (as the KJV, by supplying a future tense verb in italics) has it.   The comfort Paul speaks about will occur in the very present to those who are steadfast in their faith.

---

[27] "Firmly grounded" translates *bebaios*, a word which means "steadfast, constant, firm." George Ricker Berry, *A New Greek-English Lexicon to the New Testament* (Chicago: Wilcox & Follett, 1948), p.19.

[28] The manuscripts at this place present some variations in the order of the clauses, but the variation hardly affects the sense in any appreciable degree.   We'll comment on the phrases in the order they occur in the NASB.

[29] The circumstantial participle translated "knowing that" equals "because we know."

[30] It is this commentator's position that the Judaizers were not Christians.   They were false brethren who pretended to be Christians just to infiltrate the churches and try to make them live like Pharisees lived (Galatians 2:5).

2. God's deliverance of Paul from a recent severe affliction is the reason for the hope.   1:8-11

1:8 – For we do not want you to be unaware, brethren, of our affliction which came to us in Asia, that we were burdened excessively, beyond our strength, so we despaired even of life;

For we do not want you to be unaware, brethren - "For" seems to introduce an example from Paul's own recent experience of the kind of "comfort" the Corinthians can expect from the Lord.[31] "We do not want you to be unaware" is an expression Paul uses often[32] to call attention to the importance of what is about to be said. "Brethren" calls attention to the close relationship that exists between Paul and the faithful Corinthians because they are all sons of God by adoption (Galatians 3:26-29), and therefore brothers. It is also a way of expressing "an appeal for affection and sympathy."[33]

Of our affliction which came *to us* in Asia - The other afflictions alluded to in this context refer to attacks made upon Paul by unbelieving Jews, attacks that were similar to the sufferings of Christ (verse 5). There is no reason to believe that this one was different. "Asia" is the Roman Province that covered the whole west end of the land we know as Turkey. Since the time he wrote 1 Corinthians from Ephesus, Paul has made a sorrowful intermediate trip to Corinth and back to Ephesus, and then he traveled overland through Troas (also in the province of Asia) on his way to Macedonia, from which he is now writing this second letter to Corinth. Whatever the affliction was, it happened before Paul's recent arrival in Macedonia. Apparently, the Corinthians knew of this recent close escape from death, since Paul gives no details. It was but 200 miles across the Aegean from Ephesus to Corinth so news would soon reach Corinth. We may not be able to know with certainty to what Paul refers, but there are verses that are suggestive. Unbelieving Jews were capable of plots against Paul's life (Acts 20:3, 23:12).[34] It is not inconceivable that they made

---

[31] A less satisfactory option is to treat the "for" with which verse 8 begins as we treated the "for" with which verse 5 begins, i.e., as reasons why Paul blesses God (verse 3).

[32] See Romans 1:13, 11:25; 1 Corinthians 10:1, 12:1; 2 Corinthians 10:1; 1 Thessalonians 4:13.

[33] Alfred Plummer, *A Critical and Exegetical Commentary on the Second Epistle of St. Paul to the Corinthians,* in the International Critical Commentary Series (Edinburgh: T&T Clark, 1915), p.15.

[34] Since Paul gives so few details here, the commentators have offered other guesses concerning the specific event to which Paul alludes. Since each is open to serious objection, we will just enumerate them briefly, and then pass on. (1) The stoning at Lystra (Acts 14:6,19,20) happened too far in the past to be a viable option here. (2) The plot referred to in Acts 20:3, on the eve of the departure for Jerusalem with the offering, is still in the future, after the writing of 2 Corinthians. (3) Though Tertullian (*De Resur.Carnis.* 49) thought Paul was speaking of fighting with the wild beasts at Ephesus (1 Corinthians 15:31,32), there is no evidence that the beasts, if two-legged, were unbelieving Jews, something this context rather requires. (4) The riot of Demetrius and the silversmiths (Acts 19:23-41) does not appear to be life-threatening to Paul since his friends

such an attempt at Ephesus a few weeks or months after Paul wrote 1 Corinthians, in which he reported that he had many adversaries at Ephesus (1 Corinthians 16:9). On a later occasion, speaking to the Ephesian elders, Paul refers to the trials that came upon him through the plots of the Jews (Acts 20:19) while he was in Ephesus. Was it at the time of this recent attack on Paul by unbelieving Jews that Aquila and Priscilla risked their own lives for Paul, something that put all the Gentile churches of the whole Roman empire in their debt (Romans 16:4)? This commentator thinks so, and though Luke does not detail it in Acts, he does make allusion to it.

That we were burdened excessively, beyond our strength - The danger was so great, and weighed down on Paul so heavily, that Paul could not see any way out of the desperate situation.

So that we despaired even of life - In his own mind, as he looked at all the probabilities, he decided this was the time he was going to die. But the God who comforts had other plans, and delivered him. We think God used Aquila and Priscilla, somehow, as His tools to effect Paul's rescue.

1:9 – *Indeed, we had the sentence of death within ourselves in order that we should not trust in ourselves, but in God who raises the dead*

Indeed - "Indeed" indicates it is the intention of verse 9 to intensify the description of the desperate situation introduced in verse 8.

We had the sentence of death within ourselves - "Sentence of death" is a technical term for receiving a death sentence.[35] When Paul asked himself if he could possibly live through this attempt on his life, the only answer that came to his mind was that he was going to die. He was "convinced that in all human probability his hours were numbered."[36]

In order that we should not trust in ourselves - The final outcome of this attack on Paul's life taught him a lesson, namely, to stop trusting in his own power and resources, and instead to rely on God. Paul has told us that sharing in the sufferings of Christ (verse 5) has had two beneficial results: one was to have the ability to com-

---

discouraged him from entering the theater. (5) That Paul in Troas, where he had no rest for his spirit day or night (2 Corinthians 2:12,13), was so depressed in spirit he thought he was going to die, makes the affliction to be emotional rather than physical, and it does not directly relate to personally suffering at the hands of the Judaizers.

[35] Plumptre supposes the word is derived from the vocabulary of medicine, referring to the opinion a physician formed on his diagnosis of a case submitted to him. In this case, Paul's diagnosis was against the prospect of recovery. (E.H. Plumptre, *The Second Epistle to the Corinthians*, in the Layman's Handy Commentary series (Grand Rapids: Zondervan, 1957), p.10.

[36] Plummer, *op. cit.*, p.17

fort others in similar circumstances since he himself had received comfort (verse 4); the other was to learn to trust in God who has the power of life and death (2 Kings 5:7). When the Corinthians are in similar desperate circumstances, let them trust in God.

But in God who raises the dead - To Paul, his escape from that life-threatening situation was as though he had been raised from the dead. In Hebrews 11:17-19 we have similar language. Abraham, commanded by God to sacrifice Isaac, obeyed, because "he considered that God was able to raise men even from the dead, from which he received him back as a type." Coffman argues that the similarity of language used in 2 Corinthians and Hebrews is incidental evidence of Pauline authorship of Hebrews. "Where else in all the Bible is Abraham's reliance upon God's ability to raise the dead even hinted at? And how did Paul know it? He himself had trusted God in the same manner when death loomed as a certainty."[37] Paul's verb "raises" is a present tense in the Greek; it pictures a timeless action on God's part.[38] What He has done once, He can and will do again.

1:10 - *who delivered us from so great* **a peril** *of death, and will deliver* **us,** *He on whom we have set our hope. And He will deliver us,*

Who delivered us from so great *a peril* of death - "Delivered us" is a reference to the recent experience introduced at verse 8. "Delivered" is *errusato*, a word which favors our presentation that the great affliction in Asia was a deadly plot by the Jews to get rid of Paul permanently. The same verb appears in Romans 15:31 where Paul asks for prayers that he may be "delivered from those who are disobedient in Judea." Literally, the phrase reads "so great a death." Perhaps it says that the manner of death he was about to be subjected to was particularly frightful. We might speak of a terrible death.

And will deliver *us* - The "will deliver" of this phrase speaks of the immediate future.[39] The danger to Paul from the Judaizers was not over. He could expect their plots against his life wherever he went.

---

[37] Coffman, *op. cit.*, p.310.

[38] "Raises the dead" is a fine expression to use in a letter to the Corinthians, many of whom, at least prior to 1 Corinthians, questioned the doctrine of resurrection (1 Corinthians 15:12).

[39] This clause appears twice in the NASB, and on the surface one of them seems superfluous. Some manuscripts (A,D, Syr.ᴾ) omit this phrase completely, and those represented by the Textus Receptus have changed the verb to a present tense. The present tense then says God will deliver in the present, and the next verb (a future tense) says He will deliver on into the future. The better Greek texts have the phrase twice. The NASB solves the apparent difficulty by beginning a new sentence the second time the words appear in this verse. The sentence then continues on into verse 11.

He on whom we have set our hope - The verb "hope" is not the same verb as the one translated "trust" in verse 9. Paul would not presume that God would always protect or deliver him from danger, but he could hope for such deliverance in his life until God's great purpose for his life was fully accomplished. "We have set our hope" is a perfect tense in the Greek, indicating past completed action with present continuing results. He set his hope on God in the past; he still hopes in God. His hope is grounded on God's past performance. Not only has God raised Jesus from the dead, but He has also, in a sense, raised Paul (verse 9). Paul is confident God can be trusted.

And He will yet deliver us - In the NASB, this clause begins a new sentence that is completed in verse 11. God will deliver, Paul writes, if you Corinthians will make it a matter of your prayers on our behalf.

1:11 - *you also joining in helping as through your prayers, that thanksgiving may be given by many persons on our behalf for the favor bestowed upon us through* **the prayers of** *many.*

You also joining in helping us through your prayers - Paul has been making some specific petitions to God. The language of this request to the Corinthians implies they are already praying; he asks they add his deliverance to their prayers.[40] God's activity of delivering Paul from future life-threatening perils is pictured as happening because the Corinthians have been praying for that very thing.[41] The Corinthians are unlikely to offer such prayers on Paul's behalf unless they are completely reconciled to Paul, the very thing Paul will plead for in the first seven chapters of this letter. Other churches, on different occasions, have been asked to offer intercessory prayer for Paul's future welfare and ministry (Romans 15:30; Ephesians 6;19; Colossians 4:3; 1 Thessalonians 5:25; 2 Thessalonians 3:1).

That thanks may be given by many persons on our behalf - The picture in Paul's mind is this: when their prayers are answered and he is delivered, many will give thanks. "Many persons" is literally "from many faces." It was customary, when offering prayer, to have one's face upturned toward God.[42] Paul envisions many such faces upturned as they give thanks to God.

---

[40] The word translated "prayers" (*deēsis*) "refers chiefly to prayer for particular benefits" and is often used of prayer on behalf of the needs of others (i.e., petition, intercession). George R. Berry, *New Testament Synonyms* (Chicago: Wilcox & Follett Co., 1948), p.120.

[41] The circumstantial participle "joining" may be translated "provided you join" or "as you join." God, in His providence, intervenes in His creation because His children have asked for His special help. He does cause "all things to work together for good to those who love [Him], to those who are called according to His purpose" (Romans 8:28).

[42] Jesus was looking up to Heaven when He prayed about the raising of Lazarus (John 11:41). Folk did not look up to heaven when they were conscious of their own sin and praying for God's forgiveness (Luke 18:13).

For the favor bestowed upon us - The favor[43] in this instance is future deliverance from mortal danger, a danger like the one from which he recently was delivered (verse 10).

Through *the prayers of* **many** - There are two possibilities here since the word "many" can be either masculine or neuter. If neuter, Paul pictures himself being delivered through many things. If masculine, Paul pictures many people giving thanks after they hear about the deliverance for which they had been interceding. They give thanks because Paul still lives to preach the gospel which is God's power unto salvation. Paul's explanation of the recent attempt on his life, and how God delivered him, certainly serves as a wonderful foundation for his answer to the insinuations of the Judaizers that he was vacillating (2:17) and conducting himself according fleshly wisdom (1:12).

I. PAUL'S REVIEW OF HIS RECENT RELATIONS WITH CORINTH. 1:12-7:16

A. Defense of his Conduct. 1:12-2:17

1. With regard to his change of plans concerning a promised visit. 1:12-2:4

1:12 – For our proud confidence is this, the testimony of our conscience, that in holiness and godly sincerity, not in fleshly wisdom but in the grace of God, we have conducted ourselves in the world, and especially toward you.

For our proud confidence is this - It is unusual to begin a new paragraph with "for" as the NASB has done. Paul's first letter to Corinth has clearly marked divisions as he deals with topics learned from the household of Chloe, and as he answers questions the Corinthians had addressed to him. 2 Corinthians also deals with major topics and these topics have determined the outline being offered in these notes. Verses 12-14 are thus treated as being transitional from the reasons God should be blessed (1:3-11) to a vindication of Paul's character and recent relations with the church at Corinth. There had been a change of travel plans by Paul, and his promised visit to Corinth has been delayed. This change of plans gave the Judaizers who have recently infiltrated the church an opportunity to accuse him of fickleness as they tried to destroy the Corinthians' confidence in his apostleship. "Proud confidence" trans-

---

[43] "Favor" translates *charisma*, a word that speaks of a gift freely and graciously given by God. *Charisma* is the word used for miraculous spiritual gifts (1 Corinthians 12:4). Paul's deliverance was as miraculous as were the special gifts.

lates *kauchēsis*, the word usually translated "boasting."[44] Elsewhere Paul repudiates boasting based on human accomplishments and human pride, but he will boast in what the Lord has done (1 Corinthians 1:31). He can say he acted with integrity because the grace of God has changed his life. He does such boasting because the boasting of the Judaizers has caused him to boast in self-defense (2 Corinthians 11:17,18).

The testimony of our conscience - *Suneidēsis* can mean either "conscience" or "consciousness," depending on the context. "Conscience" is an innate faculty that prompts us to do what our mind thinks is right, and criticizes us when we do what our mind thinks is wrong. Unless one's mind is schooled and tutored in the Word of God, the conscience is not a safe guide. "Consciousness" is man's own awareness of who he is and what he has done. Paul may be saying he has searched his consciousness of his past behavior and there is no nagging accusation of improper behavior. That is one reason why he can boast.[45]

That in holiness and godly sincerity - "Godly" is a noun in Greek, and goes with both the words holiness and sincerity. Paul is saying that his upright behavior came from God. "Holiness" and "sincerity" were "God-given qualities rather than human achievements."[46] This explains how Paul could boast about them. He was boasting in the Lord. "Holiness" (*hagiotēti*) is a better attested reading than the KJV's "simplicity" (*haplotēti*).[47] "Holiness" speaks of the consecrated character that a person devoted to God should have. One whose life is dedicated to God does not use devious or underhanded actions. "Sincerity," from a Greek word which means judged in the light of the sun, speaks of transparency of character. Paul had not been a shady character as the Judaizers claimed. His behavior was such as to stand the test of the strongest light.

Not in fleshly wisdom, but in the grace of God - The preposition "in" (*en*) pictures the sphere in which one operates. The sphere of "fleshly wisdom," a wisdom which

---

[44] "Boasting" is an issue of special emphasis in 2 Corinthians. The noun and verb forms for "boasting" occur 29 times in this letter, whereas they occur but 23 times in all of Paul's other letters.

[45] In other places Paul appealed to the testimony that his conscience gave to his actions (Acts 23:1, 24:16; Romans 9:1; 1 Corinthians 4:4). To have nothing on his conscience, so that his conscience would not accuse him of having done wrong, was one of the great guiding principles of his life.

[46] Fisher, *op. cit.*, p.289.

[47] *Hagiotēti* is found in P[46], Aleph*,A,B,C,K,P. It is a rare word, occurring only in Hebrews 12:10, where it is an attribute of God that men are to develop. The word "simplicity" speaks of an uprightness, a purity of life. There was no deviousness in his actions or motives.

is merely human, is the sphere where one is guided by principles of self-interest.[48] In his first epistle to Corinth, Paul spoke of fleshly wisdom in negative terms (1 Corinthians 1:19-21) and insisted that apostles of Christ did not rely on such wisdom, but rather on the wisdom of God. This may be intended as a deliberate contrast between his behavior and that of the Judaizers. "In (*en*) grace" says the grace of God was the sphere in which Paul walked.[49] Grace (unmerited favor) led to his salvation,[50] had something to do with his calling to be an apostle, and had something to do with his every-day walk and ministry.[51] That's why his life was characterized by holiness and godly sincerity.

We have conducted ourselves in the world, and especially toward you - Conducted (*anastraphō*), when speaking of human conduct, means to "*act, behave, conduct oneself, or live* in the sense of the practice of certain principles."[52] "In the world" embraces his behavior during all his missionary efforts. "Especially toward you" has special reference to the time when he had been in Corinth. Rather than saying he had been less careful about his behavior in other places than when he was in Corinth, "especially toward you" is his rebuttal of the charges made against him by the Judaizers that he had been crafty and deceitful toward them. Not so! He insists

---

[48] Care must be taken in commenting on this word. Many commentators, holding it as a given that hereditary total depravity is a Biblical doctrine, talk about perverted human nature as they try to explain the word "fleshly." This matter of an alleged sinful nature inherited from Adam is discussed in a Special Study titled "The Doctrine of Original Sin" in the author's *New Testament Epistles: Romans* (Moberly, MO.: Scripture Exposition Books, 1996), p.231-244.

[49] "Grace" has a number of meanings in the New Testament. At this place, as they explain grace, some commentators call attention to Romans 1:5, where Paul speaks of having received "grace and apostleship." In the author's *New Testament Epistles: Romans*, in notes at 1:5, it is debated whether the expression refers to just one thing, namely, the grace of apostleship, or apostolic grace. In Romans 15:15,16, it appears that "grace' is used to refer to Paul's ministry, so it would not be unheard of if "grace" at Romans 1:5 referred to his apostolic office. If Romans 1:5 speaks of two things, then grace has reference to the forgiveness of sins at his conversion, since men are saved by grace (Ephesians 2:8). If 2 Corinthians speaks of the same grace that Ephesians 2:8 does, then Paul says he lives a disciplined and consecrated life precisely because he remembers what God and Christ have done to save him. Such "grace" just naturally leads one to live a holy life, not a life of double dealing and craftiness.

[50] As we explain "grace" in this verse, there is no need to allude to any alleged "first work of grace" – as though Paul were saying the change in his life was the result of a sovereign act of God that changed his old Adamic nature. See the Special Study titled "Call and Grace" in the author's *New Testament Epistles: Romans*, p.47-65.

[51] Grace enabled Apollos to help believers (Acts 18:28). Paul may be claiming the same thing here in 2 Corinthians 1:12. The church at Antioch commended Paul and Barnabas "to the grace of God for the work which they had accomplished" (Acts 14:26). Paul, in 1 Corinthians 15:10, says the grace of God was with him as he labored as an apostle. In 2 Corinthians 12:9, God's grace will help Paul bear the thorn in the flesh that was given to him. In Acts 6:5,8, there is very little difference between "full of the Holy Spirit" and "full of grace and power." When Paul speaks of "grace" he may be saying he has had a special leading of the Holy Spirit. When someone is going on in the power of the Spirit, there is very little room for insincerity and unholiness.

[52] Arndt and Gingrich, *op. cit.*, p.61.

he conducted himself in holiness and godly sincerity during his long ministry in Corinth. He was careful how he lived; he gave them no reason to be suspicious of him.

1:13 - *For we write nothing else to you than what you read and understand, and I hope you will understand until the end:*

For we write nothing else to you - "For" says this verse is a reason for what he just wrote in verse 12, "especially toward you." It would seem the Judaizers have charged that Paul writes words that are ambiguous or have hidden meaning so that the reader can hear what he wants to hear. Since charges of deception were made, "we write" (a present tense) probably means "I habitually write."[53] What is true of what he just now is writing was also true of 1 Corinthians.

Than what you read and understand - "You don't have to read between the lines of my letters."[54] "Read" refers to the practice of reading apostolic letters out loud to the congregation at the public assembly.[55] "Understand" says there was no hidden meaning, no weasel words. He did not evasively write one thing while intending something else. When it was read out loud, the listeners could take at face value what they heard.

And I hope you will understand until the end - "I hope you will understand fully" (RSV).[56] He knows some of them understand.   He hopes all will understand fully

---

[53] This verse is the only time Paul uses "we write" of his letters; elsewhere he uses the first person, "I write" (e.g., 1 Corinthians 4:14, 14:37; 2 Corinthians 13:10; Galatians 6:11; 1 Timothy 3:14) or "I wrote" (2 Corinthians 2:3,4,9, 7:12; Galatians 6:11).

[54] James Moffatt, *A New Translation of the Holy Bible* (New York: Harper & Brothers, 1950), p.223. "The Greek presents a play on the two words "read" (*anaginōskein*) and "understand" (*epignōskein*), which is impossible to reproduce in English" (Plumptre, *op. cit.*, p.13).

[55] Because "read" means to read out loud in public, Conybeare and Howson have assumed that Paul had been suspected of sending private letters in which he modified the statements of his public epistles. This verse is taken as a denial he has sent any private letters. W.J. Conybeare, and J.S. Howson, *The Life and Epistles of St. Paul* (London: Longmans, Green, and Co., 1873), p.441,442.

[56] Expositors and translators have not been able to agree on the meaning of *heōs telous* ("until the end").   Some have defended the idea the words are equivalent to "completely" (see the marginal reading at John 13:1).   Others defend the idea Paul means "to the end of his life," letting them know his writings will be in plain words as long as he lives. A very faulty interpretation is that Paul has reference to the second coming of Christ. The interpretation of "until the end" as referring to Christ's second coming has led some commentators to expostulate on how the apostles and early church were mistaken about the time of the second coming. Such a claim of a mistake in turn impinges on the doctrine of inspiration and inerrancy. Allo wrote, "Those who wish to understand this in an eschatological sense are not only misled by the mistaken idea that Paul and the Corinthians were expecting the end of the world as near at hand ... they also commit a serious error of literary judgment in failing to notice the intentional antithesis between *know* and *know fully*, as here, and as in 1 Corinthians 13:12." E.B. Allo, *Saint Paul: Seconde epitre aux Corinthiens* (Paris: Gabalda, 1934), *in loc.*

that they do not have to read between the lines; his words are not slippery or full of double meanings.

1:14 - *just as you partially did understand us, that we are your reason to be proud as you also are ours, in the day of the Lord Jesus.*

Just as you also partially did understand us - Verse 14 continues the sentence begun in verse 13: "I hope you will understand [fully] just as part of you did understand us." "Partially" (literally, "in part") likely means that part of the congregation understood Paul's sincerity and consistency,[57] though there was a small faction that denied it. The source of Paul's knowledge about the majority's views would have come from the report Titus recently made to Paul (7:5-16). As the sentence continues, the topic shifts from their understanding of what he wrote to their understanding of him.

That we are your reason to be proud - The majority of the church were proud of Paul. They admit he is an apostle and his message and his preaching are straightforward and come from God.

As you also are ours - Paul tells them he is proud of the faithful majority. Elsewhere in 2 Corinthians he again indicates his pride in them (7:14; 8:24; 9:3,4). He says they are his letters of recommendation (3:2). He will even feel this pride on the day of the Lord. They were the fruit of his apostleship.

In the day of our Lord Jesus - In the LXX, the expression "day of the Lord" is frequent in the Old Testament prophets. Ultimately, the reference is to the final judgment (2 Peter 3:10). Concerning the Christians at Thessalonica, Paul could say "for who is our hope or joy or crown of exultation? Is it not even you, in the presence of our Lord Jesus at His coming? For you are our glory and joy" (1 Thessalonians 2:19,20). He encouraged the Philippians to hold fast the word of life "so that in the day of Christ I may have cause to glory because I did not run in vain nor toil in vain" (Philippians 2:16). As Paul thinks of Christ's return, he pictures himself proud to see the Corinthians present and being ushered into glory. There is an implication here that there will be recognition of loved ones in Heaven. Paul would know the Corinthians and be proud of them.

1:15 - *And in this confidence I intended at first to come to you, that you might twice receive a blessing.*

---

[57] It hardly means there is something in me which none of you quite understands, for this would be to admit the charge the Judaizers were making that he wrote cleverly to conceal the truth of his intentions and actions.

And in this confidence - The words stand first in the Greek to give them great emphasis. He refers to the understanding of the majority of the church at Corinth (verse 15). What has now been said about their relationship paves the way for his explanation of his change of travel plans.

I intended at first to come to you - The verb "intended" is an imperfect tense in the Greek, indicating continuous action in the past time. We might give the words "at first" the meaning of "originally."[58] The travel plans as originally made (see verse 16) included four trips: (1) a direct trip by sea from Ephesus to Corinth, (2) a land trip from Corinth to Macedonia, (3) a return trip to Corinth to spend some time with them, and (4) a trip from Corinth to Judea with the offering for the poor at Jerusalem. Paul's original plans were to visit Corinth twice. When he wrote 1 Corinthians 16:5-9, he had already modified his original plan by deciding to go into Macedonia first. This change of plan was the basis for the Judaizers' slander that Paul could not make up his mind (verse 18).[59]

That you might twice receive a blessing - Two planned visits; two opportunities to bestow a blessing. "Blessing" translates *charin*, the word for "grace."[60] This is not boastfulness; it is a conscious statement of what an apostle of Jesus could do. Paul, filled as he was with the power of the Holy Spirit, was able to impart to his converts spiritual gifts (Romans 1:11, 15:29). That would be one way many of them would receive a blessing. Before this paragraph is finished, Paul will insist that he did not make his plans as worldly men planned (verse 17) but as a man with a commission from God (verse 21) would make his plans.

1:16 – *that is, to pass your way into Macedonia, and again from Macedonia to come to you, and by you be helped on my journey to Judea.*

That is, to pass your way into Macedonia - As detailed above, Paul's original plan was to pass through Corinth on his way to Macedonia. Macedonia in Romans times was a huge province, having Achaia on the south, Thrace and Dalmatia on the north, the Adriatic Sea on the west, and the Aegean Sea on the east.

And again from Macedonia to come to you - This was to be the second of his planned visits to Corinth.

---

[58] Kirsopp Lake, *The Earlier Epistles of St. Paul* (London: Rivington, 1927), p.226.

[59] There is no objection in this verse to the idea that an "intermediate visit" was made by Paul to Corinth since the writing of 1 Corinthians. After he had changed his plans to only one visit, he was led by circumstances to make the intermediate visit, on which, as has been shown, he was unable to impart any "benefit" at that time.

[60] There is a manuscript variation at this place.   *Charan* ("joy") is supported by Aleph[3],B,L,P,Thdrt.   *Charin* ("grace, blessing") is supported by Aleph*,A,C,D,E,F,G,K,Latt.

And by you to be helped on my journey to Judea - "Helped on my journey" (*propempein*) "is a technical term for the support of a missionary" which involved providing "food, money, and a means of travel."[61]   The purpose of the trip to Judea was to carry the offering raised by the churches of the Gentiles to the poor saints at Jerusalem (see Romans 15:25,26; 1 Corinthians 16:3,4; 2 Corinthians 8 and 9).

1:17 - *Therefore, I was not vacillating when I intended to do this, was I? Or that which I purpose, do I purpose according to the flesh, that with me there should be yes, yes and no, no at the same time?*

Therefore, I was not vacillating when I intended to do this, was I? - The Corinthians have been aware of his change of plans since they had read 1 Corinthians 16:5-9.   The Judaizers have jumped on this change of plans to make the accusation that you could never depend on what Paul says.   "Vacillating" translates *elaphria* which means, not to change one's mind, but to give no thought to something.   It pictures a man who makes promises without even thinking whether or not he can do what he promised.   The question is so worded in the Greek that it expects a negative answer.   Certainly the Corinthians did not think his change of travel plans was the result of acting on impulse rather than with careful forethought.

Or, that which I purpose - The previous question was written with a past tense verb that referred to a particular incident.   This verb is a present tense indicating what was habitual, covering his life as a whole.   'When I make my plans,' is the idea.

Do I purpose according to the flesh? - Men who do not have the Spirit of God to guide them make their plans "according to the flesh."   'Do I make my plans from worldly motives so as to suit my own convenience and selfish interest?'   Again, a negative answer is expected by the Greek wording.

**That with me there should be yes, yes and no, no *at the same time?* - *Hina* ("that") may express result at this place.   'Is it true with me, as the Judaizers have charged, that you can never depend on what I say?   Do I really say "yes" out of one side of my mouth, and "no" out of the other, all at the same time?'   In the Greek there is a "the" before "yes" and "no."[62]   Perhaps it points to something one of Paul's detractors has said.   May we picture one of the Judaizers quoting the Sermon on the Mount (Matthew 5:37; see James 5:12) and asking, "with a sneer, when the first epistle came

---

[61] Thompson, *op. cit.*, p.27. Compare Acts 15:3, 20:38 and 1 Corinthians 16:6-11.

[62] This verse has been interpreted to mean that Paul was accused of being headstrong and inflexible.   When he says "the yes" it is going to be "yes," and when he says "the no" it is going to be "no."   However, Paul has not been charged with being obstinate, but of being unthinking ("vacillating") as he makes his plans.

and showed that the original plan had been abandoned, whether Paul's actions were in harmony with Jesus' teaching."[63]   Paul, in the following verses, contends that although his plans changed, yet his principles did not; He was always loyal to the gospel and to his converts. He was not unprincipled in his dealing with them; his change of plans resulted from his desire to spare them (2 Corinthians 1:23, 2:1,2).

1:18 – *But as God is faithful, our word to you is not yes and no.*

But as God is faithful - Before he explains his change in travel plans (as he does in 1:23-2:4), Paul stops to state positively why his speech and writing had to be nothing but pure, holy truth, with no deception.   God had something to do with what an apostle spoke and wrote.   "Faithful"[64] is "a special attribute of God.   It means that God can be relied upon, that one can take Him at His word."[65]   In other instances where God's faithfulness is spoken of (e.g., 1 Corinthians 1:9, 10:13; 1 Thessalonians 5:24; 2 Thessalonians 3:3; Hebrews 10:23, 11:11; 1 John 1:9) the statement is followed by some act that God can be counted on to do.

Our word to you is not yes and no - Paul, the apostle, is here making a claim to inspiration.   His word to them is not simply human in origin, and is not inconsistent with itself (it "is not yes and no" at the same time).   The next verse shows that Paul's "word" includes his preaching of Jesus, and by parity of reasoning, his writing of letters like 1 and 2 Corinthians.

1:19 – *For the Son of God, Christ Jesus, who was preached among you by us – by me and Silvanus and Timothy – was not yes and no, but yes in Him.*

For the Son of God - "For" makes verse 19 a reason for something just said, namely that God is faithul.[66]   The same faithful God who moved Paul's preached word is the God who sent His Son.   The Son was not and could not be inconsistent.   In the lan-

---

[63] Plumptre, *op. cit.*, p.15. Plumptre also calls attention to the fact that this passage is of interest as being indirectly a reference to our Lord's teaching, showing, like Acts 20:35, that the words of the Lord Jesus were habitually cited as rules of life.

[64] The KJV reads "as God is true," but the Greek is better translated "as God is faithful."   This phrase is not an oath calling on God as his witness.   "The expression does not have the formal form of an oath in the Greek" (Fisher, *op. cit.*, p.292).

[65] Fisher, *ibid.*

[66] The Greek word order throws emphasis on "of God."

guage "Son of God" there is an assertion of Jesus' deity (cp. John 5:18).[67]

Christ Jesus - As explained in comments on verse 1, "Christ Jesus" is an affirmation that the One known as Jesus of Nazareth is the long promised Messiah.

Who was preached among you by us - "Was preached," a past tense verb, refers to the time when the church was planted at Corinth. "Preached" (*kēruchtheis*) means heralded. It is a regular word for preaching the gospel (1 Corinthians 1:23, 15:12; 2 Corinthians 4:5, 11:4; Philippians 1:15; 1 Timothy 3:16).

By me and Silvanus and Timothy - Paul here names who he means "by us." The three men here named were fellow-workers on the first visit to Corinth (Acts 18:5). A comparison of this verse with Acts 18:5 shows that "Silvanus" and "Silas" are the same person. Paul is here talking about inspiration being the evidence of the truthfulness of what is written or spoken. Since Silas is called a "prophet" in Acts 15:32, he, too, could speak by Holy Spirit inspiration. Timothy likewise evidently could speak by inspiration, ever since he had received a gift by the laying on of Paul's hands (2 Timothy 1:6). The testimony of all three preachers was consistent. Paul and his helpers spoke pure, holy truth because they were so led to speak by the God who is faithful.

Was not yes and no, but is yes in Him - Have the Judaizers, who preached "another Jesus" (2 Corinthians 11:4) made an affirmation that the Jesus who was crucified and rose from the dead was not deity, was not the promised Messiah, and was inconsistent in His message and actions? That Paul makes the three assertions he does in this verse seems to point in that direction. The "Son of God, Christ Jesus ... was not yes and no." He was not inconsistent during His earthly ministry. "Is" translates a perfect tense verb, signifying past completed action with present continuing results. Paul can affirm Jesus is (always has been, always will be) "yes" because "Jesus Christ is the same yesterday and today, yes and forever" (Hebrews 13:8).

1:20 – *For as many as may be the promises of God, in Him they are yes, wherefore also by Him is our Amen to the glory of God through us.*

---

[67] Paul often refers to Jesus as the "Son" (1 Corinthians 1:9, 15:28; 1 Thessalonians 1:10; Galatians 1:10, 4:4,6; Romans 1:3,9, 5:10, 8:3,29,32; Colossians 1:13). The term has several senses or emphases. Sometimes it is used in its *official* sense. That is, there is emphasis on the fact that Jesus is deity, co-equal with the Father. The word "Son" is used all through the book of Hebrews in this official sense. Sometimes the word "Son" is used in what is called its *ethical* sense. This means that Jesus held the same views and ideas as did the Father. There was a perfect union, absolute intimacy, and a mutual knowledge between the Father and the Son. Perhaps Matthew 11:27 is an example of this ethical use of the designation "Son." Again, the word "Son" is sometimes used in its *metaphysical* sense. When this emphasis seems intended, there is reference to Jesus' incarnation. We do not call Jesus "Son" because God the Father had a "baby" back in eternity before creation, nor does the term "Son" indicate that Jesus is less than co-eternal with the Father (John 1:1). Here in 2 Corinthians 1:19, "Son" is used in its *official* sense.

For as many as may be the promises of God, in Him they are yes - "For" introduces an explanation of in Him is "yes" (verse 19). In the context of 2 Corinthians, where Judaizers were attempting to require Gentile converts to Judaize, the "promises of God" would be the Old Testament promises that when Messiah came, He would bring salvation to all men, Jews and Gentiles (Romans 15:8,9); this salvation to all men is conditioned on faithfulness to God's revelation ("the righteous shall live by faith," Habakkuk 2:4; Romans 1:17 ASV). That Jesus is the "yes" to these promises means that in Him the promises have their fulfillment. He is the ultimate fulfillment of the history of redemption (Hebrews 1:1-4), God's last message to mankind. "He is the mediator of a new covenant in order that since a death has taken place for the redemption of transgressions that were committed under the first covenant, those who have been called may receive the promise of the eternal inheritance" (Hebrews 9:15). This new covenant is the thing the Judaizers failed to recognize.

Wherefore also by Him is our Amen[68] - The fact that there is no verb in this clause in the Greek has given rise to numerous attempts at translation. Interpretations of the Greek may be summarized under two options: (1) Christians are saying the "Amen" in their public worship assembly (1 Corinthians 4:16);[69] (2) The truthfulness of Paul's preaching is found in Christ Jesus, the Son of God.[70]

To the glory of God through us - "Glory" says that God is made to look good and is getting the praise He deserves. The context tells us that the words "through us" refer to the preachers (Paul, Silvanus, and Timothy) rather than to the hearers of the word. God gets glory, Paul says, through us gospel preachers; the implication is He gets no glory through the teaching of the Judaizers.

1:21 – *Now He who establishes us with you in Christ and anointed us is God*

Now He who establishes us with you in Christ - "Us with you (*sun humin*, in company with you)" indicates that God's establishing is something Paul and his Corinthian readers share in common. The Greek behind "in Christ" is *eis Christon*, "into Christ." God had something to do with both Paul and   the Corinthians becoming Christians

---

[68] This verse in the NASB reads differently than it does in the KJV because there is a manuscript variation.

[69] "Amen" comes from the Hebrew word which means "truth"; it has an affinity with the Hebrew verb which means "to confirm" (R.V.G. Tasker, *The Second Epistle of Paul to the Corinthians* in the Tyndale New Testament Commentaries [Grand Rapids: Eerdmans, 1971], p.48). When spoken by men in response to something preached, the word "Amen" denotes acceptance of the teaching. Perhaps the point in this context is that the Corinthians once expressed acceptance of the preaching of Paul, Silvanus, and Timothy. That being true, it is not Paul but rather some of the Corinthians who have proven to be inconsistent.

[70] Jesus often is reported to have said "Verily, verily (Amen, Amen) I say unto you ...." It was Jesus' way of declaring to His listeners "the absolute authority and immutability of His teachings" (Coffman, *op. cit.*, p.315).

("into Christ"). Scriptures everywhere speak of God's initiative in salvation. "God causes the growth" (1 Corinthians 3:7). The Corinthians were "God's field, God's building" (1 Corinthians 3:9). "He (God) brought us forth by the word of truth that we might be as it were the first fruits among his creatures" (James 1:18). "Establishes" is a present participle, indicating a continuous action of God in the lives of Christians. "Paul wanted to penetrate behind the squabbles of the church to the spiritual realities that made it a church. The Corinthians need to have their attention called to the unique character of their religion and to realize that both they and Paul shared a common spiritual foundation of life."[71]

And anointed us - The "with you" is not carried on to this clause. "Anointed" is something Paul claims for himself and his fellow preachers.[72] It was not something the church members at Corinth had received. The background of the expression "anointed" is the Old Testament custom of anointing prophets, priests, and kings to their office. The act consisted of a pouring of oil on the head, which indicated the anointed person had been divinely set apart to that office. "Christ" ("anointed," in the previous phrase) is the noun form of the participle here translated "anointed." Paul is claiming for himself and his fellow preachers who were specially gifted by the Spirit (verse 20) an anointing which Christ Himself shared, namely, the power of the Holy Spirit (Acts 10:38). Paul is in the midst of giving evidence of the truthfulness of what he has written. He claims an anointing as one of the evidences. We immediately think of the baptism of the Holy Spirit which conferred special powers on the apostles,[73] or (in the case of Silas and Timothy) of the spiritual gifts that certain men received by the laying on of an apostle's hands (Acts 8:17).[74] The aorist tense "anointed" points "to the time when the gospel preachers (verse 20) were set apart for missionary work."[75]

---

[71] Fisher, *op. cit.*, p.293.

[72] Some treat "anointing" in 1 John 2:20,27 as a confirmation that all Christians, not just Paul and his fellow missionaries, receive an anointing. However, in that place, the Greek word "anointing" is *chrisma*; ending in *-ma* the word emphasizes the result of an anointing which the apostles had received. The words of the apostles, the result of such an anointing, is why the readers of John's epistle know all things.

[73] Paul claims the same "empowerment" that was given to the apostles on the day of Pentecost. Paul even uses the same word for "power" ("strengthened" in the NASB) at 1 Timothy 1:12 that is used at Acts 1:8 when Jesus promised His apostles they would "receive power."

[74] Certain charismatics have recently begun talking about how some singers and speakers are "anointed" for their particular ministry. They seem to suppose that today's leaders have the same outpouring of the Spirit that the apostles and New Testament prophets had, an idea that has been seriously called into question both by what Paul has written in 2 Corinthians 1:21, and by what he wrote in 1 Corinthians 12-14 (on which see the comments in the author's *New Testament Epistles: 1 Corinthians*).

[75] Plummer, *op. cit.*, p.39.

Is God - The implication is that God had not established the Judaizers into Christ, nor had God anointed the Judaizers.

1:22 - *who also sealed us and gave us the Spirit in our hearts as a pledge.*

Who also sealed us - "Also" says that Paul and his fellow preachers had a measure of the Holy Spirit in addition to the anointing. Folk who become Christians receive the seal, but only God's special workers received the anointing. In Old Testament times, Abraham "received the sign of circumcision as the seal of the righteousness of faith which he had" (Romans 4:11). In New Testament times, the Holy Spirit is the Christian's seal (Ephesians 1:13,14, 4:30; cp. Revelation 7:3, 9:4, 14:1). Seals[76] in the ancient world proclaimed ownership, and the indwelling Holy Spirit shows that the person belongs to God (2 Timothy 2:19). That measure of the Holy Spirit called the indwelling of the Holy Spirit (Romans 8:9-11) is the seal. "Sealed" is an aorist tense pointing to one act in the past; this is something that happens to all who are baptized (Acts 2:38). The same thing is taught in Ephesians 1:13 which reads "when you believed in Him, you were sealed with the Holy Spirit of promise" (NASB mg.).

And gave us the Spirit in our hearts as a pledge - The aorist tense participles indicate that the sealing and giving took place at the same time, at the time a person is immersed into Christ. The "Spirit in our hearts" refers to the manifestation of the Spirit called the indwelling of the Holy Spirit.[77] While 1 Corinthians 6:19 says the Christian's body is a temple of the Holy Spirit which is in him, this verse says the Holy Spirit is in their hearts (that is, in their minds). A "pledge" (the word appears again at 2 Corinthians 5:5) was a deposit, a first installment, a down payment, a portion of the full price, a promise that full payment will be made. A "pledge" means more to come. Romans 8:23 uses the language "first fruits of the Spirit" as a promise of a glorified resurrection body. Romans 8:11 says that "He who raised Christ Jesus from the dead will also give life to your mortal bodies through His Spirit who indwells you." The Judaizers' ministry was not able to impart the gift of the Holy Spirit (Galatians 3:2, where "works of the Law" was the Judaizers' plea; there was no Holy Spirit connected with that).[78]

---

[76] In its literal sense, a "seal" was melted wax placed on a document; and then while still warm, a signet ring would be used to give an imprint to the wax. A good example would be the seals found on ancient papyri.

[77] The New Testament refers to different measures of Holy Spirit. The baptism of Holy Spirit empowered an apostle to do the work to which he was called (Acts 1:8). The gift of the Holy Spirit (Acts 2:38), His indwelling, was intended to help a man live the Christian life (Romans 8:13-17). Miraculous spiritual gifts (1 Corinthians 12:8-11,28), given by the laying on of an apostle's hands (Acts 8:17,18), were for the edification of the local congregation (1 Corinthians 14:4,5,17).

[78] The mention of God, Christ, and the Holy Spirit in this paragraph is noteworthy. Paul's language is in harmony with the triune personalities in the Godhead.

1:23 - *But I call God as witness to my soul, that to spare you I came no more to Corinth.*

But - Having shown that Holy Spirit inspiration made it impossible that an apostle like Paul made his plans or preached without giving thought to it (verse 17), from this verse through 2:4 he now reveals his true motive for his change in travel plans.

I call God as witness - The pronoun "I" is emphatic in the Greek.   Paul disassociates himself from his fellow-workers as he explains his change of plans.   Calling God as a witness (see also Romans 1:9, Philippians 1:8) is tantamount to taking an oath.   He makes a similar adjuration in 2 Corinthians 11:31.[79]

To my soul - The Greek reads "upon my soul" or "upon my life."[80]   That makes this verse "a conditional curse which Paul pronounces on himself."[81]   If he is lying about the real reason for his change of travel plans, he calls on God to punish him accordingly.

That to spare you - This is the reason Paul changed his travel plans.   Had he come immediately, he would have had to punish the unrepentant and disobedient.   He would have had to exercise apostolic discipline, which can be severe (13:10).   His delay gave them time to repent.   Then he would not have to use the rod (1 Corinthians 4:21).   "Many of Paul's opponents jumped on his change of plans to accuse him of being so weak that he would not exercise apostolic discipline (10:10).   Here and at 13:10 Paul assures his readers that, as a last resort, he can exercise his authority in a very stern way."[82]

I came no more to Corinth - This language "no more," and "again" in 2:1, harmonizes with the fact Paul made an intermediate trip to Corinth.   He was determined not to make another painful visit to Corinth.   He knew firsthand their rebellion against him, so he had sent Titus to try to lead them to repentance.   Had he come before they had been given that opportunity, his only option would have been

---

[79] When Jesus said, "Swear not at all" (Matthew 5:34 KJV), He was not prohibiting all oath taking.   Jesus, Himself, when on trial, answered under oath (Matthew 26:63), and God Himself on one occasion "interposed with an oath" (Hebrews 6:13,17).   Paul understood Jesus' rule, "Let your statement be, 'Yes, yes,' or 'No, no'" (Matthew 5:37) as teaching that a Christian's words are to be so consistently truthful that he needs take no oath to get people to believe him.   Jesus' prohibition against taking oaths (Matthew 5:33) is not an absolute rule.

[80] Alfred Marshall, *The Interlinear Greek-English New Testament* (London: Samuel Bagster and Sons, 1959), p.710.

[81] Thompson, *op. cit.*, p.30.   Not everyone agrees that this verse is a conditional curse. Instead, it is thought Paul is saying that God knows all the thoughts and intents of his heart. (Compare 1 Corinthians 4:5, and Revelation 2:23 where Christ says He is the One who searches the minds and hearts of men.)   However, such a claim would not be subject to verification by the Corinthians as would the conditional curse.

[82] Thompson, *op. cit.*, p.30.

not to spare them, and that would cause him sorrow (2:3).

1:24 - *Not that we lord it over your faith, but are workers with you for your joy; for in your faith you are standing firm.*

Not that we lord it over your faith - Realizing the Corinthians might draw a wrong conclusion from what he has just written about wanting to "spare" them (verse 23), Paul plainly states his motives.   "Faith comes by hearing the word of Christ" (Romans 10:17), and is something that is voluntary on each person's part.   It is not something that can be coerced, and Paul was not trying to violate their freedom of will.   "Servants and stewards of Christ" (1 Corinthians 4:1) try to awaken interest in the gospel, and encourage a positive response.   They do not act like tyrants or try to domineer.   Apostles did have power over the churches, but it was in matters of discipline, not of faith; he could not force them to believe or disbelieve anything.   In matters of faith, he was not a dictator but a fellow helper of their joy.

But are workers with you for your joy - "We are workers with you" is a direct contrast to the idea he wanted to lord it over them.   What Paul and the Corinthians were both working for was their joy.   This is why he changed his travel plans; he wanted them to have joy, not grief.   Paul's prayer, "may the God of hope fill you with all joy and peace in believing, that you may abound in hope by the power of the Holy Spirit" (Romans 15:13), was written in a context concerning how Jewish Christians and Gentile Christians are to live in harmony with each other.   When the Corinthians learn to do this, they will be happy in their faith.

For in your faith you are standing firm - A better translation of the Greek would be "for by faithfulness you stand."[83]   "Standing firm" is a perfect tense verb; this is how you stood in the past, and this is how you may continue to stand firm, namely, by your faithfulness.   If they are faithful to the gospel Paul and his helpers have preached to them (verse 19), they will have joy.   Paul teaches them what the Lord expects; it is up to them to be faithful.   A majority of the congregation has been faithful; a minority will be called on to repent and change their behavior in this letter. If they change, then they will stand firm in the Christian religion.   "Therefore having been justified by faith, we have peace with God through our Lord Jesus Christ; through whom also we have obtained our introduction by faith into this grace in which we stand" (Romans 5:1,2).[84]

---

[83] Compare the interlinear translation "for by faith you stand firm" in Marshall, *ibid.*

[84] The chapter break here is right in the middle of Paul's line of thought.   It would have been better to have made it between 1:22 and 1:23 or between 2:4 and 2:5.

2:1 – *But I determined this for my own sake, that I would not come to you in sorrow again.*

But I determined this for my own sake - 2:1-4 continues the sequence of thought begun at 1:23.[1] "But" introduces a second reason for the change in his travel plans. (For the first reason, see 1:15,16.)[2] His second reason was to spare them sorrow (verse 2) and to avoid sorrow for himself (verse 3). The singular "I" indicates the decision was Paul's own and did not depend on his fellow-workers, Silas and Timothy. The verb *ekrina* ("determined") excludes any possibility he was "vacillating" (1:17). The verb speaks of thinking a matter over carefully before a conclusion is reached.[3] The demonstrative pronoun "this" points to what follows.

That I would not come to you in sorrow again - The Greek word order is, literally, "not again in sorrow to you to come." Expositors have debated the meaning for years. This commentator's judgment is that the phrase means Paul has already made one sorrowful visit to Corinth; he determined he was not going to make another.[4] That is why he changed his travel plans. "If he was to cooperate with them to further their joy, he had to decide against another visit that would bring pain."[5] Whose "sorrow" Paul has in mind is explained in verse 2 as being theirs, and in verse 3 as being his. *Lupē* can be translated "sorrow, pain, grief"[6] and speaks not of physical pain in this place, but of mental anguish and turmoil.

---

[1] In the remainder of the chapter, Paul first encourages loving concern for the penitent offender who had been disciplined (2:5-11), and then introduces how he waited for Titus to bring news of how things were going at Corinth and how thankful he was for the good report (2:12-17).

[2] Some manuscripts (P46, B) read "but"; some (*Aleph*,A,C,D,G,K,P) read "for," making 2:1 an explanation of why he gave up the idea of coming to Corinth first, before going to Macedonia. The evidence is about evenly divided. Our comments are based on the reading chosen by the NASB translators.

[3] Verse 3 below must be studied carefully before a decision can be made concerning just when Paul made this determination.

[4] In the Introductory Studies, considerable attention was given to "the travels of Paul and his companions." Briefly, one decision was that regardless of how little we know about such an intermediate trip, the plain meaning of 2 Corinthians 12:14 and 13:1 is that Paul has made two trips to Corinth before he wrote 2 Corinthians. The intermediate trip is a trip about which Luke in Acts gives no record. Another decision was that the trip was made in the interval between the writing of 1 Corinthians and 2 Corinthians. The silence of Luke with regard to the intermediate trip should not be used as evidence that Luke and Paul contradict each other, and therefore, one or the other cannot be believed. Instead of so arguing and impinging on inspiration, it is important to note that Luke's record is not intended to be all-encompassing; for example, he does not record the fact that Paul wrote letters to the churches he established.

[5] Fisher, *op. cit.*, p.296.

[6] Joseph Henry Thayer, *A Greek-English Lexicon of the New Testament* (New York: American Book Co., 1889), p.383.

2:2 - *For if I cause you sorrow, who then makes me glad but the one whom I made sorrowful?*

For if I cause you sorrow - "For" introduces one reason why he decided against another sorrowful visit. The "I" is singular; Paul speaks of himself causing sorrow. The way the if-clause is written in the Greek, "if" assumes he would have had to make someone (or several some ones) at Corinth sorrowful had he followed his original travel plans.

Who then makes me glad - Paul's gladness was contingent on their being faithful (1:24). He could have no gladness if he had to discipline one or more of the Corinthians. As a result of the discipline the apostle might administer, they would be in sorrow, and so would he because he had to administer it.

But the one whom I made sorrowful? - Both "who" (previous clause) and "the one" are singular. The singular refers to any person in Corinth he has to discipline.[7]

2:3 - *And this is the very thing I wrote you, lest, when I come, I should have sorrow from those who ought to make me rejoice: having confidence in you all, that my joy would be* the joy *of you all.*

And this is the very thing I wrote you - The interpretation of "this ... very thing" depends on how "I wrote" is interpreted. "I wrote" (*egrapsa*) is an aorist tense, and may be construed either as an historical aorist or as an epistolary aorist.[8] In this commentator's judgment *egrapsa* should be treated as epistolary and would be equivalent of "I am writing."[9] "This ... very thing" thus refers to the sorrow he was seeking to avoid, which had been the reason Paul revised his travel plans.

Lest, when I come - The revised travel plans as announced in 1 Corinthians 16:5-9 are still Paul's intended itinerary (even though he has since made an unplanned "inter-

---

[7] The dual singulars "who" and "one" do not refer to the offender (see 1 Corinthians 5:1-8) because that discipline problem was a thing of the past when 2 Corinthians was written (see 2 Corinthians 2:6,7).

[8] See notes in the author's *New Testament Epistles: 1 Corinthians*, at 1 Corinthians 5:9 for details concerning historical and epistolary aorists. The historical aorist, if that is what *egrapsa* is at this place, would refer to a letter written before 2 Corinthians. Philip E. Hughes (*Paul's Second Epistle to the Corinthians* [Grand Rapids: Eerdmans, 1962], p.56) tells us that older commentators generally assumed that the letter we know as 1 Corinthians is what Paul here makes reference to, and in particular the announcement in 1 Corinthians 16:5-9 concerning his change in travel plans. In more recent times, higher critics have postulated that Paul wrote some letters to Corinth that are now lost. It is rather common to read that Paul has reference to a "severe letter" he wrote to Corinth, a letter now lost. See this discussed in the Introductory Studies under the topic "Other Critical Matters."

[9] The epistolary aorist looks at the letter from the standpoint of the readers. When they actually read this letter, the time of its writing was in the past, hence "I wrote."

mediate trip" to Corinth). His plans still are to visit Macedonia, and then come to Corinth for an extended visit, just as he said he would. He is writing this letter to prepare them for his coming visit which he hopes will be joyful.

I should have sorrow from those who ought to make me rejoice - He is writing 2 Corinthians to mend broken relationships between himself and the church (3:1-7:16), and to call for repentance from those who needed to repent (10:1-13:10). If those things occur, Paul will be able to rejoice when he makes his next visit.

Having confidence in you all - These words not only express his confidence but they also "contain a subtle invitation for them to make it true. He refused to believe that the Corinthians would want it any other way."[10] His anticipation was that those who were living immorally (2 Corinthians 12:21) and those who were embracing Judaizing tendencies (13:1-4) would repent rather than require the apostolic discipline he could and would administer if needed.

That my joy would be *the joy* of you all - The "joy of you all" is the same joy he alluded to in 1:24. If they acted positively on his instructions, he will have joy (he will be "glad," 2:2). As a result their next meeting will be one of mutual joy. That is why Paul altered his travel plans and is writing this letter before his next visit.

2:4 - *For out of much affliction and anguish of heart I wrote to you with many tears; not that you would be sorrowful, but that you might know the love which I have especially for you.*

For out of much affliction and anguish of heart - "For" introduces Paul's explanation why he had the confidence he did that they might have mutual joy. He here bares his emotional state as he writes to tell them he loves them. "Affliction" can speak either of physical pressure or mental anguish caused by outside factors. The situation at Corinth is what caused this affliction. "Anguish of heart" speaks either of the mental concern Paul felt as he wrote, or it can refer to the pressure that great emotion causes on the human heart.[11]

I wrote to you with many tears - "I wrote," as the same word was treated in verse 3, should be considered to be an epistolary aorist. Paul is referring to this very letter he is now writing. Concern for the welfare of his converts often caused Paul great

---

[10] Fisher, *op. cit.*, p.297

[11] *Sunochē* refers to the tight pressure felt around the heart that great grief can cause (A.T. Robertson, *Word Pictures in the New Testament* [Nashville: Broadman, 1931], Vol. 4, p.31). Since the word "anguish" is used only by Luke and Paul in the New Testament, some think it is one example of Luke's medical terminology adapted by Paul to express his feelings. "Anguish" was the medical term to describe a tight pressure or constriction of the heart.

heartbreak. Rehearsing his ministry at Ephesus to the Ephesian elders, Paul reminded them that "night and day for a period of three years I did not cease to admonish each one of you with tears" (Acts 20:31). Grant the unity of 2 Corinthians, and we have in chapters 1-7 and 10-13 plenty that would cause a writer anguish and tears.[12]

Not that you should be made sorrowful - He is not trying to make them feel sorry that their behavior had caused him anguish. Had he not written the next line, that may well have been the result of his letter.

But that you might know the love which I have especially for you - Here he tells the Corinthians the real reason he was writing this letter: he wanted them to know how much he loved them. In the Greek, "love" is placed first for emphasis and "for you" comes at the end of the sentence for emphasis.[13] "Love" (*agapē*) is willfully doing what is spiritually best for the other person, whatever it may cost to do it.[14] While Paul also loved the Philippian Christians (Philippians 1:7), the Corinthians had a special place in his heart. "He could have spared himself the tears; he could have come at once to deal with them harshly. He did neither. He wrote the letter and gave them time to repent because he loved them."[15]

2. With Regard to the Treatment of the Offender. 2:5-11

Summary: We are still in the midst of Paul's review of his recent relations with Corinth. First, he defended his conduct with regard to a change in his travel plans (1:12-2:4). Now he defends his conduct with regard to the treatment of the offender, whose sin and the church's toleration of it led to a break in relationship between Paul and the church. But that is past now, and should no longer be the cause of strained relations.

---

[12] It is often said, when the topic of inspiration is being discussed, that inspiration does not keep the personality of the writer from showing through. Here in 2 Corinthians 2:4 is a plain statement where Paul tells us what his personal feelings were as he wrote, and those feelings show through on every page. There are more broken sentences in 2 Corinthians than in any other Pauline letter (as can be seen by observing the number of times words are included in italics in our versions). The most satisfactory reason why Paul wrote such broken sentences is that his heart was full of emotion when he wrote.

[13] "It was the custom of Greek structure to place the word which was to be emphasized first and the word which received the secondary emphasis last" (Fisher, *op. cit.*, p.298).

[14] "True love for any person makes one seek to deliver the loved one from wrong. Sometimes people uphold their husbands, wives, children, and friends in a wrong course, and say they do it from love. This is not true and helpful love. Love says get them right and pure before God, and insists on the discipline needed to purify them. A selfish determination to uphold one's family or friends in a course of wrong is not love. It is really hatred, in a Bible sense of the word" (Lipscomb, *op. cit.*, p.37).

[15] Fisher, *ibid.*

2:5 - *But if any has caused sorrow, he has caused sorrow not to me, but in some degree – in order not to say too much — to all of you.*

But if any has caused sorrow - Here we begin to get some information concerning the trouble in the congregation at Corinth that had caused the change in his travel plans. "Some one" (*tis*) had caused sorrow to Paul and many of the Corinthians.[16] The traditional view is that the person referred to is the incestuous person of 1 Corinthians 5:1-8.[17] Some of the Corinthians, at least, were heartsick at that man's scandalous behavior.

He has caused sorrow not to me - "Not to me" is emphatic and probably means "not to me alone."[18]

But in some degree – in order not to say too much – to all of you -- "In some degree" translates a Greek expression which means "in part."[19] So, "in some degree ... to all of you" can mean either that not all the Corinthians were grieved, or it may mean that all of them were distressed to some extent. In light of verse 6, "this punishment which was inflicted by the majority," perhaps the former option is the correct one. He would have said "too much" were he to affirm that all of them were distressed to some extent.

---

[16] The if-clause in the Greek assumes that he had in fact caused sorrow. *Tis* is an indefinite pronoun. Harris calls attention to Paul's sensitivity: "he avoids naming the culprit (verses 5-8); he recognizes that Christian discipline is not simply retributive but also remedial (verses 6,7); he understands the feelings and psychological needs of the penitent wrong-doer (verses 6-8); he appeals to his own conduct as an example for the Corinthians to follow (verse 10); and he is aware of the divisive operation of Satan within the Christian community (verse 11)." Murray J. Harris, *The Second Epistle to the Corinthians* (Grand Rapids: Eerdmans, 2005), p.222.

[17] See the Introductory Studies concerning the identity of the "offender," and also see notes at 7:11,12. We have noted in the Introductory Studies that some believe the offender of 2 Corinthians 2:5-11 is not the incestuous person of 1 Corinthians 5:1ff, but rather someone (e.g., a Judaizer) who has recently attacked Paul's person and/or work. (See this view defended in Fisher, *op. cit.*, p.298-99; and C.K. Barrett, *Essays on Paul* [Philadelphia: Westminster, 1982], p.87-100). In notes on chapters 10-13 this commentator challenges the idea that verses therein refer to only the leader among the Judaizers. For a defense of the equation that 2 Corinthians 2:5 = 1 Corinthians 5:1-8 see Hughes. *op. cit., in loc.* Throughout the first 19 centuries of the church, the only dissent to the traditional view was Tertullian (*De Pucid.* 13), and it seems likely his denial of the identity of the two was based on dogmatic rather than historical evidence. Tertullian was involved in a controversy about post-baptismal sins being unforgivable (Hebrews 6:4-6). If the offender who is to be forgiven and restored to fellowship in 2 Corinthians 2 is the incestuous person, then Tertullian's position about post-baptismal sins being unforgivable was patently wrong. So, to defend his position, he argued that the two passages are not speaking of the same person.

[18] Fisher, *op. cit.*, p.299.

[19] Marshall, *op. cit.*, p.711, and the ASV.

2:6 - *Sufficient for such a one is this punishment which was* **inflicted** by *the majority,*

Sufficient for such a one is the punishment - Paul's purpose in directing the church to administer discipline had been to save the sinner (1 Corinthians 5:5). Until Titus came to Corinth, the church at first was hesitant to act. He helped guide them to practice church discipline. "Sufficient" indicates the discipline had accomplished its intended purpose. The "punishment"[20] brought the guilty man to end his immoral relationship with his father's wife, to acknowledge his sin, and to come to the congregation with a plea for forgiveness. Now, on the basis of Titus' report to Paul about the Corinthian's action taken in this case (see 7:7-11), Paul counsels the church concerning its next responsibility to the individual in question.

Which was *inflicted by* **the majority** - According to Paul's instructions in 1 Corinthians 5:4,5, the congregation was to have a meeting at which the offender was to be delivered to Satan for the destruction of the flesh. "Inflicted by the majority" indicates that the congregation did meet as instructed, and the majority voted that the discipline should be carried out.[21] The decision was not unanimous; since 2 Corinthians 12:21 indicates that a minority had not yet repented of their "impurity, immorality and sensuality which they have practiced," it would not be unlikely that these were the minority who were not in favor of disciplining the immoral one.

2:7 - *So that on the contrary you should rather forgive and comfort* **him**, *lest somehow such a one be overwhelmed by excessive sorrow.*

So that on the contrary - "On the contrary" means that now, since the offender has repented, something different than continued disciple is called for. There is no need to continue to punish and ostracize[22] him.

You should rather forgive and comfort *him* - "Rather" seems to imply that some in the congregation thought the social ostracism should continue. On the contrary, says Paul, when the disciplined person repents, the duty of the members of the congregation is clear. The forgiveness and comfort extended to the penitent is simply a reflection of what has already been done in heaven ("whatever you loose on

---

[20] The Greek word is *epitimia* ("punishment") and could also be rendered "censure" or "rebuke" (Plumptre, *op. cit.*, p.20).

[21] At the close of comments on chapter 2 is a Special Study titled "A Review of Paul's Instructions Concerning Church Discipline."

[22] "Ostracize" is an attempt to capture what "not even to eat with such a one" (1 Corinthians 5:11) and Jesus' words "let him be to you as a Gentile and a tax-gatherer" (Matthew 18:18) would have entailed.

earth shall have been loosed in heaven," Matthew 18:18[23]). The penitent has been forgiven by Christ (Colossians 3:13); can Christ's followers do less? Ephesians 4:32 ("be kind to one another, tender-hearted, forgiving one another, just as God in Christ also has forgiven you") indicates that past offenses, now forgiven, are not to be a barrier to fellowship. Restoration to fellowship is regarded as favor (the word translated "forgive" is *charisasthai*, from *charis*, favor, grace) offered by the church. "Forgiveness does not mean the offense is forgotten or belittled. It is rather an act of grace."[24] Here, as elsewhere in this epistle, "comfort" (*parakaleō,* to call alongside, to come alongside) carries the idea of encouraging, heartening, strengthening. The church body is to give encouragement and help to the penitent in his or her renewed efforts to live the Christian life.

Lest somehow such a one be overwhelmed by excessive sorrow - For "overwhelmed" the ASV has "swallowed up," which is a literal translation of the Greek. It is a strong figure of speech, perhaps "taken from a whirlpool which seems to swallow up anything that comes within reach. Excessive grief or calamity, in the Scriptures, is often compared to such waters; cp. Psalm 69:1, 124:2-5."[25] Godly sorrow led the man to repentance (2 Corinthians 7:10); if he is not forgiven and comforted his sorrow will likely turn to despair and he will give up any desire to continue being a Christian. He may even return to a reckless indulgence in sin. In 1 Peter 5:8, in a context that likely speaks of Nero's persecution of Christians, it is said that the devil is ever striving to "swallow up" men; that is, the devil put ideas into Nero's head and Nero was doing the devil's bidding. Likewise, if the Christians at Corinth did not forgive and comfort the penitent, they could be doing the work of the devil for him (see verse 11).

2:8 - *Wherefore I urge you to reaffirm* **your** *love for him.*

Wherefore - Since he has repented, and since there is danger of his being overcome by his sorrow, Paul pleads for them to reaffirm their love for him.

I urge you - "Urge" translates *parakaleō*, the same Greek word translated "comfort" in verse 7. Paul recognizes the local autonomy of the congregation at Corinth. So, rather than invoking apostolic authority and commanding them, he pleads with them. It is an appeal to their will. They may choose to heed his exhortation; they may not.

---

[23] The verb is a future perfect passive, and says the binding and loosing done on earth has already or previously been done in heaven.

[24] Fisher, *op. cit.*, p.300.

[25] Albert Barnes, "II Corinthians and Galatians" in *Barnes' Notes on the New Testament* (Grand Rapids: Baker, 1955), p.36.

To reaffirm *your* **love for him** - In Galatians 3:15 the same word here translated "reaffirm" is translated "ratified." One gets the idea that the reaffirmation of the penitent was to be as public an action as was the excommunication that led to repentance. By a public act the whole congregation restores the penitent to fellowship; the ostracism is officially ended.[26]

2:9 - *For to this end also I wrote that I might put you to the test, whether you are obedient in all things.*

For to this end also I wrote - "For" shows this verse is intended to be a reason for the admonition just given in verse 8. As was explained in verses 3 and 4, "I wrote" is to be treated as an epistolary aorist, meaning "I am writing," referring to this very paragraph he is now dictating.[27]

That I might put you to the test - "Test" (*dokimē*) is the word used for testing metals to determine if they are genuine. Paul is making his instructions concerning restoring the penitent a test of whether or not the Corinthian profession of faith is genuine.

Whether you are obedient in all things - The test is whether you will be obedient – be it to Christ (who taught about discipline, Matthew 18:15-18) or to an apostle of Christ and the gospel of Christ which he preaches. Obedience to Christ and the gospel is what Paul wants. Will you be as obedient in restoring as you were in disciplining? "In all things" says there is more for them to be obedient to than the restoration of the penitent. What some of those things are will be unfolded as he writes the next chapters.

---

[26] There are some lessons for us from these verses. We should note here that excommunication and restoration are actions of the church, and not of the officers alone. "The proper time for restoring an offender is only when the punishment has answered the purpose for which it was designed: i.e., the punishment has shown the just abhorrence of the church against the sin, and has caused the offender to repent. How can you tell if a man has repented? When it can be ascertained that the punishment has been effectual in reforming the offender may depend somewhat on the nature of the offence. In this case, it was sufficiently shown by his ceasing relations with his mother-in-law, and by the manifestations of sorrow. So in other cases, it may be shown by a man's abandoning a course of sin, and reforming his life. If he has been unjust, by his repairing the evil; if he has been pursuing an unlawful business, by abandoning it; if he has pursued a course of vice, by his forsaking it; and by giving satisfactory evidences of sorrow and of reformation, for a period sufficiently long to show his sincerity. How long must a man be repentant, before he is restored to fellowship? The time which will be required in each case must depend, of course, somewhat on the nature of the offence, the previous character of the individual, the temptations to which he may be exposed, and the disgrace which he may have brought on his Christian calling" (Barnes, *op. cit.*, p.35). A helpful resource is Earl and Sanday Wilson, *Restoring the Fallen* (Downers Grove, IL: InterVarsity, 1997).

[27] Those who take it as an historical aorist cannot agree on whether it refers to 1 Corinthians or to some hypothetical severe letter. J.H. Bernard, "The Second Epistle to the Corinthians" in *Expositor's Greek Testament* (Grand Rapids: Eerdmans, 1967), Vol. 3, p.49, is one who thinks 2 Corinthians 2:9 points to 1 Corinthians. Plummer (*op. cit.*, p.61) is one who writes at length concerning a severe letter. Neither are convincing as they to reconstruct how either of those options was a test of the Corinthians' obedience.

2:10 - *But one whom you forgive anything, I* forgive *also; for indeed what I have forgiven, if I have forgiven anything, I* did it *for your sakes in the presence of Christ,*

But one whom you forgive anything, I *forgive* **also** - In order to show the connection of verse 10 with verse 9, the Greek word *de* should be translated "and" rather than "but." "One whom" is another anonymous reference to the penitent brother. "I forgive" says "anyone who has your forgiveness has mine, too" (NEB). In fact, as the next clause shows, he had already forgiven the penitent man.

For indeed what I have forgiven, if I have forgiven anything - We may assume that when he heard from Titus that the incestuous man had repented (2 Corinthians 7:6,7), at that moment Paul forgave him. There are several places in the manuscripts the readings for this clause differ, but the NEB may have caught the idea with "so far as there is anything for me to forgive." "He is not suggesting a doubt as to whether he has granted forgiveness, but he puts the fact of there being something for him to forgive as a mere hypothesis."[28]

I *did it* **for your sakes in the presence of Christ** - One reason Paul has taken the action he has was for their benefit. Verse 11 will explain what the benefit is. "In the presence of Christ" is, literally, "in the face of Christ," the mental image being that Christ was looking on as Paul acted. Paul forgave not only for their benefit, but so that he might please Christ who was watching.[29]

2:11 - *In order that no advantage be taken of us by Satan; for we are not ignorant of his schemes.*

In order that no advantage be taken of us by Satan - The sentence begun in verse 10, "I did it for your sakes ...," is continued in this verse. Paul took the action he did in order to defeat the devil. Of the various designations for the evil one found in the New Testament, four are found in 2 Corinthians: "Satan" (2:1), "the serpent" (11:3),

---

[28] Plummer, *op. cit.*, p.62. The apostles were given the power of binding and loosing (Matthew 18:18; John 20:23). Paul here asserts that authority himself, for he, too, is an apostle of Jesus, just as much as the twelve were. He has "loosed" because heaven already had; now the Corinthians should act toward the penitent as if they recognized that were true.

[29] "In the presence of Christ" has been variously explained. Literally it reads "in the face of Christ." By the authority of Christ, is one suggestion. Acting "as Christ's representative" is the way the NEB translates it. It must be pointed out that in the Douay version (Fort Wayne, IN: George J. Phillipp & Sons, 1935), there is a note appended to this text explaining that "the Apostle here granted an indulgence or pardon, in the person and by the authority of Christ, to the incestuous Corinthian, whom he had put under penance: which pardon consisted in releasing of part of the temporal punishment due to sin." It can only be hoped that the omission of any such note in the Confraternity edition of the New Testament (New York: Catholic Publishing Co., 1950) results from a changed attitude toward finding dogmatic proof texts.

"Belial" meaning good for nothing (6:15), and "god of this world" (4:4).[30]   Satan (a Hebrew name) means "adversary"; devil (a Greek name) means "accuser" (see Revelation 12:10).   *Pleonektein* ("[take] advantage [of]") has the idea of trickery or deceit in order to gain a victory.   "Us" includes both Paul and the Corinthians.   If the Corinthians fail this test (verse 9), Paul's ministry will have been defeated by Satan.   If the penitent man is "overwhelmed by excessive sorrow" (verse 7), the devil will have won.   If the Corinthians display a lack of comfort and forgiveness (verse 7), they will have been defeated by Satan.   "A church may be overcome by evil simply by failing to do right."[31]

For we are not ignorant of his schemes - If "we" refers to the Corinthians, they learned about Satan's schemes from the apostle's preaching and teaching.   The word *noēmata* ("schemes," or evil plans, plots) at this place has adverse connotations. Though a different word (*methodiai*) is used at Ephesians 6:11, both passages warn against Satan's deceitfulness (cp. 2 Corinthians 11:3,14).   Satan had gained an advantage when he tempted the incestuous man into his sin.   Repentance had defeated Satan's scheme on that occasion.   Satan has other schemes and will use them if given opportunity.   The personality and agency of the adversary can hardly be taught in plainer terms than this passage.[32]

3.   His thankfulness at the news brought by Titus. 2:12-17

Summary: We are still in the midst of Paul's review of his recent relations with Corinth.   First he defended his conduct with regard to his changed travel plans (1:12-2:4).   Then he explained the reasons behind his instructions with regard to the treatment of the penitent offender (2:5-11).   Now he

---

[30] Satan is referred in Scripture by many other terms, such as Beelzebub (or Baalzebub, 2 Kings 1:2,3,6), prince of the powers of the air (Ephesians 2:2), Abaddon, Apollyon (both of which mean destroyer, Revelation 9:11), murderer (John 8:44), liar (John 8:44), prince or ruler of this world (John 14:30), dragon (Revelation 12:7,9).   The devil is a fallen angel (cp. Jude 6 and Revelation 12:7-9). This being is often called the tempter because of his attempts to compromise Jesus and thus disqualify Him from being our savior (Matthew 4:1-11).   It is likely that the war in heaven (Revelation 12:7-9) explains the origin of the devil's hostility to God and His plans and people.

[31] Fisher, *op. cit.*, p.302.

[32] One of the tenets of modern infidelity is the denial of the personality of the devil.   It is asserted that the idea of a devil was not known to the early Hebrews, but was borrowed from Persian dualism. The Persians held that there were two contending deities – a good one and a bad one.   The Hebrews, according to these critics, learned this doctrine from the Persians during the days of the Babylonian captivity, but modified it so the god of evil became the devil.   In reply, it must be said that such a theory is based on the absurd notion that all the books of the Old Testament were written after the return from the captivity.   Their theory requires this notion, for the books of Genesis and Job were written centuries before the Babylonian captivity and both show a knowledge of this being. In fact, Genesis connects the devil and his work to the very beginning of human history.   Those who believe in the inspiration of the Scriptures must also believe in the personality of the devil, for Scriptures plainly teach it.

> turns to the good news Titus has recently brought about the church at Corinth. He is still showing them how wrong it was to think there was any "vacillating" (1:17), or any lack of love and concern for them on his part.

2:12 - *Now when I came to Troas for the gospel of Christ and when a door was opened for me in the Lord,*

Now when I came to Troas - After a digression telling them of his love for them, and why he had urged discipline and then comfort and forgiveness, he resumes the narrative concerning his travels which he broke off at 1:16. Shortly, Paul will again break off his narrative to tell of a rush of other feelings at Titus' report, finally to resume it at 7:5. Troas refers to the Roman colony located just a few miles from ancient Troy, of Trojan horse fame in Homer's *Iliad*. It was Paul's custom to evangelize population centers, and at this time Troas was a flourishing colony favored by the Romans.[33] Since about a year after this visit to Troas there was a flourishing congregation at Troas (Acts 20:5-11),[34] there would have been someone to be Paul's host while in town. Perhaps it was Carpas (2 Timothy 4:13), who on a later occasion (about AD 66 or 67) would welcome Paul into his home. Paul had left Ephesus after the riot of Demetrius (Acts 19:23ff) intending to make his way to Macedonia. Perhaps he took the coastal road that ran northwards from Ephesus through Adramyttium to Troas. Perhaps he went by sea from Ephesus to Troas. He is beginning the journey through Macedonia that he announced at 1 Corinthians 16:5.

For the gospel of Christ - That is, "to preach the gospel (that tells) about the Christ." Paul came to Troas intending to preach the gospel and strengthen the church which already existed there. As he came to Troas, he had not intended to continue his journey on toward Corinth so quickly, but anxiety over the unresolved situation in the Corinthian church led to a change of plans. On another occasion, or in different circumstances, he might have stayed longer in Troas in order evangelize the town further.

And when a door was opened for me in the Lord - An open door is a figurative expression for an opportunity, in this case, for evangelistic endeavors.[35] He apparently

---

[33] Because the Roman colony called Alexandria Troas was a crossroads of travel (where people changed ships, and where land travel became sea travel, and vice-versa), it was a highly desirable place for missionary work, for from this urban center the message would easily spread in all directions.

[34] Paul's first visit there (on his second missionary journey) had been limited to a few days because of the call to come over into Macedonia, so there is no trace of his preaching there (Acts 16:7-9). When Luke joined Paul's missionary team at Troas at that same time, he already was famous for the gospel (2 Corinthians 8:18 probably refers to Luke). Luke likely planted the church in Troas before joining Paul on Paul's first trip into Macedonia.

[35] When Paul reported the favorable results of his first missionary journey to the sending church at Antioch (Acts14:27) he told them how God "had opened a door of faith to the Gentiles." Recent-

found people who were willing to hear the gospel. But Paul was so anxious to receive news about Corinth that he could not take advantage of the opportunity. If Titus had arrived sooner (verse 13) with good news from Corinth, perhaps Paul could have taken advantage of the "open door" to preach there for two or three months. Something caused these two men, Paul and Titus, to fail to make the expected connections at Troas, so Paul will leave Troas. Who was that someone? Did folks at Corinth, by their sin, cause Titus to delay? Is it possible that souls were lost at Troas because of somebody's failure at Corinth?

2:13 - *I had no rest for my spirit, not finding Titus my brother; but taking leave of them, I went on to Macedonia.*

I had no rest for my spirit - This is why he could not take advantage of the open door for evangelistic work at Troas. Mentally and physically, he was just not able to do so. "I had" is a perfect tense verb; he still vividly remembers how it was. "Rest" (*anesis*) is the relaxation of strings which have been drawn tight, a release from unfavorable conditions.[36] 1 Thessalonians 5:23 indicates that man is made up of body, soul, and spirit. 2 Corinthians 7:1 speaks of flesh and spirit. The "spirit" is that part of a man that gives directions to the soul which in turn animates the body.[37] Man's "spirit" is so closely associated with his mind that NEB reads "I still found no relief of mind." In 2 Corinthians 7:5, he says he had no rest for his flesh. His anxiety for the Corinthians was so great it left him incapacitated.

Not finding Titus my brother - The Greek infinitive phrase should be treated as causal, "because I did not find" (NRSV). Evidently, plans had been made that Titus would report to Paul at Troas.[38] However, Titus did not arrive as soon as Paul wished. The weeks of waiting would stretch into months before Titus would finally come, and that, not until after Paul had left Troas and crossed over into Macedonia. Calling Titus "my brother" is expressive of Paul's high opinion of Titus as an able fellow-worker in the gospel.[39]

---

ly at Ephesus, he had seen another wonderful opportunity (1 Corinthians 16:9).

[36] Berry, *Synonyms*, p.130-31. R.C. Trench, *Synonyms of the New Testament* (Grand Rapids: Eerdmans, 1966), p.146-147.

[37] It is man's "spirit" that quits functioning when he commits his first sin. Such a person is said to have died spiritually (Romans 7:9, "sin slew me"). When the new birth occurs, it is the "spirit" that is reborn (John 3:6).

[38] See the Introductory Studies (under "The Travels of Paul and his Companions") for greater detail concerning the travels of Titus.

[39] Titus, though not mentioned in Acts, is the most prominent person in this epistle; and it is evident that Paul felt for him a warm affection and respect (2 Corinthians 7:13,15, 8:16,17, 2 Timothy 4:10).

But taking my leave of them - That is, taking leave of the Christians in Troas. *Apotaxamenos* ("taking leave") in the New Testament is found in the middle voice only, and its meaning is "to bid farewell to friends." The anxiety to hear something positive from Titus about the Corinthians' response to Titus' ministry was a greater motivation on Paul's behavior than the open door of opportunity at Troas. He would move in the direction from which Titus was coming, in hope of meeting him sooner.

I went on to Macedonia - This visit to Macedonia is recorded at Acts 20:1. Perhaps at Philippi, the long awaited Titus finally arrived and made his report. That report was the occasion for the writing of this letter, 2 Corinthians, which was written from Macedonia.[40] We now must wait until 7:5 to resume the story of Titus. In the meantime, from 2:14 onward, what Paul writes reflects what Titus told him about the situation at Corinth.[41]

2:14 - *But thanks be to God, who always leads us in triumph in Christ, and manifests through us the sweet aroma of his knowledge in every place.*

But thanks be to God - At this point, Paul does not finish telling where and when he met Titus, but tells instead his outburst of feeling at the glad report Titus brought (7:5,6). The dejection and incapacitation he so well remembered (verse 13) gave way to elation. He is still giving thanks to God as he writes this letter.[42] This triumph metaphor which follows serves as a transition to the following chapters in which Paul claims authority for his gospel. All through the section he is answering objections and allegations made against him by the Judaizers, allegations which Titus has reported.

Who always leads us in His triumph in Christ - "Leads us in triumph" (NASB) gives a wholly different mental picture than "causes us to triumph" (KJV);[43] it calls

---

[40] Allusions to what the Macedonians were doing while Paul was there are found in 2 Corinthians 8-9. On the scene, Paul was reporting from first-hand knowledge.

[41] That the story of Titus is resumed at 7:5 has led Thompson to write, "In fact, 7:5 fits perfectly to 2:13. It is very understandable that many scholars observe this interruption and conclude that 2:14-7:4 is part of a separate letter, inserted here by error." (Thompson, *op. cit.*, p.37). The hypothesis that this long section was once part of a separate letter fails to satisfy external evidence concerning this letter. There are no manuscripts that have these verses by themselves; all the manuscripts have them in the letter we call 2 Corinthians. Furthermore, to call this a Pauline digression misses the point of what Paul is writing.

[42] Paul's usual word order in the Greek is, "Thanks be to God"; here he puts "to God" first, with great emphasis. (Compare 2 Corinthians 8:16, 9:15; Romans 6:17, 7:25; and 1 Corinthians 15:7.)

[43] The Greek word is *thriambeuō*. It is true that some Greek verbs ending in -*euō* have a causative sense: *matheteuō* may mean "I make a disciple"; *basileuō* may be "I make a king"; *choreuō* may mean "I cause to dance." But there is absolutely no authority for the causative meaning given to the verb in the KJV. We do not know that *thriambeuō* ever means "I cause to triumph." In Colossians 2:15 Paul uses this word in the only sense in which it is actually found, "to lead in triumph."

to mind the triumphal procession given to a victorious Roman general. Barclay's description of such a triumphal procession down the Via Sacra in Rome is this:

> First there came the state officials and the senate. Then there came the trumpeters. Then there were carried the spoils taken from the conquered land. For instance, when Titus conquered Jerusalem the seven-branched candlestick, the golden table of the shew-bread and the golden trumpets were carried through the streets of Rome. Then there came pictures of the conquered land and models of conquered citadels and ships. There followed the white bull for the sacrifice which would be made. Then there walked the wretched captives, the enemy princes, leaders and generals in chains, shortly to be flung into prison and in all probability almost immediately to be executed. Then there came the lictors bearing their rods, followed by the musicians with their lyres. Then there came the priests swinging their censers with the sweet-smelling incense burning in them. And then there came the general himself. He stood in a chariot drawn by four white horses. He was clad in a purple tunic embroidered with golden palm leaves, and over it a purple toga marked out with golden stars. In his hand he held an ivory sceptre with the Roman eagle at the top of it, and over his head a slave held the crown of Jupiter. After him there rode his family, and finally there came the army wearing all their decorations and shouting *Io triumphe!* the cry of triumph. As the procession moved through the streets, all decorated and garlanded, amid the shouting, cheering crowds, it was a tremendous day, a day which might happen only once in a lifetime.[44]

Several additional notes will fill out the picture. (1) In AD 51, just a few years before Paul wrote 2 Corinthians, the emperor Claudius had solemnized such a triumph for the general Ostorius who had conquered Britain. Ruins of the triumphal arch constructed for him are still visible in the courtyard of the Barberini Palace in Rome.[45] (2) Other animals besides horses were sometimes used to pull the victors' chariot. "When Pompey triumphed over Africa, his chariot was drawn by elephants; that of Mark Antony by lions; that of Heliogabalus by tigers; and that of Aurelius by deer."[46] (3) An issue of *Biblical Archaeology Review* (27:4 [July-Aug, 2001]) suggests that the gold plundered from the temple at Jerusalem by Titus the Roman (AD 70) was what paid for the construction of the Coliseum in Rome. Vespasian and Titus had to get the money from somewhere to erect this grand structure. (4) When the marchers reached the foot of the Capitoline hill, some of the prisoners, condemned as treacherous or rebellious, were led off to execution or thrown into the dungeons (the *Tullianum*) of the Mamertime prison, while others were pardoned and set free. In the AD 51 triumph over the Britons, their king Caractacus and his children, marching in the procession, were spared by the mercy of the Emperor (Tacit. *Ann.* XIII. 36).

---

[44] William Barclay, "The Letters to the Corinthians" in *The Daily Study Bible Series* (Philadelphia: Westminster Press, 1956), p.205.

[45] Plumptre, *op. cit.*, p.23.

[46] Adam Clarke, "Romans to the Revelation," volume 2 in *Clarke's Commentary on the New Testament* (Cincinnati: Methodist Book Concern, 1855), p.321.

There is a very good possibility that Claudia and Linus, named in 2 Timothy 4:21, were among those children so freed.[47]   (5) It would appear that "in Christ" pictures Jesus as the one being honored in the triumph.   "Always" indicates His triumph was not just a one-day affair, but would continue all through Paul's earthly life.   Wetstein worded it well: "God [in Christ] leads us around as it were in triumph, so that we do not stay in one place or move on to another according to our own will, but as seems good to our all-wise Director.   The man whom He had vanquished at Damascus He leads in triumph, not just at Rome, and not just once, but through the whole world as long as he lives."[48]

And manifests through us the sweet aroma of the knowledge of Him in every place - As he writes "through us," Paul claims to be, as it were, a priestly incense bearer in the procession of the conqueror.   He pictures the knowledge of Christ as being the sweet-smelling aroma or fragrance[49] that wafts up from the censer he carries.   The "knowledge of Him" is the knowledge about Christ that is manifested[50] when the gospel is preached.   2 Corinthians 4:6 and 10:5 picture Paul's ministry as the dissemination of knowledge about God and Christ.   "In every place" reflects the fact that by AD 57, the time Paul writes this letter, the gospel had been very widely preached in Asia and Europe (Romans 15:18,19; see also Colossians 1:23).

2:15 - *For we are a fragrance of Christ to God among those who are being saved and among those who are perishing:*

For we are a fragrance of Christ to God - "We" here, and "us" (verse 14), refer to the same people.   In verse 14 he spoke of "aroma" (*osmē*); now he speaks of fragrance (*euōdia*), with the change of words signaling a change of metaphor.   No longer does he picture himself as a priest in a triumphal procession bearing a censer and burning incense.   Now he (like all the apostles appointed by Christ, such as he is) is the smell the burning incense gives off.   God is pictured as smelling the fragrance and as being pleased by it.[51]

---

[47] See Gareth L. Reese, *New Testament Epistles: Timothy and Titus* (Moberly, MO: Scripture Exposition Books, 2007), p.547.

[48] Cited by Plummer, *op. cit.*, p.68.

[49] The word "aroma" is used at John 12:3 to denote the fragrant odor of the spices used to anoint Jesus.   At Ephesians 5:2 and Philippians 4:12, the word is used of the sweet smell that fills the air when incense is burned.

[50] The choice of the verb "manifests" is determined by "knowledge" rather than by "the sweet aroma."

[51] The word here rendered "sweet savor" (*euōdia*) occurs only here, at Ephesians 5:2, and at Philippians 4:18 in the New Testament.   All apply the word to persons or things well-pleasing unto God.   In the Septuagint *euōdia* is the word that was frequently used of the sweet smell which burnt offerings gave off (Genesis 8:21; Exodus 29:18,25,41; Leviticus 1:9,13,17).

Among those who are being saved and among those who are perishing - "In every triumphal procession some captives know they are being led to death, and others that they are approaching the moment of forgiveness and life, and of these fates the incense keeps them in mind."[52]   As the apostles evangelize from place to place, they minister among two classes, those who are being saved, and those who are perishing. It is not some eternal decree, nor the gospel itself, but men's response to it, that is the determining factor.   Both present tense participles ("being saved" and "are perishing") carry the idea of progress or movement, either from good to better, or from bad to worse.   The preaching of the gospel among the lost, if they rejected the message, only made their destiny worse.   But for those who believed and obeyed the gospel, they found they were set free from their old bondage to sin into a life of delightful spiritual growth.[53]   Every time the lost hear the gospel and reject it, they are reminded they are on the way to destruction.   Every time believers hear the gospel they would be reminded they were on the way to their deliverance.   It is implied that some would reject the gospel and perish, no matter that the preachers of the gospel labored with fidelity.

2:16 - *To the one an aroma from death to death, to the other an aroma from life to life. And who is adequate for these things?*

To the one an aroma from death to death - "Aroma" is again *osmē*, and the gospel is pictured as being like the odors one could smell during the triumphal procession. The two classes of people just mentioned, the saved and the perishing, are treated here in reverse order.   "From death unto death" pictures a transition from bad to worse.   They were dead in trespasses and sins (Ephesians 2:1) when the gospel came to them.   They rejected it with the result that, having rejected more light, now their guilt is increased and their condemnation is greater.   (Compare Luke 10:1-16. Sodom, Tyre, and Sidon had less opportunity than Chorazin, Bethsaida, and Capernaum, and so it would be more tolerable for the former on the day of judgment than for the latter; "to whomsoever much is given, of him shall much be required," Luke 12:48 ASV.)   The Bible teaches degrees of punishment and those who reject the gospel will be punished more severely than those who sinned against less light. Ultimately the death that the rejecters of the gospel will experience is the second death (Revelation 20:14).

---

[52] J.W. McGarvey, "Thessalonians, Corinthians, Galatians and Romans" in *The Standard Bible Commentary* (Cincinnati, OH: Standard Publishing Co., 1916), p.180.

[53] In the New Testament, salvation is described as:
- *Past* - aorist tense (2 Timothy 1:9, Titus 3:5);
- *Present* - present tense (here and in 1 Corinthians 1:18, 15:2);
- *Future* - future tense (Romans 5:9,10, 1 Corinthians 3:5, 2 Timothy 4:18);
- *Completed* - perfect tense (Ephesians 2:5,8).

"'Those who are perishing' (*apollumenoi*) are not merely regarded as on the road to *apoleia* (perdition); *apoleia* (perdition) is regarded as their end, unless some complete change takes place" (Plummer, *op. cit.*, p.71).   That the verb "perish" (*apollumi*) designates destruction and ruination rather than annihilation is clear from its use in 2 Peter 3:6.

To the other an aroma from life to life - The gospel produces opposite effects[54] on those who obey it when they hear it (1 Peter 2:7a). First as penitent believers are immersed, they rise to walk in newness of life (Romans 6:4). Then follows an ever-improving Christian walk (Romans 5:1-5; 2 Peter 1:5-8) and then an entrance into the eternal kingdom of our Lord and Savior Jesus Christ (2 Peter 1:11).

And who is adequate for these things? - When the eternal destinies of the listeners are involved, how can any man feel qualified to preach the gospel? In the next verse, Paul will begin to answer his own question. He will have to speak in sincerity (2:17), and not be like the Judaizers who peddle the word of God.[55] He will be adequate if the message he preaches is in harmony with the new covenant (3:5,6). He will have to have an ambition to be pleasing to Christ (5:9,10). He will have to recognize that his adequacy comes from God (3:5). With this question Paul is preparing the way for an elaborate vindication of his apostolic office and message. How wrong the Corinthians were to think of him as vacillating (1:17) in the discharge of his ministry. No one can be flippant when the outcome is the life or death of the hearers.

2:17 - *For we are not like many, peddling the word of God, but as from sincerity, but as from God, we speak in Christ in the sight of God.*

For we are not like many - The "for" indicates this is the beginning of a reply to the question "who is adequate for these things?" His answer is, we apostles are "for we are not like many." "The many,"[56] to whom he contrasts himself and his fellow apostles of Christ, are the Pharisaic Judaizers at Corinth, who preach a different gospel (2 Corinthians 11:4; Galatians 1:6).

Peddling the word of God - The metaphor of the triumph is no longer in his mind. Now the metaphor is of unscrupulous merchants (*kapeloi*, hucksters, peddlers) who dilute their wine with water in order to cheat the buyers.[57] With these words Paul throws light on the true motives of the Judaizers. They were selfishly pursuing their own personal gain at the expense of their followers. He will later openly accuse them of greedily taking all they can get from the Corinthians (2 Corinthians 11:20).

---

[54] The double working of the gospel that this verse pictures is also set forth at Matthew 21:44, Luke 2:34, and John 9:39.

[55] The Judaizers had nothing to offer that would be an aroma from life to life.

[56] The apparent harshness of "the many" (found in P[46], *Aleph*,B,C,K), as though the majority of teachers in the apostolic age dealt untruly with the word of God, led some copyist to substitute *hoi lopoi*, "the rest," and this found its way into later manuscripts (D,E,F,G,L). It was a mistake to think that Paul had any other teachers in mind than the many Judaizers who had arrived in Corinth to infiltrate the church there.

[57] Perhaps Paul had Isaiah 1:22 (LXX) in mind, for it reads "the wine merchants (*kapeloi*) mix their wine with water."

In 2 Corinthians 4:2, using a different word than "peddling," Paul will accuse the Judaizers of "walking in craftiness" and of "adulterating the word of God." "The word of God" says that God is the source of the message; the expression covers both the Old Testament Scriptures and the new covenant Scriptures (i.e., the preaching of Jesus and the apostles). The Judaizers were cheating their followers out of the truth of both old and new covenants. Who is adequate for the task? Not the Judaizers, certainly.

But as from sincerity, but as from God - "But" (*alla*, the strong adversative) introduces a quadruple contrast between the Judaizing peddlers and the true preachers of God's word. The Greek is a bit ambiguous, reading, literally, "but as of sincerity, but as of God before God in Christ we speak."[58] The sense, however is transparent; Paul is giving some reasons why true apostles of Christ are adequate for the awesome job they have been commissioned to do. "Sincerity" is the opposite of the deceit practiced by the Judaizing peddlers.[59] "From God" probably means that God is the source of the message the apostles of Jesus preach.

We speak in Christ in the sight of God - The present tense verb "we speak" indicates a habit of life for the apostles of Christ. "In Christ" may mean united with Him (e.g., branches bear fruit by being in the vine, John 15:4), or it may mean "representing Him to the world."[60] "In the sight of God" reminds us that God was watching the work of the appointed apostles, and they knew they were to appear before the judgment seat of Christ to answer for the deeds done in the body (2 Corinthians 5:10).

---

[58] Marshall, *op. cit.*, p.712.

[59] We had the word "sincerity" at 1:12. It indicates the motive of the heart which can stand to be judged in the light of the sun.

[60] Fisher, *op. cit.*, p.307.

SPECIAL STUDY #1

A REVIEW OF PAUL'S INSTRUCTIONS CONCERNING CHURCH DISCIPLINE

(The reader may wish to consult comments in the author's *New Testament Epistles: 1 Corinthians* at 1 Corinthians 5:1-8, the Special Study at the close of notes on chapter 5 of 1 Corinthians in the same source, and also the Special Study on "Church Discipline" in the author's *New Testament History: Acts*.)

I. **Overview of 1 Corinthians 5:1-8**

A. **5:1** -- Paul takes notice of the case of incest where one of the members of the church was living in adultery with his step-mother.

B. **5:2** -- The Corinthian church was filled with pride in spite of the wickedness, when they should have been brokenhearted that one of their members had sunk so low. There should have been mourning that resulted in excommunication of the offender.

C. **5:3** -- Paul here indicates that he had already made up his mind as to what ought to be done in the case. He says, "Even though I am separated by many miles from you, I would act the same way and say the same things if I were present with you."

D. **5:4** --

1. **"In the name of our Lord Jesus"** probably means by the authority of Christ, acting by His commission. It would therefore be a reference to Matthew 18:15-18.

2. **"When you are assembled"** speaks of a meeting of the church, whether a regular service, or a specially called meeting. The disciplining was to be done by the congregation.

   The passage shows discipline belongs to the church. The general doctrine of the New Testament is that the government of the church is invested in the elders. However, they do not assume dictatorial power. They rule, having been elected by the people, and as being responsible to God.

   So deep was Paul's conviction on this matter of the churches' autonomy that even he would not administer discipline without their concurrence and without the action of the church itself.

3. **"And I with you in spirit"** means "You should act in accordance with my declared conviction. You should act just as if I were with you, knowing what I would advise."

4. **"With the power of our Lord Jesus"** has been taken two ways: (1) Some think it has reference to some miraculous and extraordinary power – like in the case of Ananias and Sapphira, or Elymas. It is said that miraculous power will be shown in the case, proceeding from the Lord Jesus Himself. (2) Others think that this speaks of the fact that the assembly for disciplinary purposes would be accompanied by the power of the Lord Jesus, i.e., that when discipline is properly carried out, the action is recognized in heaven. (That which is bound on earth is bound in heaven; and that which is loosed on earth is loosed in heaven, Matthew 16:19).

E. **5:5 --**

1. **"To deliver such a one unto Satan"**[1] -- Excommunication is intended by these words. It speaks of an expulsion of the unrepentant sinner from the church, and a relegation to the region (outside the realm of the kingdom of God) where Satan holds sway.

2. **"For the destruction of his flesh"** -- It does not appear that this speaks of a miraculous affliction (like in the case of Elymas), but that this speaks of repentance. (The purpose of the excommunication was to get the offender to mortify his fleshly appetites and carnal affections.)

3. **"That his spirit may be saved"** -- That is, the man's ultimate salvation is the design behind the discipline. While he lives in sin, he is damned. But if he could be led to repent, it would bring eternal blessing.

F. **5:7 -- "Clear out the old leaven"** -- Remove from the congregation the sin of complacency toward members who continue to live in habitual sin.

G. **5:11** – In addition to excommunication, there was to be a cessation of fellowship; Christians are to be careful not to do anything that would acknowledge the excommunicated as a brother (as long as the excommunicated person remains unrepentant).

H. **5:13** -- A final commandment to excommunicate the incestuous person.

---

[1] The addition of "I have decided" in italics in the NASB obscures what Paul actually wrote. It was the congregation's action in the case that would deliver the unrepentant offender to Satan.

II. Other notes on the matter of church discipline

A. Discipline is an individual matter (local autonomy must be recognized).

B. In the Scriptures we have --
1. The divine law of admission to the church
2. The divine law of organization of the church
3. The divine law of regulation of the church
4. The divine law of exclusion from the church
We have no right to be lax on one law, more strict than on another.

C. Reasons for church discipline (from 1 Corinthians)
1. Maintain the authority of Christ
2. Maintain the purity of the congregation
3. Save the sinner

D. There are two types of church discipline.
1. *Formative* – teaching what is right, rebuking sin
2. *Corrective* – excluding the flagrant offender (until he or she repents, and then receiving the penitent one back into fellowship)

E. Concerning the spirit of the church during a person's excommunication:
1. The church might sin as much as the man being excluded.
2. It must be done in the spirit of fierceness and tenderness and love (brokenhearted that such action must be taken).

F. The Scriptural method of church discipline
1. There must first be the formative discipline before the corrective discipline can be undertaken.

    The congregation must be instructed in this matter of discipline before they will be able to discipline properly and effectively.

2. The process for corrective discipline is given in Matthew 18:15-18.

    a. First, the offended goes to the offender (or a friend goes to the one who is slipping), verse 15.

        If the proper preliminary work (formative discipline) has been done, the person will repent, before excommunication is even thought of. Of course, the offended, or the friend, must go in the proper spirit.

    b. If the offender will not repent, and the sin is flagrant, and continued, then the offended has no choice but to go to the elders, inform them, and take them to face the offender, verse 16. Very often, if the person has not repented before, when faced with the elders, the sinner will repent.

If there is a rumor of sin in the congregation, the elders may have to go to the alleged offender and talk with that person (especially if the church is going to be hurt by the rumor). Perhaps the elders can take the person spreading the rumor to the accused person and have them talk it out face to face. Or the elders may go to the rumor spreader, and say "Have you any evidence?" Also, look for a person to contradict the rumors.

   c. If the offender still will not repent, but continues in his flagrant sin, the elders must take the problem to the church, verse 17.

In the matter of discipline, the elders may take the lead, but the church still is given a voice. The elders, after thorough investigation and examination of all the facts, bring the problem before the congregation for a congregational vote. (Allow time for objections. If there are any, meet with the objector privately.) Then the decision is made.

3. Once the impenitent sinner is excommunicated, each member of the congregation must conscientiously carry out the "social ostracism."

For example, at the Morse Mission in Tibet, before he became a Christian, a man had plural wives. The Morses taught that repentance prior to his being immersed included getting rid of all his wives but one. This he did, but after some years decided he had kept the wrong one. He therefore exchanged the one he no longer wanted for the one he now wished he had kept. For this he was disciplined. As part of the social ostracism, even though he attended church he was not served the Lord's Supper, nor would any of the members shake his hand. It was this latter that finally convinced him of his need to repent. He moved wife number two out and moved wife number one back into his house.

4. Again, it should be noted that discipline, correctly administered, is nothing less than recognizing on earth what has already been done in heaven, Matthew 15:18.

G. Milligan says, "Nothing can be more plainly taught in the Scriptures, than that it is the duty of the church to withdraw her fellowship from every member who persists in a disorderly course of conduct."[2]

---

[2] Robert Milligan, *An Exposition and Defense of the Scheme of Redemption* (St. Louis: Christian Board of Publication: nd), p.529.

B. The Glory of the Apostolic Office. 3:1 - 6:10

1. The superiority of the ministry of the New Covenant to that of the Old. 3:1-11

> *Summary*: We are still in the general topic of Paul's review of his recent relations with Corinth. Not only was Paul's conduct upright and honorable (1:12-2:17), but behind his ministry as an apostle of Jesus Christ was the introduction of the long-promised new covenant, a much more glorious covenant than the one given through Moses (3:1-6:10). His dealings with the Corinthians were in harmony with his commission as an apostle of Christ.

3:1 - *Are we beginning to commend ourselves again? Or do we need, as some, letters of commendation to you or from you?*

Are we beginning to commend ourselves again? - Apparently, one of the things Titus reported to Paul was that the Judaizers at Corinth had tried to disparage Paul by saying he was always singing his own self-praises in order to gain their favor. The word "again" implies the charge had already been brought against Paul. In the closing verses of chapter 2, Paul has said he was not like certain peddlers, but spoke "as from sincerity" and with divine authority because he was sent by God. He anticipates the Judaizers will jump on these words and accuse him of commending himself again, thus robbing any such potential accusation of any credibility. Paul begins his transition to the topic of the new covenant by asking if what he is writing was only self-serving commendation so as to make him look good in their estimation? His rhetorical question suggests its own answer, 'Of course not.'

Or do we need, as some - The "some" are the Judaizers, the same people named as "the many" in 2:17. The question is so written in the Greek that it expects a negative answer. Of course, Paul did not need letters of commendation. It was outsiders and strangers who needed such letters.

Letters of commendation - Letters of introduction or commendation were common in the ancient world. In an age when there were no motels, such letters were given to people who were about to depart on a journey in order to introduce them, and vouch for them, to friends or acquaintances in the city of destination. This would thus gain hospitality for them as they were on their journey.   A Christian traveling with such a letter from any church was certain to find a welcome in any other.[1]   They were in-

---

[1] Examples of an honest use of such letters are seen in the recommendation of Phoebe (Romans 16:1,2), Timothy (1 Corinthians 16:10,11), Apollos (Acts 18:27), and Zenas and Apollos (Titus 3:13). It was only when such letters were dishonest commendations that Paul disparages their use.

tended to guarantee at once the traveler's soundness in the faith and his personal character. Disreputable folk could take advantage of the custom to gain hospitality. When the Judaizers arrived in Corinth they produced such letters of introduction to the church there. We wonder from whom the Judaizers had letters. Certainly not from the apostle James at Jerusalem. If the Judaizers who invaded Corinth are the same as those who troubled Galatia (and those latter were false brethren, Galatians 2:4), it seems hardly likely they had letters from the leaders of the church at Jerusalem. Maybe these peddlers carried fake letters which they themselves had composed; maybe they carried letters from their sympathizers in Judea, or from churches they have already duped.

To you or from you? - "To you" implies the Judaizers had gained entrance into the church at Corinth through the use of such letters. "From you" indicates they would then ask for letters when they departed from Corinth to go to another place.

3:2 - *You are our letter, written in our hearts, known and read by all men;*

You are our letter - If Paul needed any letter of recommendation, the existence of the Corinthian church would be all that was needed. The Corinthian church was the seal of Paul's apostleship in the Lord (1 Corinthians 9:2).

Written in our hearts - The Judaizers may bring their letters of commendation in their hands; Paul's letter is written on his heart.[2] "Heart" often stands for a man's mind ("with the heart man believes," Romans 10:10). When Paul thinks about the changed lives in Corinth, and the existence of the church he planted, his mind is filled with feelings of joy and accomplishment.

Known and read by all men - "Known and read" are present participles. All over the Roman world Paul's work can be seen as folk look at the church in Corinth. Implied is the idea that the letters the Judaizers carried were not so public and well known, but rather were secretly and fraudulently produced.

3:3 - *Being manifested that you are a letter of Christ, cared for by us, written not with ink, but with the Spirit of the living God, not on tables of stone, but on tablets of human hearts.*

Being manifested that you are a letter of Christ - Using "letter" in a figurative sense, Paul says the Corinthians show (*phaneroumenoi*) that they are his letter of commendation. Christ is pictured as being the author of the letter of commendation.

---

[2] A few manuscripts (*Aleph*, 33) and versions (RSV, for example) read "written on your hearts." Thompson has delightfully suggested that "written on your hearts" anticipates the coming discussion of the new covenant (3:6) under which he ministers, for Jeremiah 31:33 (part of the classic new covenant prophecy) indicates that that future covenant will be written on hearts, not on tables of stone. Thompson, *op. cit.*, p.42

Cared for by us - Perhaps Paul pictures himself as the amanuensis whom Christ used to write the letter.[3]

Written not with ink - The letters the Judaizers carried were written with black ink (*melan*[4]).

But with the Spirit of the living God - "Written" is a perfect tense verb; the letter of Christ was written in the past and still stands. "Spirit of the living God"[5] is one of the names for the Holy Spirit; the words "of the living God" suggest that the living God[6] sends the Spirit to do His convicting, converting work as the gospel is preached. The Holy Spirit, working through the preached word, had something to do with the Corinthians becoming Christians.[7] That the Holy Spirit is compared with ink which leaves something that can be seen when the writing is finished is a bold metaphor. What could be seen among the Corinthians was their changed lives, from sinners to saints.

Not on tablets of stone - The reference is to the Decalogue of Moses, written on two tablets of stone. The letters on the tablets of stone were written by the finger of God (Exodus 31:18).[8] That was old covenant times. Things are greatly different in the new covenant age. Paul is beginning to introduce his contrast between the Mosaic and Christian ministry – one based on the old covenant, the other, because it is based on the new covenant, being an infinitely superior ministry. The Judaizers, emphasizing their "works of the Law" (man-made rules based on what Moses wrote) are behind the times.

---

[3] The word "cared for," *diakonētheisais*, comes from from *diakoneō*, which picks up a theme that permeates this letter (e.g., 3:6-9), that Paul is a "minister" or "servant" (*diakonos*) of Christ, whereas the Judaizers are not.

[4] First-century letters were customarily written on papyrus or parchment with a reed pen and with a black ink made by mixing together soot, gum (perhaps egg white), and water (cp. 2 John 12).

[5] Here in verse 3 (see 1:22) we have another allusion to the Godhead -- Father, Son, and Holy Spirit.

[6] In Scripture, God is often described as the "living" God (e.g., Matthew 16:16; 2 Corinthians 6:16). Two different constructions (*theos ho zōon*, "God who lives," and the one used here, *theos zōon*). *Theos zōon* always fixes attention upon the characteristic "living"; if God lives, so also does the Spirit. That accounts for His ability to work on the hearts of men.

[7] That the Spirit works through the word in conversion can be seen by comparing verses that speak of the Holy Spirit's work in conversion (like John 3:6-8; 1 Corinthians 12:13) with verses that attribute the new birth to the word of God (such as Luke 8:11; James 1:18, 1 Peter 1:23; 1 John 5:1). One of the things the Spirit does is to produce conviction of sin (John 16:8-11) in the hearts of those who are listening to the preached message.

[8] There is a place in the New Testament where "finger of God" and the "Spirit of God" are used interchangeably (cp. Luke 11:20, "finger of God," and Matthew 12:28 "Spirit of God"). However, it is not at all certain that Paul is here saying the Holy Spirit had something to do with writing the tables of stone, like He has something to do with men becoming Christians.

But on tablets of human hearts - The material on which Christ writes His letter at Corinth was not on inanimate rock, as was the law of Moses, but rather on living tablets, sensitive human hearts. The Corinthians must not disregard the memory of the operation of the Holy Spirit in their lives when they responded to the gospel. What Christ has done at Corinth far surpasses what the Judaizing peddlers could do.

3:4 - *And such confidence we have through Christ toward God.*

And such confidence - Paul refers to the confidence[9] just expressed, viz., that he has no need of any credentials or letters of commendation other than the testimony which the existence of the Corinthian Church provides.

We have through Christ - Paul hastens at once to show that his expression of confidence was not just another attempt to commend himself (3:1). He gives the credit to Christ[10] because he recognized what his Master had taught His apostles, "Apart from Me you can do nothing" (John 15:5).

Toward God - When used with a person, the Greek preposition *pros* ("toward") means "face to face." Paul pictures himself as standing face to face with God. God is the one who rightly judges the validity of one's credentials and God is contrasted with the Judaizers in Corinth who have been judging Paul's apostolic credentials negatively.

3:5 - *Not that we ourselves are adequate in ourselves to consider anything as* **coming** *from ourselves, but our adequacy is from God.*

Not that we are adequate in ourselves - "Adequate" (*hikanos*, qualified) reminds us of the question Paul asked in 2:16, where the topic was how can anyone be qualified to preach a gospel which has such profound eternal consequences on the listeners. Here, the topic is different, but the source of the adequacy is the same.

To consider anything as *coming* **from ourselves** - Here Paul is saying he does not decide on the basis of his own judgment (*logisasthai*, "consider") the means and ways of discharging his apostolic duties.

But our adequacy is from God - In his first epistle he wrote, "We are God's fellow-workers" (1 Corinthians 3:9). Not only did the apostles belong to God and work under Him, but God was the source of their adequacy. Paul immediately goes on to

---

[9] On the word "confidence," *pepoithēsis*, see notes at 1:15.

[10] The use of the definite article before "Christ" ("the Christ," i.e., the "anointed one") is quite common in this epistle (1:5, 2:12,14, 3:4, 4:4, 5:10). Contrary to what the Judaizers were claiming, Paul does not want the Corinthians to forget that Jesus is "the" long-promised Messiah.

explain exactly what that means in their case and his.

3:6 - *Who also made us adequate* **as** *servants of a new covenant, not of the letter, but of the Spirit: for the letter kills, but the Spirit gives life.*

Who also made us adequate *as* **servants** - With these words Paul explains how the apostles' adequacy came from God.[11]   Their methods and the message alike are related to the inauguration of the new covenant which Jeremiah had predicted some 600 years before Christ (Jeremiah 31:31-34; cp. Hebrews 8:8-12).   That new covenant was inaugurated by the sacrifice of Jesus (as the cup of the Lord's Supper reminds us, Luke 22:20).   The place of the apostles in this whole program of God was that of "servants" (cp. "servants of Christ" in 1 Corinthians 4:1; also "cared for by us" in 2 Corinthians 3:3).   The point of the whole paragraph is that the Judaizers are in error because, as they formulated their man-made rules ("works of the Law"[12]) allegedly based on some passage or another from the Torah, they were acting as though the law of Moses were of perpetual validity.

Of a new covenant - "Covenant" (*diathēkē*[13]) speaks of the arrangement which God has made with men for their salvation.   "New" translates *kainos*, not *neos*:   that tells us the covenant under which Paul ministers is not brand new (*neos*, new, never existing before), but renewed (*kainos*, fresh, renewed, new in point of quality, new as compared with obsolete).   The new covenant predicted by Jeremiah (Jeremiah 31:31-34) has been inaugurated by the blood Jesus shed on Calvary (Luke 22:20). The new covenant is the good news that the Abrahamic covenant has been renewed. The Abrahamic covenant is stated in these words: "In your seed all the nations of the earth will be blessed" (Genesis 22:16; Acts 3:25,26; Galatians 3:8).   The seed is Christ (Galatians 3:16).   All nations include Jews and Gentiles.   The blessing includes having sins forgiven (Romans 4:7,8).   It quickly becomes clear (cp. 1 Cor-

---

[11] There is a repetitious use of the word "adequate" in these verses since 2:16:   "Qualified ... qualified ... qualified!"   Let no Judaizer try to convince the Corinthians otherwise when it comes to Paul's apostolic qualifications under the new covenant.

[12] See notes on Galatians 2:16 and 3:2 for further explanation of "works of the Law."

[13] "Covenant" is preferred to "testament" to translate *diathēkē*.   A *diathēkē* was an agreement between unequals (where one party with plenary power makes all the rules and conditions, and the other can either accept or reject the rules and conditions but cannot change them).   Greek has another word that can be translated "covenant."   *Sunthēkē* is an agreement between equals; this connotation makes *sunthēkē* a word wholly unsuitable for arrangements between God and men. The word *diathēkē* occurs 33 times in the New Testament, and, perhaps, only in one or two passages (Galatians 3:15 and Hebrews 9:15-17) does *diathēkē* mean "testament" (as in last will and testament).   See comments in the author's commentary *New Testament Epistles: Hebrews* at 7:22 and 9:15-17.   The word occurs about 300 times in the LXX and over 200 of these times it represents the Hebrew *berith*, "covenant."   The Jews knew nothing about making wills until they learned it from the Romans, but they did know about "covenants."

inthians 9:20,21) how completely Paul has broken with the Law of Moses.[14] Apostles of Christ are not preaching obedience to the abrogated Law of Moses (Hebrews 7:12; see also 2 Corinthians 3:11); they are preaching the good news of obedience to Christ. The "new covenant" requires a "new man" (Ephesians 2:15, 4:24) who is a "new creature" (2 Corinthians 5:17). This regenerated person has a "new name" (Revelation 2:17), observes a "new commandment" (1 John 2:7,8), sings a "new song" (Revelation 14:3), looks for a "new heavens and a new earth" (2 Peter 3:13; Revelation 21:1) where the "new Jerusalem" (Revelation 21:2) is, and where all things will be "new" (Revelation 21:5).

Not of the letter, but of the Spirit - The decision of the translators of the NASB to capitalize "Spirit" appears to be correct, if we may let the context guide us, for the context speaks of the Holy Spirit. Verse 3 has already spoken about the "Spirit of the living God"; verse 17 will allude to "the Spirit of the Lord"; verse 8 has the phrase about "ministry of the Spirit."[15] This decision about "Spirit" guides the comments offered for this chapter. One further word needs to be said since another decision made by this commentator will guide the comments offered on these verses. It is this: As one reads the whole of chapter 3, it looks as if Paul has used several different expressions to refer to the Law of Moses (tablets of stone; letter; letter that kills; ministry of death; ministry of condemnation; that which fades away; old covenant). Likewise, he has used several different and contrasting expressions to refer to the gospel of Christ (tablets of human hearts; Spirit; the Spirit gives life; ministry of the Spirit; ministry of righteousness; that which remains; new covenant). If these indeed are different ways to refer to the old and new covenants, then "letter" stands for the whole written code, the old covenant, the Law of Moses; "Spirit" stands for the new covenant wherein the Spirit is at work in ways far beyond what He did in Mosaic times (John 7:3-39; Galatians 3:2,3).

For the letter kills - What might this startling expression mean?[16] In this commen-

---

[14] The actual text of the old covenant, the Mosaic covenant, is found in Exodus 20-23.

[15] The translators of the ASV chose to use a small "s" as the translated this phrase "of the spirit." They believed Paul had reference to the human spirit that is part of the makeup of man (1 Thessalonians 5:23). Appeal may be made to similar language that fills Romans, another letter of Paul's from the same period in Paul's life. There Paul explains how the "spirit" of man is able to function after it becomes alive because of righteousness (Romans 8:10). Romans even has a contrast (as the ASV reads) between "spirit" and "letter" at Romans 2:29 and 7:6. This commentator might opt for the ASV reading if it were not for the fact that 2 Corinthians 3:8 is not easily explained were we to attempt to make that verse read "ministry of the spirit" (small "s").

[16] It was this passage, more than any other, that led Origen, Tyndale, and others, to insist that scripture must be interpreted allegorically, not literally, because "the letter kills." (McGarvey, *op. cit.*, p.184. Hughes, *op. cit.*, p.99 quotes William Tyndale's affirmation that "the literal sense [of Scripture] profits not, but is hurtful, noisome, and kills the soul.") To use this verse as justification for the allegorical method of interpretation will not do since "letter" here speaks, not of a single word which might or might not be given an allegorical meaning, but of the whole written code, the old covenant, the Law of Moses.

tator's judgment, we should turn to what Paul writes about the Law of Moses in some of his other letters from this same period of his life; namely, Romans 7:9-11, 8:2,31; 1 Corinthians 15:56; and Galatians 3:10,21. In those passages, it is explained in a much more serious sense how the Law kills – its presence gives the devil a place from which to launch his operations against men (Romans 7:9-11). And when the devil succeeds and men sin, they die spiritually. Unless men are covered by the blood of Christ, so as to be justified, they will perish. The Law was "holy and righteous and good" (Romans 7:12). We do not blame the Law, we blame sin (the devil) for causing the spiritual death of people (Romans 7:13). The letter then kills in the sense that the presence of the Law gave sin the opportunity needed to accomplish this bad end (the sting that causes death is sin, and the Law is the thing that gave power to sin, 1 Corinthians 15:56). If we didn't have Romans and 1 Corinthians to help us, this passage in 2 Corinthians would be very obscure.

But the Spirit gives life - Remember we have opted to agree with translations which capitalize "Spirit" making it a reference to the Holy Spirit. *Zōopoieō* (translated "gives life") could also be translated "makes alive" (Moffatt) or "restores to life"[17] Whatever *zōopoieō* means, it is the opposite of "kills" in the previous clause. If that clause spoke of how a man's spirit is affected by sin (men die spiritually), then this clause speaks of how the Holy Spirit can affect man's spirit. The Holy Spirit can help his spirit become alive again (viz., when the new birth takes place, "that which is born of Spirit is spirit," John 3:6). Romans 8:10 affirms that the spirit is alive because of righteousness (i.e., God's way of saving man includes making his spirit alive again). Romans 6 tells how converts come up from the waters of baptism to live in newness of life.[18] Romans 8:2 tells us that the "law of the Spirit of life in Christ Jesus" (a complex name for the gospel) has made us free from the law of sin and death (how things were under the Law of Moses). Under the Mosaic covenant men were governed wholly from without by letters written on stone or on a scroll. Under the new covenant men's lives are governed from within as the spirit, having been restored to life, is now able to function and give directions to the whole man. The Law gave no help to those who lived under it to live up to its demands and requirements. The Christian's spirit has the help and guidance of the indwelling Holy Spirit. What life we have!

3:7 - *But if the ministry of death, in letters engraved on stones, came with glory, so that the children of Israel could not look intently at the face of Moses because of the glory of his face, fading as it was,*

---

[17] Thayer, *op. cit.*, p.274, who also tells us the word can be used metaphorically of seeds germinating or growing.

[18] It might be objected that we have been too specific in our explanation of the Spirit giving life. After all we are using different expressions to refer to the old and new covenants. The new covenant deals with *pneuma* ("Spirit" and/or "spirit"). There was no indwelling Holy Spirit in the old covenant (John 7:37-39). There was no new birth in old covenant. We think that "the Spirit makes alive" would include all these benefits of the gospel that were unavailable under the old covenant.

But if the ministry of death - Under the Mosaic Law, Jewish priests ministered. However, "to be ministers of the old covenant was no great distinction; there were large numbers of them, and their duties were largely matters of routine."[19]   There were not many apostles of Jesus, and their ministries were anything but routine.   Paul has now reached the main topic in this portion of the epistle (3:1-6:10), viz., the superiority of the apostle's ministry under the new covenant to ministry under the old covenant.[20]   He will make his point about the superiority of the new to the old by calling attention to selected points that any Jew could read in the LXX of Exodus 34:29-35.[21]   Paul drives home three points as he shows the inferiority of the Law: it was a ministry of death (verse 8), a ministry of condemnation (verse 9), and a ministry which was designed to be only temporary (verse 11).   That the Law of Moses was a "ministry of death" expresses the same idea that "the letter kills" did in verse 6.   This discussion of the inferiority of the law to the Gospel is quite in place, for Paul's chief opponents were Judaizers, whose one aim it was to bind upon the church the yoke of Pharisaic Judaism.

In letters engraved on stones - "Stones" recalls "tablets of stone" in verse 3; "letters" recalls "the letter kills" in verse 6.   The Ten Commandments (the only part of the Mosaic code written on stones) are here used for the whole of the Mosaic code.

Came with glory - Paul is insisting the new covenant is superior to the old, but he does not argue that there was no glory connected with Moses' ministry.   Instead he affirms (verses 8-10) that the glory of the new far outshines the glory of the old.   Paul goes on to explain about the glory of the old covenant that he has in mind; namely, the glory that shone on Moses' face.   Perhaps we could also think of the presence of God on Mt. Sinai, the thunder and fire and earthquake, the whirlwind and the trumpet blast, all of which inspired awe in the people.   The giving of the Law on Mt. Sinai was one of the highlights of Jewish history.   It was a glorious thing, the likes of which not many peoples in the history of the world have been privileged to experience.

So that the sons of Israel could not look intently at the face of Moses because of the glory of his face - When Moses came down from the mount with the second set of the tables of stone, Exodus 34:29,30 (LXX) records that "the skin of his face shone

---

[19] Plummer, *op. cit.*, p.85.

[20] "Ministry" here and in the following verses picks up the same root word translated "cared for" in verse 3, and translated "servants" in verse 6.   The word includes the arrangements by which God's covenants were administered and maintained.   The men who administered God's covenants were no more than His servants, but they were His servants!   This is something for the Judaizers and the Corinthians to keep in mind.

[21] The presentation here of important points in an Old Testament passage differs little from the way the argument for the superiority of the new covenant to the old is presented in the epistle to the Hebrews.   There, too, Old Testament passages are recalled to mind, and their pertinent points driven home.

(was glorified[22])" and when they saw the glow on Moses' face "the people were afraid to come near him." Apparently not only were they afraid to come near, but Paul tells us they were also afraid to keep looking at him.

Fading *as* it was - Once Moses left the presence of God, the glow on his face gradually diminished[23] in brightness until the glow was all gone from Moses' face. The glory surrounding Moses at the giving of the Law was very splendid, but it was very temporary. In verse 13 below, Paul will continue his account of what happened to the "glory" that radiated from Moses' face, and use it as a parable to show the superiority of the unfading new covenant.[24]

3:8 - *how shall the ministry of the Spirit fail to be even more with glory?*

How shall the ministry of the Spirit - This is an argument from the lesser to the greater. If it was true that glory was involved in Moses' case as he administered the old covenant, how much greater glory is involved in the case of the apostles as they administer the new?[25] We might have expected the contrast to the "ministry of death" (verse 7) to be "ministry of life." Paul instead calls his ministry the "ministry of the Spirit." As the apostle Paul ministers, bringing the gospel to Corinth and other places, his ministry gives the Holy Spirit opportunity to do His convicting, converting, life- giving work (see verse 6, "the Spirit gives life").

Fail to be even more with glory? - We look to the context to explain in what way the new covenant is superior to the old. We might recall what the preceding verses have pointed out, namely that the new covenant makes alive whereas the old covenant killed. Obviously making alive is better than killing. If we look to the following verses we will see that the old was but temporary and fading away, whereas the new was to remain. Or, since the following verse begins with "for," as giving an explana-

---

[22] It may be noted that the Latin Vulgate rendering of Exodus 34:29 is "he knew not that his face was horned." It is a possible translation since the Hebrew word for "a ray of light" and "a horn" are identical. It was the Vulgate translation which gave rise to artists painting or sculpting Moses with horns, as in the matchless statue by Michelangelo in the church of St. Peter in Chains at Rome. Readers can see a picture of the statue in *Zondervan Pictorial Bible Dictionary*, p.560.

[23] The Greek participle "fading" indicates continuing action. This Greek word (*katargeō*) is the same word used of spiritual gifts in 1 Corinthians 13:8-10 (there it is translated "done away"). It also is used at 1 Corinthians 2:6 where it is said the rulers of this world were "passing away." Plumptre (*op. cit.*, p.29) calls it a favorite word of Paul's at this period of his life, since he uses it 22 times in the second group of his letters (1 and 2 Corinthians, Galatians and Romans), and only 3 times in his other epistles.

[24] In passing, it should be observed that Paul here expresses his view of the historicity of the Old Testament accounts of the giving of the Law.

[25] In the question Paul asks here in verse 8, he uses a negative adverb (*ouchi*, "not," which is untranslated in the NASB) to show he expects a strong positive answer to his question. Indeed the ministry of the Spirit has more glory. He uses the same construction in 1 Corinthians 9:1 and 10:16,18.

tion of something just said, we might understand that the reason the glory of the new surpasses the glory of the old is to be found in the contrast between "condemnation" and "righteousness."

3:9 - *For if the ministry of condemnation has glory, much more does the ministry of righteousness abound in glory.*

For if the ministry of condemnation has glory - "For" tells us that verse 9 is related to verse 8, either as a reason for something just said, or as a further explanation of something just said.   Since verse 6, Paul has been giving us ways in which the Law of Moses was inferior to the gospel.   Here is another one, namely, the Law brought condemnation, while the gospel brings righteousness.   The expression "ministry of condemnation"[26] speaks of the same covenant as did "the ministry of death" (verse 7).   "Condemnation" reminds us of the struggles a man under the Law had as he tried to meet its just demands, and found himself living in a body of sin and a slave to sin, with eternal punishment awaiting transgressors.   One is reminded of Romans 8:1, which summarizes much of what went before in that letter as being "condemnation" – a condemnation that is no longer true for those who are in Christ Jesus.   As was true in Romans, so here we must not accuse the Law of Moses, or even Moses its "minister," of deliberately causing men to come under the condemnation of God. Rather, we must recall what Romans 7 says, where Paul tells those readers how the devil[27] took advantage of the presence of the Law and tricked men into doing the very thing the Law prohibited.   Blame the devil, not the Law, for the condemnation that men experienced!   In comments on verse 7 we indicated some of the glories of the Old Testament.   See also Romans 9:4,5.

Much more does the ministry of righteousness abound in glory - "The ministry of righteousness" is another name for the gospel, the new covenant, under which Paul and the Christian preachers were carrying on their ministry.   Sometimes "righteousness" speaks of God's way of saving man (the same word can be translated "justification"), and sometimes the word calls attention to right living – how God expects His creatures to live and behave towards one another and towards Him.   Both explanations of "righteousness" have been defended at this place, but we should probably let the contrast between "condemnation" and "righteousness" guide our explanation.   Therefore we suppose that Paul is calling attention to the gospel being God's power for salvation (justification) as in Romans 1:16,17.[28]   Apostles and preachers of the Gospel, ministering under the new covenant,   are vessels who make

---

[26] The recent editions of the Greek Text (UBS[3] and later) prefer the dative "in the ministry" to the nominative reading which is reflected in our English translation.   If the dative is correct (and it is found in P[46], *Aleph*, A,C,D*,G) then the translation would read "If there was glory in the ministry that condemns men ...."

[27] "The sin" (as the Greek reads) is likely a personification of the devil in Romans 7:8 and context.

[28] See also Romans 3:21-31, 4:1-18, 4:25, 5:18-21, and 2 Corinthians 5:21.

known the terms by which sinners can be reckoned "righteous" in God's sight.   If there was glory in ministering under the old covenant which brought condemnation, much more is there glory in ministering under the new covenant which brings justification (righteousness).

3:10 - *For indeed what had glory, in this case has no glory on account of the glory that surpasses* **it.**

For indeed what had glory - "For" indicates Paul is continuing his explanation of the contrast between the glory of the old and new covenants.   The reference in "what had glory" is to the old covenant (verse 7).   The verb translated "had glory" is the very spelling of the same verb found in the LXX of Exodus 34:35, which talked about the "glory" of Moses' face.

In this case has no glory - "The splendor that once was is now no splendor at all" (NEB).   In other words, the glory that once was connected with the Mosaic covenant is so completely out-dazzled by the splendor of the gospel that, relatively speaking, it has no glory left.   So superior was the glory of the new covenant that the glory of the old faded into insignificance by comparison.

On account of the glory that surpasses *it* - This is the reason Paul says Moses has ceased to have any glory, because of the overwhelming glory of the gospel.   When the sun has risen, the brightness of the moon is no longer bright.   The more brilliant light obscures the lesser light.[29]   So it is when we compare the Law and the gospel. "The law of Moses, while it was glorious, loses all claims to glory, compared with the greater glory of the ministration of the Spirit that so exceeds it.   It is more glorious, as Jesus was more glorious than Moses; as its eternal rewards in heaven are more glorious than the temporal blessings of the land of Canaan."[30]

3:11 -- *For if that which fades away* **was** *with glory, much more that which remains* **is** *in glory.*

For - "For" (see verse 10) continues the explanation of how the new covenant surpasses the old covenant in glory.   It does so because the gospel is permanent, whereas the Law was never intended to be anything but temporary and transitory.

If that which fades away *was* **with glory** - "That which fades" is the Law of Moses. The translation "fades away" is not as strong as the present passive verb in the Greek

---

[29] Plumptre (*op. cit.*, p.30) calls attention to the imagery and symbolic meaning of the Transfiguration.   Moses and Elijah appear in glory, but the glory of the Son of man surpasses that of either.

[30] Lipscomb, *op. cit.*, p.52.

which means "is being done away." The implied agent who is doing the action is either Christ or the gospel. The same idea is expressed in Hebrews 8:13 where we are told the old covenant (Moses) is "growing obsolete" and is ready to disappear.[31] The idea in "*with* glory" is "not that it was glorious in itself, but that it was accompanied with splendor and majesty."[32]

Much more that which remains *is* in glory - The gospel is the thing described as "that which remains." Paul uses a present participle, indicating the gospel is permanent, abiding, lasting. Hebrews 12:27 ("things which cannot be shaken may remain") indicates the gospel will last to the end of the age. It is an eternal covenant (Hebrews 13:20), lasting to the end of the present Christian age. The Law of Moses was never intended to be anything but temporary. The gospel which is given to last to the end of the age is obviously superior to that which was to last only for a time and then be abrogated.[33] The change from "*with* glory" (previous phrase) to "*in* glory" may have been done purposely to indicate another difference between that which is being done away (Moses) and that which remains (the gospel). Paul's stress in these verses on the fading glory and ultimate abrogation of the Law of Moses was directly related to the problems at Corinth. The people who have come to town and attacked Paul's message and apostleship are proponents of the abiding validity of the Mosaic covenant. Paul shows the foundation on which they stood was erroneous.[34]

2. The great boldness of the ministers of the new covenant. 3:12-4:6

Summary: As Paul continues to review his recent relations with Corinth, he explains that unlike the Judaizers (and their old covenant), his apostolic ministry has been involved with the more glorious new covenant. That fact is what accounts for the boldness of the gospel preachers.

[31] "The complaint of Foy E. Wallace, Jr. regarding the RSV's rendition of this paragraph is fully justified. He said, 'They have omitted "done away" (verse 7), "abolished" (verse 13), and "is done away in Christ" (verse 14) ... This chapter clearly affirms the abolition of the *ministration of death* (the old covenant). They have clobbered the entire chapter of 2 Corinthians 3'." (Coffman, *op. cit.*, p.337) Not only does the RSV tend to downplay the deity of Jesus in numerous passages (see R.C. Foster, *The Revised Standard Version of the New Testament, An Appraisal*"), it also translates the words of Old Testament Messianic prophecy differently in the Old Testament than when those words are quoted in the New Testament Scriptures. Thus the average RSV reader sees no prediction of the coming Messiah at all in those old prophecies. Issues like these have caused this commentator to be hesitant about using or recommending the RSV to the churches.

[32] Barnes, *op. cit.*, p.58. See notes above on verse 7 concerning the glory related to the giving of the old covenant at Mount Sinai.

[33] The contrast between the temporary and the permanent is expressed by the same Greek words as were used in 1 Corinthians 13:8-11.

[34] See the notes on "The Law and the Gospel" in the author's commentary *New Testament Epistles: Hebrews*, at 7:22 and in chapters 8-10, and especially the material in the Special Study which summarizes Carl Ketcherside's *Death of the Custodian* (Cincinnati, OH: Standard, 1976).

3:12 - *Having therefore such a hope, we use great boldness in* **our** *speech.*

Having therefore such a hope - The facts enumerated in verses 7-11 give us the content of Paul's hope or confident expectation.[35] Harris words it this way: "As participants in the new covenant, Paul and his fellow apostles and fellow preachers had the confident expectation that the new covenant was a permanent and irrevocable covenant ('it remains,' 3:11), never to be superseded and never to be surpassed in splendor."[36] That is what accounted for their boldness in preaching. In the new covenant, God has reached the climax of His redemptive dealings with men. The church age is the last in the series of ages. God has appointed the apostles of Jesus to a great ministry.

We use great boldness in *our* **speech** - "Boldness" is the opposite of reticence or concealment.[37] Folk may be reticent to speak because of timidity, or because of a desire to deceive, or from a fear of the consequences of speaking out.[38] Not Paul! There was nothing in him that even came close to "peddling" (2:17). In one matter Paul had been accused of vacillating so that his word could not be relied on (1:17). Not so, says Paul. He habitually used great boldness and openness of speech precisely because he had a great hope. Ministers like Paul, who are confident God has made them "adequate" (2:16,17) and that their work will endure, have great reason to be bold.

3:13 - *and* **are** *not as Moses,* **who** *used to put a veil over his face that the sons of Israel might not look intently at the end of what was fading away.*

And *are* **not as Moses** - The italics indicate that the Greek sentence is not quite complete, but the sense is obvious. Putting verses 12 and 13 together, Paul is saying that, unlike the Judaizers, the apostles did not have to conceal anything as they preached. They do not need to act as Moses did when he concealed his face with a veil. "We make no attempt to conceal anything in regard to the nature, design, and duration of

---

[35] That Paul uses "hope" here, after he used "confidence" in verse 4, is of no great moment. One should not interpret "hope" to mean that there was some doubt concerning what he has just written about the glory or permanence of the new covenant.

[36] Harris, *op. cit.*, p.295.

[37] *Parrēsia* originally meant frankness or freedom in speaking or fearless candor. Then it came to denote boldness or confidence or openness in action as well as speech.

[38] Plummer (*op. cit.*, p.96) thinks that "it is possible that Paul is again glancing at the hole-and-corner methods of his Judaizing opponents. It was impossible for Moses to speak with the same bold plainness, and it is impossible for any proponent of the Law to speak with the same boldness as an apostle of Jesus under the new covenant can speak."

the gospel."[39]   It is very likely that Paul has in his thoughts the LXX version of Exodus 34:29-35, and especially verse 33 at this point.

***Who* used to put a veil over his face** - The verb "used to put" is an imperfect tense in the Greek which indicates continuing or customary action in the past time. When Moses came down from the mount after meeting with Jehovah, the skin of his face was glowing with a shining light.   Moses would deliver to the children of Israel the message he had received from God.   "When Moses had finished speaking with them, he put a veil over his face" (Exodus 34:33).[40]   When Moses went back up the mountain to speak with the Lord, he took the veil off.   When he came back down again to tell the people what God had said his face was again aglow.   The people saw the glow.   When he finished delivering the message from God, Moses put the veil back on again (Exodus 34:34,35).   "Apparently we are to understand that this practice was continued by Moses throughout the wanderings in the wilderness."[41]

That the children of Israel might not look intently - As time passed, the glow on Moses' face gradually diminished in intensity.   That diminishing intensity is what Moses did not want the people of Israel to see, so he put on a veil.[42]   The Old Testament does not explicitly state that the radiance on the face of Moses gradually faded, but Paul here makes plain what the Old Testament implied.

At the end of what was fading away - NASB translators apparently chose correctly when they determined to translate *telos* as "end."[43]   The glow on Moses' face slowly diminished in intensity until there was no more glow to be seen.[44]   Paul is treating

---

[39] Barnes, *op. cit.*, p.60.

[40] The statement of this verse (2 Corinthians 3:13) and the KJV translation of Exodus 34:33 are inconsistent.   The KJV reads "*till* Moses had done speaking with them he put a veil upon his face," which means he wore it all the time he was speaking with them.   This is erroneous.   The correct translation is "*when* Moses had done speaking to them, he put a veil upon his face" (see the NASB).

[41] Plummer, *op. cit.*, p.97.

[42] The Greek translated "that" is *pros to* with an infinitive, a construction in the New Testament that expresses purpose, i.e., in order that.   Paul has now given two reasons why Moses veiled his face: (1) verse 7, because the dazzling brightness made it difficult to look at Moses; and (2) the gradual diminishing of the glow was a type and kind of the Mosaic dispensation which was destined to pass away.

[43] *Telos* can also be translated "goal," i.e., that toward which something moves.   This same word occurs at Romans 10:4 and there, as here, the scholars cannot agree on whether "end" or "goal" is the better translation.   Perhaps, they affirm, Paul there meant that the Law was terminated in Christ; or, others insist, perhaps Paul meant that Christ was the goal to which the Law pointed.   Here in 2 Corinthians 3:13, it will hardly do to translate *telos* as "goal" and then think that Paul goes on to say that Moses veiled his face to prevent the Israelites from seeing Christ.

[44] As in verse 11, the verb translated "fading away" is passive voice meaning "was being done away."   The glow on Moses' face was done away just as the old covenant was done away by God. It did not just pass away with time.   Almighty God consciously abrogated it because Israel had not kept it (Hebrews 8:9).

the fading of the glow on Moses' face as symbolic of the temporary nature of the Law of Moses. Moses was aware, and even told the people, that his legislation was not final (Deuteronomy 18:15-19). Just why, then, Moses did not want them to see the fading glory, or from the very start realize the temporary nature of the old covenant, is not clear. Perhaps if they had understood from day one that the old covenant was only temporary, they would not have taken it seriously, but instead would have carelessly waited until its replacement came along.

3:14 - *But their minds were hardened: for until this very day at the reading of the old covenant, the same veil remains unlifted, because it is removed in Christ.*

But their minds were hardened - At this place, *alla* ("but") would better be translated "also," making verse 14 to be an additional factor involved in Moses' time. Not only was there a veil on Moses' face to keep the people from seeing the fading glory, "also" there was besides a veil on the hearts of the children of Israel. *Pōroō* ("were hardened") literally means hard skin, a callous (Mark 6:52, 8:17; Romans 11:7). When used in a figurative sense as here, describing people's minds or thinking, a more suitable English translation would be blinded, dulled, insensible. The true hindrance to a correct understanding of the old covenant was not the typical veil worn by Moses. The real hindrance was a veil on the minds of the people. "Were hardened" is a passive voice verb, but the agent who did the hardening of their minds is not stated. When it comes to how men's minds are hardened, it is equally correct to say a man can harden his own heart (Hebrews 3:8), or Satan can blind the minds of unbelievers (2 Corinthians 4:4), or God hardened their hearts (Romans 11:7,8).

For until this very day at the reading of the old covenant - "For" introduces an explanation of "their minds were hardened." "At the reading of the old covenant"[45] alludes to the practice in the 1st century of publicly reading passages from the Law and the Prophets every Saturday in the synagogue (Luke 4:16-19; Acts 13:15,27, 15:21). "The old covenant" is the covenant given by God to the children of Israel at Mount Sinai, the Mosaic covenant which included the Ten Commandments and the book of the covenant (Exodus 20-23).[46] That the Mosaic covenant is an "old cove-

---

[45] "At" translates the Greek *epi*. This use of *epi* to refer to the occasion on which or circumstances in which something takes place is a common usage in the New Testament (1 Corinthians 14:6; 2 Corinthians 1:4, 7:4).

[46] Technically, the pre-Mosaic covenants made and recorded in Genesis are not temporary. The Noahic covenant (no more flood, plus a rainbow in the sky) is still valid. The writings of history, poetry, and prophecy following Exodus 20-23 are, technically speaking, not the old covenant itself, but are sacred writings by people who lived under the old Mosaic covenant. The KJV reads "old testament" (where the NASB has "old covenant"). In our day, the expression "Old Testament" is popularly used for the whole collection of books from Genesis to Malachi. Therefore, care must be exercised lest we think the KJV's "old testament" is used in the modern sense, for the whole of the 39 books of the Old Testament canon; i.e., the Law, the Prophets and Holy Writings. Paul alludes only to the Mosaic covenant in verse 14. That it was the Mosaic covenant which was superseded is plainly shown in Hebrews 8:6-12.

nant" is clearly stated in Hebrews 8:13, "When He said 'A new covenant,' He has made the first obsolete. But whatever is becoming obsolete and growing old is ready to disappear." Plummer calls attention to the fact that "old covenant" and "new covenant" are such familiar expressions to us that we are apt to forget their enormous significance to these who first used their equivalents.[47] Nowhere else in the New Testament is the expression "old covenant" found, and it is possible that Paul was the first person to speak of the Mosaic code as "the old covenant."[48] But he was not the first person to declare its abrogation. Moses taught it when he said "God will raise up a prophet like me ... you shall listen to him" (Deuteronomy 18:15, and the reference is to Jesus). Jesus had taught the abrogation of Moses (e.g., "you have heard that it was said ... but I say unto you," Matthew 5:21-44. Jesus set aside Moses and put His own teaching in its place). This idea of the abrogation of the Mosaic covenant did not originate with Paul; he simply says it clearest and plainest.

The same veil remains unlifted - Paul's use of "veil" passes from its literal meaning to a figurative meaning. First, it referred to the cloth Moses used to hide the glow on his face (verse 13). In this verse it takes on a figurative sense, synonymous with hardness of the mind.[49] Moses' veil and the veil on Paul's Jewish contemporaries are different in that in Moses' case it was on his face, whereas it is on the minds of the Jews. The two veils are alike in that they had the same effect; namely, to prevent folk from recognizing a truth that was vitally important. The NASB text makes "veil" the subject of "remains unlifted," and the idea implied is that the same veil (a hardened mind) remains, without being lifted, because it is only when a man turns to the Lord that the veil (hardness of mind) is done away.[50]

---

[47] Plummer, *op. cit.*, p.99.

[48] H. Seesemann (*Theological Dictionary of the New Testament* edited by Gerhard Friedrich [Grand Rapids: Eerdmans, 1967], V.5, p.720, n. 13) has suggested that Paul coined the phrase "old covenant" to form a distinction to the "new covenant" of Jeremiah 31:31.

[49] Those who suppose Paul has reference to the *tallith* worn by Jewish worshipers as being the veil that hides Christ from their minds are hardly correct. The *tallith*, which Jews now wear as a scarf on the shoulder when worshiping in the synagogue, was formerly worn on the head. This veil was a symbol of reverence, like that of the seraphim in Isaiah 6:2, who covered their faces with their wings. Even if use of the *tallith* dates back to the time of Paul, to introduce it into the discussion here at 2 Corinthians 3 gains nothing.

[50] The ASV, "it not being revealed to them that it is done away in Christ," while a possible translation of the Greek (in technical language, the Greek can be either a nominative absolute or an accusative absolute) is probably to be rejected. The idea that the Greek word translated "unlifted" [like lifting a veil] can also be translated "revealed" cannot be defended doctrinally, since the ASV translation would affirm that the Israelites were not told that the Law of Moses was temporary, to be done away when the Messiah came. That cannot be reconciled with Moses' own statement about a coming Prophet to whom the people should listen instead of to him (Deuteronomy 18:15), or with the Old Testament prophecies that a new covenant would take the place of Moses (e.g., Jeremiah 31:31-34).

Because it is removed in Christ - Again, the NASB translators apparently have chosen correctly[51] when they translate the Greek, "because it is removed in Christ," that is, the veil which covers Jewish minds is removed in Christ. In this they are following the guidance offered by the next two verses. The present tense verb "is (being) removed" would picture what continually happens as Jewish followers of the Law of Moses turn to Christ. The veil that blinded their minds is gone.

3:15 - *But to this day whenever Moses is read, a veil lies over their heart;*

But to this day - Verses 15 and 16 make clear the point introduced in verse 14. "But" contrasts with "the veil is removed in Christ" and says that for unconverted Jewish folk the opposite of removed is still true. "This day" is the time when Paul wrote this epistle, some thirty years after Jesus died and rose again. Jewish folk like the Judaizers are still dull and insensible to who Jesus is.

Whenever Moses is read - As in verse 14 the reference is to the custom in the synagogue of reading from the Law. They also recited the Shema and sang psalms. This verse reads "Moses" in the place of "old covenant" which Paul wrote in verse 14. It makes clear that what Paul has in view is the Mosaic covenant given at Sinai.[52]

A veil lies over their heart - In verse 14 Paul wrote "their minds were hardened." Now he writes "a veil lies over their heart." The plural "their" picks up the expression "children of Israel" (verse 13). This is one of the places where we learn that "mind" and "heart" are often used interchangeably. The Biblical "heart" is the mind.[53] The veil (their hardness of heart) keeps the Jewish folk from recognizing and understanding with their minds the true significance of what Moses wrote about the temporary nature of the Law, and about the coming Christ and His gospel.

---

[51] Certain technical matters are hidden under the translation offered in the NASB. Ancient Greek was written in all capital letters with no spaces between the words. Hence, one must decide how to translate the four Greek letters HOTI at this place, whether they are *ho ti* (meaning "which") or *hoti* (meaning "because"). The verb is a third person singular verb, and can be translated "he," "she," or "it," depending on the needs of the context. As a result, in addition to the translation offered in the NASB, one finds Moffatt's translation saying the glory (of Moses) fades in Christ, and the ASV/NEB rendering that has the old covenant being done away in Christ.

[52] Paul had no question about the Mosaic authorship of the Pentateuch. Cf. Acts 26:22, 28:23; Romans 10:5,9; 1 Corinthians 9:9.

[53] Compare Romans 10:6,8,10; 1 Corinthians 2:9; 2 Corinthians 4:6; Philippians 4:7.

3:16 - *BUT WHENEVER A MAN TURNS TO THE LORD, THE VEIL IS TAKEN AWAY.*

BUT WHENEVER A MAN TURNS TO THE LORD - The words of this verse are similar enough to Exodus 34:34 that our translators have printed them in capital letters, the usual way of showing a citation from the Old Testament. The verse in Exodus actually reads, "But whenever Moses went in before the Lord to speak with Him, he would take off the veil."[54] "Turns" in this context has reference to the process of conversion,[55] and unfolds what "in Christ" (verse 14) means. "Lord" here clearly means Christ, for it balances "in Christ" of verse 14.[56]

THE VEIL IS TAKEN AWAY - When a man ceases resistance to the idea that Jesus is the promised Messiah, then the veil on his heart begins to lift.[57] Just begin to acknowledge that idea, and suddenly the Messianic prophecies in the old covenant Scriptures become crystal clear. When a man views the Old Testament through the lens of Jesus Christ, he then will recognize the true meaning of the prophecies, and the true nature of the old covenant.[58] Jesus Himself affirmed that the key to under-

---

[54] The KJV, which reads "when it shall turn to the Lord, the veil ..., " treats "Israel" as the subject of the verb "turns." If "it" is Israel which is envisioned as turning to the Lord, then Romans 11:15-27 might be a parallel passage, for there Paul certainly teaches that many Israelites will turn to the Lord at some time after he wrote Romans.

[55] The verb "turn" (*epistrephō*) often designates conversion (cf. Luke 1:16,17; Acts 3:19, 26:20; 1 Thessalonians 1:9).

[56] In Exodus 34:34, the LXX reads *kurios* ("lord") where the Hebrew has YHWH ("Jehovah"). Paul often uses *kurios* for Christ (e.g., Philippians 2:11). In Moses' case, he "turned to Jehovah." In the Christian convert's case, he turns to Christ. Here is likely another example of a New Testament writer using an Old Testament "Jehovah" passage with reference to Jesus. The same thing occurs often in Romans. This interchange is only legitimate if Jesus is God, one of the members of the self-existent Godhead. Since Jehovah passages are applied to Jesus, Paul cannot be accused of misusing the Old Testament Scriptures. It has been affirmed by some that the angel of the Lord who appeared to Moses in the burning bush was Jesus. Paul plainly affirms that Jesus provided water and manna to Israel during the wilderness wanderings (1 Corinthians 10:3,4). Did Paul here mean to affirm, as he paraphrases Exodus 34:34, that it was Jesus to whom Moses turned?

[57] The verb form can be either middle ("whenever anyone turns to the Lord *he removes* the veil") or passive ("whenever anyone turns to the Lord, the veil *is removed*").

[58] "According to this interpretation, the obscurity which rested on the prophecies and types of the Old Testament is withdrawn in Christ; and as the face of Moses could have been distinctly seen if the veil on his face had been removed, so it is in regard to the true meaning of the Old Testament by the coming of the Messiah. What was obscure is now made clear; and the prophecies are completely fulfilled in Him, that His coming has removed the covering and shed a clear light over them. Many of the prophecies, for example, until the Messiah actually appeared, appeared obscure, and almost contradictory. Those which spoke of Him, for illustration, as man and as God; as suffering, and yet reigning; as dying, and yet as ever-living; as a mighty Prince, a conqueror, and a king, and yet as a man of sorrows; all seemed difficult to be reconciled until they were seen to harmonize in Jesus of Nazareth" (Barnes, *op. cit.*, p.62).

standing the Old Testament was to see Him in those verses (John 5:39) and then come to Him.   "Few passages in the New Testament emphasize more strongly that the Old Testament scriptures are fully intelligible only when Christ is seen to be their fulfillment."[59]

3:17 - *Now the Lord is the Spirit: and where the Spirit of the Lord is,* **there** *is liberty.*

Now the Lord is the Spirit - Who the Lord was and what He did in that old covenant passage (verse 16)[60] is analogous to who the Holy Spirit is and what He does in new covenant era.[61]   To and through Moses the Lord revealed His old covenant expectations for His people.   To and through the apostles of Christ, the Spirit of the Lord does the same in this new covenant age.   The result of the Spirit's work is freedom.

And where the Spirit of the Lord is - "Spirit of the Lord" appears to be one of some 40 different names by which the Holy Spirit is known.   Apostles of Christ had a special leading of the Holy Spirit; the Judaizers had no such Holy Spirit behind their ministry.

***There* is liberty** - The gospel of Christ offers "liberty" or freedom.[62]   We recall that Jesus Himself said, "If the Son shall make you free, you shall be free indeed" (John 8:36).   "Liberty," here, may speak of freedom from the law of sin and death (Romans 8:2); the man who has died to sin in baptism is freed from sin (Romans 6:7).[63]   Or

---

[59] Tasker, *op. cit.*, p.66.

[60] "Lord" has been anarthrous throughout these verses.   Now, here in this verse, the Greek has a "the" in it.   Likely, the article here in verse 17 is the article of previous reference.   The same "Lord" that verse 16 introduced is the "Lord" about whom verse 17 speaks.

[61] The explanation offered is this commentator's attempt to explain a verse that most writers affirm is one of the most difficult in the New Testament for which to offer a satisfactory exposition. Explanations this commentator has rejected include: (1) This verse teaches the deity of the Holy Spirit.   While that is a Biblical doctrine, in this commentator's judgment the present verse is not a proof text for that doctrine.   (2) Nor is this a proof text that the risen Christ and the Holy Spirit are the same person.   This cannot be right since the Spirit is sent both by the Father and the Son (John 14:16, 15:26, 16:7).   Furthermore, Paul clearly distinguishes between the "Lord" and the "Spirit of the Lord" later in this very verse!   (3) The Lord to whom Moses turned was the third member of the Godhead, namely the Holy Spirit.   This hypothesis would require a rewriting of numerous comments offered earlier on these verses.   (4) Less likely is the conjecture that a scribal mistake has crept into the text which originally read "where the Lord (Jesus) is, there the Spirit is."

[62] On the liberty a Christian has, see also Romans 8:15; 1 Corinthians 6:12ff, 9:1,19, 10:29; Galatians 4:6,7,21-31, 5:1.   Each of these are letters written at a time nearly contemporary with 2 Corinthians.

[63] See also in the author's commentary *New Testament Epistles: Romans* the outline for Romans 8 which speaks of "freedom":   freedom from condemnation (8:1-14), freedom from destitution (8:12-17), freedom from discouragement (8:18-30), and freedom from fear (8:31-38). Indeed where the Spirit is, there is freedom!

perhaps it includes freedom from the requirements of the Law of Moses.[64]   Certainly, in the context of 2 Corinthians, "liberty" is freedom from the narrow, man-made rules for behavior which the Pharisaic Judaizers proclaimed.   When "works of the Law" become the rule of a man's life, Christian liberty is forfeited.

3:18 - *But we all, with unveiled face beholding as in a mirror the glory of the Lord, are being transformed into the same image from glory to glory, just as from the Lord, the Spirit.*

But we all - Since "we" in 3:12 and 4:1 refers to the apostles, it follows that "we" here in verse 18 does also.   Since verse 13 Paul has been comparing how things are under the gospel with how things were under the Mosaic covenant.   Here, two comparisons are found in the words "we" and "all."   "We" is emphatic and the implied contrast is with Moses;[65] a second contrast is marked by "all" which is in antithesis to one Moses.   There is a contrast between the one Hebrew leader and the whole apostolic college.   Only Moses appeared before the Lord with unveiled face and partook of His glory; in the gospel age, the apostles all, with unveiled face, stand before the Lord and partake of His glory.

With unveiled face - The participle "unveiled" shows clearly that there has been a veil, and that it has been removed (see verse 16).   We might have expected "unveiled heart" rather than "unveiled face," for the veil was on their heart before conversion (verse 15); but the comparison here is with Moses, whose face was veiled.

Beholding as in a mirror - This clause is a translation of one word in the Greek, *katoptrizomenoi*, a present participle that expresses something that continually goes on.   The word occurring here is used nowhere else in the New Testament, and in fact it is not a common word.   Paul obviously had some special reason for choosing it, instead of the more familiar words for looking into a mirror, such as *blepō* ("to see") or *katanoeō* ("looks," contemplates, James 1:23).   Perhaps Paul recalls he has used "mirror" (*esoptrou*) in 1 Corinthians 13:12 and he chooses a different word here so his readers will not think he has the same idea in mind in both passages.

The glory of the Lord - "Lord" in this verse is the risen and glorified Christ.   Think

---

[64] Christians are released from obligation to observe the Law of Moses, but they are still under law to Christ (1 Corinthians 9:20,21).   The Law of Moses repeatedly reads, "Thou shalt not ...!" Jesus also gave many negative commandments which may not be ignored by a Christian under the guise that he is "free."   There are, for example, seven negative commands in the first twenty verses of Matthew 6 (part of the Sermon on the Mount, where Jesus is teaching God's expectations for those who follow Christ).   "Freedom" or "liberty in Christ" does not mean that a man is free to do as he pleases; rather, it means that a man is free to do what is spiritually beneficial to others.

[65] Very often, when a personal pronoun is used in the nominative (the emphatic use of the pronoun), as is true here, there is an implied contrast.

of how John wrote of beholding the glory of Jesus Christ, glory as of the only begotten of the Father (John 1:14). Paul elsewhere says that in Him "dwells all the fullness of deity ... in bodily form" (Colossians 2:9) and speaks of Him as being "the effulgence of God's glory" (Hebrews 1:3 ASV). The idea of the verse so far seems to be this: 'We apostles look unto Jesus as people look into a mirror. Instead of seeing ourselves, it is His likeness that is reflected back upon us apostles.' Moses' face may have glowed in the reflected light of the Father's glory. Apostles of Christ no less are illumined by Jesus, who is the direct shining of God's glory.

Are being transformed into the same image - "The same image" means the image of the Lord Jesus Christ that was seen in the mirror. Paul's word for "image" or likeness (*eikon*) is the word used for Christ being the image of God (2 Corinthians 4:4; Colossians 1:15), and for Adam who was made in the image of God (Genesis 1:27). The effect of looking intently on the glory of the Lord is that the apostles are being transformed (the Greek is *metamorphoumetha*, from which we get metamorphosis, a change which takes place from the inside out) into Christ's likeness. First, the inner man is changed (2 Corinthians 4:16), and then a resurrection body one day (just like the glorified body Jesus now has, 1 Corinthians 15:49). Judaizers have nothing like this to offer.

From glory to glory - There is a variety of interpretations given to this phrase. We like the idea that there is a contrast between the glory on Moses' face which lost its intensity or brightness as time passed, and the glory experienced by the apostles under the new covenant, a glory which keeps on progressively increasing.

Just as from the Lord, the Spirit - "Just as" means in keeping with. The words which follow are evidently intended to explain how this marvelous transformation into the very image of Christ is possible. It is not the result of man's unaided efforts, nor was it available through the Mosaic covenant. The Holy Spirit (who is sent by the Lord Jesus Christ, verse 17) makes it possible for Christ's new covenant apostles, such as Paul and the twelve, to be transformed.[66] Some were questioning the validity of Paul's apostolic ministry (3:1). To any who questioned his ministry "his rejoinder in verses 7-18 is that his ministry is greater than the greatest of all ministers of the old covenant, Moses."[67]

---

[66] As a comparison of translations at this place will reveal, the brief explanation here offered hides the fact that there is little agreement concerning the meaning of this phrase in the Greek. This commentator's comments are based on the studied conclusion the verse says that the Holy Spirit is the agent who transforms the apostles, and that the Holy Spirit is here called "the Lord" (Jehovah).

[67] Thompson, *op. cit.*, p.55.

4:1 - *Therefore, since we have this ministry, as we received mercy, we do not lose heart,*

Therefore - "Therefore" (*dia touto*, for this cause, on account of this) points back to what has been said and connects 4:1-6 with 3:12-18. 3:12-18 spoke of the glory of the apostolic ministry; 4:1-6 answers some of the charges Paul's enemies have spoken against him and his ministry, and sometimes he brings charges against his Judaizing detractors by hinting that they do some underhanded things that he himself does not do. We are still in the outline point that stretches from 3:12 to 4:6. Here again, as between chapters 1 and 2, the division of the chapters is unhelpfully made.[1] Plummer shows the close correspondence between 3:12-18 and 4:1-6 in these words:

> In both we have the same subjects in the same order: the excellence of the Gospel ministry, the sad condition of those who are so blind as to be unable to see the excellence of the Gospel, and the Divine source of the excellence. Both passages begin with similar words expressing the rich possession of those to whom the ministry of the Gospel has been entrusted. In chapter 3 the metaphor is applied to the unbelieving Jews, and in chapter 4 the metaphor is applied to unbelievers generally, especially, but not exclusively, Gentiles.[2]

Since we have this ministry - The ministry referred to is the same one about which such great things have just been said: the ministry of the new covenant, of the Spirit, by which men are justified (3:9), a ministry that is glorious (3:9,10,11). Apostles were ministering a letter from Christ (3:2). "We" likely includes Paul and his fellow apostles, and perhaps Timothy (1:1). For the word "ministry" as applied to the apostles, see 3:8,9, and 5:18.

As we received mercy - In Paul's case, he always felt that after his persecuting the church, it was a special mercy and favor that God called him to preach the gospel. While Paul sometimes uses mercy to refer to the mercy of salvation (1 Timothy 1:13,16; Titus 3:5), and to the mercy God bestows when he heals someone critically ill (Philippians 2:27), he also uses mercy to refer to his call to preach (1 Corinthians 7:25).

We do not lose heart - The word translated "lose heart" (*egkakoumen*) means to grow weary or become discouraged so as to think of quitting. Jesus used this word when He said men ought always to pray and "not lose heart" (Luke 18:1). Criticism can cause folk to lose heart and cease being bold (3:12). Instead they take refuge in silence. Not Paul! God had granted him a privilege and a ministry that exceeded that of Moses. That knowledge inspired him to keep on speaking with holy courage and perseverance even when many who heard refused to respond positively to the in-

---

[1] Fisher (*op. cit.*, p.317) does start a new point in the outline here, treating all of chapter 4 as a separate point. He sees Paul as giving reasons why he had not become discouraged or despondent (verses 1 and 16).

[2] Plummer, *op. cit.*, p.95.

vitation to become a follower of Christ.

4:2 - *but we have renounced the things hidden because of shame, not walking in craftiness or adulterating the word of God, but by the manifestation of truth commending ourselves to every man's conscience in the sight of God.*

But we have renounced the things hidden because of shame - "But" marks a contrast with "we do not lose heart" in verse 1. Discouragement might lead to the temptation to take shortcuts and use underhanded methods, but not in the apostles' case and certainly not in Paul's case. "Renounced" translates *apeipametha* (from *apo* and *eipon*) and means to disown, to spurn, to scorn with aversion. We should most likely think that the time when shameful methods were renounced was when Paul and the others became Christians, or when Jesus called them to be apostles.[3] "Because of shame"[4] might mean the hidden things make a man ashamed of himself; or it might mean they bring disgrace when they become known; or it might mean that shame makes a man conceal things. The next two phrases give examples of the kinds of hidden things Paul has in mind. It is difficult to decide whether Paul is answering a slander his enemies have spoken about him, or whether he is accusing the Judaizers of these hidden things. The first part of verse two might be charges against them; or, since he has defended his integrity against false charges at 1:15-22, he might be doing so again.

Not walking in craftiness - This is a participial construction in the Greek and gives one example of the kind of hidden things which Paul has renounced. "Walking" is a verb often used by Paul to denote a person's daily conduct (e.g., 1 Corinthians 3:3). "Craftiness" denotes adopting any means in order to gain one's own selfish ends: trickery, deceit, underhandedness, doing anything you are capable of doing. According to 2 Corinthians 12:16, Paul had been accused of craftiness. Here he denies the accusation while at the same time, perhaps, he turns the accusation back on his detractors and their efforts to undermine his influence at Corinth. "True religion can never be advanced by trick or craftiness or underhanded methods."[5]

---

[3] The word "renounced" (an aorist tense pointing to a single time in the past) does not mean that earlier in Paul's ministry he had previously practiced what he here says he has renounced. At 1 Corinthians 2:1-5 we rejected the idea that Paul tried worldly methods at Athens, only to find that such failed, and so rejected them. Admittedly, Christians will be often tempted to use worldly methods; but if one has made a firm decision early in life that such temptations will be resisted, it is not likely that the devil will later be successful in any temptations he offers to a man to do hidden things.

[4] The KJV translation ("the hidden things of dishonesty") was not far wrong in 1611, when "dishonesty" had the connotation of "disgrace" and "honesty" meant "decorous behavior." However, as the years have passed, the word "dishonesty" has changed meanings, and its contemporary meaning of not telling the truth, or violation of a trust, is not what this verse is talking about.

[5] Barnes, *op. cit.*, p.72.

Nor adulterating the word of God - This is a second example of the kind of hidden things which Paul has renounced.   "The word of God" in this place does not refer to a collection of books included in our Bibles, but rather in the Judaizers' case it spoke of the Law of Moses, while in the case of New Testament preachers it referred to the message which centered on Christ, who is the Word (John 1:1).[6] *Dolountes* ("adulterating") means to beguile, to be deceitful, to tamper with.[7] Paul has already accused the Judaizers of "peddling the word of God" (2:17). The Pharisees (the Judaizers were Pharisees) long ago had voided the word of God (i.e., the Law of Moses) by their traditions (Matthew 15:1-9). They used fallacious arguments to explain away its requirements, and they adulterated it with purely man-made rules and regulations. Paul would never tamper with the Gospel the way the Judaizers deceitfully tampered to the Old Testament.

But by the manifestation of truth commending ourselves to every man's conscience - "But" contrasts Paul's behavior (about to be explained) with the hidden things he has renounced.   "Manifestation" (*phanerōsis*) is an open statement, undisguised, the opposite of "hidden."[8] His opponents might be deceitful; he is not. "Truth" (in the New Testament) is almost a technical term for the gospel.[9] In fact, in the next verse Paul speaks of "our Gospel" in such a way that you understand he is continuing to speak about how he handles the "truth." "Manifestation of truth" stands first in the Greek for emphasis: by an open and straightforward presentation of the gospel, and by nothing else, is how Paul commends himself to his listeners. "Commending ourselves" looks back to 3:1-6 where allusion was made to the Judaizer's claims that Paul wrongfully commended (or presented) himself to his listeners. Recognizing that God made him adequate for his apostolic work, he will present himself and his message in a straightforward and positive light. "Conscience" is probably used here in the sense of awareness.[10] As men observe his ministry they are aware he is not tricky or underhanded.

---

[6] See how "word of God" is used at 2 Corinthians 2:17, as well as Acts 11:1, 1 Thessalonians 2:13, and 1 Peter 2:23.

[7] The ASV translated this phrase as "nor handling the word of God deceitfully."

[8] Paul uses the same word (*phaneroō*) at 2:14 ("manifests") to say that the triumph God leads him in is public. In 11:6 he uses the word to say he has made things evident to the readers.

[9] Fisher (*op. cit.*, p.319) reminds us to be careful as we explain John 8:32, "the truth shall make you free." It is not truth in general that Jesus is speaking about, but the gospel truth that sets men free from slavery to sin.   "In Galatians 2:5,14, where Paul is dealing with similar opponents, we have the more definite expression 'the truth of the gospel.' Compare also Colossians 1:5. In these places the expression is a protest against misrepresentations of the gospel and spurious substitutes for it, especially such as destroyed Christian liberty" (Plummer, *op. cit.*, p.112).

[10] Sometimes *suneidēsis* is used of an innate sense that prompts a man to do what his mind thinks is right, and criticizes him when he does what his mind thinks is wrong. It is not easy to use that definition of conscience in this verse.

In the sight of God - In every self-defense, self-commendation must play some part. Paul will commend himself with God as an onlooker – that should convince folk he is straightforward in his self-defense. "This is not an oath, but simply implies that the assertion he had made, respecting his commendation of himself to every man's conscience, was entirely pure, inasmuch as he made it under a full sense of God's presence to hear him."[11]   If the verdict of men's conscience fails, Paul is not afraid to appeal to the judgment of God. Paul claims, by implication, a consciousness of God's approval of his ministry.

4:3 - *and even if our gospel is veiled, it is veiled to those who are perishing,*

And even if our gospel is veiled - "Even if" (*ei kai* with *estin* in the emphatic position in the Greek) has Paul conceding what is here stated hypothetically.   Perhaps someone objects to Paul's argument about the clearness and fullness of the presentation of the gospel in this fashion: 'If it is so clear, why has not every hearer[12] become a Christian?' To this anticipated objection, Paul replies. He and the other apostles do present the gospel openly and honestly (verse 2), but that does not mean everyone who hears it understands it and responds positively. The expression "our gospel" does not mean that what Paul preached was different from Jesus' gospel. He calls the message "our gospel" because he and the other apostles preached the same message, with all of them preaching what Jesus commissioned them to preach. If some men do not see the truth of what Paul preaches, it is not because he is presenting the gospel in obscure terms.   It is not the fault of the gospel if some do not understand it.   The problem is that the unresponsive listeners have a veil on their minds. He will shortly (verse 4) explain that the devil has had something to do with blinding the minds of the listeners.

It is veiled to those who are perishing - "Those who are perishing" is a present participle. The construction does not exclude any thought of a possible change in the future (they may by repentance get off the way that leads to hell), but it does describe the present state of the listeners who reject the gospel. "Perishing" is the opposite of being saved.   Romans 2:8,9 tells what will happen to those who perish: they will receive wrath, indignation, tribulation and distress.   The difference between perishing and being saved is the result of a person's response to the gospel (1 Corinthians 1:18).   The apostle John wrote a similar sentence at 1 John 4:6 where he notes that he and his fellow apostles receive their inspiration from God and the man who is of God listens to their message, whereas the man who is not from God does not listen.

4:4 - *in whose case the god of this world has blinded the minds of the unbelieving, that they might not see the light of the gospel of the glory of Christ, who is the image of God.*

---

[11] Lipscomb, *op. cit.*, p.58.

[12] "Every hearer" reflects the word "every" (in "*every* man's conscience") from verse 2.

In whose case the god of this world - The veiling of those who are perishing (verse 3) is here further explained. Why are some of Paul's listeners not perceiving his message and responding to it positively? They have been blinded by the activity of him whom Paul here calls "the god of this world,"[13] the one who is elsewhere called the devil and Satan. When Paul calls him "god," he is not imputing deity to the devil.[14] However, men do pay him homage; he is the being who is really worshiped by men who give their affection to idols. Unbelievers make the devil their god. The devil's being "god" is something that will last only until the end of the present age.[15] When the age to come (Luke 18:30, 20:35; Ephesians 1:21) dawns, one of the first things that will happen is the devil will be cast into the lake of fire (Revelation 20:10) and God will reign supreme (1 Corinthians 15:28). Before we judge Paul's description of the devil to be startling or inappropriate, we should note that his language has parallels in John 12:31, 14:30, and 16:11, where the devil is called "the ruler of this world (*kosmos*)," and in Ephesians 2:2, where he is called the "prince of the power of the air."

Has blinded the minds of the unbelieving - The "god of this world/age" is directly antagonistic to the gospel of Christ, and tries to keep men from the light. Implied in Paul's description at this place is the fact that there is a battle going on for the hearts of men between Satan and his hosts on one side versus God and his armies on the other side. God is ultimately in control, and Christ has won a great victory (Ephesians 1:21; Colossians 2:15), but the effects of that victory are not yet complete. The devil is still winning skirmishes here and there as he blinds the minds of unbelievers. The word translated "minds" here is *noēmata*, thoughts, the same word used at 3:14. Paul has already spoken of men's minds being hardened (3:14); the idea in "blinded"

---

[13] The Greek translated "in whose case" is *en hois*. Macknight translated this "by whom," and he understood it to mean that certain perishing men (verse 3) were used by the devil as instruments in blinding yet others. The NASB refers the action of blinding not to agents, but to the devil himself.

[14] Fear of giving Apostolic support to the Manichaean doctrine, of a good God (Jehovah) and an evil god (the devil), caused various Church Fathers, both Greek and Latin, to adopt a translation of this verse that makes it a reference to Jehovah God. That translation reads "in whom God has blinded the minds of the unbelievers of this world." Augustine (*c. Faust.* xxi.2) recognized that it was an unusual translation, but noted that others had adopted it, and so he did, too. The Bible does not teach dualism, i.e., the recognition of two gods of equal power. The devil's beginning as a fallen angel, and the fact that his power is derivative (nevertheless it is very great), are evidence that the Bible does not teach dualism. Further, the devil may be the god of this age, but he is not the God of the age to come. Hebrews 2:14 tells us that Jesus (at Calvary) rendered the devil powerless. There is little evidence on which to base a doctrine that the devil and Jehovah are "equal" gods. "Dualism is a Persian idea ... God alone is God. Satan, however, has usurped the place which God should have in some lives" (Fisher, *op. cit.*, p.320). "If Satan is the ruler of this limited age, God is the King of the countless ages which are to follow it, 1 Timothy 1:17" (Plummer, *op. cit.*, p.115).

[15] The Greek word translated "world" in the phrase "god of this world" is *aiōn*, age. Sometimes when this word occurs in the Greek Bible, it is translated "world." When it is so translated it speaks of "the wicked world, or the mass of men – the men who obey the devil's will, execute his plans, further his purposes, and who are his obedient subjects" (Barnes, *op. cit.*, p.76).

is not much different.   Romans 1:21 speaks of men's hearts being darkened.[16]   What methods does Satan use to blind men's minds?   Tertullian suggested that he uses superstition and idolatry.[17]   Jesus told of another method used by the devil when He said, "When any one hears the word of the kingdom, and does not understand it, the evil *one* comes and snatches away what has been sown in his heart" (Matthew 13:19). Satan has the ability to plant thoughts in men's minds (Acts 5:3).   Satan can use man-made religious rules (such as those the Pharisaic Judaizers taught) to blind men's minds.   He can "produce in the minds of men a wholly disproportionate view of the value of objects.   A very small object held before the eye will shut out the light of the sun."[18]   It is likely that "those who are perishing" (verse 3) and "the unbelieving" are co-extensive,[19] and can include both Jews and Gentiles,[20] anyone who has heard the gospel and rejected it.   Just as a man does not have to remain among the perishing, so a man does not have to remain among the unbelievers.   If they will quit their unbelief, God can graft them in (Romans 11:23).

That they might not see the light of the gospel of the glory of Christ - This clause states the purpose (or perhaps the result) for which the devil blinds the minds of men. He wishes to keep them from seeing the light and thus prevent them from embracing the gospel.   The English expression, "to see the light," is a common metaphor for understanding something, Fisher reminds us.[21]   The Greek construction carries the same idea.[22]   "Light" often is a metaphor for God's revelation (e.g., John 8:12).[23] The devil tries to keep men from seeing the revelation that is made in the gospel.   The

---

[16] Other verses to study concerning spiritual blindness are Matthew 23:16,17,23; Luke 4:18; John 9:39, 12:40; Romans 11:7.

[17] Cited by Coffman, *op. cit.*, p.347.

[18] Barnes, *op. cit.*, p.77.

[19] By urging that the unbelievers is a larger group than those who are perishing, this verse has been improperly pressed into the debate over the eternal destiny of the unevangelized.   The Bible just may teach judgment on the basis of available light, but nothing can be found here to document the idea that Paul knew of unbelievers who were not perishing.

[20] "Unbeliever" is used of Gentiles in 1 Corinthians 6:6, 7:12-15; on the other hand, "unbelievers" at 1 Corinthians 14:22-24 and at 2 Corinthians 6:14 may include both Jews and Gentiles.   There is little difference between a Jew who has a veil over his heart (3:15) and an unbeliever who has his mind blinded (4:4).

[21] Fisher, *ibid*.

[22] The Greek *augazō* word can either be transitive (meaning "to see") or intransitive (meaning "to dawn [upon them]," ASV).

[23] Paul's mission to the Gentiles was to "open their eyes so that they may turn from darkness to light" (Acts 26:18).

gospel specifically speaks of the glory of Christ,[24] the same glory to which 3:18 ("the glory of the Lord") has already called attention, save here it is called "the glory of *the* Christ."[25] This was precisely what the message preached by the Judaizers did not do. It did not own Jesus as the long-promised Messiah. "The rapid sequence 'see' or 'dawn,' 'glory,' 'gospel,' 'Christ,' 'image of God,' shows how anxious Paul is to give some idea of the amazing brightness and beauty which was lost when unbelievers came into the power of Satan."[26] As a blind man cannot see the brightness of the noon-day sun, so the unbelievers Satan has blinded cannot see the glory of Christ.

Who is the image of God - This clause is added in order to show what "the glory of Christ" includes. This important description of Jesus as being the "image of God" has already been introduced at 3:18. Colossians 1:15 says that Christ "is the image of the invisible God." Hebrews 1:3 affirms that Jesus is the radiance (or effulgence, ASV) of God's glory. Jesus is not just reflected light from God the Father; whatever it takes to produce the unapproachable light in which God dwells (1 Timothy 6:16) is exactly the same quality that Jesus possesses. Those who would see God may behold Him by looking at His Son, for, as Jesus said to Philip: "He who has seen Me has seen the Father" (John 14:9). "Christ is called the image of God, (1) in respect to his divine nature, his exact resemblance of God in his divine attributes and perfections, and (2) in his moral attributes as Mediator, as showing forth the glory of the Father to men."[27]

4:5 - *For we do not preach ourselves but Christ Jesus as Lord, and ourselves as your bond-servants for Jesus' sake.*

For we do not preach ourselves - "For" suggests that what was identified as "our gospel"(verse 3) is here further explained. The content of that gospel includes not only the glory of Christ (verse 4), it also includes the proclamation of Christ Jesus as Lord (verse 5). "Preach" (Greek, *kērussō*, to herald like a town crier, to declare something orally) is the public proclamation of the good news about Jesus Christ to the non-Christian world. We should supply "as Lord" from the next clause to complete the thought here introduced. Paul says, 'We do not preach ourselves as Lord.' While he does preach Christ as Lord, Paul vehemently denies that he preaches or promotes himself, though his enemies apparently made such accusations against

---

[24] The gospel has the glory of Christ for its theme and object. It weakens the force of the genitive ("of the glory") to treat it as a characterizing genitive by translating this clause as "the glorious gospel of Christ" (as the KJV did). In 1 Timothy 1:11 (ASV) Paul says he was entrusted with "the gospel of the glory of the blessed God."

[25] "Christ" has the article in the Greek, and perhaps should be taken as a title and translated "the Messiah."

[26] Plummer, *op. cit.*, p.117.

[27] Barnes, *op. cit.*, p.78.

him (2 Corinthians 5:12).   Indeed, there were times when Paul asked men to follow his example (1 Corinthians 4:16, 11:1), and he did speak about how he had received mercy from the Lord (1 Timothy 1:13), but none of these personal references were for the sake of self-aggrandizement.   He was not setting himself up before his hearers as their leader or savior even when he commended himself to every man's conscience (verse 2).

But Christ Jesus as Lord - With "but" Paul indignantly repudiates the charge that he has been preaching about himself.   All along he has been proclaiming the Lordship of Jesus the Messiah.   Scattered references elsewhere give further content of apostolic preaching: 1 Corinthians 1:23 ("we preach Christ crucified") and 15:3,4 (which give four topics included in Paul's preaching, "that Christ died for our sins according to the Scriptures, and that He was buried, and that He was raised on the third day according to the Scriptures, and that He appeared ..."), are two such references.   Romans 2:16 indicates that how things would be on the day of the final judgment also was part of his gospel.   2 Timothy 2:8 indicates that not only Jesus' resurrection but His descent from David was part of his message.   Each of the three major words in this clause need to be studied.   "Christ" says that Jesus was preached as being the Messiah long promised in the Old Testament Scriptures (cp. Acts 9:22).   "Messiah" means anointed one (Acts 10: 38).[28]   "Jesus" recalls the incarnation and the whole earthly ministry of the Son of God.   "Lord" is a rich word.   As we learned at 3:16, in the Old Testament "Lord" was the word used for God (Jehovah).   If Jesus is "Lord," He is deity.   It was a word used when someone wished to show respect (1 Peter 3:6).   It was the word used of someone who was master over slaves.[29]   During His earthly ministry (Mark 2:10; John 5:27) and in the great commission (Matthew 28:18), Jesus Himself claimed all authority in heaven and earth had been given to Him.   Peter likewise pointed out how Jesus was both Lord and Christ (Acts 2:36).   When the early church confessed that "Jesus Christ is Lord," they did so because they had learned it from apostolic preaching (Romans 10:9).   Having learned it from Jesus (John 13:13), the apostles preached that Jesus was Lord from day one.[30]   The day will come when every knee will bow and every tongue will confess that Jesus is Lord (Philippians 2:11).

And ourselves as your bond-servants - We must supply the verb "we preach" to complete the thought.   Rather than presenting the apostles as Lords, they presented

---

[28] We tend to think of "Christ" as being a proper name, but actually it speaks of an office.

[29] "Lord" is used here not as a title for the Savior.   It is used here with reference to the fact that Jesus had supreme headship, or lordship over the church and the world.   (Barnes, *op. cit.*, p.79)

[30] Not enough time has passed for a legend about who Jesus was to grow, nor would honest Christians misrepresent the truth they had learned, so that there can be any validity to the modern claim that people's idea of Jesus evolved from a Palestinian peasant to a Greek god.   Jesus called himself "Lord" ("You call me teacher and Lord, and that is right!   That is what I am!" John 13:13), and from Him (and from the Old Testament predictions of Messiah - "God with us") the first preachers of the Gospel learned it.

themselves as "bond-servants" (*doulos*, slaves). Elsewhere Paul calls himself the "bond-servant of Jesus Christ" (Romans 1:1, Philippians 1:1). Peter also called himself a bond-servant of Jesus Christ (2 Peter 1:1). This is the only passage where an apostle speaks of being a slave (bond-servant) of his converts. How it is that he is their slave (not their Lord) is explained in the last clause of this verse.

For Jesus' sake - It is because of Jesus, or on account of Jesus, that Paul is their bond-servant. His relationship with Jesus had brought him into a relationship with the Corinthians. A service to them is a service to Christ. When we do things for the least of His servants, we do them to Christ (Matthew 25:40). Jesus had expressed His wishes that His followers be slaves to others (Matthew 20:27). Paul earlier had written to the Corinthians how he had made himself a slave to all, that he might win more to Christ (1 Corinthians 9:19).

4:6 - *For God, who said, "Light shall shine out of darkness," is the One who has shone in our hearts to give the light of the knowledge of the glory of God in the face of Christ.*

For God, who said - This explains why ("for") they must preach Christ and not themselves; it is because the God who said "Let there be light" has shone in their hearts so that they can give light to others. The apostolic preachers did not press their own merits because they had none; all that is of value in the apostles is derived from God. Paul felt an obligation to others on account of what Jehovah God had done for him. If God had given His truth to Paul, then Paul must give to others what God had taught him.

"Light shall shine out of darkness," - It seems likely that there is an allusion to the history of creation recorded in Genesis 1:3. "God said, 'Let there be light,' and there was light."[31] This whole verse is a deliberate contrast to what is said in verse 4: the god of this world does his work of blinding men so they may not see the light; the true God, who called light out of darkness, is the source of spiritual revelation and knowledge, and He does His work of bringing light to places where there is darkness.

Is the One who has shone in our hearts - As all through this paragraph, the plural ("our") refers to the apostles. The baptism of the Holy Spirit empowered the apostles to be witnesses concerning Jesus. In the case of Paul, some of the details of the process of shining in the heart are told us in Galatians 1:15,16 and 1 Corinthians 2:10-13. The same God who spoke at creation is the One who has caused His light to shine in the hearts of the apostles. The apostles were not the originators of the message; they were but transmitters.

> God did not allow physical darkness to reign over the material universe He was creating. With the first utterance attributed to Him, He dispersed it. It is not likely

---

[31] There may also be an allusion to Isaiah 9:2 (cp. Matthew 4:16).

that He would allow darkness to prevail throughout the spiritual world. From the first, He provided means for dispersing that also. The old lamps, however, were going out; but better ones have taken their place, and some of them have been sent to Corinth.[32]

To give the light of the knowledge of the glory of God - This clause gives the reason why God shined into the apostles' hearts. It was so that (Greek, *pros*, with a view to) others might see the "light" as the apostles passed it on. When the risen Lord appeared to Paul on the Damascus road, He spoke of how Paul was to turn men from darkness to light (Acts 26:16-18). The genitive "of the glory" is objective: Paul came to know about the glory. "Of God" is possessive; the glory spoken of is God's own glory. To know the glory[33] of God brings spiritual light into a man's life. That's why Paul preached about the glory of Christ and the glory of God after he came to know about it. "The only true knowledge of God which is available to men is to be comprehended in the life and teachings of the Son of God."[34]

In the face of Jesus - This phrase has been given two different explanations. Perhaps Paul is again making a contrast between Jesus and Moses. The reflected glory of God was manifested to Israel in the face of Moses. In Jesus' case it was not reflected glory. It was the direct shining of the glory that characterizes Jehovah God. Or, perhaps Paul is making allusion to what happened on the Damascus road. When the light brighter than the noon day sun shone on him (Acts 26:13), Paul was seeing the glory of God in the appearance of Christ. He saw the same glory the other apostles had seen on occasion (John 1:14).

Since 3:12 Paul has been explaining the glorious ministry an apostle of Jesus had, because it involves a more glorious covenant than the Mosaic, and because the glory of Christ far surpasses the reflected and fading glory on Moses' face. Because of the superiority of the new covenant, he and the other apostles are "adequate" (2:16, 3:5-6) and qualified to deliver the message about the glory of Christ and the glory of God with boldness and openness.

3. The sufferings and supports of an apostle. 4:7-5:10

Summary: The sufferings an apostle experienced and the compensating supports that helped him through the sufferings and hardships are discussed under three aspects: (a) in reference to the power of God overruling the difficulties and hardships an apostle faced, 4:7-15; (b) in reference to the hope of the resurrection, 4:16-5:5; and (c) in reference to life, death, and judgment, 5:6-10.

---

[32] Plummer, *op. cit.*, p.121.

[33] See verse 4 and John 1:14 for "glory."

[34] Coffman, *op. cit.*, p.349.

4:7 - *But we have this treasure in earthen vessels, that the surpassing greatness of the power may be of God and not from ourselves:*

But we have this treasure in earthen vessels - "But" marks a contrast between the glory about which he has been writing and the hardships, humiliations, and sufferings that a preacher of that gospel of glory often experienced. Glory, yes; "but" a great deal also can be said about some things involved in the ministry of an apostle that are not so glorious. The thing referred to in "treasure" is the gospel of the glory of Christ (4:4). The figure calls attention to the immense worth of the gospel. It recalls an expression Jesus used when he spoke of the gospel as a pearl of great value (Matthew 13:46). In Colossians 2:3, Paul says that in Christ "are hidden all the treasures of wisdom and knowledge." "Earthen vessels" describe bowls and pitchers made of fired clay. Coins and jewels could be stored in such vessels (cp. Jeremiah 32:14). King Darius, for example (so *Herod.* iii.103 tells us), melted his gold and put it into earthen jars which could be broken when the gold was wanted. "In one Roman triumph, the silver and other precious metals looted from conquered peoples were melted down and poured into clay pots to be carried in the procession."[35] Paul likely applies the figure of earthen vessels to the physical bodies of the apostles,[36] but Paul's language should not be pressed so as to make him disparage the human body.[37] He is rather saying that the value of the contents of a vessel cannot always be determined from the kind of vessel that contains them. Paul's words about "earthen vessels" may have been a side glance at the taunts that have been thrown at his bodily infirmities (10:10). He says, if those taunts are true, it all the more helps men to see that the "surpassing greatness of the power" that accompanies and helps his ministry is something that can come from God alone.

That the surpassing greatness of the power may be of God - "May be" means may be seen to be. God used earthen vessels to carry the treasure so that it might be evident to all that the power comes from God, not from the men who preached the gospel. God chose to use humble instruments whom no one could suppose to have produced such effects by their own powers. (The Greek word translated "surpassing greatness" is *huperbolē*. The power was a great deal more than was needed for the purpose.)   The "power of God" is very much connected with the gospel message.

---

[35] Coffman, *op. cit.*, p.350.

[36] Perhaps there is an allusion to the fact that the body of man was originally formed out of the dust of the ground (Genesis 2:7).

[37] Coffman (*ibid.*) prefers not to speak about the frail and transitory nature of mortal life when he explains "earthen vessels." Instead he thinks it preferable to see the apostles (who had been fishermen and tax collectors) as remarkably ordinary men, just like clay pottery was remarkably ordinary.

The gospel is the power of God unto salvation to everyone who believes (Romans 1:16). The same power it took to raise Jesus from the dead is available to believers (Ephesians 1:19,20). In his first letter to the Corinthians, Paul has already told them that he wants their faith to be based in God's power, not in human wisdom (1 Corinthians 2:5).

> The great power referred to here was that which was manifested in connection with the labors of the apostles – the power of healing the sick, raising the dead, and casting out demons; the power of bearing persecution and trial; and the power of carrying the gospel over sea and land in the midst of danger and in spite of all the opposition which men could make, whether as individuals or as combined.[38]

Coffman[39] calls on Bible students to consider "the difficulty encountered in turning pagan worshipers away from their idols, or the power required to woo men away from the fleshly lusts in which they lived, as being simple evidence that power like God's was absolutely indispensable."

And not from ourselves - In the following verses Paul will give several examples of the afflictions suffered by the apostles, so that it can be perceived that the power does not originate in the earthly vessels. These afflictions would have been fatal to their cause had it not been for the power of God at work in and through them.

4:8 - we are *afflicted in every way, but not crushed; perplexed, but not despairing;*

We are **afflicted in every way** - The Greek presents all the clauses in verses 8-10 in a participial form, the participles being in apposition to the "we" with which verse 7 opened. The participles are arranged in pairs; the first word in each pair expressing a weakness, and the second word expressing a corresponding result because the power of God had come into play. As Paul gives these participles he has changed metaphors. No longer is he speaking of an "earthen vessel" or a "treasure." Perhaps in his mind he thinks of the apostles as soldiers active in battle where there are hardships to be endured if the victory is to be won. "Afflicted" pictures the enemies pressing upon them very closely[40] in every way, or "on every side" (ASV).[41] An ex-

---

[38] Barnes, *op. cit.*, p.95.

[39] Coffman, *op. cit.*, p.350.

[40] The same word which means to press or to press together or crowd around is used at Mark 3:9 where Jesus got into a boat so the multitude would not crowd him. It is the root word translated "narrow" (in "the way is narrow") at Matthew 7:14. The word is used of persecutions or evils that distress and afflict at 2 Thessalonians 1:6 and of sufferings at 2 Corinthians 1:6. At 2 Corinthians 7:5 Paul speaks of the afflictions he endured when he preached in Macedonia the first time.

[41] It is not possible to determine if the prepositional phrase "in every way" is to be taken only with the participle "afflicted," or whether it goes with each of the pairs of participles.

ample of such afflictions in Paul's life would be what happened in Asia (1:8-10).   It was something that continually happened in Paul's life and the lives of the other apostles.

But not crushed - The Greek word (*stenōchoreō*) means to crowd into a narrow place, to be hemmed in so as to have no place to turn.   Crowded and hard pressed, yes; but left with no place to turn, no.[42]   God constantly delivered the afflicted apostles so they could continue to proclaim the message they had been commissioned to preach.   For example, on Paul's first missionary journey, his enemies chased him everywhere but were never able to hem him in thanks to God's power at work.

Perplexed - This Greek word is *aporos* (an alpha-privitive meaning "no" and *poros* meaning way or exit) and means to be without resources, to not know what to do.   It speaks of mental perplexity rather than bodily trials.

But not despairing - It is the same word used at 1:8.   Though perplexed about what to do, they were never at their wits end, nor altogether totally without resources.   The Lord interposed and guided them in the way they should go.

4:9 - *persecuted, but not forsaken; struck down, but not destroyed;*

Persecuted - The word can be translated either pursue or persecute.   "As the hunter pursues his prey, so the enemies of Paul pursued him with the hope or destroying him."[43]   The book of Acts shows how this was true in the Apostle's case.   For example, 40 men on one later occasion made a conspiracy and bound themselves with an oath that they would kill Paul (Acts 23:12).   Jesus warned his apostles that they could expect religious persecution (John 15:20).

But not forsaken - Never forsaken by God, is the idea.   Although God allowed men to persecute Paul, and to seek to destroy his life and usefulness, yet He never deserted Paul, any more than He deserted the other apostles.   Perhaps the figure is taken from the battlefield, where the soldier is pressed on all sides in the heat of battle, but not abandoned to whatever his fate may be (like Uriah in the Old Testament, 2 Samuel 11:23,24).   The battle may be intense, but God doesn't abandon His servants, leaving them to go it alone.   God long ago promised "I will never desert you, nor will I forsake you" (Deuteronomy 31:5; Joshua 1:5; Hebrews 13:5,6).

---

[42] A note concerning Greek grammar.   Here we have the negative adverb *ou* with a participle four times in two verses.   This construction is rare in the New Testament, since the regular negative adverb to use with a participle is *mē*.   However, there are eight other examples in the Pauline epistles of this unusual construction, one example being 1 Corinthians 9:26.

[43] Fisher, *op. cit.*, p. 322.

Struck down - This figure may come from the battle field or the arena.   The apostles are dealt blows like a soldier or a gladiator.   They are knocked down.

But not destroyed - Philips translated this, "knocked down but not knocked out."   In Paul's case, the stoning at Lystra may be in the background.   He was left for dead but he rose and continued his ministry (Acts 14:19).   "When he falls, he shall not be hurled headlong; because the Lord is the One who holds his hand" (Psalm 37:24).   "Paul's situation was often desperate, but never hopeless.   God's power is capable of overcoming any human problem even when human effort cannot see how victory will come."[44]   When men seemed to have the apostles in their power, God regularly delivered the apostles from men's hands.   Those acts of deliverance made it clear and obvious that the power of God was exerted on their behalf.   The apostles were not left to their own resources.

4:10 - *always carrying about in the body the dying of Jesus, that the life of Jesus also may be manifested in our body.*

Always carrying about in the body - This comparison appears to sum up the results of the preceding four.   The idea is that Paul bore on his body scars similar to those that were left on Jesus' body after His mission on earth.   Paul was exposed to the same violence that Jesus himself endured (cp. Romans 8:36; 1 Corinthians 15:31; Galatians 6:17; Philippians 3:10; Colossians 1:24).

The dying of Jesus - The meaning of this "dying of Jesus" is explained ("for," *gar*) in verse 11.[45]   The apostles were never free from peril.   Just as was true in Jesus' case, it was true in theirs.   Because they were serving God, their enemies were constantly seeking their lives.   They were in imminent danger of being killed.   They were experiencing the same process which in Jesus' case ended in His death, and at any time might end in their deaths.   Paul wrote in 1:5 of sharing the sufferings of Christ; this verse is even stronger when it speaks of the dying of Jesus.   Paul writes "Jesus" here rather than "Christ Jesus" or "Christ" because the apostles' experiences are similar to the human Jesus' experiences, the Jesus who for a few years partook of the same flesh and blood bodies we all share.   There was one difference: Jesus knew up to the hour of his arrest in Gethsemane that His hour to die had not yet come; Paul and the other apostles (with a few exceptions) had no such knowledge.   For example, as Paul faced perilous hazards every day, he anticipated every day he might

---

[44] Thompson, *op. cit.*, p.65.

[45] The phrase "dying of Jesus" should not be interpreted to be a reference to the dying with Christ one experiences in baptism (Romans 6:3-5), nor should it be made a reference to the daily "putting to death" the desires the devil stirs up in the flesh (Romans 6:12ff, 8:13).

die (1 Corinthians 15;30,31).   As Jesus had warned His apostles (John 15:20,21) that the hatred that once was focused on Him would be focused on them, so it was.

That the life of Jesus also may be manifested in our body - As in each of the previous pairs (verses 8-9) so here, the second member is a way of expressing the surpassing greatness of the power of God (verse 7) in the lives of the apostles. Concerning the expression "the life of Jesus" several explanations have been proposed.   (1) Perhaps just as resurrection from the dead followed Jesus' death, so the future resurrection with its glorified body will be an exhibition of God's power in the lives of the apostles.   Thus understood, this passage would be similar to Philippians 3:8-11.   (2) Perhaps Paul is saying that the Christian lives which the apostles lived, lives of self-denial and perseverance in trials, was the same kind of living that characterized Jesus' life.   So interpreted, this passage would be similar to Galatians 2:20.   (3) If we allow the explanation given in the second half of the next verse to guide us, this phrase means the living Jesus is the one who repeatedly delivered the apostles from being overwhelmed and overcome by the constant dangers they faced.   Jesus is alive and His divine power is what sustained the apostles.[46]   What He does in the lives of the apostles is indication He is alive. If He were not, the kind of adversity the apostles faced would stop unaided human beings.

4:11 - *For we who live are constantly being delivered over to death for Jesus' sake, that the life of Jesus also may be manifested in our mortal flesh.*

For we who live are constantly being delivered over to death for Jesus' sake - The verse begins with "for" which makes it an explanation of what was just written in verse 10.   This first clause explains what verse 10a ("the dying of Jesus") meant. "We who live" may be an allusion to the fact that, at the time Paul writes, some of the apostles of Jesus have already been killed (James, for example, Acts 12:2).   For those apostles still living, as they went about their mission there was no guarantee today that they would still be alive physically tomorrow.   Because they were working for Jesus ("for Jesus' sake") they were constantly exposed to death.

That the life of Jesus also may be manifested in our mortal flesh - As the first half of verse 11 explains the first half of verse 10, so the second half of verse 11 explains the second half of verse 10.   The "life of Jesus," as explained in verse 10, means because He is alive, having risen from the dead, He is able to make changes in the lives of men.   To whom is the living Jesus' power manifest?   Not only to the apos-

---

[46] The passage has a certain evidentiary value, indicating that Paul viewed both the death and resurrection of Jesus as historical facts.   Modern critics who made a distinction between the "Jesus of history" and the "Christ of faith" will find no support for such a distinction in Paul!   Rather than some things being *historie*, and some *geschichte*, both the death and resurrection are viewed as *historie* by Paul.

tles, but to their converts (as verse 12 will make clear).   By supporting and helping the apostles through so many trials (men who were mere mortals – "mortal flesh" here is substituted for "our bodies" in verse 10), Jesus was making it clear to the world that they were His chosen messengers, and that He was indeed alive!   The apostles were "earthen vessels" (verse 7) and in the very element of their nature that was liable to death, namely their fleshly bodies, that is one place where Jesus displayed His saving powers.

4:12 - *So death works in us, but life in you.*

So death works in us - "So" shows us that verse 12 is a summary of all that has been said since verse 7.   "Death works in us" sums up the hardships and death threats the previous verses have alluded to.   We recall that Paul has shown that when he is comforted it allows him to comfort others (1:3-7).   In a similar way, when he is preaching and experiences all the hardships and afflictions and threats of death an apostle does, good can come out of it for his converts.   The help he receives from Jesus he can share with others.   Paul is not complaining about the hardships, but is pointing to the many preservations through dangers as being irrefutable evidence that God was with him, mercifully providing benefits to lost men.

But life in you - As the earlier pairs had a contrast between the apostles' desperate situations and the power God displayed, so does the contrast in this verse.   The contrast here is mainly verbal, since "death" is physical death, while "life" seems to be mainly spiritual involving salvation and eternal life.   The apostles have physical suffering; their converts have the blessedness of spiritual comfort and gain because Jesus is alive and empowering His apostles.   "In the resurrection of Jesus, Paul has seen a principle at work: human weakness, even death, can be transformed into life.   In his work as apostle, Paul has been given life by God in the midst of hopeless situations.   The same principle is true in Paul's relationship to the Corinthian church.   Paul's labors bring suffering to him but life to his converts.   The more he suffers, the more he is able to bring ... life to his converts."[47]   In effect, Paul says to the Corinthians, "You are now in the way that leads to life.   It is marvelous that you should owe this enormous blessing to so insignificant and depressed a person as myself; but that strange fact manifests the power of God."[48]

4:13 - *But having the same spirit of faith, according to what is written, I BELIEVED, THEREFORE I SPOKE," we also believe, therefore also we speak;*

But having the same spirit of faith - Paul is now going to give several reasons why

---

[47] Thompson, *op. cit.*, p.66.

[48] Plummer, *op. cit.*, p.132.   Serious attention should be given to Paul's rich theology of suffering elaborated in these chapters of 2 Corinthians.

he could and would still speak even though he had to undergo such sufferings and hardships.   This verse is reason number one.   "Same spirit of faith"[49] evidently means that Paul shares the same attitude that is about to be expressed in the quotation from Psalm 116, an attitude that motivates a man, an attitude inspired by faith. "Faith" in this verse is not a reference to a body of doctrine; it is Paul's personal faith or conviction or trust that even when there is adversity God will take care of him.

According to what is written - The passage about to be quoted is from Psalm 116:10. As often in his quotations, Paul seems to have the whole passage in his mind, although he quotes only a few words, for it will be noted that the context of the quotation is in harmony with Paul's feelings.   He who had been so frequently delivered from death very appropriately can use the same words the Psalmist wrote.   "The cords of death encompassed me, and the terrors of Sheol came upon me; I found distress and sorrow. Then I called upon the name of the Lord: 'O Lord, I beseech Thee, save my life!' ... I was brought low, and He saved me ... Thou hast rescued my soul from death" (Psalm. 116:3-9).[50]   The title of this Psalm as given in the NASB is "Thanksgiving for Deliverance from Death."   Paul cites the passage from Psalms as scripture ("it is written") and we wonder whether Paul has used this Psalm as his own stay and comfort as he found himself in daily affliction and persecution.

"I BELIEVED, THEREFORE I SPOKE" - As is true with most Pauline quotations from the Old Testament, this one is from the LXX.[51]   When the Psalmist uttered the words, he was greatly afflicted, much like Paul, and the Psalm describes how he maintained his faith amidst those afflictions and adversity.   While the meaning of the Hebrew text is disputed, Paul's use of the LXX here indicates the correct meaning the Hebrew writer intended.[52]   The point of the quotation is this: Paul expresses his

[49] Plummer (*op. cit.*, p.133) offers two useful comments.   "Many of the church fathers understood 'spirit' here to mean the *Holy Spirit* as the bestower of faith, but the idea is probably incorrect."   After all, faith comes by hearing the word of Christ (Romans 10:17).   Again, "Chrysostom appeals to this verse as evidence that both the Old Testament and the New Testament are *inspired* by the same *Holy Spirit*.   While this is certainly true (there being only one Holy Spirit) it is doubtful this verse should be used to prove it.

[50] Because the language of Psalm 116 is so applicable to Jesus, some have supposed that the words of the Psalmist could also be put into the mouth of Christ (verses 3 and 4 being a reference to Gethsemane, and verses 5-9 a reference to Christ's resurrection).   Paul's "spirit" (verse 13) would then be the same "spirit" Christ had, as well as the same "spirit" the Psalmist had.

[51] The Psalms are numbered differently in the LXX than in our English versions.   What is Psalm 116:10 in our English Bibles is 115:1 in the LXX.

[52] It will not do to say that the words of the LXX are certainly wrong.   The Hebrew of Psalm 116:10a can be translated in several different ways: (1) "I believed, for I will speak" (i.e., his speaking is proof of his belief).   (2) "I kept my faith, even when I said ('I am greatly afflicted' as Psalm 116:10b goes on to report)" is how the RSV and the Jerusalem Bible treat it.   (3) "I believed, therefore I spoke" (belief is the ground for speaking) is how the LXX and Paul treated it.   It certainly is no help to anyone's faith to be told that an apostle, like Paul, at times deliberately misquoted Scripture.   Has not Paul himself just said he was not like some, who "adulterated the word of God" (2 Corinthians 4:2)?   How mistaken then, to accuse him of just that a few verses later!   At times,

thoughts in Biblical language because those words exactly express his feelings and the principles by which he was motivated. What was it that enabled Paul to continue to discharge his ministry, even when it involved him in daily suffering and affliction? He shared the same conviction the Psalmist did, that faith cannot remain silent.

We also believe - The present tense indicates continuous action. If we emphasize what has already been written, "we believe" might mean we have faith in God that He will rescue us. Like the Psalmist who called on the Lord for help and received it, the same was true in Paul's life. Because of his confidence in the Lord, Paul went right on preaching. If we emphasize what he will write in the verses following, it might mean we have faith in the facts of the gospel. Believing the facts of the Gospel, Paul could not do otherwise than speak them to the world, even though it might bring persecution and death to him.

Therefore also we speak - This is also a present tense indicating continuous action. They continued to speak. This is how it comes to pass that "life [takes effect] in you" (verse 12). On the part of the preachers, faith cannot be silent. On the part of the hearers, faith comes by hearing the word of Christ (Romans 10:17).[53] In verse 13, Paul disclosed the first of several reasons which explained his endurance of so many trials: he truly believed God would take care of him.

4:14 - *knowing that He who raised the Lord Jesus will also raise us also with Jesus and will present us with you.*

Knowing that He who raised the Lord Jesus - "Knowing" is a circumstantial participle agreeing with "we speak" in verse 13. Thus, this verse gives a second reason why, in the face of adversity and afflictions, Paul continued to proclaim the good news with such boldness (verse 12): it was his firm conviction of the resurrection of Jesus from the dead, and all that entailed. He had a knowledge based on testimony that Christ's resurrection guarantees the resurrection of believers (verse

---

both Jesus and His apostles quote the LXX (even when it differs from the Masoretic text), strikingly making evidentiary use of its statements to substantiate Christian doctrine. So effective was the use of the LXX to point people to Jesus the Messiah that in the early ages of the church (c. AD 130), a Jewish scholar named Aquila put out a competing version of the Greek scriptures so Jewish people would not have to try to answer the arguments made by the Christians based on the LXX. They could say, with their new Greek version, "that's not the way my Bible reads," when Christians pointed to LXX passages to validate Christian claims.

[53] G. Campbell Morgan (*The Corinthian Letters of Paul* [Old Tappan, NJ: Fleming H. Revell, 1946], p.239) identified this verse as revealing the secret of effective preaching. Because Paul believed, his testimony had the ring of truth. Morgan concluded with the imperative: "If you do not believe, shut your mouth!" Coffman (*op. cit.*, p.352) adds this comment: "This writer would add that if men do not believe the word of God, let them refrain from wasting our time with their books on the subject."

14). In many places Christ's resurrection is attributed to God (Romans 4:24; 1 Corinthians 6:14; 1 Peter 1:21). In Romans 8:11 the Holy Spirit was also involved in raising Jesus from the dead.

Will raise us also with Jesus - Since Jesus' own resurrection from the dead occurred more than 25 years before 2 Corinthians was written, it is evident this does not mean that Paul expected himself and his readers to be raised at the same time Jesus was. The future tense verb "will raise" shows that Paul has in mind the future resurrection from the dead concerning which he wrote at length in 1 Corinthians 15,[54] and his language "will raise us" suggests that he anticipates both he and his readers will have died before that event occurs.[55] "With Jesus"[56] does not mean that Jesus will be raised again when we are raised at His second coming, but rather that our future resurrection is absolutely dependent on His. The resurrection of Jesus was called "first fruits" (i.e., more to come) in 1 Corinthians 15:20,23. The hope of the resurrection was the thing that sustained Paul and the other apostles in their ministries. They knew their earthly trials would end and then, on the great resurrection morning, they would be raised up to a world of eternal glory.

> The idea of being "with Christ" is important for Paul. The Christian will, at the end, appear "with Him in glory" (Colossians 3:4). The final state will be that of being "with the Lord" (1 Thessalonians 4:17). The very opposite of this state will be "exclusion from the presence of the Lord" (2 Thessalonians 1:9).[57]

---

[54] The resurrection will also be discussed at length in chapter 5 of this letter.

[55] Many pages have been written on the question of what was Paul's belief concerning the nearness of the second coming and of the future resurrection. As this question is pursued, 1 Thessalonians 4:15 is often appealed to as proof that Paul expected to be alive when Christ returned, while 2 Corinthians 4:14 is used to show that Paul expected to die before Christ's return (so he would need to be raised from the dead). It is reading too much into these passages to affirm that Paul's attitudes have changed in the years between the writing of 1 Thessalonians (AD 51-52) and the writing of 1 Corinthians (AD 57), and that he now expects to die before Christ's return. In fact, to affirm that Paul's thinking changed is a direct attack on the doctrine of inspiration. Further, it ignores what is written (only a few weeks or months after 1 Thessalonians was written) in 2 Thessalonians 2 concerning things that must occur before Christ's return. Paul did not mistakenly suppose the Second Advent was to occur immediately. All that can be confidently said is that the thinking of Paul seems to have included both these possibilities. He did not know the exact time of the Lord's return, so speaks of both alternatives (either living until Jesus comes, or dying before He comes) as being possible to him.

[56] The KJV at this place reads "he ... shall raise up us also BY Jesus." This reading (*dia Iēsou*) is found in *Aleph*[3], D[3], X, L, Syr., Goth., and would mean that by the power or agency of Jesus the dead will be raised from their graves. Perhaps the change to "by Jesus" originated from some scribe's desire to adopt the words to the fact that Christ had already risen long before Paul wrote. The better supported reading *sun Iēsou* ("with Jesus") is found in *Aleph**, B, C, D, E, F, G, P, Latt., Copt., Arm., Aeth.

[57] Thompson, *op. cit.*, p.68.

And will present us with you - There will come an hour when every child of God shall be presented before Him "blameless and beyond reproach" and "perfect [NASB, complete] in Christ" (Colossians 1:22,23,28). Ephesians 5:27 has Jesus presenting the church to Himself "in all her glory, having no spot or wrinkle ... but ... holy and blameless." Jude 24 speaks of standing "in the presence of His glory blameless with great joy." When writing to the Thessalonians, Paul said that his joy and crown would be to see the Thessalonian Christians among the redeemed in the presence of the Lord at His coming (1 Thessalonians 2:19,20). Here in verse 14, Paul tells the Corinthians that his anticipation of all of them being united in Jesus' presence is something that keeps him proclaiming the gospel boldly in spite of the afflictions and persecutions he suffers.

4:15 - *For all things* are *for your sakes, that the grace which is spreading to more and more people may cause the giving of thanks to abound to the glory of God.*

For all things *are* **for your sakes** - "All things" recalls all that the apostles do and suffer as recounted in verses 7-13.[58] The introductory "for" shows this verse is intended to continue the reasons why Paul and the apostles boldly proclaimed the Gospel. It was "for your sakes." By speaking boldly, he benefitted the Corinthians by promoting their salvation and that added to the host of those who would glorify God. "One cannot long continue suffering if that experience is senseless. But if the suffering serves a definite goal, man's capacity to endure is almost limitless. Paul's suffering makes sense: he is serving God and man."[59]

That the grace - People come to know about the grace of God through the gospel preached by Paul and the apostles. God's grace is both an attitude and an action. The attitude is unmerited favor towards men; the action is all that God does as He attempts to save men – the sending of His Son into the world to die for sins, the sending of preachers to share the gospel of salvation, the convicting of the hearts of the hearers as the gospel is preached, and help to live the Christian life. "For the grace of God has appeared, bringing salvation to all men, instructing us to deny ungodliness and worldly desires and to live sensibly, righteously and godly in the present age, looking for the blessed hope and the appearing of glory of our great God and Savior, Christ Jesus, who gave Himself for us, that He might redeem us from every lawless deed and purify for Himself a people for his own possession, zealous for good deeds" (Titus 2:11-14).

Which is spreading to more and more people - The marginal reading at this place ("which is being multiplied through the many"), when compared with the text, reflects the fact that the Greek construction is unclear, making several translations of the text

---

[58] As he explains "all things," Plumptre (*op. cit.*, p.42) calls attention to "the glorious words of 1 Corinthians 3:21-23."

[59] Thompson, *op. cit.*, p.69.

grammatically possible.[60] A few examples will suffice: "so that the more grace abounds, the more thanksgiving may rise to the glory of God" (Moffatt); "so that as grace extends to more and more people, it causes thanksgiving to increase, to the glory of God" (RSV); "as the abounding grace of God is shared by more and more, the greater may be the chorus of thanksgiving that ascends to the glory of God" (NEB).[61] The general idea of this phrase is clear enough: the apostles keep boldly preaching and the result is that more and more people come to know about the grace of God. More and more souls were being converted. Those conversions gave the apostles motive to keep preaching in spite of the difficulties and hardships they faced.

May cause the giving of thanks to abound to the glory of God - Like a rock thrown into a pond results in an ever enlarging circle of waves, Paul elsewhere (Romans 15:14-29; 1 Corinthians 9:19-23) pictures the results of the gospel being an ever-enlarging circle of converts. This verse seems to express the same sentiment. The more people come to know about the grace of God through the apostles' preaching, the more numerous are the thanksgivings offered up to God. When the chorus of thanksgivings grows, the praise ("glory") God receives increases. That Paul wants God to receive glory, rather than himself, may be a further reason why he boldly preaches the gospel. The fact that God was being glorified sustains and motivates the apostles. Anything that causes thanksgiving and praises to be given to God is worth all it costs.

4:16 - *Therefore we do not lose heart, but though our outer man is decaying, yet our inner man is being renewed day by day.*

Therefore we do not lose heart - Here Paul repeats the assertion with which this chapter began. "Therefore" (*dio*, on account of which) summarizes the reasons given in chapter 4 why the apostles ministered on in the face of trials and hardships instead of letting discouragement stop them.[62] They have a divine commission as ministers

[60] Technically, does the Greek "through the many" ("to more and more people," NASB) go with the verb "spreading" or with the verb "abound" (in the next clause), and is "abound" transitive or intransitive? If it is transitive it needs an object. Where do we put the word "abound"? The text of the NASB likely presents the proper answers to these questions, and so forms the basis of our comments.

[61] None of these translations quite reproduces what the Greek says, literally "through the many." Long ago, Chrysostom offered this translation, "in order that the grace, made more by means of the many (i.e., grace given to Paul in answer to the prayers of the many), causes thanksgiving to be given to God, to His glory." He apparently took "the many" to be the majority of the Corinthian church who sided with Paul (2 Corinthians 2:6). He also supposed that Paul thought that grace was given to him in answer to the prayers of the Corinthians. He treated "abound" as a transitive verb, translating it "causes" and giving it an object in "thanksgivings." Most contemporary translators favor the intransitive use of "abound."

[62] We see no reason to limit the reasons summarized in "therefore" to the four things mentioned in verses 13-15, nor to the idea of a resurrection body introduced at verse 14. The topics discussed in the remainder of this chapter and in the beginning of chapter 5 are broader than just the immediate verses preceding "therefore" in verse 16.

of the new and superior covenant; they have seen the power of God deliver them from tough situations on more than one occasion; they have the example of the Psalmist to guide them; they have the certain prospect of sharing in a resurrection like Christ's resurrection from the dead; they anticipate being presented together with the Corinthians to God; they saw the increasing number of converts who responded to their gospel preaching.   Because of all these reasons, instead of becoming discouraged, the inner man was renewed day by day.

But though our outer man is decaying - The outer man is the physical body in which the soul and spirit are housed.[63]   "Decaying" pictures the body growing old, becoming more feeble, suffering from the pressure of hard work, infirmities, and persecution.[64]   The outer man is mortal, and in spite of frequent divine deliverances, Paul knows that the process of decaying will one day end in physical death.[65]   While he didn't get discouraged at all the afflictions he faced, he did recognize that his toil and suffering had taken a toll on him physically (on his "outer man").

Yet our inner man is being renewed day by day - "Inner man" tells us there is another part to man besides his "outer man" (his mortal, physical body).[66]   If we admit trichotomy,[67]   then man's "spirit" and "inner man" seem to speak of the same

---

[63] In this place the "outer man" is contrasted with the "inner man."   The expression "inner man" is contrasted with the physical body at Romans 7:22,23.   The "outer man" and the "old man" (of Romans 6:6; Ephesians 4:22; Colossians 3:9 [ASV]) are not interchangeable terms.

[64] The Greek verb is present tense denoting a process of decaying, something that is continually going on.

[65] "Though" (*ei kai*, as it did in verse 3) concedes that what is being stated hypothetically is actually the way things are.   The outward man is decaying.

[66] "Paul was no materialist.   He has here described *two* parts as constituting man, so distinct, that while one perishes, the other is renewed; while the one is enfeebled, the other is strengthened; while the one grows old and decays, the other is invigorated" (Barnes, *op. cit.*, p.91-92).

[67] Evidently Paul believed in trichotomy, for twice he distinguishes between "soul" and "spirit" (1 Thessalonians 5:23, Hebrews 4:12).   (We also admit that there are times when it is not certain that he does so distinguish.)   This is how trichotomy defines the terms: (a) "Body" is the house of flesh and bones in which we live.   It is what Paul designates here in 2 Corinthians as his "outer man."   (b) "Soul" is an immaterial part of man's nature that is different from the body.   The soul animates the body.   It departs from the body when physical death occurs (Acts 7:60).   (c) The "spirit" is the highest part of man's tripartite nature.   God intended that the spirit direct the soul which in turn animates the body.   It is the spirit that is born again when a man becomes a Christian (John 3:6).   The spirit also leaves the body when physical death occurs (John 19:30).   In the unregenerate, it is the soul (*psuchē*) or "flesh" (*sarx*) that directs the activities of the man.   Such men are called "natural" (*psuchikos*) or "carnal" (*sarkinos*).   On the other hand, in the regenerate, it is the "spirit," the "inner man," that directs the activities (Romans 7:6, 8:4-9; Ephesians 3:16).   A good source to study these matters in detail is Lange's *Commentary on Romans*, p.232-36, an article titled, "Excursus on Biblico-Psychological Terms."   Not all writers agree with Lange.   See for example W.D. Stacey, *The Pauline View of Man* (New York: St. Martin's Press, 1956), p.211-214. The translators of the NIV use "outwardly we ..." and "inwardly we ..." (instead of "outer man" and "inner man") on the belief that Paul is not speaking of distinct parts of the human constitution, but is rather speaking of man's total existence from two different viewpoints.   This commentator does not agree, for he has found that a number of passages of Scripture that formerly were difficult to under-

thing.   It is man's spirit that is receptive of divine influences.   Though the body is constantly wearing away under the pressure of work and persecution, it is man's spirit that is renewed day by day, and motivates the man to go on boldly preaching. "Renewed" is a present tense verb form also, describing continuing action: is being renewed, is in the process of daily renewal, daily strengthening, daily invigoration.[68] This renewal takes place as Paul and the apostles contemplate the reasons (4:1ff) for not losing heart.   This renewal takes place as Paul and the apostles keep their eyes on things eternal (verses 17,18) rather than on things temporal.   Every day ("day by day") the apostles went to their work as their renewed spirits prompted them to move out.   Paul is not here talking about a gradual development of one's spiritual life.   He is still thinking about his afflictions and the temptations they offer to become discouraged.   He realizes his work has depleted his bodily resources, yet each day his inner man is renewed and strengthened to accomplish the task at hand in the face of all external pressures.

4:17 - *For momentary, light affliction is producing for us an eternal weight of glory far beyond all comparison,*

For momentary, light affliction - "For" appears to introduce an explanation of how it is (verse 16) that the apostles were being renewed daily, which was a further source of support which Paul and his fellow-laborers had in their many trials.   Verse 17, which uses superlative upon superlative, "abounds with intensive and emphatic expressions, and manifests that the mind of the writer was laboring to convey ideas which language, even after all the energy of expression which he could command, would very imperfectly communicate."[69]   There are several beautiful contrasts here: for affliction, there is glory; for light affliction, there is a weight of glory; for momentary affliction, there is eternal glory.   One surprising expression in the verse is to find that the epic sufferings the apostles experienced that took a toll on their physical bodies should be called "light affliction."   In Paul's case the afflictions consisted of lack of necessities, and danger, and contempt, and stoning, and toil, and weariness, and the scorn of the world, and constant exposure to death by land or sea (as he will enumerate in 2 Corinthians 11:23-27).   It is not that they were literally in any sense light, but when compared with the ultimate glory Christians will share, they are light (i.e., a burden easy to bear) and were but momentary (when compared with

---

stand all of a sudden speak volumes when Lange's distinction between body, soul, and spirit are accepted and kept in mind.

[68] The verb *anakainoutai* ("is being renewed") does not mean that something which had perished is restored, but that in some particular that which is "strengthened" is made as good as new.   (Plummer, *op. cit.*, p.136.)

[69] Barnes, *op. cit.*, p.92.

the duration of the coming glory).[70]   Even if the afflictions accompany Paul's ministry to the end of his earthly life, the time was short lived compared to eternity.

Is producing for us an eternal weight of glory - As he uses the word "glory" as he tries to describe heaven, perhaps Paul had in mind the Hebrew word for glory (*kabod*) which denotes weight as well as glory.   Think of "the splendor, magnificence, honor, and happiness of the eternal world."[71]   "Weight of glory" is an attempt to describe glory in the highest possible degree.   "Eternal" contrasts with "momentary," and tells us that the glory of heaven is solid and lasting; there are no limits to its duration.   The general ideas in this verse are thus far rather straightforward.   But when we come to the verb "is producing" (*katergazomai*) there is some debate as to what it says.   The verb means to work out, to prepare, to accomplish, to equip, to produce.   The Council of Trent found in this passage support for their doctrine that suffering merits a claim to heavy compensation in heaven.[72]   To say that *katergazomai* means "merit" may be more than the word will bear.   But does it mean more than simply "results in"?   It appears to this commentator that the Scriptures teach degrees both of punishment and rewards.[73]   If so, this passage may say that the suffering apostles will receive a greater degree of reward than those Christians who have not had to endure such suffering.   Passages teaching a similar idea come to mind: "I consider that the sufferings of this present time are not worthy to be compared with the glory that is to be revealed to us" (Romans 8:18); "to the degree that you share the sufferings of Christ, keep on rejoicing; so that also at the revelation of His glory, you may rejoice with exultation" (1 Peter 4:13); "if we endure, we shall also reign with Him" (2 Timothy 2:12).   For the Christian who is diligently serving God, the afflictions and troubles of this life are constantly preparing and qualifying[74] him to enjoy the greater and higher honors God reserves for the faithful in the world to come.

Far beyond all comparison - The Greek reads *kath' huperbolēn eis huperbolēn*, "ex-

---

[70] The word translated "momentary" (*parautika*) occurs nowhere else in the New Testament. We learn its meaning from classical literature where it means short lived, at this very instant, momentary.

[71] Barnes, *op. cit.*, p.94.

[72] Session VI, *De justific.* xvi.

[73] 1 Corinthians 3:14,15 hold out the prospect of some teachers losing their reward while still being saved.   Jesus also spoke a blessing on those who are persecuted for the sake of righteousness, saying "your reward in heaven is great" (Matthew 5:10-12).

[74] *Katergazomai* is present tense, signifying continuing action, a prolonged process, a constant working out.

cessively to excess,"[75] or exceeding to the superlative. Perhaps Paul has used a Hebraism, where intensity was expressed by repetition of the same word, to try to capture the superlative quality he is trying to convey. It is very possible that "far beyond comparison" goes with all three expressions used in this verse to describe heaven: the "glory" is far beyond all comparison; the "weight" is far beyond all comparison; and "eternal" is far beyond all comparison to "momentary." The glory is superlative to the superlative degree. That is the thought that sustains the apostles in their ministry.

4:18 - *while we look not at the things which are seen, but at the things which are not seen: for the things which are seen are temporal, but the things which are not seen are eternal.*

While we look not at the things which are seen - The "while we look" is, according to the Greek participial construction, the condition that must be true if what has been stated in the preceding verse about light affliction producing an eternal weight of glory is to occur.[76] The apostles[77] had to keep their eyes on things eternal, rather than on things temporal. In this context "the things which are seen" refers to the physical suffering they were called on to endure.

But at the things which are not seen - "We look" must be supplied to complete the sense, and the "look" is that of one who contemplates this or that as the end or goal for which he strives. The "things which are not seen" (of course, at the present time) are what he has described as the "eternal weight of glory far beyond all comparison," and what he will go on to describe in 5:1-10 (the resurrection body, being at home with the Lord, and anticipation of the final judgment). The very same expression "things not seen" occurs in Hebrews 11:1. If a man has his priorities right, the unseen things are more important than the things which are presently visible and being experienced.

For the things which are seen are temporal - In verse 17 he said the afflictions were "momentary." Here he says such afflictions only occur during this present, temporal age. We recall the precious promise that there will be nothing in heaven

---

[75] Alfred Marshall's interlinear translation in *The Interlinear Greek-English New Testament* (London: Samuel Bagster and Sons, 1958), p.717.

[76] The circumstantial participle might be translated 'since we do not direct our gaze,' or 'provided we do not ....' We are being told that the production of glory (verse 17) was by no means an automatic compensation for suffering. "The working of God depends on the attitude of the men in whom He works. It is not enough that men suffer evil; this, in itself, does not work glory. It does so only if the concern of the Christian is for the things that really matter. If his concern is for the material and earthly realities, his evil can only be evil; it can never be good" (Fisher, *op. cit.*, p.327).

[77] The first person plural ("we") is used by Paul sometimes of himself alone, sometimes of himself and his fellow-laborers, and sometimes with reference to all Christians. Which it is here, is not easy to tell.

to produce tears, nor will there be any hunger or thirst, nor mourning, nor crying, nor pain (Revelation 7:16,17; 21:4).

But the things which are not seen are eternal - Everything that pertains to that state beyond the grave is eternal. They are not subject to time limits, but endure through all the ages of the ages to come. Abraham was motivated to keep on being faithful because he wanted to live in that city that has the foundations whose builder and maker is God (Hebrews 11:10). Paul and the apostles likewise kept their eyes on the future kingdom of God. That goal enabled them to bear the afflictions they suffered, and made them seem to be not heavy at all. We have here the same law for the Christian which governed the life of Christ (Hebrews 12:2). If temporal afflictions are the only thing we can see, they seem heavy and profitless. Christ looked beyond the cross to the joy He would have when redeemed people join Him around the throne in heaven. If we look on our afflictions as part of God's discipline which prepares us for an unseen world, then they are light and momentary.

5:1 - *For we know that if the earthly tent which is our house is torn down, we have a building from God, a house not made with hands, eternal in the heavens.*

For we know that if the earthly tent which is our house is torn down – Again, as between chapters 1-2 and 3-4, the division of the chapters is unhelpfully made.[1] "For" shows that this verse is intended either as a reason for something just said, or a further explanation of something just said. Paul is now explaining what he wrote in 4:16-18, about the importance of focusing on things which are not seen, the eternal weight of glory far beyond all comprehension, so as to keep from losing heart. As in 4:14, what Paul is about to write he knows by revelation.[2] "That" introduces the clause (the rest of verse 1) that identifies what Paul knows as a certainty. He likely learned it from Jesus who one day contrasted His physical body with His resurrection body, saying "destroy this temple made with hands, and in three days I will build another made without hands" (Mark 14:58; John 2:19-21). Or he speaks here as a prophet who has received a revelation from God. Paul has spoken in chapter 4 of daily deliverance from afflictions and death, yet he knows that such deliverance from death may end at any moment in death. That does not deter him since death has been conquered by Christ once and for all. "If" expresses uncertainty as to the time, not doubt of the fact that human beings die. "Earthly tent" is Paul's equivalent to the fleshly body (the "outer man" of 4:16) in which we dwell while living here on earth. "Earthly" (since it stands opposed to "in the heavens" at the close of this verse) does not seem to refer to the material out of which the physical body is composed, but rather to the sphere in which it operates. "Which is our house" refers doubtless to the body as being the habitation or dwelling place of the "inner man" (4:16). To characterize the human body as a "tent" is an apt figure of speech.[3] It is the word used of the temporary, portable dwellings in which Israel lived during the wilderness wanderings while on their way to the Promised Land. Such tents were either a lean-to made of branches, or a tent made of poles and cloth or hides similar to the shelters in which a nomadic people who have no permanent dwelling live. "Is torn down" is the regular word in Greek for striking a tent in preparation to moving on.[4] The idea

---

[1] We are still in the paragraph that began in 4:7, regarding the sufferings and supports of an apostle. Paul is telling the things that motivate apostles and keep them going in spite of all the hardships they face as they serve Jesus. In 5:1-10 Paul's point is that what happens after a man dies (i.e., life after death and the final judgment) is a strong motivation to keep going in the ministry.

[2] This is not the knowledge of experience, or of human testimony, or of intuition.

[3] Paul did not invent this figure. There are numerous references in ancient literature where the human body is called a tent. For example, Hippocrates, "the father of Medicine" has "the soul has left the bodily tent" (*Aph.* viii. 18). It need not be supposed that the figure was suggested to Paul by his own occupation as tentmaker, where his own hands were making temporary shelters for travelers on earth.

[4] Some English translations (KJV, ASV) have "dissolved," a word not ordinarily used of tents, though it may be used of human bodies. Since the body without the spirit is dead (James 2:26), the choice of the word "dissolve" has caused some commentators to speak about how our present hu-

Paul conveys is that when the present physical body dies, the man's soul and spirit move on to another dwelling.

We have a building from God - We suppose that Paul calls the resurrection body a "building" because it is something more substantial than our present frail tent house. "From God" means that God provides this new building, this new body. "It is true that 'tent,' our present material body, proceeds from God (see 1 Corinthians 12:18,24), but man takes part in the production of it. The resurrection body is wholly God's creation (1 Corinthians 15:38)."[5] "We have" is a present tense verb in the Greek. In what sense can it be said that we already have our new bodies? Probably the present tense is used here of a future reality because the present tense gives vivid expression to something that is absolutely certain.[6] Everyone is going to be raised from the dead ("In Christ all shall be made alive," 1 Corinthians 15:22) though not all will go to heaven. The resurrected, glorified body is one day certain to take the place of the earthly tent we live in during this life.[7]

A house not made with hands, eternal in the heavens - Rather than a cottage in the corner of glory land, as a once-popular song worded it, each spirit has a "house" of its own. That new "house" replaces the "earthly tent" in which the inner man lived during life here on this earth. "Not made with hands"[8] affirms that human hands have no part in the production of the glorified resurrection body; that glorious resurrection body is far above and beyond anything human hands might be able to produce.

---

man body is perishable, mortal, and will return to dust, while the spirit returns to the God who gave it (Ecclesiastes 12:7). Just as earthly tents do not last long when exposed to constant use and the elements, so neither do men's bodies since physical death entered the world because of the fall and the curse (Romans 5:12).

[5] Plummer, *op. cit.*, p.143.

[6] It probably should not be inferred from this verse that glorified resurrection bodies already are in existence, having been created in the beginning and stored up in a warehouse somewhere (so to speak), until the resurrection morning when they will be gotten out and put on. Since "building" in this verse is the same word used at 1 Corinthians 3:9 of a "building" in the process of being built, some affirm that our glorified bodies do not in fact actually exist, but are in the process of being developed by God as they are needed. Back in eternity before creation, God made a plan that redeemed souls would be conformed to the image of His Son (Romans 8:29), and those future bodies like the one He now has will take form when God moves history to the goal which has been His plan all along.

[7] Or, worded another way, Christ died for body as well as for soul. When a man becomes a Christian, the inner man starts being renewed. When men get their resurrection bodies, the outer man is renewed, thus finishing the process.

[8] The same expression is used in Mark 14:58; Colossians 2:11; and Hebrews 9:11.

The new body will be deathless. It is eternal,[9] that is, it is of timeless duration and unending durability. When the inner man of the Christian is clothed with that wonderful and glorious resurrection body, decay and death will be no more. The redeemed in their glorified bodies will abide "in the heavens," that is in a renovated universe, the new heavens and new earth (2 Peter 3:13). At this point, it would be well to review 1 Corinthians 15 concerning the resurrection body. Some at Corinth denied that there was any future resurrection body (1 Corinthians 15:12). The Greeks believed in the immortality of the soul, but not in the resurrection of the body. Paul presented the Christian doctrine of resurrection in this manner: (1) He showed that the idea of the resurrection of the body is a thing that is reasonable. For example, Jesus Christ has risen from the dead, a fact shown by much evidence (15:1-11). (2) He showed the absurdity of denying that Christ arose from the dead (15:12-34). (3) Then he answered the questions how are the dead raised and with what kind of bodies will they come (15:35-50). God will raise the bodies. While our earthly bodies are exactly suited for a soul to live in, the new bodies will be exactly suited for a spirit to inhabit and be exactly suited for the environment in which it will live. (4) He then told what will become of those who are still living on earth at the time of the Second Advent (15:51-54). (5) He concluded with the practical consequences of the doctrine of the resurrection (15:55-58). Once he had established the fact of the coming resurrection, he exhorted others in light of that fact to be "steadfast, unmovable, always abounding in the work of the Lord." Here in 2 Corinthians Paul indicates that he himself has been practicing exactly what he preached.[10]

5:2 - *For indeed in this* house *we groan, longing to be clothed with our dwelling from heaven;*

For indeed in this *house* we groan - Perhaps the *kai gar* ("for indeed") is argumentative or intensive, introducing an additional reason (beyond the "knowing" of verse 1 which also began with "for") for focusing on things which are not seen (4:18). It would have been better to supply "earthly tent" (from verse 1) to complete "in this ..." rather than picking "house" as the NASB has done. The words that follow seem to show Paul is still thinking about how things are in this "tent" as he begins this verse. "Groan" means to sigh because one is in an uncomfortable situation. In Romans 8:23 Paul has described how, because of suffering we experience in this

---

[9] See what was said about "eternal" at 2 Corinthians 4:17,18. This language about a body that is "eternal" seems to answer the question about whether Paul spoke of the resurrection body or some intermediate body. While spirits may have shapes (e.g., the rich man in Hades spoke of a tongue and Abraham's finger), it appears that in the intermediate state men's spirits/souls are disembodied, rather than having an intermediate body as they are pictured in Dante's *Divine Comedy*.

[10] Perhaps here in 2 Corinthians Paul again takes up the subject of the future resurrection body because of what had happened recently in Asia where he almost met death (2 Corinthians 1:8). Such a near-death experience often causes us humans to reflect on the subject of death and what happens when we die.

earthly tent, we "groan within ourselves, waiting eagerly for our adoption as sons, namely the redemption of our body." In this context in 2 Corinthians, the groaning results from the attempts of others to hinder what the apostles were doing.

Longing to be clothed with our dwelling from heaven - The circumstantial participle "longing" explains the attitude that accompanies the groaning. Paul intensely desires[11] to be free from the bodily pains and afflictions of this life. That freedom will be realized when he puts on the new body, here called a "dwelling from heaven."[12] Paul changes metaphors from the human body being a tent or a house to a garment which may be put on or taken off.[13] Mixed metaphors like this are not uncommon with Paul, nor indeed in much popular speaking. "The Christian has already put on Christ (Galatians 3;27) and the new man (Colossians 3:16) in baptism. He has yet to put on the glorious body,"[14] the new garment which will replace the old one. There are two ways to get the resurrection body. One is to have died before the return of Christ, and to receive the resurrection body at His coming, when the dead shall be raised incorruptible (1 Corinthians 15:21-23). The other is still to be alive on earth when Christ returns, to be changed in the twinkling of an eye from living in a mortal body to living in the immortal body (1 Corinthians 15:51,52).[15]

---

[11] Everywhere else that Paul used the verb "longing" (Romans 1:11; Philippians 1:8, 2:26; 1 Thessalonians 3:6; 2 Timothy 1:4) it expresses his intense desire to see absent friends. Paul pictures himself as being "homesick" for his permanent and glorious resurrection body.

[12] "From heaven" expresses the same idea as "from God" expressed in verse 1. God provides it, God furnishes it.

[13] Before Paul spoke of the resurrection body as being a house (*oikia*). Now he speaks of the new body as being a "dwelling" (*oikētērion*). Plummer (*op. cit.*, p.145) tells us that the difference between "house" (*oikia*) and "dwelling" (*oikētērion*) is that the latter implies an inhabitant, the former does not. The inner man is the inhabitant of the dwelling, the new garment. Whether the "body" is a garment or a dwelling, each pictures a shelter in which the inner man lives. Sometimes little children fall asleep before they have their pajamas on. Their parents pick them up, put on their pajamas, and tuck them into bed. When they wake up in the morning, they are in their own bed with different clothing on than when they went to sleep. When he uses the metaphor of clothing, it is as though Paul looked upon death and resurrection as going to sleep and awaking with the new garments already on.

[14] Thompson, *op. cit.*, p.73.

[15] At 4:14 we pursued the issue of whether or not Paul was mistaken about how far in the future the return of Christ would be, and whether he would die before that occurred, or whether he would still be among the living when Christ returns. 2 Corinthians 5:2-4 has also been pressed into the debate and used by proponents of both options to bolster their argument. Barnes (*op. cit.*, p.105) quotes writers who thought Paul was picturing himself as being one of the living who would be transformed at the coming of Christ. Harris (*op. cit.*, p.365) suggests that "previously, to judge by 1 Thessalonians 4:15,17 and 1 Corinthians 15:51, he had expected to be among those Christians living when Christ returned. But now, as a result of his recent devastating encounter with death in Asia (2 Corinthians 1:8-11), he realized that he was likely to die before the Parousia, though he always entertained the hope of survival until the Advent (note Philippians 3:20,21)." Whether or not Harris' interpretation is true depends on how verse 4 is punctuated (whether "burdened" goes with "groan" or "we do not want to be unclothed." As we concluded in that earlier study, so here; we affirm that Paul's language is non-committal about his own situation (still living on earth, or having died) when the Lord returns. He really does not know when the Lord will return. Perhaps his pres-

Revelation 3:5, 3:18,6:11, 7:9,13 describe the bright white robes worn by the saints in glory in the intermediate state. It is not easy to decide if Paul's idea here of being "clothed with a dwelling from heaven" has those white robes in view, or whether he is speaking of the glorified body that is received when it is time to leave the intermediate state and enter the final abode of the redeemed. Perhaps the white robes in the intermediate state are not the same as the glorified body received at the resurrection (at which time the intermediate state gives way to the final one).

5:3 - *inasmuch as we, having put it on, shall not be found naked.*

Inasmuch as we, having put it on - "Inasmuch as" means "on the supposition that."[16] Not everyone at Corinth shared Paul's view of a coming resurrection body (1 Corinthians 15:12). He here reminds them he has not changed his views about the future from what he wrote to them a few months earlier. "Having put it on" expresses Paul's confident expectation that there really is a resurrection body, and that in the next world his soul will not be naked or disembodied.[17]

Shall not be found naked - "Naked" means bodiless in this context. The conviction Paul expresses here in verse 3 is identical with the one he expressed in 1 Corinthians

---

ent earthly tent will be taken down; perhaps he will be among the living when Jesus returns. Either way, he longs for that new body.

[16] Some versions read "if so be that." However, the Greek particles express the truth of what follows, rather than doubt (like "if so be" does). This passage has been interpreted in a great many different ways. Part of the reason for this stems from the fact that there are several different readings at this point, and several different ways of translating the different readings. *Ei ge* (Aleph,C,K,L,P) is to be preferred to *eiper* (B,D,F,G,17). *Endusamenoi* ['being clothed'] (P46, *Aleph*,B,C,D3,E,K,L,P, Vulg. Syr. Cop. Arm. Aeth. Goth) is to be preferred to *ekdusamenoi* ['being unclothed'] (D*,F,G,d,e,g, Tert.). *Ekdusamenoi* would mean 'if in reality, after *unclothing* ourselves (i.e., putting off our earthly tent as we die physically), we shall not be found naked.'

[17] A big difference of opinion is found in the commentaries when an attempt is made to answer the question, "Clothed in what?" One answer has Paul explaining what happens to the living (those still in these mortal bodies) when Christ comes. (We think Paul, instead of writing an aorist tense verb, would have written a perfect tense verb if he wished to express the idea we are still in the bodies we lived in here on earth.) Another answer has Paul picturing souls being clothed with righteousness in the next world. A third answer has Paul making reference to an intermediate body. (We have previously noted that Revelation 6:9-11 has the souls of the redeemed in the intermediate state being disembodied, while 1 Corinthians 15:20-28 indicates the resurrection body is not received until the second coming of Christ. Nor is it acceptable to suppose Paul has changed his mind so that in 2 Corinthians he has the glorified body being received the moment a man dies, whereas in 1 Corinthians and 1 Thessalonians the glorified body is not received until the final resurrection.) The correct answer is that Paul has not changed subjects. He is still writing about his expectation of receiving a glorified body when the resurrection occurs. E. Earle Ellis ("2 Corinthians 5:1-10 in Pauline Eschatology," *New Testament Studies*, 6 [Apr. 1960], p.211-214) has argued rather convincingly that the contrast here in 2 Corinthians 5 is not between the present life and the intermediate state, but between this age and the age to come. Therefore, it would be speaking of the resurrected and glorified body, rather than an intermediate body.

15:35-49 against those who, admitting the immortality of the soul, denied the resurrection of the body. Redeemed men will find that the future state is not a disembodied one, but each soul has a body, a resurrection body.[18]

5:4 - *For indeed while we are in this tent, we groan, being burdened, because we do not want to be unclothed, but to be clothed, in order that what is mortal may be swallowed up by life.*

For indeed while we are in this tent, we groan, being burdened - After the affirmative note of verse 3, this verse takes up and expands verse 2. He repeats the thought of groaning from verse 2. "This tent" is the same "tent" of verse 1, our present mortal body. "Burdened" seems to reflect the external evils and calamities the apostles constantly faced (4:8-10).[19]

Because we do not want to be unclothed - Paul seems to be saying that if it is possible for him to receive his resurrection body without going through the disembodied intermediate state, that is the way he prefers to do it.[20]

But to be clothed - The NEB reads, "Rather, our desire is to have the new body put on over it."[21] For those who are living on earth when Christ returns, Paul seems to envision their transformation into a glorified body as being one where the new body is put on over the present earthly tent.

---

[18] Perhaps this passage implies that the souls of the wicked will be naked. A similar thing might be expressed by the words "second death" (Revelation 20:14); if the first death, physical death, resulted in separation of soul and body, why would that not also be true of the "second death"? The idea would be that after all are raised from the dead (in the resurrection), and after all are judged, the wicked are stripped of their resurrection body, leaving their souls "naked." Having lived in a glorified body for a short period of time, part of the torment of the wicked would be the realization of what they could have had and lost.

[19] The cause of the groaning depends on how you understand the rest of the verse. The comments just offered treat the words "being burdened" with "groan," resulting in the idea that Paul desires to leave this world because he is being borne down by trials and toils and the calamities of this life. The RSV ("we sigh with anxiety") treats the words "being burdened" (anxiety) with what follows, with the resulting idea that Paul is expressing the anxiety which the thought of death causes. Fisher (*op. cit.*, p.332) writes instead about the "very human dread of dying." Though Paul knew that death was a gateway to a new and more glorious life, there was still a dread of the experience of dying. "The prospect of death is not a pleasant one for any human being, and it is false interpretation to try to make the Christian face death without qualms or fears."

[20] Marshall's interlinear translation (*op. cit.*, p.717) has "inasmuch as we do not wish to be unclothed."

[21] This translation follows the lead of those commentators (Meyer, Hughes) who emphasize the fact that the Greek verb is a double compound (*ep-en-dusasthai*). These interpreters suppose the reason for the double compound is that Paul is trying to say he wants to "put [his new body] on *over* the earthly body he now lives in," rather than experiencing death where the soul is separated (for a while) from the body.

In order that what is mortal may be swallowed up by life - Again, the NEB reads, "So that our mortal part may be absorbed into life immortal." Paul is explaining that when the transformation of the living takes place, only what is mortal is affected; the inner man consisting of soul and spirit survives. Paul here states in abbreviated form what he wrote earlier in 1 Corinthians 15:53,54. One ancient writer illustrated the change that takes place when the old is swallowed up by the new by reminding his readers of the way darkness vanishes when light enters.

5:5 - *Now He who prepared us for this very purpose is God, who gave to us the Spirit as a pledge.*

Now He who prepared us for this very purpose is God - "This very purpose" or "this very thing" (ASV) refers back to what has been said about the longing for the replacement of this earthly tent with a resurrection body. Our versions have translated *de* as "now," which implies a certain amount of contrast. 'Do not think that my longing for a new body is fanciful; God Himself has so formed and made us that the new body is a certainty.' Two possibilities exist for when God so "prepared us": perhaps, when He first created us, He made us so that our inner man would first be clothed in a body like Adam's, and then in a body like the one the glorified Christ now has (1 Corinthians 15:49), or perhaps it was at the time of our baptism. Commentators who opt for the latter idea point to the next clause as proof, for it is when we are immersed that we receive the pledge of the Spirit. In the Greek, the words "is God" are placed at the very close in order to give emphasis. "If God is the one who does it, there can be no doubt that it shall be done."[22]

Who gave to us the Spirit as a pledge - The indwelling gift of the Holy Spirit, received at baptism (Acts 2:38), serves as a "pledge" (a guarantee[23]) that we will be raised from the dead (Romans 8:11), thus satisfying the longing for a dwelling in which the inner man continues to live. By giving us a pledge, God has placed Himself in the position of a debtor who has made a first installment, thereby obligating Himself to pay the remainder in full.

5:6 - *Therefore, being always of good courage, and knowing that while we are at home in the body we are absent from the Lord --*

Therefore, being always of good courage - "Therefore" points back to what was said in verse 5 about how God has made us and has given us the Holy Spirit as a pledge. "Good courage" is the opposite of losing heart (2 Corinthians 4:16). The

[22] Fisher, *ibid.*

[23] On the meaning of "pledge," see notes at 2 Corinthians 1:22. Also consult Ephesians 1:13,14. Compare what is said about the Holy Spirit being "first fruits" (i.e., there is more to come) at Romans 8:23.

KJV translates the verb "we are always confident."   "Always" (*pantote,* compare 2 Corinthians 2:4, 4:21, 9:18) means "in every event," the same events he has called a "burden" in verse 4.

And knowing that - With a broken sentence in the Greek,[24] Paul here takes up the sufferings and supports of an apostle viewed from the standpoint of the coming judgment (verses 6-10).   In addition to the encouragement one gets from thinking about the resurrection body, another thing that keeps the apostles steadfast in the face of hardships and persecutions is the thought of how awesome it will be to stand at the judgment seat of Christ.   On the meaning of the word and how Paul "knows," see verse 1.   "Being of good courage" and "knowing" are both participles in the Greek and are coordinate; that is, they describe two things true of the apostles.

While we are at home in the body - "At home in the body" is the same thing as living in our earthly tent (verse 1).   It speaks about this earthly life, where the physical body provides our inner man with a "tent" in which to dwell.

We are absent from the Lord - Again there is a change of metaphors.   In verses 1-5 it was a tent or a dwelling, and clothing that could be put on or off.   Now the figure is in terms of presence or absence with someone.   Jesus Christ is the person intended by "Lord."   When Paul says we are "absent" from the Lord, he does not mean that while we are living in our physical body that we are altogether absent from or separated from the Lord.   Jesus promised to be with us to the end of the age (Matthew 28:20).   Rather Paul is speaking relatively.   The next verse explains how he is using the term "absent":   now, in this life, we do not have the full fellowship with Jesus that we will have when we see Him face to face.   "The life of faith (as he explains in the next verse) is less close and intimate than the life of sight.   While in this world, we are separate from the Lord, in spite of His constant presence (Matthew 28:20) and our union with Him (1 Corinthians 6:15, 12:27; 1 Thessalonians 5:10)."[25]

5:7 - *for we walk by faith, not by sight --*

For we walk by faith - Beginning with "for," this part of the broken sentence (verses 6-8) explains what it means to be "absent from the Lord."   Paul seems to feel that the language "absent from the Lord" (verse 6) could be misunderstood, so he hastens to explain in what sense that expression is true.   To "walk," as often in the Scriptures,

---

[24] Our English translations have tried to alert us to the fact that there is a broken sentence here in the Greek.   The KJV put the verse in parentheses; the NASB puts one dash at the close of verse 6 and another at the close of verse 7.

[25] Plummer, *op. cit.*, p.15.

denotes to live, to act, to conduct one's life in a certain way. In the background is the idea that life is a journey, a pilgrimage, that the Christian is traveling to another and better country. "Faith comes by hearing the word of Christ" (Romans 10:17). Of course, "faith" is not just wishful thinking or credulity. A person who walks by faith is constantly walking according to God's directions. Faith is habitually doing what God says. All the while a person is walking faithfully, there are things which he cannot see, but he is looking forward to all that God has promised, that will be given to the faithful. Think of Abraham who kept looking for the city which has the foundations whose builder and maker is God (Hebrews 11:10); or think of Moses who "was looking to the reward" (Hebrews 11:26).

Not by sight - The Greek word does not refer to the faculty of seeing, but rather to the form or fashion of the thing that is seen. When we have received our resurrection bodies and are together with the Lord, it will be a time of walking by sight.[26] 1 John 3:2 tells us that when Jesus appears in His second coming, "we shall be like Him, because we shall see Him just as He is." Romans 8:24 has a similar idea: "hope that is seen is not hope; for who hopes for what he sees?" (NASB mg.). Faith gives way to sight. Hope gives way to fruition. There will be a fellowship with Jesus that is not possible while we are living in this world. With Jesus in sight, no longer will we feel that we are absent from the Lord.

5:8 - *We are of good courage, I say, and prefer rather to be absent from the body and to be at home with the Lord.*

We are of good courage, I say - The sentence which began in verse 6 and was broken off, is here resumed. "Good courage" was explained in verse 6 where this sentence was begun. "I say" (meaning "I repeat") is a good equivalent for *de* at this place.

And prefer rather to be absent from the body - The earlier verses in this chapter have shown that the inner man has two bodies, a physical, earthly tent, and a glorified body which, however, is not attained until resurrection day. To be "absent from the body" means to leave this physical body behind in death. In the state between death and resurrection, of which Paul here speaks, the soul is with Christ, as we are here informed, but without a body. The apparent sense of the verse is that he prefers death to life, because it brings him into the presence of his Lord.[27] At first this seems at variance with what he had said in verse 4, as to his not wishing to put off the garment

---

[26] Belief, however strong, cannot be the same as sight; and from a Christ whom we cannot see we are to that extent separated, just as a blind man is cut off from the world to which he nevertheless belongs.

[27] The weighing of possibilities – which was best, to remain here or die and be with the Lord – reminds us of what the same apostle describes in Philippians 1:21-25. There he said the choice was one that left him "hard pressed from both directions."

of the present body. Here, however, the expression is not so strong. "We are willing, he says, if death comes before the Coming of the Lord, to accept death; for even though it does not immediately bring with it the glory of the resurrection body, it does make us at home with Christ among the souls who wait for the resurrection."[28]

And to be at home with the Lord - "At home" is the same word we had in verse 6. "With" translates *pros*, which in this construction means "face to face" with the Lord. This verse shows that the souls of the saints, when they depart this earthly body, are at once taken to heaven, where Christ is.[29] The same idea occurs in Philippians 1:23 where he wrote "to depart and be with Christ." When physical death occurs, the soul is carried by the angels to the sea of glass (Revelation 15:2) underneath the altar in heaven (Revelation 6:9-11). From that vantage point the souls are "face to face" in intimate association and fellowship with Jesus (whose near presence is described in Revelation 5:6). Revelation 3:21 describes the saints as sitting with Christ on His throne. "Even the possibility of being left bodiless for a time loses its terrors, when it is remembered that getting away from our present temporary shelter furnished by the physical body means getting home to closer fellowship with Christ."[30] "This passage assumes that the dead are conscious, conscious of the presence of the Lord (Philippians 1:20-23; Luke 23:43; Acts 7:59); otherwise departure from the body would be a worse condition, with regard to Christ, than being in the body."[31]

5:9 - *Therefore also we have as our ambition, whether at home or absent, to be pleasing to Him.*

Therefore also we have as our ambition - "Therefore" summarizes what was just said, an assurance we go to be with Jesus when we die, and the prospect beyond that of a resurrection body. "Ambition" is used of striving after some honor or prize in Romans 15:20 and 1 Thessalonians 4:11. Here Paul says he makes a constant, similar kind of effort to be pleasing to Jesus.

Whether at home or absent - "At home" picks up "at home in the body" (verse 6) and "absent" picks up "absent from the body" (verse 8). Wherever he was, whether he is still living and ministering here on earth, or whether his life on earth is finished and he is present with the Lord, Paul is going to make it his aim to so live that he meets the Lord's approval.

---

[28] Plumptre, *op. cit.,* p.46.

[29] The moment physical death occurs, the soul of the righteous man takes up permanent residence "with the Lord." We have concluded from our study of the Scriptures that souls in the intermediate state are disembodied, and will not receive their resurrection body until the second advent of Christ.

[30] Plummer, *op. cit.,* p.152.

[31] Plummer, *op. cit.,* p.150.

To be pleasing to Him - "Him" is the Lord Jesus Christ.   When it comes to a motive for living, it makes no difference to Paul whether he is here on earth or present with the Lord.   What does matter is that he pleases the Lord Jesus Christ.   If we are going to be face to face with Him in the judgment, we had better be pleasing to Him in the meantime.   There are verses that seem to say the redeemed will do service for the Lord in the intermediate state.   Two such verses are Philippians 1:21, "For me to live is Christ, to die is gain" (gain "for Him," it is implied), and Revelation 7:15, "His servants serve Him day and night in His temple."   Perhaps we may draw a conclusion from 2 Corinthians 5:9 that the service of the redeemed in the intermediate state is further opportunity to please Jesus.   We should not try to draw any conclusion from verse 9 regarding the possibility of performing actions that are displeasing to Christ during the intermediate state (i.e., when we are "absent from the body"), since verse 10 tells us that the recompense given out at the judgment seat of Christ concerns deeds done while in the body (i.e., during the life time on earth).

5:10 - *For we must all appear before the judgment seat of Christ, that each one may be recompensed for his deeds in the body, according to what he has done, whether good or bad.*

For we must all appear - "For" indicates we have good reason for making it our aim to please Christ; namely, there is a day coming when we will stand before Him as the judge of the universe.   Every man, according to Paul, will be judged (Romans 2:6-8), and that includes "we" Christians.   "Must" says that attendance at the final judgment is compulsory because God has so mandated it.[32]   Where the NASB has "appear," the ASV translation "be made manifest" is more satisfactory.   Not only will men "appear" at the final judgment, but they will have their lives laid open for scrutiny by God and all in attendance.   Things that were done in darkness will be brought to the light.   What God has seen and known all along will be public knowledge (1 Corinthians 4:5).

Before the judgment-seat of Christ - At times in the New Testament "judgment seat" (*bēma*) refers to the raised platform from which the judge presided (Acts 18:12; Acts 25:6), and at times it refers to the judge's seat (*curule*) which rested on the platform (Matthew 27:19; John 19:13).[33]   Christ is identified as the judge who con-

---

[32] When Paul says "we all must appear at the judgment seat of Christ," some have supposed that Romans 8:1, which speaks of no condemnation for those who are in Christ, is contradicted.   But the context of that passage shows it speaks of no further condemnation to a life of slavery to sin, rather than to something that happens at the final judgment.

[33] Some verses (e.g., Matthew 19:25, 25:31; Revelation 20:11) speak of the divine judgment-seat as being a "throne" rather than a *bēma*.   Certain modern premillennialists, for example, distinguish between the *bēma* ("judgment seat") and the *thronos* (throne) as though they spoke of two different judgments.   It is further urged that only Christians are present at the *bēma* (judgment) seat of Christ and the only thing done there is to pass out rewards; none is sent to Hell from the *bēma*.   On the other hand, the theory goes, only the wicked are at the great white throne judgment (Revelation 20:11-15).   But such a distinction, resulting in a plurality of future judgments, does not

ducts this final judgment.[34]   Elsewhere in his writings (e.g., 2 Thessalonians 1:7,8) Paul tells us that the time when this judgment occurs is at the second coming of Christ.

That each one may be recompensed for his deeds in the body - "Each one" corrects any false inference which might be drawn from "we must all appear."   We shall not be judged *en masse*, or in classes, but one by one.   "Recompensed" *(komidzēsthai)* carries the idea of receiving what is due, the appropriate reward or penalty for conduct ("his deeds") while in the body on earth.   "In the body" literally means "through the body."   It is not the body itself that does the deeds, but the man who lived in the body is pictured as using the body as a tool or instrument.   The recompense is for deeds done in this life, not for something done after the body is laid aside in death.   "All beyond the grave is either reward or punishment.   It is not probation.   The destiny is to be settled forever by what is done in this world of probation."[35]

According to what he has done - The recompense will be in harmony with what the man has done.   Judgment on the basis of works is completely in harmony with the doctrine of justification by faith, for "faith" never did exclude works of obedience which God commands.   Even a close study of Romans 2:1-16, where it is carefully explained that the final judgment will be according to truth, according to deeds, and without partiality, shows there is no contradiction in Paul concerning what standards will be applied to men as they are judged at the judgment seat of Christ.[36]   Paul reflects what Jesus Himself taught on this subject: "everyone who hears these words of Mine and [habitually] acts upon them" is the one who is building his house on the rock (Matthew 7:24).

---

seem to fit either 2 Corinthians 5:10 or the teaching of Scripture elsewhere. We are convinced that Scriptures such as Acts 24:25 teach that there is to be one, general judgment, when Christ returns, not several judgments. Paul might naturally use this Roman and Greek idea of judgment, being very familiar with it in his own experience (Acts 12:21, 18:12, 25:6; Romans 14:10), and mean by it the same thing as the gospel writers do when they used *thronos* to give a mental picture of what the final judgment will be like. Coffman (*op. cit.*, p.365) urges that the reason for making a distinction in the judgments (such as found in the footnotes of the *Scofield Reference Bible*) is to be found, not in what Paul taught, but in the theory of justification by "faith only." The problem these theologians have is how to harmonize the idea that men will be saved by "faith alone" but judged on the basis of their deeds. Coffman says (*ibid.*), "The blunt truth is that verse 10 is not only 'inconsistent' with the theory of justification by 'faith alone'; it is a dogmatic contradiction of it." Further, not only must 2 Corinthians be explained away but so must other passages which speak of "deeds" as being one of the criteria God looks at in the final judgment (see Romans 2:6-10; Matthew 7:21-23).

[34] According to the New Testament all judgment has been committed to the Son (John 5:22,27; Acts 10:42, 17:31).   The better manuscripts have "judgment seat of God" at Romans 14:10.   Those verses that seem to have God the Father doing the judging should be understood to mean that what He does through His agent (Christ) He is said to be doing.

[35] Barnes, *op. cit.*, p.111.

[36] For further information on what saving "faith" involves consult the special study on "Justification by Faith" later in this author's commentary *New Testament Epistles: 2 Corinthians-Galatians.*

Whether good or bad - The change to the neuter ("what he has done ... good or bad") indicates that conduct as a whole (rather than separate acts) will be judged and rewarded or punished. In Romans 2:7-10 (where the verbs are all present tense) the righteous are described as persevering in doing good, while the wicked are pictured as habitually being selfishly ambitious, as not habitually obeying the truth, but rather habitually obeying unrighteousness. In the final judgment it is the tenor of a man's life that will be judged. What was done during a lifetime is summed up and estimated as a total. "Bad" translates *phaulon*, worthless, good for nothing.[37] If a man's behavior is consistently worthless, the divine Judge will sentence the man or woman to punishment.

There is one question to which attention must be given: how shall we harmonize verses that speak of sins being forgiven and verses that speak of what we have done being made manifest at the final judgment? Scripture certainly does speak of forgiven sins: the death of Christ provides a propitiatory sacrifice (Romans 3:25; Ephesians 2:13); men's sins are forgiven (washed away) at baptism (Acts 22:16; 1 Corinthians 6:11); the blood of Christ cleanses those who habitually walk in the light (1 John 1:7). On the other hand, every thought and action is to be judged (1 Corinthians 4:5), and men shall give account for every idle word they speak (Matthew 12:36). How are these seemingly contradictory ideas to be harmonized? This commentator has often expressed the idea that after the deeds and thoughts that make up the tenor our lives have been made manifest at the judgment, and it is obvious to all that what is deserved is condemnation, then Jesus will step forward and claim the Christian for his own, rather than allowing the faithful one to go to perdition. All through eternity we will praise Him for making our salvation possible.

We have come to the close of the paragraph, begun at 4:7, which deals with the sufferings and supports of an apostle. They are supported by God's blessing, the hope of future glory, by anticipation of receiving a resurrection body, and the prospect of having to answer to Christ at the coming judgment.

4. The life (self-sacrifice) of an apostle.   5:11-6:10

Summary: We are still in the first major portion of the book in which Paul recounts his recent dealings with Corinth. He continues this rehearsal by doing three things: he calls attention to his motives, which are reverence for Christ and Christ's love for us (5:11-15); he points out that he is working un-

---

[37] There is a manuscript variation at this place. Where our Bibles read "bad," some (Aleph, C, 17, and other cursives) have the word *phaulon,* and others (P[46], B,D,F,G, K,L,P) have the word *kakon* ("evil, wicked"). *Agathon-kakon* ("good-bad") is the usual Pauline antithesis (cf. Romans 2:9,10, 3:8, 7:19, 12:21) while *agathon-phaulon* is found only once elsewhere in Paul's writings (Romans 9:11). It is likely that *phaulon* is original, for it would be more likely for a scribe to substitute *kakon* for *phaulon,* than the other way around.

der new conditions that make it possible for any man to be a new creature in Christ (5:16-19); and he calls attention to his appointment as an ambassador of Christ and to some of the things which that appointment has involved (5:20-6:10).

5:11 - *Therefore knowing the fear of the Lord, we persuade men, but we are made manifest to God; and I hope that we are manifest also in your consciences.*

Therefore knowing the fear of the Lord - "Therefore" (*oun*) builds on what was written in verses 9 and 10 concerning the coming judgment where Christ will serve as the judge. Verse 11 serves as a transition to the topic of the motives that have guided Paul's ministry as an apostle of Jesus. He defends his motives and integrity which have been attacked by his opponents. "Knowing" here has the idea of being influenced by or being motivated by. The "Lord" is the Lord Jesus, who has just been pictured as one day to be seated on the throne of Judgment, the One to whom all will give an account, and the One who will give to all their due. That awareness produces an awesome feeling of reverence and respect.[38] It is the same attitude that characterized the early churches (Acts 9:31) and is to motivate each Christian's submission to one another (Ephesians 5:21).

We persuade men - The context seems to make this mean we endeavor to persuade men concerning our good motives and that our conduct is sound and above board. Verse 12 alludes to an accusation by his opponents that he appealed to men in the wrong way. In Galatians 1:10, another letter from this same time period in Paul's life, the same word here translated "persuade" (there rendered "am I now seeking the favor of men?") reflects the charge by Paul's enemies that he was always trying to please men.[39] Perhaps this attempt by Paul to persuade men concerning his integrity is addressed to those opponents. He asserts that his sole ambition is to please the Lord (verse 9). In the close of this verse he then addresses the church members in Corinth, in case they, too, need persuading, now that some have begun to listen to what the opponents were saying about Paul.

---

[38] The KJV reads "terror of the Lord," but "terror" is too strong a word for this place; it hinders English readers from seeing that Paul speaks of the identical "fear of the Lord" which the Old Testament indicates is "the beginning of wisdom" (Job 28:28; Psalm 111:10; Proverbs 9:10).

[39] Because Paul does not specifically identify what it is that he tries to persuade men to believe, this verse has been given other interpretations, including: (1) Because there is a judgment to be faced, we try to persuade men to become Christians and thus flee the wrath to come; and (2) We try to persuade men concerning the urgency and truth of the gospel. While both of these are true statements, it appears that these suggested interpretations are both foreign to the context at this place and make the contrast between persuading men and being fully known (manifest) to God pointless.

But we are made manifest to God - "But" marks a contrast.[40]   We try to persuade men, but whether or not men recognize our claims, God sees and knows that we are upright in our aims and purposes.   We don't need to try to persuade God in this matter.   A man who holds Jesus in reverence and who knows that God is watching will not be underhanded or try to take advantage of others for his own benefit. "Made manifest" is the same verb used in verse 10 ("appear").   Here it is a perfect tense which indicates that God already knows about Paul's conduct and motives, and has for some time.   Paul has already told his readers that he always conducts himself in the awareness that God is watching (2:17).   Now Paul states that what Paul wants to be when he stands before the judgment seat of Christ he now seeks to be every day before God.

And I hope that we are made manifest also in your consciences - In 4:2 he has appealed to every man's conscience in the sight of God.   He does so here again.   This verse is an echo of what has already been said at 4:2, in which "conscience" meant "awareness" or "consciousness," rather than the innate faculty that prompts us to do what our minds think right, and criticizes us when we do what our minds think wrong. God was aware of Paul's integrity; he hoped his readers would become conscious (aware) of his integrity, also.   Paul says "consciences" (plural) and not "conscience" (singular) because he appeals to each individual convert's knowledge of him rather than to the church as a whole.   If the Corinthians consult their own personal knowledge of Paul, he is confident he will be accepted by them just as he has been known and accepted by God.

5:12 - *We are not again commending ourselves to you but* **are** *giving you an occasion to be proud of us, that you may have* **an answer** *for those who take pride in appearance, and not in heart.*

We are not again commending ourselves to you - This verse recalls what he wrote in 3:1.[41]   In 2:17 he had written something that his enemies could misconstrue, so he makes it certain he was not just praising himself.   The same is true here when we read 5:11 and 5:12 together.   His claim that God knows that his motives were honorable certainly could be twisted and made to look like a boast of self-commendation.   He writes this verse so his enemies will have no place where they can make an accusation that he is just praising himself.   Throughout this letter (3:1,

---

[40] The KJV loses the antithesis by separating this clause from the one preceding with a semicolon.   The ASV and NASB punctuate with a comma after "men" and a semicolon after "God" thus preserving the antithesis.

[41] The KJV version begins this verse with "for."   The word was likely not in what Paul originally wrote, and it is conjectured the word was added by a scribe for the sake of an apparent sequence of thought.   In reality, verse 12 is more understandable without it.

4:2, 5:12, 6:4) Paul is sensitive to the slander that he constantly commends himself.[42]

But *are* giving you an occasion to be proud of us - He tells his readers exactly why he wrote what he did.   In contrast to his opponents who regularly slandered him, Paul is giving the Corinthians a starting point for saying a good word about Paul. "Occasion" translates *aphormē,* a word used only by Paul in the New Testament.   It means a base of operations, a place to start from, and hence good grounds, or a good reason.   The readers are personally aware that they had become Christians as a result of Paul's ministry among them, but they did not have personal evidence to support any of the charges made by Paul's opponents as they denigrated Paul.   Paul therefore suggests that the next time they hear him being accused, they are to tell the accusers what their own personal convictions about Paul are.   They are to use their own estimate of him in replying to his Jewish detractors.

That you may have *an answer* for those who take pride in appearance, and not in heart - As far as grammar is concerned, something must be supplied after the verb "have" – either "something" or "something to say," or "occasion" or "a basis of being proud."   Paul wants the Corinthians to speak up in his defense when the Judaizers speak against the apostle.   Those opponents are described as "those who take pride in appearance and not in the heart."   The verb translated "take pride in" can also be translated "boast."   Is this description of Paul's opponents a critique of the Judaizers, saying they were people who boasted about things they themselves did which made a good outward impression?[43]   Or are the Judaizers being rebuked for making sneers about Paul's appearance while ignoring what was in the apostle's heart?   The next verse would cause us to adopt the second option as being the better explanation of boasting in appearance and not in the heart.

---

[42] Modern scholars who suppose Paul wrote a previous letter, or a severe letter to Corinth, will conclude that Paul commended himself and boasted about himself in one of those earlier letters. That boasting is what is supposed to have aroused the criticism his opponents then voiced (cf. 11:16-12:13).

[43] Elsewhere in the letter the Judaizers are rebuked for calling attention to their own letters of recommendation, their own training and position, their Hebrew descent, their circumcision, their relationship with Jesus that Paul did not have (2 Corinthians 5:16), their Palestinian orthodoxy (11:22), and their visions and revelations (12:1-7).   They certainly did have some serious character flaws.   If the verse is interpreted as a rebuke of the Judaizers for their own self-assertion and self-commendation, it forms the ground work for the decisive attack he makes on those opponents in chapters 10-13.   When one reads the commentaries at this place, it should be kept in mind that decisions made about the integrity of 2 Corinthians will have considerable bearing on the comments offered.   Those (e.g., Philip E. Hughes [*Paul's Second Epistle to the Corinthians* {Grand Rapids: Eerdmans, 1962}, p.189) who believe in the integrity and unity and coherence of the book will be impressed how Paul in the early chapters of the book is already preparing us for the blistering attack that will follow in chapters 10-13.   Coffman (*op. cit.*, p.369) urges that Paul never could have written the mild words of this verse if the Corinthians had already received a severe letter (made up in part of the forthright and devastating language found in chapters 10-13).   "Thus the notion (and it is only that) of those chapters being a fragment of a lost 'severe letter' Paul had delivered to Corinth in the interval between the two canonical epistles cannot be logically supported."

5:13 - *For if we are beside ourselves, it is for God; if we are of sound mind, it is for you.*

For if we are beside ourselves - "For" makes this verse an explanation of something just said, evidently "appearance." The word *exestēmen* here translated "are beside ourselves" means to be out of one's mind, to be deranged. Compare Agrippa's words to Paul in Acts 26:24, "Paul, you are out of your mind." The Jews used the same word when they charged Jesus with being mentally deranged (Mark 3:21). Apparently, Paul's enemies, perhaps observing his zeal and self-denial,[44] have accused him of being "crazy" when he was last in Corinth,[45] and here he responds to that sneering charge.

It is for God - Whatever may have been the actions or behavior that the opponents appealed to as proof Paul was mentally deranged, Paul says those actions resulted from his desire to honor God.[46] Here is one area where the opponents, looking on appearances, did not understand Paul's heart.

If we are of sound mind - If "beside ourselves" spoke of being over-zealous, then "sound mind" refers to what people called restrained zeal,[47] wise self-control, common sense.

It is for you - If he restrained his zeal, his motive was to secure their spiritual good. Whatever may be the estimate in which Paul was held by people who only looked on appearances, Paul has just revealed the two motives that resulted in how he acted: he was motivated by love to God and by love for man. It is evident, therefore, that

---

[44] In the absence of any specific explanation from Paul, commentators have attempted to explain what might have led Paul's opponents to accuse him of being crazy. (1) Perhaps Paul was so accused because of his excessive use of glossolalia (cf. 1 Corinthians 14:2,18). This interpretation relies on "tongues" being something other than a language used for evangelistic purposes, a view we have rejected as we explained 1 Corinthians. (2) Perhaps Paul was accused of being crazy because on a number of occasions when he received a revelation from the Lord he was carried away to a state of ecstasy or altered state of consciousness. This suggestion states more than we know, for 2 Corinthians 12:1-4 is the only time we know of that Paul didn't know whether he was in his body or out of it when he saw a vision. (3) Perhaps Paul's alleged repeated self-commendation was attributed to sheer lunacy by his critics. (4) Perhaps to Jewish way of thinking, Paul's conversion was evidence of his madness. (5) Perhaps his continual drive to evangelize yet more towns was cited as evidence he was mad (a fanatic). (6) Perhaps Paul's enemies have alluded to his lack of rhetorical skills for both *exhistēmi* and *sōphroneō* ("sound mind") were used in rhetorical handbooks in relation to proper oratorical style.

[45] The NASB marginal note shows the verb may well be translated "if we were beside ourselves."

[46] Just what "it is for God" means depends on the unspoken reason why men accused Paul of being crazy.

[47] Several writers have commented on the aorist tense "crazy" as compared to the "sober minded" which is a present tense. The aorist might refer to a single specific occasion in the past when Paul was thought to be "out of his mind." But since it is contrasted with a present tense, it is also possible that the aorist tense looks at habitual or intermittent conduct as a unit.

if these were his driving motives, he cannot be seeking self-exaltation nor commending himself.

5:14 - *For the love of Christ controls us, having concluded this, that one died for all, therefore all died;*

For the love of Christ controls us - With "for" Paul introduces another reason why his ministry is "for you" (verse 13), i.e., for the Corinthians. It is also another reason why a life of self-centeredness and self-pleasing was impossible for himself. It unfolds the "heart" part (verse 12) of Paul's behavior. "Love of Christ"[48] in this context points to the idea that Christ's love for us (or the love Christ showed for us) is the thing in mind, for the context speaks of His death.[49] Christ's love for mankind was manifested most clearly at Calvary (Romans 5:8). The thought of what Jesus did for him on the cross is what controls (Greek, *sunecho*, restrains or constrains or urges on) Paul's behavior. What Paul says here he also said in Galatians 2:20, that the love which Christ has for Paul keeps him back from all self-seeking, and confines his aims to the service for God and for his fellow-man (verse 13). He felt hemmed in, and without any other option than to spend himself in such service. This is one of Paul's great statements about his motivation for ministry.

Having concluded this - The aorist participle probably has a causal connotation, e.g., "because we long ago concluded this."[50] The time when he arrived at this conviction is likely the time he first learned that Christ loved him enough to die for him, i.e., back to the time of his conversion in Damascus.

That one died for all - While the general sense is clear, it is difficult to follow the thread of thought from this verse to the next. To smooth the rough spot some manuscripts read "that *if* one died for all."[51] The "one" who died for all is the Lord Jesus Christ. "For" translates *huper*, which means 'in behalf of, for the benefit of.'[52] "All" obviously means all mankind, every man. Compare 1 John 2:2, "He is the propitia-

---

[48] The Greek translated "love of Christ," like the English, can be taken two ways: either Christ's love for us (a subjective genitive) or our love for Christ (an objective genitive). However, *agapē* ("love") is a verb that seems never to be used of man's love for Christ or God.

[49] Zerwick (*Biblical Greek*, p.13) reminds his readers that when a Greek text can have two possible meanings, and both may be correct, that both should be held in the reader's mind. And certainly it is true that the Christian's love for Christ motivates his actions. However, in light of the following context which talks about what Christ has done for us, it seems best to interpret the phrase "love of Christ" in this place as His love for us.

[50] Both the KJV and ASV treat the aorist participle as being a present conclusion. The aorist participle actually speaks of completed action in past time.

[51] The manuscripts and versions that have "if" are *Aleph*[3], C*, 69, f, Vulg., Copt., Arm.

[52] Another preposition, *anti* ('in the place of, instead of'), is used to indicate that Christ's death was vicarious and substitutionary (Matthew 20:28 = Mark 10:45; 1 Timothy 2:6).

tion for our sins; and not for ours only, but also for the whole world." Christ's sacrificial death was potentially efficacious for every man, but not every man will take advantage of what Christ has done for him. It is efficacious only for believers (Romans 3:22-26). "The thought here in 2 Corinthians is the same as in the nearly contemporary passage of Romans 5:15-19, and takes its place among Paul's most unqualified assertions of the universality of the atonement effected by Christ's death."[53]

Therefore all died - As stated earlier, it is difficult to see a smooth train of thought in these verses. As a result, at this place, some want to talk about the change that should be obvious in the redeemed; that is, they have died to their own desires (cp. Romans 6:1-11; Galatians 2:19,20; Colossians 3:3) and therefore cannot (for example) go around commending themselves (verse 12).[54] Others want to postpone talking about the change that should be obvious in redeemed men until the next verse. Instead, they have chosen to read verse 14 as though it said, 'if Christ died for all, it must be assumed that all had died (spiritually) and therefore needed what Christ came to make available,' i.e., removal of the deadness that results from their trespasses and sins (Ephesians 2:1; Colossians 2:13).

5:15 - *and He died for all, that they who live should no longer live for themselves, but for Him who died and rose again on their behalf.*

And He died for all - The expression "died for all" means the same as in the previous verse.[55] The idea seems to be, "the purpose in His dying for all is ... that they should no longer live for themselves."

---

[53] Plumptre, *op. cit.*, p.50. 2 Corinthians 5:14 is one of the verses that has figured prominently in the theological debates concerning the extent of the atonement. Was it limited (say to the elect) or was it universal? In *Barnes' Notes* (p.116-121) is a running debate between Barnes, who taught universal atonement, and Robert Frew, who taught a Calvinistic limited atonement. On the nature of the atonement see notes at 2 Corinthians 5:21. For the present, let us say that Christ's death for sinners removed every obstruction that lay in the way (once they had sinned) of their becoming friends of God again.

[54] Federal theology makes use of this verse to show that Paul regarded the death of Christ as representative. Federal theology will say that as Christ had died as the head of the race, therefore all men had died with Him to their sins, and so were obligated to lead self-sacrificing, unselfish, sinless lives for the sake of Him who, on their behalf, had died and risen again. In metaphorical terms, the Bible does describe the believer's participation with Christ in terms of being crucified, buried, and raised with Christ. But it is not necessary to press this verse into service for either the truth of our participation with Christ or in defense of the questionable doctrine of federal theology.

[55] Certain neo-orthodox interpreters insist that since "Christ died for all," everyone's sins have already been forgiven (even without any faith or repentance on the part of men), and the task of the preacher is simply to go tell men what has already been done for them. Such a handling of this verse is totally unsatisfactory. Christ's redemptive death is potentially available to all, but men must respond to the gospel in faith and repentance and immersion before it becomes actually operative in their lives. Paul is not suggesting that irrespective of men's response, all men are already actually forgiven. Care must be taken lest certain Bible verses are twisted or misconstrued so as to make them teach universalism.

That they who live should no longer live for themselves - If "died" in the previous verse means to be spiritually dead because of trespasses and sins, then "they who live" are those who have "risen to walk in newness of life" (Romans 6:3-7). Perhaps this phrase shows Paul is not speaking of all men in general, but only those who "live" in union with the resurrected Christ. Paul is not teaching universalism. Paul is explaining his selfless conduct. One of the purposes for which Christ died was that those He redeemed should cease to be motivated by selfish concerns.[56]

But for Him who died and rose again on their behalf - "Him who died and rose again" is Jesus Christ. Redeemed men who have risen to walk in newness of life now live for Him. They are motivated by a desire that He receive glory and honor, not themselves. Their energies and time and talents are invested and expended to promote Him in other people's estimation. Christ died on men's behalf.[57] Now we have some explanation of what "the love of Christ controls us" (verse 14) means. Because He loved us so much that He would die for us, we cannot, without shame, frustrate the purpose of His death by living selfishly rather than living for Him. Christ lived a new life after His resurrection; so also should those who believe in Him after they have risen to walk in newness of life. Paul has now stated the motives that guide his work as an apostle. One is reverence for Christ before whose judgment-seat he must one day stand to answer for the deeds done in the body. The other is Christ's love for man which led Him to become our redeemer. Instead of being selfish, someone like that is worth honoring by how we live.

5:16 - Therefore from now on we recognize no man according to the flesh; even though we have known Christ according to the flesh, yet now we know *Him thus* no longer.

Therefore from now on we recognize no man according to the flesh - "Therefore" introduces a consequence as it connects the following verses with the foregoing (verses 14-15). Because of the stated motives that guide his work as an apostle, Paul now has new standards of judgment and new ways of looking at things.[58] "We" is

---

[56] "Paul was not writing a theological treatise, and the statement was accordingly not meant to be an exhaustive presentation of all the purposes of God in the death of Christ." Plumptre, *op. cit.*, p.51.

[57] It is likely that the phrase "on their behalf" is to be taken with both participles ("died" and "rose"). The Greek preposition is *huper*, the same preposition found in "died for all" in verse 14. In comments there it was explained that the preposition means 'in behalf of,' or 'for the benefit of.'

[58] "Recognize" translates *oida*, which here means to form an estimate of, to judge, to value, to appreciate. The verb is used with the same sense at 1 Thessalonians 5:12. J. Louis Martyn (erroneously, this commentator believes) uses this verse to claim Paul's opponents were Gnostics rather than Judaizers, and that the point of conflict was over epistemology. "Epistemology at the Turn of the Ages: 2 Corinthians 5:16," *Christian History and Interpretation*, ed. by W. R. Farmer, et al., Cambridge: University Press, 1967.

emphatic in the Greek, implying a contrast: "we" no longer[59] do what the trouble-makers still do, namely, judge men "according to the flesh."   The NASB margin reads "by what he is in the flesh," namely, the external distinctions and circumstances of the person being evaluated.[60]   If Christ died for all so that they would live for Him and for others, and cease to live for themselves, then our estimate of others is no longer based on the outward and external circumstances which the world values, but on the character of the inner man.   What is really important is the fact that Christ has died for him, and he needs to know what to do to be saved.

Even though we have known Christ according to the flesh - As usual, "even though" (*ei kai*) concedes the point which is being stated hypothetically.   The time referred to by Paul in the perfect tense Greek verb "we have known"[61] is evidently some time before his conversion.   Paul is saying there was a time in the past, before his conversion, that he did judge Christ according to the flesh.   In this commentator's judgment, when Paul writes "according to the flesh" in this phrase, he means the same thing that he stated in the previous one.[62]   He is talking about judging a person according to external circumstances.

Yet now we know *Him thus* no longer - There was a time when Paul was convinced Jesus could not possibly be the long-awaited Messiah, but that is no longer true.   He

---

[59] "Now on" translates *apo tou nun*, which means 'from the present time.'   Evidently, the context tells us that from the time the apostles recognized the true nature of Christ's death and resurrection, from "then on" they had a different view of what is important in life.

[60] For Paul, in contrast to how the Judaizers still judged people, the Jew-Gentile distinction was no longer important.   What mattered now to Paul was whether a man was a believer or an unbeliever.

[61] The change of verbs for "know" from *oida* to *ginōskō* is of little moment here; it is the change of tense that matters.   Paul wanted a perfect tense to express a completed action in the past time, and since *oida* has no perfect tense form, a change of verb became necessary.

[62] An overview of interpretations proposed for the phrase "we have known Christ according to the flesh" can be found in J.W. Fraser, "Paul's Knowledge of Jesus: 2 Corinthians 5:16 Once More," *NTS* 17:3 (1971), p. 293-313.   Among the views we have found are these: (1) Paul here claims to have seen Jesus during His earthly ministry.   But if he had seen Christ before the crucifixion, it seems reasonable that he would have mentioned it in 11:22,23, especially in the light of the claims of Paul's opponents that the original twelve were superior to Paul because they had seen the Christ, but he had not (1 Corinthians 9:1).   (2) Paul here confesses that at an immature stage of his ministry he still retained some of the low ideas about Christ which he inherited from Judaism.   The theory goes that Paul's theology developed and changed as the years passed.   This denies the claim made by Paul himself that the source of his doctrine was divine revelation (Galatians 1:12).   Paul does admit more than once that he had been a persecuting Jew, but he nowhere confesses that he had once preached a Judaizing gospel.   In Galatians 2:15-19 he declares that his message has always been the same.   (3) Paul is rebuking the "Christ party" at Corinth who seem to have boasted that they were superior to all others because they had personally seen or known the Christ when He was on earth.   This interpretation that Paul is rebuking the exclusiveness of the "Christ party" has against it the fact that Paul concedes that he, too, once knew Christ, whereas it is doubtful that he ever personally saw Christ before the Jesus appeared to him on the Damascus road (an event that was four years after the completion of Jesus' earthly ministry).

no longer thinks of Jesus as a misguided Messianic pretender whose followers must be wiped out (Acts 9:1,2, 26:9-11).[63] Jesus may have been perfectly human on the outside, but he was deity in the flesh. When you looked on the inside, you saw much more than a mere man. Since that day on the Damascus road when Jesus appeared to Paul to call him to be an apostle (Acts 26:16-18), and since his conversion in Damascus (Acts 22:14-16), Paul has changed his estimate of Jesus and he now preaches Him as the Messiah. He has learned to stop using an unregenerate standard of judgment which looks at outward appearances, and instead he focuses on men's inward spiritual life.

5:17 - *Therefore if any man is in Christ, he is a new creature; the old things passed away; behold, new things have come.*

Therefore if any man is in Christ - This is the second verse in a row that begins with "therefore."

- Perhaps this is a second consequence deduced from what was said in verses 14 and 15: verse 16 is a negative consequence resulting from the truth written in verses 14 and 15, and verse 17 is a positive consequence. Both verses 15 and 17 have the apostle speaking of all Christians (a group inclusive of the apostles), whereas verse 16 refers to Paul in particular, though what is said should be true of all Christians.
- Perhaps, verse 17 is a deduction from verse 16. In that event, Paul is saying that what was true in his case (i.e., that he has a different way of looking at things since his conversion) is also true in the case of all believers in Christ.

The expression "in Christ" has a depth that is often hastily passed over by the modern interpreters.[64] The phrase to be "in Christ" means that one has become a Christian and that he is a member of the body of Christ, a body which is composed of those who have been united with Christ in his death and resurrection (Romans 6:3,4). "It no longer matters whether a man is by birth a Jew or Gentile, bond or free; the one thing that is of weight is whether he has the right spiritual relation to Christ."[65] "Any man" says that what was true of Paul is also true for any Christian.

He is a new creature - The same expression occurs in Galatians 6:15 (though the NASB renders it "a new creation" at that place). "New" translates *kainos* (new in quality, renewed, see notes at 2 Corinthians 3:6), which calls to mind the new birth in

---

[63] It is a patent wresting of this verse to enlist it as a proof text for showing no interest in the "historical Jesus" (Christ-according-to-the-flesh) in favor of putting all emphasis on the "Christ of faith" – as certain neo-orthodox and neo-liberal scholars have been wont to do.

[64] Coffman (*op. cit.*, p.372) calls attention to the fact that Paul uses the expression "in Christ" (or its equivalent) a total of 169 times. He then expresses his astonishment that so few commentaries offer any help in answer to the all-important question, "How does one find the status of becoming 'in Christ'?" He then points to Romans 6:3 and Galatians 3:27 as being two verses where the question is answered.

[65] Plummer, *op. cit.*, p.180.

which man's spirit is renewed as he becomes a Christian. That spirit had died, or ceased to function, when the man committed his first sin.   In the process of becoming a Christian that spirit has been born again (John 3:6; Ephesians 2:10, 4:23,24; Colossians 3:3; Romans 8:10).   For each individual who becomes a Christian there is new life in Christ.   God has been at work in his life with the same power He used when He first created.[66] Ephesians 2:11-21 explains something more that is involved in this new creation.   Gentiles were once separate from Christ and excluded from the commonwealth of Israel.   They were "strangers to the covenants of promise."   But all that has changed in Christ Jesus.   His blood, shed on Calvary, has brought people together and made both groups into one by breaking down the barrier of the dividing wall ("the Law of commandments").   Christ did this so that "He might make the two into one new man, thus establishing peace" (Ephesians 2:15).   When we observe that the verb translated "make" in Ephesians 2:15 can also be translated "create," we have the key to Paul's expression "new creature/ creation."   The new creation is the society in which both believing Jews and believing Gentiles are reconciled "in one body to God through the cross" (Ephesians 2:16).   If Paul's readers will recognize God's new creation, then it won't matter whether one is circumcised and the other is not.   After all, they are no longer strangers and aliens, but are "fellow citizens with the saints," together they are "God's household" (Ephesians 2:19).

The old things passed away - In the context the "old things" would include the selfish motives that drive men who do not know Christ as their savior; estimating others according to the flesh (external circumstances); and judging Christ according to the flesh.   "Passed away" is an aorist tense, referring to one time in the past when this occurred.   When a person is immersed into Christ and becomes a new creature, that is when all these old things become a thing of the past.   Paul may still be unfolding the assertion that his sober behavior with the Corinthians that is uppermost in his mind (verse 13), is exactly what his Savior would expect.

Behold, new things have come - "Behold" expresses Paul's vivid realization of the truth he is uttering, and may echo Isaiah 43:18,19 ("do not call to mind the former things ... behold, I will do something new").[67]   Paul says the reason he is an apostle, and does as he does, is because his conversion has produced a change in him.[68]   He

---

[66] Of course, it is not affirmed that man is wholly passive as God is doing His creative work on the man's spirit.   Whether or not a man is "in Christ" is conditioned on the man's response to the gospel invitation.   As the man responds in faith and repentance and immersion, God goes about His creative work on the man's spirit.   It is wholly in error to affirm that any such response by man to God's invitation is somehow a "work" that is excluded by Ephesians 2:8,9, or is somehow to be equated with earning salvation.

[67] The words "former things" and "new" in the LXX of Isaiah 43 are the same words ("old things" and "new things") Paul uses here in 2 Corinthians.

[68] "Have come" is a perfect tense in the Greek.   It implies a past completed action with present continuing results.   It expresses his determination that the new way of living has come to stay.

has new goals, new aims, new purposes, new views of God and of Jesus Christ; new views of this world and of the world to come; new views of truth and duty; his whole soul, mind, and body are consecrated to Christ.

5:18 - *Now all* **these** *things are from God, who reconciled us to Himself through Christ, and gave us the ministry of reconciliation,*

Now all *these* things are from God - The presence of the article in the Greek ("all *these* things" is *ta de panta* in the Greek) indicates Paul is speaking of the new creation he has just mentioned (verse 17), which results in a whole new set of motives and standards of judgment. The new creation with its new way of living (verse 15) is the result of God's work just as surely as the first creation was (4:6). In addition to all the things already named as being "from God," Paul goes on to explain some additional things that have God as their source: reconciliation, the ministry of reconciliation given to the apostles (verse 18), not counting men's trespasses against them (verse 19), and His making Christ who knew no sin to be sin on our behalf (verse 21).

Who reconciled us to Himself through Christ - In the New Testament, the word "reconcile" speaks of a broken relationship being mended, or to make peace after war, or to be readmitted to the presence and favor of our rightful sovereign after we have rebelled against Him.[69] Relationships that were stressed and broken are restored by the removal of what caused the enmity. When we speak of a relationship between God and man, the idea involved is that man (as a result of his sin) had been at enmity with God, but was now (by being forgiven by the blood of Christ) brought into harmony (concord) with God.[70] Who is intended by "us"? Since verse 11 it has been necessary to identify who is meant by the plural pronouns "we" and "us." Since we are still in a paragraph that deals with the life (self-sacrifice) of an apostle (5:11-6:10), we would expect the plural pronouns in the paragraph to refer primarily to apostles. True, verse 17 has been understood to apply to all the readers (i.e., "if any man is in Christ") some of the same changes that resulted in the lives of the apostles when they became Christians. But verse 20 ("we are ambassadors for Christ") certainly speaks of the apostles, so we would expect the plural pronouns in verses 18 and 19 to do likewise. Of course, what was true of apostles concerning reconcilia-

---

[69] The word occurs four times in the New Testament – Romans 5:11, 11:15; 2 Corinthians 5:18,19. The word here translated "reconcile" (and "reconciliation") is translated "atonement" at Romans 5:11 in the KJV. It was also translated "atonement" here in 2 Corinthians in some of the older English versions such as Tyndale. In 1611, the root idea in "atonement" (at-one-ment) is that people who were at enmity with each other have been "made-at-one" again. The word "atonement" has changed meanings since 1611. Then it meant to reconcile, to make one what had been separated; now it refers to the cause that makes reconciliation possible.

[70] "It was through sin that man became alienated from God and from man (Isaiah 59:1ff). 'We were' according to Romans 5:10, 'enemies of God' (see Colossians 1:21)." Thompson, *op. cit.*, p.82.

tion is true for all men.[71]   If in the word "us" Paul is thinking of himself and his fellow apostles, he expresses his deep awareness that an apostle has as much need as anyone of the reconciliation which was effected through Christ.

It will be noted that the work of reconciliation is described as originating with God the Father. Man was in no position to bring about the reconciliation, so God took the initiative to reconcile us to Himself. He actively went about seeking to bring the estranged sinners back. Even though this verse specifically says "God ... reconciled us to Himself" there has been a long running theological debate concerning reconciliation. Greeks thought of the gods as being estranged from men, and it was the angry god who had to be appeased before the broken relationship was mended. Men had to provide the sacrifice to placate the angry god. Paul certainly has not adapted this old pagan idea, for it was not men who provided the sacrifice; it was God who sent his son to be the propitiatory sacrifice.[72] Is it God who is reconciled to man, or is it man who is reconciled to God? Does God change his attitude toward men, so that at one time it might be said He is angry with them, and on another occasion He is positively warm and friendly toward them? Or should it be maintained that God never changes? Calvinists often espouse the view that God never changes ("God is not a man ... that he should repent," Numbers 23:19), therefore all the change that takes place must take place in the heart and actions of men.[73]

Now, in this debate about who changes attitudes when reconciliation takes place, this commentator has come to believe that both sides are saying some things that are Biblically correct. We agree that God's unchanging love is always waiting for the sinner to repent. Certainly, a strong case can be made that after a man has sinned and rebelled against his Maker, he certainly needs to change. The things man has done to cause estrangement need to be removed. If "reconciliation" implies a mutual change of attitude (and we believe it does), then a case can be made that, in the light of Calvary, God can change His attitude, too. Those verses that describe unforgiven sinners as being God's "enemies" (e.g., Romans 5:10, 11:28) may well describe God's attitude towards the sinners, as well as the sinners' attitudes towards God. The same Bible that says "God so loved the world" (John 3:16) and "God dem-

---

[71] A view that is less than what the Bible teaches is the neo-orthodox view that all men are already saved because of Calvary, but just don't know it. What the preacher must do, therefore, is go tell them that (without any response to some invitation, without any change of lifestyles) they are already saved. In this scenario, "reconciliation" is little more than a discovery on man's part that God is friendly, followed by a change of attitude, entirely on man's part, toward the friendly God.

[72] Scripture speaks of propitiation as being the means to reconciliation (1 John 2:2, 4:10; Romans 3:25; Luke 18:13).

[73] A readable presentation of this view of reconciliation is Leon Morris, *The Apostolic Preaching of the Cross* (London: Tyndale, 1955), p. 186-223. Barnes (*op. cit.*, p.129) illustrates the view that God does not change thusly: "When a father sees a child struggling in the stream, and in danger of drowning, the peril and the cries of the child make no CHANGE in the character of the father, but such was his love for the child that he would plunge into the stream at the hazard of his own life to save him. So it was with God."

onstrates His love toward us ... sinners" (Romans 5:8) and "God is ... not willing that any should perish" (2 Peter 3:9; 1 Timothy 2:4) also says that God is angry with the wicked every day (Psalm 7:11, KJV).   When Christ's redemptive work is complete, God is free to change His attitude towards those who were once His enemies.   Some Bible students speak of "objective reconciliation" and "subjective reconciliation." The former speaks of what can go on in God's mind once Jesus has made atonement for sins.   God can offer forgiveness to all believers in Jesus.   His anger and wrath can give way to expressions of His love.   "Subjective reconciliation" refers to what happens in the sinner's mind.   He is aware that when he embraces Jesus as his savior, that all the sins that have separated him from God are covered.   All his feelings of rebellion are replaced with soul-stirring love for Him who loved us first.   Now there is nothing to keep forgiven men and God apart.   The enmity is gone.   Restored relationships are the order of the day.   Reconciliation has occurred as once broken relationships are mended.

That there is any opportunity for such reconciliation between a Holy God and a lost sinner to occur at all is traced directly to the action of God in sending a Savior to be an atoning sacrifice for sins.   That is what is involved when Paul tells us "God reconciled us to Himself through Christ."   Because of the death and resurrection of Christ, God regards men who are "in Christ" as reconciled to Himself.   Only through Christ, therefore, is there "peace with God" (Romans 5:1).   No longer is He "angry" with them; no longer are they liable to the "wrath" that awaits unforgiven sinners. The apostles needed this as much as any other man.   There is another possible nuance involved in the words "through (*dia*, Greek) Christ," namely, that of His work as mediator between God and men (1 Timothy 2:5).

And gave us the ministry of reconciliation - Paul here states again the reason why he and others were apostles.   God gave them the job!   In Paul's case this is a sort of climax; the one who persecuted His son and the church is the one whom God not only reconciled to Himself but also committed to him the apostolic ministry of reconciliation.   That means that God gave the apostles the job of announcing to men how God was reconciling the world to himself (verse 19).   He gave them the terms on which men could be reconciled to Him, and sent them as ambassadors to make known to men what those terms of reconciliation are.   That is Paul's ministry.   "The use of the word 'ministry' (*diakonia*) for the apostle's work[74] (here, 4:1, 6:3, Romans

---

[74] Not all expositors limit the "us" to the apostles and their fellow-workers.   Instead, this passage in 2 Corinthians 5 is used to show that all Christians (not just a selected few leaders) have a common task of evangelizing the lost.   Every Christian, they affirm, is intended to be a "minister of reconciliation."   Now we agree that the church will not grow very rapidly until all Christians share with their neighbors who Jesus is and what He has done for lost men.   But we are not convinced that 2 Corinthians 5:19,20 is a proof text that all should be personal evangelists.   This passage, instead, is Paul's insistence that he has been acting just as the One who called him to be a "minister of reconciliation" expected him to do.   "On a far lesser sense, every Christian is also a custodian of the good news; but in the original and plenary sense, this applies only to the apostles of Christ." Coffman, *op. cit.*, p.374.

11:13, 1 Timothy 1:12, and often in Acts) shows that they are not regarded as having authority in themselves. They do not act on their own independent authority, but are commissioned by God to continue Christ's 'ministry of reconciliation'."[75]

5:19 - *namely, that God was in Christ reconciling the world to Himself, not counting their trespasses against them, and He has committed to us the word of reconciliation.*

Namely - This word introduces the news they are to tell as they carry out their God-given apostolic ministry.

That God was in Christ reconciling the world to Himself - This appears to be a restatement of what was written in verse 18.[76] However the wording here ("in Christ") is slightly different from what we had in verse 18 ("through Christ"). As a result our translations offer various explanations for this verse. Some (e.g., KJV) treat "God was in Christ" as an affirmation of Jesus' deity.[77] Others (e.g., Goodspeed) treat "in Christ" as being a statement which expresses the same idea verse 18, namely, a summary of all Jesus our mediator has done to make reconciliation possible. Another way of punctuating the verse makes it read "God was reconciling to Himself the world that is in Christ," so that the verse means that only those who are "in Christ" (i.e., Christians) are the ones who are reconciled to God. A fourth punctuation makes it read "there was God, in Christ reconciling the world to Himself."[78] The "world" that was being reconciled is the world of men (like John 3:16). Potentially everyone has the possibility of being reconciled. Whether or not

---

[75] Plummer, *op. cit.*, p.182-83.

[76] What was said about reconciliation previously is true here.

[77] In the view of some older commentators, the punctuation of this verse found in the KJV makes the verse emphasize the deity of Jesus. Some modern translators deliberately punctuate this verse to make it refer to Christ's agency, because those translators have serious reservations against the deity of Jesus. If we were to affirm that "God was in Christ" stresses the deity of Christ, we would be saying no more than the Old Testament predictions did that spoke of Messiah being Immanuel ("God with us," Matthew 1:23). We would be saying nothing other than what Jesus Himself claimed on the great day of questions when He asked the religious leaders how Messiah could also be David's "Lord" (Yahweh) unless He were God in the flesh (Matthew 22:43). There are numerous passages which affirm the deity of Jesus (see, for example, Hebrews 1). For this commentator, the deity of Jesus is not an issue. It is a doctrine passionately held and taught. Should he opt for 2 Corinthians 5:19 as expressing "agency," he should not be accused of attempting to water down the deity of Jesus.

[78] This was Theodoret's way of reading the verse. The theologians who picture God as a reluctant bystander while Christ accomplished man's redemption do not have it quite right. God was actively involved in all that was happening, Paul here affirms. Or again, those theologians who picture God as regarding Jesus as "sin" and punishing Him accordingly, we think, do not have it quite right. Jesus suffered redemptively, as a "sin offering," but not penally. As Jesus suffered on the cross, the Father could not come to His help ("My God, why did you forsake me?"). But Jesus was doing what the loving Father sent Him into the world to do, and there was never a time in the life of Jesus when God was more pleased with Him than when He died on the cross.

they are actually reconciled depends on how they respond to the plea voiced by the preacher, "Be ye reconciled to God!" (verse 20, KJV). In the following clauses, two participial phrases will describe two things involved in God's reconciling work based on Christ's atoning death.

Not counting their trespasses against them - "Trespasses" (*paraptoma*), denoting a lapse from doing what is right in God's sight, is one of several synonyms for sin used in the Scriptures.[79] Paul's word for "counting" was used in the ancient world for record keeping. It was an accountant's word for the entries posted in the debit or credit columns of a ledger. It was the word used for the records which were kept by oriental monarchs by which they were reminded of the merit or demerit of their subjects (e.g., Esther 6:1-6). "Not counting" ("not reckoning," ASV) is a present participle which describes a process that is continually going on. In notes at Romans 4:3-8 it is explained how God's reckoning or counting faith as righteousness is something that occurs over and over in a man's life.[80] Now, here in 2 Corinthians, we learn that God also habitually counts or reckons or records a person's trespasses, unless they are covered by the blood of Christ. So, in a sense, "not counting" a man's sins against him is the same as forgiving or pardoning the sins. The heavenly strategy by which men could be reconciled is that men's sins would not be counted against them. This required the sacrificial death of Christ that the sins might be forgiven. It was sin which caused the alienation between God and men. If because of Calvary God can stop counting men's sins against them (that is, stop keeping a record of them), the cause of alienation is removed. This is how God reconciles men.

And He has committed to us the word of reconciliation - Another part of the heavenly strategy by which sinners could be reconciled is that God would prepare a message announcing what He had done and what His expectations were, and commissioning special messengers to carry that message to the ends of the earth. As all through this paragraph, "to us" means to us apostles. "Committed" (an aorist participle) indicates the commissioning of apostles was a completed act in the past time, completed before 2 Corinthians was written. "Committed" also describes the word of reconciliation as something which has been deposited in the hands of the apostles, just as though it were a sacred treasure. The "word of reconciliation," the message that tells men about the forgiveness that is available to them and the condi-

---

[79] See George R. Berry's "New Testament Synonyms," section #2, for the Greek synonyms for "sin." George R. Berry, *The Interlinear Greek-English New Testament with Lexicon and Synonyms* (Grand Rapids, MI: Zondervan, 1950), p.117-118. Berry tells us that *paraptoma* is used in different senses, sometimes in a milder sense, denoting an error, mistake, a fault; and sometimes meaning a trespass, a willful sin.

[80] In Romans the matter of whether "righteousness" is imputed (counted, reckoned) or infused is discussed at length. The conclusion reached was that it is imputed (or reckoned), an idea supported by the language here "not counting their sins against them."

tions on which it can be appropriated, is a precious message indeed, a pearl of great price.   Paul has a ministry of reconciliation (verse 18) and a "message of reconciliation" (verse 19), so that he pleads with men, "Be reconciled to God" (verse 20).   Romans indicates that faith comes by hearing the word, and when men respond with an obedient faith, God justifies them.   When they are justified, they are also reconciled.

5:20 - *Therefore, we are ambassadors for Christ, as though God were entreating through us, we beg you on behalf of Christ, be reconciled to God.*

Therefore, we are ambassadors for Christ - "Therefore" means "because we apostles have had committed to us the word of reconciliation (verse 19) and have been given the ministry of reconciliation (verse 18)."   In the Greek the phrase "for Christ" ("on behalf of Christ," ASV[81]) stands first for emphasis: it is on behalf of Christ that the apostles are acting as ambassadors.   The dignity, responsibility, and authority of an apostle are all expressed in the term "ambassadors."[82]   An ambassador (or "legate" in the time of the Roman emperors) was a personal representative sent by a sovereign to do and say what the sovereign himself would do or say were he personally present.   To scorn an ambassador was to scorn the sovereign who sent them.   To send them away was to break relations with the sovereign who sent them. Paul chose this word to indicate the closest possible relationship between the apostles and the Lord Christ who sent them.   Paul and the other apostles of Jesus were representatives of King Jesus, acting on His behalf and with His authority behind their mission and message as they explained and made public the terms on which man might be reconciled to God.   As ambassadors they must deliver the message exactly as it was given to them.   "They were not to negotiate on any new terms, nor to change those which God had proposed, nor to follow their own plans or devices, but they were simply to urge, explain, state, and enforce the terms on which man might be reconciled to God."[83]

As though God were entreating through us - As the apostles spoke by inspiration you heard not only the message King Jesus wanted delivered, but also you heard God speaking.   What a momentous claim, a declaration analogous to the formula of the Hebrew prophet who said "thus saith the Lord."   One of the ways God goes about

---

[81] It is the same preposition "for" that was explained in verses 14,15.

[82] Lipscomb (*op. cit.*, p.83) has a helpful note that stresses the importance of the office of an apostle of Jesus Christ.   "The apostles were and are the ambassadors of Christ.   They sustained a relation to the gospel that no other preachers in their day or since ever sustained or could sustain. They were the *revealers* of the gospel [inspired preachers of what had been revealed to them].   All others are only *proclaimers* of what the apostles revealed; no preacher today has any revelation ... He does not have the credentials of an ambassador; he cannot work miracles; and God will not work with him in signs and wonders confirming the word that he preaches ... We may not expect any more ambassadors until the Lord has a new message for mankind."

[83] Barnes, *op. cit.*, p.131.

reconciling the world to himself is to speak through His ambassadors. "This phrase presents the picture of God, after having given his Son to die to redeem man, still through His chosen ambassadors at work tenderly beseeching men to be reconciled to Him."[84]

We beg you on behalf of Christ - "We beg" ("we beseech," ASV) is one of the words regularly used for prayer. With the same intensity Paul asks for blessings from God, he begs men to respond positively to God's gracious invitation. When Paul writes "we beg you," we should not read this plea as though it meant the Corinthian Christians yet needed to be reconciled to God. There is no word for "you" in the Greek either after the verb "entreating" or after the verb "beg." Paul makes both verbs as general in their scope as possible, likely because he was thinking of a wider audience than Corinth. He was an apostle not only to the Corinthians (1 Corinthians 9:2), but to many others besides (Acts 26:17). To any unconverted people, the message the ambassador delivered was "be reconciled to God." "On behalf of Christ" says that when he thus pleaded with people, the apostle was not exhorting in his own name or on his own behalf. He was acting for Christ who had sent him. He was simply serving as Christ's ambassador, delivering the message Christ sent the apostles to proclaim.

Be reconciled to God - Sinners are at enmity with God (Romans 5:10, 8:7; James 4:4). If the enmity is not ended, the sinner is liable to suffer God's wrath. Gospel preachers plead with men to respond to God's offer of salvation so that the enmity can be ended. The aorist imperative ("be reconciled") in the Greek calls for an immediate acceptance of the offer of reconciliation. Right now, act decisively to be reconciled to God. The passive voice verb means "allow yourselves to be reconciled." In other words, respond heartily and with haste to the invitation to become a Christian. This was Paul's common appeal to unbelievers. According to Romans 5:11 reconciliation is something that must be received. There are conditions to be met if men would participate in the offer God makes to them. "Men can be reconciled to God in only one way, and that is by complying with the conditions God has laid down in the gospel, which conditions are antecedent and prerequisite to salvation."[85]

5:21 - *He made Him who knew no sin to be sin on our behalf, that we might become the righteousness of God in Him.*

He made Him who knew no sin - It appears verse 21 is part of the message spoken

---

[84] Lipscomb, *op. cit.*, p.81.

[85] Coffman, *op. cit.*, p.376.

when the apostles begged men on behalf of Christ.[86] Not only did they say "be reconciled to God!" They also explained (as Paul now states here in verse 21) what God did to make reconciliation possible. "Knew no sin" is placed first in the Greek sentence for emphasis. "Him who knew no sin" is Jesus Christ whom this verse declares to have been innocent of any sin whatever. Paul's declaration here of Jesus' sinlessness is no different from what one may read from him and others elsewhere in the New Testament (see John 8:46, 14:30; Hebrews 4:15, 7:26; 1 Peter 2:22, and 1 John 3:5). "He made Him" must not be interpreted to mean that God forced Jesus to go to Calvary against Jesus' will. Jesus voluntarily went to the cross. "No man takes my life from Me. I lay down My life on my own initiative," said Jesus (John 10:18). He also said, "Greater love has no man than this, that a man lay down his life for his friends" (John 15:13). Only by being sinless perfect did Christ qualify to be a sin offering for others.

***To be* sin on our behalf** - In the Greek the sentence reads "He (God) made Him sin (*hamartian*)."[87] What is meant by this language has been the topic of a running theological debate for centuries as proponents of one or another theories of the atonement explain the verse in such a way as to support the theory being advanced.[88] There are three major explanations offered. (1) God treated Christ who had committed no sin as though he were sin itself. He suffered the consequences of our sins for our sakes. The fact that the word "sin" occurs almost side by side in two consecutive clauses here in verse 21 leads proponents of this view to argue the word should be given the same meaning in both instances. Proponents of this theory often appeal to Galatians 3:13 as being a parallel passage. There Paul speaks of Christ being made "a curse for us." And it is certainly true that Christ died in our stead. (2) Sin in this clause refers to Jesus' human nature. Long ago, Augustine offered the view that since God cannot die, God made Jesus assume human nature so He could die. This interpretation (which identifies sin and human nature) reeks of the doctrine of total hereditary depravity and it will never do to claim that Jesus experienced this the same as all the other descendants of Adam. (3) God made Christ to be a sin offering. Support for this idea can be found in Romans 8:3, where it is certainly true that "sin" (*hamartias* in the prepositional phrase *peri hamartias*) does mean "sin offering." Other verses appealed to where "sin offering" is evidently the proper explanation are Leviticus 5:9 [LXX], Hosea 4:8, Ezekiel 43:22,25, 44:29, 45:22,23,25. The chief objection raised against this interpretation is the fact that it

---

[86] This comment is based on the fact that there is no "for" at the beginning of verse 21 in the NASB. Though the better manuscripts omit it, the KJV starts verse 21 with the word "for." That would mean that verse 21 is either a reason for or an expansion of something just said in verse 20. It is not uncommon to read that verse 21 is the strongest possible reason for being reconciled to God.

[87] The words "to be" are not in the original.

[88] There is a Special Study on "The Doctrine of the Atonement" following the comments on 2 Corinthians 5:21.

causes "sin" to be used two different ways in close proximity in the same verse.   This we admit, but we still tend to agree that 'He made Him to be a sin offering' is the easiest way to explain this clause.   "On our behalf" then says the same thing as Isaiah 53:6, "The Lord laid upon Him the iniquities of us all."   Christ was our substitute. The atonement was vicarious and substitutionary.

That we might become the righteousness of God in Him - "That" (a *hina* clause, "so that") introduces a statement either of the purpose or the result of Christ's becoming a sin offering.   "In the phrase 'righteousness of God,' there is a reference to the fact that it is *His* plan of making men righteous, or of justifying them."[89]   The best comment on the significance of this language is Romans 1:16,17, where "salvation" and "righteousness of God" are interchangeable terms, and then see Romans 3:22-25, 4:5-8, 5:19 wherein God's way of saving man is developed and explained.[90]   "In Him" limits the people covered by God's way of saving men to those who are in Christ.   If men are baptized into Christ they share in the outcome of His death and resurrection.   This clearly teaches that the benefits of Christ's sin offering, the righteousness of God, the reconciliation to God, come only to believers.   There is no tinge of universalism anywhere in Paul's writings.   God wants men to be righteous in His sight; that is why He commissioned the apostles with the "ministry of reconciliation" and gave to them the "word of reconciliation."   That is why Jesus was a sin-offering.

---

[89] Barnes, *op. cit.*, p.135.

[90] In the notes on Galatians in this volume is a Special Study on "Justification by Faith" where the whole matter of imputed righteousness is explained.   In that Special Study, an old Protestant doctrine is questioned; namely, whether 2 Corinthians 5:21 means that when God looks at us when we are in Christ, He sees only His righteousness which has been reckoned (imputed) to us.   Rather, 2 Corinthians 5:21 seems to mean that as a result of Christ's sin offering, we may be reckoned as righteous in the sight of God; it is our faith that is reckoned as righteousness, says Romans.   God can justify sinners (reckon them as righteous) because of Christ's sin offering.

SPECIAL STUDY #2

An Introduction to
THE DOCTRINE OF THE ATONEMENT

What Jesus did at Calvary is often described by three words, as His "vicarious, substitutionary atonement." It seems to this commentator that the words vicarious[1] and substitutionary[2] are used as they are normally defined, but the definition of the Hebrew and Greek words sometimes translated "atonement" is seldom in mind when the words are used. Instead, "atonement" is used as a general word to refer to what Jesus was doing for mankind on the cross without any actual thought about what the word meant in Bible times or what it means today. The word "atonement" – almost the only theological term of English origin – has changed meanings. Originally it spoke of being reconciled[3]; then it came to refer to the means which makes reconciliation possible (viz., the death of Christ somehow results in a restored relationship between God and men[4]).

Since the word "atonement" has changed meanings, it no longer represents any one Greek or Hebrew word, but is used to convey the Biblical idea of the saving or redeeming work of Christ wrought through His incarnation, sufferings, and death, as well as how His death affected both man and God. Christ offered a redemptive sacrifice once-for-all (Hebrews 10:1-14). But why was such a sacrifice necessary? How was it intended to affect man and God? It is when this latter idea of how Christ's death affected man and God comes into the picture and it is called "atonement" that the word atonement can become fraught with theological baggage. Various theories of the atonement have been advocated through the ages since Christ was here on earth.

---

[1] "Vicarious" means to act in the place of another, or on behalf of another. In the phrase "vicarious, substitutionary atonement" it alludes to the fact that Christ's sacrifice for sins was for others, for He Himself (being sinless) needed no sacrifice for His own sins.

[2] "Substitutionary" means that Christ died in the place of or in the stead of sinners themselves dying.

[3] The term atonement is derived from Anglo-Saxon words meaning "making at one;" hence, "at-one-ment." It translated Greek and Hebrew words meaning "to reconcile" or "to set at one" what previously had been severed or at odds with each other.

[4] It was man's sin that broke the personal relationship between the Creator and the creature (Isaiah 59:2, "Your iniquities have made a separation between you and God"). There was no way for man to take away the cause of the estrangement, so if there was to be reconciliation, God would have to provide the way. If sins could be covered and forgiven then there would be nothing to cause a continued rift between God and man. God graciously introduced the death of a sacrificial victim to substitute for the death of the sinner. That removed the sin-barrier that caused the separation. When blood is shed, there can be forgiveness (Leviticus 17:11; Hebrews 9:22), after which reconciliation can occur.

I. HISTORY OF THEORIES OF THE ATONEMENT[5]

A study of history will show how the several prominent contemporary theories of the atonement (i.e., about how the death of Christ saves men from their sins) grew and developed, and in some cases were disavowed after being popular for a while.

A. The Patristic Period

Irenaeus (c.130-c.202) taught that the death of Christ was a ransom which wrested men free from the grasp of the devil.[6] Men's liberation was achieved by the payment of a price. "The ransom theory of Irenaeus," Hastings Rashdall tells us, "became, and for nearly a thousand years continued as, the dominant, orthodox, traditional theory on the subject."[7] Origen (c.185-c.254) said that the ransom was paid to the Devil.[8] Athanasius (ca. 296-373) described Christ's death as a payment of a debt.[9] Augustine (354-430), while discussing the atonement, spoke of Christ's death both as a ransom paid to the devil and also as a satisfaction offered to God's justice.[10] Until the 11th century, with a few exceptions such as Gregory of Nazianzus (329-389) who raised a strong protest against the accepted doctrine that Christ's death was a ransom paid to either God or the devil,[11] soteriological thought centered in the theory that Christ's death was a RANSOM.[12]

---

[5] Sources from which notes in this study are paraphrased and/or quoted are: Vernon C. Grounds, "Atonement" in *Baker's Dictionary of Theology* (Grand Rapids, MI: Baker, 1960), p.71-78; T.H. Hughes, *The Atonement: Modern Theories of the Doctrine* (London, 1949); Leon Morris, *The Apostolic Preaching of the Cross* (Grand Rapids: Eerdmans, 1956); *idem*, "Atonement" in *The Illustrated Bible Dictionary* (Wheaton, IL: Tyndale House Publishers, 1986), Vol.1, p.147-151; *idem*, "Atonement, Theories of the," in *Evangelical Dictionary of Theology* edited by Walter A. Elwell (Grand Rapids, MI: Baker, 1984), p.100-102; David Neelands, "Substitution and the Biblical Background of *Cur Deus Homo*," *The Saint Anselm Journal* 2:2 (Spring 2005), p.80-87; Tuckett, C.M., "Atonement in the New Testament," in *Abingdon Bible Dictionary* (New York: Doubleday, 1992). Vol.1, p.518-522.

[6] See his two works, *Against Heresies* and *The Demonstration of the Apostolic Preaching*. To call Christ's death a "ransom" reflects the Biblical words "redeem" or "redemption."

[7] Hastings Rashdall, *The Idea of Atonement in Christian Theology* (London: 1919), p.247.

[8] *Comm. in Matt.* xvi.8.

[9] *On the Incarnation of the Word of God*, xx.2.

[10] See his *Enchiridion* and *On the Trinity*, xiii.12-15. Augustine pictured the devil as exercising a legitimate ownership over sinners, and thus a ransom had to be paid to the devil. "Men were held captive under the devil and served the demons, but they were redeemed from captivity. For they could sell themselves. The Redeemer came, and gave the price; He poured forth His blood and bought the whole world. Do you ask what He bought? See what He gave, and find what He bought. The blood of Christ is the price. How much is it worth? What but the whole world? What but all nations?" (*Ennaration on Psalm 95*, no.5).

[11] *Oratio* 24.22.

[12] Some early theologians taught that sinners go to hell because they belong to Satan. In this situation God offered Christ to the devil as a ransom in exchange for sinners. Satan eagerly accept-

B. The Medieval Period

In Medieval times several theories of the atonement were given expression. John of Damascus (ca.675-ca.749) summarized the theories that had been taught before his time; namely, Christ's death was a ransom to God.   It was a kind of fishing-expedition which snared the devil; and it was a victory which destroyed death, liberated captive sinners, and brought life and immortality to light.[13]

Anselm of Canterbury (1033-1109) taught a theory of the atonement that has come to be known as the SATISFACTION theory.[14]   Anselm defined satisfaction as the repayment of a debt that is owed to God.   Human sin resulted in a debt or obligation because it has robbed God of the honor which is rightfully His due.[15]   That debt must be paid.   However, man, the sinner, cannot provide the repayment price to satisfy the debt, but Christ's death did repay the debt.   Christ was sinless and didn't deserve the punishment; therefore, He deserved something from God.   Christ built up an excess of merit which was put at the disposal of sinners.

Abelard (1079-1142) advocated the view sometimes called the MORAL INFLUENCE THEORY.[16]   While Abelard did speak of Christ's death as a sacrifice

---

ed the offer realizing that he was getting far more than he was giving up, but when he got Christ down into hell he found that he could not hold Him.   On the third day Christ rose triumphant and Satan was left with neither his original prisoners nor the ransom price.   (Gregory of Nyssa [ca.330-ca.395] spoke of Jesus' humanity being bait that concealed the fish hook of His deity and of how the devil was caught for our saving good [*The Great Catechism*, chap.24].) Of course, only a little thought is needed to see that on this view God was deceiving Satan, but that did not worry the church fathers.   To them it simply showed that God was wiser than Satan.   The ransom view faded as time passed and men came up with what seemed to be better ways to explain the atonement, but the ransom theory was revived in the 20th century by Gustav Aulen (*Christus Victor*, London, 1931).

[13] See his *Exposition of the Orthodox Faith*.

[14] See his *Cur Deus Homo* 1,11.   The Latin title has been translated "Why God Became Man" or "Why the God-Man?"   In *Cur Deus Homo* II,16, Anselm pointed out that a king is in a very different position from a private citizen.   He may be ready to overlook an insult or an injury to his private capacity, but as supreme in the kingdom he cannot.   Proper satisfaction must be rendered for all that harms the kingdom.   To Anselm, Christ's death provided that "satisfaction."   Another name for the Satisfaction theory is the "Legal Theory" since it is God's justice that is thought to be satisfied. Prior to *Cur Deus Homo*, the view of Christ's death which prevailed widely was that it was a ransom paid to the devil in order to deliver the souls of men over whom he had a legal claim.   Anselm by contrast stressed the fact that the death of Christ was a satisfaction rendered to God's justice and honor.   Since Anselm's time this view has become one that is found in both Protestant and Catholic orthodoxy.

[15] The idea of sin being a "debt" is reflected in the wording of the model prayer, "forgive us of our debts as we forgive our debtors" (Matthew 6:12), and in the parable of the unforgiving servant at Matthew 18:23-25 where the servant is imprisoned until he should pay back what he owed.

[16] See his *Epitome of Christian Theology* and his *Commentary on Romans*.

offered to the Father (not a redemption price paid to the devil), he subordinated everything to the controlling idea that the cross, by demonstrating God's love, draws out man's love almost automatically.   The cross shows how greatly God loves us and this causes us to respond with an answering love.   Because we love Him, we turn away from the sin that injured Christ so severely.   The moral influence theory is also called the Socinian view, the view that Christ's work consists in influencing people to lead new and better lives.[17]   Bernard of Clairvaux (1090-1153), a fierce opponent of Abelard, revived the earlier idea that Christ's death was a ransom that freed men from the power of the devil.[18]

Thomas Aquinas (1225-1274) in his *Summa Theologica* worked out a comprehensive synthesis of his predecessor's theories, which included the patristic component of release from the bondage of the devil, the Anselmic component of satisfaction, the Abelardian component of an ethical impact, and even a penal substitution component, since Thomas held that as our substitute, Jesus Christ bore our punishment.

C. The Reformation Period

The Protestant Reformers modified the doctrine of ransom payment.   It was not God's honor that received the ransom payment, it was God's justice.   Christ's death satisfied God's justice.   Among Reformation writers, satisfaction is the preferred theological word rather than atonement when speaking of Christ's work on the cross.   Martin Luther (1483-1546) was an exponent of the DRAMATIC THEORY (or the 'Christus Victor' theory), that Christ's death was a victory over hostile powers that held men, with the victory resulting in liberation from sin, law, death, wrath, and the devil.   Luther also regarded the death of Christ as a propitiatory sacrifice.   Being somewhat nearer to Anselm's views than those of Irenaeus, Luther asserted that Christ was punished on our account ("*propter nos punitur*").   Melanchthon (1497-1560) in his *Loci Communes* explained that by Christ's death the just demands of God's law have been met and satisfied, the wrath of God has been appeased, and that the soul of the sinner has been liberated from the

---

[17] There is truth in this theory, but it is not adequate to cover all the Scripture teaches about the results of the cross.   This moral influence view of the atonement has been defended in recent times by Hastings Rashdall in *The Idea of Atonement* (1919).   Probably the best known hymn about the death of Christ in modern times is "When I Survey the Wondrous Cross," a hymn that sets forth the moral influence view of atonement.   Every line of it emphasizes the effect on the observer who is surveying the wondrous cross.   What the hymn says is true and important.   But if it is claimed that this is *all* the cross means, we must reject it.

[18] *Tractatus ad Innocentium II Pontificem contra quaedamcapitulaerrorum Abaelardi* (Ep.190). Peter Lombard (c.1100-c.1160) also taught the ransom theory with the ransom being paid to the devil.

curse.[19]

John Calvin (1509-1564) in his *Institutes on the Christian Religion*[20] taught what has come to be known as the PENAL SUBSTITUTION theory. Penal substitution sees the death of Jesus as being a vicarious, substitutionary sacrifice that satisfied the demands of God's justice that sin be punished. Christ died for man, in man's place, taking man's sins and bearing them for man. As their substitute, Christ took the punishment men would have received for their sins.[21]

What is called the GOVERNMENTAL THEORY was formulated by Hugo Grotius (1583-1645),[22] and subsequently has been found in Arminianism, Methodism, the Church of the Nazarene, and was influential in the early New England colonies. This view sees the death of Christ as demonstrating God's high regard for His own law and as demonstrating to erring man that sin is displeasing to Him. As ruler of a moral universe, God must see to it that sin's pardon will not prompt man to think it a matter of indifference, a thing to be engaged in with impunity. The death of Jesus satisfied the demands of God's justice upon sin, and Christ's penal example also serves as a deterrent from sin. When God's laws are broken a penalty needs to be paid, and that is what Jesus did. Christ's death was a precondition to forgiveness, not the direct cause of forgiveness.

D. The Modern Period

Soteriological theories in modern times have been, for the most part, restatements of one of the earlier theories. For example, Alexander Campbell was an advocate of penal substitution, while Barton Stone was an advocate of the moral influence theory, and Walter Scott taught the governmental theory.[23]

---

[19] This is a slight modification of Anselm's views. While Anselm thought that sin outraged the majesty of God, Melanchthon substituted the idea that sin is a breaking of God's law. The essence of the atonement, he thought, is that Christ took our penalty upon Himself. He stood in the place of sinners and since He bore their punishment, it no longer falls on them. Opponents of Melanchthon point out this does not take account of the fact that while some penalties, like fines, may indeed be transferred, penalties like imprisonment or execution may not be. Further, sin is not something that can be transferred from one person to another (say, from the sinner to Christ).

[20] "Christ took upon Himself and suffered the punishment which by the righteous judgment of God impended over all sinners, and by this expiation the Father has been satisfied and His wrath appeased" (*Institutes*, II, chap.16).

[21] This is an extension of Anselm's satisfaction theory, but speaks of God's justice (rather than God's honor) as being satisfied.

[22] See his *Defense of the Catholic Faith*.

[23] John M. Hicks, "What Did Christ Accomplish on the Cross: Atonement in Campbell, Stone and Scott," *Lexington Theological Quarterly* (http://johnmarkhicks.files.wordpress.com/2008/05/atonement1-article- ltq.doc).

Some soteriological theories in modern times have been new attempts to explain Christ's death. Albrecht Ritschl (1822-1889) taught a form of the moral influence theory called the Declaratory Theory, or the Demonstrative View, according to which Christ died to show men how greatly God loves them. The Accident Theory treats Christ's death as an accident, as unforeseen and unexpected as is the death of any other victim of man's hatred. The Martyr Theory pictures Jesus giving up His life for a principle of truth that was opposed to the spirit of His day.[24] These new attempts fall far short of what the Scriptures say about the death of Jesus.

II. SOME BASIC BIBLICAL WORDS USED OF CHRIST'S WORK ON THE CROSS

Whichever word a Bible writer used, several truths are understood as to why Jesus should go to Calvary. (1) *All men have sinned* (Romans 3:23). Scripture uses several metaphors to describe the predicament man was in due to sin. As a sinner, man is a slave who needs to be redeemed, an enemy who needs to be reconciled, a corpse which needs to be resurrected, a captive whose powerful oppressors need to be overthrown, a criminal who needs to be justified by his judge. (2) *The love of God for His creatures.* God's attempt to provide a means of forgiveness of sins results/proceeds from His love. "God demonstrates His love for us in that while we were sinners, Christ died for us" (Romans 5:8). "As Moses lifted up the serpent in the wilderness, even so must the Son of Man be lifted up, that whoever believes may in Him have eternal life. For God so loved the world that He gave His only begotten Son that whoever believes in Him should not perish" (John 3:14-16). "This is love, not that we loved God, but that He loved us and sent His Son to be the propitiation for our sins" (1 John 4:10). (3) *God is holy.* A holy God cannot stand or tolerate sin. God's holiness and man's sin clash, and results in God's wrath being kindled against sin. (4) *God is a God of wrath.*[25] Wrath is God's holy, settled displeasure against sin. The New Testament depicts divine wrath just as it does divine mercy. It even speaks of the wrath of the Lamb (Revelation 6:16). If wrath is to be turned away and God is to forgive, there was a divine necessity for the sacrifice Jesus made.[26]

---

[24] Notes in this paragraph are from "Atonement of Christ" in *Theopedia*, an on-line encyclopedia of Biblical Christianity. The Socinian moral influence view is that Christ's death was only the death of a martyr. That being true, all that is required for the forgiveness of sins is faith and repentance on the part of the sinner: the death of Christ has nothing to do with the forgiveness of sins. Certain Disciples of Christ have held this theory, using the Prodigal Son parable to substantiate their view.

[25] The Bible does speak of the wrath of God. Using 20 different words to express God's wrath, there are 580 occurrences of the idea in Scripture. (Leon Morris, *Apostolic Preaching*, p. 131).

[26] While God is loving, He is likewise holy. His self-integrity requires that He maintain and assert Himself as self-derived, self-sufficient, and self-giving. So, after quoting Matthew 16:21 ("From that time Jesus began to show His disciples that He must go to Jerusalem, and suffer many things ... and be killed ..."), W.J. Wolf comments, "It is in the mystery of that word 'must' that all subsequent Christian doctrines of the atonement are rooted." (*No Cross, No Crown: A Study of the Atonement*, New York, 1957, p.64).

Restoration Movement people like to use Bible names for Bible things, since such a practice helps to reduce confusion about what we are saying and what the Bible says. It seems to this commentator that it is a good rule; even when speaking of Christ's work on the cross, use Bible words for that work, and in this light to limit the use of "atonement" (as much as possible) to its Biblical sense of reconciliation.[27] The Bible writers used several different figures or metaphors to explain what God was doing as He sought to provide forgiveness for the men He had created.

A. Propitiation

Greek words thus translated (*hilasmos* and *hilasterion*) appear in several passages. Writing about Christ Jesus, Paul says that He was "displayed publicly as a propitiation (*hilasterion*) in His blood" (Romans 3:25). We find *hilasterion* at Hebrews 9:5 where it is translated "mercy seat."[28] According to 1 John 2:2, Jesus "is the propitiation (*hilasmos*) for our sins," and according to 1 John 4:10, God "loved us and sent His Son to be the propitiation (*hilasmos*) for our sins."[29]

It is difficult to find a suitable English equivalent for the *hilasmos* word family. "Propitiation" is a problem because it is a term borrowed from the vocabulary of paganism, where it speaks of appeasing or placating an angry deity by means of a sacrifice. The Biblical Hebrew and Greek words meaning "to cover" or "mercy seat" do not seem to have the same connotation as did the non-Biblical Greek word.[30]

---

[27] We say "as much as possible" since we are so accustomed to read and speak of the "Day of Atonement" (*yom kippur*) in which the English word "atonement" has been used to translate *kippur* (covering). Here is a place where our English Bibles use "atonement" as a translation for a word which means something other than "reconcile."

[28] The "mercy seat" was the lid of the Ark of the Covenant. Onto this lid, on the Day of Atonement, the high priest sprinkled the blood of the sin offerings both for himself and the sins of the people (Leviticus 16:11-15; Hebrews 9:7). "Day of atonement" (*hemera exilasmou*) might better be translated 'day of propitiation' or 'day of covering.'

[29] In addition we find the verb *hilaskomai* ('to propitiate') in the prayer of the publican (Luke 18:13) and in Hebrews 2:17. There is also an adjective form, *hileos*, found in Matthew 16:22 ("God be merciful to you Lord," NASB mg.) and Hebrews 8:12 (" will be merciful to their iniquities"). In the LXX, the Hebrew word translated by the *hilas-* family of words was the *kpr* root (see *kipper, kippurim, kaporeth* [mercy seat]), a word that means "to cover." The Hebrew root *kaphar* occurs about 110 times in the Old Testament Scriptures, principally in Leviticus and Numbers, and the root idea is "to cover" (though such English words as atonement, make atonement, appease, and pacify are found in our English Bibles). The primitive verb and its noun occur in Genesis 6:14, "*cover* it inside and out with pitch." Just as the pitch covered the ark and protected its passengers, so the shed blood of sacrifice stands between the sinner and the wrath of a holy God.

[30] Any transactional theory where an offended deity is placated by the intervention of one more merciful in character is to be repudiated. The idea that the death of Christ appeased an angry God like the angry god is appeased by the heathen woman throwing her baby into the Ganges River, is not a Biblical idea. The Scriptures explain that God is a God of love, and He Himself provided the propitiation, the covering for sin. It is not a case of one more merciful providing the sacrifice, but God Himself provided it. This much the Scriptures tell us, but what else is involved in *hilasmos* we are not told.

Neither the Old Testament nor New ever tells us that animal sin-offerings remove the divine anger. C.H. Dodd has defended the word "expiate" as a better English equivalent than propitiate. Expiate means to nullify the effects of sin.[31] Yet expiate is not quite satisfactory either. When the "covering" connotation of the original words is taken into account, it speaks about how God's wrath (rather than being appeased) is averted or turned away from the sinner.[32]

How the mercy-seat and sin-offering functioned in Old Testament times seems to point the way for us. A sacrifice was made, and blood was sprinkled on the mercy seat (covering), with the result that the punishment for sin was averted. Romans 3:21-26 indicate that there was a divine necessity for the cross. If God is going to be righteous, and at the same time justifier, there had to be the cross, with the blood being a covering for our sins. The cross will never be understood unless it is seen that Jesus was providing a covering for sins (potentially) for all mankind.[33]

B. Sacrifice

Why did people offer sacrifices in Old Testament times? Because it was the God-given way of dealing with sin. Folk accepted the idea humbly and gratefully. (1) Some sacrifices ratified covenants God was making with men. When this was the purpose of the sacrifice, the sacrifice did not automatically secure God's favor (cf. Micah 6:6-8). Instead, once the sacrifice was made and the covenant was in force, the sinner could seek God's forgiveness according to the terms and conditions which God Himself revealed are necessary. Jesus' death was a covenant-ratifying sacrifice (Matthew 26:28; Luke 22:20; 1 Corinthians 11:25). Jesus himself referred to his blood as "the blood of the covenant" (Mark 14:24). (2) Some sacrifices were related to the forgiveness of sin. "Without shedding of blood there is no forgiveness" (Hebrews 9:22). In the Mosaic dispensation, forgiveness did not occur when the sacrificial victim died. It occurred when the blood of the victim was sprinkled on the mercy seat in the Holy of Holies. Likewise with the sacrifice of Christ. Jesus

[31] C.H. Dodd (*JTS* xxxii [July 1931], p.353-356) tried to show that the LXX does not always use *hilaskomai* to translate *kipper*. When it does not, it uses words with meanings like 'to sanctify,' 'purify' persons or objects of ritual, or 'to cancel,' 'purge away,' 'forgive sins.' When *hilaskomai* is not used to translate *kipper* and its derivatives, the LXX translators used words that fall into one of two classes: (i) with human subject, 'to cleanse from sin or defilement', 'to expiate'; (ii) with divine subject, 'to be gracious,' 'to have mercy,' 'to forgive.' Dodd concluded that, when using *hilaskomai* to render the *kipper* group, "the LXX translators did not regard *kipper* (when used as a religious term) as conveying the sense of propitiating the Deity, but the sense of performing an act whereby guilt or defilement is removed." Morris (*Apostolic Preaching*, p.138) objected that Dodd ignored passages where there is explicit mention of averting God's wrath (i.e., where propitiation might be a suitable equivalent).

[32] For *hilasmos*, at Romans 3:25, the NIV has a footnote which reads, "as the one who would turn aside His wrath."

[33] Walter Elwell, "Atonement, Extent of the," in Evangelical Dictionary of Theology (Grand Rapids: Baker, 1984), p.98-100, gives all arguments pro and con for both limited atonement and universal atonement.

offers His blood in the genuine Holy of Holies (Hebrews 9:11-14). The sacrifices of the Mosaic dispensation were shadows of which the death of Christ is the substance (Hebrews 10:1). The sacrifices of the Mosaic dispensation did not take away sin (Hebrews 10:4), but the sacrifice of Christ actually does (Hebrews 10:11-12). Sins in Old Testament times were "passed over" as God waited for the sacrifice that took place at Calvary (Romans 3:25). Jesus fulfilled all that the old sacrifices had foreshadowed. Scriptures often describe Christ's death as a sacrifice. "Now once at the consummation of the ages He (Jesus) has been manifested to put away sin by the sacrifice of Himself" (Hebrews 9:26). "For He (Jesus), having offered one sacrifice for sins for all time, sat down at the right hand of God" (Hebrews 10:12). When John introduced Jesus with the words, "Behold the Lamb of God who takes away the sin of the world" (John 1:29), he was using sacrificial language based on the sacrifice of lambs in Old Testament times. Christ's sacrifice was the fulfillment of the Passover Lamb (1 Corinthians 5:7, "Christ our Passover [paschal lamb] has been sacrificed"). When the angel of death saw the blood of the lamb on the doorpost of the home, he passed over it. The lamb had died in the place of the firstborn who was spared. When God sees the blood of the Lamb in our lives (when men obey Jesus they are "sprinkled with His blood," 1 Peter 1:2), He passes over us, sparing us. Jesus is the lamb slain from the foundation of the world (Revelation 13:8, NASB mg.) Christ gave himself as a sacrifice to God (Ephesians 5:2). "Christ died for (*huper*) our sins, according to the Scriptures" (1 Corinthians 15:3). Paul tells us that Jesus loved us and gave himself up for us, "an offering and a sacrifice to God" (Ephesians 5:2).

C. Offering, Sin offering

What happened at Calvary is sometimes described as an offering. Christ loved us and gave Himself up for us "as an offering (*prosphoran*) to God" (Ephesians 5:2). Christ was "offered once to bear the sins of many" (Hebrews 9:28). That language emphasizes the finality of His sin offering, as does Hebrews 7:27, "This He did once for all when He offered up Himself." Christ "through the eternal Spirit offered Himself without blemish to God" (Hebrews 9:14). "We have been sanctified through the offering of the body of Jesus Christ once for all" (Hebrews 10:10). It also seems likely that both Romans 8:3 and 2 Corinthians 5:21 speak of Christ's death as being a sin offering.[34]

Perhaps a review of the "offerings" of the Old Testament will help us understand what is meant when Christ's death is called an "offering." Sins pollute. Offerings could bring about cleansing. The need for purification from sin or the desire of the worshiper to enter into fellowship with God underlay the prescription regarding the various kinds of offerings (sin offerings, trespass offerings, peace offer-

---

[34] If these verses do mean "sin offering" then it may be too much to say that penal substitution is a New Testament doctrine, for penal substitution says that once Jesus was made to be sin, God then punished Him as though he were a sinner. These verses may not say that at all.

ings, meal offerings, drink offerings). An offering is something presented to God.
If it were a sin offering the worshiper normally laid his hand heavily on the head of
the animal or birds being used as the offering, symbolically designating it as his
substitute in the sacrificial ritual. Whereas ceremonial cleansing was involved in
those Mosaic sin offerings, actual cleansing of sin is involved in Christ's offering
(Hebrews 9:13,14).

The activities of the Jewish high priest on the Day of Atonement are typical of
the functions of Jesus, our high priest. On the Day of Atonement, the high priest
killed the sin offerings (both for himself and the people) and took the blood into the
Holy of Holies where he sprinkled it on the mercy-seat. Now Jesus is our superior
high priest, and a priest must have something to offer (*prospherein*) (Hebrews 8:3).
Following His death and resurrection, He entered the greater and more perfect
tabernacle in heaven through His own blood (Hebrews 9:11,12), where He appears in
the presence of God for our benefit (Hebrews 9:24). In fact, heaven itself was
cleansed by Christ's blood (Hebrews 9:23). The blood of bulls and goats could never
take away sin; Christ's death does (Hebrews 10:4).

All offerings were related directly to covenantal religion, the basic principle of
which was obedience. (At Sinai, when God gave the Mosaic covenant, He did not
speak specifically about sacrifices, but about obedience, Exodus 19:4-8; Jeremiah
7:21-23). Each sacrifice was a reminder of human sin and of divine provision for
the helpless sinner. Each sacrifice was an opportunity for the faithful worshiper to
obey what God had required. Without obedience and faith the offerings were
valueless.

D. Substitution

The belief that as Jesus suffered He was suffering as a substitute for men who
had sinned is quite common. However, finding the idea of substitution specifically
stated in Scripture is not as straightforward as one might expect. What we do find
is: (1) The whole background of the Old Testament sacrificial system (Leviticus 1:4,
3:2,8,13; 4:4,15,24,29; 16:21,22; 17:11) where the slain victim was a substitutionary
representative of the worshiper. (2) There are the prepositions *anti* and *huper* which
mean "instead of" and "on behalf of" (often translated "for"). *Anti* ("instead of"[35]) is
used of Christ's death in Matthew 20:28 and Mark 10:45, where we read the Son of
Man gave His life "a ransom for many." *Huper* ("on behalf of"[36]) is used at 2 Cor-

---

[35] "The preposition *anti* characteristically has the meaning 'in the place of', 'instead of', whether
in the classics or in the Koine" (Morris, *Apostolic Preaching*, p.30). In the LXX, Abraham offered
the ram for a burnt offering "in the stead of (*anti*) his son" (Genesis 22:13).

[36] Both Thayer and BAG give "in behalf of, for the sake of" as the first meaning for *huper*. Both
also give "instead of, in place of" as a possible alternative meaning.

inthians 5:14, "one died for (*huper*) all."[37]   "For Christ also died for (*peri*, concerning) sins once for all, the just for (*huper*) the unjust, in order that He might bring us to God ..." (1 Peter 3:18).[38]   John 15:12-15 has the famous dictum that "greater love hath no man than this, to lay down one's life for *(huper)* one's friends" (that is, on their behalf).   (3) Peter's use of Isaiah 53 appears to be a passage which clearly supports the idea that Christ's death was substitutionary.   Christ "Himself bore our own sins in His body on the cross" (1 Peter 2:24).   For "bore" there is a marginal note, "He carried our sins up to the cross."   The word picture is of a priest offering a sacrifice for sins by bearing that offering up to the altar of burnt offering.[39] Isaiah 53:5 tells us that Messiah would be pierced through (wounded) for our transgressions, he would be crushed (bruised) for our iniquities; the chastening for our well-being (peace) would fall upon Him, and by His scourging (stripes) we would be healed.   Jesus got the scourging; we get the healing.   That's certainly substitution. Isaiah 53:6 goes on to say that all of us like sheep have gone astray.   Each of us has turned to his own way; but the Lord has caused the iniquity of us all to fall on Him ("the Lord has laid on Him the iniquity of us all" KJV).   Rather than being penal substitution, this language may reflect the laying on of hands on the sin offering.   If so, Isaiah was predicting that Jesus would become our sin offering.

E. Redemption/Ransom

"Ransom," "redeem," "redemption" are English words used to translate the Greek words *lutroō, lutrosis* and *apolutrosis* at Luke 24:21, Titus 2:14, Hebrews 9:12, and other passages.   This metaphor occurs at Matthew 20:28 (Mark 10:45 is a parallel), where Jesus explains that He, the Son of man, came "to give His life a ransom for (*anti*) many."[40]   Paul seems to have had Christ's words in mind when he declared that Christ Jesus "gave Himself a ransom for all" (1 Timothy 2:6).   Peter also uses the word "redeemed."   "You were not redeemed with perishable things like silver or gold from your futile way of life ... but with precious blood ... the blood of Christ" (1 Peter 1:18,19).   John records the words of the new song about Jesus sung in heaven, "Thou wast slain, and didst purchase for God with Thy blood men from every tribe and tongue and people and nation" (Revelation 5:9).

---

[37] *Huper* also occurs at 2 Corinthians 5:21 in "made Him to be sin on our behalf (*huper hemon*)." See the commentary on this verse where it is proposed to mean "a sin offering on our behalf" rather than penal substitution.

[38] There is a manuscript variation at this place.   Following the Greek of the Textus Receptus, the KJV reads Christ "suffered for sins," a reading that has been used to support the idea of penal substitution (that idea that Christ our substitute suffered the punishment that sinners deserved).

[39] Matthew 8:16,17, Christ "Himself took up our infirmities and carried away our diseases," is a fulfillment of Isaiah 53:4.   Not that infirmities were vicariously imputed to Christ at His crucifixion; rather, Christ healed the sick, thus "carrying" or "bearing" their diseases away from them.

[40] The authenticity of this ransom saying has been disputed (Rashdall, for example, *op. cit.*, p.29-37, 49-56).   Morris, *Apostolic Preaching* answers, p.27ff.

"Redemption" or "ransom" is the act of buying back. The Psalmist reminds us that men cannot ransom themselves nor ransom each other (Psalm 49:7-9). The coming of Christ into the world to offer Himself as a ransom is rooted in the absolute impossibility for man to ransom himself or his fellow-man from the bondage of sin and death. The ransom model is based on the emancipation of slaves or the ransom of prisoners taken in war, who might, in the ancient world, have been forced to become slaves. Slaves and prisoners are quite clearly unable to ransom themselves. Sin in this model is equated with slavery or imprisonment. The person whose freedom is to be purchased must rely on another to purchase and restore the freedom which was assumed to be the natural state. The purchase price to redeem men from the slavery of sin was the blood of Christ (Acts 20:28; 1 Corinthians 6:19,20).[41]

Another word (*antilutron*) is translated "ransom" in Christ "gave himself a ransom for all" in 1 Timothy 2:6. Thayer defines *antilutron* as "what is given in exchange for another as the price of his redemption." "The preposition (*anti*) emphasizes the thought of substitution; it is a 'substitute-ransom' that is signified."[42]

This ransom model, of course, invites the question "to whom was the ransom paid?" Early church fathers[43] came up with a guess. It is because it did not seem that God was the cause of the enslavement that the obvious candidate for receipt of the ransom was the devil. We have noted earlier the telling objections to this view. Nor does it seem right to say that the price was somehow paid to God. God's forgiveness is not literally purchased; there would be no forgiveness in that. Therefore, it seems right to say that while "ransom" or "redemption" does at times include the idea of a price being paid, that is not always true in the Scriptures. While God's freeing the Israelites from Egypt was called a redemption (Deuteronomy 7:8), no ransom was paid by God (the great redeemer-deliverer) to anyone (Exodus 4:22,23 and 6:6; Deuteronomy 9:26; 2 Samuel 7:27; 1 Chronicles 17:21). Another great redemptive act occurred when God redeemed His people from the Babylonian Captivity, an act that was a type of Messianic redemption (Isaiah 52:3-7). It is doubtful that Jews ever thought in terms of a price being paid *to someone* for that redemption. Rather, the word was used simply of the rescue God achieved, with no idea of a price being paid. Likewise, when speaking of the redemption that is in Christ, the main idea in the metaphor is that a prisoner has been freed. To whom a ransom price was paid is a part of the figure that is not to be pressed. "You were bought with a price" (1 Corinthians 6:20, 7:23) is the language of the slave market to emphasize the idea Christians have changed their allegiance; they are no longer under their old master (sin), but under a new one (Christ).

---

[41] Redemption is obtained even for the transgressions committed under the Mosaic covenant (Romans 3:25,26; Hebrews 9:15).

[42] Morris, *Apostolic Preaching*, p.48.

[43] See Irenaeus, Origen, Gregory of Nyssa, Augustine, Gregory the Great, Peter Lombard and Bernard of Clairvaux.

F. Reconciliation

The Greek words that the word "reconciliation" represents are *katallagē* (which means exchange, adjustment of a difference, reconciliation, restoration to favor) in 2 Corinthians 5:18ff; *katalassō* (which means to change, to reconcile) in Romans 5:10, 2 Corinthians 5:20; and *apokatalassō* (which means to reconcile) found in Ephesians 2:11ff (especially verse 16, "reconcile") and Colossians 1:19ff.[44] "The chief difficulty to be solved in the New Testament use of reconcile, reconciliation, etc., is whether, in the process of reconciliation, God can be said to be reconciled to man, or whether the process is one in which man only is reconciled."[45]

God is thought of as being angry with men because of sin. James 4:4 tells us that friendship with the world is hostility towards God, and "whoever makes himself a friend of the world makes himself an enemy of God." Romans 5:9-11 speaks of sinners as being enemies of God, and of being reconciled through Christ's death so that men are saved from the wrath of God. Without the death of Christ, God's attitude towards men would not be what it is. If God is hostile to evil, reconciliation would affect His hostility. Colossians 1:21 tells us there was a time when men were alienated from God because of their sins, but it was the Father's good pleasure "through Him (Christ) to reconcile to Himself all things ... making peace by the blood of the cross." Sin has estranged men from God, and men from men. God initiated the means of reconciliation. The death of Christ really did something to remove barriers; God made peace through the blood of the cross, and God has reconciled men in Christ's fleshly body through death (Colossians 1:20,22). Sinners were formerly "alienated and hostile in mind, engaged in evil deeds" (Colossians 1:21). Reconciliation certainly includes a change of mind on the part of former sinners. 2 Corinthians 5:19 tells us that "God was in Christ reconciling the world to Himself, not counting their trespasses against them." Not counting their trespasses against them certainly points to a change in God's attitude towards men. Because of the death of Christ the obstacle that destroyed their fellowship, namely sin, has been removed. Peace,[46] reconciliation is now possible.

Reconciliation naturally means that two, who were estranged, come together again in virtue of an inner change which takes place in both. A mutual change has

[44] At 2 Samuel 29:4 the Hebrew word *ratsah* is translated "reconcile" in the KJV ("make acceptable" in NASB). The verb speaks of the removal of enmity. The English word "reconciliation" occurs in the KJV several times (Leviticus 6:30, 16:20; Ezekiel 45:20) as the translation of the Hebrew *kaphar* (which has been shown above to mean "covering"). At these places the LXX has some form of the word for covering or propitiation (namely, *exhilasasthai, exhilaskomenos,* or *exhilasesthe*). At these places it is translated "atonement" or "atoning" in NASB, another not quite satisfactory choice of an English equivalent.

[45] Morris, *Apostolic Preaching*, p.192.

[46] The idea of "reconciliation" is sometimes present when the actual word does not appear, e.g., when "making peace" is spoken of (peace with God).

been effected – from enmity to love. Man's attitude is now right. Man accepts the way of God. God's no longer has to be angry with sinners. When man's attitude changes and he accepts Christ, God can be true to Himself and accept the reconciled back into fellowship. Right relationships now exist on both sides. While the other metaphors describing what Christ did on Calvary might be considered slightly impersonal, when it comes to the language of reconciliation we are talking in terms of personal relationships, severed and now restored.

G. The Victory Model

This metaphor is taken from war and the battlefield. "Thanks be to God, who gives us the victory through our Lord Jesus Christ" (1 Corinthians 15:57).[47] Christ is victorious. By His saving work He has accomplished a victory over their opponents for those who were embattled by inimical spiritual powers. Passages that speak of the victory won at Calvary include Romans 8:37 and 1 Corinthians 15:24-28,57, but the most important passage from which this view of Calvary is derived is Colossians 2:12-15. It tells how Christ triumphed over all a Christian's enemies at the cross. Satan has been overthrown by what Jesus did on Calvary (Hebrews 2:14; John 12:31; 1 John 3:8; Revelation 12:7-12).

This is the model Gustav Aulen chose to promote as the "classical theory" in his highly influential work *Christus Victor* (London, 1931), in which he developed his famous criticism of Anselm's model. Aulen identified how influential this view of Calvary was in patristic thought and how this view has dropped out of later theological reflection.

III. SUMMARY

The entire Bible presents the view that men's sins have alienated them from God. Something must be done to remove or pardon the sin that has brought about this estrangement.

Once Adam had sinned, the sin needed to be "covered" – and not only his but the sins of his posterity, for it soon became a fact that "all have sinned and come short of the glory of God" (Romans 3:23). God instituted a sacrificial system[48] to teach men that a sacrifice was needed to bring about the desired reconciliation. But as the

---

[47] All the New Testament verses that have the resurrection as the victory over the powers of death and enabling the Christian to share the consequences of Christ's victory may also be included in this category.

[48] That God instituted sacrifice is implied in "by faith Abel offered a more acceptable sacrifice than Cain" (Hebrews 11:4) for, after all, "faith comes by hearing the Word of God" (Romans 10:17 KJV).

years passed, the deaths of thousands of animal sacrifices made it abundantly clear that "the blood of bulls and goats could never take away sin" (Hebrews 10:4). It also became clear that man himself could not provide a suitable sacrifice. All along, God promised how in due time He would provide the needed sacrifice. The ceremonies on the Day of Atonement were even a detailed preview of what Jesus, our great high priest, would actually do, with this notable exception: unlike the Jewish priest, Jesus did not have to offer any sacrifice for His own sins. He was sinless. God has provided the needed salvation for believers through the redemption that is in Christ Jesus (Romans 3:21-28).

The New Testament writers struggle with the inadequacy of language as they seek to present to us what Calvary means. No one metaphor quite captures the full significance of Calvary. In history's most memorable moment, the Son of God died on Calvary to set a world of sinners free. God had given his only Son to be the sacrifice that would actually make a covering for sins. In no sense was the merciful Son championing the rights of humankind against the severe Father who grants forgiveness only grudgingly. "God was in Christ reconciling the world to Himself" (2 Corinthians 5:19). Jesus volunteered to be the sacrifice (if such were needed) when, back in eternity before creation, the members of the Godhead formulated their eternal purpose (or "plan" as it is translated by Beck at Romans 8:28). Jesus was a lamb slain from the foundation of the earth (Revelation 13:8).

Now, with Christ's death in the picture, God is able to forgive and restore to fellowship those men who respond positively to His invitation and live faithfully in harmony with His revealed will ("the propitiation" is available "through faith," Romans 3:25). With Christ's death in the picture, God can be just and at the same time justifier of him who has faith in Jesus (Romans 3:26).[49] The different words used to explain Christ's death vividly help us to see from a number of different perspectives how Christ's death on Calvary works. Sinners who are slaves to sin are freed. Captives of the devil are redeemed. The wrath of God is turned away from sinners. People suffering estranged relationships are reconciled.

Bearing shame and scoffing rude, In my place condemned He stood;
Sealed my pardon with His blood: Hallelujah! What a Savior![50]

---

[49] What is being presented here is a deliberate repudiation of the doctrine of "limited atonement," i.e., that Christ died only for the elect. The Bible says Christ died for all (Isaiah 53:6; 1 John 2:2; 1 Timothy 2:6, 4:10), and that potentially is true. Whether or not a man avails himself of the benefits of Christ's death is a matter of his free will and choice, not a matter decided for him by God back in eternity before creation. It is man's decision to reject the salvation God offers that brings about His condemnation.

[50] P.P. Bliss.

6:1 - *And working together* with Him, *we also urge you not to receive the grace of God in vain; --*

And working together *with Him* - The chapter break here may cause English readers to miss the thread of thought.   Paul closed chapter 5 explaining what an appointment to be an ambassador of Christ involves.   Now he opens chapter 6 with *de kai* in the Greek, which carries the idea that more is to be said on the subject.   In all the various experiences such ambassadors are called on to face (6:4-10), they do their best to give offense in nothing while doing everything possible to vindicate their claims that they are serving God in genuineness and honesty of purpose.   The words "with Him" are italicized in the NASB, indicating they are not part of the Greek text.   The Greek is simply "working together" and does not say whom the apostles are working or cooperating with in order to produce the result of the Corinthians receiving the grace of God.   When it comes to answering the question, "With whom are the apostles working?" there are several possibilities suggested in the immediate context.   Many of our English versions supply "with Him," meaning that the apostles and God are working together to secure the salvation of lost men.   This is probably the most obvious meaning since we have already read that God made His appeal through the apostles (5:20).[1]

We also urge you not to receive the grace of God in vain - "We urge" translates the same Greek word rendered "entreating" in 5:20.   "We" has Paul (God's fellow worker, verse 1a) acting as God's mouthpiece as he makes this urgent appeal.   "You" (a plural form placed in the emphatic position in the Greek) speaks to the Christians at Corinth.   This is no general entreaty to the unsaved world.[2]   "Receive" translates an aorist tense infinitive (*dexasthai*) in a construction which usually implies that the action of the infinitive is an event that happened prior to the action of the main verb

---

[1] Other answers are (1) "with Christ," which might be inferred from 5:20 if *huper Christou* means "in Christ's stead" rather than "on behalf of Christ"; (2) "with you," which would have the Corinthians cooperating with the missionaries as they listened and responded to their message of reconciliation; (3) "with other teachers," which requires us to interpret the first person plural "we" all through this paragraph as a reference to Paul alone.

[2] Defenders of unconditional eternal security must find some other explanation for "you" than the Christians at Corinth, for if their doctrine is right, it could not be said of Christians that they had "received the grace of God in vain," could it?   Tasker attempted to defend the idea the people addressed had not received the grace, i.e., had not become genuine Christians in the first place. Martin ("2 Corinthians" in *Word Biblical Commentary* [Waco, TX: Word Books, 1986], p.166) responds by asking how can someone be exhorted not to have done something?   "Receive" suggests that something has already taken place.   You cannot exhort someone to avoid something that has already transpired.   Hodge's solution (p.154) to harmonizing this verse with his belief in unconditional security insists that Paul's appeal is to mankind in general.   Both these attempts ignore how the context describes the "you" to whom this appeal is directed.   Robert Shank, who once held the doctrine of unconditional eternal security, has written a frank, scholarly, and comprehensive critique of the doctrine.   His book is titled *Life in the Son: A Study of the Doctrine of Perseverance* (Springfield, MO : Westcott Publishers, 1961).

("urge" in this this case).[3]   At the time of their conversion the Corinthians had received (i.e., welcomed[4]) the grace of God.   Writing to Titus on the island of Crete, Paul spoke of the grace of God in these words: "The grace of God has appeared, bringing salvation to all men, instructing us to deny ungodliness and worldly desires and to live sensibly, righteously and godly in the present age, looking for the blessed hope and the glorious appearing of our great God and Savior, Christ Jesus" (Titus 2:11-13).   The "grace of God" here in 6:1 evidently means the gracious offer of reconciliation and pardon.   Christ's first coming has made reconciliation possible (2 Corinthians 5:18,19), and when the Corinthians had believed and been baptized they experienced this reconciliation.   However, a good beginning does not guarantee a good ending.   If the expected life of faithfulness doesn't follow, the initial reception will prove to be "vain" (*kenos*, empty, not producing its intended effect).   Christians still have freedom of the will to choose good or evil (Romans 6:12-23); if they chose evil, they would frustrate the end which the grace was intended to produce in their lives (cp. 1 Corinthians 9:27, 15:10).

Several things may have been in Paul's mind which he feared would make the grace ineffective.   If the Corinthians embraced the false teachers who have come among them (11:11-13); if their minds should be led astray from the simplicity and purity of devotion to Christ (11:3); if, after having become obedient to the gospel of Christ which the Apostle had taught them, they should turn unto another gospel (11:4), which was really a perverted gospel (Galatians 1:7); if they failed to repudiate darkness and Belial and idols, and instead became bound together with unbelievers (6:14-18); if they failed to perfect holiness in the fear of God (7:1); or even if they rejected Paul's overtures for reconciliation with them (6:13; 7:2); then, they would have received God's grace in vain.   Paul appeals to them not to squander what grace has begun in their lives.   If they do not meet their responsibilities, their initial reception of grace will have been in vain.

One more observation is necessary to complete the comments on verse 1:   the punctuation in NASB (both verses 1 and 2 are followed by a dash in order to indicate that verse 3 continues the tread of thought begun in verse 1) suggests that this verse is beginning to lay the foundation for the stern admonitions that are given in verses 14-18.

---

[3] Instead of picturing the grace as received before the present appeal is made, some writers (often with a bias toward unconditional eternal security) propose the aorist infinitive should be treated as timeless.   This allows the receiving of grace to be something potentially occurring in the present time and the future, and Paul's appeal then is "Don't now or ever receive the grace of God in vain."   To call it a timeless aorist, in this commentator's judgment, is a case of special pleading.   The construction here is one that is called indirect discourse.   The verses appealed to where "receive" is said to be timeless (2 Corinthians 11:4; 1 Thessalonians 1:6, 2:13; 2 Thessalonians 2:10) are not examples of indirect discourse.

[4] There are two Greek words for receive: *lambanō* emphasizes the taking of the gift, and *dechomai* which emphasizes the attitude with which the gift is received, i.e., it is welcomed.   Thayer, *op. cit.*, p.131.

6:2 - *for He says, "AT THE ACCEPTABLE TIME I LISTENED TO YOU, AND ON THE DAY OF SALVATION I HELPED YOU:" behold, now is "THE ACCEPTABLE TIME," behold, now is "THE DAY OF SALVATION"; --*

For He says - With "for" Paul introduces a statement made by God Himself[5] which underscores the grand reason why the Corinthians should respond to his appeal (verse 1) not to receive the grace of God in vain. God's statement is quoted from the LXX of Isaiah 49:8. Isaiah 49:1-13 is the second of the "Suffering Servant Poems" found in Isaiah 40-66. Every time one of these five poems is quoted by the apostles in the New Testament, the servant is identified as being Jesus Messiah (e.g., Matthew 12:18, 8:17; Acts 3:13-15,24, 4:26,27,30; 1 Peter 2:24). The poems describe what Messiah would do when it finally came time for Him to come into the world. In order to appreciate Paul's citation of Isaiah 49:8, it is needful to recall the context. The Servant is speaking as chapter 49 begins. He alludes to His incarnation (the Lord formed Messiah from the womb to be His servant). The Servant is to reconcile Israel to the Lord and He is to be a light to the Gentiles, so that His salvation may be to the ends of the earth.[6] It will be Messiah's work to inaugurate a new covenant (49:8), an idea afterwards developed and elaborated in Jeremiah 31:31ff. Isaiah 49:4 has the Servant crying out to God that His work had been in vain. The words from verse 8 (cited by Paul) are God's response to those cries and include God's promise to the Servant to support Him as He carries out the task He was appointed to do in the world.

"AT THE ACCEPTABLE TIME I LISTENED TO YOU - These words from Isaiah 49:8 are God's answer to the Servant's prayer. The idea contained in God's answer is that in God's wise arrangements there was an acceptable time, both for God and for man,[7] for Messiah to come into the world to redeem Israel and to be a light to the Gentiles.

"AND ON THE DAY OF SALVATION I HELPED YOU" - God promised to sustain Messiah as He went about His mission of making salvation possible for all men.

Behold, now is "THE ACCEPTABLE TIME," behold, now is "THE DAY OF SALVATION"; - Having quoted Isaiah 49:8, Paul now applies the passage to the present situation. By saying "now" Paul meant that the wonderful era that had been predicted in the Servant poems of Isaiah has now arrived. Messiah, the Servant, has come, and the salvation and reconciliation that God makes available in Him is man's

---

[5] The NASB capitalizes "He" since the antecedent of the pronoun is involved in the "workers together with Him." "This is hardly to be classed with those rabbinic methods of citation found also in Philo, which deliberately omit the word 'God' as the speaker, and use 'He' by preference." (Farrar, *op. cit.*, p.144).

[6] At Acts 13:47 Paul cites Isaiah 49:6 as a mandate for him and Barnabas to take the gospel to the Gentiles.

[7] See how "acceptable time" is explained at Luke 4:19 and Philippians 4:18.

for the taking. How unthinkable, in light of what time it is, that men should waste the grace they have received.[8] The term "salvation" in Scripture can have a past, a present, or a future connotation: I was saved, I am being saved, I hope to be saved. Here, where initial salvation is not the topic, the present connotation likely prevails; contextually, "salvation" picks up the entreaty to not let their reception of grace be ineffective, as well as the previous emphasis on the need to live a life worthy of God (5:9,10,14,15). The Greek word translated "acceptable" is much stronger than the word used in the previous clause. The word here expresses a jubilant feeling about the present time. What a great time to be alive! What a wonderful opportunity God is offering. In this gospel era when there is opportunity to profit from God's grace, how urgent it is not to take His offer lightly. There is no time to lose. Act while you have opportunity.[9]

6:3 - *giving no cause for offense in anything, in order that the ministry be not discredited.*

Giving no cause for offense in anything - The participles of verses 3 and 4 ("giving" and "commending") resume the sentence begun in verse 1. From here to verse 10 there is a whole series of first-person plural participles which agree with the subject of the sentence found in verse 1 ("we urge you") and to 5:20 ("we are ambassadors ..."). Present tense circumstantial participles such as these often are translated by the helping word "while." Thus the thought runs "we urge you ... while giving no cause ... and while commending ourselves." It is the apostles themselves who aim at giving no cause for offense in anything whatever. "Giving" is a present tense which speaks of continuous, habitual, or customary action. The effort to avoid giving offense is how the apostles ever and always made it their aim to live. The word (*proskopē*) translated "no cause for offense" speaks of placing an obstacle in someone's path over which you know he will stumble. The Greek *en mēdeni* ("in anything") can be either masculine[10] (no obstacle "to any one") or neuter[11] ("in anything"). If we take it as a neuter, we must understand that when Paul speaks of no obstacle he means no unnecessary offense, for some are offended at the gospel (1 Corinthians 1:23; Galatians 5:11). When they were able to avoid putting an obstacle in anyone's path,

---

[8] It has been observed that the Hebrew at Isaiah 49:8 speaks of "a time of favor" which enables Paul to apply the verse to "grace" as he does.

[9] Many preachers, as part of the gospel invitation, quote this verse to their listeners to impress on them the importance of responding "now!" to God's offer, rather than thinking they can safely put off a decision until another day. This rather common application of the "now," viz. "act at once, for delay is dangerous," while true in itself, is not quite the meaning of "now." It speaks instead of a golden opportunity which may never occur again.

[10] The NIV takes it as masculine, and offers "in anyone's path" as a dynamic equivalent rendering.

[11] The NASB treats it as neuter.

Paul and the other apostles were scrupulously careful.[12]   It appears the apostles knew that men would look for an excuse to reproach the ministry and the message of Christ they preached.[13]   Well, they would not find such an excuse in the behavior of the apostles.   A fellow worker with God, an ambassador of Christ will hardly live so as to permit others to discredit the One whom they represented.   As we connect verse 3 with verse 1, we see that the example of the apostles is such that no one can use it as an excuse to go astray, the result then being that they have received the grace of God in vain.

In order that the ministry be not discredited - "In order that" indicates that this is the purpose behind the apostles' constant avoidance of giving offense.   The expression "the ministry" reminds us that in earlier paragraphs Paul spoke about the ministry of the new covenant (3:6), and the ministry of reconciliation (5:18).   That apostolic ministry is the one he doesn't want to be discredited.   The word for "discredited" (*mōmaomai*) means to blame, to vilify, or to find fault.[14]   Paul uses the word again at 2 Corinthians 8:20 as he indicates how careful he was to avoid giving any false impression that would give a handle to any adversary[15] who might wish to ridicule or malign the gospel he preaches or the Christ he represents.

6:4 - *but in everything commending ourselves as servants of God, in much endurance, in afflictions, in hardships, in distresses,*

But in everything commending ourselves as servants of God - "As servants of God" is in the nominative case in the Greek.   We catch the meaning by rearranging the English wording so that it reads "we as servants of God commend ourselves in everything."   He admits the apostles commended themselves,[16] but in ways servants of God should commend themselves, by their upright lives.   "Ourselves" includes

---

[12] Paul's language reminds us of what he wrote in Romans 14:13 and 1 Corinthians 8:9,13 and 9:19-23 about how the Christian is never to place an obstacle or stumbling block in the way of his brother.

[13] Norman Hillyer, *The New Bible Commentary, Revised* (Grand Rapids: Eerdmans, 1970, p.1081) reminds us that "There are people who will be glad of an excuse not to listen to the gospel or to take it seriously, and they will look for such an excuse in the conduct of its ministers."   That is precisely what Paul and the apostles tried to avoid.

[14] The verb here is related to the name *Mōmos* (spelled Momus in English), a figure in Greek literature who personifies fault-finding, mockery, and ridicule.

[15] "It is man's criticism and abuse that is meant, not Divine condemnation.   The Apostle is not thinking of the judgment seat of Christ (5:10); neither 'stumbling' nor 'blamed' would be used in reference to that."   Plummer, *op. cit.*, p.192.

[16] Paul still may have had in mind the Judaizers' claims that he and the other apostles improperly commended themselves (5:12) and could produce no letters of commendation like the Judaizers could (see also comments at 3:1 and 4:2).   That slur is about to be answered forcefully.

the other apostles along with Paul. "But" signals a contrast with what was said in verse 3. Rather than giving people an excuse to reject the gospel by how they lived, the apostles did everything they could to help people see they were servants[17] of God. Paul continues on in this paragraph to show how true ministers commend themselves.[18] 2 Corinthians 6:1-10 is one sentence in the Greek, held together by a series of nominative plural present tense participles modifying "we" (verse 1, "we urge"): "working together with him (verse 1), "giving no cause for offense" (verse 3), but "commending ourselves" (verse 4). The remainder of this paragraph contains a series of phrases which enumerate some of what is included "in everything." Emphasis in the Greek is on the adverbial *en panti* ("in everything") which can mean in every way or in all circumstances. Paul has already told us that the apostles tried to commend themselves and the Christian cause to "the conscience of each and every person" (4:2). Having called attention to the fact that his credentials come from God (5:18), Paul now calls attention to his life as an apostle as a way of leading up to his passionate appeal to the Corinthians for reconciliation and reciprocity of relations (6:11-13).

In much endurance - That this phrase is a general term which embraces all the particulars that follow seems to be indicated by the fact "endurance" is the only noun in the singular in verses 4 and 5, and the only noun that is qualified (he speaks of "much" endurance). Thus the idea Paul writes is this, "We commend ourselves as servants of God by our steadfast endurance." Two Greek words have been translated as "endurance" or "patience." One is *makrothumia* and denotes "putting up with people"; it is the self-restraint which does not hastily retaliate a wrong. The other word, the one used here, is *hupomonē*, which denotes fortitude, "putting up with things," the ability to stand up under the pressure of adversity, hardship, and deprivation. Barclay has given an illustration of how endurance works: "If life hands you a lemon, make lemonade!" Endurance or fortitude is an evidence that Paul is a minister of God because it is a quality which Jesus emphasized to his disciples (Matthew 10:22, 24:13; Mark 13:13; Luke 8:15, 21:19). Paul will emphasize this quality again in 2 Corinthians 12:12. Had Paul shrunk from enduring all the trials he suffered, he would have been ill-qualified to prescribe for others those rules of duty which called for self-sacrifice, one of which rules he is about to lay down for the Corinthians. Nine outward circumstances follow (verses 4b-5) in which Paul showed an attitude of endurance despite deprivations. Chrysostom called the following list Paul's "blizzard of troubles."

---

[17] The Greek is *diakonoi*. The NASB margin gives "ministers" as an alternate translation for a word that is formed from the same root as the word translated "ministry" in verse 3.

[18] There may be a side reference to the Judaizers whose behavior shows they are not ministers of God like Paul and the other apostles of Jesus are. The Judaizers commended themselves by boasting of worldly things (11:16,18), of their advantage as Jews (11:22), and of their position as apostles (11:12). As Paul goes on to show, that is not the way a minister of God commends himself.

In afflictions, in hardships, in distresses - The plurals speak of multiple instances of each trial. Paul used the haunting word "affliction" at 1:4,8, 2:4, 4:8, to speak of the internal pressures a man experiences who is greatly concerned about his ministry and the people to whom he ministers. Paul voluntarily accepted these pressures; still, endurance is needed to accept the affliction and make good come out of it. "Hardships" denotes the distress a person experiences when he is poor and in need. He is living through unrelieved adverse circumstances. "Distresses" (*stenochōriais*, literally narrowness of space) denote being in dire straits, in a tight spot where one has a feeling of being so hemmed in that there is no room left to move, no way of escape.

6:5 - *in stripes, in imprisonments, in tumults, in labors, in sleeplessness, in hunger,*

In stripes, in imprisonments, in tumults - These three troubles which give Paul and the apostles opportunity to demonstrate endurance/fortitude were inflicted on them by men. While we do not have much historical record concerning the other apostles, we do have record of some of the countless beatings (2 Corinthians 11:23) that were endured by Paul.[19] When Jews inflicted the beatings (and at least five times this happened to Paul, 2 Corinthians 11:24) they used whips. When the Romans did it (and three times this happened to Paul, 2 Corinthians 11:25), they used rods. We know about the time and place of only one of these Roman beatings (Acts 16:23). Perhaps imprisonments were more serious than beatings, since they stopped the apostles' work for a while. By the time he writes 2 Corinthians, Paul can speak of "imprisonments" plural, but we know of only the one at Philippi (Acts 16:24); the imprisonments at Caesarea (Acts 23:23-26:32) and Rome (Acts 28:16-31) were subsequent to the time of writing this epistle. Clement of Rome says Paul was thrown into prison no fewer than seven times, though he names no specific instance.[20] "Tumults" were riots or mob actions directed against the apostles. Often they caused the apostles to abandon their work altogether in the place where the tumult occurred. But fortitude led them to begin again in a new field. In Paul's case we know of such tumults at Antioch of Pisidia (Acts 13:50), at Iconium (Acts 14:5), at Lystra (Acts 14:19), at Philippi (Acts 16:19), at Thessalonica (Acts 17:5), at Berea (Acts 17:13), at Corinth (Acts 19:12, with which the readers would have been familiar), and at Ephesus (Acts 19:29).

In labors, in sleeplessness, in hunger - These three troubles seem to be things the apostles voluntarily took upon themselves as they went about carrying out their mission. The Greek word (*kopos*) translated "labors" speaks of the fatigue incurred,

---

[19] Coffman (*op. cit.*, p.383) wrote that it has often been observed that the records of the earthly ministry of Jesus (the Gospels) and the historical account of what the apostles did (Acts) are only fractional records. Any total record would have required more than a library (John 20:30; 21:25).

[20] 1 Clement 5.

the feeling of weariness and exhaustion resulting from the strenuous exertions they were called upon to make[21] while traveling and preaching and caring for the souls in the churches. It is hard work, not worldly position, that validates the apostleship of Jesus' apostles. While the word *agrupniais* ("sleeplessness") includes anything that would keep a person from sleeping,[22] the present context suggests Paul is not talking of insomnia but rather voluntarily going without sleep in order to get the job done that they were doing. Paul reminded the Ephesian elders of his toil into the night (Acts 20:31). The same word is used in the expression "through many a sleepless night" (2 Corinthians 11:27). Sleepless nights can result from concern for the converts or the need to spend time in prayer. Some of our older English versions have translated the plural Greek word *nēsteias* as "fastings" rather than "hunger" as has the updated NASB. This has led some commentators to write about fasting in the religious sense.[23] The New Testament does not teach Christians to observe regular religious fasts as the Jews were required to do, but it does assume Christians will fast from time to time (Matthew 6:16-18, 17:21; Mark 2:19,20). However, since Paul is writing about hardships the apostles have had to endure, it is doubtful he would include in such a list those fasts which may have been practiced for their own spiritual benefit. It is rather to be inferred from 2 Corinthians 11:27 that Paul is speaking of voluntarily going without meals in order to take advantage of some opportunity for evangelism or preaching or to get done whatever job he was at the moment doing for the Lord. The implication in the plurals is that these hard experiences were not isolated, but were frequent and familiar. This triplet completes the list of hardships that called for endurance/fortitude on the part of the apostles (verse 4).

6:6 - *in purity, in knowledge, in patience, in kindness, in the Holy Spirit, in genuine love*

In purity - This verse is not a continuation of the hardships that call for endurance (verses 4,5). Rather it speaks of character traits (like endurance) that apostles constantly tried to practice in everyday life so that no reproach would be brought on their ministries (verses 3,4). "Purity" (*hagnotēs*) may refer to morals (chastity) or to purity of motive (integrity).[24] It is a mindset which makes a man careful to keep a clean heart and clean hands. While the apostles were careful to be pure, such a char-

---

[21] George R. Berry, "Synonyms #53" in his *Greek-English Lexicon to the New Testament* (Chicago: Wilcox and Follett, 1948), p.135.

[22] The verb means to keep watch (Hebrews 13:17), to be vigilant, keep alert (Mark 13:33; Luke 21:36; Ephesians 6:18).

[23] "Fasting" (*nēsteia*) is used in a religious sense at Luke 2:37; Acts 13:2,3, 14:23, 27:9.

[24] Plumptre (*op. cit.*, p.58) thought that because of the general state of morals throughout the empire, and especially in writing to such a city as Corinth, Paul likely had a moral emphasis in mind.

acter trait is also expected of all Christians (2 Corinthians 11:3;[25] James 3:17; 1 John 3:3). In 1 Thessalonians 2:10 ("You are witnesses ... how devoutly and uprightly and blamelessly we behaved toward you believers") Paul calls attention to his purity in behavior.

In knowledge - Perhaps Paul is emphasizing the idea the apostles had to exercise prudence or discretion as they traveled to and ministered to various audiences in town after town. Perhaps it has reference to their divinely revealed knowledge concerning God's way of saving man, the very kind of knowledge concerning which, he says, Jewish people's zeal was lacking (Romans 10:2,3). In another place Paul speaks of his knowledge of the mysteries of God (Ephesians 3:3,4); namely, truths not clearly revealed in Old Testament times, but which now, through the apostles, are made known (Ephesians 6:19; Colossians 1:26). It was one of the privileges of the apostles to spread abroad the knowledge of God (2 Corinthians 2:14, 4:6, 10:5) which involved not only factual information but also a call to recognize and obey Him.[26]

In patience - "Patience" (*makrothumia*,[27] translated "longsuffering" in the ASV) is the quality of enduring undeserved injuries, insults, and evil deeds by other people without being provoked to anger or retaliation. This quality is a Christian virtue (Galatians 5:22; Colossians 3:12; Hebrews 6:12) which requires self-control to keep one's passions in subjection when faced with the faults and failings in the lives of those who come in contact with us. When we men exhibit patience we are reflecting the character of God who constantly is patient or forbearing towards men who are sinful and rebellious (Romans 2:4, 9:22; 1 Peter 3:20). In Philippians 1:15-18 we learn of Paul's patient endurance of insults, and in 2 Timothy 3:10, 4:2 we read that Timothy is to copy Paul's "patience."

In kindness - "Kindness" is an attitude of graciousness toward others, of looking for ways to be helpful or beneficial to others. It is opposed to severity. "It is the sympathetic kindliness or sweetness of temper which puts others at their ease and shrinks from giving pain."[28] Since this quality is also a characteristic attitude of God and Christ (Romans 2:4; Ephesians 2:7), true disciples of Jesus try to reproduce this quality in their lives (Galatians 5:22; Colossians 3:12).

---

[25] "The use of this word at 11:3 (if genuine) is the only other passage in which the word is found in either biblical or classical Greek" (Fisher, *op. cit.*, p.353).

[26] *Gnōsis* ("knowledge") is the word that will later be used for the heresy known as Gnosticism. However, at the time 2 Corinthians was written, the word had not yet acquired the negative connotation it would within a generation or so.

[27] See notes on "endurance" at verse 4, where it was explained that this word denotes "putting up with people." Literally, *makrothumia* means "long tempered," the opposite of *oxothumia*, "short tempered."

[28] Plummer, *op. cit.*, p.196.

In the Holy Spirit - Theologians and translators debate whether or not to capitalize the words "Holy Spirit."[29] Thus far in verse 6 Paul has been listing inward moral qualities he and the other apostles sought to display in their behavior. Therefore, to capitalize this phrase, thus making it a reference to the Holy Spirit, seems to be out of place.[30] But how does one explain what "in a holy spirit" might mean? We offer this suggestion: when a man becomes a Christian, his spirit is alive (Romans 8:10) and is able to direct the man's behavior. Paul would then be saying that he has made it his aim to practice those holy things his spirit has prompted. The fruit that Galatians 5:22,23 names is how a man whose "spirit" is alive chooses to live. Those who think the reference is to the Holy Spirit are not in agreement about which measure of the Spirit might be intended,[31] or how to connect these threads of thought.[32] Most speak of the Holy Spirit as being the divine source of the other virtues. The center references in the NASB point to 1 Corinthians 2:4 and 1 Thessalonians 1:5 as being analogous.

In genuine love - "Love" is doing what is spiritually best for the other person (cp. 1 Corinthians 13). "Genuine" represents the Greek word which means "without hypocrisy." It is the same Greek as "without hypocrisy" in Romans 12:9. Christ often warned against hypocrisy, so His apostles made it a priority to manifest genuine love. Since "love" is the first word in the list to be qualified ("genuine," unhypocritical), perhaps the false teachers who have come to Corinth have advanced themselves by pretending to love. What a contrast is seen in Jesus' apostles whose love has been unhypocritical. That is the proper way for an apostle to commend himself (verse 4).

6:7 - *in the word of truth, in the power of God, by the weapons of righteousness for the right hand and the left,*

In the word of truth - In the first part of this verse there a shift from inward qualities that motivated the apostles' behavior to the content and corroboration of their preaching. Elsewhere (e.g., Ephesians 1:13; 2 Timothy 2:15), "the word of the truth" is a

---

[29] The NAB, the Jerusalem Bible, Goodspeed, and the NRSV all translate with small letters, e.g., "by a spirit of holiness," "by holiness of spirit."

[30] When the Holy Spirit is intended the Greek usually has a "the" in it – *to pneuma to hagion*, or *to hagion pneuma*. Here it is simply *en pneumati hagio*.

[31] The NEB and REB have "by gifts of the Holy Spirit." Plumptre (*op. cit.*, p.58) speaks of "spiritual gifts, such as those of tongues, and prophecy" but then has difficulty differentiating this from "in the power of God" in verse 7. Barnes (*op. cit.*, p.147) alludes to the indwelling Holy Spirit who produces fruit (Galatians 5:22,23). The problem is that it may not be right to capitalize "Spirit" in the Galatians 5:22,23 passage (see the explanation in the author's *New Testament Epistles: Galatians*).

[32] Lenski's attempt (*op. cit.*, p.1068) to give us a thread of thought treats "in the Holy Spirit" as a preparation for the next three things to be listed, all of which depended on the Holy Spirit. But he, too, struggles for an explanation of "in the power of God" at verse 7.

regular expression to denote the gospel. Here in the Greek, however, there is no "the" before either "word" or "truth," and this results in a slight shade of doubt about the meaning of this phrase.[33] James 1:18 has precisely the same combination of words as here (with no "the" in the Greek) and there it speaks of the gospel. That gives us ample warrant for treating "word of truth" in this passage as referring to the apostolic preaching of the gospel. It was by such preaching that the apostles attempted to commend themselves to their hearers.

In the power of God - Jesus promised the apostles they would receive power when the Holy Spirit came upon them (Acts 1:8). Peter says that what Jesus promised actually happened (2 Peter 1:3).[34] Mark tells us that as the apostles went out and preached everywhere, the Lord worked with them, confirming the word by miracles (Mark 16:20). Paul himself affirmed that the signs of an apostle had been wrought at Corinth (2 Corinthians 12:12).

By the weapons of righteousness for the right hand and the left - Rather than the preposition *en* ("in") which has been used since verse 4, here the preposition in the Greek is *dia*, which means "through, amidst, by means of." It is our conviction that the change of prepositions at this place signals more than an attempt to relieve the monotony of repeating "in." We think it signals a slight change of thought when it comes to how apostles commend their ministry. Their weapons were not (like the Judaizers' weapons were) of the flesh (2 Corinthians 10:4).[35] The apostles used "weapons of righteousness," which can mean either (1) weapons supplied by God as a result of justification, (2) weapons used in the cause of righteousness (Romans 6:13), or (3) weapons that consist of right living toward one's fellow men. Commentators have struggled to explain the expression "for the right hand and the left." Plummer suggested it means the apostles were thoroughly equipped.[36] Since Roman soldiers carried a sword in their right hand with which to attack their foes, and a shield in their left in order to defend themselves, Lipscomb offers the suggestion that Paul assailed pagan corruption with his right hand, and defended himself by all

[33] The RSV translators rendered this phrase as "truthful speech." This is grammatically possible, and would be an affirmation that the apostles, perhaps in distinction to the false teachers who have come to Corinth, always spoke truthfully.

[34] In 2 Peter 1:3, we interpret the "us" who received "divine power" as being Peter and the other apostles.

[35] Weapons is a military metaphor often used by Paul (see 2 Corinthians 10:4; Ephesians 6:11-17; 1 Thessalonians 5:8). It should also be noted that our translators preferred "instruments" (or "tools") when translating the same Greek word at Romans 6:13. It should also be noted that the Greek word translated "weapons" (*hopla*) is not the same as the word translated "armor" (*panōplia*) at Ephesians 6:11, so it may not be that Ephesians explains what weapons Paul has in mind here in 2 Corinthians 6:7.

[36] Plummer, *op. cit.*, p.198. See also Barrett, *op. cit.*, p.188.

righteous means from every blow aimed at him in his office or person.[37]   Plumptre supposes that in the right hand Paul carried the "sword of the Spirit," and in his left "the shield of faith" that form a part of the Christian's armor (Ephesians 6:16,17).[38] Fisher, following Chrysostom,[39] offers another suggestion.   Since Greek authors used "on the right" and "on the left" for describing the results of divination, whether "favorable" or "unfavorable," this verse seems to mean that the apostles fought on in all kinds of times, whether they brought prosperity or adversity.[40]   If we understand the first two phrases in verse 8 as explaining when the weapons in the right and left hands had to be used, this suggestion may be the right one.

6:8 - *by glory and dishonor, by evil report and good report;* **regarded** *as deceivers and yet true;*

By glory and dishonor - The first two clauses of this verse allude to some of the circumstances through which (*dia*) the apostles had to pass as they went about their ministries.   In the midst of these circumstances, they had to use the weapons of righteousness in such a way as to give no offense (verse 3) but rather to commend themselves as being ministers of God (verse 4).   If they were publicly acclaimed (given "glory"[41]) they could use the weapons on the right hand.   If they suffered dishonor and ignominy which they did not deserve, that called for using the weapons on the left hand.   Paul received dishonor from the false teachers at Corinth and this calls for him to use the proper weapons of righteousness as he does in this letter.

By evil report and good report - Whereas "glory and dishonor" spoke of personal treatment the apostles received, this pair of words refers to what was said about them when they were not present.   "Evil report" (*dusphēmia*) speaks of reproach, of calling one's motives into question, of slanderous charges such as representing the apostles as deceivers and impostors who deliberately misled their converts.   For example, it was during Paul's absence from Corinth that the worst things were said about him by the false teachers.   "Good report" calls to mind the times when the apostles were commended and praised and spoken of in positive terms as being genuine ministers of God.   The choice of which weapon of righteousness to use depended on what was being said about the apostles in their absence.

---

[37] Lipscomb, *op. cit.*, p.89.

[38] Plumptre, *op. cit.*, p.59.

[39] Chrysostom, *de Sacerd.*, p.464.

[40] Fisher, *op. cit.*, p.354.

[41] We are giving "glory" (*doxa*) its usual meaning, a recognition of worth or value. Plummer (*op. cit.*, p.198) reminds us that the apostle Paul received "glory" from God and from those whose hearts God touched, especially from his beloved Philippians and the Galatians (Galatians 4:14).

Regarded **as deceivers and yet true** - With the conjunction "as" (*hōs* in the Greek[42]) Paul begins a list of examples of glory and dishonor, of evil and good report. "Deceivers" (*planoi*) combines two ideas: that the person so called is a wandering impostor or vagabond having no decent home, and that he slyly corrupts his listeners, leading them away from virtue into sin. The Jews called Christ "a deceiver" (Matthew 27:63; John 7:12) and now the term is applied to the apostles. It must have been very hurtful to Paul to have this charge flung against him, when he was conscious of his truthfulness. "True" expresses Paul's denial of the charge that he or the other apostles were "deceivers." Contrary to the false charges, they were no more deceivers than was the Lord who commissioned them.

6:9 - *as unknown yet well-known, as dying yet behold, we live; as punished yet not put to death,*

As unknown and yet well-known - The clauses from here through verse 10 are couplets, the first member of each referring to how enemies of the cross viewed the apostles, while the second member of each couplet states things as they really are. There is also a sense in which the second member of each couplet is a commendation of the apostles' ministry as being from God. "Unknown" (*agnooumenoi*) means the apostles were habitually treated by their contemptuous critics as being nonentities, men to be ignored and given no recognition.[43] However, to those who are in any way interested in the gospel of Christ, the apostles (especially those whose writings are included in the New Testament Scriptures) are held in high regard, and Paul himself is one of the most famous men of all ages, other than Jesus Christ Himself.

As dying yet behold, we live - "Dying" suggests that their enemies regarded the apostles as doomed men over whose desperate condition they rejoiced. Indeed, the apostles faced danger every hour (1 Corinthians 15:30,31) and were constantly exposed to afflictions and dangers which any day might prove fatal. To all outward appearances they were as good as dead men. Not so, says Paul. "Behold" expresses an exultant confident feeling. Surprise! "We live" expresses the true state of the case. Perhaps Paul has Psalm 118:17 in mind, "I shall not die, but live, and declare the works of the Lord" (NKJV). Divine deliverance after divine deliverance was a commendation of their ministry. God wanted the apostles to continue to minister. An example of this from the life of Paul occurred at Lystra (Acts 14:19). Unbelieving Jews "dragged Paul out of the city and stoned him, leaving him for dead. But he rose up to claim Timothy from that environment and to make letters to that

---

[42] "Regarded" is placed in italics (there is no Greek word it represents) in the NASB to help readers follow the train of thought that is obvious in the Greek.

[43] Both words in this couplet are present participles which speak of what is habitual and constant. The present tense participles continue through these two verses (9,10).

young preacher a part of the word of God for twenty centuries."[44]   Such living commends the apostles as ministers of God.

As punished yet not put to death - "Punished" translates *paideuomenoi* which means to be corrected or chastised.   The word is used of the correction a father gives to his son (Hebrews 12:7) and of the chastening which God inflicts on erring men to lead to a change of behavior (1 Corinthians 11:32; Revelation 3:19; Hebrews 12:6). In a context where we are dealing with the taunts and sneers of men that apostles had to endure, perhaps their enemies represented their sicknesses and hardships as being chastisements from God who was punishing them for their sins.   Perhaps in Paul's case, they told others that the scourgings he received were men's attempts to correct the prisoner's behavior.   After all, if he weren't a criminal he wouldn't be on the receiving end of so many attempts to correct his behavior.   In "not put to death" Paul gives the true facts of the case.   Scourgings were painful, but they were not fatal. The apostles survived them and this was evidence that God was with them.   In his own case Paul does not deny that he has been punished (whipped) but he understands that the words of Psalm 118:18 ("The Lord has chastened me severely, but He has not given me over to death" NKJV) have come true in his case.   After being punished, the apostles endeavored to reflect a behavior in harmony with the fact that they were ministers of God.

6:10 - *as sorrowful yet always rejoicing, as poor yet making many rich, as having nothing yet possessing all things.*

As sorrowful yet always rejoicing - We suppose that it is proper to treat the first words in these couplets as being the taunts and sneers against the apostles of which we have found such distinct traces in the previous verses.[45]   There was plenty of sorrow (*lupē*, grief, sadness) in Paul's life (Romans 9:2, Philippians 2:27), and no doubt in the lives of the other apostles.   All of them would feel keen sorrow when potential converts rejected the gospel invitation, when Christians defected, and when problems beset the churches.   It is always difficult not to let such sorrow show in one's outward demeanor.   Whenever they saw an apostle with a troubled soul, the enemies had a plausible ready explanation.   Did men say of them, as they did of the Suffering Servant, that they were "smitten of God, and afflicted" (Isaiah 53:4)?   Was it with them, as it was with David when he wept and fasted, that people reproached him (Psalm 69:10), or when David put on sackcloth that people insulted him (Psalm 69:11)?   We assume that what was true of Paul was true of the other apostles. Notwithstanding the fact that he had occasions for grief, Paul could find reason to re-

---

[44] Coffman, *op. cit.*, p.386.

[45] Plummer (*op. cit.*, p.200) wrote that Paul has ceased to think of the accusations and insinuations of his adversaries.   If so, both members of these couplets express what the life of an apostle was really like.

joice (Romans 5:2,3;2 Corinthians 7:4-9) and he kept encouraging other Christians to rejoice (Philippians 2:18, 3:1, 4:4; 1 Thessalonians 5:16). Christianity has a power not only to sustain the soul in trial, but to fill it with positive joy, especially when one contemplates God's goodness and lovingkindness. "Solid joys and lasting pleasures only Zion's children know."[46]

As poor yet making many rich - While they were still accompanying Jesus during His earthly ministry, the apostles had left all (houses, lands, families) behind (Mark 10:28; Luke 18:27). They had become poor in this world's goods. The same was true of Paul. At times he had to work with his own hands as a tentmaker to support himself and his follow-workers so that he could preach the gospel (Acts 18:3, 20:34). Occasionally his living expenses were supplied by offerings from churches like the one at Philippi (2 Corinthians 11:8,9; Philippians 4:16). In Plumptre's words, "we can hear his enemies taunting him about being a beggar or a mendicant."[47] Poor he may often be, but he was "making many rich." Jesus became poor that many might become rich (2 Corinthians 8:9). His apostles followed His example. Remember the day when Peter said to a lame man, "I do not possess silver and gold, but what I do have I give to you" (Acts 3:6). What the apostles had to give was spiritual riches,[48] the riches of life eternal, the unsearchable riches of Christ, to all those who accepted the offer of salvation they preached.

As having nothing yet possessing all things - We suppose it was true, in a literal sense, of most of the apostles that they had no property and little of this world's riches. Paul was no different; for Christ's sake, he had suffered "the loss of all things" (Philippians 3:8). In his case, have the false teachers pointed to his near destitution, proposing that the real reason was that he was a fraud? The true facts of the case were that the apostles had taken a secure hold on (*katechontes*, "possessing") "all things" that were really important. Jesus promised the apostles that if they left all things to follow him, they would receive one hundred times as much in this present age, and in the world to come they would receive eternal life (Mark 10:30). Paul likewise recognizes that all things belong to the Christian (1 Corinthians 1:21-23). Nothing can compare to the riches one has in Christ. They may have sacrificed all things for Christ and His gospel, but they lost nothing by the exchange; rather, they have made infinite and eternal gain thereby (Matthew 16:25).

---

[46] Coffman, *op. cit.*, p.386.

[47] Plumptre, *op. cit.*, p.60.

[48] It is true that Paul supplied physical support to his helpers (Acts 20:35), and that he took offerings to Jerusalem (Acts 11:29,39; Romans 15:25,26), but these made no one rich. Paul has in mind spiritual riches when he writes this verse in 2 Corinthians.

Paul has thus concluded the section of this letter begun at 5:11 that concerns "The Life of an Apostle." He has talked (1) about their motives (reverence for the Lord who will be their judge, and the influence of Christ's love for them as demonstrated at Calvary, 5:11-15); (2) about how they came to be apostles (God who was reconciling the world to Himself called them and committed to them the message He wanted preached, 5:16-19); and (3) about the credentials which showed them to be genuine apostles/ambassadors for Christ (God was entreating through them, He sustained and helped them, and they did all they could to commend themselves as servants of God, 5:20-6:10).

C. The Restoration of a Loving Relationship Between the Apostle and the Corinthians. 6:11-7:16

1. **An appeal to the Corinthians to love him as he has them, and to separate themselves from evil influences that would destroy such a loving relationship. 6:11-7:4**[49]

6:11 - *Our mouth has spoken freely to you, O Corinthians, our heart is opened wide.*

Our mouth has spoken freely to you - Our way of wording such appeals is slightly different from the way people in the 1st century worded them. We might say "I have spoken very openly and very frankly to you." In the previous paragraphs of this letter Paul has spoken without reserve. In earlier paragraphs in this letter we have explained the plural "we" that Paul uses as being a reference to all the apostles. In this and the following verses, the plural pronouns "our" and "us" certainly speak of himself, if not also Timothy (2 Corinthians 1:1).

O Corinthians - It is a rare thing to find Paul addressing his readers by name, there being only two other examples (Galatians 3:1; Philippians 4:5). Naming his readers at this place lends a very affectionate tone to the appeal he is about to write. Plumptre has conjectured that before writing this verse Paul has paused as the letter was being dictated. He thought back over what he had written and finds himself a little surprised at the emotion with which he has written,[50] and so goes on to explain them to his readers. He appeals to the unreserved freedom with which he has written as a reason why they should treat him with the same open, generous, unreserved love.

---

[49] A second part to this appeal is a statement that their repentance has made such a restoration possible (7:5-16).

[50] Plumptre, *op. cit.*, p.61.

Our heart is opened wide - This was the ancient way of saying "we have no reservations about saying we have great affection for you all." There may have been strained relations when they rejected his counsel and sent him away full of sorrow (2 Corinthians 2:1-9). Now, because of a change in them (they finally did discipline the erring member), Paul says that in his heart their misconduct is forgotten,[51] and he stands open and ready to receive them. "These words are a perfect example of the attitude and words which must be used for the final healing of any breach between alienated friends."[52]

6:12 - *You are not restrained by us, but you are restrained in your own affections.*

You are not restrained by us - The verb translated "restrained" means to be compressed in a narrow place. Thus Paul assures them that his affection for them has not diminished or been restricted or squeezed down to a smaller size because of recent events that have strained their relationship with each other. Paul had received the report of Titus that the Corinthians had indeed changed their attitude toward him; now he wanted to reassure them that he was ready in his heart for a renewal of the old fellowship of mutual trust and affection.

But you are restrained in your own affections - The point is that nothing prevented a restoration of an affectionate relationship between Paul his readers except their own lingering wrong "feelings" toward him.[53] They will have to quit their splitting into parties (some of whom were hostile to Paul). They will have to quit welcoming the false teachers whose sinister words had helped lead to strained relations. They will need to receive his other instructions set out in 1 Corinthians just as they recently had

---

[51] There is some question as to whether the word translated "opened wide" should be taken literally (the ASV translates it "enlarged"), i.e., in the sense that his heart is now larger than before. McGarvey (*op. cit.*, p. 202) writes, "When Paul had written his former letter (1 Cor.) his heart had been narrowed by his suspicions as to the loyalty of the Corinthians, and he had spoken to them as with compressed and guarded lips, weighing not only his words, but mindful as it were, of the tone in which he uttered them. But by their obedience to the instructions which he gave them (through Titus), his confidence in them had been restored, his heart was enlarged to its former largeness and wealth of affection toward them, and his mouth had been set free to speak to them unreservedly and openly." Lipscomb (*op. cit.*, p.92), on the other hand, does not take "enlarged" absolutely, but writes, "Not that he loved them any more dearly than he had formerly done, but his emotions had broken forth into overflowing expression, and he took opportunity to assure then of the great place they had in his heart."

[52] Fisher, *op. cit.*, p.356.

[53] "Affections" translates the Greek word *splangchna*, a word which the KJV always translated "bowels," an English word that now gives a wrong connotation since it refers to the lower viscera (the small and large intestines). The Greek word properly denotes the upper viscera: the heart, the lungs, the liver. In fact in this context the word is used interchangeably with heart as the seat of emotions, just as Theophilus (*ad Autol.* ii.10,22) used "affections" and "heart" as interchangeable terms. The reason the word is used is because when men have deep emotions, their heartbeat is affected, their breathing rate changes, they often lose appetite, and are left weak. (Think of how folk are affected just after witnessing an accident, for example.) The ancients noticed this, and so applied the word *splangchna* to deep emotions.

followed his counsel to discipline the offender (1 Corinthians 5).

6:13 - *Now in a like exchange – I speak as to children – open wide to us also.*

Now in a like exchange - Paul has opened his heart to the Corinthians (verse 11). Now he asks for a like response on their part toward him.[54]

-- I speak as to children -- The KJV reads "my children," and though there is no "my" in the Greek, the addition of the word "my" evidently expresses the right idea. Paul is speaking of the Corinthians as his spiritual children.[55] New Testament writers regularly use *tekna* ("children") in speaking of or to their spiritual children (their converts). Paul did (1 Corinthians 4:14,17; Galatians 4:19; 1 Timothy 1:2,18) and so did John (1 John 2:1,28, 4:4, 5:21). By inserting this affectionate phrase Paul mitigates the severity of "you are retrained in your own affections" which he wrote in the previous verse. Since children should return the love of their parents, Paul's request is simply a father claiming his children's affection. His tone of voice is the tender tone you use when you are dealing with your own family members.

Open wide *to us* **also** - Their hearts are not yet open to Paul, so Paul (repeating the same word he had used of his own affection for them, verse 11) pleads with them to repay him with the same kind of affection he has lavished on them. 'As I am ready to embrace you, reach out and embrace me,' he pleads. One way by which they could show they had opened their hearts to him was (as the following context shows) in separation from the unbelievers whose influence had contributed to their recent broken relationship.

6:14 - *Do not be bound together with unbelievers; for what partnership have righteousness and lawlessness, or what fellowship has light with darkness?*

Do not be bound together with unbelievers - The Greek (a present imperative with *mē*) prohibits the continuance of an action already going on: 'Stop being bound together with unbelievers,' or 'Stop being unequally yoked with unbelievers.' The Greek word translated "bound together" is the compound word *heterozugountes*, made up of *heteros* and *zugos*. A *zugos* ("yoke") was a heavy piece of timber put on the shoulders of oxen to which was attached the tongue of the wagon, plough, or sled

---

[54] A word of explanation is needed concerning the Greek grammar at this place. As Paul dictated, he failed to supply a verb to govern the beginning of this verse. The idea is obvious, however: give me the exact equivalent which I have given you.

[55] His calling them children should not be explained as meaning they were still little children in need of milk and in need of growing up. Nor is he writing to them as if they were merely children (someone else's children).

which the animals are yoked together to pull.[56] *Heteros* speaks of "another of a different kind" or "pulling in a different direction." Perhaps Paul has drawn the metaphor from God's command to the Israelites: "You shall not plow with an ox and a donkey together" (Deuteronomy 22:10). Or perhaps it comes from Leviticus 19:19 where the same word *heterozuge* is used, "You shall not breed together two kinds of your cattle; you shall not sow your field with two kinds of seed, nor wear a garment upon you of two kinds of material mixed together." When two oxen were yoked together, the yoke allowed one animal to control the other. We thus suppose that Paul speaks against a situation where the Christian is being controlled by the unbeliever. The word "yoke" is used figuratively several times in the New Testament. Compare 1 Timothy 6:1, Galatians 5:1, or Acts 15:10 – and the last two references are in a context written about Judaizers, just as is true here in 6:14. It is this commentator's judgment that "unbelievers" is a term used to characterize the false teachers who had come to Corinth. Paul often uses "unbeliever" to refer to pagans (1 Corinthians 6:6, 7:12ff, 10:27, 14:22ff). But if we immediately talk about pagans (in general) in this context, we will miss the point of the prohibition. We remember that the Judaizers in Galatia were not Christians, but "false brethren" who pretended to join church so as to be able to control it from the inside (Galatians 2:4). When we make this identification of unbelievers as being the false teachers, i.e., the ones who stole the affections of the Corinthians, there is no reason to write, as some have, about how there is no connection between this paragraph (6:14-7:1) and the rest of the letter. This paragraph is closely connected in sense with the previous verse.[57] The apostle

---

[56] When he translated "be not too much inclined to the heathen," Theophylact was offering a different explanation of the idea of *zugos* (in *heterozugountes*). He supposed it referred to the arm or yoke that connected the two pans of a balance scales which could be unfairly tipped. A useful study of this verse is W.J. Webb, "Unequally Yoked Together With Unbelievers: What is the Unequal Yoke in 2 Cor. 6:14?" *Bibliotheca Sacra* 149 (593, 1992), p.27-44.

[57] Coffman (*op. cit.*, p.388) suggests not only a connection with 6:11-13, but also a possible connection with 6:1, where Paul had just warned them against receiving the grace of God "in vain.

The NASB has a paragraph break at 6:14, and the RSV has left spaces in the text both before and after the paragraph, giving the impression that perhaps those scholars are right who think 6:14-7:1 has no connection to the thoughts being expressed on either side of this long section. We have argued in the introductory studies to this book that 2 Corinthians enjoys integrity and that this paragraph is genuine. In all the ancient manuscripts of 2 Corinthians this paragraph is found in its present position. There is no external evidence whatever to support the idea that this paragraph does not enjoy integrity. Nevertheless, not all agree. Critical scholars who, because of "the abrupt change in tone," think 6:14-7:1 is an interpolation offer two hypotheses to explain where it originally came from. (1) One is that someone else, not Paul, wrote this material. Appeal is made to the fact that in this short paragraph there are six Greek words (*heterozugeō, metochē, sumphōnēsis, sunkathesis, Beliar*, and *molusmos*, translated bound together, partnership, harmony, Belial, and defilement) not found elsewhere in the New Testament. This counts for very little, since there are more than three dozen such words (i.e., they occur but once in the New Testament) in Paul's letters to the Ephesians, Colossians, and Philippians. (2) The other hypothesis is that this paragraph is a fragment from a supposed "previous letter" (cf. 1 Corinthians 5:9). Thompson (*op. cit.*, p. 93) calls attention to the fact that this hypothesis is faced with certain difficulties. It does not tell us how such an insertion of a piece of another letter came to be included here in 2 Corinthians. New Testament letters were written on scrolls, and it would not have been easy to insert the material here. Further, it is not certain that this passage is out of place. As explained earlier, it is plausible to suppose the

is there stating the nature of the reciprocation for which he seeks.   'It will be proof of your affection for me, and it will help your attitude towards me greatly, if you quit listening to "unbelievers" and letting them influence and control you,' is the idea that Paul is expressing.[58]

For what partnership have righteousness and lawlessness? - "For" introduces a series of reasons (in the form of questions) for the admonition to end any tangling yokes with unbelievers. In these five questions, the Greek interrogative form is worded in such a way as to presuppose a negative answer. So the answer to this first question is "None!"   "Partnership" (*metochē*) speaks of having things in common, a sharing, a venture where each partner has a share.   "Righteousness" in this place (as in Romans 1:17) evidently refers to God's way of saving man.   "Lawlessness" (*anomia*) speaks of contempt for and violation of God's commandments.   Such lawlessness is what characterized the Judaizers.   Jesus accused the Pharisees of being lawless (Matthew 23:28; Mark 7:8) while teaching for doctrine the commandments of men.   Years later, the Judaizers who troubled the churches are identified as being Pharisees and false brethren (Acts 15:5; Galatians 2:4).   Like the Pharisees whom Jesus condemned, they taught man-made rules ("works of the Law," Romans 3;20,28; Galatians 3:2,5).   The lines are clearly drawn. There is no middle ground between righteousness and lawlessness.   If there cannot possibly be any partnership, then the Corinthians should quit any attempted relationship with the lawless ones.

Or what fellowship has light with darkness? - "Fellowship" (*koinōnia*), a synonym for "partnership" (*metochē*), pictures each member of the group enjoying the whole of what the group has in common.   "Light" stands for Christianity,[59] "darkness" for

---

unbelievers here spoken of have been the cause of the alienation of affections.   Instead of saying, "There is no doubt that this passage comes in very awkwardly.   When we omit it and when we read straight on from 6:13 to 7:2 we get perfect sense.   This stern section seems out of place with the glad and joyous love of the verses on each side of it" (Barclay, *op. cit.*, p.245), would not it be better to try to understand what Paul has written, for what is "perfect" about the "sense" if we omit the very reason for the broken relationship between Paul and the Corinthians?

[58] Fisher (*op. cit.*, p.357) has thoughtfully outlined this section: it consists of the plea (verses 14a), various rhetorical questions designed to show that there could be no real fellowship between Christians and unbelievers (verses 14b-16a), a medley of Old Testament Scriptures to enforce the plea which Paul made (verses 16b-18), and a final repetition of the plea in the light of the promises which God gave (7:1-4).

Of course, association with unbelievers would be inescapable as long as believers were in the world.   What is prohibited for believers is remaining in a situation where the unbeliever can control the Christian.   This passage has often been used to discourage a Christian from entering into marriage with an unbeliever.   While such a course is not well advised, this passage which says "Stop being bound together" should not be applied to initially entering into such a mismatched relationship, nor can it mean that a mixed marriage should be ended.   1 Corinthians 7:12ff tells the Christian to continue the marriage relationship with the unbeliever, if the unbeliever consents.   2 Corinthians 6:14 would hardly be a contradiction of 1 Corinthians 7:12.

[59] According to Paul, Christians are children of light (Ephesians 5:8) and sons of light (1 Thessalonians 5:5).

what the Judaizers were teaching.[60]   These two have nothing in common; there is nothing of which they can both partake; they are mutually exclusive.   To remain a Christian while attempting to have an intimate relationship with the Judaizers was as impossible as trying to combine light and darkness.   That is why Paul pleads with the Corinthians to quit their relationship with the Judaizers.

6:15 - *Or what harmony has Christ with Belial, or what has a believer in common with an unbeliever?*

Or what harmony has Christ with Belial? - Verse 15 continues the rhetorical questions intended to help the Corinthians see the reason why they should stop being unequally yoked with unbelievers (verse 14).   "Harmony" translates *sumphōnēsis*, a word transliterated into English as "symphony."   It comes from the world of music where strings of musical instruments are struck so as to play a chord thereby giving a harmonious sound.   "Christ" is Jesus Messiah, the head of heaven's society. "Belial" here is probably used as a name for the devil, the head of the kingdom of darkness.[61]   If it is a name for Satan, then the implication is that the Judaizers (Paul's opponents) were tools of their father, the devil.   That is why there is no way that Christ and Belial can produce any harmony; instead there is only discord.   That is why the Corinthians should cease to allow themselves to be influenced by the Judaizers.

Or what has a believer in common with an unbeliever? - "In common" (*meris*, to share) suggests there is a whole to be shared (Acts 8:21).   Believers (Christians, whose characteristic it is to believe in the Lord Jesus Christ) and unbelievers (the false teachers in this context, see verse 14) do not form a whole.   There are no por-

---

[60] The kingdom of darkness is the devil's domain.   Jesus said of the Pharisees that they were of their father the devil and did the desires of their father (John 8:44).   Jesus came to destroy the works of darkness (1 John 3:8).   The false teachers apparently called themselves "servants of light" (cf. 2 Corinthians 11:14; 4:6).   That was a falsehood.

[61] This is the only occurrence of this name in the New Testament, and it does not appear in the Greek version of the Old.   It is found, however, in other versions of the Old Testament and is spelled three ways – Belial (which is Hebrew), Beliar (which is Syriac), and Berial.   (The interchange of "l" and "r" when pronouncing certain Greek words was not uncommon.   Plummer, *op. cit.*, p.208, cites an example from Alcibiades who had a lisp and mispronounced these letters.)   The Hebrew word is made up of two words *bel* ("not") and *ya'al* ("useful") so the compound means literally without profit, worthless, or wickedness.   In the Old Testament the word is not used for a person's name but rather as an adjective for wickedness, vileness, or worthlessness (e.g., Deuteronomy 13:13; Judges 19:22; 1 Samuel 2:12, 25;17; Proverbs 6:12).   The word is widely used in intertestamental Jewish literature (e.g., *Jubilees* i.20) and in the Dead Sea Scrolls (e.g., *War Scroll* 13:1-4) as a proper name for the devil, the one who leads the forces of evil in opposition to God.

In the *Testaments of the Twelve Patriarchs* the word "Belial" is used of various evil spirits (Reub. iv.11, vi.3;   Sim. v.3;   Dan 1:7,8;   Levi xix.1).   Milton, in *Paradise Lost* (i.490; ii.204), treated the name "Belial" as the name of a fallen angel.   While what the Judaizers were doing is certainly in opposition to Christ, it is not at all likely that "Belial" is another name for Antichrist (1 John 2:18; 2 John 7).   The Syriac version translates "Beliar" as a Satan.

tions of a whole to be shared; there is nothing in common. Believers and unbelievers "are governed by different principles, are looking to different rewards, and are tending to a different destiny."[62]

6:16 - *Or what agreement has the temple of God with idols? For we are the temple of the living God: just as God said, "I WILL DWELL IN THEM AND WALK AMONG THEM: AND I WILL BE THEIR GOD, AND THEY SHALL BE MY PEOPLE."*

Or what agreement has the temple of God with idols? - This is the fifth and final in a series of questions intended to influence the Corinthians to stop being bound together with unbelievers (verse 14). As in the previous questions the expected answer to the question "What agreement?" is "None!"[63] The following statement shows that when Paul writes "temple of God" he has the church in mind. In 1 Corinthians 3:16,17, we learned that Christians corporately are a "temple of God" in which the Holy Spirit lives. Ephesians 2:21,22 express the same idea that Christians together form a dwelling in which God lives in the Spirit.[64] "Idols" is somehow related to what the false teachers at Corinth have been trying to do. To appreciate the point Paul is making it is helpful to recall some Old Testament history. "Manasseh had put a graven image of Asherah in the house of the Lord, and Josiah removed and burned it" (2 Kings 21:7, 23:6). Ezekiel tells of other abominations (9:3-18) for which unsparing punishments were inflicted by God. The history of Israel had shown with terrible distinctness that God allowed no agreement between His house and idols."[65] God hates idols. Paul's point is that it is as absurd for his Christian readers to make a compact with the unbelievers as it was to erect the image of a heathen god in the temple of Jehovah. Just as idols had no place in the temple of God, so enemies of the gospel have no place in the church. Were it not for the fact that believers are God's temple, there would be no propriety in this question. "A temple consecrated to the service of God is no place for idols. The service of idols and that of God cannot be combined. Idolatry is such an insult to God that when an idol comes in, God goes out."[66]

---

[62] Barnes, *op. cit.*, p.157. There is a play on words in the Greek – "believer" being *pistō* and "unbeliever" being *apistou*. The KJV translates *apistou* as "infidel," a word that has a connotation of having rejected the faith. This passage certainly speaks to the question of whether or not Christians should be involved in the Ecumenical Movement, for that movement has within it many who are unbelievers in Jesus as Lord. Believers do not select such as partners.

[63] "Agreement" translates *sungkatathesis* which refers to a compact or treaty of alliance between two otherwise antagonistic systems.

[64] In 1 Corinthians 6:19, we learned that the bodies of individual Christians also form a temple in which the Spirit dwells.

[65] Plummer, *op. cit.*, p.208.

[66] Lipscomb, *op. cit.*, p.95.

For we are the temple of the living God - "For" indicates that Paul is explaining something just said, namely, the expression "temple of God" in the previous clause. And, of course, if it is true that Christians are a temple of God, that is the basis of Paul's demand for no compromise whatever with the unbelief of the false teachers (verse 14).   The "we" is emphatic,[67] with the implied contrast being that the Judaizers are not by any stretch of the imagination the temple of God.   There are two different Greek words which are translated "temple":   *naōs*, the most sacred part of the building, the sanctuary, the place where a deity dwells, and *hieron*, the place where a priest works, the rest of the temple complex.   The word here is *naōs*, and in the person of the Holy Spirit the living God dwells in the church.[68]   The "living God," literally, "the God who lives" (see notes at 2 Corinthians 3:3) reminds us of the horrendous incongruity of trying to compare Him to the lifeless idols and the demons behind them (1 Corinthians 10:20).

Just as God said - God (Paul affirms) was the author of the Old Testament passages he is about to string together in verses 16b-18; therefore, what is said in them cannot be gainsaid.   Paul introduces this series of Old Testament quotations (a) to prove from Scripture that the church is the temple of the living God, and (b) to give Scriptural grounds for his exhortation to keep that temple pure from defilement. Citations of Old Testament texts which are grouped together around a common theme are found elsewhere in the New Testament (e.g., Romans 3:10-8; 1 Peter 2:6-8).[69]

I WILL DWELL IN THEM AND WALK AMONG THEM - This part of verse 16 is a composite of several Old Testament passages including Exodus 29:45 ("And I will dwell among the sons of Israel and will be their God"), Leviticus 26:12 ("I will also walk among you and be your God, and you shall be My people"), and Ezekiel 37:27 ("My dwelling place also will be with them; and I will be their God, and they shall be My people").   The implied premise of these verses is that wherever God

---

[67]There is a manuscript variation at this place, with a choice between "we" and "you."   There is good support for the variant "you" (*Aleph*[3],C,D[3],E,F,G,K,etc.); however in this passage "we" (supported by *Aleph*,B,D,L,P,17,67,etc.) should probably be read in preference to "you" which is the true reading of 1 Corinthians 3:16.

[68] If it read "we are temples (plural)" as some manuscripts do, then it would speak of the indwelling of the Holy Spirit in the heart of each individual believer, rather than of the church as a whole.   The Most High God does not dwell in houses made with hands (Acts 7:48), but in the congregations of followers of Jesus (1 Corinthians 3:16).

[69] To call attention to the fact that it was customary for Jewish Bible scholars to group together passages that deal with the same subject, and then to recognize that Paul is doing the same thing, is far from saying (as some modern writers have alleged) that Paul is simply using "rabbinic exegesis" (with the implied notion that he is actually mishandling the Old Testament verses as badly as some of the rabbis did).   If Paul is writing by inspiration, he will not be deliberately misleading or trying to deceive his readers!

dwells, there is His temple.[70]   Through Paul's application of the Old Testament passages to the church, God's promise to Israel in the wilderness becomes His promise to the church in the gospel era.   Dwelling in them and walking among them describes the very personal nature of the Christian's relationship with God.[71]

AND I WILL BE THEIR GOD, AND THEY SHALL BE MY PEOPLE - God promises to have a special relationship with those who willingly submit to Him. They will enjoy His favor.   This promise is certainly as true of Christians as it was of the Israelites to whom God originally spoke.   Paul has not departed from the spirit of the promise in applying it to the Church.   In fact, when one studies the classic new covenant prophecy (Jeremiah 31:31), he finds the promise "I will be their God and they will be my people."[72]   The pronouns here are emphatic, and should be qualified by "only."   Thus, "I and I only," and "they and they only."   Christians are God's own special and treasured possession (1 Peter 2:9).   God is a jealous God and will brook no rival.   When Paul calls for the Corinthians to stop being bound together with unbelievers it is much the same as if God were entreating through him (2 Corinthians 5:20).

6:17 - *"Therefore, COME OUT FROM THEIR MIDST AND BE SEPARATE," says the Lord.   "AND DO NOT TOUCH WHAT IS UNCLEAN; AND I WILL WELCOME YOU"*

Therefore - With "therefore" Paul introduces the practical application to be drawn from verses 14-16.   'Since you Corinthian Christians are the temple of God and His special possession, here is what He expects of you.'   To give his command as much weight as possible, it is stated in language taken from the utterances of Jehovah in the Old Testament.[73]

COME OUT FROM THEIR MIDST AND BE SEPARATE, says the Lord   -

---

[70] The Hebrew reads "among them" (at Exodus 29:45 and Leviticus 26:12) since the indwelling of God by His Holy Spirit belongs only to the new covenant age (John 7:35-37).   "Dwell in them" likely speaks of the indwelling presence of the Holy Spirit (see Romans 8:9-11).

[71] Revelation 2:1 has the glorified Christ walking among the churches (the "lampstands" represent the churches, Revelation 1:20).

[72] The implications of this promise are unfolded in Hebrews 8:10 and 1 Peter 2:10.

[73] Because several passages are combined, and because the passages cited are not exact quotations but include words added by Paul (e.g., "daughters," verse 18), some have been critical of what Paul here writes.   Coffman (*op. cit.*, p.391) objects to commentaries that view verses 17 and 18 as a blundering effort by Paul to quote the Old Testament.   Coffman insists, instead, that these are Paul's own inspired words.   Paul was not "quoting scripture" but was *writing Scripture*.   He did not say "Thus it is written," but "thus saith the Lord" – the very formula used a thousand times by the prophets of the Old Testament to introduce a revelation just received from God.   Coffman may be right in his explanation, though this commentator has no problem with Paul couching his inspired exhortation in the words of Scripture.

These words may reflect Isaiah 52:11, the words of which were originally applied to the Jews in Babylon.   They were a solemn call which God made to them to leave the place of their exile, to come out from among the idolaters of that city, and to return to their own land.   The passage in Isaiah contains an important principle that was just as applicable to the Corinthian Christians as it was to the Jews in Babylon.   The language of the Old Testament appropriately expresses the very idea he wished to convey to his readers.   Evidently the Judaizers who have come to Corinth are as bad an influence on God's people as was ancient Babylon.   The aorist imperative verb "come out" calls for an immediate and decisive withdrawal.[74]   The withdrawal commanded does not mean that Christians are to migrate from heathen cities (like the Jews were from Babylon); it does mean they are to get away entangling alliances with the unbelieving Judaizing opponents of Paul who have intruded into Corinth.   "Be separate" tells the Corinthian Christians to put some distance between themselves and the false teachers who have negatively influenced their attitude toward Paul.[75]

AND DO NOT TOUCH WHAT IS UNCLEAN - The verb translated "do not touch" might better be translated "stop clinging to."   When Isaiah addressed these words to the priests and Levites who were about to return from Babylon, he was telling them they were not to bring back with them any symbol of that "unclean" idolatrous ritual which they had witnessed there.   Paul pictures the influence of the Judaizers of his day as being as contaminating as the idolatry of Babylon (recall his use of the word "idols" earlier in verse 16).[76]   Paul has written, "Stop being bound together with unbelievers."   He has said, "Come out of their midst and stop clinging to that which is unclean."   He has called for separation.

Careful thought must be given as we would make application of this paragraph to our contemporary lives.   Clearly 6:14 is not an injunction against all association with unbelievers.   Remember what Paul wrote in 1 Corinthians 5:9,10 and 10:27.   Paul also encouraged the Christian partner in a mixed marriage to maintain the rela-

---

[74] "The cry 'come ye out' rings through the Hebrew history: in the call of Abraham, in the rescue of Lot, in the Exodus, in the call to depart from the neighborhood of the tents of Dathan and Abiram, etc."   Plummer, *op. cit.*, p.209.

[75] The verb *aphoristhēte* means "separate from," or to separate for a purpose (Acts 13:2; Romans 1:1).   This passage became one of the chief texts fueling the holiness movement, both in the denominational world and in the Restoration Movement.   Church members were called on to separate themselves from other believers over such issues as mixed swimming, ladies' hair styles, card playing, dancing, ownership of television sets, and the like.   As objectionable as some of these lifestyles may be, it seems to this commentator that applying Paul's words to things in the realm of Christian liberty is a misuse of what Paul is writing.   Remember, he is assailing the real reason why the Corinthians are "withholding their affection from him" – namely the fact that *unbelievers* have influenced them to treat Paul badly.

[76] As the intertestamental period passed and we come to 1st century Judaism, we find it to be a sad mixture of Old Testament and heathen religious ideas.   Zodiacs adorned the floors of 1st century synagogues.   There was something "unclean" about Pharisaic Judaism (as it had become).   Is this what the Corinthians have let influence them?

tionship as long as possible (1 Corinthians 7:12-16). 2 Corinthians 6 has a religious milieu. Judaizers were threatening to cause Christians to fall from grace. Thus, when the believer's Christianity (doctrine or practice) is liable to be compromised, that is when separation is called for.

AND I WILL WELCOME YOU - God makes two promises (verses 17b and 18) to the man who obeys His demand and separates himself from what would defile him spiritually. His first promise is that He will welcome the person who obeys with favor and approval. These words "I will welcome you," are not from Isaiah as was the first part of verse 17, but perhaps come from the Greek of Ezekiel 11:17, or 20:34,41, or perhaps from Jeremiah 24:5. If a man wants to be received by God and welcomed as His friend and adopted child, he will have to live a life separated from such unbelievers as the Judaizing opponents of Christianity.

6:18 - *"AND I WILL BE A FATHER TO YOU, AND YOU SHALL BE SONS and daughters TO ME, SAYS THE LORD ALMIGHTY."*

AND I WILL BE A FATHER TO YOU - Verse 18 contains a second promise to the man who separates himself from what would defile him spiritually; it is a promise of a close family relationship between God and his children. The language seems to come mostly from 2 Samuel 7:8-14, with phrases perhaps from a few other places in the Old Testament.[77] The original setting of 2 Samuel 7 is God's promise to David that his son Solomon would build the temple and that God would "be a father to him (Solomon) and he will be a son to Me." Since the church is now the temple of God (2 Corinthians 6:16), Paul can cite the Old Testament temple passage as containing a truth that appropriately conveys the idea he is trying to express. When God promises to be "a father" to them, He is promising His protection, guidance, and tender loving care to those who are adopted into His family. He will provide for them and cherish them and acknowledge them as His children. What an astounding privilege to be able to address the Most High God as "our Father." If the friendship of the world means enmity with God (James 4:4), it is also true that separation from the world leads to loving friendship with God.

AND YOU SHALL BE SONS and daughters TO ME - Galatians 3:26-29 explains that folk who have been baptized into Christ are sons of God by faith; they are also Abraham's spiritual offspring, heirs according to the promise. As adopted children, we Christians have a spirit of adoption whereby we cry "Abba, Father" (Romans 8:15). If Christians corporately are the temple of the living God (verse 16), individually they are the sons and daughters of the Lord almighty (verse 18). Some suppose the language about "sons and daughters" is drawn from Isaiah 43:6. Others

---

[77] Certain older speculations that Paul took these words from some apocryphal book, or from some Jewish hymn, are gratuitous.

suppose that Paul deliberately added "and daughters" to his quotation of 2 Samuel 7:14 because there were women in the church at Corinth and they were a part of the temple of God in that town, too.[78]

Says the Lord Almighty - The Greek word translated Almighty (*pantokrator*) is used in the LXX as an equivalent for "Lord of Sabaoth" (e.g., Isaiah 12:16) or "Lord of Hosts" (e.g., Hosea 12:5; Amos 3:13; Zephaniah 2:10) and in the New Testament occurs only elsewhere in the book of Revelation (1:8, 4:8, 11:17, 15:3, 19:6,16, 21:22). The word speaks of One who has all power (see Psalms 89:6-8) and can do what He promises He will do. He has hosts of angels whom He sends to minister to the redeemed (Hebrews 1;14). What a contrast to the idols that are weak and powerless. If Paul's readers will obey and stop their dalliance with the false teachers who have poisoned their attitudes toward Paul and Christianity, then they will see God 's promises fulfilled in their lives. Their loving Father with almighty power has spoken it.

---

[78] "It is characteristic of Christianity that it was the first system that ever recognized the dignity of women and raised them generally to the same moral and spiritual level with men." Lipscomb, *op. cit.*, p.97.

7:1 - *Therefore, having these promises, beloved, let us cleanse ourselves from all defilement of flesh and spirit, perfecting holiness in the fear of God.*

Therefore, having these promises - The division between chapters at this place was not well made. As the "therefore" shows, 7:1 continues the paragraph which began at 6:14. This verse is part of Paul's stern warning to the Corinthians (6:14-17) to separate themselves from the false teachers who have poisoned the earlier warm relationship between the Corinthian Christians and Paul. If the Corinthians will recognize who they are (the temple of the living God, verse 16) and if they will help keep that temple pure (by cleansing themselves of all defilement of flesh and spirit, verse 1), then it will be possible for a restored relationship between the Corinthians and Paul to occur. "These promises" refer to the chain of Old Testament quotations found in 6:16-18. "These" stands first in the Greek for emphasis, for it is what is promised that should motivate the readers to action so that friendly relations between them and Paul can be restored. The particular action Paul is calling for is explained in the verses following.

Beloved - It is either because Paul loves them, or because God loves them, or both (remember that God appeals to men through the apostles, 5:20), that Paul makes this appeal.

Let us cleanse ourselves - This is a reiteration of the Biblical command to "be separate" written in 6:17. By including himself among those who need cleansing, perhaps Paul intended to take some of the edge off the appeal. It leaves the impression that both Paul and his readers have harbored some ill feelings toward each other. They both have a need to make a clean break (*katharisōmen*, aorist tense) with all the ideas and actions that have defiled their relationship in the past. Since the temple of God (the church) must be pure (6:17), the Christians who collectively make up the temple must cleanse themselves, or the temple never will be pure.[1]

From all defilement - The Greek noun here used (*molusmos*, translated "defilement") occurs nowhere else in the New Testament,[2] but likely is intended to pick up the idea introduced in the words "do not touch what is unclean" (6:17). Whatever interferes with our relationship to God is to be removed. "The thought of 7:1 is identical with that of 1 John 3:3 ("everyone who has this hope fixed on Him purifies himself"). In each there is the contrast between the high ideal to which the believer in Christ is call-

---

[1] The word here for cleanse, *katharizein*, was also used of ritual cleansing required from temple service in the temple at Jerusalem (Thompson, *op. cit.*, p.98).

[2] The noun is used in 2 Maccabees 1:27 referring to the "pollution" of idolatry. In the LXX of Jeremiah 23:14, the word is used of the sin of Sodom and Gomorrah. The verb *molunō* occurs in 1 Corinthians 9:7 and in Revelation 3:4, 14:4. In some of these passages the context deals with the defilement that results from idolatry.

ed and the debasement into which he may possibly sink."[3]

Of flesh and spirit - One gets the impression that the false teachers who have troubled the Corinthian Christians have promoted both things that would defile the body (flesh) and things that would defile the spirit. "Flesh" (body) and "spirit" are two of the constituent parts of man (1 Thessalonians 5:23), and either of these may be defiled,[4] thus causing the temple of the living God to be defiled. "Man may be defiled in either flesh or spirit, and in either case there must be cleansing. The two together sum up human nature, and the intercommunion of the parts is so close that when either is soiled the whole is soiled."[5] Our flesh is defiled when our hands and feet and bodies do the bidding of sin. Our spirits are defiled when we think evil thoughts about another in our hearts. Speaking to the Pharisees one day, Jesus spoke of the kinds of evil thoughts that defile a man (Matthew 15:19,20). When the Corinthians harbored hard feelings against the apostle they were exhibiting a defiled spirit of the same kind Jesus warned about, and it was Judaizers (Pharisees who pretended to be Christians) who fanned those evil thoughts.

Perfecting holiness - How is the cleansing to be done? By perfecting holiness. "Perfecting" (*epitelountes*) means to bring to an end, to finish, to complete something that is already started, to bring it to its proper goal. The Greek word is a present tense participle indicating continuing action. Thus, it appears that holiness (*hagiosunē*, sanctification, consecration to Christ) is a continuing process that goes on all through one's Christian life.[6] It begins when a person is immersed into Christ (see 1 Corinthians 6:11) and is first set apart to sacred service. Because the Christian has already been set apart for Christ it is proper to speak of Christians as being saints (1 Corinthians 1:2). But the process of becoming holy is not completed at baptism. Cleansing (and being set apart to sacred service) is something that goes on during the whole remaining earthly life of the Christian. Corrupting influences such as those which the Judaizers suggested to the Corinthians must be repudiated since they would destroy a person's relationship with Christ. Perfecting holiness is important for each and every Christian to pursue since only those who are holy shall see God (Hebrews

---

[3] Plumptre, *op. cit.*, p.64.

[4] "Paul is using popular language covering the material and immaterial elements in man, and it is manifest that he is not under the influence of the Gnostic doctrine that everything material is *ipso facto* evil. He says that the flesh must be cleansed from every kind of pollution. Gnostics maintained that it was as impossible to cleanse flesh as to cleanse filth" (Plummer, *op. cit.*, p.211).

[5] Plummer, *ibid.*

[6] The present participle "perfecting" gives little support to those who would find the doctrine of sinless perfection in this verse. Among some Bible students there is a running debate about whether sanctification in the Bible is pictured as an act (that may be completed in this life) or a process (that is not completed in this life). What Paul actually wrote here has reference to an advance in holiness, not a finished product that needs no more improvement. For an in-depth study of "Sanctification," see the Special Study in the author's *New Testament Epistles: Romans*.

12:10,14).   While the Holy Spirit initiates the process of sanctification (2 Thessalonians 2:13; 1 Peter 1:2), the Christian has the responsibility to make it his steady aim to continue and grow in his dedication and consecration to Christ.   When one finds a congregation of such dedicated saints he sees a beautiful temple of the living God (6:16).

In the fear of God - The phrase is in the dative case, and could be either a dative of sphere ('in an atmosphere of reverential fear for God') or a dative of means ('by means of reverence for God').   "Fear" is the same word Paul used at 5:11.   One who fears God will have a high regard for His commandments and will be aware that God punishes sin in this life as well as in the next and is not to be trifled with.   Reverence and awe of God is the attitude that will motivate a man to perfect holiness and thus cleanse himself from every defilement.   With this appeal to cleanse themselves from all defilement of flesh and spirit Paul has driven home the point that the Corinthians should avoid all fellowship with the unrighteous people who have heretofore poisoned their relationship with him.

7:2 - *Make room for us* **in your hearts;** *we wronged no one, we corrupted no one, we took advantage of no one.*

Make room for us *in your hearts* - The Greek word *chōrēsate* means to make a space for or to make room for, and our translators are likely correct when they added the words "in your hearts."   Having finished with the reasons why there had been a breach in their relationship, verses 2-4 are the conclusion to the appeal which began in 6:11-13 in which Paul implores his readers to find room in their hearts for him.   If the Corinthians will stop being controlled by unbelievers, if they behave like a temple of God should, everything that would hinder complete reconciliation will be gone.

We wronged no one - Here begins a series of statements in which he attempts to show there is no reason they should not open their hearts to him.   In the Greek, each of the statements begins with an emphatic "no one" and each is written with an aorist tense meaning there has not been a single person nor a single case in which Paul has wronged or taken advantage of them.   Commentators are about equally divided as they interpret these statements.   Some think Paul is replying to known false statements made to the Corinthians about him by the Judaizers.   Others think Paul is calling attention to the behavior of the Judaizers which, in contrast with his own behavior toward the Corinthians, has wronged them, corrupted them, and taken advantage of them.   If the former is correct, then reference is perhaps made in the words "we wronged no one" to the Judaizers' whispered accusations that he was greedy of gain and acted from self-interested motives, a topic to which Paul does refer in 8:20 and 12:18.   If the latter, the implication is that the Judaizers treated the Corinthians unjustly or unfairly, or led them into sin.

We corrupted no one - The word *ephtheiramen* ("corrupted") can refer to money, morals, or doctrine.[7] It often carries the connotation of using misleading tactics in order to ruin or corrupt the other person.   Perhaps the Judaizers have accused Paul of corrupting the morals of Christians by his refusal to emphasize the Pharisaic works of Law.   Perhaps the Judaizers have corrupted the faith of the Corinthians by their false teaching.

We took advantage of no one - The word *pleonekteō* means to take advantage of or defraud another so as to get and have more than he has.   Perhaps Paul is answering a charge made against him by the Judaizers.   At 12:17 the word certainly suggests that Paul has been charged with taking financial advantage of the church.   Paul clearly calls attention to the fact that he took extra precautions lest anyone accuse him of absconding with the offering collected for Jerusalem (8:10,20; 12:16-17).   One could also imagine that Paul alludes to the fact the Judaizers lived well in Corinth at the expense of the Christians.   Whether Paul alludes to the false accusations made by the Judaizers, or whether he alludes to their actual behavior, either way there is nothing that should shake their confidence in Paul or stand in the way of reconciliation.   Especially if they can embrace the Judaizers who did corrupt them, certainly they should be able to make room in their hearts for one who did nothing but love them.

7:3 - I do not speak to condemn you; for I have said before that you are in our hearts to die together or live together.

I do not speak to condemn you - Aware that what he has just written could be interpreted to imply he was finding fault with them, Paul assures them that was not the idea.   If they had listened to the false things that were circulated about him, if they had made friends with the Judaizers, that was all in the past.   It was no barrier on his part to renewed fellowship and affection.   He was speaking about his attitude toward them: he loves them.   An open condemnation or censure is incompatible with such affection as he had for them.

For I have said before - Though he has not used these exact words before, he has indicated his love for them at 3:2,3 and 6:11-14.

That you are in our hearts - He does not say "I am ready to receive you into my heart." He says "You are already in my heart!"

To die together and to live together - There appears to be a rush of emotion as he tries to express the depth of his affection for them.[8]   Perhaps Paul uses a proverbial

---

[7] It is the same word translated "destroy" in 1 Corinthians 3:17.   It is the word used of sensual impurity in 2 Peter 2:12, Jude 10, and Revelation 19:2.

[8] Fisher (*op. cit.*, p.363) reminds us that "the statement is not limited to Paul, but includes his fellow-workers, as the plurals indicate."

statement to express his affection, for the words remind us of something Horace (Odes iii.9) wrote, "With thee I fain would live, with thee I fain would die," and perhaps even what Ruth said, "Do not urge me to leave you ... where you go I will go ... where you die, I will die" (Ruth 1:16,17).   The fact that Paul spoke of dying before living has caused commentators to suppose he has in mind the fact his death is a more likely prospect than is a long life (he spoke of dying daily, 1 Corinthians 15:31[9]). The unexpected word order "death-life" has parallels in ancient literature,[10] so there is no reason to look for a spiritual explanation to the words.[11]   Paul is expressing how strong his love for them is.   To tell someone you have no desire to live without them, and you are ready to die with them, is one of the strongest expressions of tender affection a person can utter.

7:4 - *Great is my confidence in you, great is my boasting on your behalf; I am filled with comfort.   I am overflowing with joy in all our affliction.*

Great is my confidence in you - As is shown by a comparison of the NASB with the KJV ("great is my boldness of speech"), the word *parrēsia* can be translated either "confidence" or "boldness of speech."   The KJV translators thought Paul was saying that it was because he loved them that he could speak freely and openly to them as he has done in this paragraph.   The NASB translators suppose the connection is that Paul's confidence in them has been restored by the good news recently brought to him from Corinth by Titus.   Either way, Paul's tone here is one of exultation as he recalls the feelings triggered by news of recent events at Corinth.   He speaks of confidence (boldness), pride, comfort, and joy.

Great is my boasting on your behalf - Our modern idiom would likely read "I have great pride in you."   Paul founded the congregation at Corinth, and when they do well he is delighted and loves to boast to others about how well the Corinthians are doing (cf. 7:14, 8:24, 9:2ff).   While Paul will not boast of himself, save what Christ has done through him (Romans 15:17ff; 1 Corinthians 15:10), and while he will not boast in such a way as to commend himself as his opponents do (3:1; 5:12), he will boast about others.

I am filled with comfort -- In the Greek, "filled" is a perfect tense verb indicating a past completed action with present continuing results.   As the following verses will show, the comfort (recall his use of "comfort" in chapter 1 of this letter) was the result of the good news recently brought by Titus that the just concluded ministry in Corinth

---

[9] See also 6:9, where he spoke of "dying, yet behold, we live."

[10] Harris, *op. cit., p.519.*

[11] Other views found in the commentaries speak of past death to sin and present spiritual life with Christ; or future physical death followed by future eternal life.   In this commentator's judgment commentators struggle to present the thread of thought when adopting either of these views.

had accomplished one of its intended goals: the Corinthians have been led to repent.

I am overflowing with joy in all our affliction - The word *huperperisseuō* ("over-flowing") here used occurs nowhere else in the New Testament except Romans 5:20 where the NASB translates it "abounded."   It is a compound verb meaning to super-abound, to abound exceedingly, to overflow.   Paul says his joy is overflowing.   In the Greek there is an article before both "comfort" and "joy," and it would be well to translate the article so that it reads "the comfort" and "the joy," namely, the comfort and the joy caused by the report brought by Titus (7:5ff).   "Affliction" (see at 1:4 and 7:5, "conflicts without, fears within") speaks of Paul's mental condition before Titus brought the good news.   That news turned his affliction to overflowing joy.   The clouds of turmoil and doubt and fears are past.   The sun is shining again, and he was encouraged about what the future could hold.

2. A statement of Paul's rejoicing over Titus' report concerning their repentance which makes complete reconciliation now possible. 7:5-16

7:5 - For even when we came into Macedonia our flesh had no rest, but we were afflicted on every side: conflicts without, fears within.

For even when we came into Macedonia - With "for" Paul takes up an explanation of what he had just written about the comfort and the joy in affliction.   At the same time this verse resumes the story (interrupted by the digression that extends from 2:14 to 7:4 in which Paul deals with matters related to the problems at Corinth[12]) of his travels and emotions prior to the writing of this letter he is now composing.   Since the writing of 1 Corinthians Paul has traveled from Ephesus to Troas.   At 2:12-13 Paul was telling about his stay in Troas while anxiously awaiting Titus to arrive and report concerning the church at Corinth.   The story left off with "taking my leave of them, I went on to Macedonia."   Paul was anxiously hoping to meet Titus sooner than would have been possible if Titus had to travel through Macedonia on his way to Troas.   Now, as he resumes the story of this travels, he tells how Titus met him in Macedonia with good news from Corinth.   Perhaps this even helps explain the unexpected thanksgiving we read at 2:14:   Titus has arrived with cheering news.   The remainder of chapter 7 can be summarized under three headings.   First, Paul tells of his anxiousness for the arrival of Titus and of his relief when Titus finally arrived bearing good news (verses 5-7).   Second, he speaks of the sorrow he had caused them by the letter he had written to them,[13] and how that letter and Titus' mission had

---

[12] In passing, if the whole of 2:14 to 7:4 is a digression, then the hypothesis that 6:14 to 7:1 is also a digression becomes very improbable.

[13] In the Introductory Studies the disputed issue of how many letters Paul wrote to Corinth has been documented.   Those who postulate a "severe letter" between our books of 1 Corinthians and

accomplished one of the desired changes in the lives of the Corinthians (verses 8-12). Third, he speaks of his joy and encouragement that the report of Titus triggered and how his confidence and boasting in the Corinthians had not been disappointed after all (verses 13-16).

Our flesh had no rest - Paul has already alluded to troubles he had in Ephesus (1:8) and in Troas (2:3,14). Now he tells them that even in Macedonia he was no less troubled and agitated as he waited for Titus and news from Corinth. At 2:13, Paul had written "I had no rest for my spirit." Now he says he had no rest or relief for his flesh (i.e., his body).[14] "Flesh" here seems to speak of the body as being affected by emotions such as anxiety and fear. The causes of his distress he immediately states.

But we were afflicted on every side - As was explained at 1:4 and 4:8, "afflicted" can speak of either physical or mental sufferings. No matter where he turned, on every side there were pressures that seemed to hem him in. In the next two clauses, he identifies two kinds of afflictions.

Conflicts without - The history found in Acts of this period of time in Paul's life gives us no details about such conflicts. It seems that in Macedonia, at this moment of time, Paul faced, as he did everywhere (e.g., Acts 16:23, 17:5; Philippians 1:30), physical threats, opposition, and persecution, though we know not who were the instigators this time, whether unbelieving Jews, or unconverted Gentiles, or false brethren.

Fears within -- "Fear" (*phobos*) here seems to refer to anxiety or alarm or foreboding over the news he was soon to hear from Titus.[15] How would the Corinthians receive Titus' mission? Titus has been gone longer than he expected. Did that possibly mean the news about the state of the church at Corinth would not be good?[16]

---

2 Corinthians refer to it as the letter about which Paul was apprehensive. We shall address this issue at the appropriate place in the notes below at verse 8.

[14] If our distinction between the constituent elements of a man is correct, then "no rest for my spirit" denotes spiritual sensitivity, and "no rest for my flesh" denotes physical suffering.

[15] Plummer (*op. cit.*, p. 218) reminds us that the fear about which the apostle John says, "Perfect love casts out fear" (1 John 4:18), though the same Greek word *phobos* is used, is not of the same kind of fear as that which the apostle Paul felt concerning the spiritual state of the Corinthians (i.e., worry that they would be subdued by the subtlety of the serpent), for love is susceptible of this fear, yea, love alone is capable of it.

[16] The words of this passage have been made very familiar to us through the words of the invitation song often sung, "Just as I am." One stanza has these words, "though tossed about with many a conflict, many a doubt, with fears within, and foes without." While the invitation song speaks of the potential convert's agitation of mind, Paul's words speak of a Christian's agitation at how others will respond to his attempts to correct a sorry situation.

7:6 - *But God, who comforts the depressed, comforted us by the coming of Titus;*

But God, who comforts the depressed - "Depressed" (or it might be translated 'downcast'[17]) describes Paul's state of mind while he was awaiting Titus' arrival. As we have seen, he was thinking that the whole effort at planting a church in Corinth possibly might come to nothing. The longer-than-expected passing of time before Titus' arrival certainly must have tended to confirm his worst fears. "Comforts" is a present tense verb; giving comfort to His servants when they are depressed or despondent is something God does regularly (cf. Isaiah 49:13). The language of this verse reminds us of the beautiful passage with which Paul began this letter (1:3-4).

Comforted us by the coming of Titus - In the midst of Paul's depression, Titus came and brought him comfort.[18] Just why Paul attributes the comfort to God is not at first obvious. Did God somehow, providentially, have a hand in the safe journey of Titus from Corinth to Macedonia? Had God aided Titus while he was trying to lead the Corinthians to repentance? Did God help Titus with the wording of his report to Paul so that Paul can say God comforted him by the coming of Titus? Each of these ideas seems to be alluded to in the following verse. The word translated "coming" (*parousia*[19]) may suggest that he remained with Paul for a while after his arrival. If so, then Paul was encouraged by Titus' company as well as by the good report Titus gave when he arrived. God used Titus as the means of encouraging Paul.

7:7 - *and not only by his coming, but also by the comfort with which he was comforted in you, as he reported to us your longing, your mourning, your zeal for me, so that I rejoiced even more.*

And not only by his coming - While Paul was anxious for Titus' report, Paul was also worried about Titus. Whenever dear friends who are traveling are later to arrive than we expect them, we begin to worry that some accident has happened, or that some harm has come to them. Titus' arrival was not as soon as expected and it was a worry, but now that worry is past. Paul's anxiety over Titus' welfare has been relieved.

---

[17] "Depressed" is a better choice of words at this place than the ASV which reads "lowly," a word that now tends to mean humble circumstances, rather than feeling low.

[18] Much has been said about Titus in the comments at 2 Corinthians 2:13 and in the introduction to the author's commentary on 1 & 2 Timothy and Titus. Not only was he a convert of Paul's (Titus 1:4) and likely a brother of Luke, Titus was a key figure at the Jerusalem conference (Galatians 2:3) and also a trusted helper whom Paul sent to various troubled churches. The reason for the suggestion that Luke and Titus were brothers is the fact that Titus is not named in Acts (of which Luke was the human author), either at the Jerusalem conference (Acts 15 compared with Galatians 2:3) or at Acts 20:4 where the listing of his name would have been very appropriate. See Wm. Ramsay, *St. Paul the Traveler* (Grand Rapids: Baker, 1960 reprint), p. xxxviii, 390. Though he is mentioned in a few other New Testament books (Galatians, 2 Timothy, and Titus), it is from 2 Corinthians that we learn the most about Titus.

[19] The word for coming (*parousia*) is often used elsewhere in the New Testament (e.g., 1 Corinthians 15:23; 1 Thessalonians 4:15) for Christ's return at the end of the age.

But also by the comfort with which he was comforted in you - Here is stated a second reason why Paul was comforted. The repentance and positive response of the Corinthians to Titus was a comfort to Titus himself. Has Paul been anxious how Titus would come through this difficult assignment? Knowing what had recently happened to Paul on his intermediate trip to Corinth, was Titus apprehensive about his mission to Corinth, as to whether or not it would be successful? The repentance of the Corinthians was a comfort to Titus as well as to Paul.

As he reported to us your longing, your mourning, your zeal for me - "As he reported to us" shows that the actual making of his report to Paul was a comfort to Titus. The present participle translated "as he reported" indicates that as Titus made his report his optimism and excitement about the response of the Corinthians (the comfort he had received) showed through.[20] The next clauses tell us three things Titus reported concerning the Corinthians, three things that inspired him with such joy. We have to guess as to the object of "your longing."[21] Perhaps it is to be on good terms with the apostle once again, or it may have been a longing to do the right thing. "Mourning" (*odurmos*) is a feeling of bitter remorse over one's actions, whether it was their tardiness in exercising discipline, or for having cause so much distress to Paul, or their readiness to listen to the false teachers who came to town. *Zēlos*, which indicates a passionate state of mind, can be translated either zeal or jealousy. Here zeal seems correct, and it may speak of zeal now for Paul rather than for those who had attacked him, or it might speak of eagerness to carry out his wishes (i.e., to put the matter right and discipline the offending party).[22]

So that I rejoiced even more -- The joy that Titus felt as he made his report to Paul was so contagious that it doubled the joy of Paul. The "even more" has been understood in several ways. (a) I rejoiced at his coming, I rejoiced even more at what Titus had to say about you Corinthians. (b) I rejoiced rather than being merely comforted.[23] (c) I rejoiced rather than being sorrowful as I was when I last wrote to you.

---

[20] In strict grammar we ought to have *anaggellōnton*, but the participle is attracted to the verb, almost inevitably.

[21] See the same word used at Romans 1:11; Philippians 1:8; 1 Thessalonians 3:6; 2 Timothy 1:4.

[22] It is not unusual, after a preacher has been rejected by the people to whom he ministers, and he has left, that the people have second thoughts about their behavior that tended to drive him away. Paul's recent intermediate trip had not gone well; Paul had been rejected by the Corinthians. When they thought about it, did they too have second thoughts about their actions toward Paul? When Titus came, did he find a people ready to do what they could to be reconciled to the one they had hurt? Or does the fact it took Titus longer than expected to deal with the problem indicate he had to change people's minds after he arrived?

[23] *Mallon* can mean "rather" as well as "more."

7:8 - *For though I caused you sorrow by my letter, I do not regret it, though I did regret it – for I see that that letter caused you sorrows, though only for a while –*

For though I caused you sorrow by my letter - "For" usually introduces an explanation or a reason for something just said. Paul seems to be explaining why he rejoiced even more at Titus' report. It removed any regret Paul had about the letter he had previously written to them. That he pained them by something he had written is treated as a fact.[24] Though some suppose the allusion is to a lost intermediate letter, "my letter," we believe, is a reference to the letter we know as 1 Corinthians.[25] In the 1 Corinthian letter, Paul had felt it necessary to reprove them for their dissensions and other disorders which had occurred and which were tolerated in the church. How did he know he caused sorrow by his letter? His intermediate trip might have been one source of this knowledge. However, we doubt that there was Godly sorrow in the hearts of the Corinthians that early; otherwise, Paul would not have left town in sorrow (2 Corinthians 2:1). Perhaps, then, the knowledge of their sorrow is something Paul has only recently learned about from the report made by Titus. Their sorrow was something that occurred after Paul's intermediate trip. What he had written had made them sorry, but it was not his purpose in writing just to make them sorry and leave it at that (compare what he wrote at 2:4). His purpose had been to produce a sorrow that would lead them to repentance.

I do not regret it - Though he did have some regret about the letter (as he explains in the next clause), as he writes this letter he no longer regrets having to write the earlier one because it did lead to their repentance as verses 9 and 10 will show. "Regret" (*metamelomai*) is an uneasy feeling concerning what has been done.[26]

---

[24] *Ei kai* rather than *kai ei* in the original concedes as true what is stated (Plummer, *op. cit.*, p.219).

[25] On the whole question of whether or not there was a severe letter written after Paul's intermediate trip to Corinth and delivered by Titus, see the Introductory Studies. It will be recalled that some think 2 Corinthians 10-13 are a fragment from that severe letter, while others are just as adamant that the whole severe letter has been lost, with none of it being now extant. The interesting thing about this speculation is that the arguments by the proponents of each of these views cancel out the arguments of the other view, leaving us with no real evidence of such a hypothetical severe letter. We are left with "my letter" being a reference to the letter we call 1 Corinthians.

[26] The KJV here has "I do not repent," but that version does not distinguish in this context between the two words *metamelomai* ("regret") and *metanoeō* ("repent") used in verse 9. *Metamelomai* speaks of a change of mind (regret or remorse), while *metanoeō* speaks of a change of mind and a change of action (repentance). While Trench (*Synonyms*, #lxix) has shown in some places no hard and fast line can be drawn between the two words, nevertheless *metanoeō* has the richer and more serious meaning. The difference between *metamelomai* (Matthew 21:30,32, 27:3; Hebrews 7:21) and *metanoeō* (Acts 2:38, 3:19; 2 Corinthians 12:21) is fairly represented by the difference between "regret" and "repent." That difference is often illustrated by Peter and Judas. Peter, after denying Jesus, went out and repented. Judas, on the other hand, merely "regretted" what he did (Matthew 27:3); in his case there was no genuine repentance.

Though I did regret it - According to 2 Corinthians 2;4, while Paul was writing 1 Corinthians, he had an uneasy feeling about the letter he was writing. That letter was intended to produce pain in them, a pain that would ultimately (he hoped) lead them to repentance. But he was aware that a rebuke like he was writing could result in a completely negative reaction accompanied by hard feelings and further alienation. Through his mind went the question, would it more likely help produce a positive response if he used different words, or a different tone?[27]

-- *For* **I see that that letter caused you sorrow, though only for a while --** With a parenthetic remark, Paul here states the reason he no longer regrets having written the letter: it brought about the kind of sorrow he desired, the sorrow (he tells us in a verse or so later) that leads to repentance. The verb *lupeō* here translated "caused you sorrow" could also be translated "caused you pain" as it awakened the Corinthians to their past sin. It is the same verb used at 2:4 where he told them his letter was not intended just to cause them pain or grief, but rather that the pain was a means to an end, an end which (through the help of Titus' mission) finally has now been attained. "For a while" says the sorrow lasted only a short while, until it resulted in the desired repentance.

7:9 - *I now rejoice, not that you were made sorrowful, but that you were made sorrowful* **to the point of** *repentance; for you were made sorrowful according to* **the will of** *God, in order that you might not suffer loss in anything through us.*

I now rejoice - Now that the Corinthians have repented, the regret that plagued Paul's mind over the writing of 1 Corinthians is past, and as he has said in verses 4 and 7 he is joyful about how things are progressing.

Not that you were made sorrowful - Paul does not want them to draw the mistaken idea that he was happy merely that they were pained by his letter, or that he was happy when he heard of their lamentation. He was rejoicing because the sorrow had led them to repentance.   Since there apparently was no sorrow on the Corinthians' part

---

[27] What is the bearing of this verse (and 2:4) on our beliefs about inspiration? If one were to hold a mechanical dictation view of how inspiration worked, these verses certainly would cause difficulty. But if we picture holy men of God speaking or writing as the Spirit moved them, what we read in these verses is perfectly harmonious. Concerning the words inspired men spoke and wrote, as explained in the author's commentary on 1 Corinthians 2:6-16, the Spirit allowed the men to choose the words they would use, as long as the words expressed the spiritual truths the Holy Spirit wanted spoken. Nor did inspiration suppress the emotions of the men who were writing or speaking. In Jesus' own case, speaking what is right did not always lead to happy results (John 6:60-68). As the case of the martyr Stephen teaches us, what inspired men spoke could get them into serious trouble (Acts 7:51-60). Thus we are not surprised to learn that Paul had some serious misgivings about how what he wrote in 1 Corinthians would be received. We don't gain anything if we think (as many do) that Paul must be referring to misgivings about some letter other than 1 Corinthians, say a severe letter written after his unsuccessful intermediate trip to Corinth. Unless we are ready to affirm that the hypothetical severe letter was uninspired, we are still faced with the question of how an apostle could regret writing an inspired letter.

when Paul last visited Corinth on his intermediate trip, the time when Paul's 1 Corinthian letter made them sorrowful must have come later. It appears that Titus must have made use of 1 Corinthians as he called upon the Corinthians to repent.

But that you were made sorrowful to *the point of* repentance - The word here rendered repentance is *metanoeō*, the word which means a change of mind and a change of actions.[28] "To the point of" translates the preposition *eis*, a word expressing motion toward or result. Godly sorrow for sins precedes any real repentance.[29] Of what had the Corinthians repented? One thing involved was certainly their careless attitude concerning the discipline of habitual sinners in the midst of the congregation, for this is the topic about which Paul goes on to write in the following verses. Perhaps they repented of their hurtful treatment of Paul during his intermediate visit. Perhaps they repented of their being all too ready to listen to Paul's detractors who have recently come into their midst.

For you were made sorrowful according *to the will of* God - "Sorrowful" still, as in verses 8 and 9, has the idea of inward pain, grief, remorse because of sin against God. In verse 10 Paul explains what he means when he speaks of sorrow that is "according to ... God." It is the kind of sorrow that God approves if it leads to repentance, or that leads one to seek forgiveness for sin which then results in a relation that is in harmony with God. Sorrow that is not "according to ... God" is being sorry that you got caught, not sorry that you did it; that is, there is no sorrow that the actions were done, or that God has been offended.

In order that you might not suffer loss in anything through us - "If Paul had not written to them to urge them to change their course, that would have been a great loss to them, and a great blame to him."[30] Godly grief has led them to repentance and repentance has saved the Corinthians from loss. What does Paul mean by "suffer loss"? The word for suffer loss (*zēmiōthēnai*) is used at 1 Corinthians 3:15 for the loss of one's reward at the final judgment.

7:10 - *For the sorrow that is according to* the will of *God produces a repentance without regret,* **leading** *to salvation; but the sorrow of the world produces death.*

---

[28] The definition we learn in Basic Bible Doctrine for repentance is this: Repentance is a change of mind and a change of action resulting from Godly sorrow for sin and including restitution where possible. The change of mind and action comes from Isaiah 55:7; Godly sorrow from this passage in 2 Corinthians; and restitution from the example of Zacchaeus (Luke 19:8).

[29] It seems to be implied that sorrow can sometimes serve no useful purpose, but can rather lead a person to being overwhelmed with excessive sorrow (2 Corinthians 2:7) with no repentance ever forthcoming. What happens instead is that such a person loses his faith.

[30] Plummer, *op. cit.*, p.221.

For the sorrow that is according to *the will of* **God** - "For" introduces an explanation of what "sorrow according to ... God" is.   To help us see its meaning, Paul contrasts two kinds of sorrow (one "according to ... God" and the other "of the world") by the results which they produce.

Produces a repentance - The kind of sorrow that could be called "Godly sorrow" produces a change of mind and action, a reformation, a reorientation of how one lives so that he lives in harmony with what God has revealed He expects of men. Repentance also includes restitution where possible (Luke 19:8).   Godly sorrow is not the same thing as repentance.[31]

Without regret - In the Greek, this adjectival phrase "without regret" may qualify either "repentance" or "salvation."   Since it is doubtful that Paul meant to say that salvation brings no regret, the NASB takes it with "repentance," thus having Paul affirm that repentance is something not to be regretted.   Indeed, whoever yet has regretted having truly repented of sin?   Here again Paul makes a distinction between repentance and regret.   One leads to God, the other does not.

Leading **to salvation** - "Salvation" is forgiveness of sins and, ultimately, eternity in the presence of God.   In the case of the Christian who sins, repentance is one condition on which salvation is based.   There is a repentance that is one of the steps in becoming a Christian in the first place (Acts 2:38, 20:21), and there is a repentance that is needful when one sins after becoming a Christian.   It is the latter that Paul has in mind in this passage.   Several important truths need to be emphasized.   (1) Christians who sin need to repent, not just feel remorse or regret.   (2) Christians who commit sin and do not repent are in danger of suffering "loss," namely, their salvation.

But the sorrow of the world produces death - "Sorrow of the world" is sorrow like the world sorrows.   It does not see sin as God sees it.   Such a worldly sorrow does not lead to repentance.   It may lead to resentment or bitterness or remorse.   You are not sorry you did the sin and offended God thereby.   You are simply sorry you got

---

[31] Some commentators have called attention to the few times Paul uses the word repent or repentance (Acts 17:13, 26:20; Romans 2:4; here in 2 Corinthians 2:10; and 2 Timothy 2:25.   We would also include Hebrews 6:1 and 6:6 as being written by Paul).   Because Paul uses the word repentance so rarely in his epistles, Fisher (*op. cit.*, p.367) thinks verse 10 is an insertion into this passage of a common Christian saying, rather than being an expansion of the thought in verse 9. He also affirms that the apostle John never used the word at all (but to do so he has to deny the Johannine authorship of Revelation – cf. Revelation 2:16, 3:19, 9:21).   Once he has called attention to the relatively few uses of repentance by Paul and John, Fisher then affirms that neither Paul nor John (apostles to the Gentiles) ever required repentance as a condition of salvation.   Instead, he affirms, all they required was faith, and, by implication, that is all we should require of those who would become converts.   In this commentator's judgment, this is a pitiable attempt to try to explain away what the Scriptures actually say is a condition of salvation.   Furthermore, the Corinthians are not just becoming converts: Paul is writing to folk who have been Christians for several years when he emphasizes their need for repentance when there has been sin in their lives.

caught, were disgraced, or ruined.   Cain, Esau, Saul, Ahithophel, and Judas are examples of this wrong kind of sorrow.   All of them regretted their actions, but none of them repented.   Their remorse did not lead them to turn back to God.   "Death" is the opposite of salvation in this verse, and is what is involved in the "loss" (verse 9) the Corinthians would have incurred if their sorrow had been only worldly sorrow. "Death" may be both temporal and eternal, as in the case of Judas where worldly sorrow produced both: suicide (Matthew 27:3-5) first, and then he went to his own place (Acts 1:25).   Ultimately, death involves spiritual death (Romans 6:21-23) and then the complete alienation from God which leaves one without hope for future fellowship with Him (cf. 1 Corinthians 6:9,10; Galatians 5:21).   What a contrast there is between Godly sorrow and worldly sorrow.   Whereas Godly sorrow promotes salvation, worldly sorrow works out or produces death.[32]

7:11 - *For behold what earnestness this very thing, this godly sorrow, has produced in you: what vindication of yourselves, what indignation, what fear, what longing, what zeal, what avenging of wrong!   In everything you demonstrated yourselves to be innocent in the matter.*

For behold what earnestness this very thing, this godly sorrow, has produced in you - John the Baptist called for his listeners to bring forth fruit in keeping with their repentance (Matthew 3:8).   From that we learn that genuine repentance can be judged by its results.   It looks like, under the direction of Paul's letter and the guidance of Titus, the Corinthians' repentance is genuine, for in this verse Paul lists seven results of their repentance that give evidence it was genuine.   We presume he learned about these results as Titus made his report to Paul.   "This godly sorrow" is the very same sorrow alluded to in "sorrow according to God," and in the "sorrow ... that produces repentance that leads to salvation."   Paul is emphasizing that in their case one can see a splendid example of Godly sorrow and its fruits.   In the phrase "what earnestness," "what" translates a Greek word which means how much or how great. "Earnestness" means eagerness, seriousness of purpose, diligence.   Where there had been indifference to evil, and even a tacit approval of it (1 Corinthians 5:2), repentance has brought a change so that now their efforts to remedy the situation and to comply with Paul's instructions are not half-hearted.   They have gone about it with holy determination.   One evidence of genuine repentance is "earnestness."

What vindication of yourselves - The word translated "what" in this clause and those following is *alla*, the force of which in such a listing is "over and above this" (i.e., the

---

[32] Fisher (*op. cit.*, p.368) tells us that "produces" in this clause (a compound verb in the Greek) is a stronger expression than in the previous clause.   The compound form means 'to work out to its completion.'   Repentance 'works' salvation, but does not 'work it out to completion.'   Repentance is only an intermediate cause of salvation.   Worldly sorrow is different.   It is an effectual cause of death.

thing just mentioned before). Paul is building to a climax in this listing.[33] Rather than "vindication of yourselves" the ASV reads "clearing of yourselves."[34] The idea is that the Corinthians were eager to clear themselves of blame, especially in the matter of the offender whose offense they once abetted and condoned. Not any more!

What indignation - "Indignation" in this context speaks of holy anger. Perhaps it was directed at the offender (2:5) whose behavior had brought shame on the congregation. Perhaps it speaks of a hatred for sin (something that true repentance produces) either in their own lives or the lives of others.

What fear - It would appear that Paul has in mind "fear of a holy God and a reverence for his sacred word"[35] rather than a fear of what supernatural measures Paul might take if he should come among them with a rod (1 Corinthians 4:21) as he had warned them he might have to do.

What longing - Although we are in a paragraph in which Paul is pleading for the Corinthians to open their hearts to him, it is doubtful that this speaks of a yearning for Paul's favor and return. Rather, we choose to explain it as meaning a hunger and thirst for righteousness (Matthew 5:6). Repentance had produced a change in this area, too.

What zeal - "Zeal for God and the apostle (verse 7) and against the evil which dishonors both."[36] Or perhaps zeal in exercising discipline as the following "avenging" might suggest.

What avenging of wrong! - The wrong that was punished or avenged was likely that done by the offender of 1 Corinthians 5:1-5 and 2 Corinthians 2:6. It included excommunication from the congregation. It was done to maintain what was right.

In everything you demonstrated yourselves to be innocent in the matter - For "in everything," the RSV reads "at every point." On each of the matters where the Corinthians were once blamable, their repentance has resulted in no blame being attached to them any longer. By the fruits of their repentance, they had removed all necessity of further blame. As the previous clauses show, "the matter" refers to the temporary failure to exercise the needed discipline of the member of the church who

---

[33] The same use of *alla* in a climax is found at 1 Corinthians 6:11. The ASV tries to catch the energy of the Greek by translating *alla* as "yea what."

[34] The word translated "vindication" is *apologia* which means literally to give a defense, as in court (cf. Acts 22:1; 2 Timothy 4:16), in order to clear one's name.

[35] Coffman, *op. cit.*, p.401.

[36] Plummer, *op. cit.*, p.223

was living in habitual sin (1 Corinthians 5:1-5). They repented; the man was disciplined; he repented; that matter is now past. Sadly, it is also true that there were other matters where repentance was still needed (cf. 2 Corinthians 12:20).

7:12 - *So although I wrote to you* it was *not for the sake of the offender, nor for the sake of the one offended, but that your earnestness on our behalf might be made known to you in the sight of God.*

So although I wrote to you - Just as he explained why he is writing this second letter to Corinth (2:3,4,9), he here explains why he wrote the letter we call 1 Corinthians, namely, to give the Corinthians opportunity to show whether or not they would be loyal to an apostle of Jesus such as he was. For what he had written, see 1 Corinthians, but especially 5:1-5.

It was **not for the sake of the offender** - We might say it was not *just* for the sake of the offender, or not primarily for his sake. Paul has already shown he had immense concern for the offender, and the one offended. He is saying that although he had concern for them, they were not the main cause of his writing. He may be using a Hebrew mode of thought where two alternatives are given, one of which is more important than the other.[37] In this case their willingness to listen to any and all of Paul's inspired instructions, rather than the misleading teaching of his opponents, was more important than any other consideration. The offender (the one who did the wrong) is the incestuous person (1 Corinthians 5:1-5, 2 Corinthians 2:5-7).[38]

Nor for the sake of the one offended - The offense was that a man had taken his father's wife as his own (1 Corinthians 5:1), and the person injured (offended), therefore, was the father.[39] Neither in 1 or 2 Corinthians is any mention made of the woman being disciplined, nor of her repentance. We infer from this that only the father and the son were members of the congregation. We also infer from this that the father was still living at the time Paul wrote this epistle. We wonder if the woman involved ever became a Christian. How sad when actions by Christians (think of the son's actions) are spiritually detrimental to the very unsaved people they should be seeking to win.

---

[37] Plummer (*op. cit.*, p.224) reminds us that in Jewish literature when two alternatives are given, one of which is stated negatively and the other positively, it does not mean the negative alternative is rejected absolutely, but only in comparison with the other alternative, which is much more important. For example, Hosea 6:1 reads, "I will have mercy and not sacrifice." That is not intended to prohibit sacrifice; rather it affirms that mercy is much the better of the two (cp. Mark 9:37, Luke 10:20, 14:12, 23:28).

[38] The identity of the "offender" was covered in notes at 2:5-8. This commentator, it will be remembered, is not in agreement with the view that the "offender" was a false teacher who recently had come to Corinth and said derogatory things about Paul, as some modern writers propose.

[39] The suggestion of some writers that the unnamed injured party (the one offended) was Paul himself is hardly satisfactory.

But that your earnestness on our behalf might be made known to you - "But" introduces the primary reason why Paul wrote: it was to get the Corinthians to realize their true state of mind respecting Paul's position and leadership. Recall all he has written in chapters 2-6 about the office and ministry of an apostle. This verse reminds us of 2:9 where Paul said that his purpose in writing was to test their obedience.[40]

In the sight of God - Placed last in the Greek for emphatic solemnity, it may mean either God is watching you, or God is watching me. If the former, it expresses the Corinthians' feeling of responsibility to act as God would have them act. If the latter, it expresses the idea that Paul wrote with a deep sense that he must be careful of his words and motives since God would judge him in this matter.

7:13 - *For this reason we have been comforted. And besides our comfort, we rejoiced even much more for the joy of Titus, because his spirit has been refreshed by you all.*

For this reason we have been comforted - To show that this clause concludes what has gone before, the NASB puts a full stop after these words and then begins a new paragraph with "And besides ...." "For this reason" refers back to the earnestness or dedication they have shown to Paul. Paul says that because the good purpose in writing the letter was accomplished, namely in bringing their loyalty to light, his anxiety about his first letter has been relieved. The perfect tense verb "have been comforted" (speaking of past completed action with present continuing results) reaches back to the time of Titus' report, and continues on to the time of the writing of this letter.

And besides our comfort - "Over and above the comfort we received personally," is the idea. The NASB starts a new paragraph here.

We rejoiced even much more for the joy of Titus - In the Greek "even much more" is expressed by the use of two comparative adjectives, a construction Paul seems fond of (cp. 12:9; Philippians 1:23). Paul experienced joy when he heard of their repentance. He had even more joy when he saw the joy and delight of Titus at the success of his mission to Corinth. Paul's joy overflowed.

Because his spirit has been refreshed by you all - Evidently Titus had some misgiv-

---

[40] Because of a manuscript variation, the KJV reads differently here. The KJV speaks of "our care for you" rather than "your care (earnestness) for me." If the reading of the KJV is right, then Paul is here affirming the motive behind his writing was his deep anxiety for the whole church, not just the offender and the offended. Actually there is a diversity of readings at this place, perhaps arising from an attempt to smooth out the apparent strangeness of the claim that his letter had been written in order that their earnestness might be manifested to themselves. Nevertheless, the better supported reading is as we read in the NASB.

ings about the mission to Corinth which Paul asked him to undertake.[41] It is not a pleasant task to be a trouble-shooter.   However, his apprehension about the unhappy circumstances he was being asked to attempt to solve is now a thing of the past. Their repentance and its evidences (verse 11) resulted in a refreshing that continues even to the time Paul is writing this letter.[42] Perhaps Paul calls attention to Titus' delight with them because he is about to ask Titus to return to Corinth to supervise the arrangements for the offering now being gathered for the poor saints at Jerusalem (8:6,16).   By a positive response to that the Corinthians can add to the delight of both Paul and Titus.

7:14 - *For if in anything I have boasted to him about you, I was not put to shame; but as we spoke all things to you in truth, so also our boasting before Titus proved to be* **the** *truth.*

For if in anything I have boasted to him about you - "For" introduces a further reason for Paul's abounding joy: all the complimentary things he said about the Corinthian Christians to Titus had turned out to be true.   At some time in the past, likely when he enlisted Titus to accept the trouble-shooting mission to Corinth, Paul had boasted about the many good traits of the Corinthians.   Reading between the lines, one gets the impression that Titus was reluctant to accept the assignment until he had some strong assurances from Paul concerning the Corinthians.   After his recent intermediate trip and rejection at Corinth it is unexpected to read that Paul could still express pride in the Corinthians, but for all their faults they also had some commendable positive traits.   In spite of the hurt he has experienced, his love for them enabled him to see their good qualities.

I was not put to shame - It was when Titus came back with his positive report that Paul was not put to shame.   If he had been utterly mistaken about how the Corinthians would respond, he would have been put to shame.   But the Corinthians' repentance had proved Paul's estimate of them to be correct.

But as we spoke all things to you in truth - There is an allusion to what Paul had already written at 1:15-19 where he responds to a charge by the troublemakers that he was vacillating in what he told them.   No, says Paul, every word he ever addressed to them, whether he was present with them or writing a letter to them, was an expression of pure holy truth.   Paul was not one who, on occasion, practiced deception.

---

[41] Some English translations choose "mind" rather "spirit" to translate the Greek *pneuma* at this place.   Concerning the "spirit" part of a man see notes at 2 Corinthians 3:6.

[42] The Greek "refreshed" is a perfect tense verb, indicating a past completed action with present continuing results.   It seems to be a favorite term with Paul (see 1 Corinthians 16:18; Philemon 7 and 20).   Involved in the word is the idea of giving rest to the weary, as in Matthew 11:28 and 26:45.

So our boasting before Titus proved to be *the* truth - Paul was accustomed to speak the truth. Paul often boasted of the qualities of the churches (see 8:24 and 9:2). He did so when speaking well of the Corinthians to Titus. Their repentance is evidence Paul had neither spoken falsely nor embellished the truth when he expressed his pride concerning their good qualities to Titus before Titus left for Corinth.

7:15 - *And his affection abounds all the more toward you, as he remembers the obedience of you all, how you received him with fear and trembling.*

And his affection abounds all the more toward you - "His heart warms all the more to you" (NEB).[43] It seems that Titus accepted the difficult assignment Paul gave him because he loved the Corinthians. Now, after his happy experience, he loves them more.

As he remembers the obedience of you all - That the Corinthians were obedient indicates that when Titus came he had certain definite demands (in harmony with the gospel) to which he called for compliance. Our English translation "you all" might be interpreted to mean that the compliance was universal. It apparently was not universal. As chapter 10 will indicate, there were still those at Corinth who were opposed to Paul, and there was still much wrongdoing in the church. On the matter of discipline of the offender, the majority of the congregation had acted in harmony. There were still things that needed correction, teaching, and discipline.[44]

How you received him with fear and trembling - It looks like the Corinthians had given up the attitude of resistance to God's messenger that they had displayed on Paul's recent intermediate visit. We do not know what led to the change, but Titus was received with respectful reverence and an anxiousness to do what God says is right.[45] How are we to harmonize Plumptre's comment (p.71) that Titus was received respectfully by the Corinthians, not with resistance, with our suggestion that it actually took Titus some time to lead the congregation to correct their errors, thus accounting for his delay in coming back to report to Paul? Did they receive him with fear and trembling from the first day? Or did that fear and trembling only come after a period of time? While it may have been over a period of time, once it has been

---

[43] The Greek again reads "bowels" as at 5:12, and with the same meaning. Our translations treat the Greek as implying a contrast with a former occasion, but it is possible that the Greek simply means "very abundantly" and implies no comparison with any other occasion.

[44] Far from meaning everybody in the church with no exceptions, the expression "you all" is a translation of a second person plural pronoun which means "you" (plural). About the only way we have in English to show that "you" is plural is to say "you all." Coffman (*op. cit.*, p.405) speaks of the terms "you all" and "in everything" as being hyperbole, rather than as being literally true. He does so in anticipation of arguments by some that chapters 10-13 cannot be part of the same letter in which were written such glowing terms as we find in 7:13-16.

[45] "No other New Testament writer uses this expression except Paul. He used it four times (here; 1 Corinthians 2:3; Ephesians 6:5; Philippians 2:12)" (Fisher, *op. cit.*, p.370).

won, Paul and Titus can look back on it with satisfaction and joy.

7:16 - *I rejoice that in everything I have confidence in you.*

I rejoice - "Rejoice" is a present tense verb.   Paul concludes this whole first section of 2 Corinthians (1:12-7:15) with an expression of his continuing joy since he has heard of their repentance.

That in everything I have confidence in you - The reason Paul is rejoicing is that the Corinthians are giving him reason to be encouraged.   "In you" means "about you" (cf. Galatians 4:20) or "in your case."   The verb behind "I have confidence" is *tharrō*, to take courage, to be of good cheer.[46]   In 2 Corinthians 5:6,8 it was translated "be of good courage," and could be so translated here.   So translated, Paul does not mean "I trust you" but rather that he is encouraged when he sees how they are responding to his instructions and directions.   The many were back on the right road and Paul was encouraged about their future.   Their obedient response to Titus encourages Paul to think that they will respond positively to his appeal to them to be involved in raising the offering for the poor at Jerusalem, the topic he is about to introduce in the next two chapters.

Tharrō can also be translated "I am bold" as it is at 2 Corinthians 10:1.   Were it so translated here it would prepare us for the change of tone we feel as we enter into the rest of this letter.   He has been using words expressive of comfort, rejoicing, glorying, boldness, and courage with surprising frequency.   Those words cease to be used as Paul changes topics to the offering and how the troublemakers should be repudiated and about other areas of failure that need attention.   He may be cautious about how he says it, but he will speak boldly to them on these topics.

---

[46] The word translated "confidence" at 2 Corinthians 7:4 was *parrēsia*, a different word than the one used here.   It is helpful if our choice of English equivalents reflects the different Greek words used.

II. PAUL ENCOURAGES LIBERALITY IN THEIR COLLECTION FOR THE POOR CHRISTIANS AT JERUSALEM. 8:1 - 9:15

A. The Example of Liberality set by the Macedonian Churches is Worthy of Imitation. 8:1-7

8:1 - *Now, brethren, we* **wish to** *make known to you the grace of God which has been given in the churches of Macedonia.*

Now, brethren - With these two words Paul transitions to a new subject that he will unfold in 2 Corinthians 8 and 9, namely, the offering for the poor saints at Jerusalem. The *de* (translated "now") may suggest a connection with the last verse of chapter 7. He trusts that his encouragement concerning the Corinthians will carry over to their participation in the offering.   The term "brethren" is the keynote of this section, since "brotherly love" is the motive of generosity in the matters of benevolence.   Although he had written to them about this offering in 1 Corinthians 16:1-4, for some reason he finds it necessary now to encourage the church to complete their part in the offering.   Perhaps the troubles at Corinth have resulted in interest in the offering being temporarily laid aside.   Perhaps the troublemakers at Corinth have said derogatory things about Paul and the offering (e.g., see 2 Corinthians 11:7-11 and 12:16-18) that make this explanation and encouragement necessary.   Paul intends to answer any doubts that have been raised about this offering.   Evidently, about the time 1 Corinthians was written, the Corinthians had shown interest in the collection, a fact which Paul had called to the attention of the Macedonians (2 Corinthians 9:2). While troubles at Corinth had caused a hiatus in participation, the Macedonians had gone on carefully accumulating what would be their part of the offering.

We *wish to* **make known to you** - When Paul uses this expression elsewhere (e.g., 1 Corinthians 12;3, 15:1; Galatians 1:11) it seems to mean "I remind you."   Perhaps here it means that Paul is about to tell the Corinthians something about which they did not yet know,[1] namely, how generously the Macedonians have responded to the needs of their brethren at Jerusalem.   The reason why Paul is telling them of the commendable liberality of the Macedonian churches was to encourage them to a similar liberality.

The grace of God which has been given in the churches - As explained in notes at 1 Corinthians 16:1,   "grace" is one of eight different Greek words which are used by

---

[1] The "We do you to wit" of the KJV (a translation first offered in Tyndale's translation) means "We cause you to know."   It is now an obsolete way of expressing the idea.   Many of our older commentaries, based on the KJV, treat *gnōridzō* here as meaning to make something known for the first time.

the New Testament writers to denote this collection.[2] A major emphasis late in Paul's third missionary journey was the organizing and completion of this offering for the poor saints at Jerusalem.[3] Of course, one of the reasons for the offering was compassion for brethren who were in need.[4] But there was another important reason for it, as explained in Romans 15:26-31 and 2 Corinthians 9:12-14: to strengthen the ties which bound the Gentile and Jewish Christians together in Christ. It does not read "the grace of God bestowed *on* the churches of Macedonia,"[5] so we should probably not explain it to mean that God's grace, operating on the Macedonian Christians, is what caused them to be generous. It reads "given *in* the churches of Macedonia," and likely reflects the idea that it is a favor from God to have an opportunity to give and to have the means to give. "The word 'grace' sometimes has the sense of 'gift,' and 'of God' sometimes has the idea of 'very great.' Some writers, therefore, have supposed that this means that the churches of Macedonia had been able to contribute a *very great gift* to aid the saints of Judea."[6] Concerning the method of the actual collection, Paul indicates in 1 Corinthians 16:1-2 that each week each Christian was to contribute in proportion to the blessings he received the past week. Each week when they assembled to worship the offering was received.[7]

---

[2] The Greek words are *logeias* (1 Corinthians 16:1), *charis* (2 Corinthians 8:1,4), *koinōnia* (Romans 15:26; 2 Corinthians 8:4, 9:3), *diakonia* (2 Corinthians 8:4, 9:1,2,13), *hadrotēs* (2 Corinthians 8:20), *eulogia* (2 Corinthians 9:5), *leitourgia* (2 Corinthians 9:12), and *eleēmosunē* (Acts 24:17).

[3] Luke refers to it in Acts 20:4 and 24:17, while in the letters written during that period of the apostle's life the offering is alluded to in Romans 15:26,27, 1 Corinthians 16:1-4, 2 Corinthians 8-9, and Galatians 6:6-8.

[4] As has been set forth in our comments at 1 Corinthians 16:1, there seems to have been a long-standing, almost chronic, need for financial help for the saints in Jerusalem. Acts 6:1 shows that early in that congregation's history, a problem arose concerning the equitable distribution of food for the widows. In the early AD 40's at Antioch, Agabus the prophet told about a coming famine during which the church at Jerusalem would need help. The church at Antioch sent relief by the hands of Barnabas and Saul (Acts 11:27-30). In the early AD 50's, at the Jerusalem Conference, Peter, James and John urged Paul and Barnabas to remember the poor as they ministered among the Gentiles (Galatians 2:9,10). Paul reminds the Galatians that he was eager to do that very thing. Now, during the third missionary journey (AD 54-58), Paul is enlisting the help of the Gentile churches in collecting another offering for the saints at Jerusalem.

[5] The KJV translation at this place, "on the churches," is not defensible.

[6] Barnes, *op. cit.*, p.178.

[7] This offering for Jerusalem was evidently a special offering, over and above their weekly giving. Giving is basic to worship, (cf. "fellowship" in Acts 2:42). Paul's instructions that the offering is to be concluded before he comes (1 Corinthians 16:2) does not mean that no more offerings would be received at the weekly assembly. It merely means that this special drive would be concluded. Their regular giving would continue. "The two chapters of 2 Corinthians that deal with the offering are, therefore, of importance to us, as we have here a statement of the duty of giving liberally to the cause of benevolence, and of the motives by which it should be done" (Barnes, *op. cit.*, p.17).

The churches of Macedonia - The only churches in the Roman province of Macedonia about which we have any details in the New Testament are those of Philippi, Thessalonica, and Berea. The congregations of Christians in Macedonia were not the only ones involved in this benevolent project; so were congregations which Paul himself had planted in Asia, Galatia, and Achaia (Acts 20:4).

8:2 - *that in a great ordeal of affliction their abundance of joy and their deep poverty overflowed in the wealth of their liberality.*

That in a great ordeal of affliction - Paul can talk about the situation of the Macedonian Christians for he was passing through Macedonia at the time of the writing of this letter, and may have been personally involved in some of the same troubles the Macedonians faced, for he writes about afflictions within and conflicts without (7:5). With two contrasts in this verse (heavy affliction and abundant joy; extreme poverty and wealth of liberality) Paul begins his account of their generosity. "Affliction," which can refer to either mental or physical pressures, is the same word which Paul has used often in this epistle (e.g., 1:4-8). "It is the verb used to describe the crushing of grapes to extract their juice."[8] The word translated "ordeal" (*dokimē*) was translated "test" at 2:9. Paul seems to be saying that the troubles they have been through served as a test of their devotion and faith. The test was severe and prolonged (*pollē*, "great"), but their Christianity proved to be genuine. Paul doesn't specify the exact nature of these afflictions, , but perhaps they were the result of persecutions against the Christians (see Acts 16:20, 17:5; 1 Thessalonians 1:6, 2:14,15; and 2 Thessalonians 1:4).

Their abundance of joy - It might be supposed that an abundance of joy is a strange thing to be found when an ordeal of afflictions is being experienced, but Christian joy does not depend on outward circumstances (Colossians 1:24). Perhaps Paul speaks of the joys of being able to serve and help others as being one motive that led them to be generous in their contribution for the poor at Jerusalem. Is Paul reminding the Corinthians that God loves a cheerful giver?

And their deep poverty - "Poverty" speaks of financial deprivation where the people had little money to buy food or clothing for themselves. The desperate financial condition of the Christians may have only reflected the depressed economy of the region. Plummer calls attention to the fact that when the Romans conquered this part of the Mediterranean world, they were very hard on the Macedonians. "The Romans had taken possession of the gold and silver mines which were rich sources of revenue, and had taxed the right of smelting copper and iron; they had also reserved to them-

---

[8] Fisher, *op. cit.*, p.373.

selves the importation of salt and timber for the building of ships."[9]   McGarvey pointed out that "Macedonia had suffered in three civil wars (between Caesar and Pompey; between the Triumvirs and Brutus and Cassius; and between Augustus and Mark Antony), and had been reduced to such poverty that Tiberius Caesar, hearkening to their petitions, had lightened their taxes."[10]   "Deep" translates *kata bathous*, literally, 'down to the depth.'   It does not mean that their poverty was getting worse and worse; it means that it had already reached its lowest stage.[11]   In the midst of "afflictions" and "poverty" like this, we might suppose that they would be unable to give, but that was not the case.   For example, from the earliest days of the church at Philippi those Christians had been generous (Philippians 4:10-19).

Overflowed in the wealth of their liberality - "Overflow" pictures a river rising until the abundance of water floods over its banks.   Verses 3-5 will identify four areas where there was overflow in the motives and actions of the Macedonians as they participated in this offering.   It is an amazing combination to say that deep poverty plus an abundance of joy can result in an overflow of generosity or liberality. What the Macedonians gave was much greater than could be expected from persons so poor.   The phrase "wealth (riches) of liberality" is a Hebraism meaning lavish open-handedness, great liberality.   The word (*haplotēs*) here translated "liberality" is translated "simplicity" (singleness of purpose) at 2 Corinthians 11:3.   How the word came to change meaning from "simplicity" to "liberality" is not obvious on the surface.[12]   Perhaps if we begin with a single-minded purpose or desire to relieve the necessities of others, we can soon understand how such a driving motive leads to generosity and liberality.   Paul likely implies that if the Corinthians will manifest such a spirit they will not be outdone by their less-fortunate brethren in Macedonia. "God does not measure the greatness of one's gifts by the amount given (consider the poor widow with her two mites, Luke 21:3,4), but by the spirit in which it is given; not by the amount given, but by the amount retained."[13]

8:3 - *For I testify that according to their ability, and beyond their ability* they gave *of their own accord,*

---

[9] Plummer, *op. cit.*, p.233.

[10] McGarvey, *op. cit.*, p.210.

[11] Macknight saw in Paul's mention of the Macedonian's poverty a delicate insinuation that the more opulent Corinthians should equal or exceed what had been given by the Macedonians. (*Apostolic Epistles and Commentary* [Grand Rapids: Baker, 1969], V.2, p.396.)

[12] *Haplotēs* is translated "liberality" at Romans 12:8 and 2 Corinthians 9:11,13; also in Josephus, *Ant.* vii.332;   *Test. Issachar* iii.8).   In Romans 12:8 where the word occurs it seems to refer to giving which was uncalculating and free of ulterior motives.

[13] Fisher, *op. cit.*, p.374.

For I testify that according to their ability - Verses 3-5 form one long sentence in the Greek.[14] The "for" (*hoti*, Greek) that introduces this sentence shows that Paul is further explaining what he had in mind when he wrote "overflowed." The fact that their gift was far beyond what might have been thought possible considering their small means, the way they spontaneously got involved, their begging to be permitted to be partners in this offering, and the way they gave themselves to the Lord and to Paul are all examples of the commendable overflow Paul has witnessed. "Testify" here has its regular meaning of telling what one knows from personal knowledge of the situation. Paul was in Macedonia when he writes 2 Corinthians. He can testify concerning the circumstances there from personal knowledge.[15] That the Macedonians did what they had the ability to do is held out as an incentive for the Corinthians to do likewise.

And beyond their ability - The Greek words translated "beyond their ability" are *para dunamin*. Perhaps it means "above and beyond their power" (i.e., the Macedonians gave beyond what it would have been thought possible in their circumstances), or perhaps it means "against their power" (i.e., it was a contradiction of their poverty to give so much).

***They gave* of their own accord** - "They gave" is the key word in the long sentence that makes up verses 3-5 in our Bibles. The Greek word *authairetoi* ("of their own accord") is a compound made up of two words meaning "self" and "choice." Their generous giving was voluntary, done on their own initiative. It was not something they had to be pressured into doing. What Paul wants is for the Corinthians to give in a similar way, without compulsion (2 Corinthians 9:7). When Timothy and Erastus passed through the area informing the churches of the need for the offering and how it was to be collected and sent (Acts 19:22), the Macedonians spontaneously determined to get involved.

8:4 - *begging us with much entreaty for the favor of participation in the support of the saints*

Begging us with much entreaty - Verse 4 is further explanation of what he just said ("of their own accord"). Since Acts 19:22 seems to exclude a reference to the Macedonians begging to be allowed to participate in the offering in the first place, verse 4 appears to be saying that when Paul recognized they were giving beyond their means he sought to restrain them. Then is when it was that they were persistent and urgent in their pleading that they might be allowed to continue giving so generously.

---

[14] The addition of words in italics in our English versions are an attempt to make clear the meaning of this long sentence which in Greek is rather awkward, perhaps due to prolonged dictation.

[15] This is hardly a proof text for "giving one's testimony" at a testimony meeting. The Greek word transliterated produces "martyr," and in later Christian history came to be used of those who were put to death because of the "testimony" they bore to Jesus.

For the favor of participation in the support of the saints - This is apparently how the Macedonians worded their urgent request to be allowed to continue giving generously. Four powerful words succinctly expressed their understanding of what they were doing. "Favor" (the Greek word *charis* is regularly translated "grace" elsewhere in the New Testament) tells us the Macedonians considered the opportunity to give to others as something God's grace had made available to them. "Participation" translates *koinōnia*, a word that speaks of participation in a common cause or being partners with someone in something. The Macedonians wanted to be partners with the other Christians in this offering being collected for the saints at Jerusalem.[16] The Greek word translated "support" is *diakonia* which is regularly translated "ministry" or "service" as the NASB margin shows. The Macedonians did not consider their offering as "charity" (in the modern sense of the word). Rather, when the Macedonians gave the money they looked on it as way they could minister to others. When the Christians in Jerusalem received the money it would render a service to them. It would be a much needed means of financial support.[17] Finally, the Macedonians identified the recipients of their gifts as being "saints."[18] They are folk who are sanctified or who are set apart for God's service; they are fellow Christians. That helps explain the Macedonians' motive for their generosity.

8:5 - *and* **this,** *not as we had expected, but they first gave themselves to the Lord and to us by the will of God.*

And *this,* **not as we had expected** - Since "they gave" is the main idea in this long sentence, we could supply that verb here so that it reads "*they gave* not as we had expected." The context makes it clear that the sum of money the Macedonians collected was far beyond Paul's expectations from folk who were so poor. Now he will call attention to how that came to be.

But they first gave themselves to the Lord - "First" seems to say that of all the areas of overflow (verse 2) being highlighted in this long sentence (verses 3-5), giving of themselves to the Lord was the most important. "To give oneself to the Lord is to

---

[16] Paul does not specifically identify the geographic location where the "poor saints" lived, but there can be no doubt they lived in Jerusalem, as the other letters written from this period in Paul's life indicate (e.g., Romans 15:25; 1 Corinthians 16:3).

[17] Paul uses the same words (fellowship and service) in Romans 15:27 as he talks about the offering to Jerusalem: the Gentiles have come to share (*koinōnia*) in spiritual blessings; they can in return be of service to them in material blessings. The collection is therefore not merely a financial matter. It expresses in a tangible way the union that existed between Jewish and Gentile churches.

[18] See comments at 2 Corinthians 1:1 for an explanation of the word "saints."

make all one's powers and resources available for His use."[19]   The Macedonian Christians recognized that since Christ has died for them, they should no longer live for themselves but for Him (2 Corinthians 5:15).   Where a people honestly and truly devote themselves to the Lord, they will keep nothing back.   Everything they have is His and is to be used where He wants and needs it.   The Macedonians' sacrificial giving occurred because their lives had already been given to the Lord.

And to us - Their devotion to the Lord resulted in their making themselves available to Paul and his fellow-workers for any service for Christ that needed to be done.   All the leaders had to do was to give instructions and the Christians were ready to act. Fisher observes that this expression states what should be the attitude of all Christians. Devotion to Christ leads Christians to place themselves at the disposal of God's leaders in order to get the work of Christ accomplished.[20]

By the will of God - Such actions as giving themselves to the Lord and to the Lord's special workers, as well as sacrificial giving in partnership with other Christians, are the very things that God wishes or desires.[21]   The Macedonians did as they had done because they had deliberately chosen to surrender to what God willed they should do.

8:6 - *Consequently we urged Titus that as he had previously made a beginning, so he would also complete in you this gracious work as well.*

Consequently we urged Titus - "Urged" translates *parakaleō*, the word that is constantly used of the missions of Titus to Corinth (1 Corinthians 16:12; 2 Corinthians 8:17, 12:18).   "Consequently" means that the example of the Macedonians resulted in Paul's determination to seek a generous offering at Corinth also, and to this end to encourage Titus to return to Corinth to finish the collection which already had been begun sometime earlier.   So great was Paul's hope for a generous offering from the Christians at Corinth that he has already boasted to Titus about them (2 Corinthians 7:4, 9:3).   Titus, who just recently had come from Corinth to Paul bearing good news, is the logical choice to return there to carry out the completion of the benevolent campaign.

---

[19] Fisher, *op. cit.*, p.375.

[20] Fisher, *op. cit.*, p.376.

[21] Some writers, persuaded that if the sovereign God wills something it is absolutely bound to happen, are anxious at this place to translate *thelēma* as "wish" or "desire" rather than "will."   In this way it can be affirmed that man is free to surrender to or to resist what God "wishes," whereas there is no such freedom in an area where God has willed something.   We do not find that such a nice distinction between "wish" and "will" can be maintained, whether the Greek word is *thelēma* or *boulēma*.   God does not "will" that any should perish (2 Peter 3:9), but some, in fact the great majority of men, nevertheless, are going to (Matthew 7:13).

That as he had previously made a beginning - These words convey the content of Paul's words to Titus. Titus is encouraged to go and finish what he began. It is not easy to date precisely when the visit to Corinth occurred during which Titus was instrumental in making a beginning of the collection for Jerusalem. According to 1 Corinthians 16:1-4 and 2 Corinthians 8:10, and 9:2, the beginning of the attempt to raise an offering for Jerusalem was a considerable time in the past, a year before the writing of 2 Corinthians. So in the Introductory Studies (in notes about the journeys and work of Titus[22]) it has been proposed that Titus had been to Corinth to begin the offering even before 1 Corinthians was written.

So he would also complete in you this gracious work as well - "In you" refers to the members of the church at Corinth. It appears that in Corinth the collecting of relief funds for the saints at Jerusalem had begun well, only to be interrupted by the crisis that led to Paul's intermediate trip to Corinth as well as Titus' just concluded visit during which he was attempting to get the church to deal with the offender (2 Corinthians 2:5-11, 7:12).[23] Now that that crisis has been resolved, Paul can encourage them to revive their interrupted participation in the offering for Jerusalem. It was now just a few more months and Paul would be embarking on his journey to Jerusalem with the offering. He did not want possible rich gifts such as the Corinthians might contribute to be lacking, nor did he want them to miss the opportunity this offering presented to them to take advantage of the gracious opportunity God was giving them.[24] "As well" means there was something else which Titus had already completed, but we are at a loss to know exactly the thing which Paul had in mind. Perhaps it refers to the gracious opportunity extended to the Corinthians by God that resulted in the repentance and loyal obedience just mentioned in chapter 7 as brought to completion through Titus' ministry among the Corinthians.

8:7 - *But just as you abound in everything, in faith and utterance and knowledge and in all earnestness and in the love we inspired in you,* see *that you abound in this gracious work also.*

But just as you abound in everything - "But" introduces another and stronger incentive to giving on the part of the Corinthians. Not only is what God has enabled the Macedonians to do an incentive, the Corinthians must also remember what God has done for them. This language in the first part of the verse reminds us of what Paul wrote in 1 Corinthians 1:4-7 where he enumerated some of the things God had done for the Christians at Corinth. Perhaps Paul lists blessings the Corinthians valued, and

---

[22] See page xvii in the Introductory Studies.

[23] When trouble strikes a congregation, the offering is one of the first things to suffer, Coffman (*op. cit.*, p.413) observes.

[24] The Greek behind "this gracious work" is the same Greek we saw translated "favor" in verse 4. See the notes at 2 Corinthians 8:1 on "grace."

then blessings he valued. From folk who have received such blessings Paul has a right to expect much.

In faith - If this list is similar to the one in 1 Corinthians 1 where Paul calls attention to the spiritual gifts that had been bestowed on the Corinthians, then "faith" speaks of the spiritual gift of faith, which includes the powers to work miracles (1 Corinthians 12:9, 13:2).[25]

And utterance - Perhaps it refers to their power of speaking foreign languages (1 Corinthians 1:5, 12:10, 14:2ff).[26]

And knowledge - Likely this is a reference to the spiritual gift called "knowledge" (1 Corinthians 1:5, 12:8, and 13:2).[27]

And in all earnestness - Now we have come to the qualities in the Corinthians that Paul specially valued. The word *spoudē* is translated "earnestness" and combines the ideas of eagerness, earnestness, and carefulness. Fisher writes about "dedication of the Corinthians to the Christian cause."[28] As he did at 7:11, Paul may have been alluding to their readiness and enthusiasm to discharge every duty a Christian should. By implication Paul is hoping that readiness and enthusiasm will carry over into their participation in the offering for Jerusalem.

And in the love we inspired in you - The manuscripts at this place vary between "our love for you"[29] and "your love to us."[30] Literally the Greek reads either "the out of us in you love" or "the out of you in us love." The sense either reading produces is awkward and must be interpreted. We suppose Paul is praising them for one of their qualities, as the NASB has interpreted by speaking of love that Paul has inspired in them. Paul's concern for them has led to their love for Paul being renewed and confirmed by their recent repentance as alluded to in 7:4,6,7,11,16. If they do love

---

[25] "Faith in Christ, such as every believer has," is how Plummer (*op. cit.*, p.238) explains this. God is the source of such faith because He sent messengers who shared the gospel (faith comes by hearing the word of Christ).

[26] Since the Greek is *logos* ("word"), some explain this expression to refer to the ability to instruct others in Christian doctrine.

[27] Those who doubt a reference to spiritual gifts explain it to mean knowledge of God learned through the Gospel.

[28] Fisher, *op. cit.*, p.377

[29] This reading is supported by P[46], B, 1739.

[30] This reading is supported in the Alexandrian, Western, and Byzantine families of manuscripts.

him as he thinks they do, they will be involved in the offering that is dear to the apostle's heart.

See **that you abound in this gracious work also** - Instead of supplying the verb "see" we could just as easily supply "I urge you" from verse 6. Just as the Macedonians abounded ("overflowed," verse 2) he wants the Corinthians to "abound" (i.e., overflow). The Macedonians were in deep poverty. The Corinthians "abound in everything." To whom much is given, much is required. He wanted the Corinthian's contribution to be generous, but he also wanted it to be voluntary. "Gracious work" is the same expression Paul used in verse 6, and carries the same meaning. This offering was a gracious opportunity extended by God to the Corinthians (verse 7) just as it was to the Macedonians (verse 6). Two words have dominated this paragraph: "overflow" (found in verse 2 and twice in verse 7) and "grace" (found in verses 1,4,6,7). Will the Corinthians experience the joy of living out of the overflow when grace presents opportunities? Paul hopes so.[31]

B. The Example of Christ, and the Proportion to Give.   8:8-15

8:8 - *I am not speaking* **this** *as a command, but as proving through the earnestness of others the sincerity of your love also.*

I am not speaking *this* **as a command** - Paul has used some very persuasive language in his appeal to the Corinthians to resume their part in the offering for Jerusalem. Lest they think he is trying to command them what to do he makes it very clear that is not trying to be dictatorial. If he were passing along a command from God he would have worded it as "a command of (from) God" (as in Romans 16:26, 1 Timothy 1:1, Titus 1:3). When Paul says what he has written is not a command he is not disclaiming inspiration or that divine authority is behind what he writes. Rather, as the similar language means in 1 Corinthians 7:6, Paul is saying that he was not trying to order them around in this matter. He does not lord it over anyone's faith (2 Corinthians 1:24). God loves free-will offerings and Paul is not intending to impinge on the Corinthian's freedom in this matter of giving. Rather than being a command, his instructions come in the form of advice (verse 10).

But as proving through the earnestness of others -- Having told them what he was not doing (i.e., he was not trying to dictate to them), he now tells them what he is trying to do as he writes. "Proving" is a common Greek word meaning to test some-

---

[31] Paul is so certain that the old loving relationship between the Corinthians and himself has been restored that he is confident he can ask a favor of them and remind them of their obligations without jeopardizing that newly restored relationship. Nevertheless, he words his appeal cautiously lest old resentments be rekindled. (Plummer, *op. cit.*, p.230).

thing to see if it were genuine or not.[32]   "The others" Paul has already called attention
to are the Macedonian Christians.   Their eagerness to be involved in the offering is
going to be used as a standard of comparison.   Will the Corinthians measure up to
that standard of earnestness and generosity?

The sincerity of your love also -- The RSV translates this clause "that your love also
is genuine."   That catches the idea in the Greek.   Christians are not to love just in
word but also in deed.   "Whoever has the world's goods, and beholds his brother in
need and closes his heart against him, how does the love of God abide in him?" (1
John 3:17).   Whether or not the Corinthians participate in the offering is a test of the
genuineness of their love for their brethren in Christ.   "The most substantial evidence
that our love is genuine, is when we are willing to part with our property, or with
whatever is valuable to us, to confer happiness and salvation on others."[33]   The
enthusiastic generosity of the Macedonian churches was a convenient standard for
assessing the genuineness of the Corinthians' professed love.

8:9 - *For you know the grace of our Lord Jesus Christ, that though He was rich, yet
for your sake He became poor, that you through His poverty might become rich.*

For you know the grace of our Lord Jesus Christ - "For" introduces a reason why
he does not need to issue orders; there are numerous incentives to be generous, the
greatest of which is the example of Christ.[34]   It is likely the Corinthians knew about
the grace of Christ from the gospel sermons they had heard.   Already in this context
(verses 6,7) the Greek word for "grace" (*charis*) has been translated "gracious work."
As Paul has Jesus' incarnation and Calvary in mind, he uses the word in reference to
the "gracious work" Christ did.   The Lord's "gracious work" is the example he wants
the Corinthians to emulate.   The full title ("Lord Jesus Christ") adds to the
impressiveness of the appeal.   When the import of each term is considered, there are
no arguments the Corinthians might give that they are above being involved in
something like a benevolent offering to Jerusalem.

That though He was rich - "Rich" was the condition of Christ's existence before His
incarnation at Bethlehem.   He was rich in the ineffable glory of heaven, and in the

---

[32] *Peirazō* ("to prove") is the common word used of placing precious ores in a crucible where
the dross was burned out, leaving only pure, genuine gold or silver.   The figure should not be
pressed to mean that the Corinthians' participation in the offering to Jerusalem might have something
to do with removing dross from their lives.

[33] Barnes, *op. cit.*, p.181.

[34] Barnes (*ibid.*) has called attention to the fact that Paul was accustomed to illustrate every
subject, and to enforce every duty where it could be done, by a reference to the life and sufferings
of Christ.   He points to examples at Romans 15:2,3, Ephesians 5:2, and Colossians 3;9,10.

independent exercise of divine attributes.   "Was" translates a present tense participle, thus "rich" is something that always was true before His incarnation.   There never was a time back through all eternity when He was not rich.[35]

Yet for your sake He became poor - The aorist tense verb "became poor" points to one act in the past, namely, the moment of His incarnation.   Coffman says Christ's becoming poor "has a double meaning, (1) referring to the contrast between His eternal state and His incarnation, and (2) also to the extraordinary poverty of his earthly state as compared with the affluence of some of his contemporaries."[36]   True as this may be, we believe the emphasis is on the riches Christ possessed in the heavenly world prior to His earthly life and ministry.[37]   Philippians 2:7,8, wherein

---

[35] The pre-existence of Christ is plainly taught here just as it is in Philippians 2:6, where we are informed that Jesus was always "existing in the form of God" before His incarnation. Passages which speak of His preexistence (some of which speak of His eternal pre-existence) are John 1:1, 8:58; Romans 8:3,4; 1 Corinthians 10:4; Galatians 4:4; Colossians 1:16; Hebrews 1:2. Jesus' pre-existence was not an idea that developed late, as certain modern theologians attempt to show, apparently in the mistaken belief that the doctrine is false, and that Jesus somehow grew in people's estimation from a Galilean peasant to a Greek god. 2 Corinthians is an early document, and it flatly affirms Jesus' pre-existence, as do claims from John the Baptist and from Jesus' own lips. (It will not pass critical examination to claim these words were mistakenly put into the mouths of John and Jesus by later writers.) 1 Corinthians 8:6 speaks of Christ's creative work, and if He was active in creation, He was pre-existent. Christians in the mid-AD 50's believed the pre-existence of Jesus because that is what was taught and believed from the first.

[36] Coffman, *op. cit.*, p.412. The word translated "poor" is used of the beggar who was laid at Lazarus' gate (Luke 16:20-22). Our word "pauper" catches the idea. This passage of Scripture was one used in the medieval controversies between the moderate and the extreme members of the mendicant orders. Francis of Assisi and others insisted they must choose the life of the poor (beggars, mendicants) in order to follow Jesus' life-style, here described as "poverty." William of Ockam and others, taking the word "poverty" in its extreme sense, maintained that the Franciscans ought to possess nothing. On the other side of the controversy was Pope John XXII and the Dominicans, who took a more rational view of the sense of this passage and of the historic facts. While Jesus' life is one Christians imitate, it cannot be demonstrated that all Jesus' followers should aim to be as poor as He was (the Greek word could be translated "beggar"). When it comes to imitating Jesus, what this passage does teach is that His followers should aim at a readiness to be helpful to others, whatever it might cost to offer such help.

[37] Adam Clarke's comment at this place on the pre-existence of Christ is helpful. "If Jesus Christ was only a man, in what sense could he be rich? Joseph and Mary were poor in Jerusalem, and poor in Nazareth; and, from the stable to the cross, Jesus never possessed any property among men, nor did he have anything at his death to bequeath, except his peace! The question of the riches of Christ, on the Socinian scheme, can never be satisfactorily answered" (*Clarke's Commentary on the New Testament* [New York: Methodist Book Concern, 1855], Vol.2, p. 349).

Coffman (*ibid.*) adds a valuable paragraph about supernaturalism. "The simple objective truth of Christianity is founded upon the conviction of the supernatural. In the final analysis, if there is no supernatural, there is no Christianity. So-called Christians who do not believe in the supernatural are unbelievers; and there can be no reconciliation of the supernaturalness of Christianity with the existential and speculative denials of it. What is affirmed in the New Testament is either true or false; and this student of the New Testament believes it to be true. Paul here assumed as fact, nor did he even pause to defend it, that Christ existed with God before the earth was created. No one can know the mind of Paul without seeing this fundamental truth."

Paul tells how Jesus "emptied Himself, taking the form of a servant," gives us a glimpse of the poverty into which Jesus voluntarily entered, a poverty that involves being subject to suffering and death, as well as being involved in serving others. "For your sake" helps us see the point of this appeal to the example of Christ. This makes what Jesus did intensely personal. Jesus was willing to become poor if He could benefit others. That is how love works. Will the Corinthians imitate the example of their Lord and Savior?

That you through His poverty might become rich - The reason Jesus gave until He became poor was so that people like the Corinthian Christians might become rich.[38] Had he not given until He had no more to give, the Corinthians (and we) would forever remain destitute – destitute of forgiveness of sins, holiness, happiness, and fellowship with God in heaven. It does not refer to being rich in this world's goods. It refers, rather, to spiritual riches in heavenly places such as Ephesians 1:3 points to. The two words "poverty" and "rich" drive home the point Paul is making. The Corinthians were relatively rich in this world's goods. He hoped to lead them to be sacrificially generous to relieve the "poverty" of the saints in Jerusalem. What better example could he find than the example of the Lord Jesus Christ? "No one can enter into the meaning of this verse or feel its power, without being thereby made willing to sacrifice himself for the good of others. It is vain for any person to imagine that he loves Christ if he does not love the brethren and is not liberal in relieving their needs."[39]

8:10 - *And I give* my *opinion in this matter, for this is to your advantage, who were the first to begin a year ago not only to do* this, *but also to desire* to do it.

And I give *my* **opinion in this matter** - The word translated "opinion" is *gnome*. Here, as at 1 Corinthians 7:26, *gnōmē* is contrasted with *epitagē* ("command"). The Latin Vulgate used *consilium* (counsel, advice) to translate *gnōmē*. He told them in his first letter to Corinth (1 Corinthians 7:40) that he believes his *gnōmē* is worth considering, because behind it is the prompting of the Holy Spirit. Rather than command them what to do, he is laying down what is the Christian thing to do, and leaves them to act upon it, or not, according to their own free will.

For this is to your advantage - "This" may point back to his giving them advice rather than commanding, or it might refer more particularly to their participation in the relief fund for Jerusalem. Or perhaps "this" points back to winning the riches of Christ by imitating His example of giving. In any case, Paul is saying that to get involved in the offering is something that will prove profitable to them, both in time and eternity.

---

[38] The dative here probably means 'as a consequence of his poverty' rather than 'by means of his poverty.'

[39] Lipscomb, *op. cit.*, p.113.

Who were the first to begin a year ago - Paul has been comparing the Macedonian Christians with the Corinthian Christians. The offering is pictured as being an honorable competition. The Corinthians had started well, but the Macedonians (starting their participation in the offering at a later time than the Corinthians) had overtaken them. Are the Corinthians now going to become bystanders and let the Macedonians continue to set the pace in this friendly competition? With all their problems (as indicated in 1 Corinthians), the Corinthians Christians have some very admirable qualities. They were the first group of Christians to desire to raise a relief fund for their needy brethren in Jerusalem, they were the first to actually begin collecting the funds that would be eventually delivered to Jerusalem. And that was "a year ago." It is not easy to fix the exact limits of the time here indicated.[40] Had an entire year elapsed since the relief project had been initiated? Perhaps so, or nearly so. 1 Corinthians was written about Passover time, AD 57. After writing 1 Corinthians, Paul remained at Ephesus a while, made his intermediate trip to Corinth, returned to Ephesus, sent Titus to Corinth, then went to Troas and Macedonia to await Titus' report. Count in the longer-than-expected time until Titus arrived to report to Paul, it is certainly the fall of the year by the time 2 Corinthians was written. Since the Corinthians apparently knew about the offering before they received 1 Corinthians (see notes at 2 Corinthians 8:6), at least 10 or 12 months must have passed since the offering was first initiated among them.

Not only to do *this*, but also to desire *to do it* - It should not be thought strange that Paul's order of words is first "do" and then "desire." Such a word order is a way to praise them for being not only the first to get involved in the offering, but also praise them for being the first even to desire to get involved.[41] Perhaps in the word "desire" lies the two notions of the cheerful giver (2 Corinthians 9:7) and the willing mind that is generous and willing to share (1 Timothy 6:17-19). Paul seems to be asking, "Have you Corinthians lost both the doing and the desire to do it?" If a year has elapsed with little or no offerings collected, there have been a lot of lost opportunities. No wonder it was expedient for them to be "doing" again!

8:11 - *But now finish doing it also; that just as* there was *the readiness to desire it, so* there may be *also the completion of it by your ability.*

---

[40] Some versions such as the NIV read "last year." Others (KJV, ASV, NASB) read "a year ago." The translations reflect the ambiguity in the way ancients reckoned time. At times they counted a part of a year as a whole year. On the other hand "a year ago" might mean a full 12 months. Then we may also need to consider the fact that the new year began in Macedonia in the month of September or October. If 2 Corinthians were written after the new year began, the previous months of January to April would be "last year."

[41] To say on the basis of the word order here that in the field of morals it is the willingness that is of value and not what is accomplished, is not satisfactory.

But now finish doing it also - Verse 11 completes the thought begun in verse 10.[42] "Now" (*nuni de*) is emphatic, "Now, this very moment."   Enough time has elapsed; no more time should be allowed to pass before they again get eagerly involved in the offering, for the poor saints in Jerusalem still have a pressing need for relief.   Rather than merely being satisfied with what had been collected in the past, Paul urges them to complete or finish what they had begun so well by again laying aside funds on the first day of the week as they had been prospered (cf. 1 Corinthians 16:2).

That just as *there was* the readiness to desire it - Paul had boasted to the Macedonian Christians (2 Corinthians 9:2) about the Corinthian's readiness to participate in the needed offering.   How sad and disappointing it would be for those who were first in desiring and actually beginning to raise funds to now show they had lost the desire to continue their participation.

So *there may be* also the completion of it - Paul urges the Corinthians to take advantage of this favorable opportunity to finish what they had promised and started.

By your ability - The Greek reads literally "out of what you have."   As the next verse goes on to explain, the point Paul is now making is that their giving is to be in proportion to what they possess.   He has been comparing the Corinthians to the Macedonians, but there is one area where he is not asking the Corinthians to be like the Macedonians.   They gave "beyond their means" (verse 3); he is not asking the Corinthians to go beyond their means like the Macedonians did.   But their giving should be in proportion to their ability to give,[43] and it should be given without further delay.

8:12 - *For if the readiness is present, it is acceptable according to what* **a man** *has, not according to what he does not have.*

For if the readiness is present - Paul here explains what he meant when in the previous verse he said "by your ability."   Verse 10 spoke about a desire to give, and verse 11 of a readiness (eagerness) to give.   God loves a cheerful giver, that is, an eager desire to give.   It is the heart that God looks at first, rather than the relative amount given.   And no donation, whether it be a small amount or even though it be a huge amount, is acceptable if a readiness/eagerness does not exist in the giver's mind.

---

[42] Three stages in their participation in the offering are distinctly marked out by Paul.   It began with a desire (the purpose in their mind to give or a readiness to give), beginning to go about giving (the beginning of the collection), and finishing what they had begun.

[43] While 2 Corinthians deals with a special benevolent offering, rather than regular giving for the cause of Christ, the principles followed in the offering for Jerusalem are in perfect harmony with what God expects in any giving.   Christians are expected to give according to their means, in proportion to what God has entrusted to them to manage.   To whom much is given, much is required (Luke 12:48).

It is acceptable according to what *a man* has - "Acceptable" refers to how the offering looks in God's eyes. Paul is not making rules about what was or was not acceptable in God's sight; rather, he is reflecting what God has revealed about giving. "What a man has" is something that is true of both the rich and the poor. "If one is able to give one dime or one cent and fails to give it, he is just as culpable before God as is the man who is able to give a thousand dollars and fails to give it to the Lord. God values, blesses, and rewards gifts according to the sacrifices made, not according to the amount given."[44]

Not according to what he does not have - No one is expected or required to give what he does not have. He may give all he has, as did the poor widow whom Jesus praised when she gave her last two small coins (Mark 12:42-44; Luke 21:1-4), but each person's obligation is proportioned to his or her ability. God considers not the magnitude of the gift, but the proportion which it bears to the means of the giver.

8:13 - *For this is not for the ease of others and for your affliction, but by way of equality* –

For *this* is not for the ease of others - "This" (added in italics to express the idea of the Greek) likely expresses the idea behind giving according to his ability. Paul tells them specifically what he is thinking as he writes what he does. He is interested in believers ministering to others when they have opportunity, for the day may come when they will need help and they, in turn, can then be ministered to by the very ones they earlier have helped. "Ease" refers to the circumstances changed for the better when the relief offering has been received, for the desperate burdens their poverty added to their lives would be lifted. Needy Jerusalem Christians are evidently the ones intended by "others."[45]

***And* for your affliction** - "Affliction" speaks of hardship or the pressure of an intolerable burden. There is no intention on Paul's part to relieve the hardships the Jerusalem Christians are enduring by plunging the donors into similar hardships that accompany poverty. As he asks for their participation in the offering, Paul is not asking them to give until they themselves are forced to live in poverty.

But by way of equality - The adversative "but" says that contrary to the idea he was trying to put an unfair hardship on them, his real goal was equality.[46]   The topic is

---

[44] Lipscomb, *op. cit.*, p.114.

[45] It is not possible to determine with certainty whether or not this disclaimer is an answer to an innuendo made by Paul's opponents (that he is just attempting to provide funds for Jewish Christians at the expense of the Gentile churches), or whether it is something the Corinthians may have raised to justify their recent lack of participation in the offering.

[46] NASB closes verse 13 with a dash, showing the flow of grammar is not smooth. The KJV and RSV close verse 13 after the word "affliction" (burden), and then connect this clause with verse

supplying material help when brethren need it.[47]   As verse 14 will show, in his mind Paul thinks of the possibility in the future when the fortunes of the brethren at Corinth and Jerusalem could be reversed.   Then the Jerusalem Christians could send financial help to their brethren in Corinth.   What Paul envisions for the church is a mutual give and take where persons who now have the means minister to those who do not; and when circumstances change, the one who received becomes the one who gets to minister.   When there is such reciprocity, the principle of proportionate giving made the burden equal on those who participate in it.[48]

8:14 - *at this present time your abundance* **being a supply** *for their want, that their abundance also may become* **a supply** *for your want, that there may be equality;*

At this present time your abundance *being a supply* **for their want** - "Your abundance" indicates that at this time in history the Corinthians were better off financially than the saints at Jerusalem who were in want and poverty.   "Want" translates *husterēma*, the same used of the destitute widow (Luke 21:4).   Since Paul in this chapter has been comparing the Corinthians and the Macedonians, perhaps "your abundance" means the Corinthians were relatively more prosperous than the Macedonians (2 Corinthians 8:2).   That being so, the Corinthians were better able to contribute a larger amount of money than were other churches.   God has supplied the Corinthians with the means to relieve their brethren.   It would be proof of a lack of gratitude for what God has done if they fail to again become involved in the offering for Jerusalem.

That their abundance also may become *a supply* **for your want** - Paul envisions the possibility that in the future there could be a change in fortune and the Jerusalem church would be expected to come to the financial relief of the Corinthians.   Paul may even imply that if he were still living he would not fail to plead with the brethren

---

14 with no dash, so that it reads, "but that as a matter of equality your abundance at the present time should supply their want, so that their abundance may supply your want, that there may be equality." Either way we punctuate it, the idea Paul is expressing is understandable.

[47] We need not bring in here the thought included at Romans 15;27, as Paul discusses this very offering for Jerusalem, of Gentiles giving material help to Jerusalem in return for spiritual help they have already received from the Jerusalem church, who gave themselves poor that the gospel might spread.   After all, it is not easy to envision a situation where Corinth might give spiritual help to Jerusalem.

[48] Some have taken the verse out of context to make it support a political philosophy that calls for an artificial equalization of all property.   This allows some who are able to work nevertheless to live off the sweat of those who do work.   Coffman (*op. cit.*, p.414) calls such a use of this passage deplorable.   Paul's object was the relief of those who through no fault of their own were in poverty. At 2 Thessalonians 3:10, "The poor are commanded 'with quietness to work, and to eat their own bread,' inculcating on the poor the duty of self-support to the extent of their ability" (Hughes, *op. cit.*, p.307).

at Jerusalem just as fervently as he now pleads of the Corinthians' assistance.[49]

That there may be equality - The idea of "equality" (spoken of earlier in this context) is repeated for emphasis. Paul's motives were not to take money from the Corinthians for the purpose of impoverishing them so as to enrich the Christians at Jerusalem. He was rather teaching a pattern for relief work, a pattern that is taught in a well-known example from the Old Testament.

8:15 - *as it is written, "HE WHO gathered DID NOT HAVE TOO MUCH, AND HE WHO gathered LITTLE HAD NO LACK."*

As it is written - The quotation is from the LXX of Exodus 16:17,18, to illustrate the idea of reciprocal sharing. There was a mutual give and take in the gathering of the manna.

"HE WHO *gathered* MUCH DID NOT HAVE TOO MUCH, AND HE WHO *gathered* LITTLE HAD NO LACK" - Commentators on the Exodus passage have been divided concerning what it actually says, whether or not God miraculously subtracted from those who gathered too much while miraculously adding to the bowls of those who had gathered too little.[50] As Paul applies the idea in the passage to sharing in an offering to needy brethren, he does not seem to treat the equality of manna for each person as something done miraculously.[51] The manna which fell around the camp of Israel was to be gathered in the morning, before the heat from the rising sun would cause it to melt into liquid. All who were able were employed in gathering it. Some were more successful than others in how much they collected. When it was brought back to the camp, the amount each person had collected was measured by an omer. If he had a surplus, it went to supply the wants of some other family that had not been able to collect a sufficiency. Thus the one who had gathered little had no lack. Those who gathered more than an omer would constantly be manifesting a spirit of benevolence. The lesson being taught is that if each will give freely to help others, none will want. From the instructions from God concerning the

---

[49] When dogmatic theology flourished and theological students were instructed to find verses in the Bible to support the dogma taught by the Roman Catholic church, this passage became one of the proof texts for works of supererogation. One wonders how it is possible to see in these verses the doctrine that men are to give to the poor so that in the hour of death and in the day of judgment the donors may receive from the recipients of the alms a transfer of their superfluous merits.

[50] Ancient Jewish interpreters understand by this statement in Exodus 16:17,18 that whatever quantity each person had gathered, when he measured it in his tent, he found that he had just as many omers as he needed for the consumption of his family. (F.C. Cook, "Exodus," in *The Bible Commentary* [London: John Murray, 1871], Vol.1, p.318.)

[51] Certainly there was miracle in the daily provision of the manna over a period of 40 years, and in how long it kept before it bred worms and stank (one day during the week, two days over Friday and Saturday). When they settled in the land of Canaan the manna ceased (Exodus 16:35-36).

manna Paul draws a lesson from the Old Testament that rich Christians at Corinth should impart freely to their poorer brethren.[52]

C. Commendation of Those Engaged in Superintending the Collection.   8:16-24

8:16 - *But thanks be to God, who puts the same earnestness on your behalf in the heart of Titus.*

But thanks be to God - Because Paul is so anxious that the Corinthian portion of the offering be generous, he now begins to tell them about the arrangements he is making to help them complete their part of the offering and to avoid any breath of scandal about how the money was handled (verse 20).   To start with, he tells them about Titus and two other brothers whom he has sent to Corinth to aid in the administration of the fund raising.   Paul begins by telling the Corinthians how he gives thanks[53] to God for Titus.

Who puts the same earnestness on your behalf in the heart of Titus - Titus (Paul tells them), the one who likely introduced the matter of the offering to the Corinthians, and who likely carried 1 Corinthians from Paul to Corinth, and who recently has been a successful troubleshooter helping the church practice needed discipline, has an enthusiastic concern[54] for the Corinthians.   That concern was given[55] to Titus by God, says Paul.   Since the present tense verb "puts" indicates continuous or repeated action, we suppose each of Titus' trips to Corinth was motivated by his God-given earnest concern.   Or perhaps "same" and "for you" may indicate that Paul's special concern at the moment of writing, namely, the important offering for Jerusalem, has now become Titus' concern also.   The Corinthians should not think that Paul and Titus are interested only in the relief of the Jerusalem poor; no, indeed, their zeal is on behalf of the Corinthians' spiritual welfare.   If the Corinthians will renew their participation in this offering, it will do much for the unity of the church.   More im-

---

[52] "Those who tried to hoard the manna found that 'it bred worms and stank' (Exodus 16:20); and this is precisely what is true of hoarded wealth in all ages" (Coffman, *op. cit.*, p.415).

[53] *Charis* is the word in the original.   The changes of meaning in this chapter with regard to *charis* should be noted.   The NIV uses "grace" (when it refers to God's generosity or to his enablement), "privilege" (referring to the honor and opportunity of participating in the offering), "act of grace" or "offering" (when referring to the offering itself as an expression of goodwill), "grace of giving" (when it refers to a virtuous act of sharing or helping), and "thanks" (when it speaks of prayer), all as translations for *charis* in this context.

[54] "Earnestness" translates *spoudē*, the word we have already had in verses 7 and 8.

[55] The word translated "puts" is the present tense of the verb "give."   God can put things in a man's heart (that is, He can plant thoughts and ideas in the man's mind).   The man will recognize the opportunity set before him and of his own free will set about to do what God has suggested.

portantly, it will also do much for the Corinthians' spiritual growth. The Corinthians will be the chief losers if they continue to fail to participate in the offering.

8:17 - *For he not only accepted our appeal, but being himself very earnest, he has gone to you of his own accord.*

For he not only accepted our appeal - Verse 6 told us that Paul requested that Titus undertake the superintending of the completion of the collection at Corinth.

But being himself very earnest - Here we learn that Titus eagerly accepted (welcomed) the invitation. "Very earnest" is the comparative adjective form of the word "earnestness" in verse 16; he was more earnest than ever about ministering to the Corinthians. Titus is coming to Corinth not only at Paul's authorized request but also because Titus himself wanted to come.

He is going to you of his own accord - The Greek verb translated "is going" is an aorist tense and is an example of what is known as an epistolary aorist.[56] As Paul was writing this letter, Titus was not already on the road, but would start for Corinth, likely carrying this letter, as soon as it was finished. At verse 3 Paul used the Greek word *authairetos* to describe how the Macedonians gave of their own accord, of their own free will. He uses the same word to describe Titus' response to his request to return to Corinth to undertake the work of finishing their offering for Jerusalem. Thus, Titus' credentials have been called to the attention of the Corinthians. Indeed, he is traveling at Paul's request, but Titus is doing something he wanted to do. The Corinthians should respond positively to the ministry of such a man with gladness.

8:18 - *And we have sent along with him the brother whose fame in* **the things of** *the gospel* **has spread** *through all the churches;*

And we have sent along with him the brother - "Have sent" is another epistolary aorist tense verb in the Greek. It looks at things from the time when the letter is read at Corinth, rather than at the time when the letter was being written. Thus, Paul introduces and commends the second of the three workers whom he is sending to Corinth to aid in the administration of the offering. Though "brother" might mean a brother in Christ, something can be said for this first helper being Titus' literal brother. Out of all the conjectures offered in an attempt to identify this brother, the best one is that this brother is Luke. In the next verse, Paul tells us that this brother had been appointed to travel with Paul to carry the offering to Jerusalem: Luke fits that criter-

---

[56] On what the epistolary and historical aorist tense verbs imply, see the Introductory Studies on 1 Corinthians and also notes at 1 Corinthians 5:9. Paul speaks of Titus' return trip to Corinth as an event already completed, because it would be completed when the Corinthians read this epistle.

ion, for he was in the company who traveled with Paul to Jerusalem (Acts 20:2ff).[57] Luke also fits what is said in the remainder of this verse, better than do some of the other conjectures. Further, an argument that Luke is the intended unnamed worker has been deduced from the fact Titus is not named in Acts which was written by Luke. Though present at the Jerusalem Conference (Galatians 2:3), perhaps the reason why Titus is not mentioned in Acts (Acts 15:1-21) is because Luke chose not to give the names of his own family members in his history book. It appears they were brothers in the flesh and brothers in the faith.

Whose fame in *the things of* the gospel *has spread* through all the churches - If we accept the words added in italics as the NASB does, this phrase is interpreted to mean that this second worker was well-known among the churches as a preacher of the gospel.[58] Of all the conjectures attempting to identify this helper, Luke fits this criterion best. The first time we are introduced to Luke in Acts is at 16:10 where Luke says, "God called us to preach." That implies that Luke too is a preacher of the gospel just as Paul and Silas were, and also that he was involved in preaching before he joined Paul's missionary team. Perhaps he was responsible for planting the congregation of Christians who lived in Troas (cp. Acts 20:6 and 2 Corinthians 2:12). The presence, then the absence, of the "we" passages in Acts indicate that Luke was left at Philippi from the time when Paul visited there on the Second Missionary Journey till the time of his return on the Third Journey, a period of 5 or 6 years. During that time, Luke might have become a favorite in Macedonia, and be an obvious person of whom it could be said he is a well-known gospel preacher among the churches.[59] Perhaps this long introduction implies the Corinthians do not know Luke personally; that being so, Paul shows he was very much respected by the churches who knew him. Plumptre calls attention to the fact that Luke would be qualified to stir up the Corinthians in this matter of the offering. In his Gospel he dwells emphatically on all parts of our Lord's teaching that point out the danger of riches and the blessedness of generous alms-giving. Not only is this so, but surely it

---

[57] Other guesses which name another one of the messengers from the churches (Acts 20:4) have no more evidence behind them than the fact that 2 Corinthians 8:19 says he had been appointed by the churches to travel with Paul as they carried the offering to Jerusalem.

[58] Adam Clarke (*op. cit.*, p.350) capitalized the word "Gospel" at this place, making it clear that in his opinion the brother sent with Titus was the author of the third Gospel. It has been customary to date Luke's Gospel about AD 60, since the two years while Paul was imprisoned at Caesarea would have given his companion Luke a window of opportunity to conduct the personal interviews that Luke 1:1-4 indicates he did in preparation to write. Further, Acts is volume 2 of the same set of history (the history of Christ and early Christianity), and it is usually assumed to have been written about AD 63, which would require volume 1 (the Gospel) to have been completed earlier. Of course, if the date we have assigned to Luke's Gospel is later than it actually was written, it would be possible that 2 Corinthians 8:18 could be a reference to that Gospel as already written and as already being well-known.

[59] "Famous for the gospel" speaks of Luke being well-known as an effective preacher of the gospel. It would be difficult to show, for example, that men such as Tychicus and Trophimus already have such a reputation by the time 2 Corinthians was written.

was Luke who guided the Philippian church to be generous in its missionary support of Paul (Acts 16:40, Philippians 4:15; 2 Corinthians 11:9).[60]

8:19 - *and not only* **this**, *but he has also been appointed by the churches to travel with us in this gracious work, which is being administered by us for the glory of the Lord Himself, and* to show *our readiness,*

And not only *this* - Assuming the second helper introduced in verse 18 is Luke, verse 19 continues listing his credentials. Not only is he highly esteemed for his gospel preaching, but the churches have honored him by appointing him to carry their portion of the collection to Jerusalem.

But he has also been appointed by the churches - Paul had directed each congregation to choose someone they trusted to convey their portion of the offering to Jerusalem (1 Corinthians 16:3). "Appointed" (*cheirotoneō*) tells us that he had been selected by public vote just as Paul directed the churches to do.[61] We are to think of Macedonian congregations as being intended by "the churches," but just which ones? We know of Macedonian congregations in Philippi, Thessalonica, and Berea. Acts 20:4 tells us the names of the representatives from Berea and Thessalonica. Perhaps, then, the churches who appointed Luke to carry their offering were those in and around Philippi.

To travel with us in this gracious work - "Gracious work" (see verses 1,4,6,7) is one of the series of words used in 2 Corinthians to refer to the offering for Jerusalem. Each church sent its own representatives with Paul, carrying the offering from each particular church. Many are named at Acts 20:4. All the messengers would travel together with Paul as they made their way to Jerusalem. While Luke is not named in Acts 20:4 as one of the messengers, the use of the first person plural from Acts 20:5 on does indicate Luke was traveling with Paul and the messengers.

Which is being administered by us - "Administered" translates the verb *diakoneō*, to minister or to serve. Paul and Titus and others have been instrumental in spearheading the drive for relief, but Paul thinks of himself and his helpers only as servants of Christ in this matter.

For the glory of the Lord Himself - The thread of thought in the Greek is a bit am-

---

[60] Plumptre, *op. cit.*, p.77.

[61] The word *cheirotoneō* (the same word used at Acts 14:23) speaks of "stretching the hands." Originally, it meant to elect by a show of hands such as would be done in a vote of the people; then it came to mean to elect in any way; finally it came to mean appoint, whether by election or not. (In this latter sense it may picture the laying on of hands as done in an ordination service.) We do not know whether or not Luke was "ordained" to this task by the churches after they chose him to be their messenger.

biguous.   Perhaps it says the brother was appointed to promote the glory of Christ. Perhaps it says the offering was being administered to promote the glory of Christ. Either way, in his mind, Paul pictures the offering as causing people to think well of Jesus, who was concerned about the needs, physical and spiritual, of His people.

And *to show* **our readiness** - The addition of "to show" in italics indicates this clause is controlled by the same Greek preposition that introduced the previous phrase.   We might offer the translation "to promote" in both clauses.   The offering would promote both the glory of the Lord and Paul's readiness.[62]   "Readiness" is the same word we had in verses 11,12, for which we have used the words eagerness and enthusiasm. Paul seems to be saying that his enthusiasm about the success of this offering at Corinth has been greatly increased by the fact that Titus has been joined by such a helper as Luke.

8:20 - *taking precaution that no one should discredit us in our administration of this generous gift;*

Taking precaution - "Taking precaution" (*stellomai*) is a nautical term used for the furling of sails which was done as a precaution in anticipation of danger.   The present tense participle indicates that Paul continually was taking precautions against any possible accusation that he misappropriated the funds.

That no one should discredit us - *Mōmaomai* can mean to condemn, to criticize, to find fault with.   Paul, who often extolled the virtue of being blameless (*amōmos*, Ephesians 1:4, 5:27; Philippians 2:15), here practices what he preached.   He took precautions lest any hint of blame be leveled against him concerning how the money was handled.   What was intended for the glory of Christ was not to be tarnished by any evil suspicion about what happened to the funds.[63]   First, the churches appointed messengers they trusted.   When the offering had been delivered, the messengers could report back to the several churches from which the money had been collected, telling them of its delivery and how it was received.[64]

---

[62] The KJV reflects the fact that some ancient manuscripts read "your" readiness, rather than "our readiness."   In this case, the meaning is, Titus and Luke are coming to give the Corinthians an opportunity to show their readiness to do good to others and promote their welfare.

[63] Paul was not secretly keeping a large portion of the offering as a commission for his services as prime mover behind the idea of the offering.

[64] As 2 Corinthians 12:17,18 show, Paul was particularly sensitive to charges that he misused funds.   Commentators at this place pause to make application to today's church leaders as they urge those leaders to exhibit the same caution Paul used in the handling and management of church funds.   Just like Paul's enemies would pounce on even the slightest appearance he was misusing funds, so, today, enemies of the cross love to raise suspicions in people's minds that the funds they entrusted to the leaders were embezzled and appropriated to personal use.   In so doing they can thereby destroy the leader's ministry.   To help administer the offering for Jerusalem, Paul involved others who had the entire confidence of the churches,   in order to make sure they were above the

In our administration of this generous gift - "Administration" is the same word found at verse 19 where the idea of "ministry" being done for Christ is involved. It covers both the collection of the gift and its delivery as something being done for the Lord. "Generous gift" translates *hadrotēs*, a word that signifies succulence or juiciness in plants or fruits. It means bounty or abundance. Paul was already aware that the offering from Macedonia was a large one; he expected the offerings from the other churches to be just as abundant.

8:21 - *for we have regard for what is honorable, not only in the sight of the Lord, but also in the sight of man.*

For we have regard for what is honorable - Paul is quoting the LXX of Proverbs 3:4 as a reason for "taking precaution."[65] He evidently has learned one of the rules by which he lives from the Old Testament Scriptures. It is a rule upon which he is acting in the present circumstances concerning the offering – everything must be above reproach. When others looked at his behavior they must see something that is *kala* ("honorable" or beautiful and attractive). Paul deliberately took steps beforehand so that his enemies would have no handle to which they might attach slanderous insinuations.

Not only in the sight of the Lord - Here is a reminder that the Lord Jesus is watching His servants. They must give thought to what He will think of their thoughts and actions. In this case, had Paul had only the judgment of the Lord to consider, he could well have taken the money up to Jerusalem by himself. It would all have been delivered to its intended recipients. In that matter, Paul had nothing to fear from the Lord.

But also in the sight of men - Proverbs 3:4, however, says more than being concerned with what the Lord thinks. It also teaches that a man must be concerned that his conduct appears honorable to men.[66] "Not to care what others think of us may be unfair to them. It would have been disastrous to his converts for them to be

---

possibility of suspicion. Coffman (*op. cit.*, p.418) makes this application: "The wise, prudent, and business-like handling of a congregation's financial affairs is without exception prerequisite to any general confidence of a congregation in its leadership." "There is such a thing as a foolish and reprehensible indifference to public opinion (1 Peter 2:12)" (Farrar, *op. cit.*, p.197).

[65] English readers may not recognize the fact, but readers of the Greek Bible would recognize at once that these words ("respect what is right in the sight of the Lord and men") come from Proverbs. It literally means to take forethought or to think ahead of time about how others will view what we are about to do. We might have expected the NASB to have these words in small caps, but those translators did not use small caps at Romans 12:17 where Paul quoted the same passage from Proverbs as a reason why Christians do not seek to take revenge.

[66] An old Chinese proverb says "In a field of melons, do not stoop to tie your shoe." The point of the proverb is that it will look to others as if you were stealing one of the melons. (Farrar, *op. cit.*, p.197)

able to suspect Paul of dishonesty."[67]   Because he was listening to the Word of God, Paul took the precautions he did concerning this offering for Jerusalem, and had each congregation choose its own trusted representatives to deliver the offering in person, and if need be, give an account for it.

8:22 - *And we have sent with them our brother, whom we have often tested and found diligent in many things, but now even more diligent, because of his great confidence in you.*

And we have sent with them our brother - Since verse 16 Paul has been introducing Titus and the men who with him who have been sent to administer the offering at Corinth.[68]   In addition to the brother (Luke) already introduced at verse 18 there is another helper who will be traveling with Titus and Luke.   It is impossible to identify with any certainty who this second brother was.   Almost all the names suggested as being the "brother" of verse 18 are again offered here.   Verse 23 indicates he, too, has been chosen by the churches to be a messenger to help carry the offering to Jerusalem.   Clement, Paul's fellow-worker (Philippians 4:3), has been proposed as being this second brother,[69] as have Trophimus and Tychicus.[70]   The Greek phrase translated "our brother" at this place is slightly different than the Greek behind "the (his) brother" at verse 18.   Paul seems to be saying that this helper is a fellow-Christian rather than a brother in the flesh.[71]   Having considered the options, it is probable that this other "brother" is Timothy who was present with Paul when 2 Corinthians was written (2 Corinthians 1:1).   If he leaves after 2 Corinthians was written and sent, it explains why he is not named in Galatians, which was likely written shortly after 2 Corinthians was sent on its way.   Timothy is named as one of the messengers of the churches (Acts 20:4) but the church which chose him is not identified.   He thus could be one who was appointed by the Macedonian churches to

---

[67] Plummer, *op. cit.*, p.250.

[68] "Have sent" is an epistolary aorist.

[69] Clement was connected with the church at Philippi. If he helped carry their part of the offering that would satisfy what is said of this brother at 2 Corinthians 8:23. If we assume the identity of this Clement with the Clement of Rome who a quarter of a century later wrote a letter to Corinth (1 Clement), we have an illustration of his diligence in many things (2 Corinthians 8:22). On the other hand, it appears that the distinction drawn in 2 Corinthians 9:4 between these "brethren" and the Macedonians may exclude Clement.

[70] Farrar (*op. cit.*, p.197) tells us that Stanley conjectured that the two who accompanied Titus were the Ephesians Tychicus and Trophimus. Plumptre (*op. cit.*, p.78) fills in the arguments given to support this guess. Tychicus and Trophimus were messengers who helped carry the offering (Acts 20:4). Paul speaks well of them in Ephesians 6:21 and Colossians 4:7. In 2 Timothy 4:12 and Titus 3:12 we have further evidence that Tychicus was on other occasions sent on a mission by Paul.

[71] While we are told Paul had a sister (Acts 23:16), we know of no physical brother. Even if he had a brother, he could not have made use of him in the administration of the offering and still kept himself free from suspicion of misappropriation of funds.

convey their portion of the offering to Jerusalem (just as verse 23 indicates). Since the two helpers are not named, it is implied either that Titus would personally introduce the two unnamed "brothers" when he and they arrived in Corinth, or else that the Corinthians already knew both of these men so well they would need no introduction when they arrived in Corinth.

Whom we have often tested and found diligent in many things - These words show that this other "brother" had been a long-time associate of Paul's, and had proven himself valuable and eager whenever he was given special tasks. "Tested" seems not to mean that Paul had deliberately and often put him to the test, but rather that as he had watched this brother carry out those tasks, he always came through. Implied is the question, Will the Corinthians keep him from doing well on this assignment? "Diligent" translates the same word that was translated "earnestness" in verses 7 and 16. In the past, when asked to do a task, he undertook his assignment eagerly.

But now even more diligent, because of *his* great confidence in you - Eager as he was to carry out past assignments, this brother was even more eager to be engaged in this ministry. Perhaps this man's eagerness concerning this relief-fund was increased when he saw that Titus was "very earnest" (verse 17, where the same word in the Greek is used of Titus). Was Titus' enthusiasm contagious? Just as Paul expressed his confidence in the Corinthians (2 Corinthians 7:4,16), this other brother likewise has confidence they will do well. If this other "brother" is Timothy, his confidence may well be the result of his own personal experiences with the Corinthian Christians (Acts 18:5; 1 Corinthians 16:10) as well as echoing Paul's confidence. By the way he introduces this second helper Paul hopes to provide further motivation for the Corinthians. Implied is the question, 'You won't disappoint this brother's confidence by failing to give liberally, will you?'

8:23 - *As for Titus,* he is *my partner and fellow worker among you; as for our brethren,* they are *messengers of the churches, a glory to Christ.*

As for Titus - There is no verb in the Greek, but the NASB catches the sense suggested by the Greek when it opens the verse with "as for Titus." Perhaps Paul's intent, as he finishes his commendation of the team of helpers whom he has sent to Corinth, is to make it clear that Titus is the leader of the team. Perhaps he is also anticipating a possible question by someone at Corinth concerning what authority these folk have to engage in the administration of the offering.

***He is* my partner and fellow-worker among you** - Titus, the team leader, can perfectly represent the wishes of Paul since he has worked right alongside Paul and knows his mind. To call Titus a partner (*koinōnos*) and fellow worker (*sunergos*) is a very meaningful commendation of Titus. Some of Titus' work is described in 2 Corinthians 2:13, 7:4ff, and 12:18. Later, he would serve at Paul's request or direction as evangelist on the island of Crete (Titus 1:5). Titus 1:5 does not say that Titus is Paul's personal representative to Crete any more than this verse in 2 Corinthians identifies him as a personal representative.

As for our brethren - The "brethren" are the two men (verses 18,22) who were to accompany Titus on this trip to Corinth.

***They are* messengers of the churches** - The churches intended are the congregations in Macedonia, the location from which Paul is writing this letter. As the footnote to the text shows, the word translated "messengers" is the same Greek word regularly translated "apostles." *Apostolos* refers to anyone commissioned to do a job or sent on a mission (see notes at 1:1). Paul does not call them "apostles of Christ."[72] The two brethren had been commissioned or chosen, not by Christ, but by the churches to convey to Jerusalem the money which the churches had contributed to the offering. To have been so selected by the churches speaks volumes concerning these men's character and abilities. Another example of an "apostle" commissioned by a church rather than personally by Christ is Epaphroditus, who is called a "messenger" (*apostolos*) of the church at Philippi (Philippians 2:25).[73]

A glory to Christ - The Greek does not say "they are a glory *to* Christ." "Christ" is in the genitive case; the messengers are "a glory *of* Christ." That is, these messengers are like Christ in their character; by reason of their integrity they reflect His glory. One may compare the similar expression at 1 Corinthians 11:7 where man is called the "glory of God."

---

[72] Apostles of Christ such as the twelve, Matthias, Paul, James the brother of the Lord, Barnabas, and perhaps a few others, all received their commission directly from Christ Himself.

[73] Lipscomb reminds us this verse has a bearing on church polity. He points out that these messengers of the churches were sent by the churches, and sustained the same relation to the churches which sent them as the apostles sent by Christ sustained to Him. The apostles of Christ were sent by Him to deliver a message. They had no authority except to deliver the message and perform the work Christ sent them to do. They had no authority as delegates. They had no right to confer one with another to determine what to do or teach. They had no right to change or modify any decision of Christ or sit in judgment upon the will or work or order of God. They had no right to legislate where God had spoken. Likewise, the messengers of the churches had no more right to assemble, confer, or determine what was best for the churches than the apostles had the right to legislate where God had already spoken. The messengers of the churches were sent to carry the message and to do the specific work the church had sent them to do, and they had no power to change the message, or do other than as directed, or to direct the churches they were visiting. The duties of these messengers are not clearly defined here, but are hinted at in the verses. They were sent by the churches to bear the gifts to Jerusalem. They were sent to learn how other churches were doing in the collection of the relief fund. But evidently they did not meet to legislate, or did not direct the collection. (Lipscomb, *op. cit.*, p.117,118). It is clear that some modern "church messengers" who do attempt to legislate and otherwise direct the work of the churches get no Scriptural mandate for their polity from this passage. Those who interpret the first part of this verse to mean that Titus is Paul's personal representative, have a ready explanation of why the other two "brothers" are sent. Those two independent "brothers" would be able to testify about Paul's honest intentions and conduct in regards to this offering.

8:24 - *Therefore openly before the churches show them the proof of your love and of our reason for boasting about you.*

Therefore openly before the churches show them - In view of the qualifications and the eagerness of the men Paul has sent to supervise and observe the collection the Corinthians will be raising, Paul makes this appeal. Paul pictures the Macedonian churches (we might think of Philippi, Thessalonica, and Berea) as in a sense being present in the person of the messengers whom they chose. It is implied that the men will certainly report back to the churches of Macedonia how the Corinthians responded to the offering. They will report either that the Corinthians met the high expectations placed before them, or they did not. How disappointed the Macedonian Christians will be if the Corinthians don't come through.

The proof of your love - There is a play on words in the Greek. The words translated "show" (previous clause) and "proof" (this clause) come from the same root. Earlier in this appeal to the Corinthians, Paul spoke of their love (verse 8). The Corinthians must do more than just say they love; they must give tangible proof of it, or their claim is hollow. Certainly love for the Judean Christians is involved; perhaps also love for Christ and love for Paul. 'Show the churches you love like you claim you do.'

And of our reason for boasting about you - At 7:14 Paul has alluded to his boasting to Titus concerning the positive qualities of the Corinthian church, and how they had proven Paul's boast to be true. Paul has boasted that the Corinthians would give liberally (2 Corinthians 9:2). Will their offering now demonstrate that Paul's boasting about the Corinthians is justified? It has become obvious that Paul's motive for sending the three brethren to Corinth was to help ensure that the Corinthian's part in the offering would be generous.

D. An Exhortation to Have Everything Ready When he Comes. 9:1-5

9:1 - *For it is superfluous for me to write to you about this ministry to the saints;*

For - Since the Greek word *gar* ("for") indicates that Paul is continuing a discussion already mentioned,[1] inserting a chapter break between 8:24 and this verse may be unfortunate, especially if it leaves the impression a new subject is being introduced as chapter 9 begins. The chapter break here is even more unfortunate if we are prompted to think that perhaps chapter 9 is a fragment of another letter that somehow or other has been inserted here.[2]

The Greek here is *peri men gar*, and that does not introduce a new subject.[3]   In the NASB, *peri* is translated "about" and the *men* is an untranslatable particle that tells us to anticipate the second part of a contrast that soon will be introduced by a *de* (one follows in verse 3). The *men* looks forward. Paul has been boasting to the three workers whom he has sent to Corinth about the Corinthians' readiness to participate in the ministry to the saints and he wants to make sure his boasting would not turn out to be unwarranted. "Now about this ministry to the saints" beautifully sums up what was just written in chapter 8.   As he comes to the conclusion of what

---

[1] "For" tells us that verse 1 continues the thought (either giving a reason for, or further explaining something) just expressed in 8:23,24.   The *gar* looks back.   Paul has been speaking of the three delegates and the Corinthian's need to welcome them warmly.

[2] As was the case at 6:14-7:1, here again the hypothesis has been advanced that chapter 9 is a fragment of another letter, sent at a different time and perhaps to a different audience than Corinth, that has somehow been inserted here. About the only arguments that have been marshaled to support this hypothesis are (1) the affirmation that 9:1 does not explain 8:24 and therefore *gar* ("for") cannot refer to 8:24, and (2) in chapter 9 we have repetition of things already said in chapter 8. As the integrity of 2 Corinthians has been defended, each of these arguments has been answered. As to *gar* ("for") looking back, it does continue the thought begun at 8:23. Without chapter 8, the statement in 9:3 ("I have sent the brethren") makes no sense (their identity would be unknown if chapter 9 were a separate letter).   There is a connection between chapter 8 and chapter 9. Plummer (*op. cit.*, p.252) observes that "repetitions in letters are common enough, especially when the writer is very much in earnest and has to feel his way with caution." Plummer adds, "Hypotheses of stray leaves from other documents being imbedded in the New Testament writings are to be received with much skepticism, unless they are supported by strong external evidence, as in the case of John 7:53-9:11.   Some critics suggest that it is chapter 8 that has been interpolated; [others that it is chapter 9].   But there is no evidence in any manuscript, or version, or series of quotations that 2 Corinthians ever existed without chapter 8 or chapter 9.   Cyprian quotes from both, and commentators both Greek and Latin comment on both without betraying any doubt about the genuineness of either.   It will be found that chapter 9 helps us to understand chapter 8.   It is more likely that the chapter division is misplaced than that this material lacks integrity."

[3] While the phrase *peri de* regularly introduces a new topic (e.g., 1 Corinthians 7:1, 8:1, 12:1, 16:1), there is no evidence in extant Greek literature that the phrase *peri men gar* ever has an introductory function. S.K. Stowers, "*Peri men gar* and the Integrity of 2 Cor. 8 and 9," *Novum Testamentum* 32 (4, 1990), p. 340-348 has shown this construction expresses close relationship to what precedes, rather than a wholly different topic.

he wants to say about the offering, Paul wishes to add two more things: (1) he gives his reasons for sending the brethren instead of coming himself (verses 1-5), and (2) he calls attention to the blessings of Christian giving (verses 6-15).

It is superfluous for me to write to you - This phrase indicates that it is really unnecessary for him to go on writing (present tense infinitive) to them about the offering. The whole matter had been brought to their attention in 1 Corinthians 16:1-4 and by all Paul has written here in 2 Corinthians 8. Little more needs to be said, yet Paul is so deeply concerned about the Corinthians that he does go on to say more.

About this ministry to the saints - The "saints" are the poor Christians in the Jerusalem church (Romans 15:26; 2 Corinthians 8:4). "Ministry" (*diakonia*) is one of the terms regularly used to describe the offering to Jerusalem.[4] Thompson has a thought provoking note at this place. He calls attention to the fact that Jesus came ministering (Luke 22:26,27) and His followers are taught to serve or minister to each other. In those verses in Luke, the English words "serve" or "minister" translate the Greek *diakoneō* or *diakonia*, the same words used here in 2 Corinthians of the offering. The offering therefore may be looked upon as a "service" or "ministry" in response to Christ, the servant.[5]

9:2 - *for I know your readiness, of which I boast about you to the Macedonians, namely, that Achaia has been prepared since last year, and your zeal has stirred up most of them.*

For I know your readiness - "For" indicates this verse gives the reason why he feels he need not keep on writing about the offering. What Paul here says reflects what he has written in 8:10-12 about the Corinthians' initial readiness, even eagerness, to help with the offering. It was no sooner suggested to them than they indicated they would be eager to help.

Of which I boast about you to the Macedonians - Paul is in Macedonia when he writes this second letter to Corinth. He tells the Corinthians that with pride he habitually speaks of their readiness to participate in the offering. Paul used the example of the generosity of the Macedonians to encourage the Corinthians (2 Corinthians 8:1-5). Now he very tactfully states that he has been using the readiness of Corinthians to stimulate the Macedonians. The Corinthians may have lagged in

[4] See the use of the term in Acts 6:1, 11:29, 12:25; and Romans 15:31. At 2 Corinthians 8:4, Paul referred to the collection as a "service" or "ministry" (*diakonia*, "support" in NASB). At 2 Corinthians 8:20, Paul used the verb form *diakoneō* to speak of the "administration" (NASB) of the offering. He will refer to the offering by using the word "ministry" in two more verses, 2 Corinthians 9:12,13.

[5] Thompson, *op. cit.*, p.121.

the gathering of the offering, but Paul could still speak of their "readiness" as he communicated with the churches of Macedonia, namely, Philippi, Thessalonica, and Berea.

***Namely*, that Achaia has been prepared since last year** - As in 2 Corinthians 1:1, "Achaia" (the Roman province) includes Corinth and the other congregations that were nearby in district (Cenchrea, Romans 16:1; and Athens, Acts 17:34). "Last year" is the same expression that is translated in 8:10 "a year ago."[6] What is meant when Paul says Achaia was "prepared"? Was he telling the Macedonians that the Corinthians already had the offering (or at least some of it) collected? Or has Paul been telling the Macedonians that the Corinthians were quick to consent to participate in the offering. In light of the present appeal to the Corinthians to "finish" the collection of the offering (2 Corinthians 8:11), we must assume that the latter interpretation of "prepared" is the correct one. Paul has been telling the Macedonians that since last year the Corinthians were ready to give.

And your zeal has stirred up most of them - The readiness of the Corinthians to participate in the offering is here called "zeal." "Stirred up" translates a verb (*ērethise*) which occurs but twice in the New Testament, here and at Colossians 3:21 where it is translated "exasperate." The word can have either a good or a bad sense; here it has its good sense. It speaks of arousing or stimulating, and pictures a healthy rivalry. The Macedonian Christians, at least a great number of them,[7] feeling their tardiness in comparison to the Corinthians, have been stirred to great activity and zeal in this matter.

9:3 - *But I have sent the brethren, that our boasting about you may not be made empty in this case, that, as I was saying, you may be prepared;*

But I have sent the brethren - "But" (*de*) tells us that verse 3 is part of the thought begun in verse 1. Together the verses say this: 'Though it is needless to go on writing to you about this collection, I sent the brethren to make sure that all I had said about you might prove to be true.' The "brethren" are Titus and his two colleagues referred to in chapter 8:16,18,22,23.[8] "I have sent" is another example of an epistolary aorist (cp. 8:18). "I am sending" is the meaning. It looks at the sending from the standpoint of the Corinthians when they received the letter.

---

[6] Some critics have tried to use the expressions about "last year" in chapters 8 and 9 as proof that both chapters could not have originally been in the same letter. Others have charged Paul with exaggeration. Neither of these critical uses of the language here is valid.

[7] "Most of them" tells us not every member of the churches in Macedonian was participating in the offering. There were some who had not yet accepted the challenge and opportunity that had been laid before them.

[8] Without 8:16-23, these verses (9:3-5) would be rather obscure. This fact argues for the unity of these two chapters.

That our boasting about you may not be made empty in this case - Paul's explains that his purpose in sending the brethren is to ensure that what he has said about the Corinthians concerning the offering should not prove to be an empty boast. He has boasted about their readiness to participate in the offering. The brethren have been sent to give some organization to their efforts lest their performance fall short of their promise.

That, as I was saying, you may be prepared - "As I was saying" indicates that Paul repeatedly told the Macedonians about the Corinthians, how they were quick to consent to participate in the offering. Paul has not been telling the Macedonians that the money had already been gathered at Corinth, since he is sending men to see that the work is resumed and accomplished. Paul is saying that, when he himself finally comes to Corinth, he wants to find that the Corinthians have already gathered the funds they are going to contribute, just as 1 Corinthians 16:2 instructed. It would be a shame if the Corinthians failed to imitate the Macedonians to whom the Corinthians had been held up as a model to imitate.

9:4 - lest if any Macedonians come with me and find you unprepared, we (not to speak of you) should be put to shame by this confidence.

Lest if any Macedonians come with me and find you unprepared - Verse 4 continues the explanation begun in verse 3. In this verse Paul makes it quite clear that he means to visit Corinth again.[9] As he writes this letter to Corinth from Macedonia, Paul's plans are to go to Corinth and then on to Jerusalem with the offering (Acts 20:3). When he finally makes his way to Corinth, he expects that some of the messengers who will be carrying the Macedonian churches' offerings will be accompanying him. Before Paul makes his trip to Corinth, Titus and the two brethren whom Paul has sent will themselves arrive at Corinth. If either of those brothers are Macedonians, it will not matter so much if they find the offering at Corinth not completed. But if when Paul finally comes to carry the money to Jerusalem, he and those accompanying him find the Corinthians have not completed gathering their part of the offering, that will matter. "Find you unprepared" means unprepared to send messengers to Jerusalem because no offering had been collected.

We (not to speak of you) should be put to shame by this confidence - "This confidence" refers to what Paul has confidently spoken to the Macedonians about the Corinthian's readiness as much as a year ago (verses 2,3).[10] After holding the Corin-

---

[9] "Lest if any come with me" is not hypothetical nor does it indicate uncertainty. Paul alludes to that forthcoming visit later in this letter at 12:14 and 13:1,2.

[10] "Confidence" translates the Greek word *hupostasis*, a word which has a number of different meanings. It is translated "assurance" at Hebrews 3:14 and 11:1, and it is used at Hebrews 1:3 to describe Jesus' divine "nature" as being exactly like the Father's. In the papyri it is the word for a

thians up as a model to be emulated, if the Corinthians fail to resume the gathering of their part of the offering, Paul will feel humiliated. Of course, as the parenthetical phrase indicates, the Corinthians, too, would be disgraced in the eyes of the Macedonians. But Paul asks them to spare him, which is a better plea than asking them to watch out for their own interests.

9:5 - *So I thought it necessary to urge the brethren that they would go on ahead to you and arrange beforehand your previously promised bountiful gift, that the same might be ready as a bountiful gift, and not affected by covetousness.*

So I thought it necessary to urge the brethren - "So" points back to verse 4 and concludes the statement of Paul's reasons for sending the three men (2 Corinthians 8:16,18,22) to expedite the collection of the offering. It was to make sure that neither he nor the Corinthians should be embarrassed or humiliated.

That they would go on ahead to you - Paul himself plans to come to Corinth in the near future. However, the need for the Corinthians to resume their gathering of funds has led Paul to send Titus and the other two brethren on ahead. The Corinthians needed to resume their laying aside on the first day of the week before Paul ever arrives in town and that was something the three men can help encourage.

And arrange beforehand your previously promised bountiful gift - There were to be no hurried and unsatisfactory attempts at collecting the relief funds after Paul got to Corinth. The offering was to be arranged or completed[11] before Paul arrives. Titus and his helpers will not be putting undue pressure on the Corinthians to give; they will simply be helping the Corinthians to do what they had previously promised they would do.[12] "Bountiful gift" is a good choice of words to translate the Greek word *eulogia*, especially in light of the fact that in the next verse the same word is translated "bountifully" as contrasted with "sparingly." *Eulogia* is a word with several meanings. Originally it meant "good words" and then came to mean "good

---

title deed to a piece of property. *Hupostasis* is a compound verb, the two parts of which mean 'to stand under;' thus, it speaks of a foundation or that on which something rests. Paul's confidence in the character of the Corinthians was based on past experiences with them. If they fail to live up to his expectations based on what he knew of them, it will mean he has misjudged their character.

[11] "Arrange" translates a compound verb made up of *katartizō* meaning to "complete" or "make up what it ought to be" and *pro* meaning "before."

[12] We understand that the participle speaks of something "previously promised" by the Corinthians. It is possible that it means "announced or promised before" by Paul, namely when he told the churches of Macedonia about the readiness of the Corinthians to participate in the offering.

deeds."   The margin has "blessing" which is the usual translation for *eulogia*.[13]   The word is very suitable for use concerning the collection, for the "gift" being collected was something intended to confer a blessing on others.   There is a triple repetition of the word "before" ("go on ahead," "beforehand," "previously promised") in this verse, which seems to imply that there has already been entirely too much delay and that prompt completion of the offering is the only honorable thing to do.

That the same might be ready as a bountiful gift, and not affected by covetousness - This is the second time in this verse that the expected Corinthian contribution has been called a "bountiful gift."   Paul thus implies the Corinthians would not be absolved from their promise to give by giving the least possible sum. He expects their gift to be generous.   In the last phrase of this verse, Paul says he does not want their contribution to be affected by *pleonexia*, a word that can be translated covetousness, avarice, or extortion.   The word pictures one who seeks to grasp things he or she does not have.   Perhaps Paul is saying that if the Corinthians' gift is small it will show their greed for riches.   Or perhaps Paul is saying if he and the other messengers reach Corinth on their way to Judea and did not find the Corinthians ready, and had to try to pry the funds out of them, the funds would seem to be extorted from unwilling hearts.[14]   A prompt response when Titus and the brothers arrived would show their gift was voluntarily made and was not a grudging contribution.

E. An Encouragement to Be Generous – Calling Attention to the Benefits of Generosity. 9:6-15

1. Their own enrichment depended on their liberality. 9:6-11

9:6 - *Now this I say, he who sows sparingly shall also reap sparingly; and he who sows bountifully shall also reap bountifully.*

---

[13] *Eulogia* is used of spoken words whereby men bless God and one another, and of God blessing men.   It is used of concrete actions by which benefits are bestowed by men or God.   When Christians have received God's blessing (Ephesians 1:3), a suitable response to God's goodness is for the Christian to be a source of blessing to others.

Plumptre (*op. cit.*, p.81) calls attention to the fact that throughout church history "blessing" came to have special meanings applied to it.   "In liturgical language, as connected with the 'cup of *blessing*,' it was applied (1) to the consecrated bread and wine of the Lord's Supper generally; (2) specially to those portions which were reserved to be sent to the sick and other absentees; (3) when that practice fell into disuse, to the unconsecrated remains; and (4) to gifts of bread or cake to friends of the poor, as a residuum of the old distributions at the Agape, or Feasts of Charity."   Paul's use of "blessing" here in 2 Corinthians has no relation to any of these later church ideas.

[14] Plumptre (*ibid.*) suggests Paul is tauntingly using the word "covetousness" of himself, as though his enemies have charged him with always "asking for more" and as always "having his hand in people's pockets."   If so, Paul is answering the taunt by saying "Don't look on this offering as a self-interested work of mine.   Think of it, in every sense of the word, as a blessing both to givers and receivers."   Coffman (*op. cit.*, p.423) comments that "extortion" is exactly the correct word to apply to all "radical and high pressure methods of fund raising."

Now this *I say* - "This" calls attention to the fact that the words which follow are worthy of special consideration.[15]   Paul devotes the remainder of this chapter to four benefits or motives for giving generously and joyfully. (1) Giving generously in a right spirit is a sure way to experience God's love, verses 6,7. (2) Scripture promises that God is able to and does provide worldly wealth to those who are benevolent so that they may continue to be generous givers, verses 8-11. (3) Such generous offerings not only provide relief to the needy recipients, but will result in thanksgivings being offered to God, and the recipients will be filled with affection for the givers, verses 12-14. (4) God Himself has given an indescribable gift, verse 15. The words which follow are in harmony with what one reads in both Old and New Testament scriptures. Proverbs 11:24 (RSV) says, "One man gives freely, yet grows all the richer; another withholds what he should give, and suffers only want." Jesus Himself promised, "Give, and it shall be given to you; good measure, pressed down, shaken together, running over, they will pour into your lap. For whatever measure you deal out to others, it will be dealt to you in return" (Luke 6:38).

He who sows sparingly shall also reap sparingly - Paul uses a figure of speech from agriculture to teach the principles of God's dealings. "Sows sparingly" is a present tense verb, pointing to a habit of life. The future tense "shall reap" points to harvest time.[16] The person who, year after year, sows a scanty amount of seed in his soil will reap a scanty harvest (whatever may be true of the growing conditions). What is true in the world of agriculture is also true in the world of benevolence. When there is an opportunity to be benevolent, the person who with a tight hand holds back what he might give will receive few blessings. "The rewards of giving are in proportion to the degree of generosity."[17]

And he who sows bountifully shall also reap bountifully - When we shift the figure of speech from agriculture to benevolence we learn this: just as the farmer can decide how much seed to plant, so each Christian can decide in his heart how much to give. "Bountifully" is the plural form of the word "blessings" (*eulogia*) used twice in verse 5. Literally, this verse reads, "He who sows in blessings shall also reap blessings."[18] Bountifulness or generosity blesses both him who gives and him who receives. Paul does not say when the harvest is. Perhaps it is in this life when God replenishes what we have given (as verses 8-11 will show).   Perhaps it is at the end

---

[15] Paul used the single word *touto*. The NASB has supplied the verb "I say" to complete the meaning. Paul used this same construction at 1 Corinthians 7:29 and 15:50.

[16] In Galatians 6:7,8, we have appealed to the similarity of language to suggest that the topic in Galatians is the offering, just as it is here in 2 Corinthians.   Both letters come from the same period of Paul's life.

[17] Thompson, *op. cit.*, p.124.

[18] The contrast with the first part of the verse where the word "sparingly" was used suggests that the plural word "blessings" here indicates abundance, and the adverbial phrase is well translated as "generously" or "bountifully."

of the age (cp. Matthew 25:34-40; 2 Corinthians 5:10; Galatians 6:7,8; Ephesians 6:8; Colossians 3:23-25). Perhaps both in this life and the next, the rewards of benevolence and the rewards of scanty sowing (giving) are received. The idea that a generous giver can expect to reap a bountiful harvest of blessings from God is not to be thought of as a low or selfish motive for giving. The poor widow gave generously and exhibited trust in God's promise to take care of her. Such trust is as exalted a motive as any taught in the Scriptures. If a man wants more money to manage for the lord, what he needs to do is show that he can be trusted to be a faithful manager of those funds.[19]

9:7 - *Let each one* do *as he has purposed in his heart; not grudgingly, or under compulsion; for God loves a cheerful giver.*

Let each one *do* **just as he has purposed in his heart** - Paul calls for each Corinthian Christian to participate in the offering. "Purposed" rules out a passing impulse or a spur of the moment decision. Instead each is to give serious thought about their circumstances and the needs of the saints, and then make a deliberate resolve as to what he or she ought to give.

Not grudgingly - Literally, the Greek reads "not of grief." Generosity depends not only on the means of the giver (2 Corinthians 8:12) but also on the giver's attitude. There is to be no reluctance, as if he or she were sorry to part with the money.

Or under compulsion - Something done by compulsion is not done willingly. A person who gives of necessity gives only because he feels he has to, but at the same time he doesn't really want to. He may feel a necessity to give because of public opinion, or the example of peers (he would be ashamed to give less than others do), or because of pressure from those arranging the offering. "The implication is the gifts which come from a reluctant heart and are begrudged are really no gifts at all in the sight of God."[20]

For God loves a cheerful giver - The words "cheerful giver" are placed first in the Greek to put emphasis on them. "Cheerful" giving is contrasted to giving grudgingly and/or under compulsion.[21] Cheerful giving is what God likes. In the LXX of Proverbs 22:9 are found these words, "God blesses a cheerful man and a giver." Paul makes "cheerful" modify "giver," and he substitutes "loves" where Proverbs had "blesses." In that substitution we see the point of the quotation from Proverbs. Al-

---

[19] The promise of a bountiful harvest should not be interpreted as being an appeal to selfish interests. The farmer is not pictured as simply wanting to get for himself, but so that he will have more to share.

[20] Fisher, *op. cit.*, p.391.

[21] The Greek word rendered "cheerful" can be transliterated into our word "hilarious." What a happy opportunity it is to be able to give away what God has granted me to manage!

though it may be true to say God loves a cheerful giver and does not love a begrudging giver, there may be more involved than simply His attitude. Rather, the cheerful giver is not only "loved" by God, he is "blessed" by God, while the grudging giver is not so blessed.[22]   The words of this verse also give us an insight into the methods of the three helpers whom Paul has sent to Corinth to administer the offering. Their job must have been to convince the Corinthians that it was right to give to this cause so that their hearts would be willing to give. Paul talks in Romans about acts of mercy being done with cheerfulness (Romans 12:8). That, too, could have been an emphasis of the helpers as they worked among the Corinthians. Nothing they did would impinge on the offering from the Corinthians being anything but voluntary and joyous.

9:8 - *And God is able to make all grace abound to you, that always having all sufficiency in everything, you may have an abundance for every good deed;*

And God is able to make all grace abound to you - The same word "grace" (*charis*) was used in 8:1,6,7,19 of the opportunity God gave the Corinthians to be generous. Here it speaks of the blessings (material and spiritual) which God bestows on men in this life. The relation of this verse to what precedes is this: if the Corinthians would generously participate in this God-given opportunity to relieve the needs of the poor they can expect God, in return, to express His love (verse 7) by giving them more than they need.[23]   He certainly is able to do that; such bestowal of what is needful to meet one's necessities is indisputably within His power. Perhaps Paul is anticipating a common objection men have voiced that if they were to be generous now, they might find themselves in want later. Paul replies that that is not the way God works. He furnishes faithful givers with what is needful now and He gives them the means to be generous on later occasions. "Few persons are ever reduced to poverty by liberality. Perhaps in the whole circle of his acquaintance it would be difficult for an individual to point out *one* who has been made the poorer by being generous. God's blessing rests upon the liberal man, and God keeps him from want."[24]

That always having all sufficiency in everything - Since it is God's grace on which the Christian relies, he should keep in mind that the supply will never be depleted. God will always be able to meet his needs   so that he will always have enough to be

---

[22] Plumptre (*op. cit.*, p.82) offers several thoughtful comments. First, he notes that as in 2 Corinthians 8:21 and 9:6, so here we have a distinct echo from the Book of Proverbs. The numerous allusions to Proverbs suggests to him that Paul has recently been studying the Book of Proverbs so that his mind was full of the teachings of that book. Second, he calls attention the fact that since Paul's language reflects the LXX (rather than the Hebrew), it suggests that Paul regularly used the LXX as his Bible.

[23] "Abound" translates *perisseuein*, the same word used at 2 Corinthians 8:7.

[24] Barnes, *op. cit.*, p.198.

content.[25]   This contentment (*autarkeia*) continues only when others have a share in what the Christian has received.

You may have an abundance for every good deed - The sense is this: if you give liberally, rather than becoming impoverished you should expect that God will furnish you with the means (not for selfish use, but) to do more good works.   Not only does Paul speak of God's gift as being "an abundance" but he uses some form of the Greek word "all" (*pas*) at least five times in verse 8[26] to express how often and how generous God is.   In this passage, as well as at Philippians 4:18,19, Paul clearly teaches that, in the New Testament dispensation, God bestows temporal blessings on those whose management of funds shows God they are good managers of what He has entrusted to them.

9:9 - *as it is written, "HE SCATTERED ABROAD, HE GAVE TO THE POOR, HIS RIGHTEOUSNESS ABIDES FOREVER."*

As it is written - The words "it is written" are Paul's regular formula for introducing a quotation from the Old Testament.   The passage he quotes is from the LXX of Psalm 112:9.   "As" says there is an exact correspondence between something just said in verse 8 and what the Psalmist wrote.   The issue we face is whether the Psalm is quoted to show how God continually makes His grace abound, or whether it gives Biblical evidence that men can always count on having abundance for every good deed.   That is, does the Psalm speak of the charitable man or of God?   We will offer both explanations for each of the lines quoted from the Psalm.

He scattered abroad - If the Psalmist is speaking of the character of the man who fears the Lord (Psalm 112:1) then one of the things such a man does is habitually and generously dispense funds to places where they are needed.[27]   If it speaks of God, it says God habitually bestows His blessings on the one who fears Him.

He gave to the poor - The word here translated "poor" is *penēs*, which does not occur elsewhere in the New Testament, refers to a moderate poverty.   Paul elsewhere (e.g., Romans 15:26) used the Greek word *ptōcheia* to describe the abject   poverty of the

---

[25] "Sufficiency" translates *autarkeia*, the word translated "contentment" in Philippians 4;11-13. Paul's contentment in the midst of privation is made possible by Christ who strengthens him. *Autarkeia* is the same word used at 1 Timothy 6:6 ("godliness with *contentment*").   It is doubtful that the word ever carries the meaning 'abundance.'   In classical times the word spoke of being independent of external circumstances, i.e., self-sufficient.

[26] Our English translation obscures this fact by using different words to translate *pas*: "all grace," "always," "all sufficiency," "everything," "every good deed."

[27] "Scattering" is the opposite of "sowing sparingly."

saints at Jerusalem.[28]   If the Psalmist is speaking of the charitable man, this clause says he sees to it that his gifts go where they will help the needy, just what the Corinthians are being asked to do.   If it speaks of God, then even the man with the funds to be generous is, in God's sight, in relative poverty.

His righteousness abides forever - If the character of the man who fears the Lord is the subject of the sentence, then "righteousness" is used as it was in Matthew 6:1 where the word is a technical term for almsgiving.[29]   However, the statement that such almsgiving "abides forever" has proven difficult for commentators to explain. "Forever"[30] is often toned down to as long as the man lives, or his good deeds are remembered among men long after he is dead.   If the sentence speaks of God, and "abides forever" might incline us to believe it does, this sentence says right actions towards men, such as making His grace abound to them, is something that God can be expected to do until the end of the age.   Generous men of God can count on God supplying their needs, so they can continue to be generous, just as verse 8 has claimed. The Scriptures say so.[31]

9:10 - *Now He who supplies seed to the sower and bread for food, will supply and multiply your seed for sowing and increase the harvest of your righteousness;*

Now He who supplies seed to the sower - Paul is continuing his presentation that Scripture promises that God is able to and does provide worldly wealth to those who are benevolent so that,   instead of generosity being ruinous to those who practice it,

---

[28] On the difference of meaning in the two synonyms, see Richard Trench, *Synonyms of the New Testament* (Grand Rapids: Eerdmans, 1966), p.128.

[29] "Righteousness" is used in the Scriptures with several meanings: sometimes of God's way of saving man (Romans 3:21-25); sometimes of a man's right relationship with God; and sometimes of man's right relationships with men.   It is the latter of these uses that we find in this place, if the subject is the charitable man.   Thus, in this place "righteousness" and "every good work" (verse 8) are synonymous, with both referring to the giving of money to the poor.

[30] Two Greek phrases are translated "forever" in our Bibles.   The shorter of the two forms, *eis ton aiōna*, literally, "unto the age," often means to the end of the [present] age, while the longer of the two forms, *eis ton aiōna tou aiōnos*, literally, "to the age of the ages," is the one that implies endlessness of time, forever and ever.   The distinction is not absolute in the New Testament, and the shorter form sometimes refers to the life to come (e.g., John 8:51, 11:26, 12:34, where "never" translates the shorter form).   Berry, *Greek-English New Testament Lexicon*, p.4.

[31] When Paul's quotation of Psalm 112 is made to refer to God, there are those who think Paul has given the Psalm passage a meaning different than it had in its original setting.   Such interpreters affirm that originally the Psalm applied to men who gave alms, whereas Paul makes it apply to God as the giver of all good.   In fact, in Psalm 112, both man's and God's righteousness are referred to. The phrase "his righteousness abides forever" occurs both in Psalm 112:3 and in Psalm 112:9, and a strong case can be made that verse 3 is speaking of God's righteousness.   Barnes (*op. cit.*, p.200) reminds us that when Old Testament passages are quoted, the key to understanding is often the whole passage, not just the verse quoted.   He calls attention to the fact that verse 9 closes with the words "His horn shall be exalted with honor," that is, the generous giver "shall be abundantly blessed with prosperity and with the favor of God."

they may continue to be liberal givers. His argument here, alluding to Isaiah 55:10 and Hosea 10:12, is that what God does in the realm of nature, he also does in a richer way in the life of the generous Christian. This language about seed for the sower and bread for food comes from Isaiah 55:10, and takes up again the figure from verse 6 about sowing sparingly and sowing bountifully. If God did not provide the seed there would be no sowing. The present tense verb "supplies" indicates the habitual action of God; the Greek word means God is lavishly generous as He provides seed for the sower.[32]

And bread for food - This clause can be taken either with what precedes or what follows. The KJV takes it with what follows, so that the verse reads that God "will supply bread for food and multiply your seed for sowing." First, at seed time, God generously provides seed to plant. At harvest time the crop is bountiful enough that there is grain to make bread and there is enough left over for seed again. Just as Isaiah called attention to God's bountiful provision, the Corinthians may be certain of God's faithfulness to provide their needs. Generous giving will not leave them bankrupt.

Will supply and multiply your seed for sowing - The verbs should be treated as a future indicative form,[33] and thus are a simple statement of what will take place. Using an example from the world of agriculture, Paul drives home the point of verse 8: if the Corinthians give generously to this offering, they need not fear the depletion of their resources. God supplies and multiplies both in the realm of nature and in the realm of His provision for the needs of the Christian. Did not Jesus instruct His followers to seek first His kingdom and His righteousness and you will then find that your every-day material needs of food, shelter, and clothing will be taken care of (Matthew 6:33)? There is a change of verbs from the compound *epichorēgeō* ("supply") to the simple verb form *chorēgeō*, but even the simple verb form suggests generous behavior. There also is a change of nouns translated "seed" from *sperma* before to *sporon* here. *Sperma* is seed in the literal sense, like grains of wheat one can sow in the ground. *Sporon* ("seed") is here used in this clause of the gifts and wealth which must be scattered generously by the Corinthians, and which God will in turn resupply and augment. Christian giving is analogous to the sowing of seed. When the harvest comes, the seeds planted have turned into whole heads of grain. They will have more finances to share in benevolent gifts.

And increase the harvest of your righteousness - In the words "the harvest of your righteousness" there is an obvious reference to the LXX of Hosea 10:12 and Amos

---

[32] The Greek verb *epichorēgeō* ("supplies") has a somewhat interesting history. From meaning to lead a musical drama or chorus, it came to mean to pay the expenses of producing the drama in the theater (a *leitourgia*, a "public service" which required a large outlay of money), and then it came to mean any lavish act where a plentiful amount of anything was supplied.

[33] The verb forms could also be optative, which would make them a wish. We doubt that this is to be understood as a wish on the part of Paul, for a wish does not suit the context.

6:12. In those passages we find God's own promise that the harvest will be greater than the amount of seed sown. "Righteousness," as in verse 10, has reference to almsgiving (participating in the offering for Jerusalem).[34] That participation was the sowing of seed, as it were. If the Corinthians give liberally, they are assured that their crop (harvest) will be more than they planted. When the harvest comes, and it will in God's own good time, God promises the generous giver that there will be an increase that will allow him or her to be continue to be generous.

9:11 - *you will be enriched in everything for all liberality, which through us is producing thanksgiving to God.*

You will be enriched in everything for all liberality - The first part of verse 11 completes the thought of what happens when God increases the harvest.[35] It also summarizes what has been written since verse 8 about God making all grace abound to those who give generously to the offering to Jerusalem. "Enriched" is *ploutidzo-menoi*, which speaks of lavish giving. When God gives, the amount is sufficient for great generosity. In this context, "in everything" points to their financial position. God pays large dividends to the generous giver.[36] The word (*haplotēs*) translated "liberality" here has the same meaning it did in 2 Corinthians 8:2. There it spoke of single-minded purpose, namely to serve Christ by participating generously in the offering. The word speaks of an absence of selfish motives so that the giver understands he has been blessed by God in order to enrich others.

Which through us - In his mind's eye, Paul pictures what will happen when he and the other messengers of the churches arrive in Jerusalem with the alms. As the alms are distributed, the saints at Jerusalem will offer up heart-felt thanksgiving to God. With these words, Paul introduces the idea that will be taken up in the next few verses.

Is producing thanksgiving to God - Thanksgiving is the proper response to the grace of God (2 Corinthians 4:15). The single-minded purpose of the Corinthians to serve Christ will have resulted in a huge offering, just what the poor saints in Jerusalem have desperately been needing. When it is announced the gifts come from their Gentile brothers and sisters in Christ, the recipients will not only thank God for the gifts, they will also thank God for the people who gave the offering.

---

[34] Perhaps benevolent giving is called "righteousness" because it is a right act toward one's fellow man; it is the right thing to do.

[35] Though the Greek participle "enriched" is not grammatically connected to the rest of the sentence, the idea seems to be a continuation of what went before.

[36] Of course, "in everything" (or "in every way") may be thought to include spiritual riches, too, as 2 Corinthians 8:9 has stated.

2. Their liberality would lead to God being glorified.   9:12-15

9:12 - *For the ministry of this service is not only fully supplying the needs of the saints, but it is also overflowing through many thanksgivings to God.*

For the ministry of this service - "For" indicates that verses 12-14 unfold or explain the idea introduced in 11b, that the offering would glorify God.   "Ministry" translates *diakonia* and "service" translates *leitourgia*.   In chapters 8-9, Paul has consistently referred to the offering as a "ministry" (*diakonia*, 8:4, 9:1,12,13).   In classical Greek, *leitourgia* ("service") referred to the aid which wealthy citizens had to render to the public in financing choruses for dramas,[37] or supplying the funds to build and man naval vessels which would help defend the town, or supplying funds to train gymnasts to represent the town in the Olympics.   When the Jews began using the Greek language, they used *leitourgia* to refer to the public ministrations performed on behalf of others by the priests and Levites in the temple (Exodus 38:21 [38:19 LXX]; Hebrews 8:6, 11:21).   Just as the noun form of the word is used here for the offering, the verb form of this word is used of the offering in Romans 15:27 ("to minister"). In the church age, every Christian is a priest (1 Peter 2:5), and priests have the privilege of voluntarily providing aid and offering service on behalf of others. "What Athenian citizens who had the means were made to do, Gentile Christians will be glad to do, in order to render service to society and to God."[38]   "For those Corinthians who were unconcerned or even adamant against the collection, Paul says that the collection is no less than the service of the "royal priesthood" (1 Peter 2:5), the church."[39]

Is not only fully supplying the needs of the saints - "Fully supplying" means helping to supply or supplying in addition.   The Corinthians were not the only contributors to the offering.   Their gifts together with the gifts of others will meet the needs of the saints at Jerusalem who are suffering from hunger.   Their needs were urgent.   Not only will this offering help relieve that, but it will do something more.

But is also overflowing through many thanksgivings to God - If the Corinthians' offering is generous, if they "overflow" in every good work (verse 8),[40] the natural result will be that Jerusalem's poor will   overflow with thanksgiving to God[41] when

---

[37] See the footnote on "supply" above at verse 10.

[38] Plummer, *op. cit.*, p.265.

[39] Thompson, *op. cit.*, p.130.   Christians, a little later, gave this word (transliterated as "liturgy") a special religious meaning in connection with the Lord's Supper as they began to think of it as being a "sacrifice to God."   It is doubtful if there is any idea of sacrifice intended in Paul's use of the word here.

[40] The word translated "overflow" here is the same root translated "abundance" in verse 8.

[41] A few manuscripts including Vaticanus read "to Christ."

they receive the offerings.   "To God" (standing last in the sentence) is emphasized in the original.   The Jerusalem Christians will trace the true source of the gifts they have received to God and thus give Him thanks.   Not only will the gifts supply the needs of the saints, they will promote the glory of God.

9:13 - *Because of the proof given by this ministry they will glorify God for your obedience to your confession of the gospel of Christ, and for the liberality of your contribution to them and to all,*

Because of the proof given by this ministry - Verses 11 and 12 both spoke of thanksgiving being given to God.[42]   Verse 13 explains why Palestinian Christians give thanks to God: the offering gives evidence or proof that the Gentile believers are Christians, and the offering is very liberal.   "Ministry" (*diakonia*) is one of the words Paul has been using to designate the offering (see 9:1).   As we saw at 2:9 and 8:24 the word *dokimē* ("proof") can also be translated as "put to the test."   The Corinthians may not have thought of their participation in the offering as a test of the genuineness of their Christianity, and of their willingness to minister to the needs of others, but that is what Paul here says it is.   And when they have given generously, the recipients at Jerusalem will see that as proof the Gentile converts are brethren in every respect.   It will go a long way to break down the old cultural barriers that have tended to separate the Jerusalem Christians from the Christians of different ethnic backgrounds.   The breaking down of these walls was one of the great results Paul hoped to achieve as he encouraged the collection of this offering for Jerusalem.

They will glorify God - "Glorify" (*doxadzontes*) is a nominative plural present tense participle, and it is unclear who the subject of the participle is; the subject is undesignated in the Greek.[43]   It could be either the Jerusalem poor who glorify God for the offering, or the Corinthians themselves who thank God for the opportunity after they have sent the offering on its way.   Because of the present tense participle, Lipscomb (*op. cit.*, p.125) writes to the effect that the Judean Christians were already rejoicing, even before they have received the money, having been made aware of it on account of the length of time during which it was collected.   Such a period of time would give news of the impending collection time to get to Jerusalem.   We rather picture continual praises being given to God because of the collection after it was received.   Perhaps we may even think of a specially-called congregational meeting at Jerusalem at which time the offering was presented and the praises began to be lifted up on high.

---

[42] The UBS Greek text has verse 12 between dashes, making verse 13 continue what was begun in verse 11 about producing thanksgiving to God.   The dashes are added because the Greek has a nominative participle (translated "glorify") that is not grammatically connected to the rest of the context.

[43] The RSV and UBS think the Corinthians to be the subject.   The NASB takes the Jerusalem Christians to be the subject.

For *your* obedience to your confession of the gospel of Christ - This is the first of two things for which the recipients glorify God. Though the Jerusalem Christians were not "Judaizers" (like the false brethren of Galatians 2:4), they were very zealous for the Law (Acts 21:20) even though it had been abrogated at the cross (Colossians 2:14; Hebrews 7:12). Practicing their freedom in Christ to do so, they have continued to eat kosher table and observe other things that were commanded in the Law of Moses. It seems to be implied that the Jerusalem Christians had been suspicious of the Gentile Corinthians' loyalty to Christ because they did not observe these old Mosaic practices. Jewish believers might think the Gentile converts were not as careful in their Christian living as they should be. This offering would help change people's minds about the quality of the Corinthians' Christianity. "Confession" is used elsewhere in the New Testament of the confession of belief in Jesus made just before a person is immersed (Hebrews 3:1, 4:14). Sometimes the wording is "I believe that Jesus Christ is the Son of God" (Acts 8:37). In Romans 10:9 Paul talks about confessing that Jesus is Lord. Here in verse 13, Paul tells us that if such a confession is meaningful it involves obedience to the Lord. In this case, obedience to the Lord includes participation in the offering; after all, Jesus did teach His disciples of the need to love their neighbor (Luke 10:25-37; Mark 12:31-34). That teaching is an important part of the gospel of Christ.[44]

And for the liberality of your contribution to them - This is the second thing for which the Jerusalem Christians would give thanks to God. "Liberality" translates the word *haplotēs*, the same word used in 8:2 and 9:11, of a gift given without any selfish holding back of what might be given. "Contribution" is the word *koinōnia*, which means fellowship or partnership together in a common cause. The generous offering given by the Corinthians would show the Jerusalem Christians that their brethren in Corinth really were partners in Christ against whom no suspicions should be harbored, especially over cultural differences. Note that there is more praise offered to God for the spiritual virtues of the donors than for the gift itself.

And to all - Perhaps this phrase was a sudden afterthought as Paul dictated this letter, but whether it was or not, it does say that Christian partnership (*koinōnia*) involved more than just the brethren at Jerusalem. Paul expected the Corinthians to be personally involved in any situation where participation together in the cause of Christ was at stake. Christians are to have care for one another (1 Corinthians 12:25,26).

9:14 - *while they also, by prayer on your behalf, yearn for you because of the surpassing grace of God in you.*

---

[44] "By virtue of one's confession, he is already pledged as a giver to support God's work." Coffman, *op. cit.*, p.440. "The doctrine is, that one evidence of true submission to the gospel – one proof that our profession is sincere and genuine – is a willingness to contribute to relieve the needs of the poor and afflicted friends of the Redeemer. Compare the same idea in James 1:27 and Romans 12:13" (Barnes, *op. cit.*, p.202).

While they also - This verse explains how the partnership would be returned.[45] While the Corinthians showed their partnership by giving money, the Jerusalem saints would show theirs by intercessory prayer and yearning to know their brethren better.

By prayer on your behalf - The Greek word "prayer" ("supplication," ASV) speaks of "prayer for particular benefits."[46]   The Christians at Jerusalem would now pray for their brethren in Corinth that God would bestow on them whatever benefits they needed.   In this Greek sentence, "prayer on your behalf" is a subordinate idea to "they will yearn for you."

Yearn for you - In his mind's eye, Paul pictures what will happen when he and the other messengers deliver the offerings into the hands of the elders at Jerusalem (Acts 21:18).   He pictures mutual distrust being abandoned and the bonds of affection between Jewish and Gentile Christians being tightened.   The Jerusalem Christians will desire to know more about the Corinthians; they will pray for their welfare; they will long for closer relationships with them.   Paul felt confident that a liberal gift from the Gentile churches he has been involved with would bring about a better understanding, and would work wonderful changes in the thinking of Jewish Christians.   The Jewish hesitancy about the genuineness of the Gentiles' Christianity certainly would be overcome.

Because of the surpassing grace of God in you - The Greek here translated "in you" (NASB) means "imparted to you" (NEB), and is not the same expression found in 2 Corinthians 8:1.   This language reminds us of 2 Corinthians 8:9 ("You know the grace of our Lord Jesus Christ, that though He was rich, yet for your sake He became poor, that you through His poverty might become rich"), of 2 Corinthians 6:1 (which indicates that grace is something one may receive), and of 2 Corinthians 1:12 (which speaks of one's conduct being guided by the grace of God).   This is the grace which the Jerusalem Christians now recognize to have been motivating the Corinthians' behavior.   They yearn to become better acquainted with such folk.

9:15 - *Thanks be to God for His indescribable gift!*

Thanks be to God - Perhaps as a final appeal to the Corinthians to be generous, Paul, with thanksgiving, calls their attention to the wonderful gift God has given.   Their gratitude will motivate them to give.

---

[45] As it has been for several verses now, the structure of the Greek at this place is somewhat ungrammatical, being a construction known as a genitive absolute.   There is little doubt, however, that the genitive absolute states the response which the Palestinian Christians will make to the generosity of their Corinthian partners.

[46] Berry, *Synonyms*, p.120.

For His indescribable gift! - "Indescribable" ("unspeakable," ASV) tells us there are no human words to properly describe the greatness of the gift God has given to men. We are left to conjecture as to what gift Paul has in mind. Perhaps it refers to the gospel which the hearers have obeyed (verse 13). Perhaps it refers to the grace of God just alluded to (verse 14), or to God's constant providing for those who share in the act of giving (9:8-10). Perhaps it refers to the spirit of love for and partnership with members of the family of God which results from obedience to the Gospel. Of course, Christ Himself is God's great gift to man (2 Corinthians 8:9 and Romans 8:32).

This thanksgiving to God closes the second main division of this epistle, the whole of which concerned the readers' participation in the collection for the poor at Jerusalem. Should anyone wonder whether or not Paul's appeals were successful, and whether or not on the first day of each week the Corinthians resumed their putting aside and saving, it should be noted that there are evidences both in the New Testament and early Christian literature that they did participate in the offering. Romans 15:26 (written only a few months later from Corinth) reports that "Macedonia and Achaia have been pleased to make a contribution for the poor among the saints at Jerusalem."[47] He could only write that if in the few months between the writing of 2 Corinthians and the writing of Romans the Christians in Corinth (and Achaia) have responded.[48] Clement of Rome, writing forty years later to the church at Corinth, praises them as "more willing to give than to receive" (1 *Clement* ii.1), which he could hardly have done had the Corinthians not participated in the offering.

---

[47] The Greek reads "a certain (*tina*) contribution" at Romans 15:26. The indefinite adjective "certain" should not be interpreted as a derogatory reference to the size of the contribution. BAGD (p.828) interpret it exactly the opposite, as referring to a not insignificant amount.

[48] If one objects that Acts 20:4 names no "messenger" who was responsible for carrying the offering from Corinth, we would respond with two candidates who might have been entrusted to that honor: (1) either Paul himself was their appointed messenger, or (2) Titus (who is not mentioned by name in Acts) was their messenger, or both.

III. PAUL'S APPEALS FOR NEEDED CHANGES AT CORINTH SO THEIR RECONCILIATION CAN BE COMPLETE.   10:1 - 13:10

A. An Appeal for the Church to Recognize his Apostolic Authority.   10:1-11

10:1 - *Now I, Paul, myself urge you by the meekness and gentleness of Christ – I who am meek when face to face with you, but bold toward you when absent! –*

Now - As it did at 8:1, *de* (translated "now") marks a transition, this time to a further defense of his apostolic authority, message, and mission. It might be said that the major topics in 2 Corinthians have dealt with the past, the present, and the future. Chapters 1-7 dealt with an issue in the past: the strained relationship between the church at Corinth and Paul which resulted from a basic failure to recognize his apostolic authority as represented by their failure to discipline the offender as Paul had taught them to do. That matter has been properly resolved and reconciliation has resulted.   Chapters 8-9 dealt with an issue in the present, Paul's pressing concern for the offering for Jerusalem and Paul's hope that the Corinthians, after a lapse, will again get involved in sharing generously in that offering.   Now, chapters 10-13 will resume the topic of most vital importance to the church at Corinth and all the saints in Achaia, a topic that poses a serious threat to their future relationships with each other.[1]   Will the Corinthians recognize Paul's apostolic authority, message, and mission, or will they be drawn away from their appreciation of Paul's apostleship and drawn away from Christianity by the claims of false apostles who have recently come to town?   Paul presents a vigorous defense of his apostolic authority and his gospel message, for appreciation of that is vital to the readers' spiritual welfare, now and hereafter.   It not only affects their newly restored relationship between the church and Paul.   The church's attitude toward Paul's apostolic message will have a bearing on their relationship to Christ, a relationship that has eternal consequences.[2]

I, Paul, myself urge you   -   Some suppose this language signals the fact that at this

---

[1] We can trace Paul's emphases as he develops two main ideas: (1) his apostolic authority and the area of his mission, 10:1-18;   and (2) an appeal to the church to esteem him more highly (and the false apostles not at all), 11:1-13:10.

[2] Such present and future consequences make the topic of chapters 10-13 to be of vital importance in the 21st century.   Today, to treat apostles and their writings as common and uninspired results in a low view of Christianity, if not of Jesus Christ Himself who sent the apostles. This commentator has in mind the negative effect on men's faith that "assured results of higher criticism" has produced.   Paul's claims to apostleship and the authority of his message cannot be harmonized with the conclusions of higher criticism.   Would that the erstwhile higher critics had listened to Paul's claims!

point Paul took the pen from the amanuensis and wrote the remainder of the letter in his own handwriting, as 2 Thessalonians 3:17 indicates was a practice he followed as his letters neared their conclusion. However, it is most likely that the place where Paul picked up the pen in this letter is at 13:11. A better suggestion is that since Paul is discussing the authority of an apostle, he no longer includes Timothy who, up to now, has been associated with him in the writing of this letter (2 Corinthians 1:1). The topic of apostleship is something that does not involve Timothy, who held the office of evangelist rather than apostle (2 Timothy 4:5). It is Paul whose apostleship has been misrepresented and denied, and it is Paul who answers those slanders.[3] The best parallel to "I, Paul, myself" is Galatians 5:2, where Paul also is asserting his apostolic authority in direct refutation of false and malicious defamation of his apostleship. "Myself" makes the refutation more emphatic.[4] It is also important to call attention to the verb ("urge," *parakaleō*) that Paul here uses. It is a present tense verb in the Greek, indicating continuous encouragement or urging. It is the same verb, and thus the same tone of voice, that Paul used earlier in this letter (2 Corinthians 2:8, 6:1, 8:6, 9:5). "You" (plural), just as it did in chapters 1-9, shows these words are addressed to the church members at Corinth.[5] He addresses the whole congregation to alert them to the insidious and subversive methods of his opponents, to whom allusion is made from time to time.

By the meekness and gentleness of Christ - As the dashes in verse 1 of the NASB show, the sentence which began with "I, Paul, myself urge you" is broken, only to resume in verse 2 with a prayer that he not have to punish disobedience when he next arrives in Corinth.[6] In the spirit of the meek and gentle Christ, or in the spirit of meekness and gentleness which Christ taught His disciples to exhibit, I appeal to you, is what Paul says. "The word 'meekness' (*praus, prautētos*) does not suggest cowardice or spineless acceptance of bad circumstances; the word suggests strength

---

[3] The pronoun usage in this part of 2 Corinthians provides some confirmation of the view that Paul is writing about himself (and not including Timothy). In chapters 1-9 he commonly uses the first-person plural ("we"), while the first-person singular ("I") is exceptional. In chapters 10-13 the singular is the rule, and the plural is exceptional. This distinction between singular and plural is not true without exception, for in this chapter the plural is still used on occasion when the reference seems to be to Paul (e.g., 11:12, 12:19, 13:4-7). However, once we get to 13:7, it is possible the "we" again includes Timothy along with Paul in their wishes and hopes for the Corinthians.

[4] "When Paul writes this expression elsewhere (Colossians 1:23, 4:18; 1 Thessalonians 2:18; 2 Thessalonians 3:17, Philemon 9,19) the purpose is to emphasize his apostolic authority" (Thompson, *op. cit.*, p.133).

[5] Some have advanced the hypothesis that chapters 10-13 are addressed to the Judaizers who have troubled the church, but those troublemakers are identified separately as "some" in verse 2.

[6] The conduct which Paul threatens to exhibit (if when he gets to Corinth he still finds disobedience) might seem incompatible with the meekness and gentleness of Christ, but it is not really so. Rather, it is a misunderstanding of the words "meekness and gentleness" that have led some to think Paul's threats are incompatible.

under control."[7]   Jesus was meek (Zechariah 9:9; Matthew 11:29), and Moses was meek (Numbers 12:3), but neither of them acquiesced to wrongdoing when they saw it.   Meekness is an important Christian virtue (Galatians 5:23).   "Gentleness" (*epieikeia*) denotes fairness, sympathetic consideration for others, sweet reasonableness.[8]   "The word is not a word for passivity. It suggests one who, although he is provoked, is able to maintain a generous attitude (see Philippians 4:5, where the word is translated 'forbearance')."[9]   "Of Christ" likely means not only that Jesus exhibited these traits, but that Jesus taught and expects such attitudes in His followers.   Paul's appeal to the meekness and gentleness of Christ implies the Corinthians already knew about Jesus' character and teachings.   They learned about Jesus during the evangelizing ministries of Paul and Peter in Corinth.[10]   Paul learned about the ministry of Jesus, His words and actions, by revelation (Galatians 1:12); what he learned by revelation he passed on to his audiences as he preached (cf. 1 Corinthians 11:23-25, 15:1-7).   Peter, having traveled with Jesus during His earthly ministry, knew about it first-hand.

Paul's own statement about his attitude as he makes this appeal certainly has bearing on the tone of Paul's voice that one should hear as he reads these chapters. Why should scholars say, as they begin to comment on chapters 10-13, that Paul's tone in these four chapters has changed from delight over reconciliation (chapter 7) and joy (chapter 9) to stern and harsh and sarcastic?[11]   Should we not, instead, hear Paul's own evaluation of his tone?   At 10:1 he uses the same verb "urge" that he used four times earlier in this same letter, and he says his appeal is in the spirit of meekness and gentleness which Jesus taught.   In 11:2 he says it is out of love for the Christians that he is doing what he can to stop the influence of those who would seduce the Corinthians away from Christ.   At 12:19 he explains that in the sight of God he has been speaking in Christ in order to build up the Corinthians.   At 13:2 it is implied that he has been sparing as he writes this letter, but he will spare no more when he gets to Corinth if changes have not been made.   He has been praying the Corinthians

---

[7] Thompson, *op. cit.*, p.135.

[8] Gentleness denotes the habit of mind which makes kindly allowance for wrong doing, and does not insist upon dealing with it according to the letter of the Law (Arist. *Nic. Eth.* vi.11).   Joseph Waite, "2 Corinthians" in *The Bible Commentary*, edited by F.C. Cook (New York: Charles Scribner's Sons, 1886), New Testament Vol.3, p.452.

[9] Thompson, *ibid.*

[10] If we interpreted 1 Corinthians 1:12 and 9:5 correctly, then some of the Corinthians' knowledge about Jesus could have come from the apostle Peter, also.

[11] Instead of interpreting certain verses (10:1, 11:4, 11:7,8, 11:11, 11:19-21, 12:13-16) as being sarcasm, picture that Paul, in order to repudiate what was being said about him, is repeating the actual misrepresentations and disparaging statements about him voiced by those who have been attacking his apostolic authority and gospel message.

do no wrong (13:7),and he rejoices when he can be weak rather than stern (13:9). In 13:10 he says he does not want to use the severity he could use because of the authority Christ gave him, though he would if he has to. The whole letter ends on a note of rejoicing (13:11). Rather than being harsh or sarcastic language, we have apostolic authority sweetly but firmly expressed. He knew he was an apostle of Christ. He knew what he taught was the truth, while his detractors were teaching false doctrine (11:4). On that issue there could be no equivocation, so Paul, as it were, appeals to the Corinthians with gracious encouragements to choose his apostleship over the claims of the false teachers, yet he is not feeble in his opposition to the Judaizers who are deceitful and doing the work of the devil (2 Corinthians 11:13,14).

-- I who am meek when face to face with you, but bold toward you when absent! -- This is the first of several places in these four chapters where Paul is quoting the derogatory words spoken against him by his opponents at Corinth. When Paul came to Corinth the first time, he was with them in weakness and in much fear and trembling (1 Corinthians 2:3). Did the Judaizers put a spin on his lack of stamina and say that cowardice or timidity[12] was what Paul's listeners were seeing? The Judaizers recognized that Paul's letters had a ring of authority to them, for one particular area where Paul could be very courageous and brave, when he was not present in person, was on paper (10:9,10). The accusation that he was a coward, if true, would have ruined his effectiveness as a minister of Christ. He answers that charge by saying apostles of Christ, such as he was, are very bold in areas where they must be. The same apostolic authority presented in their inspired letters can also be exercised in person, when such public exercise is called for.

10:2 - *I ask that when I am present I may not be bold with the confidence with which I propose to be courageous against some, who regard us as if we walked according to the flesh.*

I ask - This word takes up the broken sentence which began in verse 1, except that "ask" (*deomai*) used here is a milder verb than "urge" (*parakaleō*) used there. It would seem the language is still addressed to the Corinthians (in fact, the ASV reads "I beseech you").[13] He is beginning to present his case that it rests with them to avert any necessity of exercising his apostolic authority when he next visits Corinth.

---

[12] The Greek word *tapeinos* can be translated lowly, humble, cringing, artful, groveling, timid. Paul has already used this word of himself at 2 Corinthians 7:6 in a context where "depressed" caught the meaning. Here the antonym is "bold" or "brave." Some English versions chose the word "presence" to translate the Greek phrase "face to face" (*kata prosōpon*), thinking that here in verse 1 the allusion to what Paul's enemies said had reference to his outward bodily appearance since in 10:10 the same word here translated "humble" is translated as "unimpressive."

[13] While *deomai* is a word sometimes used to refer to prayer to God, it seems hardly probable that this verse is a prayer Paul has addressed to God.

That when I am present I may not be bold - Paul had indicated at 2 Corinthians 9:5 his plans to visit Corinth soon.   He requests the Corinthians to so respond to the false teachers that he will have no need to exercise the power which God had given him (a power similar to what any apostle of Jesus could exercise).[14]

With the confidence which I propose to be courageous against some - The word for "courageous" here in verse 2 is *tomesai* (rather than *tharrēsai* which is translated "bold" in verses 1 and 2).   Perhaps Paul chose this word to contrast his uncompromising apostolic boldness or daring with the feigned courage which the Judaizers attributed to him.   Before he ever wrote these words he had determined in his own mind that if persuasion failed to bring the congregation to a right state of mind, he would resort to that power with which God had armed him to put down all opposition, whether it be from among the members of the congregation or from the false teachers.   The people indicated by "some" certainly included those who were the cause of any lost appreciation for Paul's apostolic authority among the members of the church.   We have concluded in the Introductory Studies that the errorists attacked in chapters 10-13 are evidently the Judaizers.[15]   Paul has already alluded to the fact the Judaizers were not really Christians (6:14).   He now calls attention to the fact that what they taught was not Gospel (11:5) but instead was contrary to any real knowledge of God (10:5).

Who regard us as if we walked according to the flesh - "By the word 'us' here, Paul means himself, though it is possible also that he speaks in the name of his fellow-apostles and laborers who were associated with him."[16]   "Walk" is a word often used in its figurative sense to denote the course or manner of a person's life (cp. 2 Corinthians 5:7).   *Logidzomai*, which is translated "propose" in the previous clause and "regard" in this one, could also be translated "reckon."   The false teachers may "reckon" that he walks according to the flesh;[17] that is, he is a crafty and deceitful man (12:16) whose motives are unspiritual and whose aims are selfish.   Paul says that he "reckons" that he is daring enough to confront those who have slanderously offered that estimate of him and his ministry.

---

[14] 1 Timothy 1:12 indicates Paul had received the same empowerment that the twelve apostles were promised by Jesus (Acts 1:8).   The word translated "strengthened" at Acts 1:12 is the same word translated "receive power" at Acts 1:8.

[15] Before reading further in these comments, it would be well for the reader to review the information there given.

[16] Barnes, *op. cit.*, p.207.

[17] See notes at 1:17 for an explanation of living "according to the flesh."   Living "according to the flesh" has also been dealt with in Romans 8:12,13 and 1 Corinthians 1:26.

10:3 - *For though we walk in the flesh, we do not war according to the flesh,*

For though we walk in the flesh - There is a play on prepositions in this verse.   To walk (live) "*in* the flesh" (this clause) is different from walking "*according* to the flesh" (next clause).   He concedes that like all human beings who live "in the flesh," that is, in mortal bodies,[18] he must devote some of his time taking care of his temporal needs.   However, when it comes to his apostolic ministry, he flatly insists that those human limitations and weaknesses do not regulate or determine his conduct.

We do not war according to the flesh - Paul pictures his ministry as being like a soldier in active military service ("war" translates *strateuomai*[19]).   The metaphor of warfare is a common way of illustrating the Christian life where the forces of God and of the devil are locked in mortal combat.[20]   Paul and his helpers and converts are on God's side; the Judaizers and their followers are on the devil's.   The devil's soldiers do walk according to the flesh, and they do mind the things of the flesh (Romans 8:5); their whole outlook is prompted by worldly considerations prompted by the devil.   Christ's men walk according to the spirit as they are prompted by the Holy Spirit (Romans 8:6-14).   Perhaps in the background of what Paul here writes we can hear an allegation against Paul made by the Judaizers that he walked according to the flesh (i.e., he was dominated by worldly standards and principles and methods).   Paul repudiates that charge.   Rather, he says, as Christ's soldiers campaign, they fight with spiritual weapons rather than carnal (verse 4).   In fact, were he living according to the flesh he might be a coward like the Judaizers have tried to assert he was, and he might stay far away from the enemy camp.   But to the contrary, he indicates that he is about to carry the battle into their camp.

10:4 - *for the weapons of our warfare are not of the flesh, but divinely powerful for the destruction of fortresses.*

For the weapons of our warfare are not of the flesh - The ASV put this verse in parentheses to show English readers that verse 4 unfolds the truth of the statement just made in verse 3, that "we do not war according to the flesh."   It continues the metaphor where Paul compares his labors in the ministry to a military campaign.   Paul recognized that the "arm of flesh" will fail you, so he did not rely on such weapons.   With an allusion to the methods his opponents used when they attacked him, Paul indicates that his methods are not slander, detraction, and misrepresentation.   Unlike them, he did not appeal to pride and positions of power and influence

---

[18] The phrase "in the flesh" is generally used by Paul for the simple fact of bodily existence (e.g., Galatians 2:20; Philippians 1:22-24).

[19] At Luke 3:14 the same word is translated "soldiers" in the NASB, which has a marginal reading, "Lit., men in active military service."   There are times when the Christian minister finds himself, as it were, in a battle as fierce as any ever fought on the battlefield between opposing armies.

[20] See Ephesians 6:11-17; Philippians 1:30; 1 Thessalonians 5:8; 1 Timothy 1:18; 2 Timothy 2:3,4, 4:7.

to overcome his opponents. He does not here specify the weapons he does use, but Paul has elsewhere (e.g., 2 Corinthians 6:6,7) enumerated the weapons on which he did rely, so there was no danger of mistake.[21]

But divinely powerful for the destruction of fortresses - Where the NASB has "divinely powerful," the Greek reads "powerful to God." "To God" is in the dative case, for which there are several possible meanings.

- It might be a dative of advantage or interest, i.e., "for God" or "in His service," where one would not use weapons of flesh.
- It might be a dative of agent, i.e., "through God," where God is the one who gives the power.
- It might be a dative of respect, i.e., "before God," that is the weapons Paul uses are powerful in His estimate.[22]

The antithesis between "of the flesh" and "powerful" is unusual. We might have expected Paul to write "spiritual." When he chose "powerful," Paul likely was answering a false charge made against him by the Judaizers. Using human eyes, they judged Paul's meekness and gentleness as weakness. However, Paul is aware that when he is weak, that is when God's power is available to him (1 Corinthians 1:27; 2 Corinthians 12:10, 13:14). He has been empowered (1 Timothy 1:12) by God, just as were the twelve (Acts 1:8), and he knows how God works mightily though him. Since Paul was born in Tarsus of Cilicia, perhaps his language ("destruction of fortresses"[23]) is colored by memories of recent history, such as Pompey's victorious wars against the Cilicians. Using the "crow" (a large military engine which operated a great claw) to break into walled cities, Pompey destroyed 120 military strongholds and fortresses, and carried off 10,000 as prisoners. The crow was in general use in Roman armies, so even the readers outside Cilicia would get a good mental picture of what Paul is saying when he uses this figure. The word here for "destruction" (*kathairein*, used also at 10:8 and 13:10) signifies one facet of the work of an apostle. Just like the prophet Jeremiah's ministry was two-fold, "to destroy ... and to build" (Jeremiah 1:10), so was the work of an apostle (2 Corinthians 10:8). God gave powers to the apostles both to build and destroy. Paul would rather use the power to build up (2 Corinthians 13:10), but he will use the God-given power to destroy when the occasion or situation calls for it. The fortresses which Paul is bringing down are

---

[21] Paul also names the weapons he uses at 1 Thessalonians 5:8. (Ephesians 6:11-16 deal with weapons used against demonic attack, rather than against attacks from false teachers like his opponents at Corinth.)

[22] A Greek dative case is not well translated as an adjective ("divinely"). Those versions which do so treat this expression as a Hebraism, as though behind the dative is a Hebrew way of speaking when one wants to express a superlative idea. Thus "to God" in this place is thought to mean the strongest power available, namely divine power.

[23] The language comes from the military world, being used there of the capture and destruction of fortified cities (cp. Lamentations 2:2; Proverbs 21:22; 1 Maccabees 5:65, 8:10).

those in which evil is entrenched and from which the progress of the gospel is hindered. Examples of the kind of fortresses which he specifically has in mind are identified in the next verse.

10:5 - We are *destroying speculations and every lofty thought raised up against the knowledge of God, and* **we are** *taking every thought captive to the obedience of Christ,*

We are **destroying speculations** - This verse begins Paul's application of his military metaphor to his own ministry and the situation at Corinth. "Destroying" is a nominative plural participle and so agrees with the "we" of verse 3 that is the subject of the sentence. One of the enemy fortresses Paul has to pull down as he goes from place to place with the gospel is "speculations" (*logismous*) which men raise up (the verse goes on to say) against the knowledge of God. Included in such speculations would be systems of false philosophy, and in this particular case, the plausible arguments by which the Judaizers were attempting to lead the Corinthians astray. Paul says the "weapons of God" he used (verse 4) are mighty enough to overcome even the reasonings by which Jews and Gentiles tried to evade the teaching of the apostles.

And every lofty thing raised up against the knowledge of God - The noun "lofty thing" probably, like "fortresses" in verse 4, continues Paul's use of military metaphor to describe his ministry. "Lofty" calls to mind fortresses such as the ones at Gamla or Megiddo, where walls and towers were erected on rocky hilltops to check the progress of the enemy. In this case it is the devil who has erected these lofty places, and the knowledge of God is the enemy he is trying to stop. The "knowledge of God" is the true knowledge of Him that comes through knowing His Son Jesus Christ (2 Corinthians 4:4). Apostles of Jesus such as Paul were the God-chosen agents to spread that knowledge. The Judaizers were disparaging Paul's apostolic authority, and therefore Paul looked on their teachings as hindrances to the gospel, hindrances which needed to be destroyed. In this attitude he agrees with Jesus who denounced the Pharisees and their teaching (Matthew 15:3-9: 23:1-39).

And *we are* **taking every thought captive** - The military metaphor continues. Having destroyed the fortress, the victorious army takes captive the survivors. "Every thought" indicates that the conflict in which Paul is engaged is not physical, but is in the realm of ideas which are contradictory to the truth of the gospel.[24] Paul was not trying to forcefully subjugate people (who, even though conquered might still be rebels in thought to their captor), but he wanted to win their loyalty by capturing their thoughts. Using God's weapons to change men's thoughts, Paul is able not only to win submission but also loyalty.

---

[24] *Noēma*, translated "thought" is used five times in 2 Corinthians, and usually the word signifies man's unredeemed state of mind (2:11, 3:14, 4:4, 10:5, 11:3). "Neither here, nor in 1 Corinthians 4:4, does Paul express disapproval of human reasoning, or deny the right to think for oneself. It is those reasonings and thoughts which oppose or corrupt the truth to which he declares hostility" (Plummer, *op. cit.*, p.277).

To the obedience of Christ - There is little doubt that "the obedience of Christ" means "obedience to Christ." If we continue the military metaphor, submission to Christ (in all their thoughts) is the new land into which Paul wants to carry the captives. In that land, the old hostile thoughts and plans promoted in men's minds by the evil one have been removed and replaced with whole-hearted allegiance to Jesus Christ.[25] The Judaizers were not teaching obedience to Christ, so the Corinthians ought not listen to them.

10:6 - *and we are ready to punish all disobedience, whenever your obedience is complete.*

And we are ready to punish all disobedience - Not only will Paul (in the confidence that for the most part he will prevail) wage a battle for truth and his apostolic authority, he is also prepared to use whatever measures his apostolic office required to deal with folk who continue to fight against that truth.[26] Some have supposed the military metaphor continues, and Paul is threatening a court-martial. Be this true or not, Paul is threatening the disobedient with serious consequences. When he speaks of his readiness "to punish all disobedience," he certainly did not have in mind the majority of those in the Corinthian church to whom he writes, and whose recent repentance and obedience have filled him with so much joy (2 Corinthians 7:6-13). He rather is warning either a minority in the church who continue to resist his apostolic authority, or the Judaizers who are fomenting that rebellion. If it is the Judaizers he has in mind, then the threatened punishment may be some severe discipline such as the apostle exercised in the case of Elymas (Acts 13:6-12). If it is Corinthian Christians he has in mind, then the threatened severe punishment may be akin to "delivery unto Satan" (1 Corinthians 5:5; 1 Timothy 5:20), with a view, if it were possible, to their ultimate restoration (2 Corinthians 13:3-10). If all we read in this verse is a threat of punishment, then we might say Paul's tone is harsh or severe.

---

[25] If we continue the military metaphor, this clause describes Paul's ministry objectives. Those who think the military metaphor ended earlier in the verse will often comment on this verse as though it speaks of each Christian's effort to control all his own thoughts so that they are pleasing to Christ. It is certainly true that once a man has become a Christian, he will have to work on his thoughts. Lipscomb (*op. cit.*, p.130,131) has a thoughtful paragraph: "This brings out the truth that the lifework of the Christian is to cast down all the imaginations and everything that exalts itself against the knowledge of Christ and casting these out of his heart; to bring every thought of his heart to the obedience of Christ. No heart is actually clean in the sight of God until the very thoughts and feelings and impulses of the heart are brought into subjection to the will of Christ. It takes a lifework to accomplish this, but too often the Christian life is so neglected that the heart never becomes purified for a habitation of God through the Spirit. ... The end sought is to bring every thought of the heart and mind into obedience to Christ, which is a difficult thing to do. Evil thoughts will arise in our minds, excited by fleshly lusts, yet by constant prayer, watchfulness, and persevering effort, the very thoughts that spring from the heart can be brought into subjection to the will of Christ. The heart can be so trained that the thoughts that arise in it will be of God, of our duties and obligations to Him, and of the high and exalted privileges blessings that are bestowed on us as His children."

[26] "We are ready" is an idiom meaning "I am prepared to act if necessary."

But if Paul is trying to lead them to repentance, trying to bring their thoughts into harmony with Christ, then the tone is solemn but loving and compassionate.

Whenever your obedience is complete - The words translated "disobedience" and "obedience" are both formed off a Greek root which means "to listen" or "to hear." Obedience means to listen and do.   Disobedience means failure to listen. "Whenever your obedience is complete" implies that their obedience, even at the present moment as this letter is being written, was approaching completeness.   He hopes that all the members of the congregation will repudiate the Judaizers' false claims and acknowledge his apostolic authority.   He will allow an interval to give the minority more time to listen and do, but his language also implies that he expects there may be some exceptions.   Those disobedient cases he will punish and people in Corinth will see that he is not, as has been charged, a coward.   What they will see is an apostle of Jesus in action using methods that are "divinely powerful."

10:7 - *You are looking at things as they are outwardly.   If anyone is confident in himself that he is Christ's, let him consider this again within himself, that just as he is Christ's, so also are we.*

You are looking at things as they are outwardly - The NASB treats the Greek verb *blepete* as being an indicative[27] form by means of which Paul makes a charge which he will press home in the following verses.   The phrase "things as they are outwardly" (literally, "according to the face") occurs first in the Greek sentence for emphasis.   Judgments based merely on outward appearance very often prove to be wrong.   The Judaizers have been trying to cause the Corinthians to doubt Paul's apostolic authority by an appeal to outward appearances instead of calling attention to what was the essence of a true apostolic ministry.   Paul here charges the Corinthians with having too readily listened to such superficial arguments.   Now, Paul has no problem with examining a man's credentials, provided the examiner uses correct criteria.   So Paul here begins a list of his actual (not superficial) apostolic credentials.

If any one is confident in himself that he is Christ's - The indefinite pronoun *tis* ("any one"), like the indefinite *tinos* ("some") in verse 2, points to the apostle's opponents.[28]   The Judaizers have made a claim that they belong to Christ in an exclusive sense in which Paul did not; therefore, they argued, the Corinthians should listen to them and dismiss Paul as having any authority.   Paul begins his refutation

---

[27] The Greek verb form can be either an interrogative ("Do you look?" KJV), imperative ("Look at what is before your eyes!" RSV), or indicative (ASV, NASB). If we accept the verb as being imperative, the command is addressed to the congregation, as Paul instructs them to "Take a look at what is obvious!"

[28] The singular need not be interpreted to mean that Paul is now thinking of a particular individual, say the ringleader of his opposition.

of this claim of exclusivity by saying it was just in the Judaizers' minds[29] that they had this special relationship to Christ, i.e., that they were the true apostles of Christ (2 Corinthians 11:13,23).[30]

Let him consider this again within himself - "Let him consider" is an imperative in the Greek. This is a command from Paul. "Consider" translates the same Greek word that "reckon" did in verse 2. The Judaizers reckoned that Paul walked according to the flesh, and they reckoned themselves to be Christ's apostles. This is what they thought in their minds. Well, Paul says, they need to think again. They need to take another look, a serious look, at the evidence to see if there is any valid reason to exalt themselves and disparage him at the same time.

That just as he is Christ's, so also are we - This is a denial that the Judaizers had any *exclusive* claims to be apostles of Christ. At this point, Paul only claims bare equality; as the argument advances, he will claim more than equality.[31] "Paul will proceed to prove that he is Christ's servant and apostle by the fact that he was the founder of their congregation (10:13-18); that he had always acted with absolute disinterestedness (11:1-15); that he had lived a life of toil and suffering (11:21-33); and that he had received special revelations from God (12:1-6)."[32] Is there any way his opponents can make credible claims to such evidences for their authority? Hardly! It should be remembered that all of this is not just an attempt at personal vindication, but was intended to guard the Corinthian church from the danger of apostasy (11:2,3).

---

[29] "Confident in himself" means confident in his own mind. "Confident" is a perfect tense verb which implies a long-time confidence that still exists. The Judaizers were evidently in error in this confidence.

[30] The expression "that he is Christ's" requires some special attention. (1) Some have supposed it means simply "he is a Christian." It is true that the word "Christ's" (literally, "of Christ," a genitive of possession) is another way of saying in Greek what is expressed by the word "Christian," namely, one who belongs to Christ (the suffix -*ian* shows possession). But it is difficult to explain the remainder of this verse ("just as he is Christ's, so also are we") under this hypothesis. In fact, if the Judaizers at Corinth were like their contemporaries at Galatia, they were *not* Christians, but were false brethren who sneaked into the church to spy out the liberty Christians have in Christ (Galatians 2:4). (2) Perhaps the Judaizers were claiming a special, exclusive relationship to Christ. It will be recalled that there was a "Christ party" in the church at Corinth (1 Corinthians 1:12), people whose rally cry was "I am of Christ" ("of Christ" being the same Greek we have here in verse 7). That party claimed some exclusive relationship to Jesus that none of the other groups in the Corinthian church could claim. Did that party trace its roots to the Judaizers who came to town and claimed a special relationship with Jesus? This interpretation of what Paul writes here in verse 7 is hard to accept, for again when Paul says "so also are we" would he not be including himself among those who made such narrow, exclusive claims, and even be giving legitimacy to that party? (3) Those who supply a noun after "Christ's" seem to be on the right track – e.g., "Christ's servant" (manuscripts D,E,F,G, read "a slave of Christ") or "Christ's apostle." The Judaizers apparently came to town claiming to be apostles of Christ, and it is this claim that Paul is refuting.

[31] Paul will give various criteria by which they may test his apostolic credentials at 10:8, 11:23-28, 12:9,10,12-15, 13:5,6.

[32] Farrar, *op. cit.*, p.239.

10:8 - *For even if I should boast somewhat further about our authority, which the Lord gave for building you up and not for destroying you, I shall not be put to shame.*

For even if I should boast somewhat further about our authority - "For" shows this is a reason why Paul could say (verse 7) "so also are we." Apostolic authority was the issue. The Judaizers made empty boasts about having such authority. Paul really does have apostolic authority, and if he should boast about it, his boasts would not be empty. In fact, even if he should use stronger language than he has done in verses 3-6 about his authority, there is not the least prospect that he will be put to shame because his claims proved to be false. There will be ample justification of his claims. The word "boast" occurs eighteen times chapters 10-13. "Boast, boast, boast" seems to reflect what the Judaizers are doing, making numerous empty boasts. Because some of the Corinthians have been impressed by such boasting, Paul feels compelled to adopt the same method (2 Corinthians 11:16, 12:1,6), though one feels as he reads these boasts that Paul is embarrassed about doing so.[33] "Our" may be an editorial plural by which Paul refers to himself,[34] or he may be connecting himself with the other apostles whom Jesus chose. Christ's apostles had authority (*exousia*) to be Christ's ambassadors who urged their listeners to be reconciled to God. They had authority to direct the affairs of the church. They had authority to administer discipline (even, on occasion, supernatural chastisement). Paul is claiming for himself the same apostolic authority.[35]

Which the Lord gave for building you up and not for destroying you - While apostolic authority could be used to punish disobedience (verse 6),[36] Paul makes it clear in this clause that he was not threatening the faithful majority at Corinth. In their case (he twice writes "you") he will use apostolic authority to build them up.[37] There likely is intended a deliberate   comparison with the Judaizers when Paul says

---

[33] In chapters 10-13, Paul uses the word "boast" with a different sense than we saw in chapters 1-9, where he used the word to describe his glad confidence in his readers (7:4,14; 8:24).

[34] "A mixture of singular and plural persists through this chapter; then the singular becomes dominant in the remaining chapters of this letter" (Fisher, *op. cit.*, p.401).

[35] In Galatians, when refuting the Judaizers, Paul emphasized the divine origin of his call and gospel. Here in Corinthians, against similar opponents, he emphasizes the origin of his authority, and its employment for the up-building of the Corinthian church. How different from the Judaizers, whose presence and influence had produced only friction and division.

[36] "Destroy" is the same root word used in verses 4 and 5.

[37] The Greek word behind "building up" is regularly translated "edification," and is a metaphor for the promotion and preservation of the community. He will use his apostolic endowments to help them continue to grow in Christ.

his authority came from the Lord.[38]   Theirs did not, no matter what they may have boasted.   "The Lord gave" protects Paul from any hint of egotism as he makes this boast about authority.   In the words "destroying you" there seems to be another deliberate comparison between his ministry and that of the Judaizers whose influence on the church has only been harmful.

I shall not be put to shame - Can the Judaizers say that the things they have boasted about will never prove false?   No, they will be disgraced when the day comes on which it is obvious their boasts were hollow.   Paul knew his powers were God-given and God-approved, so he here (using an indicative verb) expresses confidence that he will not be shown to be a pretentious boaster.

10:9 - *for I do not wish to seem as if I would terrify you by my letters.*

For I do not wish to seem as if I would terrify you - Verse 9 is a purpose clause in the Greek that may be translated "in order that I may not seem as though to terrify you."   Paul has interjected the note about building up the believers (verse 8) precisely so they will not be frightened by what he has been writing concerning his powers to destroy and his readiness to use them.   It is not the faithful majority but the disobedient whom Paul wishes to frighten into action.   Paul uses this language, he goes on to explain in verse 10, because he is aware of and is heading off the disparaging allegation made by the Judaizers that he could be terrifyingly forceful in his letters, but was afraid to press his authority when face to face with men.

By my letters - While the plural "letters" in this verse and the next has been used as proof there must have been a "previous letter" (see notes at 1 Corinthians 5:9), no such hypothesis as a lost severe letter is required to explain the plural "letters."[39]   1 Corinthians and the letter now being written would satisfy the plural "letters." Besides these two letters, the Corinthians must have known about the letters to Thessalonica which were written from Corinth.

10:10 - *For they say, "His letters are weighty and strong, but his personal presence is unimpressive, and his speech contemptible."*

For they say, "His letters are weighty and strong -   While it is difficult to decide

---

[38] It was on the Damascus road that Jesus called Paul to be an apostle (Acts 26:16-18), and on another occasion, perhaps during Paul's stay in Arabia, he was also given the same apostolic powers that had been given to twelve.   (Cp. also 1 Timothy 2:12 and Acts 1:8.   The word translated "empowered" in Timothy is the same translated "power" in Acts.)

[39] Those who believe there was a previous letter and a severe letter in addition to 1 Corinthians write how the more Paul writes to Corinth, the more forceful his letters become.

whether Paul wrote "they say" or "he says,"[40] it is obvious that here we have an actual quotation of the very words Judaizers used to disparage Paul's apostolic authority.[41] What they said about Paul's letters was exactly right: they are weighty (impressive[42]) and they are strong (powerful in the effects they produced; they abounded with strong argument, manly appeals, and impressive reproof). His critics could not deny the solid and effective character of Paul's letters,[43] for the Corinthians had already been moved to grief by one of them (2 Corinthians 7:8).[44]

But his personal presence is unimpressive - Just as there was truth in their statement about Paul's letters, there must be some truth in this statement about his "bodily presence" (ASV) or his personal appearance. Some folk exude an air of authority by their outward appearance, their size or stature, the way they carry themselves, or the way they take charge. Not Paul. "Unimpressive" translates the word *asthenēs*, a word often used to denote weakness or infirmity of body, sickness, or disease.[45] How sick a man was Paul when he came to Corinth to minister? On his first missionary journey, it was because of a bodily illness that Paul preached to the Galatians the first time (Galatians 4:13). On his second missionary journey, when he did come to Corinth, Paul says that he was with them in weakness (*asthenēs*) and in fear and in much trembling, and his preaching was not punctuated with the flowery oratory the Corinthians were so delighted to hear from public speakers (1 Corinthians

---

[40] The manuscript evidence seems to favor the singular reading "He says" (Aleph,D,E,F,G,K,L,P) rather than the plural (B, f,g,r,Vulg.) so that recent Nestle-Aland and UBS Greek texts uniformly read "he says." Paul has used a singular ("any one," verse 7) and will use another singular ("such a person," verse 11) to refer to his Judaizing opponents. Thus the suggestion that at this place Paul is quoting the very words of the *leader* of the Judaizers may be overstating the case. It just might be the case that some scribe altered Paul's plural to a singular to match the singulars in verses 7 and 11. On the other hand, a singular might have been changed to a plural by a scribe who noted that the context seems to show that the criticism of Paul was not confined to one individual.

[41] Before this (at 1:17, 3:1, and 5:12,13) we have had allusions to what the Judaizers had said about Paul, but not actual quotations.

[42] The same word *bareiai*, which can mean weighty or impressive, is used at Matthew 23:23. While it is possible the two epithets the Judaizers used to describe Paul's letters are not meant to be complimentary (as though they said his letters are tyrannical and violent), the translation of our version seems better.

[43] The plural "letters" referred to here are the same letters spoken about in the previous verse.

[44] We, too, agree with this assessment of Paul's letters that they are weighty and strong. "Paul's letters comprise a considerable portion of the New Testament; some of the most important doctrines of the New Testament are those which are advocated and enforced by him; and his letters have done much to shape the theological doctrines of the Christian world. Take away Paul's letters, and what a chasm would be made in the New Testament Canon!" (Barnes, *op. cit.*, p.211)

[45] See Matthew 25:39,43,44; Luke 10:9; Acts 4:9, 5:15,16.

2:3,4). Even if this is a true description of Paul's bodily presence, and it may be,[46] it was very cruel of the Judaizers to call attention to his infirmities just to raise questions about his apostolic authority.[47]

And his speech contemptible" - While the first two quoted statements in this verse may have been accurate, this one is not, unless one was judging merely by worldly standards. Greek audiences delighted in oratorical flourishes and rhetorical eloquence. Paul himself acknowledged that when he preached, he did not use "cleverness of speech" (1 Corinthians 1:17), nor "persuasive words of wisdom" like Greek orators did (1 Corinthians 2:4). However, he insists that when he preached the gospel, the word of the cross, he preached by inspiration and he demonstrated the power of God (1 Corinthians 2:1-5, 13). The word here translated "contemptible" is translated "despise" in Galatians 4:13,14, where Paul observes the Galatians did not despise nor loath him because of the sickness that had brought him to their region. How Paul might wish for a reception at Corinth like he received in Galatia. To say his speech was contemptible is a mean insult the Judaizers have spoken.[48] The scorn conveyed in them must have deeply wounded Paul, especially if people were persuaded by such observations to reject Paul's apostolic authority.

10:11 - *Let such a person consider this, that what we are in word by letters when absent, such persons* we are *also in deed when present.*

Let such a person consider this - This is Paul's response to anyone[49] who tries to undermine his apostolic authority in the minds of folk by saying he is incapable of showing that authority in person. Authority to destroy he has, and the next time he

---

[46] The Judaizer's characterization of Paul is not quite the same as the description given in *The Acts of Paul and Thecla* (a uninspired document from the 2nd century AD). There the description of Paul is "a man of middling size, and his hair was scanty, and his legs were a little crooked, and his knees were projecting (bowlegged); and he had large eyes, and his eyebrows met, and his nose was somewhat long (aquiline); and he was full of grace and mercy; at one time he seemed like a man, and at another he seemed like an angel." (*The Ante-Nicene Fathers*, edited by Roberts and Donaldson [Grand Rapids: Eerdmans, 1951], Vol.8, p.487.)

[47] In this commentator's judgment, the Judaizers have made allusion to the physical appearance of Paul, that he was a sick man much of the time. Because *asthenēs* can also mean 'without strength,' and because of what Paul writes in verse 11 following, a case could be made that the contrast intended is one between the character of his letters and the character of the man himself. In his letters he was bold as a lion and firm as a rock; when he came face to face with you, he was mild, and gave way as much as possible, trying to please everybody. Face to face, he was a weakling, his enemies said. Perhaps there is even a reference to the recent unsuccessful intermediate visit Paul made in person to Corinth. His enemies have used his defeat to taunt him.

[48] It should be remembered that this disparaging word about Paul's speech was spoken by a servant of Satan (2 Corinthians 11:15) and should not be accepted as though it were gospel truth.

[49] "Such a person" (like "some" in verse 2 and "any one" in verse 7) refers to anyone who questions his apostolic authority by making such a remark as quoted in verse 10.

comes to Corinth and finds disobedience, they will learn that he is not hesitant to exercise it when the need calls for it. They will find that his deeds will compare favorably with the threatenings and warnings penned in his letters. Twice more before this letter is finished he will repeat this warning (cp. 12:20, 13:2,10). "Consider" is the same verb used at verses 2 and 7. In verse 7 he asked his detractors to think again. Once more he commands them to think again about what he is really like.

That what we are in word by letters when absent - The detractors' charge was that Paul was more brave and courageous in his letters than he was in person.

Such persons *we are* **also in deed when present** - The words "we are" in italics show that some verb must be supplied, since the Greek has none. The KJV supplied a future tense verb ("will we be") which makes this a reference to his intended visit to Corinth. The ASV/NASB have supplied a present tense verb, which makes the statement not so much a threat of what will happen in a particular instance, say, the next time he comes to Corinth; rather it becomes a statement of the general consistent character of his life, day in and day out. Whether it is building up or destroying, whether in person or in letter, the exercise of apostolic authority was consistent. There was no discrepancy between his words and his deeds. Instead of thinking he is inconsistent, they should be thinking that what he threatens in his letters will certainly be executed against the unrepentant. This is Paul's reply to the charge of weakness and lack of courage.

B. An Appeal for Them to Recognize his God-Assigned Area of Mission, and to Help Him Cover It.   10:12-18

10:12 - *For we are not bold to class or compare ourselves with some of those who commend themselves; but when they measure themselves by themselves, and compare themselves with themselves, they are without understanding.*

For - We are following the lead of the UBS Greek text which begins a new paragraph at this verse. This verse forms a transition to the new topic, namely, whether or not Paul even had a commission to come to Corinth to preach. In language similar to verse 12, verse 18 closes this paragraph.

We are not bold to class or compare ourselves - "We" is emphatic in the original, indicating a sharp contrast between Paul and the Judaizers when it came to boasting. "Paul's enemies had accused him of a lack of courage, a lack of boldness, when present with them, 10:1,2.   Here, in a strain of severe but delicate irony, he says he was too timid to do things which they had done."[50]   There is a play on words in the Greek behind "to class or [to] compare" (Greek, *enkrinai, sunkrinei*).   If we were to translate these verbs as "pair or compare," we would preserve the similarity in sound and yet not change the meaning conveyed by the original.   "I could not venture to pair myself with, or even compare myself to" is Paul's declaration.[51]

With some of those who commend themselves - Paul had been accused by the Judaizers of singing his own praises (3:1, 4:2, 5:12, 7:11).   Whereas, before, he defended himself against the charge of self-commendation, now Paul affirms that such self-commendation is precisely what his critics are fond of doing.   "To do this, Paul says, required greater boldness than he possessed, and on this point he yielded to them."[52]

But when they measure themselves by themselves, and compare themselves with themselves - The repeated plurals in this verse (just as in 3:1 and 4:12) point to several false apostles who have come to Corinth.   Paul accuses them of having formed a mutual admiration and self-admiration society.   In order to "measure themselves by themselves," they would have to set up their own conduct as the standard of excellence; then constantly "comparing themselves with themselves" they would find their conformity to their own standard of conduct to be eminently satisfactory and admirable.   "Only those who judge by worldly standards would become involved in such comparing."[53]

They are without understanding - The Greek verb express the idea that all power of spiritual discernment is missing.   It is very far short of wisdom or spiritual discernment to set up one's own standards of conduct as normative, and then find great satisfaction in always measuring up to that standard.   If "the value of a comparison depends on the standard,"[54] then wise men of God need an external standard by which to compare themselves.   Such a proper standard would be the will of God (what God requires), the character of Christ the Redeemer,   and the message

---

[50] Barnes, *op. cit.*, p.213.   In verses 12 and 13 there are a number of different textual readings. For example, the Western Text manuscripts omit "they are without understanding, but."   All other manuscripts retain these words.   Some manuscripts read "not boasting" instead of "we will not boast."   In addition, since early manuscripts had no accent marks, it is not possible to determine whether *suniasin* (the last word in verse 12) is a third person plural indicative active verb, or a dative plural participle agreeing with "themselves."   Plummer, *op. cit.*, p.285,286 has well described how adopting one or another of these readings changes the meaning of the passage, sometimes significantly.   Having examined the evidence and the probabilities, in this commentator's judgment, the NASB gives substantially the meaning of the original.

[51] Plummer, *ibid.*

[52] Barnes, *ibid.*

[53] Thompson, *op. cit.*, p.143.

[54] John W. Russell, *Compact Commentary on the New Testament* (Grand Rapids: Baker, 1964), p.452.

Christ spoke, which, after all, will be the standard of judgment on the last day (John 12:48).

10:13 - *But we will not boast beyond* **our** *measure, but within the measure of the sphere which God apportioned to us as a measure, to reach even as far as you.*

But we will not boast beyond *our* measure - "We" is emphatic in the Greek and draws a sharp contrast between Paul and his critics. They are boasting beyond measure, not he.[55] The language is indefinite. In what area were the Judaizers' boasts excessive? Was it what they claimed after they had measured themselves by themselves (verse 12), the idea being that there was no limit[56] to how much they would praise themselves? Was it what they claimed concerning the area to which they had been assigned (verse 13), the idea being that they boasted that their assigned sphere of ministry included Corinth while Paul's did not? Was it boasting in "other men's labors" (verse 15), the idea being that they were boasting of what had been done in Corinth as if it were their own work? In none of these areas did Paul make boasts like the Judaizers did. We will interpret in light of the immediate context which speaks of their sphere of labor.

But within the measure of the sphere which God apportioned to us as a measure - While the Judaizers who set their own standards boast beyond measure, Paul does not set the standards. God does. And when he boasts, Paul has a settled determination never to exceed the limits which God has fixed for him. Literally, Paul wrote, "according to the measure of the canon which the God of measure has apportioned to us." "The God of measure" tells us that it is God's prerogative to set the standards or areas in which Paul will minister. *Kanon*, translated "sphere" here and at verses 15 and 16 in the NASB, was originally a reed used as a measuring rod or to determine straightness.[57] The ASV chose "province" to translate *kanon* since the word speaks of an area definitely marked out. In stark contrast to the Judaizers' commission (if

---

[55] In this section, each of Paul's denials ("we are not, we will not, we are not") are his accusations against the intruder(s) from Palestine. He does not behave like they have behaved. When the Corinthians are weighing the claims to authority given by both the intruders and Paul, who has been the most straightforward and openhanded with them?

[56] The word translated "beyond measure" is *ametron*, literally 'no limit.'

[57] To be a measuring rod, the reed first had to be measured against an absolute standard; then the measured rod became a standard by which other things could be measured. The word *kanon* has an interesting history. It is used in Philippians 3:16 of the standard of life and doctrine by which Christians are expected to live. In the 2nd century, *kanon* came to refer to the "rule of faith" by which all religious ideas were measured. In the 4th century, *kanon* also came to be used of the inspired books included in our Bibles. Those books were measured to ascertain that they came from God, and they then became the standard by which all other religious books are measured. So, when we speak of the canon of the New Testament, we are alluding to books that are an authoritative standard for Christian faith and practice.

indeed they had one), Paul says his sphere of ministry was assigned to him by the God of measure.[58]

To reach even as far as you - Jesus called Paul to be an apostle to the Gentiles (Acts 26:17,18). At the Jerusalem Conference (Galatians 2:7-9) the apostles Peter, James, John, and Paul all recognized the sphere of ministry assigned to each of them, and in Paul's case it was to "go to the Gentiles."[59] Since the whole country of Greece was predominantly Gentile, Paul rightly regarded that region falling within the sphere assigned to him by God.[60] If the Judaizers claimed that Corinth was theirs and he was an intruder because he came to Corinth, they were wrong. If they asserted Paul had gone beyond the area assigned to him by God, they were wrong.

10:14 - *For we are not overextending ourselves, as if we did not reach to you, for we were the first to come even as far as you in the gospel of Christ;*

For we are not overextending ourselves - Paul appears to be answering an accusation against him made by the Judaizers, that he has no right to be there in Corinth.[61] Either they said he had no commission, or that he had exceeded the limits of his commission when he presumed to enter Corinth. Paul replies that he did have

---

[58] It is better to speak of God mapping out the area Paul was to evangelize rather than appealing to the agreement made at the Jerusalem Conference (Galatians 2:7-9), where Paul (and his helpers) would go to the Gentiles while Peter, James and John would go to the Jews. Since the Judaizers were false brethren and not even a part of that agreement, it is difficult to think that Paul is here accusing them of having trespassed on his sphere of operation in defiance of that agreement (as Harris, *op. cit.*, p.712, suggests).

[59] That God had assigned Paul a people to evangelize is not to be confused with man-made comity agreements, where a certain territory (say Achaia, in Paul's case) is assigned exclusively to some missionary as the region in which his actual ministry should be confined. The attempt to impose comity agreements on the mission fields of the world in the mid-20th century was a cause of great evil when some of the parties to the agreement were non-immersionist denominations.

[60] In Romans, which Paul writes from Corinth at the end of his labors in this area, Paul alludes to his mission as being to go where other apostles had not been (so we interpret Romans 15:20 to mean). He also indicates that he is free to go to Rome and to Spain only after he has thoroughly evangelized other areas between Jerusalem to Illyricum (Romans 15:19-23).

[61] Behind our NASB translation lie some difficult technical matters. Did the original text contain the negative "not"? How shall we punctuate the verse (punctuation marks have been invented and added by men; they do not occur in the ancient manuscripts)? Concerning the text, some manuscripts (*Aleph*, D, F, G, K, L, M) read just as does our English text – making this verse a statement of fact. A few manuscripts (B and 2 cursives) omit the negative "not." This requires the sentence to be treated as a question, "Are we overextending ourselves, as though we had no commission to come to Corinth?" with an implied answer of "No!" This reading has proven attractive because it carries with it the implied question, Where did the Judaizers get their authority? Then there is the question how the verses should be arranged. It is doubtful that verse 14 should be considered as a parenthetical explanation of verse 13, though Westcott and Hort so treated it. We agree with our translators that verse 14 is not a parenthetical statement. Furthermore, since verse 15 begins with a participle in the Greek, we will connect it to verse 14 rather than to verse 13. This decision requires us to begin a new sentence with verse 14.

a commission from God (verse 13) and he was well within the limits of the area assigned to him to evangelize. It was the Judaizers who were the intruders at Corinth, just as they were intruders years earlier in Antioch (Acts 15:1; Galatians 2:4) and more recently in the churches of Galatia (Galatians 1:6-8).[62] They had not been sent by God as Paul the apostle was.

As if we did not reach to you - As Paul alludes to a claim made by the Judaizers that by going to Corinth he had crossed over into territories in which he had no business, there is a subtle implication that the Judaizers themselves were intruders. They had not been sent by God. Paul had been. Corinth was included in his God-assigned field of work.

For we were the first to come even as far as you in the gospel of Christ - "For" tells us this clause is intended as a reason why Paul can say Corinth was included in his God-assigned field of work. Paul was the first[63] to preach Christ in Corinth because that is the way God so ordained it. When we remember that the very missionary tour that eventually brought Paul to Corinth was directed by the Holy Spirit (Acts 16:6-10), and when we recall that once Paul got to Corinth that Jesus told Paul to go on preaching (Acts 18:9-11), there is no question but that God wanted Paul in Corinth. Paul was not the intruder. Corinth was within the sphere to which God had called Paul to evangelize. Furthermore, as Paul went from place to place preaching, it was the gospel of Christ that was his message. The implication is that the Judaizers have a different message, one that is *not* gospel.[64]

10:15 - *not boasting beyond* **our** *measure,* **that is,** *in other men's labors,* **but with the hope that as your faith grows, we shall be, within our sphere, enlarged even more by you,**

Not boasting beyond *our* **measure** - Again, Paul contrasts his behavior with that of

---

[62] Did the Judaizers have a commission? As the Sanhedrin once commissioned Paul the persecutor of Christians to go to foreign cities (Acts 9:1,2, 22:5) seeking them out, have they commissioned the Judaizers to go to Corinth? Was the Sanhedrin the source of their letters of commendation (2 Corinthians 3:1). Even if the letters the Judaizers had were not fake, such a commission from men would be less than worthless compared to a commission from God such as Paul had.

[63] There is no word in the Greek that corresponds to "first" but the verb translated "come" is *phthanō* (not the usual *erchomai*) which in classical Greek had the sense of anticipation, i.e., to get somewhere before others came, to arrive first in a place.

[64] It is implied that the Judaizers who have invaded Corinth have wrongly been teaching what God expects of Gentiles in this church age, and that Paul is reminding his readers (who certainly knew of the decision of the Jerusalem Conference, Acts 15 and Galatians 2) that God accepts Gentiles on the basis of their obedient faith, not on works of the Law (Pharisaic halakhic rules, cf. Galatians 2:16). The Judaizers at Corinth were as crossways of the gospel as were the Judaizers who had invaded Antioch years earlier, and should be repudiated just as firmly.

the Judaizers.   They are the ones intruding on the labors of others and boasting about it beyond measure.   Paul does boast,[65] but he never boasts in the labors of someone else.

That is, **in other men's labors** - To boast in another man's labors is to take credit for what the other person did.   The Judaizers have accused Paul of boasting in other men's labors, i.e., of intruding into an area not assigned to him and taking credit for evangelistic work others had already done.[66]   Paul's rebuttal of their false accusation presses home the charge that it is they, not he, who were guilty of such boasting beyond measure.   He has done nothing of the kind.   These are the facts: after Paul labored a year and a half (Acts 18:11) planting the church in Corinth (he was the first to come to Corinth, verse 14), the Judaizers arrived in town.   They did not begin any new work; they simply moved in and claimed the results of Paul's work as their own. If the Corinthians wish to identify who it is that is working in some other man's sphere, they should think carefully concerning who were the intruders.

But with the hope that as your faith grows - Paul boasts about what the Lord has sent him to do in Corinth (verse 13) with the hope that their faith would grow.   Paul uses a present tense verb, "as your faith grows."   He expresses his confidence in them that growth in faith will begin immediately and continue.   Perhaps the particular area of "faith" this context requires is belief in Paul's apostolic authority.   He is the messenger from God, not the Judaizers.   Their continuing growth in faith will free him from needing to spend time with them giving them constant care, thus freeing him up to carry the gospel of Christ to other unevangelized areas.

We shall be, within our sphere, enlarged even more by you - Here Paul begins to hint at his future plans.   He had been commissioned to go to the Gentiles, and there were more of those to be reached with the gospel.   If and when he goes to them, he will still be working within the sphere which God assigned to him.   From his letter to the Romans, written from Corinth only a few months after this letter, we know that Paul dreamed of going on further west, to Rome and to Spain with the gospel (cf. Romans 15:24,28).   At the time Paul was writing this letter, Corinth was the Western

---

[65] Not all boasting is bad.   Paul can boast about the things pertaining to God and what Christ has accomplished through him (Romans 15:15-17).   He speaks of God's grace bestowed on him that allowed him to labor more than all of the other apostles (1 Corinthians 15:10).   He has boasted of the Corinthians' willingness to give (2 Corinthians 9:3).   He boasts of visions and revelations from the Lord (2 Corinthians 12:1).

[66] The Judaizers could marshal certain evidence that on the surface might appear to substantiate their accusation about Paul.   Had not Paul worked at Antioch where the gospel had already been preached (Acts 11:20-26) by someone else?   Did he not come to Ephesus after Priscilla and Aquila had already been laboring there (Acts 18:24-19:8)?   Is this charge by the Judaizers behind Paul's explanation written a month or so after 2 Corinthians (Romans 15:20) that he endeavored to preach the gospel where Christ was not already named, lest he build upon another man's foundation (an expression, it has already been noted, likely means he does not go where another apostle of Jesus has already been)?

limit of Paul's missionary work.   Before Paul can do anything else, the problems at Corinth must be satisfactorily settled.   He could not leave in his rear an unstormed fortress of opposition to the gospel.   Then he can, perhaps even with their help,[67] go to lands yet unevangelized.   So this verse contains an appeal to the Corinthian church to set their house in order, for if they did not, they would become a hindrance to the mission work God would do in His world.

10:16 - *so as to preach the gospel even to the regions beyond you, and not to boast in what has been accomplished in the sphere of another.*

So as to preach the gospel even to the regions beyond you - Having delicately suggested that the Corinthians might help him on his way (verse 15), Paul now gives them the gist of his future plans for areas to evangelize.   It will be in regions west of Corinth, regions beyond the territory already covered by the three missionary journeys recorded in Acts 13-21.   If we take as a beginning point of Paul's evangelistic work either Jerusalem or Antioch of Syria, then Western Greece,[68] Italy, or Spain,[69] would all be regions beyond Corinth.   By pointing to regions beyond Corinth, Paul is telling them he has no intention of settling down in Corinth to exploit them, as the Judaizers were doing.   When the disorders there were corrected, he was going to move on to evangelize other parts of the world.

And not to boast in what has been accomplished in the sphere of another - With an implied criticism of the Judaizers, and using some of their very words of accusation against him, Paul says his plans are to go to areas no one has yet evangelized (cp. Ro-

---

[67] Most translations take the dative *en humin* at the close of the verse as a dative of agent, "through you," "with your help," "by you" (NASB).   The NIV treats it as a dative of sphere, "among you."   The resultant meaning is that rather than financial help, Paul hopes to receive from them the apostolic esteem he deserves.

[68] A few weeks or months after writing 2 Corinthians, Paul will say he has fully preached the gospel from Jerusalem as far as Illyricum (Romans 15:19).   His previous preaching in Macedonia would have brought him to the province that bordered the east side of Illyricum.   Perhaps that is all that is intended in Romans 15:19.   No evangelistic work in Illyricum is recorded in Acts.   If Paul actually evangelized in the province of Illyricum itself, we must suppose he made a trip there between his writing of 2 Corinthians from Macedonia and his subsequent arrival in Corinth just before he wrote Romans.

[69] In this commentator's judgment, in light of what Paul wrote to the church at Rome, he had Italy and Spain in mind when he spoke of the "regions beyond" Corinth.   While Paul did get to Rome (Acts 28:14,16), whether Paul ever went to Spain has been a much-debated question.   In the Introductory Studies in the author's commentary on 2 Timothy and Titus, it is concluded that the first Roman imprisonment changed Paul's plans, and rather than going to Spain when released from that imprisonment, he revisited the churches of Asia Minor and Macedonia, as he indicated in the Prison Epistles he intended to do when released.

mans 15:20).[70]   If he does that, no one can claim he is working in another man's sphere.[71]   Can the Judaizers say they are free from that very charge during their stay in Corinth?   If they really are apostles of Jesus like they claim to be, why are they not, like those genuine apostles, out doing new church evangelism instead of merely intruding into churches already established.   If the Corinthians will consider all this for a moment, it should quickly become evident who has genuine apostolic authority. It is Paul, not the false apostles.

10:17 - *But HE WHO BOASTS, LET HIM BOAST IN THE LORD.*

But - As a Scriptural rebuke of the Judaizers, Paul is about to paraphrase some words from Jeremiah 9:23,24.[72]   They have not been giving the Lord the credit He should be given.

HE WHO BOASTS - The thrust of the Old Testament passage is that boasting is illegitimate unless it is boasting in what the Lord has done.   The boasting of the intruders (they boasted in themselves and in other men's labors as though they had accomplished what others had actually done) is certainly condemned by this very familiar passage from the Word of God.   The Judaizers could never quote this passage about the only proper kind of boasting as a criticism of Paul.   In this very letter, Paul ascribed all his power to God (10:5), and insisted that God had apportioned to him the very sphere in which he has been working (10:13).   A study of 1 Corinthians 15:10, Romans 15:17, and Galatians 2:8, will show that, whatever Paul has accomplished, he only boasts in what the Lord enabled him to do.

LET HIM BOAST IN THE LORD - It is likely that in the Old Testament "the Lord" refers to God the Father.   While it is possible "the Lord" (both here and at 1 Corinthians 1:31) refers to Jesus Christ,[73] the context here has been talking about God apportioning fields of work.   The Judaizers have been violating this fundamental, Biblical rule about boasting.   They have not been giving God the credit He is due.

---

[70] "What has been accomplished" is a good rendering of the Greek which literally reads "things ready to hand," i.e., something already done by someone else.

[71] "Sphere" (the same word used in verses 13 and 15) recalls all that has been said about how God apportions spheres of labor.   Paul was not going to do what the false apostles had done, go to an area which God had appointed to another, and boast that they had done what someone else actually had accomplished before them.

[72] The same words were already quoted in 1 Corinthians 1:31.

[73] "It is remarkable with what readiness that New Testament writers transfer what in the Old Testament is said of Jehovah to Jesus Christ, and this may be a case in point." Plummer, *op. cit.*, p.290. To boast in Jesus Christ, if, indeed "the Lord" refers to Him, is something the Judaizers will find it impossible to do as long as they continue to reject Jesus as the Messiah and champion their works of the Law.

10:18 - *For not he who commends himself is approved, but whom the Lord commends.*

For not he who commends himself is approved - Here Paul makes application of the passage just quoted from Jeremiah. He has referred a number of times to the Judaizers' custom of commending themselves (3:1, 4:2, 5:12, 10:12), that is, of advertising their own virtues and accomplishments. Jeremiah 9:23,24, which calls on men to boast in the Lord, not themselves, shows that folk who commend themselves do not have God's approval. *Dokimos,* here translated "approval," was a word commonly used of metals that have been tested and found to be pure. The test that shows the Judaizers to be in error is the passage from Jeremiah.

But whom the Lord commends - How do we know whom the Lord commends? Jeremiah has told us that it is the one who boasts in the Lord, not the one who commends himself. Paul's point is this: if the Lord does not commend the Judaizers, then neither should the Corinthian Christians. If people (like the intruders) who praise themselves disqualify themselves for the Lord's approval, then by parity of reasoning they disqualify themselves from receiving the approval of the Lord's people. If the Corinthians carefully consider this Biblical truth, surely there will be no question which leadership – the apostle Paul's, or the false apostles' – the Corinthians will choose to accept and follow.

C. An Appeal for the Church to Esteem him More Highly (than the False Apostles Esteemed him).   11:1-13:10[1]

1. The Reasons for this Appeal.   11:1-4

> *Summary:*   Both verses 2 and 4 begin with "for" and are thus to be understood as being reasons why Paul wishes the Corinthians would bear with him in a little foolish boasting.[2]

11:1 - *I wish that you would bear with me in a little foolishness; but indeed you are bearing with me.*

I wish that you would bear with me in a little foolishness - *Ophelon* (translated "I wish") is an interjection in the Greek.   "O that!" catches the earnest wish that Paul is expressing.[3]   Paul is going to continue the comparison of himself (an apostle of Jesus) with the Judaizers (false apostles), but first (11:1-4) he justifies making this comparison.   The Corinthians have been impressed by such boastings when the Judaizers commended themselves.   Since the Corinthians have shown such toleration for them, he now asks them to show a little toleration[4] for him if he wishes to indulge in a little foolishness.   Paul knows that boasting[5] is "foolishness;" if by such means a battle is one, it really would not be wining at all.   Throughout this section he keeps repeating the word "fool" or "foolish" (verses 1,16,17,19, 21, 12:6,11) because it was distasteful and embarrassing to speak of his own labors and sufferings; but he is willing to make a fool of himself (if that is what it takes) to save them from disaster.   God's word commands that a fool should be answered according to his folly (Proverbs 26:5).   That is what Paul is about to do here.   He will meet the Judaizers on their own ground.

---

[1] This appeal is the heart of these last four chapters of 2 Corinthians.

[2] It will be observed that verse 2, verse 4, and verse 5, all begin with "for."   Some treat all three as being reasons for asking them to bear with him in a little foolishness.   We think it best to treat verse 5 as the beginning of a new paragraph, since no new thought begins after verse 5 until we get to verse 16 of this chapter.

[3] Berry, *Lexicon*, p.73.   As the words "to God" (see KJV) are not in the Greek, it is better to treat the words of verse 1 as a wish.   The interjection is a way of expressing a wish that is almost too good to become true.

[4] "Bear with" (or "tolerate") is used often in this chapter (see verses 1,4,19,20).

[5] For a number of verses now, Paul has been writing about "boasting" (10:8,13,15,16,17).   It is, of course, foolish to boast (i.e., commend one's self, 10:12,18).   In fact, he has already emphasized that self-praise is inadmissible and worthless (3:1, 5:12, 10:12).   But since the Corinthians looked on outward things (10:7), Paul feels forced to do what the Corinthians evidently like to listen to (12:11).

But indeed you are bearing with me - The Greek verb can be either indicative or imperative. Taken as a simple statement of fact (indicative), Paul would be saying that the Corinthians have already been humoring a little of his foolishness (6:3-10, 10:13-17). Taken as in imperative, Paul would be repeating his wish in the form of a prayer ("Please do bear with me," NEB, NASB mg.). To treat it as an imperative makes it easier to explain the next verse.

11:2 - *For I am jealous for you with a godly jealousy; for I betrothed you to one husband, that in Christ I might present you as a pure virgin.*

For I am jealous for you with a godly jealousy - "For" shows Paul is here giving his first reason for asking them to bear with him. He loves them fiercely, and so is anxious for them because they were in danger (verses 2 and 3). "You" in this verse is plural and indicates Paul has in mind, not the Judaizers, but the Christians at Corinth. The word *zēlos* translated "jealous" can also be translated "zeal"; it speaks of a "passionate commitment to a person or a cause."[6] At each place the word occurs in the Greek, the precise meaning must be determined from the context. Since Paul is using a metaphor of a marriage, "jealous" is a good choice to convey the idea. The Greek behind "godly jealousy" is, literally, "jealousy of God." The exact meaning for "of God" is not certain. Perhaps it is a Hebraism, so that like "mountains of God" means very lofty mountains, "jealousy of God" means very great jealousy. Perhaps we are to see a contrast intended between Paul's jealousy and the "jealousy" the Judaizers have for the Corinthians; there is nothing "Godly" about their desires for the Corinthians! Instead it was purely selfish and mercenary. Perhaps Paul means that his jealousy for the Corinthian church is like God's jealousy for Israel in Old Testament times. The Old Testament characterizes God as a jealous God who was provoked when Israel was unfaithful to Him by going off after other gods (Exodus 20:5; Ezekiel 16:38, 23:25). Paul seems to be saying that he was as anxious for the faithfulness of his converts to Christ, as Jehovah in Old Testament times was anxious for Israel to be faithful to Him.[7]

For I betrothed you to one husband - "For" says here is why Paul was jealous over them. In the metaphor Paul uses, the Corinthian congregation is pictured as Paul's spiritual daughter. Like fathers arranged the betrothal and marriage of their daugh-

---

[6] Thompson, *op. cit.*, p.147.

[7] "Human jealousy is a vice, but to share divine jealousy is a virtue. It is the motive and object of the jealousy that is all-important. There is a place for a spiritual father's passionate concern for the exclusive and pure devotion to Christ of his spiritual children, and also a place for anger at potential violators of that purity."

ters in the ancient world, so Paul pictures himself as arranging an engagement[8] of the Corinthian believers to the heavenly bridegroom, Jesus (Mark 2:19,20; John 3:29).[9] Paul spoke of himself as their spiritual father (1 Corinthians 4:15); when the Corinthians responded to the gospel they[10] had become betrothed or engaged to Christ.[11] The indwelling Holy Spirit is a "pledge" of more to come (2 Corinthians 1:22, 5:5). "Pledge" pictures the gift of the Holy Spirit (Acts 2:38) as the engagement ring.

That to Christ I might present you as a pure virgin - In the ancient world, a certain period of time elapsed between the betrothal and the wedding ceremony. During that time the father committed himself to guarding her virginity until the day of the wedding. Likewise, Paul pictures himself as being committed to guarding the virginity of the Corinthian Christians, that is, their undivided loyalty to Christ, until the day of Christ's second coming when they are presented to the bridegroom at the marriage supper of the Lamb (Revelation 19:7-9).[12] When those wedding festivities begin the holy bride (the church) will enter her bridegroom's home. That's when the believers' wedding ceremony takes place. Paul hopes to present (*parhistēmi*) the church to Christ, the bridegroom, at that time.[13] He wants the bride to be "pure," and such purity is maintained only by the Corinthians' loyalty to the one Husband to

---

[8] Contemporary usage is "engaged" instead of "betrothed." Some authors, mistakenly in this commentator's judgment, have suggested that Paul pictures himself as the friend of the bridegroom. The Greek word *hērmosamēn* (from *harmodzō*) is not found elsewhere in the New Testament, though it does occur in the LXX. Strictly speaking, it is used of the act of the father arranging for the coming marriage of his daughter. So we explain this passage. In the Greek the word translated "betrothed" is in the middle voice. In classical Greek the middle voice would be used of the man betrothing himself, and in Proverbs 19:14 it is used of the woman betrothing herself. The active voice would have been used of betrothing another person, say a father giving his daughter to be engaged (see G.B. Winer, *A Grammar of the Idiom of the New Testament* [Andover: Draper, 1872], p.323). But in the Semitic societies, fathers arranged for the marriage of their sons or daughters. The use of the middle voice in this context perhaps suggests that Paul was acting in his own interest when he betrothed the Corinthians to Christ.

[9] See Ephesians 5:25-32 for an extended presentation of the metaphor of the church being the bride of Christ.

[10] Here again, as in the concluding verses of chapter 10, it is clear that Paul, by using "you" (plural), is addressing the whole congregation, and not the Judaizers.

[11] There are some who, when preaching, illustrate the relation between the Christian and Christ as that between *married* people, whereas this passage speaks of that relation as being an *engagement*. Ephesians 5:22 is sometimes appealed to as proof that the Christian is already married, because the term "wife" is used. But the apparent discrepancy might be reconciled by remembering that the ancient custom was to call the *betrothed* woman a "wife" (see Deuteronomy 22:24 and the case of Mary by comparing Matthew 1:20 with Luke 2:5) and the *betrothed* man a "husband" (see the case of Joseph, Matthew 1:19).

[12] Compare also Jesus' parable about the marriage feast, and the man with the improper garment (Matthew 22:1ff).

[13] Because Paul did not live until the second coming, some have looked for a different explanation for the time of "presentation." Because the word "present" is elsewhere used for offering up a sacrifice to God (the same word *parhistēmi* is translated "commend" at 1 Corinthians 8:8), some think Paul mixes metaphors at this place. No longer is he using marriage customs as

whom they are betrothed.   If they listen to the Judaizers and turn to "another Jesus," they will have become unfaithful, and that will result in a breaking of the engagement. The jealousy which Paul had for the church was that nothing should interfere with the marriage.   For that to happen, the Christians must be faithful to Jesus, and not allow their affections to be turned aside to another.

11:3 - *For I am afraid, lest as the serpent deceived Eve by his craftiness, your minds should be led astray from the simplicity and purity* **of** devotion *to Christ.*

But I am afraid - Paul had just compared the church to a betrothed virgin, soon to be presented as a bride to the Redeemer.   There is one, the devil, who does not want this to happen, and he is at work in Corinth (2 Corinthians 11:14,15).   Jealous as he is for the Corinthians, Paul harbors some apprehension about what the devil and his helpers might do to the bride.   "I am afraid" is a present tense verb in the Greek.   It implies a continuous fear, something Paul is constantly worried about.

Lest - The Greek is *mē pōs*, which is better translated "lest somehow."   The expression is indefinite and it suggests Paul's ambivalence that the devil may be successful at Corinth, and then, again, perhaps he may not be successful.

As the serpent deceived Eve by his craftiness - Paul here writes about what is recorded in Genesis 3:1-16, just as he did in Romans 16:20.   "Serpent," here and in the Old Testament, refers to the one who is called the Devil and Satan (Revelation 12:9, 20:2) and who was the agent by whom Eve was deceived.   "Deceived" translates a compound verb which is strong in meaning.   It would be proper to say that Eve was utterly or completely deceived.[14]   She was fooled, tricked, deceived intellectually.[15]   How could the devil deceive Eve so thoroughly?   Because of his

---

his metaphor; instead, he is speaking of what he is doing during his earthly ministry, namely, offering up the Corinthian Christians as a sacrifice to God. (See his use of similar language in Romans 15:16.) If it be thought that the marriage metaphor is continued, with the presentation taking place at the second coming, appeal for a parallel idea of what occurs at the second coming might be made to 1 Thessalonians 2:19,20, where faithful Thessalonian Christians in the presence of the Lord will be Paul's joy and crown.

[14] In 1 Timothy 2:14 the same compound verb marks a distinction between Adam and Eve; she was "quite deceived," but he was not even "deceived." What he did, he did to please himself and his wife. (Plummer, *op. cit.*, p.294)

[15] H. St. J. Thackeray (*The Relation of St. Paul to Contemporary Jewish Thought* [London: Macmillan, 1900], p.55), we believe, goes too far in saying that in these verses (2 Corinthians 11:3-15) we have very strong reason to believe Paul was being influenced by the Rabbinical legend found in the *Apocalypse of Moses*, and elsewhere, that the serpent seduced Eve to unchastity and that Cain was their child. Paul doesn't say "seduced"; he says "[utterly] deceived." It is certainly possible that Paul was acquainted with the legend, but there is no evidence that he accepted it, or that he intended to give his approval to it in the language here used. It is difficult to believe Paul would allude to such Jewish legends when writing to Gentiles.

"craftiness,"[16] a word that means he uses trickery and is willing will do anything, however mischievous and underhanded, in order to achieve his ends. In passing, it should be observed that here is another place where the inspired New Testament writers accept the historical facticity of the Genesis record. They do not treat it as myth, or allegory, or fiction, or poetry. The account in Genesis 3 is a true record of what actually happened in the early history of mankind.

Your minds should be led astray - This is a very appropriate analogy, for as Eve was the wife of the first Adam, so the church is the betrothed wife of the second Adam. If the Corinthian church becomes unfaithful to Christ, it will be because their minds are led astray (or corrupted) just as was Eve's. Paul is fearful the devil would try to do to the Corinthians exactly what he did in Eve's case. The devil got Eve to be disloyal to God. The devil would now make an effort to get the Corinthians to be disloyal Christ. At the time of Paul's writing, only a few of the Corinthians were under the influence of the Judaizers. But there was a risk that large numbers of the church might be led astray by these agents of Satan (verses 14,15), especially if his apostolic authority is not recognized by them.

From the simplicity and purity *of devotion* **to Christ** - The addition of the words in italics, "of devotion," after the words "simplicity and purity" likely expresses the thought Paul was writing. "Simplicity" has a connotation now which does not represent what Paul is saying. *Haplotētos*, here translated "simplicity," means single-minded.[17] The one who is betrothed to Christ must have his or her mind focused solely on Him. If the Corinthians turn to "another Jesus" (verse 4), their single-minded devotion will be gone. Christ will allow no sharing of affections. The one who is betrothed to Christ must be pure in devotion; that is, she must have in her intended husband the only object of her affection. The bride's great danger was intellectual deception that would lead to spiritual apostasy.[18]

11:4 - *For if one comes and preaches another Jesus whom we have not preached, or you receive a different spirit which you have not received, or a different gospel which you have not accepted, you bear* **this** *beautifully.*

For - As "for" in verse 2 introduced a first reason why the Corinthians should bear

---

[16] "Craftiness" is a stronger word than "subtlety" that was used in the Genesis 3 account to describe the Devil. At 2 Corinthians 4:2 Paul has already used this "craftiness" to describe the methods of the Judaizers.

[17] See at 2 Corinthians 8:2 where the word "liberality" in our NASB reflects the same Greek word *haplotēs*.

[18] The Corinthians were not the last church which faced danger of apostasy. Down through the years, numerous congregations have been seduced by servants of Satan. It still happens in the 21st century.

with Paul (verse 1), so "for" here introduces this verse as being a second reason why they should bear with him. The general idea is that if the Corinthians were willing to listen to the Judaizers who came to town, should they not be willing to listen to a genuine apostle of Christ?

If one comes - The singular "one" is used like the "any man" and "such an one" in 10:7,11 to indicate any one of the Judaizers who have come to Corinth after Paul started the church there. "If" is the Greek word that assumes the truth of what is being said. That these false apostles "came" to Corinth reminds the readers that the Judaizers were outsiders who were causing the trouble and raising doubts about his apostolic authority. It is also clear from the way Paul describes the Judaizers at Corinth (verse 4,13,15) that they are no more genuine Christians than were the "false brethren" who sneaked into the Galatian churches in an attempt to spy out those Christians' liberty (Galatians 2:4).

And preaches another Jesus - "Another" in the Greek is *allos*, a synonym which means another of the same kind.[19] The Judaizers habitually preached[20] a Jesus who, in some respects, at least, was just like the Jesus whom Paul preached. During His earthly ministry, the Pharisees rejected Jesus' claims to deity and being the Messiah. They, of course, did recognize His human side. Perhaps the Judaizers who were Pharisees were telling only about His earthly ministry and then using His crucifixion (something that was a stumbling block to Jews) to claim He couldn't possibly be the long-awaited Messiah. Whereas the Judaizers preached "Jesus," Paul preached "Jesus Christ as Lord" (4:5) and Christ "who is the image of God" (4:4). What is at stake is the validity of Paul's ministry. If the Judaizers are correct in their view of Jesus, then what Paul preaches must be in error. He could not then be an apostle of Jesus.[21]

Whom we have not preached - The past tense verbs "preached," "received," and "accepted" refer to the time when the apostle Paul converted the Corinthians and planted the church at Corinth.

Or you receive a different spirit which you have not received - "Different" in the

---

[19] Berry, *Lexicon*, p.6.

[20] "Preaches" is present tense in the Greek, indicating something that is continuous or repeated or customary action.

[21] We live in a day when form and redaction critics affirm there were several different gospels at the beginning of the Christian era, and that the one we have in our Bibles is the one which won out over the others. It is mistaken to claim that the message of the Judaizers about Jesus was legitimate. We must recall that the Judaizers were not Christians. Their doctrine was not apostolic. Therefore, this verse is not to be taken to prove that Paul's opponents were correctly preaching an "historical Jesus" – a sort of primitive type of gospel – in distinction to the "heavenly Christ" that Paul preached. This verse is no proof text that Paul's doctrine about Jesus was different from that generally held by all the apostles of Jesus and by the early Christians.

Greek is *heteros*, the synonym which means another of a different kind.[22]   The Greek word translated "spirit" in the NASB is *pneuma*.   When *pneuma* refers to the Holy Spirit, the word "holy," or some other descriptive term, indicates this.   But where *pneuma* is used by itself, as it is here, it is sometimes difficult to determine whether it is Holy Spirit,[23] the human spirit, an angel or evil spirit,[24] or an attitude that is intended.   In this place the explanation that is easiest to see is to treat "spirit" as though it refers to an attitude.   The "different spirit" the Judaizers taught would be a spirit of bondage and fear (Galatians 4:24; Romans 8:15), and of fear (Romans 8:15), while the spirit the gospel produced is a "spirit of adoption as sons" (Romans 8:15), a spirit of freedom (2 Corinthians 3:17; Galatians 5:1,15) and of joy (1Thessalonians 1:6; Galatians 5:22; Romans 14:17).

Or a different gospel which you have not accepted -- "Accepted" translates *edexasthe*, a verb which means "welcomed," something done voluntarily.   It pictures the Corinthians' early response to the gospel of Christ.   Again, "different" is *heteros*, another of a different kind than the gospel Paul preached when he planted the church at Corinth.   This "gospel" that is "different" from the one Paul preached and the Corinthians accepted is the message of the Judaizers.   In Galatians 1:6-9, Paul accuses the Galatians to turning to a "different gospel" which in fact is no gospel at all.   His words to the Galatians throw light on the message preached by the false teachers who came to Corinth.   Paul's gospel was one of pardon conditioned on obedient faith to what God has commanded.   The Judaizer's "gospel" was based on punctilious observance of the old Pharisaic works of the Law, an observance which substituted man-made rules for God's rules.   We recall how Jesus, during His ministry, denounced the Pharisees' rules as making void the word of God (Matthew 15:1-9).   In the years since, the Pharisees have not changed.[25]

You bear *this* beautifully - "You" is plural.   As before, this section is addressed to

---

[22] Berry, *ibid*.

[23] Moffatt and the NEB treat this as a reference to the Holy Spirit, but attempts to explain how the Judaizers offered a different Holy Spirit than the gospel does have not proven convincing.   The most believable of these attempts is the one that has Paul referring to miraculous spiritual gifts (1 Corinthians 12:1-11) and has him asking whether the Corinthians received these to a greater degree from the Judaizers than they did from him.   After all, the signs of an apostle are the miracles they performed (2 Corinthians 12:12).

[24] If "spirit" is speaking of a demonic spirit, then the inspiration claimed by the Judaizers for their teaching was a counterfeit or demonic inspiration (similar to what 2 Peter 2:1 and 1 John 4:1-3 warn against).   1 Corinthians 12:3 also indicates that unholy spirits can inspire false cries.

[25] Plummer (*op. cit.*, p.296) conjectures that "Jesus," "spirit," and "gospel," which are a somewhat strange triplet, were leading terms in the teaching of the Judaizers.   If so, it shows that men may use the language of Scripture and pour into their words whole different meanings so as to actually pervert the glorious gospel and make it a gospel that actually is no gospel at all.

the congregation as a whole. The KJV ("ye might well bear with him"[26]) and the ASV ("ye do well to bear with him") seem to treat this clause as a positive statement, but that cannot be right, since the very thing Paul is writing to stop was their "bearing with" the Judaizers. In order that English readers will not think it is a positive statement, the NASB adds a demonstrative pronoun, "you bear *this* beautifully." Still, it is difficult to determine whether Paul meant to speak sarcastically or seriously. We doubt Paul is being sarcastic for sarcasm ("You manage to put up with that well enough," NEB) is hardly a winsome tone. If we take Paul seriously, and if we treat verse 4 as a reason for his plea in verse 1 to bear with him, then in this closing clause of verse 4 he is asking the church to give him at least as much consideration as they gave his opponents, for, after all, he has proven that he is a genuine apostle of Christ. It was from Paul they first heard about Jesus. What reason have they for not listening to him now?

2. As a basis of his appeal to esteem him more highly he calls attention to his credentials. 11:5-12:13

a. His knowledge was one credential. 11:5-15

11:5 - *For I consider myself not in the least inferior to the most eminent apostles.*

For I consider myself - "For" gives a reason why they should give him as much consideration as they do the Judaizers, that reason being his superior credentials. The verb translated "consider" is the same verb used several times in these chapters (see 10:7,11). In his mind, Paul has totaled up the real facts of the case and this is the result: by his reckoning he is not inferior to the apostles whom the Judaizers idolized. Before he has finished with this paragraph, he will show he was superior in knowledge (11:5-15), in the matter of service and suffering (11:16-23), and when it came to visions and revelations (12:1-10). These superior credentials certainly gave him a right to be heard.

Not in the least inferior to the most eminent apostles - At Jerusalem, a few years before, Judaizers held the apostles Peter, James, and John in high repute (Galatians 2:6) and spoke of them as "pillars" (Galatians 2:9). The Judaizers treated the three as being higher in rank than Paul. It appears that the Judaizers who have come to Corinth are making the same argument. They have called those three, or perhaps the twelve, by the title "most eminent apostles" as they tried to destroy the Corinthians'

---

[26] The KJV, following a different manuscript tradition, makes all of verse 4 entirely hypothetical. "If he that cometh preacheth ... ye might well bear with him."

confidence in Paul and his gospel.[27]   The Greek word translated "most eminent" is *huperlian*, a word that occurs in the New Testament only here and at 2 Corinthians 12:11.   It carries the idea of extra special, super, extraordinary.   The possibility is to be considered that the Judaizers coined this phrase to speak of Jesus' original apostles whose authority the Judaizers illegitimately invoked in support of their denial of Paul's apostolic authority.   Paul is picking up their term and refuting it.[28]

11:6 - *But even if I am unskilled in speech, yet I am not* so *in knowledge; in fact, in every way we have made* this *evident to you in all things.*

But even if I am unskilled in speech - *Kai*, with which this verse begins in the Greek, should be translated as "and" rather than "but."   Using *ei kai* (translated "even if"), Paul is conceding as a fact what is stated in the "if-clause."[29]   Paul here makes an admission that there is one particular that was true in the Judaizers' statements which were intended to defame him,[30] namely he was no trained rhetorician or professional orator.   He was unskilled in that kind of speech,[31] and deliberately so.   He has called attention to the fact that he did not use "superiority of speech or of wisdom," nor did he use "persuasive words of wisdom" (1 Corinthians 2:1-5), and that Christ sent him "to preach the gospel not in cleverness of speech, that the cross of Christ should not be made void" (1 Corinthians 1:17).   All these expressions refer to Greek oratory or

---

[27] Those who write about how chapters 10-13 are harsh in tone have drawn some of their evidence from this very unusual expression.   First, it is concluded the "most eminent apostles" are not the twelve but the Judaizers who have come to Corinth.   Then "most eminent" is said to be an expression by Paul of extreme sarcasm.   In notes on 10:1 we have seriously questioned the whole idea that chapters 10-13 are harsh in tone.

[28] Baur and many others have supposed that, instead of being an attack on the Judaizers, Paul here has mounted an attack on the twelve, or at least on the three "pillar-apostles" (Peter, James and John) of Galatians 2:9.   Once this identification of Paul versus the twelve is made, it is alleged that we have here a powerful piece of evidence from Paul's own pen in support of the theory that in the Apostolic Age there was strong opposition or cleavage between Petrine and Pauline factions of the church.   Baur's hypothesis about the conflict between the Petrine and Pauline tendencies in the Apostolic Age, based as it was on Hegel's dialectic philosophy, is now almost everywhere abandoned.   The student who wants more information on this matter should consult the introductory notes in the author's commentary on Acts where he discusses the alleged purpose behind the writing of Acts as being an *eirēnikon*, i.e., a "peace maker" between the two factions.

[29] Dana and Mantey, *A Manual Grammar of the Greek New Testament* (New York: Macmillan, 1927), p.292.

[30] In 2 Corinthians 10:10 Paul has already made allusion to the Judaizer's claim that Paul's "speech is contemptible."

[31] The word translated "unskilled" is *idiōtēs*, the same as that translated "untrained" at Acts 4:13, where it speaks of a lack of professional training.   Paul had professional training under Gamaliel (Acts 22:3).   It is one thing to understand that Paul was unskilled in using rhetorical flourishes; it is quite another to suppose Paul here admits that he was a poor public speaker.

rhetoric.[32]   Had Paul used that, the faith of the Corinthians would have rested on the wisdom of men rather than on the power of God (1 Corinthians 2:5), something which was totally undesirable.[33]

Yet I am not *so* in knowledge - Perhaps this language reflects another defamatory claim made by the Judaizers against Paul.   They said that Paul preaches the way he does because his knowledge is lacking.   Paul flat out repudiates the idea that he is unskilled when it comes to "knowledge."   Paul did claim to have insight into the mysteries of God (Ephesians 3:3,4), to know things because he had received the Spirit of God (1 Corinthians 2:12), and that he had received his gospel by revelation from Jesus Himself (Galatians 1:12).   So his "knowledge" is no doubt the knowledge of God, of Jesus Christ, and of the truth of the gospel.   Paul might also have in mind a knowledge of what is spiritually best for the Corinthians.

In fact, in every way we have made *this* evident to you in all things - His knowledge ("this") was the thing he had made manifest to the Corinthians.   "To you" says Paul and his fellow workers manifested the knowledge of God in every way with the intention of bringing this knowledge to the Corinthians.[34]   "In every way" says that at all times "he made known to them the full truth" (NEB).   "In all things" says that Paul's behavior was compatible with the message he preached.   He has left no grounds for suspicion of his ministry or apostolic authority.   Such a "knowledge" as Paul had to impart was something the Judaizers could not claim.   Paul's credentials were superior to theirs.   Why would the Corinthians want to listen to the Judaizers?

11:7 - *Or did I commit a sin in humbling myself that you might be exalted, because I preached the gospel of God to you without charge?*

Or did I commit a sin in humbling myself - "Or" introduces another negative state-

---

[32] Greek speakers "constructed their speeches with all kinds of decorative phraseology, gloried in balanced phrases and clauses, sought stunning effects by the use of alliteration, used words which sounded good, no matter their meaning, ... and paused at predetermined intervals to receive the applause of their hearers" who appreciated their good performance.   Coffman, "A Treatise on Greek Oratory," *op. cit.*, p.459-50.

[33] We think that modern scholars who pursue rhetorical criticism as a means of interpreting and understanding what Paul is trying to say should hear Paul's own dismissal of such speech!

[34] Students who compare the reading of the KJV and the NASB observe a variation.   The KJV has a passive voice verb in this clause, "But we have been thoroughly made manifest among you in all things," a clause which speaks of Paul working openly and without secrecy among the Corinthians.   The NASB follows a better-attested Greek text (supported by *Aleph*, B, F, G, 33) which has an active verb, "we have made known to you."   "The apparent awkwardness of having a transitive verb without an object in the Greek text probably led to the substitution of the passive participle that is reflected in the KJV" (Plumptre, *op. cit.*, p.100).   P[46] omits all of verse 6b.

ment the Judaizers made as they attempted to spoil the Corinthians' attitude toward Paul and his apostleship.[35]   It is not unusual to introduce a question with the word "or" (cp. 1 Corinthians 6:2; Romans 2:4, 3:29, 6:3).   It serves to introduce an alternative to something just said.   If they are not ready admit that "in every way" and "in all things" his life was in harmony with the gospel he preached, would they be prepared to assert (as the Judaizers had done) that Paul did wrong when he humbled himself by refusing to take financial support from them.   When Paul talks about degrading himself by working for his bread with his hands, he was alluding to the eighteen months he spent in Corinth when the church was first being established. For a while, he supported himself by "tent-making" (Acts 18:3), and all the while he refused to accept wages from his Corinthian converts.   "Did I commit sin" means "Did I do wrong when I gave you God's gift for nothing?"[36]   When Paul wrote 1 Corinthians 9:3-18, he did so because someone had already used his practice to raise questions about him (verse 3) in his listener's minds.[37]   In that first letter to Corinth he told them his reason for refusing to take pay from the people to whom he was preaching.   His enemies seem to have said that was not the real reason.   The Judaizers tried to raise prejudice against Paul by alleging that the real reason Paul did accept any wages from the Corinthians is because he knew that he was not an apostle, and so was hindered by his conscience from taking the wages of an apostle.

That you might be exalted - The exaltation Paul has in mind is in the spiritual realm. God has done for the Corinthians what He did for the Ephesians: he blessed them with "every spiritual blessing in the heavenly *places* in Christ" (Ephesians 1:3). They were brought out of the degradation of idolatry and lifted up to be adopted children of God.

---

[35] Thinking these words are not a quotation of what the Judaizers said, but something Paul is saying, commentators write about the tone as being bitter sarcasm or bitter irony.

[36] This comment interprets the synonym word Paul uses for "sin" (*hamartanō*, which means "to miss the mark") in a figurative sense (making this verse similar to 2 Corinthians 12:13 where Paul pleads, "forgive me this wrong!").

[37] "Greek sentiment would not allow a free citizen to undertake manual labor for anything less than dire necessity (Arist. *Pol.* iii.5), and there was also a general feeling that teachers ought to be paid.   The professional teachers of philosophy in Greece took large fees, and for this turning of instruction into a trade and selling wisdom for money, Socrates (*Mem.*I.vi.1), Plato (*Gorg.* 520, *Apol.* 20), and Aristotle (*Eth.Nic.* IX.1.5-7) condemned them.   The sophists replied that those who taught gratuitously did so because they knew that their teaching was worth nothing" (Plummer, *op. cit.*, p.302).   To the professional orator (just alluded to in verse 6), working with one's hands, especially making tents, to support himself would be to dishonor himself.   Paul did not mean to imply that working with one's hands was demeaning.   He was meeting his detractors on their own ground. Greek sentiment was that traveling teachers were suspect if they did not demand fees.   In the light of this fact, at Corinth it would be easy for the Judaizers to arouse prejudice against Paul's lifestyle. In passages like Ephesians 4:28 and the Thessalonian letters, Paul spells out the fact that, for an able-bodied person, working to support one's self is honorable and expected by Christian ethics.

Because I preached the gospel of God to you without charge - "Because" introduces an explanation of the expression "humbling myself." Paul put in emphatic juxtaposition *God's gospel* (that most precious thing) and *for nothing* ("without charge"). "Without charge" says that Paul received no money from the Corinthians while he was evangelizing in the city of Corinth.[38] To be an unpaid missionary was Paul's "reward" (1 Corinthians 9:17; see also 2 Corinthians 12:14; 1 Thessalonians 2:9; 2 Thessalonians 3:8,9). He could say that he "coveted no man's silver or gold" (Acts 20:33).

11:8 - *I robbed other churches,* **taking wages** *from them to serve you;*

I robbed other churches - Using these words, as they took note of how he was supported during the 18 months he was planting the church in Corinth, the Judaizers made a charge that they had detected what they looked on as evidence he was not a genuine apostle. They used a strong term (which Paul here repeats) to describe what in their eyes was Paul's bad behavior. They said he "robbed"[39] other churches, taking money from them while working for someone else.[40] They saw what he was doing and put a negative spin on it. As verse 9 will indicate, the "other churches" are those in Macedonia. The ones we know about were in the towns of Philippi, Thessalonica, and Berea (Acts 16:19-40, 17:1-9; 17:10-15). Acts 18:5 tells of Silas and Timothy coming from Macedonia to join Paul in Corinth, and 2 Corinthians 11:9 tells us the brethren brought what was required to supply Paul's need. That offering permitted him to cease laboring to support himself and allowed him to devote his whole time preaching. We may believe that Philippi was one church involved in this offering to Paul, for it was their practice to make contributions to his needs (Philippians 4:15,16).

Taking wages *from them* **to serve you** - This was where the charge of "robbery" came in. The Corinthians got Paul's services, and others were allowed to pay him. The word for wages (*opsōnion*), used for the daily rations a soldier received (Luke 3:14; 1 Corinthians 9:7), does not imply any abundance of funds, just enough to live on. "To serve you" says the result of Paul's acceptance of wages from Macedonia

---

[38] There may be an intended contrast to the Judaizers who preach what is not God's Gospel, and take remuneration for so doing (2 Corinthians 11:20).

[39] The verb is *sulaō* which means "to rob or despoil [someone]" (Thayer, *op. cit.*, p.595). The word picture is that of stripping a fallen foe of his armor and valuables (Robertson, *Word Pictures*, V.IV, p.258). Moulton and Milligan give the word "pillage" as a translation (*The Vocabulary of the Greek New Testament*, p.596).

[40] Writers who think "robbed" is Paul's own way of expressing what he was doing as he took wages from the churches of Macedonia, speak of the irony or deliberate hyperbole of the expression. So interpreted, it becomes one more evidence of the alleged harsh tone in chapters 10-13, an idea we have rejected (see notes at 10:1). If this was Paul's own word choice, it would be difficult to explain why Paul used "robbed" since he certainly did not think of himself as obtaining something from someone else in a violent manner, or that the givers were not giving voluntarily. So we treat this language as another slander made by the Judaizers.

was that he could minister to the Corinthians.   "The Corinthians had not only Paul to thank for their hearing of the gospel, but other churches a well."[41]

11:9 - *and when I was present with you and was in need, I was not a burden to anyone; for when the brethren came from Macedonia, they fully supplied my need, and in everything I kept myself from being a burden to you, and will continue to do so.*

And when I was present with you and was in need - Paul continues setting the record straight concerning his acceptance of money from other churches while he was in Corinth.   There was a time when, despite working at the trade of tent-making (Acts 18:3), he was in desperate need.   "The tense and mood of the Greek imply that he ran short of money and felt it."[42]   The time when he "was present" at Corinth was during the second missionary journey, when the church at Corinth was being established.   The aorist tense verb "was in need" shows that this falling behind in needed finances was a crisis, rather than chronic.   At that moment of desperate need, he did not tell them he was hurting, nor did he ask them for help.

I was not a burden to anyone - The word translated "burden" comes from the Greek word *katenarkaō* from whence we get our word narcotic.   It is used of the benumbing shock one experiences when the electric eel called the "torpedo fish" touches you.[43]   He is saying, "I didn't leave you numb, or drain your vitality from you."   There is, likely, in the use of "burden," a subtle accusation against the behavior of the Judaizers in Corinth.   If so, Paul is saying that the Judaizing teachers have drained the Corinthians of all they could get.

For when the brethren came from Macedonia - We may suppose the brethren from Macedonia either were Silas and Timothy (Acts 18:5), or some Macedonians who accompanied those two.   As he wrote about the offering to Jerusalem, Paul has already described the generosity of the Macedonians (8:1,2).   That generosity led the Macedonians to support Paul the missionary.

They fully supplied my need - "Fully supplied" is a good translation of the compound verb *prosanaplērōsan*, which means "to fill up."[44]   The offering got him out of a deep hole financially.   While his custom was not to accept financial support

---

[41] Fisher, *op. cit.*, p.411.

[42] Plummer, *op. cit.*, p.304.

[43] Aristotle, *Anim. Hist.*, vi.10.

[44] Arndt and Gingrich, *Lexicon*, p.718.

from the people to whom he was currently preaching, he did welcome free-will offerings and regular support from other churches and previous converts. On occasion he even asked churches to "send him on his way," that is, to help him financially so he could get to the next place that needed to hear the gospel. He did so in order to avoid all suspicion that he was just preaching for the money. It also precluded any thought that he must say only what would please the people who were supporting him.

And in everything I kept myself from being a burden to you - "Burden" in this clause is another Greek word which means "to place a weight on." This was true the whole year and a half he was there.

And will continue to do so - The future tense obviously points to a resolution that he will continue to act in harmony with his declared statement in 1 Corinthians 9:15-18 that he would preach the gospel without accepting pay. "He had acted on this principle of financial independence early in his ministry in Macedonia (2 Thessalonians 3:8), during time when he was planting the church at Corinth (1 Corinthians 9:1-18), and more recently at Ephesus, which he had just left (Acts 20:34)."[45] His resolution was to continue to offer the gospel *gratis* to those to whom he was currently preaching.

11:10 - As *the truth of Christ is in me, this boasting of mine will not be stopped in the regions of Achaia.*

As **the truth of Christ is in me** - There is no word corresponding to "as" in the original Greek. The KJV and NASB translators added it because of the belief Paul is here taking a solemn oath. Though Paul elsewhere took an oath (e.g., Galatians 1:20; 1 Timothy 2:7) not all commentators agree that Paul is here taking an oath. Omitting the "as," it reads "The truth of Christ is in me." That is a claim of inspiration for what he is writing.[46] What he writes cannot, therefore, be called empty boasting.

This boasting of mine will not be stopped in the regions of Achaia - His boast was that he preached the gospel without cost to them. Since *phrassō* ("stopped") means "to fence in, block up, stop up, close up"[47] or "to stop the mouth,"[48] the metaphor is

---

[45] Plumptre, *op. cit.*, p.100.

[46] Paul claimed inspiration in 1 Corinthians when he claimed to have the "Spirit of God" (1 Corinthians 7:40).

[47] Thayer, *op. cit.*, p.657.

[48] Arndt and Gingrich, *op. cit.*, p.873.

uncertain.   Chrysostom thought the metaphor comes from the damming of rivers.[49]
Plummer thinks it comes from barricading a road.   The verb is used of stopping the
mouths of lions (Hebrews 11:33).   Paul may be saying concerning his boast that his
mouth will not be sealed.   Judaizers may have used Paul's practice of preaching the
gospel without cost to raise doubt in people's minds about his apostolic authority, but
he will not let their innuendoes deter him from his resolution (verse 9).   Frequently
throughout 2 Corinthians Paul has rejected the boasting which characterizes the
Judaizers (3:1, 5:12, 10:12,18).   But there is nothing wrong with boasting in the Lord
(1 Corinthians 1:31).   "In the regions of Achaia"[50] may indicate that the Judaizers
had not confined their operations to the city of Corinth.   He would not bow to their
pressure anywhere in the province.   Since Corinth was the capital of Achaia,[51] if his
boast was not stopped in Achaia, it would not be stopped in Corinth.

11:11 - *Why?   Because I do not love you?   God knows I do!*

Why? - Knowing that the Judaizers have suggested wrong reasons why he refused
maintenance from them, he raises the question himself, so that he may answer the
false accusations.

Because I do not love you? - The Judaizers have said or malevolently insinuated that
his refusal to take their money was proof he did not love them.   In the rest of the
verse, Paul dismisses this charge, and then in verse 12 gives his own explanation.

God knows *I do!* - The Greek has only "God knows," but the added words "I do" are
probably justified.   Fisher says, "The expression is almost an oath."[52]   The NEB
reads "God knows I do love you!"   If we omit the "I do," then perhaps Paul is saying,
'God knows the real reason I don't accept your money.'   It was not lack of love.

11:12 - *But what I am doing, I will continue to do, that I may cut off opportunity from
those who desire an opportunity to be regarded just as we are in the matter about which
they are boasting.*

But what I am doing, I will continue to do - If we translate *de* as "and" (rather than
"but") we have Paul's own explanation of why he did not accept payment for preach-

---

[49] Cited by Plummer, *op. cit.*, p.306.

[50] "Regions" (*klimata*) literally means coastlands (see notes at Galatians 1:21 and Romans
15:23).   The land called Achaia was bounded on all four sides by water.

[51] 2 Corinthians 1:1 has this letter addressed both to Corinth and to the saints throughout
Achaia.

[52] Fisher, *op. cit.*, p.412.

ing the gospel.   It was not that he didn't love them (verse 11) but because he wished to undermine the claims of the Judaizers.   For that reason he will continue to preach *gratis* as he had done all along.

That I may cut off opportunity from those who desire an opportunity - One motive for his conduct is "that he may silence the tongues of those who seek opportunity to detract him."[53]   "Those who desire an opportunity" were the Judaizers. When Paul uses the verb "cut off"[54], he is saying that he is putting an end to any opportunity the Judaizers might seize to cause the Corinthians to doubt his apostolic authority.   They were claiming that their acceptance of wages was proof they were true apostles, while Paul's refusal to accept wages proved he was not.   That claim was just flat wrong.   Before this paragraph is finished Paul will assert that their taking money was a sign of selfish grasping (11:20).   Fisher calls this "a head-on meeting between the embattled apostle and the Judaizers.   Paul frankly admitted that he was out to undermine their claims, and to show them up in their true colors to the Corinthians."[55]

To be regarded just as we are in the matter about which they are boasting - The Greek literally reads: "in order that in what they boast, they may be found just as also we are."[56]   The verb "may be found" is *heuriskō*, which means to be regarded

---

[53] McGarvey, *op. cit.*, p.228.   This clause is the first of two which begin with *hina*, "in order that."   The first is "in order that I may cut off...," and the second introduces the verb "to be regarded." It has not proven easy to decide whether the two *hina* clauses are parallel to each other, or whether the second depends on the first.   We judge that the second *hina* does depend on the first, and gives a reason for his aim of cutting off opportunity.   It is thus a second and final aim of "What I am doing, I will continue to do."

[54] Elsewhere in the New Testament *ekkoptō* ("cut off," cut down") is used of limbs that are amputated from a body (Matthew 5:30), or branches that are removed from a tree (Romans 11:22,24), or of a tree that is felled (Matthew 3:10).

[55] Fisher, *op. cit.*, p.412.

[56] It has been said that "there is no real answer to the problem of the meaning of this verse" (Fisher, *op. cit.*, p.413).   Fisher is reflecting the fact there is little agreement among the commentaries concerning the meaning.   Harris (*op. cit.*, p.769) lists seven different proposals that have been made to clarify the meaning of this verse.

1. Their "mission" (RSV, NAB[2]) or "ministry" (NAB[1]).
2. Their claimed apostleship (Moffatt, Goodspeed, NEB, REB).
3. The legitimacy of their Corinthian ministry, Corinth as their legitimate field of operation (cf. 10:15-16) (Martin, p.348-9).
4. "The apostolic right to support by the churches" (G. Bertram, TENT 5.473).
5. "The dignity of being Apostolic missionaries" (Plummer, p.307).
6. Their superiority to Paul in authority and message (Plummer [CGT] p.170).
7. Financial support from the Corinthians as proof of their being recognized as genuine "apostles of Christ" (cf. 11:13) (Hughes).

We have offered the one that seems to be correct.   Paul correctly thought of himself as an apostle of Christ and the Judaizers as servants of Satan.   Comments on this verse must not contradict that truth.

or recognized.[57]   It speaks of what the Judaizers wished the Corinthians to think, namely, that they were apostles.   "Just as we are" means we (Paul and the other apostles of Jesus) are genuine apostles.   They boasted that they were apostles; Paul actually is an apostle of Jesus.

11:13 - *For such men are false apostles, deceitful workers, disguising themselves as apostles of Christ.*

For such men are false apostles - "For" introduces Paul's reason for not giving the Judaizers any opportunity (verse 12).   If it were not for his "knowledge" (verse 6), Paul's language as he describes the character and true identity of the Judaizers might be called harsh.   As it is, it is an inspired judgment upon them.   First he calls them "false apostles."   Missionaries they may be, but they have no divine commission from Christ.   Their claim to be apostles of Christ is false, and their message was "a different gospel" (verse 4).   They are proven false by their methods, specifically, their deceitfulness and their disguising of themselves.

Deceitful workers - Workers they certainly were,[58] but they did an immense amount of damage as they led men astray from the truth.   *Dolioi* ("deceitful") means "treacherous, dishonest."[59]   It is built on a stem that means a lure or a snare.[60]   It speaks of cunning or stealth.   "Lies and deception were their stock in trade."[61]

Disguising themselves as apostles of Christ - Either "disguising" or "masquerading" or "pretending" catches the meaning of *metaschēmatizō*.   They used a disguise to deliberately hide who they really were.   By the use of this word, Paul rips away the false front they had put up.   Whatever pretenses they might have, they were really impostors, agents of Satan, and the enemies of Christ.

11:14 - *And no wonder, for even Satan disguises himself as an angel of light.*

And no wonder - If the prince of darkness can disguise himself as an angel of light,

---

[57] *The Analytical Greek Lexicon*, p.176.   Also see Thayer, *op. cit.*, p.362.

[58] "Worker" (*ergatēs*) was applied to Jesus' apostles who were being sent on a mission to the house of Israel (cf. Matthew 10:10, "the worker is worthy of his support"; Luke 10:7).   The Judaizers may have been on a mission, but they were not Jesus' apostles.

[59] Arndt and Gingrich, *op. cit.*, p.202.

[60] Robertson, *op. cit.*, p.259

[61] Coffman, *op. cit.*, p.465.

it is certainly not surprising to find that his servants use deceit and masquerade as ministers of Christ.

For even Satan disguises himself as an angel of light - The present tense verb ("disguises") points to what Satan habitually does, rather than to any one particular occasion recorded in the Old Testament or in tradition.[62]   The thought is that this is Satan's habitual practice.   This is one of Satan's devices (2:11).   The point made here may be no more than that evil is often made to look like innocence or like virtue, or else the devil would not make any headway as he tempts us.   If we were to look for an occasion when Satan disguised himself, we might find it in the words "though we, or an angel from heaven ..." (Galatians 1:9), a verse which infers the Judaizers claimed angelic visions as the source of their message.   If this suggestion is true, then the Judaizers have had a satanic or demonic revelation, and were mistaking it for an angelic visitation.[63]

11:15 - *Therefore it is not surprising if his servants also disguise themselves as servants of righteousness, whose end shall be according to their deeds.*

Therefore it is not surprising - Since it is true of Satan that he disguises himself as an angel of light, it is not a strange thing that his servants, following his example, disguise themselves as something they are not.

If his servants also disguise themselves - Paul here characterizes the Judaizers as servants of Satan.   Again, this is not unloving denunciation but an inspired statement of fact.[64]

As servants of righteousness - "Righteousness" has been explained in two ways: (1)   It refers to the "righteousness of God" (Romans 1:17),   God's way of justifying

---

[62] There is no necessity to suppose that Paul is here alluding to some Rabbinical legend, similar to the one about Eve and the Serpent, in which Satan (after the incident in the Garden) is said to have taken the form of an Angel, or that the angel who wrestled with Jacob was Satan, and this is what Paul refers to.   We doubt that the Corinthians, few of whom were Jews, would understand any such allusion to Jewish legends.   Some think that Satan fashioned himself as an angel of light when he appeared before God as one of the "sons of God" as narrated in Job 1:6 and 2:1.   Still others have suggested that Paul may have known the story of our Lord's temptation in a form which suggested to him that the devil appeared to Jesus in the form of an angel to tempt Him.

[63] Paul seems to emphasize his visions and revelations (2 Corinthians 12:1) to remind the Corinthians that there can be false visions and revelations.   During 2000 years of church history, how many heretics have affirmed that new light has been revealed to them which supersedes the revelation of God made through Jesus Christ?

[64] Paul has been somewhat severely criticized for the (alleged) bitter controversial style of his denunciation of his opponents, but perhaps it should be recognized that the modern critics do not view false apostles and different gospels the way God does.   Paul's language is hardly more severe than Christ's description of some Jews as being a "synagogue of Satan" (Revelation 2:9, 3:9), nor is it more harsh that Jesus' words to some Jews, "You are of your father the Devil" (John 8:44).

sinners, the very thing on which Satan and his servants are making war.   Understood in this way, the Judaizers pretend to be preachers of God's way of salvation.   (2) "Righteousness" should be given the definition the Judaizers would have given it. They claimed that righteousness comes by works of the Law (Galatians 2:21) whereas what Paul preached promoted licentiousness.   To say that Paul's message of Christian liberty promotes licentiousness, and to call the uncompassionate Pharisaic traditions and rules of living "righteousness," is a spin worthy of the one who masquerades as an angel of light.

Whose end shall be according to their deeds - Perhaps the "end" Paul has in mind is what will happen to them the next time he comes to Corinth.   He has said he is ready to punish all disobedience (2 Corinthians 10:6).   He intends to put certain men to the test (13:5), and will inflict some kind of punishment on them (13:2).   A better explanation is that Paul has in mind the sentence that will be pronounced on them at the final judgment.   That God renders to every man "according to his deeds" is clearly stated in Romans 2:6 and 2 Corinthians 5:10, as well in the Old Testament (Jeremiah 17:10; Psalms 61:5).   What the deeds of the Judaizers were has been stated in verse 13, to which may be added the charges in verse 20.   As preachers of a different gospel (verse 4) they stood under the anathema of Galatians 1:8,9.   It is the Corinthians Paul cares about.   Paul cannot ask the church to excommunicate these Palestinian intruders since they were not members of the congregation there (and perhaps only pretended to be Christians).   So Paul will have to destroy them in the estimation of his readers, so that they voluntarily will quit giving them a hearing.

b.   His service and suffering for Christ are a credential.   11:16-29

11:16 - *Again I say, let no one think me foolish; but if* you do, *receive me even as foolish, that I also may boast a little.*

Again I say - "Again" looks back to 11:1, where he made a similar request that they not refuse to listen to him.   He has shown he is superior in knowledge to the Judaizers (verses 5-15).   Now he is going to highlight another area where his credentials are superior to those of the Judaizers.

Let no one think me foolish - "Foolish" is *aphrona*, a word that means "without reason, senseless, without reflection or intelligence."[65]   Though he is about to do something that some at Corinth might think foolish, that is not the truth of the matter. There was a reason behind what he writes, as he goes on to explain.

But if *you do* - Some Corinthians, at first, may think so, but Paul was not being foolish.   He was deadly serious in this attempt to win their renewed acceptance of his

---

[65] Thayer, *op. cit.*, p.90.

apostolic authority. Paul is about to do more boasting, but it is something the Judaizers have forced him to do (12:11). Since the Corinthians have listened to the Judaizers' boasts, which certainly were foolish, he asks the Corinthians to give his boasting a hearing.

Receive me even as foolish - "Receive me" probably equals 'give me a hearing.' Perhaps they will think him foolish. So be it. All Paul wanted them to do was to listen and consider the implications of what he says.

That I also may boast a little - Paul had not started this foolish boasting; the Judaizers had. "I also" is emphatic. "He meant: You listen to them, now listen to me. It is my turn to boast."[66] "A little" may mean that Paul intended to restrict his boasting, something the Judaizers have not done.[67]

11:17 - *That which I am speaking, I am not speaking as the Lord would, but as in foolishness, in this confidence of boasting.*

That which I am speaking, I am not speaking as the Lord would - Verse 17 does not mean that Paul is denying inspiration for the words which follow.[68] If such were the interpretation, then other questions must be asked. If these words that follow are not inspired, what other parts of the Bible are merely human (not inspired)? How many verses following are included in what is uninspired? Are there things in this section contrary to the inspired portions? Similar words in 1 Corinthians 7:12 (where Paul means Jesus Himself never spoke on this subject during his earthly ministry) were not a denial of inspiration. They should not be so interpreted here. Verse 17 does not imply that Paul is disobeying a command from the Lord. Rather, "As the Lord would" means "according to (*kata*) the example of the Lord." Paul's answer to his opponents is not like Jesus answered his opponents. We have no record of Jesus boasting. "It was not the Lord's usual method; but Paul speaking by inspiration certainly had the Lord's approval. The Lord granted this use of boasting because it was the best weapon to use in the situation Paul faced."[69]

---

[66] Fisher, *op. cit.*, p.414.

[67] The language should not be construed as being sarcastic; it is a statement of what Paul intends to do. He leaves it up to the Corinthians to recognize the difference between his boasting and that of the Judaizers.

[68] Dummelow's comment reads, "I am not speaking now under the inspiration of Christ" (J.R. Dummelow, ed., *Commentary on the Holy Bible* [New York: Macmillan, 1927], p.941). The RSV reads, "What I am saying I say not with the Lord's authority." The RSV treats verses 17-18 as a parenthesis because the translators assume Paul is here denying these words are inspired.

[69] Raymond Kelcy, *Second Corinthians* (Austin: R. B. Sweet Co, 1967) p.66. "The view advocated by Kelcy goes all the way back to Chrysostom and has been known for ages as the correct view of what is here said." (Coffman, *op. cit.*, p.468).

But as in foolishness - Notice that Paul does not say he was speaking "in foolishness" but "as in foolishness." In that distinction lies the understanding of this phrase and makes it unlikely that Paul is speaking sarcastically. He will state in the next verse that the Judaizers actually were in the habit of indulging in such foolishness.

In this confidence of boasting - "Boasting" refers to the boasting which Paul is about to do. "Confidence" (*hupostasis*) is the same word used in 9:4 where this same phrase occurs.

11:18 - *Since many boast according to the flesh, I will boast also.*

Since many boast according to the flesh - When Paul says "many," he certainly had the Judaizers in mind, though what he says is true of many people. This is not sarcasm, but a statement of fact. "Boast" is a present tense verb in the Greek; they made a habit of boasting. We might use the word "bragging" to convey what the Judaizers were doing. There is a deliberate contrast between "according to the Lord" (verse 17) and "according to the flesh" which Paul wrote here. To "boast after the flesh" (see this language explained at 2 Corinthians 5:16) is to lay stress on things which are the by-products of living in this body – such as physical descent, prerogatives, rank, reputation, and the like – all of which are not the real essence of living a life for God.

> Nowhere else does Paul insert the article ("the") in this phrase, a phrase which is very frequent in his writings, and this fact may have led to the omission of the article in some manuscripts. If the article is original, the difference may be that, while "according to flesh" means "from a human point of view," "according to *the* flesh" may mean "from their human point of view".[70]

I will boast also - Paul is hardly to be understood here as if he were saying he was going to follow the carnal example of the Judaizers.[71] He says he intends to boast. But instead of boasting according to the flesh about what he has done, beginning in verse 23 he will boast about what he has suffered.

11:19 - *For you, being so wise, bear with the foolish gladly.*

For you, being so wise, bear with the foolish gladly - "Gladly" stands first in the Greek sentence for emphasis. The primary meaning of *phronimoi* ("wise") is "intel-

---

[70] Plummer, *op. cit.*, p.214.

[71] Paul's language should not be understood to mean that he plans to sink to the level of the Judaizers.

ligent, prudent (mindful of one's own interests)."[72] "Although you are" is a good way to translate the circumstantial participle *ontes*. He compliments them for being mindful of their own interests. By so doing, the clause serves to soften the rebuke about their bearing with the foolish, namely the Judaizers.

11:20 - *For you bear with anyone if he enslaves you, if he devours you, if he takes advantage of you, if he exalts himself, if he hits you in the face.*

For you bear with anyone - Paul here gives a reason why they should bear with him. He certainly has as much right to a hearing as did the Judaizers. "Anyone" (*tis*) as before (verse 4) refers to the Judaizers. Any and all such false teachers at Corinth are included.   In the phrases that follow, as Paul describes how the Judaizing teachers have been treating the Corinthians, he gives us insight into their character and behavior. "Every word clearly points to something that Titus had told him of the action of these rival teachers."[73] Perhaps the Corinthians have not recognized what the Judaizers were doing, but this is Paul's inspired statement of the facts.   Will they listen to an apostle when he speaks?

If he enslaves you - The Greek word *katadouloi* (describing abject slavery) is found only here and at Galatians 2:4 where it refers to the efforts of the Judaizers in Galatia to rob Christians of their liberty which they had in Christ. It was by demanding observance of "works of the Law" that the Judaizers were enslaving the Corinthians.[74] Just like the Pharisees in Jerusalem (Matthew 23:4,14,25), the Pharisees in Corinth were trying to put heavy burdens on men's backs (2 Corinthians 12:16).   In Galatians 4:8,9 Paul indicates that bondage to works of the Law (such as the Judaizers advocated) was as much bondage to the elemental spirits of the world as was paganism.

If he devours you - *Katesthiein* ("devour"), literally "to eat up," means the Judaizers "took as much money from the Corinthians as they could lay hold of."[75] As traveling teachers were wont to do in the ancient world, they claimed payment for their teach-

---

[72] Thayer, *op. cit.*, p.658. If we accept the translation "wise" for *phronimoi*, which is a possible way to render the word, then Paul is chiding the Corinthians because they thought they were wise, just as he did at 1 Corinthians 4:10 where the same word was used. However, we are not prepared to say, as has one commentator, that "This is perhaps the most sarcastic sentence ever penned by the apostle Paul" (cited in Barnes, *op. cit.*, p.232). As stated earlier, sarcasm is not a way to win a sympathetic hearing, which is the thing Paul is pleading for at this place.

[73] Plumptre, *op. cit.*, p.104.

[74] "A false religion always makes slaves. It is only true Christianity that leaves perfect freedom." Barnes, *op. cit.*, p.232.

[75] Coffman, *op. cit.*, p.469. Barnes (*op. cit.*, p. 233) offers the colloquial expression "they eat you out of house and home" in an attempt to catch the meaning.

ing, greedily accepted all that was offered to them, and then took more. Their grasping behavior reminds us of the way the Pharisees in Jerusalem acted as the devoured widows houses while at the same time, for a pretense, made long prayers (Matthew 23:14; Mark 12:40).

If he takes advantage of you - Since the verb (*lambanein*) has the meaning of "catching birds in a snare, or fish with bait,"[76] the translation found in the ASV, "if he taketh you *captive*," is helpful. There is trickery implied in the language. The Judaizers who have come to Corinth have used deceit ("bait") in their effort to "catch" the Corinthians. Coffman's comment on this phrase is intriguing. "This suggests 2 Timothy 2:26, where Paul spoke of Satan's taking people 'captive' to do his will."[77] The false teachers were leading the people back into slavery to the devil.

If he exalts himself - The Judaizers had "put on airs" (RSV) of superiority when they claimed to be apostles. Coffman (*ibid.*) thinks 1 Corinthians 10:5 ("every lofty thing raised up against the knowledge of God") explains this language, and that the Judaizers were placing their own words above the word of God, just as did the Pharisees in the land of Israel.

If he hits you in the face - Though it has been disputed whether this is to be taken literally or figuratively,[78] in this commentator's judgment there is no reason to take it figuratively. Plumptre thinks "it is obvious that Paul has heard of instances when this had actually been done at Corinth,"[79] when the Judaizers at Corinth had used blows to silence their opponents. To smite on the face was the highest indignity. "The conduct of the Sanhedrin in the case of Christ (Mark 14:65), and of Paul (Acts 23:2) shows that this may be understood literally."[80] "From the accounts in Josephus and the Talmud there is evidence the priests made free use of their fists and staves."[81] Do the Corinthians not recognize how anti-Christian and contrary to the Holy Spirit the outrageous behavior of the Judaizers was? One of the qualifications for leaders

---

[76] Plummer, *op. cit.*, p.316.

[77] Coffman, *op. cit.*, p.469.

[78] It is possible this metaphor means "insults you grossly." Whether literal or figurative, the Judaizers have treated the Corinthians with contempt.

[79] Plumptre, *op. cit.*, p.104.

[80] Plummer, *ibid.*

[81] Farrar, *op. cit.*, p.265.

in the church was that they be "no striker" (1 Timothy 3:3; Titus 1:7 [ASV]).[82]

11:21 - *To* my *shame I* must *say that we have been weak* by comparison. *But in whatever respect anyone* else *is bold (I speak in foolishness), I am just as bold myself.*

To *my* **shame I** *must* **say that we have been weak** *by comparison* - The Greek reads, literally, "According to dishonor I am speaking, as that we have been weak" (Marshall). What Paul means by this terse expression has proven difficult to determine.[83] The "we" (*hēmeis*) is in emphatic opposition to some people who are not regarded as weak; and these can hardly be any but the Judaizing teachers. "According to dishonor" may speak of the Judaizers attitude toward Paul who was disgraced or dishonored according to their point of view. Allusion has already been made to their disparaging estimation that he was weak (10:10). Almost with tongue-in-cheek Paul grants he has been weak. If you think about the Judaizers' abusive behavior toward the Corinthians as indicated in verse 20, Paul admits he was too weak to behave like that.

But in whatever respect anyone *else* **is bold** - Paul's "anyone" speaks of the whole class of false teachers as if they were a single individual. When the Judaizers make claims that are true, Paul can match such claims.

(I speak in foolishness) - He parenthetically protests once more that this comparing himself with others who commended themselves is folly. By this parenthesis Paul shows that his behavior at this moment is not something the Corinthians should emulate.

---

[82] Some accuse Paul of being unmindful of Jesus' rule about turning the other cheek (Matthew 5:39), or as writing for the moment something that is uninspired, when he rebukes them for submitting to the Judaizer's blows. However, when Jesus was teaching, the context (and the application of His teaching elsewhere in the New Testament) indicates it is towards a brother in Christ that the Christian turns the other cheek. When the Judaizers do the striking, the Christian is not obligated to meekly submit.

Commentators have speculated as to why the Corinthians allowed such brutish behavior. Farrar (*in loc.*), for example, calls attention to the social status of many of the converts. They were downtrodden slaves and artisans and he thinks this fact would make them less likely to resent conduct to which they were duly accustomed among the heathen. Neither Greeks nor Orientals felt to anything like the same extent as ourselves the disgrace of a blow. That sense of disgrace which we feel, Farrar suggests, rises from the freedom which Christianity has gradually wrought for us, and the deep sense of the dignity of human nature which it has inspired.

[83] The difficulty can quickly be ascertained by comparing how the Greek words have been translated:

"I speak as concerning reproach, as though we had been weak" (KJV).

"And we, you say, have been weak! I admit the reproach" (NEB).

"To our shame, I say that we are too weak for that!" (NKJV)

"I speak by way of disparagement, as though we had been weak" (ASV).

"I am quite ashamed to say I was not equal to that sort of thing" (Moffatt)

I am just as bold myself - After the somewhat long prelude from 10:8 onwards, in which Paul has stated repeatedly (11:1,16) that he must embark on the foolish project of boasting, he at last lets himself go.[84]   When the Judaizers make boasts that are true, Paul here says he could match those boasts with a counter boast of his own. Point by point their boastful claims are matched (verse 22).   Then in the next 21 verses we have a summary of his career as an apostle, in which he lists over 20 items which he is confident the Judaizers cannot match.   After listing his credentials in the area of suffering and humiliation, Paul emphasizes especially his concern for all the churches (verses 28,29).   He will finish his presentation of his credentials as he calls attention to the visions and revelations which were granted to him (12:1-10).

11:22 - *Are they Hebrews?   So am I.   Are they Israelites?   So am I.   Are they descendants of Abraham?   So am I.*

Are they Hebrews?   So am I. - Each of Paul's four questions in this verse and the next are echoes of what the Judaizers had claimed as they tried to impress the Corinthians with their credentials.[85]   When men claimed they were "Hebrews," it is not entirely clear what it was they were claiming.   Acts 6:1 reflects on broad lines the groups into which Jews of the 1st century were divided, namely, "Hebrews" and "Hellenists."   This commentator once thought that the Hebrews of Acts 6:1 were native Palestinians whose native language was Aramaic, while the Hellenists were Jews born outside of Palestine and whose native language was Greek, but this explanation cannot be squared with Philippians 3:5, where Paul claims to be a Hebrew, yet he was born outside of Palestine in Tarsus of Cilicia.   He has tried the hypothesis that Hebrews were the old-line conservatives when it came to observing the Law of Moses, while the Hellenists were culturally more contemporary in their attitudes and life-style.   That has not proven entirely satisfactory either, since the Judaizers with their emphasis on "works of the Law" were not observing the Law.[86] The suggestion which rings true about "Hebrews" v. "Hellenists" is the one which makes a distinction only in language.   "Hebrews" were those who still understood and spoke *hebraisti* (the word can designate either Aramaic or pure Hebrew), not "Hellenists" who no longer knew the Aramaic/Hebrew language.   Did the Judaizers boast that they could read the Law and the Prophets in the original?   With "So am

---

[84] Lenski (*op. cit.*, p.1266) pictures Paul's thoughts as having been dammed up, and now burst forth in a flood.

[85] Plummer (*op. cit.*, p.319,320) affirmed that the three terms used in this verse (Hebrews, Israelites, descendants of Abraham) cannot be meant to be mere synonyms.   He also thought it likely that the terms are arranged in an ascending scale of values.   The last seems to form a climax.

[86] For a while, in the older commentaries, it was proposed that there was a difference between Palestinian Judaism and what used to be called Diaspora Judaism.   Some have tried to explain the difference between "Hebrews" and "Hellenists" along these lines.   However it has now been shown that there was little difference between Judaism (the religion of the Pharisees) in Palestine and the Judaism in all the countries around the Mediterranean to which the Jews had been dispersed.   See E.P. Sanders, *Paul and Palestinian Judaism* (Philadelphia: Fortress Press, 1977).

I!" Paul claims he is as good as they when it comes to being "Hebrew." Though born in Tarsus, he speaks and reads the Hebrew vernacular (Acts 21:40, 22:2) as they do.[87] Another view that has believability is that the Judaizers used "Hebrew" to refer to blood lines. The Judaizers may have insinuated that because Paul was born in Tarsus and was a Roman citizen, there was a possibility he might not be a full-blooded Hebrew like they were themselves. Might he not be the grandson of a proselyte?[88] Paul's response was that he, too, was a Hebrew, or as he puts it in Philippians 3:5, "A Hebrew (born) of Hebrews." There were no Gentiles among his ancestors.

Are they Israelites? So am I. - A second claim made by the intruders from Judea was that they were Israelites, while perhaps Paul was not. The name Israelite denoted one descended from Jacob (who was given a new name "Israel," Genesis 32:28).[89] These descendants were God's chosen people, chosen to do a special job in the world (Romans 9:4,5). One could be a descendant of Jacob and not be a true Israelite (Romans 9:6, 11:1). To be an Israelite in the sense God intended, one had to be true to the covenant God had made with Israel. Though they were not true to the covenant, the Judaizers claimed to be involved in preserving the idea of the sacredness of the nation whose God was Jehovah. Their implication was that Paul was an enemy of that sacredness. Paul's counter-claim is "So am I!" If "Israelite" expresses a special interest in the nation of Israel, Paul is certainly not one whit behind the Judaizers. In Romans 9:1-5 he expresses his deep concern for their salvation and in the rest of chapter 9 recalls their special privileges. They had been chosen to do a special service in the world for God. In Romans 11 he looks forward to the conversion of large numbers of Israelites to Christianity. Granted, this spiritual interest may not be quite the same as the Judaizer's interest in the nation of Israel, but Paul could certainly claim to be equal with his rivals when it comes to a strong interest in Israel.

Are they descendants of Abraham? So am I. - From the Gospels we learn that the Jews prided themselves on their physical descent from Abraham. When some Jews visited the site where John the Baptist was preaching repentance, they rejected his call to repentance because they thought, being Abraham's physical offspring, they were already saved (Matthew 3:9). Later, during Jesus' ministry, they kept insisting that "We are Abraham's offspring" (John 8:33). That, basically, they thought, was all that was needed to insure entrance into heaven. It appears the Judaizers thought

---

[87] The word *hebraisti* can be translated either as "Aramaic" or "Hebrew." In Paul's case we think it points to pure Hebrew.

[88] The Ebionites (a Jewish-Christian sect which existed during the first six centuries) asserted that Paul was a Gentile by birth, and that he had accepted circumcision only so that he might marry the high priest's daughter (Epiphanius, ·*Haer*. xxx.16). Did they get such an idea from the old whispering innuendoes of the Judaizers?

[89] Rather than using "Israelite" to speak about blood lines, we have usually understood "Hebrew of Hebrews" to mean there were no proselytes in Paul's family tree, nothing but pure-blooded Hebrews.

their zeal for the Law was what was involved in being one of Abraham's offspring. They told the Corinthians that since Paul taught that the Law was abrogated and that "works of the Law" would not save, he could not possibly be a son of Abraham. Paul's counter-claim is "So am I." He, too, is of the seed (a descendant) of Abraham. One can be a descendant of Abraham physically, or one can be a descendant of Abraham spiritually. It takes more to be pleasing to God, in this Christian age, than simply physical descent from Abraham! Verses that speak of Abraham's spiritual children are John 8:39, "Jesus said to them, 'If you are Abraham's children, do the deeds of Abraham'"; Romans 9:7, "Neither are they all children because they are Abraham's descendants, but: 'THROUGH ISAAC YOUR DESCENDANTS WILL BE NAMED'"; and Galatians 3:29, "If you belong to Christ, then you are Abraham's offspring, heirs according to the promise."

11:23 - *Are they servants of Christ? (I speak as if insane) I more so; in far more labors, in far more imprisonments, beaten times without number, often in danger of death.*

Are they servants of Christ? - Just as the questions "Are they?" in verse 22 reflected claims the Judaizers had made, it is obvious this one does, too. Our problem is that we cannot tell from "servant" exactly what they were claiming. The most plausible explanation is that *diakonos* ("servant," "minister") is used here of the work of an apostle. They called themselves apostles and ministers of Christ; Paul called them false apostles and ministers of Satan (verses 13-18). We have argued elsewhere (see at Galatians 2:4) that the Judaizers were not Christians. That makes it difficult for them to be servants of Christ.

(I speak as if insane) - The word translated "insane" is not merely as before *aphron*, "foolish" (verse 16), but *paraphronon*, "delirious." He has just called them "sham apostles" and "ministers of Satan" (verses 13,15). He may have granted their claims alluded to in verse 22, but he would be delirious or out of his mind were he to grant their claim to be servants of Christ.

I more so - On Jewish grounds (verse 22), Paul claimed equality. But as a servant of Christ, he no longer is satisfied to claim equality; rather, he claims superiority (verses 23-28). He has a greater claim to recognition than they. The reason he has a greater claim follows from the list of hardships and sufferings he has endured, which they have not. When we compare what Paul here writes with what Luke writes in Acts 13-19,[90] it becomes clear that Luke's record is wholly reliable but fragmentary, and that Paul's life was even more eventful and colorful than Acts describes for us.

.

---

[90] 2 Corinthians (with the offering for Jerusalem not quite completed) fits into the Acts record just before at Acts 20:3-4. So all the things Paul here talks about occurred before the close of his third missionary journey.

In far more labors - Paul has reference to labors in the service of Christ, labors needed to spread the gospel. Paul labored until he was exhausted more times than the Judaizers have ever worked. (The word Paul chooses for work is *kopoi* which stresses the exhaustion and fatigue of the laborer, rather than the results of his work.[91]) Rather than working to produce their own fruit, they claimed the fruits of Paul's labors (10:15,16). The Judaizers have never distinguished themselves by working until they were fatigued.

In far more imprisonments - Were the Judaizers ever imprisoned for their work? Paul was. In Acts, Luke identified one imprisonment of Paul (the one at Philippi, Acts 16:23) before the time when 2 Corinthians was being written. From the New Testament writings after 2 Corinthians, we know of an imprisonment at Jerusalem, one at Caesarea, and two at Rome. Clement of Rome (who may have been the Clement who is named as one of Paul's fellow workers at Philippians 4:3) says that Paul was imprisoned seven times.[92] Perhaps there were more than seven since this verse speaks of several imprisonments before 2 Corinthians was written.

Beaten times without number - Since the next verse specifies beatings by the hands of the Jews, this phrase may refer to scourgings inflicted by the Romans. Such Roman scourgings were not limited to forty stripes save one, to which the Jews were restricted. Of such Roman scourgings we have no other record. When had the Judaizers ever been scourged?

Often in danger of death - Paul indicates he had numerous narrow escapes from death. One such incident is recorded at 1:8, where he "despaired of life itself." See also 4:10. The following verses indicate it was human violence and accidents that nearly cost Paul his life. Had anything like that ever happened to the Judaizers?

11:24 - *Five times I received from the Jews thirty-nine* **lashes.**

From the Jews - "Of the Jews" is placed first in the Greek sentence for emphasis. Jews like the Pharisaic Judaizers would have been the ones who administered the lashings. Jesus warned his disciples that they might suffer such lashings: "Beware of men," he said, "for they will ... scourge you in their synagogues" (Matthew 10:17). One who fulfilled Jesus' prediction was Paul himself, as we learn from Acts 22:19, where he said to Jesus, "In one synagogue after another I used to imprison and beat those who believed in Thee." The time came when Paul the Christian was on the receiving end of Jewish lashings.

Five times I received ... thirty-nine *lashes* - The punishment was so severe that Paul could easily remember how many times he had suffered it. The word "lashes" does

---

[91] Thayer, *op. cit.*, p.355.

[92] *1 Clement* V.

not occur in the original, but is necessarily understood. The Greek reads "forty save one." The Law of Moses (Deuteronomy 25:3) expressly limited the number of stripes that might be inflicted to a maximum of 40. Josephus (*Ant*. IV.viii.21) tells us that in light of this law, the Jews took care that the number not exceed 39. A single stripe in excess subjected the executioner to the same punishment. Two-thirds of the thirty-nine lashes were given across the back, and one-third across the chest.[93] While there is record of the Sanhedrin ordering such a punishment (Acts 5:40), such punishments were administered by local synagogue officials to Jews for religious offenses (Deuteronomy 25:1-3). While the whip was being applied, passages from Deuteronomy and Psalms were read. The punishment was intended to be remedial (to get the offender to stop his contrary-to-the-Law behavior), not fatal.[94] Provisions were made to apply oil to the wounds opened by the lashes to hasten healing. The occasions when Paul suffered these Jewish floggings are not recorded either in Acts or in the Epistles. Perhaps they occurred in the early years of his work in Cilicia (between Acts 9:30 and 11:25, a period whose details are not recorded in Acts, yet whose results are implied at Acts 15:41 which speaks of churches in Cilicia). We may picture Paul going to the synagogue to preach. When his message proved objectionable, the religious officials seized him and administered the lashing.

11:25 - *Three times was I beaten with rods, once I was stoned, three times I was shipwrecked, a night and a day I have spent in the deep.*

Three times I was beaten with rods - The rods were similar in size to our broom sticks or hoe handles. As a sign of their authority, lictors carried a fasces which was an axe and a number of rods bound together. This was a Roman style of punishment and usually was inflicted after being ordered by city magistrates. Unlike the Jewish scourging which had a limited number of stripes, there was no limit to the number of strokes laid on the victim. Of the three Paul here mentions, we know of only one, that inflicted at Philippi, in violation of Roman law (Acts 16:22,23,37). In Acts 22:24, Paul's Roman citizenship prevented such a beating.[95] The magistrates at Phil-

---

[93] Commentators' descriptions of the whip differ. This commentator has always understood that the Roman scourge, like the one used on Jesus, had three loaded strands, while the one used by Jews consisted of but one strand. Plumptre's graphic description (*op. cit.*, p. 106) of a Jewish scourging has a leather scourge of three knotted thongs. This appears to confuse the Jewish and Roman scourge. Wouldn't thirteen strokes on the chest equal 39 stripes, the legal Jewish limit?

[94] In the Mishna, in the section called *Makkoth*, Rabbinical thoroughness provided for the possibility that death from heart failure might be caused by the lashing, but such deaths cannot have been common.

[95] "Cicero says that to beat a Roman citizen was a crime, but that reckless and ruthless magistrates sometimes committed the outrage (*In Verr*. v.62,66). Gessius Florus, who succeeded Albinus as procurator of Judea, AD 64 or 65, caused persons of equestrian rank to be scourged and crucified, ignoring their rights (Joseph. *BJ*. II.xiv.9). The fact that Paul was thrice treated in this way is evidence that being a Roman citizen was an imperfect protection when magistrates were disposed to be brutal" (Plummer, *op. cit.*, p.324-25).

ippi apparently did not even check to see if he was a Roman citizen before ordering the beating.

Once I was stoned - This was the usual mode of capital punishment among the Jews, and it was inflicted especially as the penalty for blasphemy (cf. Leviticus 24:16), idolatry (Deuteronomy 13:6-10), desecration of the Sabbath (Numbers 15:32-36), occultism (Leviticus 20:27), and adultery (John 8:5). We should picture the stones used as being large enough to require both hands to pick them up and to hurl them from overhead. It was at Lystra, during Paul's first missionary journey, as the result of a riot, that he was stoned and left for dead (Acts 14:19). He barely avoided being stoned earlier in Iconium (Acts 14:5-6).

Three times I was shipwrecked - Luke in his Acts tells us that Paul made no less than nine voyages before these words we call 2 Corinthians were written. There will be more afterward. The one shipwreck we know about (Acts 27) happened after 2 Corinthians was written, and that would have been shipwreck number four. Paul's ministry for Christ began in AD 34 with his call to be an apostle. After 3 years in Arabia, we find him ministering in Cilicia and Antioch of Syria, and after that traveling around the Mediterranean basin. So these three shipwrecks have occurred in the 20 years between AD 37 and AD 57 (the time of writing of 2 Corinthians).[96]

A night and a day I have spent in the deep - "In the deep" pictures Paul as being in the water, far from any land, after one of the shipwrecks just mentioned.[97] "A night and a day" is a very rare compound Greek word, meaning a complete night and day, 24 hours. It also suggests that the ship was wrecked late in the day, so that first the night time, and then during much of the next day, too, he had to keep himself afloat (either swimming or on a plank or by clinging to flotsam), before he was rescued. Paul has been writing past tense verbs until here, where he uses a perfect tense verb. The change to perfect tense indicates that the experience was still vivid in Paul's mind. Perhaps those twenty-four hours of struggle for life occurred during his recent "inter-

---

[96] Archaeology has shown how dangerous travel by ship was in the ancient world. Hundreds of wrecked first-century ships have been located, and some excavated. See G.L. Reese, "Underwater Archaeology and Paul's Travels," 1992 *North American Christian Convention Manuscripts* (Cincinnati, OH: NACC, 1992). Also, Lionel Casson, *Ships and Seamanship in the Ancient World* (Baltimore: John Hopkins University Press, 1995).

[97] "In the deep" translates a word which originally meant "the bottom of the sea." The Vulgate translation led to an extraordinary belief that the apostle had spent 24 hours under water (like in the case of Jonah), but is a poor translation. A figurative meaning also has been assigned to this passage. Theophylact quoted a tradition that after the stoning at Lystra Paul lay concealed in an underground pit which was called "the deep." The tradition is difficult to square with the account in Acts 14:19,20.

mediate trip" from Ephesus to Corinth and back.[98]   Paul experienced such dreadful things because he was traveling in service of Christ.   Even if they were in the service of Christ (which they were not) what can the Judaizers show to match this?

11:26 - I have been *on frequent journeys, in dangers from rivers, dangers from robbers, dangers from* **my** *countrymen, dangers from the Gentiles, dangers in the city, dangers in the wilderness, dangers on the sea, dangers among false brethren;*

I have been **on frequent journeys** - Paul now turns to dangers he faced and privations he endured as he was constantly on the road as a missionary.   Much of the time he traveled by foot, walking thousands of miles, over the interior of Cilicia, Galatia, Asia Minor, Macedonia and Greece.   These overland journeys, of course, necessitated crossing several mountain ranges and numerous rivers.

In dangers - In the rest of the verse he lists eight dangers or perils into which his travels as an apostle of Christ brought him.

From rivers - In the spring time, swollen torrents that rush down from the mountain heights of the Taurus and other ranges in Galatia and Asia Minor render the steams unfordable.   A sudden rainstorm in the mountains can cause a wall of water to rush down the creek and rivers.   Sudden death can occur if one is not cautious when crossing creek and river beds.[99]

Dangers from robbers - The setting of the parable of the Good Samaritan (Luke 10:30) is the road from Jerusalem to Jericho in the land of Israel.   The mountains of Galilee were a hideout for robbers.   Asia Minor, too, was troubled by highwaymen, as the story of John and the young robber attests.[100]   Paul is saying that he has been attacked at times by robbers as he was journeying from town to town.[101]

Dangers from *my* **countrymen**   - In many of the towns Paul entered to evangelize,

---

[98] At least three times, the apostle heard the dreadful cry, "Abandon ship!"; and anyone who ever heard it once knows the soul-chilling terror of such an experience.   (Coffman, *op. cit.*, p.472).

[99] In the Kiamichi Mountains of Oklahoma, Harold Dunson's car was swept off the concrete slab that served as a bridge across a creek near Nashoba, and washed 300 feet downstream.   It had rained up in the mountains earlier in the day, and now the torrent of water was rushing downstream with great force.   He learned that you always stop and look upstream to see if a wall of water is rushing down towards you from the mountains.   Only when you are sure it is safe do you drive on across the slab.   In Paul's time, bridges were few, and slabs non-existent.   You simply forded the rivers as best you could.

[100] Eusebius, *HE.* iii.23.

[101] The Morses, in Tibet and China, were more than once attacked by robbers as they journeyed to the next mission station.

the first to start opposition against him and excite mob action against him were his own Jewish countrymen. In the book of Acts we have numerous examples: at Damascus (9:23), at Jerusalem (9:29), at Antioch in Pisidia, Iconium, Lystra (Acts 13:50, 14:5-19), at Thessalonica, and at Corinth (Acts 17:5-13, 18:12). One wonders whether the Jews might have been the initiators of the "affliction" that befell Paul recently in Asia (2 Corinthians 1:8).

Dangers from the Gentiles - Of such dangers, we find examples at Philippi (Acts 16:19, 20) and Ephesus (Acts 19:23).

Dangers in the city - All the cities listed in the above two statements of dangers would be included.

Dangers in the wilderness - A "wilderness" was an uninhabited area. In Bible times, since people lived in towns and cities, rather than in the countryside, most rural areas were "wilderness." Deserts, too, which were "wilderness, would have their own peculiar dangers of heat and thirst. Wilderness areas could call out a man's survival skills.

Dangers on the sea - On the Mediterranean Sea he certainly encountered storms, leaks, and benumbing calms. Pirate attacks were another danger faced on the Mediterranean.

Dangers among false brethren - In both Galatians and 2 Corinthians, the "false brethren" were none other than the Judaizers, who pretended to be Christians (cp. Galatians 2:4). One might expect danger from the first seven items listed, but not always from those who pretend to be your friends and brothers when they first come to meet you. The first seven imperiled life, limb, and property. This one was more distressing because it was an attack on his life's work for Jesus.

11:27 - I have been *in labor and hardship, through many sleepless nights, in hunger and thirst, often without food, in cold and exposure.*

I have been **in labor and hardship** - Having alluded to dangers while traveling, he now adds a series of difficulties and hardships he endured as an apostle of Christ. If Paul's enemies ruined his work and he had to rebuild it, that would add to his work load.

Through many sleepless nights - Already mentioned at 6:5, this probably does not refer to involuntary insomnia, but sleeplessness caused by the necessity of working late into the night while others slept, or staying up to read and write a book (cp. the prologue to Ecclesiasticus and 2 Maccabees 2:26), and even to preach (Acts 20:7-11).

In hunger and thirst - Hunger and thirst are named as privations incident to his journeys or his labors, when for one reason or another (e.g., the water holes were dried up, or the journey took longer than expected and the provisions he took along ran out before the journey was completed, or all was lost during the shipwrecks) he ran short of rations.

Often without food - In the previous phrase he spoke of hunger caused by shortness of rations. Now he tells us there were times he went without anything at all to eat, either because there was nothing left to eat, or because he was so absorbed in the missionary work he was doing he simply worked or traveled on when others would have been eating.[102]

In cold and exposure - This would happen when he was thrown into prison, or was drenched by rain, or was stripped by robbers, or was caught with old and threadbare clothing when crossing high mountain passes, or had to stay in lodgings without fire. One gets the idea that when his clothes wore out, he had no money to buy new ones. All these experiences in pursuit of service for Christ are in strong contrast to what the Corinthians knew of the comfortable life of the Judaizers in Corinth, who, if they were anything like their brethren in Judea, walked in long robes, and loved the chief places at the feasts (Matthew 23:6).

11:28 - *Apart from* **such** *external things, there is the daily pressure upon me* **of** *concern for all the churches.*

Apart from *such* **external things** - Paul now turns from the physical trials related to his service for Christ to those which were mental.[103] Think of the list of sufferings just enumerated as being "external." "They were not essential to the conduct of his ministry for Christ, but arose incidentally as he conducted his work. [Now he turns to] those things which come from the ministry itself, being essentially connected with it."[104]

There is the daily pressure upon me - None of the hardships and afflictions men-

---

[102] The ASV reads "In fastings often," and this has caused some to suppose Paul here refers to religious fasting (i.e., fasting as a means of spiritual self-discipline). But even if New Testament Scripture speaks of such fasts, would such fastings be included in a list of hardships?

[103] The Greek reads *tōn parekton* and its meaning is debated. The article *tōn* can be either masculine or neuter, and *parekton* can be translated "without" ("external," NASB) or "omitted." Debated also is whether the phrase goes with what precedes, or what follows. The NASB, in this commentator's judgment, has made the correct choices. It treats the article as neuter, *parekton* as meaning "external," and takes the phrase with what follows.

[104] Fisher, *op. cit.*, p.421.

tioned in verses 23 to 27 were everyday experiences. But the "pressure" was.[105] What the daily pressure was is explained in the next clause.

Of concern for all the churches - This phrase explains what he meant by "pressure." "Concern" translates *merimna*, a word that can be translated "anxiety" (cf. 1 Peter 5:7).[106] When news came to Paul about folk in the churches who were struggling spiritually, it caused him anxiety. Do the Corinthians hear Paul saying that he had anxiety caused by just the sort of thing that was happening in Corinth right at this very moment. Would the converts stand firm in the gospel? Will they recognize his apostolic authority? That was a grave concern!

11:29 - *Who is weak without my being weak? Who is led into sin without my intense concern?*

Who is weak without my being weak? - In this verse, Paul gives two examples of the "concern" about which he has just spoken.[107] One concerns the weak brother. Paul has written much in the letters from this period in his ministry about the "weak" brother (i.e., those who do not have the courage to stand for their convictions).[108] Paul has written in 1 Corinthians 9:22 how he deliberately accommodated himself to other's weaknesses and became all things to all men in order to win them if they were unsaved, or to keep his Christian brothers from being tempted to sin. That accommodation, we here learn, did not come automatically. It was something that produced "anxiety" in Paul's mind. Perhaps the Judaizers, in contrast, instead of showing concern, were impatient with those who did not conform to their own ideas about how men should walk.

---

[105] The KJV reads "that which cometh upon me daily" because it translates the Greek word *episustasis* (to "rush upon") found in a few manuscripts (K, L, M, P) and the Textus Receptus. Commentaries based on this reading speak of the daily rush of the crowd and the daily rush of business that made demands on his time and energy. The NASB translates the Greek word *epistasis* found in the better manuscripts (*Aleph*, B, D, F, G, 17). It means "pressure" or "to conspire against." In addition, some manuscripts have "me" in the genitive case, and some have it in the dative case. If the genitive is read, it is Paul's own daily concern or attentiveness or anxiety. If the dative is right, the pressure comes "to Paul" from what is going on in the churches.

[106] "Anxiety in the form of earthly 'cares' is condemned in the New Testament because it betrays a lack of trust in God (Matthew 6:25-34; Philippians 4:6; 1 Peter 5:7). But anxiety on behalf of others is to be commended (1 Corinthians 12:25)." Thompson, *op. cit.*, p.165. Because the KJV reads "care of all the churches," the passage has been interpreted to mean that Paul, as an apostle, claimed responsibility for and jurisdiction over all the churches, whether founded by himself for not. While it is true that the authority of apostles was not limited to a single congregation, this may not be the passage to prove it.

[107] Paul is not disobeying Jesus' teaching about "anxiety" (*merimna*) in Matthew 6:25-34. There is a difference between anxiety about such everyday matters as food and clothing, which Jesus does forbid, and anxiety over the spiritual welfare of fellow Christians, about which Jesus and His servants are rightly concerned.

[108] See 1 Corinthians 8:7-12, 9:22; Romans 14:1-15:13.

Who is led into sin without my intense concern? - The ASV reads "Who is caused to stumble ...?" A stumbling block is a temptation to sin. Jesus warned about causing one who believes in Him to stumble (Matthew 18:6). In 1 Corinthians 8:9,13 Paul has already warned the Corinthians about so behaving as to become a stumbling block to others. He will say the same thing to the Romans (Romans 14:13). Paul here is thinking about one of his Christian brethren being seduced into sin by the Judaizers. The Greek translated "intense concern" (*poroumai*) is literally "I burn" or "I am on fire," and the "I" is emphatic, causing us to think of a contrast with the Judaizers. They do not have any such intense concern as this. The exact meaning of "burn" depends in each case on the context wherein it appears (see 1 Corinthians 7:9; Ephesians 6:16; 2 Peter 3:12; Revelation 1:15, 3:18). Commentators have offered several options for this verse. Perhaps when a brother stumbles into sin, Paul is set on fire with grief[109] or "filled with distress" (TEV). Perhaps when he hears of what the Judaizers are trying to do in places like Corinth, he burns with indignation (NEB). Whichever way we treat "burn," we should hear that what the Judaizers were doing was seducing the Corinthian Christians into sin.

c. God's sustenance when Paul was weak was a credential. 11:30-12:10

11:30 - *If I have to boast, I will boast of what pertains to my weakness.*

If I have to boast - Paul has been rehearsing the hardships and sufferings he experienced as an apostle traveling to unevangelized places in order to preach the unsearchable riches of Christ. He here states he really did not get any pleasure out of that rehearsal, but it was something he has been compelled to do. The word *dei* translated "have to" speaks of boasting as being something that is a necessity growing out of the nature of things, rather than being a personal obligation.[110]

I will boast - This future tense verb and the rather abrupt change of subject in the verses which follow have led us to begin a new paragraph with verse 30.[111] As he relates his escape from Damascus, and the thorn in his flesh, he will show how God has unexpectedly sustained him even in circumstances which otherwise would have been overwhelming. When the Judaizers itemize their credentials, can they claim any such sustenance from God?

---

[109] A.T. Robertson, *op. cit.*, p. 263.

[110] Berry, *Synonyms*, p.137.

[111] In UBS[1-4] verse 30 begins a new paragraph, but not in Westcott & Hort or Nestle Aland[27].

Of what pertains to my weakness - The Judaizers have accused him of being weak (10:10). When a man recognizes he is weak he then will depend more on the Lord. When the Lord comes to the rescue, that is something to boast about. One example of such weakness and deliverance was the time when Paul had to flee from the city of Damascus at night through a hole in the wall. In that ignominious flight there was not much courage about which he could boast. But he recognized that God had orchestrated his successful escape. Jesus had promised to deliver Paul from the Jewish people (Acts 26:17), and God was keeping His promise.

11:31 - *The God and Father of the Lord Jesus, He who is blessed forever, knows that I am not lying.*

The God and Father of the Lord Jesus - Paul here repeats an expression he used at 2 Corinthians 1:3. Lord Jesus is not something the Judaizers could affirm, nor the idea that God was His Father. Nevertheless, that God is the one on whom Paul calls as he takes an oath concerning the truthfulness of what he is about to say. How verse 31 is related to what Paul is here writing is debated. Is this oath retrospective? So understood, verse 31 is an appeal to God's omniscience as a witness that all those things he has described in verses 23-29 did actually happen. In this commentator's judgment the oath Paul is taking should be treated as prospective, as pertaining to 11:32-12:10. Paul is calling on God as a witness there really was danger and humiliation in what happened at Damascus and to the truth of the fact that he has received superior visions and revelations (12:1-10).

He who is blessed forever - The Greek (*ho ōn eulogētos*) is not easily translated into smooth English. The article and participle (*ho ōn*) means "He who is" and in this place the expression ascribes "being" to God, and may well be the equivalent of the Hebrew name for Jehovah, "He who is," the great "I AM." The adjective *eulogētos* (which modifies "He") is a compound Greek word which is made up of two words: one meaning "well" and the other "to speak." Thus, it means to speak well of someone, in this case the One "who is." We are reminded of the Jewish habit when speaking God's name of saying, "Blessed be He!" We might render it, "The God ... Who Is (blessed is He forevermore) knows ...."

Knows that I am not lying - "God knows" reminds us of verse 11. Paul was accustomed to make solemn appeals to God for the truth of what he said, especially when what he is saying is likely to be called in question (see 1:18,23, 11:10).[112] This oath introduces what follows. Paul says he is not lying either about what happened at Da-

---

[112] Jesus had forbidden the use of evasive distinctions (Matthew 5:33-37) and in their place taught his disciples to always speak the truth ("Let your yes be yes, and your no, no"). Paul's taking of oaths here and elsewhere (Romans 9:1; Galatians 1:20; 1 Timothy 2:7) are not violations of what Jesus taught, but rather help show the real intent of His prohibition.

mascus or about the visions and revelations and the resulting thorn in the flesh. We do not know what the Judaizers have said about what happened at Damascus, though they have said Paul is a crafty fellow who practiced deception (12:16). The omniscient God knows there is no lie in what Paul writes here. He is not trying to lead the Corinthians astray.

11:32 - *In Damascus the ethnarch under Aretas the king was guarding the city of the Damascenes in order to seize me,*

In Damascus the ethnarch under Aretas the king - Paul now introduces the first weakness he indicated in 11:30 that he was going to talk about. This event, which occurred early in Paul's Christian ministry, is also recorded at Acts 9:23-25.[113] It seems likely the Judaizers have used this event to expose Paul to ridicule and that Paul here sets the record straight. Damascus, located about 50 miles north east of the Sea of Galilee, because of numerous springs and two rivers watering it, is an oasis in the desert. The Greek word "ethnarch" properly means "a ruler of a people."[114] We do not know the name of this man, nor do we know whether he ruled the whole city of Damascus or just one ethnic group (the Jews). Whichever it was, he seems to have been delegated the responsibility of ruling by Aretas the king of the Nabatean Arabs and whose capital city was Petra. This Aretas[115] is Aretas IV who ruled within the rough limits of 9 BC to AD 40.[116] Paul's description of this man as "king" helps us solve some New Testament chronological questions. The earliest that Aretas could be called "king" of this region is after the death of Tiberius, for Tiberius was a

---

[113] By beginning a new paragraph at verse 30 we have defused all the objections heretofore raised that verses 32 and 33 are out of place here, and in fact were a later addition to the book. Such objections and replies to them can be studied in detail in Plummer, *op. cit.*, p.332; Harris, *op. cit.*, p.820; and Martin, *op. cit.*, p.384.

[114] "Ethnarch" was a common title of a subordinate provincial governor. It had been borne by Judas Maccabaeus (I Maccabees 14:47, 15:1,2) and by Archelaus (Jos. *Wars* ii.6.3).

[115] The Greek word transliterated "Aretas" has a rough breathing mark because the original form of the man's name was Haritha, which in Greek becomes *Harethas*.

[116] He was the father of the first wife of Herod Antipas, tetrarch of Galilee and Perea. When Herod repudiated Aretas' daughter in order to marry Herod Philip's wife, Herodias, Aretas was infuriated and made war on Herod. This occurred about AD 28. (John the Baptist, who was imprisoned in AD 28 and beheaded in AD 29, condemned Herod for his actions, Luke 3:18-20). Aretas' war against Herod continued, and by as early as AD 32 Aretas had captured Damascus, a town that had been in Roman hands since 63 BC and was then currently ruled for them by Herod Antipas. We suppose it was at this time that an ethnarch was appointed by Aretas to administer the affairs of the city for him, while he went on to fight more battles against Herod. He watched for a suitable time and invaded Perea and utterly defeated Antipas. "Antipas desperately invoked the aid of the Roman Emperor, Tiberius, who in a rage sent Vitellius to capture Aretas and bring him alive to Rome or send his head." Vitellius was proconsul of Syria, and a personal friend of Aretas, and was in no hurry to carry out the emperor's orders. "In the course of his march against Aretas, Vitellius went up to Jerusalem near Pentecost in 37 AD, where he heard news of the death of Tiberius and of the accession of Caligula, and he at once stopped his expedition against Aretas, for the new emperor Caligula liked Antipas as little as Vitellius did." (The words in quotation marks are from Plummer, *op. cit.*, p.333, who cites Jos. *Ant.* 18.5.)

tyrant who permitted the title "king" to be given to himself alone.   Once Tiberius was dead, as long as subordinate rulers recognized Caligula's authority, Caligula did not care what title they took for themselves.[117]   So we date Paul's escape from Damascus as being in AD 37.[118]

Was guarding the city of the Damascenes - Ancient cities were surrounded by high walls which served as part of the city's defenses against invading armies. A few gates, at most, would have pierced the walls on each side of Damascus.   There is no discrepancy between the statement here that the ethnarch guarded the city and the statement in Acts 9:24 that the Jews watched the gates day and night so as to capture Paul.   We may suppose that it was the Jews who urged the ethnarch to so act against Paul.[119]   If the ethnarch is the administrator of the Jewish ethnic group, we can easily see why he would be involved in this effort by the Jews to get Paul.

In order to seize me - What has Paul done to raise the ire of the Jews so that they were determined to arrest him?[120]   Acts shows that once he was apprehended, they planned to kill him.   This is what was done to Stephen who preached Jesus in the synagogues of Jerusalem (Acts 6:8ff).   Paul has been preaching Jesus in the synagogues of Damascus (Acts 9:20-22).   Do the Corinthians recognize that the Jews who years ago tried to get Paul killed at Damascus taught the same things as the Judaizers who have recently come to Corinth?

11:33 - *and I was let down in a basket through a window in the wall, and* **so** *escaped his hands.*

And I was let down in a basket through a window in the wall - Acts 9:23-25 also give an account of this escape from the Jews who were intent on killing him. Somehow their plot became known to Paul,   but the usual ways of escape from the

---

[117] It is possible that Caligula, the new emperor, wishing to settle the troubled affairs in Syria, freely gave Damascus to Aretas, inasmuch as Aretas had captured it, and it formerly belonged to his territory.

[118] Once 2 Corinthians 11 has helped us date Paul's escape from Damascus, we can also date his Damascus road call to be an apostle at AD 34 since that event occurred three years before his escape (Acts 9:19-26; Galatians 1:15-18).   For further details, see under "Aretas" in "Chronology of the Apostolic Age," in the introduction to the author's *New Testament History: Acts*.   This phrase about "Aretas the king" gives us one of the few solid dates on which to hang the chronology of Acts and the Pauline letters.   "A coin found in Damascus has an image of King Aretas and the date 101 inscribed on it.   If that date points to the era after Pompey captured this area for Rome, it equals AD 37.   This is further confirmation of the above dating scheme that has Paul's escape in AD 37 and his call/conversion in AD 34" ("Aretas" in *ISBE*, Vol.1, p.240).

[119] That there was collaboration between the Jews and the ethnarch is a better explanation than the suggestion that the Jews were watching for Paul inside the walls, while the soldiers of the ethnarch were on the outside.

[120] The verb *piasai* is used in John's Gospel of attempts to arrest Jesus (John 7:30,32, 8:20, 10:39).

city were blocked.   They were watching the gates to arrest him anytime he tried to leave the city.   The Christians at Damascus came up with a way to help Paul escape the trap he was in.   Houses were often constructed along the inside of city walls. The upper story of such homes might have an opening through the wall, high enough to make it difficult for enemy attackers on the outside to easily gain access.   The basket is mentioned in Acts 9:25, but the information about the window in the wall is only supplied in italics.   The word Paul uses for basket is *sarganē*, while the word Luke used at Acts 9:25 was *spuris*.[121]   Both words refer to a basket or hamper woven of rope or wicker.   Such baskets might be used for the storing of grain or provisions and would be large enough to hold a man.   A suggestion sometimes made is that such baskets were used to put trash and garbage outside the city walls.   In just such a basket Paul was let down outside of the wall.[122]

And *so* escaped his hands - Does Paul now look back on this escape from life-threatening trouble as just the prelude to a long line of such hardships and sufferings he has had to undergo.   While the Judaizers may see what happened to Paul as an example of his weakness, not Paul.   In that event, and all those since, Paul can see God's providential care and blessing.

---

[121] As with "needle" (in the verse about a camel going through a needle's eye) where the Holy Spirit allowed the inspired writers to use words from their own vocabulary (i.e., Luke uses a different Greek word for "needle" than Matthew does), so here.   Under the inspiration of the Spirit, Paul can use one word, and Luke another, since either word would convey the correct meaning to the readers. Compare what was said in 1 Corinthians 2:13 about how inspiration worked: writers, under the guidance of the Holy Spirit, searched their own vocabularies for just the right word.

[122] Did the Christians in Damascus get their idea from some stories in the Bible?   In a similar fashion the spies escaped from the house of Rahab (Joshua 2:14) and David escaped from the pursuit of Saul (1 Samuel 19:12).   Modern Christian tourists to Damascus are shown a small opening "in the wall" and told that it is the little window through which Paul escaped.   The tourists are not told that Damascus has been destroyed and rebuilt many times since Paul's day, and that the window is Moslem architecture.

12:1 - *Boasting is necessary, though it is not profitable; but I will go on to visions and revelations of the Lord.*

Boasting is necessary, though it is not profitable - Here, as at 11:16ff, Paul speaks with regret about his boasting. He would never have publicly spoken about these experiences if his opponents had not forced him to.[1] This chapter opens with a continuation of Paul's appeal for the church to esteem him more highly than they do the false apostles, because his apostolic credentials were superior to theirs. 11:30-12:10 gives the third area where his credentials were superior (see 11:5 and 11:16). Since Paul is talking about his weaknesses (verse 10), the main point of 12:1-10 is not the visions and revelations, but the thorn in the flesh, and God's grace and power which enabled him to carry on in spite of such weaknesses. When Paul wrote that boasting "is not profitable," he is not saying there is nothing to be gained from boasting. Instead, he is saying that the kind of boasting he is about to do is not the best way of promoting the gospel.

But I will go on to visions and revelations - Visions and revelations were two ways by which God communicated divine information to the minds of the apostles and prophets in Bible times. When God used visions (*optasia*), he caused a scene to pass before the mind so that the messenger could actually see (in his mind's eye) what was going to occur. Revelation (*apokalupsis*, a thought being planted in the mind of God's messenger) could occur without a vision, but the apostle or prophet would, nevertheless, receive a disclosure of truth or instruction concerning God's will and His plans which He wanted delivered to men.[2] The plurals "visions" and "revelations" indicate that for Paul these means of receiving information from the Lord took place numerous times. Acts is full of such visions (9:12; 16:9,10; 18:9,10; 22:17-21 [trance]; 26:19),[3] so the plural "visions" does not surprise us. Galatians 1:12 speaks of how Paul received the gospel he preaches via revelation. Galatians 2:2 speaks of another such revelation made to Paul. Here in Corinthians we learn of still another. Of all the revelations he has received, Paul chooses to talk about just one in this context.

---

[1] "Necessary" translates the same word *dei* that Paul used at 11:30, and again indicates that the necessity was brought on by the circumstances of the case. There is a manuscript variation at this place. The Textus Receptus reads "to boast indeed is not profitable for me." The Nestle-Aland[23] text on which the NASB is based seems best attested. It reads *dei* ("it is necessary") rather than *de* ("indeed" or "doubtless").

[2] The definition of "revelation" given at 1 Corinthians 2:10,11 is "The act of the Holy Spirit making known to God-chosen messengers truths they were incapable of discovering by unaided human research."

[3] We do not treat Acts 9:4-6 as a vision since the risen Lord actually appeared to Paul on the Damascus road. What happened on the road was not simply something he just saw in his "mind's eye." Likewise, there may be something far more objective recorded in Acts 23:11 and 27:23 than what would qualify as simply a "vision."

Of the Lord - The genitive case here means "from the Lord" (NASB margin) or "granted by the Lord" (NEB), rather than visions and revelations in which the Lord is seen and revealed. "The Lord" is most likely a reference to Christ rather than to God the Father. "From the Lord" is the difference between Paul's visions and those of the Judaizers.[4] It is implied that the Judaizers have pointed to self-induced ecstatic experiences which they called visions from God as authenticating their teaching (see comments on 5:13).[5] There was one significant difference between Paul's visions and theirs: Christ was the source of Paul's visions and revelations. His visions were so real that one of them resulted in permanent impairment (another "weakness" for Paul).

12:2 - *I know a man in Christ who fourteen years ago – whether in the body I do not know, or out of the body I do not know, God knows – such a man was caught up to the third heaven.*

I know a man in Christ -The man about whom Paul is talking is Paul himself, as verse 7 shows.[6] The Greek verb translated "I know" is a perfect tense verb, indicating present continuing results from some past completed action. He does not say he had known the man, but that he still knows him. Paul the writer is the man whose experience is here related. The meaning of "in Christ" is not clear. Perhaps, in a deliberate aside at the Judaizers, Paul is saying a man has to be "in Christ" (i.e., a Christian) to have such visions and revelations. Perhaps "in Christ" should be taken with the verb "caught up." If so, this verse says Christ was the One who initiated the vision.[7] The latter interpretation would have Paul boasting in the Lord as he writes about this experience.

Who fourteen years ago - Just like the Old Testament prophets dated the revelations they received,[8] Paul here dates the revelation he received. Putting a date on the event is one way of indicating it was not simply an imaginary thing that never actually

---

[4] It is important to recall that men can have visions which are self-induced, and which can be deluding. "From the Lord" guards us against thinking Paul's was self-induced.

[5] Plumptre (*op. cit.*, p.111) calls attention to the fact that in the Clementine *Homilies* we find similar claims made by Simon Magus, claims to visions and dreams and revelations, in order that his life might compare more favorably with that of Peter. Somehow in all the controversy it is conveniently forgotten that Peter, too, had visions (remember the sheet full of clean and unclean animals, Acts 10) through which revelation was made to him.

[6] Ancients often spoke about themselves using the third person. We recall that Jesus often did this using the phrase "the Son of Man" for "I" (Matthew 8:20).

[7] It is possible for pagan holy men to enter into self-induced trances (by fasting, dancing, hanging suspended by hooks placed under the skin, etc.) where they see "spirits" and get information about the future. But we can hardly lower Paul's visions and revelations to something self-induced.

[8] See Amos 4:7; Hosea 1:1; Zechariah 1:1, 7:1; Isaiah 6:1; Jeremiah 1:2, 26:1, 42:7; Ezekiel 1:1.

happened.   If our chronology of the apostolic age[9] is correct, we have Paul writing this letter in AD 57.   Counting back 14 years brings us to AD 43, roughly the time when Paul and Barnabas were working for a year in Antioch of Syria (Acts 11:26).[10]

-- Whether in the body I do not know, or out of the body I do not know, God knows - Paul is not indicating a doubt as to the fact of the vision, but ignorance as to whether his body may have been caught up to heaven,[11] or whether it may have been left behind on earth while Paul had an out-of-the-body experience.[12]   Only God, who knows all things, knew exactly how this "catching up" was done.   It has been deduced from Paul's not knowing whether or not his body was caught up that he must have been alone at the time of the vision.   Had others been present, all he would have had to do is ask whether his body had disappeared for a while.

Such a man was caught up to the third heaven - "Caught up" is a passive verb which stresses the fact that the one who had this experience exercised no initiative in himself.   He was "caught up" by Christ himself; this vision was not self-induced. *Harpadzō* ("caught up") suggests he was suddenly seized and rapidly taken up to the

---

[9] The chronology of the apostolic age can be studied in detail in introductory studies in the author's commentary, *New Testament History: Acts* (Moberly, MO : Scripture Exposition Books, 2002).

[10] There were visions Paul received on other occasions, none of which quite fit the date given as "fourteen years ago." Acts 22:17 tells us of a trance Paul fell into about the year AD 37.   That was more than 14 years before he wrote 2 Corinthians.   What happened to Paul on the Damascus road, AD 34, was not a trance but was an actual appearance of the risen Lord to Paul.   Besides, that was more than 20 years before the writing of 2 Corinthians.   What was said to Paul on that occasion is told to us, and it does not match 2 Corinthians 12:4.   A closer match, date wise, would be the stoning of Paul at Lystra (Acts 14:19) when Paul was left for dead.   As that would have taken place late in AD 44, or early AD 45, it might be close enough (in round numbers) to "fourteen years ago" to be given some consideration.   If it is the same event, even Paul didn't know if he were dead or alive (2 Corinthians 12:2,3).

[11] Translation to heaven of a person in his body is familiar from the examples of Enoch and Elijah.

[12] Plumptre is confident that Paul is here explaining the "state of mind" (a trance) one is in when he has a vision.   "No words can describe more accurately the phenomena of consciousness in the state of trance or ecstasy.   It is dead to the outer world.   The body remains, sometimes standing, sometimes recumbent, but, in either case, motionless.   The man may well doubt, on his return to the normal condition of his life, whether his spirit has actually passed into unknown regions in a separate and disembodied condition, or whether the body itself has been also a sharer in its experiences of the unseen.   Compare Ezekiel's visions on the banks of the Chebar River where he was transported to Jerusalem (Ezekiel 8:3, 11:1)" (Plumptre, *op. cit.*, p.112).   On page 113 of the same work, Plumptre also notes that many well-known men have had such experiences – Epimenides, Pythagoras, Socrates, Mohammed, Francis of Assisi, Thomas Aquinas, Johannes duns Scotus, George Fox, Savonarola, Immanuel Swedenborg.   This commentator would not lump all these famous people in the same group, if such a lumping implies that their visions or trances were all legitimate avenues of contact with God.   Some of the people so named have, as a result of the visions, started religions that are detrimental to Christianity.   This being true, those visions were hardly from God!   If God can produce genuine "trances," it stands to reason that Satan, the great counterfeiter, could produce similar experiences in the minds and spirits of men to keep them deceived and enslaved.

third heaven.[13]   Scriptures both Old and New uniformly speak of but three heavens:[14] first, the heaven of the clouds and atmosphere; second, the heaven of the sun and stars; and third, the heaven in which God dwells.   The Hebrew word *rakiah* is used at Genesis 1:20 of the heavens where the birds fly.   Jesus also spoke of "the birds of the air" (the Greek reads, 'of the heaven', Matthew 8:20).   *Shamayim* is the Hebrew word used for the second heaven, in which the sun, moon, and stars appear to be situated (Deuteronomy 18:3; Matthew 24:29).   The third heaven, the place beyond the stars where God dwells, is designated in the Hebrew by *shamayim ha-shamayim* ("the heavens of the heavens," Deuteronomy 10:14; 1 Kings 8:27; Psalm 148:4). Jesus spoke of the Father being in heaven (Matthew 5:16,45, 6:10).   The third heaven is also the residence of the angels and the spirits of the departed righteous, the place where, since His ascension and coronation, Christ is seated at the right hand of the Father (Ephesians 4:10; Hebrews 4:14).   Biblical cosmology speaks of three heavens.[15]

12:3 - *And I know how such a man – whether in the body or apart from the body I do not know, God knows –*

And I know how such a man - Scholars have struggled to understand the relationship between verses 3-4 and verse 2;   there are both similarities and differences between

---

[13] The same word "caught up" is used of what will happen to believers at the *parousia* (second coming) of Christ (1 Thessalonians 4:17).

[14] The popular notion that there are seven heavens is likely a pagan idea.   "Among the Babylonians, a sevenfold division of heavens seems to have prevailed ... In Zoroastrian books ... we find the idea of a succession of seven heavens" (S.D.F. Salmond, "Heaven," *Hastings' Dictionary of the Bible*, V.2, p.322).   Salmond argues (p.321) that it was from the Babylonians and Persians that the Rabbis' notion of seven heavens was derived, a notion we find given a large place in Rabbinical literature (e.g., Talmud, *Bereshith Rabba* 19.19.3 [a legend about the Shekinah moving step by step through the seven heavens down to earth and then back again, step-by-step, as sin got worse; only to reverse course until it rested on the tabernacle Moses built]).   The pseudepigraphic books (e.g., *Testament of the Twelve Patriarchs* (Levi ii and iii), the *Ascension of Isaiah* (6:13, 7:13-9:18), and the *Slavonic Secrets of Enoch* (viii.1-3, xlii.3) give the same enumeration of seven heavens and describe them at length, with Paradise being the third one.   It apparently was from similar pagan or Rabbinical sources that Mohammed borrowed the idea of seven heavens (Koran, *Sura*, lxvii). Dante's speculations also included 7 heavens (see "Dante's Guide to Heaven and Hell," *Christian History* XX:2 [Issue 70, 2001]).   Early Christian literature shows the Gnostics held a view of seven heavens (Tert. *Adv. Valent.* 20; Irenaeus *Adv Haer.* I.xxx.4,5; Origen *Cont. Cels.* vi.31; Epiph. *Haer.*, xxvi.10).   Origen denied that Paul had any idea of seven heavens (*Cont. Cels.* vi.31).   "Irenaeus (*Adv. Haer.* II.xxx.7) has good sense on his side when, in arguing with Valentinus, he rejects the notion that Paul was raised only to the third heaven in a series of seven, leaving the four highest heavens still beyond him" (Plummer, *op. cit.*, p.343).

[15] Modern men, with their growing knowledge of the immensity of space, have had some difficulty accepting the idea that "Heaven" (God's abode) is somehow "up" above the earth we live on. Faced with what their telescopes have revealed, modern men are all too ready to abandon the Biblical view of the cosmos.   But there is one direction that is always "up" no matter where a man is on this globe, and that direction is north.   Perhaps it is not so surprising, if God's abode is out beyond the stars, to the north of our globe, that certain Old Testament sacrifices required the worshipper to face north as he offered them, nor is it surprising that Ezekiel saw the glory of the Lord unfolding "in the north" (Ezekiel 1:4), while Psalm 48:2 speaks of the city of the great King "in the far north."

the two descriptions penned by Paul.   Is he recording a second experience unrelated to the one fourteen years ago, or giving further details about the one that happened fourteen years ago?   Arguments that Paul was "caught up" on two separate occasions include: (1) If he twice uses the expression "to keep me from exalting myself" in verse 7, it must be true that he was caught up twice. (2) The conjunction "and" which begins verse 3 is said to be strongly in favor of verse 3 being a second vision or revelation. (3) Having introduced what he writes in verses 2-4 by speaking of "visions and revelations" plural, would he then give only one example?   Arguments that there was but one occasion when he was "caught up" include: (a) *Kai* with which verse 3 begins may be translated "also" ("I also know that ...") or emphatic as "indeed" ("Indeed I know that ... such a man was caught up to Paradise"). (b) The same verb "caught up" is used in both verses 2 and 4. (c) The repetition about "in the body or apart from the body" seems to indicate the same experience is being elaborated. (d) If verses 2 and 4 speak of the same destination, then the third heaven and Paradise are interchangeable terms.   Scripture elsewhere pictures Paradise and heaven alike as being the abode of God, not two different places.   Jesus, too, is now in the Paradise of God (Revelation 2:7), yet He is said in Hebrews 9:24 to have entered into heaven itself.   In this commentator's judgment it is better to treat the wording of verse 3 as an elaboration of what Paul introduced in verse 2.

-- Whether in the body or apart from the body I do not know, God knows -- The condition Paul describes himself being in is the same as verse 2, though here he uses a Greek word that means "apart from" whereas before he wrote "out of."

12:4 - *was caught up into Paradise, and heard inexpressible words, which a man is not permitted to speak.*

Was caught up into Paradise - If we are correct that verses 3-4 are an elaboration of verse 2, then Paradise is a synonym for the third heaven.[16]   In the LXX, "Paradise" (a word meaning a grand enclosure, a preserve, a pleasure ground, a delightful region) occurs often as the translation of the Hebrew word "garden" (e.g., the garden of Eden, Genesis 2:8, 3:1).   According to Luke 16:22,23, in the ages before the cross and the resurrection of Jesus, the intermediate place of the dead had two compartments – one for the righteous (Abraham's bosom) and one for the wicked (Hades).   Jesus' words to the penitent thief suggest that the compartment for the righteous is also called Paradise (Luke 23:43).   In Ephesians 4:8, there is the statement that on the day of His resurrection, when Jesus ascended to His Father, He took captivity captive with Him.   That means that the compartment of the righteous changed places; that is, the souls of the redeemed accompanied Jesus to the presence of the Father, and are now

---

[16] Did Paul single out the event that happened fourteen years ago in order to make a deliberate correction of the Judaizers' teaching (see footnote #14 above about Rabbinic thinking) concerning seven heavens, with Paradise being the third heaven, and therefore a rather inferior place?

on the sea of glass underneath the altar before the throne (Revelation 6:9, 15:2). Until Christ died the sins of the righteous had only been passed over, not pardoned (Romans 3:25). At Calvary, sins are atoned for and righteous people are welcome in God's presence. We may say that Paradise changed places. Paradise is now in the third heaven, or is a part of the third heaven, and that is the place to which Paul was "caught up."

And heard inexpressible words - *Rhēmata* ("words") may refer to words or a message spoken by God or the angels. "Inexpressible" (*arrētos*) means either cannot be or must not be expressed in human language.[17]

Which a man is not permitted to speak - This clause may define what is meant by inexpressible, or it may give a second characterization of what Paul heard. The meaning of the Greek verb hovers between "it is not lawful" (ASV) and "it is not possible" (i.e., human words are inadequate to express what he heard). Just as the apostle John was not permitted to write some of the things he saw (Revelation 10:4), so Paul is not permitted to relate what he heard.[18] Paul may be deliberately contrasting what God permitted him to do after he had a genuine experience with God and the unbridled way the Judaizers boasted of what they had seen and heard in their self-induced experiences.[19] The question, "What was the use of the revelation if Paul

---

[17] The adjective "inexpressible" was used in the Greek mystery religions of secrets told only to the initiates, secrets they were forbidden to tell others. Paul has been accused of borrowing language from the mystery religions. Could he not be using a term long-familiar from classical Greek?

[18] Other Biblical characters (e.g., Enoch, Elijah, Lazarus, and the many saints who slept in their graves only to arise after Jesus did [Matthew 27:52]) had a personal experience connected to heaven, and none of them tell us about what they saw or heard.

[19] "There is a marked contrast, when we compare the elaborate details given us (in the Apocrypha) about the experiences of Enoch and others when translated into heaven, with the brief and restrained statements made by the Apostle in these few verses. He does not tell us what he saw in the third heaven, still less what he saw in the first and second while on his way to the third. He does not even tell us that he was conscious of passing through other celestial regions. The condensed intensity of the narrative leaves little room for the idea that Paul is just being fanciful, or that his imagination is overworked as he writes this section" (Plummer, *op. cit.*, p.342).

How different is the reticence in Scripture as compared with the wild exuberance of some pretenders of heavenly visions.

Mohammed indeed feigned that he had made a journey to heaven, and he attempts to describe what he saw; and the difference between true inspiration and false or pretended inspiration is strikingly shown by the difference between Paul's dignified silence and the puerilities of the prophet of Mecca (see the *Koran*, chap. xvii). He solemnly affirmed that he had been translated to the heaven of heavens; then on a white beast, smaller than a mule, but larger than an ass, he had been conveyed from the temple of Mecca to that of Jerusalem; had successively ascended the seven heavens with his companion Gabriel, receiving and returning the salutations of its blessed inhabitants; had then proceeded alone within two bow-shots of the throne of the Almighty, when he felt a cold which pierced him to the heart, and was touched on the shoulder by the hand of God, who commanded him to pray 50 times a day, but with the advice of Moses he was prevailed on to have the number reduced to five; and that he then returned to Jerusalem and Mecca, having performed the journey of thousands of years in the tenth part of a night. (Barnes, *op. cit.*, p.249-50).

cannot make known what was revealed?" can be answered. The resulting thorn in the flesh, a weakness, and God's provision to strengthen Paul in his weakness, was just a harbinger of God's future sustenance when Paul in weakness needed strength from God.

12:5 - *On behalf of such a man will I boast; but on my own behalf I will not boast, except in regard to* **my** *weaknesses.*

On behalf of such a man will I boast - "Of such" means "one of such a kind."[20] It can be either masculine or neuter.[21] We take it as masculine, just as we did in verses 2 and 3, since Paul is talking about himself and the visions and revelations which have been granted to him. Those visions and revelations are credentials that authenticate his apostleship. They need to be highlighted for they came from the Lord. He is still attempting to guide the Corinthians away from listening to the boasts of lesser "apostles," namely, those Judaizing false apostles.

But on my own behalf I will not boast - There was nothing to boast about in the experience of being caught up to Paradise. "In his everyday existence he was not the kind of person who walked around in Paradise."[22] Since it was not something he did, but something done to him, there was nothing to boast about. He had not done anything special that made him superior to other Christians.

Except to boast in regard to *my* **weaknesses** - In 11:30 Paul announced that he would boast in what pertains to his weakness. Now he shows how the visions and revelations granted to him actually relate to his weaknesses. "Notice he did not say he would boast of himself as the kind of man who was victorious in spite of weaknesses. That would have been egotism. Rather, he boasted of his weaknesses themselves as evidence that he was in himself nothing at all."[23]

---

[20] Per Plumptre (p.114,115), the old Indian medicine man will, with sadness, reflect how he no longer sees visions like he did in his youth. And he also writes eloquently about how the vision drives the young man, and how the old man simply lives on fading memories. But it would not be right to say that there was one Paul, 14 years ago, who had visions, and an old Paul, now, who no longer has such revelations from the Lord. Paul's visions did not end years ago. There have been more, and there will be more (cp. Acts 27:23) to encourage and guide Paul.

[21] If we were to treat it as neuter, it would be translated "of such a thing" he would boast, i.e., that he had been caught up into heaven, for such a boast would bring honor to Christ and would enhance his claim to apostolic authority. It did not, however, add to his own personal status or importance.

[22] Fisher, *op. cit.*, p.427.

[23] Fisher, *ibid.*

12:6 - *For if I do wish to boast I shall not be foolish, for I shall be speaking the truth, but I refrain from this, so that no one may credit me with more than he sees in me or hears from me.*

For if I do wish to boast I shall not be foolish, for I shall be speaking the truth - Paul says parenthetically, that if he had a wish to boast like other men boasted of their honors and privileges and attainments, there would be many wonderful experiences and revelations which he could rightfully mention. As indicated in 11:1,16, there is such a thing as foolish boasting. Were Paul to boast like others, he would not be foolish. What he would say could not be categorized as folly for he would be relating only what was the truth, plain and simple. One gathers the idea that Paul's opponents have been boasting about imaginary visions and the stupendous exploits they claimed to have done before their arrival at Corinth. But unlike Paul's boast, they were not telling the truth. Their alleged experiences were folly and their claims braggadocio.

But I refrain *from this* - Paul could have boasted truthfully of things other than his weaknesses had he chosen to do so, but he deliberately chooses not to do so. The reason he chooses not to boast is given in the next clause.

So that no one may credit me with more than he sees *in* me or hears from me - Paul refrains from boasting lest anyone form an improper estimate of him. When the Corinthians form an estimate of him, he wants that estimate to be based on their own personal contact with him – his conduct, his preaching, the signs and wonders and miracles he worked while he was among them – rather than on claims of exceptional private spiritual experiences. He wanted them to base their estimates on what they could see for themselves,[24] not on what someone simply claimed had happened in the past. Their estimate of the authority of an apostle should not rest on unprovable claims of mysterious private experiences; after all, a fraud can delude people by making such claims. If the Corinthians form their estimate based only on what they themselves see, there is less chance for fraud.

12:7 - *And because of the surpassing greatness of the revelations, for this reason, to keep me from exalting myself, there was given me a thorn in the flesh, a messenger of Satan to buffet me – to keep me from exalting myself!*

And because of the surpassing greatness of the revelations - Paul has said in verse 5 he was going to boast in his "weaknesses." In pursuit of that intention, he is about

---

[24] The translation offered by the KJV, "or that he heareth of me," can be misleading. Paul does not desire to be judged by what people say of him. Rather, it is by the words that come from him that he wishes to be judged.

to lay bare one of the greatest of all those weaknesses, and how he came to have it.[25] The word translated "surpassing greatness" (*huperbolē*) can point to either their great quantity or to their outstanding quality. The revelations granted to Paul were extraordinary. "Revelations" is plural here just as it was in verse 1. This does not prove that verses 2-4 describe different revelations. As noted earlier, Paul has received numerous visions and revelations during the course of his ministry. Out of all these he has chosen one to call to the attention of his readers.

For this reason, to keep me from exalting myself - The outstanding revelations could easily have become the source of pride on Paul's part.[26] As the verse goes on to say, the thorn was given to him to keep him from arrogant self-exaltation (*huperairōmai*).[27] Is this another reference to the false apostles? Have they been exalting themselves? We think so. What happened to Paul is how God handles genuine apostles. What do the Judaizing pretenders have to match this?

There was given me - Even though he later calls the thorn a messenger from Satan, Paul apparently means that, because it was a deterrent to spiritual pride, he views the thorn as a gift from God. Evidently the thorn was given immediately or shortly after the visit to Paradise described in verses 2-4. We wonder if the devil made accusation in the courts of heaven after Paul had been caught up, and God granted the devil permission to afflict Paul with the thorn. Something like that is what happened to Job (Job 2:1-7).

A thorn in the flesh - The Greek is *skolops tē sarki*. Scholars have written many pages in an attempt to explain these three words. The dative *tē sarki* may be translated either "in the flesh" (meaning a physical ailment, rather than mental) or "for the

---

[25] Bible translators and expositors are not in agreement concerning the punctuation of the text at this place. Two options have been defended. (1) The first clause of verse 7 completes the thought of verse 6 so that the passage says "I refrain from this, so that no one may credit me with more ... and because of the surpassing greatness of the revelations." (I.e., he is giving two reasons for refraining from boasting). This is the way the passage is punctuated in the Westcott & Hort, UBS and Nestle-Aland Greek texts. (2) The first clause of verse 7 is the beginning of a new thought. This is the way the NASB punctuates it. Our translators understood the sentence to say that he can talk about the thorn in pursuit of his intention to boast only about his weaknesses.

[26] Up until now, Paul has written "such a one ... such a one." In verses 7-10 Paul uses the first person ("me" and "I") to describe what happened. He can write in the first person because there was no danger of his reputation being illegitimately enhanced by describing the thorn in the flesh.

[27] The verb is in the middle voice in the Greek, which pictures Paul doing something for his own benefit. It is present tense which indicates continuous action. The only other place the verb occurs is 2 Thessalonians 2:4 where the man of lawlessness is described as "one who exalts himself against every so-called god or object of worship ...."

flesh" (meaning the thorn was to last for the duration of Paul's physical life).   Since the regular meaning of the word *skolops* in the koine Greek of the 1st century was "thorn" the NASB translation is acceptable.[28]   What was the thorn in the flesh?   Out of the multitude of hypotheses offered, we think there are two reasonable options.[29] If we accept "in the flesh" for the dative, then Paul is describing a very painful bodily illness.[30]   If "for the flesh" is how the dative is to be translated, then Paul refers to

---

[28] In classical Greek *skolops* was a pointed stake, used either to build a palisade, or to impale the body or head of a criminal.   The word became a very vivid metaphor for intense physical suffering.   In the koine Greek period, the papyri and inscriptions use the word to mean either thorn or splinter.   In the LXX it is usually thorn (Numbers 33:55; Ezekiel 28:24; Hosea 2:6; Ecclesiasticus 43:19).   In the medical writers, such as Dioscorides (ii.29; iv. 176) and Artemidorus (p.181[11]), *skolops* is used for what we would call a "splinter" which getting into the flesh causes acute inflammation.

[29] There are two popular conjectures about what the thorn was which are not live options: (1) We reject the attempt to identify the thorn in the flesh of 2 Corinthians 12:7 with the sickness that caused Paul to go to Galatia the first time (Galatians 4:13-15).   In this commentator's judgment, it is not proper to identify Paul's sickness in Galatians 4 as being ophthalmia, even though we are told the Galatians would have gladly given Paul their eyes (Galatians 4:15) and that Paul wrote with large letters (Galatians 6:1).   (See comments *in loc.* in the author's commentary *New Testament Epistles: Galatians*.)   Nor, in this commentator's judgment, is Paul's first entrance into Galatia to be dated as many as fourteen years before the writing of 2 Corinthians (2 Corinthians 12:2).   (2) We reject the rather standard explanation that the "thorn" was some recurring lustful thoughts or sensual passions. Plummer explains the origin of this oft-given interpretation:

> When a knowledge of Greek became rare in the West, the New Testament was studied in the Vulgate in which Jerome had left *stimulus carnis* uncorrected.   He understood the thorn to mean bodily pain, but the Latin suggested to others temptations to impurity.   The idea of sensual passion became almost universal in the West, until Cornelius a Lapide (d.1637) says that it is *communis fidelium sensus*.   Luther's rejection of this theory is well known, and Calvin condemns it as ridiculous.   No Greek father adopted this view, and it is doubtful whether any Latin writer of the first six centuries did so.   The statement that Jerome, Augustine, and Salvian do so is erroneous. Jerome says it is bodily pain, Augustine says it is persecution, and Salvian nowhere explains the passage.   (Plummer, *op. cit.*, p.350)

Medieval ascetics and Monastics often had trouble with such temptations, and so were sympathetic to this interpretation.   There is no evidence that "thorn" was ever used by any Greek writer to refer to sensual impulses.

[30] A good case can be made for the "thorn" being a painful bodily illness: The devil can cause physical sickness.   Such sickness could be described as a messenger from Satan because it proved to be a hindrance to the spread of the gospel.   The use of the word "difficulties" (verse 10) would fit physical infirmities.   Conjectures concerning the sharp pains include migraine headaches (Tert. *De Pudic.* xiii.16); Malta fever (W.M. Alexander, "St. Paul's Infirmity," *The Expository Times*, Vol.10 (1904); kidney stones (Baxter, cited by Barnes, *ibid.*, p.254); epilepsy (advocated by Lightfoot, Schaff, and Findlay); or malarial fever (William Ramsay, *St. Paul the Traveller and Roman Citizen*, p.97).   We rather agree with Ramsay that Paul did come down with malaria in the lowlands of Pamphylia during his first missionary journey, and, in fact, that he went to Galatia the first time in order to get relief from the fever in the highlands of Galatia.   But we doubt that recurring attacks of malarial fever constitute the thorn, if for no other reason than the "fourteen years ago" of 2 Corinthians 12:2 does not fit the chronology of Paul's first visit to Galatia.   The fact is, we just do not know which, if any, of these, was the cause of the thorn-like pain.

the persecutions he suffered at the hands of the unbelieving Jews.[31]   Either of these would remind Paul that he was a very weak human in need of the strength which God provides.

A messenger of Satan to buffet me - In God's providential government of His people and His world, Satan is sometimes permitted to afflict bodily suffering upon men (Job 2:7; Luke 13:16; Acts 10:38; 1 Corinthians 5:5).   That is apparently how Paul viewed this case: God permitted Satan to bring this calamity to keep Paul spiritually humble. God so works things that what Satan means for harm God can turn into spiritual good. Nevertheless, the thorn was a messenger from Satan since it brought hindrance to his preaching.   "Buffet" (*kolaphizō*) means to smite with the fist, to maltreat.[32]   It speaks of blows to the body, rather than affliction of the mind.   The present tense, expressing continuing action, likely speaks of frequent attacks inflicted from time to time, not something suffered 24/7.   From time to time Paul received a disciplinary reminder that he needed to beware of spiritual pride.[33]

To keep me from exalting myself! - The fact that he repeats what he wrote earlier in this verse[34] suggests that Paul recognized a real danger that he might exalt himself unduly.   Just like "buffet" was present tense indicating what was continually going on, so "exalting myself" is present tense indicating a very frequent temptation.[35]

---

[31] A good case can be made for the "thorn" being persecution by his Jewish enemies. Such was the view of some of the early church fathers.   The verb "buffet" (*kolaphizō*) means to strike with the fist, and was used to describe the punishment Jesus received (Mark 14:65). Paul specifically speaks of persecution in verse 10. He could call it a messenger from Satan since the devil was behind those persecutions.   Such attacks against him by unbelieving Jews were recurrent, occurring in almost every town he entered.   Paul's prayer that the thorn be removed could not be answered without taking away the enemies' freedom of the will.   See Terrence Y. Mullins, "Paul's Thorn in the Flesh," *Journal of Biblical Literature* (Dec. 1957), p.299-303, who argues that Jewish usage of this language (such as the Canaanites being thorns in the sides of the Israelites, Numbers 33:55) points to a personal enemy.

[32] The fact that "messenger" immediately precedes this clause saves us from a mixture of metaphors. A stake or thorn cannot 'strike with the fist'; but a messenger can.

[33] It was in this aspect that Jerome compared Paul's thorn to the slave riding behind the victorious commander in his triumphal chariot, whispering at intervals, "Remember you too are human" (*Ep.* xxxix.2).

[34] A manuscript variation exists at this place, but the evidence for including this phrase a second time here in verse 7 is found in P[46], B, ψ, 1739, Syr. Copt.

[35] Plumptre (*op. cit.*, p.118), who treats Paul's "in the body or out" as a trance or ecstasy, comments here, "The man who is so exalted is in danger of sensual passions. The ecstatic is on the borderland of the orgiastic. He needs a check of some kind ... What more effective check could there be than the sharp pain of body, crucifying the flesh with the affections and lusts (Galatians 5:24), with which we have seen reason to identify the 'thorn' of which Paul speaks?" While what he says about "ecstasy" leading to sensual temptations is true, Plumptre's identification of Galatians 5:24 with 2 Corinthians 12:7 is exceptionally difficult to accept.   In 2 Corinthians 12:7 the "messenger" was given to Paul.   In Galatians 5:24 Paul says the Christians themselves "crucified" the flesh; it is not something just given to them.

12:8 - *Concerning this I entreated the Lord three times that it might depart from me.*

Concerning this - Paul prayed concerning the "thorn" or "messenger".

I entreated the Lord three times that it might depart from me - "Entreated" is the word for earnest prayer.   In the light of verse 9 which speaks of the "power of Christ," "Lord" here likely is Jesus.[36]   Prayers addressed to Jesus are not uncommon in the New Testament (John 14:14; Acts 1:24, 7:59; 1 Corinthians 1:2; 1 Thessalonians 3:12,13).[37]   Rather than three prayers on one occasion (like Jesus in Gethsemane, Matthew 26:36; Luke 22:42-45), it seems that Paul on three separate occasions earnestly prayed for the removal of this "thorn."   Paul wanted to be rid of the thorn – whether it was bodily suffering or the persecutions from the Jews – because it seemed to him to be a hindrance to his ministry.

12:9 - *And He has said to me, "My grace is sufficient for you, for power is perfected in weakness."   Most gladly, therefore, I will rather boast about my weaknesses, that the power of Christ may dwell in me.*

And He has said to me - Jesus replied to Paul's prayer.   How Jesus spoke to Paul, we do not know.   Perhaps Jesus appeared to Paul and spoke to him in an audible manner, as happened on the Damascus road (Acts 26:15).   Perhaps it was in a vision, as happened during Paul's initial evangelization of Corinth (Acts 18:9,10).   "Said" is a perfect tense verb, and Jesus' answer still holds good at the time Paul writes this letter.   His grace is still sufficient.

"My grace is sufficient for you, for power is perfected in weakness." - Paul here repeats the exact words Jesus spoke to him.   "Sufficient for you" is placed first in the Greek for emphasis.   Jesus says, in effect, What you are asking for will not be granted, but something better than what you have asked for is being granted to you. Instead of thinking his ministry is dependent on his own human resources, Paul is to learn that his ministry depends on the gracious power of the Lord.   "Grace" is used in the Bible to designate a number of different spiritual blessings.[38]   Here it is synonymous with Christ's power (i.e., empowerment to help His apostle do the work

---

[36] In Paul's writings, as here, *ho kurios* refers to Jesus, and *kurios* to the Father.   *Kurios* is the term the LXX used to translate Yahweh (Jehovah).

[37] If this refers to Jesus, this is but another evidence that it is proper to go to Jesus for help in times of trouble.   We may pray to Him as much as to the Father.

[38] See the special study on "Grace" in the author's *New Testament Epistles: Romans* (Moberly, MO: Scripture Exposition Books, 1996), p.52-65.

to which he had been called[39]), since Jesus spoke both of "grace" and "power" in his response to Paul's prayer.[40] "Grace" here speaks of the help Christ would give to assist Paul so that the "thorn" would not be an impossible hindrance to his ministry. The weakness in Paul to which the Judaizers have called attention was really an opportunity for Christ's power (grace) to operate. "Perfected" means "brought to completion." There is no indication that Christ's power is ever less than perfect. When men are able to operate in their own strength, there is little opportunity for others to see the Lord's power at work in their lives. When it is obvious men are weak, and great things for God are still accomplished, then is when it is obvious that more than human strength has been involved.

Most gladly, therefore, I will rather boast about my weakness - These are Paul's words of comment on Jesus' answer to his prayer. Paul no more asks for the thorn to be removed because Christ has promised to take advantage of it in the furtherance of God's purpose. If such a weakness (or indeed the weaknesses itemized in the next verse) gives the Lord opportunity to display His power, then Paul would rather see the power at work than have the thorn removed.

That the power of Christ may dwell in me - The word picture Paul uses here is delightful. The Greek behind "may dwell in me" literally reads, "may tabernacle over me."[41] The power (grace) of Christ is pictured as surrounding Paul like a tent or a shelter. Christ's special grace to Paul will be provided as often as needed. No wonder Paul can gladly boast of his weaknesses.

12:10 - *Therefore I am well content with weaknesses, with insults, with distresses, with persecutions, with difficulties, for Christ's sake; for when I am weak, then I am strong.*

Therefore - Since my "weaknesses" are an occasion for the power of Christ to surround me.

I am well content with weaknesses - When Paul says he is content with weaknesses, or bears weaknesses cheerfully, he is not stating a passive attitude but a positive one. Paul immediately lists four examples of the kinds of weaknesses he has in mind, hardships that are signs he is a true apostle (6:4,5). Coffman uses this verse to corroborate his view that the "thorn" Paul had in mind is persecution by the unbelieving

---

[39] Elsewhere Paul claimed the same power the apostles received on Pentecost (cp. 1 Timothy 1:12 and Acts 1:8).

[40] The better Greek manuscripts read "the power." Perhaps this is a case where the article "the" serves as a personal pronoun, or perhaps the scribes who added "my" to the text were correct. Jesus is speaking of His power being made available to Paul. Furthermore, later in this verse Paul himself speaks about "the power of Christ."

[41] The same word is used at John 1:14 and Revelation 7:15, 21:3.

Jews.   He wrote, "This verse describes Paul's living with the thorn unremoved; and there is not a word about sickness, disease, or near-sightedness, or anything of the kind.   It is 'injuries, persecutions, etc.' of which he speaks."[42]   Fisher, on the other hand wrote, "If the thorn in the flesh was a physical malady, this word would include it."[43]

With insults - *Hubresin* ("insults" or "injuries [ASV]) can refer to verbal attacks or physical assaults and maltreatment.   Perhaps Paul has in mind the taunts and sneers and contempt of the Judaizers that have been alluded to in 1:17, 2;1, 7:8, 8:2, 10:10, 11:6,8,16.   Perhaps Paul refers to the confiscation of his property since the same word is used in Acts 27:10,21, where it describes the loss of material goods (the ship and its whole cargo) in the storm and wreck.

With distresses - See 6:4,5, and 11:26,27 where such distresses and hardships have been enumerated.

With persecutions - The history of Paul given in Acts records that he faced numerous persecutions.   He has already called attention to these at 2 Corinthians 4:9.   Jesus promised His disciples they might expect persecutions (Mark 10:30).   Instead of meeting them with dogged resistance as a strong man might, he endured them as a weak man, waiting to see what good Christ would bring out of them.

With difficulties - At 6:4 Paul used the same word, which speaks of someone who is in a tight place, where he has little room to maneuver, but plenty of room to suffer.

For Christ's sake - He is content for Christ's sake to bear all these hardships to which he is exposed as he makes his missionary journeys.   After all, Christ died for his sake (5:14).

For when I am weak, then I am strong - "For" introduces the reason why he is "well content."   When his human strength and human resources fail, when he has no way to resist the persecutions and difficulties men heap upon him, then the Lord goes to work exerting His power.   Jesus keeps his promise (verse 9) and that is something exciting to see.   Philippians 4:13 likewise speaks of Christ's power: "I can do all things through Christ who strengthens me."

With these triumphant words Paul has finished calling attention to the credentials that prove him to be a genuine apostle of Christ.

---

[42] Coffman, *op. cit.*, p.488.

[43] Fisher, *op. cit.*, p.431.

3. The necessity for this appeal – the Corinthians have failed to commend his apostolic office. 12:11-13.

12:11 - *I have become foolish; you yourselves compelled me. Actually I should have been commended by you, for in no respect was I inferior to the most eminent apostles, even though I am a nobody.*

I have become foolish - He had warned the Corinthians (11:1,16) he was going to do some foolish boasting. Looking back, using the same word "foolish," he says he has done it.

You yourselves compelled me - It was because the Corinthians, listening to the sneers and insinuations of the Judaizers, had failed in their loyalty to him that he has had to boast, calling attention to his apostolic credentials.

Actually I should have been commended by you - The "I" is emphatic; the implied contrast is with the Judaizers who spoke disparagingly concerning Paul, and to whom the Corinthians have been listening. "You" is plural and the Greek word translated "should" is *ōpheilo*, which speaks of moral obligation. All the Corinthian Christians, Paul says, had a moral obligation to defend him and his apostleship when the Judaizers made their false claims. To speak out in this way was a debt they owed to Paul. If Paul had been commended by the Corinthians, as he should have been, he would not have needed to write chapters 10-13 of this letter.

For in no respect was I inferior to the most eminent apostles - "For" introduces the reason they should have commended him. As indicated at in comments at 11:5, the Judaizers have held the twelve (or at least Peter, James, and John, Galatians 2:6-9) in higher esteem than Paul. Paul says the Corinthians might have rightly commended him because he was inferior to the twelve in not one single thing.[44] When it comes to being called to be apostles, Paul and the twelve all were called by Jesus himself. When it comes to being empowered by the Holy Spirit, they were all equal. When it comes to being sent to their respective fields of service, all went where Jesus (or the Spirit of Jesus) sent them.

Though I am a nobody –Paul is likely repeating the insulting words the Judaizers have spoken about him. Or perhaps Paul is speaking truthfully of his own self-assessment; he recognizes that all his work was due to God's grace (verse 9; 1 Corinthians 15:9,10). Either way, Paul claims equality with the twelve when it comes to apostolic authority.

12:12 - *The signs of a true apostle were performed among you with all perseverance, by signs and wonders and miracles.*

---

[44] "In no respect" is emphatic. The Greek word *ouden* says "in no single thing."

The signs of a true apostle - This is the reason Paul gives why the Corinthians should have rushed to his defense when the Judaizers came to town and claimed he was inferior to the twelve chosen by Jesus. The miracles he had worked when he was in Corinth were obvious indicators or evidence[45] that he was equal to the twelve in apostolic position and authority. If the Judaizers had come to Corinth before the writing of 1 Corinthians, and spoke in derogatory terms of Paul's apostleship, the brethren at Corinth already had an affirmation from Paul that he was an apostle of Jesus. 1 Corinthians 9:1, "Am I not an apostle?" expects a yes answer. He went on to say, "If to others I am not an apostle, at least I am to you; for you are the seal of my apostleship in the Lord" (1 Corinthians 9:2).[46] The signs of an apostle are enumerated in the last part of this verse.

Were performed among you - The verb Paul uses here is passive voice with the agent being only implied. He does not say that he performed the miracles; rather he says God was working them through him. He was only God's instrument. Other than Paul's claim here, we have no record of such miracles wrought at Corinth. Luke in Acts does not record any miracles wrought there, but this only shows the abbreviated character of the account in Acts. It is not a proof that miracles do not actually happen.[47]

With all perseverance - *Hupomonē* (translated "perseverance") speaks of patience under trials and emphasizes the things which cause the trials.[48] Perhaps Paul is alluding to the fact that while he was in Corinth, even though he was in need financially (2 Corinthians 11:9; 2 Corinthians 13:13) the miracles kept coming. "All

---

[45] The word "signs" apparently is used with two different meanings in this verse. First, in the sense of "identifying mark" or "token." Later in the verse, in the sense of "miracle" or "supernatural power."

[46] As was documented in notes on 1 Corinthians 12-14, this commentator is a "cessationist" when it comes to the question of miracles today (that is, genuine sign miracles like one reads about in the New Testament). Here is one reason: if the "signs and wonders" observed in the "Signs and Wonders Movement" of the late 20th century are genuine as their workers claim, what "signs" would we have to see to be able to recognize a genuine apostle? Would not the claims of the modern miracle workers (who are not apostles) cause Paul's argument here in 2 Corinthians 12 to be robbed of all force?

[47] Coffman (*op. cit.*, p. 489) has a well-written paragraph at this place concerning the proof for miracles in Bible times. He notes that Luke the physician documents several of the miracles. He then notes that the enemies of Christ also had to admit the validity of the apostolic miracles. "Paul was writing to a congregation that contained bitter and unscrupulous enemies of the truth; yet Paul dared to call attention to his miracles in this letter. Could he possibly have done such a thing unless they were indeed legitimate, accepted and proved miracles? Every logic on earth answers NO." Floyd Filson (*Interpreter's Bible* [Nashville: Abingdon, 1953], V.10, p.411) has added, "Writing to churches that would have challenged him if he had falsified facts, Paul unhesitatingly refers to such miracles; he knows that even his enemies cannot deny their occurrence." The student who wishes to pursue this matter of the validity of miracles further might consult C.S. Lewis, *Miracles: A Preliminary Study* (New York: Macmillan, 1948).

[48] Berry, *Lexicon*, p.10.

perseverance" seems to say the signs of an apostle were worked numerous times while Paul was in Corinth.

By signs and wonders and miracles - By these three terms, Paul does not mean three different kinds of miracle. The terms are three ways of describing any miracle. Miracles in Bible times were "signs" because they pointed to something, namely, the validity of the messenger or the message he was delivering. Miracles were "wonders" because they excited amazement or awe in those who witnessed them. "Miracles" (*dunameis*) are called "mighty works" (ASV) because it took the mighty power of God to work them. Jesus promised the twelve they would work miracles and with them confirm the word (Mark 16:20). Like the twelve did, so Paul always attested the validity of his message by miracle (this verse; Acts 15:12; Romans 15:19; Galatians 3:5; Hebrews 2:4). In fact, in the Bible, miracles were always wrought to credential the message (John 2:11,18,23; Acts 2:22).[49] Exactly what these miracles at Corinth were, we are not distinctly informed. We might think of miracles like he wrought at other places: healing the sick (Acts 18:8), casting out demons (16:18), raising the dead (Acts 20:9), and speaking in tongues (1 Corinthians 14:18).

12:13 - *For in what respect were you treated as inferior to the rest of the churches, except that I myself did not become a burden to you? Forgive me this wrong!*

For in what respect were you treated as inferior to the rest of the churches - The "rest of the churches" would be those founded earlier by Paul on his first and second missionary journeys, or those founded by any other apostle. The idea that they might be "inferior" to other churches had been planted by the Judaizers. However, he so fully gave evidence of his apostleship when he was among them, they had no reason to feel that they were somehow at a disadvantage because Paul, rather than some other apostle, planted the church at Corinth.

Except that I myself did not become a burden to you? - He comes back to the subject of refusing to accept financial support from them while working among them. It was the chief argument of the Judaizers as they spoke derogatively of Paul's apostleship (see at 2 Corinthians 11:9). "I myself" contrasts his behavior to that of the Judaizers who made slaves of the Corinthians by demanding support (2 Corinthians 11:20).

Forgive me this wrong! - When Paul speaks of his behavior as being "wrong," he is quoting what the Judaizers have affirmed. They accused him of sin because he did not take wages (2 Corinthians 11:7). Paul's prayer for forgiveness rests on this idea: If my refusal to take wages is what has caused you to doubt for a moment that I am an apostle, equal in authority with the twelve, please forgive me for giving a wrong

---

[49] Preachers are judged now by their conformity to the gospel. But when the gospel was first being preached there was a real need for miraculous authentication.

impression.[50]

Paul has appealed for them to recognize his apostolic authority (10:1-11), to recognize his God-assigned area of mission (10:12-18), and to esteem him more highly than the false apostles esteemed him (11:1-12:10). Having called attention to the reason he had to make this appeal concerning his apostolic authority (12:11-13), Paul has one more appeal in this third section of his letter.

D. An Appeal to be Ready for his Third Visit.   12:14 - 13:10

1. Basis for the appeal – exceptional love characterizes his dealings with them.   12:14-18

12:14 - *Here for this third time I am ready to come to you, and I will not be a burden to you; for I do not seek what is yours, but you; for children are not responsible to save up for* their *parents, but parents for* their *children.*

Here for this third time I am ready to come to you - According to 13:1,2, Paul is about to make his third actual visit to Corinth. His first visit was when he planted the church (Acts 18:1); his second visit was the intermediate trip that proved to be sorrowful (2:1, 12:21).[51] Three times in this paragraph, Paul calls attention to his forthcoming visit (12:14, 13:1,10). They could be "ready" for his coming visit if they submit to his apostleship and reaffirm their belief in Jesus and the lifestyle He taught (as compared to the Jewish lifestyle advocated by the false teachers who have come to Corinth). If these things were done, they would be ready, and he would be spared the necessity of severe action when he arrived.

And I will not be a burden to you - "Not a burden" is an expression used before (11:19 and 12:13). It means to refuse to demand wages from them. Paul here announces that on this third visit he intends to live by his stated principle not to accept financial support from the people among whom he is living and ministering. He will maintain himself without their support.   Romans 16:23 indicates he did accept the

---

[50] Older writers who spoke of the harsh tone with which Paul writes chapters 10-13 call this verse a striking mixture of sarcasm and bitter irony (e.g., Barnes, p.261). In this commentator's judgment this is a wrong interpretation given to the verse. Those who do take it as irony speak of the privilege it is to contribute to the support of the gospel, and how it would have been best for the church at Corinth if he required them to help him financially from the beginning. In this commentator's judgment, while the idea that it is a privilege to contribute to the support of the gospel is a correct and Biblical idea, this is just not the verse to prove it. The idea that Paul now regrets and apologizes for living by his stated resolve to offer the gospel *gratis* (1 Corinthians 9:18) when he was at Corinth is a mistaken idea since 2 Corinthians 12:14 indicates he intends to be as independent on his coming visit as he was earlier.

[51] See the Introductory Studies for a detailed discussion of Paul's visits to Corinth.

hospitality of Gaius while he visited Corinth. That should not be thought of as a deviation from his stated purpose of not being a burden on them. There is a vast difference between accepting a gracious offer of a place to stay, and a demand for wages.

For I do not seek what is yours, but you - "For" indicates this is one reason why he plans not to be a burden to them. "Seek what is yours" defines the meaning of "burden." He does not want their money or their possessions for himself. There is an implied contrast with the Judaizers and what they desired. The present tense ("seek") indicated his habitual aim; he is always seeking what is best for them. "Some of them had thought that it was because he cared so little about them that he would not accept anything from them (11:11); here he says that he cares too much about *them* to care about their *possessions*."[52] He is concerned about their souls (12:15). He is concerned only with their loyalty to Christ, since he wants to present them to Christ as an unspotted bride (2 Corinthians 11:2). In view of the fact that at this very time, in this very letter, he was soliciting a contribution of money to help the poor saints in Judea, some have had trouble reconciling this statement that he is not interested in their money. But such a comparison is not proper. To seek funds for the poor at Jerusalem is one thing. To seek funds for himself is another.

For children are not responsible to save for *their* parents, but parents for *their* children - This phrase, like the previous one, begins with "for," and states a second reason he has no plans to be a "burden" on them when he makes his third visit. When children are grown up and their parents are old or widowed, the children have a responsibility to take care of their parents (1 Timothy 5:3,4). But when the children are small, it is God's expectation that parents take care of their young children.[53] Paul is their spiritual father (1 Corinthians 4:15), and his spiritual children are only about six years old when he writes this letter. The word translated "save" is the same word Jesus used in the Sermon on the Mount when He said, "Do not lay up for yourselves treasures on earth" (Matthew 6:19). We suppose Paul used this word because the Judaizers expected the Corinthians to lay up treasures and accumulate money for them. Paul says he has no such expectation, and implies that such an expectation is not right.

12:15 - *And I will most gladly spend and be expended for your souls. If I love you the more, am I to be loved the less?*

And I will most gladly spend and be expended for your souls - "'I' is very emphatic.

---

[52] Plummer, *op. cit.*, p.361.

[53] Jesus rebuked the Pharisees for calling their possessions "corban" and thus not using the means they had to take care of their parents (Mark 7:11,12). Neither Jesus nor Paul expected that parents are responsible to financially support children who are mature and able-bodied, but who are too lazy to support themselves.

In contrast with the attitude of others (the Judaizers) he is ready to do more than a parent's duty, and to do it with delight. He will spend all he has, and exhaust all his energy and strength for his children."[54]   Paul will do this because he loves them, and because one who has accepted Christ no longer lives for himself (2 Corinthians 5:15). "For your souls" means for your spiritual good, for the salvation of your souls. To another church Paul wrote of a similar love: "Having thus a fond affection for you, we were well pleased to impart to you not only the gospel but also our own lives, because you had become very dear to us" (1 Thessalonians 2:8).

If I love you the more, am I to be loved the less? - The Greek construction of this "if-clause" assumes the "if" is true. Paul does love them more.[55]   Again, Paul answers the question that was raised at 11:11. Emphatically he says that his dealings with the Corinthians have always been motivated by his love for them, and that includes his refusal to accept support from them. Paul's question asks the Corinthians if they are going to continue to believe the accusation of the Judaizers that his refusal was a sign he didn't love them. That accusation had led to a cooling of the Corinthians' affection for Paul.

12:16 - *But be that as it may, I did not burden you myself; nevertheless, crafty fellow that I am, I took you in by deceit.*

But be that as it may, I did not burden you myself - "Be that as it may" ("Let it be," the Greek says) seems to mean 'Grant for the moment that the Judaizers' claim that I don't love you is true.' "I" is emphatic in the Greek, marking a contrast between his behavior and that of the Judaizers. They were a burden to the Corinthians, weighing them down[56] with demands for money; but not Paul! Paul took no money for his own needs when he was at Corinth.

Nevertheless, crafty fellow that I am, I took you in by deceit - These words are a quotation of what the Judaizers have said as they accused Paul. The Greek behind "crafty fellow that I am" is a participial phrase, "being crafty"; the word for "being" means "being by my very nature."   "Crafty" translates *panourgos*, which means ca-

---

[54] Plummer, *op. cit.*, p. 362. The verb translated "expended" speaks of spending down to the last penny. He will exhaust all his resources.

[55] Fisher (*op. cit.*, p.435) observes, "It is worthy of note that this verse speaks with tenderness and affection for the whole church, thus belying the usual contention that this whole section is a diatribe against the church and belongs in another letter." He has not been using irony and sarcasm against his beloved Corinthians. Indeed, there are strong words in these chapters, but any strong words Paul has written in chapters 10-13 are an apostle pronouncing God's judgment on the Judaizers, similar to what he wrote in Galatians 1:8,9.

[56] The word here translated burden (*katebarēsa*) is different from the word (*katenarkēsa*) translated burden in verses 13,14.

pable of doing anything underhanded, or being thoroughly unscrupulous.[57] The Judaizers have attacked Paul's very character, accusing him of having ulterior motives in his refusal to accept maintenance. The metaphor behind "I took you in by deceit" comes from the world of hunting and fishing. "Deceit" in this context is the bait used to catch fish or to lure game into a trap. Paul's refusal of maintenance, they said, was just bait to catch a bigger prize. The Judaizers were accusing Paul and his helpers of skimming some of the money he was collecting for the poor at Jerusalem. Or some of his helpers took maintenance and shared with Paul what they got. He was very shrewd and deceitful in his methods of obtaining money, they alleged.

12:17 - Certainly *I have not taken advantage of you through any of those whom I have sent to you, have I?*

***Certainly* I have not taken advantage of you through any of those whom I sent to you, have I?** - This is the first of three questions in which he asks the Corinthians whether they really believe he was getting their money under false pretense, as the Judaizers have insinuated. "Paul pursues every accusation that has been made against him in order to clear himself."[58] One charge the Judaizers made, this question implies, is that Paul used the helpers whom he had sent[59] to take unfair advantage of them in order to get their money for him. Some of the ones whom Paul had sent to Corinth were Timothy (who had been sent before 1 Corinthians was written, 1 Corinthians 4:17, 16:10,11) and Titus (who had been sent to Corinth after Paul's sorrowful intermediate trip, 2 Corinthians 2:13, 7:6,13-15). Can any evidence be produced, he asks, to show any of these have been asking for money on Paul's behalf? "Certainly" (added by the NASB translators) helps English readers to know the question in the Greek expects a negative answer, "No, I did not!"

12:18 - *I urged Titus* to go, *and sent the brother with him. Titus did not take any advantage of you, did he? Did we not conduct ourselves in the same spirit* and walk *in the same steps?*

I urged Titus *to go*, and sent the brother with him. - There seem to have been three missions made by Titus to Corinth. (1) According to 2 Corinthians 8:6, Titus was the one who started the collection for the saints in Jerusalem. That was almost a year before the writing of 2 Corinthians and likely occurred even before 1 Corinthians was written. That was his first mission to Corinth. (2) Titus' second mission to Corinth,

---

[57] We have had the root word translated "crafty" at 4:2 and 11:3 where the word was used of Satan's cunning. That Paul has been accused of taking advantage of the Corinthians is evident from 7:2.

[58] Thompson, *op. cit.*, p.179.

[59] "Sent" is the word from which we get "apostle." "It means that Paul had sent his fellow-workers on a definite mission" (Fisher, *op. cit.*, p.436).

alluded to in 2 Corinthians 2:13 and 7:6,13, was the one Paul urged him to make after Paul's own intermediate trip ended in sorrow for Paul. Titus' mission was to bring about some repentance among the Corinthian Christians.[60] It was Titus' report back to Paul about the Corinthians' repentance that was the occasion for Paul to pen 2 Corinthians and express his "comfort" (2 Corinthians 1:3-6). (3) As Paul writes 2 Corinthians 8:16-22, Titus' third mission to Corinth has not yet begun. So his upcoming trip cannot be the one referred to here since the next phrase of this verse indicates the mission in question was already in the past. In this commentator's judgment we should opt for the view that Paul has reference to Titus' first mission to Corinth. This conclusion requires us to understand that Titus was accompanied by an unnamed brother on that occasion.[61] It also requires us to understand that Titus worked for his own maintenance while he was in Corinth the first time. We may also conjecture that Titus' part in the early stages of the offering is what gave the Judaizers occasion to implicate Titus in Paul's crafty plot to get money for himself from the Corinthians.

Titus did not take any advantage of you, did he? - Like the preceding one, the way the question is written in the Greek shows it also expects a negative answer. No, Titus had not actively taken advantage of the Corinthians when he was there before. Titus' reputation was above suspicion. Nevertheless, we read between the lines that the Judaizers have accused Titus of being in collusion with Paul's underhanded scheme to get money from the Corinthians. Paul's question asks the Corinthians if they really believe the accusations made by the Judaizers.[62]

Did we not conduct ourselves in the same spirit *and walk* in the same steps? - The

---

[60] This commentator holds the view that 2 Corinthians enjoys integrity, and that chapters 10-13 are not to be thought of as part of a severe letter sent to Corinth after 1 Corinthians had been delivered. Writers who defend the idea that chapters 10-13 are a fragment of some other letter than the one we call 2 Corinthians tend to choose Titus' second mission to Corinth as the one being referred to here in verse 18. However they have struggled to make the details match. There were two unnamed brothers on that journey; one is referred to here. It requires us to believe that Paul saddled Titus with two disparate tasks: that of putting down a rebellion against Paul's apostolic authority, and at the same time broaching Paul's request for money. How much more convincing it is to hold to the unity and integrity of 2 Corinthians, and understand that in verse 18 Paul has reference to Titus's first mission to Corinth.

[61] Though there is no way for us to know whom the unnamed brother was, expositors offer conjectures. Acts 19:22 indicates that Timothy and Erastus were sent to Macedonia, apparently in order to help the Macedonians get involved in the offering for Jerusalem. Perhaps from there Erastus is the one who accompanied Titus to Corinth to do the planning and organization of the offering in its early stages. According to 1 Corinthians 4:17 and 16:10 Timothy had also been sent to Corinth before 1 Corinthians was written, but would arrive after 1 Corinthians had been delivered. Thus, he cannot be the unnamed brother. 2 Timothy 4:12 and Titus 3:12 indicate Tychicus was one whom Paul sent on missions, so perhaps he accompanied Titus to Corinth that first time.

[62] The question, "[he] did not take advantage of you, did he?" is not repeated for the unnamed brother who accompanied Titus, likely because the unnamed brother was not accused by the Judaizers as was Titus.

way this question is worded in the Greek shows that the expected answer is "Yes!" Paul's thinking and behavior and Titus' thinking and behavior had been in perfect harmony.[63]   Neither one of them had been a "burden" to the Corinthians. If Titus was guiltless, so was Paul, since both were governed by the same principles.

2. Reason for this appeal – he intended to deal harshly with the unrepentant when he arrived. 12:19 - 13:4

> *Summary:* 12:19-21 speak of his fears that he will find them unrepentant when he arrives in Corinth this third time.   13:1-4 speak of his intention to deal severely with those who remained unrepentant.

12:19 - *All this time you have been thinking we are defending ourselves to you. Actually, it is in the sight of God that we have been speaking in Christ; and all for your upbuilding, beloved.*

All this time you have been thinking that we are defending ourselves to you. - The NASB marginal reading makes this sentence a question, "Have you been thinking?" This seems the best way to translate the Greek.[64] "All this time" is *palai*,[65] and *dokeite* ("you have been thinking") is a present tense verb in the Greek. "*Palai* with a present tense verb is an elegant classical idiom, and means 'You have, perhaps, been imagining all this time that all I am doing is pleading with you by way of self-defense. Do not think it!'"[66] "All this time" likely refers to all Paul has written since 10:1, though he defended himself occasionally in earlier verses (1:15-24, 8:20-24, 11:7-12). There is no doubt Paul has defended himself against the defamatory remarks made by the Judaizers, and there is no doubt he has been defending his apostolic authority. But the Corinthians must not think that his only purpose was purely self-vindication. What he actually was doing was trying to change their negative attitudes towards an apostle of Jesus Christ. Unless their attitudes are changed and there is some repentance, their chances of being built up are slight. When he comes to town this third time, he will discipline those who habitually continue to sin (13:1-4), but there is no guarantee that will result in their repentance.

---

[63] In our judgment, the NASB translators were correct in writing the word "spirit" with a small "s." The rest of the question seems to require that this not be a reference to the Holy Spirit.

[64] Since Wycliffe's days, some Bible students have treated this portion of verse 19 as a categorical statement of fact, but that makes his language more severe and less tactful.

[65] There is a manuscript variation here, with many (*Aleph*[3],D,E,K,L,P,g, Syr. Copt.) reading *palin* ("again.") This is the reading found in the KJV, and commentaries based on the KJV will give a different explanation of this sentence than we have offered. The text we are following (*palai*) is supported by *Aleph*[*],A,B,F,G,17,d,e,f, Vulg., and is the preferred reading.

[66] Farrar, *op. cit.*, p.292.

***Actually,* it is in the sight of God that we have been speaking in Christ** - "In the sight of God" pictures God as being in the audience when Paul speaks. His awareness that God is watching is a deterrent to being untruthful. "Speaking in Christ" is likely a claim to inspiration. Jesus' apostles spoke and wrote by inspiration (1 Corinthians 2:13). The Greek verb translated "we have been speaking" is a present tense verb ("we are speaking") and indicates what Paul does habitually. God cannot lie, so one speaking by inspiration cannot lie. When Paul tells of his real motive for defending his apostolic authority, he is writing nothing but pure holy truth.[67]

And all for your upbuilding, beloved - "All [is spoken[68]] for your upbuilding" is the real reason behind his vindication of his apostolic authority. It was for their benefit, not his. If possible, he wants to lead them to repentance by his written defense ("all he has been speaking"), or by disciplining them if necessary (13:1-4). Speaking by inspiration, with God as his witness, every word he has written was for the purpose of their edification.[69] They needed to grow in faith, for Judaizers had diminished their earlier convictions. "Beloved" says that whether the readers belong to the faithful majority, or to the minority who have been negatively influenced by the Judaizers, Paul loves them. He has been writing in love,[70] because he is concerned about their spiritual welfare.

12:20 - *For I am afraid that perhaps when I come I may find you to be not what I wish and may be found by you to be not what you wish; that perhaps* **there may be** *strife, jealousy, angry tempers, disputes, slanders, gossip, arrogance, disturbances;*

For I am afraid - "For" shows this verse gives the reason for his previous assertion that the reason for writing was to build them up. "'I fear' is a present tense verb, indicating a constant dread that haunted Paul's mind as he thought of his coming visit."[71] Verses 20 and 21 express three reasons for this fear: (1) concern for the outcome of the impending visit, (2) that the Corinthians will not yet have repented of some of their besetting sins, and (3) that he will be humiliated like he was when he made his intermediate trip to Corinth.

---

[67] In this commentator's judgment, Paul's language here (God is watching, and my words are inspired) is hardly to be treated as so harsh it borders on being unchristian. We do not agree with those who affirm chapters 10-13 are harsh and sarcastic and cannot be a part of the same letter that started with chapters 1-9.

[68] We must supply the verb from the previous clause to complete the thought here.

[69] The same word "build up" or "edify" was used in 1 Corinthians 14:12-26 and at 2 Corinthians 10:8.

[70] This word is another evidence that chapters 10-13 were not written in a harsh tone of thundering condemnation of the whole church. Coffman, *op. cit.*, p.492.

[71] Fisher, *op. cit.*, p.437.

That perhaps when I come I may find you to be not what I wish and may be found by you to be not what you wish - Paul's first reason for fear is that the coming visit to Corinth will not be as pleasant as both he and they might desire. "Not what I wish" says that if they have not repented of their wrong behavior toward each other, and if they have not repudiated the Judaizers, then they will not be what Paul wishes them to be. "Not what you wish" says that, since no discipline at the moment seems joyful, the Corinthians will be wishing he were not administering the discipline he finds he must.

That perhaps *there may be* - Paul's second reason for fear is that he will find[72] the Corinthians sinning in their relationships to one another.[73] It seems obvious that the wrong behavior about to be highlighted in the rest of the verse resulted from the Corinthians having listened to the Judaizers' doctrine that unless one keep the works of the Law there is no salvation (cp. Acts 15:1). Years earlier, in the church at Antioch, the infiltration of the Judaizers into the church led to cessation of table fellowship between Christians who were ethnically Gentile and Christians who were ethnically Jewish (Galatians 2:11-13). Hard feelings resulted both in the accusers' minds and in the minds of the accused. Wherever the Judaizers went, the result was the same: broken fellowship and hard feelings, and the sins Paul is about to list here.[74]

Strife, jealousy - The Greek word translated "strife" is *eris*.[75] Eris was the Greek god of discord. Quarreling had already characterized the Corinthians when 1 Corinthians 3:3 was written. Such behavior is sin (Galatians 5:20). The Greek word translated "jealousy" is *zēlos*,[76] which in this context seems to mean passionate commitment for one's side over against the other in a dispute.

---

[72] We mentally supply the verb "found" from the previous clause to fill out the sense of what Paul was writing.

[73] The eight sins about to be listed all deal with personal relationships.

[74] It is a low view of Scripture, and how it came to be written (i.e., God breathed), that leads some writers to affirm Paul is just inserting a vice list common among the Greeks and Romans. The idea that such lists as those found in Galatians 5:20, Romans 13:13, and Ephesians 4:25-31 were just copied from existing lists and thoughtlessly included is a denial of inspiration, and a denial that the vices warned about were exactly pertinent to the readers and the situation in which they lived. This subtle denial of inspiration must be repudiated.

[75] The KJV translators chose "debates" as the meaning of *eris*. In 1611 the word "debates" had a different meaning than it does now. "Debates" spoke of a "battle for one's life." When men are in a heated argument over theological issues it often becomes a battle for one's life. It may be a good way of picturing what was happening at Corinth since the Judaizers came.

[76] This same word occurs at 2 Corinthians 11:2 and 1 Corinthians 3:3.

Angry tempers, disputes - "Angry tempers" translates the Greek word for anger (*thumoi*), a word which pictures a sudden, impulsive boiling over of temper.[77]   It is a good word to describe the angry animosity between contending factions. *Eritheia* ("disputes"), a work of the flesh (Galatians 5:20), denotes personal rivalry, self-seeking, selfish ambition. Fisher observes that the word is found only in Aristotle prior to New Testament times. In his writings it spoke of the "self-seeking pursuit of political office by unfair means."[78]   That is exactly the situation Paul would face if the Judaizers still have a foothold in the congregation when he gets there.

Slanders, gossip - *Katalalia* ("slanders") means to speak against another with hostile intent, open abuse, hostile invective. This is something the Judaizers have done as they disparaged Paul and his apostolic authority. While such behavior is found among the unconverted (Romans 1:30), this is a sin Christians are to avoid (James 4:1; 1 Peter 2:1). The Greek word *psithurismoi*, translated "gossip" ("whisperings" ASV), is onomatopoetic. It imitates the sound made when people, who do not have the courage to say something openly, whisper innuendoes and insinuations against someone else. It is the kind of thing that has filled the church, and would continue to fill it, if the Judaizers are still welcome on the scene when Paul gets there. They and their followers would be the ones whispering into the ears of those who would listen.

Arrogance, disturbances - "Arrogance" (*phusiōseis*) denotes conceit, a swollen idea of self-importance, pompous egotism. One with a bloated idea of self-importance is disposed to look on others with contempt, and will often seek to humiliate them. In 1 Corinthians 14:33, Paul used the same word, though there it is translated "confusion." It pictures the disorder and chaos into which a public meeting can sometimes fall. It is difficult to want to attend a congregational meeting where you know disturbances are likely to occur. What a sad picture of congregational life Paul has just described, and all because of the influence of the Judaizers.

12:21 - *I am afraid that when I come again my God may humiliate me before you, and I may mourn over many of those who have sinned in the past and not repented of the impurity, immorality and sensuality which they have practiced.*

I am afraid that when I come again - Here is Paul's third reason for fear ("I am afraid" is supplied from verse 20). He is apprehensive that the needed repentance will not happen in spite of all his efforts to lead them to repentance.   "Again" may

---

[77] Berry, *Lexicon*, p.47.

[78] Fisher, *op. cit.*, p.438. The Greek word *eritheia* begins with the same three letters as the word for "strife" (*eris*) and until recently it was supposed that the two words were related in meaning. That is probably why the KJV has "strifes" at this place. *Eritheia* is now known to have a very different history and meaning than *eris*.

allude to the fact he has been there before and is about to make his third trip to Corinth (13:1).[79] "Again" may also say he was humiliated on his intermediate trip to Corinth (because of their failure to repent) and he is afraid it might happen again.[80] It was not a pleasant experience trying to deal with rebellious and unrepentant people. Paul hopes he won't have to experience it again, but he knows it is very possible since they are free to choose to whom they will listen (whether the genuine apostle, or the false apostles).

My God may humiliate me before you - How can Paul speak of God humiliating him? Probably by allowing Paul to accept defeat. Paul would take decisive action on this visit, but there was no guarantee the Corinthians would respond in repentance. If the unrepentant offenders cannot be restored, Paul will feel humiliation over his failure. "There is something almost plaintive in the tone in which the apostle speaks of the sin of his disciples as the only real humiliation which he has to fear."[81]

And I may mourn over many of those who have sinned in the past - "Mourn" expresses the kind of sorrow that one has when a loved one has died. Spiritually dead will become their condition if the Corinthians fail to repent (Romans 6:23), and then Paul will mourn over the loss of those he loves. The Greek perfect tense verb "sinned" speaks of the persistence of the Corinthians in the transgression. "Sinned in the past" is literally "who have sinned beforehand," which leaves it uncertain what time is referred to. Perhaps he refers to what they were doing when he wrote 1 Corinthians 6:9-11. Perhaps he has reference to when he made his intermediate trip to Corinth. Some were still living in immorality. "Over many" indicates it is a significant minority of the church members who have not repented. The sins itemized in verse 20 were the result of the Judaizers coming to town; the sins about to be itemized apparently were not the result of something the Judaizers did.

And not repented - In notes at 2 Corinthians 7:10, repentance was defined as a change of mind and a change of action resulting from Godly sorrow for sin, and including restitution where possible. A change of mind in this context is a change of attitude toward immorality. A change of action would be an immediate cessation of immoral practices. "Repented" (aorist tense), a single act of repudiation of immor-

---

[79] In Greek word order "again" precedes the participle "coming."

[80] Both those who write comments and those who read and accept what is written must be especially careful here. It must be remembered that 2 Corinthians 12:20-21 are identified as "one of the strongest arguments" why the integrity of chapters 10-13 must be denied. Involved, too, is any attempted reconstruction of Paul's journeys at this time in his life. Those who affirm there was no intermediate trip are most adamant that "again" must be taken with "come" and not with "humble." This way they can more readily deny there was an intermediate trip that ended with the apostle being humiliated.

[81] Plumptre, *op. cit.*, p.125. "Members of the church should walk uprightly lest they overwhelm the ministry in shame" (Barnes, *op. cit.*, p.265).

al practices, could have occurred any time since Paul called for repentance in 1 Corinthians. Sadly, it has not, not even at the time of his intermediate trip. That many have not repented indicates that on his previous visit to Corinth Titus had been able to correct only one or so of the problems that 1 Corinthians indicates existed in the congregation. The lingering problem of licentious living still remains and Paul is worried the Corinthians will persist in their impenitence even until he gets to town on his third visit.

Of the impurity, immorality and sensuality which they have practiced - These three words refer to "the sexual sins which were so common in Corinth"[82] and in which some of the church members were involved. The Greek says they have not repented "over the impurity, immorality, and sensuality." It is not an unusual construction to speak of a sin over which repentance is needed. In this context "impurity" would be sexual impurity of any kind. "Immorality" ("fornication," ASV) is a broad general term covering "promiscuous sexual indulgence and prostitution."[83] "Sensuality" ("lasciviousness," ASV) refers to sexual behavior done in wanton defiance of public decency. Earlier in this part of the letter (10:2,6,11) Paul has hinted that he may be compelled to adopt severe measures with the Corinthians. Now, in a context where repentance is needed for strife (verse 20) and for immorality (verse 21), he now speaks of those measures more fully (13:1-4).

13:1 - *This is the third time I am coming to you. EVERY FACT IS TO BE CONFIRMED BY THE TESTIMONY OF TWO OR THREE WITNESSES.*

This is the third time I am coming to you - As chapter 13 opens, we are still in the section that began at 12:14, which is an appeal to the Corinthians to be ready for his approaching third visit. 12:19-13:4 give the reasons why he made this appeal. Paul is hoping to avoid having to use his apostolic power to deal harshly with an unrepentant minority. Paul's first trip to Corinth was when he planted the church (Acts 18:1-18; 1 Corinthians 3:6). An intermediate trip, not recorded in Acts, ended with Paul in sorrow (2 Corinthians 2:1,5) because he could not get one of the Corinthians to repent.[84] As he now sets forth what they may expect of him, he writes two warnings: (1) every fact will be established by the testimony of two or three witnesses, and (2) he will not spare those who continue to sin.

EVERY FACT IS TO BE CONFIRMED BY THE TESTIMONY OF TWO OR THREE WITNESSES - If we omit the chapter break found between 12:21 and 13:1 in our Bibles, we will easily see that there is a close connection between 12:20,21 and

---

[82] Fisher, *op. cit.*, p.439. The same three words occur at Galatians 5:19 and are listed as "deeds of the flesh."

[83] Coffman, *op. cit.*, p.494. The same word occurs at Matthew 19:9 and 1 Corinthians 6:13.

[84] See the Introductory Studies concerning "The Travels of Paul and His Companions."

chapter 13:1-4. Comments made on this verse should reflect that fact. First, it is to be observed that Paul does not introduce this language with "it is written," the regular way he introduces quotations from the Old Testament.[1] Paul very well may be quoting the words of Jesus which Matthew also quoted (Matthew 18:16). On that occasion, Jesus spoke of two or three witnesses when church discipline is administered; Paul says he will practice church discipline when he gets to Corinth just as Jesus taught it should be done.[2] In 1 Corinthians 5, when he called on the congregation to discipline the immoral offender, he speaks of being present in spirit (1 Corinthians 5:4). This time he will be present in person. Though an apostle could unilaterally discipline unrepentant sinners (Acts 13:8-11; 1 Timothy 1:20), this language indicates when he comes to Corinth this time he will ask the faithful members of the congregation to do the discipline. "He will preside over the congregation as they acted."[3] The persons to be disciplined are those whose interpersonal relationships were sinful (12:20), and those who had not repented of their immorality (12:21). Because those sins were well-known to the members of the church at Corinth, witnesses should not be difficult to find. The requirement for two or three witnesses precludes someone with a score to settle from being able to accuse the person and get an unfair judgment against him. However, when two or three witnesses have testified, if the accused remains unrepentant, then discipline will follow, apparently from the hand of Paul himself (verse 2). The church had gone too long without practicing discipline on habitual sinners. My next visit is the time to take action, says Paul.

13:2 - *I have previously said when present the second time, and though now absent I say in advance to those who have sinned in the past and to all the rest as well, that if I come again, I will not spare* anyone.

---

[1] The words printed in capital letters in the NASB are found in Deuteronomy 19:15.

[2] Some scholars have thought this to be a strange quotation which Paul has inserted at this place, and they have struggled to decide why Paul introduces what they interpret to be a quotation from Deuteronomy 19:15. They first of all wonder why an apostle would need witnesses. Then they note the juxtaposition of "the third time" and "three witnesses." This has led to the strange suggestion that Paul's three visits to Corinth are his three witnesses. "It is fatal to this view that it turns the judge into a prosecutor, and makes him appeal to his own reiteration of his charges as evidence of their truth" (Plumptre, *op. cit.*, p.127). Or if not three visits, then perhaps three letters written by Paul to Corinth are the witnesses (a view requiring either a previous letter or a severe letter besides our two canonical letters). Though this commentator has rejected the idea that Paul wrote any more letters to Corinth than the two canonical ones we have, if the idea were granted, it would appear that Plumptre's objection to three visits can also be applied to three letters. If Paul is following Jesus' instructions for discipline, the witnesses are to be personal, human eye-witnesses.

[3] Fisher, *op. cit.*, p.439. Some have supposed that Paul is announcing his intention to set up court in Corinth when he arrives, and conduct a formal investigation by calling witnesses to testify as to the misconduct of those who were being tried. In the centuries following the writing of 2 Corinthians, men have set up church tribunals and inquisitions and have used this verse as justification, wrongly in this commentator's judgment.

I have previously said when present the second time, and though now absent I say in advance - Plummer gives the sense in these words: "When I was present the second time, I gave a warning which still holds good (perfect tense); and now that I am absent, I repeat the warning."[4]   The warning he gave them during his intermediate trip concerned his intended action if he came again and found them still sinning, rather than repentant.   Perhaps his failure to take action on that occasion led to the Judaizer's accusation that he lacked the authority to take action.

To those who have sinned in the past, and to all the rest as well - "Those who have sinned in the past" are the ones indulging in immorality (2:21).   "All the rest" are the church members who are displaying angry tempers and animosity toward those who do not agree with them and who are creating disturbances (2:20).   Both groups have received their final warning.   If they remain unrepentant, Paul would use his apostolic authority and power to punish them.

That if I come again, I will not spare *anyone* - The "if" does not imply doubt about a coming visit.   Instead, Paul is here quoting the warning he gave them on his second visit.   He said that if he comes again and finds sin and failure to repent, he would certainly use his apostolic powers to inflict punishment on the impenitent offenders.   They did not heed his warning when he was with them the second time.   They have had ample time to repent.   "I will not spare" probably means he will restrain himself no longer from taking appropriate action.   We do not know exactly what punishment he intended to inflict, but some kind of supernatural physical punishment is surely intended, for the next verse says that his actions would be ample proof of his apostolic authority and power.   Two other instances in the New Testament where physical punishment was miraculously applied come to mind: Ananias and Sapphira (Acts 5:1-11) and Elymas (Acts 13:6-12).

13:3 - *since you are seeking for proof of the Christ who speaks in me, and who is not weak toward you, but mighty in you.*

Since you are seeking for proof of the Christ who speaks in me - "Verse 3 is more closely connected with verse 2 than the dash between the verses might indicate.   A semicolon would be better."[5]   He "will not spare anymore" because the impenitent Corinthians themselves have made it impossible for him to do so.   Perhaps the ones who continued to sin (12:21) and cause confusion (12:20) were the ones claiming to

---

[4] Plummer, *op. cit.*, p.373.   The Textus Receptus, and so the KJV, read differently here, resulting in a garbled sentence.   We may ask with Denney, "Who would ever say 'I tell you as if I were present with you a second time, although in point of fact I am absent'?   Such mention of the absence is so needless as to be grotesque" (James Denny, *The Second Epistle to the Corinthians* (London: Hodder and Stoughton, 1894), cited by Plummer, *ibid.*).   Those who deny that any intermediate visit ever occurred adopt the pointless reading of the KJV.

[5] Fisher, *op. cit.*, p.441.

need proof from Paul. After all, the Judaizers had sown seeds of doubt about his apostolic authority and power. They said, 'It is just Paul himself talking; Christ isn't speaking through him.' Well, not only has Christ been calling them to repentance through the words of the apostle Paul,[6] but Christ would empower Paul when the time came to inflict punishment on the impenitent. This seems to point to the supernatural infliction of physical suffering as the threatened punishment on the impenitent.

And who is not weak toward you, but mighty in you - Paul may be thought of as weak (10:10), but Christ is not weak. He wasn't in the past; He will not be when Paul next visits. Christ is described as being "mighty." The word translated "mighty" is used only by Paul in the New Testament and "he always used it for divine power."[7] "In you" likely is a statement that Christ is mighty in their midst. The Corinthians should not forget that miraculous spiritual gifts had been bestowed upon many of them in the church by the Lord (1 Corinthians 1:7, 12:7). The signs of an apostle had been performed among them (2 Corinthians 12:12). No one should think of Jesus as being weak. Paul is again affirming that he surely is an apostle of Christ. He personally may not have great powers, but Christ who works through him has the power of God (verse 4). If they are looking for mighty power, they will witness the Lord's mighty power on Paul's third visit to Corinth. Those who refuse to repent will experience it.

13:4 - *For indeed He was crucified because of weakness, yet He lives because of the power of God. For we also are weak in Him, yet we shall live with Him because of the power of God* **directed** *toward you.*

For indeed He was crucified because of weakness - Verse 3 has characterized Christ as "mighty." Verse 4 anticipates a Judaizer objection that someone who could not save Himself from crucifixion cannot have much might. They would be voicing the fact that for the Jews a crucified Messiah was a stumbling block (1 Corinthians 1:23). The "weakness" of Christ is related to His incarnation. He emptied Himself when he took on the likeness of men in order that by dying He might make propitiation for their sins (Philippians 2:7,8; Hebrews 2:14-18; 1 Peter 3:18). That Jesus should become like a weak human was all part of the eternal purpose willed by the Godhead (Revelation 13:8 KJV). As He was being tried and crucified He did not choose to exert His power by calling on twelve legions of angels (Matthew 26:53).

Yet He lives because of the power of God - The resurrection of Jesus is indicated in this phrase. The verb tenses here are important. His crucifixion took place once for

---

[6] In the words "Christ ... speaks in me" is a direct assertion of inspiration. Rejection of Paul's words were tantamount to rejection of Christ who commissioned him.

[7] Fisher, *op. cit.*, p.441.

all (aorist tense), and now through the power of God, Christ lives (present tense) for evermore. Jesus is no longer dead, says Paul, who elsewhere wrote that God raised Jesus. "God ... has raised the Lord" (1 Corinthians 6:14). God "raised Him from the dead and seated Him at His right hand in the heavenly places" (Ephesians 1:19,20). "Christ was raised from the dead through the glory of the Father" (Romans 6:4). Because Jesus lives by the power of God, He is capable of exerting God's great power. In the remainder of this verse Paul will affirm that the risen Lord exerts His power through His apostles of whom Paul is one.

For we also are weak in Him - Paul here affirms that a parallel exists between the life of Jesus and his own life.[8] In this context, Paul's hesitation to discipline the impenitent on an earlier visit to Corinth has been mistaken for weakness by the Judaizers. Perhaps if he were judged merely by worldly standards this might be so. But his actions were representative of how Jesus acted toward sinners. In His parable of the barren fig tree (Luke 13:6-9), Jesus pictured the vineyard-keeper as making a strenuous effort for a year to revive the fig tree. "If it bears fruit next year, fine; but if not, cut it down." The Corinthians year-long opportunity to repent is about at its end.

Yet we shall live with Him because of the power of God *directed* **toward you** - Here is another parallel between Jesus' life and his own.[9] Just like Jesus lives by the power of God, so the power of God will flow through Paul the apostle of Jesus toward the impenitent Corinthians. The same power of God that raised Jesus from the dead will be demonstrated as Paul disciplines the impenitent. As the Corinthians feel God's power in punishment they will recognize that Paul's claim to being an apostle of Jesus is vindicated.

3. **The purpose for this appeal – Paul hoped they would repent and thus avert any need for severe discipline.   13:5-10**

13:5 - *Test yourselves to see if you are in the faith; examine yourselves!   Or do you not recognize this about yourselves, that Jesus Christ is in you – unless indeed you fail the test.*

Test yourselves *to see* **if you are in the faith** - He has said what he will do (13:1-4). Now he identifies what they must do to avoid the threatened discipline. It is likely this first clause of verse 5 is addressed to the Christians who have been negatively influenced by the Judaizers (12:20). The pronoun "yourselves" is very emphatic. Examine yourself, not someone else. The folk thus addressed have been testing Paul

---

[8] "We" means either "we apostles" or Paul refers to himself in particular.

[9] To refer the words "we shall live" to the future life resulting from the final resurrection of the dead is to ignore the context. It is a true idea, but this is not the verse to use to teach it.

when they should have been testing themselves. There is no contradiction between this verse ("if you are in the faith") and 1:24 ("for in your faith you are standing firm"). That was addressed to the faithful majority; this verse is addressed to the minority who have doubted Paul. "Faith" in this passage is a body of Christian doctrine which Christians must believe. To be "in the faith" is to be faithful to the Lord, both in doctrine and practice.[10] The verb "test" (*peiradzete*) is a present tense imperative, a command from an apostle of Jesus that Christians must continually compare their beliefs with the faith once for all delivered to the saints.[11] This testing is something Christians are to do continually, and something the Corinthians have not been doing.[12] When, because of the test, a Christian becomes conscious of deviations from the faith, repentance is called for.

Examine yourselves! - "Yourselves" is again emphatic, and the verb *dokimadzō* ("examine") is present imperative, calling for continuous examination. The verb *dokimadzō* is regularly used for assaying or testing metals in a crucible with the intention of finding the metals to be genuine. It suggests the Corinthians are to be very serious and thorough when it comes to making their own self-examinations. After all, the testing of one's faith is more precious than the testing of gold to see if it is genuine (1 Peter 1:7).

Or do you not recognize this about yourselves, that Jesus Christ is in you - "Or do you not recognize this" gives a reason to dissuade them from thinking there was no need to test and examine themselves. As long as it is true that Jesus Christ is in them, that is how long it is true they need to test and examine themselves. The exact meaning of "Jesus Christ is in you" is hard to determine. Can "Jesus Christ" stand for the truth of Christianity, something the Corinthians already had from the apostles? They did not get Christian truth from the Judaizers. "Christ in you" may mean that their lives have been changed by the power of the Gospel that Paul preached. They are Christians now, but if they don't repent, the day will come they are no longer Christians. Or perhaps Christ "in you" means that each Christian is a temple where Christ dwells (John 15:4,5; Galatians 2:20; Ephesians 3:17; 1 John 3:24). "The one who keeps His commandments abides in Him, and He in him" (1 John 3:24). "Christ in you" reminds us of what Paul wrote to the Colossians, "Christ in you, the hope of glory" (Colossians 1:27).

Unless indeed you fail the test? - "If they are to pass the test, they must repent before Paul arrives by putting away the sins mentioned in 12:20,21 and by withdrawing from

---

[10] The immoral folk (2 Corinthians 12:21) are not in harmony with Christian practice.

[11] Berry (*Lexicon*, p.28) tells us the difference between the synonyms *dokimazō* and *peirazō*. "*Dokimazō* means to test anything with the expectation of finding it good; *peirazō*, either with no expectation, or of finding it bad."

[12] If they are following the Judaizer's teachings they are not in the faith.

the Judaizers."[13]   If they "fail the test"[14] because they do not repent, or if they fail the test because they think that what the Judaizers teach is acceptable Christian doctrine, then it follows that Paul will need to so act that the power of God will punish them after the church has disciplined them.   That will result in their repentance; or if there is no repentance, Jesus Christ will no longer be in them.   Paul himself tells us that he practices strict self-control so that he will not be disqualified (*adokimos*, "fail the test", 1 Corinthians 9:27).

13:6 - *But I trust that you will realize that we ourselves do not fail the test.*

But I trust that you will realize - The thread of thought would be easier to follow if we translated *de* as "and" instead of "but."   "I trust" translates *elpidzō* which here seems to mean "I anticipate" or "I expect."[15]   As they do their self-testing and self-examination (verse 5), Paul anticipates that it will become evident to them that he, too, passes the test.

That we ourselves do not fail the test - There are several possibilities for the "test" Paul is confident he will pass.   He may be thinking of the "proof" that Christ was speaking through him and that he has the power to administer discipline (verse 3).   He may be thinking that they will have evidence that he has been commissioned by the Lord Jesus to be His apostle.   He may be thinking that they will realize that his gospel is the correct one, not the different gospel (Galatians 1:7) which the Judaizers preached.

13:7 -- *Now we pray to God that you do no wrong; not that we ourselves may appear approved, but that you may do what is right, even though we should appear unapproved.*

Now we pray to God that you do no wrong - "We pray," a present tense verb, shows this is Paul's constant prayer.   It would be doing "wrong" if they refuse to repent of sin (12:20,21) or if they fail to repudiate the Judaizing intruders from Palestine.   His prayer is that they will do both lest they do even one thing wrong.

Not that we ourselves may appear approved -   One thing that would have proved

---

[13] Thompson, *op. cit.*, p.187.   The KJV reads "except ye be reprobates."   The word *adokimos* really means that which fails to stand the test (cp. Jeremiah 6:30, "they call them rejected [*apodokimazō*, LXX] silver").   Nevertheless, Calvinistic theology has attached to the word "reprobate" ideas that are foreign to its true meaning.   There is no allusion here to what is sometimes called "double predestination," the doctrine that back in eternity God decreed that certain people were predestined to be saved, and certain (the reprobate) predestined to be lost, a destiny in no way related to how the men have lived.

[14] The Greek word *adokimos* which is translated "fail the test" comes from the same Greek root that is behind the command to "test" yourselves, which refers to the process of testing metals to find out whether or not they are genuine.

[15] "The rapid changes between first singular (verses 2 and 6) and the first plural (verses 4 and 7) should be noted.   In all these cases he probably means himself only" (Plummer, *op. cit.*, p.377).

his apostolic power was if he were to demonstrate with the power of God that he could punish unrepented sin (verse 3). He would rather not have to make use of that criterion.

But that you may do what is right - This clause, too, is governed by "we pray." Paul's prayer is that they do not do one thing wrong, but habitually do (a present tense verb) what is right. Habitually doing "what is right" would include repentance where needed, but even more, it would speak of habitually living the new kind of life Christians are born again to live, so there would be no need of repentance. "Right" translates *kalon*, a word that means honorable or "beautiful by reason of purity of heart and life."[16]

Even though we should appear unapproved - If they were habitually to do what is right, he would never have to exercise the God-empowered discipline that would prove his apostolic power. That is what he prays will happen. If they repent and do what is right, the discipline test of his genuine apostolic authority would never have to be applied by Paul; there would be no need for it. In this case, "even though" the Corinthians might not witness this evidence from Paul, there were other indisputable evidences of his apostleship, just as he has made plain for four chapters now.

13:8 - *For we can do nothing against the truth, but only for the truth.*

For we can do nothing against the truth - "Truth" here refers to the gospel truth which Paul had been sent to preach. In the context the topic is whether the Corinthians will repent, or whether Paul will have to use his miraculous power to discipline.[17] He here says he cannot exercise miraculous power in such a way that would be in opposition to what the gospel is intended to accomplish. The miraculous power given to the apostles was always to be used in support of the gospel. If the Corinthians repent, there is no need to use his miraculous power to discipline.

But *only* for the truth - All the displays of supernatural power must be used in the furtherance of the gospel. Should the folk who have been called to repent (12:20,21) do so, "the cause of truth would thus be reestablished, and his power of chastening would be nullified, because it is, in its very nature, to be applied only for and never against the truth."[18]

13:9 - *For we rejoice when we ourselves are weak but you are strong; this we also pray for, that you be made complete.*

---

[16] Thayer, *op. cit.*, p.322.

[17] It is taking this verse out of context to make it mean that no one can be successful in opposing the truth.

[18] Lipscomb, *op. cit.*, p.172.

For we rejoice when we ourselves are weak but you are strong - Both verses 8 and 9 begin with "for," thus giving further explanation of what was said in verse 7. "When we ... are weak" means when we appear weak because we are not demonstrating miraculous power. The Corinthians are "strong" when they do what is right (verse 7), which includes expelling the Judaizers (6:14-7:1) and repenting of the sins called to their attention (12:20,21). They are "strong" when they are doing nothing that would require censure or deserve disciplinary punishment. Even if it makes him look weak in their sight (10:10), he will gladly forego demonstrating miraculous power when he next visits Corinth.

This we also pray for - Also" says that in addition to what Paul says he prays for in verse 7, here is one more thing for which he prays.

That you be made complete - The Greek word is *katartisin*,[19] the noun form of the word used of the fishermen mending their nets (Matthew 4:21), or setting broken bones,[20] or pulling a dislocated limb back into place.[21] Ethically the word means to "strengthen, complete, make one what he ought to be,"[22] or to "complete what is lacking in your faith" (1 Thessalonians 3:10). Paul is praying for their restoration, that they may be brought back to sound spiritual health.[23] Coffman again calls attention to the fact that chapters 10-13 are not a blanket indictment of the whole congregation. "The body had not at this point been destroyed, although some of its members needed 'restoration' or 'perfecting' (ASV)."[24]

13:10 - *For this reason I am writing these things while absent, in order that when present I may not use severity, in accordance with the authority which the Lord gave me, for building up and not for tearing down.*

For this reason I am writing these things while absent - "For this reason" points to what follows. Paul was in Macedonia when he writes this letter. His next destination is Corinth. He is writing this letter before coming to Corinth because he desires not to have use severity when he does come. "These things" embrace all the

---

[19] This is the only place the noun form of the word occurs in the New Testament, but the corresponding verb form occurs at Matthew 4:21, Mark 1:19, and Galatians 6:1 ("restore such a one in a spirit of gentleness").

[20] Liddel and Scott, *Lexicon*, p.729.

[21] Donnegan, *Lexicon*, p.735.

[22] Thayer, *op. cit.*, p.336.

[23] The ASV words Paul's prayer as being for "even your perfecting." Holiness is a process, and "perfecting" catches this idea very well.

[24] Coffman, *op. cit.*, p.501.

appeals he has written in chapters 10-13. He is encouraging those who need to repent to do so quickly in order to bring about their restoration. He does not wish to have to use stronger means than his letter to try to persuade them to action.

In order that when present I may not use severity - "In order that" expresses purpose. He writes to spare himself the pains of disciplining them when he arrives in Corinth. "Severity" comes from an adverb (*apotomos*) which means "to cut off."[25] Church discipline cuts one off from the body of Christ.

In accordance with the authority which the Lord gave me for building up and not for tearing down - At 10:8 Paul has claimed the Lord gave him authority; now he makes the claim again. The miraculous powers, resulting from the baptism of the Holy Spirit which the apostles received were given to them for men's good. If he were to have to exercise discipline and cut off a member from the body, that would be tearing down. Christ had invested him with such power, but he would rather not have to use it. Instead, he would rather use his other powers to build up the congregation. He spoke much about the church being edified (built up, see 1 Corinthians 14:3,5, 12,17). It was his constant concern. "The idea of building up is a metaphor taken from the activity of building houses or temples and other buildings. In the New Testament this metaphor is used in describing the church as something which is in the process of being built. Thus Jesus 'will build [His] church' (Matthew 16:18). Paul, as apostle, laid the foundation at Corinth, and others built upon it (1 Corinthians 3:10-15)."[26]

CONCLUSION. 13:11-14

A. Final Appeal. 13:11

13:11 - *Finally, brethren, rejoice, be made complete, be comforted, be likeminded, live in peace; and the God of love and peace shall be with you.*

Finally, brethren, rejoice - *Loipon*, the Greek word translated "finally," means, literally, "the remaining." All that remains to be said are a few exhortations and a closing prayer. The concluding verses are brief and affectionate in tone.[27] Paul has

---

[25] Robertson, *op. cit.*, p.271.

[26] Thompson, *op. cit.*, p.190.

[27] Those who interpreted chapters 10-13 as being harsh and severe in tone must offer an explanation for the affectionate tone of these verses. One is to defend such a change of tone as being natural and very similar to what one reads when 2 Thessalonians 3:10-15 are compared with verses 16-18. It has, of course, been the thrust of the comments in this book that the tone of chapters 10-13 is winsome because Paul is guided by "the meekness and gentleness of Christ" (2

used the term "brethren" four times in this letter (1:8, 8:1,23 and 13:11). He is saying that he and the Corinthians are brothers in Christ. It is because of that loving relationship that he speaks to them as he does. Next, Paul writes five present tense imperatives to sum up all he has been saying in this letter.[28] The first one (*chairete*), translated "rejoice," because it is a present tense imperative, means keep on rejoicing. Paul has just said he rejoices when he doesn't have to exercise discipline (verse 9). He encourages the Corinthians likewise to rejoice.

Be made complete - "Be made complete" also reminds us of what was written in 13:9. The word here is the verb form of the noun used there. Lightfoot speaks of two technical uses of the Greek word: (1) for reconciling factions in a political dispute, and (2) for setting bones by a surgeon.[29] Either idea would fit the situation in the church at Corinth. The Judaizers have created factions, and the fellowship has been broken. The Greek verb can be either middle or passive voice. The NASB treats it as passive. If that is correct, the unspoken agent who brings about the completion would be Paul himself. In this commentator's judgment, treating it as middle voice fits the context better. The middle voice indicates the subject acts for his or her own benefit. Paul says, "Restore yourselves," or "Mend your ways" (RSV). Continue to do it for your own eternal benefit. It was the responsibility of each individual Corinthian to see that it was done in his or her own case.

Be comforted - *Parakleisthai* may be translated "be comforted," in which case it picks up the same note that was sounded as Paul opened this letter (1:4,7). It might also be translated "be exhorted;" that is, listen to my exhortations and entreaties, heed my appeals. Harris thinks this is an exhortation for them to heed his call to reaffirm their love to the penitent wrongdoer (2:8), to break with idolatry (6:14-7:1), to show warm hospitality to the three delegates (8:6:ff), for a generous and prompt contribution to the Jerusalem relief fund (chapters 8 and 9), and for a changed attitude towards him as an apostle of Jesus Christ (chapters 10-13).[30] Another possibility for translation is to take it as a middle voice meaning "encourage one another" (as in 1 Thessalonians 5:11); that is, encourage one another to heed what Paul has written.

Be like-minded - When 1 Corinthians 1:10 was written, Paul urged the Corinthians to all be of the same mind, to eschew the wrong of choosing to join one or another of

---

Corinthians 10:1). Commentators who treat 10-13 as part of a severe letter, sent separately from chapters 1-9, are obliged to say that verse 10 was the end of that fragment, and that verses 11-13 belong to some other letter. There is no need for such a hypothesis, for there are too many thoughts found in all thirteen chapters that are reflected in this final appeal (13:11-14).

[28] Plummer (*op. cit.*, p.380) says that the present tense imperatives mean "the good points to which they are exhorted are to be lasting. 'Continue to do all these things!'"

[29] J.B. Lightfoot, *Notes on the Epistles of Paul* (Grand Rapids: Zondervan, 1957), p.47.

[30] Harris, *op. cit.*, p.933.

the parties or cliques that had formed in the congregation. By the time he writes 2 Corinthians, the teachings and actions of the Judaizers have introduced a divisive spirit into the life of the congregation (12:20). Paul here calls for the Corinthians to "think the same thing" (the literal Greek behind "be like-minded") about the error of such divisiveness and to repudiate it so that they can live in harmony in action and doctrine.

Live in peace - Be at peace with each other, seems to be the idea. Let contentions and strifes cease.

And the God of love and peace shall be with you - The words "God ... shall be with you" are a promise. "And" means "and then, if you do these things constantly." God's presence and blessing on the church depended on their positive response to Paul's five exhortations. If the Christians continue in their strife and angry tempers and disputes (12:20), if they continue in their doctrinal deviations by embracing a different gospel (11:4), and immorality (12:21), they will shut God out of their midst. The expression "God of love" does not appear elsewhere in the New Testament, but the Bible clearly says "God is love" (1 John 4:8) and that He "demonstrates His own love toward us" (Romans 5:8). That's the God who wants to be with the Christians at Corinth. "The God of peace" is an expression Paul has used elsewhere (Romans 15:33, 16:20; Philippians 4:9; Hebrews 13:20). God is the author of peace. Ephesians 2:13,14 speaks of how Christ Himself is our peace, for He broke down the dividing wall between Jews and Gentiles, and has made both groups into one. Gentiles do not have to keep Pharisaic traditions in order to be acceptable to God (cp. Galatians 2:11-21.) The God who has made such an astounding attempt to bring peace among men is the God who wants to be with Corinthians. Paul prays they will meet His conditions.

B. Salutations. 13:12,13

13:12 - *Greet one another with a holy kiss.*

Greet one another - Papyri show that such salutations at the close of a letter were a common feature in ordinary correspondence, and "greet" is commonly the verb used.[31] The aorist tense of the Greek verb "greet" indicates Paul is giving directions for one act, rather than directions for a habitual practice each time the congregation assembles.[32] The direction given here assumes this letter will be read out loud at the

---

[31] Plummer, *op. cit.*, p.381.

[32] The same direction asking for a one time greeting was given at the close of 1 Corinthians (16:20).

public assembly.   When the reading was finished is when those who were listening would obey this exhortation.   If the custom prevailed in the church that prevailed in the synagogue, "one another" means the men would greet the men, and the women would greet the women.   The warm acceptance of brothers and sisters in Christ which was expressed in this greeting was to continue long after the letter was read.

With a holy kiss - In the Eastern world of the Bible, a kiss on the cheek was and still is a common salutation among kindred and near friends.   In the church, the holy kiss was given in this way: the men would embrace each other and kiss each other's cheeks.   The women would do likewise.   "It may be called a 'holy' (*hagios*) kiss because it was exchanged by saints (*hagioi*)."[33]   Such a kiss was a "token that all offenses were forgotten and forgiven, and that there was nothing but peace and goodwill between them."[34]   Each Christian would, as far as his own attitude was concerned, have to bring to an end his or her part in the strife and disturbances that had broken relationships among brethren.   It is doubtful that verse 12 was intended to make the holy kiss an ordinance for the church, to make it something to be observed in the assembly every Lord's Day, as the Lord's Supper is.   To be an ordinance of Jesus that is observed in the church, three things must be true: it must have been commanded by Jesus; we should see in the book of Acts examples of congregations practicing what Jesus had commanded; then we should also find specific commands in the epistles for observing them.   When it comes to the holy kiss, these three criteria are difficult to find.   Though the fact that Judas chose a kiss to identify Jesus to the mob who came to arrest Him indicates that such a kiss was in frequent use among Jesus and His apostles, and though Jesus rebuked a Pharisee for failing to give him such a greeting (Luke 7:45), we have no command from Jesus telling his followers to "do this" after His earthly ministry was concluded.   In situations outside the public assembly, we have examples of such a greeting in the book of Acts (e.g., Acts 18:22, Acts 20:1, 20:37, 21:7) but it appears we have no example in the Sunday assembly. There are five references to the holy kiss in the epistles (Romans 16:16; 1 Corinthians 16:20; 2 Corinthians 13:12; 1 Thessalonians 5:26; 1 Peter 5:14) but in each case the verb "greet" is an aorist tense, indicating a single act at the conclusion of reading the letter out loud in the public assembly.[35]   If the "holy kiss" were intended as an ordinance of Christ for the church to observe at each Sunday assembly, this commentator does not see why it was treated so differently from His other ordinances and commands during the early history of the church.[36]

---

[33] Thompson, *op. cit.*, p.191.

[34] Plumptre, *op. cit.*, p.130.

[35] If "greet" were present tense, we might take this to be an ordinance that was to be continually repeated, but since it is aorist, we take the position that Paul is speaking of a single act to be done at the close of the public reading of this epistle.

[36] By the 2nd century AD, congregations were pausing in their regular public assemblies to give the worshipers an opportunity to greet each other with a holy kiss.   Justin Martyr (*Apol.* 1:65), tells how the holy kiss was practiced just before the prayers which consecrated the bread and cup for the

13:13 - *All the saints greet you.*

All the saints greet you - "All the saints" are all the Christians who live in the place where Paul was at the time of the writing this letter, which according to 2 Corinthians 7:5 was somewhere in Macedonia.   As is true in 1 Corinthians 16:20 ("all the brethren greet you"), so here, "all" comes at the end of the sentence for emphasis. "All the Christians with whom he is in touch in Macedonia desire to 'send their love' to the brethren in Corinth."[37]   "This phrase, familiar as it is, is not without interest, as showing that Paul, wherever he might be, informed the Church of one locality when he was writing to another, and so made them feel that they were all members of the great family of God."[38]   Implied is the idea that "other churches are watching to see how you respond to my appeals in this letter."

C. Benediction.   13:14

13:14 - *The grace of the Lord Jesus Christ, and the love of God, and the fellowship of the Holy Spirit, be with you all.*

The grace of the Lord Jesus Christ - If Paul has dictated this letter to an amanuensis, perhaps it was at this place where he took the pen in his own hand.   It is likely this verse is intended as a prayer of benediction.   There is no Greek word that represents "be" in "be with you," but readers of the letter would mentally supply "may they be,"

Lord's Supper. In the early 3rd century AD, Tertullian tells us that the African church suspended observance of the holy kiss on "good Friday" since it was thought unsuitable for a day of mourning (*De Orat.* c.14).   Clement of Alexandria, c. AD 200, wrote about the need to keep the kiss of love pure (*The Instructor*, iii.11 [ANF, v.2, p.291]). In the 4th century, Cyril of Jerusalem explains how the holy kiss practiced in the churches differs from kisses given in public by common friends.   The congregation was called upon to greet each other before the consecration of the loaf and the cup. Christ's command at Matthew 5:23,24 ("If you are presenting your offering at the altar, and there remember that your brother has something against you, leave your offering before the altar, and go your way, first be reconciled to your brother, and then come and present your offering") was pressed into service to justify the practice (*Catech.*, Lecture xxiii.3).   This is a doubtful justification, for the Lord's Supper and "presenting your offering at the altar" are not the same topic. In the *Apostolic Constitutions*, a 4th century collection of rules of Christian faith, life, and worship, there are instructions about how the holy kiss was to be done, as well as safeguards that were put in place to prevent abuses of the practice (ii.57; viii.11).   Apparently because of continued abuses of the kiss, the practice of kissing a pax-board (a marble or ivory tablet on which some sacred object, such as the crucifixion, had been carved) was introduced in England by the Archbishop of York in AD 1250. The board was first kissed by the church leaders and then passed around among the congregation from one member to another.   Disputes about Biblical precedence caused the congregational use of these tablets to be abandoned.   Perhaps the custom in some religious circles of kissing holy things (the cup, the table, or the deacon kissing the stole hanging over his left shoulder) at some time in the public assembly is a faint recollection of the ancient practice of greeting with a holy kiss.

[37] Plummer, *op. cit.*, p.381.

[38] Plumptre, *op. cit.*, p.131.

so that it reads "may the grace ... be with you." This is the only one of Paul's benedictions that includes a request for a blessing from each member of the Godhead,[39] though the order of the names of the three are not the usual "Father, Son, and Holy Spirit." The names of each of the members of the Godhead are written in the genitive case. In this commentator's judgment, it is best to treat all three as subjective genitives; that is, the different members of the Godhead are the source of the blessings for which Paul prays.

Paul's benedictions usually summarize key ideas that have been expressed in the whole letter. Since the Judaizers have been preaching "another Jesus" (11:4), Paul has been emphasizing that Jesus Christ is Lord.[40] Unless the Corinthians get this right, all else is lost. What is the grace that comes from the Lord Jesus Christ? Lipscomb has written, "grace pardons the guilty, restores the fallen, delivers the captive, sanctifies the sinner, sustains and supports the believer."[41] Paul had spoken of the comfort brought to his own soul by the words which he heard from Jesus, "My grace is sufficient for thee" (12:9). The Corinthians, too, may have such comfort if they stay true to Jesus.

And the love of God - This clause in Paul's benedictory prayer likely means "may the love which God inspires in the hearts of his children" be yours. If such love is there, then jealousy and anger and divisiveness will be put to flight.

And the fellowship of the Holy Spirit - "Fellowship" is mutual participation in a common cause. Paul prays that such a spirit of fellowship which the Holy Spirit inspires may flood the church. Individual Christians are members of the body. The members ought to have a "the same care for one another" (1 Corinthians 12:25).

Be with you all - No member of the Corinthian church is excluded from Paul's prayer. He prays this blessing upon every one of them, even to those who were in the minority deluded by his opponents. If they will repent, they can share in the blessing. The faithful majority will have to remain faithful to share in the blessing. Paul closes the letter with the same tone of loving affection with which he began it.

---

[39] This verse furnishes evidence that in the apostolic age the doctrine of the tri-personality of the Godhead was regularly taught. On the supposition that there are three persons in the Godhead, this prayer of benediction makes beautiful sense. But if it be believed that Jesus was a mere man, or an angel, and that the Holy Spirit is but an attribute of God or a holy influence He can exercise, then the prayer becomes strange and questionable. The Bible indicates Jesus was deity, and that the Holy Spirit is a person, not just a force. If all three, Father, Son, and Holy Spirit, are not equally deity, then Paul was asking for blessings from someone less than the Father, yet putting them on an equality with the Father. This will never do.

[40] Since the LXX translators used "Lord" to represent the four-letter sacred name (YHWH), we may affirm that Paul is calling attention to Jesus' deity by his use of "Lord."

[41] Lipscomb, *op. cit.*, p.176.

Several matters yet need attention.   (1) At an early time in the Eastern churches (such as Antioch, Jerusalem, and Caesarea) the very words of Paul's benediction were adopted for the benediction at the close of worship services.   The Church of England has included them in their Prayer Book since the 1600s and, thus, many preachers in the Protestant world have adopted the habit of reciting this verse as the "benediction" at the close of the service.   (2) The KJV closes the letter with the word "Amen."   It is found in the manuscripts behind the Textus Receptus, but it is not found in the older manuscripts behind the Nestle-Aland and UBS Greek texts.   It is likely that it was added by copyists at an early date.   When the letters were read out loud in the public assemblies, it was usual for the listeners to respond with an "Amen," a word meaning "so be it," or we agree with what has been read.   The addition of the word reminded the hearers when to respond to the reading of God's word.   (3) In the Textus Receptus and the KJV, after this verse there appears in smaller type what is called a subscription. It reads, "The second to the Corinthians written from Philippi of Macedonia by Titus and Luke."   These subscriptions were added by men and were intended to be a sort of introduction to the book.   Many of the subscriptions are right; a few have details that are wrong.   2 Corinthians was written from Macedonia (though we are not sure that Philippi was the town), and it likely was carried to Corinth "by Titus" and the two unnamed brothers (2 Corinthians 8:16-22).   It is even possible that "Luke" was the brother who was famous for the gospel.   The better manuscripts simply read "Second to the Corinthians" (*pros Korinthious B'*).

When readers have finished this letter addressed by Paul to the Corinthians, the question certainly comes to mind, how was his letter received?   There is evidence that it was well-received.   When Paul does make his third visit to Corinth and stayed for three months (Acts 20:2,3), he found a welcome in the home of Gaius (Romans 16:23). When he wrote to the Romans from Corinth, he can write that the "whole church" at Corinth sends their greetings to Rome (Romans 16:23).   It is recorded that the Corinthians did participate generously in the offering (Romans 15:26).   In light of the fact that each church was to choose delegates to carry their part of the offering, and in light of the fact that Paul indicated he would go to Jerusalem only if the offering was generous (1 Corinthians 16:4), it is a very probable conjecture that the Corinthians delegated Paul himself and Luke to carry their part of the offering to the saints at Jerusalem (see the "we" passages beginning at Acts 20:5,6 as the journey to Jerusalem begins).   When we are told in Acts 20:3 that "a plot was formed against him by the Jews as he was about to set sail for Syria," we may assume that the Jews were likely none other than the Judaizers who had been expelled by the Corinthians, just as Paul had told them to do.   It would be their way of retaliating against the apostle whom they had always belittled.

The grace of the Lord Jesus Christ, and the love of God, and the fellowship of the Holy Spirit, be with you all.

2 CORINTHIANS BIBLIOGRAPHY

Alford, Henry, "2 Corinthians," in *Alford's Greek Testament*, Vol. 2. London: Rivingtons, 1871. Revised and reprinted by Moody Press, Chicago.

> It is probably still the best commentary on the complete Greek Testament by a single author. Has a critically revised text, a digest of various readings, marginal references, introductory studies, and a critical and exegetical commentary. Students will need to be able to read Greek and Latin to handle all the notes. (*Alford's Greek Testament for English Readers* will help with the translation of some of the Greek and Latin notes for those not fluent in those languages.)

Bahr, Gordon J., "The Subscriptions in the Pauline Letters," *Journal of Biblical Literature* 87, (March 1968), p. 27-41.

> Concludes that for 2 Corinthians, Paul personally took the pen in hand at 10:1 to add remarks in his own handwriting as was his custom.

Baker, Bill, "2 Corinthians," in *College Press NIV Commentary Series*. Joplin, MO: College Press, 1999.

> Hesitatingly advocates the literary unity of 2 Corinthians after giving a thorough presentation of the arguments for and against its integrity.

Barclay, William, *The Letters to the Corinthians*. Philadelphia: Westminster Press, 1964.

> A popular treatment of selected passages. Tends to be neo-liberal in theology.

Barnes, Albert, "2 Corinthians," in *Barnes' Notes on the New Testament*. Grand Rapids, MI: Baker Book House, 1955. (Reprinted many times.)

> Includes a verse-by-verse coverage of the text plus practical application of the teachings of Scripture to everyday life. Barnes preached for First Presbyterian Church of Philadelphia for over 35 years. He had a habit of studying and writing from 5-9 AM each day. His "notes" were part of his sermon preparation before preaching from the book.

Barnett, Paul, "The Second Epistle to the Corinthians," in the *NICNT* Series. Grand Rapids, MI: Eerdmans, 1997.

> Intended to be a replacement for the original commentary in this series by Hughes. Comments in this verse-by-verse treatment are based on the NIV with careful attention to the Greek text. Barnett, who defends the integrity of the letter, makes a deliberate effort to show how each section contributes to the overall flow of thought. He presents a rhetorical outline of 2 Corinthians, but rhetorical criticism does not receive any further attention in the commentary itself. At the close of each section Barnett offers perceptive pastoral and timeless spiritual applications particularly for the modern church. Readers will find extended thoughtful treatment of most of the problem verses in 2 Corinthians. Paul's opponents are seen to be newly arrived Judaizers from Jerusalem. Generally recognized as one of the better commentaries on 2 Corinthians. The reader without a good knowledge of Greek will find this commentary tough going.

Barnett, P.W., "Opposition in Corinth," *Journal for the Study of the New Testament* 22 (1984), p. 3-17.

> While concurring with C.K. Barrett's central thesis that Paul's opponents in Corinth were Judaizing Jews from Jerusalem, this article argues against Barrett's subsidiary view that

the "most eminent apostles" (11:5) are to be distinguished from the "false apostles" (11:13). Barnett thinks the mission of the Judaizers in Corinth was similar to that of the Judaizers in Galatia – to force converts to Christianity to embrace the tenets of Judaism as taught by the Pharisees.

Barrett, C.K., *A Commentary on the Second Epistle to the Corinthians*. London: A. and C. Black, 1973. New York: Harper New Testament Commentary series, 1973.
> Barrett concludes that our 2 Corinthians comprises two successive letters, chaps. 1-9 and 10-13. (Chapters 10-13 are written shortly after 1-9. Titus had led Paul to think more happily of the situation in Corinth than the facts warranted and now, by some means, Paul has discovered the truth, and so this dramatic letter must be sent to undermine the intrusive false apostles' control of the congregation.) Barrett also concludes that the "severe letter" has disappeared without a trace. Barrett's conception of the intruders at Corinth (they were Jewish Christians who aimed to Judaize Paul's converts but not demand circumcision or Sabbath observance) will not be convincing to many readers. Barrett also fails to find any reference in 2 Corinthians to the problems addressed in 1 Corinthians.

Barrett, C.K., "Paul's Opponents in II Corinthians," in *New Testament Studies* 17 (3, 1971), p.233-254.
> The intruders were Jews from Jerusalem. He distinguishes between the "superlative apostles" back in Jerusalem and the false teachers in Corinth who were their agents, but were not quite as strict in their Jewish demands as the "superlative apostles."

Barrett, C.K., *The Signs of an Apostle*. Philadelphia: Fortress, 1972.
> This material is an in-depth treatment of what was involved in apostleship in the 1st century AD. Who were apostles? What did they do? Did they faithfully hand on the message of Jesus?.

Bates, W.H., "The Integrity of II Corinthians," *New Testament Studies* 12 (1, 1965), p.56-69.
> A defense of the integrity of 2 Corinthians. Since the unity of the letter is disputed on internal grounds, the unity can only be defended on internal grounds, argues Bates. He deals with the linguistic and psychological arguments often raised against the integrity of 2 Corinthians. He concludes 2 Corinthians was written from Macedonia to announce Paul's third visit to Corinth, where the situation had improved since the second visit and the (alleged) severe letter, but there was still some suspicion in Paul's mind.

Bernard, J.H., "The Second Epistle to the Corinthians," *The Expositor's Greek Testament*, v.3, edited by W. Robertson Nicoll. Grand Rapids, MI : Eerdmans, 1970. Reprint of 1903 edition.
> Special emphasis on Greek grammar.

Bieringer, B., "Der 2. Korintherbrief in den neuesten Kommentaren," *Ephemirides Theological Lovanensis* 67 (1, 1991), p. 107-130.
> Developments in research on 2 Corinthians as reflected by commentaries written in the 1980's (by V.P. Furnish [1984], M. Carrez [1986], F. Lang [1986], R.P. Martin [1986], F.W. Danker [1989] and C. Wolff [1989]) show the major issues are the prehistory of 2 Corinthians, partition or literary integrity, the authenticity and integrity of 6:14-7:1, the identity of Paul's opponents, date and place of composition, and the letter's concerns.

Borchert, G.L., "Introduction to 2 Corinthians," *Review and Expositor* 86 (3, 1989), p. 313-324.

> This introduction to 2 Corinthians discusses the context of the letter (Corinth and the Corinthians, Paul and the Corinthians), the canonical form of the letter, and the goals of the letter. A brief selected bibliography for further study is included. The same issue contains expositions by S. Hafemann on chaps. 1-3 ("the comfort and power of the gospel"); J.B. Polhill on chaps. 4-7 ("reconciliation at Corinth"); C. H. Talbert on chaps 8-9 ("money management in early Mediterranean Christianity")' and D.E. Garland on chaps. 10-13 ("Paul's apostolic authority – the power of Christ sustaining weakness"). Also included are expository articles on 2 Corinthians 4:7-15, 5:14-21, and 11:1-21.

Bratcher, Robert G., *A Translator's Guide to Paul's Second Letter to the Corinthians*. New York, NY: United Bible Societies, 1983.

> One of the "Helps for Translators" series, the volume quickly introduces the variant readings and gives helpful suggestions for translation of the important Greek words.

Bray, G., 1-2 Corinthians, *Ancient Christian Commentary on Scripture: NT 7*. Downers Grove, IL: InterVarsity, 1999.

> Each pericope of Corinthians is presented with an overview of the patristic commentaries on it, with quotations from the most important fathers keyed to specific words and phrases.

Carson, D.A., *A Model of Christian Maturity: An Exposition of 2 Corinthians 10-13*.   Grand Rapids: Baker, 2007.

> Originally published in 1984 under the title *From Triumphalism to Maturity: An Exposition of 2 Corinthians 10-13*, this book is a readable, applicable exposition. This section of 2 Corinthians speaks to the modern church on such issues as obedient faith (chap.2), the danger of "one-upsmanship" (chap.3), false apostleship (chap.4), and suffering and boasting in weakness (chap.6). Carson states that these four chapters are "arguably, the most intense chapters in all of Paul's writings ... Certainly they reveal more about Paul himself – his sufferings, values, motives, wrestlings, and self-perceptions – than any other four chapters of comparable length. Yet far from promoting egocentricity, they point unerringly to Jesus Christ and to what it means to be a Christian" (p.9). Carson discusses the nature of Christian leadership, the need for Christian maturity, the reality of suffering for Christ, and the responsibility of individuals and churches to follow Paul's example of spiritual growth.

Coffman, James B., *Commentary on 1 and 2 Corinthians*.   Austin, TX: Firm Foundation, 1977.

> A Church of Christ writer quotes the better comments from several classic sources as he produces this verse-by-verse explanation.

Denney, James F., *The Second Epistle to the Corinthians* in the Expositor's Bible. London: Hodder and Stoughton, 1894.

DeSilva, David A., *The Credentials of an Apostle: Paul's Gospel in 2 Corinthians 1-7.* N. Richland Hills, TX: Bibla Press, 1998.

> This work aims to be a contribution to the debate over the integrity of 2 Corinthians. DeSilva purports to find in ancient rhetorical theory explanations of the discontinuities that have led interpreters since Semler (1776) to advocate finding fragments of several letters in our 2 Corinthians. DeSilva relies on the appearance of common vocabulary and themes to demonstrate the coherence between the "parts" of the canonical text.

DeSilva, David A., "Recasting the Moment of Decision: 2 Corinthians 6:14-7:1 in Its Literary Context," *Andrews University Seminary Studies* 31 (1, 1993), p. 3-16.

> Instead of the arguments that this paragraph is a non-Pauline interruption to 2 Corinthians, those arguments for considering it as integral to the letter are deemed stronger. In its original context, 6:14-7:1 is a climactic appeal to the Corinthians to dissolve any ties with Paul's rivals and to open up their hearts again to him.

Duduit, Michael, *Joy in Ministry: Messages from 2 Corinthians.* Grand Rapids, MI: Baker, 1989.

> Twenty carefully outlined expository sermons reflect Paul's major themes in 2 Corinthians. Topics such as stewardship, servanthood, sufficiency of grace, and commitment are discussed. The volume is intended for preachers who are looking for preparation ideas.

Dunn, James D.G., "2 Corinthians III.17 -- 'The Lord is the Spirit'," in *Journal of Theological Studies* 21 (2, 1970), p. 309-320.

> In order to understand 2 Cor. 3:17, Dunn emphasizes the immediate context (2 Cor. 3:7-18) as well as employing the view that Paul's argument in this paragraph takes the form of a Christian midrash on Ex. 34:29-35, with emphasis on the words "glory" and "veil." Dunn urges that "Lord" in 3:17 refers back to the *pneuma* about which he spoke in 2 Cor. 3:3,6,8. All these considerations lead Dunn to the conclusion that Paul does not identify the risen Jesus with the Holy Spirit in 3:17.

Ellis, E.E., "II Cor. V. 1-10 in Pauline Eschatology," *New Testament Studies* 6 (1959), p. 211-224.

> Alleges that Paul does not discuss the intermediate state at all in these verses, but contrasts this age with the age-to-come.

Fisher, Fred, *Commentary on 1 and 2 Corinthians.* Waco, TX: Word, 1975.

> Defends the integrity of 2 Corinthians while commenting on the English text of the Revised Standard Version. Does not hesitate to correct the RSV when the Greek requires it. He shows rather strong dependence on Plummer.

Fraser, J.W., "Paul's Knowledge of Jesus: II Corinthians 5:16 Once More," *New Testament Studies* 17 (3, 1971), p. 293-313.

> The various interpretations of the verse given by a long series of distinguished scholars (Bultmann, Allo, Kasemann, Georgi, Martyn, et. al.) are examined and evaluated. The writer then proposes his own interpretation, that Paul the Christian uses different criteria for judging than did Paul the Jew. He sees Jesus in a different light now than he did before the Lord appeared to him on the Damascus Road.

Furnish, Victor Paul, "2 Corinthians" in the *Anchor Bible* series, vol. 32A.   Garden City, NY: Doubleday, 1984.
> Like most of the Anchor Bible series, this volume is more theologically liberal than conservative.   Views chapters 1-9 and 10-13 as separate letters.

Garland, David E., "2 Corinthians," in the *New American Commentary*, Vol. 29. Nashville, TN: Broadman Press, 1999.
> Advocates the integrity (i.e., the literary unity) of the epistle.

Georgi, Dieter, *The Opponents of Paul in Second Corinthians*.   Philadelphia: Fortress, 1986.
> The English translation of a work originally published in German, this investigation of Paul's opponents in 2 Cor. 1:14-7:4 and 10:1-13:14 considers the missionary role of those opponents, with particular attention to their self-designations for their task and origins. Georgi concludes the opponents were migrant Christian preachers of Jewish origin who were working for the early church at Jerusalem.   Despite the lack of information from the 1st century, and despite his theory's failure to come to grips with certain verses where the "Christianity" of the opponents is flatly contradicted by Paul himself, Georgi's thesis has been well-nigh accepted as a self-evident premise of all 2 Corinthian studies since.

Georgi, Dieter, *Remembering the Poor: The History of Paul's Collection for Jerusalem*.   Nashville, TN: Abingdon, 1992 (1965).
> A critical reconstruction of the history alleged to stand behind 2 Corinthians 8-9.

Goulder, M., "2 Cor. 6:14-7:1 as an Integral Part of 2 Corinthians," *Novum Testamentum* 336 (1, 1994), p. 47-55.
> 2 Cor. 6:14-7:1 is an integral part of the letter and belongs in its present context.   It supplies the appeal for holiness and the requirement of discipline that form the culmination of similar passages in 1 Cor. 4-6 and 2 Cor. 10-13.   Goulder solves what he calls the problem of the flat contradiction between the policy of 2 Cor. 6:14-7:1 and 1 Cor. 5:9-13 by proposing that the *apistoi* are not pagans but immoral/non-Pauline Christians.

Gromacki, Robert G., *Stand Firm in the Faith: An Exposition of II Corinthians*. Grand Rapids, MI: Baker, 1978.
> The thirteen chapters are designed for Sunday school classes or adult Bible study groups. The author uses the KJV but also makes careful usage of the Greek text.   Non-technical vocabulary.   Discussion questions included with each chapter to stimulate personal inquiry toward making God's truth relevant to our day.

Gunther, J.J., *St. Paul's Opponents and their Background: A Study of Apocalyptic and Jewish Sectarian Teachings*.   Leiden: Brill, 1973.
> This monograph presents "data from non-conformist Judaism and apocalypses to illumine what may be deduced concerning the doctrine and life of Paul's opponents."   The major topics Gunther singles out as he treats the parallels between the views of Paul's opponents and those of extra-biblical sources are legalism, asceticism, sacerdotal separatism, angelology, messianism and pneumatology, apocalyptic and mystic Gnosticism, apostolic authority, and the views contained in 2 Corinthians 6:14-7:1.   Gunther concludes that "Paul's literary adversaries were believers whose background was a mystic-apocalyptic, ascetic, non-conformist, syncretistic Judaism more akin to Essenism than to any other well-known 'school' or holiness sect."

Hafemann, Scott J., "2 Corinthians," in *The NIV Application Commentary*. Grand Rapids, MI: Zondervan, 2000.

> In the introductory studies the standard problems are discussed, with the positions defended by recent writers. Hafemann decides for the literary unity of 2 Corinthians. Ideas for application of ideas in the Biblical text to contemporary life. Helpful in sermon preparation.

Harris, Murray J., *The Second Epistle to the Corinthians. A Commentary on the Greek Text* in the New International Greek Testament Commentary series. Grand Rapids: Eerdmans, 2005.

> Harris deals with literary issues, historical issues, chronology, various approaches to analysis of the text, and theology in his introduction to 2 Corinthians. Included is an excursus on Paul's affliction in Asia (2 Corinthians 1:8-11) as the personal background to 2 Corinthians. Harris argues that the text of 2 Corinthians is a unified whole. He meticulously rehearses the debate (p.8-51), concluding that "there are fewer difficulties with the hypothesis of the letter's integrity" than occur with competing theories. Harris does accept the idea of differences in tone between the various sections of the letter, but instead of seeing these as discrete fragments of Pauline correspondence joined together by a later redactor, he suggests "[w]hat remains perfectly feasible is that, though sent as a single letter, 2 Corinthians was composed in stages, not at a single sitting" (p.51). Harris also provides an extremely detailed survey of theories surrounding Paul's opponents. He offers two proposals as the solution. First, Harris proposes that some members of the Corinthian church were "proto-gnostic" in their denial of the resurrection and in their pride in *gnōsis* (p.80). Second, a group of Palestinian intruders who claimed to be Christian but were in reality Judaizers had infiltrated the church after 1 Corinthians had been received (p.85). As he writes his comments, Harris first seeks to analyze the grammar of the Greek text as a vehicle for probing its theological meaning.

Harris, Murray J., "2 Corinthians" in *The Expositor's Bible Commentary*, Vol. 10, edited by Frank E. Gaebelein. Grand Rapids: Zondervan, 1976.

> The introductory studies are very readable and conservative in their conclusions.

Harris, Murray J., "Paul's View of Death in 2 Corinthians 5:1-10," in *New Dimensions in New Testament Study*, edited by R.N. Longenecker and M.C. Tenney. Grand Rapids: Zondervan, 1974, p. 327-328.

Harvey, A.E., *Renewal Through Suffering: A Study of 2 Corinthians*. Edinburgh: T&T Clark, 1996.

> Between the writing and sending of 1 and 2 Corinthians, Paul underwent a personal disaster in Ephesus (2 Corinthians 1:5-12) – either a severe illness or the infliction of a particularly severe flogging – that nearly ended his life. Harvey postulates that this experience changed Paul's view about possibly living to see the Second Advent of Christ, and changed his view of suffering. The influence of this near-fatal episode permeates the whole 2 Corinthian letter.

Hughes, Philip E., "Paul's Second Epistle to the Corinthians," in the *NICNT Series*. Grand Rapids, MI: Eerdmans, 1962.

> A careful exegesis of the epistle based on the ASV, but with reference to the Greek text. Defends the integrity (unity) of the letter. Excellent treatment of the flow of Paul's argument. Many consider this volume the finest conservative exposition of this letter.

Hughes, R.K., *2 Corinthians. Power in Weakness* in Preaching the Word series. Wheaton, IL: Crossway, 2006.

> Thirty brief sermons with titles like exalted identities (2 Cor. 1:1,2), integrity and ministry (1:12-2:4), forgiveness and ministry (2:5-11), credentials of ministry (3:1-3), a more glorious ministry (3:7-18), and doing ministry (4:1-6).

Kent, Homer A., Jr., *A Heart Opened Wide: Studies in II Corinthians*. Grand Rapids, MI: Baker, 1982.

> Charts and maps enhance the value of this volume. Kent brings to the study information from Near Eastern geography, literature, and archaeology.

Kistemaker, Simon J., "Exposition of the Second Epistle to the Corinthians," in the *New Testament Commentary* Series. Grand Rapids, MI: Baker, 1997.

> A fresh translation of each section of text is followed by verse-by-verse analysis. Doctrinal considerations, linguistic notes, and homiletic applications are included. Continuing the series begun by Hendriksen, this volume features the Reformed viewpoint in both text and footnotes. Kistemaker argues cogently for the unity and integrity of 2 Corinthians, and answers the question of "Who are Paul's Opponents?" by deciding in favor of the Judaizers over the gnostics and others.

Kreitzer, Larry J., *2 Corinthians*. Sheffield: Sheffield Academic Press, 1996.

> This volume in the *New Testament Guides* series explores the controversial place that 2 Corinthians has within Pauline studies, at least in the minds of contemporary writers. (2 Corinthians is a document that has been attracting much recent attention, and not all of it helpful to one's faith, for the conclusions often reached tend to destroy the foundations of faith.) Kreitzer gives special attention to the contribution this epistle makes to our understanding of Paul's views on such matters as his apostolic ministry, his interpretation of Scripture, and his ecclesiology.

Kruse, Colin, "2 Corinthians," in the *Tyndale New Testament Commentaries* series. Grand Rapids, MI: Eerdmans, 1987.

> Intended to update the older volume by Tasker. The commentary takes the book section-by-section, attempting to draw out its main themes.

Lambrecht, J., *Second Corinthians*, vol.8 in Sacra Pagina. Collegeville, MN: Liturgical Press, 2006.

> Provides a sixteen-page introduction, a translation of the Greek, notes and interpretations for each pericope. He maintains that 2 Corinthians was one letter, and that with it Paul sought to bring about lasting reconciliation with the Christians at Corinth.

Lipscomb, David, edited with additional notes by J.W. Shepherd, "Second Corinthians," in *New Testament Commentaries* Series. Nashville, TN: Gospel Advocate Co., 1960.
> This volume was prepared for use by Sunday school teachers when preparing their lessons.

Long, F.J., *Ancient Rhetoric and Paul's Apology. The Compositional Unity of 2 Corinthians*. New York: Cambridge University Press, 2004.
> This volume contends that Paul composed 2 Corinthians as a rhetorically unified apology drawing on the well-known Greco-Roman forensic tradition. Presented in the introduction is a survey of ancient forensic discourse including forensic rhetoric, forensic exigency, forensic invention, forensic disposition, and apologetic letters. Several of these points then become the topics for a rhetorical analysis of 2 Corinthians. Long concludes that Paul constructed an official apologetic letter to respond to damaging charges about his methods and growing suspicions about his motivations.

Martin, Ralph, "2 Corinthians," in the *Word Biblical Commentary,* V.40. Waco, TX: Word Books, 1986.
> Rich bibliographies are included for each section of the text. Three excurses cover the idea that chapters 10-13 were written about a year after chapters 1-9; the collection; and the salvation of Israel. His handling of 6:14-7:1 (that Paul borrows an Essene writing and puts some finishing touches on it) does not seem plausible. His handling of Paul's opponents (that they have a Jewish-Jerusalem connection) and 5:1-10 (Paul is participating in a debate with those who held a Hellenistic mindset by documenting that there is a distinction between soul and body, and what happens to them) will find more supporters.

Matera, Frank J., *II Corinthians* in the New Testament Library series. Louisville, KY: Westminster John Knox, 2003.
> In his introduction, Matera describes 2 Corinthians as the most personal and revealing of Paul's letters, argues for its literary integrity, and suggests that Paul wrote it for three reasons: to bring to a close the crisis over the sorrowful visit, to encourage the Corinthians to resume the collection for Jerusalem, and to resolve a second crisis caused by some intruding false teachers. This volume is a very helpful synthesis of recent scholarly conclusions concerning 2 Corinthians. Matera does not identify the offender of the early chapters of 2 Corinthians as the immoral person of 1 Corinthians 5. Paul's sorrowful visit to Corinth (not mentioned in Acts) took place between the writing of 1 and 2 Corinthians. Matera rejects the idea the false teachers were Judaizers. While he does refer to some of the recent major socio-rhetorical works on 2 Corinthians, Matera resists the trend to understand the letter exclusively in sociological terms. Paul is presented as an apostle preaching the gospel of Christ, not as an orator teaching philosophy.

McGarvey, J.W., and Pendleton, P.Y., "Thessalonians, Corinthians, Galatians, and Romans," in the *Standard Bible Commentary*. Cincinnati, OH: Standard, 1916.
> Intended to help Sunday school teachers prepare their weekly lessons as these books were studied.

Mills, Watson E., *2 Corinthians*, Bibliographies for Biblical Research, NT Series 8. Lewiston, NY: Mellen Biblical Press, 1997.
> An index to journal articles, essays in collected works, books and monographs, dissertations, commentaries and encyclopedia and dictionary articles published in the 20th century.

Mullins, Terrence Y., "Paul's Thorn in the Flesh," *Journal of Biblical Literature* 76 (December 1957), p. 299-303.
>   Argues that the context and Jewish usage indicate the "thorn" was a personal enemy of Paul's.

Murphy-O'Connor, Jerome, "The Date of 2 Corinthians 10-13," *Australian Bible Review* 39 (1991), p. 31-43.
>   Contrary to Watson (see below), 2 Corinthians 10-13 does not fit the description of the "severe letter" (see 2 Corinthians 2:4) since the two letters do not deal with the same problem. Moreover, 2 Corinthians 10-13 cannot be dated before 2 Corinthians 1-9 and therefore cannot be identified with the severe letter.

Murphy-O'Connor, Jerome, *The Theology of the Second Letter to the Corinthians*. NTT. Cambridge: University Press, 1991.
>   This first volume in a new series edited by J.D.G. Dunn that tries "to bridge the gap between too brief an introduction and too full a commentary," discusses life at Corinth and the background of 2 Corinthians. Each section of the letter is given a chapter in the book. Murphy-O'Connor also attempts to explain what went wrong at Corinth, the relation of 2 Corinthians and the New Testament, and the significance of 2 Corinthians for today.

Nickle, K.F. *The Collection*. Naperville, IL: Allenson, 1966.

Plummer, Alfred, *A Critical and Exegetical Commentary on the Second Epistle of St. Paul to the Corinthians,* in the ICC series. Edinburgh: T&T Clark, 1915.
>   Based on the Greek text, this volume has long been recognized as one of the leading commentaries ever published on 2 Corinthians.

Plummer, Alfred, *The Second Epistle of Paul to the Corinthians* in the Cambridge Bible for Schools and Colleges. Cambridge: At the University Press, 1950.

Plumptre, E.H. "The Second Epistle to the Corinthians," *The Layman's Handy Commentary Series,* edited by C.J. Ellicott. Grand Rapids, MI: Zondervan, 1957. Reproduction of 1903 edition.
>   An old classic commentary, with notes on Greek grammar, various ancient translations, and with allusion to comments by early Christian writers.

Scott, James M., "2 Corinthians," in the *New International Biblical Commentary*. Peabody, MA: Hendrickson, 1998.
>   Based on the NIV, it is evangelical in its perspective. Scott views 2 Corinthians as a unity. Background material is drawn from the Old Testament and Judaism. Focuses on Paul's understanding of what an apostle is.

Staton, Knofel, "Second Corinthians," in *Unlocking the Scriptures for You* series. Cincinnati, OH: Standard, 1988.
>   Contains 13 lessons. A workbook accompanies this volume to help introduce the Scripture to small groups.

Stephenson, A.M.G., "A Defence of the Integrity of 2 Corinthians," in *The Authorship and Integrity of the New Testament.*   London: SPCK, 1965, p. 82-97.

Sumney, Jerry L., *Identifying Paul's Opponents: The Question of Method in 2 Corinthians.* Sheffield: Sheffield Academic, 1990.
> An insightful analysis of the pitfalls encountered while trying to determine the identity and theology of Paul's opponents.   Were they Judaizers, gnostics, divine men, or pneumatics? He offers a critique of past methods used to answer this question and then proposes three tools to use instead: historical reconstructions, sources other than the primary text, and assessing passages within the primary text. Having concluded that 2 Cor. 1-9 and 10-13 are two different letters, he arrives at the conclusion Paul faced the same opponents in both letters.   He agrees with Kasemann that the opponents are "pneumatics" (folk enamored with mystical visions) rather than Judaizers or Gnostics.

Tasker, R.V.G., *The Second Epistle of Paul to the Corinthians*. Grand Rapids, MI: Eerdmans, 1958.
> A popular but scholarly treatment of the letter, this is a volume in the Tyndale New Testament Commentary series.

Theissen, G., *The Social Setting of Pauline Christianity: Essays on Corinth.* Philadelphia: Fortress, 1982.
> For those who are convinced social science criticism is a rich vein to be mined as one comments on Bible books, this volume will be comforting.

Thompson, James, *The Second Letter of Paul to the Corinthians,* in the Living Word Commentary Series, edited by Everett Ferguson. Austin, TX: R.B. Sweet, 1970.
> Based on the RSV, with frequent reference to the Greek text.

Thrall, Margaret E., *A Critical and Exegetical Commentary on the Second Epistle to the Corinthians,* Volumes 1 and 2, in the International Critical Commentary Series. Edinburgh: T&T Clark, 1994, 2001.
> This two-volume set (v.1 covers 2 Cor. 1-7; v. 2 covers the rest of the epistle) is intended to be a replacement of Plummer in this series. There are seven excurses in volume 1 covering "the church of God" in Paul, Paul's literary plurals, the mirror-vision and transformation in 3:18, etc. Thrall makes too many concessions to higher criticism in these volumes. E.g., 2 Corinthians as we have it is a compilation of at least three different letters [chaps 1-8, 9, and 10-13] written on different occasions; the doctrine of the incarnation (5:19a), though being a possibility she admits, is not the conclusion she follows in her comments. She does insist that Paul's opponents at Corinth are Jewish non-Christians (earlier commentaries have tended to see them as Jewish Christians). Her suggestion about the "offender" in 2:5-11 and 7:8-12 (someone has stolen some offering money already handed over to Paul and Paul had trouble both proving his own innocence in the matter, and in getting the thief's confession, and his eventual punishment by the congregation) is entirely innovative.

Waite, Joseph, "2 Corinthians," in *The Bible Commentary*, edited by F.C. Cook. New York: Charles Scribner's Sons, 1886. Reprinted many times.

Watson, F., "2 Cor. X-XIII and Paul's Painful Letter to the Corinthians," *Journal of Theological Studies* 35 (2, 1984), p. 324-346.
> Watson defends the identification of 2 Cor. 10-13 as being Paul's "painful letter" (allegedly alluded to in 2 Cor. 2:4,9; 7:8,12). All that has been lost from this letter is the initial greeting and perhaps the conclusion, he contends. After reviewing the scholarly debate about the unity of 2 Corinthians, the article shows that the arguments for regarding chapters 10-13 as being later than chapters 1-9, and for regarding 2:14-6:13; 7:2-4 as a fragment of an earlier letter, are unconvincing. Watson then attempts to marshal evidence to show that chapters 10-13 fit the description of the painful letter.

Wiersbe, Warren W., *Be Encouraged (2 Corinthians)*. Wheaton, IL: Victor Books, 1985.
> Subtitled, "God can turn your trials into triumphs," this volume contains 12 sermons by Wiersbe.

Wilson, Geoffrey B., *2 Corinthians: A Digest of Reformed Comment*. London: Banner of Truth, 1973.

Witherington, Ben, III., *Conflict and Community in Corinth: A Socio-Rhetorical Commentary on 1 and 2 Corinthians*. Grand Rapids, MI: Eerdmans, 1995.
> Witherington provides students of Paul's Corinthian correspondence with an introduction to how Paul's writings are viewed by scholars who have embraced modern sociology as a tool to understanding Biblical literature. Emphasizes the alleged social and cultural background of Paul's thought, and treats the text in terms of rhetorical categories, rather than hearing his intrinsic argument.

Wright, N.T., *Paul for Everyone: 2 Corinthians*. Louisville, KY: Westminster John Knox, 2004.
> Wright observes that in 2 Corinthians Paul goes down deeper into sorrow and hurt, and what to do about it, than he does elsewhere, and emerges with a deeper and clearer vision of what it meant that Jesus suffered for and with us and rose again in triumph. In the body of this book, Wright presents an exposition of each pericope in 2 Corinthians. The format makes it appropriate also for daily study.

SUNDAY SCHOOL LESSONS IN THE INTERNATIONAL STANDARD SERIES.

The Annual Lesson Commentary published by the Churches of Christ (Nashville: Gospel Advocate Co.) has lessons on 2 Corinthians in the 1956, 1963, and 1968 books.

Hill, Joseph, *Whole Bible Study Course* (Kempton, IN: Mission Services, 1965) has a series of 14 lessons on 2 Corinthians.
> Joseph Hill preached at Latonia, KY, and produced Sunday school lessons for each Sunday to complement the day's sermon from the same passage. 2 Cor. 1 was included in Year 5, Quarter 4's book, while the rest of 2 Corinthians appears in the book for Year 6, Quarter 1. Included are outlines of the chapters, discussion questions, and comments on the verses included in each day's lesson.

2 Corinthians did not often appear in the International Standard Bible Lesson series before 1951.   Since then, the whole book has not been covered.   Four to six lessons once every six or seven years is about all that's covered, but the material available is helpful in lesson and sermon preparation.

One lesson on "Christian Stewardship" was included in the 1929 *Tarbell's Teacher's Guide*.

Peloubet's Notes has a four-lesson overview of 2 Corinthians in the 1963 edition.

One could consult the *Standard Lesson Commentary's* volumes for 1954-55 (lessons by Enos E. Dowling), 1963 (lessons by Lewis A. Foster), 1965 (lessons by Dowling), 1966 (lessons by R.C. Foster), 1978-79 (lessons by Don Sharp), 1983-84 (lessons by Orin Root), 1990-91 (lessons by Knofel Staton), 1994-95 (lessons by Roger Thomas and Edwin Hayden), and 1999-2000 (lessons by John W. Wade).

2 CORINTHIANS INDEX

Roman numerals italics refer to pages in the introductory studies. Chapter and verse references refer to comments in the commentary section of this book.

Condemn, Paul did not speak to, the Corinthians, 7:3

Condemnation, ministry of, 3:9

Conducted, we, ourselves in holiness and sincerity,   1:12

Conference at Jerusalem. See: Jerusalem Conference

Confession,
> glorify God for your obedience to your, 9:13
> of the gospel, 9:13

Confidence, 1:12, 2:3, 3:4
> great is my, in you, 7:4
> in everything I have, in you, 7:16
> we should be put to shame by this, 9:4
> we have, through Christ, 3:4

Confident, if anyone is, that he is Christ's, 10:7

Conflicts without, fears within, 7:5

Conscience, 1:12
> testimony of, *xii*, 1:12
> behavior guided by, 1:12
> commending ourselves to every man's, 4:2
> we are made manifest to your, 5:11

Consider, I, myself not inferior, 11:5

Constrained, the love of Christ, Paul, 5:14

Content, I am, with weaknesses, insults, 12:10

Contentment, 9:8

Contribution, the liberality of your, 9:13

Conversation, old English word for conduct, 1:12

Conversion, 3:16, 11:2

Corinth, church at, 1:1
> planted by Paul, *ii*
> Timothy and Silas preached to, *ii*, 1:19
> not all the evils corrected, *iv*, 12:20, 13:9,14
> problems in, 4, 16, 1:1, 7:15

Corinthian Christians,
> abound in everything, faith, etc., 8:7
> a letter, of Christ, 3:2,3
> betrothed to one husband, 11:2
> to die before the second coming, 4:14

Corinthian Christians, *continued*
> had a knowledge of Jesus' earthly ministry, 10:1
> obedience tested, 2:9
> longed to see Paul, 7:11
> loved by Paul, 2:4, 11:11
> obeyed Titus, *v*, 7:15
> began the offering for Jerusalem, *vi*, 8:1,10, 9:2
> begged to open their hearts to Paul, *xiii*
> had reason to be proud of Paul, 1:14, 5:12
> Paul boasts about the, 9:2
> Paul spoke to upbuild the, 12:19
> Paul's spiritual children, 6:13, 12:14
> seeking proof of the Christ who speaks in Paul, 13:3
> signs of an apostle worked among the, 12:12
> standing firm in their faith, 1:24
> to be presented to Christ as a pure virgin, 11:2
> to help Paul on his journey to Judea, 1:16
> too easily tolerated false teachers, 11:4
> standing firm in the faith, 1:24
> were Paul's letter of commendation, 3:2

Corinthian correspondence, Paul's, *v, vi, xxi*
> reasons for the severe tone of 1 Corinthians, 2:9
> see also: Previous letter (alleged)
> "his letters are weighty and strong," *xxi*, 10:10
> results of 2 Corinthians, 13:14

Corrupted, we, no one, 7:2

Corrupting, the sin of, the word of God, 2:17

Countrymen, dangers from my, 11:26

Courage, being of good, 5:6,8

Courageous, I propose to be, against some, 10:2

Deliver, delivered,
>   God, us from so great a peril of death,
>   1:10
>   He will, us, 1:10

Demetrius, hostility of, against Paul, *ii, ix, xi,* 1:8

Demons and demon possession, 11:4, 12:7

Depressed, God comforts the, 7:6

Descendants of Abraham, are they? 11:22

Despair, afflictions never drove Paul to, 4:8

Destination of 2 Corinthians, *i*, 1:1, 6:11

Destiny of the unevangelized, 4:4

Destroying,
>   not for, you, 10:8
>   we are, speculations, 10:5

Destruction of fortresses, 10:4

Determined, I, this, 2:1

Devil.   See: Satan

Devours, if he, you, 11:20

Dictation of letters, *xii*, 6:11, 9:6, 10:1, 11:33, 12:11

Died, all, 5:15

Discipline.   See: Church discipline

Discredit, discredited,
>   that no one, us in the administration of the offering, 8:20
>   that the ministry be not, 6:3

Disembodied spirits, 5:4,8

Disguise,
>   themselves as apostles of Christ, 11:13
>   Satan, himself, as an angel of light, 11:14

Disobedience, we are ready to punish all, 10:6

Dishonor, by glory and, 6:8

Disputes, 12:20

Distresses, in, 6:4, 12:10

Disturbances, 12:20

Divination, 6:7

Divinely powerful, our weapons are, 10:4

Division of chapters, bad.   See: Chapters, bad division of

Door, was opened, 2:12

Doxology, 13:14

Dualism, Bible does not teach, 4:4

Dwell, I will, among them, 6:16

Dying,
>   as, yet we live, 6:9
>   bearing in his body, the, of Jesus, 4:10

Earnest of the Spirit.   See: Holy Spirit, earnest

Earnestness,
>   produced by godly sorrow, 7:11
>   for Paul, demonstrated by the Corinthians, 7:12
>   Corinthians abounded in, 8:7
>   God puts the same, in the heart of Titus, 8:16

Earthen vessels, 4:7

Earthly house, 5:1
>   the body, 5:1,2
>   to fail, 5:1

Eased, not that others be, and you distressed, 8:13

Ebionites, 11:22

Ecstasy, 12:1,8

Emotions, 6:12

Emphatic pronouns, 1:23, 3:18, 13:5

Empty, that our boasting be not made, 9:3

Emulation, if properly used, is a great principle, 8:1,8

Encouragement.   See: Comfort

End,
>   of the glory that was fading, 3:13
>   their, shall be according to their deeds, 11:15

Endurance.   See: Patience

Engraved in letters on stones, 3:7

Enemies at Corinth, few, 11:1

Enoch, translated into heaven, 12:2

Enriched, you will be, for all liberality, 9:11

Enslaves, if he, you, 11:20

Entreat, entreated, entreaty
>   God, through the apostles, 5:20
>   the Lord, I, three times, 12:8
>   Macedonians begged with much, 8:4

Ephesus, riot at, *vi*

Epistolary Aorist.   See: Aorist tense

Insane, I speak as if, 11:23

Inspiration, 1:19, 2:4, 3:6, 6:16,17, 7:8, 11:33, 12:19

    false teachers act under false, 11:4

    not disclaimed by Paul, 8:8, 11:17

    not mechanical dictation, 7:8

    guarantees the truthfulness of those who speak by, 1:20,21, 6:16

Insults, I am content with, 12:10

Integrity of this epistle, x, xviii, xxi-xxiii, 2:1, 5:12, 6:14, 9:1, 11:32, 12:21, 13:5

Intermediate body, 5:1,3

Intermediate state, 5:8,9, 12:4

Intermediate trip to Corinth, xvi, xviii, 1:8, 2:1, 7:8, 11:15,25, 13:2

    objections to the idea of, 1:16

Interpolation, 6:14-7:1 alleged to be, 6:14, 7:5

Interrogative or categorical, 11:4,22, 12:19

Intruders. See: Judaizers

Invisible, seeing the, 4:18

Invitation, gospel, 6:3

Irony, 4:12, 10:7,12, 11:4,5,19,23,30, 12:13

Israel, future restoration of(?), 3:16

Israelites, are they? 11:22

Italy, 10:16

Jealousy, 12:20

    a godly, 11:2

Jerusalem Conference, 10:13,14

Jesus Christ. See: Christ

John,

    apostle, 11:26, 12:4

    the Baptist, 11:32

Jonah, 13:9

Journeys, on frequent, 11:26

Joy,

    abundance of, in Macedonia, 8:2

    my, will be the, of you all, 2:3

    of Titus, 7:13

    Paul's, enhanced by the coming of Titus, 7:13

Joy, *continued*

    I am overflowing with, in our affliction, 7:4

Judaism,

    low ideas about Christ, 5:16

    Palestinian and Diaspora, 11:22

    Pharisaic, xx, 3:7, 6:17, 11:20,22

Judaizers, *xiv, xxiii, xxv*, 2:6, 3:1,7,12, 6:17, 10:1

    accepted pay from their students, 11:12, 12:16

    boastful, 10:1,15,16, 11:18

    not Christians, 25, 6:14,15

    deceitful workers, 11:13

    disguised themselves as apostles of Christ, 11:13

    disguised themselves as servants of righteousness, 11:15

    motivated by demons, 11:4

    corrupt the gospel, 11:4

    exploited the churches, 10:16, 12:16

    had a leader, 2:5, 10:1,7,10,11, 11:4,20,

    how they treated the Corinthians, 11:20

    insolent, rapacious, violent, 10:1, 11:20

    intruded into other people's territory, 10:14, 11:15

    claimed to be apostles extraordinary, 11:5

    false apostles. See: Apostles, false

    false brethren, 11:26

    contemptuous criticism of Paul, *xiv, xxv*, 1:1, 4:1,7, 5:13,17, 6:9,10, 10:1, 11:7, 8,22, 12:10-14,16

    were Pharisees, 4:2, 10:14, 11:15,20

    needed letters of commendation, 3:1

    servants of Satan, 6:15, 11:15

    wrong about the gospel, 10:14, 11:4,15

    preached another Jesus, 11:4

    their end according to their deeds, 11:15

    used hole-in-the-corner methods, 3:12

    were not "ministers of God," 6:4

    voided the Word of God by their traditions, 4:2

Sphere,
> accomplished in the, of another, 10:16
> which God appointed, 10:13

Spirit, spirit,
> capitalized or not, 3:6
> in, 6:6
> defilement of, 7:1
> did we not conduct ourselves in the same, 12:18
> a different, someone preaches, 11:4
> earnest of. See: Holy Spirit
> human, 3:6, 4:16
> ministry of the, 3:7
> no rest for Paul's, 2:13
> an attitude, 4:13, 6:6
> gives life, 3:6
> of the Lord, 3:17
> of Titus refreshed, 7:13

Spiritual gifts. See: Gifts, spiritual
Spiritual warfare, 10:3
Steps, did we not walk in the same, 12:18
Stewardship, Christian, *xii*
Stones, engraved in letters on, 3:7
Stoned, once I was, 11:25
Strife, 12:20
Strike on the cheek, 11:20
Stripes, in, 6:5
Strong,
> we rejoice when you are, 13:9
> when I am weak, then I am, 12:10

Strongholds. See: Fortresses
Struck down, but not destroyed, 4:9
Stumbling, give no occasion of, 6:3
Subscription of this epistle, *v, x*, 13:14
Substitutionary atonement: see Special Study #1
Suffering, sufferings,
> of Christ, are ours in abundance, 1:5
> patiently endured, 1:6
> possible beneficial effects of, *xii*, 1:6
> and comfort related, 1:7
> Paul was called to experience the same, which Christ endured, 1:5
> Paul's theology of, 4:13

Sufficient. See: Adequate

Summary of epistle, 13:11
Supernaturalism, 8:9
Surprising, it is not, 11:15
Swallowed up, that which is mortal, is, 5:5

Tabernacle, earthly,
> the body is, 5:1
> torn down, 5:1

Tablets,
> of stone, 3:3
> of human hearts, 3:3

Talmud, 1:3, 12:2
Tallith, 3:14
Tears, I wrote with many, 2:4
Temple,
> of God and idols, 6:16
> we are the, of the living God, 6:16

Temporal, things which are seen are, 10:18
Ten Commandments, 3:7
Tent, while in this, we groan, 5:4
> the earthly, which is our house, 5:1

Tentmaker, 11:9
Terrify, I do not wish to seem to, you, 10:9
Tertullian, xxii, 2:5
Test,
> unless you fail the, 13:5
> we do not fail the, 13:6
> yourselves, 13:5

"Testament" or "covenant." See: Covenant
Testify, I, 8:3
Testimony of our conscience, 1:12
Text of 2 Corinthians,
> manuscript variations, 1:7,20, 2:1,7, 3:9, 5:3,10,21, 7:12, 8:7,10,19, 10:10, 12,14, 11:1,6,28, 12:7,11, 12:19, 13:14

Thanks, thanksgiving,
> abounds to the glory of God, 4:15
> for the favor bestowed on Paul, 1:11
> to God, 2:14, 8:16, 9:15
> usual Pauline, in letters, 2, 1:3
> gifts brought, to God, 9:11,12

Thessalonian letters, written from Corinth, 21

Truth,
>	as the, of Christ is in me, 11:10
>	boasting about the Corinthians to Titus was, 7:14
>	consistency, a test for, 1:19
>	I will be speaking the, 12:6
>	manifestation of, 4:2
>	refers to gospel, 4:2, 6:7
>	only, spoken by inspiration, 1:19
>	spoken to Corinthians, 7:14
>	technical term for the gospel, 4:2
>	we can do nothing against the, 13:8
>	word of, in the, 6:7

Tumults, in, 6:5
Turns to the Lord, whenever a man, 3:16
Twelve. See: Apostles
Tychicus, 8:22

Unapproved, though we should appear, 13:7
Unaware, we do not want you to be, 1:8
Unbelievers, unbelieving
>	do not be unequally yoked with, 6:14
>	what has a believer in common with? 6:15
>	minds of, blinded by Devil, 4:4

Unclean, do not touch what is, 6:17
Unclothed, we do not want to be, 5:4
Unconditional eternal security, 6:1
Unction, 1:21
Understand,
>	we write what you, 1:13
>	you partially did, us, 1:14

Understanding, they are without, 10:12
Unequally yoked, 6:14
Unevangelized, fate of, 4:4
Union with Christ. See: In Christ
Unity, of 2 Corinthians, 2:1,4, 6:14, 12:11
Unknown, and yet well known, 6:9
Unskilled in speech, 11:6
Unveiled, we all with, face behold the Lord, 3:18
Upbuilding, we have been speaking for your, 12:19

Urge,
>	I, you by the meekness and gentleness of Christ, 10:1
>	we, you not to receive grace in vain, 6:1

Use of the Old Testament, Paul's, 3:7, 6:18, 8:15,21, 9:5, 10:7,9
Utterance, Corinthians abound in, 8:7

Vacillating, Paul accused of, 1:17
Vain, do not receive the grace of God in, 6:1
Veil, Veiled,
>	on the heart, remains unlifted, 3:14
>	put on by Moses, 3:13
>	the face of the Jew, to this day, 3:15
>	if our gospel is, it is, to those who perish, 4:3
>	removed in Christ, 3:14,16

Victory through repentance, 7:11
Vindication of yourselves, 7:11
Visions from the Lord, 12:1,5

Wages, taking, from them to serve you, 11:8
Walk, walking,
>	according to the flesh, 10:2
>	by faith, not by sight, 5:7
>	I will, among them, 6:16
>	in the flesh, 10:3
>	not, in craftiness, 4:2

Wall, window in the, let down through, 11:33
Want, your abundance supplies their, 8:14
War, warfare,
>	we do not, according to the flesh, 10:3
>	weapons of our, 10:4
>	spiritual, 10:3

Watchings, in, 6:5
>	often, 11:27

Commentary On

Galatians

PREFACE

What is involved in the faith that God looks for as He would justify men who have sinned? Is it faith alone (i.e., knowledge, assent, and trust), or is it a faith that includes obedience to what God has said?

Paul's words to Peter – "a man is not justified by works of the Law but through faith in Christ Jesus" (Galatians 2:16) – have long been a key Biblical text to which appeal is made by those who would champion faith alone.

But such faith-alone interpreters have failed to take into account what the language "works of the Law" signified in the 1st century world. As will be explained in the commentary on Galatians, there are verses that all along would have helped point us in the right direction. But it was the discovery of 4QMMT, one of the Dead Sea Scrolls, that has illumined for us what the expression "works of the Law" signified in the 1st century. The expression "works of the Law" signified man-made religious rules based on passages in the Law. It was man-made rules such as these that Jesus condemned when He spoke of the "traditions of the elders." It was man-made rules such as these that Jesus said voided the Law of Moses.

So the faith-alone explanation of the faith that saves is in error. According to Paul as he spoke to Peter, the faith that saves is habitually doing what God says, not walking by some man-made religious rules. The Judaizers, who championed rules like the Pharisees taught, were distorting the gospel message as preached by the apostles of Jesus (Galatians 1:7), and it is obedience to rules like those of the Judaizers that does not save. Saving faith includes not only knowledge, assent, and trust, but also obedience to what God has said.

The thrust of this commentary is not only to explain what verses in Galatians mean, but it is also an appeal to cease preaching and teaching the doctrine that is called faith alone, or faith only.

GALATIANS

TABLE OF CONTENTS

Introductory Studies

Commentary

INTRODUCTORY STUDIES

A. HISTORICAL ALLUSIONS

The historical-grammatical method of interpreting Scripture requires identification of the historical setting of the particular book or letter being studied. To determine the historical setting of Galatians one must read through the book looking for information or historical allusions that can provide insight about authorship, date, destination, and purpose of writing. Most often, in the case of the New Testament epistles, such allusions occur at the very beginning of the letter and again at the close, with an occasional allusion to be found in the heart of the letter.

1. Historical Allusions found in the beginning of the letter to the Galatians

1:1 – The letter is signed by Paul, who calls himself an apostle.

1:2 – "All the brethren who are with me" does not give any very conclusive information. Are these "brethren" fellow missionaries with Paul, or simply church members? Are they accompanying Paul as he is traveling, or is Paul temporarily settled in some city working with the local church?[1] Are these brethren unnamed because they were unknown to the Galatians,[2] or were they so well-known to the Galatians that there was no need to call them by name?[3]

1:2 – The destination of this letter is given as "to the churches of Galatia." Since the Romans had conquered the ancient world and redrawn many of the maps, "Galatia" was a huge province in the middle of the land we now call Turkey. Which towns and cities in that huge province had churches? When were those churches first planted? The answer to this question will help determine the date of writing of this letter to the churches of Galatia. This will require a careful study of the record of Paul's missionary journeys found in the book of Acts.

---

[1] In his letter to the Philippians, written from Paul's first Roman imprisonment, Paul writes, "The brethren who are with me greet you."   So we cannot say for sure that Paul was traveling when he wrote "all the brethren who are with me."   Yet it is also true that there is nothing akin to 1 Corinthians 16:19 ("The churches of Asia greet you. Aquila and Priscilla greet you heartily in the Lord, with the church that is in their house") in the Galatian letter.

[2] Galatians is a contrast to the Corinthian letters in which men who were well-known to the Corinthians were named in the opening of those letters (e.g., Sosthenes and Timothy at 1 Corinthians 1:1 and 2 Corinthians 1:1).

[3] If this opinion is correct, the brethren could be Timothy and Erastus who were with Paul on his third missionary journey (Acts 19:22). Someone has reported to Paul concerning the developing problem among the churches of Galatia. Was that report carried by the brethren who are with Paul when he writes this letter to Galatia?

1:3-5 – At its beginning, this letter essentially follows the regular format of ancient letters, which began with a signature, address, and greeting, followed by a thanksgiving, and then the body of the letter. Note, though, that Galatians does not have the usual thanksgiving following the greeting. Also, the usual 1st century greeting is greatly expanded by Paul as he writes his words of greeting in verse 4 and 5. Why did he elaborate and expand the greeting? Does this expansion about how Jesus came to deliver us "out of this present evil age" portend some of the emphases we shall find later in the letter? The fact that Jesus has already given himself for our sins (a reference to Calvary, which occurred in AD 30) gives us a clue about the date of this letter to the Galatians. It cannot be dated earlier than AD 30.

1:6 – "So quickly" sounds like Paul has been there among the churches of Galatia not too long before the writing of this letter. The Christians are thinking of deserting Christ for a different gospel, for a message contrary to the gospel preached by Paul and his helpers when they planted the churches in Galatia (verse 9). Paul is getting involved in a situation which threatens the truth of the Gospel.

1:7-9 – It appears that a number of people have come to Galatia and are disturbing the churches. The message they preach distorts the gospel of Christ. Paul pronounces God's "anathema" on such troublemaking preachers.

1:10 – Have the preachers who brought the different gospel also insinuated that the reason Paul did not preach like they did was because he was "seeking the favor of men" and "striving to please men"? We need to choose a term by which to call these preachers. "Different" (in "different gospel," verse 6) is *heteros* in the Greek, from which we get "heterodoxy." Shall we call them Paul's opponents? Shall we call them "Judaizers"? Shall we call them "false brethren" (cp. 2:4)? Shall we call them disturbers (see "those who are disturbing you," 1:7, 5:10)? Shall we call them distorters of the gospel (verse 7)? Shall we call them enchanters (see "bewitched" in 3:1)? Shall we call them troublemakers?

1:11 – Paul documents that his gospel was "not according to man" but that he received it "through a revelation of [from] Jesus Christ." Is the "not according to man" an allusion to the real source of the message preached by the preachers of the "different gospel"? Is the affirmation of a revelation from Christ a reply to false charges made against Paul by the false brethren who had disturbed the Galatian churches?

1:12-2:21 – This is an autobiographical section:

- 1:13 speaks of his "manner of life in Judaism" and his persecution of the church. This reminds us of the persecution led by Paul (Saul) that arose after the martyrdom of Stephen (Acts 8:1ff, 9:1ff).
- Paul's words in 1:16 that "[God] revealed His Son in [to] me" reminds us of Jesus' appearance to Paul on the Damascus road (Acts 9:3ff, 22:6ff, 26:12ff) in order to call Paul to be an apostle.
- Following Jesus' calling of Paul to be an apostle (Acts 26:16-18), Paul tells us in 1:17,18 that he went to Arabia and at a later time returned to Damascus. We sup-

pose it was on the occasion of his return to Damascus from Arabia that he was forced to flee for his life, being let down in a basket out a window in the wall of the city (2 Corinthians 11:32,33; Acts 9:23-25).

- Then Paul went to Jerusalem where he became "acquainted with Cephas, and stayed with him fifteen days." The 15-day visit to Jerusalem was not long enough to learn the Christian doctrine that Paul subsequently preached. His affirmation in verse 12 that the source of his doctrine was a "revelation of [from] Jesus Christ" is not vitiated by this time of getting acquainted with Peter.
- Paul continues his autobiographical sketch in verses 21-23, "Then I went into the regions of Syria and Cilicia." The ministry there was not long enough for Paul to become known by sight to the churches of Judea, but the churches kept hearing that "he who once persecuted us is now preaching the faith which he once tried to destroy."[4] This historical note matches what we know from Acts 9:30.

These too are clues concerning the date of writing. Galatians is written after Paul's ministry in Cilicia and Syria (Acts 11:25ff).

2:1 – "Then after an interval of fourteen years I went up again to Jerusalem with Barnabas, taking Titus along also." As will be demonstrated later in these notes, it is very likely that the Galatians 2 visit to Jerusalem is to be harmonized with the Jerusalem Conference described in Acts 15. The "fourteen years" is likely to be calculated from the time of the visit to Jerusalem alluded to in verse 18. If so, Galatians 2 occurred 17 years after the Damascus road appearance of Jesus to Paul.

2. Historical allusions found in the close of the epistle to the Galatians.

6:1 – Who were the folk "caught in" a "trespass"? Have some Galatian Christians begun to defect by adopting the teachings and practice of the false teachers? Are these the ones who, having repented, are to be restored in a spirit of gentleness?

6:6-10 – Goodspeed translates verse 6, "Those who are taught the message must share all their goods with their teacher." And verse 10, "So then, whenever we have an opportunity, let us do good to all men, especially those who belong to the family of faith." What is Paul talking about? At first sight, the language is rather general; it is applicable to any number of situations. Perhaps 1 Corinthians 16:1 ("as I directed the churches of Galatia, so do you also") supplies an answer to the question.[5] 1 Corinthians 16 then goes on to talk

---

[4] "He who once persecuted us is now preaching the faith which he once tried to destroy" strongly affirms that Paul's gospel was the very same message the early church believed and lived. His gospel was not different from what Jesus and the twelve preached.

[5] Any appeal to 1 Corinthians 16 to help explain Galatians 6 assumes the two letters were written from the same general time frame in Paul's life and ministry.

about the offering being collected for the poor saints in Jerusalem.   Paul had solicited alms from the Galatians for their suffering brethren in Judea.   May we suppose that the same person who brought the news to Paul concerning the troublemakers that formed the occasion for this letter also brought word that the brethren in Galatia were not participating in the requested offering?   The words of Galatians 6:6-10, which match an appeal to Corinth concerning the same offering (2 Corinthians 9:6ff), are an appeal to the Galatian Christians to give liberally.   Paul is carrying out the exhortation of Peter, James, and John, that he continue to remember the poor (Galatians 2:9,10).

6:11 – "See with what large letters I am writing to you with my own hand."   Is Paul saying he wrote the whole letter by his own hand, rather than using an amanuensis (i.e., a professional scribe)?[6]   Why would he call attention to this fact?   Why does he call attention to the size of the handwritten letters that form the words of this letter?

6:12-16 – These verses give us a picture of what was happening in the Galatian churches. Judaizers, identified as false brethren at Galatians 2:4, were coming into the Galatian communities.   Probably they came from Palestine, and (not having been silenced by the Jerusalem Conference) were teaching that Gentile Christians had to be circumcised (i.e., become a proselyte to the Jewish religion) or there could be no association with them.   In these verses Paul unmasks the real motives of the troublemakers, pointing out that they themselves do not observe the Law of Moses, and concludes by saying that neither circumcision nor uncircumcision amounts to anything, but what is of paramount importance is the "new creation" (verse 15).   We think it proper to appeal to Ephesians 2 to get an understanding of what is involved in this concept called "new creation."

6:17 – "From now on let no one cause trouble for me."   Is it the false teachers or the Galatian Christians who are thought of as causing trouble for Paul?

6:17 – "I bear on my body the brand-marks of Jesus."   During his missionary journeys Paul endured beatings and a stoning.   It sounds like these have left scars on his body.   It looks like Paul calls attention to them to enlist the sympathy of his Galatian readers.

3. Historical allusions found elsewhere in Galatians.

The historical allusions at the beginning and closing of the letter provide very little specific information regarding the setting for this writing.   So we must carefully search the rest of the letter to gather any helpful bit of information we can find.

---

[6] It would not impinge on inspiration for Paul to dictate his letters to a secretary who actually did the writing.   At times one of Paul's associates (e.g., Timothy or Luke or Tertius) might serve as secretary. Not only was Paul inspired as he spoke, but each of the secretaries had the possibility of having received miraculous spiritual gifts by the laying on of an apostle's hands, and so be able to speak by inspiration in their own right.   If Paul's amanuensis followed the customary procedure, they would have taken down what Paul dictated with a stylus on wax tablets, possibly using some system of shorthand, and then would have transcribed the text in longhand onto a papyrus sheet or roll.

2:1-10 – This describes a trip to Jerusalem and a meeting there between Paul, Barnabas, and Titus with Peter, James and John concerning whether or not Gentile Christians were required to be circumcised. When we turn to the book of Acts to see if we can find a parallel record of such a trip and meeting, we are presented with two possibilities. One is the Jerusalem Conference (Acts 15), and the other is the famine visit (Acts 11:27-12:25). For reasons which will be laid out later in these Introductory Studies, it is this commentator's studied conclusion that Galatians 2 and Acts 15 describe the same visit to Jerusalem.[7] The Jerusalem Conference of Acts 15 is dated about AD 51.[8]

2:1 – Titus is mentioned. May we assume the Galatian churches were acquainted with this man? If so, we gain some valuable information about the date of writing, for the only time the churches might have met him is during Paul's third missionary journey. Titus was with Paul on that journey, being sent to Corinth from Ephesus to attempt to solve the Corinthian church's vexing problems (2 Corinthians 2:13, 7:5-16). We recall that at the beginning of that third journey, Paul passed through the Galatian region and Phrygia, strengthening all the disciples (Acts 18:23).

2:1,9,13 – Barnabas is mentioned. Apparently the readers of this letter knew Barnabas. From the record in Acts, which churches in Galatia were likely to have known Barnabas? As far as the record goes, Barnabas was in the area called Galatia only during Paul's first missionary journey.

2:5 – Paul tells us that he had the Galatian Christians in mind when he attended the Jerusalem Conference. He tells us here that he endeavored to retain for them the truth and freedom of the gospel. He had already worked among the readers by the time of the Jerusalem Conference. This rather requires that Galatians be dated after the first missionary journey of Paul, the first time the gospel came to any part of the Roman province of Galatia. The dates for the first missionary journey are AD 45-48.

2:11 – The Galatian letter was written after Peter's hypocritical behavior at Antioch of Syria. It is generally agreed that the events recalled in Galatians 1 and 2 are given in their historical order. If so, Peter's hypocrisy (Galatians 2:11ff) took place after the Jerusalem Conference (Galatians 2:1-10).[9]

---

[7] Outstanding scholars have differed on the matter. J.B. Lightfoot, R.C.H. Lenski, and H.A.W. Meyer have seen Galatians 2 as Paul's account of what went on behind the scenes at the Jerusalem Conference in Acts 15. Others, such as W.M. Ramsay and F.F. Bruce, correlate Galatians 2 with Paul's famine visit to Jerusalem. Some scholars have adopted the identification of Galatians with the famine visit of Acts 11 because it provided an alternative to the Tubingen School who a century ago pitted Acts 15 against Galatians 2 as Pauline and Petrine interpretations of the same event.

[8] See "New Testament Chronology" in the author's *New Testament History: Acts* (Moberly, MO: Scripture Exposition Books, 2002), p.x-xxii.

[9] *Ibid.*

2:16 – What are "works of the Law"? Does it mean to obey the Law of Moses, or does Galatians 3:10-12 indicate that "works of the Law" and practicing the Law of Moses are two different things? Do "works of the Law" have any relationship to compelling "the Gentiles to live like Jews" (Galatians 2:14)? Whatever "works of the Law" are, there was no gift of the Holy Spirit connected with such a practice (Galatians 3:2). What is "faith in Christ"? What does it mean to be "justified"?

4:10 – "You observe days and months and seasons and years." It seems the troublemakers have gotten the Galatians to begin observing these Jewish feasts and fasts.

4:11 – Paul has done evangelistic work among the readers.

4:13 – "I preached the gospel to you the first time." According to this translation, Paul has been in Galatia at least twice before he writes this letter to them.[10] This bit of information drives us back to the book of Acts to see if we can find two visits to Galatia, following which we could begin to pin down the date of the writing of this letter with more confidence.

- Paul visited the area that might be called *south* Galatia on both the first and second missionary journeys. Acts 13 and 14 tell about the first journey. Acts 16:1-6 tells about a visit at the beginning of the second journey.[11]
- Later verses in Acts have been interpreted to say Paul visited what might be called *north* Galatia on at least two occasions. Acts 16:6 is said to be the first visit to north Galatia, and Acts 18:23 is said to allude to the second visit.
- If the letter is addressed to north Galatia, the earliest Galatians could have been written (after Acts 18:23) would be from the close of the third missionary journey, AD 57 or 58.

Also of note, the first time Paul visited Galatia to preach the gospel to them, he did so because of a bodily illness he suffered (4:13).

---

[10] The Greek words Paul uses here (*to proteron*) which are translated "the first time" can have the meaning "formerly," where there is no idea of the earlier of two instances (see John 6:62, 9:8; 1 Timothy 1:13). Scholars who try to equate Galatians 2 with the famine visit find it almost a necessity to give the words this "formerly" meaning. Even so, as we shall see, the attempt to equate Galatians 2 and the famine visit must contend with some other weighty objections. Since the famine visit is dated AD 44, the year Herod Agrippa I died (Acts 12:1-23), and Paul has not even been to Galatia at that early juncture in his life, it is difficult to treat Galatians 2 as being the same as the famine visit of Acts 11 and 12. All this makes it highly improbable that Galatians is to be dated as early as AD 45, as some commentators have attempted to do.

[11] One might find two visits to most of the churches as having occurred during the first journey, for Acts 14:21 shows Paul doubled back through the churches at the close of that first journey. Appeal to Acts 14:21 for two visits to Galatia would require a date for the writing of Galatians of no earlier than AD 48.

4:14 – "You received me as an angel of God, as Christ Jesus Himself" has reminded some writers of Paul's reception at Lystra, where the populace would have sacrificed to him. The impulsive citizens of Lystra enthusiastically welcomed Paul and Barnabas, supposing that the gods had come down in the flesh (Acts 14:8ff). But notice, it is the non-Christians of Lystra who received Paul on that occasion, not the Christians to whom this letter is being written.

4:20 – "I could wish to be present with you." What was keeping Paul from going to Galatia, so he could be with them in person?

4:30 – Is "cast out the bondwoman" a call for the Galatians to rid themselves of the trouble-makers?

5:2 – "I Paul." The writer of the letter names himself for a second time.

5:3 – The troublemakers must have been insisting that the Galatian Christians be circumcised. Why is such a message of circumcision so appealing to the Galatians who, after all, are Gentiles?

5:12 – "Would that those who are troubling you would even mutilate themselves." Portions of Galatians are as emotional and passionate in tone as is 2 Corinthians 10-13. Is that because the same troublemakers are being attacked?

Now we can attempt to put together all we have learned from the historical allusions. We must do so in order to appreciate the message of the letter to the Galatians.

B. AUTHORSHIP AND ATTESTATION

Evidence that points to the authorship of the books of the New Testament are of two kinds: internal and external.

1. Internal evidence points to Paul as the author.

Twice the writer calls himself "Paul" (1:1, 5:2). Galatians' autobiographical section contains numerous historical references which are all capable of being harmonized with what the book of Acts tells us about the apostle Paul. From his days as a persecutor of the church, to the call to be an apostle that occurred on the Damascus road, to the events at the Jerusalem Conference, to his ministry in Syria and Cilicia, to the allusions to his sufferings for Christ, all these ring true to what we know of Paul's life.

There is less doubt about the genuineness[12] of this epistle than any of the other of Paul's epistles – including from the negative minimalist critics. Even the Tubingen School accepted Galatians as genuine. A popular approach in 21st century scholarship is to label many of the letters that bear Paul's name as pseudonymous. Yet this letter to the Galatians has escaped such an ignominious fate.[13] The internal evidence indicates this is a genuine letter from the hand of the apostle Paul.

2. External evidence points to Paul as the author.

No hint of suspicion as to the authorship, integrity, or apostolic authority of the epistle to the Galatians has reached us from ancient times. Allusions show the book existed and was familiar to the writers who made the allusions. Annotated quotations name either the author or the book. Canonical listings are important because, for the most part, only Scripture was included in these listings.[14]

a. Allusions[15]

1) Clement of Rome (AD 96) may allude to Galatians 3:1 and 1:4.

There may be a reference to Galatians 3:1 in the words "His sufferings were before your eyes" (1 Clement, cap.2). 1 Clement, cap.49, "Christ our Lord gave His blood for us, by the will of God, and His flesh for our flesh, and His spirit for our spirits," is seen to be a reflection of Galatians 1:4.

---

[12] A work is considered "genuine" if it was written by the person whose signature is found on the work. J. Knox has written, "There can be no serious question about the authorship of this letter." ("Letter to the Galatians," *Interpreter's Dictionary of the Bible* [NY: Abingdon, 1962], E-J, p.338.)

[13] What purpose would a forger have had for writing this epistle, asks Thiessen. We have difficulty attributing it to a Gnostic writer, for a Gnostic writer would have avoided representing Paul as showing deference to the original apostles, as he does in Galatians 2. An Ebionite would have shrunk from any seeming depreciation of the Jewish customs and leaders. A harmonizer of the supposed Pauline and Petrine factions (of Tubingen School fame) would have avoided intimating that there was any conflict between them. It is clear, also, that the special themes of Galatians (e.g., Paul's apostleship, and the question of circumcision for Gentile Christians) were burning issues in the AD 50's and 60's, but they had become dead issues by the end of the 2nd century. Redaction critics can come up with no reason why a 2nd century redactor would have produced this writing. (H.C. Thiessen, *Introduction to the New Testament* [Grand Rapids: Eerdmans, 1954], p. 213,214.)

[14] A detailed listing of early references to Galatians found in the writings of the apostolic and early church fathers is given in the work of J.B. Lightfoot, *The Epistle of St. Paul to the Galatians* (Grand Rapids: Eerdmans, reprint ed.), p.58-62.

[15] These allusions and quotations which follow can all be studied in A. Roberts and J. Donaldson, eds., *The Ante-Nicene Fathers* (Grand Rapids: Eerdmans, 1953). 10 volumes.

2) Ignatius (AD 115)

The epistles of Ignatius contain several coincidences with the epistle to the Galatians. In his letter *to Polycarp*, chapter 1, in the words "Bear with all men, as the Lord beareth thee ... Bear the infirmities of all men," there may be a resemblance to Galatians 6:2. In his letter *to the Romans*, chapter 7, "My passion is crucified," recalls Galatians 5:24 and 6:14. In his letter *to the Philadelphians*, chapter 1, the words "Which bishop I know obtained the ministry for the public, not of himself, nor by men, nor out of vain-glory, but by the love of God the Father, and the Lord Jesus Christ" are an obvious reference to Galatians 1:1. Again, in the letter *to the Romans*, chapter 2, "I would not have you to be men-pleasers but to please God," resembles Galatians 1:10. In his epistle *to the Ephesians*, chapter 18, "The cross a stumbling block" may be a reminiscence of Galatians 2:21. Again, in his letter *to the Ephesians*, chapter 16, the expression "Shall not inherit the kingdom of God" is probably derived from Galatians 5:21. In his letter *to the Magnesians*, chapter 8, there is an allusion to Galatians 5:4.

3) Polycarp (AD 115)

Polycarp, in his epistle to the Philippians, more than once adopts the language of Galatians. In chapter 3, "Building you up in that faith which has been given, and which ... *is the mother of us all* ..." recalls Galatians 4:26. In chapter 5, "Knowing then that *God is not mocked*, we ought ..." recalls Galatians 6:7. In chapter 6, "Zealous in pursuit of that which is good" may be taken from Galatians 4:18 (but also compare Titus 2:14 and 1 Peter 3:13).

4)   The Epistle of Barnabas (AD 130)

The passage in Barnabas cap.19 which is said to reflect Galatians 6:6 reads, "Thou shalt communicate in all things with thy neighbor."

5) The Shepherd of Hermas (AD 140)

"They that have believed in God through his Son and are clothed with these spirits" (*Sim*. ix.13) may allude vaguely to Galatians 3:26,27.

6) Justin Martyr (AD 150)

In his *Discourse to the Greeks* (cap.5), Justin alludes to Galatians 4:12. His words are "Be as I am, for I was as ye are." In his *Dialogue with Trypyo* (cap.xcvi) he alludes to Galatians 3:10-13 as he writes "For the statement in the law, 'Cursed is everyone that hangeth on a tree,' confirms our hope which depends on the crucified Christ ...."

b. Annotated quotations

1) Marcion (AD 140)

One of the early heretical writers, Marcion is the first to refer to Galatians by name. (So we are told by Tertullian, *Against Marcion*, book 5, chap.3; and by Epiphanius, *Haer.*, xlii.) Marcion included ten books in his *Apostolicon*, and the ten were in this order: Galatians, 1 & 2 Corinthians, Romans, 1 & 2 Thessalonians, Laodiceans (Ephesians?), Colossians, Philippians, and Philemon. The reason Marcion placed Galatians first in his canon seems to have been because of its antagonism to Judaism. It does not appear that Marcion's listing was intended to be chronological. Marcion did omit two important passages in Galatians which contradicted his tenets.

2) Irenaeus (AD 180)

Irenaeus wrote (*Adv. Haeres*, 3.7), "The apostle [Paul] in the epistle to the Galatians says, 'Of what use then is the law of works? It was added until the seed should come to whom the promise was made'." (Cp. Galatians 3:19)

3) Clement of Alexandria (AD 190)

In *Stromata*, 3.5, are these words, "Wherefore Paul also writing to the Galatians says, 'My children, of whom I travail again, until ...'." (Galatians 4:19)

4) Tertullian (AD 200)

In *De Praescript. Haeret.* C.6 is this testimony to the Pauline authorship of Galatians: "But no more need be said on this head if it be the same Paul, who, writing to the Galatians, reckons heresies among the works of the flesh." (Galatians 5:19)

With all the internal and external evidence to guide us, the least controversial matter in the study of Galatians is the matter of authorship.[16] All the available evidence leads to the conclusion the letter was written by the apostle Paul.

The only dispute in this area is whether or not Paul wrote the whole letter himself or whether he used an amanuensis. Longenecker[17] gives us a good glimpse of how writing skills among amanuenses varied. He tells us shorthand notation was developed by Cicero

---

[16] H. Ridderbos, "Galatians, Epistle to the," in the *New International Standard Bible Encyclopedia* (Grand Rapids: Eerdmans, 1982), vol.2, p.385, outlines the few critical attempts to deny the genuineness of Galatians. He concludes that "none of this criticism has been able to hold its ground."

[17] Richard Longenecker, "Galatians" in *Word Biblical Commentary* (Dallas, TX: Word Books, 1990), p. lix-lxi.

(106-42 BC) so that good scribes could take down dictation. Other amanuenses were given freedom to put into their own words the ideas the letter's sender wished to send.[18] What was Paul's practice?

- He wrote Philemon all in his own hand, as he also did Hebrews (Hebrews 13:22).
- For some of his letters, Paul did use an amanuensis. 2 Thessalonians 3:17 indicates Paul used an amanuensis for that letter, and added a personal subscription in his own hand. Likewise, the words of 1 Corinthians 16:21 and Colossians 4:18 ("I write this greeting in my own hand") suggest that the subscriptions were distinguishable in handwriting from the material that preceded, which the professional scribe had penned.
- In Romans 16:22 the scribe who penned the letter for Paul names himself.

So Paul used both methods. Some letters he wrote himself; for some he used amanuenses. Which is true for Galatians? Though Galatians 6:11 has been interpreted to support both views, in this commentator's judgment the verse means that Paul wrote the whole letter in his own hand. "If he used an amanuensis for Galatians, the secretary did little to moderate the apostle's expressions (e.g. 5:12) or to buffer his emotions."[19]

C. MAPS AND HISTORY

The letter is addressed to churches in "Galatia." What territory in the ancient world went by the name "Galatia"? Just as the boundaries of countries in Europe changed during the wars of the 20th century, so the area in Asia Minor (modern Turkey) called "Galatia" varied as time passed and wars were won and lost.

1. How Galatia became a distinct territory

The name "Galatia" is derived from the Gauls or Celts (cp. the Latin *Gallia*, Gaul) who migrated from the regions we call France and Germany toward the region we call Greece. About 300 BC, three tribes that came from Europe – the Trocmi, the Tolistobogi, and the Celtic or Germanic tribe Tectosagi – attempted to enter Greece and were repulsed at Delphi in 279 BC. A portion of them broke off from the main body and settled in Thrace.[20] In 279 BC, Nicomedes, King of Bithynia in northern Asia Minor, invited the other tribes of Gauls to assist him in a war against his brother. So the Gauls crossed the Hellespont and helped Nicomedes win his war. After the war was over, they refused to go home, and settled instead in Bithynia. They continued to wreak havoc and plunder the

---

[18] We infer from the excellent Greek found in 1 Peter that Silas put down Peter's ideas. Yet this would not impinge on the inspiration of 1 Peter since Silas himself was a prophet (Acts 15:32), i.e., Silas too could speak by inspiration.

[19] Longenecker, *ibid*.

[20] See Pausanius, *Attic.*, cap. iv.

cities of Bithynia in every direction. There was a rich and fertile mountain region just to the south of Bithynia, which the Gauls seized. Not satisfied with the territory they occupied, from time to time they would go off in various directions to plunder and capture another city or area. This went on until about 232 BC when Attalus I, the king of Pergamus in western Asia Minor, drove the Gauls back into that rich and fertile territory that surrounds the cities of Tavium, Ancyra, and Pessinus. Because the Gauls lived there this valley became known as "Galatia." So for a hundred or so years, the map of Asia Minor looked like this:

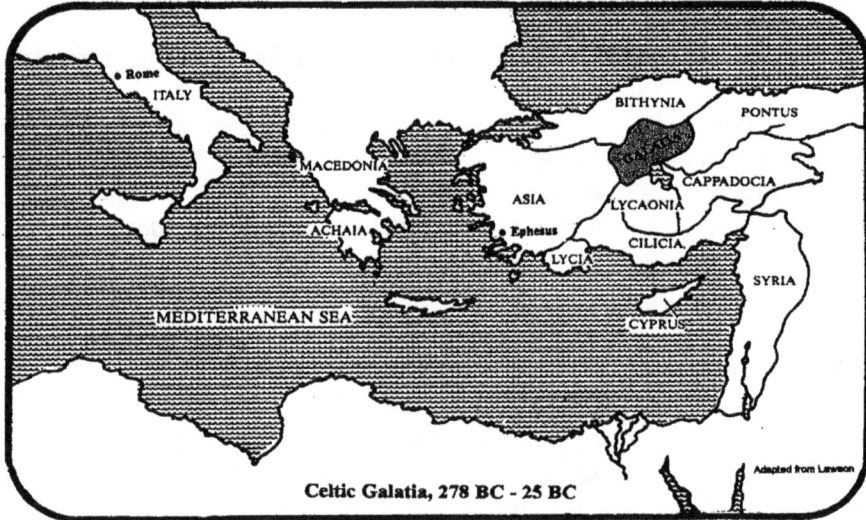

Celtic Galatia, 278 BC - 25 BC

MAP OF ASIA MINOR IN HELLENISTIC TIMES

2. How the boundaries of countries were changed

In the year 189 BC, this area was brought under Roman domination by the general Cornelius Manlius Vulso. In those early years of Roman domination, the Romans still allowed the peoples of Asia Minor to have their own kings and princes. These kings and princes continued to attempt to enlarge their own territories at the expense of their weaker neighbors. Galatia's borders continued essentially as they were in Hellenistic times. But in 25 BC, all that changed.

In 64 BC, the Romans under Pompey defeated Mithridates VI, king of Pontus (an area in northern Asia Minor), who had dominated the area. In return for the Galatians' loyalty to Rome, Galatia was made a client kingdom, retaining this status until the death in battle of her last king, Amyntas, in 25 BC. Amyntas (36-25 BC), appointed by Mark Antony, was the last independent ruler of old Galatia. In his will he bequeathed his kingdom to Rome. During his reign, parts of Pisidia and Isauria, as well as parts of Lycaonia and Phryrgia and Cilicia, were given to Amyntas as reward for his part in helping win some civil wars. So the boundaries of the kingdom of Galatia had been extended considerably by the time of Amyntas' death. Of particular importance were such major extensions as Paphlagonia in the north, and parts of Pisidia, Lycaonia and Phrygia in the south, along with the cities of Pisidian Antioch, Iconium, Lystra, and Derbe. When Amyntas was murdered in battle, the Romans reorganized the kingdom of Galatia into an imperial province under a Roman governor.[21] Phrygia, a war-like region, was divided up in an effort to make it easier to enforce the peace. The Roman province of Galatia now included the old territory of Galatia in the north, plus parts of Pisidia, Phrygia, and Lycaonia, which were all areas where people who were not ethnically Galatians (Celts) lived. Now the map of Asia Minor looked like this:

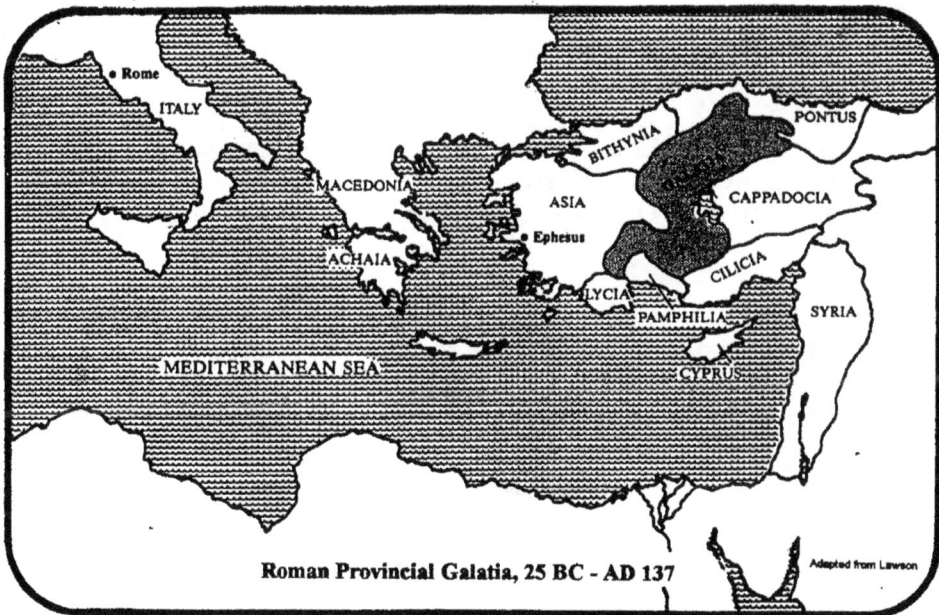

Roman Provincial Galatia, 25 BC - AD 137

Adapted from Lawson

ROMAN PROVINCIAL MAP OF ASIA MINOR

---

[21] So Dio Cassius tells us in *Roman History* 53.26.3.

3. What's in a name?

As a result of provincial boundaries being enlarged by the Romans, during the 1st century AD the term "Galatia" had two different senses. Some used the word to refer to the Galatia of Hellenistic times (i.e., North Galatia, the territory settled by the old Celtic tribes). Others used the term "Galatia" in its Roman provincial sense. The territories added to the province by the Romans (Pisidia, Lycaonia, and a portion of Phrygia) are sometimes called South Galatia.

D. DESTINATION

Paul addresses this letter "to the churches of Galatia." It is a circular letter to a number of congregations of Christians in Galatia. There is some value in determining the destination to whom this letter was sent. Certain characteristics were true of the Gauls in northern Galatia that were not true of the folk in southern Galatia. It will not do to attribute the characteristics (e.g., fickleness, devotees of Cybele) of the northerners to the readers if the readers lived in southern Galatia. In addition, the decision concerning destination can have a bearing on the date assigned to the writing of this letter. Choosing a northern Galatian destination commits us to a later dating, not earlier than the middle AD 50s. The matter of dating will be taken up in due course.

Remembering that the term "Galatia" can include a large amount of territory, what do we know about any churches being established by Paul in this whole area, to whom this epistle might be addressed? Galatians 4:19 indicates the recipients of this letter had been converted by Paul.

That any churches were planted in northern Galatia is only an inference from two passages, Acts 16:6 and Acts 18:23.[22] In this commentator's judgment, these verses will not support the conclusion that churches were planted in northern Galatia at that time.[23] As Paul and Silas begin the second missionary journey, Acts 16:6 reads, "They passed through the Phrygian and Galatian region, having been forbidden by the Holy Spirit to speak the word in Asia." That is, Paul, Silas, and Timothy passed through "Phrygian Gala-

---

[22] The northern Galatian view is defended by many of the 19th and early 20th century commentators on Galatians, including J.B. Lightfoot (1910), J. Moffatt (*An Introduction to the Literature of the New Testament* [Edinburgh: T&T Clark, 1915]), and Davidson (*An Introduction to the New Testament* [London: Samuel Bagster and Sons, 1849], Vol.2, p.286-91).

[23] At the close of the 3rd century AD and afterwards, there were Christians and churches in northern Galatia. We find reference to them during the time of Diocletian (AD 284) and Julian (AD 361). There were church councils held at Ancyra in the 4th century. But these late references would not prove that Paul planted the churches in northern Galatia and wrote to them in the 1st century. There is as much or more evidence that Peter was the founder of these churches in northern Galatia than that Paul was (1 Peter 1:1).

tia." It does not at all appear that churches were established on this journey. The Greek at Acts 16:6 reads "the Phrygian and Galatian country." There are two nouns connected by "and" with only the first noun having an article ("the") in the Greek. This is a Greek sentence construction that shows both terms refer to the same thing.[24] Thus we speak of "Phrygian Galatia," i.e., the region that was both Phrygian and Galatian. So Acts 16:6 does not refer to a trip to northern Galatia.

Acts plainly tells us a great deal about churches that were established in southern Galatia. The churches of Derbe, Lystra, Iconium, and Pisidian Antioch were established by Paul and Barnabas on the first missionary journey recorded in Acts 13-14. On the second missionary journey, in which Paul and Silas were the missionaries, the churches established on the first missionary journey were revisited (Acts 16:1,2). On the third missionary journey, we again find Paul coming to Galatia. Acts 18:23 reads, "And having spent some time [at Antioch of Syria, at the close of the second journey], he departed and passed successively through the Galatian region and Phrygia, strengthening all the disciples." Sharp's rule of grammar applies here also. Paul is passing through the region that is both Galatian and Phrygian, i.e., southern Galatia. Further, the word "strengthening" presupposes that those visited had already been converted to Christianity before Paul visited on this third journey. This verse does not speak of new churches being planted in northern Galatia.

If neither Acts 16:6 nor 18:23 refers to northern Galatia, there is no record in Acts of churches being planted in that area.

If this letter is addressed to southern Galatia, it would be addressed to people who lived in Pisidia and Lycaonia. It is asked, "Would Paul call Pisidians 'Galatians'?" The answer is yes! Though it be true that the addressees lived in the areas that once were called Pisidia and Lycaonia and Phrygia, they are now a part of the Roman province of Galatia. He would be right in calling them by the all-inclusive term "Galatians". Similarly, Paul calls folk in Ephesus "Asians" at 1 Corinthians 16:19 without making ethnological distinctions. He also refers to people from Philippi, Thessalonica, and Berea as "Macedonians." It therefore appears that Paul regularly used the Roman provincial titles (as did Peter in 1 Peter 1:1). He speaks of Achaia, Macedonia, Illyricum, Dalmatia, Judea (in the Roman sense of all of Palestine), Arabia, and Asia – all of them Roman provinces. By parity of reasoning, when Paul says "Galatia" he is using a Roman provincial name.

---

[24] This rule is called "Sharp's Rule of Grammar." "When two nouns in the same case are connected by the Greek word 'and,' and the first noun is preceded by the article 'the' and the second noun is not preceded by the article, the second noun refers to the same person or thing to which the first noun refers, and is a further description of it." H.E. Dana and J.R. Mantey, *A Manual Grammar of the Greek New Testament* (New York: Macmillan, 1927), p.147. Ernst Haenchen (*Acts of the Apostles* [Oxford: Blackwell, 1971], p.483) attempted to argue that *Phrygia* ("Phrygia") at Acts 16:6 is an adjective of two terminations and cannot qualify *chora* ("region"). Colin Hemer has shown conclusively that it has three terminations and thus may well qualify *chora* ("The Adjective 'Phrygia'" *JTS* 27 [1976] p.122-26).

It is asserted that no one until recent times argued for a southern Galatian destination. (E.g., Ramsay,[25] though not the first to suggest the idea, did make it popular.) Instead, it is affirmed the ancients all wrote supporting the northern Galatian theory. However, this statement needs to be put into perspective. Those of the ancients who touch upon the subject of destination wrote after AD 350, and were possibly misled by the fact that since AD 297 Galatia had again been reduced to the old territory that was once dominated by the Celtic tribes (i.e., Hellenistic Galatia). Bruce reminds us that Lycaonia was detached from the Roman province of Galatia about AD 137, and around AD 297 the reminder of southern Galatia was made into the new province of Pisidia, with Pisidian Antioch as the capital and Iconium as its second city. Thus in the days of the church fathers, "Galatia" meant northern Galatia only, and they would naturally interpret Galatians in that manner.[26]

Barnabas is mentioned several times (Galatians 2:1,13). The people of southern Galatia would know him, whereas those in northern Galatia would not. Barnabas was with Paul when they went through the cities of southern Galatia on the first missionary journey (Acts 13-14). As far as the Acts record goes, while in Paul's company, Barnabas never visited northern Galatia.

In Galatians 4:13 the record says Paul came into Galatia the first time because of "a bodily illness."[27] What happened in Phrygia and Pamphylia on the first missionary journey? John Mark turned back (Acts 13:13), though Acts gives no reason for his departure. The most common illness along the lowlands of Perga is malaria. If Paul contracted this disease in the lowlands, according to Ramsay[28] there were only two alternatives open to Paul in his fight against the disease. He could go back home, or he could go up into the highlands. Perhaps the missionaries had not originally planned to go into the southern highlands of the Roman province of Galatia. Because they are now going on a longer journey than originally planned, John Mark chose not to continue with them further, and John Mark made that decision right at a time when a "helper" would have been more sorely needed than ever. Malaria fever has recurrences. Paul might be well enough to preach one day, and be down sick the next. "Bodily illness" fits many diseases, but it does very well fit malaria, where a man is left weak for a long time.

---

[25] William Ramsay, *The Church in the Roman Empire* (London: Hodder and Stoughton, 1893), p.3-112.

[26] F.F. Bruce, "Galatian Problems. 2. North or South Galatians?" *BJRL* 52 (1970), p.247.

[27] Luke does not record any such bodily sickness. It could be inserted into the Acts record at Acts 13. Alternatively, it could be inserted at 16:6 if it is supposed that verse alludes to northern Galatia, a supposition already shown to be doubtful.

[28] William Ramsay, *St. Paul the Traveller and Roman Citizen* (Grand Rapids: Baker, 1960 reprint), p.94-97.

Galatians 2:5 is perhaps the strongest argument for the southern Galatian destination of the letter. In this verse we have Paul's assurance that at the Jerusalem Conference he had in mind the readers addressed in Galatians, endeavoring to retain for them the truth and freedom of the gospel. At the time of the Jerusalem Conference (Acts 15), the only part of Galatia visited by Paul the missionary is southern Galatia, on the first missionary journey (Acts 13,14). This of itself is sufficient proof the "churches of Galatia" to which the letter is addressed were primarily the churches of southern Galatia.[29]

If the "churches of Galatia" of Galatians 1:2 are the churches we can read about in the book of Acts, then this epistle is addressed to the churches of southern Galatia.

E. DATE OF WRITING

The question of the date when Galatians was written is one of the most controversial issues in Pauline studies. The difference of opinion is so great that the letter has been placed at both extremes in point of date: to some it was the first letter Paul wrote, to others it was the last, while yet others place it almost everywhere in between the first and last. To scholars trying to reconstruct the history of early Christianity, the conclusions reached concerning the date of Galatians have far-reaching consequences. For example, were there two conferences in Jerusalem dealing with the issue of whether or not circumcision was required of Gentile converts to Christianity? When did it begin to become obvious that Christianity was not just another sect of the Jews, with the result that the two religions began to go their separate ways?

Any decision about the date of writing depends on several other decisions and conclusions: (1) The decision made about the key passages at Acts 16:6 and 18:23. (2) The conclusion about the destination of the letter, whether northern or southern Galatia. (3) The verdict reached concerning whether the autobiographical section of Galatians is given in chronological order. (4) The determination made about *to proteron* at Galatians 4:13, whether it should read "previously" or "the first time." (5) The conclusion about whether Galatians 2 is the famine visit of Acts 11-12 or the Jerusalem Conference of Acts 15. (6) The implications of the parallels between Romans, 2 Corinthians and Galatians.

1. Two key passages in Acts, 16:6 and 18:23

As already explained, if Acts records any missionary activity in northern Galatia, these two passages are the only possibilities. Sharp's Rule of Grammar applied to the pas-

---

[29] This argument assumes, of course, that Galatians 2 and Acts 15 record the same conference. This is a matter that needs further elucidation, which will be forthcoming in later notes.

sages shows that any reference to northern Galatia is out of the question. Even were we to grant that Acts 18:23 is northern Galatia, there is not enough time to plant churches there (to which the epistle to the Galatians could subsequently be addressed). The time to plant a church in Thessalonica was perhaps 6 months duration (though Acts records only what happened in 3 weeks). We do not have 3 months or 6 months' time during Paul's second and third journeys for evangelism and church planting in each of the major towns in northern Galatia, so that this letter could be addressed to the "churches" (plural) of Galatia.

2. The destination of the letter

While a northern Galatia destination requires a late date for the writing of Galatians, the conclusion already reached concerning destination (i.e., southern Galatia) gives a rather large window of time during which this letter could have been written. The earliest possible date would be after Paul's first missionary journey, a journey that resulted in churches being planted in southern Galatia. The latest possible date would be just before Paul's death in AD 68. With more information we may be able to narrow down the time frame in which the letter was likely written.

3. Are the autobiographical sections of Galatians in chronological order?

At least until 2:11, there is every reason to treat the account as chronological. The account starts out with his activity as a persecutor of Christianity and then speaks of his call to become an apostle. Paul uses the word *epeita* ("then", at 1:18) to describe what happened next in his life. He tells how many years were involved between visits to Jerusalem. Even 2:11ff can be chronological. If we translate the *de* with which verse 11 begins as "and," then the passage reads "and when Peter came." I.e., the event in 2:11ff followed the Conference recorded in 2:1-10[30] Yet whether or not Peter's withdrawal from association with Gentile Christians at Antioch followed the Conference of 2:1-10, the rest of the passage certainly is chronological. The "three years" (1:18) and "fourteen years" (2:1) must be counted from his call to be an apostle (AD 34).[31] Fourteen years after AD 34 brings us to AD 48 as the earliest possible date for the writing of Galatians. If, as is likely the case, the three years and the fourteen years should be added together, thus making seventeen years between his call and the conference, the Conference of 2:1-10 occurred no earlier than AD 51. This, in turn, means we cannot date Galatians earlier than AD 51.

---

[30] As will be noted in the comments below, scholars who have doubted the Peter incident is related in chronological order do so because they cannot conceive of Peter behaving so badly after the Jerusalem Conference recorded in Acts 15. See C.H. Turner, "Chronology of the New Testament," *Hastings' Dictionary of the Bible* (New York: Scribner's, 1909), vol.1, p.424.

[31] How the date of Paul's call on the Damascus road is calculated is explained in the commentary following.

4. What does *proteron* (Galatians 4:13) mean?

How *proteron* in Galatians 4:13 is to be translated has considerable impact on the date of writing. The NASB has translated it, "It was because of a bodily illness that I preached the gospel to you the first time (*to proteron*)." It is, of course, inferred from this translation that Paul made two visits to the Galatians before he wrote this letter. However, scholars have been debating whether *to proteron* must be restricted to the meaning "the first time," or whether it might mean "previously" or "formerly." If it could mean the latter, then Galatians 4:13 requires only one visit before Paul wrote this letter to the Galatians. The leading lexicons are not in agreement. Moulton and Milligan remark "we are probably right in understanding *to proteron* in Gal 4:13 in the general sense of 'previously,' 'originally,' rather than 'on the former of two visits'."[32] Arndt and Gingrich favor the translation "the first time" but add this note: "But naturally the translation *once* is also possible, and from a lexical point of view it is not possible to establish the thesis that Paul wished to differentiate between a later visit and an earlier one."[33] Therefore the Greek expression *to proteron* cannot be used either to prove or disprove how many times Paul had been to Galatia before writing this letter. Advocates of a northern Galatia destination prefer "formerly" as the translation for *to proteron*.[34] Advocates of a southern Galatia destination are satisfied that "the first time" is the preferred translation.[35] In view of the fact that in 1:9 and 5:3 Paul speaks of having given the Galatians certain warnings, it seems simplest to suppose at least two visits to the Galatian area had been made before this letter was written.

While the problem of the date of writing remains unresolved, it begins to look like the early AD 50s are the earliest possible choice for a date.

---

[32] J.H. Moulton and G. Milligan, *The Vocabulary of the Greek Testament* (London: Hodder and Stoughton, 1963), p.554.

[33] W.F. Arndt and F.W. Gingrich, *A Greek-English Lexicon of the New Testament and Other Early Christian Literature* (Chicago: University of Chicago Press, 1957), p.729.

[34] On the hypothesis that Acts 16:6 records Paul's first visit to northern Galatia, and with one visit to northern Galatia implied by Galatians 4:13, the earliest date for the writing of Galatians would be AD 51 or 52, soon after Paul arrived in Macedonia, or soon after he went to Corinth. With two visits to northern Galatia implied by Galatians 4:13, the earliest date for the writing of Galatians would be soon after Paul arrived at Ephesus at the beginning of this third missionary journey (cp. Acts 18:23 with 19:1) in AD 54 or 55.

[35] If Galatians 4:13 is translated "formerly" one could date the letter from any time after the churches in southern Galatia were planted by Paul during his first missionary journey in AD 45-48 (Acts 13-14). This would give us a date of c. AD 49 for the writing of Galatians. This conclusion would make Galatians the earliest of Paul's letters. (One difficulty with such an early date is how to harmonize it with the probable date of the Jerusalem Conference, concerning which we shall speak in a moment.) If Galatians 4:13 is translated "the first time," then the letter could be dated from any time after the beginning of Paul's second missionary journey, since Acts 16:6 records his second visit to Galatia. We date the second journey AD 51-54. "The 'first time' is the preferable reading since 'formerly' would be somewhat superfluous in this context" (Ridderbos, *op. cit.*, p.379).

5. Which visit of Paul to Jerusalem is detailed in Galatians 2:1-10?

After his call to become an apostle of Jesus, Paul made several visits to Jerusalem. The first three are recorded in Acts 9:26, 11:29ff (the famine visit), and 15:2ff (the Jerusalem Conference).[36] There is agreement among Bible students that Galatians 1:18 and Acts 9:26 are two records of the same visit. However, Bible students disagree about Galatians 2:1-10. Is this the famine visit, the Jerusalem Conference visit, or a visit not even recorded in Acts? This is the most difficult problem faced by those who try to determine the chronology of the New Testament. It will take some detailed notes to sort through our options.

a. Both Acts and Galatians record events in their correct chronological order.

That Galatians records events in chronological order has already been shown in notes above.

We can see no need to devise a rearrangement of Acts 11-15, or of Galatians 1 and 2, as though this is necessary to keep the accounts from being hopelessly contradictory. Attempts to rearrange Acts have proven unconvincing. For example, to attempt to date the famine journey (Acts 11:29-12:25) after the first missionary journey (Acts 13-14) produces a problem.[37] At the end of the famine trip, Mark accompanies Paul and Barnabas (Acts 12:29). However, on the first journey, Mark deserted the missionary team (Acts 13:13) and Paul refused to take him along on a subsequent journey (Acts 15:38). How can we harmonize this refusal to take Mark along with Acts 12:29 if we were to try to rearrange the famine trip so it follows the first missionary journey? While Acts does not contain a complete history of the first thirty years of the church, nor even a complete record of Paul's ministry,[38] the current widespread skepticism concerning the historical reliability of what Acts does record is ill-founded. Luke is a trustworthy historian.[39]

---

[36] There were also later visits to Jerusalem. Acts 18:22 ("they went up and saluted the church") speaks of a fourth visit to Jerusalem at the close of the second missionary journey. Acts 21:17ff tells of a fifth visit to Jerusalem at the end of the third journey when an offering was brought from the churches of Greece and Asia Minor to the poor saints at Jerusalem (Acts 24:17; Romans 15:25-33; 1 Corinthians 16:1-4; 2 Corinthians 8-9).

[37] The rearrangement is part of an attempt to make Galatians 2 reference the famine journey while at the same time allowing for churches to already be in existence in Galatia, something which, at its earliest, happened on Paul's first missionary journey.

[38] See for example 2 Corinthians 11:23-27. Not many of those dramatic and traumatic events that happened to Paul are recorded in Acts. Even where the same events are recorded by both Luke and Paul, each writer records information not given by the other (e.g., cp. Acts 9:26-30 with Galatians 1:18-20).

[39] See "Trustworthiness" in the Introductory Studies of the author's *New Testament History: Acts*, p.xxvi-xxxiii. Another treatment of Luke's historical reliability is Richard Longenecker, "The Acts of the Apostles" in the *Expositor's Bible Commentary* series (Grand Rapids: Zondervan, 1981), Vol.9, p.208-211.

b. Both Acts and Galatians are historically accurate.

Until the beginning of the 20th century, the traditional view was that Galatians 2 = Acts 15. In the 20th century several hypotheses were advanced, attempting to identify Galatians 2 with the famine visit of Acts 11:27-12:25. To make this new identification, one of two things was required:

- We must deny the historical accuracy of the book of Acts, or
- We must treat the account of trips to Jerusalem in Galatians as being an incomplete record of such trips.

Attempting to build a case for the first of these options, scholars began to question the historical reliability of Acts. Paul's writings are treated as primary sources, while Luke's writings are treated as secondary sources. Then, Paul's writings are treated as being historically accurate, whereas Luke's are not, because they are based on secondary sources. However, such a reconstruction undervalues an important fact. Certainly, Luke examined eyewitnesses (Luke 1:2,3) as he wrote a history of the life of Christ, but for much of Acts he did not need to question others or rely on secondary sources. He himself was there and was a participant in much of what happened; he himself was a primary source.

Regarding the second of the options given above, certainly there are details in Acts that are not found in Galatians, and vice-versa. For example: What led to the trip to Jerusalem? Was it a revelation from God, or did the church at Antioch send them? Acts does not name Titus in its account (it just says that "certain others" accompanied Paul and Barnabas), whereas Titus figures prominently in the Galatians account. Was the meeting at Jerusalem public or private? Acts 15:5 is asserted to be more reticent than Galatians 2:3ff about the unpleasantness at Jerusalem. The decision of the council (Acts 15:22-29) contains more than one would guess from the summary in Galatians 2:7-9. Was Paul a major participant or did Barnabas, Peter, and James play the leading role?

While the two accounts do provide different details, it is not impossible to harmonize the two records. That is, the differences in the accounts do not require us to abandon the hypothesis that Galatians 2 = Acts 15. Finding details in one account that are not found in the other is not proof that one or the other of the accounts is in error. In fact, if all the details matched exactly, then we would be suspicious of one or both.

c. The parallels between Acts 15 and Galatians 2

The many similarities in the accounts surely favor the identification of Galatians 2 with Acts 15.[40]

---

[40] The following list is adapted from Lightfoot, *op. cit.*, p.123-128. See also Pierson Parker, "Once More – Acts and Galatians", *JBL* 86 (June 1967), p.175.

1) Paul and Barnabas attend the council together (15:2, 2:1)
2) They travel from Syria. (14:26-28, 1:21)
3) They go to Jerusalem (15:2-4, 2:1)
4) They are accompanied by others (15:2, 2:1)
5) Paul faces opposition from Judaizers before the meeting begins (15:5, 2:3-5)
6) The apostles meet (15:6-29, 2:6-10)
7) A prominent role is taken by Peter (Acts 15:7-11,14, 2:7-9)
8) A prominent role is taken by James (15:13-21, 2:9)
9) Paul reports about his mission to the Gentiles and defends it (15:4,12, 2:2ff)
10) Much discussion ensues (15:6,7, 2:6,7)
11) The council arrives at a decision (15:13-29, 2:7-10)
12) Paul and Barnabas are given the right hand of fellowship, and encouraged to continue their work (15:22-29, 2:7-9)
13) A few requirements are imposed on the Gentile converts (15:28ff, 2:10).
14) Paul continues to act as though he is in the right (15:30ff, 2:9,11ff)

It certainly looks as though these accounts cover the same meeting, "for it would be hard to imagine two such councils, on the same subject, involving the same people, with the same sequence of events, and held in the same place."[41]

d. Those who identify Galatians 2 and the famine visit can make a plausible case.[42]

The following points can be adduced as supporting the identification of Galatians 2 with the famine visit of Acts 11-12.

1) The same two churches were involved, with the trip being initiated at Antioch.
2) Paul's use of *epeita* ("then") at 2:1 leaves no hint that any trip to Jerusalem after Paul's call to become an apostle has been omitted.[43] The use of *epeita* would lead us to treat Galatians 2 as Paul's second trip to Jerusalem, and according to Acts that is the famine visit.
3) No public meeting is described in Galatians 2 like the one described in Acts 15:4 and 15:6.[44]

---

[41] Parker, *ibid.*

[42] The following points are adapted from Homer Kent, *The Freedom of God's Sons: Studies in Galatians* (Winona Lake, IN: BMH Books, 1976), p.21,22. Calvin linked Galatians 2 with Paul's famine visit of Acts 11. So did Ramsay ("On the Interpretation of Two Passages in the Epistle to the Galatians," *Expositor's.*, 5th series, 2, 1895, p.1-3-115). See also Bruce, Tenney and Stott in their commentaries.

[43] This statement, in this commentator's judgment, is only a partial truth. More will be said on this matter in the notes following.

[44] In the author's commentary on Acts, the reconstruction of the events at Jerusalem is made in this fashion: it began with a first public meeting (Acts 15:4,5), followed by a private meeting (Galatians 2:1-10), and concluded with a second public meeting (Acts 15:6-29) at which the apostles attempted to bring the church into harmony with what they and the Holy Spirit had been teaching all along. See also Lightfoot, *op. cit.*, p.125-126. This was the view of Irenaeus in his work *Against Heresies* 12.12 and 13.3.

4) According to Galatians, the "only" exhortation given to Paul and Barnabas was that they continue remembering the poor. This is said to fit Acts 11 better than Acts 15 since there was a decree published by the Conference in Acts 15.

5) The Acts 11 visit names only two delegates from Antioch, and Galatians 2 agrees, for Titus is described in terms suggesting he was a subordinate (*sumparalabōn*, Galatians 2:1). Acts 15:2, however, informs us that "certain others" were delegated to go with Paul and Barnabas.

6) The Galatians 2 visit was made in response to a divine revelation. This could be understood as the prophecy made by Agabus that led to the famine visit (Acts 11:27-30).

e. Obstacles to identifying the famine visit of Acts 11 with Galatians 2

(a) According to Galatians 2:2, Paul related to the apostles at Jerusalem an account of the gospel he had been preaching to the Gentiles. If Galatians 2 = Acts 11, what Gentile converts (other than the few in Antioch, Acts 11:19) to Christianity are there at the time of the famine visit since that visit occurred before Paul took his first missionary journey?

(b) When the famine visit occurred (Acts 11-12), Paul has made no missionary journeys to Galatia. His journey to Galatia is not recorded until Acts 13-14. Galatians 2:5 and 4:13 require that Paul has already evangelized among the readers before the conference alluded to in Galatians 2:1ff. At the time of the famine visit there have been no visits to Galatia.

(c) In Acts 11-12, Paul meets no antagonism at Jerusalem. In Galatians 2 he meets a great deal.

(d) There is nothing said at Acts 11:29ff about seeing Peter and James and John (as Galatians 2:9 has it). Acts tells us Paul met with "the elders" (Acts 11:30).

(e) According to Acts, the famine visit occurred before Agrippa died in AD 44. Paul's call occurred in AD 34. Galatians 2 must be dated either 14 or 17 years after Paul's call. Even if we treat the 3 years of Galatians 1:18 concurrently with the 14 years of Galatians 2:1, the resulting date will still not allow us to treat Galatians as being the famine visit. 14 years after Paul's call is AD 48 AD – or 4 years after the death of Agrippa.[45]

(f) To identify Galatians 2 with Acts 11 makes circumcision an acute problem years before Acts 15, a view for which there is no evidence in Acts. "It would be strange indeed if the same question of circumcision of Gentile believers had twice within a few years been raised by Antioch, to be twice carried to Jerusalem and twice over decided there by the same parties – Barnabas and Paul, Peter and James – and with no reference made in the second discussion (that of Acts) to the previous compact (Galatians 2)."[46]

---

[45] Recognizing the problem, some have attempted to work out a chronology using a method of computation wherein parts of years are counted as full years. In reply, we are still two years off – if the 14 years is really only 12 – for 12 + 34 = 46, which is still two years after the Famine visit.

[46] George G. Findlay, "Galatians, Epistle to the," *International Standard Bible Encyclopedia*, edited by James Orr (Grand Rapids: Eerdmans, 1949), V.2, p.1160. See also James Moffatt, *An Introduction to the Literature of the New Testament* (Edinburgh: T&T Clark, 1918) p.92.

f.   Obstacles raised by those who wish to deny Galatians 2 = Acts 15

(a) One question often asked is this: if the council described in Galatians 2 is the same one reported in Acts 15, why doesn't Paul cite the decree (Acts 15:23-29) in his impassioned argument against the Judaizers?   Why would Paul omit any allusion to the decree since it dealt with precisely the issue faced by the Galatian churches?   *Reply:*   If the Galatian letter is dated in the late AD 50's, it has been 6 or 7 years since the Jerusalem Conference and the delivery of the decrees of the Conference to the churches in southern Galatia per Acts 16:4.   Instead of asking why Paul doesn't cite the decree, would it not be better to say that his allusion to the Conference in chapter 2 would remind his readers of that very decree?

(b) The most serious obstacle in identifying Galatians 2 with Acts 15, and the most difficult to answer to everyone's satisfaction, is the apparent discrepancy concerning the number of trips Paul made to Jerusalem after his call on the Damascus road.   "It is hardly an answer to suppose that Paul just ignored or forgot one visit.   His whole argument, in Galatians, depends on listing *all* of his contacts with the Jerusalem leaders."[47]   *Reply:*   We would word it differently.   Paul's argument in Galatians depends on listing *all his visits at which it might be affirmed he got his gospel from men* (Galatians 1:11).   "Since the point of Paul's autobiography was to record his relationship with the original apostles in Jerusalem, not simply his visits to Jerusalem, it was not necessary for him to refer to the famine-relief visit (Acts 11:27-30) since he did not met with the apostles then."[48]   The famine visit, as recorded in Acts 11:29-12:25, presented no opportunity to study intensely under any of the original apostles.   James, the son of Zebedee had just been executed (Acts 12:2).   Peter had been arrested and put in prison (Acts 12:4), and upon his release hurriedly left town (Acts 12:17).

g.   This commentator adopts the traditional view that Galatians 2 = Acts 15

The parallels between the two accounts and the obstacles to identifying Galatians 2 with Acts 11 have led this commentator to accept the traditional view, even though a number of contemporary scholars reject it.[49]   The arguments against the traditional view

---

[47] Parker, *op. cit.*, p.179.

[48] G.W. Hansen, "Galatians, Letter to the," in *Dictionary of Paul and His Epistles*, edited by Gerald Hawthorne, et.al. (Downers Grove, IL: Inter-Varsity Press, 1993), p.327.

[49] A solid reply to those who reject the traditional view can be found in R.H. Stein, "The Relationship of Galatians 2:1-10 and Acts 15:1-35:   Two Neglected Arguments," *JETS* 17 (1974), p.239-242.

are certainly to be excluded if those arguments require skepticism about the historical accuracy of Acts.[50]

Further, the traditional view also helps us to reconstruct when the opposition of the Judaizers first began to be felt *in the churches*. (Galatians 2:4 describes them as false brethren who infiltrated the church to "spy out our liberty." Acts 15:6 refers to these Judaizers as "certain ones of the sect of the Pharisees.") It was in the early AD 50s, about the time of the Jerusalem Conference (Acts 15). To be sure, unbelieving Jews have opposed the apostles from shortly after Pentecost (Acts 2). And when Peter immersed Cornelius and then stayed in his house, that raised questions in the mind of Jewish Christians (Acts 11:1-2), but that was shortly a thing of the past (Acts 11:18). So from AD 30 (Pentecost) until at least AD 40 or 41 (Cornelius), we read nothing of the Judaizers *in the churches*. It is unbelieving Jews who encourage Agrippa to assassinate the apostles (Acts 12:1-3). It was unbelieving Jews who opposed Paul during his first missionary journey (Acts 13-14). The first we hear of Judaizers *in the churches* is about the year AD 51 at the Jerusalem Conference.

One more line of evidence must be referenced in order to make a final decision concerning the date of writing.

- Seventeen years (i.e., the 3 years of 1:18 plus the fourteen years of 2:1) added to AD 34 (the date of Paul's call) would bring us to AD 51 for the Galatians 2 visit to Jerusalem. This corresponds beautifully with what Acts tells us happened after Acts 15.
- Following the Jerusalem conference (Acts 15), and after brief ministries in Philippi and Thessalonica, Acts has Paul in Corinth after the Emperor Claudius' decree requiring all Jews to depart from Rome (Acts 18:1,2).
- That decree is dated in the ninth year of Claudius' reign as emperor – i.e., somewhere between January AD 49 and January AD 50.

---

[50] Among such rejecters of Luke's historical reliability are these: F.W. Beare (*JBL* 62 [1942], p.298) and R.W. Funk (*JBL* 75 [1956], p.130-36) who suggested the famine visit of Acts 11:27ff is misplaced in the book of Acts, it being a report of the collection brought to Jerusalem at the close of Paul's third missionary journey. This is how Beare and Funk are able to assert that Galatians 2 = Acts 15, and that Acts 15 is really Paul's second trip to Jerusalem after his call. Or there is Parker, who tells us "The Jerusalem visit of Acts 9[:26-30] did not occur. Luke has simply imagined the Jerusalem visit of Acts 9, constructing it out of what he heard about other visits of Paul to Jerusalem. The visit of Acts 11:29-12:25 was Paul's first after his conversion, that of Acts 15 his second" (Parker, *ibid.*). Parker also proposes that we harmonize Acts 11:29ff with Galatians 1:18. Thus, in his view, Galatians 2 and Acts 15 are the same visit. Thus would Parker harmonize Galatians' two visits with the book of Acts. This is surely extreme! It will hardly do to accuse Luke, the A-1 historian, of getting his facts wrong. Such a hypothesis, in fact, impinges on the idea that Luke was an inspired writer! Likewise, it does little for our faith to conjecture, as do Lake and Haenchen, that Acts 11:29ff and Acts 15:2ff are the same incident, but Luke confused them because he got his stories from different sources. See K. Lake, "The Apostolic Council of Jerusalem," in *The Beginnings of Christianity, Part I: The Acts of the Apostles*, ed. F.J. Foakes-Jackson and K. Lake (London: Macmillan, 1922), Vol. 5, p.201; and E. Haenchen, "The Book of Acts as Source Material for the History of Early Christianity," in *Studies in Luke-Acts*, ed. L.E. Keck and J.L. Martyn (Nashville: Abingdon, 1966), p.271.

- Shortly thereafter, Acts tells of Paul's trial before Gallio (Acts 18:12). Coins found at Delphi date Gallio's proconsulship in Achaia from July AD 51 to July AD 52.

Such dates in the AD 50s do not fit well with the attempts to make Galatians 2 = the famine visit to Jerusalem in AD 44 (Acts 11). But these dates in the AD 50s can be harmonized with the events recorded in Galatians 1-2, the Jerusalem Conference of AD 51 (Acts 15), and the subsequent chronology of events recorded in Acts.

6. The implications of the parallels between Romans, 2 Corinthians, and Galatians.

Many have followed the reasoning of Lightfoot who believed that, because of the similarity in their subject matter, 2 Corinthians, Galatians and Romans must have been written at about the same time.[51] There is a correspondence of ideas and style, and also a correspondence of historical allusions in Galatians, 2 Corinthians, and Romans. These similarities help substantiate the conclusions regarding the date and place of writing. It may now be regarded as generally accepted that Paul's epistles fall chronologically into four groups,[52] each group separated from the next by an interval of approximately six years, and distinguished from one another by their internal character. Group 2 is comprised of (excepting, for the moment, Galatians) the two letters to Corinth and the epistle of Romans, which were written at the close of the third missionary journey in the years AD 57 and 58. While the epistle to the Galatians possesses no special features in common with those of Group 1 or Group 3, in style, subject matter, general tone, and treatment, it closely aligns with the epistles of Group 2.[53]

Concerning the date of the writing of Galatians, the conclusion to which this long study has led us is that Paul wrote this letter to the Galatians in AD 57 or 58. It is after the Jerusalem Conference, and it is after Paul's second visit to southern Galatia (made during his second missionary journey). It comes from the same time in Paul's life as the other letters designated as Group 2 by Lightfoot.

---

[51] Lightfoot, *op. cit.*, p. 42-56. Lightfoot's conclusions about the dating of Galatians were accepted by Conybeare and Howson, *The Life and Epistles of St. Paul* (London: Longmans, Green, & Co., 1873), chapters 17, 18 and 19. More recently, Lightfoot's conclusions have been reaffirmed by Charles H. Buck, "The Date of Galatians," *JBL* 70 [June 1951], p.113ff. "As for the relationship between Galatians and Romans, Lightfoot's demonstration of the priority of the shorter letter has never been seriously questioned from that day to this; Romans has become the accepted *terminus ad quem* for the date of the composition of Galatians" (Buck, p.113).

[52] The four groups are: *Group 1* = 1 & 2 Thessalonians; *Group 2* = 1 & 2 Corinthians, Galatians and Romans; *Group 3* = Ephesians, Philippians, Colossians, and Philemon; *Group 4* = 1 & 2 Timothy and Titus. (If Paul wrote Hebrews, as we have concluded, it was written from Rome about the same time as the letters in Group 3.)

[53] Lightfoot calls attention to the matter of the collection for the poor at Jerusalem, the treatment of stumbling church members, Paul's own personal sufferings, the persons and places mentioned, and resemblances on the treatment of doctrine substantiated by quotations from the Old Testament.

F. PLACE OF WRITING

Because the destination is disputed, and because the date of writing is disputed, the suggestions concerning the place of writing have become numerous. Let us briefly enumerate the options that have been suggested.

Antioch of Syria has been suggested.

If Galatians 2 = Acts 11, then it could be maintained that Galatians was written after the first missionary tour was completed but before Paul and Barnabas went to the Jerusalem Conference (Acts 15). [54]   For reasons given above, this view has not commanded widespread acceptance.

Macknight (who treats Galatians 2 = Acts 15) thinks Galatians was written from Antioch after the Jerusalem Conference, but before Paul set out on his second missionary journey (Acts 15:30). [55]   To reach this conclusion, Macknight must reject Lightfoot's argument based on the doctrinal similarity pertaining to each of the groups of Paul's letters, and he must explain Galatians 4:13 either as meaning "formerly" or find the second visit to the Galatian churches in Acts 14:23.

Thessalonica has been suggested.

This suggestion rests mainly on three assumptions:

- Galatians 2 = Acts 15
- Galatians 4:13 indicates two different trips to Galatia
- Galatians 1:6 ("so quickly") is interpreted to mean that the letter to Galatia is written very shortly after Paul's second visit to the area.

Very shortly after leaving Galatia on that journey, Paul is in Philippi (Acts 16:12) and then in Thessalonica (Acts 17:1). This reconstruction would yield a date of AD 51 or 52 for the writing of Galatians.

---

[54] Ramsay's original view was that Galatians was written just before the third missionary journey began. He later changed his view. In the preface of the 14th edition of his *St. Paul the Traveller and Roman Citizen* (London: Hodder and Stoughton, 1920), Ramsay suggested that Galatians was written from Antioch before the Jerusalem Conference of Acts 15. Calvin arrived at a date before the Jerusalem Conference purely on internal evidences (see Calvin's commentary on Galatians 2:1-5.), but he did not follow through the implications as to the destination of the letter. (Calvin taught a northern Galatia destination.)

[55] Cited in Albert Barnes, "2 Corinthians and Galatians" in *Barnes' Notes* (Grand Rapids: Baker, 1995, p.280).

It is correctly objected to this view that Paul says the Corinthians started the offering for the poor at Jerusalem about one year before 2 Corinthians was written (2 Corinthians 9:2). That means the offering was started about AD 56. It was about AD 57 that Paul sent instructions to Galatia about the offering (1 Corinthians 16:1-3). If Galatians 6:6-10 speaks of the progress of the offering for the Jerusalem church among the Galatian churches, there is no way Galatians could have been written in AD 51 or 52. The Galatian letter could not have been written before AD 56.

Corinth has been suggested.

Paul was in Corinth twice, on both his second and third missionary journeys. Several commentators suppose Galatians was composed at Corinth during Paul's 18-month residence there in the midst of his second missionary journey (Acts 18:1).[56] The Jerusalem Conference antedated the second missionary journey, so if Galatians was written from Corinth during Paul's second journey, that would coincide with Galatians 2 = Acts 15. However, the second missionary journey dates from AD 51-54. The same argument concerning the Jerusalem offering that ruled out Thessalonica (see above) as the place of writing would also be against Corinth on the second missionary journey.[57]

Lightfoot asserted that Galatians was written from Corinth during Paul's 3-month stay there at the close of his third missionary journey (Acts 20:2,3).[58] This date and place (AD 58, from Corinth) is a possibility,[59] but we believe there is a better suggestion.

---

[56] Theo. Zahn (*Introduction to the New Testament* [Grand Rapids: Kregel, 1953], v.1, p.193-99), F. Rendall ("Galatians" in *Expositor's Greek Testament* [Grand Rapids: Eerdmans, 1967], v.3, p.144-47), and R.C.H. Lenski (*Interpretation of St. Paul's Epistle to the Galatians* [Columbus, OH: Wartburg Press, 1946], p.13-15) hold that Galatians was written during the early part of Paul's stay at Corinth during the second missionary journey, before the arrival of Silas and Timothy (Acts 18:5).

[57] Hendriksen has Galatians written from Corinth, and though he does not explain the reference in Galatians 6 concerning the offering for Jerusalem, he does reply to other objections to the view that Galatians was written about AD 52 from Corinth.

[58] W.C. Allen and L.W. Grensted (*Introduction to the Books of the New Testament*, 3rd ed. [Edinburgh: T&T Clark, 1936], p.138) have Galatians written from Corinth, but after the letters to the Thessalonians. This gives time for the Judaizers to do their work, and for messengers to come to Corinth from Galatia. Since the Lord had definitely instructed Paul to remain at Corinth (Acts 18:9,10), this would account for his inability to go to Galatia to deal with the problem (4:20).

Others who have opted for Corinth as the place of writing are Berkhof, Hiebert, Ridderbos, and Robertson. Some have chosen this possible place of writing after defending a northern Galatia destination for the letter. A northern Galatia destination almost requires a date of writing late in the third missionary journey.

[59] It is after the Jerusalem Conference. Paul has made at least two visits to Galatia. It allows for Group 2 of Paul's letters to be kept together. It allows for Galatians 6:6-10 to be a reference to the offering for Jerusalem.

Ephesus has been suggested.

Paul was at Ephesus twice during his missionary journeys. Some have proposed the idea that Galatians was written from Ephesus during Paul's short stay there on his way to Jerusalem at the close of his second missionary journey (Acts 18:19-21). Other proponents of an Ephesian location for the writing of the letter have it written during the third missionary journey, when Paul spent three years at Ephesus. Paul says, "I am amazed that you are *so quickly* deserting Him who called you ... for a different gospel" (Galatians 1:6). It is asserted that this means Paul has just recently visited the churches of Galatia, perhaps just a few months before. Therefore, it is argued, the letter must have been written from Ephesus, the place where Paul settled just after traveling through the Galatian region on his way from Antioch of Syria (Acts 18:23-19:1).[60]

However, Galatians 4:20 indicates that Paul would have wished to make a quick trip to Galatia, but he plainly shows that he does not plan to come to Galatia in the near future. If the letter to Galatia was written from Ephesus, Paul could have made a quick trip to visit the Galatian churches to follow up any good effects this epistle may have had. The fact that Paul contemplates no trip may imply that he was much farther away from Galatia than Ephesus, and in the midst of a work that could not be interrupted by a journey to Galatia.

Troas has been suggested.

Writers who offer this hypothesis suppose the letter to the Galatians was written from Troas as Paul was on his way to Jerusalem with the offering (Acts 20:6). *Objection:* When Paul arrived at Troas, the offering had already been collected. The men who were carrying the gifts were with Paul (Acts 20:4), and their number included some from the churches of Galatia. Galatians could not have been written from Troas at this late date if, in fact, the reference in Galatians 6:6-10 is to the Jerusalem offering.

Rome has been suggested, in spite of the fact that the words of the subscription in the KJV which have it written from Rome are spurious.

The claim that Galatians 4:20 ("I could wish to be present with you now") and 6:17 ("I bear on my body the brand-marks of Jesus", which are interpreted to refer to the beatings Paul allegedly had received while in prison) are appealed to as evidence that Paul is in prison when he writes Galatians. It is assumed that it is his first Roman imprisonment.

---

[60] "So quickly" ("so soon," ASV), however, is a relative term. It may mean any interval from a few minutes to one or more centuries. The context must decide. A thing might be described as taking place "soon" if it is brought about in a space of time conspicuously shorter than might have been expected. In this context, Paul is indicating that he might have expected more time for the apostasy of a whole community to take place than it actually took.

In answer to this theory, there are other possible interpretations of these verses that are just as plausible, and perhaps more so. The language of Galatians is totally unlike how Paul words it in the Prison Epistles when he does tell of his being a prisoner in Rome. And by the time Paul was imprisoned in Rome, the offering to Jerusalem was an event already in the past. The mention of the offering in Galatians 6:6ff would thus be meaningless.

Macedonia is the best suggestion for the place of writing.

Lightfoot's reconstruction of the writing of Paul's letters in Group 2 cannot be improved upon, in this commentator's judgment.[61]

- While in Ephesus on his third missionary journey, Paul wrote 1 Corinthians.
- Towards the close of the third missionary journey, after Paul has left Ephesus because of the riot, and having waited at Troas for Titus who did not arrive as expected, Paul pushed on into Macedonia.[62]
- Paul had just recently communicated with the Galatians about the offering for Jerusalem (1 Corinthians 16:1,2).
- In Macedonia, Titus arrives with good news that the sinful person at Corinth has been disciplined and has repented. Paul writes 2 Corinthians in a feeling of relief.
- Then, just when he thought his problems were over, Paul hears of the trouble in the churches of Galatia.

As he sits down and starts writing to the Galatians, you can just see Paul's rush of thoughts. He does not complete his sentences. He is elliptical (though the meaning and the power are still there). He even omits the section of thanksgiving that he usually puts in his letters. He sends his greeting, and then says, "I am amazed that you are so quickly deserting Him ... for a different Gospel."

Remember, Paul had just recently communicated with the Galatians about the offering for Jerusalem, and at that time he had no misgivings about his converts in Galatia. Now, just a few weeks later, he will write "I marvel that you are so quickly deserting Him ...." Thus, we would pick somewhere in Macedonia as the place of writing for the letter to the Galatians.[63]

---

[61] Lightfoot, *op. cit.*, p.43-56.

[62] Acts 20:2 speaks of his passing through this area. See also the discussion of Paul's life as seen in Acts and the Corinthian correspondence in the Introductory Studies to 2 Corinthians.

[63] The historical references in Galatians fit this conclusion. It is after the Jerusalem Conference (Galatians 2). Paul has been through Galatia at least twice (Galatians 4:13). Paul is traveling, and not settled at a church (Galatians 1:2). Of the seven suggestions as to the place of writing, only those three which occur on Paul's third missionary journey (i.e., Ephesus, Corinth, and Macedonia) fit with all of the historical allusions.

G. THE TROUBLEMAKERS

A number of verses in Galatians indicate that someone is causing problems in the churches of Galatia.

- "There are some who are disturbing (*tarassō*, agitate, trouble) you" (Galatians 1:7).
- "Those who are troubling you" (Galatians 5:12).
- "False brethren who had sneaked in to spy out our liberty" (Galatians 2:4).
- "They wish to shut you out" (Galatians 4:17).
- They were "disturbing" the Galatians (5:10).
- The troublemakers will eventually have to bear a judgment from God (5:10) whose verdict will be condemnatory ("anathema," accursed, 1:8,9).

Galatians 6:13 as well as the allegory in 4:21-31 seem to indicate the troublemakers are Jews.[64]

What can we learn about these troublemakers from Galatians and Acts?[65] They are preaching a different gospel (Galatians 1:6) and they are distorting the gospel of Christ (1:7). Their message is different from the gospel preached by Paul and his helpers (1:8). It is implied that the troublemakers, in contrast to Paul himself, got their message by oral tradition from men (1:12). The troublemakers in Galatia are like the false brethren who infiltrated the churches of Syria and Judea to spy out the liberty Christians have in Christ (2:4). The troublemakers are identified as "certain of the sect of the Pharisees who had believed" (Acts 15:5). Acts 15:24 uses the same verb (*tarassō*, "disturbed") we find applied to the troublemakers in Galatia (1:7). The troublemakers held the original apostles in higher esteem than they held Paul (2:6,9). "Behold, I, Paul, say to you" (5:2) also implies his apostolic authority had been undermined by the troublemakers. The troublemakers emphasized "works of the Law" (2:16, 3:10). Paul tells the Galatians that the troublemakers were courting the favor of the Galatians, but their motives were not honest; instead, they intended to shut the Galatians out, to isolate them (4:17). The troublemakers were hindering the Galatians from obeying the truth of the gospel (5:7). What they were trying to persuade the Galatians to do did not come from God (5:8). The troublemakers have apparently claimed that Paul preached and practiced circumcision just like they were teaching the Galatians they needed to do (5:11). The troublemakers were

---

[64] J. Munck (*Paul and the Salvation of Mankind* [Richmond, VA: John Knox, 1959], p.87-132) pointed to the present participle at Galatians 6:13 and argued the verb "receive circumcision" is a middle voice; that is, it refers not to the troublemakers but to converts already won by the troublemakers from among the Gentile members of the Galatian churches. Against Munck's hypothesis, it has been pointed out that it is difficult to make much sense of "[they] try to compel you to be circumcised" (6:12), nor is it easy to explain who would persecute the Galatians if they did not get other Christians to be circumcised (6:12).

[65] Galatians 1:6-9 and 6:11-18 are the clearest indicators of who the troublemakers were and what they taught. We are using a type of mirror reading when we infer information about the troublemakers from other passages in Galatians. Caution is advised here. Mirror readings work best when the passage used as a mirror is an attack against the troublemakers or a defensive response to something the trouble-makers taught. Mirror readings are not always trustworthy when the passage used as a mirror is a straightforward presentation of Christian doctrine.

trying to get the Galatian Christians to accept circumcision (6:12,13). One would also infer that the troublemakers taught the Galatians to observe Jewish calendar dates – i.e., days, months, seasons, and years (4:10). It has been inferred that the troublemakers insisted the only good way to insure careful living was by observing their works of the Law (5:13ff), even though the troublemakers themselves did not carefully keep the Law of Moses (6:13). Finally, Paul indicates one motive that drove the troublemakers was selfish – they were trying to avoid being persecuted (6:12).

Generally accepted conclusions drawn from these passages about the troublemakers include:

(1) Since Paul regularly distinguishes between the Galatians and those who are disturbing them, the troublemakers appear to be outsiders who have come as missionaries to Galatia, rather than being local converts[66].

(2) The troublemakers were plural in number (see 1:7, 4:17, 6:12-13), though there may have been one of their number who was a prominent leader[67].

(3) If the troublemakers in Galatia were like the troublemakers who years earlier came to Antioch, they were Pharisees (Acts 15:5) who pretended to become Christians in order to infiltrate and take over control of the churches (Galatians 2:4, 4:17[68]). Pharisees, as we shall learn, championed "works of the Law." They had their own calendar (which differed from the calendar observed by the Sadducees and Essenes) for determining "days, months, seasons, and years" (4:10). Pharisees did try to "compel the Gentiles to live like Jews" (2:14). If the troublemakers in Galatia were like those in Antioch of Syria, they may have come from Jerusalem, but had been given no orders or commission by the apostles (Acts 15:24), whatever they might claim to the contrary.[69]

---

[66] Because there is no specific statement that the troublemakers came from outside of Galatia, Ropes proposed the view that the troublemakers were local synagogue Jews in Galatia. However, Ropes' reconstruction has been criticized for not offering any clear an explanation of the emphasis on Jerusalem found in 1:11-2:20 and 4:31,32. J.H. Ropes, *The Singular Problem of the Epistle to the Galatians* in Harvard Theological Studies 14 (Cambridge: Harvard Univ. Press, 1929), p.44,45.

[67] The singular verbs and pronouns in 1:8-9, 3:1, and 5:7 might point to a leader of the troublemakers, though the singular verbs and pronouns "can be understood as literary devices for purposes of simplification and illustration" (Kent, *op. cit.*, p. 23).

[68] "Wish to shut you out" (4:17) reminds us of Jesus' condemnation of the Pharisees, when He charged them with perverse obstructionism (Matthew 23:13).

[69] Each of the generally accepted conclusions has been the topic of scholarly debate. Students who wish to pursue a brief history of scholarly discussion may consult Longenecker, *op. cit.*, p. lxxxix-xcvi; F.J. Matera, *Galatians* in the Sacra Pagina Series (Collegeville, MN: The Liturgical Press, 1992), p.2-6; or E.E. Ellis, "Paul and His Opponents: Trends in Research," in *Christianity, Judaism, and Other Greco-Roman Cults* (Leiden: Brill, 1975, p. 264-298). Issues discussed include whether or not the troublemakers came from Jerusalem or perhaps were native Galatians; whether or not they were Christians; whether or not there was one sect of them, or two; who might have been their potential persecutors; what was their relationship to the church at Jerusalem; and when did they embark on their mission.

What designation shall we use as we refer to the troublemakers in our comments? "Judaizers" has been the name long-given to these false brethren.[70] Where did this term come from? The suffix -izo added to a Greek root word means to do what the rest of the word says. The verb *ioudzaīzein* ("live like a Jew") occurs at Galatians 2:14. Its normal meaning is "to live as a Jew in accordance with Jewish customs."[71] At Galatians 1:14 Paul the Pharisee spoke of his advancement in "Judaism" (*'Ioudaīsmo*, the "Jews' religion" ASV). The term identifies his way of life prior to his conversion to Christ, and being a Pharisee of Pharisees the term covers the ancestral traditions of the Pharisees.[72] So a Judaizer was someone who tried to make others observe the Jews' religion.[73] "Judaizer" is a term that expresses well who the troublemakers were and what they were doing. So we will continue to use it since no better or more descriptive term exists. Throughout this commentary, we shall alternate between the terms Judaizers, false teachers, and trouble-makers.

Galatians indicates the Judaizers, while demanding the observance of works of the Law, did not keep the Law of Moses themselves. In order to get a right understanding for the situation in Galatia, it may prove helpful to study what we can learn about the Pharisees from the Gospels.

Pharisees in the Gospels

The Pharisees first appear as a distinct party or sect of Jewish people in the intertestamental period. They adhered to and handed down "from the fathers" a distinct body of traditional material (*paradosis*) which defined what a man's behavior should be (Heb. *halakhah*, how to walk). It is usually said that after AD 70 Pharisaism became normative Judaism.

John the Baptist denounced them as a "brood of vipers" (Matthew 3:7-9). Jesus had many critical things to say about them. After saying, "Unless your righteousness surpasses that of the scribes and Pharisees, you shall not enter the kingdom of heaven" (Matthew 5:20), Jesus goes on to illustrate how the Pharisees did not have right rela-tionships with men. Jesus characterized them as evil at heart while attempting to appear

---

[70] Ignatius (Mag. 10:3) identifies them as Judaizers. So did Chrysostom, *Commentary on Galatians* 1:1-3.

[71] W.S. Campbell, "Judaizers," in *Dictionary of Paul and His Letters*, edited by Gerald Hawthorne, et al. (Downers Grove, IL: InterVarsity Press, 1993), p.513. Originally the Greek word "to Judaize" was used to describe the adoption of Jewish customs by Gentile converts to Judaism.

[72] The word "Judaism" first appears in intertestamental literature, 2 Maccabees 2:21, 8:1, 14:38; 4 Maccabees 4:26.

[73] In this age of political correctness, scholars have tended to avoid the term "Judaizer." In its place scholars have come to use designations such as Paul's opponents, agitators, teachers, false brethren, troublemakers, and false teachers.

good (Matthew 12:33-37). He applied Isaiah 29:13 ("this people honors Me with their lips, but their heart is far from Me") to the Pharisees (Mark 7:1-23; Matthew 15:1-20). The long list of "woes" He pronounced on the Pharisees ("hypocrites") gives a correct picture of Pharisee beliefs and practices (Matthew 23:1-25). In His denunciation of the Pharisees, Jesus delineates the "heavy burdens they bind on others," their ostentatious works, petty legalism, evasive distinctions in oaths, tithing, and mere external purifications. Jesus, the founder of Christianity, denied that traditions of men (Heb., *halakhah*, how to walk) were equal in authority with the revelation from God (Mark 7:1-23). The Pharisees' practice of fasting twice a week (Luke 18:12) and their petty rules about Sabbath-keeping (Matthew 12:2; Mark 3:2, 2:24) were other than what the Law required or taught. Jesus objected to their neglecting the commandments of God, while holding on to the traditions of men (Mark 7:9), and illustrated this with His famous "Corban" lesson (Mark 7:11). "Why do you yourselves transgress the commandment of God for the sake of your tradition?" He asked (Matthew 15:3). "Neglecting the commandment of God, you hold to the traditions of men," said Jesus as He rebuked them (Mark 7:8).

Judaism (Pharisaism) and the Law of Moses Compared

On the following pages, the column on the left is a picture of Pharisaism/Judaism[74] taken from the Gospels and Acts. We, of course, are taking the trustworthiness and historical character of these narratives for granted.[75] The column on the right is evidence that 1st century Judaism (Pharisaism) was greatly different than what God had originally revealed to Moses.[76]

---

[74] No 1st century AD Jewish source describes or even alludes to Galilean Judaism as being somehow truncated or deviant from the Judaism as practiced in Judea or elsewhere in the Roman Empire. So there is no reason to distrust the picture of Pharisaism given in the New Testament.

[75] Leonard Swidler, "The Pharisees in Recent Catholic Writing," *Horizons* 10 (2, '83), p.267-287, tells us that two events in 20th century Catholicism have led to the beginning of a radical shift away from viewing the Pharisees as hypocrites by Jesus, and toward understanding them as Jesus-like criticizers of hypocrites: (1) the revolutionary move from diatribe to dialogue at Vatican II; and (2) the acceptance of critical Biblical scholarship.

[76] A straightforward reading of the Gospels and Acts gives evidence about the beliefs and practices of the Pharisees. It is noteworthy that on almost every occasion that Jesus confronts the Pharisees, He shows that their beliefs cannot be reconciled with the Law of Moses they profess to be interpreting.

PHARISAIC JUDAISM

John the Baptist called them a "generation of vipers," and indicated they were in need of repentance (Matthew 3:7-9). They claimed their "descent from Abraham" made them special and exempted them from John's call.

Jesus talked about the need for a "righteousness" that exceeded that of the Pharisees (Matthew 5:20). In Matthew 6:1 Jesus objected to just showing off when practicing "righteousness" as "Hypocrites do in the synagogues" (6:2), and about "neglect[ing] their appearance in order to be seen [to be] fasting by men" (6:16).

The Pharisees objected to Jesus eating with tax-gatherers and sinners (Matthew 9:11; Mark 2:16).

The Pharisees practiced "fasting" twice a week (Matthew 9:14, Mark 2:18, Luke 18:12).

The Pharisees were familiar with the casting out of demons by the power of Beelzebul, the ruler of the demons (Matthew 9:34, 12;24-27).

Pharisees had certain things they believed were "Not lawful to do on a Sabbath" (Matthew 12:2, Mark 2:24, 3:2).

WHAT DID MOSES SAY?

"Righteousness" has to do with right relations to God and to fellow men. See how Jesus objected to anyone "who annuls one of the least of these commandments, and so teaches others" (Matthew 5:19), and then to illustrate His point He called attention to certain Mosaic commands (5;21,31,33,38,43) where their idea of "righteousness" needed to be surpassed.

Jesus defended His behavior, and by implication condemned theirs, by appealing to Hosea 6:6 on two different occasions (Matthew 9:13, 12:7).

The Old Testament (Leviticus 6:29,20,24) required fasting but once a year, on the Day of Atonement.

Jesus showed this "tradition" to be erroneous by making appeal to David's example, and by an appeal to Hosea (Matthew 12:3-8).

PHARISAIC JUDAISM

The Pharisees had a persistent desire to be shown "signs" (Matthew 12:38, 16:6-12).

The Pharisees wanted to know why Jesus and His disciples did not "walk" (*halak*) according to the tradition of the elders" (Matthew 15:1-20, Mark 7:1-23, especially verse 5). To illustrate what they meant, they called attention to certain rules about purification (Mark 7:1-3).

Some Pharisee teaching about divorce permitted "divorce ... for any cause at all," as long as the proper "bill of divorcement" was given (Matthew 19:3-12).

On the Great Day of Questions (Matthew 21:18ff) as they struggled with Jesus for control of the popular mind (Matthew 21:46), Jesus suggests the Pharisees are thinking "the inheritance will be ours" (Matthew 21:38).

In Matthew 23, Jesus expresses His sadness ("woe") about the hypocrisy of the Pharisees as He delineates the heavy burdens they bind on others, their petty legalism, their evasive distinctions in oaths, their tithing, and their mere external purification.

WHAT DID MOSES SAY?

"The sign of the prophet Jonah" was to be the sign they sought, said Jesus. In a tone He never used of the Law of Moses, Jesus specifically warned against the "leaven (teachings) of the Pharisees" (Matthew 16:12).

When followed, the "tradition of the elders" caused men to "transgress the commandment of God" (Matthew 15:3). Jesus illustrates this by appealing to the very Old Testament passages that were nullified not only by their purification rules but by their "Corban" rulings (Mark 7:11).

Note carefully that Jesus says that the 'plant' called Pharisaism is something God had not planted (Matthew 19:4-8).

Jesus appealed to several passages in Moses to show how their traditions were contrary to the will and intent of God as revealed in Moses (Matthew 19:4,5,7,8).

The Pharisees were embarrassed by the fact that they had not submitted to John the Baptist's divinely given instructions (Luke 7:30), something symptomatic of their regular refusal to hear what God said through heaven-sent messengers (Matthew 21:33ff).

Jesus laments that in their bowing and scraping to men, they fail to acknowledge God's authority. Sadly, they are not in the kingdom of God, and they are perversely obstructing the way of those who would like to enter the kingdom (Matthew 23:13).

PHARISAIC JUDAISM

WHAT DID MOSES SAY?

In their scrupulous effort to tithe more than the Old Testament itself required, they had neglected to practice Micah 6:8.

Something was sadly wrong with the Pharisees' ideas of purification if they missed the internal moral and ethical cleansing that the Old Testament every-where expected (Matthew 23:25,26).

Pharisees pretended to honor the "prophets" and holy men of old by building elaborate tombs and monuments for them, thus attempting to show their disapproval of the way the prophets and holy men were treated by a previous generation (Matthew 23:29ff).

Jesus, looking into the future with divine foresight, sees that they, too, will act just as did their ancestors. When Jesus sent prophets to them after His resurrection, they would lead out in the persecution and execution of those gospel messengers (Matthew 23:34).

"While Jesus violated no specific command in the Law of Moses, He refused to allow the Pharisaic principle of separation or the scribal interpretations of ceremonial defilement and the eating of untithed foods to impede His ministry to sinners and Samaritans."[77] Longenecker has quoted two sources to fill in the details of this claim:

Note Jesus' ministry to those at Levi's feast (Mark 2:15, par.), to the sinful woman who shocked the Pharisaic sense of ceremonial propriety in her anointing of Jesus (Luke 7:37ff), to the tax collectors and sinners who drew near to Jesus and possibly ate with him (Luke 15:1), to Zacchaeus (Luke 19:5), and to the Samaritans (John 5). Such actions quite naturally raised in Pharisaic minds the objection: He befriends the *am haaretz*! (Mark 2:16, par.; Matthew 11:19, Luke 7:34, Luke 7:39, Luke 15:2, Luke 19:7). In all of these contacts "Jesus probably ate no prohibited foods – custom and ordinary courtesy to a great religious teacher would take care of that – but he did run the constant risk of ceremonial defilement and of eating untithed foods." (B.H. Branscomb, *Jesus and the Law of Moses* [London: Hodder & Stoughton, 1930], p.135).

Thus Jesus ignored the Pharisaic principle that "one does not stay as a guest with an *am haaretz*" (Mish. *Dem.* 2:2-3, Tos. *Dem.* 2:2) and probably broke rabbinic rulings in (1) eating untithed food in the house of an *am haaretz* (Tos. *Dem.* 2:2), (2) allowing His disciples to buy food in a Samaritan village (Mish. *Dem.* 2:3), and (3) talking with the Samaritan woman and actually drinking from her vessel (Mish. *Kel.* 1:1ff) since "daughters

---

[77] R.N. Longenecker, *Paul, Apostle of Liberty* (Grand Rapids: Baker, 1976), p.140,141.

of the Samaritans are menstruants from their cradle" (Mish. *Nid.* 4:1). (D. Daube, *The New Testament and Rabbinic Judaism* [London: Athlone Press, 1956], p.173-74.)

The more this commentator studies the Pharisees and then compares that learning with what is read in Galatians (especially 2:4 compared with Acts 15:5), the more he is convinced that a key to understanding Paul's argument in Galatians is to recognize that Paul is combating Pharisaism. Jesus and Paul are in perfect agreement about the danger of Pharisaism.

H. OCCASION AND PURPOSE OF WRITING

Pharisees who pretended to become Christians (if we may harmonize Acts 15:5 and Galatians 2:4) have come to Galatia and disturbed the Gentile Christians with demands that they must keep the Pharisaic "works of the Law" – including circumcision, observance of special days on the Jewish calendar, and a refusal of table fellowship with uncircumcised Gentiles. The Galatians have been deceived by the arguments of these Pharisees:

- That Paul relaxed the requirements of the gospel when preaching to Gentiles, lest some of the Jewish emphases cause the Gentiles to reject his message.
- That the original apostles were more reputable sources of doctrine than Paul.
- That without "works of the Law" to order a man's life he was liable to descend into loose living like "sinners" among the Gentiles.
- They may have insisted that the Law of Moses was still valid for Christians just as for Jews if they wished to enjoy Messianic privileges.

These troublemakers have arrived among the Galatian churches since the last time Paul himself had visited Galatia. The disturbance they have caused in the churches is the occasion for the letter.

Having arrived at conclusions about destination, date of writing, and place of writing, our reconstruction of the occasion for the writing of Galatians is this:[78] About AD 56 or 57, from Ephesus Paul sent someone to Galatia – just as he did to Macedonia and Corinth – to organize the collection for the poor Christians at Jerusalem (1 Corinthians 16:1, Acts 19:22). This messenger returns to Paul, bearing news of the condition of the Galatian churches since the Judaizers have arrived. So Paul sits down and writes this letter. Barclay has said, "Someone has likened the letter to the Galatians to a sword flashing in a great swordsman's hand. When Paul wrote it, both he and the gospel he preached were under attack."[79] The letter is a masterful defense both of his apostleship and the gospel he

---

[78] For a possible reconstruction of the occasion based on the view the letter was written before the Jerusalem Conference, see D. Guthrie, "The Epistle to the Galatians" in *New Testament Introduction* (Chicago: Inter-Varsity, 1961), p.84-85.

[79] William Barclay, *The Letter to the Galatians* in the Daily Study Bible Series (Philadelphia: Westminster, 1956), p.1

preached.   In contrast to the bondage of one who was under the Law (Galatians 3:23, 4:2,3) and the even more galling yoke of slavery one found himself in when trying to observe "works of the Law" (Galatians 4:9,25; Acts 15:10), Galatians is a defense of the freedom we have in Christ Jesus from both these bondages (Galatians 4:31, 5:1).

I. TEXT

The epistle is found in P[46].   Also, it appears in whole or in part in nearly two dozen uncial manuscripts, including Aleph, A, B, C, D, E, L , Ψ.[80]

Occasional phrases from Paul's other letters have crept into the text of Galatians (4:17; 5:19,21; 6:15).   At 3:1 we have the later insertion of "that ye should not obey the truth" (KJV) from 5:7."[81]   "There is some confusion between the Aramaic name Cephas and the Greek name Peter in 1:18 and 2:9,11,14, but in each case there seems to be nothing more than the substitution of the better-known Greek name for the unfamiliar Aramaic form."[82]   Marcion excised several passages when he included Galatians in his canon, and J.C. O'Neill attempted to remove approximately one third of the letter as being later glosses or interpolations,[83] but neither has gained much of a following for their mutilated epistle. Certain contemporary writers are proposing that Galatians 2:7b-8 is either taken from an official transcript of the Jerusalem Conference, or else is a non-Pauline interpretation,[84] but their arguments have not convinced this commentator that those verses do not enjoy integrity.

---

[80] A picture of page one of Galatians in P[46] is included in H.N. Ridderbos, "Galatians, Epistle to the" in *The New International Standard Bible Encyclopedia,* edited by Geoffrey Bromiley (Grand Rapids: Eerdmans, 1982), V.2, p.384.

[81] R.T. Stamm, "The Epistle to the Galatians" in *The Interpreter's Bible* (New York: Abingdon, 1953), v.10, p.442

[82] D.A. Carson and D. Moo, *An Introduction to the New Testament* (Grand Rapids: Zondervan, 1992), p.297.

[83] J.C. O'Neill, *The Recovery of Paul's Letter to the Galatians* (London: SPCK, 1972).

[84] W.O. Walker, "Galatians 2:7b-8 as a Non-Pauline Interpolation," *CathBibQuart* 65:4 (2003), p.568-87, calls attention to the problems that confront the interpreter in Galatians 2:7b-8, then discusses the history, main features, and possible weaknesses of the "protocol" (Paul is citing some official or quasi-official record) and "interpolation" hypotheses, respectively.   Then Walker describes the problems presented by these verses (i.e., the name *Petros,* the peculiar construction with *energein,* the distinction between two "gospels," the parallelism between Peter and Paul, the treatment of "apostleship," the relation of verses 7b-8 to the immediate context), and concludes that this material was composed by someone other than Paul and somewhat arbitrarily inserted at its present location.   (I.e., the interpolation hypothesis is inherently less problematic than the protocol hypothesis.)   An addendum points out that no attestation of 2:7b-8 has been found prior to Irenaeus, but this observation fails to note how few are any allusions and attestations to Galatians in early Christian literature.

"Galatians contains an average number of minor variants, but on the whole there are no serious doubts about the text of the letter, as is shown by the fact that in UBS[3] there are only five passages graded D."[85]

The reconstructed text, given the present knowledge of how such reconstructions are made, found in NA[27] and UBS[3] is as close an approximation to the original as is possible. We have the letter substantially as Paul wrote it.

J. GALATIANS IN RECENT STUDY

This material is presented to help readers understand what they may encounter in other commentaries and studies on Galatians.[86]

Each time *the current popular philosophy* gives way to a new one, the new philosophy spawns new methods of Biblical interpretation. Why? Because the writers of commentaries hope to make their works match the current popular philosophy so that the conclusions presented will prove acceptable to the masses who live by the current popular philosophy. A brief review of some of the changes in Biblical interpretation in the past century will be helpful.

- About the time of World War I, Kierkegaard's existentialism (the popular philosophy) gave rise to the method of Scripture interpretation called neo-orthodoxy. It made use of form criticism to try to explain our Bible books.[87]
- After World War II, Heidegger's existentialism became popular, and neo-liberalism arose, using redaction criticism as the new method of Biblical interpretation.[88] Redaction critics working with Galatians and Acts tended to find historical mistakes in

---

[85] *Ibid.*

[86] A major shift in the study of Paul and the doctrine of justification by faith was triggered by the publication of E.P. Sander's book *Paul and Palestinian Judaism: A Comparison of Patterns of Religion* (London: SCM Press, 1977). The resulting shift is called the "new perspective on Paul." We shall deal with this matter in a special study on "Justification by Faith" later in this book.

[87] Form criticism is a modern method of Bible study that asks two questions of the paragraphs of Bible books. (1) What is the literary form of a particular unit of gospel tradition? I.e., is it a saying, a legend, a miracle story, etc.? (2) What is the pre-gospel history of such a unit? The intent is to determine the original data behind our present text. Form critics believe the early church played a significant role in adapting and shaping the earlier data into its present form, and that the present text of our New Testaments reflects the beliefs of the early church rather than what Jesus or the apostles actually taught and did.

[88] "Redaction" is a scholarly term for the *editing* that has come to be widely imagined to have taken place in the preparation of the books in the form they now have in our Bibles. The theory is that the editors pieced together, adapted, modified, and unified many original literary strands into our final composite document. Bible study then becomes an attempt to identify the original sources and strands of material, and to attempt to determine why the editor made the changes in his sources that he did. It also attempts to reconstruct the community that produced the text being studied. This method of study leaves us with no message from God in our Bible books.

Acts because Luke, in their view, had problems sorting out his sources.[89]
- For a short while structuralism became the philosophy of interest, and literary/rhetorical criticism became the accepted method of Bible study.[90]
- When post-modernism began to become the ascendant popular philosophy, social-science criticism became the new way to do Bible study,[91] and a whole new flood of commentaries began to appear in the book stores.

For a while, *literary criticism* tried to impose a chiastic outline (i.e., the literary pattern A-B-B-A) on each of the books of the New Testament. For Galatians, one such chiastic outline[92] was produced for the whole book. It looked like this:

A. Prologue, 1:1-12
  B. Autobiographical Section, 1:13-2:10
    C. Justification by faith, 2:11-3:4
      D. Arguments from Scripture, 3:5-3:29
        E. Central Chiasm, 4:1-4:10
      D'. Argument from Scripture, 4:11-4:31
    C'. Justification by Faith. 5:1-5:10
  B'. Moral Section, 5:11-6:11
A'. Epilogue, 6:12-6:18

Such attempts failed because of disagreement about where paragraphs begin and end, and because of the arbitrary titles assigned to some of the paragraphs.

[89]John Knox, *Chapters in the Life of Paul* (Nashville: Abingdon, 1950), treats Galatians 2 as the Jerusalem Council visit of Acts 15, with Acts 11:27-30 being an invention of Luke, and with the Jerusalem Council actually taking place during the hasty visit to Jerusalem recorded at Acts 18:22. This view depends on a denial of the historical reliability of Acts.

[90] The methods used to study folklore are applied to the Bible by literary critics. Literary criticism asks what audience the authors wrote for, their presumptive purpose, and the development of the text over time. Literary critics analyzed the text to determine possible use of sources, and whether the text is a composite or not. Secular literary critics had a category they called rhetorical criticism which concentrated on identifying and explaining the stylistic markers of the text, and asks how the rhetoric functions in discourse, and how it affected the original audience, rather than on the meaning of the text itself. When Bible scholars became interested in rhetorical criticism this is the approach their studies took.

[91]Social-science criticism will attempt to draw on insights that might be learned from cultural anthropology, sociology, economics, political science, and linguistics to understand the historical world behind the text. A typical investigation may draw on studies of contemporary nomadism, shamanism, spirit-possession, millenarianism, politics, and ethics in an attempt to reconstruct what the society was like in the 1st century. (While we do need to know about the 1st century world in order to use the historical-grammatical method of interpretation, is there anything to make us think contemporary and 1st century cultures are alike?)

[92] John Bligh, *Galatians: A Discussion of St. Paul's Epistle* (London: St. Paul, 1969), p.37-42.

Epistolary analysis has also been tried as a tool to explain Galatians. It has been observed that Hellenistic letters followed a certain form: an epistolary opening (signature, address, greeting), thanksgiving, body of the letter, words of encouragement or exhortation, and closing (greeting, doxology, benediction). It has been claimed that Paul's letters, like other 1st century letters found by archaeologists, contain "standard epistolary formulae" and that clusters of such formulae mark transitions from one section of a letter to the next.[93]

H.D. Betz's *Galatians* (1979) was the first modern commentary to employ *ancient rhetorical theory* (as found in the ancient rhetorical handbooks[94]) in the interpretation of a Pauline letter. Since then the method has been applied to numerous Biblical books. Betz, using rhetorical language, outlined Galatians[95] as follows:

I.   Epistolary Prescript (Galatians. 1:1-5)
II.   *Exordium* ("introduction," Galatians 1:6-11)
III. *Narratio* ("narration," Galatians 1:12-2:14)
IV.   *Propositio* ("proposition," Galatians 2:15-21)
V.   *Probatio* ("confirmation," Galatians 3:1-4:31)
VI.   *Exhortatio* ("exhortation," Galatians 5:1-6:10)
VII. Epistolary Postscript with *Peroratio* ("conclusion," Galatians 6:11-18) included

- Betz insisted the rhetoric in Galatians is *forensic* rhetoric, the kind of persuasive argument addressed to a judge or jury as the attorney seeks to defend or accuse someone with regard to certain past actions. Betz says that in antiquity rhetoric "has little in common with the truth; rather, it is the exercise of those skills which make people believe something to be true."[96] Betz did admit that he is not able to cite parallels to the exhortation section from the classical rhetorical handbooks.

---

[93] See examples in Longenecker, *op. cit.*, p.*cv-cix*. The weaknesses of the 'formulae' thesis of White and others – e.g., J.C. O'Neil's review of J.L. White, *The Form and Function of the Body of the Greek Letter: A Study of the Letter-Body in the Non-Literary Papryri and in Paul the Apostle* in JTS NS 25 [1974], 173-76) - are not interacted with by Longenecker.

[94] Ancient handbooks on rhetoric by Aristotle *(Rhetoric)*, Cicero *(De Inventione* and *De Optimo Genre Oratorum)*, Quintillian *(Institutio Oratoria)*, and the anonymous *Rhetorica ad Herennium* all tell us about the basic elements of rhetoric (i.e., persuasive arguments). Longenecker (*op. cit.*, p.cx) tells us the basic elements of rhetoric are:

1. *Exordium* (introduction) – tells character of speaker and defines central issues being addressed.
2. *Narratio* (narration), a statement of the facts that relate to the issues of the case.
3. *Propositio* (proposition), which states the points of agreement and disagreement and the central issues to be proved.
4. *Probatio* (confirmation), which develops the central arguments.
5. *Refutatio* (refutation), which is a rebuttal of the opponents' arguments.
6. *Peroratio* (conclusion), which summarizes the case and evokes a sympathetic response.

[95] H.D. Betz, *Galatians: A Commentary on Paul's Letter to the Churches in Galatia*, in the Hermeneia Series (Philadelphia: Fortress, 1979), p.14-25.

[96] Betz, *op. cit.*, p.24.

- Longenecker sees it as *deliberative* rhetoric.[97]   Deliberative rhetoric is an attempt to persuade the listener.
- G.W. Hansen thinks it best to classify Paul's argument in Galatians as *a mixture of forensic and deliberative* rhetoric, with the major shift taking place at 4:12.[98]   He thus offers a two part outline to the book – *Rebuke* (forensic rhetoric in 1:6-4:11) and *Request* (deliberative rhetoric in 4:12-6:10).
- Another option advanced has been *epideictic* rhetoric, the kind that is adapted to display or exhibition, as an orator sometimes does.

M.P. Surburg has offered a critical assessment of this entire approach twenty-five years since Betz's work. He concludes that the vast majority of rhetorical analysis in Galatians has been of little tangible benefit.[99]   Rhetorical critics spend more time trying to classify the sentences and paragraphs than they do explaining their meaning then and/or now.   One wonders if "in the excitement and urgency of the crisis with which he was suddenly confronted Paul would have been consciously careful to construct his letter according to the canons of the rhetorical schools."[100]   Louis Martyn has called for a moratorium "of some length" on research in rhetorical analysis.[101]

Ben Witherington III is a writer who tries to **combine rhetoric and social-science criticism** as he writes his commentaries.[102]   Some of the interests of social-science critics include: (1) How one gets in, stays in, and what goes on in the community?   What sorts of rites of passage are involved?   (2) Honor and shame issues.   (3) The status of Jews in

---

[97] Longenecker, *op. cit.*, p.cxiv-cxix.

[98] Hansen, *op. cit.*, p.329.   Deliberative rhetoric is interested in persuading listeners to adopt a certain course of action, rather than accuse or defend as forensic rhetoric does.

[99] M.P. Surburg, "Ancient Rhetorical Criticism, Galatians, and Paul at Twenty-five Years," *Concordia Theological Journal* 30 (1-2, '04), p.13-39.

[100] F.F. Bruce, *The Epistle to the Galatians* in the New International Greek Testament Commentary Series (Grand Rapids: Eerdmans, 1982), p.58.

[101] J. Louis Martyn, *Galatians*, v.33a in the Anchor Bible Commentary series (New York: Doubleday, 1998), p.21, note #26.   Philip Kern, *Rhetoric and Galatians* (New York: Cambridge University Press, 1998) has argued that not one of Paul's writings follows the pattern of classical rhetoric such as was developed by Greek and Roman writers including Aristotle, Cicero, Quintillian, and others.   Another source for information about the inherent weaknesses of attempting to analyze the New Testament letters according to rhetorical genres is Abraham Malherbe, *Ancient Epistolary Theory*, edited by B.B. Scott (Atlanta: Scholars Press, 1988), p.2-3.

[102] The brief overview of social-science criticism's interests is adapted from Ben Witherington III, *Grace in Galatia: A Commentary on Paul's Letter to the Galatians*, (Grand Rapids: Eerdmans, 1998), p.41ff. Many of Witherington's books are subtitled *"A Socio-Rhetorical Commentary on ...."*   Witherington explains his willingness to use rhetorical analysis as he interprets the Scriptures in "Rhetorically Writing," *Bible Review* (Dec.2002), p.12 and 62.

Roman colonies. (4) The cult of the emperor. (5) Leadership issues (i.e., who is recognized as an authority figure) and power structures in the early church. (6) Social networks between Jerusalem and Antioch, and between Paul and his converts. (7) In-group and out-group language. The concern of social-science commentators is to discover what Paul was up to within the social setting of his society by examining the typical eastern Mediterranean social behaviors witnessed in his letters.[103]

Reader Response criticism, another social-science approach to interpreting Scripture, is interested in how the reader responds, not what the author intended when he wrote. Dieter Mitternacht, for example, writes from the standpoint of the speechless, as the title indicates, to allow the letter's recipients and Paul's opponents to have their say.[104]

There are a number of reasons to be hesitant about the social-science approach to interpreting Scripture.[105] It is true that most contemporary readers no longer share the customs, values, worldviews, or rural milieu of the original readers of the Bible. These have to be explained so that readers understand what is being read. (E.g., not many modern readers have seen a chicken gathering her brood, or a sower sowing, or a farmer winnowing his wheat.) And if this were what social-science criticism was doing, we would have little objection to the method. But in fact, this is not what social-science critics are doing. For the social-science approach, the New Testament is no longer studied in terms of a history of ideas (i.e., its theology), but as a history of communities. The Biblical documents are assumed to be contentious presentations of positions intended either to defend or change the tensions that were found in society (e.g., whether between haves and have-nots, or those created by Roman rule). The text itself and how it has been traditionally interpreted are not at the center of attention in social-scientific studies. Some socio-linguistic studies focus on the social dynamics that produced the text and the meanings given to words in the text;[106] as a result, the Holy Spirit's role in the task of in-spiration is diminished. N.K. Gottwald has said, "The question of which social structures and behaviours were the 'right' ones in Biblical times and which are the 'right' ones for us

---

[103] See for example, B.J. Malina and J.J. Pilch, *Social-Science Commentary on the Letters of Paul* (Minneapolis: Fortress, 2006).

[104] Dieter Mitternacht, *Forum fur Sprachlose: Eine kommunikationspsychologische und epistolar-rhetorische Unterschung des Galaterbriefs* (CB NT 30, Almquist & Wiksell International, 1999).

[105] Sources for further study include Kenneth Berding, "The Hermeneutical Framework of Social-Scientific Criticism: How Much Can Evangelicals Get Involved?" *EQ* 75:1 (2003), p.3-22, who submits social-scientific criticism to careful scrutiny. See also Louis Jonker, "The Influence of Social Transformation on the Interpretation of the Bible: A Methodological Reflection," *Scriptura* 72 (2000), p.1-15. See also D.J. Tidball, "On Wooing a Crocodile: An Historical Survey of the Relationship Between Sociology and New Testament Studies," *Vox Evangelica* 15, p.95-109.

[106] The social-scientific method "seriously considers texts as socially and culturally conditioned documents," wrote David May, *Social Scientific Criticism of the New Testament: A Bibliography*, NABPR Bibliographical Series, 4 (Macon, GA: Mercer University Press, 1991, p.1.

will always remain a matter of dispute. There simply is no 'neutral' or 'objective' Biblical social ethic."[107] All such approaches to Scripture simply leave little room for a God who has spoken and objectively, understandably revealed Himself to us and revealed His will for us.

This commentator urges extreme caution concerning the use of all such recent approaches to the study of Galatians. As soon as the current popular philosophy changes, all the commentaries that have been previously written will now be wrong, and a new set of commentaries will have to be written – which themselves are soon likely to be just as wrong. The recent approaches to the study of Galatians do not allow us to hear the voice of God in Scripture – and in final analysis, this is the most disconcerting and disappointing thing about the methods of interpretation based on men's philosophy.

K. OUTLINE

The attempts at outlining offered by redaction and social-science critics have not reached a consensus, so this commentary chooses to follow the traditional method of indicating the structure and flow of Paul's argumentation in the book of Galatians.

INTRODUCTION. 1:1-12

    A. Paul Affirms His Apostolic Credentials. 1:1-5
        1. The Source and agency of his apostleship. 1:1
        2. His associates in the gospel, and address of the letter. 1:2
        3. Salutation. 1:3
        4. His message. 1:4
        5. His motive. 1:5

    B. Occasion of the Epistle. 1:6-10
        1. He expresses his anxiety over the beginning defection of the Galatians. 1:6,7
        2. He pronounces divine judgment upon the distorters of the gospel. 1:8,9
        3. He declares his passion to please God. 1:10

I. *APOLOGETIC PORTION*: PAUL'S DEFENSE OF HIS APOSTLESHIP AND GOSPEL MESSAGE. 1:11-2:21

    A. The Divine Source of His Call to be an Apostle and of His Gospel Message. 1:11,12

---

[107] N.K. Gottwald, "Sociology (Ancient Israel)," *Anchor Bible Dictionary* (New York: Doubleday, 1992), V.6, p. 88.

B. Proof of Its Divine Origin.   1:13-2:21
   1. He did not learn it from his youth – very much to the contrary.   1:13,14
   2. He did not learn his gospel at his call to apostleship, and immediately after his call he did not confer with men to learn it.   1:15-17
   3. His first visit to Jerusalem was not long enough for instruction in the gospel.   1:18-20
   4. Christians in Judea glorified God because of what Paul was preaching in Syria and Cilicia.   1:21-24

C. The Other Apostles Acknowledged Paul's Gospel.   2:1-10

D. Rather Than Learning from the Apostle Peter, Paul Corrected Peter When He Was Trying to Judaize.   2:11-21
   1. A brief account of the incident at Antioch.   2:11-13
   2. Paul's reprimand of Peter – the five basic doctrines jeopardized.   2:14-21
      a. The unity of the church.   verse 14
      b. Justification by faith.   verses 15,16
      c. The very teachings of Jesus.   verses 17,18
      d. The new life we have in Christ.   verses 19,20
      e. The grace of God.   verse 21

II. *DOCTRINAL PORTION*:   PRESENTATION OF THE TRUTHS OF THE GOSPEL THAT SHOW THE JUDAIZERS WERE IN ERROR.   3:1 - 4:31

A. The Argument from the Readers' Personal Experience.   3:1-5

B. The Scriptural Argument.   3:6-14

C. The Logical Argument.   3:15-29
   1. The Law cannot set aside or alter God's own covenant.   3:15-18
   2. The Law, given as an added revelation to man, is not greater than the promise (covenant with Abraham).   3:19,20
   3. The Law is not contrary to the promise (Abrahamic covenant).   3:21-29
      a. One great lack in the Law was its inability to provide life.   verse 21
      b. Scripture shuts up everyone under sin.   verse 22
      c. The Law was given to lead men to Christ for forgiveness.   verses 23,24
      d. The Law was but temporary while the promise (Abrahamic covenant) continues; therefore, the Law cannot be contrary to the promise.   verses 25-27
   4. The Law could not do what the promise (Abrahamic covenant) can.   3;28,29
      a. The Law didn't make people "one."   That's a thing of the past.   verse 28
      b. The Law didn't make people "heirs of God."   verse 29

D. The Argument from Absurdity. 4:1-11
  1. Before their conversion, they were all slaves. 4:1-3,8
  2. In Christ they have been redeemed (freed) and adopted. 4:4-7
  3. It is folly to regress into bondage. 4:9-11

E. The Sentimental Argument. 4:12-20

F. The Allegorical Argument. 4:21-31
  1. The historical facts. 4:21-23
  2. The spiritual truths taught by this allegory. 4:24-27
  3. The practical application of the spiritual truths taught in the allegory. 4:28-31

III. *PRACTICAL APPEAL* TO THE GALATIANS. 5:1 - 6:10

A. Since Christ Has Set You Free, Stay Free! Keep Living Like Free Men! 5:1-12
  1. If you turn to man-made religious rules and regulations, you lose your liberty.
     5:1
  2. ... you lose your wealth and become a debtor. 5:2-6
  3. ... you lose your direction and run the wrong way. 5:7-12
     a. Five things said about the Judaizers
     b. Doctrinal indifference can have devastating consequences.

B. Safeguards to Ensure Wholesome Use of Christian Liberty. 5:13-6:10
  1. Through love to serve one another. 5:13-15
  2. Walk by the Spirit, not by the flesh. 5:16-24
  3. Respond to the needs of others as the Spirit prompts. 5:25-6:5
     a. Do not become boastful. verse 26
     b. Attempt to restore those who are caught in any trespass. verses 1-3
     c. Let each one examine his own work and bear his own load. verses 4,5
  4. Be generous when there is opportunity to share with those who are in need. 6:6-
     10

CONCLUSION. 6:11-18

A. Final Warning Against the Judaizers. 6:11-16

B. Appeal Enforced by Reference to His Own Sufferings. 6:17

C. Paul's Final Prayer for the Galatians. 6:18

L. INFLUENCE OF THIS EPISTLE

It is only by inference that we can assess the influence of this letter upon *the churches of Galatia*. After Galatians was sent on its way to the churches, there are no other letters written to Galatia, and very little information about the Galatian churches, either in Acts or in early church history. In the middle AD 60s, 2 Timothy 4:10 tells us that "Crescens has gone to Galatia," but this Galatia is likely the land we call France, from which some of the Gauls originally migrated to Asia Minor. The epistles of Peter are addressed to Christians living in Galatia (among other places), but detailed information about the Galatian Christians is difficult to glean from anything Peter says in his letters. Several things lead us to believe the apostle's rebuke was successful, that his apostolic authority was restored, the Judaizers' teachings were repudiated, and the churches returned to their allegiance to the gospel of Christ. Had the Galatians rejected this letter, we could see it being destroyed. The fact that copies were made and that Galatians eventually is included in the canon of New Testament Scriptures is an evidence of its acceptance by its first readers. The fact that some Galatian churches are included in the offering to Jerusalem (Acts 20:4) indicates they did carry out Paul's instructions concerning participation in that offering (Galatians 6:6-10). Finally, the fact that the history of Christianity would have been significantly different than it has been, had the Judaizers won, is compelling evidence the directions in the letter were followed.[108]

Several prominent men in *the post-apostolic era* made use of Galatians. Interestingly, the Gnostics tried to find Biblical warrant for some of their doctrines by putting a peculiar slant on certain passages in Galatians. Gnostics claimed the source of their doctrine was revelation, just as Paul claimed revelation as the source of his gospel (Galatians 1:11,12). However, in an attempt to justify their different doctrines, the Gnostics put a spin on Paul's claims so that they became proof that one does not need to listen to the traditional Christianity of the original apostles like Peter and John. Gnostics made a distinction between "psychics" and "pneumatics" (the latter being a term they applied to themselves because with their superior knowledge they had gone beyond being mere "psychics"), and appealed to Galatians 4:29 (with its distinction between Jews, born according to the flesh, and Christians, born according to the Spirit) to prove such distinctions were Biblical. When the Apologists came along, in order to defend orthodox Christianity against the Gnostic claims they were obliged to demonstrate that the message of Paul and the message of the original apostles were not different messages. A message that differs from the old Jerusalem gospel cannot be a true message. The Apologists had to show Paul's application of the allegory in Galatians 4 was not compatible with Gnostic claims at all.

---

[108] Of course, the argument against the Judaizers is not limited to the letter to the Galatians. We find apostolic doctrine in many of the New Testament letters, and if it had not prevailed, then Christianity would not be a religion materially different from what Judaism has become.

The catechetical schools at Alexandria and Antioch emphasized different methods for interpreting the Scripture. The Alexandrian school emphasized the allegorical method and leaned heavily on the allegory of Hagar and Sarah (Galatians 4:21-31) as the Biblical proof text that such a method was proper. Origen, a prominent teacher at Alexandria, used Galatians 2:15 to support his view that Paul was mightier than the original apostles, and used 2:12 to explain the reason as being the twelve were not using the allegorical method of interpretation.[109] When it came to explaining the relationship of the Law to the gospel, Origen separated the Law into two parts, the moral and ceremonial. He then insisted only the ceremonial has been abrogated, whereas the moral requirements were retained and amplified by Christ. Since Origen's day, not a few commentators have repeated these same ideas as they try to explain the Biblical teaching concerning Law and gospel. The school at Antioch flatly rejected the allegorical method and emphasized the historical-grammatical method of interpretation. Chrysostom (c. AD 395), who wrote a commentary on Galatians, is an example of what was taught at Antioch. His comments identify the troublemakers as being Jewish believers who were still wedded to Judaism. The original apostles did not initially oppose them since their emphases on circumcision and special days were in the realm of Christian liberty. (In fact, Paul himself, when with Jews, observed those special Jewish customs.) It is when their Jewish behavior began to reflect badly on uncircumcised and unkosher Gentile Christians that Paul and the apostles had to take note. Chrysostom treated Galatians 2 as referring to the same Jerusalem Conference recorded in Acts 15, a view that all interpreters of his day, including those at Alexandria, held. He treated Galatians as being written toward the close of Paul's third missionary journey (AD 56-57). In contrast to Alexandria, Antioch saw the whole Law as being abrogated. Now that faith in Christ has come, we are no longer under the tutor (Galatians 3:25).

Galatians and Romans both played an important role in the controversy between Augustine and Pelagius. Jerome also wrote a commentary on Galatians, being heavily dependent on the work of Origen.

16th century studies on Galatians helped trigger *the Reformation*. About 1518 or 1519 Erasmus wrote and published his *Paraphrase on Galatians*. He was heavily dependent on Origen and Jerome. Then in 1531 Luther delivered a series of lectures on Galatians. His lectures and writings drew heavily on the earlier works of Jerome and Erasmus. On Galatian introductory matters, Luther was quite traditional, accepting the conclusions arrived at by the church fathers who preceded him (e.g., he equated Galatians 2 with Acts 15). The Antioch episode (Galatians 2:11-21) influenced Luther's behavior

---

[109] See *Contra Celsus*, 4.44; 7:21 and 2:1.

in the years leading up to his break with Rome. What Luther did that was explosive was to equate what the leaders of the Roman Catholic Church of his day did and taught with what the Judaizers of Paul's day did and taught. In Luther's preaching, if the Judaizers were wrong, so was the Roman Catholic Church. The deeds of penance required by the Catholics were no different that the "works of the Law" that the Judaizers championed. Men are justified by faith alone, not by any works they may do, insisted Luther. Luther, of course, was correct in his view that works required by men (even if they are church leaders) are not a condition of salvation. When Luther added the word "only" to the text of Romans 3:28 (so that it read, "we maintain that a man is justified by faith *only* ...") he was objecting to works Rome required, not to works of obedience that the Scriptures require. While other reformers joined Luther in opposing the errors of the Catholic Church, not all arrived at the same theological conclusions on certain topics. For example, Lutherans are still concerned to emphasize the forensic nature of justification and the imputation of a righteousness to the person who has faith. Reformed theologians are not certain about the imputation of an "alien" righteousness to the believer, even though they treat justification as a forensic concept.[110]

In response to the Protestant presentation of justification by faith, the Roman Catholic Church attempted to answer at the Council of Trent. They, too, appealed to Paul's letters to Rome and Galatia as they formulated their doctrines on justification. Until Vatican II, Catholic commentators tended to read Galatians and Romans through the glasses produced at the Council of Trent. Justification was seen as an infused righteousness, an act of God which effects the sanctification of the believer. Since Vatican II, Lutherans and Catholics (in 1985) issued a common statement on justification which has not satisfied the purists in either camp. But as a result, scholars in both groups no longer feel compelled to hurl anathemas at each other for teaching a different gospel.

In the theological world of *the 20ᵗʰ and 21ˢᵗ centuries*, the advocates of both *sola gratia* (grace alone) and *sola fides* (faith alone) find their proof texts in the epistle to the Galatians. If men are justified by faith alone and not by works, then of course baptism, for example, is not a prerequisite for salvation/justification. By grace alone indicates that salvation is monergistic (God does it all) and not synergistic (man cooperates with God to arrive at the condition on which God pronounces justification). Protestant commentators regularly treated "works of the Law" as being synonymous with obeying what the Law of Moses commanded. The discovery of the Dead Sea Scroll 4QMMT ("Some [pertinent] Works of Law") has called into question the long- held Protestant definition of what "faith"

---

[110] More will be said about this continuing controversy in Protestant theological circles in the special study on "Justification by Faith."

(as in "justification by faith") actually means.[111] Perhaps *sola fides* has been a serious theological error. Throughout the last quarter of the 20th century, Galatians became prominent in various liberation theologies, whether in Latin and South American liberation theology,[112] or black liberation,[113] or women's liberation.[114] The discovery of the Dead Sea Scrolls also triggered a new study of 1st century Judaism. The old perspective on Paul and Judaism pictured Judaism as teaching justification on the basis of works of Law. This old perspective has been called into question in the last part of the 20th century by scholars who have been given the title "the new perspective on Paul."[115] Some of these scholars have tried to make the case that 1st century Judaism did not think salvation could be conditioned in any way on the good works a man might do. Of course, what Paul has written in Galatians lies right at the heart of this whole discussion.

Pharisaic Judaism is a dead end! The Law of Moses has been abrogated and replaced with the new covenant and the high priesthood of Jesus (Hebrews). If Jesus was crucified, and if the tomb is empty, then Christianity is the only valid religion in the world. This certainly needs to be trumpeted abroad!

Gentile Christians did not have to adopt the culture of the Judaizers in order to be accepted as one of Abraham's spiritual children and thus to belong to the Israel of God. This raises the question whether cultural assimilation is required today in order for people from different ethnic backgrounds to be welcomed into the fellowship of the local congregation. Are immigrants to America to be coerced to become Americanized in order to enjoy full membership in the local congregation in the town in which both live? Not if we read Galatians aright. Such fellowship is not dependent on whether one is Jew or Greek, Hispanic or Asian. Justified believers are to keep in step with the Spirit, demonstrating the fruit of the Spirit as they interact with their brethren. This, too, is an emphasis that cries for dissemination and understanding and practice.

---

[111] "With renewed appreciation of first century Judaism (since the discovery of the Dead Sea Scrolls), the historical circumstances surrounding the letter to the Galatians become clearer, and the theological stance of the 'false brethren' becomes more understandable." (Frank J. Matera, *Galatians* in the Sacra Pagina Series [Collegeville, MN: Liturgical Press, 1992], p.30.)

[112] See G. Gutierrez, *A Theology of Liberation* (Maryknoll, NY: Orbis Books, 1973).

[113] See J.H. Cone, *Black Theology and Black Power* (Maryknoll, NY: Orbis Books, 1979).

[114] R. Scroggs, "Paul and the Eschatological Woman," *JAAR* 40 (1972), p.283-393.

[115] It is this commentary's intention to explain the new perspective on Paul, and to show who the proponents are and what they have said, in the special study on "Justification by Faith."

COMMENTARY ON GALATIANS

INTRODUCTION. 1:1-10

Summary: As Paul begins this letter, he starts without hesitation to establish his apostolic authority. He gives the reasons why he can speak with authority on behalf of Jesus. He will declare his apostolic *credentials* (1:1-24). He will affirm his apostolic *commendation*. (2:1-10). He will describe his apostolic *confidence* (2:11-21).

A. Personal Greeting. 1:1-5

1. Source and agency of his apostleship. 1:1

1:1 - *Paul, an apostle (not* sent *from men, nor through the agency of man, but through Jesus Christ, and God the Father, who raised Him from the dead),*

Paul – First century letters began with the signature of the author, an address, and a greeting. The author of this letter signs his name, "Paul." He is the famous 1st century missionary to the Gentiles. Much of his life story can be read in the book of Acts, chapters 7,9, and 13-28.

An apostle – The word "apostle" means a commissioned messenger, an official envoy, one sent on a mission. Such messengers were dispatched to deliver a specific message from the sender. They had no authority of their own, but had delegated power from the one who sent them. Elsewhere (e.g., 1 Corinthians 1:1) Paul explains that he was an "apostle of Jesus Christ." That is, he was sent on his mission by Jesus.[1]

(Not *sent* from men, nor through the agency of man - Using several phrases that are unique to this letter, Paul begins explaining what kind of apostle he was. If our inference

---

[1] There were two kinds of apostles in the early church: those sent by Jesus, and those sent on a mission by local churches (see 2 Corinthians 8:23 and Philippians 2:25). The apostles of Jesus included the twelve, Matthias (Acts 1:24-26), Paul (Acts 26:16,17), Barnabas (Acts 14:14), James, the Lord's brother (1 Corinthians 15:7, Galatians 1:19), and perhaps Andronicus and Junias (Romans 16:7). We commonly call this group "the apostolic college." In the church, these apostles of Jesus were first in rank, first in time, and first in dignity. The apostles of Jesus had administrative functions in the whole church. They had authority over the whole church. They were not limited to any one congregation, as were elders and deacons.

is correct that Judaizers[2] have attacked his apostleship and his teaching, then these opening words, the likes of which are not found in many Pauline letters, are the beginning of Paul's response to that attack.   Perhaps the troublemakers asserted that Paul did not meet the qualifications to be an apostle (Acts 1:21-22), or perhaps they insisted instead that he was sent out by the church at Antioch (Acts 13:1-4).   Perhaps they called attention to the fact that when the first missionary journey was complete, Paul and Barnabas reported back to the church at Antioch (Acts 14:26-28).   Is not all this proof, they might ask, that he is but an apostle of a church?   As they put their spin on their presentation, how easy it was to suppress the fact that the church at Antioch acted on direct orders from the Holy Spirit (Acts 13:2,4).   The prepositions "from men" and "through man" imply respectively the primary and intermediary source of his authority.   When Paul writes "nor through ... man" he seems to be answering the misrepresentations of the Judaizers concerning who sent him. "Not ... from men" says that the source of Paul's authority did not lay in any body of men – not the church at Antioch, nor the church at Jerusalem, nor the original 12 apostles such as Peter, nor from James the brother of the Lord who ministered at Jerusalem.

But through Jesus Christ - The reference in "through Jesus Christ" is evidently to Paul's original commission, recorded in Acts 26:16-18, which took place on the Damascus road. On that occasion, Jesus appeared to Paul and specifically commanded him to go to both the Jews and to the Gentiles.   Jesus Himself called Paul to be an apostle.

And God the Father, who raised Him from the dead) - If the Judaizers should question who Jesus is, Paul here implies that Jesus' Sonship (i.e., His deity) is documented by the fact that God has raised Him from the dead.   Paul has been sent on his mission by the highest possible authority.   Paul's calling to the apostleship was part of God's grand plan, a design set in motion when God the Father raised Jesus from the dead.   If the Judaizers have claimed, "You are no apostle.   You never saw Christ while He was on earth, nor were you taught by him," Paul responds with a reminder that he knows about the resurrection of Jesus.   If one were to ask how did he know, he could respond that the risen Lord had appeared to him (1 Corinthians 9:1; see also Acts 9:5).   Paul was commissioned by the same risen and glorified Christ who commissioned all the other apostles of Jesus.

2.   His associates in the gospel, and address of the letter.   1:2

1:2 - *and all the brethren who are with me, to the churches of Galatia:*

And all the brethren who are with me - "Brethren" indicates they are fellow Christians (cp. 2 Corinthians 8:18,22).   Who these fellow Christians may have been is dependent on

---

[2] See the section concerning "The Troublemakers" in the Introductory Studies.

one's view of the time and place of writing. If our conclusions in the Introductory Studies as to the time and place of writing are correct, those with Paul could also have included some of the company mentioned in Acts 20:4; namely, Sopater of Berea, Aristarchus and Secundus of Thessalonica (maybe), Gaius of Derbe, Tychicus and Trophimus of Asia, and probably Timothy and perhaps Titus.

We doubt that attention is called to Paul's companions as though he needs to fortify himself and his teaching with their sanction. Has not Paul just set aside all human authority? Nevertheless, if some of the brethren are from the Galatian churches, Paul's calling attention to them as he writes would express their concern over what is happening in the churches.

With this one allusion to the "brethren," they are dismissed, and Paul uses the singular "I" throughout the rest of the epistle. "Paul's authority has been challenged, and Paul alone answers the challenge."[3]

To the churches of Galatia - It has been argued in the Introductory Studies that the churches so addressed here are those of southern Galatia, the ones founded during Paul's first missionary journey (Acts 13:14-14:25). There were at least four congregations in southern Galatia, the towns in which they were located being tied together by the Roman highway. The readers to whom this letter was addressed were members in the local congregations in those towns. The plural "churches"[4] shows this is a circular letter meant to be read in several Galatian congregations.[5] A messenger sent by Paul would have carried this letter to each of the congregations, where it would have been read out loud in the public assembly of Christians. It would then be carried on to the next town, until all the Galatian churches had heard its contents.

3. Salutation. 1:3-5

1:3 - Grace to you and peace from God our Father, and the Lord Jesus Christ,

---

[3] J.B. Lightfoot, *The Epistle of Paul to the Galatians* (Grand Rapids: Zondervan, 1957), p.73.

[4] The plural "churches" here in Galatians 1:2,22 is an interesting contrast to the singular form "church" at Galatians 1:13. Actually, "church" (*ekklēsia*) may be used in both a local (1 Corinthians 16:1; 1 Thessalonians 1:1) and universal (Ephesians 1:22) sense. Evidently, Paul's concept was that the various congregations were but local manifestations of the one body, the church. Paul also recognizes the autonomy of the local church, so he writes to each one, expecting each one to act upon his directions.

[5] Paul apparently did not send several copies, a separate one for each congregation. His words in 6:11 imply that each congregation would see the one copy that he had sent and take note of the "large letters" that characterized his handwriting. If each congregation wished to have a copy of the letter for themselves, they could no doubt make a copy before the messenger carrying the letter went on to the next church.

Grace to you and peace - The words of Paul's salutation, or greeting, are equivalent to a prayer by Paul that grace and peace would be bestowed on the readers. Scripturally, the word "grace" speaks of unmerited favor, bestowed upon man by God. It refers to God's offer of salvation, with all that offer implies. It takes in Calvary's cross with all the personal sacrifice that included. It takes in the forgiveness of sins even to those who deserved nothing but punishment, a forgiveness given out of the bounty and free-heartedness of the Giver. It involves all God thinks and does to save a man. "Peace" wishes the recipient nothing less than one's total well-being for time and all eternity.[6]

From God our Father, and the Lord Jesus Christ - "The grace and peace come from the same two persons from whom Paul's apostleship came."[7] During Jesus' ministry, the Pharisees had difficulty with the idea of the deity of Jesus because of their belief that there is only one person in the Godhead (i.e., Jesus on earth couldn't be God, they thought, if God were in heaven). Perhaps the Judaizers who have come to Galatia, being kin to those Pharisees (Acts 15:5), also need to be reminded that there is a distinction between God and Christ, and at the same time an equality of deity.[8] Perhaps it is also a subtle reminder to the Galatians that God and Jesus dispense grace and peace through the apostles of Jesus, rather than through the Judaizers, who are false brethren and false apostles. Or, perhaps, the distinction between "Father" and "Lord" is in relation to the Galatian Christians. To the receivers of grace and peace, God is in the relation of *Father*; to the same subjects Christ is in the relation of *Lord*. God is *Father*, having made them children through adoption. Christ is *Lord*, being constituted head of the church, and having won the right to their loving obedience and honor.[9]

1:4 - *who gave Himself for our sins, that He might deliver us out of this present evil age, according to the will of our God and Father,*

Who gave Himself for our sins - "Gave Himself" tells us that what Jesus did as He gave

---

[6] LeRoy Lawson, "Galatians" in *Unlocking the Scriptures* series (Cincinnati, OH: Standard, 1987), p.19. The Greek noun (*eirēnē*, which is equivalent to the Hebrew *shalom*) is from the verb *eirō* which means "to join." That is, when things are disjointed, there is lack of harmony and well-being. When they are joined together, there is both. The Judaizers were sowing seeds of disharmony among the churches. Paul prays for their unity.

[7] R.C.H. Lenski, *Interpretation of St. Paul's Epistles to the Galatians, Ephesians, Philippians* (Columbus, OH: Wartburg Press, 1946), p.26.

[8] In associating these names together as Paul does, the conclusion is inescapable that the Lord Jesus must be Very God of Very God Himself, possessing co-eternally with God the Father the same essence, that of deity.

[9] We must not overlook the importance of this passage where Paul wrote "Lord Jesus Christ." Whatever date we give to the writing of Galatians, it is evidence that repudiates the modern claim that the early church did not begin to think of Jesus as "Lord" until around AD 96. If we credit the Gospel record, Jesus called Himself "Lord" while He was here on earth (John 13:13).

His life on Calvary was voluntary.[10]   Though there is a manuscript variation here, the better supported reading behind "for" is *huper* (in behalf of, in the interests of).   That there is an idea of substitution in the preposition can be seen in its use by professional letter writers who would close their documents with their names, adding "I wrote on behalf of (*huper*) him who does not know letters."[11]   Paul's statement about the substitutionary death of the Lord Jesus Christ was evidently something the Galatian Christians needed to keep in mind, especially when they were hearing the pronouncements of the Judaizers about "works of the Law."   What the Judaizers were doing is slurring the greatness and magnanimity of Christ's sacrificial death.   When that fact is realized, what the Galatians ought to do is repudiate the enormous error of the Judaizers.

That He might deliver us out of this present evil age - It is implied that Jesus gave Himself to deliver us from the very thing into which the Judaizers were trying to get the Galatian Christians to revert.   In this word "deliver"[12] we have our first intimation of one of the emphases in this letter – *freedom*.   A bit of thought may help us see the point in the expression "present evil age."   In Old Testament times, men looked forward to "the age to come," the very age we live in since Messiah appeared and inaugurated it.   If one is in Christ, he is enjoying the blessings of the "age to come."   If he leaves the church by reverting to the religion the Judaizers are espousing, he will be going back to the "present evil age."   That would be to frustrate the purpose for which Christ died!

According to the will of our God and Father - The same expression is used in 1 Corinthians 15:24.   As there, we suppose "God and Father" refers to the Godhead.[13]   According to Romans 8:28, before He ever created, God purposed or planned how He would do things.   It was determined between the Father and Jesus that if the man they were about to create should sin, Jesus would be the One who would come to be the sin offering and redeemer of that fallen creature.   Revelation 13:8 (mg) speaks of the lamb slain from the creation/foundation of the world.   The Godhead conceived the plan and put it into action.   The point is this: the Judaizers and their converts were setting themselves in opposition to what God Himself had planned and willed from before the beginning of time.

---

[10] See also 1 Timothy 2:6 and Titus 2:14.   The same Greek phrase occurs in 1 Macc. 6:44, with reference to the Eleazar who rushed upon certain death to kill the elephant which was carrying the king, Antiochus: "He gave himself to save his people."   Edgar Huxtable, "Galatians" in *The Pulpit Commentary* (Grand Rapids: Eerdmans, 1962), p.5.

[11] J.M. Boice, "Galatians" in *Expositor's Bible Commentary* (Grand Rapids: Zondervan, 1976), p.427. At times another preposition (*peri*, concerning, relating to) is used of Christ's death.   For example, *peri hamartias* (concerning sin) means "as a sin offering" (see Romans 8:3 NASB and Hebrews 10:6,8).   Some verses picture Jesus dying as a substitute for the sinner, and some picture Him as the sin offering for those sinners.   The redemption that is in Jesus Christ is what makes it possible for God to justify sinners who believe in Jesus (Romans 3:22-24).

[12] This is the only occurrence of *exhaireō* in the Pauline writings.   It is in the middle voice, which suggests that Jesus was acting for His own benefit when He delivered or rescued us.

[13] The Greek reads "the God and Father" with a "the" before God and none before Father.

1:5 - *to whom* be *the glory forevermore.   Amen.*

To whom *be* **the glory forevermore.   Amen**. - To whom is this doxology addressed? The nearest antecedent is "God and Father." The further antecedent is "the Lord Jesus Christ." What the Judaizers are teaching will not bring glory either to the Father or to Jesus. Paul closes his salutation by saying, in effect, "Galatians, praise God/Jesus with me by allowing His will and purpose – rather than the will of the Judaizers – to have full sway among you."[14] "Forevermore" translates a Greek expression that means 'to the ages of the ages.' The corresponding Hebrew expression denotes "a period of long undetermined duration."[15]   That's how long God should be praised!   "Amen" transliterates the Hebrew noun meaning 'truth.' It is a solemn affirmation of what has just been written.[16] Where "amen" appears in Paul's letters, it marks the place where the early church would show their agreement with what has just been read to them. They would respond with a hearty "Amen!"

B. Occasion of the Epistle.   1:6-10

> *Summary*: These verses are the reason the letter is being written now. Something inimical to the gospel is being listened to in Galatia. They are giving serious consideration to defecting.

---

[14] Lenski, *op. cit.*, p.31.   The "will" Paul has in view is the will just talked about in verse 4.

[15] Huxtable, *op. cit.*, p.9.

[16] The opening verses of Galatians are rich in theology.   Read it carefully and summarize <u>what it says about God</u>.   (Adapted from Richard Longenecker, "Galatians" in *Word Biblical Commentary* [Dallas, TX: Word, 1990], p.100.)
- God is the source of Paul's apostleship (verse 1).
- God raised Jesus Christ from the dead (verse 10).
- God is the source of the Christian's grace and peace (verse 3).
- God's will and plan are the basis for Christ's work and mankind's salvation (verse 4).
- Praise and worship are God's due (verse 5).

Then summarize <u>what it says about Jesus Christ</u>.
- "Jesus" = Jehovah saves (Matthew 1:21).
- "Christ" = the long promised Messiah (1 Kings 19:16; Isaiah 61:1; Exodus 29:21; 1 Samuel 9:16; Isaiah 53).
- Son of God since God is called "the Father".
- "Lord" = majesty and authority (He runs the universe for the Father).
- He rose from the dead – else our faith is vain and worthless.
- He gave Himself for our sins = vicarious atonement as He lays down His life for us, and offers Himself as our Savior.
- Grace and peace find their source in Him.
- In Him is deliverance from the present evil age.
- He is to be worshipped forevermore.
- He was the agent who called Paul to be an apostle.

1. The beginning apostasy/defection of the Galatians.   1:6,7

l:6 - *I am amazed that you are so quickly deserting Him who called you by the grace of Christ, for a different gospel;*

I am amazed - The verb *thaumazō* can express disappointment, astonishment, rebuke, surprise, and even indignation or irritation.   Perhaps Paul was both surprised and irritated; he was certainly agitated.[17]   This is the sole example in Paul's letters where he omits any word of thanksgiving in his opening.   He is so disturbed by the news from the churches in Galatia that he plunges at once into the topic for which he writes this letter.

That you are so quickly deserting - The Greek word *metatithesthai* denotes a change of position.   "The Greek word is one regularly used for a 'deserter,' 'turncoat,' or 'apostate,' either in war, politics, or religion."[18]   The middle voice of the Greek verb means the Galatians were doing this "deserting" for their own benefit.   The Greek verb is in the present tense which means the desertion was in its initial stages, it was just beginning to happen.[19]   The decisions made about date and place of writing have some bearing on how "so quickly" is explained.[20]   In harmony with the decisions made in the Introductory Studies, we suppose "so quickly" means "so quickly after my last visit among the Galatian churches" or "so quickly after the false teachers arrived in town."   Either way, it is implied that "when Paul last visited the churches all was well with them.[21]   Then came the Juda-

---

[17] Hansen, "Galatians" in *The Dictionary of Paul and His Letters* (Downers Grove: InterVarsity, 1993), p.329, tells us that the expression "'I am astonished [amazed]' was used in letters of the time as a rebuke for not meeting the expectations of the writer."   The usual letter style of the 1st century was to include a word of thanksgiving between the salutation and the body of the letter.   In Paul's letters he often gives thanks for something God has done for the readers (if their behavior is faulty), or for something the readers are doing for God (if their behavior is commendable).   There is no word of thanksgiving in opening of Galatians.

[18] William Sanday, "The Epistle to the Galatians" in *Layman's Handy Commentary* Series, edited by Charles J. Ellicott (Grand Rapids: Zondervan, 1957), p.16.

[19] An aorist tense verb would imply the change/desertion was a completed act.

[20] Those who date the letter early suppose it means so soon after their initial conversion.   Those who date the letter sometime after the churches were first planted must give a different explanation for "so quickly."   Longenecker (*op. cit.*, p.14) suggests there may be an allusion to some familiar Old Testament passages in the language "so quickly."   Recall that at the golden calf the people turned "quickly" away from what God had commanded (Exodus 32:8 LXX).   And in the time of the judges the people fled "quickly" from the way in which their fathers had walked (Judges 2:17 LXX).   Did the Galatians know their Old Testament well enough to grasp the connection that Paul is attempting to make, that he is picturing them as doing what the people of ancient times did when they went away from the Lord?

[21] In the Introductory Studies, we suggested that a few weeks earlier and before the writing of Galatians, when Paul had sent instructions to the churches of Galatia concerning the offering for Jerusalem (1 Corinthians 16:1ff), he had no reasons for misgivings about his Galatian converts.   How quickly that has now changed!

izers, and instead of being promptly escorted to the door, all these churches began to listen to them and to find something attractive in their false gospel."[22]

Him who called you by the grace of Christ - Whichever way we take "him," be it a reference to God, or to Christ, or to Paul who was God's gospel messenger, the thrust of this passage is that the Galatians are about to accept something that has not come from God! They will be in revolt against God (Christ) if they continue their path of defection away from the gospel. The "call" or invitation into the Messianic kingdom comes from God through the preachers of the gospel (2 Thessalonians 2:14). The dative construction (*en chariti Christou*) can be translated "in the grace of Christ" or "by the grace of Christ."[23] "In the grace of Christ" (ASV) suggests that God's call/invitation to men to become Christians depends on what Christ has done to save them.[24]

For a different gospel - The Greek is *eis heteron euaggelion*. "Gospel" is sometimes used to identify the first four books of the New Testaments; we call them "Gospels." However, the word simply means "good news"[25] and at the time Galatians was written the good news had been delivered to them by word of mouth rather than in written fashion. The Greek language has two synonyms which might be translated "another": *allos*, mean-

---

[22] Lightfoot, *op. cit.*, p.33.

[23] The KJV translation "into the grace of Christ" is hardly defensible. The preposition *en* hardly is to be translated "into."

[24] Other interpretations are offered for this phrase. (1) The grace of Christ is the instrument by which God calls men (i.e., what theologians call the first work of grace). (2) One Covenant theologians see a reference to the one covenant of grace, which in their view has been available ever since Adam sinned. What God did through Abraham, Moses, and Jesus was simply a renewal of that one covenant of grace. (3) Since there is no article in the Greek, the phrase simply means that God has "graciously" called them when they didn't deserve it. (4) The "grace of Christ" denotes the state of acceptance with God into which Christians are brought by Christ through faith in Him. (5) The genitive "of Christ" denotes the author of the grace. Each of these alternate interpretations is flawed, in the judgment of this commentator. So is the view that "by the grace of Christ" means the call was effectual. The Calvinistic doctrine that some calls are effectual and some not, because that is the way God has predestined things to be, is to be avoided.

[25] The word "gospel" (*euaggelion*) is found in Greek writers from the days of Homer. In the classical period it often meant "reward for good news." In the Septuagint it is used in the plural with the same meaning (2 Samuel 4:10; 18:22), and perhaps once in the singular in the sense of "good news" (2 Samuel 18:25). In the New Testament "gospel" is found only in the singular and only in the sense of "good news." In most cases "gospel" is used in a doctrinal sense, having reference to the good news of salvation as announced by Jesus or signifying the great body of teaching concerning salvation. Paul uses the word about 60 times in his letters. He occasionally calls it "the gospel of God" (1 Thessalonians. 2:2,8,9; 2 Corinthians 11:7; Romans 15;16); sometimes it is "the gospel of Christ" (2 Corinthians 9:13; Galatians 1:7; Philippians 1:27); or again, Paul will say "my" or "our gospel" (1 Thessalonians 1:5; 2 Corinthians 4:3; Romans 2:16). In a few instances "the gospel" is used to denote certain historic events or a series of events and teachings which are a central part of or which constitute the good news (1 Corinthians 15:1; Mark 1:1, 14:9; 2 Timothy 2:8). (Adapted from Robert Johnson, *The Letter of Paul to the Galatians* in the Living Word Commentary Series [Austin, TX: R.B. Sweet Co., 1969], p.42-43.)

ing another of the same kind, and *heteros*, meaning another of a different kind.[26]   *Heteros* is the word used here.   The message to which the Galatians were beginning to listen is different in kind from the gospel Paul and the other apostles preach.   There is no similarity between the message of the Judaizers and the message the apostles preach.   The Judaizers may have tried to make their teachings sound like gospel, but it was not really the gospel!

1:7 - *which is* **really** *not another; only there are some who are disturbing you, and want to distort the gospel of Christ.*

Which is *really* **not another** – The relative "which" (*ho*) in the phrase *ho ouk estin allo* refers to the "different gospel."[27]   *Allo* says it is not really another of the same kind.   There cannot be two gospels.[28]

Only there are some who are disturbing you – For the first time Paul mentions the troublemakers/agitators who are causing the turmoil in the churches.[29]   No one except the

---

[26] While the distinction of terms was true in classical Greek, the tendency among scholars today is to regard the words *heteros* and *allos* as synonyms, and thus to deny any recognizable difference between them in Koine Greek.   See BAGD, p.315; H.W. Beyer, *"heteros"* in Kittel's *Theological Dictionary of the New Testament*, Vol.2, p.702-704, and in Blass, DeBrunner, & Funk 306 (4) who all see no essential distinction.   Moulton and Milligan (p. 257) give many references where the terms may be studied.   J.K. Elliott, *ZNW* 60 (1969), p.140-141 concluded there is a recognizable distinction between these synonyms in the LXX and in the New Testament.   The context here seems to suggest that in this place Paul does use the old classical meaning of these synonyms, just as he did at 1 Corinthians 15:39-41.

[27] How to translate the first clause of verse 7 has troubled the translators.   The NASB adds the word "really" in italics.   The KJV rendered both adjectives (*allos* and *heteros*) by the same English word "another," which certainly does not aid the reader to come to an understanding of what Paul wrote. Lightfoot argued the first clause in verse 7 means "that it is no gospel at all."   A footnote in Boice (*op. cit.*, p.429) tells us that Ramsay and Lightfoot had a debate on the meaning of the two adjectives.   The problem for many of these commentators results from trying to make *ho* the subject of the sentence, rather than treating it as a relative pronoun.   "If the clause be rendered 'whereas there is no other gospel (i.e., than the true),' the sense becomes perfectly clear, and it forms an appropriate introduction to the succeeding anathemas by its emphatic testimony to the one true Gospel."   (Fredric Rendall, "The Epistle to the Galatians," Vol.3 in *Expositor's Greek Testament* [Grand Rapids: Eerdmans, 1967], p.152.)

[28] If Paul hadn't added this verse, readers of Galatians might get the idea that in the early days of the church there were various gospels making the rounds, among which a Christian might choose.   Such a view is not so.   The faith (singular) was once-for-all delivered to the saints (Jude 3).   Various heresies were making the rounds, but there was only one true gospel.

[29] The Judaizers (i.e., the preachers of this "different gospel") are styled as *hoi tarassontes* – "some who are disturbing/troubling you."   That is not how the Judaizers would have viewed themselves, but it certainly is an accurate description of them that Paul here gives.   Paul will use this same descriptive term of the false teachers in Galatians 5:10 and 6:17.   Compare the use of the same verb in Acts 15:24, where the same group of troublemakers is alluded to. The same verb is used to describe the feelings of Jesus' disciples in the ship during the storm (Matthew 14:26).   It also describes the feelings of King Herod when he heard that a new king had been born (Matthew 2:3).

Judaiazers[30] would think of calling the message they were preaching a "gospel." The plural "some" indicates a plurality of troublemakers.[31] The present participle *tarassontes* ("disturbing") indicates the troublemakers are already at work. The word pictures turmoil, alarm, disquiet, or mental confusion being caused by the agitators. The teachings of the Judaizers have filled the minds of the Galatian Christians with uneasiness and apprehension, perhaps by telling them they were not saved as they currently are living. Perhaps the Galatians were being told that they need to begin to practice "works of the Law" in order to be sure of Divine favor. What the Judaizers were doing would eventually result in schism and division.

And want to distort the gospel of Christ - The Greek word *metastrephō* means to reverse, to turn about, to corrupt. The phrase seems to be Paul's estimate of the ideology that drove the Judaizers. They didn't like the gospel as Jesus and the apostles presented it. They wanted to twist it to suit themselves and their own views.[32] The "gospel of Christ" can be the gospel *about* Christ (objective genitive) or it can be the gospel which was given *by* Christ (subjective genitive). The gospel of Christ is the message Paul and all the apostles of Jesus preached as they went from place to place obeying the Great Commission.[33]

2. Pronouncement of Divine judgment upon the distorters of the gospel. 1:8,9

1:8 - *But even though we, or an angel from heaven, should preach to you a gospel contrary to that which we have preached to you, let him be accursed.*

But even though we - So evil it is to distort the gospel the way the Judaizers are trying to do, that if even Paul and his helpers ("we," i.e., Barnabas and Silas; or perhaps the "we" covers all the apostles of Jesus) were to do something like that (i.e., preach a "different gospel"), they would deserve to be sentenced to hell.

---

[30] The word "only" in our text represents *ei me*, a construction that has the force of "except." 'No one *except* the troublers themselves' is the idea.

[31] The singular *tis* ("any man") of verse 9 seems to be generic.

[32] Remember that Jesus one day accused the religious leaders of trying to twist the gospel of the kingdom (Luke 16:16).

[33] As noted above in footnote #25, the characterization of the apostolic message as being "the gospel of Christ" is found in many passages in the New Testament (Romans 15:19; 1 Corinthians 9:12; 2 Corinthians 2:12, 4:4, 9:13; Philippians 1:27; 1 Thessalonians 3:2). According to Mark 1:1, the book of Mark is concerned with the gospel which has Jesus Christ as its focus and God as its source. It is also called "the gospel of God" (Romans 1:1-3, 15:16; 1 Thessalonians 2:2, 2:8,9; 1 Timothy 1:11).

Or an angel from heaven - We do not know why Paul added this word here. Was it because the Judaizers were appealing to angels as the origin of their doctrine? Or is this simply the strongest way to express a hypothetical supposition?

> Paul draws an impossible picture to impress upon his readers the impossibility of an altered gospel. He has preached the true gospel of Christ to them. Any message that contradicts it must be rejected, even if preached by Paul himself. And what if someone should come claiming higher authority than his? Regardless of who he is, even if he is an angel from high heaven itself, if he preaches a gospel different from the true gospel already received, let that person be accursed.[34]

Should preach to you a gospel contrary to that which we have preached to you - The Greek preposition *para* can mean "in addition to" or "contrary to." Perhaps the Judaizers' message was an "addition to" the gospel. Perhaps it was "contrary to" the gospel. Either way, the Galatians should have evaluated the troublemakers' message by comparing it to the apostolic preaching they heard[35] when Paul and Barnabas planted the churches, and they should have rejected that which did not match. "It is the message, not the messenger, that ultimately matters."[36]

Let him be accursed! - The marginal note informs us that the Greek word translated "accursed" is *anathema*. There are two ways to spell the word in the Greek: (a) *Anathema* (short "e"), which means an object on which God's wrath rests (Leviticus 27:28; Joshua 7:1; Acts 28:14), and (b) *Anathēma* (long "e"), which means an object dedicated to God as a gift (2 Maccabees 9:16; Luke 21:5). Here the spelling with the short "e" is used, so the NASB translates it "accursed." There can be little doubt that *anathema* involves a reference to eternal perdition, but how does being *anathema* differ from being condemned? Do we make reference to degrees of punishment, with *anathema* being greater than condemned? Though the NASB reads "let him be accursed," scholars have objected since they think this is not a wish, but a verdict similar to the one Jesus pronounced on the Pharisees (Matthew 23:13-39, especially verses 15,33). "The apostle, as Christ's fully authorized representative, is pronouncing God's curse upon the Judaizers."[37] Their mes-

---

[34] R.C. Foster, 1963 *Standard Lesson Commentary* (Cincinnati, OH: Standard, 1962), p.426.

[35] The aorist tense "preached" speaks of the time past, when Paul and his helpers worked to spread the gospel among the readers. If our conclusions about time and place of writing are correct, this can include preaching among the readers in southern Galatia on both Paul's first and second missionary journeys.

[36] F.F. Bruce, *The Epistle to the Galatians*, in The New International Greek Testament Commentary series (Grand Rapids, MI: Eerdmans, 1982), p.83.

[37] William Hendriksen, *Galatians* in the New Testament Commentary series (Grand Rapids: Baker, 1968), p.41.

sage puts the souls of men and women in jeopardy. No wonder they fall under the judgment of God.[38]

1:9 - *As we have said before, so I say again now, if any man is preaching to you a gospel contrary to that which you received, let him be accursed.*

As we have said before - Lest the Galatians fail to grasp the seriousness of the matter, Paul repeats his *anathema* by calling attention to the fact that it had been uttered before he wrote this letter. Rather than "before" being a reference back to what was just written in verse 8, it is more likely that on some visit previous to the writing of this letter Paul had solemnly warned against any who would distort the gospel or preach a different gospel. When Paul speaks of "we," he seems to be recalling a visit when he and his fellow workers voiced this warning. Perhaps it was on the first missionary journey when he and Barnabas helped plant the churches. Perhaps it was during the second visit, at a time when Judaizers had already appeared in Syrian Antioch where they troubled the church, during which visit Paul and Silas delivered the decrees of the Jerusalem Conference (Acts 16:4). Perhaps the reference is to a recent visit at the beginning of the third missionary journey.

So I say again now - In effect, Paul says, "I am repeating right now the same solemn warning we issued before." Paul is probably writing this sentence in his own hand, and he speaks as an apostle of Jesus, clothed with His full authority.

If any man is preaching to you a gospel contrary to that which you received - The singular "any man" is probably generic.[39] The Judaizers, each and every one of them, whoever they may be, the ones who are currently preaching to the Galatian churches,[40] are the ones in view. The type of conditional question in the Greek in verse 8 differs from the type here in verse 9. That change brings the denunciation of verse 8 down out of the region of mere hypothesis, and gives it a present reality and application. The previous verse reads "that which we have preached" while this one reads "that which you received." By this change of expression Paul reminds them they had at one time solemnly professed to embrace the apostolic gospel. "It had not only been preached among them, it had been

---

[38] This commentator rejects the view that *anathema* ("accursed") is a word of excommunication, either from the synagogue or the church. In later ecclesiastical use, the word may have had that meaning, but there is no evidence it meant such in Paul's day. In fact, in our judgment, the significant addition of "from Christ" in Romans 9:3 associates *anathema* with separation from Christ rather than excommunication from church.

[39] Rather than taking the singular in a generic sense, some commentators suggest that the singular "any one" here and the singular "who" in Galatians 5:7 may refer to the ringleader of the Judaizers. We tend to believe that Paul's *anathema* is intended for more troublemakers than just their leader.

[40] "Is preaching to you" translates *humas euaggelizetai*. In classical writers this verb takes only a dative of the person; in later Greek it has indifferently a dative or an accusative (Lightfoot, *op. cit.*, p.78). The construction found here, *euaggelizetai* with the accusative of the person to whom the message is brought, is common in New Testament Greek. Cp. Acts 13:32, 14:21.

embraced by them."[41]   Again it should be noted there is only one gospel, one faith delivered to the saints.[42]

Let him be accursed - The words of explanation given in verse 8 hold true for the repetition of *anathema* here in verse 9.   "The ringing words of Paul (preached earlier, and re-emphasized here again) should cause every reader of Galatians to consider most carefully the purity of the gospel which he receives and promotes.   It is no small matter. The eternal destiny of man is at stake.   If we do not feel as deeply about it as Paul did, perhaps we do not understand the issues as clearly as he."[43]

3. Paul's passion to please God.   1:10

1:10 - For am I now seeking the favor of men, or of God?   Or am I striving to please men? If I were still trying to please men, I would not be a bond-servant of Christ.

For am I now seeking the favor of men, or of God? - It would appear that the Judaizers had slandered Paul, telling the Galatians that Paul was not consistent, but rather was a man-pleaser.   They said that when Paul comes to town, lest he offend his Gentile listeners, he deliberately leaves out of his "gospel" certain things that are really necessary.   To answer that slanderous false representation Paul asks, "At this moment, does my word of *anathema* sound like I am a man-pleaser?   Does it not rather sound like my aim is to please God?"[44]

---

[41] Albert Barnes, "Epistle to the Galatians" in *Barnes' Notes on the New Testament* (Grand Rapids: Baker, 1955), p.291.

[42] "Contrary to" in verse 9 translates the same Greek we just had in verse 8.   It is an emphasis of the Restoration Movement that we should return to the message and the way of doing things as they were done from the beginning by Jesus and His apostles.   Something of this very sort is what Paul expects of the Galatians as he calls attention to the apostolic preaching.   If there is only one gospel, then the oft-repeated dictum "It doesn't make any difference what one believes, as long as one is sincere" is patently false.

[43] Paraphrased from Homer Kent, *The Freedom of God's Sons: Studies in Galatians* (Winona Lake, IN: BMH Books, 1976), p.36.   Some readers have wondered whether the language of Paul at this place gives us the right to "curse" false teachers.   Huxtable (*op. cit.*, p.14) offers a prudent answer.   "It is lawful also to us individually and right, that we should add to the utterance of each sentence our hearty 'Amen,' and thus take part with God and His Law, not only against sins committed by our neighbors, but most especially and above all against willful transgressions of our own.   But beyond this, none who are *not special organs of inspiration* may venture to go, whether acting individually or in any corporate capacity."

[44] The Greek of this verse presents problems to translators.   (1) It begins with the words *arti gar* ("for now").   "Now" apparently refers to the *anathemas* he has just uttered.   *Gar* is used in many different ways. It can be translated "yes, indeed," "certainly," or even translated as an exclamation ("there!") so that the verse reads "There!   Does that sound like I am a man-pleaser?"   (2) The fact that *gar* appears here has affected how men outline the letter to the Galatians.   Some think verse 10 is the conclusion of the first paragraph in the letter; others think it is the first verse in the new paragraph that follows.   (3) How shall we translate *peitho*?   Does it mean appeal or persuade (as we find it used in Acts 26:26), or does it mean to strive to please or curry favor with someone?   The following phrases here in verse 10 suggest the latter is the correct idea.

Or am I striving to please men? - This phrase evidently echoes the charges the Judaizers have made to discredit Paul and his message.[45]   In the exercise of his Christian liberty, Paul's actions could well look like inconsistency on his part.   At the Jerusalem Conference, Paul had refused to circumcise Titus.   Yet shortly after that, at the beginning of the second missionary journey, when they were in southern Galatia, Paul had circumcised Timothy as a concession to Jewish feeling.   It would have been easy for the Judaizers to put a spin on Paul's actions, as though he were inconsistent because he was a man-pleaser.   When it was a matter of Christian liberty, Paul did enter into the customs of the people with whom he was living.   "To the Jews I became a Jew ..." (1 Corinthians 9:20ff).   But where a question of Christian doctrine was at stake, he knew how to take his stand.   The refusal to circumcise Titus (Galatians 2:3-5) was a matter of principle, a matter of right doctrine.   To have done so in Titus' case would have compromised the gospel.   The circumcision of Timothy (Acts 16:3) was done as a matter of liberty, and that in order to try to win unbelievers to Christ (1 Corinthians 9:22, "that I may by all means save some").

If I were still trying to please men, I would not be a bond-servant of Christ - This is a contrary-to-fact condition implying that he is not still trying to please men.   Perhaps those were his motives when he was a zealous Pharisee,[46] but all that is in the past.   Now, his one goal was to please his master, Jesus Christ.   God's Old Testament mouthpieces, the prophets who by inspiration spoke God's message, were often styled "servants."[47]   Paul here claims to have stepped into the role of the prophets of old as he delivers God's message, the gospel of Christ.[48]

---

[45] If the Judaizers are going to win over Paul's converts to their different gospel, they first must destroy the Galatians' confidence in the apostle.

[46] It is perhaps not without reason to suppose Paul already has in mind the charge he will make in Galatians 6:12 concerning the Pharisaic troublemakers, where he tells us that one of their motives was to "make a good showing" before men, just like Paul the Pharisee used to do before Christ met him on the road to Damascus.   Observe carefully: Paul is not here speaking against being pleasing to others for the sake of the gospel (cf. 1 Corinthians 10:33), but is speaking against currying the favor of others for one's own selfish advantage.

[47] Amos 3:7; Jeremiah 7:25; Isaiah 20:3; and "My servants the prophets" in Jeremiah 44:4.

[48] Some commentators call attention to Paul's attitudes elsewhere – an attitude "of openness, tolerance, and accommodation to issues in the churches (e.g., 1 Corinthians 7-14), a breadth of spirit (e.g., Philippians 1:15-18; 4:8-9) – and have contrasted those attitudes to the emotion, indignation, force, and unyieldingness that we find here in Galatians.   When issues are really matters of Christian liberty (*adiaphora*), Paul can be magnanimous, because those are not fundamental issues.   Where fundamental issues are at stake, Paul is prepared, without hesitation, to draw clear lines and to speak with fervor in defense of the 'truth of the gospel.'   That is exactly what he is doing here (as also 2 Corinthians 11:13-15; Colossians 2:8)."   Longenecker, *op. cit.*, p.19.

I. *APOLOGETIC PORTION*: PAUL'S DEFENSE OF HIS APOSTLESHIP AND GOSPEL MESSAGE. 1:11 – 2:21

Summary: First, Paul claims a divine source for his apostleship and gospel message. He then sets about to prove the truth of that claim by rehearsing the key and salient historical events of his life.

A. The Divine Source of his Apostleship and Gospel Message. 1:11,12

1:11 - *For I would have you know, brethren, that the gospel which was preached by me is not according to man.*

For - Paul seems to be saying in verses 11 and 12 that he is a bond-servant of Christ, and his message came directly from Christ.[49]

I would have you know - *Gnōrizō*, here as in 1 Corinthians 12:3 and 15:1, has the force of reminding, rather than initially making something known. Paul is calling their attention to truths they seemingly have forgotten.[50]

Brethren - The people alluded to as "brethren" in verse 11 are church members in general, whereas in 1:2 the "brethren" were likely Paul's co-workers in the mission work. If we are Christians, we are brothers because we have the same Father. The address "brethren" conveys a good deal. The Christians in Galatia may be wavering in their beliefs and were in great danger, but they are still Paul's "brothers" in Christ.

That the gospel which was preached by me - The Greek is a restrictive attributive, and

---

[49] There is a manuscript variation here, some reading *gar* ('for') and some reading *de* ('and/but'). *De* is the slightly better supported reading. *De* could be resumptive, picking up the argument of 1:1-5. It could be mildly adversative, standing in contrast to something said in 1:6-10. Taken as mildly adversative, it suggests that a new section of the outline begins here at verse 11.

[50] "In the verses that follow, the apostle is not trying to present a complete autobiography. He chooses from his career only those events which support his main contention with reference to the source of his calling as an apostle and of the message which he proclaims. Hence, when he omits an event mentioned elsewhere – for example, in Acts or in Paul's letters to the Corinthians – this must not be charged against him, as if he were purposely suppressing certain facts in order to win the argument against the Judaizers. On the contrary, he is deeply conscious of telling the truth (Galatians 1:20). The omitted incidents are left unmentioned for the simple reason that they have nothing to do with the point which Paul is trying to prove." Hendriksen, *op. cit.*, p.47.

reads, "the gospel, the one preached by me."[51]   There is a deliberate contrast to the different gospel the Judaizers have been preaching.   In Romans 2:16 and 16:25 Paul speaks of his preaching as being "my gospel."   In 1 Corinthians 15:1-4 he tells us his gospel included the death, burial, resurrection, and post-resurrection appearances of Jesus. In Galatians 3:1 he indicates that he stressed "Christ ... crucified."   Paul's preaching was identical with the message of the original twelve apostles (1 Corinthians 15:1-11).   As we look at examples of apostolic preaching in Acts, we find that men, Jews or Gentiles, who believe in Jesus (i.e., who are obedient to Jesus) are accepted by God apart from any Pharisaic rules or rituals.   Apostolic preaching also made it clear the Law of Moses had been abrogated (Acts 13:39).   No matter who the audience was, since Christ called him to be an apostle, there was only one gospel preached by Paul.

Is not according to man - "Apparently another attack against Paul has been the claim that he is dependent upon other men for the gospel he preaches.   He was not a disciple before Jesus died, so he must have learned about Jesus from others.   His is only a secondhand gospel, or so his accusers say."[52]   Perhaps "not according to man" means his gospel was not a human invention.[53]   The phrase then would speak of the origin of the gospel.   In Romans 15:20, Paul uses "man" ("man's foundation") as though it referred to an apostle. If "man" has the same connotation here as in Romans, then perhaps the troublemakers in Galatia have been saying Paul is dependent upon the original apostles for his message. Such a charge Paul vehemently denies and in the verses following gives reasons for the denial.

1:12 - *For I neither received it from man, nor was I taught it, but* **I** received it *through a revelation of Jesus Christ.*

For I neither received it from man, nor was I taught it - "For" seems to introduce a reason for what was just said.   "I" is emphatic in the Greek, and there is an implied contrast with the Judaizers and where they got their teachings.[54]   For generations the Pharisees have

---

[51] What Paul here calls "the gospel which was preached by me" is elsewhere called "the gospel of God" (1 Thessalonians 2:8,9; 2 Corinthians 11:7), because God is its author; "the gospel of Christ" (1 Thessalonians 3:2; 2 Corinthians 2:12; Romans 15:19), because Christ is its subject-matter; or, more comprehensively, "the gospel of God concerning his Son" (Romans 1:1-3). (Adapted from Boice, *op. cit.*, p.84.)

[52] Foster, *op. cit.*, p.246.

[53] So explained, this statement could be an aside at the Judaizers about the source of their message. Was not their message "simply human" in its origin?   Their message certainly was not from God as was Paul's.

[54] According to Gerhardsson and others of the Scandinavian school who have been doing a study on oral tradition in the ancient world, the expressions used in this clause belong to a set of technical words used of the process of memorization by which rabbis passed along rabbinic traditions to students (Boice, *op. cit.*, p.431).   The Jews learned under rabbinic teaching.   The teacher would speak and then the student would repeat.   They memorized the opinions and interpretations of famous rabbis before them, and then repeated them to their students, who in turn taught the people.

been handing down their teachings by word of mouth from teacher to pupil. Their doctrines were the commandments of men (Matthew 15:9, KJV), and they were passed along to the next generation by men. To complete the thought in "nor was I taught it," we should mentally add the words "by man."[55] The verb "received" (*paralambanō*), in a context of oral transmission of information, speaks of something being transmitted from one person to another by word of mouth.[56] "Taught" pictures a formal school or formal instruction, the way most people learn. It is also not possible to claim Paul received his gospel from Ananias who baptized him (Acts 9:17,18 and 22:14-16). The only instruction he received from Ananias was how to become a Christian.

But *I received it* through a revelation of Jesus Christ - "But" is the strong adversative (*alla*) and means "on the contrary." As explained in 1 Corinthians 2:10-12, revelation is the act of God imparting to the Bible writers and preachers truth that they were incapable of discovering by a man's unaided reason. They had to have divine help to know the things of God. Such divine help Paul here claims for his gospel. The words "of Jesus Christ" are in the genitive case. The majority of older writers take this to be a subjective genitive[57] which means Jesus Christ did the revealing, and we agree. The context has been talking about where his message came from. It was not from men, but from Jesus Christ. When this revelation was made to Paul is a matter of debate. Some would point to what happened to Paul on the Damascus road, but does the language of Acts suggest that the whole "sum of Christian doctrine" was impressed into Paul's mind in a moment of time? Later, in verse 17, Paul will lay stress on his trip to Arabia, and in so doing he seems to be saying that the gospel he preached was revealed to him while he was in Arabia. Perhaps, as Paul persecuted Christians, he heard some of the historical facts of the gospel from his

---

[55] Redaction criticism, which claims Paul was dependent on those who were believers before him for much of what Christianity taught, and that he repeatedly made use of early Christian creedal statements for his teaching, is in error. Here in Galatians Paul himself flatly insists that he was not dependent on his Christian predecessors for his message. To say he was dependent on his predecessors is to deny any role for revelation and inspiration as the source of his message. See 1 Corinthians 2:6-13 where Paul explains how through Holy Spirit-inspired words the message got from the mind of God to the minds of his hearers.

[56] Compare 1 Corinthians 11:23, "for I (emphatic) received (*egō parelabon*) from the Lord that which I also delivered (*paradidōmi*) to you." According to the usual language of oral transmission, *paralambanō* speaks of receiving (from predecessors), *paradidōmi* speaks of delivering (to successors). The use of *paralambanō* at 1 Corinthians 11:23 (concerning the Lord's Supper) and at 1 Corinthians 15:3 (with regard to information about the death, burial, resurrection, and post-resurrection appearances of Jesus) should not be explained as meaning Paul received those messages from *human* predecessors. He did not get his gospel from men, but from the Lord. He specifically says this in 1 Corinthians 11:23.

[57] Many contemporary writers treat it as an objective genitive, a revelation "about Jesus Christ." Verses 15 and 16 are then used by these contemporary writers to corroborate this idea, after they are explained as teaching that God was the revealer and it was Jesus Christ who was revealed to Paul's mind.

victims.   And surely he heard confessions of the Lordship of Jesus Christ from those who were about to die for Christ, as they insisted the crucified One had risen from the dead. And Paul was also present and heard the testimony when Stephen was being stoned (Acts 7:58).   But what did those historical events mean?   Their meaning would make up some of the revelation Jesus gave him.   Paul's knowledge of the gospel came by a direct revelation given by Jesus Christ, just as was true in the case of the twelve.   But how is Paul going to prove to the Galatians that he did not get his gospel from any human teacher? Answer: by an appeal to his personal history, which he now relates.

B. Proof of its Divine Origin.   1:13 - 2:14

Summary: From 1:13 through 2:21 Paul calls attention to a number of incidents in his life previous to the writing of this letter, none of which furnished the slightest opportunity to learn his gospel from men.   Furthermore, some of those events show that his gospel was the same as the gospel the original apostles preached.

1.   He did not learn it during his youth – very much to the contrary. 1:13,14

1:13 - For you have heard of my former manner of life in Judaism, how I used to persecute the church of God beyond measure, and tried to destroy it;

For you have heard of my former manner of life - Paul's manner of life in the days before he became a Christian was something already known to the Galatians.   "The word Paul used for his former 'manner (way) of life' (*anastrophē*) is singularly appropriate to the Jewish faith.   Judaism was not a mask to be donned or doffed at will, as was the case with so many of the pagan religions.   Judaism was a way of life, involving all of life, and Paul is correct in describing it as his exclusive sphere of existence before his conversion."[58] Paul certainly did not derive his knowledge of the Christian religion from his schooling under Gamaliel.   In those days Paul was a Pharisee of Pharisees (Acts 23:6).   He would have been immersed in the very doctrines the troublemakers were now trying to impose on the Galatians.   Paul has been there; he can speak with authority on matters of the Jews' religion.

In Judaism - "Judaism" is a proper term to describe Pharisaism, for it refers not to the religion of Moses as revealed in the Old Testament scriptures, but to the whole Jewish sys-

---

[58] Boice, *op. cit.*, p.432.

tem of religion and life as it was practiced at that time, especially by the Pharisees.[59]   That system of religion included the *halakhah* – i.e., the oral law, or the traditions of the Pharisees – which Jesus said (Matthew 15:6) voided the written Law.   Jesus also said the laws of the Pharisees are the doctrines of men, not the commandments of God (Matthew 15:3,9).   Paul goes on to emphasize two aspects of his life while he was immersed in Judaism.   First, he persecuted the church.   Second, he advanced in those traditions well beyond what others did.   Neither of these two aspects could have contributed to the gospel which he has been preaching since Jesus called him.   In those days before he became a Christian, Paul thoroughly understood that Pharisaic Judaism and Christianity were irreconcilable enemies.

How I used to persecute the church of God beyond measure - The Galatians knew how Paul persecuted Christians before his call and conversion.   "Beyond measure" describes the persecution as excessive, far beyond what might ordinarily be expected.   The imperfect tense verb "used to persecute" recalls the fact that the persecution went on over a rather long period of time, and was not limited just to Jerusalem.[60]   There certainly is a vivid contrast between "Judaism" and "the church of God."[61]   It calls to the attention of the churches in Galatia (who at the time of writing are also part of the church of God) that there is a remarkable difference between Christianity and the Pharisaic Judaism which Paul had abandoned because of Christ's call.   Before they embrace what the Judaizers are teaching, the Galatian Christians should be perfectly aware that Judaizers are not part of the church of God, nor will they be if they join them.

And tried to destroy it - The imperfect tense says Paul kept trying to destroy the church. The word translated "destroy" is *porthein*, a word used of devastating a city with fire and sword.   Paul was trying to wipe the church off the face of the earth.   His intention was to root out and destroy the Christian religion.

---

[59] The term "Judaism" is used in 2 Maccabees 2:21, 8:1, 14:38, and 4 Maccabees 4:16 to distinguish between the way of life a strict Pharisee would live and the way of life found in Seleucid Hellenism. Ignatius (*Ad Magn*. 8) also uses the term.   Galatians 1:13,14 are the only uses of the term in the New Testament.

[60] See Acts 9:1,2, 22:4, and 26:11 for a record of the persecution led by Paul.

[61] At Galatians 1:2, attention was called to the fact that Paul can speak both of local churches and of the church universal.   "Church" here in verse 13 is singular, referring not to a local congregation but to the Christian community at large.   Perhaps the different names given to the body of believers are significant. "The church" (Acts 9:31) calls attention to its universal nature.   "Church of God" (1 Corinthians 1:2 and Galatians 1:13) may call attention to her Planner.   "Church of the first born [ones]" (Hebrews 12:23) calls attention to the new birth, and to the special responsibilities believers have.   "Body of Christ" (1 Corinthians 12:27 ASV) may emphasize the activity of the different members of the body.   "Churches of Christ" (Romans 16:16) speaks of ownership.   "Churches of the saints" (1 Corinthians 14:33) talks about the character of those who make up the congregations.   "Churches of the Gentiles" (Romans 16:4) takes cognizance of the ethnic background of the majority of the members of those congregations.

1:14 - *And I was advancing in Judaism beyond many of my contemporaries among my countrymen, being more extremely zealous for my ancestral traditions.*

And I was advancing in Judaism beyond many of my contemporaries among my countrymen - Not only was he totally committed to Pharisaic Judaism, he saw himself as a kind of "pioneer who was cutting his way through a forest, destroying every obstacle in order to advance."[62]   "He was rapidly becoming an outstanding man among the Jews."[63] When Paul says "contemporaries" (*sunēlikiōtas*, people of his own age group), he likely is thinking of his Jewish schoolmates who were studying at the feet of Gamaliel or some other eminent rabbi.

Being more extremely zealous for my ancestral traditions - Paul, whose father was a Pharisee, was but one in a long line of Pharisees (Acts 23:6).   The traditions he refers to are "the whole hedge of 613 human commandments which the rabbis had built around the law, and which the Pharisees made it the business of their party to maintain at all costs."[64] "Zeal" is a neutral word and only its context can determine if it is used in a good or bad sense.[65]   A person's zeal can be misdirected, and Paul's certainly was when he was zealous for his ancestral traditions.   Since Christianity and Judaism are not compatible, it is rather quickly evident that Paul's avid promotion of Jewish traditions in his pre-Christian life is hardly the source for his gospel message.

> This provides a blade that cuts two ways.   First, Paul is well acquainted with the kind of things the Judaizers are trying to bind on the Gentile Christians; second, he received his Jewish training from men, but he received his Christian instruction from Christ.[66]

2. He did not learn his gospel at his call to apostleship, and immediately after his call he did not confer with men to learn it. 1:15-17

---

[62] The verb translated "advancing" is *prokoptō*, to "cut forward, to push forward."   Hendriksen (*op. cit.*, p.521) is the one who suggested the picture of the pioneer.

[63] Orrin Root, *1984-85 Standard Lesson Commentary*, p.13.

[64] Lenski, *op. cit.*, p.53.   The expression "ancestral traditions" ("traditions of my fathers," ASV) is likely coterminous with the expression "traditions of the elders" (Matthew 15:2 and Mark 7:3,5).   These are the Jewish oral laws devised to apply the written Law to new circumstances, which laws today are known as the *halakhah* and are collected in the Talmud.

[65] The word, sometimes translated zealous and sometimes as jealous, is used with an honorable connotation in Romans 10:2; 2 Corinthians 11:2; Numbers 25:11; and 1 Kings 19:10,14.   It is used in a bad sense in Romans 13:13; 1 Corinthians 3:3; and 2 Corinthians 12:20.

[66] Foster, *op. cit.*, p.247.

1:15 - *But when He who had set me apart,* even *from my mother's womb, and called me through His grace, was pleased*

But - "But" highlights the abrupt change in Paul's way of life that resulted from God's calling him to be an apostle. Here in verse 15, Paul will emphasize three things about his commission to be an apostle. First, it happened because God was pleased to do it that way. Second, before he was born, God had set him apart for a special service. Third, in harmony with God's good pleasure and choice for service, the day came when God called him into that service.

When He ... was pleased - What happened to Paul on the Damascus road was the result of God's good pleasure. God was moved to so act simply because it seemed to Him a good way to do things. "To emphasize the role of God in preparing him for his Christian work, Paul draws attention to God's foreknowledge and foreordination."[67]

Who had set me apart, *even* **from my mother's womb** - A careful study of Acts chapters 9, 22, and 26 will show that Paul was called to be an apostle before he was baptized into Christ (Acts 26:16). Now we see that God's choice of Paul to be an apostle was much earlier than His call. The participle "set me apart" has the sense of setting aside for service. God had chosen Paul to be an apostle before he was born. God worked the same way with several others of His special servants. In Jeremiah 1:5, God said to Jeremiah, "Before I formed you in the womb I knew you, and before you were born I consecrated you; I have appointed you a prophet to the nations." God worked the same way with Isaiah (see Isaiah 49:1-6) and John the Baptist (see Luke 1:13-17). God's predestination to service spoken of in Romans 9 was true in Paul's case, too.[68]

And called me through His grace - Krister Stendahl has rightfully identified this as Paul's "call rather than conversion."[69] On that occasion Jesus said to him, "... for this purpose I

---

[67] Foster, *ibid.*

[68] What God did on the Damascus Road was to "separate" Paul for the task which God had all along planned for Paul to do. Romans 9 tells how God in His sovereignty chooses certain men to be vessels of mercy, that is, men through whom His mercy becomes known to others. What God did in Old Testament times, He did with Paul, too.

　　　Caution should be exercised here. Predestination to service is not the same doctrine of predestination that Augustine and Calvin taught. Theirs was a predestination to salvation or damnation, and their idea was mistaken. God has determined that those who are in Christ are saved, but whether or not a man is in Christ is his own choice, not God's predestination.

[69] K. Stendahl, *Paul Among Jews and Gentiles* (Philadelphia: Fortress Press, 1976), p.7-23. Caution is needed here when one consults the commentaries, especially those written from a Reformed standpoint. In the opinion of many Reformed writers, "called me" is a reference to Paul's conversion rather than his call to apostleship. And the writers of that persuasion usually emphasize that the conversion of Paul was all *God's doing*, without any works, etc. We must be careful how we word our explanation, lest we simply repeat such erroneous monergistic ideas.

have appeared to you, to appoint you a minister and a witness not only to the things which you have seen, but also to the things in which I will appear to you: delivering you from the *Jewish* people and from the Gentiles, to whom I am sending you" (Acts 26:16-17). Jesus did not appear to Paul to convert him, but to call him to be an apostle. "The theme of [Paul's apostolic] calling by God plays an important role in this letter" (see 1:6, 5:8,13).[70] "The implacable foe certainly did not deserve God's favor [grace], but God wanted this man to preach the gospel, not among the Jews with whom he was reared, but among the Gentiles."[71]

1:16 - *to reveal His Son in me, that I might preach Him among the Gentiles, I did not immediately consult with flesh and blood*

To reveal His Son in me - "Two possible interpretations suggest themselves for the expression 'to reveal his Son in me.' Possibly, Paul was describing his job, to reveal Jesus to others. Or, perhaps, 'to reveal his Son in me' refers to the revelation made about Jesus to Paul."[72] We see no reason why this revelation cannot be a reference to what happened *after* Paul's call to be an apostle. Verses 16 and 17 together present this idea: when God was pleased to make a revelation about Jesus to Paul, Paul went away to Arabia (not to Jerusalem) to receive it. While Paul was away in Arabia, he was receiving revelations 'in his mind' (i.e., "in me") concerning Jesus' earthly ministry – what His life, death, and resurrection signified, as well as what Jesus taught while He was on earth. "Not only did God determine that Paul would bring the gospel to the Gentiles; it was God who determined *when* He would reveal His Son to Paul."[73] This is the first time in Galatians that Jesus is

---

[70] Frank J. Matera, *Galatians* in the Sacra Pagina Series (Collegeville, MN: Liturgical Press, 1992), p.59.

[71] Root, *op. cit.*, p.13. "By his grace" translates *dia tēs charitos*. *Dia* and the genitive does not seem to say that "grace" was the means of the call. It was "through" God's grace that the call came to be extended to Paul.

[72] Foster, *op. cit.*, p.247. Caution again is urged. Those who teach that faith is a gift of God are likely to insist that "reveal His Son in me" means "in my mind" or "in my consciousness." God did that, it is supposed, and the faith produced in Paul by that revelation resulted in Paul's conversion. Calvinists, who posit an effectual call by which a man becomes a Christian, have their own explanation of "revealed in me." To them, it speaks of the moment, in conversion, when a man becomes aware of God's work inside of him (in his mind). If we take it as an inward revelation to Paul's mind or consciousness, it certainly cannot be a reference to his conversion. Paul will write in 1 Timothy 1:12-16 that his conversion was an example of how all men are converted. We are hardly ready to say that God gives an inward revelation of Jesus Christ to all men as part of their conversion process. "Faith comes by hearing the word of Christ" (Romans 10:17).

[73] Matera, *op. cit.*, p.63. Lightfoot (*op. cit.*, p.83) understands that "reveal His Son in me" means "by means of Paul's preaching."

called God's "Son."[74]   We call Jesus God's "Son" because of the incarnation (Luke 1:35). The language also carries the connotation of deity.   As a result of the incarnation, Jesus was God in the flesh.

That I might preach Him among the Gentiles - This clause states the purpose of the revelation to Paul.   It was 'in order that' Paul might preach Him among the Gentiles. Paul's commission to proclaim the gospel did not originate with man, but with God. "Preach" translates *euangelizōmai*, preach the gospel.   The present tense verb indicates Paul was called to do a continuous preaching of the good news.   This is the most important phrase in verses 15,16 as it emphatically refutes the Judaizers' claims that there was something faulty with Paul's preaching when the audience was Gentile.   Isaiah 49:1-6 had predicted that Messiah would have a ministry among the nations (i.e., the Gentiles).   Paul's commission to be an apostle of Jesus was in part a fulfillment of that prediction.   "Preach Him" is an expression that causes us to pause.   Elsewhere Paul speaks of "preaching the gospel" (Romans 1:15, 15:20; 1 Corinthians 1:17, 9:16) and "preaching the ... faith" (Romans 10:8).   These three ideas – Christ, gospel, and faith – are closely connected, even equated.   The "faith" certainly includes instruction concerning Jesus that would lead listeners to express their belief in these words, "I believe that Jesus is the Christ, the Son of the living God."   The "gospel" (see notes at Galatians 1:7) is the good news about this Jesus, that in Him remission of sins is proclaimed to all the nations (Luke 24:47).

I did not immediately consult with flesh and blood - Commentators are divided concerning with which verb to attach the word "immediately."   It can go with "did not ... consult," or it can go with "went away" (in verse 17).   "Consult" translates *prosanethemēn*, a compound verb that means to gain authoritative information.   "I did not ... consult with flesh and blood" sounds like a refutation of a lying report made about Paul by the Judaizers.   "Flesh and blood" is a Semitism and has reference to human authorities (mortal humanity/human beings) who might have issued orders to Paul or instructed him about Jesus.[75]   "No Christian in Damascus, not even Ananias, was consulted by Paul so as to provide instruction or grant any sort of authorization to him."[76]   In fact, we find Paul

---

[74] Other references to Jesus as the Son of God are Romans 1:3,9, 5:10, 8:3,29,32; 1 Corinthians 1:9; 2 Corinthians 1:19; Galatians 2:20, 4:4,6; and 1 Thessalonians 1:10. In the author's commentary on Romans, he has called attention to the fact that Jesus is officially, ethically, and metaphysically the Son of God. The title "Son of God" for Jesus Messiah was derived by Paul from the Jewish Scriptures. Paul was not alone in the ascription of this title to Jesus. For example, see Mark 1:1, with the recollection that tradition says Mark's Gospel reflects Peter's preaching.

[75] Compare Matthew 16:17, where Jesus says to Peter that "flesh and blood" had not revealed the true identity of Jesus to him. In that verse humans are compared to "My Father who is in heaven."

[76] Kent, *op. cit.*, p.44. "Ananias of Damascus had told Saul to be baptized and wash away his sins. It would seem natural then for Saul to ask more information and instruction from him, or from the other brethren in Damascus. But that was not God's plan for teaching Saul" (Root, *op. cit.*, p.13-14).

preaching Jesus in the synagogues of Damascus right after his conversion in Damascus, and his preaching was so powerful that he confounded the Jews who lived there (Acts 9:19-22). Paul has a proper knowledge of who Jesus is from Jesus' appearance to him on the Damascus road. At Acts 19:22, in the word "*proving* that this Jesus is the Christ," it is understood that what Paul did in these early days of his preaching was to take what he knew of Jesus and 'lay alongside' the Old Testament Messianic prophecies he also knew well from his rabbinic training. The perfect match proved Jesus had to be the Messiah.

1:17 - *nor did I go up to Jerusalem to those who were apostles before me; but I went away to Arabia, and returned once more to Damascus.*

Nor did I go up to Jerusalem to those who were apostles before me - "This verse seems designed especially to answer the false teachers' claim that Paul learned the gospel from the other apostles, but did not learn it very well. In the verses following, Paul enumerates the only times he has come into contact with the other apostles, either in Jerusalem or in Antioch. Rather than seek the wisdom of men, he has sought communion with God."[77] "It might seem natural, too, for a new apostle to be guided by the earlier apostles. But no, Jesus meant to teach this new apostle personally."[78] "The usual phase is to 'go up to Jerusalem,' because the city stood on high ground, and was approached from all sides by an ascent."[79] In "apostles before me," Paul fully acknowledges them as such. The original apostles plus Matthias (Acts 1:13 and 1:26) were apostles before Paul was ever called to be one.[80] Paul's language here also implies that he regarded himself to be an apostle just like those earlier ones. He did not go to Jerusalem to be instructed by the apostles in regard to the nature of the Christian religion. That his gospel did not originate from them is the point of this section.

But I went away to Arabia - Over against the false reports that the Judaizers were spreading, Paul states the facts regarding what he did do in the early days after his call. At

---

[77] Foster, *ibid.* "'Immediately' (it will be recalled) may be construed also with this clause. Paul did not hurry to Jerusalem to get anything, whether information or instruction or corroboration or approval, from any of the twelve." Lenski, *op. cit.*, p.59.

[78] Root, *ibid.*

[79] Sanday, *op. cit.*, p.22. There is a manuscript variation at this place. Several manuscripts (P^{51}, B,D,G) read *apēlthon* ('go away,' 'go') in place of *anēlthon* ('go up'), the reading of Sinaiticus, A^{vid}, et al. P^{46} simply has *ēlthon* ("go," "went"). There is another variation concerning the spelling of the name of the city. "Only in v.17ff and 2:1 does Paul use the Hellenized neuter plural *Hierosoluma* for Jerusalem; in seven other places he uses the Septuagintal *Hierousalem*" (Bruce, *op. cit.*, p.94). "If the spelling of the city's name (*Hierousalem*) at Galatians 4:25-26 has any significance, it might be in that context that Paul is thinking of the religious significance of the city, rather than simply the geographical site" (Longenecker, *op. cit.*, p. 34).

[80] "Before me" is temporal, rather than affirming status.

this early time (mid-30s AD) the original apostles are all still working in the Jerusalem area (Acts 8:1). In Arabia, therefore, Paul had no opportunity to meet any of Jesus' apostles. The Nabatean kingdom, founded in the 2nd century BC, had its capital at Petra. The region was ruled by Aretas IV from 9 BC to AD 40. The borders were not clearly defined, but the kingdom stretched from the Red Sea on the southwest to the Euphrates River on the northeast, and from the Jordan rift on the west side, to the desert on the east. At times it included the area around Damascus (2 Corinthians 11:32), and at times it apparently did not. Perhaps Paul's language ("I went away [from Damascus] to Arabia") indicates that when Galatians was written (after AD 40), that Damascus was at that time no longer part of the Nabatean kingdom.

Were it not for this mention of Arabia, we would not know Paul had ever been there. We place this trip between Acts 9:22 and 9:23.[81] Exactly where Paul went[82] and what he did there[83] have both been the subject of much conjecture. We see little reason for conjecture about what he did. "We have no information other than here in Galatians about what he did there, but it seems probable that he received the revelation (verse 12) that fitted him for his new work. It was three years before Paul returned to Damascus, and he then went to Jerusalem to see Peter (verse 18). His three years of learning from the Master (in Arabia) matched the three years of training the other apostles received."[84]

And returned once more to Damascus - When the trip to Arabia was finished, Paul did not go to Jerusalem or anywhere else to consult with the apostles. Rather than go else-where, he went back to Damascus. After his trip to Arabia, Damascus was his first appointed sphere of labor. "With all he learned in Arabia, Paul still had some bitter lessons to learn from experience. When he returned again to Damascus, he plunged eager-

---

[81] See the comments at Acts 9:23 in the author's *New Testament History: Acts* (Moberly, MO: Scripture Exposition Books, 2002), p.364-65.

[82] One Arabic translator (of the Polyglots) gives El Belka, the region lying to the east and northeast of the Dead Sea, as the place to which Paul went. Another suggestion is that he spent time in the Sinaitic Peninsula, the scene of the giving of the law. (Paul notes in Galatians 4:25 that Mt. Sinai is located in Arabia.) Rendall argues against a trip to Sinai. "Had the apostle been granted communion with God at Mt. Sinai, the name would have constituted too effective an argument in favor of his divine commission to be suppressed here. And a journey from Damascus to Sinai was at all times dangerous, and may not have been possible in the years AD 34-37 because of the war between King Aretas IV and the Herodian armies (and later the Roman armies)." Rendall, *op. cit.*, p.155.

[83] One suggestion is that he was "working out his conception of Christianity", which seems to be contrary to the idea of Divine revelation. This commentator has never been convinced by the suggestions often read (cf. Bruce and Longenecker) that Paul's understanding developed throughout the course of his Christian life – that controversies forced his theology to crystalize and evolve as he tried to meet those controversies head on. This leaves us with a naturalistic Christianity, rather than a divinely-given Christianity. A second suggestion, made by the patristic writers and some modern writers, is that Paul went there to preach to the Gentiles who were living there (Sanday, *op. cit.*, p.24).

[84] Root, *ibid.*

ly into the work of teaching the faith he had received by revelation.   But he now was on the receiving end of the persecution and he barely escaped with his life (Acts 9:20-25)."[85]   According to Acts 9:24,25 and 2 Corinthians 11:31,32, Paul was driven out of the city of Damascus at this point, having to flee for his life.

We learn from 2 Corinthians 11:32 that Damascus was at this time in the possession, or under the rule, of Aretas IV, the Arabian king (9 BC-AD 40).   Aretas IV had been embroiled in a war with his western neighbor, Herod Antipas, tetrarch of Galilee and Perea (4 BC-AD 39).[86]   The most probable date of Paul's return to Damascus and of his being let down through the wall in a basket would be soon after the death of the emperor Tiberius (AD 37).   At the time of Paul's escape, Aretas was called "king" (2 Corinthians 11:32).   The earliest Aretas could be called "king" would have been AD 37, the year of the death of the emperor Tiberius, who would never have allowed any vassal ruler like Aretas to call himself "king."[87]   An absence of Roman coins from the years AD 36-61 has been used to show that for these years the city of Damascus was controlled by the Nabateans.

The point of importance in all this is that there was no apostle in Damascus either at the time of Paul's conversion or when he returned.   And in Arabia there certainly was no apostle with whom it was possible for Paul to confer.   His message, therefore, came not from human authorities.   It must have come from Jesus Himself.

3.   His first visit to Jerusalem was not long enough for instruction in the gospel.   1:18-20

1:18 - *Then three years later I went up to Jerusalem to become acquainted with Cephas, and stayed with him fifteen days.*

Then three years later I went up to Jerusalem - "Then" is *epeita*.   The word is repeated three times, at 1:18, 1:21, and 2:1.[88]   It singles out the three important times in Paul's life when he not only was in Jerusalem but also could have had opportunity to "consult" with one or more of the original apostles of Jesus.   "Three years later" apparently means three

---

[85] Root, *ibid.*

[86] The cause leading to the war was an insult offered to his family some years earlier when Antipas divorced Aretas' daughter so as to be free to marry Herodias (Josephus, *Ant.* 18.109-115).

[87] The principate of Gaius Caligula (AD 37-41), who re-established a system of client-kings in that part of the world, provides the setting for 2 Corinthians 11:32ff, where Aretas is called "king." Bruce, *op. cit.*, p.96.

[88] Paul's use of *epeita* suggests he is giving a careful chronology of events. In these three *epeita* statements, Paul is paying particular attention to his contacts with the Jerusalem leaders. The *epeita* statements assure his readers there are no gaps in his account of contact or consultation with the Jerusalem apostles.

years after Paul's call to become an apostle.[89]   The Judaizers have apparently been claiming that Paul was dependent on and subordinate to the Jerusalem apostles.   Paul's rebuttal to that claim is to lay out an account of his life since Christ stopped him on the way to Damascus to call him to be the apostle to the Gentiles.   The visit alluded to here in verse 18 is described in detail in Acts 9:26-30.   On this occasion the Christians at Jerusalem were afraid of him.   Barnabas befriended Paul and got the Christians to accept him.   But his former Jewish friends were now his mortal foes.   After little more than a fortnight in the city, he was forced to flee, barely escaping with his life.   However, that visit afforded Paul an opportunity to get acquainted with some of the Jerusalem apostles.

To become acquainted with Cephas - Cephas is the apostle whom Jesus renamed "Peter."[90]   Paul here uses a word (*historeō*) that in Hellenistic Greek means "to become acquainted with;" it does not mean, as was true in Classical Greek, "to get information from."[91]   Paul would have told his story, Peter would have told his life story, and so the two apostles would have become acquainted for the first time.   Perhaps they compared their experiences of seeing the resurrected Lord (1 Corinthians 15:5, "He appeared to Cephas").   Paul has already been preaching the gospel for at least three years before he ever met Peter.   Paul no more got his gospel from Peter on this occasion than Peter got his from Paul.

And stayed with him fifteen days - Huxtable thinks Paul stayed in Peter's house at Jerusalem, or else he would have said "I stayed in Jerusalem."[92]   "Only a small portion of this time can have been actually spent in the company of Peter, as we gather from Acts

---

[89] The construction of a detailed New Testament chronology is rendered difficult by the lack of precise data.   We have no way of knowing for certain whether the "three years" are a full three years or one full year and parts of two others.   If we are correct that Paul's escape from Damascus while Aretas was "king" occurred in AD 37, then 3 years before would lead us to date Paul's call in the year AD 34.

[90] The true reading here is undoubtedly "Cephas" (P[45], P[51*], Aleph*, A, B) though some manuscripts (Aleph[c], D, E, F, G, K, L, P) have "Peter" (see the KJV).   "Cephas" is the Aramaic word for rock, or stone; "Peter" is the Greek equivalent.   "The Aramaic name Cephas is used in the New Testament only in the writings of Paul (1 Corinthians 1:12; 3:22; 9:5; 15:5; Galatians 1:18; 2:9,11,14), except for the instance when Jesus bestowed the name "Cephas" on Simon son of John (John 1:42), and in that case the Gospel writer explains the meaning of the Aramaic name by saying 'which translated means Peter.'   The more familiar Greek name Peter occurs 153 times in the New Testament, but only twice is used by Paul (Galatians 2:7,8)" (Kent, *op. cit.*, p.45).

[91] For the Hellenistic usage and meaning "to become acquainted" see Josephus, *Wars* 6.81; Plutarch, *Theseus* 30, *Pompey* 40, Epictetus, *Diss.* 1.14.28; 3.7.1.   (See Wm. Arndt and F.W. Gingrich, *A Greek English Lexicon of the New Testament* [Chicago: University of Chicago Press, 1957], p.383.)   If we were to give the term its Classical meaning of "to get information from," it would be a contradiction of what Paul has already affirmed at verse 12.   Nevertheless, many Roman Catholic writers (who have a mistaken notion that Peter was the first pope) prefer the Classical meaning since it allows them to have Peter taking the lead in this meeting with Paul.

[92] Huxtable, *op. cit.*, p.33.

9:28-29, where we are told Paul spent time in public disputations with the Hellenists."[93] Fifteen days would be a rather brief time for instruction if that had been what Paul was seeking. Jesus taught His disciples about three years before they were qualified; if that had been Paul's intent, how could he expect to become qualified in fifteen days under Peter's teaching? Such a comparatively short time, and not even full time during those 15 days, shows how inconceivable it is that Paul was a disciple of Peter. Neither subordination nor dependence can be drawn from this short visit.[94]

1:19 - *But I did not see any other of the apostles except James, the Lord's brother.*

But I did not see any of the other apostles - During these brief days in Jerusalem, Paul did not see even one of the other[95] twelve apostles. Consequently, he could not have received his gospel from them.[96]

Except James, the Lord's brother - It appears likely that James is here called an apostle. That would be possible as long as we do not think of him as one of the original twelve apostles. James was called "the Lord's brother" to distinguish him from James the son of Zebedee, and from one of the original apostles who was known as "James the less," a.k.a. "James the son of Alphaeus" (Mark 15:40; Acts 1:13).

> That James is here called "the Lord's brother" because he sprang from the same womb as did Jesus, according to the latter's human nature, would seem to follow naturally from such passages as Matthew 13:55,56 and Mark 6:3, where the names of the other brothers are also mentioned, and the presence of sisters is also indicated. The burden of proof rests en-

---

[93] Sanday, *op. cit.*, p.25.

[94] Assuming the Pauline authorship of Hebrews, we can affirm that Paul acknowledges his gospel was "confirmed" by those who personally witnessed Jesus' ministry (Hebrews 2:4). Thus, when Paul visits with Peter, we could picture Peter telling Paul of his personal time with Jesus, and Peter's account would match exactly the revelation of Jesus that Paul had received while in Arabia. It is not that Paul learned details from Peter that he didn't already know about Jesus life and message. It is rather that the account Peter gave matched exactly what Paul already knew. Whatever happened at that visit, Paul insists that his gospel did not come from men, not even Peter!

[95] In a long note on *heteros* ("other," the word used here) and *allos* ("another," see notes at Galatians 1;6,7), Burton shows that the distinction usually made between the two words – differentiation v. simple enumeration – wasn't always observed. About 1 out of every 8 times *heteros* is used it means simple enumeration, not differentiation. Burton argues that here it is simple enumeration. E.D. Burton, *A Critical and Exegetical Commentary on the Epistle to the Galatians* (Edinburgh: T&T Clark, 1959), p.420-21.

[96] The charge is sometimes made that Galatians 1:19 and Acts 9:26-29 are in hopeless conflict. Luke's statement in Acts that Paul was brought "to the apostles" (plural) does not conflict with Paul's own declaration here in Galatians 1:19, for we have plural "apostles" (plural) if we treat James the Lord's brother as an apostle.

tirely on those who defend the idea that "brother," as used here, means *step-brother* (son of Joseph by an earlier marriage) or *cousin*.[97]

During much of Jesus' ministry, his half-brothers were unbelievers (John 7:5). Someone who did not believe on Him could hardly be one of his original apostles. But then Jesus made a post-resurrection appearance to James (1 Corinthians 15:7) and he and the rest of the family soon became involved with the believers who lived in Jerusalem (Acts 1:14). We may picture Jesus commissioning him to be an apostle sometime between His resurrection and the departure of Peter from Jerusalem (Acts 12:17). His holding the office of an apostle of Jesus would explain how James is the recognized leader at Jerusalem.[98] He served in that capacity until he was martyred in AD 62 as a result of a persecution against the church led by Annas the high priest. There is not a hint of any clash between Paul and James. Judaizers cannot claim James as being on their side, in any actuality.

1:20 - *(Now in what I am writing to you, I assure you before God that I am not lying.)*

(Now in what I am writing to you - He has been writing about seeing only Peter and James at Jerusalem on this visit three years after his call to be an apostle. He is giving evidence that he had not learned his gospel from Jesus' original apostles, nor received his commission from them. Knowing that this presentation of the facts is likely to be challenged in the future, if indeed it has not already been told differently to the Galatians

---

[97] Hendriksen, *op. cit.*, p.62. The New Testament speaks of several persons named James. Concerning the problem of the identification of this James, and the question of his relation to Jesus, see the special study at Acts 1:14, entitled "The Brethren of the Lord," in the author's *New Testament History: Acts.* Lightfoot (*Galatians*, p.252-291) also has a study on the "The Brethren of the Lord." He calls the three principal views the Epiphanian, the Helvidian, and the Hieronymian. The so-called Helvidian view, that James, being the son of Joseph and Mary, is an actual half-brother of Jesus, is the correct view in this commentator's judgment.

[98] In comments offered at Galatians 1:1, a distinction between apostles of Jesus and apostles of churches was noted. A much-disputed issue of church polity lurks just under the surface here. Was there a group of sub-apostles whose position in the church was not quite as authoritative as that of the original twelve? The Restoration Movement, trying to do Bible things in a Bible way, has struggled with this issue of polity. For example, Alexander Campbell rejected any hierarchical form of church government, yet accepted the presidency of the American Christian Missionary Society, and defended his decision by appealing to the fact that James the Lord's brother could be a commissioned leader at Jerusalem, holding a leadership position other than that of apostle or prophet or evangelist or elder. (Earl I. West, *Search for the Ancient Order* (Nashville: Gospel Advocate, 1964.) The whole matter hinges both on the force of *heteros* ("other") and on whether or not "except" refers to the whole previous clause, or just to the verb. Lightfoot argued that "except" refers to the whole clause, and concluded that "James is here called an apostle, though it does not therefore follow that he was one of the Twelve" (Lightfoot, *Galatians*, p.85). The whole matter has been argued by L.P. Trudinger in *NovT* 17 (1975), p.200-202. Trudinger insisted that James is excluded from being an apostle. George Howard answered Trudinger in *NovT* 19 (1979), p.63-64, and showed that Trudinger's examples (all from classical literature) were not rightly applicable to this passage in Galatians. Howard affirmed that had Paul intended to exclude James from being an apostle, he would have used *heteros* in combination with *para* ('than') or the dative case, neither of which is the construction here in Galatians.

by the Judaizers, Paul adds a solemn affirmation.

I assure you before God that I am not lying) - The Greek simply reads, "Behold, before God I am not lying."   "Paul goes so far as to give an oath ('before God') that his testimony is true.   This is clear indication that Paul was responding to some very specific accusations made by the Judaizers."[99]   In the 1st century world, when one took an oath outside of a courtroom, it was understood in Roman law that the person was prepared to go before a Roman court to have the veracity of the statement demonstrated by witnesses.[100]   Paul is prepared to challenge the Judaizers' claims to the contrary in any court.   Paul appeals to the highest court he can think of to assure the Galatians that he is telling the truth about his apostolic authority and the source of his message.   He takes an oath before God; he is swearing as to the truthfulness of his historical review.   To make such a statement under oath, knowing the statement is false, is to invite God's judgment and wrath.

4. Christians in Judea glorified God because of what Paul was preaching in Syria and Cilicia.   1:21-24

1:21 - *Then I went into the regions of Syria and Cilicia.*

Then I went - In the corresponding narrative in Acts 22:17-21, at the end of the fifteen days in Jerusalem, the Lord appeared to Paul and told him to leave because Jews would seek his life.

> Strict chronology is not the main concern in this verse; if that were so, the correct order of the areas visited by Paul would be Cilicia and then Syria, as indicated by Acts 9:30, 11:25,26.   Actually, Paul is merely indicating that in the next period of his life he worked, not in the immediate area of Jerusalem – in Judea, where one might suppose him to have been under the authority and subject to the review of the other apostles – but far away from Jerusalem in the regions of Syria and Cilicia.[101]

Into the regions - 'Districts' or 'territories' might be a preferable translation for *klimata,* since the word pictures the areas sloping down from the mountains inland to the sea coast. (Cp. 2 Corinthians 11:10, where it refers to the coastlands of Achaia.)   Another Greek word (*chora*) is the word for "regions," the administrative subdivisions of a Roman province.

---

[99] Moises Silva, "Galatians" in the *New Bible Commentary*, edited by G.J. Wenham, et al. (Downers Grove, IL: InterVarsity, 1994), p.1211.

[100] See J.P. Sampley, *NTS* 23 [1977], p.478-82.

[101] Boice, *op. cit.*, p.436.

Of Syria and Cilicia - In Acts 9:30 Paul is sent forth to Tarsus, a city of Cilicia. In Acts 11:25-26, he is brought by Barnabas to Antioch, a city of Syria. When Paul ended his first visit to Jerusalem after his call to be an apostle, he went to places so remote that the possibility of contact with any of the original apostles is excluded. The whole of Syria became a Roman province in 64 BC. The province was bounded on the north by the Taurus Mountains, on the east by the Euphrates River, on the south by Judea/Palestine, and on the west by the Mediterranean Sea. Its capital was Antioch on the Orontes River. Cilicia lay to the north and west of Syria. Its capital was Tarsus, the birth place of Paul (Acts 22:3). At Acts 15:41, Syria and Cilicia are coupled together as forming a single region; there is only one article with two nouns connected by *kai*. Here in Galatians, we have an article before each country's name, suggesting that two geographical areas or districts are in view. Certainly the ministry in and around Tarsus was distinct from that at Antioch. One evidence, perhaps, of Paul's ministry in Cilicia is the fact that there were churches in Cilicia (Acts 15:41) to which were delivered the decrees of the Jerusalem Conference (Acts 16:4). What Paul did in these regions is signified by the words which follow. Folk in Judea were hearing news of Paul's preaching the gospel in those regions.

1:22 - *And I was **still** unknown by sight to the churches of Judea which were in Christ;*

And I was *still* unknown by sight to the churches of Judea - Rendall argues that the correct translation (of this periphrastic construction of the imperfect tense of *eimi* plus a present participle) is not "I was unknown," but "I was *becoming* unknown."[102] At the time he led the persecution against the Christians, and even at the time of his visit with Peter and James, he was a familiar figure in Jerusalem. But now at least ten years have passed since his last visit to Jerusalem, and in that time he was gradually becoming a stranger to the Christians of Judea. He was gone from the city so long that folk at Jerusalem didn't even know what Paul looked like. "Churches of Judea" would include not only the church at Jerusalem, but also those congregations outside of Jerusalem.[103] During those ten years the people of Syria and Cilicia saw a great deal of Paul, but the churches of Judea saw him hardly at all (the famine visit being the lone exception). How will the Judaizers harmonize this fact with their claim that Paul was dependent upon Jerusalem for his apostleship and message?

---

[102] Frederic Rendall, "The Epistle to the Galatians" in *The Expositor's Greek Testament*, edited by W. Robertson Nicoll (Grand Rapids: Eerdmans, 1967), V.3, p.157.

[103] This passage speaks of "churches" (plural) in Judea, and 1 Thessalonians 2:14 also speaks of "churches" (plural). In Acts 9:31 (in the better manuscripts), it speaks of "the church (singular) throughout all Judea, and Galilee, and Samaria" – i.e., all the congregations in these geographical areas are taken together as forming the one body of Christ. The use of the plural "churches" in Galatians 1:22, compared with the singular "church" at Galatians 1:13, is another evidence (see also 1:2) that Paul thought of the church in both senses, as the church universal and as a collection of local churches.

Churches ... which were in Christ - "Churches" designates groups of gathered/assembled believers in Jesus in any geographic locality. The expression is parallel to 1 Thessalonians 2:14, "the churches of God in Christ Jesus that are in Judea."[104] Recalling that the Israelites during the wilderness wanderings were called "the congregation in the wilderness" (Acts 7:38), perhaps the addition of "in Christ" was necessary to distinguish congregations of Christians from congregations of Jews.

1:23 - *but only, they kept hearing, "He who once persecuted us is now preaching the faith which he once tried to destroy."*

But only, they kept hearing - "Only" limits what was said in the previous clause. Paul may have been becoming unknown to the Judean churches by face, but they were not totally without information about him. "They were continually hearing reports of the startling change in the former persecutor."[105] One can imagine these reports were carried by visitors who came from those regions to Jerusalem for one of the feasts.

"He who once persecuted us - "Once" shows the persecuting was a thing of the past. Paul is, of course, the former persecutor now turned preacher.

Is now preaching the faith which he once tried to destroy." - "What was said about Paul in all these Judean churches? Anything derogatory? Any criticism of his gospel, or of his apostleship, or of his relation to the other apostles? Not a word. On the contrary, everyone was hearing time and again the astounding news that their one-time persecutor was preaching the very faith he at one time tried to wreck."[106] Notice carefully. What faith was it that Paul preached? The same faith the twelve preached.[107] His preaching was not a different message than the primitive apostolic faith. It was the very same faith. The Judaizer's claims that Paul was a man-pleaser who modified his message to please his

---

[104] For a people interested in calling Bible things by Bible names, what to call the church so that it has a Biblical name becomes a matter of importance. In addition to what was written earlier in footnote #61 at verse 13, it is instructive to compare various English translations here at verse 22. REB translates this "the Christian congregations in Judea," and NEB has "Christ's congregations." Moffatt renders the passage "Christian churches of Judea." RSV has "churches of Christ."

[105] Kent, *op. cit.*, p.49-50.

[106] Lenski, *op. cit.*, p.64.

[107] This is another case where "the faith" is used in the objective sense as equal to "the body of Christian doctrine." "Faith" here seems to be a synonym for the gospel. Compare Acts 6:7 where "priests became obedient to the faith." Compare Jude 3, the faith which was once for all delivered to the saints. "Paul often uses *tēn pistin* ("the faith") as a synonym for the Christian gospel (Galatians 3:23,24; also Philippians 1:27), and in Galatians 6:10 it is a descriptive phrase for Christians" (Longenecker, *op. cit.*, p.42). What is written in this verse certainly causes us to be dubious of the modern conception that to begin with in the history of Christianity there were competing faiths, and that the faith represented in the Bible is the one that won out in the end.

audience could be flatly shown to be wrong by any church in Judea which heard the report of his preaching. "The faith" Paul and the other apostles preached allows Gentiles to associate themselves with the Israel of God, without observing works of the Law, or even living by the Law of Moses.

1:24 - *And they were glorifying God because of me.*

And they were glorifying God because of me - The Judean Christians recognized Paul's message as the truth, and they were praising God for Paul's ministry and message. Instead of running down Paul as the Judaizers in Galatia did, every time the Judean churches heard news about Paul they kept on glorifying God for Paul. What is wrong with the Judaizers that they are not doing the same? The Judean Christians praised God, not because Paul preached works of the Law as the Judaizers did, but because he preached "the faith," the gospel of Christ.[108]

The autobiographical notes we've been studying here in Galatians 1 form one of the strongest arguments for apostolic authority anywhere in the New Testament.

---

[108] LeRoy Lawson asks a sobering question here, "'They praised God because of me,' Paul says of his early years of serving Christ. That raises a question for every Christian [preacher], doesn't it? Has anybody congratulated God recently because of me?" (Lawson, *op. cit.*, p.34).

5. The other apostles acknowledged Paul's gospel. 2:1-10

Summary: In chapter 1 Paul made it clear that his gospel was of divine origin, not human origin.   The subject matter of chapter 2 is slightly different.   His apostleship was independent of the original apostles, but those apostles recognized and sanctioned the message he preached.   This occurred at a time when they had to deal with the heresy now troubling the Galatian churches.

2:1 - *Then after an interval of fourteen years I went up again to Jerusalem with Barnabas, taking Titus along also.*

Then after an interval of fourteen years - This is the third time Paul uses *epeita* ("then") as he rehearses his life after his call to be an apostle.   The repetition of this adverb assures Paul's readers there are no gaps in the record of visits to Jerusalem when he might have had any contact with the Jerusalem apostles, either to learn from or to be dependent on them.[1] "From what date shall we reckon the fourteen years?   While it might be reckoned from his call to be an apostle, the phrase following, 'I went up *again*' seems to be decisive in favor of reckoning it from the visit to Jerusalem just mentioned in chapter 1."[2]   Fourteen years after AD 37 would bring us to AD 51 for the Jerusalem Conference about to be described. A review of Acts 15 informs us that Judaizers had come from Jerusalem to Antioch and had begun teaching the Christians there that "Unless you are circumcised according to the customs of Moses, you cannot be saved."   The troublemakers created no small disturbance.   The church at Antioch determined "that Paul and Barnabas and certain others of them should go up to Jerusalem to the apostles and elders concerning this issue" (Acts 15:2).

I went up again to Jerusalem - The trip talked about here in Galatians 2 is the same trip recorded by Luke at Acts 15:2, at which the Jerusalem Conference occurred.[3]   The fact

---

[1] Caution must be observed here. As indicated in the Introductory Studies, "no gaps in the record" can be appealed to as though it proved that Galatians 2:1-10 is the same as the famine visit of Acts 11:27-12:25. In the Introductory Studies, it was also indicated that it is our judgment Paul is not talking about any and every visit to Jerusalem, but visits when there was interaction of any kind between him and the original apostles of Jesus.

[2] Sanday, *op. cit.*, p.27. The decision made on this question affects one's understanding of the chronology of the book of Acts and especially the life of Paul. If we count the 14 years from Paul's call to be an apostle, AD 34, then we could date the Jerusalem Conference as early as AD 48. (For a detailed chronology of the life of Christ and the apostolic age, see the author's *New Testament History: Acts*, p.i-xxi.)

[3] See this matter covered in detail in the Introductory Studies. If we were to construe the word "again" in Galatians 2:1 with the words "with Barnabas," as a few manuscripts read, then we would have an allusion to the previous famine visit to Jerusalem, for the famine visit was the only other time we know about when both Paul and Barnabas went together to Jerusalem (Acts 11:30). Thus, we would have further confirmation of the conclusion that Galatians 2 harmonizes with Acts 15.

that the topic of chapter 2 is apostolic sanction, rather than the origin of his gospel, explains why the famine visit of Acts 11 is not referred to in Galatians. On that visit, neither was Paul taught, nor was he sanctioned. Besides, the imprisonment of Peter at the time of the famine visit, and the events involved in Peter's escape, would preclude any idea either that Paul got his gospel from Peter during that famine visit or that Peter had any opportunity to do what he is pictured doing in Galatians 2:1-10.

"This [Jerusalem Conference] visit was by no means an easy visit. Even as he writes about it, years later, there is an agitation in Paul's mind. There is a disorder in the Greek which it is not possible fully to reproduce in the English translation."[4] The Galatians knew all about this Conference and what was decided there. After it took place, Paul started on his second missionary journey, and began it by visiting the Galatian churches, delivering to them the decrees produced by the Conference (Acts 15:23-29, 16:4,5). Paul has only to remind the Galatians of the vital points of the Conference; he does not have to tell the whole story. If the Galatians had just remembered what Paul had told them then, the Judaizers certainly would have been repudiated when they came to town.

With Barnabas, taking Titus along also - Paul went up to Jerusalem "with (*meta*, 'in company with') Barnabas."[5] He and Barnabas were both apostles of Jesus (Acts 14:14). They were the two main members of the delegation which was sent from Antioch to the Jerusalem Conference (Acts 15:2). Kent urges that the verb "taking along" (*sumparalambanō*) implies Titus was taken along "in a somewhat subordinate capacity."[6] 'Taking Titus along as well,' would catch the idea. "With 'taking along' being singular, it is implied that it was Paul who took the initiative to bring Titus along to Jerusalem."[7] Titus is not named in Acts 15, though we are told that others accompanied Paul and Barna-

---

[4] See Wm. Barclay, "The Letter to the Galatians" in the *Daily Study Bible Series* (Philadelphia: Westminster Press, 1957), p.16. More will be said about the rugged grammar at verses 4,5.

[5] Barnabas appears frequently in the book of Acts. For example, in Acts 4:36,37, we are told Barnabas was a Levite who sold a tract of land and donated the proceeds to the church. Soon he became a prominent member of the Jerusalem church and later the church at Antioch. After Paul's escape from Damascus, it was Barnabas who introduced Paul to the apostles at Jerusalem (Acts 9:27). It was Barnabas who at a later date brought Paul, after Paul's stay in Tarsus and Cilicia, to Antioch (Acts 11:22-26). The church at Antioch entrusted Barnabas and Paul with famine relief to the church of Jerusalem (Acts 11:27-30). Later the church at Antioch, under the direction of the Holy Spirit, set him and Paul apart for the mission to the Gentiles that resulted in what we call Paul's first missionary journey (Acts 13:1-14:28), and the beginning of the churches in Galatia to whom this letter is written.

[6] Kent, *op. cit.*, p.54.

[7] Longenecker, *op. cit.*, p.47. Luther suggested that Paul was making clear the liberty he had in Christ: he could travel with Barnabas (a Jewish Christian) and Titus (a Gentile Christian) at the same time. (Luther's Works, 27:200).

bas to Jerusalem (Acts 15:2).[8]   The reason Paul took Titus along is best explained by Paul's desire to use him as a test case, as indicated in verses 3-5.   Being a Gentile Christian, Titus was just like the Galatian Christians.   Would works of the Law be demanded of him?   If not, then neither were works of the Law necessary for the Galatians.

2:2 - *And it was because of a revelation that I went up; and I submitted to them the gospel which I preach among the Gentiles, but I did so in private to those who were of reputation, for fear that I might be running, or had run, in vain.*

And it was because of a revelation that I went up - According to Acts 15:1-5, Judaizers came from Jerusalem to Antioch and caused a dispute in the Antioch church.   According to Acts 15:2, Paul and Barnabas opposed the Judaizers.   In an effort to learn the truth, the Antioch church sent Paul and Barnabas and certain others to Jerusalem about the question. No mention is made in Acts about any "revelation."   The question is, where does this revelation fit into the narrative?   The revelation either prompted the decision or confirmed the decision that a delegation should be sent to Jerusalem concerning the issue raised by the Judaizers.   Being an apostle, Paul could have received this revelation directly.[9]   Or a prophet like Agabus could have conveyed to the church a revelation he had just received.[10] Had the Judaizers put a spin on the Conference, arguing that at one time in his ministry Paul had been required to attend a meeting in Jerusalem, and had to submit in private to Peter, James, and John, and had proved his willingness to obey their instructions by collecting funds for the Christians in Judea?   If so, then perhaps Paul calls attention to this

---

[8] Luke does not ordinarily name those related to himself in Acts.   Ramsay suggested Titus was Luke's brother. (*St. Paul the Traveller & Roman Citizen* [Grand Rapids: Baker, 1960], p.390).   So did A. Souter, "A Suggested Relationship between Titus and Luke," *Exp.Tim.* 18 [1906-07], 285, p.335-336.   Titus' name occurs several times in 2 Corinthians (2:13; 7:6; 8:6,16,23; 12:18) written just shortly before our letter to the Galatians (cf. Introductory Studies).   This man also is the one, when he was serving as evangelist to the island of Crete, to whom the epistle to Titus is addressed (Titus 1:4,5).   He is also named in 2 Timothy 4:10.   Titus evidently was converted by Paul, for Paul calls him his own son (Titus 1:4).

Matera has an excursus entitled "Galatians and the Acts of the Apostles" (*op. cit.*, p.105-111).   He presents the current debate amongst scholars about whether Paul and Luke are contradictory in their accounts of what happened, with scholars making decisions to trust one rather than the other (since Luke, after all, wasn't there personally at the Jerusalem Conference).   Or, as Matera puts it, "Paul and Luke present the facts to suit their needs" (p.110).   What Matera presents reflects modern historiography, which arbitrarily assumes that each writer of history manipulated the account to support the bias from which each writer writes.

[9] Revelations were given to Paul in various ways: in dreams or visions (Acts 16:9; 18:9; 23:11; 27:23), in a state of trance (Acts 22:17; 2 Corinthians 12:2-4), and in other undefined modes (Acts 16:6,7; 20:22,23).   Sometimes these revelations communicated truth to the apostles (1 Corinthians 2:10; Ephesians 3:3), and sometimes they were given to encourage or give directions about a particular course of action (Acts 16:9,10; 18:9; 22:17-21; 27:23).   What particular form this revelation took is not defined. In this author's commentaries on Acts and at 1 Corinthians 2:10, we have defined revelation as "the act of the Holy Spirit making known to God-chosen messengers truths they were incapable of discovering by unaided human research."

[10] Defenders of the view that Galatians 2 is the famine visit observe that that visit was prompted by a prophecy made by Agabus (Acts 11:28).

revelation lest anyone think the trip was made because of "pressure from the apostles (or anyone else) to get his doctrine straightened out,"[11] or to be confirmed in his apostolic office by the Jerusalem apostles. Paul asserts there was no more human motivation behind this visit to Jerusalem than there was behind his call and commission to be an apostle.

And I submitted to them the gospel which I preach among the Gentiles - "Them" probably refers to the Jerusalem church generally (Acts 15:4). Elsewhere, we have proposed that there were three meetings at the Jerusalem Conference: a public one (Acts 15:4,5), a private one recorded here in Galatians 2:3ff, and a second public one (Acts 15:6-29).[12] The purpose of that second public meeting was not to hammer out a position, but rather to enable the apostles to bring the whole church into agreement with themselves. Before that second public meeting, Paul submitted[13] the gospel[14] he regularly preached[15] to the leaders, Peter, James, and John, as he will describe in the following phrases and verses here in Galatians.[16] It was Paul's "gospel ... among the Gentiles" that the Judaizers

---

[11] John MacArthur, Jr., *Liberated for Life: A Commentary for Laymen/Galatians* (Glendale, CA: Regal Books, 1976), p.28.

[12] Reese, *Acts*, p.534f.

[13] "Submitted" (*anethemēn*), when used in the middle voice as here, means to declare, communicate, refer, with the added sense that the person to whom a matter is referred is asked for an opinion (Arndt-Gingrich, Lexicon, p.61).

[14] At Galatians 1:11-12 is an explanation of how Paul uses the word "gospel." It is good news about how God has been at work in Jesus to provide salvation for lost men, the conditions on which men may share in the benefits of Christ's sacrifice on Calvary, and the world-wide scope of the message ("go into all the world and preach the gospel to every creature" [Mark 16:15 KJV]).

[15] The present tense ("which I preach" or "which I am preaching") should be noticed. The gospel which Paul had been preaching since the day he was called to be an apostle, the same gospel he preached in Syria and Cilicia, the same gospel he preached when he planted the churches in Galatia, the same gospel he had been preaching up to the time of the Jerusalem Conference, was the same gospel that he was still preaching at the time he wrote this letter to the Galatians. Matera notes that "in the letter opening of Romans, Paul summarizes his gospel as 'the gospel concerning His Son who was descended from David according to the flesh and was declared to be the Son of God with power according to the Spirit of holiness by resurrection from the dead.' 1 Thessalonians 1:9b-10 contains a summary of the message Paul brought to the Thessalonians and other Gentiles: God has raised His Son from the dead and the Son will soon return to judge the world. Therefore, turn from idols to serve the living God if you wish to be saved from the coming wrath" (Matera, *op. cit.*, p.73). 1 Corinthians 15:1-5 summarizes the gospel under four points: that Jesus died, was buried, arose, and appeared. In none of these summaries is there any word that one must keep observing the Pharisaic works of the Law such as the Judaizers were demanding. When Paul preached to people living in Gentile lands, his message was always the same. A typical example of his sermons, Paul's first recorded sermon, can be read in Acts 13:16-41.

[16] We should be careful in our comments at this place that we do not leave the idea that Paul is setting the theological agenda for the church. It was the Holy Spirit who did that, as He worked through both Paul and the twelve (Acts 15:28).

had been criticizing.   Apparently, as noted earlier, they accused Paul of watering down his message when his audience consisted of Gentiles.

But *I did so* in private to those who were of reputation - Paul seems to be speaking of two events in this verse: one when he appeared before the whole church and submitted to them the gospel which he was preaching (verse 2b), and the other when he met privately with the Jerusalem leaders (verse 2c).   It was the results of this private meeting especially which Paul wants the Galatians to know about, for those results completely refute the contentions of the Judaizers.   The Jerusalem leaders who met in private with Paul, Barnabas, and Titus, were Peter, James, and John (Galatians 2:9).   The phrase "those who were of reputation" occurs three times in this passage (verses 2,6, and 9)   The verb in each case is present tense, 'those who are [considered to be] of reputation.'   It was the Judaizers and their converts who considered Peter, James, and John to be the "pillars," i.e., those who gave stability to the church.   The repetition of this designation probably shows that Paul is quoting it from the lips of the Judaizers in Galatia.   "Who," they said, "is Paul when compared with men like James, Peter, and John?   These are the men of standing in the church."[17]

For fear that I might be running, or had run, in vain - The Greek that begins this phrase, *mē pōs*, 'lest somehow' or "lest by any means" (ASV), expresses misgiving or apprehension on Paul's part.   But for what?[18]   Paul knew the gospel message he had been preaching was precisely what had been revealed to him by revelation from Christ.   What Paul did not know was what the Jerusalem apostles have been preaching in the years since they last conferred with each other.   If indeed they have been requiring works of the Law as the Pharisees insisted they did, then Paul's ministry was all for nothing.   Folk would do what the twelve said, not what Paul taught, and Gentile liberty in Christ would be a thing of the past.   From the world of athletics Paul uses the metaphor about "running" to describe his ministry, something he had worked hard at.   The first verb is present tense[19] and speaks of Paul's ministry at present.   The second verb "run" is aorist tense and looks back at his missionary work since his call on the Damascus road.

---

[17] "Paul does not begrudge the three the honor that is bestowed upon them by the Judaizers" (Hendriksen, *op. cit.,* p.84).   Paul is not speaking of them in a disparaging sense, nor is he belittling them. That would not have helped his argument, for the point of these verses is that he and they were in complete agreement as equals.

[18] To give this phrase an interpretation that makes Paul fear lest he was mistaken about the gospel he preached "is inconceivable in view of Paul's previous insistence upon the divine source and truthfulness of his teaching" (Boice, *op. cit.*, p.439).   Yet, that is the way Tertullian interpreted it (*Adv.Marc.* i.20, v.3, iv.2).

[19] It can be either present indicative ('I am running') or a present subjunctive ('I might be running').

2:3 - *But not even Titus who was with me, though he was a Greek, was compelled to be circumcised.*

But - "But" is set squarely against the idea Paul was running in vain. Titus, the test case, proved decisively that circumcision and works of the Law were not required of Gentiles converts to Christianity.

Not even Titus, who was with me, though he was a Greek, was compelled to be circumcised - "Paul made Titus an open challenge to the Judaizers. They might have *allowed* other Gentiles who were living in distant places to remain uncircumcised."[20] But here was a Gentile right in the midst of the Jerusalem Conference! Being a "Greek" indicates he was born of Gentile parents who had not circumcised him. The case of Titus, as it was presented at the Jerusalem Conference, was exactly the situation the Galatian Christians found themselves in. They were believers in Jesus, but not keeping the traditions of the elders, nor had they submitted to circumcision. Whatever was required of Titus, therefore, is exactly what the Galatian Christians can expect to be required of themselves. The verb "compelled" seems to suggest someone had demanded that Titus be circumcised. It is likely the pressure came from the Judaizers who before the Conference had stirred up trouble at Antioch.[21] Whether it was at the first public meeting that the demand was made, or whether it had been made at Antioch before the folk ever made the journey to Jerusalem for the Conference, we are not able to ascertain. "A minor operation involving the cutting and removing of the foreskin of the male penis, circumcision was a rite of high significance to Israel,"[22] the origin of which can be traced to the covenant God made with Abraham (Genesis 17:10,11). Of course, it was not just the act of circumcision the Judaizers were interested in. To them, circumcision was the critical test, or evidence, by which one showed he had fully and unequivocally embraced the whole Pharisaic system they were trying to enforce. That's what Paul refused to do in Titus' case.[23] If the apostles in the home church at Jerusalem did not require circumcision

---

[20] Lenski, *op. cit.*, p.75.

[21] This commentator doubts (as some commentators have suggested) that it was the Jerusalem leaders who at first urged Paul to concede to the demands of the Judaizers, hoping perhaps to thus disarm the opposition.

[22] MacArthur, *op. cit.*, p.10.

[23] On the second missionary journey (AD 51-54), just after the Jerusalem Conference, Paul had Timothy circumcised (Acts 16:1-3). Is this not inconsistent? How do you explain this seeming inconsistency, especially in the light of the decision of the Jerusalem Conference against the necessity of circumcision for salvation? To a reader not fully informed as to Paul's position in regard to circumcision, it seems very strange that he circumcised Timothy so soon after refusing to do the same with Titus in Jerusalem (Galatians 2:3). Further, such a course of action as Paul took with Timothy seems to conflict with the statements of Paul in several of his epistles, especially that in Galatians 5:2-4.

The terms of the Galatians 5 passage show that Paul is contemplating one who receives circumcision in order that he may come under the system of works of the Law being advocated by the troublemakers. To cases such as Timothy's, where there was no thought of his being circumcised because it was needful for salvation, the censure written in Galatians 5:2-4 did not apply. In the case of Timothy, this was an act of expediency for the sake of peace with the Jews, and was in accordance with

of Gentile believers, how could the non-apostolic Judaizers require it of Gentiles outside of Jerusalem?

2:4 - *But* it was *because of the false brethren who had sneaked in to spy out our liberty which we have in Christ Jesus, in order to bring us into bondage.*

But *it was* **because of the false brethren who had sneaked in** - Verses 4 and 5 seem to be an elaboration of the word "compelled" introduced in verse 3.[24]   It apparently was the Pharisees ("false brethren," Galatians 2:4) at the Jerusalem Conference who were demanding Titus be circumcised.   Acts 15:5 tells us that certain ones of the sect of the Pharisees who had believed, stood up saying, "It is necessary to circumcise them, and to direct them to observe the Law of Moses."   It is the Judaizers, not the Jerusalem apostles, who are designated as "false brethren."   To all outward appearances they must have appeared to be orthodox Jewish Christians.[25]

Paul's uniform and avowed principle of conduct (1 Corinthians 9:20), "And to the Jews I became a Jew, that I might win the Jews."   Paul did all he could to win the Jews, short of compromising the gospel.

If Paul had circumcised Titus, men would have construed that as evidence of the necessity of circumcision for salvation.   No one, however, would so misunderstand the circumcision of Timothy – in fact, uncircumcision in him would have been a stumbling block, especially to the Jews.   "Circumcision was a matter of Christian liberty to Paul, 1 Corinthians 7:19.   He performed it with regard to Timothy because it would prove a help in the work" (Lenski, *op. cit.*, p.75).   Paul became all things to all men if it would help win them for Christ (1 Corinthians 9:22).   In the historical circumstances surrounding Timothy's being circumcised, no one would have understood it as indispensable to his salvation (Barnes, *op. cit.*, p.307).   The circumstances in Titus' case, however, would have been construed as meaning that circumcision was obligatory.   Paul therefore refused to so use his liberty so as to set a wrong example.   "The moment any liberty is demanded as being necessary to salvation (as circumcision in the case of Titus), it ceases to be something in the area of Christian liberty, and becomes, instead, a vital issue on which we dare not yield" (Lenski, *ibid.*).

[24] This verse, a would-be sentence which extends through verse 5, is never completed.   For those who wish to pursue this matter in detail, Hendriksen has a long footnote (#52, *op. cit.*, p.78-79) explaining some of the attempts to complete the abbreviated expression.

[25] "The designation 'false brethren' after the analogy of 'false apostles,' 'false prophets' (2 Corinthians 11:13; 2 Peter 2:1), were those who were not really brethren in Christ ... they only simulated faith in Christ" (Huxtable, *op. cit.*, p.72).   Acts 15:1 says "some men came down from Judea and began to teach the brethren" at Antioch.   It does not say the "some" were brethren.   Luke (Acts 15:5) calls them "Pharisees who had believed" yet who demanded that it was necessary to circumcise them and to direct them to observe the Law of Moses.   Does "believed" (at Acts 15:5) mean mental assent to Christianity, without actual obedience to the gospel?   Conversion usually is indicated by the verb "believed," followed by a preposition ('in' or 'on').   At Acts 13:12, the proconsul of Cyprus "believed."   Does that mean converted, or simply gave mental assent?   Thayer tells us, "*Pseudadelphous* is a 'lying [?] brother,' one who ostentatiously professes to be a Christian, but is destitute of Christian knowledge and piety: 2 Corinthians 11:26; Galatians 2:4."   H. Thayer, *A Greek-English Lexicon of the New Testament* (Chicago: American Book Co., 1889), p.675.   "The term 'false brothers' (*pseudadelphous*) is used only twice in the New Testament (here and in 2 Corinthians 11:26).   In each case Paul uses the term of those who are not in fact Christians, though they were pretending to be so" (Boice, *op. cit.*, p.440).

Who sneaked in - The time and place when the false teachers "sneaked in"[26] is not stated. Perhaps they slipped into the Conference at Jerusalem. Perhaps, as Luke seems to tell of the event (Acts 15:1), they sneaked into the congregation at Antioch and thus precipitated the dispute that led to the Jerusalem Conference. The antecedent of "who" is the "false brethren." *Hoitines* ("who") emphasizes a characteristic quality of the false brethren. "Sneaked in" (*pareiselthon*) has an overtone of being a traitor or a spy. They infiltrated the church, coming in by stealth. They professed to be Christians, but were really Jews of the narrowest sort (i.e., Pharisees), who only entered into the church to do dirty work.

To spy out our liberty which we have in Christ Jesus - "Spy out" translates *kataskopēsai*. In 2 Samuel 10:3, this word is used of the servants of David who, according to his enemies, had come "to search the city, to spy it out and overthrow it." Similarly, Paul characterizes what the Judaizers were doing. The false brethren clandestinely were making an effort to learn where Christianity disregarded the traditions of the Pharisees, and in these points attempt to restrict its freedom. Freedom – Christian liberty – is an important theme in Galatians (3:28; 4:22,23,26,30,31; 5:1,13), and in numerous other places in the New Testament (Romans 6:18; 8:2,21; 1 Corinthians 7:22, 9:1,19).[27] This freedom, our liberty, is described as being "in Christ Jesus." Believers have been baptized "into Christ" (Romans 6:3). In this place it is freedom from works of the Law that is the topic. Works of the Law, from which Gentile Christians are free from any obligation to observe, include circumcision, observance of the Sabbath and other Jewish special days, dietary regulations (e.g., clean and unclean), etc. Paul writes "*our* liberty" for the matter concerned the congregation at Antioch, the delegation from Antioch (Paul, Barnabas, Titus), the Galatian churches, and Gentiles the world over. In fact, "this freedom extends to Jews as well as Gentiles."[28]

In order to bring us into bondage - "The 'bondage' is, in the first instance, that of the Pharisaic traditions of the elders, and through that to the Mosaic Law, and through it the personal domination of the Jewish partisans."[29] It is spiritual slavery that is indicated by the word "bondage." It is the worst kind of slavery to be forced to try to observe all the minute traditions of the Pharisees.

---

[26] The updated NASB reads that the false brethren were "secretly brought in." Perhaps the Greek says that someone was to blame for bringing them in. Or perhaps the Greek word simply means they "sneaked in under false colors" on their own accord. (Thayer, *op. cit.*, p.487, gives both meanings for the Greek word.)

[27] The chart included in the author's *New Testament History: Acts* at Acts 15:31 helps explain the matter of Christian liberty.

[28] Matera, *op. cit.*, p.75.

[29] Sanday, *op. cit.*, p.30. There is a manuscript variation at this place, some reading *katadoulōsontai* (Textus Receptus), and some reading *katadoulōsousin*. The *-ontai* ending would picture the false teachers bringing their converts into bondage to themselves. Compare 2 Corinthians 11:20 "where Paul complains that the Corinthians too willingly accept enslavement from false apostles" (Matera, *ibid.*)

2:5 - *But we did not yield in subjection to them for even an hour, so that the truth of the gospel might remain with you.*

But we did not yield in subjection to them - "We" apparently speaks of the apostles who met in private, and "them" refers to the false brethren who were demanding that Titus and Gentile Christians be circumcised. "We did not yield"[30] indicates that from the very beginning the leaders at Jerusalem were in agreement concerning the question of whether or not Gentiles who accepted Christ were also obligated to observe the works of the Law.

For even an hour - We would say, "we didn't yield for a minute." Do the Galatians who are in the process of yielding to the demands of the Judaizers get the point?

So that the truth of the gospel might remain with you - This is the reason Paul and the others did not yield. They were thinking of (among others) the Galatian Christians who had already been evangelized.[31] "Truth" is a vivid contrast to the falseness of the false brethren (verse 4). The *"truth"* taught by the gospel is that in Christ men are *free*. "If therefore the Son shall make you free, you shall be free indeed" (John 8:36). In this context, the truth contained in the gospel is that God has provided a way of salvation for Gentile believers that does not require circumcision, or any works of the Law. That's what Paul wanted the Galatians – and all Christians – to continue to enjoy!

2:6 – *But from those who were of high reputation (what they were makes no difference to me; God shows no partiality) – well, those who were of reputation contributed nothing to me.*

But from those who were of high reputation - *De* ("but") would better be translated "and" so that we see verse 6 continuing the thought begun in verse 2, which was interrupted by

---

[30] There is a manuscript variation here, plus the grammar is broken. Both of these facts have contributed to confusion as to what Paul was actually saying. The Western text (the Old Latin version, Irenaeus, Tertullian, and Codex D) omit the words "to them" and "not even" so that the passage reads "because of false teachers ... we yielded for an hour." If "to them" is omitted it would do away with the broken grammar. If "not" is omitted the passage says that the Jerusalem apostles did make a temporary concession to the Judaizers and did circumcise Titus. The reading of the Western text has weak textual support, and the resulting meaning gives a conclusion that would contradict what Paul has just written in verse 3. It also would be hard to see how Paul could say he temporarily yielded to the demands of the Judaizers, and at the same time affirm that he always maintained the truth of the gospel.

[31] This verse strongly supports the southern Galatian destination for this letter. The readers had already been evangelized before the Jerusalem Conference. If the apostles meeting in Jerusalem had yielded to the Judaizers, the truth of the gospel would have been lost to the Galatians. Paul and Barnabas would have had to go back to Galatia and undo all that they had done. "If Titus had been circumcised, then all Gentile believers would have to do the same" (Matera, *op. cit.*, p.75).

the explanatory remarks in verses 3-5.   Verses 6-10 highlight three results of the Jerusalem Conference:

(1) The Jerusalem apostles did not add any new stipulations to the gospel Paul was preaching.
(2) The Jerusalem pillar apostles extended the right hand of fellowship to Paul and Barnabas, thereby showing they were in perfect agreement with the missionary activity and message being preached among the Gentiles.
(3) One thing the Jerusalem apostles asked Paul to do was to continue to remember the poor.[32]

As it did in verse 2, "those who were of high reputation" reflects the high esteem in which Peter, James, and John were held by the Judaizers.[33]

(What they were makes no difference to me - Paul now adds two brief, parenthetical remarks concerning the designation for the Jerusalem apostles used so pointedly by the Judaizers.[34]   This phrase is not intended to be derogatory to James or any of the twelve, as though Paul cared nothing for them or their standing.   It is the Judaizers' claims for these men (versus their deprecation of Paul) that Paul here disparages.   The Greek reads *pote ēsan*, "what they once were."   The reference is apparently to the background of the men before Jesus called any of them to be apostles.   One might draw the inference that the Judaizers had extolled the personal relationship the twelve had with Jesus when they attempted to show that Paul, who had no such relationship, was inferior to the twelve.

God shows no partiality) - By this short phrase Paul reminds the Galatians that in God's sight he and the twelve were equal in apostolic authority.[35]   The twelve were not elevated above Paul merely because they had known Jesus during His earthly ministry.   He was not inferior to the twelve because he was once a persecutor of the church and was not called

---

[32] Marcion omitted verses 6-9a.   Robert L. Johnson (*The Letter of Paul to the Galatians* [Austin, TX: R.B. Sweet, 1969], p.59) comments that verses 6-10 form one long sentence (94 words) in the Greek. Paul's style is erratic here with a number of relative pronouns, participles, and parentheses holding the sentence together.   The broken grammar as Paul writes may reflect the agitation of mind that was triggered by recalling what happened at the Conference.

[33] Boice's suggestion (*op. cit.,* p.443), that the repetition of the terms about "those who were of high reputation" reflects the fact that as far as Paul is concerned the Jerusalem apostles did not perform well in the crisis, appears to be a flawed explanation based partially (1) on the reading that implies it was the apostles who urged that Titus be circumcised, and (2) partially on verse 7, interpreted to mean that the twelve had a change of mind.

[34] Here we have a broken sentence.   In the Greek text, the first six words in this verse start the sentence, then the thought is interrupted, and the sentence is begun over again.   By putting his thoughts in a broken sentence, Paul is able to express what otherwise would have taken several statements.

[35] Acts 10:34 and Romans 2:11 call attention to some other matters in which God does not show partiality.

to be an apostle until years after Jesus' ascension.[36]   "God is able to make an apostle of whomever He will – faces, names, persons, backgrounds are not important for Him."[37]   If God doesn't play favorites, then why should the Judaizers exalt the twelve to a favorable, preferential position?   It isn't right.

– well, those who were of reputation contributed nothing to me - The dash shows the broken sentence is being resumed.   "Paul has begun this verse as if he intends to say, "From them I on my part received nothing."   But if he had finished thus, it might sound as though these men of repute tried to impart something to him."[38]   By writing a broken sentence, Paul is able to deny both that the Jerusalem apostles were superior in authority and that they tried to impart something to him.   That those apostles "contributed nothing" to Paul means they found nothing defective in Paul's gospel message.   The Judaizers' assertions to the contrary are patently false.   The apostles at Jerusalem did not advise Paul to add something to his gospel message, namely, an additional requirement that his converts from among the Gentiles must observe works of the Law.   For seventeen years Paul has been preaching the truth of the gospel.   The Jerusalem Conference confirmed that Paul's message was not a heretical message or a truncated gospel.   It was the same as the other apostles preached.

2:7 - *But on the contrary, seeing that I had been entrusted with the gospel to the uncircumcised, just as Peter* **had been** *to the circumcised*

But on the contrary - The thread of thought in verses 7-9 is this: "having seen – and having realized – they gave."   The Jerusalem leaders did the complete opposite of making any extra demands concerning Paul's message; instead, they endorsed Paul and his gospel.

Seeing that I had been entrusted - The language implies that the fact of different spheres of ministry – some to Jews and some to Gentiles – was new to them.   It does not indicate a change of mind as the result of the report given by Barnabas and Paul.   It rather speaks of coming to recognize something for the first time, of gaining a new insight.   The perfect tense verb "entrusted" speaks of a past act with present continuing results.   Jesus commissioned Paul to go to the Gentiles, and that is what Paul will continue to do.

With the gospel to the uncircumcised ... the gospel to the circumcised - This does not indicate a different content of the gospel for the Gentiles (uncircumcision) compared with

---

[36] Barnes, *op. cit.*, p.309, calls attention to the fact that Paul is saying the apostles are equal in regard to their authority.   God has not favored one above another.   The idea that Peter was pope with authority over the other apostles is erroneous.

[37] Lenski, *op. cit.*, p.83.

[38] Lenski, *ibid.*

the gospel for the Jews (circumcision). "The gospel is identical for all nations and all times."[39]   The phrase does indicate that different audiences or different nationalities may be targeted for one's particular sphere of labor.   These separations in spheres of ministry were not ironclad separations.   Paul regularly preached first in synagogues whenever he began evangelizing a new area; in fact, both Gentiles and Jews were named in his commission (Acts 9:15).   And Peter preached to Gentiles (Cornelius, Acts 10) as well as Jews, and even wrote to churches that were, perhaps, predominantly Gentile (1 Peter).

Just as Peter *had been* to the circumcised - We may supply the verb and object that are missing from the previous clause.   Peter "had been entrusted with the gospel" to the circumcised.   The circumcised are a class of people, those who are ethnically Jewish.   The reason Paul uses the name "Peter" in this verse and the next, while he uses "Cephas" elsewhere, has called forth various conjectures.   It is likely Jesus was speaking Aramaic when He gave the name "Peter" (Greek) to this apostle.   If so, Jesus said "you are Cephas."   In light of this fact, Kirsopp Lake was probably correct when he suggested that Paul "used 'Cephas' and 'Peter' indifferently, and on no fixed principle."[40]

2:8 - *(for He who effectually worked for Peter in* **his** *apostleship to the circumcised effectually worked for me also to the Gentiles),*

(For He who effectually worked for Peter in *his* apostleship to the circumcised effectually worked for me also to the Gentiles) - "Peter is not named with the idea of excluding the eleven but as representing them."[41]   "Apostleship" (*apostolē*) refers to the apostolic office.[42]   The point of this parenthetical note, with the repeated verb "effectually worked", is that God has been doing the same for Paul as He has been doing for the twelve. God worked miracles through Peter (Acts 3:6,7) and did the same through Paul (Acts 15:12).   Through both apostles the laying on of hands was the means of imparting spiritual gifts.   Both men received revelations from God (Peter in Acts 11:5-18; Paul in Acts 18:9-10 and Galatians 2:2).

---

[39] Lenski, *op. cit.*, p.86.   Paul has already emphasized there is only one gospel (1:6-9).   He will do so again later, in chapter 2, verses 11-16.

[40] Kirsopp Lake, *Earlier Epistles of St. Paul* (London: Rivingtons, 1911), p.116.   Redaction critics, who are constantly ferreting out alleged sources for the Bible writings, have suggested that the name change here reflects the fact that verses 7b and 8 were extracted from the official minutes of the Conference.

[41] Lenski, *ibid.*

[42] The only other uses of *apostolē* ("apostleship") in the New Testament are Acts 1:25, Romans 1:5, and 1 Corinthians 9:2.   The omission of "in ... apostleship" in the clause about Paul does not mean that Paul has an inferior position as compared with Peter.   Rather, the missing words in an ellipsis may be supplied mentally from the preceding clause.   Both had the same apostolic office.

2:9 - *and recognizing the grace that had been given to me, James and Cephas and John, who were reputed to be pillars, gave to me and Barnabas the right hand of fellowship, that we might go to the Gentiles, and they to the circumcised.*

And recognizing the grace that had been given to me - After several digressions and explanations, we have come to the key point being made by this rehearsal of what happened at the Jerusalem Conference. The key point is that the Jerusalem apostles did not side with the Judaizers (as the Judaizers seem to have claimed was so before the Conference), but gave formal recognition to Paul's Gentile mission and message. The participle "recognizing" is parallel, it seems, to "seeing" in verse 7. It is not implied that the Jerusalem apostles changed their minds. It rather says they have come to a new understanding of what the facts involved mean. The Greek reads "the grace," so it is not just grace in general, but to a particular divine grace, what might be called "apostolic grace."[43] The separation in the spheres of ministry was not arbitrarily assigned at some apostolic meeting. It was assigned by God Himself.

James and Cephas and John - Having spoken several times of "those who were of reputation," Paul now names them.[44] "James," whom we have already met at Galatians 1:19, is perhaps named first because he presided at the Jerusalem Conference.[45] Peter is named next though he is called by his Aramaic name "Cephas," perhaps because that is what he was commonly called in Jerusalem. Third to be named is John. This is the first time the son of Zebedee has been named in Galatians. We know of John's presence at the Jerusalem Conference only from what Paul states here. We read their two names together ("Peter and John") so often in the Scriptures[46] that we are not surprised to find them together on this occasion.[47]

---

[43] The expression "the grace that was given unto me" occurs also in Romans 12:3, 15:15 and 1 Corinthians 3:10. Compare Romans 1:5, 1 Corinthians 15:10, and 2 Corinthians 12:9. "Grace" in verse 9 corresponds to "entrusted with the gospel" in verse 7.

[44] Several things may be observed about the sequence of names. One observation is that later in church history the order of names became Peter, James and John, "though the reading (which is found in Tertullian and Origen, and therefore must run up into the 2nd century) is too early to be directly connected with the pretensions of the papacy" (Sanday, *op. cit.*, p.32). The sequence given in our text is found in Sinaiticus, B, C, and P46, which reads "James and Peter and John." A second observation is that it has often been noted that this passage of Scripture may account for the order of the catholic epistles of James, Peter, and John in our collections of New Testament Scriptures.

[45] Scholars have hypothesized that because Peter was named before James at Galatians 1:18,19, he was recognized as the most important man in Jerusalem in AD 37. But by the time of the Conference in AD 51, since James is here mentioned first, James had become increasingly the more influential in the Jerusalem church.

[46] They are often mentioned together in the Scriptures (Matthew 17:1; Mark 3:16,17, 9:2, 10:35-45, 14:33; John 21:2; Acts 1:13, 3:1-11, 4:13-20,23, 8:14-25).

[47] One wonders where the other original apostles were. Jesus had told them to "go into all the world." The absence of their names at the Jerusalem Conference may be an indication that by AD 50 or 51 they have begun to carry out that commission. We may suppose they were away on mission trips.

Who were reputed to be pillars - This is the fourth time "reputed" has been used in this paragraph. As before, it indicates the deference granted to James, Peter, and John by the Judaizers. Since it was common practice among the Jews to use the word "pillars" in a metaphorical sense to designate the great Rabbinical teachers,[48] it looks like the Judaizers have applied to the apostles a term they were used to using of those whom they held in high esteem as teachers.

Gave to me and Barnabas the right hand of fellowship - James, Peter, and John can recognize God's handiwork when they see it. James, Peter and John took the initiative in offering their right hands to Paul and Barnabas. The Greek is plural, "right hands." Each of the three took turns clasping Paul and Barnabas by the right hand. They shook hands as equals in the work of the Kingdom.   Such an act is a symbol of mutual agreement and acknowledgment;[49] in this case, it is an acknowledgement of their mutual fellowship and partnership in the gospel.   *Koinōnia*, here translated "fellowship," could also be translated 'partners.' They were participating in a common cause. Paul never had to submit to the three pillar apostles; they were already in perfect harmony.   That is what the right hand of fellowship implied.   Perhaps this public acknowledgment took place at the close of the second public meeting of the Jerusalem Conference just after James offered his judgment concerning what should be done (Acts 15:19-21).   We can only "imagine what the Judaizers must have thought when this letter was read in Galatia, and they heard that the Jerusalem apostles took Paul's hand and said, 'we are partners.' It was all over for the Judaizers."[50]

That we *might go* to the Gentiles and they to the circumcised - When they clasp each other's hands,   the partners were agreeing to their respective fields of labor as they all con-

---

[48] Johanan ben Zakkai, a prominent rabbi, is called a "pillar" in *Bab. Berakoth* 28b. It is in *Pirke Aboth* that we find such men as Antigonus listed as a "pillar" in Pharisaism.   "Pillar" is a common Greek architectural term denoting the supporting columns in a building. The figure suggested by "pillars" (*stuloi*) states outright what being "of high reputation" (verse 6) means: columns that support the "building" of Pharisaism.   "The men named were pillars indeed although the Judaizers used the expression to deny such importance to Paul" (Lenski, *op. cit.*, p.87-88).

[49] In the Western world we often "shake hands" to finalize an agreement.   So did the ancients. For example, a clay image of clasped right hands might be sent to a neighboring country as a means of asking for an alliance with that country (cp. Xenophon, *Anab.* ii-4,1; Tacitus, *Hist.* i.54; ii.8). On one occasion the Roman general Vespasian sent two tribunes to Josephus. As ordered, the tribunes offered their right hands to Josephus as a statement that Vespasian would guarantee the security of Josephus if he were to come to Vespasian's camp (*Wars* III.8.1 and *Ant.* xviii.9.3).

[50] MacArthur, *op. cit.*, p.32.

tinued to preach the truth of the gospel.[51]   Paul and Barnabas would concentrate on evangelizing Gentiles.   The Jerusalem apostles would concentrate on evangelizing the Jews in the empire.   They preached the same gospel, just to different audiences.   The Judaizers, who had appealed to the example of the Jerusalem leaders, turn out to be the ones violating the Jerusalem agreement by demanding that the Gentile converts to be circumcised.

2:10 - They *only* asked *us to remember the poor – the very thing I also was eager to do.*

***They* only *asked* us to remember the poor** – "Only" indicates there was one matter suggested by the "pillars" to which Paul and Barnabas agreed.   However, carefully observe that it had nothing to do with the content of the message he and Barnabas preached or would continue to preach.   In fact, it is not even a new activity being asked for, since the present tense participle implies "continue to remember."   This participle suggests the poor[52] at Jerusalem had already been remembered by Paul and Barnabas, and this might well point to the famine visit (Acts 11:29-30).[53]   Peter, James, and John are not begging. The Jerusalem church in her earlier years, when they had the means, was famous for its benevolence (Acts 4 and 5).   Now the Jerusalem church had needs, and Gentile Christians had the means.   There was to be no division of spheres when it comes to benevolence.

The very thing I also was eager to do - Perhaps "the transition from the plural 'that *we* should remember' to the singular 'I was eager' is significant.   Before Paul had any opportunity of filling the request, he had parted from Barnabas (Acts 15:39)."[54]   "The energy with which, in the following years, Paul organized a relief fund in his Gentile churches for their brethren in Jerusalem (1 Corinthians 16:1-4; 2 Corinthians 8:1-9:15; Romans 15:25-

---

[51] This agreed-to division of labor should not be interpreted to mean that the apostles are modifying the mission assigned to them in Jesus' Great Commission.   Both the original apostles and Paul and Barnabas will all go to "all nations," but they may well target certain ethnic groups as they go.   As noted earlier, Peter did not limit his ministry just to Palestine.   From 1 Corinthians 1:12 and 9:5 (Peter has been to Corinth) and 1 Peter 1:1, it seems clear that Peter did not limit his ministry just to the land of Israel, nor did he limit his preaching to those who were ethnically Jewish.   The churches in Pontus, Galatia, Cappadocia, Asia and Bythinia, to whom he wrote 1 Peter, were comprised largely of Gentile Christians. From 1 Corinthians 9:20-21, it also seems clear that Paul preached to Jews as well as Gentiles, though he often went to the Jew first and then to the Greek (Romans 1:16; Acts 18:5-11) since there were large Jewish colonies in most of the major cities of the Empire.   In passing, notice the beautiful picture of New Testament unity – not the theology of Paul, not the theology of Peter, not the theology of James or John. Instead, it was the theology of God, delivered by Jesus Christ, and harmoniously represented by all these apostles.

[52] "The poor" (or perhaps it should be translated "their poor") referred to are the poor among the Palestinian churches.   "*Ptōchōs* speaks of those who are economically deprived" (Matera, *op. cit.*, p.78).

[53] Acts 11 is before Acts 15, or we have no recorded example of such a ministry to the poor at Jerusalem spearheaded by Paul and Barnabas.

[54] Lightfoot, *op. cit.,* p.111.

28) is an eloquent commentary on this statement."[55]   Whether there were other acts of aid between the time of the Jerusalem Conference and the writing of Galatians we do not know.

In Galatians 2:1-10 we have seen Paul looking back on a key event in his life – a showdown with the Judaizers before the apostolic leaders of the church at Jerusalem (Acts 15). The Judaizers lost! All the apostles were in agreement, and even tried to bring the church into agreement on this matter.[56]

6. Rather than learning from the apostle Peter, Paul maintained his gospel in direct confrontation with Peter. 2:11-21

Summary: Paul's final apologetic calls attention to a time when Peter and Barnabas began to practice the very thing the Judaizers in Galatia wanted the Galatian Christians to do, and Paul corrected them!   Paul demonstrates his consistency in behavior, something he wants the Galatians to be.   When the truth of the gospel was at stake, Paul would confront even one of the original apostles. On that occasion when Paul corrected Peter, he did so not with a new doctrine, but with the very doctrine of justification by faith which he had preached to the Galatians.

a. A brief account of the incident at Antioch. 2:11-13.

2:11 - *But when Cephas came to Antioch, I opposed him to his face, because he stood condemned.*

But when Cephas came to Antioch - This is certainly the same "Cephas" who was one of

---

[55] Bruce, *op. cit.*, p.126.

[56] In verses 2 through 10, Paul has done several things: (a) He has indicated that the "false brethren" at Jerusalem had the same agenda as did the Judaizers of Galatia, and both were in opposition to the gospel of Christ.   (b) He has recognized the position and authority of the Jerusalem apostles without diminishing his own authority.   (c) He has indicated, in opposition to the exaggerated claims made about them by the Judaizers, that the Jerusalem apostles were not superior to Paul in authority.   His going to Jerusalem was in response to a revelation from God, not a request from the Jerusalem apostles to submit to them.   (d) He has decisively separated the message and practice of the twelve from the message and practice of the Judaizers.   (e) He has taken note of the fact that he and the twelve, rather than the Judaizers and the twelve, stood together.   (f) He has told us something about *freedom*, too.   There is freedom from the demands of the Judaizers concerning works of the Law.   And there is freedom to help others.

Perhaps it should be added that the issue between Judaizers and Gentile Christians involved more than simply a clash of cultures.   If the Judaizers were Pharisees who pretended to become Christians, their points of emphasis were ideologically driven, and the ideology was man-made and false.   Remember, according to Jesus' own words, they voided the Law of Moses with their traditions.   When the truth of the gospel is involved, suddenly we are no longer in the realm of opinion or Christian liberty.

the pillars at Jerusalem (Galatians 2:9).[57] "Antioch" is evidently Antioch of Syria.[58] Peter's journey from Jerusalem to Antioch was over 300 miles. Boice sets the stage for us. "For some reason[59] Peter had left the Jewish community at Jerusalem and had gone to the Gentile city of Antioch in Syria ... Whatever the reason, at Antioch Peter discovered a community of Jewish and Gentile Christians living together and, in particular, eating together in apparent disregard of Jewish dietary customs."[60] Just as he had done in Cornelius' home (Acts 11:3) years earlier, Peter does at Antioch. He joins with the other Jewish Christians in eating with his Gentile brothers and sisters in Christ. When this episode occurred is a matter of dispute.[61] We believe it belongs to a time following the Jerusalem Conference.[62] Perhaps it happened "in the interval described in Acts 15:35,

---

[57] Kent (op. cit., p.67) tells us that this identification of "Cephas" as being the apostle Peter has proven embarrassing to those who hold extravagant views about the infallibility of the apostles. So embarrassing that some early interpreters explained this "Cephas" as being some other person besides Peter – perhaps one of the seventy who had the same name (Clement, Hypotyposes, book 5, quoted by Eusebius, HE. 1.12). There is a manuscript variation here, some reading "Cephas" (Aleph, A, B, C, H, P, vg) and some reading "Peter" (D, F, G, TR, Marcion, Victorinus).

[58] Matera (op. cit., p.85) gives us some useful background information. Syrian Antioch was located in the northwest corner of the province of Syria. The third largest city in the empire, it was the capital of the province and a center of culture. Christianity was brought to Antioch by Hellenists about AD 40 (Acts 11:20-26), and it was there that Hellenists from Cyprus and Cyrene converted Gentiles without demanding circumcision. Paul ministered there in the early years of the church, and he and Barnabas were sent on the first missionary journey from this place (Acts 13:1-3). Archaeological digs were conducted here in the 1930s, and Bruce Metzger has written about them in "Antioch-on-the-Orintes" in Biblical Archaeologist 11 (1948), p.69-88.

[59] Guesses as to the reason are numerous. Perhaps because he was apostle to the Jews, he was visiting Antioch to evangelize Jews. Some, who identify the conference in Galatians 2:1-10 with the famine visit of Acts 11:29-30, suggest Peter came to Antioch seeking refuge from the persecution initiated by Herod Agrippa I after being miraculously released from prison (Acts 12:1-19).

[60] Boice, op. cit., p.445.

[61] Some, including Augustine, Zahn, Bruce, and Longenecker, place it before the Jerusalem Conference; others, including Bo Reicke [who places it at Acts 18:22,23], place it after the Jerusalem Conference. The incident at Antioch is not introduced by epeita (next in a series of events) as were the other historical events Paul has used in his defense, but rather by hote ('when'). This is what allows scholars to conjecture that this event is not related in chronological order.

[62] The vast majority of commentators treat the material in Galatians 2:11-21 as chronological, whether they see the meeting of Galatians 2:1-10 as being the famine visit (Acts 11) or the Jerusalem Conference (Acts 15). Matera (op. cit., p.88) is correct when he notes that dating the Antioch incident before the Jerusalem Conference raises as many issues as it allegedly solves. For example, do we have Judaizer problems as early as Acts 13? Modern higher critical scholars are anxious to fill in details as they attempt to reconstruct the development of early Christianity. Were there competing faiths, with the one represented in our New Testaments being the one that survived? Modern higher critical scholars are operating from the presupposition that our New Testament books contain three levels of material: they want to know how long did it take for the teachings of Jesus to be modified by the apostles, and how long did it take for the early church to modify the teachings of the apostles.

shortly before the separation of [Paul and Barnabas] and the departure of Paul on his second missionary journey (Acts 15:40-41)."[63]

I opposed him to his face - "To his face" indicates Paul's rebuke of Peter was public (see also verse 14, "in the presence of all").   "The clash between Peter and Paul at Antioch must surely rank as one of the most intriguing episodes in New Testament history.   These two dynamic leaders among Christ's apostles are in face-to-face confrontation, and one of them boldly rebukes the other in the presence of the whole church!"[64]   In verse 12, Paul explains what Peter did that was so condemnable.

Because he stood condemned - "He stood condemned" because he had done something wrong.   His conduct was glaringly wrong.   It is apparently in God's sight that Peter stood condemned.[65]

2:12 - *For prior to the coming of certain men from James, he used to eat with the Gentiles; but when they came, he* **began** *to withdraw and hold himself aloof, fearing the party of the circumcision.*

For prior to the coming of certain men from James - The explanatory "for" shows that verse 12 gives the reason why Peter was in the wrong and stood condemned before God. At Antioch, Peter behaved the same way Judaizers in Galatia were asking the Christians there to do.   The first half of this verse sets the scene; the last half tells about what Peter did and specifies why he acted as he did.   The "certain men"[66] are likely not Judaizers.[67]

---

[63] Sanday, *op. cit.*, p.33.

[64] Kent, *ibid.*   "In the 19th century these verses became a primary basis for the historical reconstruction of early church history by Baur and others of the Tubingen school.   According to this school, the gospels of Peter and Paul were in antithesis in the Hegelian sense and were synthesized into early Catholicism. This view is unsupported by the context" (Boice, *op. cit.*, p.447).   See the author's *New Testament History: Acts* (p.xxii-xxiii) for further details about Baur's theory.

[65] Longenecker (*op. cit.*, p.72) tells us that Wilckens (*TDNT* 8:568, n.51) shows the term means to "be condemned before God," and not just "be blamed" (KJV) or "in the wrong" (JB, NEB, NIV), or "self-condemned by the inconsistency of his own actions" (as Lightfoot, Burton, Bruce).   Kenneth Wuest (*Galatians in the Greek New Testament* [Grand Rapids: Eerdmans, 1944], p.70) is likely mistaken when he suggests that "stood condemned" means there was a public and official action, an adverse judicial pronouncement by the church at Antioch.

[66] The accusative plural masculine reading *tinas* ("certain men") is well-supported, being found in Aleph, A, B, C, D, G, P[46].   A few old Latin manuscripts and Irenaeus read *tina* (accusative singular masculine), "before a certain one came from James."   The plural reading perhaps became a singular because some scribe accidentally (or deliberately) dropped the sigma off *tinas*.

[67] They likely are to be distinguished from the "false brethren" of Galatians 2:4 who were members of the Pharisee sect and who had attempted under false colors to infiltrate the church.   (See Introductory Studies, "Identity of the Opponents.")

However, these new visitors who have recently come from Jerusalem to Antioch behaved just as the Judaizers insisted church members should behave when it comes to obeying Pharisaical rules about table fellowship between Jewish Christians and uncircumcised Gentile Christians. "James" (who was introduced at Galatians 1:19), being an apostle, is the leader of the church at Jerusalem (Acts 12:17). These "certain men" could be members of the congregation there, or they could be on a special mission on orders coming from James. While James may have sent these men, we doubt that James is to be blamed for the attitude of exclusiveness these visitors quickly exhibit.[68]

He used to eat with the Gentiles - In the Pharisaic view, eating with Gentiles would result in ceremonial defilement since the food served by Gentiles was not likely to be kosher.[69] Strict Jews were afraid of becoming ceremonially unclean by associating with Gentiles (see Acts 10:28). Though He was criticized for it by the Pharisees, our Lord Himself set the example of eating together with those whom the Pharisees stigmatized as sinners (Luke 15:2). In fact, during His earthly ministry, Jesus declared all foods clean (Mark 7:19). For His followers, He ended the Old Testament distinction between clean and unclean foods. In the light of Jesus' example and Jesus' teaching, it is unacceptable for a Christian to refuse to eat with another simply because of different ethnic backgrounds or from a mistaken notion of what is clean and what is not. Peter knew this. At least as long ago as the conversion of Cornelius, Peter learned not to call unclean anything that God has cleansed (Acts 10:9-23). He regularly ate with the Roman centurion while he stayed with him after Cornelius' conversion (Acts 11:3). "With the Gentiles" gives us a glimpse of the make-up of the church at Antioch. Acts 11:20-26 tells us both Jews and Gentiles were converted to Christ.   Perhaps this resulted in numerous house churches scattered all over

---

[68] We recall that at a later date, James and the Jerusalem church are still observing many of the Jewish religious practices (they all were "zealous for the Law," Acts 21:20) common in the town in which they lived (Acts 21:17-26). It would not be out of the question that the visitors from Jerusalem could have said, "We are simply asking you to do what all the folk in the church at Jerusalem do." On the other hand, there is no certain proof that the Jewish Christians in Jerusalem held themselves aloof from their Gentile brethren. In fact, at a later date, when the delegation from Gentile churches came to Jerusalem bearing the offering for the poor, we are told "the brethren [at Jerusalem] received us gladly" (Acts 21:17). There is no reason to conclude that James prompted or approved the assault against Gentile freedom at Antioch. Scrupulous as he was about observing the Law himself (as was his privilege in the realm of Christian liberty), he had taken a large part at Jerusalem in leading the congregation there into agreement with the apostles, and (unless his behavior was as inconsistent as was Peter's on this occasion) he would be the last man to sanction an evasion of the terms of the decree sent to the churches, or to encourage others to disobey them.

[69] It is most likely that the image intended to be portrayed is that of eating common meals in people's homes, or eating the love feast at the assembly of the brethren. For the love feast all the members save the poor brought their own food. Jewish folk likely brought the kosher food they were accustomed to eat. The Gentiles brought the foods they were accustomed to eat. In a sort of "basket dinner" style, all shared the food that had been brought, whether by Jews or Gentiles, and dined in groups, families together with friends. We are not convinced that eating the Lord's Supper is the thing referred to, though the love feast usually concluded with an observance of the Lord's Supper (see 1 Corinthians 11:17-34).

the city, many of them ethnically mixed. Perhaps there was one large congregation made up of both Jews and Gentiles. Whichever the setting, for a while at least, Peter has no qualms about enjoying table fellowship with Gentile Christians at Antioch. The church at Antioch understood the far-reaching implication of the *freedom* endorsed by the Jerusalem Conference. They continued to live in that freedom until these folk from Jerusalem showed up.[70]

But when they came, he *began* to withdraw and hold himself aloof - "When they came"[71] talks about the folk who came from James. Their presence led to a change of behavior in Peter. The two verbs are both imperfect tenses in the Greek, which pictures a timid and gradual withdrawal that finally ended in a complete separation from the Gentile Christians. Peter evidently at first declined some invitations to eat with Gentiles. Soon he was declining all such invitations. People saw what he was doing and his actions sent a message. It said "we Jewish Christians are more Christian than you non-Jewish Christians." That was bad.

Fearing the party of the circumcision - Peter acted as he did because he was afraid. Fear made him act against his own better convictions.[72] But who are "those from the circumcision" (as the NASB margin indicates is a literal translation of the Greek)? Was Peter afraid of the powerful Pharisees who were back in Jerusalem?[73] Was he afraid of

---

[70] One more thing needs to be called to our attention: the freedom that the Jerusalem Conference tried to promote was equally true for both Jewish believers and for Gentile believers. The Gentile Christians were free to ignore kosher-food rules, and eat with whatever Christian brothers they desired to eat. The only limitation was if their eating would cause a brother to stumble (1 Corinthians 10:23-33). The Jewish Christians were just as free to continue to observe kosher-food rules, as long as they did not by their actions demonstrate that exclusivistic and better-than-thou attitudes the Pharisee's rules promoted. In fact, had Peter chosen to eat kosher food and only with Jewish brethren, he could have still insisted he was but exercising the liberty he had in Christ. Whether he ate or didn't eat, and with whom, was in the realm of liberty.

[71] "They came" is the reading supported by A, C, D^c, it^r, vg, syr^{p,h}, cop^{sah, boh}. Some manuscripts (P⁴⁶, Sinaiticus, B, D*, F, G, 33) read "when he came"" (rather than "when they came"). Origen knew of the singular reading and supposed it meant that James himself came from Jerusalem to Antioch (*C.Cels*. ii.1). The "he came" would match the "one" who came as found earlier in this verse in P⁴⁶. See footnote #66 above.

[72] Not even apostles are sinless perfect. Before Pentecost (Acts 2), Peter is often depicted as being impetuous, and making foolish decisions and taking foolish actions. And it is often depicted that after Pentecost Peter is "rock" stable in his character. Well, here at Antioch is one place where Peter the "rock" was not so solid in his behavior! Fear (we suppose) led Peter to deny His Lord when a maid-servant challenged him while Jesus was on trial (John 18:15-18). Now it is fear again, fear of the circumcision party, which leads Peter, in a sense, to deny His Lord again.

[73] About seven years before this incident at Antioch, Peter was arrested and nearly executed at the instigation of Jews at Jerusalem (Acts 12). James, the son of Zebedee, was executed, and Peter would have been, too, but for the intervention of an angel who engineered Peter's escape from jail. Peter went into hiding (or at least got out of the country) after that incident (Acts 12:1-17). The problem with the suggestion that Peter feared the Jerusalem governing authorities is this: would the "certain men from James" (verse 12) be likely to inform the governing authorities of what Peter was doing?

the "certain men from James" who were visiting Antioch?[74] Was he afraid of the Jewish Zealots who, already as early as the mid-40s AD, Josephus tells us,[75] had begun to intimidate any Jew who had Gentile sympathies or had begun to associate with Gentiles?

2:13 - *And the rest of the Jews joined him in hypocrisy, with the result that even Barnabas was carried away by their hypocrisy.*

And the rest of the Jews joined him in hypocrisy - The "rest of the Jews" are converts to Christianity from among Jewish people in Antioch. Peter's actions, a misuse of his liberty in Christ, caused the Christian Jews at Antioch to stumble. They became co-hypocrites with Peter.[76] Neither Peter nor the Jewish Christians at Antioch believed in the validity of the dietary restrictions or in the need to not associate with uncircumcised Gentiles, but they pretended to do so apparently because they too feared the party of the circumcision.[77]

With the result that even Barnabas was carried away by their hypocrisy - "Even Barnabas" reflects Paul's thinking (before the event happened) that Barnabas was the last man from whom such conduct could be expected. Had it not been for the example of Peter and the other Jewish believers at Antioch, Barnabas would never have made such a grievous mistake.[78] He and Barnabas have been through many things together. Paul took Barnabas' defection very hard.[79] Observe that Peter and Barnabas are charged with hypoc-

---

[74] What could they do to cause Peter to be afraid? Perhaps they would report to the Jerusalem church and the church would again call him on the carpet as they did after he was found eating with Cornelius (Acts 11:1-18).

[75] Josephus, *Wars* II.8.1; *Ant.* XVIII.1.6 in *The Life and Works of Flavius Josephus,* translated by William Whiston (Philadelphia: John C. Winston Co., nd).

[76] Some have thought Paul too severe to label their behavior "hypocrisy." However, the gift of discerning of spirits would give Paul the ability to read their hearts and thus know their actions were hypocritical. But there is no real need to posit a supernatural source of information. Paul knew what Peter had done earlier in his life at Cornelius' house. He knew that Peter's behavior was at total odds with what had been affirmed at the Jerusalem Conference. Knowing by observation what Peter really believed, it was easy to see that Peter's actions were pretense intended to convey an impression he believed something else. In light of their earlier behavior (eating with Gentile Christians), the same can be said for the other Jewish Christians at Antioch.

[77] Or did the Jewish Christians follow Peter's example because of who he was?

[78] The verb "carried away" (*sunapagō*) often carries the idea of irrational action or irrational emotion.

[79] From this time on Paul and Barnabas do not appear associated together in missionary work. In fact, Acts 15:39 tells us the two separated over the matter of whether or not to take John Mark with them on the second missionary journey, but many wonder if Paul's disappointment with Barnabas' hypocrisy didn't contribute to their going separate ways. While they no longer worked together as a team, they remained friends. Whenever Paul mentions Barnabas, it is always with respect (cp. 1 Corinthians 9:6 and Colossians 4:10).

risy, not heresy. Their actions are completely inconsistent with what they taught at the Jerusalem Conference.

b. Paul's words of reprimand to Peter. 2:14-21

2:14 - *But when I saw that they were not straightforward about the truth of the gospel, I said to Cephas in the presence of all, "If you, being a Jew live like the Gentiles and not like the Jews, how is it that you compel the Gentiles to live like Jews?*

But when I saw that they were not straightforward about the truth of the gospel - What Peter was doing and the bad influence of his behavior were not immediately obvious to Paul. But when they did become obvious, Paul acted. Perhaps it was when Barnabas joined the defection that Paul became aware of what was going on. "Were not straightforward"[80] means they were not on the right road; they were not going in the straight direction the gospel pointed. As before[81] when we encountered this expression "the truth of the gospel," we are convinced the particular "truth" is the *freedom* men in Christ are to enjoy. In this context "truth of the gospel" is synonymous with freedom to eat together and share one another's food. Peter and Barnabas were acting as though the gospel did not teach that. When a man's conduct, especially in the realm of Christian liberty, becomes a stumbling block for others, he is sinning.

I said to Cephas[82] in the presence of all - "In the presence of all" points to a public assembly of the Christians at Antioch.[83] In the light of Matthew 18:15 ("If your brother sins, go and reprove him in private"), Bible expositors have wondered whether Paul should have gone to Peter privately. Perhaps Paul did go to Peter in private before rebuking him publicly. Perhaps in this case a public wrong (i.e., others in the church have been adversely affected by Peter's behavior) cannot just be corrected in private. We have no doubt that Paul's rebuke, strong and pointed as it is, was spoken "in a spirit of gentleness," just as Galatians 6:1 calls for.

---

[80] The verb (*orthopodousin*) is a compound verb derived from two words meaning "straight feet." Our modern word "orthopedics" comes from this Greek word. Peter and Barnabas were not walking with a straight step.

[81] The phrase, "the truth of the gospel," occurred earlier at Galatians 2:5.

[82] "Cephas" is attested by P[46], Aleph, A, B, C, vg., while "Peter" is how D, F, G, TR read. On Paul's use of "Peter" or "Cephas" in his letters, see notes at Galatians 1:18 and 2:7-8.

[83] "In the presence of all" reminds us of 1 Timothy 5:20, where Paul writes these instructions to Timothy, "Those [elders] who continue in sin, rebuke in the presence of all."

"If you, being a Jew, live like the Gentiles and not like the Jews - Paul words the beginning of his rebuke in the form of a question. If Peter gives a correct answer to the question, he will thereby condemn himself for his hypocritical behavior. The form of the conditional sentence assumes the truth of what is stated. Peter was a Jew by birth, but since the conversion of Cornelius, he had lived like a Gentile when he was with Gentile believers.[84] He lived with them and ate with them. He did not insist that the Gentiles acquiesce to Jewish dietary rules while he was with them. He did not hold himself aloof from them as though they weren't quite equal as Christians. Living "like the Jews"[85] pictures living like the Pharisees insisted men should live, observing clean and unclean dietary rules, and refusing table fellowship with Gentiles who are unclean because they do not observe such laws. This helps us see the reason why Paul alludes to this incident in his letter to the Galatians. Peter and Barnabas were doing the very thing the trouble-makers in Galatia wanted the Christians there to do. Peter was wrong when he did it, and the Galatian Christians likewise will be wrong if they do it.

How *is it that* **you compel the Gentiles to live like Jews?** - We might have expected the question to end with "how can you separate yourself from the Gentile Christians now?" Instead, Paul goes right to the heart of the matter by asking, 'How can you compel the Gentile Christians to Judaize?'[86] The verb "compel" is present tense and indicates the ongoing effect of Peter's behavior. Folk who saw his continuous withdrawal from Gentile believers were continually being influenced to behave in a similar manner. Of course, Peter had not been teaching such a doctrine by word of mouth, but his *actions* in changing groups with whom he ate spoke volumes. Put into words, Peter's conduct said, "If you will live like a Jew, I will be happy to join you. But if not, well, you are just a bit beneath me, and therefore I cannot join you." Paul's rebuke of Peter should have a telling effect among the Galatians, especially in regard to the Judaizers' contention of the necessity of observing Jewish customs.

2:15 - *We* **are** *Jews by nature, and not sinners from among the Gentiles;*

"We *are* **Jews by nature** - In the judgment of this commentator, the translators of the NASB were correct to include verses 15-21 in quotation marks, as though the rest of chap-

---

[84] The verb "live" is present tense, indicating continuous action.

[85] The word *Ioudaïkōs*, ("like a Jew") occurs only here in the New Testament. It comes from the same family of words that was translated "Judaism" at Galatians 1:13,14.

[86] The verb translated "to live like Jews" is *Ioudaidzein*, from the same word family as noted in the previous footnote. The verb "to Judaize" occurs in the LXX of Esther 8:17 ("Many of the Gentiles had themselves circumcised and Judaized [*Ioudaidzon*] by reason of their fear of the Jews"). *Ioudaidzein* ("to live like Jews") refers to the Pharisees' religion, what Paul will shortly identify when he writes about "works of the Law."

ter 2 contains Paul's words to Peter;[87] the comments that follow will reflect this choice.[88] "We" (in the Greek this word is emphatic, "we ourselves," indicating this may be part of Paul's reply to Peter) means "I Paul, and you Peter." "By nature" implies more than just physical birth. It means both descent and long-time practiced religious customs.[89]

And not sinners from among the Gentiles - As Paul continues his rebuke of Peter, he refers to those born of Gentile parents by using the word "sinners" in the same sense the Pharisaic Judaizers who treated others with contempt would have used the word.[90]

2:16 – nevertheless, knowing that a man is not justified by the works of the Law but through faith in Christ Jesus, even we have believed in Christ Jesus, that we may be justified by faith in Christ, and not by the works of the Law; since by the works of the Law shall no flesh be justified.

---

[87] We do not start a new point in our outline of Galatians here at verse 15. We have tried to draw the outline from the material in Galatians rather than trying to impose one on the book, e.g., the way rhetorical critics try to do. It soon becomes obvious that one's interpretation of the verses may become seriously tainted by that imposed outline if one is not extremely careful.

[88] Because of the change of pronouns from "you" in verse 14 to "we" in verse 15 and following, some interpreters believe verses 15-21 are Paul's words to the Galatians, intended to drive home the point of the rebuke to Peter as related to the situation among the Galatian churches. To whom the words are addressed is of some importance for the interpretation of several of the clauses.

Wycliffe offered four rules for the interpretation of Scripture. Pay attention to (1) who is speaking, (2) to whom, (3) for what age, and (4) for what purpose. Applying those rules to this passage: (1) Paul, the author of the letter, is speaking. He has been giving a historical account of his message and mission. (2) In verse 14, Paul has been speaking words of rebuke to Peter in front of a congregation of believers. The thoughts introduced by the pronouns "we" and "I" in the remaining verses make good sense if Paul's rebuke to Peter is continuing in those following verses. (3) Bible history is divided into three dispensations, or ages – patriarchal, Mosaic, and Christian. The words here in Galatians are for the Christian age. (4) If one has his doctrine right, there is a good possibility his behavior will be right. This is true in the matter of Peter's behavior toward his Gentile brethren.

[89] That the two expressions "by nature" and "by birth" are not convertible terms is evident from Galatians 4:8 and Romans 2:14. The former covers a wider ground than the latter. The prerogatives attaching to the natural position of a born Jew were higher than those which appertained to a circumcised proselyte. (Hendriksen, *op. cit.*, p.84.) Adam Clark has offered additional comments: "Some suppose that 'by nature' here refers to some natural corruption which every man brings into the world by inheritance from one's parents. Such a doctrine can neither be supported by this verse, nor at Ephesians 2:3. See also notes at Romans 2:14." (Adam Clarke, "Galatians" in *Clarke's Commentary* [New York: Methodist Book Concern, 1855], p.394.)

[90] Pharisees used the term to denote all who made no attempt to keep their man-made traditions. Compare Matthew 26:45 (sinners) and Mark 14:41 (sinners) with Luke 18:32 (Gentiles), and compare Luke 6:32 (sinners) with Matthew 5:47 (Gentiles, NASB). Paul does make a long argument in Romans 1:18-32 that Gentiles really were sinners in God's estimation, but that seems not to be how the term "sinners" is used here in Galatians.

"Nevertheless, knowing that a man is not justified by the works of the Law - "Knowing" is a perfect tense[91] circumstantial participle in the Greek. Its subject is "we" of verse 15. The sense of the whole sentence is, 'Because we [you and I, Peter] have known [and still do know] ... we have believed in Christ Jesus in order that we may be justified by faith.' What Paul and Peter have known that led them to transfer their allegiance away from works of the Law is that "a man (i.e., any man, be he Jew or Gentile) is not justified by the works of the Law." Here in Galatians we meet for the first time the words "justified,"[92] "works of the Law,"[93] and "faith" (faithfulness). Each of these terms requires special attention.

In the word "justified" we have one of the great words of the Pauline vocabulary. We find it in his first recorded sermon (Acts 13:38,39) and frequently in his epistles. Briefly, it is a word borrowed from the law courts.[94] It speaks of a judge passing sentence on the person standing before the bar. It means to be *declared* righteous, not *made* righteous. The opposite of 'to justify' is 'to condemn' or 'to pronounce guilty.' God is the implied judge in the passive voice verb "justified." The verb is present tense in the Greek, indicating continuing action. Perhaps it speaks of a general principle true every time God justifies a man. Perhaps it speaks of something God does several times in the course of each person's life.

"The works of the Law" is one of the great phrases of the Pauline vocabulary. At least since the Reformation, this expression "the works of the Law" has been explained as

---

[91] The fact about to be specifically stated is something the apostles have known for a long time, and still do know it. The perfect tense denotes past completed action with present continuing results.

[92] The verb *dikaioō* occurs three times in verses 15 and 16, four more times later in Galatians, and numerous times in Romans, 1 Corinthians, 1 Timothy, and Titus. The word has been explained in detail in the author's *New Testament Epistles: Romans* (Moberly, MO: Scripture Exposition Books, 1987) at Romans 1:17, 3:24,27, and 6:7. As will be detailed in a Special Study later in this volume, "Justification by Faith" is one of the major topics that led to the Reformation because the Reformers were convinced the Catholic Church had been wrongly teaching the whole doctrine of what is required of a man for salvation. In Catholic and Protestant circles, there has been a long, extensive, and complex discussion about the meaning of this word. Catholics used to insist the word speaks of *infused* righteousness (i.e., when they are justified, sinners are actually *made* righteous). Protestants insisted the word speaks of *imputed* righteousness (e.g., like when a judge *declares* someone to be not guilty). More will be said about this in the Special Study. But for now, it should be noted that the English word often used to translate the noun *dikaiosunē* (a word in the *dikaio-* stem family) is "righteousness." Thus "justified" and "righteousness" denote the same idea.

[93] In Romans 3:20 and 28, Paul uses "works of the Law," and in other places Paul simply speaks of "works" (Romans 4:2,6, 9:32, 11:6). (The language at Romans 2:15, "the work of the Law" is a different topic than "works of the Law.") See also the outline from the author's workshop at the 1996 North American Christian Convention held in Dallas, Texas, entitled "4QMMT and Paul's 'Works of Law'." That presentation is included as a Special Study at the end of these comments on chapter 2.

[94] In our literature, "forensic" is often the term used to denote something connected with law courts.

synonymous with keeping the Law of Moses.[95]   That in turn became the basis of *sola fides* ("faith only") as the condition of justification.   The idea was that nothing a man might do, even doing what God required in the Law, was a pre-condition of salvation.   Since the discovery of the Dead Sea Scrolls, and in particular with the publication of 4QMMT, it has become obvious that the Reformation definition of "the works of the Law" was erroneous.[96] Perhaps, in hindsight, we didn't need to wait for the discovery of the Scrolls.   Since Paul is rebuking Peter for his table-fellowship behavior toward Gentile believers, it looks as though the behavior of Peter and Barnabas is a typical example of "works of the Law" (i.e., Pharisaical rules[97]).   That seems to be why Paul here speaks of "works of the Law."   A guiding principle to help us understand this Scripture is this: "works of the Law" and keeping or observing what the Law of Moses required are not the same thing.[98]

But through faith in Christ Jesus - While "but" is offered for the Greek *ei mē*, it would be better to use "except."   "The sense, therefore, must be, 'A man is not justified by works

---

[95] The NIV continues this line of interpretation when it offers the translation "by observing the law" here at 2:16.   This choice of translation should immediately cause us to wonder about the contradiction this creates with Romans 2:13, which flat out states that "doers of the Law will be justified."   According to Matthew 7:21, Jesus said "he who [habitually] does the will of my Father" is the man who will enter the kingdom of heaven.   There obviously is something wrong with the translation "by observing the law" as is found in the NIV.

[96] 4QMMT is the sigla (shorthand) by which one refers to the manuscript entitled *Miqsat Ma'aseh ha-Torah* found in cave 4 at Qumran.   The Hebrew title might be translated "some significant legal rulings." The scroll contains over 20 *halakhic* rules of conduct expected by the authors of the manuscript.   The Greek equivalent of the Hebrew *Miqsat Ma'aseh ha-Torah* is *ergōn nomou* ("works of the Law").   One sentence in 4QMMT reads "the works of the Law ... will be reckoned to you as righteousness, in that you have done what is right and good before Him ..." (Craig Evans, quoted in "The War of the Scrolls," written by Kevin D. Miller [*Christianity Today* 41 {October 6, 1997}, p.44).   In this context, "what is right and good before Him" are the peculiar *halakhic* rulings contained earlier in the scroll.   Evans goes on to say, "Located in 4QMMT, the phrasing is the same as that found in Galatians, where Paul writes that Abraham's *faith* was 'reckoned to him as righteousness' (3:6).   Paul, in contrast to MMT, insists that 'by the works of the law shall no flesh be justified' (2:16)."

[97] To recall what some of these 613 rules were, remember all the times the Pharisees criticized Jesus for breaking one of their rules.   Observing such man-made rules, even if based on the Law of Moses, is not the same as "faith," which is doing what God says.   Jesus, it will be remembered, told the Pharisees that their man-made rules led them to pay no attention to what Moses taught (Matthew 15:3-6).

[98] This can be seen clearly by reading Galatians 3:5,6.   Faith, which is doing what God says, is contrasted with "works of the Law," and Abraham is given as an example of such faithfulness (vis., "Abraham believed God ...").   Galatians 3:10-12 teaches the same thing when "works of the Law" and "practices [what the Law commands]" are contrasted.   "Works of the Law" and the failure to "abide by all things written in the book of the Law" are treated as opposites.   "Works of the Law" and performing the things written in the Law of Moses are opposites.   Romans 3:20,28 also show this distinction between "works of the Law" and keeping the Law of Moses.   Failure to keep this important distinction in mind has plagued the interpretation of this passage for centuries!

[of the Law], nor is he justified at all, *except* by faith in Christ'."[99]   Peter and Paul both knew perfectly well that it was through faith, and not by works of the Law, that men are justified in God's sight.   "The term *pistis* is to be understood in terms of the Hebrew term *emuna*, which means both 'faith' and 'faithfulness'."[100]   There is a vast difference between works of the Law (i.e., man-made rules based on the Law) and "faith" (i.e., faithfulness to what God has revealed).   The words "Christ Jesus" are in the genitive case in the Greek. Literally it is "(the) faith of Christ."   The NASB translators treated the construction as an objective genitive when they rendered it "in Christ Jesus."[101]   Messiah Jesus is the object of our faith.   He is the one to whom we are to be faithful.   The next clause appears to explain this clearly.

Even we have believed in Christ Jesus, that we may be justified by faith in Christ - Stripped of all the subordinate clauses, these words form the main point of the sentence. "Even we" includes Peter and Paul, just as it did in verse 15.   "Believed in Christ Jesus" translates the verb *pisteuō* plus a prepositional phrase (*eis Christon Iēsoun*).   *Pisteuō* followed by the simple dative case denotes belief in what the person said.   *Pisteuō* followed by a prepositional phrase, as it is here, denotes an obedient faith.[102]   "Believed" is an aorist tense which points back to the time of their conversions.   "That" is a *hina* clause which can express either purpose or result.   It expresses either the purpose Peter and Paul had in mind when they believed in Christ Jesus, or it expresses the result of that belief.   What it means to be "justified" has been explained earlier in the notes on this verse. "Faith" certainly has the same meaning it did in the previous clause.   "Faithfulness" (i.e., not just a one-time belief) is a legitimate translation of *pistis*.   "By faith in Christ" (*ek pis-*

---

[99] Sanday, *op. cit.*, p.37.   The debate here is whether "except" refers to the whole previous clause, or just its principal part, namely, how a man is justified.   If "except" modifies the whole clause the sense might be, "no one is justified by the works of the Law except these works be accompanied by faith."   J.D.G. Dunn (*BJRL* 65 [1983] 112-113) defended this interpretation.   On the one hand, Dunn correctly identified "works of Law" not as good works but as circumcision and Jewish dietary rules, and explained Paul to mean that a man could be justified by "works of the Law" *if* (*ean mē*) these "badges of covenantal nomism" (as Dunn calls them) are accompanied by faith in Jesus the Messiah.   On the other hand, such an explanation of the first part of verse 16 is totally at variance with the last part of verse 16.

[100] Longenecker, *op. cit.*, p.87.   The LXX generally uses *pistis* to translate the Hebrew *emunah*.

[101] If it were taken as a subjective genitive, the phrase would denote the faith/faithfulness which Jesus Christ exercised.   A majority of the commentaries written before 1980 take the phrase as an objective genitive.   More recent writers have asserted that the phrase elsewhere in Paul (e.g., Romans 3:22,26; Galatians 2:20, 3:22; Philippians 3:9) makes eminent sense if we take it as subjective.   Thus our salvation is based on Christ's faithfulness manifested in His obedience to God by His death upon the cross.   See M.D. Hooker, "PISTIS CHRISTOU," *NTS* 35 (1989), p.321-342.   Matera (*op. cit.*, p.100-101) gives six reasons why he thinks it should be treated as a subjective genitive.   For a contrary view, see A.J. Hultgren, "The PISTIS CHRISTOU Formulation in Paul," *NovT* 22 (1980), p.248-263.   Those who treat the genitive as objective also affirm that without the cross there could be no justification pronounced by God.   The question is simply which verses are used to prove that point.

[102] Leon Morris, *The Gospel According to John* in the New International Commentary on the New Testament series (Grand Rapids: Eerdmans, 1971), p.335-337.

teōs christou) is another genitive construction. The same issue raised by the genitive construction in the previous clause carries over to this one.[103]

And not by the works of the Law - As if to drive home his point, three times Paul says "not by works of the Law." There was a time in Paul's life when he was a Pharisee, deeply involved in observing "works of the Law" (i.e., the Pharisaic traditional rules). Did Peter, too, once practice works of the Law, only to learn from Jesus that these man-made rules were not necessary to salvation? Again, notice that "works of the Law" and obedience to the Law of Moses are two different things. Having missed this distinction, Protestantism has generally interpreted passages like this one in Galatians 2:16 as proof that there is a vast difference between "faith and works" or between "grace and legalism." Having wrested the passage out of its context (which addresses the question, What are the conditions of continuing fellowship in the church? and/or Are the Judaizers correct in their exclusivistic attitudes?), interpreters then make the passage prove that any and all human actions are excluded by a salvation based on faith and grace. If we are correct in our exposition of these clauses, Protestantism has interpreted this passage incorrectly. As we have explained it elsewhere,[104] God looks for faithfulness (though not sinless perfection) in the persons who would be justified. God looks to see if individuals are doing what He said. Is he or she being faithful to what God has revealed? If so, then justification results. And justification (being declared by God to be "just" or "not guilty") is something that occurs several times during a man's lifetime.

Since by the works of the Law shall no flesh be justified - Perhaps this last phrase of verse 16 is a loose quotation of Psalm 143:2 (142:2 LXX). If so, Paul is citing the authority of Scripture to cap his argument.[105] "The future 'shall no flesh be justified' means that no case of this kind will ever occur ...."[106] In verses 15 and 16 Paul has established the common ground between himself and Jewish Christians like Peter: all have come to realize that they are justified by faith in Christ, and not by works of Law.

2:17 - *"But if, while seeking to be justified in Christ, we ourselves have also been found sinners, is Christ then a minister of sin? May it never be!*

---

[103] The change of prepositions employed by Paul perhaps should be noted. Earlier in the verse, Paul wrote *dia pisteōs* ('through faith'). After that he wrote *ek pisteōs* ('by faith') or *ex ergōn* ('by works'). Should the exegete make a sharp distinction between the two different prepositions? Perhaps what Paul means is that when one "believes in Christ" God justifies him because of the faithfulness of Christ. Christ's sacrifice on the cross atones for the sins the believer has committed.

[104] See Reese, *New Testament Epistles: Romans*, especially comments on Romans 3:20-28 and 4:1-23.

[105] In Romans 3:20, Paul quotes this Psalm in the same fashion to explain why no one is justified by works of the Law. "The sentence indeed would be an unmeaning repetition of what has gone before unless Paul were enforcing his own statements by some authoritative declaration" (Lightfoot, *op. cit.*, p.115). In fact, Psalm 143:1 talks about "God's righteousness" apart from which (verse 2) no flesh shall be justified.

[106] Lenski, *op. cit.*, p.108.

"But if, while seeking to be justified in Christ - This repeats the main point of verse 16 ("we have believed in Christ Jesus, that we may be justified by faith in Christ"), apparently to drive home a new point.[107]   "While seeking to be justified in Christ" is not limited to the time of one's conversion, for that was past for both men at the time Paul is reprimanding Peter.   It describes the continued experience of Christians.   Believers are justified over and over again during their Christian lives.   The condition God looks for is faithfulness![108]

We ourselves have also been found sinners - Just who is it that would accuse Paul and Peter of being "sinners" when they did not keep the works of the Law?   Why, the Pharisees (i.e., the troublemakers in Galatia), of course.   Now, why is it that Paul and Peter have not preached works of the Law?   Because they were delivering the truth of the gospel just as Jesus gave it to them.[109]

Is Christ then a minister of sin? - The NASB treats this as a question.[110]   The thread of thought seems to be this: 'Jesus taught us that works of the Law are not necessary for salvation.   We don't demand works of the Law, like the Judaizers do.   If we are sinners (as the Judaizers say) for not demanding such works, then Jesus must be thought of as promoting sin.   Is that possible?'

May it never be! - The Greek is *mē genoito*, literally, 'O let it never be.'   "By no means"

---

[107] Bible expositors have struggled to follow Paul's trend of thought in this verse.   Many questions arise.   Is the entire sentence a statement or is it a question?   Are all the ideas true, or is just the first clause true?   Is Paul responding to a charge made by the Judaizers, and if so, in which clause?   What is it that would make Christ a minister of sin, or a promoter of sin?   In our notes we shall give the conclusions to these questions to which we have come, without calling attention to many of the other possibilities.   For those interested in pursuing the matter in detail, E.D. Burton (*Galatians* in the International Critical Commentary series [Edinburgh: T&T Clark, 1959], p.127-130) gives an excellent summary of the ways verse 17 has been interpreted.

[108] See Romans 4:5 where "justify" is a present tense verb, and 4:24 where "(righteousness) will be reckoned" is a future tense verb.   See also Hebrews 4:13 and 1 Corinthians 4:4, where examination by God is are every-day thing.

[109] Had not Jesus declared all foods clean (Mark 7:19)?   Jesus did not observe the Pharisees' rules (*halakhot*).   Did Jesus not eat with publicans and sinners (Matthew 9:10-13)?   Did Jesus not also defend His disciples when the Pharisees objected to their actions on the Sabbath (Mark 2:23-28)?

[110] The first word of this clause in the Greek is *ara*, and that word can mean different things depending on the accent mark put upon it.   If we put a circumflex accent on it, it is a question.   If we put an acute accent on it, it is an inferential particle.   If we read the word as an inferential particle, then "May it never be!" is Peter's response to Paul's statement of the necessary implication of Peter's behavior.   The next verse then becomes Paul's affirmation that Peter's answer is correct.   Before we choose this as the possible thread of thought, it must be taken into account that every other instance of *mē genoito* ("May it never be!"), as an independent sentence, follows a question.   That is strong circumstantial evidence that in this place *ara* should be treated as a question.

(TEV), or "Perish the thought," or "God forbid!" (KJV) are attempts to catch the force of this expression. Any idea that Jesus' teachings and actions encourage others to sin is to be unequivocally rejected. Would Christ, who gave His life as a sin offering (Hebrews 9:28), encourage others to sin? Of course not!

2:18 - *For if I rebuild what I have* once *destroyed, I prove myself to be a transgressor.*

"For if I rebuild what I have *once* **destroyed** - Using "I," Paul uses himself as an illustration of the enormity of what Peter has been doing. Peter was rebuilding the works of the Law (Pharisaic rules)[111] that he had repudiated when he became a Christian (or when the Lord granted him a vision prior to the conversion of Cornelius, Acts 10:9-16). Paul says, "If I did that, I'd be a sinner!"[112]

I prove myself to be a transgressor - "Transgressor" (*parabatēs*), one of the Biblical synonyms for 'sin,'[113] does not picture a perchance breaking of one of God's laws. It speaks of a willful and deliberate violation, a deliberate crossing over the line from right to wrong. "Prove" (*sunhistēmi*) means to put something forward in clear light. If I repudiated the old Pharisaic system because Jesus directed me to, then it is quickly obvious that I am sinning if I rebuild it, for I am acting contrary to what Jesus wants.

2:19 - *"For through the Law I died to the Law, that I might live to God.*

"For - Beginning with "for," this verse assigns another reason for the use of the word "transgressor" (*parabatēs*) in the previous verse. Not only am I repudiating what Jesus taught about Christian liberty, but I also am rejecting the fact that the Law of Moses taught that such works of the Law are worthless when it comes to justification.

Through the Law I died to the Law - With the emphatic "I" (*egō*), Paul now refers to himself. The emphatic "I" implies a contrast, likely between Paul and the Judaizers. Whatever may be the case with the Judaizers (yea, and perhaps with Peter), Paul declares he is not even under the Law of Moses (let alone under the man-made works deduced from that Law).

---

[111] Commentators who treat "works of the Law" as being synonymous with keeping the Law of Moses will offer a comment here on this fashion: to go back to the Law after having become a Christian would make a man a sinner (a lawbreaker). This calls to mind the central thesis of Hebrews.

[112] In fact, as we read on, we find other enormously wrong consequences if he were to encourage the observance of Pharisaism's works of the Law. 'Not only would I be a sinner,' Paul says, 'but I'd be repudiating the truth that the Law of Moses has led me to see that works of the Law are worthless. I'd no longer be taking my orders from Christ. I'd be no longer living by faith in the Son of God. I'd be nullifying the grace of God. I'd be saying Christ died needlessly.'

[113] It is a different word from "sinner" used in verses 15 and 17, and so apparently is not used here in a pejorative sense – as repeating the language of the troublemakers – as was true in those earlier verses.

As the marginal note in the NASB tells us, there is no article in the Greek before the second occurrence of *nomos* ("Law") in this verse. It is just possible that anarthrous *nomos* here in the second half of this phrase is shorthand for "works of the Law." If so, the verse then says, "The Law of Moses taught me that such 'works of the Law' were worthless."[114]

"Died" is a powerful figure of speech. "To die to a thing is to cease to have any relation to it, so that it has no further claim upon or control over someone (Romans 6:2,10,11, 7:1-6)."[115] The time when Paul "died" was likely when he was immersed, as Romans 6:2-4 explains.

That I might live to God - Romans 8:10 explains that Paul's spirit is alive because of righteousness/justification. A man dies spiritually when he commits his first sin (Romans 7:9-11). The old Pharisaic works of the Law gave him no help to get his spirit alive. It is when a man becomes a Christian that his spirit has come to life again ("that which is born of Spirit is spirit," John 3:6). Since the Pharisaic rules void the word of God (Matthew 15:5, 6), it is very hard to "live to God" (i.e., live to please Him) when one is doing "works of the Law." But when a man's spirit is alive, that spirit can direct his behavior so that he does do what God requires. Paul says in effect, "Peter, if you submit to the Judaizers' rules, you will be living to the Pharisees, not to God."

2:20 - *"I have been crucified with Christ, and it is no longer I who live, but Christ lives in me; and the life which I now live in the flesh I live by faith in the Son of God, who loved me, and delivered Himself up for me.*

"I have been crucified with Christ - Six words are needed in English to translate two Greek words, *Christo sunestaurōmai*.[116] Paul's crucifixion with Christ corresponds to his

---

[114] We recall the fact that the last clause of verse 16 was an allusion to a passage from Psalms 143:2. When we come to chapter 3 of Galatians we will have more verses quoted from the Old Testament to show that "works of the Law" are worthless.

If anarthrous *nomos* ("law") is not shorthand for "works of the Law," then this verse says that the Law of Moses has been abrogated – just like the Law of Moses itself predicted would occur. Paul has accepted the truth that the Law of Moses is no longer a valid covenant now that Messiah has come and Calvary has happened. While it is true the Law of Moses looked forward to its own abrogation, it is difficult to follow the thread of thought in this paragraph if that interpretation is given to this verse.

[115] David Lipscomb and J.W. Shepherd, *Second Corinthians and Galatians* in the New Testament Commentaries series (Nashville, TN: Gospel Advocate Co., 1960), p.214.

[116] "The versification of the KJV has accustomed Protestants to read the words 'I have been crucified with Christ' as the beginning of verse 20, and that tradition has been followed by many modern Protestant translations. Critical editions of the Greek text, however, are almost unanimous in placing *Christo sunestaurōmai* ('I have been crucified with Christ') with the material of verse 19" (Longenecker, *op. cit.*, p.92). Its location may affect how many arguments Paul gives to show the wrong consequences of observing works of the Law. The new English Standard Version puts the clause in verse 19 and punctuates it so that "I have been crucified with Christ" is a complete sentence by itself.

death to the Law. This, of course, is metaphorical language. "What occurred in a physical way in the case of Christ, Paul predicates of himself in whom it occurred in a spiritual way."[117] The Greek verb is in the perfect tense, indicating a past completed act with present, continuing results. The thought of participation with Christ in the experiences of His redemptive work is a favorite one with Paul (Romans 6:3-8, 8:17; Philippians 3:10; Colossians 2:12-14,20-22, 3:1-4). When Christ died on the cross, He was no longer subject to temptations from the devil. His resurrected life was lived in a completely different sphere. So it is with Paul. From the time of his conversion on, the interests and allurements of the old life in Pharisaism were past. He had risen to walk in newness of life, and live that new life he would!

And it is no longer I who live - Paul has been crucified, yet he is still living. Strange language. The order of the Greek is, 'And live no longer I, but lives in me Christ.' Instead of Paul's inner man ("I") giving the orders in his life, Paul "will ever respond to Christ in thought, word, and deed."[118]

But Christ lives in me - "When Paul was alive to the Law his self (*egō*, "I") was the controlling factor in his life. But now that he is alive to God, Christ has replaced that self."[119] In Romans 8:9-11, Christ indwelling Paul and the Holy Spirit indwelling Paul are presented as interchangeable expressions. Perhaps "Christ living in me" is another way of saying the indwelling Spirit helps direct Paul's life.[120]

And the *life* which I now live in the flesh - "'Now' is his present condition as a Christian as opposed to his old life before his conversion."[121] "Life" is in italics. "That which I am living" (as the Greek reads) speaks of the whole of this life, as it manifests itself day by

---

[117] Lenski, *op. cit.*, p.115.   In Romans 6:6, Paul words it that "our old self was crucified with Him."

[118] Lenski, *op. cit.*, p.116. S. McKnight, in "The Ego and 'I': Galatians 2:19 in New Perspective," *Word & World* 20:3 (2000), p.272-280, examines Paul's statement ("I have been crucified with Christ") in the light of the new perspective on Paul and Judaism, in its context in Galatians 2:15-21, and with reference to the three contemporary interpretations offered for *egō* in 2:19 (universalistic, autobiographical, Peter and Paul as Jewish Christians).   He concludes that the interpretation of *egō* that views Paul as a representative Jewish convert to Jesus Messiah is most likely.

[119] Matera, *op. cit.*, p.96. "Christ lives in me" should not be treated as a proof text for Christian mysticism.

[120] Those who think chapters 3 through 5 unfold the terse statements (Galatians 2:15-21) of Paul's rebuke to Peter could well point to Galatians 5:18-26 to explain what "Christ lives in me" involves.

[121] Sanday, *op. cit.*, p.42.

day. "In the flesh" (*sarx*) denotes the physical, mortal body one's soul and spirit inhabit here in this world.[122]

I live by faith in the Son of God - Paul's life is now a life of faithfulness to Christ. He thinks and acts as such faithfulness guides and controls him. Not only is a man's initial justification conditioned on "faith in Christ" (2:16), so is to be the rest of his earthly life. Another way to word this is that not only is initial justification conditioned on faith, so is sanctification; not only is initial justification conditioned on faithfulness, so is continuing justification.[123] Since "Son of God" is in the genitive case, again we face the question of objective or subjective genitive.[124] This one is an objective genitive; Messiah Jesus is the object of our faith. Paul is now describing the faith he lives by. "Son of God" speaks of the deity of Christ. Paul often speaks of Jesus Christ as being God. "Christ, then, is Paul's master and Lord. Paul lives for Christ, but Christ does not control him by threats of legalistic rules. Paul is controlled and motivated by the love of Christ as demonstrated on the cross."[125]

Who loved me, and delivered Himself up for me - These two phrases qualify the "Son of God" and give a reason why Paul lives by faith in Him.[126] "Loved" and "delivered" are both participles in the Greek, and they are aorist tense. This signifies that both refer to the great, supreme act of love, the death of Christ. "Loved" says He was doing what was spiritually best for others when He went to Calvary. "Delivered Himself" tells us that Jesus' role in redemption was active. He Himself asserted as much: "I lay down my life for the sheep ... I lay down My life that I may take it again. No one has taken it away from Me, but I lay it down on My own initiative ..." (John 10:15-18). The preposition behind "for me" is *huper*, which has been explained at Galatians 1:4. Christ died 'on behalf of' Paul. His death was vicarious.

---

[122] Reformed theologians have a problem here, and at 3:3. They regularly are accustomed to use the expression "old sinful nature" to translate "flesh (*sarx*)." But they can't use "old sinful nature" here and have the passage make any sense. In this commentator's opinion, to ever translate *sarx* as "old sinful nature" is a blatant example of the translator thrusting his theology on the reader of the translation, which ought not be done.

[123] In Roman Catholic theology justification includes sanctification. In Protestant theology justification precedes sanctification. (Both have verses they can appeal to that seem to justify the position they have taken.) As one reads the commentaries, it is instructive to note how comments at this place tend to defend the theological position held by the respective commentators.

[124] See the discussion at verse 16.

[125] Mark S. Krause, *Standard Lesson Commentary*, 11-09-08, p.86.

[126] Paul words it vividly in 2 Corinthians, "the love of Christ constraineth us; because we thus judge, that one died for all ... and ... he died for all that they which live should not henceforth live unto themselves, but unto him who died for them, and rose again" (2 Corinthians 5:14,15 KJV).

2:21 - *"I do not nullify the grace of God; for if righteousness* comes *through the Law, then Christ died needlessly.*

"I do not nullify the grace of God - We have come to the final reason why Paul tells Peter he would not encourage the observance of Pharisaic works of the Law. To do so would nullify all that God has been graciously doing in His world to save men.[127] The following clause shows that Christ's death was a significant exhibition of God's grace. "Nullify" (*athetō*) means 'to make void' or 'frustrate' or 'to disdain or scorn.' That's what the Judaizers were doing.

For if righteousness *comes* **through the Law, then Christ died needlessly"** - "For" shows that the remainder of this verse gives a reason why Paul can say he does not nullify the grace of God. He would be if he demanded works of the Law from his converts. This is the first occurrence of *dikaiosunē* ("righteousness") in Galatians. It will occur again at 3:6,21 and 5:5. As we learned earlier, "justified" (verses 16,17) and "righteousness" (verse 21) are translations of the same *dikaio-* stem family of words. "Through the law" (*dia nomon*) could also be translated "through law" as the NASB margin shows. We think it means the same in this verse that it did the second time "Law" appeared in verse 19, where it was explained to be an abbreviated way of saying "works of the Law." If man-made religious rules will suffice to receive God's pronouncement of "justified," then Christ died for no reason,[128] and God has been wasting His grace.

Paul has finished his apologetic section. The incident between Paul and Peter is a reminder that the principle of justification on the condition of faithfulness is too important to compromise. No "works of the Law," no man-made rules, may be substituted as a condition. Paul now turns to his doctrinal presentation as chapter 3 begins, wherein he will unfold in no uncertain terms some of the ramifications of what he said to Peter.

---

[127] For the meaning of "grace," see notes at Galatians 1:3 and 15, and also the special study on "Call and Grace" in the author's *New Testament Epistles: Romans*, p.47-65.

[128] The Greek reads *dōrean*, "as a gift." This expression, used adverbially, comes to mean "without a cause" or "without a reason." See John 15:25, Ezekiel 6:10 (LXX), 1 Samuel 19:5 (LXX). See also Romans 3:24 and 2 Corinthians 11:7.

Nothing is said about Peter's reaction to this public reprimand.[129]   Peter apparently repented and corrected this error in his conduct, inasmuch as we hear no more about it.   It is a compliment to his Christian character that he bore Paul no ill will as they continued to serve Christ as faithful apostles (2 Peter 3:15).   Barnabas, too, must have repented, and so, we suppose, did the members of the Antioch church who had been temporarily influenced adversely by Peter's behavior.

---

[129] Scholars have debated what the lasting results of this confrontation with Peter were.   One argument is that the matter was not yet settled when Paul wrote Galatians, or he would have specifically spoken of Peter's change.   Another hypothesis is the church at Antioch sided with Peter in this matter, so that all Paul can report is what he said and the logic of his case.   Both these guesses appear to be wrong-headed, for they would tend to undermine Paul's apologetic.   If these guesses were accurate, the Judaizers in Galatia would have been able point to the lack of settlement with Peter or the actions of the Antioch church as supporting what they had been teaching all along.

SPECIAL STUDY #1

4QMMT AND PAUL'S "WORKS OF THE LAW"

INTRODUCTION

4QMMT is the sigla scholars use to refer to one of the Dead Sea manuscripts. 4Q refers to Cave 4 and to Qumran where this manuscript was found. The acronym MMT are the first letters of the Hebrew words in the name assigned to the manuscript, *Miqsat Ma'aseh ha-Torah*. Translated, the words mean "a selection of the works of the Law" or "significant works of the Law."[1] "Works of the Law" is a phrase used by Paul several times in the New Testament. It is the thesis of this Special Study that "works of the Law" is a phrase that has been misunderstood and misused in theological circles for several hundred years. The Dead Sea Scrolls may throw light on what this phrase meant in the 1st century. If so, it will help us understand what Paul was saying when he used the phrase, and also help us to correct several centuries of misuse of this language in theological discussions.

1. THE ORIGINAL DISCOVERY OF DSS MANUSCRIPTS (Cave 1). 1947

The goatherder and his stone throwing. The first Qumran cave to yield ancient manuscripts was discovered in 1947-48. The discovery of the Dead Sea Scrolls was made in cliffs near Wadi Qumran, overlooking the Dead Sea just south of Jericho. A young goatherder was throwing rocks into a cave opening and heard a "crash" sound. The Scrolls were subsequently found.

Kando the "Antiquities Dealer" and the seven scrolls. The first seven scrolls were sold by their Bedouin finders to Kando, a Christian Arab cobbler and part-time antiquities dealer. The Bedouin suggested Kando might use the old leather in his shoe business. Kando then sold four of the scrolls to Athanasius Yeshue Samuel, of the Syrian Metropolitan of St. Mark's Monastery, in Jerusalem, for $100. The other three were acquired by Eliezer Lipa Sukenik, a professor at Hebrew University, and soon became the property of the new state of Israel. Archbishop Samuel took his four scrolls to the United States where they were exhibited with much fanfare. (For example, the 24'-long Isaiah

---

[1] See Martin Abegg, "Paul, 'Works of the Law' and MMT," *Biblical Archaeology Review* 20:6 (Nov-Dec. 1994), p.52-55,82. James D.G. Dunn, "4QMMT and Galatians," in *New Testament Studies* 43 (1997), pp.147-53. M. Bachman, "4QMMT und Galaterbrief, *Ma'aseh ha-Torah* und EPГA NOMOΥ," in *Zeitschrift für die neutestamentliche Wissenschaft* 89 (1998), pp.91-113.

scroll was unrolled on a table in the Library of Congress.) Eventually, the scrolls were purchased for $250,000 and returned to Israel after Yigael Yadin saw an ad in the *New York Times*, with Yadin employing an intermediary to make the purchase of the scrolls. With the four scrolls now returned to Israel, the Shrine of the Book was constructed to house all seven.

Archaeologists conducted a professional dig at Cave 1 from February 15 to March 5, 1949. This dig turned up hundreds of fragments the Bedouins missed. The archaeologists thought there could be no other cave like it in the area. What a mistake! Most of the materials from Cave 1 were published by 1956.

2. 1952-1956 -- MORE CAVES ARE DISCOVERED!

Stories began to appear about the fabulous value of old manuscripts. The Bedouins saw a way to become rich if they could find more manuscripts.

Caves 2 and 3 were discovered in March 1952. Caves 7-10 were discovered in 1955. Cave 11 was discovered in 1956. Late in 1951, in some large caves at Murabba'at (18 km south of Qumran), the Ta'amireh Bedouin located a deposit of inscribed leather and papyrus. By January 21, 1952, archaeologists were working the same area, and did so until March 3, 1952. Then news came about the discovery of another cave at Qumran, close to Cave 1. G. Lankester Harding immediately went there on his own, and, not far from the site of the first cave, he saw a cloud of dust from high up on the cliffs which betokened the activities of the Ta'amireh "archaeologists." There was nothing he could do on his own, so, returning to his car, he drove as quickly as possible to Jericho and begged the services of two soldiers of the Arab Legion. With these, he was able to round up four of the diggers, but the rest melted away, taking with them any fragments they may have had. By March 10 Harding had set up a small archaeological camp at Qumran, and several archaeologists (i.e., Milik, de Vaux, de Contenson, Barthelemy) and 24 Bedouins were employed. They searched 275 caves and crevices, locating 39 that contained traces of habitation and household objects, like wooden poles, bronze rings, fragmentary cooking pots and lamps. The most important object discovered at that time was the Copper Scroll, discovered on March 20, 1952, in Cave 3 north of Qumran. The Copper Scroll was a list apparently of hiding places of the Temple treasure; the treasure had been hidden to keep the Romans from confiscating it if Jerusalem were destroyed by Roman armies who were attempting to put down a Jewish revolt (AD 66-70).

The Discovery of the Cave of the Wounded Partridge (Cave 4). "One evening in one of their tents, a group of Ta'amireh were discussing the recent finds which were winning world-wide fame ... and substantial income. A remark roused a venerable grey-beard from his somnolence, recalling to his mind something which might be of interest to keen cave hunters. It happened long ago, during his youth. He was following a wounded partridge when, suddenly, it disappeared into a hole not far from the ruins [of Qumran]. With great difficulty he reached his prey which had fallen into a cave, and there he collected also an old terracotta lamp and a few potsherds. The younger tribesman noted carefully the topographical details that the old man gave, equipped themselves with a bag of flour, ropes, and primitive lamps, and went down to Qumran. Using their ropes, they finally climbed into the right cave and set to sifting its earth. They had already turned over several cubic meters of earth, when suddenly their hands came upon a compact layer of thousands of [leather and papyrus] manuscript fragments. Their courage and perseverance had its reward."[2] Soon there were more Ta'amireh "volunteers" working at the "dig." "The news [of the discovery] spread also among the members of the [Ta'amireh] tribe and numerous volunteers – they say about 100 – who claimed a part in the work and in the booty. Organized in teams which planned to make joint profit, they had strictly determined sectors in the cave where they worked in sequence, resting and sleeping on the neighboring [Qumran] plateau, where [Roland de Vaux] saw their campfires. They gained access to the cave by extending a hole washed out by the rains on one side of the chamber. They made their entry very close to the original entrance, which had been filled and not recognized by them."[3]

Manuscripts for sale, but not cheap! The first two fragments were offered for sale by the Bedouins as early as September 18, 1952, at the doors of the Palestine Archaeological Museum (now Rockefeller Museum) in Jerusalem. Two days later, very early in the morning, a dozen Bedouin knocked on the door of the Ecole Archeologique Francaise and presented many manuscript fragments, which R. de Vaux immediately recognized as Qumranian on paleographic grounds. The guests confirmed his identification. They bargained all morning, until an agreement on price was reached. A few minutes later the conservator of the Palestine Archeological Museum was offered a lot of new documents.

The professional archaeologists spring into action. They "find" Caves 4,5,6.[4] It was obvious that it was necessary for archaeologists to act quickly. Harding in Amman was alerted, and he alerted the police post in Jericho, and about 3 pm the same day a few policemen came to Qumran. Seeing the soldiers, the Bedouins left the cave and fled the area. A guard was posted for the next day, with no one allowed to enter the cave. Caves

---

[2] Josef T. Milik, *Ten Years of Discovery in the Wilderness of Judea*, translated by James Strugnell (Naperville, IL: Alec Allenson, 1959), p.16-17.

[3] Roland de Vaux, *Discoveries in the Judean Desert*, VI (New York: Oxford University Press 1977), p.3.

[4] The archaeologists had earlier in 1951 and 1952 spent nearly 40 days in the Qumran area.   None of them noticed caves 4,5,6.

4 and 5 had been artificially carved out of the terrace of marl and fitted with wooden shelves.   In Cave 4, as later in Cave 11, archaeologists found regularly spaced holes in the walls where supports for shelves were once anchored.   Whether or not the cave was originally intended for use as a library, or perhaps simply a storage room, is debated. Whatever its original purpose, it appears that nearly 600 different scrolls were placed on the shelves, which over the years collapsed.   The scrolls ended up on the floor of the cave where the Bedouins and the archaeologists found them.   Early in the morning of September 22, 1952, a rescue expedition arrived in the Qumran area (including Milik, de Vaux and Harding).   By that time the Bedouins had removed more than half the contents of the cave – including many thousands of small fragments of ancient documents. However, the Bedouins had not touched the lowest strata of the cave, nor found the underground chamber.   The tribesmen had worked so neatly that only a few fragments were found in the earth they had already moved.   The rescue expedition found about 1,000 more fragments of about 100 different manuscripts.   They also located Caves 5 and 6, which the Bedouins had already been through.

The Jordanian Government enters the picture.   Realizing that the lot of fragments offered on September 20 were only a very small part of what the Bedouins had in hand, the archaeologists went to work to find enough money to purchase all that the Bedouins had. Negotiations with the Bedouins to purchase the fragments and documents they had discovered took years.   Making a long story short, over $43,000 was raised, much of it from the Jordanian government, and eventually some 15,000 fragments were purchased, with some of the purchases occurring as late as the summer of 1958.   The Bedouins requested one British pound (at the time, $2.80) for each square centimeter of manuscript with a written text on it.   The Jordanian Government selected an "International Team" made up of 8 men to examine and sort the hundreds of tiny fragments and attempt to assemble them together into their original shape and place.   The Jordanians relied on de Vaux to assemble the team since he was the local archaeologist involved in much of the digging in Jordan.   All of the original 8-member team were paleographers.   Eventually, they became able to recognize a certain scribe's handwriting style, etc.   They'd pick up a new piece, examine it, and exclaim "Here's ...." and name the scribe whose handwriting they had come to recognize.   They would then carry it across the room, and place it with the plate(s) of that scribe's work.   Old lantern slides had two plates of glass with a piece of film between; the scrollery team adapted this idea to preserve the fragments of manuscripts now in their possession.   Using plates of glass a bit over a foot square, the team members would put the matching scraps between two plates of glass, making a kind of sandwich.

Now the fragments began to trickle in to the Rockefeller Museum in East Jerusalem, 1953-59.   It is interesting to note progress in the identification and collation of the manuscripts from Cave 4.   In 1953, 70 manuscripts were identified.   By August 1955, 330 manuscripts had been isolated on 420 plates, and 80 plates remained unidentified.   By summer 1956, the number of identified manuscripts had increased to 381 on 477 plates, while only 29 plates were without attribution. By June 1960, 511 manuscripts on 620 plates were ready for study, with only 25 plates of small isolated fragments remaining. Today, there are 574 manuscripts on 752 plates, with 41 plates of miscellaneous texts and fragments which have not been identified.[5]

The fragments purchased from tribesmen generally came in boxes: cigarette boxes, film boxes, or shoe boxes, depending on the size of the fragments. The precious leather and papyrus had been delicately handled by the Bedouins, for the value of the material was all too keenly appreciated. Often cotton, wool, or tissue paper had been used by the Bedouins to separate and protect the scraps of scrolls. On occasion they even applied bits of gummed paper to pieces which threatened to crack apart or disintegrate.

3. WHAT A HUGE JIGSAW PUZZLE WE HAVE!

My grandfather had pieces of 6 different jigsaw puzzles all in one box, all intermixed. In early grade school, on rainy days when I had to stay indoors, I often remember trying to put the puzzles together. Some people get help assembling a puzzle by looking at the picture on the cover of the box. Well, there were no such pictures at granddad's! There was one helpful factor: the back side of the pieces of each puzzle had a different pattern. Before trying to assemble the puzzle, you made 6 different piles of pieces, depending on the pattern on the back of the pieces. But that alone didn't solve all the problems. Some of the pieces were damaged, making it hard to find where they fit as one tried to assemble the puzzle.

At the Rockefeller Museum, there were 15,000 pieces from nearly 600 "puzzles" all in one room! The pieces did not all arrive at the same time; they trickled in from 1953-1959. There was precious little to help the team members know which pieces went with which puzzle. Frank M. Cross has written a memorable description of the work during the 1950's. Unlike the several scrolls of Caves 1 and 11 which are preserved in good condition, with only minor lacunae, the manuscripts of Cave 4 are in an advanced state of decay. Many fragments are so brittle or friable that they can scarcely be touched with a camel's-hair brush. Most are warped, crinkled, or shrunken, crusted with soil chemicals, blackened by moisture and age. The problems of cleaning, flattening, identifying, and piecing them together are formidable.   To soften the leather fragments so they could be

---

[5] The original sigla for the manuscript fragments of 4QMMT, i.e., 4Q394-399, say something about the size of the 4Q archive. The highest numbered sigla is something like 4Q590, implying that there are 590 manuscripts of which characterizable fragments have survived.

unrolled, the scrollery team used a tobacco humidor. After a half hour or so in the humidor, the team would return to see what they could unroll, and what they had found.

The scrollery team worked from 1953-1959 – reading, sorting, arranging together pieces that seemed to belong to the same manuscripts. Fragments were placed between two 12 x 15-inch plates of glass, taped together at the edges with the fragments between. They made a card index of the words on each fragment. They took photographs of the plates of fragments. Most of this sorting, arranging and cataloging work was done by 1959. Mr. Rockefeller, who had been funding the work, died in 1960. Without money to support them, the team disbanded and went home. Each member of the team took some of the photographs with him as he went. The plan was for each man to publish the manuscripts of which he had photos.

4. ARCHAEOLOGISTS ARE USUALLY QUITE SLOW TO PUBLISH THEIR FINDINGS.

With one or two exceptions, that surely is true of the materials found in Cave 4. Because of their failure to publish, criticisms of the scrollery team members became heated in the late 1980's and early 1990's. Then some exciting things began to happen.

First came the announcement by John Strugnell and Elisha Qimron in 1985 of the existence of 4QMMT. Though recognized as being a very important manuscript, few scholars even had had an opportunity to look at it. Partly in response to increasing scholarly pressure, by 1988 the official editors had agreed to a limited release of a Preliminary Concordance of the Scrolls, all the while keeping the majority of the actual documents unpublished and under a tight seal. Next, photocopies of a preliminary edition of 4QMMT began to circulate. Z.J. Kapera, a Polish Qumran scholar, noted that every other well-known Qumran scholar had seen a copy of that photocopied edition, but none had been given to him. Shortly, one showed up in his mail – anonymously, with no return address. Kapera published it as Appendix A of Volume 1 of his *Qumran Chronicle*, Krakow No 2, December 1990, p. 1-9. This "preliminary edition" is sometimes referred to as the "anonymous copy" of 4QMMT. The team members' infuriating practice of writing articles on unpublished scrolls long before their actual publication had led to a growing impatience among Qumran scholars who were barred from access to these materials. Consequently, in the late 1980's, "underground" (i.e., "pirated," "bootlegged") copies of the manuscript now known as 4QMMT began to proliferate within the academic community. Perhaps Qimron himself made the original copies, intended for the eyes of certain trusted associates. One of them made additional copies for his friends. These bootlegged copies of Qimron's conjectures continued to be distributed.

A preliminary edition of the fragments was published, including 4QMMT. Strugnell earlier had given a copy of the Preliminary Concordance to Ben Zion Wacholder of Hebrew Union College in Cincinnati, Ohio. Wacholder enlisted the help of a student, Martin G. Abegg, to enter the concordance material into a computer, in an effort to produce a computer-generated reconstruction of the manuscripts from Cave 4. It took two years to enter the material into the computer, and then it took the computer just 15 minutes to reconstruct the first manuscript, a text of the scroll 4QMMT. Then in 1991, amidst a fanfare of publicity, the Biblical Archaeology Society (publishers of *Biblical Archaeology Review*) published the results of the computer reconstruction made by Wacholder and Abegg, under the title *A Preliminary Edition of the Unpublished Dead Sea Scrolls, The Hebrew and Aramaic Texts from Cave Four, Fascicle One* (Washington: Biblical Archeology Society, 1991). Hershel Shanks, editor of *Biblical Archaeology Review* (BAR), included in the preface a printed copy of the "anonymous" 4QMMT. Because of this publication, Qimron sued BAR for copyright infringement. (Incidentally, Qimron won the case in an Israeli court, and subsequent editions of the now 3-volume work do not have the original preface.)

Thus was broken the publication team's monopoly on access to the original text. This extraordinary accomplishment held out the possibility that the texts of other unpublished scrolls could be produced in a similar manner. Computer generated Dead Sea Scroll texts are 98% accurate. (The original concordance was based on pre-1960 versions of the manuscripts. Some of these early readings have been improved in the intervening years.)

Pictures of all the plates of fragments were made available by the Huntington Library, San Marino, California. In September 1991, shortly after the BAR publication, the director of the Huntington Library in San Marino, California announced that the library's complete set of photographs of the scrolls and fragments would be available to virtually anyone with a serious interest in them. The library had come into possession of these photographs when E.H. Bechtel provided a second set of photographs for this library, after providing the first set for the Ancient Biblical Manuscript Center in Claremont, California.

BAR then published an edition of the photographs. By June 1989, BAR had entered the campaign to free the scrolls; in fact, Hershel Shanks' efforts had been picked up by the international press. Robert M. Eisenman, who repeatedly had been denied permission to even see some of the unpublished manuscripts, was identified publicly as the scholarly point man in this struggle for publication. In September 1989, photographs of the remaining unpublished Dead Sea Scrolls began to be made available to Eisenman. At first they came in small consignments, then more insistently, until by the autumn of 1990 photographs of virtually the entire unpublished corpus – nearly 1,800 in all – had been provided to him. Eisenman and James Robinson made use of these to publish the two-volume *Facsimile Edition of the Dead Sea Scrolls,* published by the Biblical Archaeology Society. E.J. Brill was to have published the work, but about a week before it went to press, because of pressure from the International Team and the Israelis, Brill decided not to publish it.   So the Biblical Archaeology Society did the publishing, late in 1991.   The photographs, and also a microfiche edition, were then used by Eisenman and Michael Wise to make translations of 50 key documents from Cave 4, which were published in 1992 in their book *The Dead Sea Scrolls Uncovered.*

All of this has helped call 4QMMT to the attention of the scholarly world.   The importance of 4QMMT for New Testament studies was almost lost in the sectarian wrangling and legal maneuvering.   Martin Abegg helped to show its importance for New Testament studies.[6]

5.   WHAT DO WE HAVE IN 4QMMT – *Miqsat Ma'aseh ha-Torah*?

Description of the fragments.   A multi-volume series, *Discoveries in the Judean Desert* (DJD), is the official publication of many of the finds from Qumran.   In 1994, Volume 10 in the DJD series was released (Oxford: Clarendon Press), relating the finds from Cave 4.   For 4QMMT, it shows 8 plates with a total of 52 fragments.[7]   These fragments, on fairly thin leather, form two groups.   One group is in color, a light buff ranging to grey (red where stained) with its back a coarse grey.   The other group is light brown which stains to a darker or reddish brown, with a glossy back, bluish to light brown in color.   In both groups the surface is glossy; all fragments have a tendency to lose the topmost layer of surface, leaving apparently uninscribed spaces which in fact once bore writing.   There are both horizontal and vertical dry lines.   The writing, though irregular in its relation to the horizontal lines, is most frequently suspended from them.   The leather pages would have been about 6.75 inches high, with 20 lines of writing.   Column width was about 4.5 inches.   The letters are about 3/8 of an inch high.   Distance between the columns is about 1/2 inch.   There were no "rolling" or "handle sticks" at the beginning and end of the scrolls in Qumran times, only blank "handle sheets" (at both beginning and end).   When rolled up, the text itself faced inward.   Sometimes a title was written on the outside of the first layer.

Some assembly required!   When the scrolls from Cave 1 were published, little assembly was needed.   Only two of the seven scrolls were partially broken into fragments that had to be restored.   One of these fragmented scrolls was a second copy of Isaiah, but even the smallest fragments of that second Isaiah scroll could be realigned in their original position with the help of the parallel biblical text.   The second fragmented scroll from Cave 1, the so-called *Hodayot (Thanksgiving) Scroll*, presented the text of many non-biblical hymns.   To date, the *Hodayot Scroll* has not been reconstructed into one scroll since we just do not know in what order to place some of the fragments.

---

[6] Martin Abegg, "Paul, 'Works of Law' and MMT," *Biblical Archaeology Review* 20:6 (1994), p.52-55.

[7] Photos: PAM 40.618*, 41.372*, 41.375*, 41.462*, 41.594*, 41.760*, 41.780*, 42.056*, 42.472, 42.815*, 43.477, 43.492, 43.521.

The reconstruction of the 4QMMT fragments is analogous to the *Hodayot Scroll*. To date, there is no single complete manuscript of 4QMMT. There are six or more extremely fragmentary copies of MMT, with only occasional overlaps. Thus, it is necessary for scholars to arrange the fragments in an order they think suitable.[8] The problem at hand is how to reconstruct a scroll from scattered fragments, when no parallel text exists that might help in arranging its remains according to their original sequence. Qimron and Strugnell's arrangement has been circulating for some years, but we do not know for certain if the different fragments have been arranged correctly.

Some conjectural emendation is required. Lacunae (i.e., gaps in the text) must be filled; in fact, whole phrases must at times to be supplied to finish out the thoughts. The words scholars guess should be used to fill the gaps are printed in [brackets]. DJD-10 has 33 pages of notes explaining the readings now printed in the official edition of the text. In 1993 a group of experts began using multi-spectral imaging (MSI) techniques to read the manuscripts. A computer imaging technique, MSI allows the photographer to enhance contrasts between different parts of an image since each part has a unique spectral signature. MSI allows the ink and writing surface of a fragment to be presented in far greater contrast with one another than is visible to the naked eye. The results have been astonishing. A good example is a previously illegible fragment of the Genesis Apocryphon. With MSI technology, the writing on the fragment is now clearly legible; even some letters that had been covered by another piece of leather which had become stuck to the surface of the first are now legible.

The 4QMMT fragments may be paleographically dated from 50 BC to AD 50. Philip Callaway follows Frank M. Cross's dating. "According to the paleographical analyses in the official edition, 4Q394-399 [the fragments of 4QMMT] are all Herodian and date roughly in the period 50 BCE into the 1st century CE. The youngest manuscript, 4Q399, was copied in the early 1st century CE. 4Q398 is 50 or so years older. 4Q397, which presumably overlaps with 4Q398, falls much closer to the copying of 4Q399. Until it is demonstrated that these fragments are all copies from an original document that was *much* older, one should treat them as artifacts from the 'Herodian' period – i.e., mid-1st century BCE to mid-1st century CE."[9]

Structure and content of the Composite Text of 4QMMT. The composite text, a mere 135 lines, consists of 3 parts: (1) A calendar section, based on a 364-day solar year, of 21

---

[8] MMT is reconstructed from six surviving Qumran fragments (numbered 4Q394-99), none of them complete. Most scholars believe it is a letter, written in the middle 2nd century BC, from the leader of the Qumran group to the head of a larger group, of which the Qumranites were once a part. Norman T. Wright, "Paul and Qumran," *Bible Review* (Oct. '98), p.8.

[9] Philip Callaway, "4QMMT and Recent Hypotheses on the Origin of the Qumran Community," *Mogilany*, 1993 (Krakow: Enigma Press, 1996), p.28-29.

lines.   (2) A list of approximately 20 religious laws (*halakhot*), 82 lines in length.   (3) A concluding section that discusses the separation of the sect that writes MMT from those who disagree with their *halakhic* laws, of 32 lines.   Perhaps there was an opening formula (i.e., an epistolary beginning), but it has not survived.   This commentator has examined 4 different translations of 4QMMT: the "anonymous" 4QMMT, Dombrowski's annotated translation, one published in the BAR, and the official version in DJD-10.   The translations are all very close to one another.[10]

(1) The *calendar* is a typical Sadducean calendar for the dating of religious festivals. In at least one of the six manuscripts (4Q394 3-7 i), the text proper (containing *halakhot*) is copied immediately after a 364-day solar calendar of the type known from some of the Qumran scrolls, Enoch and Jubilees.[11]   Pharisees and Sadducees did not agree on which calendar to use – the lunar or the solar.   There was a famous dispute between Pharisees and Sadducees about the celebration of Pentecost "on the day after the Sabbath" (Leviticus 23:15).   Sadducees understood the verse to refer to the Sabbath after Passover.   Pharisees understood it to refer to any day after Passover, regardless of what day of the week that was.   So for the Sadducees, Pentecost always fell on Sunday.   In the Pharisee calendar, "Pentecost" could fall on any day of the week.   As long as the Sadducees were in power in the Temple, Pentecost would be observed on Sunday.   When the Pharisees came into power, Pentecost was observed on whatever day of the week happened to be exactly 50 days after Passover.   There was a similar concern within "Second Temple Judaism to ensure that the observance of the set feasts was in accord with the heavenly calendar – the result being a factional dispute between those who calculated the dates of the feasts by the sun and those who calculated by the moon (see particularly *Jub.* 6:32-35; *1 Enoch* 82:4-7; 1QS 1:14-15; CD 3:14-15)."[12]   Perhaps the point the author of MMT was making was that the Sadducean solar calendar was the only correct one to follow.

A point of contact with Galatians may be seen in this 4QMMT calendar.   There was a concern about observance of days (Galatians 4:10) in the teachings of the troublemakers

---

[10] For translations of the text, see Elisha Qimron and John Strugnell, *Qumran Cave 4 V: Miqsat Ma'ase Ha-Torah*, Discoveries in the Judean Desert 10 (Oxford: Clarendon Press, 1994).   Geza Vermes, *The Complete Dead Sea Scrolls in English* (Harmondsworth: Penguin, 1997), p.22-228.   Michael Wise, Martin Abegg, Jr., and Edward Cook, *The Dead Sea Scrolls: A New Translation* (San Francisco: Harper San Francisco, 1996), p.358-64.   Florentino Garcia Martinez, *The Dead Sea Scrolls Translated: The Qumran Texts in English* (Leiden: Brill, 1994), p.77-83.   Bruno Dombrowski, *An Annotated Translation of Miqsat Ma'aseh ha Tora (4QMMT)* (Krakow: Enigma Press, 1993).   Idem., "Miqsat Ma'aseh ha-Torah (4QMMT) in English," *Qumran Chronicle* 4/1-2 (June 1944), p.28-38.

[11] See Shemaryahu Talmon, *The World of Qumran from Within: Collected Studies* (Jerusalem: Magnes Press 1989).

[12] James D.G. Dunn, *The New Perspective on Paul* (Grand Rapids: Eerdmans, 2005), p.345.

who disturbed the Galatian churches.   That Jewish feasts were in mind is almost certain. Observance of the proper calendar day was consistent with the emphasis on "works of the Law" both in MMT and in the teaching of the troublemakers who came to Galatia.

(2) ***Halakhot*** (Heb., "how to walk") are "religious laws" one is obligated to observe. Every Jewish sect had its own list of rules, and tried to convert the other sects to their way of thinking.   In MMT a list of 20 or so rules is introduced by the word "legal rulings" (Hebrew, *Ma'asim*).   These laws involve mostly ritual purity, especially in connection with the Jerusalem temple.   Each is related to and gives a contemporary interpretation of a verse in the Torah (Pentateuch).   The following *halakhot* are extant, and are given in the order of their appearance in the reconstructed MMT text:

1.   Grain should not be brought into the temple by Gentile proselytes.
2.   A fragmentary *halakhah* about the cooking of sacrificial offerings in impure vessels
3.   A fragmentary *halakhah* about sacrifices by Gentile proselytes
4.   Cereal offerings should be eaten the day they are sacrificed, and not be left overnight.
5.   The purity of those preparing the red heifer (whose ashes were used in "holy water")
6.   Several *halakhot* concerning the purity of animal hides
7.   The place where sacrificial animals should be slaughtered and offered
8.   Concerning the slaughtering and sacrificing of pregnant animals
9.   Intermarriage with Ammonite and Moabite converts is forbidden, and so is the entry of those people into the sanctuary.
10. Concerning the non-admission of the blind and the deaf into the temple
11. The purity of the streams of liquids (*musaqoth*) poured from a pure vessel into an impure one
12. The ban on bringing dogs into Jerusalem
13. The fruit of the fourth year is to be given to the priests.
14. The cattle-tithe is to be given to the priest.
15. Several regulations about the impurity of the leper and about his isolation during the period of purification until final purification
16. The impurity of human bones
17. The intermixture of wool and linen clothing (*sha'atnez*)
18. Plowing with diverse animals (*qilayyim*)
19. Marriages between priests and common Israelite people are forbidden.

The position taken in all these "religious laws" in MMT was the position advocated by the Sadducees (as we know from the Mishna).   The position rejected was the way the "*halakhic* laws" were formulated and applied by the Pharisees.

The *halakhot* of the Pharisees is encountered in a study of the Gospels; these Pharisaic "rulings" are called the "traditions of the elders."   Such *halakhot* were "man-made rules" but were thought to be implied in Old Testament Scripture.   Some typical examples from Qumran are these:

(a) *Concerning ritual impurity after the preparation of the red heifer.*   Since touching a dead body rendered a person ceremonially unclean, the question was raised about the priest who touched the body of the heifer.   Did he become unclean and if so, how long did the uncleanness last?   The ruling was, Just until sunset of the day the animal was killed.

(b) *Concerning streams of liquid poured from pure to impure containers.*   The ruling was that the ceremonial impurity from the receiving container would travel up the stream of water being poured from a ceremonially pure container, thus defiling that container.

(c) *Concerning inter-racial marriages.*   Since in the Old Testament prohibition about intermarriage a masculine noun is used in the Hebrew, Jewish men may not marry Moabite women.   However, Jewish women may marry Moabite men.

These purity rules were so important that a lack of consensus on these *halakhot* would make it impossible for disagreeing groups to coexist within a single religious community.   The same would be true concerning which religious calendar was followed. (E.g., if Passover fell on two different days in the same year, one group would be working on the other's Passover day and thus profaning it, and vice-versa.)   The strict observance of such *halakhot* automatically precluded fellowship with every other group.[13]   The thrust of the compilation of rules in MMT is this: the MMT writer complains that the establishment (in Jerusalem) is not observing the ritual purity laws as they were meant to be observed.

(3) The words that have become the title of this work come from ***the concluding section***.   "We have written to you some of the works of the Law (*miqsat ma'aseh ha-Torah*) ... " one line reads.

(a) First, the MMT author(s) states that by accepting the rulings listed in the previous section, they have separated themselves (*parashnu*[14]) from the mainstream of the people (*rov ha-'am*), and accordingly have had to withdraw from participation in these rituals as performed by the majority of the people.

(b) There follows an affirmation that the members of the dissident group strictly observe the rules just listed in the previous section; the members are "reliable and honest."

---

[13] As a contemporary illustration about how such rules can divide people, consider the problems that worship on Saturday or Sunday can cause.   Consider also the issues raised by the mode of baptism, whether by immersion or sprinkling, and whether believers or infants are the proper subjects.

[14] The writer of MMT tells us "we have separated ourselves from the multitude of the people [and all their impurity]."   The separation was motivated by purity concerns.   "Separated" (*PRS*, Hebrew) forms the root from which the name "Pharisees" (*prusim* = "separated ones") is generally derived.   Is what Peter did at Antioch (separated himself, Galatians 2:12), the same kind of separation the writer of MMT speaks about, that for reasons of purity he avoided association with certain other people?

(c) Next follows an explanation of the document's purpose.   The writers want the reader(s) to investigate the words of the Torah (Moses), the Prophets, and David and the day-to-day chronicles – i.e., the three-fold canon of Hebrew Scriptures (the Law, the prophets, and the writings).   The first point the reader is to see in these Scriptures is the prediction that the addressee would turn aside from the path of righteousness and as a result suffer misfortune. Then, based on some verses taken from Deuteronomy, the point is made that the Scripture foretells that in the end of days the reader would return to God.   Appeal is made to the Old Testament kings to show that the people who were spared misfortune and whose transgressions were forgiven were those who observed the laws of the Torah.

(d) The writer of MMT then sums up why this letter was sent to the addressee.

> Moreover we have written to you *some of the works of the Torah* that we thought would benefit you and your people, because we saw that you have wisdom and knowledge of the Torah.   Understand all these [things] and ask Him to set right your counsel and remove far from you any evil thought and the counsel of Belial so that you may be glad at the end of time when you discover that some of our words are so/true/correct and it may be reckoned to you as righteousness when you do what is right and good before Him, to benefit you and Israel.

This is the "penultimate line" of 4QMMT, says Dunn[15].   Men will be reckoned righteous at the end of time if they do what is upright and good (i.e., obeying the *halakhic* rules just enumerated) before Him.[16]   The writer of MMT appeals to blessings and cursings written in the book of Moses – cf. Deuteronomy 27-30.[17]   MMT recalls that curses have fallen on Israel in the past: "we know that some of the blessings and the curses have [already] been fulfilled."[18]   The writers of MMT were confident of their own status and acceptance before God, and still held out the hope that others in Israel would return to the Lord and to his Torah.

Note once more: There is enough overlap in the fragments of MMT to be able to say that "*halakhot*" and the words *Miqsat Ma'aseh ha-Torah* refer to the same things.

---

[15] Dunn, *op. cit.*, p.343.

[16] What the writer of MMT says about righteousness being reckoned to doers of *halakhic* rules is similar to what the troublemakers in Galatia were teaching, a teaching Paul repudiates when He says "by the works of the Law shall no flesh be justified."   The language "reckoned ... as righteousness" in MMT reflects Genesis 15:6 – "[The Lord] reckoned [Abraham's faithfulness] to him as righteousness."   "Doing what is right" (MMT) and "faithfulness" (Genesis 15:6) were treated as interchangeable ideas in MMT. The same phrase from Genesis 15:6 is used at Galatians 3:6.

[17] We recall that Galatians 3:10 also appeals to this same section of Deuteronomy.

[18] See "For This You Waited 35 Years," a reprint of MMT as reconstructed by Elisha Qimron and John Strugnell, c.20, printed in *BAR* 20/6 (Nov-Dec. 1994), p.60-61.

6. HOW 4QMMT ILLUMINES PAUL'S "WORKS OF THE LAW."

"Illumination" is defined as "clarifying the meaning of what was previously obscure, or the full force of something imperfectly understood."[19]   The official publication of 4QMMT (DJD 10) does not discuss the importance of MMT for New Testament studies since the current generation of Jewish scholars are delighted to find written materials that help fill the gap in the history of the development of *halakhah* between the exile and the writing of the *Mishnah* in AD 220.   But 4QMMT and Paul use the very same phrase, "works of the Law."   Thus, the Dead Sea Scrolls can help us understand exactly what Paul was talking about as he wrote.

Paul uses the expression "works of the Law" (Galatians 2:16, 3:10; Romans 3:20,28) as he writes about "works of the Law" that are not a condition of salvation, in contrast to "faith in Jesus Christ" which is!

If the conclusions above are correct, MMT should enable us to understand in its historical context what Paul refers to as he wrote Galatians and Romans.   This is important because, since the Reformation, these very passages in Galatians and Romans have been used to show that "faith alone" (and no works – not baptism nor even works of love or good works) is the sole condition of salvation.   For centuries, Protestants have emphasized "faith alone" – in spite of certain Biblical difficulties encountered.   The Reformation era "faith alone" approach causes scholars to spend pages explaining away verses where such an interpretation of "works of the Law" seemingly makes Paul contradict himself (e.g., Romans 2:6-16[20]) and seemingly makes James difficult to harmonize.[21]   The Reformation explanation contradicts what one reads regularly in Scripture (e.g., Matthew 7:21, 25:31-46) – that faithfulness to what God has commanded has always been the condition of salvation being imputed ("justification").   Faithfulness to God's revelation, not faithfulness to man-made laws, is what the Scriptures everywhere teach!

In short, *Ma'aseh ha-Torah* is the Hebrew equivalent of a phrase Paul uses in his letters, what our English translations render as "works of the Law."

The usual translation of *Miqsat Ma'aseh Ha-Torah* obscures its relationship to what we read in the New Testament in Paul's letters.   Scholars have varyingly translated the He-

---

[19] Kitchen quoted in Mattingly.

[20] In addition, when Romans 4 tells us that Abraham and David were not justified by "works" we are talking (in context) about *halakhic* kind of works.

[21] Beware!   The NIV does not use the phrase "works of law" at Galatians 2:16 and 3:10 or at Romans 3:20,28.   The NIV simply reads "observing the law," leaving the reader with the very mistaken notion that it is the Law of Moses Paul writes about, rather than the "traditions of the elders."   The reader of the NIV is led to completely miss the point of what Paul writes.

brew phrase as "some precepts of the Torah" or "some legal rulings pertaining to the Torah." Such translations cause us to miss the connection with any phraseology found in the New Testament Scriptures with which we may be accustomed.[22]

A review of the Hebrew words in this phrase would be helpful. (1) *Miqsat* does not mean simply "some." The same word is used in Genesis 47:2, where Joseph presents five of his brothers to Pharaoh. In Genesis, the word could be understood to mean the most important of the brothers, or perhaps the choice or select. In other words, when the word is used in MMT, it does not refer to some random laws; instead, these laws are important to the writer. The Hebrew word should be rendered 'some important' or 'pertinent' ... or 'most important ....' (2) *Ha-Torah*, of course, is translated "the Law," and refers often to the five books of Moses, Genesis through Deuteronomy. (3) *Ma'aseh* is the word the Jews used to refer to "*Halakhic* rulings."[23]

What Greek phrase would translate these Hebrew words *Ma'aseh ha-Torah*? A few minutes with a concordance of the LXX (the Greek translation of the Hebrew Bible) leaves little doubt that the Greek equivalent of *Ma'aseh ha-Torah* is likely *ergōn nomou*. The most common Greek word for *ma'aseh* is *ergōn*. The Greek word *nomos* most commonly translates *torah*. It is striking that when the British Bible Society translated the New Testament into modern Hebrew in 1976, at a time when the text of MMT was known to only a half a dozen scholars, they consistently translated *ergōn nomou* ("works of the law") as *ma'aseh ha-torah*.

In our English versions of the New Testament, *ergōn nomou* is commonly translated as "works of Law" or "works of the Law." This well-known Pauline phrase is found in Romans 3:20,28 and in Galatians 2:16, 3:2,5,10.

MMT has helped illumine Paul's phrase "works of law." Now we understand Paul's meaning in the verses in Romans and Galatians.

MMT is a document that details examples of "works of law" – man-made *halakhic* rulings or interpretations based on certain verses of Scripture. When Paul writes in Ro-

---

[22] For 4QMMT Eisenman and Wise choose the title "... Letter on Works Reckoned as Righteousness" (*Dead Sea Scrolls Uncovered*). This comes closer to language we are used to reading in the New Testament. Dunn (*op. cit.*, p.342) tells us that F. Garcia Martinez (at the Chicago SBL meeting, November 1994) acknowledged that the printed translation of (his) line 113 was less satisfactory, and that *ma'aseh* should after all be rendered "works of" as elsewhere in the Dead Sea Scrolls. The ambiguity arises because *ma'aseh* can signify a "deed" prescribed (hence "precept") as well as a deed carried out. Elisha Qimron and John Strugnell, *Qumran Cave 4 ... MMT* (Discoveries in the Judean Desert X [New York: Oxford University Press, 1994]) p.139 n.41, note that the LXX translates *ma'aseh* in Exodus 18:20 as *ta erga* ("works").

[23] S. Lieberman ("Sefer Ha-Ma'asim--Sefer Ha-Pesaqim," *Tarbiz* 2 [1931], p.377) demonstrated that in Palestinian literature the expressions *ma'aseh* and *sepher ha-ma'asim* were used in the sense of "*halakhic* ruling" and "*halakhic* work." *"Ma'asim* stands for legal institutions: those of the law of sacrifices (*qorbanot*), tributes for the temple and priests (*mattanot*), the purity ritual (*tohorot*), etc." (Stanislaw Medala, "The Character and Setting of 4QMMT," *QumChron.* 4:1-2 [July 1994], p.10).

mans and Galatians that "works of law" are not a condition of salvation, we can now understand that he is talking about "*halakhic* rulings" like those typified by the 20 or so examples in MMT. For the first time in years, we can with confidence put ourselves back into Paul's 1st century world and understand what he was actually writing about. We find both Pharisees and Sadducees making their own distinctive *halakhic* rulings. Both Galatians and Romans tell us that such rulings, whether they be Pharisee or Sadducee, are not conditions of salvation. "Faith," which is habitually doing what Jesus says, is the condition of salvation!

SUMMARY AND APPLICATION

Summary

4QMMT helps us see that Jewish "*halakhic* rulings" and Paul's expression "works of the Law" refer to the same thing.[24]   4QMMT enables us to illustrate what Paul meant when he wrote that "works of the Law" do not save; therefore, we no longer have to struggle with passages that for 400 years have been thought to contradict.

Application

Now we can see clearly that the Protestant dogma that no "works" are included in the "faith" that saves is a grave error! To the contrary, the condition of salvation called "faith" means precisely doing what God says – rather than getting all wrapped up in man-made rules like the *halakhic* laws of the Jews.

With this better understanding of 1st century phraseology, there should be an end to the thoughtless repeating of denominational preacher's sermons with their unbiblical ideas. Such repeating provides no way for our people to get help putting the Bible verses together into a consistent, whole pattern so as to understand God's revelation.

With this better understanding of 1st century phraseology, there should be no more "faith-only" presentations to the seeking sinner! We should cease asking a seeker to pray the "sinner's prayer" and giving him assurance when he completes it that he is already saved. We should cease using Paul's "works of the Law" as proof that immersion is an unnecessary extra in the salvation of a man. Instead, we can now present the faith once for all delivered to the saints (Jude 3) in all its pristine purity. We can use the New Testament expressions exactly as we find them when we explain to lost men the way of salvation.

---

[24] This does not mean, of course, that Galatians was written with a knowledge of MMT, or that the "certain men from James" (Galatians 2:12) were themselves Qumranites or influenced by Qumran.

SELECTED BIBLIOGRAPHY

Abegg, Martin, "Paul, 'Works of the Law' and MMT," *Biblical Archaeology Review* 20:6 (Nov-Dec 1994), p.52ff.

_____, "4QMMT C 27,31 and Works Righteousness," *Dead Sea Discoveries* 6 [1999] p.139-47.
> Abegg contends that Paul was responding to a position like that in 4QMMT, where the author sees in the Law Judaism's distinctiveness before God, not the Jewish way to earn final salvation. This interpretation is suspect. One text 4QpapMMT^c (4Q398) frag.2 col.2 (=4QMMT 111-118) is clear. In it the expression "works of the law" is used, and the observance of such works is held to pay off at the end of time: "It shall be reckoned to you as justice when you do what `is upright and good before Him" (trans. Watson, *Dead Sea Scrolls Translated* [ed. Garcia Martinez], 84-85).

Dunn, James D.G., "4QMMT and Galatians." *NTS* 43 (1997), p.147-53.

Eisenman, Robert, and Wise, Michael, *The Dead Sea Scrolls Uncovered*. Rockport, MA: Element, 1992.   Published by Penguin Books, 1993.
> A translation and interpretation of 50 key documents from Cave 4.   Eisenman had access to the set of photographs that were anonymously mailed to him, and also to the photographs and the microfilm edition in the Huntington Library, San Marino, CA.

Kapera, Zdzislaw J. ed., "Qumran Cave IV and MMT.   Special Report," *Qumran Chronicle* I:2-3 (Krakow: Enigma Press, 1991).
> The first part of this volume presents Kapera's 49-page narrative of the "unfortunate story" of the Qumran Cave 4 manuscripts.   The second part contains articles on 4QMMT: Kapera on the history of its non-publication; Piotor Muchowski on its content and character according to Jacob Sussman; Kapera on bibliography between 1956 and 1991; Lawrence H. Schiffman on its nature as a basic sectarian text; Philip R. Davies on Sadducees in the Dead Sea scrolls; Robert Eisenman on Schiffman's interpretation; James C. VanderKam on the Qumran residents as Essenes rather than Sadducees; George J. Brooke on the significance of the kings in 4QMMT; Hans Burgmann on a historically justifiable dating of the work; and Joseph M. Baumgarten on Qumran law and the identification of the sect.

Porter, Nancy, *Secrets of the Dead Sea Scrolls*, a 58-minute VHS production by NOVA, made in 1951 and distributed by PBS Video, 1320 Braddock Plce, Alexandria, VA.
> A good visual history of the discovery and publication of the manuscripts, plus a presentation of the "scandal" about the publication of Cave 4 manuscripts until late 1951.   Photos and video clips from some of the principal International Team members, as well as from second generation Dead Sea Scroll scholars.

Qimron, Elisha, and Strugnell, John, *Qumran Cave 4:   Miqsat Ma'ase ha-Torah*, Vol. 10 in Discoveries in the Judean Desert Series. Oxford: Clarendon Press, 1994.

Schiffman, Lawrence H., "The Significance of the Scrolls," *Bible Review* 6:5 (1990), p.18-27,52.

> After describing the discovery of the Dead Sea Scrolls, the article reviews the debates about dating and the identity of the people who wrote them. Then taking its starting point from 4QMMT, it discusses the various movements in Second Temple Judaism: the Pharisees as precursors of rabbinic Judaism, the Sadducees as aristocratic literalists, apocalyptic Jewish sects, and in a section that is hardly satisfactory Schiffman believes he can find Christian roots (or sources) in sectarian Judaism. Finally, it looks at the Qumran texts for the light they can shed on the history of Biblical texts.

SPECIAL STUDY #2

JUSTIFICATION BY FAITH

INTRODUCTION

A. Why This Study?

This topic was the key theological issue at the time of the 16th century Reformation between Protestants and Catholics. Protestants maintained that righteousness (justification) was imputed; Catholics taught that righteousness was infused. Protestants maintained that faith was alone (without works) while Catholics insisted that faith included works (at least works of love).

This topic has again become perhaps the number one topic of furious debate among New Testament scholars, both Protestant and Catholic, since E.P. Sanders in the late 1970s began writing about what has come to be called the "new perspective on Paul." As the debate continues, and scholars try to look at what Paul wrote through 1st century glasses, several Protestant doctrines have come under attack. (1) Is justification a forensic term (a judge pronouncing sentence)? Is man justified just once when he becomes a Christian, or is there a future, final justification, too? (2) Is *sola fides* (faith alone[1]) the condition upon which God justifies? The long-held Protestant doctrine of the relation between faith and works in the thought of Paul (namely, that faith alone initially gets you into God's favor; and that good works follow which keep you in God's favor) is under attack. (3) Is Christ's righteousness imputed to the sinner when God justifies him or her? Where in the Protestant presentation of justification, if it is by faith alone, does one find any motive for Christian living or any reason for the appeals for spiritual growth and mortifying the deeds of the flesh that one finds in the New Testament Scriptures?

It is in the letters to the Galatians and the Romans that one most often finds the terms justify, justification, and righteousness in the New Testament.[2] Since Luther developed his doctrine from a study of Galatians, it certainly is appropriate to include a study on *Justification by Faith* in a commentary on Galatians.

If all men have sinned (something all above the age of accountability do, Romans 3:23), and if sin separates a man from a holy God (Isaiah 59:2), and if justification by faith

---

[1] "Faith alone" means that saving faith is composed of knowledge, assent, and trust, with no human actions being involved.

[2] Paul uses the term "justify" (verb form) 15 times in Romans, 8 in Galatians. His use outside of these two books is found at Acts 13:39; 1 Corinthians 4:4, 6:11; 1 Timothy 3:16; and Titus 3:7. He also uses the noun "righteous" or "righteousness" numerous times.

is something that allows God to no longer reckon a man's sins against him (Romans 4:8), then justification is certainly a subject of supreme interest.

B. Preview of This Study

There are four parts to this special study: (1) An overview of the conclusions reached by this commentator as he prepared and wrote commentaries on the Scriptures that form the heart of this debate.[3]   (2) A brief historical overview of the direction theologians have gone on these topics during the course of past church history.[4]   (3) An overview of the contemporary scene.   (4) An evaluation and reply to the contemporary scholarly consensus on these debated matters in light of the conclusions previously reached.

Is it too much to ask people to rethink a 500-year-old tradition, known to us as Reformation theology?   If Luther and Calvin asked people to rethink traditions and theology that were far older than that, then it cannot be too much to ask!

C. A Glossary of Key Terms

Certain terms are regularly used in a discussion of justification.   It will help our understanding of the debate to pause to define the technical words we are using.

Augustinian – After his dispute with Pelagius, Augustine (AD 354-430) taught that salvation is totally from God.   That is, salvation is monergistic.

Covenantal nomism – This is the view that one's place in God's plan is established on the basis of covenant and that the covenant requires as the proper response of man his obedience to its commandments.   The covenant also provides a means of atonement for transgression.[5]

Grace – As defined by many Protestants, *grace* means that, in salvation, God does it all.   He provides the sacrifice, He gives faith, He justifies – man does nothing, man is wholly passive.   Scholars will use the words "grace v. legalism" to describe two opposing views of how salvation/justification works.

---

[3] This topic is treated first because it is our studied conclusion that our convictions and beliefs should be informed by the Word of God.

[4] Such historical studies often help us understand how doctrines developed as we come forward to the current situation.

[5] E.P. Sanders, *Paul and Palestinian Judaism* (London: SCM, 1977), p.75.

Halakhah – A Hebrew word which literally means "to go" or "to walk." It refers to the rules by which a Jewish person's life was to be guided.

Infuse – To instill, to implant.   In Roman Catholic theology, God transmits and instills virtues (such as faith or love) when a person is justified.

Impute – To attribute or ascribe (something) vicariously to someone else.

Legalism – As used in this study, *legalism* has the idea that a condition of salvation, a prerequisite to justification, is the doing of what the Law of Moses says. Salvation is not by faith only, but requires "works." The pejorative term "legalism" usually denotes something like self-conscious striving for the accumulation of merit independent of some divine assistance in order to make a claim before God for vindication.

Monergism – God saves man by fiat. Man is wholly passive, contributing nothing. "The very essence of 'Lutheranism' is that 'humans can contribute nothing to their salvation'."[6]

Ordo salutis – The "order of salvation;" that is, the order in which regeneration,[7] justification, sanctification, and other steps in the process of salvation take place. Much theological controversy has arisen over the correct order.

Pelagian – Pelagius (c. AD 360-c.420) taught that salvation is totally man's own doing.

Semi-Pelagian – Semi-Pelagianism teaches that salvation is a combination of the efforts of both man and God. Salvation is accomplished when man decides to co-operate with God and accepts the grace God offers him. This view is sometimes called synergism.

Synergism – Man cooperates with God in salvation. God has set forth conditions which man must meet before God reckons the man as just.

Works – In denominational thinking, a "work" is any activity a man might do.[8]

---

[6] Stephen Westerholm, *Perspectives Old and New on Paul* (Grand Rapids: Eerdmans, 2004), p.351.

[7] The term "regeneration" is used twice in the New Testament and in neither place does it function in the way it has come to be used in Reformed systematics for a 'transubstantiated heart.'

[8] We will argue that this definition is flawed. We will also use "works" in a good sense, as in James 2:14ff, "as a result of works (deeds) faith was perfected (completed)."

I. AN OVERVIEW OF THE CONCLUSIONS TO WHICH MY STUDIES HAVE LED[9]

Three different major topics are presented in detail: (A) The meaning of the term "justification." (B) The meaning of the term "faith." (C) Whether or not Christ's righteousness is imputed to the sinner. (D) Brief conclusions are given for several other topics of interest to contemporary scholars.

A. The Meaning of The Term "Justification"

The standard meaning of the verb **"to justify"** (*dikaioō*) is a verdict, a sentence pronounced by a judge. It is a term used in the law courts. "Justification" as a theological concept has its metaphorical roots in legal language; it is a forensic term. After a careful and detailed presentation of the use of the verb "justify" in classical literature,[10] in the LXX (where it is used to translate the Hebrew *tsadeq*[11], and in the New Testament, D.W. Simon summarizes his findings with these words:

> In the New Testament the sense (determined largely by the LXX) is (1) to show one to be righteous, 1 Cor. 4:4, Lk 7:35; (2) to pronounce righteous, as a judicial act, Luke 16:15, 7:29; (3) the judicial act of God whereby he declares men "righteous" in His eyes, free from guilt and punishment, Rom. 4:5, Gal. 2:16, *et al.*[12]

We are told in 1 Kings 8:32 (in an attempt to reproduce in English the play on words in the Hebrew) that God, the Judge, pronounces condemnation on the condemnable and justification on the justifiable. "To justify is not to *make* righteous but to *pronounce* righteous, to acquit one of a charge of guilt."[13] *Dikaioō* ("to justify") is what is called in Greek a contract verb. Contract verbs in the -oō class are commonly causative, but it is

---

[9] Rather than simply interacting with what other New Testament scholars are saying, but who never get into the text, we instead will begin by working with the relevant New Testament passages.

[10] Godet says there is not a single example in the whole of Classical Literature where the word *dikaioō* ("justify") = to *make* righteous. Frederick L. Godet, *Commentary On Romans*, English translation by Custin (Grand Rapids: Zondervan, 1956 reprint), p.95. To "justify" is not to *make* a man righteous; it is to *declare* or *pronounce* him righteous.

[11] "In the LXX (both Old Testament and Apocrypha) *dikaioō* is used to translate the Piel and Hiph'il of *tsadeq* (Qal stem = *dedikaiosthai*) ... The root meaning everywhere seems to be 'to set forth as righteous,' to justify, in a legal sense." D.W. Simon, "Justification," in *Hasting's Dictionary of the Bible* (New York: Scribners, 1909), Vol.2, p.826.

[12] *Ibid.*

[13] Edmund P. Clowney, "The Biblical Doctrine of Justification by Faith," in *Right with God*, edited by D.A. Carson (Eugene, OR: Wipf and Stock, 2002 reprint), p.45.

now widely granted that *dikaioō,* influenced by the Old Testament background,[14] means "to declare [someone] righteous," not "to make [someone] righteous."[15] "In the Scriptures, the terms 'justification' or 'to justify' are used in a special Biblical, forensic, or judicial sense, 'to declare or pronounce righteous,' not to make righteous."[16]

A similar expression is **"to reckon righteous"** (*logizetai eis dikaiosunē,* which in the KJV was translated "counted for righteousness" at Romans 4:3). "Reckon" is a metaphor taken from bookkeeping. Romans 2:26 provides an example of what "reckoned" means. In Romans 2:26, Paul says a man's uncircumcision is regarded (reckoned, *logizesthai)* or counted as circumcision. It is the same word in the Greek that is translated "reckoned" at Romans 4:3. In other words, one thing is simply counted for another, or a person is regarded as something he really is not.[17]

There is a whole family of words built on the Greek *dikaio-* stem: (1) *dikaiokrisia* (righteous judgment); (2) *dikaioma* (righteous statute, an ordinance, a verdict of acquittal or condemnation); (3) *dikaioō* (to declare righteous or to justify, or to free); (4) *dikaios* (just, right, righteous); (5) *dikaiōs* (justly, righteously, uprightly); (6) *dikaiōsis* (justification), and (7) *dikaiosunē* (righteous, justice). There is a semantic relationship between the Greek words translated into English as "righteousness" and "justification" that is not immediately obvious to most readers. In our English Bibles, when we read about righteousness and/or justification, we are often dealing with the same theological topic.[18]

---

[14] "In the LXX (both Old Testament and Apocrypha) *dikaioō* is used to translate the Piel and Hiph'il of *tsadeq* (Qal stem = *dedikaiosthai*) ... The root meaning everywhere seems to be "to set forth as righteous," to justify, in a legal sense" (D.W. Simon, *ibid.*).

[15] "Verbs ending in *-oō,* derived from adjectives of *moral* meaning, never have this *efficient* signification" (Simon, *ibid*). However, see Chris VanLandingham, *Judgment and Justification in Early Judaism and the Apostle Paul* (Peabody, MA: Hendrickson, 2006), who has argued that the *dikai-* word group referred not to forensic justification, but to the initial state of salvation when one is "made righteous" (chapter 4). But this argument by VanLandingham is apparently erroneous. Even the Roman Catholic scholar Joseph Fitzmyer insists on the declarative or forensic force of *dikaioō* (Joseph Fitzmyer, *Romans* [NY: Doubleday, 1993]. p.117-118).

[16] L.M. Peterson, "Justification" in the *Zondervan Pictorial Encyclopedia of the Bible* (Grand Rapids: Zondervan, 1978), V.3, p.764. Since the English word "justification" is derived from two Latin words, *justus* and the verb *facere,* which together literally mean, "to make righteous" or "to do righteousness" (*justificare*), it looks like the Latin Vulgate is the source from which the Roman Catholic doctrine of infused righteousness derives.

[17] This expression "reckoned as righteousness" is one of the sources from which theologians have deduced the idea of "imputed righteousness," a topic about which more will be said below.

[18] English has two words regularly used to translate the single Greek word *dikaiosunē* and the Latin word *iustitia*: "righteousness" and "justice." This being true, we could translate Romans 1:17 as "the justice of God." But such a rendering might give the English reader the wrong idea because, in English, these words "righteousness" and "justice" have two different connotations. "Justice" is usually thought of in the sense of an authority acting towards another in a fair, impartial, and deserving manner. "Righteous" regularly has the connotation of good and upright conduct. Neither of these English connotations quite catches the meaning of the Greek words whose stem is *dikaio-*. (A.E. McGrath, "Justification" in the *Dictionary of Paul and His Letters* [Downers Grove: InterVarsity, 1993], p.520.)

Further, that the same English words are used to describe different topics is not always immediately obvious to Bible readers. "Righteous" is used of (1) one of God's attributes, i.e., He always does what is right (Psalms 31:1, 36;6,10, 72:2, 89:10; Isaiah 42:21); (2) of God's way of saving men (Matthew 3:15; 5:6; 21:32); (3) of right living by men, of adherence to norms set by God, i.e., either right relationships with other men, or right relationships with God (Matthew 5:10,20; 6:1,33); and (4) of the resurrection of the body (Romans 4:25).

Man who has sinned cannot justify himself in God's sight.[19] The justification of men before God is often referred to in the Bible, but only to be characterized as impossible. See Psalms 143:2 ("Do not enter into judgment with Thy servant; for in Thy sight no man living is righteous [shall be justified, KJV]") and Job 25:4 ("How then can man be just with God?"). In the New Testament, the same thing is everywhere affirmed. E.g., see Galatians 2:16, "because by works of the Law shall no flesh be justified." No man can make amends or atonement for his own sin.

Only God can justify men who have sinned. See Acts 13:39, "through [Jesus Christ] every one who believes is freed (*Greek*, justified) from all things from which you could not be freed (*Greek*, justified) by the law of Moses." In Old Testament times, sins were only passed over, not actually forgiven, until Christ died (Romans 3:25). Now, since Calvary, those sins from the Old Testament are actually forgiven. God made such actual forgiveness possible by providing the atoning sacrifice Himself. Romans 3:20-26 is the clearest and best exposition of this truth in the New Testament. God not only provided the sacrifice, but made a revelation to men about His intentions and purposes, and the conditions He expected men to meet if they would be recipients of His justification.

God is both just and justifier of the ungodly person who has faith in Jesus (Romans 3:22-26). Paul speaks of God as "Him who justifies the ungodly" (Romans 4:5). At first

---

[19] Simon (*op. cit.*, p.526-27) points out that (1) Man can justify his own behavior *to himself*. Something of this kind is reflected in 1 Corinthians 4:4,5 where Paul writes, "I am conscious of nothing against myself; yet I am not by this acquitted (justified); but the one who judges me is the Lord"; and in 1 John 3:19,20, "We know by this that we are of the truth, and shall assure our heart before Him, in whatever our heart condemns us, because God is greater than our heart, and knows all things." There is such a thing as mistaken self-judgment. When we have done wrong, we call such self-justification rationalization. (2) Men may justify themselves with *other men.* If a man has been misrepresented, to justify himself is to clear or vindicate himself in the particular respect in which he has been misjudged. If on the other hand, he is guilty of wrong in thought or word or act, the wrong relation thence arising or thereby constituted, has to be rectified by some sort of expiation or good-making of the wrong. It may be by confession of fault, or by an expression of regret, or of payment of a fine, or of loss of liberty, or endurance of suffering. In the legislation of Israel, as set forth in the Old Testament, provision was made both for the vindication of the innocent (Numbers 5:18ff) and the making good of real wrong doing (Exodus 21:19-30, 22:14). (3) Men are sometimes set right or justified *by other men.* This, too, can be in one of two senses: the vindication of innocence (as Deuteronomy 25:1, "if there shall be a dispute between men, and the judges decide their case, and they justify the righteous and condemn the wicked ...") or by the making good of and atonement for a real wrong doing. Justification of the wicked for a bribe is denounced, as in Isaiah 5:23.

this delightful truth seems at variance with Scripture, since the very same Greek phrase is used in the LXX of the kind of corrupt judgment that God will not tolerate (Exodus 23:7, Isaiah 5:23).

> Indeed, that God "justifies the ungodly" seems at variance with the Old Testament presentation of God's essential righteousness. The Old Testament insists that God is "righteous in all His ways" (Psalms 145:17), a God "who does no wrong" (Deuteronomy 32:4; cf. Zephaniah 3:5). "God is a righteous judge, a God who expresses His wrath every day" (Psalms 7:11). At first, it seems unthinkable that a God who is righteous should justify the ungodly.[20]

How God can justify the ungodly and at the same time still be righteous is explained in Romans 3:24-26. He can do this because of the "redemption which is in Christ Jesus" (3:24). Christ's blood was a "propitiation" for sins (3:25). With Calvary in the picture, God can be "just" (an attribute, "righteous") while at the same time He is justifying the person who has faith in Jesus (3:26). Though such justification is available to all men, whether Jew or Gentile, slave or free, male or female (Galatians 3:28), it is not just any and all sinners whom He justifies; it is something He does for those who have faith in Jesus. "I most certainly understand now," says Peter regarding God, "that God is not one to show partiality, but in every nation the man who fears Him and does what is right is welcome (acceptable, KJV) to Him" (Acts 10:34-35). To be "welcome" or "acceptable" is to be no longer separated by sin from God, but rather to be in a close relation to Him, i.e., to be justified. Note, too, that "justification" was a common experience in the Patriarchal Age (Abraham, Romans 4:1-3) and in the Mosaic age (David, Romans 4:6-8). Such justification occurred when men obeyed what God told them to do (e.g., Abraham, James 2:21-23). The frequent injunctions to trust in the Lord point the same direction.

Justification as Paul uses it. When Paul preached the doctrine of justification/righteousness in the ancient Roman world, though he did not take pains to define his terms, it would seem that his words were readily understood by both Jew and Greek (Romans 1:14,16). Where he does explain his terms, this is what he said. When God justifies the sinner, the penitent sinner is "reckoned" (*logizomai*) as righteous (Romans 4:5), and his sins are not taken into account (*logizomai*, "reckon" NASB mg., Romans 4:8). Romans 4:11 speaks about righteousness being "reckoned" to "all who believe" (the Greek verb is present tense, indicating continuous action). When a person has been justified he becomes a "son of God," a member of Abraham's spiritual family (Galatians 3:24-29), and enjoys participation in the covenant promise made to Abraham that in his Seed all the nations of the earth would be blessed (Galatians 3:14-16).

---

[20] James I. Packer, "Justification" in *Evangelical Dictionary of Theology*, edited by Walter Elwell (Grand Rapids: Baker, 1984), p.645.

Initial justification. When a penitent believer in Jesus is immersed, at that moment God justifies that person, i.e., judges or declares him to be "righteousness" or "saved" or "forgiven" (Romans 6:17,18). We call this initial justification. Romans 6:7 says that "he who has died (in baptism) is freed (justified) from sin." This apparently says justification includes some kind of deliverance from sin's reign and misery. Justification does not promote licentiousness (i.e., forensic righteousness is not just a legal fiction as Roman Catholic theology insists it is[21]), because the justified person has been delivered from the reign of sin. Now that he is free/justified, he is to stop presenting his body to sin (the devil) as an instrument/tool (Romans 6:12-13).

God's justification of a man happens over and over again during the man's life. "Justification" (God's justification of the faithful believer) is not a one-time thing.[22] The case of Abraham as unfolded in Romans 4 shows this to be true, and Abraham is the father of the faithful (i.e., what was true in his case is true in ours). Let us study the matter of justification in Abraham's life. The first time we are introduced to Abraham was the occasion when God called him out of Ur of Chaldees. (Such a call is implied at Genesis 11:31 and stated in Acts 7:2,3.) According to Hebrews 11:8, Abraham was already a man of faith, for it was "by faith" (i.e., because he was determined to be faithful) that he left Ur when God called him. Some time passes, and Abraham was 75 years of age when God called him again out of Haran (Genesis 12:1-3; Acts 7:4). "In you all the families of the earth will be blessed," God promised Abraham (Genesis 12:3). When he arrived in the land we now call Israel, Abraham camped at Shechem, where he built an altar and called on the name of the Lord (Genesis 12:6-9). Ten years after he left Haran, God called the 85-year old Abraham out of his tent. God pointed Abraham's attention to the night sky and promised him descendants as numerous as the stars of the heavens. We are told that on that occasion "Abraham believed God and it was counted to him for righteousness" (Genesis 15:6).[23] When Ishmael was born (Genesis 16), Abraham was 86 years old. When Abraham was 99 years old God promised him that Sarah would have a son next year at this time (Genesis 17:1-21). Isaac was conceived when Ishmael was 13 or 14 years old.

---

[21] Catholics regularly dismiss Protestant explanations of justification as being legal fiction because justification as the Protestants explain it does not (in Catholic opinion) deal with the heart of human sinfulness. See K. Keating, *Catholicism and Fundamentalism: The Attack on "Romanism" by "Bible Christians"* (San Francisco: Ignatius, 1998), p.167-68. Catholics insist that justification is something by which men actually come to be (i.e., are made to be) righteous. In their view, if men are just declared righteous, what incentive is there for the person actually to be or become righteous?

[22] Many contemporary Protestants think of justification as a one-time thing – happening at the beginning of one's Christian life.

[23] Paul tells us that Abraham was justified by faith, not by works (of the Law). Genesis 15:6 is quoted at Romans 4:3 to prove it.

After Isaac was born, Ishmael was expelled in harmony with God's directive to Abraham (Genesis 17:15-21). Genesis 17:5 ("a father of many nations") is the passage referred to in Romans 4:13-22. Abraham had grown stronger in faith (Romans 4:20) in the years since Genesis 15, therefore "it (his growing faith) was reckoned to him for righteousness" (Romans 4:22).[24] For a second time in his life, we are told that God justified Abraham.

Abraham is about 125 years old (Josephus says) when he was commanded by God to sacrifice Isaac. Abraham was justified/saved/reckoned righteous on this occasion, too (by his works,[25] James 2:21-23 tells us). At the sacrifice of Isaac, God renewed His covenant with Abraham, "In your seed all the nations of the earth will be blessed" (Genesis 22:18).[26] This brief review of Abraham's life shows that he was justified on three or four different occasions during his life. We are convinced the same thing is true for Abraham's spiritual children, for Romans 8:33 tells us that "God is the one who justifies" (*ho dikaiōn*, present participle, continuous action) "God's elect" (i.e., folk who are already Christians).

Final Justification occurs at the last judgment. At the final judgment (Romans 2:1-16) it is not hearers of the Law who are just before God, but the habitual doers of the law who "shall be justified" (2:13). God's judgment will be righteous (2:5). Such final justification will happen on the day when God judges the secrets of men through Christ Jesus (Romans 2:16). Jesus spoke of this day: "I say unto you, for every careless word that men shall speak, they shall render account for it in the day of judgment. For by your words you shall be justified, and by your words you shall be condemned" (Matthew 12:36-37). Final justification, God's final verdict, takes in not only "well done, good and faithful servant," but also "Come, blessed of My Father, inherit the kingdom prepared for you." Justification is not a one-time thing in a believer's life.

B. The Meaning of the Term "Faith"

The words "by faith" in the expression "justification by faith" are just as vital as the term "justify" if we are to understand the nature of justification as taught in the Scriptures.[27] Numerous times we read that "faith" is what God looks for before He will reckon a man as

---

[24] There is no way that Romans 4:22 and Genesis 15:6 are the same instance of justification being reckoned. Romans 4:22 is a reference to Genesis 17, as Romans 4:17 shows by quoting "a father of many nations have I made you."

[25] "Works" in James are works of faith – obedience to what God had commanded.

[26] Galatians 3:16 is the apostle's explanation of Genesis 22:18. The "Seed" (singular) is Christ. "All nations" includes Jew and Gentile. "Blessed" means sins are forgiven/covered. "If you are Christ's you are Abraham's seed, heirs according to the promise" (Galatians 3:29).

[27] Peterson, *op. cit.*, p.768

righteous/justified.[28]   Exactly what is the meaning of the term "by faith"?

Is that condition 'faith only'?   "A long and distinguished tradition of interpretation, drawing its inspiration largely from Luther, has seen an absolute contradiction between faith and works.   They are held to be mutually exclusive entities designating two radically opposed ways of thinking about and responding to God."[29]   *Sola fides* became a slogan that encapsulated the Protestant presentation of what "faith" is.[30]   There is in the background of Protestant usage the influence of Augustine, who championed the idea as he reacted to Pelagianism.   *Solifidianism* is a word that means "faith only."   In this writer's judgment, that tradition is wrong-headed and does not present what the Word of God actually says.[31]   Scripture indicates that the faith that saves is made up of knowledge, assent, trust, and obedience.[32]   "Faith and obedience are in no way antithetical.   The noun *pistis* implies faithfulness and obedience."[33]   The faith that saves cannot be mere mental assent.

Let us examine the evidence that **faith is doing what God says**.

(1) We begin with the quotation of Habakkuk 2:4 at Romans 1:17, "The righteous man shall live by faith."   "Faith" is *emunah* in the Hebrew, "faithfulness."[34]   Paul chose

---

[28] Here are a few examples.   "The righteous man shall live by faith" (Romans 1:17).   "The righteousness of God is revealed from faith to faith." (Romans 1:17.   Perhaps this means that justification is on the condition of faith[fulness] to encourage us to believe.)   "We maintain a man is justified by faith ..." (Romans 3:28).   God is "justifier of the one who has faith in Jesus" (Romans 3:26; mg. "the faith of Jesus").   "Faith is reckoned as righteousness" (Romans 4:5,9).   Righteousness is reckoned "to all who believe ... who follow in the steps of Abraham's faith" (Romans 4:11,12).   Righteousness is "by faith, that it might be in accordance with grace" (Romans 4:16).

[29] McGrath, *op. cit.,* p.521.   Lutheranism is not alone in defining 'faith' as something exclusive of anything a man might do.   Reformed theology and Wesleyanism teach the same doctrine of "faith alone" (*sola fide*).

[30] The slogan had a long and well-established history prior to Luther.   It is found in Origen, Hilary, Chrysostom, Augustine, Bernard, and Aquinas, though obviously without Luther's specific nuances. (Michael F. Bird, *The Saving Righteousness of God: Studies on Paul, Justification and the New Perspective* [Carlisle, PA: Paternoster, 2007], p.9.)

[31] The key language used to deny that faith includes any works is "works of the Law."   However, Special Study #1 has already shown that Paul's phrase "works of the Law" refers to man-made religious rules (like those presented in 4QMMT).

[32] See Special Study #16, "The Faith that Saves," in Gareth L. Reese, *New Testament History: Acts* (Moberly, MO: Scripture Exposition Books, 2002), p.598ff.

[33] John MacArthur, *The Gospel According to Jesus* (Grand Rapids: Zondervan, 1988), p. 175, 219, 233.   See also Rudolph Bultmann, *Theology of the New Testament* (New York: Charles Scribner's Sons, 1951), V.1, p.314-15.

[34] See Edmund Perry, "The meaning of *emunah* in the Old Testament," *JBR* 21 p.255,56.

the Greek word *pistis* to translate *emunah*: *pistis* may be translated either "faith" or"faithfulness."[35]

(2) In a number of passages "faith" and "practice" are interchangeable/synonymous terms. See Hebrews 10:36 and 38, where "having done the will of God" and "faith" are interchangeable expressions. Or see Galatians 3:11 and 12, where "faith" (3:11) is interchangeable with "practice" (3:12). Or see Galatians 3:26 and 27, where "sons of God through faith" is explained as involving being "baptized into Christ." Or see Galatians 5:6 and 7, where "faith" and "obeying the truth" are interchangeable ideas. At Romans 10:4,5 we find "everyone who believes" explained by the words "the man who practices the righteousness based on law." In Romans 10:5 Paul wrote words very similar to what he wrote in Galatians 3:12, where he quotes with approval Leviticus 18:5, "he who practices them shall live by them." See also Hebrews 3:18 and 19, where "unbelief" and "disobedience" are synonyms. By parity of reasoning "faith" and "obedience" would thus be synonyms.

(3) In several passages "belief/faith" and "disobedience" are antonyms. They can hardly be antonyms unless belief includes obedience. See at John 3:36; Acts 14:1,2 (where "believed" and "disobeyed" [in Greek] are antonyms); and 1 Peter 2:5,8.

(4) Paul uses "faith" and "obedience" interchangeably in parallel passages in Romans:[36]

> 1:8 – your *faith* is being proclaimed in all the world
> 16:19 – your *obedience* is made known to all.
>
> 10:16a – but all have not *obeyed* the gospel (KJV)
> 10:16b – for Isaiah says, "Who has *believed* our report?"
>
> 11:23 – if they do not continue in their *unbelief*
> 11:30 – because of their *disobedience*
> 11:31 – so these also now have been *disobedient*
>
> 1:5 – the *obedience of faith* among all the Gentiles
> 15:18 – resulting in the *obedience* of the Gentiles

(5) Paul uses the expressions "work of faith" (1 Thessalonians 1:3) and the "obedience of faith" (Romans 1:5, 16:26). Don Garlington has told us faith and obedience are synonyms in Paul.[37] He renders *hupakoē pisteōs* as "believing obedience" (Garlington

---

[35] The two possibilities for translating *pistis* can be seen by comparing translations at Matthew 23:23. Where the KJV has "faith," the NASB has "faithfulness."

[36] This table is modified from C.E.B. Cranfield, *A Critical and Exegetical Commentary on the Epistle to the Romans* (Edinburgh: T&T Clark, 1974), V.1, p.66, n.3.

[37] Don Garlington, "The Obedience of Faith in the Letter to the Romans, Part I: The Meaning of *hupakoē pisteōs* (Rom. 1:5; 16:26)," *WJT* 52 (1990), p.201-224.

calls it an adjectival genitive),[38] or we might translate it "faith's obedience."

(6) At Romans 4:3, Paul alludes to Genesis 15:6 where we are told "Abraham believed God and it was reckoned to him for righteousness." "Now we know how that text was interpreted in Paul's time: 1 Maccabees 2:52 and James 2:23 are clear and sufficient evidence at this point. It was taken as a reference to Abraham's *faithfulness* in obeying God's commands (even if that meant sacrificing his son Isaac)."[39]

On the basis of all of these passages, we reiterate our affirmation and definition that "faith is doing what God says."

C. Is Christ's Righteousness Imputed to the Sinner as God Justifies Him?

What is meant by "Christ's righteousness"? Christ's righteousness is His perfect obedience to God, with the climax of that obedience being Calvary.[40] The imputation of Christ's righteousness is supposed to solve a key problem. It is a crooked judge who acquits the guilty, and men are obviously guilty ("all have sinned ... "). How can God remain righteous Himself and at the same time "justify" (acquit) the sinner? The answer: because Christ's righteousness (having been imputed or transferred to the believer) is what God sees, rather than the man's sins.

Luther helped spread the idea that justification follows as a consequence of *iustitia Christia aliena* (the "alien righteousness of Christ"[41]). Commenting on Titus 1:14, Luther declared, "Our faith depends solely on Christ. He alone is righteous, and I am not; for His righteousness stands for me before the judgment of God and against the wrath of God ... for foreign righteousness has been introduced as a covering."[42] Melanchthon further de-

---

[38] Kline R. Snodgrass, "Justification by Grace – To the Doers," *NTS* 32 (1986), p.87, likewise uses "believing obedience" when he speaks of people being "incorporated into Christ by believing obedience." That said, note that there is no agreement concerning what kind of genitive "obedience of faith" is. Possibilities proposed include: (1) An objective genitive ('obedience to the faith' where "faith" is a body of doctrine). (2) A subjective genitive ('the obedience required by faith'). (3) A genitive of source ('the obedience that springs from faith'). (4) A genitive of apposition ('the obedience that is involved in faith'). This fourth interpretation is the one that commands the most respect among commentators, including Barrett, Cranfield, Calvin, Murray, Käsemann, Ridderbos, Schlier, Sanday/Headlam, and Wilckens.

[39] James D.G. Dunn, *The New Perspective on Paul* (Grand Rapids: Eerdmans, 2008 revised edition), p.47.

[40] John Piper, *Counted Righteous in Christ: Should We Abandon the Imputation of Christ's Righteousness?* (Wheaton, IL: Crossway Books, 2002), p.41,42. *Idem., The Future of Justification: A Response to N.T. Wright* (Wheaton, IL: Crossway Books, 2007), p.125. In Romans 5:18 Christ's death at Calvary is called an "act of righteousness" and is further identified as "obedience" in Romans 5:19.

[41] Since the righteousness is transferred from Christ to the sinner, that righteousness is thought of as being "alien" righteousness, someone else's righteousness, not the sinner's.

[42] Martin Luther, "Lectures on Titus," in *Luther's Works*, ed. Jaroslav Pelikan (St. Louis: Concordia, 1968), v.29, p.41.

fined and crystallized the doctrine.[43]   Calvin argued with equal vigor for the imputed righteousness of Christ as constituting the material cause of justification.[44]

Since the Reformation, many Protestants[45] came to think that not only were our sins imputed to Christ (a view that is Biblical, cf. 2 Corinthians 5:19-21, "He [God] made the One [Christ] who did not know sin [to be] sin on our behalf"), but that His righteousness is in return imputed to us who believe in Him.[46]   The Westminster Confession helped popularize the idea in the statement "Those whom God effectually called he also freely justified ... not by imputing faith itself, the act of believing, or any other evangelical obedience to them, as their righteousness; but by imputing the obedience and satisfaction of Christ unto them."[47]   Wesley issued conflicting statements on the doctrine.   He could speak both about faith being imputed,[48] and about the imputed righteousness of Christ.[49]   Protestants still issue conflicting statements as they debate whether or not Christ's righteousness is imputed to the sinner, and, if it is, "whether imputed righteousness is fictive, forensic or transformative."[50]

---

[43] Clyde L. Manschreck (trans.), *Melanchthon on Christian Doctrine: Loci communes 1555* (Grand Rapids: Baker, 1965), p.155,156.

[44] John Calvin, *Institutes of the Christian Religion*. 3.11.2. Library of Christian Classics.   Translated by Ford L. Battles, edited by John T. McNeill, 2 vols. (Philadelphia: Westminster Press, 1960), V.1, p.760. In almost every one of the Reformers' statements on imputed righteousness there is an emphatic denial of "works."   Was the intended foil the works of supererogation emphasized in Catholic teaching?   Did this constant denial of such works eventually lead to the expression 'faith alone' taking on another character where all human activity was severed from the faith that saves?

[45] Imputed righteousness was not universally taught by Protestants.   The Augsburg Confession reads, "This faith God imputes for righteousness before Him" (*The Augsburg Confession*, Article 4, "Of Justification").   Many of the Puritans (including, for example, Richard Baxter, Christopher Cartright, John Goodwin) disputed the notion of justification being comprised of the imputation of Christ's righteousness. They insisted instead that *faith* was the thing God reckoned as righteousness (Bird, *op. cit.*, p.63).

[46] See James Buchanan, *The Doctrine of Justification: An Outline of Its History in the Church and of Its Exposition from Scripture* (Edinburgh: T&T Clark, 1867), pp.131,32.   See also *Diognetus* 9:1-5.   See also *The Apology of the Augsburg Confession*, Article XXI (p.347).

[47] *The Westminster Confession of Faith*, Chapter 11.1, "Of Justification."

[48] John Wesley, "Justification by Faith," in *The Works of John Wesley* (Grand Rapids: Baker, 3rd ed. 1978), Vol.5, p.62.

[49] See the citation in W.W. Whidden, "Wesley on Imputation," *Asbury Theological Journal* 52 (1997), p.64.

[50] Mark Husbands and Daniel J. Trier, eds., *Justification: What's at Stake in the Current Debates* (Downers Grove, IL: InterVarsity Press, 2004), p.7.   R.C. Sproul, *Faith Alone: The Evangelical Doctrine of Justification* (Grand Rapids: Baker, 1995).   Wayne Grudem, *Systematic Theology: An Introduction to Biblical Doctrine* (Grand Raids: Zondervan, 1994), p.726-29.   James White, *The God Who Justifies* (Minneapolis: Bethany, 2001).   And Philip Eveson, *The Great Exchange: Justification by Faith Alone in the Light of Recent Thought* (Kent: Day One Publications, 1996).   All have written defending the traditional Reformed view of the imputation of Christ's alien righteousness.

Since the Bible speaks often about *faith* being reckoned as righteousness (e.g., Romans 4:3,4,6,9,11,22-24; Galatians 3:6) and perhaps not at all about Christ's righteousness being reckoned, the idea of Christ's righteousness being imputed is losing support among contemporary Bible scholars.[51] These verses speak of *faith* being counted or reckoned as righteousness: "righteousness comes into view not as what is counted, but as what God counts faith to be."[52]

At this point, a brief study of the classic proof texts traditionally used to prove the imputation of an alien righteousness is needed.

(1) Romans 4:3-22 does not speak of *Christ's righteousness* as being reckoned. (*Logizomai* is translated "take into account" at Romans 4:8; as "counted" or "counting" at Romans 2:26 and 2 Corinthians 5:19; as "regarded" at Acts 19:27 and Romans 9:8; and as "credit" at 2 Corinthians 12:6.[53]) Rather, these verses speak about *Abraham's belief* (Hebrew, *emunah*) being reckoned as righteousness. Even Romans 4:6,11, which do speak of righteousness being reckoned to believers, do not specify it as being Christ's righteousness. *Abraham's faith*, not *Christ's obedience*, is the subject of *logizomai* in the context. Throughout the passage it is "faith" that God is "regarding," not something Jesus has done.

(2) Romans 4:24,25 is often cited as a proof text for alien righteousness being imputed. The KJV reads that Christ "was delivered for our offences and was raised again for our justification." We have argued elsewhere[54] that "justification" (*dikaioma*) at this place refers not to forgiveness of sins (*dikaiosune*), but rather to our future resurrection body. Jesus' rising from the dead as a sort of first-fruits of other people being raised from the dead makes possible their resurrection (1 Corinthians 15:23).

(3) 1 Corinthians 1:30 reads "Christ Jesus ... became to us wisdom from God, and righteousness, and sanctification, and redemption." We agree with N.T. Wright who has affirmed it makes little sense to say God "like a judge, imputes, imparts, bequeaths,

[51] Robert Gundry, "The Nonimputation of Christ's Righteousness" in *Justification*, ed. by Mark Husbands and Daniel J. Treier (Downers Grove, IL: InterVarsity Press, 2004), p.18. Gundry goes on to advocate that the doctrine of the imputed righteousness of Christ should be abandoned as unbiblical (p.24). If he is right, there is much that is familiar that will need to be rethought. Recall the picture in *Pilgrim's Progress* where Christian is clothed with the righteousness of Christ. Recall that Wesley's hymns like "And Can It Be?" are permeated with the doctrine of imputed righteousness. There is a lot to give up if the doctrine proves to be unbiblical.

[52] *Ibid.*

[53] On occasion (e.g., Romans 4:8,11; 2 Corinthians 5:19; James 2:23), both the KJV and Douay use "imputed" to translate *logizomai*. Familiarity with the KJV has, in the past, led this commentator to use "reckon" and "impute" as interchangeable terms, though he attempted to carefully define how he was using "impute." (E.g., to attribute, or ascribe, or credit – not to instill or implant.)

[54] Gareth L. Reese, *New Testament Epistles: Romans* (Moberly, MO: Scripture Exposition Books, 1996), p.178.

conveys, or otherwise transfers His righteousness to either the plaintiff or the defendant."[55]   If 1 Corinthians 1:30 means Christ's righteousness is imputed to the sinner, then by parity of reasoning the rest of the verse would mean wisdom, sanctification [holiness], and redemption are likewise imputed – all rather strange ideas.   In a context where Paul is comparing the wisdom of the world with the wisdom of God, the passage says Christ has become to us the wisdom from God, a wisdom that includes (*te kai*, "even") righteousness, and sanctification, and redemption.   God's wisdom includes His way of saving man ("righteousness"), holiness ("sanctification"), and ultimately a resurrection body ("redemption").

(4) 2 Corinthians 5:21 says "[God] made Him who knew no sin to be sin on our behalf, that we might become the righteousness of God in Him."   The words "that we might become the righteousness of God in Him" are said to teach that Christ's righteousness is transferred to the person being justified.   Piper has written recently that 2 Corinthians 5:21 is about how reconciliation happens (not about what Paul is trying to do in his ministry – i.e., reconciling men to God), and this requires the old Reformed doctrine of imputation.   He states, "We 'become' God's righteousness the way Christ 'was made' our sin."[56]   A much better exposition of 2 Corinthians 5:21 is to say that just as "Christ became a curse for us" (Galatians 3:21) means that He became the object of God's curse, so the phrase "we become the righteousness of God" in 2 Corinthians 5:21 means that "we become the objects of His salvifically active righteousness."[57]

(5) Philippians 3:9 reads, "not having a righteousness of my own derived from *the* Law, but that which is through faith in Christ, the righteousness which *comes* from God on the basis of faith."   Philippians 3:4-18 does not say we have Christ's faithfulness (or obedience, Philippians 2:8) credited to us, thus overcoming and canceling out whatever debts we might owe because of our sin.   It says God's righteousness (His way of saving man) is made possible through faith in Christ whose obedience led Him to die on the cross.

Our brief study of the key proof texts for imputed righteousness has led us to doubt that any verse in Scripture indicates that the righteousness of Jesus is imputed or attributed or transferred when a man is justified.[58]   To talk about the alien righteousness of Christ being imputed when we are speaking of justification/ righteousness may just add confusion to our understanding of justification by faith.

---

[55] N.T. Wright, *What Saint Paul Really Said* (Grand Rapids: Eerdmans, 1997), p.98.

[56] Piper, *Counted Righteous*, p.69.

[57] Gundry, *op. cit.*, p.41.

[58] Had Paul wanted to say that Christ's righteousness is imputed to sinners, he could have done so only with the change of a single word.   He could have written in 2 Corinthians 5:21, "in order that we might become the righteousness of *Christ*."   Or he could have written in Philippians 3:8-9, "in order that I may gain Christ and may be found in Him, not having a righteousness of my own derived from the Law, but [having] *His* righteousness on the basis of faith."   It is significant that Paul did not so write.

If we reject the language about Christ's righteousness being imputed, what language shall we use? If we were to use Biblical language, "propitiation" is one such word. Instead of Christ's righteousness being that which the Judge sees before He acquits the sinner, it is the propitiatory, atoning death of Christ that God the Judge sees (Romans 3:24). That is what covers our sins. "Redemption" is another Biblical word. Romans 3:24 (KJV) tells us that believers are "justified freely ... through the redemption that is in Jesus Christ." The substitutionary atoning death of Christ makes redemption of the penitent sinner possible. 1 Peter 3:18 ("Christ died, the righteous for (*huper*) the unrighteous, that He might bring us to God" [ASV]) connects the righteousness of Christ with His death for the unrighteous. Isaiah 53:11 (ESV) predicted what Messiah would do in these words, "The Righteous One, my Servant, [shall] make many to be accounted righteous, and He shall bear their iniquities." "Christ died for our sins according to the Scriptures" (1 Corinthians 15:3). According to Romans 5:6, in due season He died for the ungodly (Romans 5:6); while we were yet sinners He died for us (verse 8); we are justified in His blood (verse 9), and it is through Him that we are saved from wrath (verse 9). While we were enemies we were reconciled to God through the death of His son (verse 10).

D. Brief Statements on Other Topics Sometimes Brought in as Arguments in the Debate on Justification by Faith

We have been giving the conclusions which result from our lifetime of studies of New Testament writings in order to have criteria by which we may evaluate some contemporary emphases in New Testament studies. Space permits only a brief summary of topics other than the three already presented in detail.

(1) The thrust of Romans 9-11 is that Israel was elected by God for service, not for salvation. God had a special job for them to do in being the channel through whom Messiah (according to the flesh) came into the world.
(2) A summary of the epistle to the Hebrews is this: The New Testament is better than and takes the place of the Old (i.e., the Mosaic covenant) because the Messenger (God's Son Jesus) who gave the new is superior to the messengers (prophets, angels, Moses) who delivered the old.
(3) It was certainly Jesus' judgment that 1st century (Pharisaic) Judaism had departed significantly from what the Law of Moses taught (Matthew 15:3-9 = Mark 7:16-13).[59]
(4) God's intentions were to unite Jews and Gentiles into one body (Ephesians 2:14-18), one new man (Ephesians 2:15), one "olive tree" (Romans 11:17-24). This means Gen-

---

[59] This commentator takes the Gospel accounts at face value; namely, that the record of what Jesus said is accurate and true. But even if we were to grant, which we do not, that some redactor in the early church was responsible for putting these words in Jesus' mouth, it still reflects a criticism of Palestinian Judaism held by the followers of Jesus, and where did they get their ideas if not from the Master Himself?

tiles do not have to become Jews and Jews do not have to become Gentiles, but rather that both must become part of Abraham's spiritual descendants by faithfulness to Jesus Christ.

II. HISTORICAL HIGHLIGHTS – HOW THE DOCTRINE OF JUSTIFICATION BY FAITH HAS BEEN INTERPRETED THROUGH THE CHRISTIAN CENTURIES.

The meaning of the topics introduced above – justification, faith, and imputed alien righteousness – have been debated, and they have developed a history and meaning as a result of that ongoing debate.   To be acquainted with the history of doctrines often proves helpful to a correct understanding of Biblical teachings.

A. Justification/Righteousness

On this topic, the interpretation of Augustine of Hippo seems to have dominated Western theological discussion until the 14th century.[60]   Augustine argued that the expression "the righteousness of God" did not refer to an attribute of God (i.e., that He Himself personally is always righteous) but rather it refers to the righteousness which He bestows upon sinners, in order to justify them; in other words, it is a righteousness which comes from God.[61]   Working with the Latin, Augustine gave *iustitia* its classic jurisprudential notion of 'justice,' i.e., the "rendering to each one his due." Augustine treated *iustificare* as the process by which men are made just.   Human beings, he thought, neither merit God's approbation or even desire His mercy, so God takes the initiative, operating on the human soul so that it will cooperate with God in the process of restoration (i.e., first work of grace).   In Augustine's system, justification was a causative process whereby the sinner is made righteous.

Augustine's influence can be seen in Roman Catholicism where justification is something God does to a person. It *makes* men righteous. Righteousness is *infused* into their soul. Medieval Catholicism continued to teach an *infused* righteousness. Thomas Aquinas' teaching on justification (i.e., infused righteousness, an effect of grace on the soul that he called "healing,"[62] a remaking of the soul after the image of God) was what Luther

---

[60] The decisive emergence of justification as a major theme in Western theology comes with Augustine.   Then much of medieval and Reformation discussion of justification developed within an explicitly Augustinian framework. (David Fink, "'The Doers of the Law will be Justified': The Exegetical Origins of Martin Bucer's *Triplex Iustificatio*," *JTS* 58:2 (October 2007), p.489.)

[61] McGrath, *op. cit.*, p.520.

[62] *Summa Theologica* Ia2ae, Q.111, art.2.

and the Reformers objected to. To Aquinas, justification, or the making just of human nature, is something that is repeated throughout the Christian life as men and women make use of the means of grace – especially the grace given through the sacrament of penance and the performance of meritorious good works.[63] The Council of Trent, following the trajectory begun by Augustine and encouraged by Aquinas, decried the teachings of the Reformers which emphasized the monergistic operation of grace and the efficacy of faith alone.

In the 14th century certain theologians began to reinterpret the "righteousness of God" in terms of an attribute of God.[64] Justification was seen to be something God pronounces, something God reckons or imputes to men. The Reformers eventually came to proclaim that justification is by grace alone through faith alone on the ground of Christ's righteousness alone, and they embodied this doctrine in their full confessional statements.

(a) Luther understood the "righteousness of God" in Scriptural statements as being one of God's attributes, but during his debate with Melanchthon on justification, Luther changed his views so that righteousness is something God imputes to sinners when He justifies them. That imputed alien righteousness is what enables God to count them as righteous in His sight *(coram Deo)*.[65]

(b) Calvin, in his debate with Osiander, developed the Reformed alternative to Aquinas' theology. He presented justification in terms of a two-fold imputation – the remission of sins and the imputation of Christ's righteousness.[66] In Calvin's presentation, justification is by faith alone and it is strictly forensic and judicial in character. He employs the term "acquittal." "'To justify' means nothing else than to acquit of guilt him who was accused, as if his innocence were confirmed."[67] How can this happen? How can the sinner who is obviously guilty be seen as innocent before the judgment seat of God? Calvin answered, By means of the imputation of Christ's perfect righteousness. "Therefore, since God justifies us by the intercession of Christ, he absolves us not by the confirmation of our own innocence but by the imputation of righteousness, so that we who are not righteous in ourselves may be reckoned as such

---

[63] Bruce McCormack, "What's At Stake in Current Debates Over Justification?" in *Justification*, edited by Mark Husbands and Daniel J. Trier (Downers Grove, IL: InterVarsity, 2004), p.89.

[64] McGrath, *op. cit.*, p.520.

[65] McGrath, *op. cit.*, p.520. Just as Luther's views changed, it is a fact well known that Melanchthon's understanding of justification underwent significant development between 1530 and 1534. Early, he could speak of justification as a "being made righteous" as well as a "being pronounced righteous." Later he spoke of justification in purely forensic terms over against his earlier writings. See Mark Seifrid, "Luther, Melanchthon, and Paul on the Question of Imputation," in *Justification*, edited by Mark Husbands and Danaiel J. Treier (Downers Grove: InterVarsity, 2004), p.139-142.

[66] See McCormack, *op. cit.*, p.91-92.

[67] Calvin, *Institutes*, 3.2.3.

in Christ."[68]   In Calvin's view, God's verdict differs from the verdict pronounced by human judges.   Human judges can only pronounce on what is supposed or hoped to be the real state of affairs; the human verdict does not create the reality it declares. God's verdict differs in that His divine word creates the reality it declares.   God's verdict is itself thought to be transformative.   The debate between Lutherans and Reformed theologians concerning the "righteousness of God" (i.e., is it an attribute of God or something God does, and if it is something He does just what is included) has continued in 19th and 20th centuries.   There has even been debate within the two traditions.   Two influential Lutheran scholars, Bultmann and Käsemann, debated the topic of justification.   To Bultmann, the "righteousness of God" is a genitive of authorship, i.e., it is a righteousness that is imputed to believers in the present time.   Käsemann, while severely criticizing Bultmann's view, makes the "righteousness of God" to be a reference to God in action, rather than an attribute of God.[69]

(c) Wesley and the Anglicans both have issued conflicting statements about the nature of justification.   Sometimes it is a simple verdict; sometimes it involves imputed righteousness.[70]

As we have studied the history of the debate up to recent times, we have seen that Catholics treat justification as a continuing process, while Protestants treat it as a one-time thing, a verdict pronounced by God the judge at the beginning of a person's Christian life. Furthermore, there is no agreement about the relationship of regeneration to justification. Is one regenerated before he is justified, or after?   In Calvin's arrangement, regeneration follows justification, since the bestowal of the Spirit of adoption (Romans 8:15) follows justification, and, as Calvin saw it, it is this Spirit of adoption that is the means by which the believer is regenerated.[71]   Nor is there any agreement about the relationship of justification and sanctification.   Does justification include sanctification, as the Roman Catholic view has it, or does Scripture teach that sanctification must follow justification? In fact, do the Scriptures even teach that sanctification follows justification, as Calvin taught?   Or again, what is the relation, if any, between justification and conversion?

B. Faith

Not only has "justification" been debated, so has the meaning of the word "faith." Examining early Christian literature for a definition of faith,   it becomes quickly evident

---

[68] Calvin, *Institutes,* 3.2.4.   This is the presentation of justification that Catholics insist is simply "legal fiction."

[69] McGrath, *op. cit.*, p.520.

[70] See Kenneth Collins, "The Doctrine of Justification: Historic Wesleyan and Contemporary Understandings," in *Justification*, ed. Mark Husbands and Daniel J. Treier (Downers Grove: InterVarsity, 2004), p.187ff.

[71] McCormack, *op. cit.*, p.100.

that Clement of Rome (*1 Clement* xxxii.3ff, and xxxv), Ignatius (*Tral.* 2.1), Barnabas (ch. 5 & 19), Shepherd (1.3.8), and *Didache* (16.5) do not present "faith" in the form that today is called "faith only" or "faith alone."[72]   The Roman Catholic Church still continues to teach that the faith that saves is a faith that includes human actions, that saving faith is completed or made perfect by acts of love (Galatians 5:6).

Where then did *solifidianism* ("faith alone") arise?   Augustine interpreted "justified by faith apart from works of the Law" in Romans as being "faith alone" during his debate with Pelagius, who treated human good deeds as leading to salvation.[73]   Luther picked up Augustine's treatment of faith as being "faith alone."   Because of Luther's influence, it became the rather widely accepted Protestant definition.[74]   Thomas Cranmer, archbishop of Canterbury, dealt with justification in his "Homily on Salvation."   In his view, salvation is by faith only, without works; repentance precedes this lively faith and good works flow from it.   Though sinners are justified by faith alone, it is by a faith that is never alone.[75] John Wesley became a champion of *sola fides*.   After Wesley's visit to the Moravian community at Herrnhut in the fall of 1738, he began to teach justification by faith only and that faith was an instantaneous act.[76]   Numerous contemporary writers[77] still insist that initial justification is by faith alone, though this initial faith may lead to good works – in fact, the very good works which God is said to take into account at the final judgment when men will be justified by works (Romans 2:6-10).

---

[72] John A. Faulkner, "Justification" in *The International Standard Bible Encyclopedia*, edited by James Orr (Grand Rapids: Eerdmans, 1949), V.3, p.1786.

[73] Richard Hays, "Justification" in *Anchor Bible Dictionary*, edited by David N. Freedman (NY: Doubleday, 1992), V.3, p.1133.

[74] Paul Westerholm (*op. cit.*) has "The 'Lutheran' Paul and His Critics" as the subtitle of his book.   He explains that the word 'Lutheran' in the subtitle designates "one for whom the doctrine of justification by faith is central and deliberately excludes any role for human 'works'" (p.xvii).   The religious milieu in Luther's time was Tetzel's selling of indulgences to build the cathedral of St. Peter's in Rome.   Luther saw the earning (by such purchases) of an early release from Purgatory as being the same kind of meritorious achievement Jews used to teach and to which Paul vehemently objected.

[75] Cranmer insisted that the faith that saves is a lively faith, including repentance antecedent to it, as well as all the good works that flow from such a faith.   It does not exclude "repentance, hope, love, dread, and the fear of God," but it does exclude them "from the office of justifying."   J. Edmund Cox, ed., *Miscellaneous Writings and Letters of Thomas Cranmer* (Vancouver, BC: Regent College Publishing, nd), p.129.

[76] Kenneth J. Collins, "The Doctrine of Justification: Historic Wesleyan and Contemporary Understandings," in *Justification*, edited by Mark Husbands and Daniel Trier (Downers Grove: InterVarsity, 2004), p.191-95.

[77] For example, see Zane Hodges, *The Gospel Under Siege: A Study of Faith and Works* (2nd ed: Dallas: Rendencion Viva, 1991) who intensely defends faith-only as the condition.   "Paul is adamant that it is faith alone which justifies here and now," says Don Garlington, *Faith, Obedience, and Perseverance: Aspects of Paul's Letter to the Romans* (Tubingen: Mohr, 1994), p.44.   "Initial justification is by sheer, naked faith.   The sinner has no works to offer; he simply lays hold of Christ by faith," says Richard Lusk, *"Miscellanies on the 'New Perspective' and Pauline Theology,"* Fall 2003-Spring 2004 (Trinity Presbyterian Church, Birmingham, AL: Pastor's Page), #30, pt.6.

In contrast to faith only is the definition of faith championed by folk in the Restoration Movement, namely, that faith is doing what God says. The Old Covenant required faith, specifically keeping the requirements of the Mosaic Law. The New Covenant requires faith, specifically obedience to the law of Christ. Paul never pits faith against "obedience," nor does he pit faith against love for God and neighbor. When faith is contrasted with works, it is contrasted with "works of the Law" which, we have shown elsewhere, are not the same thing as the (good) works God has commanded, and by which men will be judged.

C. The Imputation or Non-Imputation of Christ's Righteousness

As noted above, the idea of the *imputation* of Christ's righteousness was introduced by Luther and Calvin, and then came to be incorporated into some of the famous confessions of faith.

Some still teach it. Systematic theologies by Reformed theologians, from Beza to Berkhof, "have regarded the doctrine of the imputed righteousness of Christ as being the defining mark of justification for Protestantism."[78] Some Protestants, as they have explained imputed righteousness, have come very close to teaching a doctrine that is hard to distinguish from the Catholic view of infused righteousness.[79] This lack of distinction between Catholic and Protestant views has led others to reject the doctrine of imputed righteousness altogether. In its place the affirmation is made that the righteousness of God refers to His covenant faithfulness to Israel, or to His treatment of both Jews and Gentiles as being right and fair.[80] N.T. Wright understands God's righteousness as His covenant faithfulness.[81] Wright defines God's righteousness by saying that it *keeps* covenant, *judges* impartially, *deals* properly with sin, *advocates* for the helpless. Wright is at odds with the Reformed view of imputation of alien righteousness.[82]

---

[78] Bird, *op. cit.*, p.64.

[79] As long ago as 1918, James Denney asked whether or not the distinction between *imputed* righteousness (as taught by some Protestants) and *infused* righteousness (as taught by the Catholics) is an unreal distinction. James Denney, *The Christian Doctrine of Reconciliation* (London: James Clarke and Co, 1959 reprint), p.164-65.

[80] Timo Eskola, *Theodicy and Predestination in Pauline Soteriology*, WUNT 2/100 (Tubingen: Mohr Siebeck, 1998).

[81] "God's righteousness is his faithfulness to the covenant." N.T. Wright, *Justification* (Downers Grove: InterVarsity, 2009), p.67.

[82] Bird, *op. cit.*, p.38.

John Piper and Robert Gundry have debated the idea of the imputed righteousness of Christ. In 1999, *Christianity Today* published an article entitled "The Gospel of Jesus Christ: An Evangelical Celebration." Gundry thought it advocated an overemphasis on imputed righteousness, and published an article contending such a doctrine flies in the face of Biblical testimony.[83] In 2002, John Piper presented a rigorous defense of imputed righteousness,[84] wherein he used Gundry as his foil as he developed his thesis that Christ's righteousness is imputed to believers.

As noted above, some reject the idea as being an unbiblical use of Bible language. For example, "There simply is no text in the New Testament which categorically states that Christ's righteousness is imputed to believers."[85]

III. HISTORICAL HIGHLIGHTS CONTINUED – THE CONTEMPORARY SCENE

A. The First Half of the 20th Century

1. Religious liberalism. James I. Packer recounts how liberal theologians in the early part of the 20th century spread the notion that God's attitude towards all men was one of paternal affection, not one conditioned by the demands of His law. Hence, interest in the sinner's justification by the divine judge was replaced by the thought of the prodigal's forgiveness and rehabilitation by his divine Father. The validity of forensic categories for expressing God's saving action towards man was widely denied.[86]

2. Neo-orthodoxy. In the 1920's, neo-orthodoxy became the scholarly passion. Packer summarizes how neo-orthodox theologians minimized any legal categories. Such legal, forensic qualities tended to downplay the personal nature of the relationship between God and man. And it was the quality of that personal relationship that neo-orthodox theo-

---

[83] Robert H. Gundry, "Why I Didn't Endorse 'The Gospel of Jesus Christ: An Evangelical Celebration' ... Even Though I Wasn't Asked to," *Books and Culture* 7:1 (January-February 2001), p.6-9.

[84] John Piper, *Counted Righteous in Christ: Should We Abandon the Imputation of Christ's Righteousness?* (Wheaton, IL: Crossway, 2002).

[85] Michael Bird, *The Saving Righteousness of God*, (Eugene, OR: Wipf & Stock, 2007), p.2. This statement was written by a self-confessed "card-carrying Calvinist" (p.2) who knew by heart the passages which purportedly teach such a doctrine (e.g. Romans 4:4-5; 2 Corinthians 5:21; Philippians 3:7-9).

[86] Packer, *op. cit.*, p.646.

logians thought better represented what the Bible says, rather than a presentation emphasizing how God expects His laws to be obeyed.[87]

3. Neo-liberalism. By mid-century, a new approach to explaining the New Testament was being promulgated. In previous notes we have already alluded to the debate between Bultmann and Käsemann over justification. Bultmann, Gunther, Bornkamm, and Käsemann all stood within the Lutheran tradition.

4. Since Vatican II. Since the Second Vatican Council (1962-65), there have been various attempts to try to reconcile Protestants and Catholics on the doctrine of justification.[88] For example, since 1967 Methodists and Catholics have been participating in a joint commission to engage in theological dialogue and to explore common understandings and purpose. Meetings have been held in Ariccia in 1967, in Denver in 1971, in Nairobi in 1986, and in Singapore in 1991. No major agreements were reached. Since 1994, a group called Evangelicals and Catholics Together (ECT) has been attempting to see if an ecumenical agreement could be reached on the long divisive issue of justification.[89] In 1994 the group issued a statement in which several prominent Roman Catholics affirmed "justification by faith alone" – however, the document was so worded that Catholics could deny meritorious works while still affirming that faith was made perfect through love, and Protestants could affirm it was "faith only."[90] One ECT statement, "All who accept Christ as Lord and Savior are brothers and sisters in Christ," led R.C. Sproul to respond with a book critiquing ECT, titled *Faith Alone: The Evangelical Doctrine of Justification* (Grand Rapids: Baker, 1995). In 1997, in response to the very point Sproul objected to, the ECT produced another ecumenical document titled "The Gift of Salvation." This document proved no more acceptable to some evangelicals than the 1994 statement.[91] Then in 1999 came the agreement signed by representatives of the Vatican and the Lutheran World Federation called "The Joint Declaration on the Doctrine of Justification." Both sides agreed to cease the anathemas hurled at each other ever since the Council of Trent. The

---

[87] *Ibid.*

[88] This brief review of Catholic-Protestant interaction is abbreviated from Collins, *op. cit.*, p.195-210.

[89] This study group was formed largely at the instigation of Prison Fellowship founder Charles Colson and Catholic priest Richard John Neuhaus. See Colson and Neuhaus, *Evangelicals and Catholics: Toward a Common Mission* (Dallas: Word, 1995).

[90] Colin Hansen, "Not All Evangelicals and Catholics Together," *Christianity Today* 53:11 (November 2009), p.19,20.

[91] Timothy George ("Evangelicals and Catholics Together: a New Initiative," *Christianity Today* 41:14 [December 8, 1997], p.34-35) argued that the language about justification which the Catholic participants in ECT agreed to was not an acceptance of justification by faith alone, but was an echo of the Thirty-Nine Articles of the Church of England: "We are accounted righteous before God, only for the merit of our Lord and Savior Jesus Christ by faith, and not for our own works or deservings."

anathemas of Trent do not apply to Protestants who agree with the joint declaration.[92]   The official statement is capable of whatever interpretation the reader wishes to see in them, and D.A. Carson has offered the opinion that Catholics (in the official teachings of the church) and Protestants are as far apart on the doctrine of justification as they were at the time of the Council of Trent.[93]

B. Last Half of the 20th Century and Into the 21st Century

1. *Krister Stendahl.*   Stephen Westerholm has offered this assessment: "No article published in the 20th century on a New Testament topic garnered more attention, provoked more debate, or exercised greater influence than Krister Stendahl's 'The Apostle Paul and the Introspective Conscience of the West',"(*Harvard Theological Review* 56 (1963), p.199-215).[94]   Two key ideas suggested by Stendahl are: (a) Luther and Protestants have been trying to read Paul using 16th century glasses instead of seeing him through 1st century glasses. As a result, they have indeed given a distorted picture of what Paul taught. To understand what Paul wrote we must try to understand his 1st century context.[95]   (b) As the title of the article indicates, the thrust had to do with the introspective conscience. Stendahl insisted it was Augustine – not Paul– who was given to introspection (i.e., a keen consciousness of personal sin and alienation from God), and who emphasized the question that tormented Luther, "How can I find a gracious God?" Luther found his answer in Romans and Galatians, even though these books, when first written, may not have specifically dealt with that question.

2. *The New Perspective on Paul.*   The so-called new perspective,[96] launched by E.P. Sanders in the late 1970s, and developed and refined particularly in the extensive writings

---

[92] Hansen, *op. cit.*, p.20. For further details about the Lutheran/Catholic rapprochement, see more below under the "Post-New Perspective."

[93] D.A. Carson, "Reflections on Salvation and Justification in the New Testament," *JETS* 40:4 (December 1997), p.606.

[94] Stephen Westerholm, "Justification by Faith is the Answer: What is the Question?" *CTQ* 70:3/4 (July/October 2006), p.197. Not even the writing of Albert Schweitzer, *The Mysticism of Paul the Apostle* (New York: Seabury, 1931), or George Foote Moore's *Judaism in the First Centuries of the Christian Era: The Age of the Tannaim* (3 volumes, Cambridge: Harvard University Press, 1927-30), both of whom advocated some of the same points that Stendahl does, had such an impact on scholarly consensus.

[95] The Restoration Movement has long championed a return to the 1st century church, not to the 4th century church and theology.

[96] See James D.G. Dunn, "The New Perspective on Paul," *BJRL* 65 (1983), p.95-122. See also chapter 1, in "The New Perspective on Paul: Whence, What, and Whither" in James Dunn's *The New Perspective on Paul*, 2nd ed. (Grand Rapids: Eerdmans, 2008). It is an extended effort to explain the origins of the NPP and to respond to critics, and is an attempt to advance the discussions surrounding the NPP. The NPP is not a single school of thought with set boundaries (since Sanders, Dunn, and Wright disagree on many issues) but rather a trajectory.

of James D.G. Dunn and N.T. Wright, has posed a significant challenge to the traditional reformed understanding of justification by faith. E.P. Sanders published two major writings addressing the theme of the relation of Paul's thought to the then contemporary Second Temple Judaism: *Paul and Palestinian Judaism* (1977) and *Paul, the Law and the Jewish People* (1983). In these two works he urged scholars to do two things: (a) Stop reading Paul through glasses tinted by a Reformation Lutheran interpretation of Paul. (b) Stop the wrongful presentation of what 1st century Judaism was like that resulted from a mirror reading of Paul's objections to Judaism as seen through 16th century glasses. Judaism, Sanders affirmed, was not a salvation-earned-by-works religion as Luther portrayed it.[97] According to Sanders, Palestinian Judaism (which, he affirmed, did not differ to any degree from Diaspora Judaism) should instead be characterized as a form of "covenantal nomism."[98] The Law was intended to spell out clearly and precisely the forms of conduct that were acceptable to God within the context of the covenant He had made with Israel through Moses the mediator. The "works of the Law" were not the means by which one became a member of the covenant community. One got in by grace, and stayed in by works. "Works of the Law," in Sanders' view, are not to be understood as the condition for getting into a covenant relationship with God, but rather of maintaining that covenant relationship once one was in it.[99]

Not quite satisfied with Sanders' explanation, James D.G. Dunn, utilizing insights suggested by social science criticism, has hypothesized that "justification" is Paul's special word to express the idea that the inheritance promised to Abraham (which was never superseded by the Law of Moses, Galatians 3) embraces Gentiles apart from the Law, or apart from works of the Law. "Works of the Law" are seen to be "boundary markers" that keep Jewish and Gentile believers apart, and this is why they were rejected by Paul.[100]

---

[97] When Sanders makes this affirmation he is arguing against the prevalent view of much New Testament scholarship that says "Judaism was a religion in which one must earn salvation by compiling more good works ('merits') whether on his own or from the excess of someone else, than he has transgressions" (*Paul and Palestinian Judaism*, p.38). The idea that 1st century Judaism taught meritorious works resulted from two sources: treating 5th century AD Jewish writings as though they accurately reflected 1st century Judaism, and supposing the 16th century Catholic system of merit was like the religion of the Pharisees which was attacked by Jesus and Paul. The old Protestant caricature had Judaism demanding perfect obedience to the Law as the condition of salvation. Sanders argued that the Law of Moses never demanded complete (perfect) obedience, and that forgiveness was available through repentance and the sacrificial system.

[98] It appears to this commentator that both Luther and Sanders, as well as Käsemann and Bultmann, have erred in treating "works of the Law" as being the same as carefully practicing the Law of Moses. Does this reflect one-covenant theology, where Moses and Christianity are but different dispensations of the same covenant?

[99] If Sanders is correct, the basic features of Luther's interpretation of Paul are shown to be incorrect, and this in turn would require a radical revision, a new perspective, on Paul. (McGrath, *op. cit.*, p.519)

[100] What Dunn emphasizes (i.e., that both Gentiles and Jews are included in the promise to Abraham) is a truth, but is "justification" the Biblical word best suited to express this idea? We think not.

Before Sanders' books were published, though few listened to them, Jewish scholars familiar with Jewish writings from around the time of Christ had long objected to the false picture or caricature that Christian theologians gave of Second Temple Judaism.[101] If the new perspective is correct, then the traditional Lutheran/ Reformed perspective was "all a big misunderstanding"[102] of what Paul meant when he spoke of justification by faith apart from the works of the Law. Defenders of Lutheran theology and of Reformed theology both consider that the new perspective on Paul has launched a broadside against their doctrine.

The new perspective on Paul begins with the epistle to the Galatians. First, scholars must reinterpret Galatians so that "works of the Law" actually reflects the beliefs and practices of Second Temple Judaism. Then, scholars must apply what has been learned from Galatians to the rest of the New Testament. This surely is a good approach to take.[103] Nevertheless, the new perspective's views about the nature of Judaism have not gone without challenge.[104] If the challengers can show that Sanders' arguments are flawed, then the traditional explanation of justification by faith may still be correct.

---

[101] See Donald A. Hagner, "Paul in Modern Jewish Thought," in *Pauline Studies* edited by D.A. Hagner and M.J. Harris (Grand Rapids: Eerdmans, 1980), p.143-165. Following the precedent set by Luther, New Testament scholars in the late 19th and the first three-quarters of the 20th centuries were influenced by the 1880 book on rabbinic Judaism by Ferdinand Weber (*System dswee altsynagogalen palastinischen Theologie aus Targum, Midrasch und Talmud*) in which the Judaism that Paul knew and critiqued was depicted as fundamentally legalistic, a religion of works-based righteousness. Weber apparently was not conversant with ancient Jewish writings, and this was said to have led to his mistaken presentations. Jewish writers objected to the picture of Judaism the Lutherans and Weber imagined by their mirror image reading of Paul. They wondered how Paul could characterize the Judaism of his day so misleadingly. One Jewish writer styled it as being "the imaginary Rabbinic Judaism, created by Christian scholars in order to form a suitably lurid background for the Epistles of St. Paul" (C.G. Montefiore, *Judaism and St. Paul* [London: Max Goschen, 1914], p.65). In 1969 Samuel Sandmel protested against the article on the "Pharisees" in *Interpreter's Dictionary of the Bible*, which characterized Pharisaism as "the immediate ancestor of Rabbinical (or normative) Judaism, the arid and sterile religion of the Jews after the fall of Jerusalem" (*The First Christian Century in Judaism and Christianity: Certainties and Uncertainties* [NY: Oxford U, 1969], p.101). Some Christian writers, such as G.F. Moore, in both his three-volume *Judaism in the First Centuries of the Christian Era: The Age of the Tannaim* (Cambridge, MA: Harvard University Press, 1927-30), and in his "Christian Writers on Judaism," *HTR* 15 (1922), p.41-61, also objected to the unfair caricature of Judaism by the Christians. Despite repeated critiques by Jewish scholars, Christian scholars, for the most part, did not themselves study the Jewish writings from the Second Temple era, but continued to apply anachronistically the 5th century AD writings to the 1st century, until the publication of Sanders' *Paul and Palestinian Judaism.*

[102] The phrase comes from R.B. Matlock's critical review of Dunn's work *The Theology of Paul*, titled "Sins of the Flesh and Suspicious Minds: Dunn's New Theology of Paul," *JSNT* 72 (1998), p.67-90, 72.

[103] See this commentary on Galatians concerning who the false teachers were and the message they presented to the Galatian Christians as they tried to recruit those church members for Pharisaic Judaism. The reconstruction in this commentary differs greatly from the scenario supposed by most new perspective advocates, but it does follow the same approach to understanding the books of Galatians and Romans and what "justification by faith" really means.

[104] One of the leaders of the challenge is Seyoon Kim. See especially his *Paul and the New Perspective: Second Thoughts on the Origin of Paul's Gospel* (Grand Rapids: Eerdmans, 2002). See also *Justification and Variegated Nomism. Volume 1: The Complexities of Second-Temple Judaism*, ed. D.A. Carson, P.T. O'Brien, and Mark A. Seifrid, *WUNT* 2/140 (Grand Rapids: Baker Academic, 2001).

What especially has given Lutheran and Reformed writers an opening is the fact that Sanders apparently overstated the case when he insisted 1st century Jews did not require works of some kind, that 1st century Jews never believed salvation was conditioned somehow on works. Two sources give us a glimpse into the mind of Second Temple Judaism: Jewish literature from the time, and the picture of the Pharisees in the Gospels. The theme of judgment according to works is one of the most frequent theological statements in Judaism.[105] Jesus' conversation with the rich young ruler (Matthew 19:16-29; Mark 10:17-30; Luke 18:18-30) is a case in point. "Good teacher, what good thing shall I do to inherit eternal life," he asked of Jesus. The rich young ruler understood that some action was required on the part of people who would be saved. Jesus' answer pointed him to the Law of Moses. That was what he was to "do." "Continue to do it, and you will live," said Jesus. Jesus' answer was not that rabbinic rules had to be observed, but that God's rules are to be habitually kept. In Jewish eyes and in Jesus' explanation, these actions/works are not meritorious, but are the condition on which God graciously grants justification. And Jesus' story about the Pharisee and the publican (Luke 18:9-14) surely captures the essence of Pharisaism. The Pharisee in his prayer spoke of how he had gone beyond what the Law demanded, and boasted he was not like other men (sinners). He thanked God for what he was doing. In Luke 18:11 Jesus allows us to overhear the Pharisee listing his score of deeds – his virtues of tithing and fasting and his scrupulous avoidance of adultery and theft. In his own estimation, the Pharisee believed he had met the conditions of salvation.

The debate spawned by the new perspective on Judaism and on Paul has taken a number of turns and twists during the last decade of the 20th century and into the first decade of the 21st century.

3. *The Post-new perspective.*   Some Finnish scholars, the most significant being Timo Laato and Timo Eskola,[106] have been championing an alternative view to Sanders' new perspective. Based on the supposition that justification is by faith alone, they see something radically wrong with Sanders' presentation that one gets in by faith alone,   but

---

[105] In a lengthy footnote, Snodgrass (*op. cit.*, p.90, n.38), from all strata of Jewish literature, gives references where works were required. It reads: "E.g. 1QS IV.6f.; X.16-18; CD VII.9f.; 1QH XVIII.12f.; IVQPs[f] VIII.4-5 (see J. Starcky, 'Psaumes Apocryphewde la Grotte 4 de Qumran', RB LXX, 1963, 256); 1QpHabv VIII.1f.; X.3; XII.14-XIII.4; Ps of Solomon 2.17f., 38; 9.4; 2 Bar. 13:8; 44.4; 54.21; 85.15; 4 Ezra 6.19; 7:17,33-44, 104f.; 8.31; 12.31f.; 14.32; Jub. 5.13-18; 21.4; 33.18; Test of Levi 3.2; 4.1f.; Test of Gad 7.5; Test of Benjamin 10.7f.; 1 Enoch 1.7-9; 16.2; 25.4f.; 41.2 & 9; 50.1-4; 60.2f.; 63.8; 100.7; Secrets of Enoch 50.1-5; 52.15; Assumption of Moses 12.10; Sibylline Oracles IV.183; Pirke Aboth I.3f.; II.1; III.15; IV.22; RH 16b; Hag. 5a; AZ 18a; Philo, *de Paemiis*, 126 *et passim*.

[106] See Timo Eskola, "Paul, Predestination and Covenantal Nomism – Reassessing Paul and Palestinian Judaism," *JSJ* 28 (1997), p.390-412. Timo Laato, *Paul and Judaism: An Anthropological Approach* (South Florida Studies in the History of Judaism 115: Atlanta, Scholars, 1995). A helpful introduction to these Finnish writers and their views is Brendan Byrne, "Interpreting Romans Theologically in a Post-'New Perspective' Perspective," *HTR* 94 (2001), p.227-41; and *idem*, "Interpreting Romans: The New Perspective and Beyond," *Interp* 58 (2004), p.241-52.

stays in by works. What is this, they want to know, if it is not a synergistic presentation of salvation? In their view, what is wrong with the new perspective is that its covenantal nomism is essentially a synergistic theology – men's works (i.e., observing the Law) have something to do with being justified. The Finnish scholars insist that what Paul fights against in Romans and Galatians is any idea of synergism. These Finnish scholars' treatment of justification is closely related to Eastern Orthodox notions of *theosis*, or "divinization" or "ontological healing" being involved in justification. The new Finnish reading of Luther has found a warm reception in the "evangelical Catholic" wing of the Evangelical Lutheran Church in America. A journal called *Pro Ecclesia* promotes it. The Finnish theologians also contributed appreciably to the final received text of the *Joint Declaration on the Doctrine of Justification* signed by representatives of the Lutheran World Federation and the Roman Catholic Church at a great celebration in Augsburg, Germany, on Reformation Day, 1999.[107] Some Lutherans in America are attacking the Joint Declaration.[108] In 2002, the 10th International Congress on Luther Research was held in Copenhagen. Two theologians, Simo Peura of Helsinki, representing the Finnish school, and Wilfried Härle of Heidelberg, representing the older Lutheran view, presented their interpretations of Luther's understanding of justification in the context of contemporary discussions of its significance.

4. *The Federal Vision*. In January 2002, a conference was held at the Auburn Avenue Presbyterian Church (PCA) in Monroe, Louisiana. The title of the conference was "The Federal Vision: An Examination of Reformed Covenantalism." The theological views presented there have come to be known as Federal Vision theology, or Auburn Avenue theology.[109] The organizers of the conference expected the conference to provide a positive federal (covenantal) view (vision), but when the conference was over, critics of the four main speakers charged them with a "fundamental denial of the essence of the Christian Gospel in their denial of justification by faith alone"[110] and in their denial of the imputation of Christ's righteousness.

---

[107] McCormack, *op. cit.*, p.95.

[108] Collins, *op. cit.*, p.199ff.

[109] Proponents of the Federal Vision insist the source of their ideas is not to be found in the New Perspective on Paul. There may be some similarities between the two theologies, but leaders in the Federal Vision movement insist they were discussing these issues long before any of them ever heard of E.P Sanders, J.D.G. Dunn, or Norman T. Wright.

[110] In June 2002, the Reformed Presbyterian Church in the United States issued a public call to the conference speakers (Douglas Wilson, John Barach, Steve Wilkins, Steve Schlissel) to repent. In 2004, the Confederation of Reformed Evangelical Churches (founded by Doug Wilson) examined Wilson regarding his views on justification and other topics, and came to a unanimous decision his theology was orthodox. In 2006 the Orthodox Presbyterian Church did agree that aberrant views on justification were promoted by the conference speakers. In 2007, the Presbyterian Church in America produced a report concluding that the teachings of Federal Vision on justification and other doctrines are contrary to the Westminster standards. In June 2009 the Reformed Presbyterian Church in the United States rejected Federal Vision theology as not in accordance with its doctrinal standards. A rejection of Federal Vision theology is found in Gary L.W. Johnson and Guy P. Waters (editors), *By Faith Alone: Answering the Challenges to the Doctrine of Justification* (Crossway Books, 2007).

The case can be made that Reformed theologians have not always rightly represented the views of Calvin as they presented their theological conclusions. The case can be made that many of the views presented at the 2002 conference were a return to Calvin's original views. Hear the Federal Vision's statement on baptism, a statement that is difficult to harmonize with faith only. Richard Lusk, for example, has written:

> Obviously, for Reformed Christians, the ultimate test of any doctrine is its fidelity to the whole counsel of God, revealed in the pages of Scripture. What does the Bible actually teach about the efficacy of baptism? ... In baptism, we are united (or married) to the crucified, buried, and risen Christ (Romans 6:1ff), though we can be cut off (or divorced) from him if we are unfaithful (Romans 11:17ff; cf. John 15:1ff). We are forgiven (Acts 2:38, 22:16); we receive the Holy Spirit (Acts 2:38); we are cleansed (Ephesians 5:26); we are regenerated and renewed (Titus 3:5); we are buried and resurrected with Christ (Colossians. 2:11-12); we are circumcised in heart (Colossians 2:11-12); we are joined to the body of Christ (1 Corinthians 12:13); we are clothed with Christ (Galatians 3:27); we are justified and sanctified (1 Corinthians 6:11); we are saved (1 Peter 3:20-21); we are ordained as priests with access to the heavenly sanctuary (Hebrews 10:19-22). Of course, the ultimate proof of baptism's efficacy rests in the baptism of Jesus himself. Here, we have the ultimate paradigm for understanding God's work in baptism. Jesus received the Spirit in fullness at his baptism, and was declared to be the beloved Son of the Father. With appropriate qualifications, this is what God does in our baptisms as well: He pours out His Spirit upon us and declares us to be His dearly loved children. In context, none of these passages teach baptism automatically guarantees salvation. But they do teach that God does a great work in baptism, a work that may be considered the beginnings of salvation for those God has elected to preserve to the end.[111]

Because of their emphasis on obedience, Robbins has characterized the views expressed by Norman Shepherd and Steven Schlissel at the 2002 conference as being "Neolegalism."[112]

5. *The Fresh Perspective.* There is a distressing attempt by some scholars to attempt to make the Bible match the current popular philosophy. One encounters a wide-spread use of reader-response methodologies as a tool to interpret Scripture.[113] In harmony with post-modernism and deconstructionism, it is rather common to read that a counter-imperi-

---

[111] Richard Lusk "Baptismal Efficacy and the Reformed Tradition: Past, Present, and Future." http:www.hornes.org/theologia/content/cat_sacraments.htm. (Certainly some erroneous ideas are taught by Lusk in this article, e.g., paedobaptism, paedocommunion, and election, but this paragraph on the efficacy of baptism is thoroughly accurate.)

[112] John W. Robbins, "Justification and Judgment," *Journal of the Grace Evangelical Society* (Spring 2002), p.71.

[113] Reader-oriented hermeneutics inevitably subject the Biblical message (the Authorial intent) to distortion. Conservatives prefer to ground our interpretation on the intended meaning of the Biblical authors, not in the shifting opinions and deconstructions of the reader. (Denny Burk, "Is Paul's Gospel Counter-imperial? Evaluating the Prospects of the 'Fresh Perspective' for Evangelical Theology" *JETS* 51:2 [June 2008], p.325.) Conservatives prefer exegesis (i.e., identifying the author's intent) to eisegesis (i.e., reading our own presuppositions, agendas, and biases into the text).

al, or an anti-colonial, thrust is the driving force behind the Pauline writings. Instead of Paul being against the religion of Judaism, Paul was taking a stand against Roman imperial ideology.[114] Paul allegedly borrows language from the imperial cult but gives it a radical new meaning. (For example, to call Jesus "Lord" is committing a calculated act of treason against Caesar by affirming that Caesar is not "lord".)[115]

N.T. Wright has spent much of the last 30 years engaging and critiquing the views of North American liberal scholarship.[116] As he has weighed in against some of the conclusions reached by other new perspective advocates, Wright has tended to move into the anti-imperialistic camp,[117] though he is more nuanced in his appeals to sources from the ancient world; he finds sources *both* in the LXX *and* in anti-imperialism. Still, Wright has some things right. In 2005, he published *Paul in Fresh Perspective* (London: SPCK), in which he correctly argues the New Testament should be read in light of 1st century data. The new perspective tends to treat Christianity and Judaism as different dispensations of the same covenant. As he attempts to correct those new perspective advocates who make little difference between the Abrahamic covenant, the Mosaic covenant, and the new covenant, Wright presents a covenant theology that appears to be more in harmony with the New Testament. (For example, Hebrews 7:12 and chapters 8-10 have the Mosaic covenant abrogated in favor of the new covenant.) But in this commentator's judgment, Wright errs when he attempts to say justification confers "status" – that it is a declarative act of God by which people are declared to belong to the covenant people of God (the covenant made with Abraham).[118] There is no doubt that if one is in Christ, he is thereby counted as one of Abraham's spiritual descendants. But is "justifica-

---

[114] Richard Horsley, ed., *Paul and Empire: Religion and Power in Roman Imperial Society* (Harrisburg, PA: Trinity Press International, 1997), p.140. Horsley, distinguished professor at the University of Massachusetts in Boston, is the driving force behind the "Paul and Politics" group at the Society of Biblical Literature. The reason for existence of this group, and the methodologies used to study the New Testament, are explained in *Paul and Politics* (Harrisburg, PA: Trinity Press International, 2000), p.10-14.

[115] It is claimed by proponents of counter-imperialism that the source of many of Paul's words is found in the imperial cult – including such words as *parousia* and *epiphaneia* (1 Thessalonians 4:15; 2 Thessalonians 2:8), *apantesis* ("meeting," 1 Thessalonians 4:17), *eirēnē kai asphaleia* ("peace and safety," 1 Thessalonians 5:3), *soteria* and *elpis* ("salvation" and "hope," 1 Thessalonians 5:8-9).

[116] Bird, *op. cit.*, p.193.

[117] See his comments on "'God's Righteousness' as the theme of Romans" in his commentary on "Romans" in *New Interpreter's Bible*, (Nashville: Abingdon, 2002), p.404,405. "God's *dikaiosunē* [righteousness] must also be read as a deliberate challenge to the imperial pretension." In his 160 page *The Last Word: Beyond the Bible Wars to a New Understanding of the Authority of Scripture* (NY: HarperSanFrancisco, 2005), Wright repeatedly offers his thesis that Paul's writings offer a critique of the pagan empire (e.g., p.13,47,89,99,100,112,115,131). However, Wright's conclusions will never do. Paul's language is shaped by the LXX; see Richard Hays, *Echoes of Scripture in the letters of Paul* (New Haven: Yale U. Press, 1989). But Paul also carefully defines his terms throughout Romans so the listeners won't be tempted to put their own interpretation on the apostle's words.

[118] Carson, *op. cit.*, p.586. McGrath, *op. cit.*, p.519.

tion" the word to express this idea?   "Wright's definition of justification is so far removed from Old Testament and Second Temple Judaism sources as to be frankly unbelievable."[119]

IV. CONTEMPORARY ISSUES RELATED TO JUSTIFICATION BY FAITH

Since the new perspective studies have triggered a review of doctrine, here are some of the topics the contemporary theologians are debating.

A. When did Paul first "formulate" his doctrine of justification?

The very wording of the question suggests a naturalistic source rather than a revelatory source for Paul's teachings.   Such a notion is certainly unacceptable when Paul specifically says he got his doctrine by revelation from Jesus Christ (Galatians 1:12). Notwithstanding Paul's own statement, modern scholars debate how and when the doctrine of justification by faith came into being.   We often read that Paul, years after his call on the Damascus road, hammered out his doctrine of justification by faith in the midst of an emergency and as a deliberate polemical response to the Judaizers, either at Antioch (Galatians 2:11ff) or at Jerusalem (Acts 15).   For example, Dunn has us watching Paul formulate his new doctrine at Galatians 2:16 as he reprimanded Peter.[120]   If Paul first formulated the doctrine late in his ministry, and in the midst of attempting to deal with an emergency, this is a subtle denial of the importance of the doctrine of justification by faith as Luther conceived it.

Was the problem in Galatia the catalyst for the invention of Paul's doctrine?   No! The allegation that Galatians 2:16 is the first time the theme of justification by faith is sounded by Paul ignores Acts 13:39, where "freed" in the NASB translates the verb "justified."   Furthermore, the doctrine of justification by faith was taught in Old Testament times; according to Romans 4:1-8 both Moses and David taught it and understood it.   Was Paul's doctrine of justification by faith a spur of the moment invention to deal with a problem?   Was it then soon forgotten when the problem was past?   No!   Jesus taught about justification.   In the parable of the Pharisee and Publican, the Publican went down to his house "justified" (Luke 16:15) in the sense that he stood in right relation to God. Several times in the Sermon on the Mount (Matthew 5:6,10,20; 6:1,33; cf. 3:15) Jesus spoke of righteousness (*dikaiosunē*).   In Matthew 12:37 the word is used in regard to the final judgment: "I say to you, that every careless word that men shall speak they shall render account for it in the day of judgment.   For by your words you will be justified, and

---

[119] Carson, *ibid.*

[120] Dunn, *op. cit.*, p.114,115.

by your words you will be condemned" (12:36-37). The word picture of the law court is projected into a vision of final divine judgment (Matthew 25:31-46). Paul certainly did not invent or formulate his doctrine in the AD 50s, a quarter century after Pentecost.

B. What was 1st century Judaism like?

"Judaism" is a proper term to describe 1st century religious practice in the Holy Land.[121] The term "Judaism" came into currency during Second Temple Judaism. In 2 Maccabees 2:21, 8:1, 14:38 and 4 Maccabees 4:26, the term appears in a context where the author uses two other *-ismos* words: *hellenismos* ("the Greek way of life") and *allophylismos* ("the Gentile/foreign way of life"). The word "Judaism" (*ioudaismos*) occurs in the New Testament only at Galatians 1:14 where the term appears to describe the Jewish way of life as a whole, as distinct from that of other religions.[122] Observe too, according to Acts 22:3, 23:6, 26:5, and Galatians 3:5, that Paul was the strictest of Pharisees when he was advancing in "Judaism" (or "the Jews' religion," Galatians 1:14 KJV). All this allows no room to distinguish between Pharisaism proper and the Judaism against which Paul objected,[123] as if they were two different and separate strains.

Our sources for information concerning 1st century Judaism are Josephus, the New Testament texts (especially the Gospels[124]), the Dead Sea Scrolls, and (if used with caution) early rabbinic literature.[125] Josephus depicts the Pharisees as the most influential of the Jewish parties, though the Sadducees (the priestly aristocracy) were still the organs of power in Jerusalem and the temple. Josephus calls attention to the Pharisees' reliance on

---

[121] In harmony with how "Judaism" is used in its modern sociological sense to describe something broader than one factional party, some contemporary scholars prefer to speak of "Judaisms," especially since the New Testament and Josephus tell about rival sects (Pharisees, Sadducees, Herodians, Zealots, Essenes) each with their own emphases and distinguishing characteristics. However, it is this commentator's judgment that there was a relationship between Pharisaic beliefs and what the Judaizers in Galatia were demanding. We are told that Pharisees sneaked in to spy out Christian liberty (Acts 15:5) and that Peter's Pharisee-like actions (Galatians 2:14) were compelling the Gentiles to live like Jews (*Ioudaizein*, to Judaize). So it will not do to attempt to make a distinction between the "Judaizers" to whom Paul objected and 1st century (*aka* Second Temple) Judaism as represented by the Pharisees. Other "Judaisms" there may have been, but all were as much man-made religions, rather than divinely-revealed religion, as was Pharisaism.

[122] Compare the use of "Judaism" in Ignatius *Philad.* 6.1, where it appears as opposite to Christianity, *christianismos*.

[123] This note reflects "a call to take Paul seriously as a first-hand witness to the Judaism of the first century, at least as seriously as other Jewish documents." Seyoon Kim, *Paul and the New Perspective: Second Thoughts on the Origin of Paul's Gospel* (Grand Rapids: Eerdmans, 2002), p.295.

[124] The Gospels and Paul's writings must both be given historical credibility concerning what 1st century Judaism was like.

[125] S. Mason, "Pharisees" in *Dictionary of New Testament Background*, ed. by Craig Evans and Stanley Porter (Downers Grove, IL: InterVarsity, 2000), p.782-787, gives a good overview of what can be learned from these early rabbinic sources.

extra-biblical tradition ("the traditions of the elders") as being as important as Scripture. Early in the Gospels, the Pharisees take the lead in opposition to Jesus. They are presented as hostile to Jesus from the outset because He did not observe their traditions. Jesus denounced their traditions as merely human rules that voided the Law of Moses (Matthew 15:3-20; Mark 7:5-8). The Dead Sea Scrolls present the kind of man-made rules that distinguished each of the Jewish sects one from the other. Just how much the complex and multilayered rabbinic literature that was written down in the AD 500s reflects how things were in the 1st century is difficult to determine. At places in the literature famous figures such as Hillel and Shammai and Gamaliel are quoted, so one would suppose in those places the literature accurately reflects 1st century practice. After the destruction of Jerusalem in AD 70 the Pharisees became the recognized power brokers within Judaism.[126] One matter of dispute is whether the Pharisees of Bible times are related to the rabbis of the 2nd and 3rd centuries, or whether 'rabbi' in the 1st century had a different connotation than it did in the 2nd and 3rd centuries. From the 1800s until the late 1960s there was a growing consensus concerning the Pharisees that they were the authorized teachers (rabbis) of Jesus' time, exercising their influence through the Sanhedrin, the synagogues (held to be Pharisaic institutions, whereas the temple was controlled by the Sadducees), and the schools (such as the schools of Hillel and Shammai). In the 1970s, having rejected the Gospel records as being unreliable sources of information, Jacob Neusner and E. Rivkin challenged the traditional view.[127] Neusner has argued that the synagogues before AD 70, of which not many have been found by archaeologists, were not Pharisaic institutions.

First-century Judaism, while often talking about the grace and mercy of God, did emphasize "works" as a condition of salvation. First-century Judaism took this emphasis from the Old Testament Scriptures, which frequently emphasize the need for Israel's obedience. Both Moses (e.g., Exodus 20:2ff and Leviticus 18:5) and the prophets insisted on practical works of righteousness (Micah 6:8, "what does the Lord require of you but to do justice, to love kindness, and to walk humbly with your God?").[128]

---

[126] The Pharisees survived the war better than any other groups among the Jews and became the sole recognized religious leaders. This was due, in part, to the fact that after Jerusalem fell in AD 70, there was an absence of priestly, Essene, Zealot, or scribal alternatives vying for leadership of the defeated peoples. Survivors of those other religious groups joined the Pharisees, which in turn led to the Pharisees' consolidation of power in the time of Rabbi Judah, toward the end of the 2nd century. After the founding of the academies such as the one at Yavneh post AD 70, we may speak of rabbinic Judaism instead of Pharisaism. For details concerning this development, see B.D. Collins, "Rabbinic Traditions and Writings" in the *Dictionary of Jesus and the Gospels* (Downers Grove, IL: Intervarsity Press, 1992), p.651-660.

[127] Jacob Neusner, *From Politics to Piety* (Englewood Cliffs, NJ: Prentice-Hall, 1973), E. Rivkin, *A Hidden Revolution: The Pharisees' Search for the Kingdom Within* (Nashville: Abingdon, 1978).

[128] Earlier we have given our studied conclusion that Sanders apparently overstated the case when he insisted that 1st century Jews did not require works of some kind as a condition of salvation. Scholars have taken Sanders to task for quoting rabbinic literature to prove his point that Judaism emphasized grace, while at the same time telling us we should not appeal to rabbinic literature to give us a picture of 1st century Judaism as Luther and others had done. Thomas Schreiner, *The Law and Its Fulfillment: A Pauline Theology of Law* (Grand Rapids: Baker, 1993), has found evidence that Palestinian Judaism was legalistic (emphasizing "works") in the same Jewish writings Sanders cited to show it was not.

C. Does Paul represent contemporary Judaism objectively and correctly?

Not a few contemporary scholars affirm that Paul deliberately misrepresented ancient Judaism.[129]   How do these scholars arrive at such a conclusion?

Scholars who begin with the preconception that Paul taught "faith only by grace only" and who then attempt to demonstrate that Paul mischaracterized 1st century Judaism by picturing Judaism as irredeemably legalistic will necessarily reach the conclusion that Paul misrepresented the truth.   Some scholars also picture Paul, in the midst of a life-or-death fight, exaggerating or giving a biased picture of his opponents, the Judaizers.

The real problem is that it is Paul who has been misrepresented. Elsewhere, this commentary has shown that Paul is not being presented objectively and correctly on the topics of "faith" and "works of the Law." Further, many arguments made by modern scholars impinge on the idea that Paul was inspired, that he simply wrote pure, holy truth.[130]

Dare we claim that Paul's letters are a reliable source of information about ancient Judaism? Alan Segal does.[131]   Segal says that "Paul should be treated as a major source in the study of first-century Judaism," (p.xi); that he gives "the only witness to a world of everyday Hellenistic Judaism now vanished" (p.xiii); that he is "our best witness to the issues that affected first-century Jews" and "one of the most fruitful and reliable sources for first-century Jewish religious life" (p.xvi). Far from misrepresenting ancient Judaism, the converted Pharisee Paul accurately represents what that religion actually was teaching.

D. To what in 1st century Judaism did Paul object?

When Paul championed faith and objected to "works of the Law" as qualifying a man to be acceptable in God's sight, what were "works of the Law"? The answer the Protestant Reformers gave to this question was that "works of the Law" refers to anything the Law of Moses required of a man. That "faith only" definition, however, required its proponents explain away all the verses that show God expects habitual obedience to His commands. To smooth over this apparent contradiction,   it has also been proposed that "works of the

---

[129] E.P. Sanders has affirmed that Judaism was not legalistic and Paul or his interpreters got it wrong. Marvin Wilson and Hiekki Raïsänen say that the Apostle did not oppose Jewish legalism because Jewish legalism did not exist, or if he did oppose it, he was misrepresenting ancient Judaism. See Marvin R. Wilson *Our Father Abraham: Jewish Roots of the Christian Faith* (Grand Rapids: Eerdmans, 1989), p.20-21, who describes the Reformation's view of the Judaism Paul opposed as a caricature, a misrepresentation, and bearing false witness. Heikki Raïsänen tells us that Paul misrepresents and distorts the Judaism of his own day in his "Legalism and Salvation in the Law," in *Die Paulinische Literatur und Theologie*, edited by S. Peterson (Aarhus: Aros, 1980).

[130] Lewis A. Foster was a strong proponent of the fact that the inspired Bible writers are objective, not subjective, in their presentations of both their own doctrine and that of their adversaries.

[131] Alan Segal, *Paul the Convert: The Apostolate and Apostasy of Saul the Pharisee* (New Haven: Yale University Press, 1990).

Law" is the same as perfect obedience, with Galatians 3:10 ("ALL the things written in the book of the Law") and 5:3 ("under obligation to keep the whole Law") being used to prove the proposition.[132] The reason then assigned why "works of the Law" will never save is because no one is sinless perfect.[133]

New Perspective advocates have set forth several proposed explanations of "works of the Law," but none has gained a consensus among scholars. It is not Jewish nationalism and exclusivism that is meant by the phrase "works of the Law,"[134] though that was a problem. It is not the refusal of equality (table fellowship) that is meant,[135] though that was a problem in some early congregations (Acts 11:3; Galatians 2:12). Neither is it Jewish boasting that is meant, though that was a problem (Romans 3:27; Philippians 3:3,19). Nor is it the Jewish failure to accept Jesus as the long-promised Messiah that is meant, though that was a problem (Romans 11:32,22; Galatians 3:29). We also dismiss the modern sociological explanations of Paul's controversy with Judaism.[136] Such hypotheses receive attention because there are verses dealing with each of these problem

---

[132] Thomas R. Schreiner, *The Law and Its Fulfillment: A Pauline Theology of Law* (Grand Rapids: Baker, 1993). The definition of "works of the Law" as synonymous with perfectly keeping the Law of Moses is a faulty starting point from which to argue.

[133] This view is flawed because the definition of "works of the Law" as perfect obedience is faulty. The Old Testament taught justification by faith (= faithfulness), not justification on the condition of perfect obedience.

[134] This is the thrust of the writings of Sanders (*Paul, the Law, and the Jewish People*, p.154-55) and Wright. The Law of Moses was a barrier between Jew and Gentile ("the barrier of the dividing wall," Ephesians 2:14). Paul found it necessary to preach that "everyone (whether Jew or Greek, Romans 1:16) who believes" is justified, and if so, Jews have no special privileges. Membership in the covenant is open to all who have faith in Christ and who thus are spiritual descendants of Abraham (Romans 4:16-18). A flaw in Sanders' presentation is that he seems to confuse the covenant with Moses (which is the basis of "works of the Law") with the covenant made with Abraham, treating them as though they were the same, when they are not (Galatians 3:15-18).

[135] This is the thrust of the writings by Dunn. He calls "the works of the Law" (which he identifies as circumcision, Sabbath observance, dietary laws, all of which distinguish Jews from Gentiles) "boundary markers." Paul's polemic is against Jewish exclusiveness toward Gentiles; it is not an argument against the role of human effort in salvation. (Charles Talbert, "Paul, Judaism, and the Revisionists," *CBQ* 63:1 [January 2001], p.1-22, especially p.13.)

[136] See Watson, Francis, *Paul, Judaism and the Gentiles: A Sociological Approach* (SNTSMS 56; Cambridge: Cambridge University Press, 1986). Watson insists that it is impossible to understand properly the theological component of Paul's controversy with Judaism without understanding its underlying social situation. Two sociological models are utilized to accomplish this goal. The first model derives from studies of how new religious movements (like early Christianity) begin as reform movements and are transformed into sects. The second model deals with how a sectarian group establishes an ideology which legitimizes its separation from the parent group. The models are then applied to three of Paul's letters (Galatians, Philippians, and Romans). Watson's view of the origin and development of the Pauline churches is that Paul began his missionary career as a preacher to the Jews. The Jews, however, rejected his message, and Paul began to preach to the Gentiles. To make it easier for Gentiles to accept Christianity, Paul decided to lay aside the requirement that they must be obedient to the Law. In social terms the question raised by Paul's mission to the Gentiles was whether the church should continue as a reform movement within the larger Jewish community, or should separate itself and become a sect. Paul's controversy was primarily with Jewish Christians who wanted to remain a reform movement, and the main function of Paul's writings was "to legitimate the social reality of sectarian Gentile Christian communities in which the Law was not observed" (p.178).

issues; however, none deals with the problems using the language "works of the Law."

To what, then, did Paul object?   The proper answer to the question may be discerned in this fashion.   If we are permitted to call attention to both terms in the phrase "works of the Law" it could be affirmed that there were two things emphasized by Judaism to which Paul objected:

(1) The Jewish belief in the abiding validity of the Law of Moses.
(2) The Jewish idea that "works of the Law" were the way to observe/obey what God
      had required in the Law of Moses.

Paul's first objection will be dealt with below in the next section.   Regarding Paul's second objection, our proposal for how "works of the Law" should be understood[137] does not match either the Protestant Reformers' views or the attempted explanations by proponents of the new perspective.   As shown in the beginning of this Special Study, "faith" is habitually doing what God commands.   That definition of "faith" helps us understand why Paul objects to "works of the Law."   Those man-made rules, drawn from some or other passage in Moses' Law, are the very sort of rules ("the traditions of the elders") which Jesus said led men to actually ignore and violate the Law of Moses.   Since the expressions "works of the Law" and "works of the flesh" (Galatians 5:19) are related by the term "works," and since "works of the Law" are man-made rules, one wonders if we could equate "works of the Law" with "works of the flesh."

Paul can rightly stand in opposition to "the works of the Law" because Paul stands in continuity with the Hebrew Scriptures (and with any of his Jewish contemporaries who were strong Bible people), but Paul stands in opposition to those who made their own religious rules (which negated the Law).

E. Was Paul against the Law of Moses?

To Paul, there was a right use and a wrong use of the Law (1 Timothy 1:8).   If men used it aright, Paul wasn't against the Law.   One of the purposes of the Law was to point men to the coming Messiah ("Christ was the goal of the Law," Romans 10:4 NASB mg.).   Contained in the Law are examples that can teach us (1 Corinthians 10:6-11).

But the Law was nailed to the cross (Colossians 2:14).   According to Galatians, the function of the Law was to serve as a guardian, a manager, a pedagogue – functions that have ceased since Calvary (Galatians 3:23-4:2).   2 Corinthians 3 shows that Paul considered the Law (i.e., the Mosaic covenant) to be obsolete; he and other Christian preachers were now ministers of the new covenant.   Hebrews 7:12 tells us that if Jesus serves as our high priest it can only mean that there has been a "change of law also."   That

---

[137] See Special Study #1 on 4QMMT.

is, the Law that provided for the Aaronic priesthood has been abrogated. The former commandment of the Mosaic covenant has been set aside (Hebrews 7:18). God took away the first (Moses) to establish the second (the new covenant, Hebrews 10:9).

Kevin Bywater has nicely illustrated how the Law was good and necessary for a season, but now its time has come to an end:

> Just as milk is health-giving and nourishing for a time, but then goes bad and becomes deadly poison after its expiration date, so it is with the Torah. The Law was healthful for Israel until its purpose in God's economy came to full realization. For Israel to continue clinging to Torah after Christ has come is to drink a fatal potion. In the New Covenant, we are not under Torah, but under grace; not under Moses, but under Christ (Romans 6:14; Hebrews 3:5,6; 1 Corinthians 9:20,21). Torah's expiration date came in the "fullness of time;" Christ redeemed us from Torah and brought us into His kingdom (cf. Galatians 4).[138]

Nor should we continue the tradition that categorizes the Law as moral, ceremonial, and judicial,[139] for that seemingly nice distinction just will not work exegetically. Paul treats the Law of Moses as a seamless robe, as a covenantal dispensation (Galatians 5:3; Hebrews 7:12). Paul says that we who have entered the new age, the Messianic age, are not under the Mosaic covenant. Period. Not just part of the Law of Moses, but all of it. The Mosaic Law completed its divinely appointed purpose and is no longer in effect. Believers are subject to the "law of Christ" (1 Corinthians 9:20), a "law" which repeats some of the commands found in the Mosaic code while excluding others. The content of the "law of Christ" is found in the teachings of Christ as recorded in the Gospels.

F. What is the relation of faith and works?

The first part of this study has shown from numerous passages that faith is doing or practicing what God says. The faith that is the condition of salvation/justification is *not* faith alone ("alone" meaning that no human actions involved).

Where did the idea that *sola fides* (faith alone) is all God the Judge looks for come from? (1) Partly from the verses where we are told that no one will be justified by "works of the Law."[140]   (2) Partly from the verses where "works" are mentioned but the context

---

[138] Quoted by Lusk, *op. cit.*, #7.

[139] The classic tripartite distinction – namely, moral, civil and ceremonial law – received its first systematic treatment as a key to explaining the relationship between the Old Testament and New Testament by Thomas Aquinas, and then later became a commonplace in Protestant theology. (Carson, *op. cit.*, p.590)

[140] Paul speaks of "works" in twelve passages – Romans 3:20-28, 4:2, 4:5-6, 9:11, 9:30-33, 11:6; Galatians 2:15-16, 3:2-5, 3:10; Ephesians 2:8-10; 1 Timothy 2:9; Titus 3:5. In five of these (all in Romans and Galatians) "works" are expressly called "works of the Law." In another five (the remaining ones in Romans and Galatians plus Ephesians 2) "works" is shorthand for "works of the Law."

does not specifically talk about the Law of Moses. Let us pursue each of these subjects in order to see if *sola fides* (faith alone, with no works) is what the Bible teaches.

(1) In Special Study #1 we have shown that the "works of the Law" which are not the same as faith (Romans 3:28, 10:32; Galatians 2:16) are man-made religious rules similar to the strictures taught in the "traditions of the elders" (Mark 7:5) or in 4QMMT. "Faith" is obeying God-made rules. When Paul used the word "faith" he did not disparage human deeds/works. He never did disparage the idea that while it was valid men should do what the Mosaic Law said (cf. Romans 2:13,26,27; Galatians 5:14, 6:2). Thus, the "works of the Law" which do not justify are not to be identified with doing/ practicing those things which the Mosaic Law certainly said were required by God ("doers of the Law shall be justified," Romans 2:13). Romans 3:20 ("no one will be declared righteous in His sight by works of the Law") does not contradict Romans 2:6-16 ("doers of the Law will be justified" at the judgment when God renders to every man according to his deeds, Romans 2:6). Those who would defend the idea that the faith which is the condition of justification is only a mental assent or trust (with no corresponding actions) cannot appeal to Paul's words about "works of the Law" as proof for their definition.

(2) Protestants, in order to prove their doctrine of *sola fides* (faith alone), have tended to point to "not of works" in (a) Ephesians 2:9, (b) 2 Timothy 1:9, and (c) Titus 3:5. Those verses need attention.[141] So does (d) Galatians 3:12.

(a) Ephesians 2:8,9 read "For by grace you have been saved through faith; and that not of yourselves, *it is* the gift of God; not as a result of works, that no one should boast." In both Galatians and Romans, Paul wrote that we are "justified by faith;" here he wrote that we are "saved by (through) faith." We understand that though the language is different, the same topic is involved. "Faith" and "works" are set forth in bold contrast. Is this contrast proof that "faith alone" is the condition of salvation? If we look carefully at what Paul wrote in Ephesians 2:1-10, we will see that it is very likely that "not of yourselves" and "not as a result of works" are Paul's way of saying to an audience that was not being troubled by Judaizers the same thing he said to an audience that was.[142] In both, Paul teaches that man cannot invent or devise a religion that will provide salvation – only God has done such a wondrous thing. If we wish to be justified or saved, we are limited to doing things God's way (i.e., "by faith," or doing what God says). If we try man-made religious rules, we'll glory in human achievement. If we do things God's way, we'll glory in God (Romans 3:27).

---

[141] These verses do not read "works of law" – therefore these are the verses where the casual reader might think that any and all works are excluded from faith.

[142] Paul added "of the Law" to "works" when he repudiated man-made rules to an audience – i.e., the Galatian church – being encouraged to embrace such rules.

Ephesians 2:1-10 summarizes what Gentiles (verses 1,2) and Jews (verse 3) were in the past, what they are in the present (verse 4-6), and what they shall be in the future (verses 7-10). Gentiles (verses 1,2) were spiritually dead because of their own trespasses and sins; they lived as the devil prompted them to live. Jews (verses 3) were little better in how they lived, since they too behaved as the desires of the flesh and mind (excited by the devil) prompted them to live and behave. But God, Who is rich in mercy and great in love, went to work to do something about mankind's lost condition. "Made alive" (verse 5) is the verb in the long sentence (2:1-10). God made believers – i.e., those who were "in Christ" (verse 7) "through faith" (verse 5) – to be spiritually alive with Christ.

What God desires is that in the ages to come (verse 7) "the surpassing riches of His grace in kindness toward us in Christ Jesus" might be shown. He desires the praise due to His name. If men go about trying to do religion their own way, all of a sudden God gets no glory. "By grace you have been saved" (verse 5) is a perfect tense verb; it expresses past completed action with present continuing results. God's grace, what He does to save a man, is not limited to the time of a man's regeneration ("made us alive"). There is continuing help given all through the Christian's life. The parenthetical reminder found in verse 5 vindicates the expression "God made us alive."

The doctrine of salvation by grace is further explained in verses 8-10. The word "grace" in verse 5 lacks an article in the Greek; in verse 8 there is an article, and it is likely what is called "the article of previous reference." That is, the same grace spoken about in verse 5 is the topic of verses 8 and 9.[143] "Raised us up with Him and seated us with Him in the heavenly places" may refer to our rising to walk in newness of life, or it may refer proleptically to our future resurrection. Either way, Christians are pictured as sharing in Christ's glories. So close is our connection with Him that we share in His glory, now and/or in the ages to come after His second coming. "Through faith" (verse 8) tells us the reception of the benefits of God's grace is conditional; it is the same word used in Romans and Galatians when justification is conditioned on faith[fullness]. On the part of God salvation is made available because of His grace; the part of man is conditioned on faith[fullness]. In the phrase "and that not of yourselves," to what does the demonstrative pronoun "that" point? Is it faith (a feminine word in the Greek)? Is it grace (a feminine word in the Greek)? Neither, since "that" is neuter. The grant of salvation on the condition of faith is the thing that is the gift of God. Even the marginal note in the NASB makes it plain that it is "that salvation" (not grace or faith) which is the gift of God.

How can we talk about "man's part in salvation" and yet at the same time affirm that the grant of salvation is "not of yourselves" (verse 8)? The words "not a result of works,

---

[143] Note, we must be careful in our comments on this passage so that we may walk the fine line between the extremes that man is wholly passive in salvation ("God made you alive" and "by grace are you saved" are often interpreted to say man is passive) and the idea that man's response to God's invitation is somehow meritorious (i.e., man's obedience puts God in debt so that God owes the man salvation because the man has earned it).

that no one should boast" (verse 9) unfold what is meant by "not of yourselves" (verse 8). The word "boast" (*kauchēsetai*) is an everyday Greek word designating an excessive or undue evaluation of one's self or one's accomplishments. It is used in the LXX to denote the basic attitude of an ungodly man who trusts in himself rather than in God. There is no faithfulness to what God has revealed, just man trying to do it his own way. The man who boasts in his own actions is thwarting the very thing God desired, that men glory in what He has done. The Old Testament protest against glorying in any but the Lord and the prophet's jealousy for the honor of God (see Jeremiah 9:23,24; Isaiah 52:8,14) appears with even more intensity in Paul, most of all when he touches the great theme of man's salvation. When it comes to salvation, God desires that all glorying for it belongs wholly to Him. Verse 10 ("we are His workmanship ...", i.e., we are something God has made) is proof that salvation is not something of our making; it is not of ourselves, nor our workmanship. If our being spiritually alive is God's handiwork, our salvation is not by our own achievement (i.e., man-made methods and rules and rites).[144] "Created in Christ Jesus" (verse 10) tells us that it is through our union with Christ that this new creation by God's hand has taken place.

The expression "for good works" (verse 10) tells us something else God had in mind when He went to work to make salvation possible. Not only did He have His own honor and glory in mind, He also had in mind that redeemed folk would habitually do good works ("walk in them"). The "good works" of verse 10 and the "works" rejected in verse 9 are not the same kind of works. The works of verse 9 are parallel to "that not of yourselves." The good works the person who is alive in Christ are to do are in vivid contrast to the worldly walk in trespasses and sins that characterized the person's life before he was born gain. "Prepared beforehand" tells us that the new life style and behavior of the believer is also an essential part of God's plan, purposed "before the foundation of the world" (1:4).

(b) 2 Timothy 1:9, speaking about God, says He "has saved us, and called us with a holy calling, not according to our works, but according to His own purpose and grace which was granted us in Christ Jesus from all eternity." Having studied Ephesians 2 in detail, it is clear that the phrases of this verse in 2 Timothy speak to the same topic. Salvation is available to mankind only on God's terms, not on the basis of man-made religious rules and rites. The terms of salvation were determined back in eternity when God planned how He would do things in the world He was about to create. If a man is in Christ, he has God's approbation and blessing. There is no other way. Men are invited to become Christians through the Gospel (He calls us with "a holy calling"). Faith comes by hearing the word of Christ (Romans 10:17).

---

[144] Similarly "by grace" contrasted with "not of yourselves" (verses 8 and 9) should help us to see that God's way is being compared and contrasted with man's way (when the man all the while is ignoring what God has said).

(c) Titus 3:4-7 gives the same basic message: "But when the kindness of God our Savior and His love for mankind appeared, He saved us, not on the basis of deeds (works) we have done in righteousness, but according to His mercy, by the washing of regeneration and the renewing by the Holy Spirit ... so that being justified by His grace we might be made heirs according to the hope of eternal life." "Appeared" speaks of Jesus' incarnation, when God became visible in the flesh. That's how God went about providing the salvation men needed. His method of salvation is compared to attempts by men ("deeds" or works) to implement their own method of salvation. There is a new birth involved, and the help of the Holy Spirit to live the Christian life. Those are some of the benefits of being justified by God. Men's works (men's religions) have no such blessings or benefits to offer, no do they give hope of eternal life.

(d) Galatians 3:10-12 has also been pressed into use to show that faith alone is what God looks for in a man before He pronounces him justified. In Galatians 3, Paul repudiates works of the Law and champions faith. He opens by speaking about the curse of the Law which falls upon those who do not habitually abide by what is written in the Law,[145] and closes by saying "the Law is not of faith; on the contrary, 'HE WHO PRACTICES THEM SHALL LIVE BY THEM'." The words in capital letters are taken from Leviticus 18:5. "Them" are things in the Law (Leviticus 17-26). "Practices" calls for habitual practice. "Live" includes a right relationship with God. Leviticus clearly portrays such life as resulting from habitual obedience[146] to God's commandments.[147]

These verses in Galatians contain a contrast between "works of the Law" (the full expression found at verse 10 is abbreviated to "the Law" in verses 11 and 12) and faith. Three passages from the Old Testament are used to show that "works of the Law" are not acceptable to God precisely because God's Law was being habitually ignored. Deuteronomy 27:26 ("abide by all things written in the Book of the Law, to perform them") calls for habitual 'abiding' and 'performing' of what the Law requires. The Judaizers with their "works of the Law" were not doing what God prescribed in Deuteronomy. Habakkuk 2:4 ("The righteous man shall live by faith") is quoted because "faith" and "the Law" (*halakhic* "works of the Law") are not the same things. Then Leviticus 18:5 is quoted to show that "the Law" (*halakhic* "works of the Law") is not the habitual practice of God's laws that God looks for.

---

[145] Deuteronomy 27:26 does not require sinless perfection in order to be saved. It does require habitual performance.

[146] The verb "practices" shows that God did not require perfect obedience. What God looked for was a habitual, consistent practice. Sacrifice was available to give opportunity for forgiveness of those lapses in practice.

[147] Faith-only writers have tried to establish that Leviticus 18:5 is antithetical to Habakkuk 2:4 (at Galatians 3:11,12). In Romans 10:5 it is likewise argued that Leviticus 18:5 is antithetical in soteriology to Deuteronomy 30:12-14. It is this commentator's position that Leviticus 18:5 is not antithetical to what is involved in "faith." It has been shown earlier that faith is doing what God says. Leviticus is in perfect agreement with this.

Properly understood, Galatians 3:10-12 does not produce a "faith only" definition of the faith that is a condition of justification/salvation. Denominational explanations have been in error for 500 years.[148] Faith is doing what God says. Without the doing there is no faith, and without faith there is no justification.[149]

G. How do we harmonize "justification by faith" and "judgment according to works"?

Judgment according to works is a theme sounded in a number of passages of Scripture. It is plainly taught in Romans 2:6-16. It is a doctrine that both Jews (Psalm 62:12; Proverbs 24:12) and Christians (Matthew 16:27; 2 Corinthians 5:10; Colossians 3:25; 2 Timothy 4:14; 1 Peter 1:17; Revelation 2:23) understood and accepted.[150]

One of most important issues to emerge from recent Pauline studies concerns the relationship between faith and works as attempts are made to clarify the relationship between "justification by faith" and "judgment by works." The connection here is that the "works" in 4QMMT ("works of the Law") and the "works" in the formula "judgment according to deeds/works" (Romans 2:6) are the same word. How can Paul write "not according to works" in some passages (Romans 3:20,28; Galatians 2:16), yet also write about judgment according to works in others (Romans 2:6, "God will render to each man according to his works," ASV)? Romans 2:13 plainly says "the [habitual] doers of the law will be justified." That the last judgment is according to works/deeds is true also for believers (2 Corinthians 5:10).

Protestants who espouse faith alone find themselves struggling to harmonize the ideas of "justification by faith" and "judgment by works." A number of these attempts at harmonization are to be rejected: (1) Paul's writings are irreconcilable because they are

---

[148] The faith-only definition of faith "is not adequate. It fails to do justice to the nuanced understanding of the relation of faith and works within Paul's thought, most notably expressed in the terse statement that 'not the hearers, but the doers of the Law will be justified' (Romans 2:13)." McGrath, *op. cit.*, p.521.

[149] Instead of pressing the word "justification" to make it include a life of right living, why not define "faith" to be "faithfulness"? Right living is then inextricably involved with the doctrine of justification by faith. If we were sinless perfect, we wouldn't need to be counted as righteous. But if we are penitent sinners, we need to have righteousness imputed to us – God's verdict of acquittal. That verdict is pronounced when God finds faithfulness. Repentance is something man does, and it is a condition of salvation even in the so-called faith-only camp, yet it is not called a "work." How can this be? Where are the verses that teach justification by faith alone, entirely on the basis of grace, quite apart from any obedience whatever?

[150] Passages outside the writings of Paul which teach that salvation is contingent upon "works/deeds" or "righteousness" include Matthew 7:21, 12:36-37, 25:31-46; John 3:20-21, 5:28-29; James 1:25, 2:14-26; Revelation 14:13, 20:11-15, 22:12. Passages where Paul places side by side *justification* by faith and *judgment* according to works include Romans 8:13, 14:10-12; 1 Corinthians 3:10-15; 2 Corinthians 9:6, 11:15; Galatians 6:7-8; Ephesians 2:10, 6:8; 1 Timothy 5:24-25.

inconsistent and contradictory.[151]   (2) The passages that teach judgment according to works are hypothetical rather than being true to life,[152] or they deal with rewards not with salvation. (3) The passages about judgment according to works are vestiges of Paul's old Jewish theology.[153]   (4) It is only the non-Christians who will be judged by their works. (5) Initial justification is by faith only while at the final judgment God judges according to deeds those whom He saves by His grace. All of these attempts at harmonization are faulty. The doctrine of judgment according to works appears in too many passages to say the idea is just hypothetical. To say that Paul's writings contain erroneous vestiges of old Jewish theology is a denial of the inspiration of Scripture written by Paul. 2 Corinthians 5:10 indicates that Christians will give an account for the deeds done in the body, so the idea that only non-Christians are judged by their deeds is not correct.

However, if we accept the idea that faith is doing what God says (rather than being faith only) then the two ideas of "justification by faith" and "judgment by works" are not out of harmony. God initially justifies when He sees an active faith, He judges faith's actions several times during a man's life, and He again justifies a man at the final judgment. If "faith" is doing what God says, then it is possible for God to inquire into whether or not a man has faithfully practiced what God revealed He requires and expects of men.

As was true for Abraham,[154] justification occurs several times during our lifetimes here on earth, as well as at the final judgment (Romans 2:13, 8:33; Galatians 5:4,5). What God looks for is not sinless perfection, but the tenor of a man's life. Is the man habitually obeying, or habitually disobeying?[155]

---

[151] Bird, op. cit., p.158, tells us that Nigel Watson (in "Justified by Faith, Judged by Works: An Antimony?" NTS 29 [1983], p.209-21), Sanders (Paul, the Law and the Jewish People [Minneapolis: Fortress Press {1983}], p.123-36) and Raïsänen (Paul and the Law [Tubingen: Mohr/Siebeck, 2nd edn {1983}], p.101-7) all think Paul was inconsistent.

[152] Douglas Moo (Romans in NICNT [Grand Rapids: Eerdmans, 1996], p.142) is one who so explains the passage.

[153] Bultmann and Sanders seem to suggest this is a 1st century Jewish attitude which is not quite in harmony with New Testament teaching on the subject of justification by faith (McGrath, op. cit., p.521).

[154] Above, in point 1 of this Special Study, it was shown that justification was not a one-time event in Abraham's life, and he is the father of the faithful. What was true of him is true of his spiritual descendants.

[155] Faith-only advocates have been closely questioned concerning whether their doctrine leads to or could encourage a libertine lifestyle. If a man is justified by faith only, what reason does he have to be careful in how he lives? Faith-only advocates have struggled to answer this question. Some (e.g., Martin Dibelius, From Tradition to Gospel [NY: Scribners, 1935], p.238-40, and J.C. O'Neill, The Recovery of Paul's Letter to the Galatians [London: SPCK, 1972]) try to say Paul was not interested in ethics, but rather that the final chapters of Galatians (which are an appeal to holy living) did not belong to the original letter Paul sent to the Galatians. Others admit that justification by faith does not of itself lead to a holy life, but we must remember that the Holy Spirit is given, and it is He who prompts the Christian to live aright. But does appeal to the work of the Holy Spirit allow us to teach "faith only"? Does the Spirit automatically produce fruit in converts to Christ? Do those converts "do" anything to co-operate with the Spirit? If they "do," are they not being saved by "works"? But if faith is doing what God says, none of these expediencies is needed. Once Paul's theology of "faith" is understood – that it is faithfulness to what God has revealed – there is no reason to wonder if living by faith might encourage a libertine lifestyle. Of course it doesn't. There is no coexistence between a life of faithfulness and a libertine lifestyle.

H. What was the center of Paul's theology?

This is perhaps another way of asking how important was the doctrine of justification by faith in Paul's thought? Was it a summarizing principle? Was it the key idea around which everything else in his theology revolves?   Many Protestants, following Luther's lead in their running debate with Catholic doctrine, have tended to make justification by faith the center of Paul's theology.   Others have proposed that the redemption that is in Christ, or reconciliation with God,[156] or the grace of God, or the dying and rising of the believer with Christ[157] is more properly viewed as the center of Paul's theology.

If we must talk about the center of Paul's theology, the key idea around which everything else revolves, would not a better answer be the way he valued certain covenants God has made with man, and not others?[158]   Paul doesn't say anything at all about the covenant made with Noah (Genesis 9:1-17).   Only twice does Paul even allude to the covenant God made with David: once at Romans 1:3-4 ("of the seed of David according to the flesh"), and again at Romans 15:12 where he quotes Isaiah 11:10 ("the root of Jesse will come, He who rises to rule the Gentiles: in Him shall the Gentiles hope").   The covenants that receive special attention in Paul's letters (including Hebrews) are the covenant with Abraham of Genesis 22:16 ("In your Seed all the nations of the earth shall be blessed"); the Mosaic covenant given at Mt. Sinai (made when God took Israel by the hand and led them out of Egypt, as alluded to in Jeremiah 31:31-32); and the new covenant of Jeremiah 31:31ff (cf. Hebrews 8:8-12; 2 Corinthians 3:6-11; and Galatians 3:15-18).   Of these covenants, the new covenant (i.e., the Abrahamic covenant renewed) is central to Paul's theology.   The Law which came 430 years after the promise to Abraham did not set aside that promise/covenant (Galatians 3:15-18).   That covenant with Abraham is the one God continues to live by, while the Mosaic covenant has been abrogated, as shown earlier in this Special Study.[159]   The sacrifice of Jesus which validated or inaugurated the

---

[156] Ralph Martin, *Reconciliation. A Study of Paul's Theology* (Atlanta: Scholars, 1981), p.5.

[157] This was Albert Schweitzer's view.   He thought justification by faith was a "subsidiary crater" in Paul's thought, an idea "incomplete and unfitted to stand alone."   A. Schweitzer, *The Mysticism of Paul* (Baltimore: John Hopkins University Press, 1998 [1931]), p.220, 225-26.

[158] Here is a place to take issue with certain new perspective presentations.   Paul was not interested in "getting in" or "staying in" the Mosaic covenant.   In fact, men did not "get in" the Mosaic covenant by faith alone as the new perspective has supposed.   Entrance into the Mosaic covenant was by physical birth.   You "stayed in" by faithfulness to the covenant obligations.

[159] This emphasis, too, is crossways with rabbinic Judaism which saw the new covenant as a return to keeping the Law of Moses.   See how the expression "new covenant" in the Dead Sea Scrolls (CD A 6.18-19; 8:20-21; B 19:33-34; 20:11-13; 1QpHab 2.3) is used to refer to the original intentions of the Law of Moses.   See *Sifra* on Leviticus, which has Jeremiah 31 juxtaposed with Leviticus 26:9 in order to clarify the latter verse.   The result of these rabbinic interpretations: the promise to maintain the covenant in Leviticus 26 is identified with the making of the new covenant in Jeremiah 31.   In later Judaism, Jeremiah 31:33-34 is understood to refer to the study of the Torah rather than observance of the Torah.   Neither of these Jewish explanations of Jeremiah 31:31ff are in tune with what the New Testament says about that classic new covenant prophecy.

new covenant makes it possible for God to forgive sins, not just pass over them as he did in Old Testament times (Romans 3:25). Jesus' sacrifice makes it possible for God Himself to be just while at the same time justifying sinners by faith (Romans 3:26). The sacrifice of Jesus makes possible all the blessings promised to Abraham and his spiritual descendants.

CONCLUDING SUMMARY

The major ideas treated in this Special Study include:

1. "Righteousness" is a term applied to different topics in the Scriptures. It is an attribute of God, it speaks of man's relationship to God, and man's relationship to his fellow men.

2. "Justification" is forensic and not transformative (i.e., it is *reckon* as righteous or *declare* to be righteous, not *make* righteous).

3. The "righteousness of God" in Romans 1:16,17 is God's way of saving man.

4. God's way of saving man includes the possibility that all men, both Jews and Gentiles, may be saved. And it includes a glorified resurrection body and the delivery of creation from its slavery to corruption, resulting in a new heavens and a new earth in which dwelleth righteousness.

5. God is able to justify penitent sinners because of the propitiatory sacrifice of Christ and His resurrection for our justification (i.e., our new body).

6. There are several places where 500 years of Reformation theology needs a corrective:

   a. The emphasis on salvation being monergistic (by grace alone, *sola gratia*)

   b. The emphasis that it is faith alone (*sola fides*) that justifies. *Instead, faith is doing what God says.*

   c. The idea that after one is justified by faith alone, good works then follow – but that the good works are in no way a condition of final justification at the judgment.

   d. The idea that Christ's righteousness is *imputed* to believers needs to be recognized as being an unbiblical use of language.

   e. The "works of the Law" which do not justify are man-made religious rules based on this or that passage in the Old Testament. The expression is not, as Reformation scholars explained it, a shorthand way of saying "obeying what the Law of Moses requires" (perhaps even perfectly, or one is condemned).

7. Christianity is intended to have societal as well as soteriological aims.

    One new man, where there is neither Jew nor Greek, slave or free, male or female, one shepherd and one fold, one olive tree into which believers are grafted – are all pictures of the sociological consequences.

8. The position this commentator advocates provides an explanation for several of the disputed points in Pauline studies:

    a. The alleged differences between Jesus and Paul. Paul did not distort what Jesus taught, so as to become the founder of Christianity.[160]

    b. The alleged differences between Paul and James.

    c. Paul does not give a distorted picture of 1st century Judaism as some allege.

    d. Judgment passages are given their rightful place, and the understanding of what the final judgment will be like is more nuanced.

    e. The relation between justification and ethics (i.e., the need for right living and obedience) in Pauline theology has been troublesome for some. This issue is resolved by the position advocated in this Special Study.

    f. The confusion about continuity with the Mosaic covenant on this side of the cross has been corrected.

    This whole study concerning what the Scriptures teach about "Justification by Faith" has an everyday importance. God loves the world, but many of the people in the world are unrepentant sinners and are lost now, and will be in the world to come, unless someone points them to what God has said are the conditions on which He forgives men, by which He treats them as justified. How terrible to give the wrong directions to a seeking sinner. Peter's first presentation of what men must do to be saved is a beautiful summary in easily understood terms of all that is involved in Justification by faith. Peter said, "Repent, and let each one of you be baptized in the name of Jesus Christ for the forgiveness of your sins; and you shall receive the gift of the Holy Spirit" (Acts 2:38). God looks for faithfulness to what He has revealed. As the Scriptures say, "The just shall live by faith." Jesus is the source of salvation to all those who obey Him (Hebrews 5:9).

---

[160] See Donald Hagner, "Paul in Modern Jewish Thought" in *Pauline Studies* ed. by D.A. Hagner and M.J. Harris (Grand Rapids: Eerdmans, 1980), p.143ff.

II. *DOCTRINAL*: A PRESENTATION OF THE TRUTHS OF THE GOSPEL THAT SHOW THE JUDAIZERS WERE IN ERROR. Galatians 3:1-4:31

Summary: Paul uses six different arguments to defend the gospel of Christ against the Judaizers: (1) An argument from the readers' personal experience. (2) A Scriptural argument. (3) A logical argument. (4) An argument from absurdity. (5) A sentimental argument. (6) The allegorical argument.

A. An Argument From the Readers' Personal Experience. 3:1-5

Summary: Paul asks the Galatians to compare the Holy Spirit's absence from the works of the Law with the help of the Holy Spirit they had actually experienced in connection with their Christian walk (hearing with faith). The troublemakers have nothing like the gift of the Holy Spirit and His miracles to offer to their converts.

3:1 - *You foolish Galatians, who has bewitched you, before whose eyes Jesus Christ was publicly portrayed* as *crucified?*

You foolish Galatians - Paul's account of his reprimand to Peter is finished. Now he addresses his next words to the Galatian Christians themselves. Paul calls them "foolish" or thoughtless. *Anoētoi* means they were not using their minds (*nous*); they were not stopping to think. In calling them "foolish" Paul is not violating Christ's words in the Sermon on the Mount (Matthew 5:22) because two different words are used and two different ideas are expressed.[1] Paul's words to Peter (Galatians 2:14-21) were the truth. Just a little reflection on the subject should make it obvious that the gospel offers blessings which a life of works of the Law could never provide.[2]

Who has bewitched you - This is like our "What has gotten into you?"   Most likely the

---

[1] "'Foolish' is the same word as that which is used in Luke 24:25 (the Lord's word to the two disciples on the road to Emmaus); it is the word found in Romans 1:14; 1 Timothy 6:9; Titus 3:3, but not the same word (*moros*) as that which is used in Matthew 5:22, 7:26, 23:17; Luke 11:40; Romans 1:22; 1 Corinthians 1:20, 4:10; 2 Corinthians 11:19." (Sanday, *op. cit.*, p.43) "Foolish" (*anoētēs*) in Galatians 3:1 means "illogical" while the word (*moros*) Jesus prohibited has the connotation of obstinate, a "godless person."

[2] In Ephesians 4:23, Paul wrote, "be renewed in the spirit of your *mind*." Many people who profess Christ as their Savior by faith get sidetracked into man-made systems and cults because they fail to use their brains to examine Scripture and to think things through.

word is used here metaphorically,[3] with the meaning to lead astray. The answer to the question "who?" of course, is the troublemakers who have come to Galatia.   If "bewitched" comes literally from the world of the occult, then Paul may even be suggesting that behind the troublemakers is none other than the devil.   Jesus once said to the Pharisees, "You are of your father the devil" (John 8:44).[4]

Before whose eyes Jesus Christ was publicly portrayed *as* crucified? - As Paul calls attention to their personal experience, he asks the Galatians to recall the content of many of the sermons preached to them.   What did that preaching say about Christ?   The idea being driven home here in verse 1 is likely the same point Paul made while reprimanding Peter (Galatians 2:21).   If it is public knowledge that Christ died for us, then we should take our marching orders from Him, not from mere men who have made up some "works of the Law."   "Publicly portrayed" (*prographō*) is used in Greek writings with the meaning "to write beforehand."   If that is the meaning here, Paul is pointing to Old Testament Messianic prophecies that Messiah would be crucified.   "Publicly portrayed" can also have the idea of putting a government proclamation up on a poster (or we might say, display it on a billboard).   When Paul and Barnabas preached, their presentation of Christ crucified was as clear as any government's proclamation ever was.   If we were to connect this verse with the thought presented in 2:21, it says this: "Jesus was *crucified* as part of saving mankind in God's way.   Would He have been crucified if man-made religions, like that of the troublemakers, were any good?"   Indeed, the Galatian Christians were not thinking clearly.

3:2 - This is the only thing I want to find out from you: did you receive the Spirit by the works of the Law, or by the hearing of faith?

This is the only thing I want to find out from you - "This ... only" implies that a proper answer to this next single question would be enough to settle the matter.   "If they conceded this point – and in light of their experience they could do no other – they had conceded Paul's case: the ground was taken away from the Judaizing argument."[5]

Did you receive the Spirit - This is the first time Paul has used the word *pneuma* ("Spirit" or "spirit") in Galatians, and the general consensus is that the Holy Spirit is intended.   Since

---

[3] In its literal meaning, *baskaineō* means to put under a spell or to be hypnotized. If the term "bewitched" were taken literally, Paul is suggesting that some magician had influenced the Galatians by putting them under some sort of demonic spell. In such a state the victim loses self-control and submits to what the magician (or demon) suggests.

[4] Some versions translated from the Textus Receptus add the phrase "that you should not obey the truth" at this juncture.   That line is evidently an interpolation by scribes from a similar phrase in Galatians 5:7.

[5] Bruce, *op. cit.*, p.148-9.

verse 3 speaks about "having begun by the Spirit" we judge that the reference in both verses 2 and 3 is to the time of their conversions. The Holy Spirit works through the Word, at the time of conversion, to bring about a belief in the message preached,[6] and a conviction of sins that desperately need to be forgiven. Then, as the believer is immersed, he or she receives the indwelling gift of the Holy Spirit (Acts 2:38) to help him or her to live the Christian life (Romans 8:4-27). As Paul writes to all the Galatian Christians, he can assume they, each and every one, have received the Holy Spirit, for that was true of any and all who were immersed into Christ. Paul knew it and his Galatian readers knew it.

By the works of the Law - In the comments at Galatians 2:16 it has been explained that the phrase "works of the Law" refers to man-made religious rules based on various passages in the Law of Moses, the kind of rules the Pharisees were accustomed to make.[7] Not only was there no indwelling of the Holy Spirit attached to observing such man-made rules of the Law, there was no Holy Spirit available to the Jew who was obeying the Law of Moses (John 7:37-39).

Or by hearing with faith? - The answer to this question which the experience of the Galatians would supply is "by hearing with faith." Commentators have struggled to explain what these words mean. At Romans 1:5 we have *hupakoēn pisteōs* translated as the "obedience of faith." The Greek here is *akoēs pisteōs* and likewise could speak of harkening to or obeying the faith.[8] "From Peter's Pentecost sermon (Acts 2:38) on through the life of the early church, the Holy Spirit was offered in Christ's name to those

---

[6] Caution is needed here. Calvinistic writers often find the "first work of grace" in this verse. They speak of the regenerating work of the Spirit (which makes it possible for a totally depraved person to even want to believe) rather than the gift of the Holy Spirit. There is a difference between the Spirit's convicting work on the heart as the gospel is heard (which is the Biblical view), and the "first work of grace" view which has the Spirit working on the sinner's heart without any gospel being preached.

[7] We object to any translation that reads "was it by doing what the Law demands?" because such a translation obscures any reference to the Judaizers' theology. Let it be noted that the 1963 NASB margin reads "by works of law" (small "L"). The NASB uses "Law" (capital "L") when reference is obviously to the Law of Moses. Some think the marginal reading is to be preferred since it does not immediately cause the reader to assume that "works of law" and obeying the Law of Moses are interchangeable expressions. "Works of law" and obeying the Law of Moses are not interchangeable expressions, as will be demonstrated in Galatians 3:6-14.

[8] The Greek phrase "the hearing with ("of," ASV) faith" can be variously translated, depending on whether "hearing" and/or "faith" is taken either actively or passively. If taken actively, meaning "hearing" or "listening," then the phrase could mean "hearing characterized by (accompanied by) faith" (i.e., as an objective genitive) or "hearing that comes from, or is inspired by, faith" (i.e., as a subjective genitive). "Hearing" can also have a passive meaning, "that which is heard, the report, preaching, message," particularly with reference to the "gospel message." The phrase could then mean "the gospel message which demands faithfulness." See the extended discussion in S. Williams, "The Hearing of Faith: AKOE PISTEOS in Galatians 3." *NTS 35* (1989), p.82-93.

who believed and repented and were baptized into Him."[9]   What the apostles Paul and Barnabas had taught the Galatians during their first coming among them was not any system of "works of the Law."   They had taught the Galatians about faithfulness to Christ, about doing what Christ says.   When they responded to the invitation to submit their lives to Christ, God gave them the gift of the Holy Spirit.

3:3 - Are you so foolish?   Having begun by the Spirit, are you now being perfected by the flesh?

Are you so foolish? - See notes at verse 1 on "foolish."   Paul asks, are you really so thoughtless?   We suppose this question goes with what follows, so it means, 'Do you think you can start one way and finish by another?'

Having begun by the Spirit - It might be better to translate *pneuma* "spirit" (with a small "s") since in this verse "spirit" is contrasted to "flesh."   "Begun," of course, is a reference to the beginning of each one's Christian life.   When a man becomes a Christian, his spirit becomes alive again (Romans 8:10).   Now that it is alive, his spirit can direct his behavior as the indwelling Holy Spirit prompts.   That is how the Galatian Christians have been living since their conversion.

Are you now being perfected by the flesh? - "The Judaizers in Galatia, it seems, claimed not to be opposing Paul but to be supplementing his message, and so to be bringing his converts to perfection."[10]   "Works of the Law" appeal just to the flesh.   They give no help to the spirit.   Therefore it is "foolish" to think that by embracing "works of the Law" you will be a better Christian.[11]   A man relying on "works of the Law" would be without the prompting of the Holy Spirit, and perhaps he has even quenched the Spirit.   He finds himself living again as his "flesh" (as its desires are stirred up by the devil) prompts.[12]

---

[9] Lawson, *op. cit.*, p.54.

[10] Boice, *op. cit.*, p.106.

[11] The verb "being perfected" is present tense.   The perfecting has not yet been completed.   "The words Paul uses are the normal Greek words for beginning and completing a sacrifice.   The first one (*enarchesthai*) is the word for scattering the grains of barley on and around the victim, which was the first act of sacrifice.   The second one (*epiteleisthai*) is the word used for fully completing the ritual of any sacrifice.   By using these two words, Paul shows that he looks on the whole Christian life as a sacrifice to God" (Barclay, *op. cit.,* p.26).

[12] "Flesh" here is another place in Galatians where Reformed theologians have to struggle to explain *sarx* ("flesh").   They cannot very well insist that *sarx* here has reference to an "old sinful nature" as they are often wont to do when this word is encountered elsewhere in the Biblical text (e.g., Romans 7:5).   If it is interpreted to mean "old sinful nature," then it follows that Christians have not been redeemed from the old nature (allegedly) inherited from Adam.   This will hardly do!

3:4 - Did you suffer so many things in vain – if indeed it was in vain?

Did you suffer so many things in vain – This question continues Paul's appeal to the readers' personal experiences. The word *epathete,* translated "suffer," could also be translated "experience." Paul asks, 'Have you, since you became Christians, experienced so many things in vain?' Just after their beginning, the churches of Galatia did experience persecution (Acts 14:2) and were told by Paul about the time of the close of the first missionary journey that they would face tribulation in the future (Acts 14:22). If "so many things" refers to persecutions, then a good translation would be "endure." Notice, though, that Paul has just written about benefits the Galatians received from the Holy Spirit when they became Christians. If "so many things" refers to the experiences of the Holy Spirit, it is best translated "experience." "Arndt and Gingrich suggest that only once in the New Testament (here in Galatians 3:4) does *paschō* have the meaning of a pleasant or 'remarkable' experience, but they are quick to acknowledge that even in this passage other scholars do not agree that *paschō* has this meaning."[13] When Paul asks if it was in vain[14] he is asking, 'Have your experiences taught you nothing, for it certainly looks that way if you are considering embracing works of the Law?'

If indeed it was in vain? - The words express Paul's hope that the readers are not going to adopt the Judaizers' view.

3:5 - Does He then, who provides you with the Spirit and works miracles among you, do it by works of the Law, or by hearing with faith?

Does He then, who provides you with the Spirit - "Then" is *oun* ("therefore") in the Greek. This verse draws a conclusion from what has just been written in this chapter. The topic is still the Holy Spirit, and "He" is likely a reference to God.[15] Verse 2 looked at the question about the Holy Spirit from the Galatians' point of view. Verse 5 looks at the matter from God's point of view. When God provides something, He does it lavishly and with an open hand.[16] In this first clause, the indwelling of the Spirit, given when a

---

[13] Johnson, *op. cit.,* p.78.

[14] The Greek word, *eikē,* means for no cause, to no good.

[15] The Greek is written with an article and a participle, and would be translated by a relative clause such as "the one who" or "he who." While some think "he" points to Paul as the giver, the NASB translators (using "He," capital "H") follow the consensus among commentators that the reference is to God. See Galatians 4:6 and 1 Thessalonians 4:8, where God is the One who gives the Spirit. See similar language in 2 Corinthians 9:10, Colossians 2:19, and 2 Peter 1:5,11 which strongly suggest that God does the supplying of the Spirit that Paul has in mind.

[16] The verb "provides" (*epichorēgeō*) was used of what was required to be a patron at the public festivals where a chorus (a type of stage play) had to be trained, costumed, and staged. The patron had to exhibit generosity to a great degree. The word is also used of the support that a husband, out of love, promised to give his wife (Barclay, *op. cit.,* p.26).

person is immersed, seems to be in view.

And works miracles among you - Both "provides" and "works" are present tense participles which imply that the divine activity still continues at the time Paul is writing this letter to the Galatians. Indeed, in the early church, miraculous spiritual gifts lasted until about the turn of the century. When Paul was among them, the Lord worked miracles through him (Acts 14:3 and 15:12).[17] According to 1 Corinthians 12:10, the "effecting of miracles" was one of the spiritual gifts received by the laying on of an apostle's hands (Acts 8:17,18; 2 Timothy 1:6). "Among you" suggests public miraculous manifestations.[18]

Do it by the works of the Law, or by hearing with faith? - "Works of the Law"[19] are *halakhot* (rules such as the Pharisees loved to make) as was learned in Galatians 2:16. "Hearing with faith" has the same meaning it carried in Galatians 3:2. "Who ever knew a Judaizer to whom the Lord granted a single work of power? But wherever the apostles went, these works followed – an abundance granted lavishly by God (Acts 14:3)."[20] If miracles credential the message (Matthew 11:4; Mark 16:20; John 20:30; Acts 2:22, 8:6; 2 Corinthians 12:12; Hebrews 2:4), then which message has God's imprimatur? Works of the Law? No, for there were no miracles there. Hearing with faith? Yes! It stands to reason that the method taught by the Judaizers does not have God's approval.

B. The Scriptural Argument.   3:6-14

> *Summary*: Since arguments from Scripture carry more weight than arguments only from personal experience (3:1-5), six Old Testament passages are quoted to prove the point that salvation is conditioned on faith in Christ (Genesis 12:3, 15:6; Deuteronomy 21:23, 27:26; Habakkuk 2:4; Leviticus 18:5). Remember, such faithfulness is in antithesis to "works of law."

---

[17] That Paul worked miracles we would expect, since such miracles were one proof the apostles could give that they were indeed apostles (2 Corinthians 12:12, "the signs of a true apostle").

[18] The Greek is *en humin*, literally "in you." However, a translation like "in your midst" or "among you" is to be preferred since works of miraculous power were never wrought simply "in men's hearts."

[19] As at 2:16 and 2:21, there is no "the" before "law" in the Greek. As was true in those verses, so here. If we capitalize "Law," we are likely to miss completely the allusion to man-made Jewish rules, and think of the Law of Moses instead. We thus miss the point of the whole passage.

[20] Lenski, *op. cit.*, p.131.

3:6 - Even so Abraham BELIEVED GOD, AND IT WAS RECKONED TO HIM AS RIGHTEOUSNESS.

Even so - The NASB margin reads "just as." The thread of thought is this: "hearing with faith" (3:2,5) brought blessings to the Galatians "just as" it did in Abraham's case.[21] The Galatians and Abraham are parallel cases in the matter of justification (righteousness): both are saved and blessed by faith – by doing what God says, rather than doing what men say (works of the Law). Also important to the whole discussion is the fact that the Abrahamic blessing (verses 8,9,13) includes Gentile believers, just like the Galatian Christians were.

Abraham BELIEVED GOD - The connection between verse 5 and verse 6 is this: "faith" (verse 5) is *pistis*, while "believe" (verse 6) is *pisteuō*. The Greek words behind "faith" and "believe" are formed off the same stem. The theme of justification by faith which was introduced in 2:16 is continued in 3:6,8,11,13. In fact, verses 6-9 epitomize Romans 4.[22] The two letters were probably written at nearly the same time, and Romans 4 helps unfold what Paul means here in Galatians. Paul uses Genesis 15:6 (LXX version) to make his point about Abraham's faith.[23] Since Abraham was faithful to God before God called him out of Ur of the Chaldees (Genesis 12:1-9; Hebrews 11:8), we may be certain that the time in Abraham's life alluded to in Genesis 15:6 was not the first time in Abraham's life that he was justified. The verb tense of "believed" in the Hebrew indicates continuous action, not a one-time belief. Abraham's continuing belief (faith, faithfulness to what God said) was the thing God was looking for.[24]

AND IT WAS RECKONED TO HIM AS RIGHTEOUSNESS - "It" is Abraham's faith, as Romans 4:5 makes plain. We learned what "righteousness" is in notes at Galatians 2:21.

---

[21] How to relate this verse to the context is a disputed matter. *Novum Testamentum Graece*, RSV, NRSV, REV, and NJB make verse 6 the beginning of a new paragraph. The *Greek New Testament*, NEB and NAB make verse 6 the conclusion of the previous paragraph, and begin a new paragraph with verse 7. The NASB makes no break until verse 15. We have chosen to treat verse 6 as the beginning of a new argument wherein Paul appeals to Scripture. As he writes Galatians, the only Scripture available to Paul was the Old Testament (as only Matthew, 1 & 2 Thessalonians, and 1 & 2 Corinthians had been written before Galatians), and he uses it as the supreme evidence of the condition on which salvation is conditioned.

[22] Marcion omitted verses 6-9 (Tert. *Adv. Marc.* 5:3) because he was opposed to any relation between what is Jewish and what is Christian. His omission led to erroneous beliefs.

[23] The same passage, Genesis 15:6, is cited in both Romans 4:3 and James 2:21ff. Paul bases his argument upon it in Romans 4:3 as proof that God imputes righteousness on the condition of faith, not on works of law (cp. Romans 4:2 with Romans 3:20,28). James guards Genesis 15:6 against misinterpretation by teachers who degraded faith into a barren assent of the intellect (James 2:17-23).

[24] To the Jew, trust (faith) in God and obedience to His laws were inseparable. See Genesis 26:4,5.

It is the same thing as being justified in God's sight, counted as righteous. "Reckoned" translates *logizomai*, a word used in bookkeeping for crediting something to someone's account.[25] "Reckoned" is the word that led to the doctrine of imputed righteousness.[26] If the forensic (i.e., legal) use of the term predominates, then the verse says this: because of Abraham's faithfulness, God thought of him as righteous and declared him "righteous." Abraham wasn't sinless perfect, but God treated him as righteous (i.e., forgiven). In Romans 4:4-12, Paul interprets this language about reckoning faith as righteousness to mean that when God reckoned righteousness to Abraham, He granted it as a free gift, not something earned. Not even faithfulness earns salvation, though it is the condition without which no one will be justified. In addition, had it not been for Calvary, there is no way God's grace is so generous that He could think of justifying even the faithful ones (Romans 3:24).

3:7 - Therefore, be sure that it is those who are of faith who are sons of Abraham.

Therefore, be sure - "Therefore" translates inferential *ara*. Since Genesis 15:6 speaks of justification by faith, there are several inferences to be drawn. The faith of Abraham becomes the basis of Paul's argument for several verses to follow. The verb *ginōskete* may either be indicative ('you know') or imperative ('be sure!'). If we follow the NASB, this verse becomes an exhortation to the Galatians to learn or to recognize something. The verb is also present tense, saying that this realization is to be an enduring one. Such a realization is exactly what the Galatians need as ammunition against the Judaizers.

That it is those who are of faith - To be "of faith" means to be characterized or controlled by faith.[27] Those who are "of faith" are those (like Abraham) whose characteristic it is to walk by faithfulness to what God says (rather than by works of the Law).

Who are sons of Abraham - What Paul is here writing is nothing new. The promises to Abraham concerning his descendants were misinterpreted by the Jews into an emphasis on physical descent. They came to think that their relationship with Abraham, a mere physi-

---

[25] *Logizomai* means to evaluate, estimate, think (something) about, consider, reckon. In the LXX it is used to translate the Hebrew word *hasab*, which means "think" or "account" or "credit."

[26] Since the time of Augustine, the Roman Church taught a doctrine of infused righteousness; that is, when God justifies a man, he puts "righteousness" in him so as to guide his behavior. (In this age of computers, think of exchanging one operating system for another.) Thomas Aquinas had defended the doctrine of infused righteousness in the Middle Ages. Luther and the other Reformers came along and objected to "infused" righteousness, instead contending for "imputed" righteousness. As the Special Study on *Justification By Faith* has shown, this "imputed" righteousness doctrine led to further controversies, even among the Protestants themselves. But without the doctrine of imputed righteousness, there would have been no Reformation.

[27] For the genitive *ek pisteōs* ("of faith"), see notes at Galatians 2:16.

cal descent from him, guaranteed eternal salvation. That the promise was spiritual and not physical was a hard idea to get into their minds. John the Baptist had taught it, when he warned the Jewish religious leaders that their *physical* descent did not guarantee them *spiritual* life (Matthew 3:9; Luke 3:8). Jesus also made a clear distinction between "Abraham's seed" physically and "Abraham's seed" spiritually (John 8:37-47). Paul's point is that the true sons of Abraham[28] are those who share his faithfulness, and he will go on to show that this sonship was true not only for folk of Jewish descent but for Gentiles like the Galatians, too. They do not need works of law to make them Abraham's sons.[29]

3:8 - And the Scripture, foreseeing that God would justify the Gentiles by faith, preached the gospel beforehand to Abraham, *saying*, "ALL THE NATIONS SHALL BE BLESSED IN YOU."

And the Scripture - "And" is continuative. Paul has more Scripture to call to the attention of the Galatians. The first point (verses 6,7) Paul made in this Scriptural argument is that the condition on which Abraham was saved was faithfulness to God's revelation, not faithfulness to some man-made system. The second point (verses 8,9) is that this same kind of salvation is meant for the Gentiles, too. Gentiles, too, are justified by faith, not by works of the Law. "Scripture" in the singular, as here, usually denotes a particular passage of Old Testament Scripture, in this case, either Genesis 12:3 or 18:18. "Paul's quotation from Moses ... proves that, from the very beginning of Abraham's relationship with God, the blessing of salvation was promised to all the nations of the world."[30]

Foreseeing that God would justify the Gentiles by faith - Scripture is personified.[31] It was actually the author of Scripture who did the foreseeing and announcing. "What Scrip-

---

[28] The phrase "son of ..." was a common Semitic expression to denote special characteristics that match those of the parent. When we call Jesus "Son of God," we are saying He has all the characteristics of God the Father. When men were called "sons of Belial," it indicates their evil characteristics match those of Belial. So "sons of Abraham" emphasizes characteristics like Abraham's. The form of the expression is precisely the same as Romans 8:14, "For all who are being led by the Spirit of God, these are sons of God." In each of these cases, the absence of the article before "sons" indicates the apostle has a class of folk in mind.

[29] Not a few writers believe Paul is here replying to an argument made by the Judaizers who were causing trouble in Galatia. Paul's appeal to Abraham then says, "There is no need for the Galatians to take up works of the Law, for they are already sons of Abraham by faith. Works of the Law can add nothing to that."

[30] W. Wiersbe, *Be Free* (*Galatians*), (Wheaton, IL: Scripture Press, 1974), p.69.

[31] Another example of such personification is found in Romans 9:17, "Scripture says to Pharaoh." This unusual way of citing the Old Testament makes these passages of great value to see how Paul and other New Testament writers viewed the Scriptures. Scripture speaking is virtually equivalent to God speaking. That's a high view of the inspiration of the Old Testament. See B.B. Warfield, *The Inspiration and Authority of the Bible* (Philadelphia: Presbyterian and Reformed, 1948), p.299-348.

ture promises God promises, for He is the speaker."[32]   The translation "would justify" treats all of this as a prediction of the future.   What God told Abraham He would do, did not actually happen until Christ came.   Yet there is another way to translate the Greek. Since it is present tense, it could be translated 'is justifying.'   Paul would thus be stating the simple fact of something he sees day to day with his own eyes.   God is doing just what He said he would do.   He is justifying Gentiles as well as Jews, and it is on the condition of their faithfulness to what He has commanded.

Preached the gospel beforehand to Abraham, *saying* - How can Paul say the Scripture preached to Abraham when the Scripture was not written until long after Abraham's time? We've already observed that Scripture and God cannot be separated.   What God said to Abraham eventually became inscripturated, and through the Scriptures God still speaks. When we hear "preached the gospel," we are accustomed to think of a preacher making a formal, public announcement of the truths of Christianity.   God apparently did not make known to Abraham all the truths Christianity teaches, but He did make known to Abraham the "good news" that a Savior was coming who would redeem lost men, and that is any and all lost men (not just Abraham's physical descendants).   "Beforehand" evidently means long before it actually happened.[33]

"ALL THE NATIONS SHALL BE BLESSED IN YOU" - The quotation is drawn either from Genesis 12:3 or 22:18.[34]   The same Greek word translated "nations" can also be translated "Gentiles,"[35] and that is the point of the passage.   "In you" means in union with Abraham, as the next verse will clearly say.   The circle drawn by "in you" has within it Abraham himself, all the Jews who believe in Christ, and all the Gentiles who believe in Christ.   When Abraham received this promise he was as much a Gentile as the Gentile Galatians, a point which Paul drives home so forcibly in Romans 4:10-12.   Note how "blessed" in the passage from Genesis 22:18 is parallel with "justified by faith" in the pre-

---

[32] Hendriksen, *op. cit.,* p.124.

[33] Romans 4 argues that "beforehand" means before the Law of Moses was given.   There is a correction here of Mormon doctrine.   The gospel was preached before Christ ever came.   Compare Romans 16:25,26 which also tells us that the gospel to the Gentiles was a mystery kept hidden in times past (that is, it was not clearly revealed to men, but it was there all the time).

[34] Genesis 22:18 also reads "In your seed all the nations of the earth shall be blessed."   Galatians 3 tells us that the singular word "seed" points to Christ.   "Nations" includes all ethnic groups.   "Blessed" includes the forgiveness of sins.   The words of Genesis 22:18 are the words of the new covenant (the renewed covenant) under which Christians live.   This is of prime importance to this whole Scriptural argument against the Judaizers.   Judaizers' claims are not compatible with the words of the new covenant. Therefore, the doctrines of the Judaizers are anti-Scriptural and false!

[35] "All the nations [families: Hebrew, *mishpechoth*; LXX, *phulai*] of the earth shall be blessed" (Genesis 12:3).   The Hebrew word "families" is broad enough to include "Gentiles" (nations).   Paul's *ethnē* ("nations") is coextensive with *phulai* (families).

vious clause here in Galatians 3:8. In God's gospel message to Abraham, "blessed" involves the forgiveness of sins.

3:9 - So then those who are of faith are blessed with Abraham, the believer.

So then those who are of faith - Verse 9 states the conclusion of the argument from Scripture thus far. If anyone, Jew or Gentile, is reckoned as just by God, it will be as a result of faithfulness, not as a result of doing the works of the Law. The same point has already been made in verse 7. "So then" means because of God's promise to Abraham. Those who are *of faith, they alone* but also *all of them* without exception, are sons of Abraham.

Are blessed with Abraham, the believer - The passive "blessed" has God as the one doing the blessing. As the parallel phrases in the previous verse taught, "blessed" and "justify by faith" are interchangeable terms. The Greek adjective (*pistis*),[36] here translated "the believer,"[37] is a word for which it is difficult to find an equivalent English expression. "The faithful Abraham" might come about as close as we can to translating *tō pistō Abraam*. It was *faithful* Abraham who received the blessing. It is *faithful* Abraham whom the Galatians should strive to emulate.

3:10 - For as many as are of the works of the Law are under a curse; for it is written, "CURSED IS EVERYONE WHO DOES NOT ABIDE BY ALL THE THINGS WRITTEN IN THE BOOK OF THE LAW, TO PERFORM THEM."

For as many as are of the works of the Law are under a curse - Paul continues his argument from Scripture. The third major point Paul develops is that those who do not live by faith, but who advocate living by works of the Law,[38] are under a curse from God.[39]

---

[36] This adjective is used to describe a characteristic of God (1 Corinthians 1:9, 10:13; 2 Corinthians 1:18; 1 Thessalonians 5:24); in each case, the word is translated as "faithful." It is also used of human beings (1 Corinthians 4:2,17 and 2 Corinthians 6:15); depending on the context, the word is translated as "trustworthy" or "believer" or "faithful."

[37] "The believer" pictures a lifestyle, rather than a one-time belief.

[38] For "works of the Law," see notes at Galatians 2:16. Such "works" (Pharisaic rules) were those "how to walk" (*halakhah*) rules the Judaizing troublemakers who had come to Galatia were demanding.

[39] Some commentators insist it is the curse of the Law, rather than the curse of God, that rests on those who do not abide by all the things written in the Law. We see nothing to be gained by this distinction, but it is to be noted that such a distinction is made in arguments concerning exactly what justification by faith means. Some want to treat justifying faith as though no actions are involved in it. Then when they read this verse that talks about a curse, it is not the curse of God if one doesn't do all that is written, they affirm. Rather, it is just the curse of the Law. Thus they would defend their doctrine of faith-only. However, failure to keep the Law in Old Testament times did bring men under God's wrath. Is His wrath somehow qualitatively different from a "curse"? We think not.

Not only are those who are of faith (verse 9) blessed of God, but those who try works of the Law (doing something other than what God says) are cursed. In verses 10-12 Paul quotes Old Testament scriptures three times to make his point. The "as many as" would include the troublemaking teachers plus any of the Galatians who followed their lead.[40] The reason for the curse is that the Law is being ignored as men pursued their man-made rules. In this, Paul's assertion is just as Jesus taught (Matthew 15:6). Men must be faithful to what God has said,[41] or the Scriptures teach they are under a curse which includes ultimately the punishment of hell, to be under divine wrath.

For it is written - The first of the three passages Paul uses to make his point is the LXX of Deuteronomy 27:26.[42] This verse from Deuteronomy is the solemn close of a series of twelve curses (Deuteronomy 27:15-26) in which Moses denounces the violators of the Law. These twelve curses were to be repeated by the Levites on Mt. Ebal in Israel's annual renewal of the Mosaic covenant. Each year, the Levites closed the ceremony with this ringing statement, "Curses on all those who do not continue in all the things written in the book of the Law."

"CURSED IS EVERYONE WHO DOES NOT ABIDE BY ALL THINGS WRITTEN IN THE BOOK OF THE LAW, TO PERFORM THEM" - What is the point of this quotation? That those who were championing "the works of the Law" were the very people who were not abiding in all the things written in the Law.[43] Pharisees ignored many of the Mosaic Laws,[44] and the troublemakers who had come to Galatia did likewise (Galatians 6:13). Even the Jewish Scriptures taught that righteousness does not come through works of the Law, but through faith ("abide by all things written in the book of the

---

[40] The Judaizers, of course, would not see themselves as being under a curse. They would see themselves as God's best children because of their scrupulous observance of the traditions of the elders.

[41] The curse seems rather to be directed against those who thought they could pick and choose which parts of Moses (for example) they should enforce, and which they could explain away and therefore ignore. No! That treatment of God's revelation brings a curse. Men are to keep the whole revelation God has given!

[42] The Hebrew is, "Cursed he who does not confirm the words of this law by doing them," i.e., he confirms them by continuing to obey them. When Paul says in in Romans 3:31, "we establish law," he may have Deuteronomy 27:26 in mind, for "establish" would match the Hebrew "confirm."

[43] The phrase "book of the Law" does not occur in the passage in Deuteronomy 27:26. The LXX reads "all the words of the Law." The sense is not affected by Paul's substitution of "book of the Law." Also, the word "all" does not appear in our present Hebrew text of Deuteronomy 27:16, but the word is found in the LXX and the Samaritan Pentateuch. The Greek text of Galatians that reads "all" is not in doubt. That is what Paul wrote.

[44] Pharisaic Judaism had no conscience against explaining away, or simply ignoring, certain of the laws found in Moses. Recall what Jesus said to the Pharisees about the law of Corban (Matthew 15:3-6; Mark 7:11-13).

Law, to perform them"). "All things written in the book of the Law" are distinguished from "works of the Law."[45] We shall see, before we have finished verse 12, that "faith" is equivalent to doing what God says. "To perform them" ("to do them," ASV) must be given some clarification. The New Testament elsewhere clearly teaches that *doing* ("to perform them"), namely, habitual obedience to the revelation a man has, is the very standard God applies in the final judgment (cf. Romans 2:6-16; Matthew 25:31-46). Note, we said "habitual doing" – not sinless perfection or perfect obedience. Faithfulness and sinless perfection are not synonymous, interchangeable expressions. Galatians 3:10 must not be interpreted in such a way that it contradicts what the New Testament says elsewhere about "doing" (i.e., the obedience of faith).

3:11 - Now that no one is justified by the Law before God is evident; for, "THE RIGHTEOUS MAN SHALL LIVE BY FAITH."

Now that no one is justified by the Law before God - The argument Paul is pursuing, that the Scriptures themselves show "works of the Law" will not justify, is here enforced by a second quotation from the Old Testament. As at Galatians 2:16 and 3:2,5, there is no "the" before *nomos* ("law") in the Greek; the NASB margin at this place notes that *nomos* ("Law") has no article. We suppose "Law" here ought to be understood as shorthand for "works of the Law." The phrase "before God" is used figuratively of God's estimation or judgment, or as God looks at it. Verse 6 has said justification is something "reckoned" by God. "Justified before God" is another way of saying the same thing. Verses 10 and 11 make a comparison. The one who does not abide in all the things written in the Law is cursed in God's estimation. The one who is faithful to God's revelation is justified in God's estimation.

Is evident - This is evident because God has said in most simple words how a man receives the verdict of righteousness, namely, in consequence of faith.

For, "THE RIGHTEOUS MAN SHALL LIVE BY FAITH" - This quotation to show that God's estimation is based on faith comes from Habakkuk 2:4.[46] "Righteous" in Habakkuk corresponds to "justified" in the words by which Paul introduces this Old Testament passage. The statement from Habakkuk is so important the Holy Spirit inspired three New Testament passages to explain it. *Romans 1:17* explains "the righteous man" and tells how God has provided a way of salvation and how the sinner can be justified or reckoned as righteous before God. *Galatians 3:11* explains how the righteous man "shall live" in freedom. And *Hebrews 10:38* discusses "by faith", showing it to be faithfulness

---

[45] Those commentaries and versions that treat "works of the Law" as being synonymous with observing the Law of Moses are misleading. That is not a legitimate explanation of "works of the Law."

[46] In its original setting, "Habakkuk was thinking of temporal ills resulting from the Chaldean invasion. Paul is thinking in a more general spiritual context." Boice, *op. cit.*, p.459.

over a lifetime.[47] "This *living* consists in such things as: *a.* enjoying the peace of God which passes all understanding (Philippians 4:7), in the knowledge that in the sight of God's holy majesty the believer is righteous (Romans 5:1; 8:15); *b.* having fellowship with God 'in Christ' (John 17:3); *c.* 'rejoicing greatly with joy unspeakable and full of glory' (1 Peter 1:8); *d.* 'being transformed into the image of the Lord from glory to glory' (2 Corinthians 3:18); and *e.*, last but not least, striving to be a spiritual blessing to others to the glory of God (1 Thessalonians 3:8)."[48]

3:12 - However, the Law is not of faith; on the contrary, "HE WHO PRACTICES THEM SHALL LIVE BY THEM."

However, the Law is not of faith - Paul continues to press his argument by quoting a third passage from the Old Testament to show that "works of the Law" will not save. The passage this time is Leviticus 18:5, a passage Paul also quotes in Romans 10:5. Instead of translating the Greek word *de* as "however," we prefer the NASB margin which reads "and."[49] As it was in verse 11, "the Law" is shorthand for "works of the Law."[50] Thus, verse 12 says that "works of the Law" and "faith" (doing what God says) are mutually exclusive.[51]

---

[47] The idea of "three New Testament writers" is adapted from Wiersbe, *op. cit.*, p.70. "A translation closer to the Hebrew of Habakkuk would be 'the just shall live by his steadfastness.' The prophet was mainly thinking in terms of right living in this present world" (Johnson, *op. cit.*, p.85). "Steadfastness" or faithfulness in Habakkuk 2:4 is synonymous with "abide by all things written in the book of the Law, to perform them." This helps us to understand what "faith" is. It is right living. It is doing what God says. It is not sinless perfection that God looks for; instead, the tenor of a man's life is what God looks for. Recall also that Jesus said to His disciples, "By your endurance you will gain your lives" (Luke 21:18). One more note of a technical sort on the Habakkuk passage: the Hebrew (Masoretic Text) reads "by his faith." Therefore, the LXX that Paul quotes, which reads "by my faith", must mean 'by the faith that I (God) require.'

[48] Hendriksen, *op. cit.*, p.127.

[49] Those commentators who regularly explained "works of the Law" as being synonymous with obedience to the Law of Moses have run into a snag at this verse. They all insist it is difficult to ascertain Paul's train of thought in the verses we are presently considering. One says that under the Law of Moses there was no place for faith (Barnes, *op. cit.*, p.333). Another's opinion is that "the Law is not of faith" means that for Gentiles their "faith" does not include keeping the Law of Moses. While this latter is true, and is an idea that will be unfolded at Galatians 3:15ff, we doubt it is the point here at verse 12.

[50] The Greek here does read *ho nomos* ("the Law"), but we would treat "the" as an article of previous reference, i.e., the same "law" we have been talking about since verse 10.

[51] Leviticus 18:5 is not quoted so as to be in contrast to what Habakkuk 2:4 says (the NASB translation notwithstanding). The passages from Deuteronomy 27:26 and 21:23 confirm the view that Leviticus is not a contradiction to Habakkuk. Caution must be exercised by commentators and translators at this place, lest the explanation here flat-out contradict what Paul has written elsewhere. The Law of Moses did demand "doing," and the importance of "doing" must not be dismissed in an attempt to prove salvation is monergistic (all done by God, with no conditions to be met by man). It must also be remembered that when men stand in the final judgment, the standard by which they will be approved or condemned is whether or not they have habitually done what was revealed to them they should do (Romans 2:6-16). It will not do to interpret Galatians in a way that contradicts Romans, when the two books were written during the same time frame in Paul's life (assuming our dating of Galatians is correct). Paul does not here in Galatians contradict what he wrote in Romans 2:13 and 10:5,6. Reformed theology, which often finds its radical distinction between "faith" and "works" (Law) in this verse from Galatians, is in error.

On the contrary - After "on the contrary," we should mentally supply "it is written." What Paul is now going to quote from the Old Testament concerning "practices them" (i.e., the things commanded in the Law of Moses) is "contrary" to the "Law [that] is not of faith." In other words, "works of the Law" (the Pharisee's traditions) are not "faith." Indeed, Pharisaic "works of the Law" are not even in harmony with Leviticus 18:5.

"HE WHO PRACTICES THEM SHALL LIVE BY THEM" - This is a quotation of Leviticus 18:5.[52] This quotation, like Deuteronomy 27:26, contains the word *poieō* ("perform, practice"), and like Habakkuk 2:4 contains the word *zēsetai* ("shall live"), which allows Paul to bring the two texts together and compare them. Some have interpreted Leviticus 18:5 to teach that sinless perfection was the only way to salvation. We doubt that such a lofty requirement is what Leviticus 18 demands. Faithfulness, not sinless perfection, has always been the condition of salvation. "By 'them' is meant the 'statutes' and 'judgments' mentioned immediately before in the verse from which the quotation is taken."[53] Again we call attention to the fact that "practices" in this clause matches "faith" in the clause which Paul used to introduce this passage. Faith is habitually doing what God says. The words from Leviticus 18:5 are commented on at Romans 10:5: "Moses writes that the man who practices the righteousness which is based on law shall live by that righteousness." "Live" is used in the sense of justification.

3:13 - Christ redeemed us from the curse of the Law, having become a curse for us – for it is written, "CURSED IS EVERYONE WHO HANGS ON A TREE" –

Christ redeemed us from the curse of the Law - There is no connective word here, so Bible students do not have Paul's help as they attempt to follow his thread of thought. We propose to do it this way: we have come to another point being made in the Scriptural argument. First, we learned that all men are justified by faith just as was Abraham. Then Paul wove together three Old Testament passages to show that folk who try "works of the Law" are under a curse. Now, Paul goes on to give a reason why the Gentiles no longer even have to worry about that curse. The reason (verses 13,14) is that Christ has redeemed us from any such obligation to keep all the things written in the Book of the Law.   If the

---

[52] The MT, LXX and the Targums all read "the man (*anthrōpos*) who ...." According to the better supported reading here at Galatians 3:12, Paul apparently left out the word *anthrōpos* which occurs in Leviticus 18:5 in the Old Testament texts to which he had access. It is this commentator's judgment that Paul's "he who" speaks of anyone. Barth (CD II/2 English translation [Edinburgh, 1957], p.245) and Cranfield (*Romans*, p.521) think that Paul's expression "he who" is a reference to Jesus, the only One who ever kept the Law perfectly. This view is based partially on a faulty explanation of Leviticus 18:5 (since that passage does not require sinless perfection), and this view fails to give any coherent thread of thought to this passage in Galatians 3.

[53] Sanday, *op. cit.*, p.50.

Law of Moses has been abrogated (as Hebrews 7:12,18 and 10:9 affirm), then there certainly is no need to insist on "works of the Law" (man-made rules based even tangentially on that abrogated system). "Redeemed" translates *exagorazō*,[54] to buy out of the marketplace, to free from (slavery). Twice in Galatians, at 3:13 and 4:5, when Paul uses "redeemed" he does so with reference to the Law of Moses. Paul will speak of those under the Law of Moses as being in a kind of slavery from which they must be freed. The aorist tense "redeemed" points back to the historical event of Christ's death on the cross. "This is a crucial point in this passage about justification by faith. All the faith in the world could not save us if Jesus had not actually given His life to atone for our sins."[55] The word "us" here must refer to all Christians, whether Gentiles or Jews by race. The "curse of the Law" has already been introduced in verse 10, where Deuteronomy 27:26 pronounces a curse on everyone who does not practice what the Law of Moses requires.

Having become a curse for us - This is how Christ redeemed us. Compare 2 Corinthians 5:21, "[God] made [Jesus] who knew no sin to be sin on our behalf." "Christ had no sin of his own, but He took upon Himself the curse we earned by our sinning. Thus He made us free from that curse."[56] We likely have a Hebrew idiom here. Just like the Old Testament sin offering was identified with sin (see Leviticus 4:21-25, and cp. Romans 8:3 where the ASV reads "sin" while the NASB reads "an offering for sin"), so we suppose the curse and the curse offering were identified. Thus, this verse in Galatians would say Christ became a curse offering on our behalf.[57]

For it is written - The fact that a "curse" is involved in Christ's death is substantiated by Deuteronomy 21:23.[58]

---

[54] This is one of three words used in the New Testament to denote redemption. The other two are *lutroō,* which speaks of the payment of a ransom in order to loose or set free, and *agoradzō,* which means to purchase or to buy in the marketplace. Christ bought us with a price, viz., His blood (Acts 20:28; 1 Peter 1:18,19).

[55] Orrin Root, *1976-77 Standard Lesson Commentary*, p.13.

[56] Root, *ibid.* Many theologians have entered into the attempt to explain in what sense Jesus became a curse. They have debated whether it is the "curse of the Law" or the "curse of God" that rested on Jesus. If men's sins were laid on Christ, the theologians have wondered whether God at that moment thought of Jesus as the "greatest transgressor" (Luther). They have speculated whether He was in some sense displeasing to God when Jesus was bearing our sins, for, after all, a holy God cannot stand sin.

[57] "For us" translates the preposition *huper*, a word that includes the sense of substitution.

[58] The better reading is *hoti gegraptai* ("because it is written"), rather than *gegraptai gar* ("for it is written"). "Because it is written" justifies what was said about Christ becoming a curse.

"CURSED IS EVERYONE WHO HANGS ON A TREE" - Deuteronomy 21:23 originally referred to executed criminals whose dead bodies were then vindictively nailed up (or impaled on a stake or gibbet) in a public place to further disgrace it (Joshua 10:26ff; 1 Samuel 31:10; 2 Samuel 21:10). God's law said the dead carcass had to be taken down and buried before sunset lest it defile the land. When the Deuteronomy passage was written, the Jews knew nothing of crucifixion, but by New Testament times "hangs on a tree" was also applied to crucifixion.[59] Paul's use of Deuteronomy says this: when Deuteronomy says "cursed," it is vitally related with Jesus being a curse offering as He is crucified.

3:14 - in order that in Christ Jesus the blessing of Abraham might come to the Gentiles, so that we might receive the promise of the Spirit through faith.

In order that in Christ Jesus the blessing of Abraham might come to the Gentiles - Here in verse 14, Paul seems to be telling us of two results that flow from Christ's being a curse offering.[60] The first result allows the blessing of Abraham to come to the Gentiles. The Law of Moses, a great barrier which excluded Gentiles (Ephesians 2:14-18), is done away in Christ (Galatians 3:13). Now the blessing of Abraham (Galatians 3:8,9), the blessing of forgiveness in Christ the Seed, to wit, being justified by faith, is available to Gentiles. "In Christ Jesus" may say that those Gentiles who are united with Christ (see Galatians 2:4,17) are the beneficiaries of His death.[61]

So that we might receive the promise of the Spirit through faith - This is the second result that flows from Christ's curse offering.[62] "We" includes Paul and his readers, whether Jews or Gentiles. "The promise of the Spirit" could be either an objective or subjective genitive. If subjective, it speaks of something the Holy Spirit promised, namely, the blessing of Abraham. Because Christ has died, the thing the Spirit promised to Abraham now can come true. If objective, it speaks of the Spirit Himself being received by those who become Christians. If we adopt the latter, verse 14 has returned to the thought introduced in verses 2 and 5, namely, how the Galatians received the indwelling

---

[59] By the time the Dead Sea Scroll known as the *Temple Scroll* was written, the language from Deuteronomy was applied to crucifixion, and spoke of the crucified as "cursed by God and men" (11QTemple 64:6-13). Cited by Longenecker, *op. cit.*, p.122. The LXX at Deuteronomy 21:23 reads "because *cursed by God* is every one hung upon a tree."

[60] There are two *hina* clauses in the Greek. One is translated "in order that" and the other is translated "so that" in the NASB. *Hina* can express either purpose or result.

[61] This whole matter of being "in Christ" is another facet of the current debate about justification. See the Special Study on justification at the close of notes on chapter 2 above.

[62] This explanation treats the two *hina* clauses in verse 14 as coordinate. Some have treated the second as subordinate to the first, explaining that the second specifies some details not found in the first clause.

gift of the Holy Spirit and continued to enjoy miraculous spiritual gifts. It is not by works of law, but it is "through faith," the same kind of faith spoken of in verses 7,9,11. Faithfulness is a condition that opens righteousness (justification) to all the world.

C. The Logical Argument. 3:15-29

> *Summary*: In this logical argument Paul reasons with his readers on the basis of what a covenant is and how a covenant works. In this paragraph, Paul makes four statements that help us understand the relationship between the "covenant" (the promise made to Abraham) and the Law, and in doing so shows that the Judaizers who exalt the Law above the promise (covenant) are in error.

1. The Law cannot set aside or alter God's own covenant. 3:15-18

3:15 - *Brethren, I speak in terms of human relations; even though it is* only *a man's covenant, yet when it has been ratified, no one sets it aside or adds conditions to it.*

Brethren, I speak in terms of human relations - The vocative "brethren" suggests the beginning of a new point in the argument, so we have begun a new point of the outline at this place. With a word of affection Paul reaches out to win his readers. The Greek is literally "I speak according to man" and indicates he is going to draw an illustration from everyday life among men.[63] Like Jesus did, Paul is using an earthly story to illustrate heavenly realities.[64]

Even though it is *only* **a man's covenant** - Instead of "covenant," the NASB margin offers the other possible meanings of *diathēkē* as "will" or "testament."[65] Since *diathēkē* can

---

[63] This expression has been found nowhere else in the New Testament, the LXX, or other Greek literature. Paul, however, uses it several times in his letters (here, Romans 6:19 in a slightly variant form, and 1 Corinthians 9:8). Translators have struggled to find a suitable English equivalent. The KJV "I speak after the manner of men" might lead the readers of that version to think Paul is disclaiming divine inspiration, which is not what the Greek means at all.

[64] C.H. Cosgrove ("Arguing Like a Mere Human Being: Galatians 3:15-19 in Rhetorical Perspective," *NTS* 34 (1988) p.536-549) offers a different explanation. He thinks the "human being" Paul alludes to are the Judaizers, and he attributes to them the argument that by issuing the Law, God annulled the promise He made to Abraham.

[65] The Greek language had two words for "covenant" or "agreement." One was *sunthēkē*, an agreement between equals. The other is *diathēkē*, an agreement between unequals, where one party with plenary power can make all the rules, and the other party to the agreement can either accept it or reject it, but cannot change the terms of the agreement. It is always this second term that is used when the Old Testament speaks of a *covenant* (*berith*, Heb.) made by God with men. It is especially at Galatians 3:15 and at Hebrews 9:15-17 that commentators debate which English word to use. Wills or testaments were not known in the ancient world until the Romans introduced them. Eventually, koine Greek came to give a different meaning ('testament') *to diathēkē* than did classical Greek ('covenant'). Josephus, for ex-

mean either testament or covenant, perhaps it makes it easiest to follow Paul's thread of thought if we translate it "testament" here in verse 15 and then "covenant" in verse 17 when it speaks of God's dealings (the promise) with Abraham.[66]   Paul calls attention to how a human testament works, and then shows that the principles are even more true in the case of a divine covenant.[67]

Yet when it has been ratified - If we are talking about a will or a testament, we would say when it has been probated, when it has been executed, and the inheritance distributed.

No one sets it aside or adds conditions to it - Neither ancient nor modern legal practice allows any alteration to a will that has been duly executed, nor can fresh conditions be added to it.[68]   "Adds conditions" translates *epidiatassetai,* which means to add a codicil. In the following verses, Paul makes a specific application of the analogy he is drawing: the Mosaic Law *cannot* have affected the basic provisions of the covenant with Abraham. One could not argue, for example, that the Law of Moses somehow qualified the covenant made with Abraham, so that the benefits of Abraham's covenant accrue only to persons ceremonially clean (as the Judaizers seem to have been arguing).

3:16 - *Now the promises were spoken to Abraham and to his seed.   He does not say, "and to seeds," as referring to many, but rather to one, "and to your seed," that is, Christ.*

Now the promises were spoken to Abraham and to his seed - Here begins Paul's application of the analogy about a will or testament.   First, here in verse 16, Paul identifies which of God's covenants it is to which one cannot add conditions: it is the one made with

---

ample, uses the word 32 times, always with the meaning of 'testament' or 'will.'   The Greek word is suitable for a will or testament since the will is often made by the testator, with the heirs having no input into the terms and conditions of the will.   For an in-depth study of the issues involved in choosing a proper English translation, see Gareth L. Reese, *New Testament Epistles: Hebrews* (Moberly, MO: Scripture Exposition Books, 1992), p.118.   It is partly from this passage (which reads "testament" in the NEB), partly from Hebrews 9:15ff, and partly due to the influence of the Latin version, which ordinarily rendered *diathēkē* by *testamentum*, that the idea grew that our Bible contains and is called an "Old Testament" and a "New Testament" (rather than "old covenant" and "new covenant").

[66] "In English one has to choose between [the words "testament" and "covenant"] simply because there are two separate words.   But in the Greek language, with one word, it is possible to use both ideas." Boice, *op. cit.*, p.462.

[67] The covenant made with Abraham ("In your seed all the nations of the earth shall be blessed") is God's last covenant, His last will and testament.   The "new covenant" (Jeremiah 31:31-33, as explained in Hebrews 8-10) is a renewal of this covenant.

[68] Roman law permitted a testator to cancel or modify a will (by codicils or otherwise) at any point during his lifetime.   But once the testator had died and the will executed, the testator was not in a position to change it, nor was anyone else.

Abraham.   Since Paul usually uses the singular "promise" when referring to God's covenant with Abraham,[69] we may believe that the plural "promises" points to the several renewals of the promise first recorded in Genesis 12:1-3 and culminating in Genesis 22:18 ("in your seed all the nations of the earth shall be blessed").   Paul is going to show that "seed" really pointed to none other than Jesus Christ.   When God made the covenant with Abraham, not only was Abraham promised something (a family as numerous "as the sand of the sea"), but Christ (the "seed") also was promised something (a family of brothers and sisters, Hebrews 2:11).

He does not say "And to seeds," as *referring* **to many, but** *rather* **to one, "And to your seed," that is, Christ** - Paul's argument turns upon the fact that both in the Hebrew and LXX the word translated "seed" is singular (*tō spermati*, a dative singular) rather than plural (*tois spermasi*).   Paul is telling us that God had one particular seed in mind, namely, Christ, when He made the covenant with Abraham.[70]   It is because Christ went to Calvary that all the families of the earth can be blessed.

3:17 - *What I am saying is this: the Law, which came four hundred and thirty years later, does not invalidate a covenant previously ratified by God, so as to nullify the promise.*

What I am saying is this - Having identified which one of God's covenants he had in mind, Paul now drives home the point of the analogy made in verse 15.   The Law of Moses, which came years after the covenant made with Abraham, does not set aside the covenant God made with Abraham nor add a codicil to it.

The Law, which came four hundred and thirty years later - The "Law" refers to the Law of Moses.   The giving of the Law at Mount Sinai is said to have taken place 430 years

---

[69] See Galatians 3:17,18,22,29.   Compare Romans 4:13,14,16,20.

[70] The key to understanding this passage is the fact that Paul is interpreting the original promise to Abraham in the light of Genesis 22:18, where Christ is in view.   When the idea is rejected that Paul may be giving an inspired explanation of the covenant made with Abraham, commentators quickly become agitated about what Paul wrote.   Some accuse him of being ignorant of the fact that the word "seed" can be either singular or collective.   But such critics ignore that Paul does himself use the singular noun in a collective sense in Galatians 3:29 (and in Romans 4:16-18 and 9:6-8), so he surely knew it could be either.   Furthermore, in Genesis 4:25, 21:13; 1 Chronicles 17:11; 1 Samuel 21:11; and 2 Samuel 7:12, the word "seed" ("descendant" in some English versions) is used to refer to one person.   Paul is not doing something unheard of when he calls attention to its singular use in Genesis 22:18.   Again, Paul surely knew that God had consistently led Abraham to think not in terms of *all* his offspring, but of a certain one.   Abraham was told that his seed would be found in Isaac, not Ishmael (Genesis 17:20,21).   Isaac and Rebekah were likewise told that there would be a distinction made between their two sons, Jacob and Esau (Genesis 25:21-23).   In the light of all this, those (such as Barclay, *op. cit.*, p.29) who have disdainfully accused Paul of forced exegesis, similar to what he would have learned in rabbinical school, are certainly in error.   This would be a low view of inspiration, to have the truth of Christianity rest on a feeble Jewish method of interpretation.

after the promise to Abraham was ratified.[71]   "Which came" is *ginomai*, a word that can mean to appear in history.[72]

Does not invalidate a covenant previously ratified by God - What earlier was called the "promise" to Abraham is here called a "covenant."[73]   "Ratified" is the same word used in verse 15.   Not only was it ratified, but God confirmed with an oath (Hebrews 6:13-18). "Previously" means before the giving of the Law on Mt. Sinai.[74]

So as to nullify the promise - "Nullify" equals to do away with.   The preposition *eis* with the articular infinitive (*to katargēsai*) speaks of purpose.   When God added the Law, it was not His purpose, Paul tells us, to do away with the promise, the Abrahamic covenant.

3:18 - *For if the inheritance is based on law, it is no longer based on a promise; but God has granted it to Abraham by means of a promise.*

For if the inheritance is based on law, it is no longer based on a promise - "For" shows this verse is intended to explain in even greater detail the point Paul is making.   In this verse, Paul wrote a contrary-to-fact condition: "if the inheritance were based on law, but, of course, it is not" is what this conditional statement implies.   The idea of "inheritance," which is introduced into this discussion here for the first time, subsequently plays a major role in Paul's argument.   Included in "inheritance" are all the blessings promised to Abraham and his seed.   Involved is the forgiveness of sins, the justification of Jews and Gentiles by faith.   We observe that the NASB does not capitalize the word "law" in this verse.   If we follow this lead, and if we remember how (at 2:16 and 3:2,5) anarthrous *nomos* was shorthand for "works of the Law" demanded by the Judaizers, then Paul pointedly says justification and the blessings of Abraham do not depend on a man carefully observing the man-made traditions of the Jewish elders.   Those man-made rules are based

---

[71] This verse has raised some difficulties in Old Testament chronology.   The "four hundred thirty years" comes from Exodus 12:14.   Now in the Hebrew, that verse reads as though that is the length of time during which the Hebrew people were slaves in Egypt (that is, the Egyptian captivity was 430 years long).   However the Greek text (both LXX and Samaritan Pentateuch) as well as Josephus (*Ant.* ii.15.2) give the 430 years as the time between the promise to Abraham and the time of the exodus, which results in a 215 year-long captivity.   Because of this verse written by Paul, this commentator opts for a short, 215 year-long captivity.   See his comments in a special study at Acts 7:6 in his *New Testament History: Acts,* p.247 and 307ff.   These chronology and dating problems do not affect the point of Paul's argument, which is that the covenant antedates the giving of the Law.

[72] See the word *ginomai* used with this sense at Mark 1:4; John 1:6,17; and 1 John 2:18.

[73] The Hebrew word *berith* (*diathēkē*, LXX, "covenant") appears ten times in Genesis 17:1-14 to speak of the covenant God established with Abraham.

[74] Some manuscripts (D, E, F, G, K, L, most minuscules, Textus Receptus) add the words *eis Christon*, "unto Christ" ("ratified by God unto Christ," i.e., with a view to Christ, or to find its fulfillment in Christ).   The words "unto Christ" are omitted in the group of oldest manuscripts (P[46], Aleph, A, B, C, P, 17), and evidently are an interpolation.

on a Law that was but temporary (i.e., lasting until Christ died on the cross) and that Law did not set aside the promise (covenant) made with Abraham. All this means that the inheritance is still based on the Abrahamic covenant.

But God has granted it to Abraham by means of a promise - "But" says that any idea that the inheritance is based on law is contrary to the way things actually are. "God" is in the emphatic position in the Greek. Whatever the Judaizers may say, here is the way *God* is doing things! The verb translated "granted" (*kecharistai*) has the word grace (*charis*) in it. God's provision for the inheritance (i.e., the promise made to Abraham) is a gracious offer. The verb "granted" is a perfect tense in the Greek, meaning that the inheritance was granted in the past and continues to be so granted.

We have now concluded the first point in Paul's logical argument. The Law did not set aside or alter God's covenant of promise to Abraham. If the covenant with Abraham is valid (and, of course, it is!), the Law cannot possibly be used in any way as a codicil to it.

2. The Mosaic Law, an added revelation to man, is not greater than the promise (i.e., the covenant with Abraham). 3:19,20

3:19 - *Why the Law then? It was added because of transgressions, having been ordained through angels by the agency of a mediator, until the seed should come to whom the promise had been made.*

Why the Law then? - "Then" (*oun*) is inferential, connecting the question to what precedes. It appears that Paul is meeting an anticipated objection to the line of reasoning he has been pursuing. If the Law, which came later, did not set aside or add conditions to the promise, why was it ever given? If it came later, doesn't that mean it is superior to the promise? First, in verse 19a, Paul gives a reason why it was added. Then in the remainder of verse 19 he gives two reasons why the Law is inferior to the promise.

It was added because of transgressions - When Paul says the Law "was added" (or appended), this cannot mean it was added as an amendment or a codicil to the testament. The word translated "adds conditions" in verse 15 was *epidiatassetai*; the verb here is *prosetethē*.[75] Thus Paul is not retracting in verse 19 what he said in verse 15. Verse 19 does say the Law "was an additional arrangement on the part of God for great and important purposes,"[76] but the Law's purpose was totally different from that of the promise/covenant

---

[75] *Prosetethē* is found in P[46], Aleph, A, B, C.

[76] Barnes, *op. cit.*, p.344.

with Abraham. "Because of transgressions" identifies that totally different purpose, but what does this phrase mean? The word "transgressions" (*parabasis*) speaks of a deliberate crossing the line, as contrasted with, say, "sin" (*hamartanō*), which means to miss the mark. The whole clause might mean that the Law was added so men could know what acts God calls "transgressions."[77] Or the whole clause might mean the Law was added to restrain sin. Paul's choice of this synonym (*parabasis*) for sin suggests that there was too much deliberate sinning, so the Law was given to restrain sin.[78] As a deterrent, each law was accompanied by the appropriate penalty for breaking it. (Cf. Hebrews 2:2, "every transgression and disobedience received a just recompense.")

Having been ordained through angels - "God" is the implied agent in the passive verb "ordained." God gave the Law. The mediation of angels is introduced here (as also in Hebrews 2:2) as a mark of the inferiority of the Law. Angels were but instruments to transmit it to Moses. Two other times in the New Testament we are told about how angels were involved in the giving of the Law (Acts 7:53, Hebrews 2:2).[79] Exactly what the angels did at Sinai, we do not know. Since "ordained" (*diatassō*) means to "dispose of [something] in order," perhaps what God did at Sinai was similar to how the message of the book of Revelation came from God to John through an angel (Revelation 1:1).

By the agency of a mediator - Having received the message from angels, Moses was the

---

[77] This understanding of the phrase treats Galatians 3:19 as similar to Romans 7:7, "I would not have come to know sin [i.e., what sin is], except through the Law."

[78] In passing, Galatians 3:19 is not the only reason for the adding of the Law. The Law segregated the nation, was a strong hedge about it, and kept it from mixing with other nations. It helped to preserve the Jehovistic religion. The Law helped men to realize they needed help with their sin problem. To accomplish this, the Levitical priesthood was established, as were the sacrifices and the cleansings, all of which were faint previews of the Christ. The Law was a tutor to bring men to Christ (Galatians 3:24-29). The Law also helped to develop thought patterns and a relevant nomenclature. If God were going to make a revelation in words, He must be able to get His ideas across. When one reads the New Testament, if it were not for the Old Testament nomenclature, one would not get the impact and force of books like Peter, Hebrews, etc. Alexander Campbell, *The Christian System* (Cincinnati, OH: Standard Publishing, nd), page 119, develops this idea.

[79] The fact that angels were involved in the giving of the Law at Mt. Sinai is also found in the Old Testament. For example, in the LXX of Deuteronomy 33:2, there is a phrase added which places myriads of angels at the Lord's right hand as He came to Sinai for the giving of the Law. Psalm 68:17 (which speaks of God being accompanied by myriads of chariots) also may be a reference to the involvement of angels at the giving of the Law. We must be careful in our comments here since higher critics, believing in the evolutionary development of Bible doctrine, are wont to say that the idea that angels helped in the giving of the Law was a human invention much after the Old Testament recorded how it really happened. Any such inference based on the few references to angels in the Old Testament is overdrawn. Again, because early Christians made use of the mediation of angels to prove the Law was inferior to the new covenant (which Hebrews 1:1-4, Hebrews 2:2, and Hebrews 10:9 indicate was given by God's Son, Jesus Christ), efforts were made within certain circles of Judaism to belittle the role of angels at Sinai. In fact, the newly produced post-Christian (and anti-Christian) Greek texts of Aquila and Symmachus changed the wording at Deuteronomy 33:2 so it no longer made reference to angels.

mediator between God and the people (Deuteronomy 5:5).[80]   He delivered the message to the people.   The Greek behind "by the agency of" means literally "by the hand of." Numerous times the mediatorial work of Moses is designated by exactly these words ("by the hand of Moses").[81]   This feature of the Law, that it was given through a mediator, is developed in the next verse and it is intended to show the subordinate place of the Law in relation to the covenant made with Abraham.

Until the seed should come to whom the promise had been made - As we were told in Galatians 3:16, the seed is Christ.   Not only did the Law come in 430 years after the promise, the Law was never intended by God to be anything but temporary; it was to be in force only until Christ should come.   At verse 16 we commented on the phrase "the promises were spoken ... to his seed."[82]   "The historical mission of the Law ended when the promise to Abraham was fulfilled in Christ, who is here called 'the seed'."[83]

3:20 - *Now a mediator is not for one* **party only;** *whereas God is* **only** *one.*

Now - It looks as though Paul is here unfolding some of the hidden truths in the word "mediator" that he used in the previous verse.[84]   When one compares the promise to Abra-

---

[80] Origen, misled by 1 Timothy 2:5 ("For there is one God, *and* one mediator also between God and men, *the* man Jesus Christ"), understood the "mediator" here to be Christ, and thereby carried a vast number of later commentators with him (e.g., Chrysostom, Jerome, Luther, Calvin).   Certainly, this commentator does teach that Christ was active in the Old Testament times, even during the wilderness wanderings of the Israelite people (1 Corinthians 10:4).   But did Christ have anything to do with the giving of the Mosaic covenant?   The argument of the epistle to the Hebrews, that the new covenant is superior to and takes the place of the old because the Messenger who gave the new is superior to the messengers who gave the old, would seem to say Jesus did not have part in the giving of the Law.   The "mediator" to whom Paul refers in this verse is Moses, not Christ.

[81] Leviticus 26:46;   Numbers 4:37,41,45,49,   9:23,   10:13,   15:23, 27:23,   33:1, 36:13;   Joshua 21:2, 22:9;   Judges 3:4;   1 Kings 8:53,56;   2 Chronicles 33:8; Psalms 77:20.

[82] In both places (verses 16 and 19) we have been careful to avoid the dogma of one-covenant theology, which has God making a covenant with Jesus concerning man's redemption just after Adam sinned.   One-covenant theology teaches that there was a covenant of works with Adam.   When Adam failed, God made a covenant of redemption with Christ and a covenant of grace with mankind.   Mankind has been living under that one covenant of grace ever since.   A corollary of this view is that all of the covenants we read about since Adam are simply renewals of that one covenant of grace.   A serious problem for this system of theology is the classic new covenant prophecy of Jeremiah 31:31ff.   God predicts "I will make a new covenant ... not like the covenant I made with their fathers" (at Mt. Sinai).   Romans 9:4 distinguishes between "the covenants" and the Law.   This, too, is hard to square with the idea of one-covenant theology.

[83] Lenski, *op. cit.,* p.168.

[84] The interpretations offered for this passage number over 300 (Sanday, *op. cit.,* p.58).   "Many of these arise out of an error as to the Mediator (where he is thought to be Christ); many more disregard the context; and not a few are quite arbitrary" (Lightfoot, *op. cit.,* p.146).   In addition, part of the problem arises from the fact that we must add words to complete the sentence Paul wrote (see the italics in the NASB). If we add the wrong words, we get the wrong interpretation.   It has not proven useful to give the pros and cons of each of these proposed explanations.   In the comments, we have offered the one that seems most consistent with the context.

ham (where no mediator was used), there is something about the use of a mediator in the giving of the Law that reflects negatively on the Law.

A mediator is not for one *party only* - The Greek reads "the mediator." The article *ho* is likely an article of previous reference, pointing us to the mediator just talked about in the previous verse, namely, Moses. Since "mediator" signifies a middle person, there must of necessity be two parties between whom the mediator stands. In the case at Sinai, unlike when He made the promise to Abraham, God did not speak directly to the people of Israel. The Old Testament plainly records how Moses went up on the Mountain, got the Law from God, and returned and read the rules to the people. They responded, "All the words which the Lord has spoken we will do" (Exodus 24:1-7). Moses thus mediated between God and the people.

Whereas God is *only* **one** - God who gave the promise is one (party). When God made His covenant with Abraham, He did it personally, without a mediator.[85] The promise was not third-hand like the Law of Moses was; therefore, the promise is superior to the Law. The statement that "God is one" reminds us of the Shema (Deuteronomy 6:4), "THE LORD (Hebrew, *YHWH*) our God (Hebrew, *elohim*) ... is one (Hebrew, *ehad*, a unity)."

Verses 19 and 20 have told us that, in comparison with the promise to Abraham, the Law was given for a very different purpose. Further, the manner in which the Law was given and the intended duration of the Law make the Law decidedly inferior when compared with the promise made to Abraham.

3. The Law is not contrary to the promise (i.e., the covenant with Abraham). 3:21-29

> *Summary*: The logical argument begun in verse 15 continues.

a. One great lack in the Law was its inability to provide life. v.21

3:21 - *Is the Law then contrary to the promises of God? May it never be! For if a law had been given which was able to impart life, then righteousness would indeed have been based upon law.*

Is the Law then contrary to the promises of God? May it never be! - "Then" connects this verse to what was just written. In verses 19-20, Paul was anticipating and answering an objection to his logic likely to be raised by the Judaizers. We treat verses 21-29 as Paul's answer to another anticipated objection. "Is the Law contrary to the spirit and pur-

---

[85] The unspoken, but understood idea is that the quality of the messenger is directly related to the importance of the message. No doubt, God is a superior messenger to Moses.

pose of the promises[86] to Abraham?" they might ask.   To this question Paul answers with an indignant "of course not!"[87]   "Well, if it wasn't contrary, then why do you insist the Law is inferior to the promise?" they might retort.   Paul has a ready answer.   The Law was inferior because it couldn't impart life.

For if a law had been given which is able to impart life - This contrary-to-fact condition means there never was such a law given.   The Law of Moses[88] never did help a man become spiritually alive, like the features of the covenant made with Abraham do.   In the Old Testament, there was no new birth whereby a man's spirit is born again (John 3:6).[89] "Impart life" is virtually equivalent to being "justified" or declared "righteous," as the last clause of this verse shows.   He who is justified is spiritually alive (Romans 8:10), having risen to walk in newness of life (Romans 6:5,6).   In addition to one's spirit becoming alive, it is also entirely possible that "to impart life" envisions resurrection life (as Romans 8:11 goes on to say).   No law was able to raise a man from the dead, let alone in a glorified body, but the Spirit received when a man is justified can give life to mortal bodies.

Then righteousness would indeed have been based on law - This is the last part of the contrary-to-fact condition contained in this verse.   In fulfillment of the promise about the coming "seed," God's righteousness is based on what the Seed did on Calvary.   If, while waiting for the Seed to come, a law had ever been given by God that was the basis of His justification of men, *then* the promise would have been contradicted.   But the fact is, no such law was ever given.   Never did God give a law which would be the basis of justifi-

---

[86] Here, as in verse 16, we have a plural, because the promise to Abraham was several times repeated, and afterward was ratified to his descendants.

[87] See notes at Galatians 2:17 on *mē genoito*, "May it never be!"

[88] We observe that the NASB has small "l" here ("law") whereas they had a capital "L" ("Law") in the first clause of this verse.   Perhaps the NASB translators thought there never was such a "law" given, whether one think of the Law of Moses or the works of the Law demanded by the troublemakers.   Neither one could help a man be born again spiritually.   That "works of the Law" could not justify has been shown in Galatians 3:11 and in Romans 3:20.

[89] Men are spiritually alive until they commit their first sin.   When that first sin occurs, their spirit dies (Romans 7:9).   Now the presence of the Law gave the devil opportunity to tempt and kill man's spirit.   No law ever helped get man spiritually alive again after his spirit died because that was not the function of law.   What the Law does is shut men up under sin (verse 22), not help them to become spiritually alive.

Numerous writers offer a paragraph here to explain that Paul does not contradict what the Scripture says elsewhere.   For example, Deuteronomy 30:15-20 pictures the Law as having something to do with life ("I have set before you ... life and death ... so choose life in order that you may live").   In Galatians 3:12 Paul quotes from Leviticus 18:5 ("keep My statutes and My judgments, by which a man may live if he does them").   A man's spirit continues to live if he keeps God's rules.   He dies spiritually when he disobeys.   Once a person had died spiritually, the Law could not make a man or a woman alive spiritually.   Nor is there a contradiction between what is here written and what Paul writes in Romans 7:10 ("this commandment ... was to result in life"), for as Romans 2:7 had already indicated, "life" in Romans 7:10 is "eternal life," not spiritual life.

cation.[90] It wasn't the Law's purpose to be the basis on which God could justify. What the purpose of the Law was is stated in the next verse.

b. Scripture shuts up everyone under sin. v.22

3:22 - *But the Scripture has shut up all men under sin, that the promise by faith in Jesus Christ might be given to those who believe.*

But the Scripture has shut up everyone under sin - "Shut up ... under sin" is contrasted to what was written in verse 21 concerning imparting life and being justified. Paul's change of wording to "Scripture" instead of "law" has raised all sorts of questions in the commentaries. Is Scripture in this verse synonymous with Law in the previous verse? If it is, should we look for a string of passages in the Law (like Romans 3:9-18) where all men are shown to be sinners? If it is not, should we look for one particular passage Paul may have had in mind, say either Psalm 143:2 (cf. Galatians 2:16) or Deuteronomy 27:26 (cf. Galatians 3:10)?[91] Or if Scripture is differentiated from Law, is Scripture a metonymy for God Himself (as at Galatians 3:8)?[92] It is difficult to sort out all this and choose one over the others. Out of all the options, we think these best help us see what Paul is saying:

(1) Scripture includes all the 39 books of our Old Testament. As the string of Scriptures in Romans 3:9-18 demonstrates, all have sinned and come short of the glory of God. Perhaps Paul does not say that "the Law" locked up everything, but that "the Scripture" did so, because the Law extended only back to Moses. Scripture, which includes more than the Law of Moses, covers all the time back to Adam when sin came into the world (Romans 5:12), and includes more than just the folk who had the Law of Moses.

(2) "Shut up" *(sugkleiō)* means to lock up, to hem in, to confine, to imprison.[93] By way of personification, sin is pictured as the power that holds men captive. The Bible elsewhere speaks of lost men being slaves of sin.

(3) Scripture does show that all men are sinners. Unless the sin is forgiven, sinners are not justified and are not spiritually alive (i.e., their spirits died when the first sin was committed and remain dead). Without the new birth, their captivity to sin continues.

---

[90] We have been substituting "justification" for the word "righteousness" that Paul wrote at this place. It has been noted earlier that "righteousness" and "justification" are translations of the same root word in Greek.

[91] So Lightfoot and Burton. Lightfoot gives several arguments to show that "Scripture" in the singular in the New Testament always means a particular passage of Scripture.

[92] So B.B. Warfield, *Inspiration and Authority of Bible* [Philadelphia: Presbyterian & Reformed, 1948], p.299-348.

[93] The word was used to describe how Jericho was "tightly shut" so that no one could go in or out (Joshua 6:1). It was used of the catch of fish which had been trapped in the disciples' nets (Luke 5:6).

Men need the provisions of the Abrahamic covenant to be freed from their captivity to sin.

That the promise by faith in Jesus Christ might be given to those who believe - This clause seems to point to what results from all being shut up under sin. The result is that God's promise of life and righteousness is good, not to everyone, but to those who believe. "The promise" gathers up all that has been said about the promise to Abraham that in his seed all the nations would be blessed. The thing promised comes as a consequence of "faith in Jesus" or as a consequence of the "faithfulness of Jesus."[94] The promise (of justification, of life) is given only to those who believe. "To those who believe" is present tense in the Greek, implying that it takes continual belief (continued faithfulness) to be a recipient of the thing promised in the "seed (Christ)."

c.   The Law was given to lead men to Christ for forgiveness.   v.23,24

3:23 - *But before faith came, we were kept in custody under the law, being shut up to the faith which was later to be revealed.*

But before faith came - We are still unfolding the logical argument begun at verse 21 that the Law is not contrary to the promise made to Abraham. Instead of the Law being contrary to the promise, it served a beneficial purpose. Whereas verse 22 pictures everyone without distinction (i.e., "all men" and "those who"), the "we" of verse 23 speaks of the Jews. (See also the shift back to the pronoun "you" in verse 26.) By definition, of course, Jews were included in "all men" in verse 22. But God did something for the Jews He did not do for other men when He gave them the Law at Mt. Sinai. The Greek reads "the faith." The article before the word faith in the Greek is likely the article of previous reference. Verse 22 spoke of "faith in Jesus Christ." Thus we say that "faith" here is taken in its objective sense,[95] meaning "before Christianity came," or "before Jesus Messiah came."

We were kept in custody under the law - "We" evidently means we Jews. The verb "kept in custody" pictures a protective custody. The Jews were being guarded to keep them out of greater trouble. The custodian was the Law of Moses.[96] The imperfect tense

---

[94] The Greek construction is a genitive case, literally, "the faith of Jesus." As was true at Galatians 2:16 it can be either an objective (faith in Jesus) or a subjective (the faith of Jesus) genitive.

[95] Compare notes at Galatians 1:23 and 3:25 where "faith" has an objective sense. If we were to give a subjective sense to "faith," it would cause this passage to conflict with what Scripture elsewhere says about many people who lived before Christ. Abraham, for example, had faith (Galatians 3:6) and so did many other Old Testament saints (Hebrews 11). Even during the old dispensation, people's salvation was conditioned on faith (Galatians 3:6,11,17,18).

[96] We observe that the NASB has "law" (small "l") at this place. Certainly, "under the Law" (*hupo nomon*) is not the same as "[works] of the Law" (*ek [ergon] nomou*). Surely the same "Law" is spoken of in both verses 23 and 24. Both times the word should be capital "L."

verb "were kept in custody" reaches back to Sinai and covers that entire period from then until Calvary.

Being shut up to the faith - "Shut up" here is the same verb used in verse 22; it means to hem in, imprison, confine, constrain.[97]   "The faith" (the Greek includes a definite article) in this clause is the same faith alluded to at the beginning of this verse.   Instead of the Law being in competition with or antagonistic to the Abrahamic promise, it served a beneficial purpose.   It kept Jews from straying, it allowed them to remain the people through whom the fulfillment of the promise made to Abraham would come.

Which was later to be revealed - Paul's point is that the Law was intended to function only during the 1500-year period between Sinai and the introduction of Christianity into the world.   That time is now past.[98]   While it was here, however, it did serve a purpose. That purpose was to hold us (Jews) in protective custody, protecting us until Christ should be revealed.

3:24 - *Therefore the Law has become our tutor* **to lead us** *to Christ, that we may be justified by faith*.

Therefore - With "therefore" (*hōste*) Paul introduces a fresh figure of speech to illustrate the Law's beneficial purpose.

The Law has become our tutor - "The Law" is a reference to the whole Mosaic Law.[99] There is no English word perfectly equivalent to the Greek word (*paidagōgos*), which was translated "tutor" by the NASB.[100]   In addition to "tutor,"[101] several English words have

---

[97] Under the Law, men were "locked up" – they were not FREE!   There is a manuscript variation here. The present tense participle *sugkleiomenoi* is better attested (Aleph, A, B, D*, F, G, P, 17) than is the perfect tense participle *sugkekleismenoi* (C, D³, E, K, L).   The present tense clearly describes a continuous process from generation to generation of being "shut up."

[98] What folly for the Judaizers to claim that the custodian was still on duty now that Christ has come. It is even greater folly for them to invent some duties (works of the Law) the custodian never required.

[99] "Law," in this context, is what was given to the Jewish people by God through the hand of the mediator (Galatians 3:19).   To see what that was, start reading at Exodus 20.   "Law" here refers to the moral, ceremonial, and judicial parts of that Law.   This passage affirms several times that the "Law" was temporary, until Christ came.   That is true of all three parts.   As commentators try to explain the relationship between the old and new covenants, it is often affirmed that only the ceremonial and judicial parts were temporary.   In his *Sermon on the Law*, Alexander Campbell denied that this distinction between moral, ceremonial, and judicial is valid.   Said he, "This division of the law was unknown in the apostolic age ... and can serve no valuable purpose in obtaining a correct knowledge of the doctrine delivered by the Apostles respecting the Law" (*Historical Documents Advocating Christian Union*, [Chicago: Christian Century Co., 1904], p.228).

[100] We might transliterate the Greek word and have "pedagogue," but that word has the connotation in modern English of "teacher."   That is not the right idea here.

[101] "Tutor" in contemporary English is a *private instructor*.   Such a connotation will not satisfy the meaning of this passage, unless we give "tutor" a special definition.

been pressed into duty, including "schoolmaster" (KJV),[102] "strict governess" (Phillips),[103] and "disciplinarian" (NAB and NRSV). "Custodian" is perhaps the nearest English equivalent. The Confraternity edition has "the slave who leads a child to the house of the schoolmaster." That succinctly catches the meaning of the Greek word.[104]

To lead us to Christ - If the proper words are supplied by the NASB,[105] the verse says this: like the slave/custodian took the child to the teacher (*eis didaskalos*), so the Law of Moses was intended to take the Jews to Christ (*eis Christon*).

That we may be justified by faith - This clause is important. "By faith" stands in the emphatic position. Contrary to the claims of the Judaizers that "works of the Law" (their Pharisaic rules) were obligatory for salvation, Paul emphatically says "by faith" (i.e., doing what God says). Justification by faith (on the condition of faithfulness to what God has revealed) is the heart and soul of both Romans and Galatians. God is the One who justifies (passive voice), and "faith" is the condition. All of this shows the Law was not contrary to the promises of God (verse 21).

> **d. The Law was but temporary while the promise (i.e., the covenant with Abraham) continues. Therefore, the Law cannot be contrary to the promise. v.25-27**

3:25 - *But now that faith has come, we are no longer under a tutor.*

But now that faith has come - The two most important points in the previous verses are repeated again for emphasis: the tutor is no longer required, and faith that was later to be revealed has been revealed. "Now that faith (there is an article before "faith" again) has come" is equal to "now that Christ has come."

---

[102] "Schoolmaster" has the connotation of master teacher. A *paidogōgos* was not a teacher.

[103] *Paidagōgos* is the masculine form of the word that would be translated "governess." But if Phillips had used "governor," that might give the wrong idea to an English reader who uses "governor" as the title for the highest governing official in one of our states.

[104] *Didaskalos* is the Greek for teacher. *Paidagōgos* literally means "boy's leader." He was an attendant, generally a slave (sometimes a freedman), whom wealthy parents provided for their son while he was between seven and seventeen years of age. This attendant was not the boy's teacher. His job was to take the boy to school (where the teacher would teach the boy) and to gymnastic practice and see that he got home safely. He watched to keep the boy from associating with youth of bad reputation, and he also discouraged foolish or hurtful actions. His primary task was preventive and protective. He did not administer punishment; the boy's father did that.

[105] Some modern versions, giving a temporal significance *to eis Christon*, read "until Christ should come."

We are no longer under a tutor - "We" (Jews) encompasses the same people that "we" in verse 23 does.   This passage plainly says that now that Christ has come, the Old Testament is no longer a binding statute.   The Law by its very nature was temporary.   This verse "delivers the *coup de grace* to the Judaizers' argument"[106] that Gentile Christians must observe "works of the Law" since the very Law from which they derive their rules is no longer valid, having been nailed to the cross (Colossians 2:14).[107]

3:26 - *For you are all sons of God through faith in Christ Jesus.*

For you are all sons of God - This verse gives evidence of the statement just made that they are no longer under a tutor.[108]   The reason they are no longer under a tutor is because they are no longer "children" (*nēpios*) but "sons" (*huios*) who have come of age.[109]   The "we" forms occurring in verses 23-25 spoke of the Jews.   Now Paul uses the second person "you" in verses 26-29.   "You" includes any Galatian who has been baptized into Christ, and "all" says this is true whatever the person's ethnic background.   Galatians 4:6-7 will say more about this sonship.

Through faith in Christ Jesus - The NASB translates the best attested Greek text of *dia tēs pisteōs en Christō Iēsou*.[110]   The ASV adds two commas to its translation, "Ye are all sons of God, through faith, in Christ Jesus."[111]   So punctuated, it means you who are in connection with Christ are sons of God.   Verse 27 then tells how one gets to be "in Christ."   The KJV and NASB have no commas in this clause.   So punctuated, it means you become sons of God by believing in Christ Jesus (the object of faith).   "Faith in Christ" (*pistis* fol-

---

[106] Longenecker, *op. cit.*, p.149

[107] One could, as a matter of Christian liberty, continue to observe religious festivals and dietary rules prescribed in Moses, but they were not requisite for the Jewish Christian any more than they were for the Gentile Christian.

[108] Verse 26 begins with "for."   Verse 27 begins with "for."   Verse 28c begins with "for."   Verse 29b concludes with an inferential "then" (*ara*).   This series of connecting particles must be accounted for as we comment.

[109] "'Sons' is the significant term, mature, full-grown sons, who are in possession of the inheritance, the fulfillment of the promise (3:18)" (Lenski, *op. cit.*, p.185).   The KJV translation "children" at this place is unfortunate, as the point to be brought out is that the Christian is no longer in the condition of children, but in that of grown-up sons.

[110] P46 reads *dia pisteōs Christou Iēsou* ("through faith of Christ Jesus").   Note the article before "faith" is omitted and Christ Jesus is in the genitive, rather than in the dative, after *en*.

[111] The RSV arrives at the same meaning by shifting "in Christ Jesus" from the end of the sentence to the beginning, "For in Christ Jesus you are all sons of God through faith."

lowed by a preposition) is an obedient faith, as verse 27 goes on to explain.[112]   Faithfulness to what Jesus has said is the condition of being sons of God.

3:27 - *For all of you who were baptized into Christ have clothed yourselves with Christ.*

For all of you who were baptized into Christ - "For" shows verse 27 is an explanation of something just said.   If the ASV has the punctuation right, this verse explains how one comes to be "in Christ."   If the NASB has the punctuation right, this verse explains that baptism is included in the faith that God reckons as righteousness.   Baptism is justification by faith.[113]   The same people are included in "all of you" (*hosoi*, in the Greek, "as many as") as are included in the words "you all" in verse 26.[114]   Whether formerly Jews or Gentiles matters not.   They have been immersed into Christ.[115]   The verb "you ... were baptized" undoubtedly refers to the baptism commanded in the Great Commission (Matthew 28:18-20), i.e., immersion in water, for this is the uniform meaning of the term in Paul (cf. Romans 6:3; 1 Corinthians 1:13-17, 12:13; 15:29).[116]   Paul's words here in Galatians imply that baptism was an adult experience, done to one who could exercise faith, not something done to infants.

---

[112] For *pistis* followed by *en* ("in") see Ephesians 1:15; Colossians 1:4; 1 Timothy 3:13; 2 Timothy 1:13.   For *pistis* followed by *eis* ("in") see Colossians 2:5.

[113] If the "faith-only" interpreters are right when they say that the "faith" that saves includes no works of any kind (and in earlier verses of the chapter they have striven to show their faith without works is right), why should Paul add this closing argument about baptism?   If the faith-only teachers are correct, Paul's argument is complete without this reference to baptism.

[114] The NASB words it so the equality is obvious.   It uses "all" in both verses.

[115] In Romans 6:3 Paul describes baptism into Christ as baptism into His death.   The passive form of the verb suggests that baptism is something that is done to the candidate by someone else.

[116] Faith-only writers struggle with this verse because it is difficult to harmonize this verse with their notes earlier on no "works" (nothing a man does) being included in the "faith" that saves.   Nevertheless, they try to find a way to make this verse fit their definition.   MacArthur (*op. cit.*, p.68) tries to do it by saying that "water baptism is not in view in verse 27."   Debbie Hunn, "The Baptism of Galatians 3:27: A Contextual Approach," *Exp. Times* 115/11 (Aug. 2004), p.372-375, makes an attempt to defend "Spirit baptism" rather than water baptism.   She also calls attention to interpretations by other contemporary scholars, among whom are F.F. Bruce, Ronald Fung, J.D.G. Dunn.   Since in the New Testament, at times, the Greek preposition *eis* has the meaning of "in" rather than "into" or "unto," others will insist that *eis Christon* ("into Christ") really should be translated "in Christ."   They then affirm that one who is already "in Christ" by faith alone may later be immersed, but immersion is not involved in the faith that saves.   They want to treat baptism, at best, as an outward sign of an inward grace.

But can we really think that verse 27 says "all of you who are in Christ (by faith only) put on (clothe yourselves with) Christ at some later time (when you were baptized)?"   If you are already "in Christ," what does it mean to "put on Christ" (ASV)?   The context here is against using "in" to translate *eis* at this place.   Would it not be more productive to abandon the faith-alone definition for faith that resulted from a faulty explanation of "works of the Law" back at 2:16?   We think so.

Paul could assume that all the Galatian church members had been immersed. How sad that we can no longer assume that all church members have been immersed. Baptism has fallen on hard times in some circles, and many voices are raised against it, voices that insist that baptism is a kind of "salvation by works." Yet Paul, who could never be accused of teaching that salvation is by works ... takes baptism for granted. He treats immersion as the means through which one "puts on" and is "united with Christ."[117]

The immersion of a penitent believer for the remission of sins puts that person into Christ. That is the point at which he is initially said to be justified by faith.[118]

Have clothed yourselves with Christ - Baptism is the moment when Christ, like a garment, envelops the believer.[119] The verb is a middle voice verb which indicates that baptism/clothed is something the believer did for his own benefit. We are not certain from whence Paul draws this figure of speech. Perhaps it is from Greek customs. If from Greek custom, then to clothe yourselves with Christ means to have reached maturity. The sons of Greeks and Romans were invested with garments that marked them as adults when they reached maturity.[120] If taken from the Old Testament, clothed with Christ means to receive justification. For example, see Isaiah 61:10, "I will rejoice greatly in the Lord ... for He has clothed me with garments of salvation, He has wrapped me with a robe of righteousness ...."[121]

---

[117] Lawson, *op. cit.*, p.72.

[118] "Now we see that we do not come into Christ by faith only, but by baptism also. We are baptized into Him. Some of us are familiar with an old sermon that presents the way into Christ under four headings: faith, repentance, confession, and baptism. We have to look at Scriptures other than Galatians 3:27 to fill out that outline. In Acts 2:38 we read, 'Repent, and be baptized every one of you in the name of Jesus Christ for the remission of sins'; and Romans 10:10 says, 'With the heart man believeth unto righteousness; and with the mouth confession is made unto salvation.' Thus Jews and Gentiles alike come into Christ" (Root, *op. cit.*, p.20). See also J.S. Sweeney's sermon, "Baptism for Remission of Sins is Justification by Faith," in Vol. I of *New Testament Christianity* (Columbus, IN: Printed for the editor, 1953), p.391-401.

[119] Perhaps this metaphor suggested the post-apostolic practice of putting on white baptismal robes before the candidates were immersed. Justin Martyr, *Dial.c.Tryph*, chap. 116, may speak of such baptismal garments, and, if so, this is the first reference to such in Christian literature.

[120] See more on this idea of reaching maturity in what Paul writes in Galatians 4:1-7.

[121] Other passages of Scripture to study in this regard are Psalm 132:9,16; Matthew 22:11; Luke 15:22; 2 Corinthians 5:21; Ephesians 4:24; Colossians 3:10. The relationship between life "in Christ" and "putting on Christ" (ASV) to justification by faith is a topic of current debate. Are they two ways of saying the same thing, or is it better to maintain a distinction between justification by faith and participation (incorporation) into the body? Faith-only scholars are especially wont to discuss this matter, for if the two are the same, it tends to look like there is more to justification by faith than simply faith alone. Note how Bruce (*op. cit.*, p.184-85) has Paul instantly and simultaneously justified by faith and incorporated into the body on the Damascus road. Then Paul must live out in his life what that incorporation involves. But the living was not made automatic with his justification, in Bruce's view. This matter was discussed at length in the special study on "Justification by Faith" included at the close of comments on chapter 2.

e. The Law's exclusiveness is a thing of the past.   v.28,29

3:28 - *There is neither Jew nor Greek, there is neither slave nor free man, there is neither male nor female; for you are all one in Christ Jesus.*

There is neither Jew nor Greek - We are nearly at the end of the logical argument.   In these two verses Paul explains what all this means for the issue raised by the Judaizers regarding Gentile Christians' relationship with Jewish Christians and with Abraham.   He zeroes in on those very areas where the Judaizers were likely to have a prejudice they held dear.   During the time the Mosaic Law was in force, the Law itself recognized and maintained differences.   It had provisions for Jews versus Gentiles.[122]   Such distinctions are not recognized in Christ.[123]   Since we are no longer under the tutor in the Christian age, it follows that for those who are in Christ there are no earthly distinctions based on race.   To be "in Christ" (verse 27) means you are one with everybody else who is in Christ!   The Judaizers' attempts to exclude some just because they are Gentiles are a great mistake.

There is neither slave nor free man - The Law of Moses had provisions for free men versus those who were slaves.   In the church there may be members who are slave and members who are free, but the old inferiority stigma on slaves must not be allowed to continue.   See this spelled out at 1 Corinthians 7:20-22.   "This is not meant to deny that in actual fact there are social distinctions among men.   It is merely meant to affirm that for those who are united to Christ these things do not matter."[124]

There is neither male nor female - The Law of Moses also had provisions for males versus females, and so did the Pharisees.[125]   In the body of Christ these old class distinctions are of no special moment.   You do not exclude someone from fellowship because she is female, or he is a slave, or ethnically because one happens to be a Gentile.

---

[122] "The spread of the Greek race through the conquests of Alexander, so that Greeks lived all over the known world, and the use of the Greek language as a universal medium of communication, led to the name 'Greek' being applied to all who were not Jews (Sanday, *op. cit.*, p.61).

[123] A technical note: the Greek reads *ouch eni*.   *Eni* is likely an emphatic equivalent of *estin*.   By derivation, *eni* was a strengthened form of the preposition *en*.   In time it came to be a variant of *enestin*, *"it is possible."*   It then came to be used as an emphatic equivalent for "it is" ["there is"].   The form occurs several times in this verse.

[124] Boice, *op. cit.*, p.469.

[125] For example, the Pharisees had a prayer they would pray each morning that went like this: "I thank Thee, God, that Thou hast made me a Jew, not a Gentile; a man, not a woman; and a freeman, and not a slave."   In Pharisee thinking, to be a Gentile, a woman, or a slave disqualified you from several religious privileges which were open to free Jewish males.

Neither being male nor female gives one any peculiar advantages for salvation. When it comes to the opportunity to become immersed into Christ, both sexes are, in this respect, on a level. When it comes to fellowship in the body of Christ, male or female is no more a limitation to fellowship than is slave or free, Jew or Greek.[126]

For you are all one in Christ Jesus - This clause gives a reason why Paul could say that the old distinctions, based on race, social class, or sex, have come to an end. "In Christ" speaks of being a participant in His redeeming work or being a part of His body, the church.[127] "You" (*humeis*) has the emphatic meaning "You, being what you are, believers baptized into Christ." "One" (*heis*) is masculine in gender. We must supply the noun. "One body" is a good suggestion.[128] "One" says that all who are in Christ Jesus are on the same level. Contrary to the Judaizers' dogma, Gentile Christians do not have to embrace works of law before they are fit to associate with.

3:29 - *And if you belong to Christ, then you are Abraham's offspring, heirs according to the promise.*

And if you belong to Christ - "You" (plural) includes Jew or Greek, bond or free, male or female. The Greek literally reads "to be of Christ." This is a Greek idiom meaning to belong to him (as the NASB has it). If they were in Christ, if they belonged to Christ, they were made so by an obedient faith.

---

[126] If we have understood the passage correctly, what Paul rules out for Christians is the kind of "with whom do I associate" taboos that the Pharisees regularly imposed. In our church associations, we do not discriminate on the basis of race, class, or sex. We do not (for example, like the Judaizers did) make people feel unwelcome simply because they are Greeks, or women, or slaves. "We must be careful not to read into the Scripture more than the writer intended. A Jew or a Greek, a Scot or a Hopi may still take pride in his human ancestry and heritage. A citizen of Christ's kingdom can still be a citizen of the United States or Ghana, and he owes allegiance to his earthly nation (Romans 13:1-7). Christian slaves were still slaves and Christian owners were still slave masters, and Paul gave instructions to each class (Ephesians 6:5-9). Christian men and women were still men and women, and Paul had different instructions for husbands and wives (Ephesians 5:22-33). But in the matter of justification there is no difference. All who come to Christ come in the same way. All of them alike are children of God" (Root, *op. cit.*, p.20). 1 Corinthians 11:2-16 indicates that Paul certainly did not intend to abolish gender roles between men and women. In the last quarter century, what the Bible teaches about the roles of men and women has been debated. Feminism's use of Galatians 3:28 to abolish such gender roles is possible only if one drags the passage out of context. See Richard Hove, *Equality in Christ? Galatians 3:28 and the Gender Dispute* (Wheaton, IL. Crossway books, 1999). Hove argues his case well, and he is fair and charitable toward those with whom he disagrees, namely, those who hold the egalitarian position. "This does not mean that all (men or women) could indiscriminately perform all the work and duties in the church" (Lipscomb, *op. cit.*, p.237). If that is so, this verse is not to be twisted, for example, into a proof text that women may occupy the office of elder (when 1 Timothy 3:2 indicates otherwise).

[127] See notes at Galatians 2:17 and 3:14 concerning being "in Christ."

[128] Elsewhere, Paul compares the church to a body (Romans 12:4-8; 1 Corinthians 6:15-17, 12:12-27). Like a human body has many members, so the church is a body of people who are its members.

Then you are Abraham's offspring - With "then" (*ara*) Paul states the conclusion to his logical argument against the Judaizers. The NASB margin shows that the Greek word translated "offspring" could also be translated "seed."[129] The prize the Judaizers had been holding before the eyes of the Galatian Christians, and by which they hoped to win them over to embracing "works of the Law," was the possibility of becoming part of the seed of Abraham. They meant physical seed. Paul now replies that the Christians already have something better. They are already the spiritual seed of Abraham.[130] If you are in Christ, you have already become part of that huge body of people who make up Abraham's children. You do not have to add "works of the Law" to become one of Abraham's spiritual descendants.

Heirs according to promise - The promise to Abraham (see Galatians 3:8) concerning the inheritance (see Galatians 3:18) was not set aside by the Law given through Moses. "Heirs" – here is something else the Law could not do for a man. Only the Abrahamic covenant can make a person an heir. Heirs of God, rather than heirs of Abraham, is the idea. This is in accordance with Romans 8:16,17, "we are children of God: and if children, heirs also, heirs of God, and fellow heirs with Christ."

---

[129] "Seed" is evidently used with a different connotation than it was used in verse 16 (where it referred to Christ).

[130] Paul has earlier alluded to Abraham's sons (3:7) and to the fact that those who are of faith are blessed with Abraham, the believer (3:9).

D. The Argument From Absurdity.   4:1-11

Summary: It is absurd to exchange one bondage for another. Whether Jew or Greek, before you were converted to Christ and became free, you were in bondage. What good was it to become a free man if now you are voluntarily going to submit to being enslaved in another form of bondage? Why exchange one form of bondage for another? Though there is a chapter break, there is no break in the argument at this point. Paul is still trying to persuade the Galatians that they can only lose if they agree to embracing works of the Law.

4:1 - *Now I say, as long as the heir is a child, he does not differ at all from a slave although he is owner of everything.*

Now I say - This is the expression Paul uses when he wishes to make a further explanation of a thought already introduced. "Let me put it this way" is how Bruce attempts to catch the meaning.[1] Paul introduces a slightly different analogy from the one used in 3:22-29 to contrast the readers' previous spiritual immaturity to their coming of age when they are in Christ. In chapter 3 he pictured readers as being kept in custody under a tutor. Now he will picture them as having been under guardians and managers.

As long as the heir is a child - "Heir" serves to tie chapter 4 to 3:29. "Child" (*nēpios*) seems to be here a minor child in any stage of his minority, naturally subject to the control of guardians. The child may be the heir of the estate, but as long as he is legally a minor he is under the control and direction of others.[2] The heir in his minority represents the spiritual state of Jewish people before the gospel.

He does not differ at all from a slave - When the child is a minor he does not differ from

---

[1] Bruce, *op. cit.*, p.192.

[2] In the ancient world, the process of growing up was much more definite than it is with us. The modern reader will miss the flavor of these verses unless he realizes that the moment of growing up was a very definite one in antiquity and that it involved matters of religious and legal importance. Barclay (*op. cit.*, p.36,37) has shown that the figure of a minor child reaching the age of his majority would have been familiar the world over. In the Jewish world, when a boy was twelve years of age he became a *Bar Mitzvah*, a son of the covenant. The father uttered this benediction, "Blessed be Thou, O God, who has taken from me the responsibility for this boy." The boy offered a prayer in which he acknowledged his own responsibility to keep God's commandments. In the Greek world the boy was under the father's care until he became eighteen years of age. A festival was held to initiate the boy into adulthood. In the Roman world, when the boy was somewhere between fourteen and seventeen, he was liberated from his minority in a festival held on the seventeenth of March. He discarded his childhood clothing (*toga praetexta*, a toga with a narrow purple band at its foot) which he had previously worn, and put on the *toga virilis*, which was a plain toga which adults wore. Lloyd Douglas in *The Robe* describes the moving nature of this moment in his description of the coming of age of Marcellus.

a slave in this one aspect; namely, he has to take orders, not give them.[3]   Both were subject to the same restraint, discipline, and correction.   Someone else was their master.

Although he is owner of everything - "Though the child is the prospective owner[4] of all the estate he is not yet old enough to enter into possession of it.   The inheritance is in reserve for him but he has not yet come into his rights."[5]

4:2 - *But he is under guardians and managers until the date set by the father.*

But he is under guardians and managers - Paul names two classes of superiors because in his analogy the inheritance is a large one (as befits the great spiritual inheritance he is illustrating).   "Under" has the sense of being subject to their control and direction.   The guardian (*epitropos*) was usually a friend or relative of the father who had responsibility for the person of his ward.   The manager or steward (*oikonomos*) would have been appointed to manage the household or property of the minor heir.   Stewards, who often were trusted slaves, were of lower social standing than guardians, but they had considerable financial and administrative powers as they managed the master's property.[6]   Though Paul has changed figures of speech from tutor to guardians and managers, the idea being illustrated is much the same.   While they were under the Law of Moses, Jewish people were in their spiritual minority.

Until the date set by the father - The term "date set" (*prothesmia*) is a legal term referring to a day appointed beforehand.   The illustration is most readily understood if it is assumed that the father had died and had left instructions in his will for the care of his son and the management of his estate.[7]   In any case, the period of the spiritual minority of the Jewish race was fixed by the heavenly Father.

---

[3] The child did differ from a slave in many ways: he differed "in prospects of inheriting the property, and in the affections of his father, and usually in the advantages of education, and in the respect and attention shown him."   Barnes, *op. cit.*, p.357.

[4] *Kurios* (here translated "owner") is used here, as often in the Scriptures, to denote master or owner. See Matthew 20:8 for a similar usage.

[5] Johnson, *op. cit.*, p.103.

[6] *Oikonomos* is used of one who manages another's property in Luke 12:42 and 16:1,3,8.

[7] Earlier in a footnote we saw that the age when a child reached majority was settled by Roman law. Yet the statement here suggests that the father could stipulate how long his heir would have to be under guardians and managers.   This looks like a contradiction.   Ramsay proposes to solve the difficulty by insisting that Paul here follows Galatian inheritance laws rather than Roman.   But the source Ramsay quotes (Justinian, *Inst.* 1.14.3) comes from 500 years after Paul's day (Longenecker, *op. cit.*, p.163). Burton (*op. cit.*, p.214,215) imagines the case of a father away on a journey who anticipated delay in returning and left explicit instructions regarding his young son.   He calls attention to the case of Antiochus Epiphanes, who on his departure for a military campaign in Persia, left his son Antiochus Eupator in the care of Lysias as steward and guardian of that son until a specified time (1 Maccabees 3:32,33; 6:17).

4:3 - *So also we, while we were children, were held in bondage under the elemental things of the world.*

So also we - With "so" Paul introduces the great spiritual truth he has just illustrated by means of the minor heir. Until Christ came, at the right time appointed by the Father, the Jewish people ("we") were like minor children, under the guardianship of the "rudiments" of the world. "We" (emphatic in the Greek, *hēmeis*) alludes to Jews in particular.[8]

While we were children – The word translated "children" is *nēpioi,* children in a state of minority. Paul is speaking of himself and his Jewish brethren from the Christian point of view. Before we Jews became Christians, we were children spiritually. Jewish folk had been in their spiritual childhood in the generations before the advent of Christ. The time between Moses and Christ, for the Jewish people, is compared to the period of childhood. Just like children in the ancient world were under guardians or managers because they needed time to gain information and experience and develop sound judgment, so the Jewish people needed a "tutor" or "guardian" and the Law of Moses served this purpose.

Were held in bondage - "In bondage" says they were being treated like slaves or like minor children. The passive nuance in the verb "held" suggests that God is the One who so stipulated that the Jewish people were held in bondage.[9]

Under the elemental things of the world - This phrase has proven difficult to interpret. The word *stoicheia* ("elemental things") has a wide range of meanings.

> Etymologically it means anything placed in a row [like stakes on which to hang fishing nets]: then it came to be applied to the letters of the alphabet, the ABCs, or a file of soldiers; since Plato's time it was used to refer to the basic elements of which the world is composed [earth, air, fire, water]; in animistic religions, it was used to designate the elemental spirits [angels or demons] associated with the physical elements; metaphorically it designates any elementary teaching or knowledge.[10]

---

[8] That Gentiles also were in bondage appears from verses 8-9. Note the change from "we" here to "you" in verse 8.

[9] *Ēmen dedoulōmenoi* (pluperfect periphrastic using the active [Classical] first plural form of *eimi*) occurs in A, B, C, TR, and most Mss. *Ēmetha dedoulōmenoi* (pluperfect periphrastic using the middle [Hellenistic] first plural of *eimi*) is found in P[46], Aleph, D*, G, and 33. This periphrastic construction emphasizes the state in which "we" were "while we were children" more than the simple pluperfect form alone would have done.

[10] Lenski, *op. cit.,* p.195.

Commentators have picked first one, then another, of these options for *stoicheia*.

- In the latter sense it denotes the elementary forms of religion or stages of religious experience.

- Ancient commentators called attention to the elements of nature, the heavenly bodies that marked the times for Jewish festivals.

- Not a few early church fathers declared that the Jews were in fact worshippers of spirits/demons/angels.[11] Archaeology has tended to confirm the eastern religions' influence on the Jews as nearly every early synagogue excavated has a mosaic zodiac on the floor.[12] The RSV translation here is "elementary spirits of the universe."[13] If we accept what the ancients said, then we are being told by Paul that the Pharisees' religion (Judaism) was heavily involved with the occult, at least in its origins.

- In other places in the New Testament (Colossians 2:8,20; Hebrews 5:12) the word has reference to the basic elements of religious teaching.[14] In Hebrews, for example, the elementary things were the Messianic prophecies of the Old Testament. The revelations given by God through Moses were valuable religious ABCs intended to educate the Jews and through them the rest of the world.

How *tou kosmou* ("of the world", which can also be translated "of the universe") is explained depends on which option is chosen for "elemental things." If we choose the option that speaks of the Law of Moses being religious ABCs, then it does not seem to mean that they were in themselves evil, or had their origin from this world, but rather that they (if they were Jews) had to submit to regulations about food and drink, washings and purifications, sacrifices of all kinds, rules about places, times, bodily actions of all kinds, all of which pertained to this world.

4:4 - *But when the fulness of time came, God sent forth His Son, born of a woman, born under the Law,*

---

[11] So Hilary, Pelagius, Chrysostom, Theod. Mops., Theodoret, Victorinus, and Augustine. This agreement seems to be because of the influence of Origen (*in Ioann* 4.22), who says the Jews were in fact worshipers of angels and archangels, months, and moons.

[12] A. Kloner, "Ancient Synagogues in Israel: An Archaeological Survey," in *Ancient Synagogues Revealed*, edited by L.I. Levine (Jerusalem: Israel Exploration Society, 1981), p.11-18. Hershel Shanks, "Synagogue Excavation Reveals Stunning Mosaic of Zodiac and Torah Ark," *BAR*, 10:3 (May-June 1984), p.32-44. Such zodiacs imply a surprising involvement with the world of the occult.

[13] There is no word for "spirits" in the Greek of this verse. All we have is a neuter plural noun (*stoicheia*) – "elemental (something neuter plural)." We must supply a noun, and any neuter plural noun that is consistent with the context is permitted.

[14] Ramsay, Lightfoot, Burton, Matera, Stott, and Tenney opt for this interpretation.

But when the fulness of the time came - The phrase "fulness of the time" in verse 4 corresponds to "the date set by the father" in verse 2.   That is when the minor son comes of age.   In the illustration, it was said that the minor has guardians and managers only until he reaches maturity.   So with those under the Law.   It was a temporary arrangement, to last only until the date fixed by the Father.   "After many centuries under the Law, there came a time that God had set, the time when Abraham's children might receive the full blessing promised to Abraham."[15]   God in His infinite wisdom knew when the proper time for the appearance of His Son had come, the proper time for men's spiritual minority to become spiritual maturity.[16]

God sent forth His Son - Galatians 3:16 spoke of Christ being the "seed" of Abraham. When the time was right, the "seed" was sent forth by God to make it possible for the blessing of Abraham to come to all believers (see Galatians 3:29).   Christ's preexistence is strongly suggested here;[17] so is His deity, for the Son is not only sent by God, but is "sent forth (*exapesteilen*, out from) from" God.[18]   The Son's purpose in coming into the world was to procure the adoption as sons for us.

Born of a woman, born under the Law - Jesus' perfect humanity is the thing emphasized in the words "born of a woman," yet it is implied He had another nature which was not de-

---

[15] Root, *76-77 Standard Lesson Commentary*, p.21.   "Here we have a very clear expression of the conception of religion as progressive, divided into periods, and finding its culmination in Christianity" (Sanday, *op. cit.*, p.64).

[16] We do not know what God saw that He regarded as being the fulness of time.   Since Gentiles, too, were to be included in Abraham's spiritual descendants, many have enumerated some of the providences which helped open the way for the spread of the gospel, such as the vast extent of the Roman Empire which united the ancient world under one government and built a remarkable system of roads which greatly facilitated travel; the universal use of the Greek language making evangelism more convenient; the Jewish diaspora with the presence of synagogues throughout the empire which provided a base for Christian preaching of the Old Testament Messianic prophecies as now fulfilled in Jesus of Nazareth.   Through the centuries, God had been nurturing and guarding men until in His inscrutable wisdom it was the right time for man's spiritual minority to end.

[17] Modern scholars have questioned the idea that the language presupposes Jesus' preexistence. See Dunn, *Christology in the Making*, p.39-43, where it is denied that preexistence is here implied.   To say that Jesus is God's "Son" only functionally, and not ontologically, is less than what Scripture presents the Son as being (see Hebrews 1:1-3).

[18] "The Greek verb *exapesteilen* is a double compound, signifying that God 'sent forth from' Himself. Christ is clearly conceived as divine" (Johnson, *op. cit.*, p.103-4).   That the divine Christ was pre-existent before the incarnation and birth at Bethlehem is clearly taught (John 1:1,14; Romans 8:3; 1 Corinthians 8:6; Philippians 2:6-8; Colossians 1:15,16).   When Paul refers to Jesus as God's "Son," he is not talking about Christ's essence, His nature as God.   Paul is referring to His role of submission in the Incarnation. We would not call Jesus "Son" save but for the incarnation (Luke 1:35).   See further comments concerning this designation "Son" at Galatians 1:16.

rived from the woman.[19]   God's sending forth of His Son on a mission is something that became visible to human eyes when Jesus became a man.[20]   One wonders why it is essential to Paul's argument to note that Christ was born of a woman.   Perhaps it is mentioned to call attention to the promise made at Genesis 3:15 about the seed of the woman.   "Born under the Law" tells us that Jesus was born into the world at a time when the Law of Moses was still in force (at least for the children of Israel), though He Himself was destined to put an end to that dispensation.[21]   The phrase also points to Jesus' Jewish lineage.

4:5 - *in order that He might redeem those who were under the Law, that we might receive the adoption as sons.*

In order that He might redeem - "Redeem" is the same word used at 3:13, and this verse expresses the same thought there unfolded.   Men were in bondage,[22] but Christ came and

---

[19] The verb translated "born" in both phrases is *ginomai* (which means be, become, come to be, be made, as well as be born) rather than the usual word for "born" which is *gennaō*.   There has been a long-running debate about the precise meaning of the two words.   Both words are used of John the Baptist (*ginomai* at John 8:58; *gennaō* at Matthew 11:11).   *Gennaō* is used with reference to Christ's conception and birth at Matthew 1:16, 2:1.   It was used in Gabriel's message to Mary (Luke 1:35).   Jesus Himself, speaking to Pilate about His own birth, used *gennaō* when He said "For this *I have been born*, and for this I have come into the world ..." (John 18:37).   Elsewhere, such as at John 1:14 ("the Word *became* flesh") and Romans 1:3 ("*born* of the seed of David according to the flesh", KJV), *ginomai* is used of Jesus.

   The real issue in dispute is whether or not Paul's use of *ginomai* (rather than *gennaō*) in Galatians 4:4 is an affirmation of Jesus' virgin birth.   J.G. Machen wrote, "This passage [Galatians 4:4] has sometimes been held to show that Paul did not believe in the virgin birth and sometimes also has been held to show that he did so.   As a matter of fact both opinions are probably wrong; the passage does not enable us to draw any conclusion with respect to Paul's belief in the matter one way or another" (*The Virgin Birth of Christ* [NY: Harper, 1930], p.259).   The virgin birth of Jesus is plainly taught in Matthew 1:18-25 (cf. Isaiah 7:14) and Luke 1:34,35.   Lenski and James Orr (*The Virgin Birth of Christ* [New York: Charles Scribner's Sons, 1927.   Reprint, Joplin, MO: College Press, 1972) have strongly argued Paul's language here affirms Jesus' virgin birth.   Hendriksen *(op. cit.*, p.158) has said "the Holy Spirit has seen to it that Paul expressed himself in a way which causes Galatians 4:4 to be in full harmony with the teaching elsewhere of the doctrine of the virgin birth."   "'His son ... out of woman' pointedly omits mention of a human father.   Why?   Because this is God's Son.   He became man by woman alone" (Lenski, *op. cit.*, p.200).

[20] "He did not cease to be the Son of God when he became man.   He did not drop his deity.   He remained what he was and added on what he had not had, namely, a human nature, derived out of a woman, a human mother" (Lenski, *op. cit.*, p.199).   Paul's words in Philippians 2:7,8 suggest Jesus' perfect humanity: "made in the likeness of men" and "appearing in human form (Moffatt)."   Hebrews 2:14 also emphasizes Jesus' likeness to humans in that He shared the same flesh we share.

[21] Law is anarthrous, yet the reference seems to be to the fact that Christ was born under the Mosaic Law.   The Law of Moses was valid until Calvary.   It did not cease when the "seed" (Christ) came to Bethlehem.   The old distinction drawn by theologians between the articular and anarthrous use of *nomos* (as though the first means "the Law of Moses" while the second means law in general) has been discredited, says Longenecker (*op. cit.*, p.171) correctly.

[22] Galatians has spoken about tutors, guardians, managers, about being kept in custody under the Law, and about being held in bondage under the elemental things of the world.

died and rose and set men free. This is why God sent His Son. Jesus purchased us and freed us, not to make us slaves, but to make us "sons." The two clauses here in verse 5 match two found in verse 4 ("God sent forth His Son" and "born under the Law"). Cancel His deity, consider God's Son a mere human son, and there can be no redemption. Cancel His subjection to the Law, and He is not our redeemer any longer, for redemption required a sinless perfect sacrifice.

Those who were under the Law - Again it is anarthrous *nomos* but Paul refers to the Mosaic Law. Now if Jesus by His death redeemed Israelites from their bondage under the Law, it should be obvious that Gentiles (such as the Galatians) who had never been under the Law of Moses would certainly not be obligated to that Law now. No, the Judaizers were wrong in their teaching!

That we might receive the adoption as sons - "We" means we Jews, the same people identified in the previous clause as "those who were under the Law." Redemption (freedom) is followed by adoption. Adoption is something that must be received; that is, it is conditional. Humanity must respond by faith in Jesus Christ (Galatians 3:26,27). The New Testament word for adoption (*huiothesia*, the legal term for adoption in the Greco-Roman world) means "to place as an adult son."[23] It has to do with our standing in the family of God: we Jews who have become Christians are no longer little children and minors, but adult sons with all the privileges of sonship.[24]

4:6 - *And because you are sons, God has sent forth the Spirit of His Son into our hearts, crying, "Abba! Father!"*

And because you are sons - If the word *hoti* is translated "because" (as the NASB does), verse 6 is given as a proof to support Paul's statement that "you are sons," that proof being that God has sent the Spirit. Romans 8:14,15 has been said to teach this same idea. If we translate *hoti* "as a result of," then verse 6 explains one of the consequences of being an adult son; namely, God sent the Spirit. Either translation is Scriptural, and either makes sense here. The shift in the personal pronouns in this passage from "we" (4:3,5) to "you" (4:6) should be noticed. By changing to "you," Paul now applies what he has been teaching in the earlier verses of chapter 4 to the Galatian Christians. Whether Jew or Gentile, every Christian believer has the position of an adopted adult son in God's family.

God has sent forth the Spirit of His Son into our hearts - The verb "sent forth" (*exapes-*

---

[23] See also Romans 8:15,23; 9:4; Ephesians 1:5 for other instances of "adoption" being used to describe how believers become God's sons. "In Paul's writings, 'adoption' is used with various connotations: of the Christian's present sonship (Romans 8:15); the Christian's future resurrection body (Romans 8:23); Israel's past special relationship with God (Romans 9:4); and that predestined by God for believers 'through Jesus Christ' (Ephesians 1:5)" (Longenecker, *op. cit.*, p.172).

[24] We do not *enter* God's family by adoption, but by being born again (John 3:3-5; Titus 3:5).

teilen) is exactly the same verb used in verse 4 where God "sent forth His Son." The Son was sent forth into the world, the Spirit of the Son was sent forth into the hearts of believers in the Son. "Spirit of His Son" is one of the numerous names for the Holy Spirit in the New Testament.[25] He is called the "Spirit of His Son" because He proceeds from the Son (John 15:26), as well as from the Father, and because He glorifies the Son (John 16:14). "All three persons of the Holy Trinity are indicated in [verse 6], and their harmonious co-operation as the one true God is beautifully set forth."[26]

The time of the sending forth here spoken of is disputed. The reference is hardly to Pentecost when the baptism of the Holy Spirit empowered the apostles, for this verse says "into our hearts" (i.e., the hearts of all believers). "Into our hearts" seems to refer to the time of our baptism, when believers receive the indwelling gift of the Holy Spirit (Acts 2:38).[27] When a penitent believer is immersed, his spirit is born again (John 3:6), he receives the gift of the Holy Spirit (Acts 2:38), and he is adopted into the family of God.

Sonship and receiving the Spirit are intimately related. How shall we explain the difference between this verse, and the one in 1 Corinthians 6:19,20, which says our *bodies* are the temple of the Holy Spirit? The Spirit takes up residence in our bodies, and then has something to do with our *thoughts* (hearts). He provides some kind of internal prompting to direct our living. With "our" Paul claims the same indwelling gift of the Spirit the Galatian Christians had received. When he was baptized by Ananias, Paul received the Spirit whom Ananias was sent to help Paul receive (Acts 9:17,18).

Crying, "Abba! Father!" - *Abba* is the Aramaic, and *patēr* the Greek, for "Father." Both words are understood to be in the vocative case (the way one addresses another when

[25] P[46] does not have *tou huiou* ("of His Son"). In 2 Corinthians 3:17 Paul does speak of "the Spirit of the Lord," and in Philippians 1:19 of "the Spirit of Jesus Christ." In Romans 8:9,10 the expressions "Spirit of God," "Spirit of Christ," and "Christ is in you" all refer to the same reality.

[26] Hendriksen, *op. cit.*, p.160.

[27] Paul, here, seems to say sonship occurs first, then the reception of the Spirit. However, in Romans 8:15-17 the order is the reception of the Spirit and then sonship. Galatians 3:2-5 has spoken of the Spirit being given when there is obedience to the faith ("hearing of faith," ASV). Longenecker (*op. cit.*, p.173) tells us that as a result "the argument as to whether the proper order is first sonship and then the gift of the Spirit, or first the reception of the Spirit and then sonship, has been heated (cf. e.g., Lightfoot, *Galatians*, p.169)."
Longenecker thinks the perceived awkwardness results from Paul's using an early church confessional statement here. In verses 4-6 source and redaction critics believe they have discovered a "confessional formula" drawn from the early church. When the critics are done, sadly, another high Christological passage has been gutted of any significant meaning. This is not the path of sober exegesis.
Some deduce another, entirely different emphasis from this passage. Reading it as though sonship comes before the reception of the Spirit (i.e., reading it "because you are sons"), not a few have argued for the doctrine of subsequence in all cases of the reception of the Holy Spirit; that is, the person first is immersed and becomes a son, and then some time later receives the gift of the Spirit. Such a subsequent time of reception of the Spirit is not demanded by this passage. It can just as well be defended that the reception of the gift of the (indwelling) Holy Spirit is simultaneous with their becoming sons. "The presence of the Spirit is ... a witness of their sonship" (Lightfoot, *op. cit.*, p.169).

speaking to him). Jewish Christians may say "*Abba*" when they call on God to listen to their prayers. Gentile Christians may say "*patēr*" when they speak to God using the Greek language. Whether we speak Greek or Aramaic, it is the indwelling Spirit who prompts us sons of God to so address God as our Father.[28] "The primary function of the Spirit in one's life is not to cause a believer in Jesus to become a 'spiritual' or a 'charismatic' person, as is so often popularly assumed, but to witness to the filial relation between the believer with God that has been established by the work of Christ."[29]

4:7 - *Therefore you are no longer a slave, but a son; and if a son, then an heir through God.*

Therefore - What Paul has said so far in chapter 4 is now summarized and applied to each individual Christian reader.

You are no longer a slave - "You" is singular so it speaks to each individual Christian who hears what Paul has written.[30] The Gentile Christians in Galatia had never been under

---

[28] Technically, "the Spirit" is the subject of the verb "cry." However, in Romans 8:15,16, it is "we" Christians who by the Spirit cry "Abba, Father!" The Spirit is in our hearts as a result of our sonship, and His presence makes this cry possible. He prompts it.

　　　Boice (*op. cit.*, p.474-75) has a long footnote on calling God "Father." "It is not always recognized how unusual the addressing of God as 'father' was in antiquity nor what an unforgettable impression Jesus' habitual mode of praying made on his followers. Lohmeyer, in a book called *Our Father* (New York: Harper & Row, 1965), and Jeremias, in an essay entitled 'Abba' in *The Central Message of the New Testament* (New York: Charles Scribner's Sons, 1965), both point out that in Jesus' day (1) no one ever addressed God directly as 'My Father' because it would have been thought disrespectful; (2) Jesus always used this form of address in praying, much to the amazement of his disciples; and (3) Jesus authorized His disciples to use this form of address after Him, and they did. In one sense, of course, the title 'Father' for God is as old as religion. Homer wrote of 'Father Zeus, who rules over the gods and mortal men.' Aristotle explained that this was right, for 'paternal rule over children is like that of a king over his subjects' and 'Zeus is king of us all.' In Israel God was called 'Father' of the nation and the nation His child (cf. Exodus 4:22; Psalm 103:13; Isaiah 64:8; Jeremiah 3:19; Hosea 11:1). The point, however, is that none of this was *personal*. God was never considered to be the father of the individual. And in Christ's day the distance between man and God was actually widening in popular thought rather than growing narrower. Jesus completely reversed this trend. This so impressed the disciples that, not only do all four Gospels record his use of this address, they also report that He did so in all his prayers (Matthew 11:25; 26:39,42; Mark 14:36; Luke 23:34; John 11:41, 12:27, 17:1,5,11,21,24,25). The only exception is one that actually enforces the significance of the phrase, for it was the cry wrung from Christ's lips at the moment in which He was made sin for mankind and in which the relationship to the Father that had been his was temporarily broken (Matthew 27:46). It may be sentimentalizing the word '*Abba*' to translate it 'Daddy,' but it should not be forgotten that the word is diminutive and implies intimacy. The early church fathers – Chrysostom, Theodor of Mopsuestia, and Theodoret of Cyprus, who came from Antioch (where Aramaic was spoken and who probably had Aramaic-speaking nurses in their childhoods) – unanimously testify that Abba was the address of a small child to his father (J. Jeremias, *The Lord's Prayer*, transl. J. Reumann [Philadelphia: Fortress Press], p.19)."

[29] Longenecker, *op. cit.*, p.174.

[30] First, Paul wrote "we" meaning we Jewish Christians (verses 3-5). Then he wrote "you" meaning all his Galatian converts (verse 6). Now here, the "you" in Greek is singular.

the Law of Moses, but they had been enslaved "to those which by nature are no gods" (verse 8). Like the Jews, they had been redeemed and reborn as God's children. They were no longer slaves. They were free. They too were adult children ("sons").

But a son - Instead of being in bondage under the elemental things of the world (verse 3), instead of being under the Law (verse 4), instead of being slaves to those which by nature are no gods (verse 8), Christians are now adult sons and daughters of God; "they have been given their freedom and the power to use it responsibly."[31] This answers why the Law is not binding on Christians: the time of men's minority is past, whether he be a Jew (under Moses) or a Gentile (under those which by nature are no gods). You are adult sons now!

And if a son, then an heir through God - We may translate the Greek if-clause as "since you are a son." The true reading here appears to be "through God" (rather than as the King James Version, "an heir of God through Christ"), since it is supported by P[46], Aleph*, A, B, C*. A comparison of a similar construction at Galatians 1:1 suggests these words are an abbreviation of "through God who adopted you."[32] In the ancient world adopted sons were treated as equal heirs with any son or daughter naturally born into the family.[33] As an heir of God, the Christian receives the same inheritance Jesus received once He had died and risen from the dead. Or, in this context, "heir" may be synonymous with "son" (adult child) – no longer under guardians and managers (verse 2). Compare this verse with what was said in verse 1 about the "heir" being temporarily a minor child. When he is in Christ, a man's spiritual minority is a thing of the past. He is free and has all the responsibilities of an adult son![34]

4:8 - *However at that time, when you did not know God, you were slaves to those which by nature are no gods.*

However at that time - "At that time" refers to the state of the Gentiles before they became

---

[31] Bruce, *op. cit.,* p.200.

[32] Lightfoot, *op. cit.,* p.170.

[33] See notes at Galatians 3:29 on "heirs."

[34] "Verses 4-7 contain the sum and marrow of Christian divinity: (1) The determination of God to redeem the world by the incarnation of His Son. (2) The manifestation of this Son in the fulness of time. (3) The circumstances in which this Son appeared: sent forth; made of a woman; made under the law; to be a sufferer; and to die as a sacrifice. (4) The redemption of the world, by the death of Christ: He came to redeem them that were under the law, who were condemned and cursed by it. (5) By the redemption price He purchases sonship or adoption for mankind. (6) He, God the Father, sends the Spirit, God the Holy Spirit, of God the Son, into the hearts of believers, by which they, through the full confidence of their adoption, call Him their Father. (7) Being made children, they become heirs, and God is their portion throughout eternity. Thus, in a few words the whole doctrine of grace is contained" (Clarke, *op. cit.,* p.408).

Christians. Jews (verse 3) while still under the Law were like heirs in their minority. They had guardians and managers to look after them, to whom they were subject. But just what had been the position of the Gentiles before they became Christians? This Paul now sets about to show.[35] They didn't know God, and they were in bondage to their "gods."

When you did not know God - Note the change of pronouns from "we" (verse 3) to "you" at this place. Verse 3 spoke of Jewish people. Verse 8 speaks of Gentile people. Not knowing God certainly does not speak of Jews (whatever we may think is the subject of verses 1-6). It encourages us to think that chapter 4:8-11 speaks of *Gentiles*. "Know" is *oida*, a knowledge gained by mental processes – i.e., what is sometimes called "head knowledge." It is a simple fact that the Gentiles of Galatia, like many other Gentiles,[36] did not have any mental perception about the true God.

You were slaves to those which by nature are no gods - "Slaves" helps us to see that just as the Jews were in bondage (verse 3) so were the Gentiles, but to a different master. "No gods" is a reference to idols. "By nature" is probably equal to "really" (Moffatt) or they are in fact not deity at all.[37] 1 Corinthians 8:4,5 tell us that in the ancient world there were many that were called gods, though there is no such thing as an idol in the world (that is, there is no real being whose image the statue or bust pretends to represent). Behind the idols were demons (1 Corinthians 10:20), and it was to these malevolent beings that the Gentiles were in bondage. To recognize how galling such slavery can be, think of the slavery to the spirits one observes among voodoo peoples of Jamaica or Haiti. "The beings which the Galatians had served in their former pagan days were at that time reckoned by them to be gods, but they were not really so."[38]

---

[35] Because of the *alla* ("however") some have begun a new paragraph with verse 8, as indeed does the NASB. We treat verses 8-11 (a separate paragraph in NASB) as part of the argument from absurdity introduced at 4:1. Paul is still trying to change the Galatian Christians' minds so that they will reject the overtures of the Judaizers. He closes the paragraph by speaking directly and personally of his concern for them.

[36] 1 Thessalonians 4:5 and 2 Thessalonians 1:8 characterize Gentiles as those who know not God. As to the spiritual darkness of the Gentiles see also Romans 1:18-32. Romans 1 indicates that originally men knew the truth, and the ordinances of God, but they deliberately repudiated what they knew and went into idolatry. Then as the years passed, the succeeding generations knew less and less about God. As they worshiped the idols, their minds quit working right (Romans 1:21,28) and their behavior deteriorated into habitual unrighteousness.

[37] There is a manuscript variation here. The Textus Receptus reads *tois mē phusei ousi theois* which would suggest "which are not gods by nature, but only in your imagination." The Greek text behind the NASB reads *tois phusei mē ousin theois*. REB translates this phrase "to gods who are not gods at all." So translated, *phusei mē ousin* is construed as an adjectival phrase limiting *theois*. The NASB treats the participle *ousin* substantively and *theoi* as its predicate. *Ousin* can be translated as "beings" (RSV, NRSV, NEB) or as "things" (NAB, NJB). Matera, *op. cit.*, p.152.

[38] Bruce, *op. cit.*, p.201.

4:9 - *But now that you have come to know God, or rather to be known by God, how is it that you turn back again to the weak and worthless elemental things, to which you desire to be enslaved all over again?*

But now that you have come to know God – Expanded, this verse would be translated, "Now that you are Christians, now that you have (*ginōskō*) gained a knowledge of God by personal experience."[39]   The temporal phrase "but now" contrasts with "at that time" (verse 8), indicating the Galatians' present condition in Christ.   To "know God" is the very essence of eternal life (John 17:3), and this had come about in Galatia when Christ had been preached by Paul and Barnabas, and the Galatians had abandoned their idolatry as they accepted the gospel.[40]   The God the Galatian Christians know is the God of Israel revealed in Jesus Christ.

Or rather to be known by God - "Or rather" introduces a slight correction to the previous statement.   Perhaps in "known by God" there is the idea of approved by God.   God approves the Galatians who are in Christ by faith, and who therefore are God's adopted sons.[41]   Expanded, the phrase would read, "Not only have you come to know the one true and living God, you even have His approval."

How is it that you turn back again to the weak and worthless elemental things - The question ('How can you do it?') implies surprise and indignation that they should even think of doing it.   Whatever "elemental things" meant in verse 3 it means here.   Paul seems to have the Judaizer's doctrines in view, particularly as he speaks of "weak and worthless elemental things."   The "elemental things" are disparaged as "weak" in comparison with the power of the gospel and the teaching and leading of the Spirit.   They are "worthless" in comparison to the wealth ("the unfathomable riches of Christ," Ephesians 3:8) that heirs of God inherit.

To which you desire to be enslaved all over again? - The Galatian Christians, who had once been slaves to idols, were now free in Christ.   Were they now going to exchange their freedom for another slavery?   How absurd!   When he writes "all over again," Paul seems to be saying that the Pharisees' works of Law were really demonically inspired, just

---

[39] The gift of the Spirit (verse 6) is one of the ways a person can know God by experience.

[40] "It is only through Christ as proclaimed in the gospel that they had come to know and serve the living and true God (1 Thessalonians 1:9; Acts 14:15)" (Bruce, *ibid.*).

[41] Caution is needed here.   Calvinism finds its first work of grace in the words "rather to be known by God."   This is the proof text that they say shows knowing God is in no way the product of man's own efforts, but rather the product of God's foreknowledge and election.   If this passage does stress God's initiative in salvation, we should remember that God first revealed Himself in the sending of His Son to be our redeemer (verse 4).   Then, God had something to do with the gospel preachers coming to Galatia in the first place.   The Galatians' acquaintance with the true God was not something solely attributable to themselves.

as pagan religions were.   It is possible to return to slavery to sin again (Romans 6:16-23).
So, religiously, it is possible to revert to bondage again.[42]

4:10 - *You observe days and months and seasons and years.*

You observe - Paul here gives an example of the kinds of things to which they will be in
bondage if they become what the Judaizers want them to be.   The word "observe"
(*paratēreisthe*) carries the idea of minutely, scrupulously observing, carefully keeping.[43]
"Observe" is a present tense verb, showing that the movement toward adopting Jewish
ceremonies was already going on, and had proceeded this far.[44]   The Judaizers have had
some success among the Galatians.   Since the Judaizers were Pharisees, are the calendar
items about to be enumerated counted and observed as Pharisees would fix the dates, rather
than say an Essene or Sadducean calendar?   We think so.   Pharisees would certainly
emphasize such observances as evidence their lives were what God expected.

Days - While the reference may be to the Jewish Sabbaths, and other fasts or festivals
which occupied a single day, one wonders if observing "days" is not tantamount to
observing Pharisaic rules about Sabbath observances, and about fasting two days a week
(Luke 18:12).

And months - Certain months in the Jewish calendar were special: the Passover fell in
Nisan, the first month of the Jewish ecclesiastical year; and the Day of Atonement and
Feast of Tabernacles fell in Tishri, the seventh month.   Careful observance of the heavens
was required to determine when the new moon occurred with which each month began.
Numbers 10:10 mentions the festival of the new moon.   Numbers 28:11-14 lists the
offerings to be brought on that day.

And seasons - Seasons might include not only the Biblically mandated feasts such as
Passover, Pentecost, and the Feast of Tabernacles, but also the festivals added later by the
Jews, such as Purim and the Feast of Dedication.   Some of these "seasons" were week-
long events.   There were also seasons of prayer and fasting.[45]

---

[42] The verbs "desire" and "enslaved" are both present tense verbs in the Greek, indicating matters in
progress.   It is not yet an accomplished enslavement, but if they continue on, it will be.

[43] The prepositional prefix *para* could imply that the observance was amiss, or beside what was right.
It may also refer to close, intent observation.   Think of the tyranny to the calendar and the hour of the day
that was required of one who would observe days and months and seasons and years.

[44] Galatians 5:1-3 will indicate the movement had not gone so far as to include submission to
circumcision, yet.   It will, unless Paul can nip this false practice and doctrine in the bud.

[45] This passage certainly should serve as a corrective to those groups (such as Seventh Day
Adventists and the World-wide Church of God) which have insisted Christians must observe these Old
Testament days and seasons.

And years - It might speak of observing Rosh Hashanah, the beginning of the Jewish New Year. Other "years" are sabbatical years (Leviticus 25:2-7) and the Year of Jubilee. We cannot know whether the Galatians recently have observed each of these Jewish calendar events or whether Paul is simply giving an exhaustive list of all the Jewish observances the Judaizers demanded of their followers.[46]

4:11 - *I fear for you, that perhaps I have labored over you in vain.*

I fear for you - Paul is saying he feels some serious alarm about his Galatian converts. In verse 11 Paul voices his greatest discouragement over the situation in Galatia.

That perhaps I have labored over you in vain - The word "perhaps" qualifies the otherwise bleak outlook, showing that in Paul's mind the situation was not entirely hopeless. The emphasis is on "in vain" (as shown by its placement before the verb in the Greek) and on "over you" which is placed at the end of the sentence. Paul had worked long and hard to evangelize the Galatians.[47] If the Galatians give up their freedom in Christ for a new slavery to the weak and worthless elemental things advocated by the Pharisees, then all of Paul's labors would have been wasted. The final result is yet to be determined. Paul's fears may or may not be confirmed.

E. The Sentimental Argument.   4:12-20

> *Summary*: Paul's earlier arguments against the Judaizers have been theologically oriented. This paragraph is full of personal and emotional appeal.[48] In verses 12-16, Paul appeals to the Galatian Christians to remember their happy relationship

---

[46] J.A. Bengel (*Gnomon of the New Testament* [Edinburgh: T&T Clark, 1860], v.4, p.35) supposed that AD 48 was a year of Jubilee, so he finds in this verse an argument for an early date for the writing of the letter to the Galatians. George Barton ("The Exegesis of *eniautous* in Galatians 4:10 and Its Bearing on the Date of the Epistle," *JBL* 33 [1914], p.118-116) has urged that AD 53-54 was a sabbatical year and so supposes the epistle to the Galatians was composed shortly thereafter. On the Christian observance of days in the light of Paul's objection here, see Origen, *Contra Celsus*, 8:21-23. This commentator has a certain reservation about Christians observing special days (think of Christmas or Easter) but he does not think it is proper to use either Galatians 4:10 or Romans 14;4,5 as proof texts against them. The observance or nonobservance of Pentecost (the birthday of the church) or Thanksgiving (for the blessing of the harvest in autumn) and other such days is something that falls into the realm of Christian liberty. It is when observance of such special days is demanded so that one becomes enslaved to a system like the Judaizers taught that such observances are condemned.

[47] The Greek verb *kekopiaka* (from *kopiaō*) denotes trying labor, hard labor.

> to him in days past, and asks if their attitude toward him has changed. Then in verses 17-20 Paul contrasts his relationship with them in the past and present to the self-interested actions of the Judaizers.

4:12 - *I beg of you, brethren, become as I* am, *for I also* **have become** *as you* are. *You have done me no wrong;*

I beg of you, brethren - Paul may be afraid for them (verse 11), but he will not give them up. Perhaps old friendships will yet prove decisive. He calls them "brethren" because he feels a strong personal affection for them (compare notes at 1:11). On the basis of that affection he *begs* them to listen.[49]

Become as I *am* - Not enough is said to know what Paul means exactly. Perhaps it is an appeal to cast off Pharisaic Judaism as Paul himself has done. Formerly he was carefully observant of works of the Law (man-made *halakhic* rules). Then he became a believer in Christ and abandoned that old system. Perhaps Paul is urging the Galatians to drop their observance of Jewish calendar days and "become" like Paul when it comes to the matters advocated by the Judaizers. The imperative verb Paul uses indicates that at the moment the Galatians were not like Paul. He wants them to remain free just as he is free. It is a call for their loyalty to the truth of the Gospel.

For I also *have become* **as you** *are* - Paul means that when he visited Galatia, as he planted churches, he had laid aside his Jewish practices and lived as a Gentile. He did not rigidly cling to the old Pharisaic practices (though before his call and conversion he had lived as a Pharisee, Acts 23:6, 26:5). His laying aside of those old practices was an example of the exercise of his Christian liberty (cp. 1 Corinthians 9:20-22, "I became ... like one not having the law ... so as to win those not having the law" [NIV]).

---

[48] Before the days of rhetorical criticism, commentators attributed the somewhat erratic style of verses 12-20 to Paul's passionate and emotional state at the time he writes the letter. That is how this present commentator explains the erratic style. However, rhetorical critics, like H.D. Betz (*Galatians*, p.220-221), argue the style would not be called erratic if one understood the nature of the rhetorical character of this passage. However, rhetorical critics have not been able to agree on the kind of rhetoric we meet in Galatians. Deliberative rhetoric seeks to exhort or dissuade an audience about adopting some future action by showing that those actions are expedient or harmful. Forensic rhetoric takes a judicial or defensive stance. Betz has attempted to show that all of Galatians is forensic rhetoric. Longenecker disagrees. Some treat 1:6-4:11 as forensic rhetoric, and the verses from 4:12 on as deliberative rhetoric. G.A. Kennedy (*New Testament Interpretation through Rhetorical Criticism* [Chapel Hill, NC: University of North Carolina Press, 1984], p.145) argues that only 5:1-6:10 is deliberative rhetoric. This commentator has not been able to get excited about all these technical arguments, which spend more time trying to determine the kind of rhetoric than is spent unfolding the message Paul wrote.

[49] In the Greek the last word in the current sentence is "beg." Thus it is emphasized.

You have done me no wrong - According to the punctuation of the NASB, this phrase begins a new sentence which runs through the next three verses. In this commentator's judgment, this whole sentence refers to the treatment they gave him when he first evangelized their cities.[50] Expanded, the phrase would read, "You did me no wrong then,[51] and I am confident you will do me no wrong now." "If one holds to the South Galatian theory for the destination of the epistle, the record of hostility in that area on Paul's first journey is quite clear (Acts 13:45,50; 14:4-6,19). Though some Gentiles were involved, it was mainly unbelieving Jews who stirred up the hostility (Acts 14:2). Many Jews and Greeks became disciples during that period (Acts 13:48,52; 14:1), and it is primarily these people to whom Paul is now addressing his remarks. They had not wronged Paul."[52]

4:13 – *but you know that it was because of a bodily illness that I preached the gospel to you the first time;*

But you know - As Paul writes about the reason that led to his first visit to the Galatians, he would cause the scenes and experiences of those days to flash vividly across their memory. That was one instance where the Galatians did him no wrong.

It was because of a bodily illness that I preached the gospel to you - The reason Paul came to the Galatians the first time was because he was ill, seriously ill. Because of some kind of bodily illness Paul's original travel plans were changed. He was left no choice but to go to Galatia, and the eventual result of his change of plans was the conversion of the Galatians. This verse lends great support to Ramsay's conclusion that Paul's illness was malaria which he contracted in the low marsh lands where Perga of Pamphylia was located.[53] The only known way to recuperate from malaria in that age before the advent of quinine or primaquine drugs was to get away from the marshy lowlands and into the highlands. "I preached" (*euangelizo*) is commonly used by Paul for preaching the gospel. So our NASB renders it.

The first time - It is implied that Paul has visited the Galatians twice, on two separate mis-

---

[50] Burton (*op. cit.*, p.237) gives a different scenario. He supposes Paul has picked up on something the Galatians have said, to the effect of 'Paul, our growing interest in what the Judaizers are teaching should not be taken as a personal affront.' To this then, Paul supposedly accedes. Thus he is making it plain he is not speaking out of a sense of personal resentment.

[51] "The verb *adikein* can mean to injure someone physically, or to treat someone unjustly. The latter makes better sense here as the following verses will show" (Matera, *op. cit.*, p.159).

[52] Johnson, *op. cit.*, p.114.

[53] See Ramsay, *St. Paul the Traveller and Roman Citizen*, p. 92-97. Ramsay's suggestion rightly treats the account in Acts as being historically correct and it assumes the southern Galatian hypothesis. In comments on the next verse here in Galatians, we shall make allusion to several other attempts to identify the bodily illness that led to Paul's first visit to Galatia.

sionary journeys.[54]   His first visit to Galatia is recorded in Acts 13:13-14:24.   His second visit is recorded in Acts 15:40-16:6.   As Paul writes in verse 13, he refers to what happened during the first of these two visits.

4:14 - *and that which was a trial to you in my bodily condition you did not despise or loathe, but you received me as an angel of God, as Christ Jesus* **Himself.**

And that which was a trial to you in my bodily condition - The Greek is awkward grammatically, and as early as the 3rd century there were copyists who tried to smooth out the awkward grammar.   Thus some manuscripts read "my trial" and some read "a trial to you."[55]   "My trial" is a touch of self-commiseration.   Paul really struggled with his illness. "A trial to you" says Paul's bodily condition[56] left a bad first impression, one likely to tempt the hearers to pay no attention to his message.

You did not despise or loathe - "A sick man is never very impressive or assuring."[57]   But the messenger's illness was soon forgotten in the excitement and delight over the heavenly message he preached.   "Despise" says Paul's illness had some unpleasant symptoms that might make him repulsive.   Was he so weak from fever that he had difficulty even sitting to speak?   "Loathe" (*ekptuō* is almost onomatopoetic) literally means to spit out, to disdain, to reject.   Spitting is sometimes an expression of disgust.[58]   The Galatians could

---

[54] In the Introductory Studies we have explained the scholarly debate over the words *to proteron*, whether it means "the first time" or "formerly."   If the word retained its Classical Greek meaning, "the first time" is the correct translation.   Because Paul visited the Galatian churches twice on the first missionary journey, once when he planted the churches, and again as he retraced his steps on his way back to Jerusalem and Antioch, it might be said that visits on two separate journeys are not absolutely required by this language.   While this whole issue has some bearing on the possible date of writing of Galatians, in this commentator's judgment there is no reason to compress the two visits into one journey.   As also indicated in the Introductory Studies, those who hold the northern Galatia theory make reference to Acts 16:6 as the first visit, and to Acts 18:23 as the second visit.

[55] The reading represented by the NASB is attested by Sinaiticus (in the first hand), A, B, C², D*, F, G, 33.   It is the more difficult of the readings.   P⁴⁶ reads "you did not despise *my* trial in my flesh" (and omits "or loathe").   Sinaiticus (in the second hand), 81, 104, 326, all omit *humōn* ("your") so the text reads "that which was a trial in my bodily condition."

[56] The NASB margin shows that the Greek reads literally "in my flesh."   He is talking about his human body, or his bodily appearance.

[57] Lenski, *op. cit.*, p.220.

[58] What Paul's illness was has perplexed Bible students for centuries.   The Galatians, of course, knew exactly what Paul was talking about, so he did not have to give details.   It is the lack of detail that opens the door for conjecture by modern readers.   Barclay (*op. cit.*, p.42) recounts how in the ancient world it was the custom for a man to spit when he met an epileptic, to avert the influence of the evil spirit which they believed to be resident in the sufferer.   Some have used the word *ekptuō* in this verse as evidence Paul was an epileptic (or suffered from prostrating headaches which would affect the person similar to an epileptic collapse).   Another suggestion is that Paul's "thorn in the flesh" (2 Corinthians 12:7) is somehow related to the bodily illness of Galatians 4:13,14.   However, it appears that this "illness" is not to be identified with the "thorn in the flesh."   The thorn which he received fourteen years before he wrote 2 Corinthians (2 Corinthians 12:1-7) would have occurred before the first missionary journey began, where-

have rejected Paul because of his illness, but they did not.

But you received me as an angel of God, as Christ Jesus *Himself* - "A sick man who claims miraculous powers and heals others while he himself remains sick would certainly raise serious doubts regarding any message he might bring. Yet, the Galatians received Paul as if he were an angel of God [i.e., a messenger from God], yea, as if he were Christ Jesus Himself."[59] They showed to the ambassador of Christ as much enthusiasm, as much deep affection, as they would have shown to Christ Himself had He come to their town. One wonders whether one example of such an enthusiastic reception is recounted in the event at Lystra (Acts 13:43-48).

4:15 - *Where then is that sense of blessing you had? For I bear you witness, that if possible, you would have plucked out your eyes and given them to me.*

Where then is that sense of blessing you had? - The inferential particle *oun* ("then") looks back on the former days when the relations between Paul and his converts were joyous. At one time the Galatians had considered Paul's coming to them to be a great spiritual blessing. They felt a sense of joy as a result of his presence and the message he preached.[60] Now Paul wants to know what has happened to this earlier sense of religious joy which a saved person has. How completely different was their growing attitude toward the gospel now that they were listening to what the Judaizers were saying.

For I bear you witness - So great was their feeling of being blessed by the gospel that they would have made any sacrifice if it would help Paul. Paul is reminding them of their former attitude toward him.

That if possible, you would have plucked out your eyes and given them to me - We agree with Lenski's explanation here, that "the expression about digging out the eyes and

---

as this illness occurred during that first journey. The stoning at Lystra (Acts 14:19) cannot have resulted in some permanent bodily illness to which Paul makes allusion here in Galatians, for Paul was already in Galatia when that stoning occurred, whereas the "illness" was the cause of his coming to Galatia. See notes below on verse 15 for another guess concerning the nature of Paul's bodily illness.

[59] Lenski, *op. cit.*, p.220.

[60] "*Ho makarismos humōn* can be interpreted as an objective or subjective genitive. In the first instance, it means the happiness or blessedness Paul ascribed to the Galatians for the way in which they received him. In the second, it refers to the happiness or good fortune the Galatians ascribed to themselves that Paul fortuitously preached the gospel to them. Since Paul is speaking of the Galatians' former attitude toward him, the later choice seems preferable" (Matera, *op. cit.*, p.160).

giving them to another is surely proverbial for making a sacrifice of something that is really priceless."[61]   Nothing they had was considered too great a price to repay the messenger who had come to them.   To Paul, it was distressing that the joyful attitude they once had toward him was now in danger of being a thing of the past.

4:16 - *Have I therefore become your enemy by telling you the truth?*

Have I therefore become your enemy by telling you the truth? - In the Greek the verse begins with *hōste* ("so") which is left untranslated in the NASB.   *Hōste* at the beginning of an independent clause usually introduces an inference drawn from something just said.[62] "Telling you the truth" is evidently a reference to the gospel he preached to them.   If the Judaizers are right that works of the Law are required, then Paul really was an enemy to their souls when he misled them by preaching justification by faith.[63]   Is that what the Galatians are now willing to affirm?   Telling someone the truth is a very poor reason for assuming that person is hostile to the hearer.   We summarize verses 12b-16 in this way: 'You did me no wrong once – please do not wrong me now by defecting to the Judaizers. You received my message gladly then – please continue to do so now.'

4:17 - They eagerly seek you, not commendably, but they wish to shut you out, in order that you may seek them.

They eagerly seek you, not commendably - The unexpressed subject of this verse ("they") is the Judaizing teachers.   From their past relationships (verses 12b-16), Paul now turns to his present relationship with the Galatians and how it differs from that of the Judaizers who are wholly selfish in their motives.   Paul, in telling the truth to the Galatians, was the truest friend they ever had.   In contrast, their real enemies were the Judaizers.   To "eagerly seek" someone is to court their favor, or to take a personal interest in that person.   "Not

---

[61] Lenski, *op. cit.*, p.221. A similar idiom in our language is "you would give your right arm" for something.   Taking the language literally, some have concluded Paul's bodily illness had somehow affected his eyes or his eyesight (see Randall, *Exp.Grk.Test.*, 178-79).   We are slow to accept this idea, for a permanent handicap like ophthalmia would have precluded any synagogue leader ever giving Paul permission to address their assembly.

[62] Burton, Rendall, and Longenecker (*in loc.*) argue that verse 16 should not be read as a question but as a declaration, because *hōste* (translated "so that") is not used elsewhere in the New Testament to introduce a question.   In spite of this fact, the clause is treated as a question in KJV, ASV, NASB, Nestle, and UBS texts.

[63] This difficult passage has been given other interpretations also.   One suggestion is that something happened on Paul's last trip among the Galatians.   He told them the truth about something and this caused them to change their feelings toward him.   Or perhaps "telling you the truth" is not a reference to his original preaching, but rather is a reference to this very letter he is now writing in which he reaffirms what he originally preached.   "The participle 'telling the truth' is present tense.   An action which has been continuous to the present hour and is still going on" (Hendriksen, *op. cit.*, p.195).

commendably" means in not a good way. In the Judaizers' case it was by flattery and feigned friendship, not out of love for the Galatians. To court someone's favor is not bad, unless the motives behind the zeal are bad.

But they wish to shut you out - It does not say from whom the Galatians will be excluded or isolated if they heed the call of the Judaizers. Perhaps the Judaizers were trying to isolate the Galatians from Paul and his fellow preachers so that Paul and company would no longer have any influence over the Galatians. Perhaps the Judaizers were trying to isolate the Galatians from other Gentile Christians who did not observe the Pharisaic works of the Law (remember Peter's withdrawal, Galatians 2:12). Or perhaps Galatians 5:4 fills out the unexpressed idea; namely, to separate them from Christ.

In order that you may seek them - This is the clause that tells us the Judaizers' motives were not good. They were courting the Galatians out of selfish motives. 'They want you to court them and show them the deferential zeal of devoted followers.'[64] The Judaizers, like the Pharisees in Jesus' day, still loved the chief places in the synagogues, greetings in the market place, and to be called Rabbi.

4:18 - *But it is good always to be eagerly sought in a commendable manner, and not only when I am present with you.*

But - The meaning of this is, "Understand me; I do not speak against zeal or admiration. I have not a word to say in its disparagement. In itself, it is good; and their zeal would be good if it were in a good cause."[65] Paul urges the Galatians to consider carefully the motives of the troublemakers.

It is good always to be eagerly sought in a commendable manner - Paul does not want it thought that he was moved to write what he does because of jealousy that some of his converts had begun looking to other teachers, so he clarifies the principle involved. He himself had sought their favor, though not selfishly; he was happy when others courted him, as long as their motives, too, were right. For example, Titus told Paul of the Corinthians' zeal for him (2 Corinthians 7:7). Remember also that the Galatians had courted Paul's favor at the time they would have given their eyes for him.

---

[64] The position of "them" in the Greek shows that it is emphatic. They are not interested in you, Paul says, but only in themselves. It should be observed that there is a manuscript variation at this place. *Hina autous zēloute* ("in order that you will seek them" or earnestly court them) is well attested. However, D*, G, and *it* read *zēloute de ta kreitto charismata* ("but be zealous for, or earnestly court the better gifts"), a reading evidently influenced by 1 Corinthians 12:31.

[65] Barnes, *op. cit.*, p.367.

And not only when I am present with you - Paul wishes their attempts to court him were as intense now as they had been when he was with them. He had gone on to other mission fields and what had they done? They had begun to listen to men whose motives and intentions were dishonorable, and who wanted to isolate them. Does the fact that he is absent end their attempts to please him? How sad, if so.

4:19 - *My children, with whom I am again in labor until Christ is formed in you –*

My children - The grammar is broken here, and NASB shows this by putting a dash at the end of verse 19. The manuscripts vary between "my children" (*tekna mou*) and "my little children" (*teknia mou*), although either would be an expression of endearment and would heighten the tenderness of Paul's appeal to them. The Galatian Christians were Paul's "children" because he is the one who initially won them to Christ (cp. 1 Corinthians 4:15; 1 Thessalonians 2:7; Philemon 10). "Because Paul had brought the Galatians into the world as spiritual children, he had a greater claim upon them than the new teachers who had followed."[66] Grammatically, "my children" can be either vocative, a form that indicates direct address to the person named (as the translation NASB has chosen), or it can be indicative, so that it further identifies whom Paul is addressing when he uses the pronoun *humas* ("you"). If we opt for the indicative, the verses would read in this way: 'It is good to be eagerly sought ... not only when I am present with you, my children, with whom I am again in labor ....' The *de* ("but"), with which verse 20 begins, would mark the beginning of a new thought. This results in verses 19 and 20 being a part of the same sentence which began in verse 17.

With whom I am again in labor - "Labor" is the word for the labor pains a mother endures when a child is born. By this metaphor Paul is saying, 'My anxiety for you compares to the deepest sufferings which human nature endures.' "Again" says this is the second time he has experienced great pain waiting for them. The first time was when he was waiting for their conversion. Now he is feeling pain as he waits for them to return to an uninterrupted relationship with Christ.

Until Christ is formed in you – Continuing the metaphor drawn from a woman giving birth, Paul pictures Christians growing just as an embryo, by degrees, takes the shape and form of a person. Insomuch as they were Christian believers, Christ was already "in" them (Colossians 1:27). Christians continue to grow until their likeness to Christ becomes more and more defined and the Christian, at last, reaches the "stature of the fulness of Christ" (Ephesians 4:13 ASV).[67] See also 2 Corinthians 3:18, where believers in Christ are described as being changed into His likeness from one degree of glory to another through the operation of the Lord who is the Spirit. The word "formed" (*mōrphothē*) denotes the

---

[66] Johnson, *op. cit.*, p.122.

[67] This language does not mean Paul is giving the Galatians a new birth a second time, as though their spiritual life had ceased and they had to be conceived and brought forth again.

development and display of an outward appearance which properly represents the inner nature. The aorist tense of "formed" is important. The idea is that Paul wants Christ to be completely formed in them so that no Judaistic ceremonialism or works of the Law will ever affect them. Unlike the Judaizers who selfishly had come among the Galatians in order to build up their own personal following, Paul had come to help them. He would help them to know Christ and be built up in Christ.

4:20 - *but I could wish to be present with you now and to change my tone, for I am perplexed about you.*

But I could wish to be present with you now and to change my tone - "How I wish I could be with you now," is how we might say it. Were it not for something that unavoidably made it impossible, Paul would be there "now" *(arti)* rather than waiting for some future opportunity. We do not know for certain what it was which left Paul unable to visit Galatia again at this time. According to the date assigned to this epistle in the Introductory Studies, the problems in the church at Corinth were so serious that they demanded Paul deal with them, rather than personally returning to Galatia. Furthermore, there is the important offering for the poor at Jerusalem that is demanding Paul's attention, time, and energy. If Paul were present with them in Galatia, and could see their reaction to his words, he would know how to change the tone of his voice in order to appeal to them in the most convincing way possible. Or, perhaps, he is saying he would rather speak with them face to face rather than depend on written communication.[68]

For I am perplexed about you - "Perplexed" *(aporoumai)* is in the middle voice, and so denotes an inward distress of a mind tossed to and fro by conflicting doubts and fears. "If the apostle had been present, so as to see what effect his words were having, he would know what line to take. As it is, in writing to them, he is at a loss, and fears to make matters worse instead of better."[69]

F. The Allegorical Argument. 4:21-31

> *Summary*: Paul's sixth argument against the Judaizers is in the form of an allegory based on the life of Abraham and his relationships with Sarah and Hagar, and especially the status of their respective sons. In this allegory, Paul (1) lays out the historical facts, verses 21-23; (2) calls attention to the spiritual truths contained

---

[68] The verb *allassō* can mean either to "change" or "exchange," and thus Paul has been understood to be saying either that he wished to "change" his tone to a gentler or more persuasive one, or else to "exchange" his pen for the living voice by his actual presence.

[69] Sanday, *op. cit.*, p.71.

> in the historical facts, verses 24-27;   and (3) makes the practical application ("Expel the children of the slave woman!"), verses 28-31.

1. The Historical Facts.   4:21-23

4:21 - Tell me, you who want to be under law, do you not listen to the law?

Tell me - "Tell me" is an affectionate appeal to their reason, and it serves to introduce a new argument against the Judaizers.   Paul may be at a loss to know what tone of voice to use, but he can appeal to Scripture and let the Holy Spirit impress the message concerning what to do with the Judaizers.   He will call attention to a story recounted in the Biblical history that illustrates the truth he is trying to teach.

You who want to be under law - Perhaps "under law" (anarthrous *nomos*) in this verse is shorthand for "works of the Law" (i.e., a system of rules), a state which these Galatians would be in if they subscribed to what the false teachers were wanting them to do.   "Under law" also describes a slavery just as the similar expression in verse 9 did.   The participial phrase "you who want to be" indicates the Galatians have not yet entirely adopted the system of works of the Law.   Compare what was said at 1:6, 3:3, 4:9,10, 17, about how far the Galatians had gone in adopting the Judaizers' system.   They were just beginning to show an interest.   The wavering Galatian Christians were not yet "under law" but for some reason they were desiring to be.

Do you not listen to the law? - *Akouō* ("listen") means both to hear and to understand.[70] There are times when *nomos* ("law") refers to the Mosaic Law given at Mt. Sinai (Exodus 20 and following), and there are other times when "law" refers to the whole Old Testament collection of Scriptures (i.e., a descriptor applied equally to Genesis or the Psalms or the books of the prophets).[71]   Paul is about to relate the story of Hagar and Sarah recorded in Genesis 16.   Now Hagar and Sarah lived long before the Decalogue was given through Moses (Galatians 3:17), so it is obvious that "the law" here refers to the Pentateuch (or Torah).   The Law and the Prophets were read in Jewish synagogues every Sabbath (Acts

---

[70] "'To hear' in Jewish thinking is not just a physical activity. In Isaiah 1:10 and 6:9-10, 'seeing,' 'hearing,' 'understanding', and 'repenting' are used synonymously.   To a Jew, 'hearing' God's word meant to internalize it, understand it, and obey it" (Longenecker, *op. cit.*, p.207).

[71] In Romans 3:19, after a catena of quotations (3:10-18) drawn from the Psalms and Isaiah, Paul applies the quotations particularly to the Jews because "whatever the law (*ho nomos*) says, it speaks to those who are under the Law (*tois en tō nomō*)."   There are also time the Old Testament canon is referred to as "the Law, the Prophets, and the Psalms" (Luke 24:44), in which case the "Law" refers to the Pentateuch (i.e., just the first five books written by Moses).

15:21; 2 Corinthians 3:14,15).[72]   It seems that the early Christian congregations continued this practice at their Sunday assemblies, reading passages from the Old Testament Scriptures until the New Testament Scriptures gradually became available for such public reading.[73]   In this way Christians (most of whom could never afford their own personal copy of the Scriptures), even those from Gentile backgrounds, became familiar with the Old Testament Scriptures.

4:22 - *For it is written that Abraham had two sons, one by the bondwoman and one by the free woman.*

For it is written - With "for" Paul introduces the section of the Law which he wished to call to their attention.   One must read Genesis 16 through 21 to get all the details.   Earlier, when Paul took a passage from the Old Testament, he introduced it with the same expression (3:10,13).[74]   The words Paul writes are gathered out of the LXX in much the same way as the story of Melchizedek (Hebrews 7:1-4) is sketched in words drawn from the LXX.

That Abraham had two sons - Ishmael and Isaac are the two sons Paul has in mind.[75]

---

[72] The Books of Moses were constantly read in the synagogues; they were divided into *paraschas*, or regular lections.   The other Old Testament books were likewise divided into sections, their lections being called *haphtharas*.   Early in the history of synagogue meetings it was just the Law of Moses that was read.   Then about 175 BC Antiochus Epiphanes forced the Jews to stop reading the "Law" in the synagogue meetings.   Since Antiochus had said nothing about reading the Prophets, the Jews divided the Old Testament prophetic books into *haphtharas* and began to read them on the Sabbath.   Once Antiochus was dead, the Jews resumed the reading of the sections from the Law, and so thereafter both were read on the Sabbath.

[73] Here at Galatians 4:21 a few Manuscripts (D, F, G, 104, 1175) read *anaginōskete* (read out loud in the assembly) rather than *akouete* ("listen").   Colossians 4:16 alludes to the Christian practice of reading Scripture in the public assembly.   Justin Martyr tells us it was customary from Sunday to Sunday to read the memoirs of the apostles in the church assemblies (*Apol.* I.67).

[74] The words, "it is written" (*gegraptai*), usually introduce a quotation of an Old Testament verse; here they introduce a brief summary of several chapters of Old Testament history.   C.K. Barrett has argued that this departure from Paul's usual exegetical procedure is a hint that Paul is here responding to arguments the Judaizers have made as they were teaching the Galatians.   According to Barrett, what Paul is doing in this passage is asking his Galatian readers whether or not they really understood that Old Testament passage which had been read or quoted to them. (C.K. Barrett, "The Allegory of Abraham, Sarah, and Hagar in the Argument of Galatians" in *Rechtfertigung*, a festschrift in honor of E. Kasemann, ed. J. Friedrich, et al. [Tubingen: Morh-Siebeck, 1976], p.9.)   This commentator is not convinced that such a large theory can be constructed from the difference between a single verse and a summary of verses.   It is this commentator's judgment that Paul uses "it is written" here in a way similar to Romans 3:10 where the expression introduces a number of passages from the Old Testament.

[75] Abraham subsequently had six sons by Keturah after the death of Sarah (Genesis 25:1-6), but this fact lies outside the events which furnish Paul with the information he needs for his allegory.

One by the bondwoman – Ishmael was the son of Hagar. The Egyptian girl Hagar was a slave who served as Sarah's handmaid.[76] When it became obvious Sarah was going to have no children, Sarah suggested that Abraham father a child with Hagar so that he would not be wholly without posterity. "Perhaps the easiest way to grasp the historical account is to trace briefly Abraham's experiences as recorded in Genesis 12 through 21. We will use his age (75, 85, etc.) as a guide, and trace the events on which Paul is basing his argument for Christian liberty.

75 – Abraham is called by God to go to Canaan, and God promises him many descendants (Genesis 12:1-9). Both Abraham and his wife, Sarah, wanted children, but Sarah was barren. God was waiting until both of them were "as good as dead" before He would perform the miracle of sending them a son (Romans 4:16-25).

85 – The promised son has not yet arrived, and Sarah becomes impatient. She suggests that Abraham "go in to" Hagar, her maid, and try to have a son by her. This act may have been acceptable in that society (Genesis 30:3-13), but it was not in the will of God that the promised seed should come through Hagar. Abraham followed her suggestion and went in unto Hagar (Genesis 16:1-3).

86 – Hagar became pregnant and Sarah becomes jealous! Things are so difficult in the home that Sarah throws Hagar out. But the Lord intervenes, sends Hagar back, and promises to take care of her and her son. So, when Abraham was 86, Hagar's son was born, and he named him Ishmael (Genesis 16:4-16).

99 – Some years later, God speaks to Abraham and promises again that he will have a son by Sarah and says to call his name Isaac. Later, God appears again and reaffirms the promise to Sarah as well (see Genesis 17-18).

100 – The son is born to Abraham and Sarah (Genesis 21:1-7). They named him Isaac ("laughter") as commanded by God. But the arrival of Isaac creates a new problem in the home: Ishmael has a rival. For 14 years, Ishmael has been his father's only son, very dear to his heart. How will Ishmael respond to the presence of a rival?

103 – It was customary for ancient peoples to wean their children at about the age of three, and to make a great festal occasion of it. At the feast, Ishmael starts to mock

---

[76] The word (*paidiskē*) translated "bondwoman" in the NASB in classical Greek did denote a slave girl. The contrast in this verse between Hagar and Sarah, who is called a "free woman," shows that Hagar was not a free woman.

Isaac (Genesis 21:8-11), creating trouble in the home.   There is only one solution to the problem, and a costly one at that: Hagar and her son have to go.   With a broken heart, Abraham sends his son away, because this is what God tells him to do (Genesis 21:12-14).   Ishmael eventually had twelve sons (Genesis 25:13-18) who are the ancestors of the Arab tribes which occupied the desert in Syria between the Euphrates and the Egyptian frontier.

"On the surface, this story appears to be nothing more than a tale of a family problem, but beneath the surface are meanings that carry tremendous spiritual power.   Abraham, the two wives, and the two sons represent spiritual realities; and their relationships teach us important lessons."[77]

And one by the free woman – Isaac was the son of Sarah, whose birth is recounted in Genesis 21:1-7.   "The word 'freewoman' is never applied to Sarah in the story in Genesis; but it was obviously a true description, and with perfect fairness introduced in antithesis to Hagar."[78]   The main point of contrast is that one mother was a slave, the other a freewoman.   And because of this, one son was a slave, and the other free.   The mother and not the father determined the status of the sons.   The slave gives birth to a slave.

4:23 - *But the son by the bondwoman was born according to the flesh, and the son by the free woman though the promise.*

But the son by the bondwoman was born according to the flesh - Both boys were sons of Abraham, "but" there were marked differences between them.[79]   One of the differences was how each was born.   The birth of Ishmael ("the son by the bondwoman") was a normal birth just like other human babies are conceived and born.[80]   There was nothing supernatural about Ishmael's birth.   "Born" is a perfect tense verb.   The aorist tense would have been sufficient if Paul only wanted to record the historical fact of being born.   His use of the perfect tense causes us to stop and ask what point he was trying to get across.

---

[77] Wiersbe, *op. cit.*, p.100-102.

[78] Hendriksen, *op. cit.*, p.200.

[79] In the Greek text there is a word in brackets, the particle *men*.   The brackets indicate there is doubt as to whether or not it was a word written by Paul.   In an earlier footnote we alluded to Barrett's opinion that Paul is answering something the Judaizers in Galatia had taught.   If we were to assume the *ad hominem* presentation, if the particle *men* is read, it acknowledges that the Judaizers were right in emphasizing the differences between the births of the two sons, but they were wrong in the application they drew from the differences.

[80] *Gegennētai* ("born," NASB) can refer either to conception or to birth.

That which is born of flesh was and continues to be only of the flesh, seems to be the point Paul is making.[81]

And the son by the free woman through the promise - There was something supernatural about Isaac's birth: direct supernatural intervention resulted in a restoration of procreative powers in the bodies of both Abraham (Hebrews 11:12) and Sarah (until the time of this birth Sarah was sterile, Genesis 11:30; Romans 4:19).   Isaac's birth was as physical as was Ishmael's, but it had an added element that it was attended by a promise (Genesis 18:10) made by God concerning that birth.[82]   Furthermore, we would not be surprised if the word "promise" is intended as a deliberate reminder of the covenant made with Abraham (see Galatians 3:16-19).   The differences between the sons (slave and free) and the manner of conception (one natural, the other supernatural) lend themselves well to the very point Paul is making concerning a religion characterized by works of the Law (natural, man-made, and resulting in slavery) and one characterized by doing things as God says (producing freedom).

2.   The spiritual truths taught by this allegory.   4:24-27

4:24 – This is allegorically speaking: for these **women** *are two covenants, one* **proceeding** *from Mount Sinai bearing children who are to be slaves; she is Hagar.*

This is allegorically speaking - "This" (*hatina*, literally, which things[83]) includes all Paul has said in verses 22 and 23 concerning Abraham, Sarah, Hagar, and their two sons.   The 1960 edition of NASB translated the Greek *hatina estin allēgoroumena* by "This contains an allegory."   "Allegory" says there is more to the historical facts just narrated than first meets the eye.   "Used as an exegetical tool, allegory views the persons, places, and events within the narrative as pointing to, or corresponding to, another reality which has a deeper,

---

[81] Some commentators want to talk about an inherited sinful nature when they see the word "flesh" here.   Ishmael's birth is not merely the product of human physical action, but the product of sinful scheming (triggered by the old sinful nature), is the way comments are worded.   Believers in an inherited sinful nature from Adam keep looking for verses to prove that this Greek philosophical idea is acceptable Biblical doctrine, but such verses are not to be found!   Abraham and Sarah may have gotten impatient as they waited for God's promise, and may have taken matters into their own hands, but that is not in any way proof that their actions were the result of an old sinful nature at work.

[82] In commenting on the words "thru (*dia*) the promise," *Expositors Greek Testament* urges that in this case *dia* and the genitive describes the attendant circumstance under which the birth took place.

[83] *Hatina* is a neuter plural relative pronoun and means things of this nature or character.

religious meaning."[84]   While the allegorical method is normally not a legitimate method of Scripture interpretation, Paul (writing under inspiration of the Holy Spirit) tells us there is a legitimate allegorical interpretation of these Old Testament events.   It is the only stated allegory in all of Scripture; it is the only time the verb *allēgoreō* is used in the New Testament.[85]

It is proper to call this paragraph an allegory; however, we must be careful how we explain the term allegory.   Paul has sometimes been accused of resorting to a method of exegesis he learned when he was studying to be a Jewish rabbi.   What is implied in this accusation is that Paul's argument here is fallacious and worthless.   Hendriksen has well-said that those who accuse Paul of rabbinical exegesis at this place "do him an injustice, and are themselves guilty of misinterpretation, for they misinterpret the apostle."[86]   Origen and others used the word "allegory" in a bad sense; to them something allegorical was not

---

[84] Matera, *op. cit.*, p.169.   "The difference between a *parable* and an *allegory* is said to be, that a parable is a *supposed* history to illustrate some important truth, as the parable of the Good Samaritan ... an allegory is based on *real facts*" (Barnes, *op. cit.*, p.370).

[85] Though not specifically so identified, perhaps Romans 11:17-24; 1 Corinthians 5:6-8, 9:9-10 (about muzzling the ox), and 10:4, are other examples where allegory is used by Paul.   "Paul is not supporting the idea that there are hidden and unrelated 'spiritual' meanings to be found beneath the plain sense of every passage of Scripture (such as Philo did with the Old Testament, and Origen did with the New)" (Kent, *op. cit.*, p.131).

[86] Hendriksen, *op. cit.*, p.180.   Lenski (*op. cit.*, p.236) has a helpful explanation: "The rabbis were great allegorizers, namely, inventors along this line.   Rabbi Akiba found a mystical sense in every hook and crook of the Hebrew letters; but these were mere fancies.   Philo, the past master of allegory, called what he found the spiritual sense.   Wherever it suited him, he made free with the historical data.   One should know that only traces of Messianic ideas are retained by Philo, among them neither the person nor name of the Messiah.   The Alexandrines copied his method and carried it still farther.   We see at once that when Paul uses this verb, he has in mind something that is far different from the method of interpretation devised by those ancient Jews and any of their followers.   Their allegories dissipate the original sense of Scripture.   The simplest and the plainest things no longer mean what is said about them but something the allegorizer's fancy distills from them.   The ordinary reader is completely disconcerted; he finds that he cannot understand a thing in Scripture until the allegorizer offers him his distillation.   There is an air of mystery, of profound learning, of deep spirituality about such allegorizing; but the most of it is mere fancy which is often unwholesome.   The worst feature about it is the fact that solid Scripture facts are turned into curling vapor."
    The rabbis were fond of allegorizing Scripture, and using this procedure to extract all sorts of teachings from the ritual or historical passages.   Often the interpretations so devised were fanciful and utterly foreign to the meaning of the text under study.   Such interpretation was not actually derived from the text but imposed on it.   Barclay (*op. cit.*, p.44,45) helps us understand what they did.   "For the Jewish rabbis, any passage of Scripture had four meanings: i. *Peshat*, which is the simple or literal meaning;   ii. *Remaz*, which is the suggested meaning;   iii. *Derush*, which is the meaning evolved and deduced by investigation;   and iv. *Sod*, which is the allegorical meaning.   The first letters of these four words – P R D S – are the consonants of the word 'paradise' and when a man had succeeded in penetrating into these four different meanings, he had reached the joy of paradise.   Now it is to be noted that the summit and peak of all meanings was the allegorical one.   It therefore happened that the rabbis would take a simple bit of historical narrative from the Old Testament, and would read into it inner meanings, which often were fantastic, but which were very convincing to the people of their day."   Paul is not giving a fantastic allegorical interpretation to this passage, but one of sober truth and judgment.

necessarily history. Paul uses the word in a good sense. While the Genesis account is history, it also contains a spiritual lesson/truth.

For these *women* are two covenants - With "for" Paul begins to explain what the spiritual lesson is. The word covenant(s) is the same used in Galatians 3:15,17 and other places (Luke 22:20; 1 Corinthians 11:25; Hebrews 8-9). What "covenants" he has in mind, Paul goes on to explain. One was the covenant made with Abraham (Galatians 3:17) and the other was made at Mount Sinai. The latter one, made at Mount Sinai, was with the Jews.[87] The former one, which is made with the New Testament people of God, was ratified at Mount Calvary, where the covenant sacrifice died (Hebrews 9:16-20). It is called the "new covenant" (Jeremiah 31:31-34) and in 1 Corinthians 11:25 the new covenant is spoken of as being ratified by the blood represented in the cup of the Lord's Supper. This "new covenant" is none other than a renewal of the covenant made with Abraham (Galatians 3:15-17), that in his seed (Christ) all the nations would be blessed.[88]

One *proceeding* from Mount Sinai - Exodus 19-20 tell of the giving of the Law (the Mosaic covenant) at Mount Sinai.[89] By naming this place, Paul reminds us of the later date (Galatians 3:17) for this covenant as well as its temporal nature as compared with the covenant of promise made with Abraham (Galatians 3:15-4:11).

Bearing children who are to be slaves - Folk who were under the Law were in bondage and slavery (Galatians 4:3,7). The present tense participle "bearing" indicates that at the time Paul writes it is true that folk who are under the old covenant are still in bondage.

She is Hagar - That is, Hagar represents or symbolizes the covenant (the Law) given on Mt. Sinai.[90]

4:25 - *Now this Hagar is Mount Sinai in Arabia, and corresponds to the present Jerusalem, for she is in slavery with her children.*

---

[87] The Mosaic Law is called a covenant in Jeremiah 31:31-34 and Hebrews 8:9.

[88] One-covenant theologians (e.g., Hendriksen) struggle to defend their theology in light of the fact that Paul here says "two covenants." Romans 9:4 ("covenants," plural) also makes it difficult to be a one-covenant theologian.

[89] The exact location of Mount Sinai is still debated. "The earliest witness to the traditional identification of Mount Sinai with Jebel Musa [at the south end of the Sinai peninsula] comes from Egeira's *Peregrinatio* [AD 383/4]; she was assured of the identification by local monks" (Bruce, *op. cit.* p.220).

[90] The Greek word translated "she" is *hētis* (which) and here it means, "which being such in character as it is, is Hagar" (Hendriksen, *op. cit.*, p.202).

Now this Hagar is Mount Sinai in Arabia - The first part of verse 25 evidently is intended to be a justification of the identification of Hagar with Sinai, with the Law, and with slavery (verse 24). There is a manuscript variation at this place and the wording of this phrase in the NASB indicates the longer of the several variants has been chosen.[91] The phrase begins with a neuter article (*to*, "this") followed by the feminine name "Hagar." Such a construction indicates that Hagar is regarded as an object of thought or of speech. It is not "the woman Hagar" (*hē*, feminine), but "the thing Hagar" (the Hagar of the allegory, the Hagar under discussion). The Hagar of the allegory represents Mount Sinai where the Law was given, and Sinai is in Arabia, the land of Hagar and her descendants.

And corresponds to the present Jerusalem - The conjunction is *de*, and if we translate it "but" then this clause says that even though Sinai is in the land of Arabia, it corresponds to Jerusalem which is now. This is the only time the word *sustoicheō* ("corresponds to") is used in the New Testament. When used as a military term, it refers to soldiers of the same height, size, and skill being lined up together because they were all alike. When used in a philosophical sense, the word was applied to columns containing antithetical pairs. In the following chart, the vertical columns are *sustoichos* (answering to), and the horizontal pairs are *antistoichos* (contrasting, antithetical).

Hagar, the bondwoman	Sarah, the freewoman
Ishmael, the child after the flesh	Isaac, the child of promise
The old covenant *(Mosaic)*	The new covenant *(Christian)*
The earthly Jerusalem	The heavenly Jerusalem
Those enslaved under the Law *(Pharisaic Judaism)*	Those born free in Christ *(Christianity)*

---

[91] The longer reading (found in A, B, D, E, 37, 73, 80, lect.40, and UBS[3]) is preferable on intrinsic grounds as there would be little point in one of the shorter readings (which omits the name "Hagar") and so says "Sinai is a mountain in Arabia." Conceivably the point of this longer reading (if it is original) was to remind the readers that there is a connection between Hagar and Mt. Sinai since that is where Hagar found a home for herself and her children after she and Ishmael were sent away by Abraham (Genesis 16:7, 21:21, 25:18). This shorter reading is well-attested, being found in P[46], Aleph, C, F, G, 17, Old Lat., Vulg., Aeth., Arm., Goth. (omitting *gar*), Thebaic, Orig., Epiph., Cyril, Victorinus, Hilary, Augustine, Jerome. Another of the shorter readings is "For Hagar is a mountain in Arabia." Though Chrysostom has remarked that "Hagar is the word for Mt. Sinai in the language of that country," it has never been demonstrated that Arabs call Mt. Sinai by the name "Hagar." Matera (*op. cit.*, p.170) tells us the Arabic word for rock or cliff is *hajar*, not *hagar*. The Ishmaelites who eventually lived in the Sinai area were called "Hagrites" in Psalm 83:6 and 1 Chronicles 5:10,19.

Hagar, Sinai, the present Jerusalem – are all part of the same vertical column. They "correspond." It is not so much the literal city that is meant, but the whole contemporary system of Pharisaic Judaism which had its world-center in Jerusalem. We recall that the Judaizers who came to Galatia apparently came from Jerusalem.[92]

For she is in slavery with her children - This explains why Hagar and the "present Jerusalem" are in the same column. Jerusalem is, as it were, personified, and her children are the converts to the Pharisees' system of works of the Law. She and her children were slaves. Those under the Law of Moses were in bondage (Galatians 4:3,7). Those who tried works of the Law also were in bondage (Galatians 4:9). Paul knew by personal experience how the religious life of Pharisaic Judaism consisted of a servile obedience to works of the Law.

4:26 - *But the Jerusalem above is free; she is our mother.*

But the Jerusalem above is free - If the "present Jerusalem" stands for a community of religious people, then we suppose that "Jerusalem above" likewise stands for a community of people; namely, those living under the new covenant. It is the Jerusalem in which Christ reigns. Compare Hebrews 12:22, where "You have come to ... the heavenly Jerusalem," Mount Zion, the city of the living God.[93] "Above" likely is not to be taken literally, but figuratively as speaking of the heavenly origin, the spiritual nature of the church. "Free" says that for Christians there is no slavery or bondage as was true of the present Jerusalem.[94] There is a liberty in Christ, not the life of adherence to human precepts and prohibitions. See Galatians 5:1.

She is our mother - Here is evidence that the "Jerusalem above" is here and now. In "*our*

---

[92] When Paul spells the name of the city *Ierousalēm* (a fairly close transliteration of the Hebrew) as he does here in verses 25 and 26, it is likely because there is a special religious significance to the city. When he spells it *Hierosoluma* as he does at 1:17,18 and 2:1, he simply has reference to the geographical site. Romans 15:19 and 1 Corinthians 16:3 may be exceptions to this rule. (A. Harnack, *The Acts of the Apostles* [London: 1909], p.76, studies this matter in detail.)

[93] The reference is not to the "*New* Jerusalem" of Revelation 21:2. "New Jerusalem" (the city with the foundations, Hebrews 11:10) and "heavenly Jerusalem" do not seem to be the same thing. "Heavenly Jerusalem" is heaven as it is now (described in Revelation 4-8). "New Jerusalem" is heaven as it will be after our Lord's second coming. The epistle to the Hebrews views the heavenly Jerusalem from a different standpoint than does Revelation 21-22. Whereas Revelation depicts its buildings, streets, and rivers (as did Ezekiel), Hebrews describes the throng of angels, the assembly of the firstborn, the spirits of departed saints who are gathered there around the throne of God.

[94] Perhaps Paul's image here in Galatians is taken from the background of a purely Greek ideal of a city, the mother and home of freemen. Those free citizens maintained justice and order in perfect peace. So Jerusalem above is a place where Christians (free citizens) dwell in peace together, and are independent of all restraints of law because they themselves do the will of God from the heart.

mother"[95] Paul includes himself plus the Galatian Christians, whether they be former Jews or former Gentiles. Perhaps the thought of Psalm 86:5 (LXX) lies behind this expression, *Meter Sion, erei anthrōpos*: "A man shall say, 'Zion is my mother'." Remember how heavenly Jerusalem is also called "Mount Zion" in Hebrews 12:22. It is not so important who your father was ("Abraham is our father" the Jews one day said to Jesus, John 8:39); it is more important, allegorically speaking, who your mother was, for that determines your status, whether slave or free.

4:27 - *For it is written, "REJOICE, BARREN WOMAN WHO DOES NOT BEAR: BREAK FORTH AND SHOUT, YOU WHO ARE NOT IN LABOR: FOR MORE ARE THE CHILDREN OF THE DESOLATE THAN OF THE ONE WHO HAS A HUSBAND."*

For it is written - Using the Scripture found in Isaiah 54:1, Paul corroborates what he has just said about "the Jerusalem above" being "our mother." "The object of the apostle in introducing this Old Testament scripture seems to be to prove that the Gentiles as well as the Jews would partake of the privileges connected with the heavenly Jerusalem."[96] Isaiah 54 is a Messianic prophecy. In Isaiah 54:1 the prophet addresses Israel after the Messiah, the great servant of Jehovah, has died and risen again (Isaiah 53). The rejoicing of Isaiah 54 is based on Messiah's death and resurrection; hence, the fruitfulness mentioned must have reference to the host of believers who would be justified by faith in Christ.

"REJOICE, BARREN WOMAN WHO DOES NOT BEAR - In its original setting, Isaiah 54:1 was written when Jerusalem was desolate and in ruins, and predicted the day would come when the exiles in Babylon would return to the city. When the people return to the city, it shall become greater and more populous than ever it had been in its best days before, the prophet foretells. The prophet's imagery seems to have been taken from Sarah's case, she who could not bear children because she was sterile. Like Sarah rejoiced at the birth of Isaac, people returning to Jerusalem would rejoice.

BREAK FORTH AND SHOUT, YOU WHO ARE NOT IN LABOR - The Hebrew has "break into singing," so we understand the shout to be a cry of joy and exultation. "Labor" speaks of the labor pains that accompany the birth of children. The earlier verb "does not bear" and this verb "are not in labor" are both present tense describing a condition that last-

---

[95] Evidently Polycarp changed the original "our mother" to "the mother of us all" and this change then began to appear in manuscript copies until it came to be included in the Textus Receptus. "Our mother" is supported by P[46], Aleph*, B, C*, D, G, whereas "the mother of us all" is supported by Aleph[c], A, C[2], K, P, and Byzantine manuscripts in general.

[96] Barnes, *op. cit.*, p.373.

ed a long time.[97]

FOR MORE ARE THE CHILDREN OF THE DESOLATE THAN OF THE ONE WHO HAS THE HUSBAND" - The imagery is taken from Sarah ("the desolate") and Hagar (who had the husband), i.e., she temporarily cohabited with Sarah's husband. The application to the case at hand in this letter is easy to see. There would be far more people in the "Jerusalem above" (the church) than there were in the "present Jerusalem" (the Judaizers' system). There were to be more spiritual children for Sarah than there were slaves from Hagar. Jewish Christians and Gentile Christians take their place in God's family and before long they outnumber Jewish people like the Judaizers. "Likely, the Judaizers did not appreciate Paul's application of the text at this point."[98]

3. The practical application of the spiritual truths taught in the allegory. 4:28-31

4:28 – And you brethren, like Isaac, are children of promise.

And you, brethren - In the light of the passage just quoted from Isaiah 54, Paul begins the application of the allegory to the readers. "You"[99] is emphatic; it contrasts all the Christians in Galatia with the Judaizers (who are the children of the present Jerusalem). The address "brethren" is significant. All these children of the once barren Sarah are indeed brothers, one family in Christ.

Like Isaac - The Greek for "like" is *kata*, meaning in accord with Isaac, in the line of Isaac.

Are children of promise - Just like Isaac was a child of promise, so Christians are children of the promise, born according to the prediction made through Isaiah the prophet. There is also the promise made to Abraham concerning all the nations being blessed in his seed (Christ, Galatians 3:7-9,16). Paul now itemizes four results of being a child of promise: (1) There is persecution from the children born after the flesh, verse 29. (2) There is an obligation to cast out the handmaid and her son, verse 30a. (3) There is a priceless spiritu-

---

[97] The grammar here is unusual. It has the negative *ou* with a participle, whereas the usual Greek is to use the negative *mē* with a participle. For some reason the LXX regularly used *ou* when translating the Hebrew word for "not" (*lo*). Thus the unusual grammar is a Hebraism.

[98] Johnson, *op. cit.*, p.129.

[99] "And you brethren" (NASB) follows the preferred reading. *Humeis* ("you") is supported by P[46], B, D*, and is adopted by Nestle and UBS. The KJV, following Sinaiticus, A, C, D[2], reads "we." If Paul wrote "we," he means we Christians are children of promise like Isaac.

al inheritance for the son of the freewoman, verse 30b.   (4) There is an obligation, if we are born free, to live free, verse 31.

4:29 - *But as at that time he who was born according to the flesh persecuted him* **who was born** *according to the Spirit, so it is now also.*

But as at that time he who was born according to the flesh - As Paul makes further application of the allegory, he notes not only how Isaac and Ishmael were born, but cites the treatment that Isaac received from Ishmael (the one "who was born according to the flesh").

Persecuted him *who was born* **according to the Spirit** - Isaac was the one persecuted. "According to the Spirit" in this verse matches "of promise" in the previous verse and "through the promise" in verse 23, where the same contrast "according to the flesh" occurs. One gets the idea that the Holy Spirit was involved in making the promise concerning the birth of Isaac, and perhaps was also involved in ending Sarah's sterility.   In the word "persecuted" there is apparently a reference to what is recorded in Genesis 21:9.[100] According to Genesis 21:8-14, when Isaac was weaned, Ishmael "mocked" Isaac, not in mere playfulness, but in scorn of Isaac's being the heir.[101]   "Ishmael was 14 years older than Isaac (Genesis 16:16, 21:5), and at the weaning feast he may have been about 17.   His mocking was apparently much more serious than innocent teasing."[102]   Jewish traditions added that Ishmael took out the child Isaac and "shot at him with arrows under pretense of sport" (*Bereshith Rabb.* 53.15).   It was apparent playfulness, but with murderous intent.[103] "Ishmael may well have realized that Isaac's presence dashed any hopes he may have had of being Abraham's heir."[104]

So it is now also - Ishmael's persecution of Isaac centuries before had its counterpart in Paul's day.   The early chapters of Acts show the Jewish religious leaders persecuting the

---

[100] Actually the word "persecuted" is an imperfect tense in the Greek.   That would describe continuous action in the past.   It might describe a tendency or disposition of Ishmael.   It might describe actual continuous persecution.

[101] The Hebrew verb translated "mocked" is used of insult and disrespect in Genesis 39:14.

[102] Kent, *op. cit.*, p.135.

[103] Hendriksen (*op. cit.*, p.186) has pointed out that the same Hebrew verb (*sahaq*) was used to denote "jesting" which was the response of Lot's prospective sons-in-law to the prophecy of Sodom's doom (Genesis 19:14); it names the accusation against Joseph by Potiphar's wife (Genesis 39:14); the idolatrous and immoral behavior of the Israelites around the golden calf (Exodus 32:6); and the amusement of the Philistines with their prisoner Samson (Judges 16:25).   None of these instances was mere playfulness, says Kent, *ibid.*

[104] *Ibid.*

newly established church (Acts 4:1-2, 5:17-18,40, 6:9-14, 7:54-60, 8:1-3, 9:1-2,29). In Asia Minor, Paul's persecutors were at first Jews, afterward Judaizers (Acts 13:45-51, 14:19, 17:5-7,13, 18:12-17, 20:3, 21:7-36, 23:12-13, 24:1). 1 Thessalonians 2:14-16 and Revelation 2:9 also document persecution of Christians by the Jews. As Isaac was persecuted, so at the time Paul writes the church of God (who are also those born after the Spirit) is persecuted by the children after the flesh. The Judaizers were harassing those who did not observe their works of the Law.

4:30 - *But what does the Scripture say? "CAST OUT THE BONDWOMAN AND HER SON, FOR THE SON OF THE BONDWOMAN SHALL NOT BE AN HEIR WITH THE SON OF THE FREE WOMAN."*

But what does the Scripture say? - What lesson does the Old Testament teach concerning what should be done with the persecutors? What is the Scripture presently saying to us in this day (since "say" is present tense)? "The Scripture" likely points to a specific passage, rather than to Scripture in general. Paul completes his argument against the Judaizers by appealing to one more passage, the verse which contains the command to cast out Hagar and Ishmael. As he quotes the verse he is using language from the very narrative from which he made his allegory.

"CAST OUT THE BONDWOMAN AND HER SON - These words form the punchline of Paul's allegory. "In Genesis 21:10 the words are put into the mouth of Sarah, but they are afterwards endorsed by the divine command, Genesis 21:12."[105] Hence, this demand for expulsion was no mere jealous petulance, but it had the authority of God to support it, and Abraham complied with it. The aorist tense "cast out" is decisive. This command is not aimed at all Jews. Paul's attitude toward Jews in general is expressed in Romans 9:1-5, 11:13-32 and 14:1-15:13. This command is aimed at the Judaizers (i.e., the bondwoman) and their system of works of the Law (i.e., her son) which leads to slavery. Applied to the Judaizers in Galatia, the passage says they are to be repudiated.[106] Perhaps it also calls for the excommunication of any Christians in the Galatian churches who embrace the teaching of the Judaizers.

FOR THE SON OF THE BONDWOMAN SHALL NOT BE AN HEIR WITH THE SON OF THE FREE WOMAN" - This is the reason why the handmaid and her son are

---

[105] Sanday, *op. cit.*, p.75.

[106] Paul is not to be accused of being inconsistent as he writes Galatians and Romans. There is a difference between what the Christians in Galatia would be doing and what the Christians alluded to in Romans 14:1-15:13 were doing. The ones in Rome were impinging on Christian liberty – and were to be treated kindly. What the Judaizers in Galatia were doing led to bondage – what they were advocating was not something in the realm of liberty. They were to be cast out.

to be cast out: they are not co-heirs with Isaac.[107]   Paul knows that if the Galatians Christians defect over to the Judaizers, they will be trading their Isaac-heritage of freedom for an Ishmael-heritage of bondage.   They will trade the Promised Land for Arabia.   They will exchange the Jerusalem that is above for an earthly Jerusalem.   What a price to pay for becoming one with the Judaizers!   "This is a bold declaration of the incompatibility of Judaism with Christianity, and clinches Paul's argument against the practices which the Judaizers were trying to introduce."[108]   Paul's application of the allegory should teach the Galatians to recognize the incompatibility of man-made and God-made religion, and respond by casting out the man-made one.   Christians are to reject both man-made religions and those who teach them.

4:31 - *So then, brethren, we are not children of a bondwoman, but of the free woman.*

So then, brethren, we are not children of a bondwoman - Here is one more lesson the Galatians are to learn from Paul's allegory, namely, that Christians are freeborn.   The Greek text the NASB follows has *dio* ("so then"), which suggests that the inference Paul draws is self-evident.[109]   The use of "we" rather than "you" (verse 28) associates Paul and other Jewish believers with the Galatian Christians.   "No slave mother for us" is the conclusion at which the Galatians ought to arrive.[110]

But of the free woman - This is an emphatic assertion of the point on which the whole gist of the previous allegory consists – that the essential character of the Christian church is freedom.   Christians have a liberty in Christ, a thought that will be developed in chapter 5ff.   Observe the absence of the article before "bondmaid" ("a bondmaid") and the presence of the article before "free woman" ("the free woman").   "There may be many slaves, but one true wife, one freewoman.   So there are many ways along which men seek acceptance with God; there is but one of His appointment,   and by it alone men may draw

---

[107] The Greek ("The son of the bondwoman shall *in no way* inherit...") has a double negative, an emphatic way of saying no (not ever, never).

[108] Sanday, *ibid.* Paul is confidently repudiating Pharisaic Judaism at the very time Judaizers were influential enough to undermine his influence in many of the churches and endanger his life, too.

[109] There is considerable variation in the manuscripts at this place.   The reading finally accepted has a bearing on paragraph division.   This will be explained in detail in our comments on Galatians 5:1.

[110] "There is no article with 'slave woman,' and thus Paul has in mind not just the particular woman Hagar, but any slave woman of any kind.   It is the fact of 'slavishness' that is emphasized" (Kent, *op. cit.*, p.137).

near to him."[111]   The Jews historically interpreted the Genesis account of God's rejection of Ishmael to mean God had rejected the Gentiles.   Paul, however, uses this passage from Genesis as an allegory of God's rejection of any Jews who have the Ishmael mentality (i.e., doing things man's way).   It is only those who continue to do things the way God has revealed them who are the children of the free woman.

Paul has thus concluded six arguments by which he defended the gospel against the Judaizers.   His broadside against them included a personal argument, a Scriptural argument, a logical argument, an argument from absurdity, a sentimental argument, and an argument based on an allegorical interpretation of an Old Testament historical incident.

Several times, now, Paul has introduced the idea of the *freedom* of God's new covenant children.   What does it mean to be free?   Paul has plenty to say about that subject, and he does so in the last portion of this epistle.

---

[111] David Lipscomb and J.W. Shepherd, *Commentary on the Epistle to the Galatians* (Nashville, TN: Gospel Advocate Co., 1960), p.256.

III. PRACTICAL APPEAL TO THE GALATIANS. Galatians 5-6

> *Summary*: As is usual in his letters, after a doctrinal section Paul offers a practical section, giving some specific instructions how a person should live who believes the doctrines just presented. A preview of the emphases in this practical section include: (a) Since Christ has set you free, stay free and live like free men, 5:1-12; (b) Some safeguards to keep one's liberty from becoming an excuse for licentiousness, 5:13-6:10; and (c) A final loving appeal to heed what Paul has written to them, 6:11-18.

A. Since Christ Has Set You Free, Stay Free! Keep Living Like Free Men! 5:1-12

> *Summary*: "Keep standing firm in your liberty!" Why should they refuse to adopt the works of the Law? The Christian, if he is not careful, can become a slave again. The Christian would lose his wealth and become a debtor, obligated to keep the whole Law. The Christian would lose his direction and go the wrong way. Doctrinal indifference can have devastating consequences.

5:1 - *It was for freedom that Christ set us free: therefore keep standing firm and do not be subject again to a yoke of slavery.*

It was for freedom that Christ set us free - "Freedom" seems to pick up the idea in 4:22-31 where Christians are children of the free woman. Earlier, Paul also spoke of the freedom we have in Christ Jesus and equated it with "the truth of the gospel" (2:4-5). Freedom in Christ is one of the basic teachings of this letter (cf. 3:13,23-25, 5:13; see also John 8:36).[1] When Paul talks about freedom in this passage, he does not mean freedom from literal prison bars, or freedom that comes when an occupation army is driven from the land. It is freedom from slavery to sin. It is freedom from a multitude of rules for living, like the Judaizers were trying to impose on the Galatian converts. Lawson calls Galatians 5:1 "the theme of the entire letter. Christ has set us free."[2]

---

[1] *Tē eleutheria* ("for freedom") is in the dative case. We often use "to" or "for" to help translate the dative. Two other places Paul writes in a similar way about freedom. The Greek at Romans 8:21 is *eis tēn eleutherian*, "into the freedom." The Greek at Galatians 5:13 is *ep' eleutheria*, "to freedom." Westcott and Hort conjectured that *tē eleutheria* here at Galatians 5;1 is a "primitive error" or early scribal corruption for *ep' eleutheria*, and many have followed their influential lead. Some have proposed to treat this dative as a dative of purpose ("for freedom"), i.e., Christ set us free for the purpose of being free from the Law of Moses. A. Deissmann found an example where *tē eleutheria* was a formula used when slaves were freed to indicate the purpose or destiny for which they were set free (*Light From the Ancient East*, p.326-328).

[2] Lawson, *op. cit.*, p.85.

The NASB treats verse 1 as a paragraph all by itself.   There are variations in the text at this point.   Depending on which one is accepted in turn determines how the phrases are to be punctuated and interpreted, which in turn affects how the paragraphs are divided.[3] Treating 5:1 as a separate paragraph (as does the NASB) or as the beginning of a paragraph that extends to 5:12 will make little difference in the interpretation of the verses.

---

[3] The text (supported by Aleph*, A,B,P) translated by the NASB reads *tē eleutheria hēmas christos ēleutherōsen: stēkete oun ....*   There are, however, a number of variations in the textual evidence, with the data being, as Burton observes, "so complex as to make clear exposition of them difficult" (*Galatians*, p.270).   The chief variations have to do with (1) whether 4:31 has *ara* ("so then") or *dio* ("wherefore") as the connective, (2) the association of an article and/or a relative pronoun with *eleutheria*, "freedom" (i.e., whether *tē eleutheria*, or *tē eleutheria he*, or *he eleutheria*),   (3) the position of *hēmas*, "us" (i.e., whether *eleutheria hēmas Christos*, or *eleutheria Christos hēmas*, or *Christos eleutherosen hēmas*), and (4) the presence and position of *oun*, "therefore" (i.e., whether after *stēkete*, or after *eleutheria*, or omitted entirely). All of the variations apparently stem from the syntactical difficulty of *tē eleutheria* ("for freedom") as a limitation of *eleutherosen* ("set ... free") and the absence of any transitional phrase or particle in 5:1a to connect with 4:31.   (This summary of the matter has been adapted from Longenecker, *op. cit.*, p.220.)

Ignoring for the moment the variant readings for "the freedom", the possible translations (including differing punctuation options) of the variant texts include:

a. "So then (*ara*) brethren, we are not children of a bondwoman, but *children* of the free woman: stand fast then (*oun*) in the freedom with which Christ set us free; and do not again get entangled in a yoke of bondage."   (Textus Receptus, KJV)

b. "Wherefore (*dio*), brethren, we are not a bondwoman's children, but *children* of the free woman; in the freedom with which Christ set us free stand fast, therefore (*oun*), and ..."   (Lachmann, Tischendorf, Tregelles, WH text).

c. "Wherefore (*dio*), brethren, we are not a bondwoman's children, but *children* of the free woman. With freedom did Christ set us free; stand fast therefore (*oun*) and ..."   (Ellicott).

d. "Wherefore (*dio*), brethren, we are not a bondwoman's children, but *children* of the free woman by [i.e., by virtue of] the freedom (or, '*children* of her who is free with that freedom') with which Christ set us free; stand fast, therefore (*oun*), and ..."   (Lightfoot).

e. "So then (*dio*), brethren, we are not children of a bondwoman, but of the free woman. It was for freedom that Christ set us free: therefore (*oun*) keep standing firm and do not be ...."   (NA[21], NASB).

There were no punctuation marks in the original Greek manuscripts.   The punctuation marks in the above examples have been added by the translators.   The Greek texts for (c) and (d) are identical, save for punctuation.   The construction of the dative *eleutheria* ["freedom"] with *stēkete* ["stand fast"] in forms (a) and (c) is difficult to account for.   To find *oun* so late in the sentence (as in (b), (c), and (d)) is most unusual. Winer, *Grammar* §61, finds no example elsewhere of *oun* being later than the fourth word of a sentence.

A careful study of the above examples will show how one reading has 4:31 introducing the new paragraph that continues in 5:1ff.   Another reading treats 4:31 as the conclusion of the paragraph that began at 4:21, and this results in 5:1 being the beginning a new paragraph.   The KJV reading has 5:1 being the conclusion of the section begun in chapter 3, with a new section beginning at 5:2.   The NASB treats 5:1 as a separate paragraph, a sort of transitional note that summarizes 4:21-31 and also introduces 5:2-12.   Longenecker and Matera, using rhetorical criticism to determine the structure and outline of Galatians, treat 5:1-12 as the conclusion of the preceding section which began with chapter 3.   Actually, the debate has been extensive as to whether the section of exhortations and practical application begins at 4:12, 4:21, 4:31, 5:1, 5:7, or 5:13.   We have chosen to treat 5:1 as the beginning of the practical section.

Therefore keep standing firm - "Keep standing firm!" is a present imperative verb. Keep on standing firm! They must never waver in their determination to be free from the enslaving works of the Law such as the Judaizers were promoting and insisting upon. Earlier, Paul asked the readers why they wanted to turn back to slavery/bondage (4:9). Now he no longer asks. He commands them, 'Don't go back! Take a firm stand in the liberty which Christ has given you!'

And do not be subject again to a yoke of slavery - The present imperative with *mē*, "do not be subject,"[4] commands the cessation of an action that has already begun. The Galatians had begun their Judaizing but now were to stop submitting to such a yoke. "Yoke" has no article ("the") in the Greek: Paul wrote "a yoke", be that any kind of yoke of bondage – Mosaic, Pharisaic, pagan, or any other. The adverb "again" recalls the Jews before their conversion being under the weak and worthless elemental things (3:3,9), and the Gentiles before their conversion being slave to those which by nature were no gods (4:8). If they continue to follow what the Judaizers want them to do, the Galatians will shortly be under slavery to the elemental things. Peter used the same imagery at the Jerusalem Conference (Acts 15:10) when he spoke of the Pharisee's rules as being a "yoke which neither our fathers nor we have been able [i.e., had the strength enough] to bear." "How different is the 'yoke of Christ,' for it brings ease and rest, not bondage (Matthew 11:28-30)."[5]

5:2 - *Behold I, Paul, say to you that if you receive circumcision, Christ will be of no profit to you.*

Behold I, Paul, say to you – The NASB reads "behold;" the NIV reads "Mark my words!" This introductory particle (in the imperative mood) calls attention to what Paul is about to write. In verses 2-6, Paul draws out the consequences the Galatians will face if they submit to circumcision and thereby to the other works of the Law the Judaizers were propounding. There are several such consequences: (1) Christ will be of no benefit to them, verse 2. (2) They will be obligated to keep the *whole* Law, verse 3. (3) They will be severed from Christ, verse 4. (4) They will have fallen from grace, verse 4. (5) There will be no verdict of acquittal at the great judgment day, verse 5. Paul's appeal to his own name ("I, Paul") can have several implications. Perhaps it is a reminder of his apostolic authority. This is Paul speaking to you, the Paul who is an apostle through Christ (1:1), the Paul who received his gospel by revelation (1:12), the Paul who first brought the gospel to Galatia (4:13, 19). Perhaps it is a refutation of what others have falsely said about him.

---

[4] *Enechomai* can be translated "entangled" as it is in Herod. ii.121 of being caught and held fast in a man-trap.

[5] Kent, *op. cit.*, p.143.

It may be that the Judaizers have circulated reports that Paul sanctioned what they were teaching. "Well, that's not so! Here is my own account of what I teach. Don't harbor any doubts that this is my real view!" What follows is intended to make perfectly clear Paul's view of circumcision.

That if you receive circumcision - Verses 2 and 3 are our first explicit indication that the Judaizers in Galatia were demanding the Gentile Christians be circumcised. While observance of special days had already begun (4:10), the if-clause here implies the circumcision of the Gentiles was still pending. The passive verb "receive" seems to have the sense "allow oneself to be."[6] Of course, Paul was in no sense condemning those Jewish Christians who had always, as it were, been circumcised. His advice to such is given in 1 Corinthians 7:17-20. Nor is he saying that circumcision is no longer in the realm of liberty. He is not contradicting in verse 2 what he will write in verse 6. Instead, he is here saying, if you receive circumcision as the Judaizers are demanding it,[7] Christ will be of no benefit to you. Pharisaism did not save in the ages before the cross (since their rules voided any keeping of the Law of Moses), and Pharisaism will not save now that Christ has died. Pharisaism is not being faithful to God or Christ, and without faith, it is impossible to be saved.

Christ will be of no benefit to you - The future tense marks the certain result of their being circumcised and embracing works of the Law: Christ (you will find) will never profit you anything because for Him to profit you, you need to be living by faith (i.e., doing what God says). After all, men are justified by faith, not by works of the Law (Galatians 2:16). "We may compare [these verses in Galatians with] the awful passage referring to the consequences accruing to Jewish Christians from their relapsing into Judaism, in Hebrews 10:26-30."[8]

---

[6] BDF, 314.

[7] According to Jewish thinking, whether or not a potential convert to Judaism was circumcised made the difference between that person being a proselyte of the gate or a proselyte of righteousness. Without circumcision the proselyte of the gate was still considered to be an outsider. In contrast to Gentiles who received circumcision, the God-fearers (Acts 13:26) were only obligated to observe the code of Noah. (According to rabbinic interpretation of Genesis, these Noahic laws were: obey civil authorities, no idolatry, no profaning God's name, no fornication, no murder, no theft, no eating of meat with blood in it ["Noachide Laws," *Universal Jewish Encyclopedia* (New York: Universal Jewish Encyclopedia Inc., 1942), VIII, p.227,228]). But when a Gentile received circumcision and thereby became a proselyte of righteousness, he was obligated to keep other elements of the Law. It is in the light of this fact that some contemporary students of Pharisaic Judaism have called circumcision an "identity marker" distinguishing who was in the party and who was not. (The language "identity marker" is drawn from social science criticism.) Circumcision was the crucial test that determined whether or not one accepted the religion the Judaizers were promoting.

[8] Hendriksen, *op. cit.*, p.239. Hebrews 6:4-6 has sobering words along the same line.

5:3 - *And I testify again to every man who receives circumcision, that he is under obligation to keep the whole Law.*

And I testify again - "Testify" means to speak in the presence of a witness. Perhaps, as in Ephesians 4:17, Paul is thinking of the Lord Jesus being the witness to what he is about to say. "Again" says that Paul has presented this same testimony to the Galatians at some previous time. There are several possibilities as to the time when this was done. Paul could be alluding to what he wrote at 3:10, "cursed is everyone who does not abide by all things written in the book of the Law, to perform them." This testimony could have been given on a former occasion when he spoke the truth to them (4:16). This testimony could have been given when Paul came through Galatia after the Jerusalem Conference, delivering the decrees the Holy Spirit had prompted the apostles and elders to teach (Acts 15:28; 16:4,5). As he delivered those Holy Spirit-inspired decrees, Paul certainly told the Galatians how the decrees came to be written, and how the Judaistic demand for circumcision of Gentile converts to Christianity and a demand that those converts observe the Law of Moses had been rejected (Acts 15:5).[9]

To every man - Paul wrote "you" (plural) in verse 2; now he writes "every man" (singular). What Paul testifies as being true for the Galatians is true for every Christian no matter when or where he may be living. Each one who hears these words is to take it personally and individually.

Who receives circumcision - One might be circumcised involuntarily – as, of course, every male Jewish infant was. But for a Gentile Christian to accept circumcision by choice (the verb here is middle voice), as a matter of religious duty (accepting what the Judaizers were teaching about it), implied a further obligation.

That he is under obligation to keep the whole Law - This verse seems to imply that the Galatians who contemplated converting to Pharisaism did not intend to keep the whole Law, any more than the Judaizing teachers were keeping the whole Law (6:12,13). "The whole Law" is the Law of Moses. One cannot pick and choose like the Judaizers were doing and still be faithful to God.[10]

---

[9] Note how the dating of this letter, i.e., before or after the Jerusalem Conference, can influence how this verse is explained. If written before the Jerusalem Conference, one is almost forced to opt for Galatians 3:10 as being the previous time when Paul emphasized the connection of submitting to circumcision with the corollary requirement for keeping the whole Law.

[10] The "obligation" rests on these facts. The Pharisees got the idea of circumcision from the Law of Moses. In its symbolic significance, circumcision was an entrance into covenant relationship with God under the terms of the old covenant. That covenant embraces not just parts but the whole Law. So, if one is going to circumcise like the Law taught, one was obligated to keep the covenant like the Law itself taught. The same Law taught both.

5:4 - *You have been severed from Christ, you who are seeking to be justified by law; you have fallen from grace.*

You have been severed from Christ - The idea of the whole verse is this: in being circumcised for the purpose being proposed by the Judaizers, you would become guilty of complete apostasy because works of the Law and faithfulness are antithetical. There is no longer any justification for you, for you are not under the grace of Christ, but rest under the condemnation of the Law (Galatians 3:10,11).[11] We might think of the agent who severed them (passive voice, agent implied) from Christ as being the Judaizers who came among them and led them away. The preposition "from" (*apo*) says they have moved way away from Christ.

You who are seeking to be justified by law - We have regularly (e.g., 3:11,12) been treating "by law" (anarthrous *nomos*) as being shorthand for "works of the Law." "Who" (*hoitines*) pictures a class of people: whoever, everyone who. "Seeking to be justified" is an attempt to translate one Greek word, the present tense verb *dikaiousthe*. The NASB translators have treated it as a conative present, which would mean "trying to be justified," or "seeking to be justified." In Romans and Hebrews we have learned that a man is justified several times during his walk here on earth. Abraham was declared righteous at least four times in his life. Perhaps this present tense pictures the same idea of repeated times of being justified. The Pharisees knew justification was not a one-time thing in a man's life, so they were diligent at keeping their works of the Law, supposing this would put them in good standing with God each time He came to judge their case.

You have fallen from grace - The aorists ("severed," "fallen") represent the consequences as instantaneous; you are then and there severed; you are then and there fallen. The moment you are circumcised (thereby accepting the works-of-the-Law religious system) is the moment you fall from grace and are severed from Christ.[12] The Greek here reads "the grace" and likely refers to the same grace spoken of in Galatians 1:3,6. Faithfulness to the revelation *God* has given is the condition of benefiting from Christ, and of continuing

---

[11] It is difficult to translate the Greek word *katargeō* ("severed") in a way that simultaneously conserves the force of the verb, the tense (aorist passive), and the preposition ("from"). We had the same Greek word at 3:17 where it was translated "invalidate." In Romans 7:2,6 it is "released from." "Disconnected" or "severed" catch the idea. Works of Law and Christ have nothing to do with each other.

[12] Those who hold the doctrine of unconditional eternal security have difficulty harmonizing this passage with their doctrine. Wiersbe is typical: "to be 'fallen from grace' does not mean to lose salvation ... [rather, the tragedy is] they would rob themselves of all the good things Jesus Christ can do for them [in this life]" (*op. cit.*, p.119). Of course, Paul is speaking here of something potential. He does not actually say this has already happened. But this fall from grace certainly would be the result of their defection to the camp of the Judaizers. Also, they would be severed from Christ. Can that occur and a person not lose salvation? We think not.

in the blessings from God's grace.[13]   Without the help of God's grace, a man is surely lost. God's grace does not cooperate with man-made religions. God's grace is available only through the channel He Himself has made available, the great salvation made available through His Son.

5:5 - *For we through the Spirit, by faith, are waiting for the hope of righteousness.*

For we through the Spirit - "For" (*gar*) seems to show this verse is an explanation of (or a reason for) something just said.   Even though there is no "the" in the Greek, we believe the translators were correct to capitalize "Spirit."[14]   Perhaps it explains what Paul meant when he used the word "grace" in the previous verse.   The indwelling of the Spirit is one of the manifestations of God's grace in this life.   We Christians expect our salvation to be aided by the indwelling Spirit (Romans 8:4ff).   Already here in Galatians (3:2-5,14; 4:6), the presence of the Holy Spirit has been described as a distinguishing blessing enjoyed by believers in Christ.   In 5:18-25, Paul will unfold in greater detail how the Holy Spirit helps believers live in harmony with God's will.   The indwelling Holy Spirit is a pledge or first installment of greater glories to come (Ephesians 1:13,14).   "'We' includes Paul and the Galatian Christians.   He has not written off any of his readers as yet."[15]

By faith - This letter has already introduced the idea of justification by faith (2:16, 3:6), or, as 3:11 is translated, "righteousness ... by faith."   "Faith" equals faithfulness to Jesus Christ.   "Faith" is habitually doing what God says (see notes at 3:11,12).[16]   That is the condition on which God grants continuing justification.   The point of these two words is that Christians are justified by faith, not by works of the Law.   There is a contrast between followers of Christ and followers of the Judaizers.   This verse is the last full statement of the principle of justification by faith in this epistle.

---

[13] In his *New Testament Epistles: Romans* (Moberly, MO: Scripture Exposition Books, 1987), p.52ff, this commentator has included a special study on Grace. It includes information about grace in Roman Catholic theology, in Lutheran theology, in Reformed theology, in 20th century religious liberalism and neo-orthodoxy, and, finally, in Biblical theology.

[14] *Pneuma* can be rendered either *spirit* (6:1,18) or *Spirit* (i.e., the Holy Spirit, 3:2). Some are of the opinion that here, as at Galatians 3:3, there is no reference to the Holy Spirit – among them, Lenski.   But if rendered *spirit*, the idea produced by this verse – i.e., that Christians rely on the inward, spiritual things, whereas the Judaizers rely on the outward, fleshly things – seems a bit forced.

[15] Kent, *op. cit.*, p.145.

[16] In Old Testament times, once the Law had been given at Mt. Sinai, faith (for a Jew) was doing what the Law of Moses required.   In Patriarchal times, faith (think of Abraham) was doing what God told him to do.   On this side of Calvary, the teachings of Jesus and the gospel which the apostles preached outline God's requirements for this church age.   On this side of Calvary, faith is practicing what God has said through Jesus and the apostles.

Are waiting for the hope of righteousness - "Waiting" (*apekdechomai*) denotes eager expectation. Such an expectation would vividly contrast with a "certain terrifying expectation of judgment" (Hebrews 10:27) that is the lot of those who abandon Christ. Does Paul mean righteousness is the thing hoped for, or does he mean the hoped-for reality (the object hoped for[17]) results from righteousness? "Righteousness," of course, is the divine verdict of acquittal when God the Judge passes sentence on us. "Righteousness" (*dikaiosunē*) and "justification" come from the same root word. To be sure, one verdict of acquittal by God had already been pronounced when the Galatians became Christians (cp. Habakkuk 2:4; Romans 5:1 and 8:1). How then can such a man still be waiting and hoping for righteousness? As the days pass, God continues to justify men in whom He finds faithfulness to His will. Finally, at the judgment, the day will have come when the final favorable verdict will be handed down (Philippians 3:9, 2 Peter 3:14; also see Matthew 7:21-23, 25:31-40; 1 Peter 1:9; 2 Peter 1:9,10; Revelation 2:17).[18] Paul has now given the last of the negative results of following a man-made religion like the one the Judaizers were teaching. There will be no verdict of acquittal at the great judgment day, no heavenly home.

5:6 - *For in Christ Jesus neither circumcision nor uncircumcision means anything, but faith working through love.*

For in Christ Jesus - This verse is a further explanation of the emphatic "by faith" of the previous verse. Barnes suggests that "in Christ Jesus" means "in the religion which Christ came to establish."[19] It might also speak of being in union with Christ (versus being severed from Him, 5:4). John 15:1-4 quickly comes to mind, where Jesus spoke of abiding in the vine.

Neither circumcision nor uncircumcision means anything - The claims of the Judaizers notwithstanding, in this new covenant era it makes no difference in God's sight whether a man is circumcised or uncircumcised. God has handed down no rules concerning this rite for this new dispensation, so a man can be faithful to Him whether he is circumcised or not.[20]

---

[17] Romans 8:24; Colossians 1:5; Titus 2:13 all use "hope" in the sense of the object hoped for.

[18] Contemporary theologians are debating what they call initial justification and future justification. Some speak of private justification (the verdict for the time present is only in God's mind) and public justification (when the Judge publicly pronounces His verdict to us with the whole universe looking on). See the special study on "Justification by Faith" at the close of chapter 2.

[19] Barnes, *op. cit.*, p.378. See notes at Galatians 3:28 where we had this expression before.

[20] "The statement that for Christians neither circumcision nor uncircumcision has any religious validity appears in two other places in Paul's writings – Galatians 6:15 and 1 Corinthians 7:19" (Bruce, *op. cit.*, p.232).

But faith working through love - This passage has been a famous battleground for Catholic versus Protestant theologians. "Love" (*agapē*) can be either love for God or love for man. The participle *energoumenē* can be taken as a middle voice ("working") or as a passive voice ("made effective"). Catholic scholars have tended to treat the participle as passive, and have thought Paul had love for one's neighbor in view (see 5:14 and 6:10).[21] Protestant theologians have tended to treat the participle as middle voice (see the NIV, "faith expressing itself through love"). This allows them to continue to teach justification by faith only. "After one is justified by faith, he is then expected to behave as love would lead him to behave," is how they would teach the passage. By this means of explanation, faith is related to love as cause and effect: the faith that saves is not an obedient faith, but the obedience follows the faith. We will speak concerning this matter in a moment. Or some have tried to explain the passive as meaning that love comes first, with faith stemming from it. Opponents of this explanation have written at length showing this is not possible since faith comes by hearing (Romans 10:17).[22] With all this acrimonious debate leaving us to wonder what Paul intended when he wrote this clause, perhaps Scripture elsewhere can guide us to a proper understanding.

In two other passages (Galatians 6:15 and 1 Corinthians 7:19) Paul makes a statement very similar to what we read here in Galatians 5:6. Galatian 6:15 reads, "For neither is circumcision anything, nor uncircumcision, but *a new creation*." 1 Corinthians 7:19 reads "Circumcision is nothing, and uncircumcision is nothing, but *what matters is the keeping of the commandments of God*." The wording of what really matters in God's sight for our spiritual well-being varies in these three passages, but the underlying idea does not. "Faith working through love," becoming "a new creation," and "keeping the commands of God" are three ways of saying the same thing. It is a faith that expresses itself through loving

---

[21] The fact that the Roman Church has built a doctrine on this verse has caused many Protestant commentators to give a false definition to "faith" in order to oppose Rome. James I. Packer ("Faith" in *Baker Dictionary of Theology* [Grand Rapids: Baker, 1960], p.210) explains the Roman doctrine as formulated by the scholastics. The Roman church has insisted that this is a passive participle and has distinguished between two kinds of faith. He tells us there is "*fides informata* (unformed faith, bare orthodoxy) and *fides caritate formata* (faith 'formed' into a working principle by the supernatural addition to it of the distinct grace of love). Both sorts of faith, Catholic doctrine held, are meritorious works, though the quality of merit attaching to the first is merely congruent (rendering divine reward fit, though not obligatory), and only the second gains *condign* merit (making divine reward due as a matter of justice). Rome still formally identifies faith with credence (i.e., mental assent), and has distinguished between 'explicit' faith (*belief* which knows its object) and 'implicit' faith (uncomprehending assent to whatever it may be that the church holds). Only the latter (which is evidently no more than a vote of confidence in the teaching of the church, and may be consistent with complete ignorance of Christianity) is held to be required of laymen for salvation." "Rome still hurls its anathema against the Protestant teaching that faith consists of knowledge, assent, and *fiducia* (confidence or trust). Rome cancels the first and third factors, especially the third. It leaves only assent; namely, blanket assent to whatever Rome teaches. Such assent is indeed *informata* and needs something to make it *formata*, to give it form and substance" (Lenski, *op. cit.*, p.261). How Rome gets "the supernatural addition to it of the distinct grace of love" out of verse 6 is difficult to imagine.

[22] See Boice, *op. cit.*, p.491, and Hendriksen, *op. cit.*, p.242. Hendriksen writes passionately that the participle cannot be passive, the idea that love is the "*genesis* of faith" being "preposterous." In the light of Packer's explanation (see the earlier footnote), in this commentator's judgment, it is a mistake to explain Catholic doctrine as teaching love produces faith.

acts. James also affirms that faith alone is not enough (James 2:24); the faith that justifies is a faith that shows itself in actions like lovingly meeting a brother or sister's needs (James 2:14-17).[23] "The thing that really is important in God's sight is a faith that demonstrates its existence by love to God and benevolence to man."[24] In this Galatians context, where the Judaizers treated uncircumcised Gentile Christians as inferior and refused table fellowship (Galatians 2:12), this instruction about "love" might just pointedly have love for the brother particularly in view.[25]

5:7 - *You were running well; who hindered you from obeying the truth?*

You were running well - Beginning at this point and continuing through verse 12, Paul wrote a number of rather short, disconnected sentences. Some speak to his readers; some deal with his own personal position; some are directed against the Judaizers; and at the end is an expression of sharp sarcasm. "Running well," as in chapter 2:2, is a metaphor taken from foot-racing in which the Christian life is represented as a race. Christians are like runners striving to reach the finish line, and the imperfect tense "you were running" pictures the Galatians, under Paul's teaching, as having started the race well and making fine progress. When Paul last visited them their progress in Christianity was encouraging. But recently something had happened to interfere with their progress toward the finish line.

Who hindered you from obeying the truth? - As he did in Galatians 3:1 and 4:9, Paul again asks who is causing the Galatians to falter. The picture is not that of making the runners stop, but rather of throwing them off their course.[26] Runners were assigned lanes in the races. If, for some reason, a runner got out of the assigned lane he was automati-

---

[23] Protestant commentators have tended to treat the participle as middle voice, "faith working through love." This allows them to teach that "faith" is composed of knowledge, assent and trust (the faith-only definition of faith). Faith-only writers regularly contradict at this place what they wrote earlier when commenting on justification by faith, not works (Galatians 2:16). Typical is this comment: "Faith is no mere intellectual conviction ... it must issue in a genuine and self-denying love for others" (Boice, *op. cit.*, p.489). One would think that this verse (Galatians 5:6) would help faith-only commentators to see that something is badly wrong with their definition (given earlier in comments on Galatians) of the faith that saves. This faith-only definition is not quite in line with Galatians 3:2 where we learned that the hearing (obedience) of faith is the condition of justification and receiving the Spirit.

[24] Barnes, *op. cit.*, p.378.

[25] In other words, the *dogma* Rome has built on this verse is wrong. Their initial *interpretation* of it may be right.

[26] Hendriksen (*op. cit.*, p.243) tells us that the reading of the Textus Receptus (*anekopse*) would mean, as in the margin of the English Bible, "Who has driven (or beaten, struck) you back." But the reading of the present day text (*enekopse*) comes from a verb that means "to hamper, shackle, impede."

cally disqualified.   Someone has cut in front of the Galatian runners, or bumped them, so they are in danger of being thrown off course.[27]   This is what the Judaizers were doing to the Galatian Christians.   The tenses are important here, an aorist in the main verb "hindered" and a present infinitive "obeying."   The truth is something that must be habitually obeyed.   In a letter that has spoken of being justified "by faith," this language ("*obeying* the truth") is instructive.[28]   The "truth" Paul refers to is "the truth of the gospel" (2:5,14), the special revelation (1:12) which Paul had spoken to the Galatians (4:16).   If Paul has in mind a specific "truth" found in the gospel, it might be either (1) the truth of salvation; namely, justification by faith, not by works of the Law, or (2) the truth of Christian living.   Paul's question "who" does not so much expect the Galatians to name the false teacher as it asks them to think about his character (see 6:12,13).[29]

5:8 - *This persuasion* **did** *not* **come** *from Him who calls you.*

This persuasion - "This persuasion" refers to the arguments used by the Judaizers intended to persuade the Galatians to begin observing the works of the Law (Pharisaic *halakhic* rules).   Greek language scholars have not been able to determine the exact force of the word, whether it speaks of the act of persuading or the disposition one would hold who has already been persuaded.   The NEB chooses the former, "Whatever persuasion he used, it did not come from God who is calling you."   This appears to this commentator as being the proper way to understand the word; it is a reference to the persuading activity of the Judaizers, rather than the obedience on the part of the Galatians.   Recall that Galatians 1:7 says the Judaizers were perverting the gospel of Christ.

Did not **come from Him who calls you** - "Him who calls you" plainly means God (cp. Galatians 1:6 and 1 Thessalonians 2:12, 5:24).   "Calls" is present tense; He is calling them even now through the gospel Paul preached.   "Day by day His sweet voice soundeth, saying, 'Christian, follow Me!'" (Mrs. Cecil F. Alexander).   Paul categorically says the Judaizers are not God's agents or messengers.   Their message was altogether different (Galatians 1:6) from the gospel preached by the apostles of Christ.   Paul's message was

---

[27] Remember the Olympic games in which Mary Slaney was tripped?   Remember the look on her face as she watched the other runners speed away from her as she lay spiked in the cinders of the track?

[28] "Obeying the truth" (verse 7) and "faith" (verse 6) are interchangeable ideas.   Faith is doing what God says.

[29] MacArthur (*op. cit.*, p.99-100) finds five things said about the Judaizers (false teachers) in verses 7-12:   (1) They hinder obedience to the truth, verse 7.   (2) Their doctrine has not come from God, verse 8.   (3) Their doctrine tends to contaminate the whole church, verse 9.   (4) They will be judged by God, verse 10.   (5) They disturb and trouble the church, verses 7,11.

accompanied by gifts of the Spirit; the Judaizers' message had an anathema on it. Since their message did not come from God, at best it came from the world. There is also the likelihood it came from Satan, whose messengers the false teachers were (2 Corinthians 11:14,15), and whose message led men into bondage to elemental things (Galatians 4:3,9).

5:9 - *A little leaven leavens the whole lump* of dough.

A little leaven leavens the whole lump *of dough* - In ancient times, housewives kept a small batch of dough from a previous baking, allowed it to ferment, and then kneaded it with the flour as they prepared a batch of dough for their next bread-making. The fermented dough (leaven) would result in the new dough rising, thus making leavened bread. Just a little lump would leaven the whole next batch. In the Bible, leaven is sometimes a symbol of good (Matthew 13:33; Luke 13:20,21) and sometimes a symbol of evil (Matthew 16:11; 1 Corinthians 5:6; and here). Using what seems to have been a 1st century proverb, Paul warns the Galatians that the doctrine of the Judaizers was an evil thing. Jesus warned His disciples to "beware of the leaven of the Pharisees" (Matthew 16:6). Does Paul perhaps have Jesus' warning in mind when he warns the Galatians about the Judaizers/Pharisees? Wrong obedience had only begun in Galatia. At present the doctrinal deviation in Galatia was small ("little"). The Galatians had begun to observe times (4:10). Before long the Judaizers would be making more demands, which, if not checked, would corrupt all the churches' beliefs and practices.[30]

5:10 - *I have confidence in you in the Lord, that you will adopt no other view; but the one who is disturbing you shall bear his judgment, whoever he is.*

I have confidence in you in the Lord - "I" is emphatic, implying a contrast, but we do not know with whom Paul contrasts himself. Huxtable proposed that "The pronoun 'I' prefixed to the verb, perhaps, distinguishes the writer from some about him, particularly those who just before had brought that unfavorable report of the state of affairs in Galatia which had prompted the writing of this letter."[31] Paul's confidence concerning the Galatians' ultimate behavior[32] rested ultimately "in the Lord." Jesus would so help His own, to keep and protect them, that they could successfully oppose and refuse to adopt the false teaching and practices of the Judaizers.

---

[30] "Paul's homely warning should be heard by us. This proverb should still be death to doctrinal indifference" (Lenski, *op. cit.*, p.267). Even little deviations in doctrine should not be thought of as innocent or as producing no harm. It only takes a little leaven to leaven the whole lump.

[31] Huxtable, *op. cit.*, p.245.

[32] "This expression of confidence implies, of course, a measure of underlying apprehension; it also in effect is an admonition, couched in an affectionate form, designed to rally them back to their true allegiance." Hendriksen, *op. cit.*, p.245.

That you will adopt no other view - Each Christian is thus charged with the responsibility to watch for the *beginnings* of doctrinal error in his own heart and mind. By "adopt no other view" (literally, think no other thing), Paul probably means no other view than what they have been taught by him. He is confident the Galatians will see that a little Judaistic leaven can infect the fellowship and eventually grow into a congregation-shattering problem.

But the one who is disturbing you shall bear his judgment - While Paul is confident the Galatian Christians will return to a right mind, he holds out no such hope for the Judaizers who have been troubling the churches.[33]   What the future holds for them is a condemnatory verdict (*anathema*) at the final judgment (1:8,9).[34]   The guilty, Paul threatens, shall bear his own guilt. A man who creates chaos and confusion in the church is going to receive punishment from God.

Whoever he is - The meaning of this phrase depends on what we did with the words "the one who is disturbing you" in the previous clause. If "one" is generic, then all are going to be condemned. If "one" is a particular ringleader of the Judaizers, there is nothing he can plead that will shield him from being punished by God. Paul is challenging the Galatians. If the troublemakers are going to be punished by God, will the Galatians continue to listen to them? Will they not share the same punishment if they do?

Verses 8-10 might be summarized as giving the *origin* (it is not from God), the *results* (it spreads, it is permeating, insidious, and therefore dangerous), and the *end* (condemnation in the final judgment) of the Judaizing doctrine.

---

[33] When speaking of the troublemakers in Galatia, twice (1:7, 5:12) Paul spoke of them in the plural. Here he uses the singular ("the one who"). Either the singular means anyone who might be described as a disturber or troubler, or it points to one particular ringleader of all the troublemakers.

F.C. Baur of the Tubingen School identified the unnamed "one who is disturbing you" as being Peter. This became the basis of his theory about an alleged conflict between Paul and Peter that permeated the early church and all our New Testament writings. Baur proposed that some New Testament writings are rather "Gentile" in character (reflecting Paul); some are rather "Jewish" in character (reflecting Peter); and some are half-way between (peacemakers). It has been satisfactorily shown, a number of times, that any attempt to interpret the New Testament along such Hegelian lines – Peter vs. Paul, and "peacemakers" – is doomed to failure for lack of evidence.

[34] In this commentator's view, "judgment" is the final judgment rather than, for instance, church discipline (could the church discipline outsiders such as the Judaizers were?), and rather than apostolic judgment (instances of which are seen in Acts 13:11 and 1 Timothy 1:20). However, a case could be made for apostolic judgment by appealing to 2 Corinthians 13:2,3,10.

5:11 - *But I, brethren, if I still preach circumcision, why am I still persecuted? Then the stumbling block of the cross has been abolished.*

But I, brethren - It is not clear why Paul so abruptly switches subjects. The personal pronoun "I" again is emphasized. This suggests someone (in contrast to what Paul actually does preach) has made the allegation among the Galatian churches that Paul himself preached circumcision. That someone is likely the "one" (verse 10) who was disturbing the churches with Judaizing doctrine.

If I still preach circumcision - It is here implied that Paul has been accused of preaching circumcision just like the Judaizers did.[35] On what the Judaizers founded their assertion is not known. It may have arisen from the fact that Paul had circumcised Timothy (Acts 16:3), who, it will be remembered, was a Galatian. Acts 16 is part of the second missionary journey, which occurred 6 years before the writing of Galatians. Or the Judaizers may have inferred that Paul, since he in general complied with the customs of the Jews when he was with them (1 Corinthians 9:20), preached circumcision in practice if not in actual sermons.[36] Paul answers the false charges with two arguments: (1) If he is preaching circumcision, why is he still being persecuted? (2) Why, if he is preaching circumcision, do Jews still look at the cross as a stumbling-block (scandal)? Paul's on-going persecution by Jews and their view of his preaching about the cross are both evidences he does not preach circumcision like the Judaizers have claimed. When had Paul ever preached circumcision? Not, we may be sure, since Jesus called him to be an apostle.

Why am I still persecuted? - That is, persecuted by the Jews. 'If I am preaching the same message and urging the same practices the Judaizers teach, why are the Jews opposing me?' In comments on 3:29, we noted that before the writing of Galatians Paul had been harassed and persecuted continually by unbelieving Jews. 2 Corinthians 11:26 speaks of continuing dangers from his own people, from Gentiles, and from false brethren (read Judaizers, as they were identified in Galatians 2:4). Would the Judaizers not have ceased their opposition to Paul if he were one of them?

Then the stumbling block of the cross has been abolished - Depending on how the Greek

---

[35] "Preaching circumcision" is a succinct summary of the Judaizers' message, just as "preaching Christ" was a grand summary of Paul's gospel message.

[36] It might, at first sight, seem that Paul was inconsistent when he had Timothy circumcised but refused to do it in Titus' case at the Jerusalem Conference. If the Judaizers pointed to Timothy as proof Paul taught circumcision, what they failed to understand was that while Paul saw it as perfectly legitimate for Jewish Christians to express their faith in Jesus through the traditional Jewish practices, he strenuously opposed the imposition of those practices on Gentile Christians as the normative way of life on which fellowship and close association depended.

word is accented, *ara* ("then") can be either inferential or interrogative.[37]   Treating it as an interrogative is more appropriate to this context.   To answer the accusation that he preached circumcision, Paul asks, "Has the stumbling block of the cross been taken away?" "Stumbling block" translates *skandalon*, the word for the trigger stick on an animal trap, which, if touched, results in the animal being caught; this in turn, of course, eventually proves fatal to the animal.   As Paul preached it, there was something about the cross that made it fatal to the Jewish religion (Colossians 2:14),[38] and thus it was a stumbling block. The cross was an offense because it brought an end to the entire Mosaic system.   Recall how the Jews charged Stephen with saying that "this Nazarene, Jesus, will ... alter the customs which Moses handed down to us" (Acts 6:14).   All those exclusive rules and feelings the Jews embraced were shown to be false!   This was hard for the Jews to accept. To the Judaizers, the scandal of the cross was this: if Calvary is true, then their whole man-made system was not.   The fact that the Jews still did not accept Paul's preaching was evidence that he did not preach circumcision.   The "stumbling block of the cross" had not been abolished from his preaching, and therefore the allegation that he preached circumcision was totally without merit.

5:12 - *Would that those who trouble you would even mutilate themselves.*

Would that - The word in Greek is the adverb *ophelon*.   Coupled with a future tense verb, as it is here, it expresses an unattainable wish.

Those who are troubling you - "Troubling" (*anastatountes*) is a different word from the one used of the Judaizers in verse 10.   *Anastatountes* is used at Acts 21:38 of causing a revolt.   It means to "uproot and overthrow," or "to cast out of country and home."[39]   The word picture is quite expressive: the Judaizers are pictured as compelling the Galatian Christians to abandon their proper country and liberty and heavenly kindred; the Galatians were being cast out of the "heavenly Jerusalem," and were being led to seek life in a strange and alien country.

Would even mutilate themselves - The verb here (*apokopsontai*, the future middle of *apo-*

---

[37] Greek in Paul's time had no accent marks.   Accent marks were invented by men to help put down on paper what speakers of Greek did with tone of voice.   With an acute accent *ara* is inferential. Inferential *ara* has been used elsewhere in Galatians to conclude entire sections (cf. 2:21; 3:29; 6:10). With a circumflex accent it indicates a question follows.

[38] The idea here in Galatians 5:11 is not quite the same as "Christ crucified" being "to Jews a stumbling block" (1 Corinthians 1:23).   In that passage the thing the Jews struggled with and stumbled over was the idea of Messiah being crucified.   In their conceptions Messiah was to be a secular king and a conqueror, a world ruler like David or Solomon.   They could not stomach the idea of a crucified Messiah.   Thus, there were two things about the cross that caused stumbling: (1) a crucified Messiah?!? and (2) the end of the Mosaic system.   Both were unthinkable to 1st century Jews.

[39] Sanday, *op. cit.*, p.80.

koptein[40]) is the regular term for "to castrate"[41] or to make someone a eunuch.   "With very deep irony, Paul is saying, 'Let them carry their self-mutilation still further, and not stop at circumcision'."[42]   That Paul would use such a sarcastic/ironic expression has proven surprising to some readers of Galatians.   Such an expression by a public speaker or writer to his audience would be thought crude and vulgar in our society.   But must we either criticize or defend Paul at this place?   Sarcasm can at times be an effective means of argument.   If the Judaizers were castrated (not just circumcised), would the Galatians then admire them and follow them?[43]

B. Christians Need to be Careful Lest They Abuse Their Liberty.   5:13-6:10

> *Summary*: Paul emphasizes four safeguards to ensure wholesome use of one's Christian liberty: (1) Through love serve one another, 5:13-15. (2) Walk by the Spirit, not by the flesh (5:16-24). (3) As the Spirit prompts, try to restore those who are caught in any trespass, 5:25-6:5. (4) Be generous when you have opportunity to share with those who are in need, 6:6-10.

1. The first safeguard to ensure wholesome use of Christian liberty is through love to serve one another.   5:13-15

5:13 - *For you were called to freedom, brethren; only* do *not* turn *your freedom into an opportunity for the flesh, but through love serve one another.*

For you ... brethren - "For" at the head of this paragraph means 'In order to explain still

---

[40] The translators of the Holman Christian Standard Bible treat the verb form as passive when they offer this reading, "I wish those ... might also get themselves castrated!"   The KJV also took it as passive, "I would they were cut off which trouble you."   The KJV translators thought Paul was wishing the Judaizers would be cast out of the church.   Stott thinks Paul is wishing the Judaizers might cease from the land.   Paul's words sound coarse and almost out of place.   However, "if we were as concerned for God's church and God's word as Paul was, we too would wish that false teachers might cease from the land" (John R. W. Stott, *The Message of Galatians*, "The Bible Speaks Today" series, [Downers Grove: Inter-Varsity, 1968], *in loc.*).

[41] Arndt and Gingrich, *op. cit.*, p.82.

[42] Sanday, *ibid*.

[43] It is somewhat common in the commentaries to find reference to the worship of Cybele in northern Galatia.   It was a practice of the priests and worshipers of Cybele to be castrated as a sign of their devotion.   If we were to suppose Galatians is written to northern Galatia, then Paul's sarcasm means "[let] the Judaizers quit playing around.   They should go the whole route, castrate themselves, and become full-fledged pagans" (MacArthur, *op. cit.*, p.101).

further.' Having urged the Galatians to keep standing fast in their freedom, the explanation now offered concerns the proper use of Christian liberty. One problem always accompanies freedom – how are we to be sure the freedom will not be misused, squandered, wasted, or used selfishly? If a man does not have the Law of Moses, or rules like the Pharisees made ("works of the Law"), are there any safeguards that will keep one from being as sinfully unrestrained as the licentious pagan? Is Paul responding to another of the Judaizers' reasons why they insisted it was necessary for the Galatian Christians to have some rules to live by, otherwise their lives would be filled with sin? The Judaizers thought a man's conduct should be controlled by external rules, that conduct could be controlled from the outside. Christianity teaches a man's conduct is to be controlled from the inside, by love and the help of the Holy Spirit. Note the emphatic use of the Greek pronoun for "you" (*humeis*). There is an implied contrast with the way the Judaizers would live. The Judaizers would urge a bondage to the tyranny of their works of Law; Christianity teaches freedom and gives some simple guidelines within which a man is free to act.[44]

Were called to freedom - The Greek preposition translated "to" is *epi*, with "freedom" being in the dative case. *Epi* plus the dative indicates goal or purpose. The Galatians were called with this goal, that they might be free. 2 Thessalonians 2:14 indicates men are called to become Christians through the preaching of the gospel as invitations are extended to men to accept the offer of forgiveness made possible because of Calvary. The idea of freedom has been introduced before in Galatians at 4:21-31 and 5:1. James 1:25 and 2:12 speak about the gospel of Christ being the perfect law of liberty. "Everyone who answers the call of Christ is made free, and he ought to treasure his freedom. It was bought for him with the priceless blood of Christ our Savior."[45]

Only *do* not *turn* your freedom into an opportunity for the flesh - Freedom in Christ, as wonderful and refreshing as it is, is open to abuse if the Christian is not diligent about self-control. How he uses his liberty is something over which a Christian has control. "Freedom in Christ does *not* mean a man is free to sin. Rather, he is free *not to sin*."[46] "Opportunity" translates *aphormē*, which denotes a starting point, an opportunity or pretext,

---

[44] See the author's *New Testament Epistles: 1 Corinthians* (Moberly, MO: Scripture Exposition Books, 2004), p.194-195 where four guidelines or limitations on our liberty are pictured on a chart. The references on the points following are from 1 Corinthians 6. Christian liberty is limited by: 1) The law of expediency, 6:12a. 2) The law of self-control, 6:12b. 3) The law of self-preservation, 6:19. 4) The law of duty to God, 6:20. "Liberty" means we are free to do what is spiritually best for ourselves and for others. There is no Christian liberty apart from Christian love (1 Corinthians 10:24).

[45] Root, *76-77 Standard Lesson Commentary*, p.35.

[46] Barclay, *op. cit.*, p.50.

a base of operations for an expedition.[47]   A few months after he wrote to the Galatians, in Romans 7:8 Paul will write how the Law gave "sin" an opportunity to act, and sin produced all kinds of evil desires (which when indulged resulted in "deeds of flesh," Galatians 5:19). In the unredeemed, the flesh can be taken captive by sin (Romans 7:14).   In Romans 7:14-28, Paul describes how things were before he became a Christian.   He could not make himself habitually do the right, and he could not habitually avoid the wrong.   When he became a Christian, the old slavery to sin was broken (Romans 8:1-3), and he must no longer walk according to the flesh (Romans 8:4).   Once a man is freed from sin (Romans 6:7), he can stop sin from reigning in his mortal body (Romans 6:12); he can instead present the members of his body to God to be used as instruments of righteousness (Romans 6:13). This elucidation of "an opportunity for the flesh" makes it clear the "flesh" (i.e., a man's physical body) is not the culprit.[48]   Instead, the enemy is sin (a personification of the devil).   The devil can stir up the desires of the body and thus lead a person into actions that will satisfy the evil desires he has prompted.   That is what the Christian is not to allow to happen when the devil tempts him to abuse his liberty.   No one has a right to do wrong just because he is free.[49]   Paul will give two exhortations (imperative verbs) to help his readers govern their lives so they do not let their freedom become an occasion for the flesh: "through love serve one another" (verse 13) and "walk by the Spirit" (verse 16).

But through love serve one another - "But" (*alla*) is the strong adversative.   This is the positive statement that contrasts with the negative one in the previous clause.   "This sets freedom in the right direction: away from self and toward others.   Christ has made me free, not to get all I can for myself, right or wrong, but to do all I can for others without any wrong."[50]   "One of the fruit the spirit produces is love.   Because of love, Christians

---

[47] Arndt and Gingrich, *op. cit.*, p.127.

[48] Commentators and translators have always had trouble with the term *hē sarx* as used in 5:13-6:10. Before this in Galatians, the translators regularly write "the flesh" (cf. 1:16, 2:16,20, 3:3, 4:13-14,23,29), and they do so again in 6:10-18.   But there is a dogma learned from Augustine concerning humanity's corrupt or sinful nature inherited from Adam since the fall, a nature distinguished from human nature as God originally created it.   Commentators writing from the Augustinian/Calvinistic theological standpoint therefore commonly say that *sarx* in Galatians 5:16,17,19,24 and 6:8 is used in an "ethical sense."   We object!   When the doctrine about total hereditary depravity is still a point to be proven Biblically, translations ought not thrust such a doctrine upon their readers by inserting an adjective like "sinful" or "corrupt" before "flesh" (as does the NIV, "sinful nature").

[49] Many parallel Scriptures come to mind.   Peter, in his first epistle, which was addressed to, among others, the Galatian Churches, has a number of passages which apparently take up sentiments and even expressions found in Paul's writings (cp. 1 Peter 5:12).   And possibly he has an eye to the present verse when he writes (1 Peter 2:16) "Act as free men, and do not use your freedom as a covering for evil, but use it as bondslaves of God."   Or perhaps both had an eye on Jesus' teaching found in Matthew 17:24-27, that sons are exempt from the king's rules, but they must be careful that they don't give offense.

[50] Root, *ibid.*

should choose to serve one another. This will be a safeguard against any idea that 'now that I am free in Christ, I can do whatever I like and it will be considered acceptable in the grace of God'."[51] In the Greek, the words "love" and "serve" are side by side. It is because one loves that he is able to serve (slave) for the other person. Recall that in 5:6 Paul has just written about "faith working through love." "Serve" is a present tense verb and it is imperative. 'Be continually serving others,' is the command. "One another" is a reciprocal pronoun: I serve you – you serve me. Paul did not write that we are slaves of each other: Christians are God's and Christ's bondservants. But Christians can slave "*for* each other" ("one another" is in the dative case) because they love each other. Christ has set us free (Galatians 5:1), but that does not mean a Christian is free from all restraints. They govern their behavior by the law of love. They may not be under the Law of Moses, but they are "under the law of Christ" (1 Corinthians 9:20, 21).[52] The next verse will explain the special kind of love Paul has in view: love for the neighbor. Love is doing what is spiritually best for the other person.

5:14 - *For the whole Law is fulfilled in one word, in the* **statement,** *"YOU SHALL LOVE YOUR NEIGHBOR AS YOURSELF."*

For the whole Law is fulfilled - With "for" Paul introduces a reason why love through which they serve one another is a suitable guideline for the Christian's behavior. What Paul here writes to the Galatians is worked out in greater detail in Romans 13:8-10. The Decalogue is divided into two parts – duties to God and duties to man. Both here and in Romans 13 the context is discussing duties to our fellow man. Thus what Paul means is the spirit and intention of the Law[53] pertaining to human relationships is obeyed[54] when one loves his neighbor. Since Paul has argued throughout this letter that the Law of Moses has been abrogated (e.g., 3:25), it has been thought surprising that he should appeal to the

---

[51] R.C. Foster, *1963 Standard Lesson Commentary*, p.441.

[52] On one thing Paul and the Judaizers were agreed, namely, that obedience to the Lord carries with it a certain expected lifestyle. Where they differed was how one determined what that lifestyle should be. For the Judaizers their "works of the Law" provided what they thought were acceptable guidelines. For Paul, it was the inner man (renewed by means of the new birth) and the Holy Spirit prompting the Christian's spirit that gave proper direction. As it relates to our fellow man, the proper direction can be summed up in this single statement, "through love serve one another." In this Paul is reflecting what Jesus Himself taught, for the Master spoke (Mark 7:17-23) of what comes from within a man either defiling or blessing the man.

[53] "Whereas *holos ho nomos* ["the whole Law"] in Galatians 5:3 is the sum-total of the precepts of the Law, *ho pas nomos* ["the whole Law"] here is the law as a whole – the spirit and intention of the law" (Bruce, *op. cit.*, p.241).

[54] A comparison with Romans 13:8-10 shows "fulfill" here in Galatians carries more of the idea of actually obeying than of the idea of "summed up." There is a word (*anakephalaioutai*) in Romans 13:8-10 that is translated "is summed up," but it is a different word than the one here (*peplērōtai*) translated "fulfilled." *Peplērōtai* ("is fulfilled") is in the perfect tense and could be translated, "the whole Law has found its full expression ..." (Arndt and Gingrich, *op. cit.*, p.677). The perfect tense says this was true in the past and is still true.

Law to make his point.[55]   We must remember the points Paul makes are direct answers to the arguments used by the Judaizers.   Here is a simple way to fulfill the Law, says Paul, and you do not have to become a Pharisee (Judaizer) to do it.[56]

In one word, in the *statement* - Paul is about to quote Leviticus 19:18.   "Jesus quoted this same passage in His answer to a lawyer concerning what one should do to inherit eternal life (Luke 20:27).   Jesus Himself listed this Scripture as second only to the commandment on the love of God (Matthew 22:39).   Paul made more than one reference to this Leviticus Scripture, and his usage in Romans 13:9,10 is helpful to the meaning of this passage in Galatians: 'If there is any other commandment, it is summed up in this saying, "You shall love your neighbor as yourself." Love does no wrong to a neighbor; love therefore is the fulfillment of the law'."[57]   "One word" means one precept, one maxim.[58]

"YOU SHALL LOVE YOUR NEIGHBOR AS YOURSELF" - The Hebrew parallelism at Leviticus 19:18, which compares "the sons of your people" and "neighbor" shows that "neighbor" was apparently restricted to the Jewish people.   However, Jesus, in the parable of the Good Samaritan (Luke 10:25-37), gave the word "neighbor" a wider significance, the same wider sense that Paul here gives it.   "Neighbor" is any brother in Christ, anyone you can help.   Now that the old slavery is broken, the Christian is free, not

---

[55] Longenecker (*op. cit.*, p.242) has succinctly summarized the current debate concerning Paul and the Law.   He tells us that E.P. Sanders (*Paul, the Law, and the Jewish People*, p.4) speaks of an apparent fundamental inconsistency in Paul's argument and thinking, but at the same time there is an underlying consistency in his arguments if one takes into account that the "the different things which Paul says about the Law depend on the question asked or the problem posed."   That is, does the passage deal with "getting in" or "staying in" covenantal relationship with God?   Longenecker tells us that "H. Räisänen dispenses with Sander's attempts to find coherence, and insists there are flat contradictions in Paul's statement about the Law" (*Paul and the Law*, p.199).   Betz (*Galatians*, p.275) posits there is a difference between "doing the Law" and "fulfilling the Law."   The "doing" of the Law is not for Christians, but the "fulfilling" is.   What is obvious is that each of these accusations of inconsistency or contradiction is the result of treating "works of the Law" as being synonymous with obeying the Law of Moses.   It is not Paul who is inconsistent; it is his interpreters who have missed what he was really saying.

[56] The possibility should also be considered that Paul is quoting the words of Jesus (Matthew 2:39,40; Mark 12:31; Luke 10:27), the very words James calls the royal law (James 2:8).   In other words, it is possible we are misled by the fact that "Law" is capitalized in our NASB into thinking the reference is to some Old Testament passage.   If indeed the passage in Leviticus 19:18 is in view here in Galatians, we ought to consider the strong likelihood that New Testament writers learned about the value and meaning of this passage from Jesus who often alluded to it.

[57] Foster, *ibid.*

[58] "The phrase 'in one word' (*en eni logō*) employs *logos* ('word') in the sense of 'commandment,' much as does the Hebrew *dabar*" (Matera, *op. cit.*, p.193).

to do selfishly what he wants, when he wants, and where he wants, but to fulfill what God wants.   Love in the heart is better than any set of laws or penalties for breaking those laws, when it comes to the way to control a man's behavior for the good.

5:15 - *But if you bite and devour one another, take care lest you be consumed by one another.*

But if you bite and devour one another - With "but" Paul presents an ugly contrast that can result when people fail to love their neighbor.   Instead of loving his neighbor, a free man can injure his neighbor, but if he does, both of them will suffer.   The figure of speech "bite and devour" is "taken from the jungle and forest where tooth and claw reign and the denizens are exterminated by each other."[59]   Church members – think of that! – are pictured in the act of rushing at each other like wild beasts!   These two verbs are present tense: "If you keep on biting and devouring."   The Greek construction is a first class conditional sentence.   Such a construction might imply the bickering was already presently going on in the churches of Galatia.   Any of us who have experienced the heart-breaking divisions false teaching can bring about in a congregation do not find it hard to imagine the kind of strife that must have engulfed the whole church in Galatia.   Any of us who have had to deal with a neighbor who has used his freedom to injure us can well understand the initial reaction to get even that we are likely to feel.   Selfish misuse of Christian liberty can have devastating results on men's spiritual life.

Take care lest you be consumed by one another - "Consumed" (*analisikō*) means to utterly destroy, annihilate.   Wild beasts contending with each other have been known to lock horns resulting in the death of both.   When folk fail to practice love for one another they can destroy one another spiritually and, at times, physically, too.   Perhaps we should also think of the whole congregation's losing its reputation, influence, and its effectiveness as a result of its members using their freedom selfishly.   Fellowship disintegrates and the churches disappear.   "Is it possible for two church members to battle so long and so bitterly that both are lost to Christ and to the church?   Wrath and strife are among 'the works of the flesh' listed in this chapter with the warning that 'they which do such things shall not inherit the kingdom of God' (verses 19-21)."[60]   Love for one's neighbor is a safeguard to ensure wholesome use of one's Christian liberty.

---

[59] Lenski, *op. cit.*, p.278.   *Daknō* ("bite") was used of the serpents which bit the Israelites in the wilderness (Numbers 21:6).   *Katesthiein* ("devour") speaks of wild animals devouring (consuming) the carcasses they have killed.   This second word is used in the papyri for damage caused to pasturage by sheep that "overran, cropped, and utterly destroyed it."   In another place the word is used of "officials who were swallowing up the ... treasury with its surplus."   J.H. Moulton and G. Milligan, *The Vocabulary of the Greek Testament* (London: Hodder and Stoughton, 1963), p.336.

[60] Root, *ibid.*

2. A second safeguard to ensure wholesome use of Christian liberty is to walk by the Spirit, not by the flesh.   5:16-24

5:16 - *But I say, walk by the Spirit, and you will not carry out the desire of the flesh.*

But I say - "But" takes us back to the words of verse 13, "do not turn your freedom into an opportunity for the flesh." In that verse "but" introduced one safeguard to ensure wholesome use of Christian liberty. "But" in this verse introduces a second safeguard.

Walk by the Spirit - "Walk" is often used by Paul in a figurative sense to denote daily living. The present tense verb, keep on walking, aptly pictures "the progressive round of activities which comprise the routine of life (Romans 6:4, 8:4, 13:13, 14:15; Ephesians 2:2,10, 5:2,8,15; Colossians 3:7)."[61] The verb is in the imperative mood which, requires each reader to make a choice. Such walking is something that a person can will to do, or not. The Judaizers had a list of rules (Heb. *halakhah*, "to walk," or how to conduct one's life[62]) by which they expected their followers to walk. Paul offers a much more satisfying way to walk.

The word *pneuma* ("Spirit") occurs seven times in verses 16 to 25. Translators and expositors must make a decision whether or not the reference each time is to the Holy Spirit (the third person of the Godhead) or whether, at least in some instances, the reference is to man's human spirit.[63] Now the truth of the matter is that our understanding of the actions done by a man walking according to the flesh, versus the actions done by the man walking according to the spirit (Spirit), will not be greatly different whichever way we translate *pneuma*. What will differ is how we explain how these actions are triggered or motivated. Just how does the *pneuma* produce fruit? Does the man have to cooperate, or does the *pneuma* do it all for him? Does the flesh automatically lead to certain sins, or does it so lead only after being tempted and agitated by the devil? The approach adopted in these notes is to treat *pneuma* in verses 16,18, and 25b as a reference to the Holy Spirit, and in verses 17,22, and 25a as a reference to the human spirit. The verses dealing with the man's spirit refer to the born-again spirit (John 3:6) being able to direct the person's life. The verses dealing with the Holy Spirit tell of the help the indwelling Spirit gives to a man's

---

[61] Kent, *op. cit.*, p.156.

[62] "*Halakhah* became the generic designation for all of the rabbinic ethical and social legislation" (Longenecker, *op. cit.*, p.244).

[63] Lenski (*op. cit.*, p.278-83) takes *pneuma* in all these verses as being the human spirit. He did so because in his judgment "flesh" and "Holy Spirit" would be an unusual contrast, whereas "flesh" and "spirit" would not be. The majority of Bible translations this commentator has reviewed capitalize "Spirit" in all the places where it occurs in these verses. The translation by Knox sometimes uses capital "S" ("Spirit") and sometimes small "s" ("spirit").

spirit.[64]   If this approach is correct, then verse 16 is telling us Christians that we are to walk constantly as the Holy Spirit directs; but the passage does not tell how the Holy Spirit directs the Christian, whether directly or through the Word.   Verses such as Hebrews 3:7, 9:8, 10:15, Revelation 2:1 and 7 show the Spirit can and does work through the Word.   Verses like Luke 11:13, Ephesians 4:23, and Philippians 2:13 seem to indicate the Spirit can also work apart from the Word but in harmony with it as He prompts and plants thoughts in our minds.

And you will not carry out the desire of the flesh - Paul now attaches a promise to the exhortation of verse 16a.[65]   Were a man to carry out the desires of the flesh he would be misusing his liberty (verse 13).   "Carry out" (*teleō*, the same verb translated "fulfilled" in verse 14) equals obey.   Until we come to the next verse, where there are further notes of explanation about the "flesh," let us say that "desire (lust) of the flesh" equals those desires and cravings in our physical bodies which are stirred up or prompted by the devil, and which, therefore, are not pleasing to God.[66]   The Christian, now that he is a free man, must decide which prompting to obey – the prompting of the Spirit or the prompting stirred up in his body by the devil.   As long as he follows the Spirit, he will not ever, never (emphatic double negative in the Greek) carry out the desire of the flesh.

5:17 - *For the flesh sets its desire against the Spirit, and the Spirit against the flesh; for these are in opposition to one another, so that you may not do the things that you please.*

For the flesh sets its desire against the Spirit - With "for" Paul introduces a reason why his readers should "walk by the Spirit" as he commanded in verse 16.   There is a contest going on inside the Christian.   His spirit[67] wants to do one thing, but the flesh (prompted

---

[64] Verse 25b is where we learn the Holy Spirit who helped us become a Christian (1 Corinthians 12:13, "by one Spirit were you baptized into one body," i.e., the Holy Spirit led you to the place where you wanted to be immersed), also helps our "spirit" (so we would translate *pneuma* in 25a) to guide us so we live right.

[65] There is some dispute as to whether this construction is imperative or indicative.   The RSV translates the clause as a negative command: "do not gratify the desires of the flesh."   To translate it as an imperative requires us to ignore a fact of Greek grammar: "not" translates a double negative (*ou mē*).   While the future tense verb with *ou* ("not") is often used for an imperative, there is no instance found of *ou mē* being used in the New Testament in this sense.   For this reason most grammarians treat the verb here as indicative.

[66] In an earlier footnote we have called attention to how misleading it is to translate *sarx* ("flesh") by the term "sinful nature" as the NIV does at this place.   One result of such a misleading translation is the idea that even though one has been redeemed (freed) there is something from which he was not redeemed – as if when a man became a Christian nothing was done about the old inherited sinful nature.   Thus, some have invented a second work of grace by which, after one becomes a Christian, something is finally done about the old sinful nature.   So we hear the language "saved and sanctified."   In this commentator's judgment, this doctrine causes us to fail to understand what Paul actually wrote about how sin works in the Christian, and how the Christian is called on to choose which master he will obey (Romans 6:12-23).

[67] Because there is no article before *pneuma* in the Greek, it seems we should read "spirit" (small "s") both times *pneuma* appears in this verse.

by the devil) wants to do the opposite. Without the spirit getting some divine help from the Holy Spirit, the flesh is likely to win.[68] We explain the terms "flesh" and "spirit" here the same as we explain the terms at John 3:6.

And the Spirit against the flesh - We supply the verb ("sets its desire") from the previous clause. A man's spirit (his "inner man," Romans 7:22) can have desires for what is holy and good; in fact, Paul will shortly enumerate some of these (Galatians 5:22,23).

For these are in opposition to one another - "These" (*tauta*, neuter plural), these things or these entities, refers back to flesh and spirit. The verb *antikeimai* ("in opposition to") denotes opposing action, and its tense (present) denotes an ongoing opposition between the two. There would be no continuing war going on inside of us if the devil would quit trying to entice us to do evil. But that is something that will not happen in this life.

---

[68] We are interpreting this passage in Galatians in the light of the antithesis between flesh and spirit as explained in greater detail in Romans 8:5-13. We offer the NASB reading of these verses save we suggest changing "Spirit" to "spirit" in Romans 8:5,6,9. Thus the passage reads, "For those who are according to the flesh set their minds on the things of the flesh, but those who are according to the spirit, the things of the Spirit. For the mind set on the flesh is death, but the mind set on the spirit is life and peace, because the mind set on the flesh is hostile toward God; for it does not subject itself to the Law of God, for it is not even able to do so; and those who are in the flesh cannot please God. However, you are not in the flesh but in the spirit, if indeed the Spirit of God dwells in you ... the spirit is alive because of righteousness ... so then, brethren, we are under obligation, not to the flesh, to live according to the flesh ... if by the Spirit you are putting to death the deeds of the flesh, you will live."

First, we need a brief review of Biblical psychology as this commentator teaches it. Man is body, soul, and spirit (1 Thessalonians 5:23). God intends that the spirit control the soul which in turn animates the body. When man commits his first sin, the spirit dies; that is, his spirit is no longer able to control the house we live in. The "body" and the "soul" do as they wish, and often the spirit must stand by and watch helplessly (wishing it were different, but unable to do anything about it, Romans 7:14-23). The devil tries to influence people's behavior by stirring up the desires of a man's body (see Romans 7:5), or planting thoughts in the man's mind (see Acts 5:3). He is very often successful; in fact, the non-Christian (after he has committed his first sin) is what the Bible calls a slave of sin (Romans 6:6), and he lives in a body of sin (Romans 6:6).

When a person becomes a Christian, the old slavery to sin is broken. When a person becomes a Christian, his "spirit" is born again (John 3:6), or as Paul words it, "the spirit is alive because of righteousness (i.e., God's way of saving man)" (Romans 8:10). Because it is alive, the spirit prompts a man to do what is right, while the desires stirred by the devil would urge a man to do things that are wrong. When a man chooses to do what is right, or determines to avoid the wrong (putting to death the deeds of the body, Romans 8:13), the indwelling Holy Spirit (received as a gift when he became a Christian (Acts 2:38; Galatians 3:2) helps him live the Christian life. We would compare Romans 8:13 ("if by the Spirit you are putting to death the deeds of the body") with Galatians 5:16 ("walk by the Spirit, and you will not carry out the desire of the flesh"). Romans 6:23 tells us that if one who has become a Christian continues to walk by the flesh, it leads to spiritual death and eternal punishment. If one who has become a Christian continues to live by the spirit and walk by the Spirit (Galatians 5:25), he will continue to live spiritually and eternally.

This commentator teaches that the human body is *not* inherently sinful; it is neutral. A person's behavior (after he becomes a Christian – a free man, a new creature) depends on who is giving the orders. The devil will offer his promptings to the flesh, in hopes that we will behave in a way contrary to the will of God. The Holy Spirit will offer His aid to our spirit, in hopes that our behavior will be in harmony with the will of God. Which one we do depends on our own will – what do we want to do with our freedom (our liberty).

So that you may not do the things that you please - The KJV translation "cannot do" is much stronger than the Greek subjunctive mood will allow. In the Greek there is no declaration about the *impossibility* of doing these things.[69] Rather, the present subjunctive (continuous action) says we sometimes do and sometimes we do not do these things. The "things that you please" may refer to the evil which the desires of the flesh want us to do, but which the spirit's influence seeks to prevent. Or it may refer to the good the spirit prompts us to do, but which we fail to accomplish because the desires of the flesh hinder. Whichever way we interpret the passage, whether "the things that you please" refer to the desires of the flesh or to the desire of the spirit, the struggle goes on. That's why the help the Holy Spirit can give (verse 16) is so desperately needed.

5:18 - *But if you are led by the Spirit, you are not under the Law.*

But if you are led by the Spirit - We think the conjunction should be translated "and" so that this verse gives a second result of walking by the Spirit (verse 16). First, we do not carry out the desire of the flesh, and second, we are not under the Law. The parallel passage in Romans 8:14 shows that *pneumati* here denotes the Holy Spirit. It is instructive, too, that both passages about being "led by the Spirit" (Romans and Galatians) are in a context dealing with self-control. The dative case for "Spirit" must be a dative of agent. How the Spirit leads was discussed in verse 16. The passive verb "led" involves an element of submission on the part of the Christian. The Christian must choose to follow the Spirit's promptings.

You are not under the Law - "You are not under law, on the one hand, because there is now no need of its restraints, nor on the other hand, because it finds nothing, in the one led by the Spirit and walking by love, to forbid or condemn."[70] "If the Spirit has won out in this conflict within us, then the constraint of the law will not be felt in our decisions. We have a freedom in which righteousness is done because we desire it, not because the law requires it."[71]

5:19 - *Now the deeds of the flesh are evident, which are: immorality, impurity, sensuality,*

Now the deeds of the flesh are evident - The thread of thought is this – if one wishes to

---

[69] Of course, translated as the KJV does, Calvinists find proof for their doctrine of total inability.

[70] Lipscomb and Shepherd, *op. cit.*, p.265. As on several other occasions in Galatians, we must decide whether to translate *nomos* as "Law" or "law." For anarthrous *nomos*, see 3:18 and 4:4,5,21. Perhaps Paul has the Law of Moses in mind (Christians are no longer under the tutor, 3:25). Perhaps he has in mind the works of the Law the Pharisees were demanding. Led by the Spirit, Christians do not need such rules to keep them from lapsing into libertinism. Of course, Christians do have certain precepts and prohibitions found in the law of Christ (1 Corinthians 9:21).

[71] R.C. Foster, *op. cit.*, p.442.

ascertain whether he is walking by the flesh or by the spirit, all he needs to do is check his behavior against the following lists of actions and feelings typical of each.   "Deeds of the flesh" means actions which result from the desires and thoughts the devil has prompted in our bodies and minds.[72]   The noun "evident" (*phaneros*) means open to public observation, obvious.   Paul does not mean that all the actions and feelings of the flesh are committed in public where they may be seen, but that such standards have been known from Patriarchal times (cf. Romans 1:24-32).

Which are - The following list of fifteen behaviors is not exhaustive; instead, these are typical or representative (*hatina,* "which," of such sort as[73]) of the evil effects which result when the devil has stirred up appetites.   Since virtue and vice lists were popular in the ancient world,[74] source critics have said that Paul likely copied his list from some pagan source.[75]   But this is incorrect; if Paul is a mouthpiece for God (which is involved in the definition of being an apostle), then the list Paul gives reflects God's standards, rather than being a man-made list.[76]

As we examine the words in the list, we observe that some words appear in the singular and some in the plural.   This is not due to different manuscript readings, nor is it due to error or inaccuracy in translation.   These words are abstract nouns, and in Greek, when an abstract noun occurs in the plural it gives an example of the quality which the singular noun denotes.   For example, *thumos*, the singular form, means temper; *thumoi,*

---

[72] In Romans 13:12 and Ephesians 5:11 they are styled "deeds of darkness." They are actions that result from the devil stirring up the desires of the body, or planting thoughts in the man's mind. The "flesh" by itself does not produce evil actions, we affirm. It must be acted on and stimulated by the devil – temptations, thoughts planted, desires triggered – before the flesh so begins to act.

Likewise, a man's spirit must also be acted on before it produces fruit. The word of God is one of the prompters to positive actions. A man's spirit delights in the word of God (and from the word learns what is right and pleasing to God), then the spirit knows how to act. The indwelling Holy Spirit also acts as a prompter to man's spirit, the indwelling gift thus helping to produce behavior pleasing to God. (This is what Paul says in 5:25.)

[73] In the Greek we have a neuter plural subject (*hatina*) with a third person singular verb *estin*. This construction serves to gather all of the items involved into one complex of ideas.

[74] Pagan moralists as early as Plato (427-347 BC) were making lists of things offensive to pagan morals. Aristotle's *Nicomachaean Ethics* has a famous list of virtues and vices. Stoics drew up lists to provide their audiences with specific examples of virtues to be imitated or vices to be avoided. Examples of vice lists also are found in the Dead Sea Scrolls (1QS 4:2-14), in the Didache (1:1-6:3), and in the Epistle of Barnabas (18:1-21:9).

[75] To give but one example: "It is now generally recognized that the catalogues of virtues and vices in the New Testament are derived ultimately from the ethical teaching of the Stoa" (B.S. Easton, "New Testament Ethical Lists" in *JBL* 51 (1932), p.1).

[76] In fact, this commentator would affirm that even the pagan lists ultimately had their source in a revelation made by God to the Patriarchs and then handed down orally from generation to generation. As far as the lists in various New Testament books are concerned (e.g., 1 Corinthians 6:9,10; Ephesians 5:3-5; Colossians 3:5-9; 2 Timothy 3:2-4), if readers of the epistles had memorized those lists, it would have gone a long way toward helping a man judge whether or not his behavior is pleasing to God who makes the rules and sets the standards.

the plural form, means outbursts of temper. *Phthonos* means envy; *phthonoi* means displays of envy. Many of the words in this list of works of the flesh are actually plural forms, and mean displays or acts of the quality/vice which they denote. Attempts to arrange the vices into groups or classifications have not proven totally successful. Perhaps a four-fold classification – sexual sins, sins of idolatry or superstition, sins of personal animosity and conflict among people, and sins of self-indulgence – is easiest to remember.

Immorality, impurity, sensuality - These are the sexual sins to be avoided. The KJV version adds a fourth word to this first group, "adultery;" however, the word is omitted in the best manuscripts. The word translated "immorality" (*porneia*) can include fornication (illicit sexual relations between unmarried people), adultery (a married person engaging in sexual relations with someone other than their spouse), and even prostitution. "Impurity" (*akatharsia*[77]) covers a wide range of sexual irregularities, both in deed (self-abuse, bestiality, sodomy) and in thought (pornography, lust [Matthew 5:28]). A person who is impure may hide this thoughts and his sin from others, but the person who is sensual (*aselgeia*) has ceased to care what others may think of his or her actions. They parade their wanton behavior, unawed by shame or fear and with no regard for self-respect or the rights and feelings of others or for public decency.[78]

5:20 - *idolatry, sorcery, enmities, strife, jealousy, outbursts of anger, disputes, dissensions, factions,*

Idolatry, sorcery - These are sins that violate a man's proper relationship with God. "Idolatry" (*eidōlolatreia*) is the worship of idols and includes participation in the idolatrous feasts and rites in honor of the different gods and goddesses (1 Corinthians 8:1-10:14) as well.[79] Where the NASB has "sorcery" to translate *pharmakeia*,[80] the *Living Bible* reads

[77] *Akatharsia* is a compound word made up of *katharos* ("pure") and an alpha privative (which negates what the rest of the word says). Barclay (*op. cit.*, p.51) tells us that in the Greek language *katharos* was used of that ceremonial cleanness which entitles a man to approach his gods. "Impurity (sexual impurity and looseness), then, is that which makes a man unfit to come before God."

[78] There is no English word that carries the nuance of the Greek. We use lasciviousness, debauchery, wantonness, shamelessness, and the like, but none quite communicates the idea the Greek expresses.

[79] Idolatry was a constant temptation and danger in the ancient world. "When the Christian is warned against idolatry, it is not, of course, systematic idolatry that is meant, but that occasional compliance with idolatrous customs, such as taking part in the idol feasts, or eating things offered to idols in the idol's temple, which he might easily be led into by his association with his heathen neighbors" (Sanday, *op. cit.*, p.83). Trade unions had their tutelary deities, and to keep a job men were expected, once a year, to offer incense to the gods. Refusal to do so would cost the Christian his job. The worship of the Roman emperor as a god was beginning to be expected in the 1st century world. Idolatry is also a constant temptation and danger in the modern world. In some places the images of idols dominate the countryside. The atmosphere in such places is pervaded by encouragements to be involved in acts of worship to the god. But that is not all: "The Christian who devotes more of himself to his car, house, or boat, than he does to serving Christ may be in danger of idolatry (Colossians 3:5)" (Wiersbe, *op. cit.*, p.131).

[80] "The term *pharmakeia* originally meant medical treatment with drugs (cf. the English word "pharmacy"), but it developed the meaning of witchcraft because sorcerers often used potions in practicing their evil art" (Kent, *op. cit.*, p.158). In Exodus 7:11, 8:7,18, the word is used with reference to Pharaoh's

"spiritism;" that is, encouraging the activity of demons. "'Sorcery' is the use of magical enchantment, divination by supposed assistance of evil spirits, witchcraft."[81] "Witchcraft is a claim to put the heavenly powers [spirits] under one's control, either to benefit himself or to injure others. The presence of astrologers and fortune tellers in our society shows the need for this warning from Paul."[82]

Enmities, strife, jealousy, outbursts of anger - Here begin the sins of personal animosity and conflict among people that are works of the flesh. It should be pointed out that sins of the flesh can be found in the mind and attitude as well as in actions. "Enmities" (*echthrai*), the first of the plural words in this list of works of the flesh, is giving vent to the hostile feelings and actions which the mind harbors. A man can have enmity toward God (Romans 8:7), there can be enmity between Jew and Gentile, there can be hostility between people (the word is used of the hostility between Herod and Pilate in Luke 23:12).[83] "Strife" (*eris*) is discord, bickering, the acts of contention to which enmities lead. "This is seen in church troubles when men take opposite sides, not so much from different convictions, as from personal dislike and the disposition to thwart an opponent."[84] "Strife" led to splits into parties and cliques and bickerings within the ranks of the church members at Corinth (1 Corinthians 1:11, 3:3; 2 Corinthians 12:20).[85] "Jealousy" (*zēlos*[86]) suggests an attitude of rivalry and selfish concern for personal advancement. It is sad when

---

magicians. In Isaiah 47:9,12, the word is used with reference to magic practiced by Israel (magic is calling on demons for super-human powers). In Revelation 9:21, 18:23, 21:8, 22:15, one finds this same word for "sorcery" (drugs), and we are told such behavior results in repentance being needed, or the person is lost. In the light of these verses about drugs one wonders, in the midst of almost uncontrollable traffic in addictive drugs in contemporary society, whether it would not be proper to identify the sale and use of such drugs a work of the flesh.

[81] Lipscomb and Shepherd, *op. cit.*, p.267.

[82] Foster, *op. cit.*, p.443.

[83] This work of the flesh can be neutralized by love (the first of the fruit listed in verse 22). Jesus told His disciples to love their *echthroi* (Matthew 5:44; Luke 6:27,35). At Romans 12:20, Paul quotes Proverbs 25:21, "If your *echthroi* is hungry, give him food to eat."

[84] Lipscomb and Shepherd, *ibid*. *Eris* (strife, singular) is well-attested, though the plural *ereis* (discords, contentions) is supported by C, D², G, Byzantine.

[85] The fruit called "peace" (Galatians 5:22) is the cure for strife.

[86] At Galatians 1:14 we learned that zeal is a neutral word, and the context must describe whether it is an honorable or a dishonorable thing. Here, within a list of vices, the context requires us to think of zeal in its bad sense, namely, selfish jealousy. Sinaiticus, C, D², F, G have the plural *zēloi* (jealousies).

Christians compete with one another and try to make one another look bad in the eyes of others. Jealousy is often the motive that leads to ill will and strife. "Outbursts of anger" (*thumoi*, fits of rage) "are the open eruption of anger, which, when powerless to inflict injury, will find vent in furious language and menacing gestures."[87] "Outbursts of anger" (plural) depicts repeated displays of animosity.

Disputes, dissensions, factions, envyings (verse 21) - With these works of the flesh Paul continues his list of sins of personal animosity and conflict among people. When the KJV was translated scholars imagined that etymologically "disputes" (*eritheiai*) was related to "strife" (*eris*), but no longer. The noun *erithos* and the verb *eritheuō* mean a day laborer who labors for hire. The word came to denote selfish ambition, a mercenary spirit, "a self-seeking pursuit of political office by unfair means."[88] Displays of selfishness (getting as much as one can for oneself) is a translation that fits all New Testament occurrences of *eritheiai*. The word "dissensions" (*dichostasiai*, divisions) refers to the attitudes that lead to the splintering of groups, attitudes which are the inevitable result when selfish personal conflicts run their course.[89] "Factions" translates *hairēseis*, a word that means to choose sides. "This is the next step after dissensions. The division becomes crystallized and people prefer to split into their own sects."[90] "Envyings" (*phthonoi*, from verse 21) means

---

[87] Lipscomb and Shepherd, *ibid*. This word, too, is neutral and can be used either in a noble or ignoble sense. In the good sense, "courage" is sometimes the translation used for *thumos*. Paul uses *thumos* of God's retribution against those who habitually obey unrighteousness (Romans 2:8). In other passages, as here, Paul uses the word in its bad sense (2 Corinthians 12:20; Ephesians 4:31; Colossians 3:8). A comparison of synonyms will help us fix the meaning of *thumos*. *Thumos* is impulsive, turbulent anger. *Orge* is anger as a settled habit. Both may be right or wrong. *Parorgismos* is the bitterness of anger, and is always presented as wrong. G.R. Berry, "New Testament Synonyms," in *A New Greek-English Lexicon to the New Testament* (Chicago: Wilcox and Follett, 1948), p.47.

[88] Arndt and Gingrich, *op. cit.*, p.309.

[89] The other time this word occurs in the New Testament is in Romans 16:17, where Paul puts his readers on their guard against those who cause "dissension" likely by introducing divisive teaching in the congregation. Judaizer's teachings were likely to cause dissension at Rome just as they have caused trouble in the churches of Galatia.

[90] Foster, *ibid*. The same word is elsewhere translated "sect" and "heresy." Thus, the Pharisees had their opinions (choices) and formed a sect, a sect with peculiar views and doctrines; and they aligned themselves against the Sadducees, another sect who had their own opinions (choices). See Acts 5:17, 15:5, 26:5, where *hairēsis* is translated "sect." In 1 Corinthians 11:19 it denotes the factions into which the Corinthian church was splitting (i.e., per 1 Corinthians 1:12, the groups favoring Paul, Apollos, Cephas, or Christ). In Acts 24:5,14 and 28:22, the word is used to designate folk who have chosen to be Christians. In this Galatians passage, it is difficult not to think of the Judaizers whose work has tended to cause the church to split up into parties. It is sobering to find "disputes, dissensions, factions" in so black a list, and coupled with so clear a declaration that these sins exclude the perpetrator of them from the kingdom of God. Verily, all professing Christians would do well to take heed to what the Bible designates as sins, and not to trust too much to their own fallible sentiment and judgment in such matters.

displays of envy. "Jealousy" (*zēlos*, verse 20), which is the desire to be as well off as another, differs from "envy," which is the desire to deprive another of what he has.[91]   Envy is more than begrudging looks; it is hostile deeds intended to end someone else's prosperity.

5:21 - *envyings, drunkenness, carousing, and things like these, of which I forewarn you just as I have forewarned you that those who practice such things shall not inherit the kingdom of God.*

Drunkenness, carousing - This group of works of the flesh we have chosen to call sins of self-indulgence.[92]   "Drunkenness" (*methai*, intoxication; the Greek word here is plural) is the result of excessive indulgence in alcoholic beverages, leaving people's rational control over their words and actions weakened and imperiled.   "Drunkenness lies behind a great many other crimes.   The drink that reduces man's power to resist the temptations of life, that makes it more difficult to say no, is the poison that leads not only to drunkenness, but also to wrongdoing of all kinds."[93]   The exact connotation of "carousing" (*komoi*, plural) is disputed.   *Komos* originally referred to a festal procession or parade in honor of Dionysus (the Greek name; Bacchus is the Roman name), the god of wine.   At the end of the procession was a boisterous meal or banquet, which often ended in insobriety and wanton behavior (orgies), that in turn would invite moral censure even from the pagans.[94]

And things like these - The fifteen works just named are not all the possible works of the flesh.   A simple way to determine whether something not included in either list here in Galatians 5 is either good or bad is this: set down side by side in two-columns the things Paul names.   Now compare the unnamed action in question with each list.   Which one is it most like?   That will help to determine whether it is a work of the flesh or not.

Of which I forewarn you – That Paul is telling them before the event (i.e., the Day of Judgment) proves his words to be true.   *Prolegō*, here translated "forewarn", is used of a predictive warning in 2 Corinthians 13:2 and 1 Thessalonians 3:4.

---

[91] Aristotle, *Rhet.* ii.9-11.   The plural form *phthonoi* is attested by P[46], Aleph, B.

[92] The King James Version has "murders" before "drunkenness."   There is considerable doubt as to whether this word ought to stand in the text since it is lacking in the two oldest manuscripts.   Perhaps it is an interpolation from Romans 1:29.

[93] Foster, *ibid*.

[94] Should we think of Mardi Gras as a typical modern example?   Revelry such as the Oktoberfests and Maifests and the drunken parties at some fraternity houses would be other examples.

Just as I have forewarned you - Warnings against such sins (works of the flesh) had been the staple of many sermons from the very first day the gospel had been preached in Galatia.[95]   Paul certainly did not hesitate to warn people about the judgment to come.

That those who practice such things - Note it well that this warning is written to Christians.   Paul warns that those who *habitually practice* (a present participle conveying the idea of habitual, customary, or repeated action) such deeds as these will not inherit the kingdom of God.   Paul is not talking about the occasional act of sin, but the habit of sin. "Such things" (*ta toiauta*) refers to the works of the flesh just listed beginning with verse 19.

Shall not inherit the kingdom of God - Since it is written to folk who were already in the church (Galatians 1:2), "kingdom of God" here must be a reference to heaven.[96]   Any Christian who continues to indulge in the works of the flesh will miss heaven.[97]   Freedom in Christ does not mean freedom to habitually commit sin.

---

[95] In post-apostolic times new converts were given catechetical lessons before their baptism.   Such lessons did include ethical teaching (*Didache* 7:1; Justin Martyr, *Apology*, 1.61).   In the book of Acts we do find sermons preceding baptism, but not much evidence of a series of catechetical lessons. Nevertheless, Longenecker (*op. cit.*, p.258) gives several arguments he thinks point to this vice list as being other than Paul's own style and vocabulary.   He thinks that *hoti* ("that") which begins the next clause introduces indirect discourse where Paul is quoting a standard early church pre-baptismal catechetical lesson just as did other early gospel preachers.   This commentator's study has led to the conclusion that such detailed catechetical lessons were developed after the age of the apostles had passed.

[96] This is the first time the expression "kingdom of God" is used in this letter.   We may assume the Galatians were familiar with the concept, since Acts 14:22 tells us that at the close of the first missionary journey Paul and Barnabas warned their Galatian converts that "through many tribulations we must enter the kingdom of God."   Further, if Paul has forewarned his converts about the danger of works of the flesh, we may presume he also spoke of the kingdom of God in the same context.   The kingdom or rule of God was a theme of Old Testament prophecy.   The kingdom of God or kingdom of heaven (the two expressions being interchangeable) is a major theme in the Gospels.   The expression occurs numerous times in Paul's writings (Romans 14:17; 1 Corinthians 4:20; 6:9,10; 15:24,50; Galatians 5:21; Ephesians 5:5; Colossians 1:13; 1 Thessalonians 2:12; 2 Thessalonians 1:5; 2 Timothy 4:1,18).   In these passages different aspects of God's rule are emphasized.   For example, in Jesus' Sermon on the Mount, obedience to the rule of God is the emphasis ("Thy kingdom come, Thy will be done ...," Matthew 6:10).   Other times the emphasis falls on the community of men who in their hearts have recognized God's rule (e.g., Matthew 16:18,19 where "kingdom" and "church" are used interchangeably).   In many passages the emphasis is on the new heavens and earth in which God's rule will be finally and completely realized (e.g., "inherit the kingdom prepared for you ...," Matthew 25:34; Peter writes of an "entrance into the eternal kingdom of our Lord and Savior Jesus Christ," 2 Peter 1:11).

[97] How do proponents of a "once saved, always saved" doctrine explain this amazing verse written to Christians?   That Galatians is written to Christians, there is no doubt.   It is Christians who were pictured as abusing their freedom so as to produce "deeds of the flesh."   A few weeks before he wrote to the Galatians, Paul used the same words (1 Corinthians 6:9,10) when writing to the Corinthians about the sins that were common in their community.

5:22 - *But the fruit of the Spirit is love, joy, peace, patience, kindness, goodness, faithfulness,*

But the fruit of the Spirit is - If one wishes to ascertain if he or she is walking by the Spirit (verse 16), here is a list of attitudes and actions that would characterize a man of God. These virtues ("fruit") are the very things which the Holy Spirit has revealed are pleasing to God. When Paul wrote about "deeds of the flesh" he used the same word (*erga*, "works," "deeds") that he used when he wrote about "works of the Law" (2:16). One might draw the inference that there is some relationship between the two; neither comes from a good source. Deliberately, then, Paul does not say "works of the Spirit;" he uses the word "fruit" because these attitudes and actions are qualitatively different from those designated as "works (deeds)." "Fruit" is singular, although it is a collective noun. Works (deeds) of the flesh spread out in many different directions and actions; the "fruit" is only good; its actions and attitudes are a unity (like a bunch of grapes), a beautiful whole. "Fruit" may be the term chosen to characterize how the Christian lives because whatever is going on inside (a transformed nature) will produce on the outside (like fruit on a tree).[98]

In the notes on verse 16 we set forth the idea that *pneuma* here in verse 22 is a reference to man's renewed spirit (the "spirit" that is alive because of righteousness, Romans 8:10), rather than to the Holy Spirit (as the capital "S" "Spirit" in our translations – KJV, ASV, NIV, NASB – would lead us to believe). The reason for choosing "spirit" is explained in this fashion. This commentator confesses that for years – both in his own personal growth and for how-to-do-it sermons to benefit his parishioners – he has found it difficult to explain how, if it is fruit of the "Spirit", the Holy Spirit goes about producing such fruit in believers. Is it automatic? If so, then why do we not see this fruit in every baptized believer? Must the believer cooperate with the Spirit? If so, in what way? Perhaps we can get help from parallel passages elsewhere in the New Testament. Are there any verses parallel to Galatians 5:22-23 that specifically say that some fruit is the work of the *Holy* Spirit, rather than the spirit of man? In the epistle to the Colossians (3:12-15) we have a similar list of virtues, but with this difference – in Colossians the readers are commanded to "put [these] on." This is important. Someone walking as his renewed spirit prompts could be commanded to do something; but it is not easy to see how we could command the Holy Spirit to do something, were we to translate *pneuma* as "Spirit." The list of fruit in Paul's writings is similar to the list of virtues found in 2 Peter 1:5-7, where Christians are commanded to "supply" ("add," KJV) these virtues; that is, there is a cooperation on our part expected in 2 Peter. In the Peter passage, each new virtue develops as the previous one is exercised. Galatians 5:25 seems to explain in more detail how this works. The renewed spirit, the inner man, prompts us to think and act in a way that would be well-pleasing to God.

---

[98] Cp. Romans 7:4 ("that we might bear fruit for God") and John 15:8 ("that you bear much fruit").

The desires of flesh prompted by the devil tend to overwhelm the better wishes prompted by the spirit (Galatians 5:17), and would do so were it not for the indwelling Holy Spirit making it possible for us to carry out what the renewed spirit wants us to do. After all, "greater is He who is in you (the Holy Spirit) than he who is in the world (the devil)" (1 John 4:4). If any of us wants to demonstrate the fruit of the spirit, before any of us makes behavior choices, we will have to listen for the promptings of the inner man.[99] We shall have to have a knowledge (especially from the Word) concerning what the Spirit wants. Then, when opportunities present themselves, we can choose to act in the proper manner in ways that God has told us are well-pleasing to Him.

Attempts have been made to arrange the nine qualities about to be listed into general groupings, though it has not proven to be an easy task.[100] While the middle three might be said to be qualities that affect man's everyday relationships with his neighbor, and while the last three might be principles of character that guide a Christian's conduct (as Lightfoot suggested), what title will cover the first three? In the comments herein, we shall treat each of these virtues in Galatians 5 in the light of how others are affected by our behavior (as contrasted with the selfish deeds of the flesh).

Love, joy, peace - Is the first quality love for God, or love for man, or both? Since Paul has already spoken of love as one of the ways faith expresses itself (5:6), of love for one's neighbor as being the fulfillment of the whole Law (5:14), and of serving one another through love (5:13), we choose to treat it as love for man.   1 Corinthians 13 describes how such "love" (*agapē*) behaves.[101] It seeks the highest good of its object and does not cease or change, even when it is rebuffed. "Joy", if we may let Romans 14:17 guide us, may be a motive opposite of selfishness (getting what you want to eat or drink), a motive that seeks to produce joy in the other person. In the Romans 14 passage, attempting to produce righteousness, peace, and joy *in the other person* is something the Holy Spirit prompts a Christian to do.[102]   "Peace" suggests harmony with one's fellow man because we are at

---

[99] Elsewhere, Paul urges Christians to "consider" themselves to be dead to sin (Romans 6:11). It is only as we fail to listen to our inner man (the spirit), as prompted by the Holy Spirit, and instead heed the stirrings prompted by the devil in our minds and physical bodies, that we continue to produce the works of the flesh.

[100] A division of the nine virtues into three groups was popularized by Lightfoot (*Galatians*, p.212). The punctuation of Nestle-Aland[26] (but not of UBS[3]) divides these nine virtues into three groups of three.

[101] "As distinguished from *philia*, the love of mere liking and affection, *agapē* is the love of intelligent comprehension united with corresponding blessed purpose. So God loved the world, understood all its sin, and purposed to remove it. He could not embrace the foul, stinking world in *philia*, but He did *agapē* it and sent His Son to cleanse it. We cannot offer affection (*philia*) to our enemies who would smite us in the face; Jesus did not love the Pharisees with *philia* and does not ask us so to love our enemies. It is *agapē* that He asks, the love that understands the hatefulness of the enemy and purposes to remove it" (Lenski, *op. cit.*, p.291).

[102] If the fruit is emphasizing our behavior toward our fellow man, then joy would seem to be more than a feeling of happiness that results from pleasant circumstances. While joy can be the result of contemplating the hope of heaven (Romans 12:12), we are not sure that is the idea found in Galatians 5.

Page 239   Galatians 5:22,23

peace with God.   In Romans 14:17, "peace" that characterizes the kingdom of God is doing such things as make the other person feel at peace.   "Let us pursue the things which make for peace and the building up of one another" (Romans 14:19).   As Boice notes, "Peace should be seen in the home (1 Corinthians 7:12-16), between Jew and Gentile (Ephesians 2:14-17), within the church (Ephesians 4:3; Colossians 3:15), and indeed in the relationships of the believer with all men (Hebrews 12:14).   Moreover, Christians are to strive for it (1 Peter 3:11)."[103]   Jesus spoke of the spiritual prosperity of those who were "peacemakers" (Matthew 5:9).

Patience, kindness, goodness - "Patience" (*makrothumia,* sometimes translated "long-suffering") speaks of "putting up with people"[104] who are difficult to please or get along with.   It is patience with people who injure you.   It is the person who could retaliate or revenge himself, but does not because he chooses not to.   Such a person keeps himself under control for a long time.   It is a virtue for which Christians are to strive (Ephesians 4:2; Colossians 1:11, 3:12).   Christians are Godlike when they exhibit patience.[105] Etymologically, "kindness" (*chrestotēs*) means useable, willing to be of service to others. This also is a quality of God (Psalm 34:8 [LXX 33:8]; Romans 2:4, 11:22; 1 Peter 2:3). God is good (kind) all the time.   "Goodness" (*agathosunē*) has the sense of active benevolence, generosity.   It is the opposite of *phthonos* ("envyings," one of the works of the flesh).   "Goodness" tries to bestow on others what is good and beneficial.

5:23a – *faithfulness, gentleness, self-control;*

Faithfulness, (and in verse 23a) **gentleness, self-control** - Lightfoot called this trio "principles that guide a Christian's conduct."[106]   If we are still talking about our relationships to our fellow men and how our behavior affects them, then "faithfulness" is reliability

---

Because Christians do rejoice in God through our Lord Jesus Christ, through whom we have received the reconciliation (Romans 5:11), such a joy should manifest itself in its behavior toward one's fellow man.

[103] Boice, *op. cit.,* p.498.   "The word stands in contrast with those sins of malignity and strife noted before among the works of the flesh.   If the peace of God rules, is arbitrator (*brabeuei*) in our hearts individually, if it holds guard over our hearts (2 Corinthians 13:11; Colossians 3:14,15), it cannot fail to produce and maintain harmony amongst us toward one another" (Hendriksen, *op. cit.,* p.262).

[104] Berry, *op. cit.,* p.10.   The other synonyms for "patience" are *hupomonē*, putting up with things that are trials, and *anochē*, which is forbearance temporary in its nature.

[105] The adjective form (*makrothumos*) of "patience" appears in the LXX as an attribute of God (Exodus 34:6; Psalm 103:8 [102:8 LXX].   In the New Testament it is used of God and Christ in their attitude toward people (Romans 2:4; 9:22; 1 Timothy 1:16; 1 Peter 3:20; 2 Peter 3:15).

[106] Lightfoot, *op. cit.,* p.212.

or dependability, honesty, fulfilling our promises to them, keeping our word, a person to be trusted. Another possibility is faithfulness to the gospel, for that would mightily affect our relationships to our fellow men. "Gentleness" (*praütes*) describes a tractable spirit, compliant to the teaching of the divine word (cp. James 1:21, "in humility [*en praüteti*] receive the word implanted ....").[107] Is there an intended contrast with the Judaizers who were not submissive to the teachings of divine revelation, but rather were self-reliant and headstrong? "Gentleness" was taught by Jesus and exhibited by Him (Matthew 11:29; 2 Corinthians 10:1). In Galatians 6:1 "gentleness" is the spirit in which discipline must be applied and faults corrected. In 1 Peter 3:15,16, "gentleness" is the spirit in which a defense of the faith is given when Christians are asked to do so. "Self-control" (*enkrateia*) is a compound word made up of *en* (in, with) and *kratos* (strength). It speaks of controlled power. As Aristotle explains the word, the man who is *enkratēs* has powerful passions, but keeps them under control.[108] The last word in the virtues list contrasts markedly with the first (immorality, impurity, sensuality) and last words (drunkenness, carousings) in the vice list. The fruit of the spirit in Galatians are so incredibly *doable* for the Christian. The very familiarity of the words tends to obscure how astoundingly simple they really are for the man whose spirit is alive after he has risen to walk in newness of life.

5:23b - *against such things there is no law.*

Against such things there is no law - "Such" (*tōn toioutōn*) can be either masculine, "such persons", or neuter, "such things" (i.e., 'such fruit'); the NASB treats it as neuter. Just as "such things" in verse 21 indicated that the list of deeds of the flesh were representative, so "such things" here indicates that the list of fruit is viewed as representative rather than exhaustive. Laws are made to restrain evil; the fruit of the spirit are not evil and hence there is no need of any law concerning such. "Neither God nor man makes laws against such qualities and virtues as these, because they work good to all, and ill to none."[109] It seems to this commentator that Paul is substantiating the proposition he wrote in verse 18, "If you are led by the Spirit, you are not under the Law." If so, we should capitalize "Law" here just as it was in verse 18, or we should make both small "l" (law) in both verses. One does not need a set of rules to live by, such as the Judaizers were proposing, if he is living as the spirit prompts, all the while demonstrating the fruit of the spirit.

---

[107] "'Meekness' [gentleness] does not describe a person docile and weak, willing to be blown about by every wind that comes along. Rather, it is a word used elsewhere to describe a spirited warhorse, full of energy and life, but one that is especially responsive to the rein of his rider. The meek Christian is (1) submissive to the will of God, (2) teachable, not too proud to learn, (3) considerate of the rights and needs of others" (Foster, *op. cit.*, p.443, 444).

[108] Aristotle, *Nic. Eth.*, 7.1145bff.

[109] Lipscomb and Shepherd, *op. cit.*, p.272.

5:24 - *Now those who belong to Christ Jesus have crucified the flesh with its passions and desires.*

Now those who belong to Christ Jesus - We believe the ASV is better when it translates *de* as "and." The connection then is this: there is another reason why Christianity does not encourage libertinism. Christians ("those who belong to Christ Jesus"[110]) serve one another through love (verse 13); they walk by the Spirit and do not carry out the desires of the flesh (verse 16); and they have crucified the flesh with its passions and desires. What is true of those who belong to Christ is not true of those who were under the Law of Moses or who were advocating the works of the Law.

Have crucified the flesh with its passions and desires - Lightfoot explained the aorist tense (pointing to one act in the past) as being explained (1) by reference to the time of their becoming members of Christ in baptism, as in Romans 6:6, and (2) as denoting that the change is complete and decisive.[111] Getting control of the flesh with its passions and desires[112] requires the death and burial of the old man and rising to walk in newness of life. The description given here reminds us of what Paul wrote in Romans 6:1-11. Christians do not continue in sin, are not libertine in their behavior, precisely because they have been baptized into death – both His and their own – and then have risen to walk in newness of life. In that immersion into Christ, the old man was crucified with Christ, in order that the body of sin might be done away and we should no longer be slaves of sin. "If we have died with Christ, we believe that we shall also live with Him." Christians know they are not to continue in sin. Men who are free in Christ are not under obligation to the flesh to live according to the flesh (Romans 8:12-14); instead, they are instructed to stop making provision for the flesh (Romans 13:14), and are to stop letting sin reign in their mortal bodies, to obey its lusts (Romans 6:12).

---

[110] Some manuscripts (P46, D, F, G) omit "Jesus" but it is well-supported in the manuscripts since it is found in Sinaiticus, A, B, C, P. The Greek which reads "the Christ Jesus" is not common in the New Testament. Perhaps the article introduces an official description, "the Messiah Jesus" (similar to "the Lord Jesus"). The Scriptures elsewhere describe Christians as belonging to Christ; in fact, the word "Christian" means 'belonging to Christ.' See 1 Corinthians 3:23; Romans 8:9, 14:8; Ephesians 1:14; 2 Timothy 2:19; Titus 2:14.

[111] Lightfoot, *op. cit.*, p.213.

[112] "Flesh" has the same meaning here as found throughout this section beginning with verse 13. "Passions" (*pathēma*) may be passive, the susceptibility of our bodies to evil impressions. "Desires" (*epithumia*, used here in its bad sense) are active, the desire for that which is forbidden. As learned in earlier notes, these evil passions and desires are the result of the tempting work of the devil.

3. **A third safeguard to ensure a wholesome use of Christian liberty is to restore, as the Spirit prompts, those who are caught in a trespass. 5:25-6:5**

Summary: The Spirit-led Christian thinks of others and how he can minister to them. He is not boastful, he makes an effort to restore those who occasionally fall into sin, and in the process he examines his own work and bears his own load. Freedom in Christ has its corresponding responsibilities.

5:25 - *If we live by the Spirit, let us also walk by the Spirit,*

If we live by the Spirit - "We" and "those who belong to Christ" (verse 24) are the same persons. As explained in the comments on verse 16 above, it is our judgment that *pneuma* here in verse 25a should be translated "spirit" (small "s").[113] "Live" speaks about our ruling choices which result in everyday actions. Living by the spirit is the same as allowing the fruit of the spirit to be our motivation.

Let us also walk by the Spirit - "Spirit" in verse 25b is the Holy Spirit. In verse 16 the verb translated "walk" was *peripateō*, the ordinary word for "walk." But here, the word translated "walk" is *stoicheō*, which means "to keep in line, to march in rank and file."[114] In the following verses Paul gives some specific situations where men can keep in step with the Spirit.[115] The instructions Paul is about to write are what the Holy Spirit teaches is expected of Christians.[116] In passing, Paul's exhortation recognizes the fact that sometimes Christian conduct does not always conform to the ideal. Christians do not always keep in step with the Spirit.

---

[113] Those commentators who prefer to capitalize the "S" here, making it a reference to the Holy Spirit, are not able to agree what activity of the Spirit Paul has in mind. Some allude to the work of the Holy Spirit in conversion (similar to "born of the Spirit" in John 3:5,8). Others think the Spirit's help to live the Christian life, alluded to in Romans 8, is in Paul's mind here at Galatians 5:25.

[114] Lenski, *op. cit.*, p.295. The cognate noun *sustoichoi* (corresponds) occurred at Galatians 4:25. The verb *stoicheō* is also used at Romans 4:12 of those who "follow" in the steps of Abraham's faith, and in Galatians 6:16 where Paul offers a prayer for those who "walk" by this rule.

[115] This note assumes that 5:24 closes the paragraph about deeds of the flesh and fruit of the spirit, and that a new paragraph begins at 5:25, as the paragraphing of the NASB indicates. It also assumes the paragraph extends through 6:5 (whereas the NASB treats 6:1 as the beginning of a new, separate paragraph). There are several other paragraphing options, but none is quite as attractive as the one we have adopted. One of those treats 5:25-26 as the close of the exhortation that began at 5:16. Another treats 5:25 as the conclusion of the paragraph that began in 5:16, and 5:26 as the opening of a new paragraph that extends on into chapter 6.

[116] If we treat verse 25 as the conclusion of the previous paragraph, we would be led to believe that the Holy Spirit can plant thoughts in the believer's mind, can help the believer understand the written revelation God has given, and thus give the man's "spirit" some guidelines to know how to walk. Paul's emphasis would be this: With the spirit alive, and the indwelling Holy Spirit to help, who needs a set of rules (laws) like the Judaizers were insisting men needed to remain Christians in good standing with God?

a. If in step with the Spirit, the Christian does not become boastful. 5:26

5:26 - Let us not become boastful, challenging one another, envying one another.

Let us not become boastful - Here is practical instruction #1 that walking in step with the Spirit would demand. "Become" indicates this is a danger a Christian faces. The adjective "boastful" or vainglorious (*xenodoxos*) occurs only here in the New Testament, and the noun from the same root occurs only in Philippians 2:3. It is a compound made up of *doxa* (glory) and *xenos* (strange, foreign, alien[117]). It seems to speak of an empty pride or conceit. It would be a boasting in something other than in Christ. If individual Galatians have been embracing the Judaizing doctrines, they would have thereupon found it easy to polarize over the issue, and become conceited and boastful about their own (exalted) position and to disparage others (who have rejected the Judaizers' doctrine). On the other side, it could be just as easy to picture some, having rejected what the Judaizers taught, boasting in their liberty. The rest of this verse explains what can happen when someone comes to think of himself as better than others.

Challenging one another - "Challenging" (*prokaloumai*) occurs only here in the New Testament.[118] When a person is full of empty pride, he is likely to treat those he regards as inferiors in a contemptuous manner, or pass them by with scarcely concealed disdain. The one who is treated as though he was beneath notice is challenged to respond. He'll show the haughty one that he, too, is somebody, whether the haughty one knows it or not. Kent offers another possible explanation of how some Galatians might be provoking others. He pictures some of the liberal members boldly exercising their freedom in Christ, perhaps causing weaker brothers to stumble (cp. Romans 14-15).[119]

Envying one another - We had a cognate form of "envying" at 5:21. The disdained brother (or the weaker brother in Kent's illustration) will do what he can to deprive the critic of his or her felt advantage. Boastfulness, challenges, and envy are all out of step with what the Holy Spirit teaches.

---

[117] Berry, *op. cit.*, p.68.

[118] The KJV translation "provoking" does not mean "to make angry" as the word now does. In 1611 the word reflected the Latin verb *provocantes*, challenging, e.g., to legal controversy, or to battle, or to mutual comparative estimation in any way. Hendriksen, *op. cit.*, p.265.

[119] Kent, *op. cit.*, p.164.

b. If in step with the Spirit, the Christian will make an effort to restore those who occasionally fall into sin.   6:1-3

6:1 - *Brethren, even if a man is caught in any trespass, you who are spiritual, restore such a one in a spirit of gentleness;* **each one** *looking to yourself, lest you too be tempted.*

Brethren - This verse introduces the second in a series of exhortations which spell out in practical terms what it means to keep in step with the Spirit (5:25), which itself was a safeguard intended to help Christians avoid misusing their liberty.[1] A whole argument may lie hidden in the one word "brethren," which describes their mutual relationship in the Lord. Those who are not brethren are not possible projects for restoration (1 Corinthians 5:12).

Even if a man is caught in any trespass - The introductory words *ean kai* ("even if") have the effect of making the following situation to be an exception that is in some sense extreme. It is not something expected to happen every day. The context indicates the "man" (*anthrōpos*) is a Christian brother or sister.[2] The precise force of *prolambanō* ("caught") is uncertain. Perhaps it means the man was overtaken; that is, he was involved in the sin before he was aware what it really was he was doing. He is surprised by the force of the temptation ("overtaken" is used with temptation in 1 Corinthians 10:13). Perhaps it means the man was surprised by being caught red-handed in his sin by someone else (cp. John 8:4).[3] Although every believer should walk by the Spirit and not yield to the impulses of the flesh (5:16), the fact remains that we do not do so as consistently as we should. "Trespass" (*paraptōma*, to fall when one should have stood upright) is one of the New Testament words for sin.[4]   It indicates not a settled course of action but an isolated

---

[1] It is because of the word "brethren" that the men who divided the Bible into chapters made a chapter break at this place. But Philippians 3:13,17 suffice to show that the occurrence of "brethren" at the beginning of a sentence does not necessarily indicate the commencement of a new section of discourse. How the topics in 5:25-6:10 are related to each other has proven to be a problem for commentators. Redaction critics find no connection at all.   "There is no connection between one admonition and the next ... the collector is not pursuing a connected argument" (J.C. O'Neill, *The Recovery of Paul's Letter to the Galatians* [London: SPCK, 1972] p.67). J.M.G. Barclay (*Obeying the Truth* [Edinburgh: T&T Clark, 1988], p.149-50) and Longenecker try to build an outline on the basis of the plural and singular verbs found in the passage. In this commentary we are relying on the imperative verbs to give us some guidance concerning topics.

[2] Some manuscripts read *anthropōs ek humōn* (a person from among you) or *tis ek humōn* (someone from among you).

[3] The Greek word employed (*prolambanō*) is not used elsewhere in the New Testament with this sense of surprise. However, the meaning of "surprise, overtake, or to detect" is found in the papyri and LXX. (Arndt and Gingrich, *op. cit.*, p.715.)

[4] Berry, *op. cit.*, p.118.

act.[5]   Trespass is used of a breach of the law of God – including the instruction given to Adam (Romans 5:15), or that given through Moses (Romans 5:20), or the laws that regulate human society (Matthew 6:14,15).

You who are spiritual - This part of the sentence explains what is to be done when a fellow believer is caught in a trespass.   The spiritual man is one whose spirit is alive, who walks by the Spirit (5:16,25), and who himself manifests the fruit of the spirit in his own life.[6]   "You" is emphatic in the Greek; the implied contrast is to someone who is carrying out the desire of the flesh (5:16).   How easy it is to think of oneself as superior to the stumbling brother.   With a little smirk of self-righteousness, there is no attempt to help the sinning brother.   'Treat him like an outcast.   Push him down.   He made his own bed; let him lie in it,' is the attitude of the flesh.   "If another man is caught in a fault, what a chance that is, if we are walking by the flesh, to build up our self-esteem by putting him down! But if we are spiritual, walking in the Spirit, we do not want to put the man down.   We want to lift him up, to restore him to right living."[7]   The Christian uses his freedom to help his fallen brother.   "You" is plural.   This is something for all the Galatian Christians to do, not just one individual member (say the one who caught the sinner sinning).   Each Christian should be one of the "spiritual" ones.

Restore such a one - "To 'restore' (*katartizete*) is to straighten out the problem, repair the damage, and thus equip the offender for renewed usefulness in the church."[8]   The present tense of the imperative seems to mean try to restore, try to rehabilitate.   The actual achievement of the restoration may not be in their power.   You cannot make an offender repent, and without repentance there can be no restoration.   When it comes to the means by which such a restoration is accomplished, Paul probably has in mind our Lord's instructions on reconciliation found in Matthew 18:15-35.   Go to the person privately.   If he does not respond, take two or three witnesses.   If he still does not respond, take it to the church.   If he still does not respond, he must be excommunicated in the hope that such action will bring the offender to repentance.   When the offender has repented, he is to be restored into their community.

---

[5] Habitual sin when no repentance occurs is to be dealt with in a different way. See 1 Corinthians 5.

[6] In 1 Corinthians 2:14-15 the person who is *pneumatikos* ("spiritual") stands in contrast to the "natural man" (*psuchikos anthrōpos*).   The latter is a person who is nothing more than an ordinary human soul; the former is the person whose spirit is alive because of righteousness (Romans 8:10).

[7] Root, *op. cit.*, p.36.   Call to mind the Pharisees who dragged a woman taken in adultery before Jesus (John 8).   There was no gentleness there.

[8] Kent, *op. cit.*, p.168.   The same word (*katartizete*) is used for "mending" the nets in Matthew 4:21 and Mark 1:19.   It is also found as a medical term for setting a fractured bone/dislocated limbs (Liddell and Scott, *Greek English Lexicon* [New York: Harper and Brothers, 1836, p.729).

In a spirit of gentleness - "Gentleness" is the attitude a person who demonstrates the fruit of the spirit (5:23) would show. No matter what the circumstances may be, one who is truly spiritual will still deal gently with the offender – even if he is caught in the very act! A spirit of gentleness is the opposite of arrogance and harshness. "How much we appreciate it when the doctor uses tenderness as he sets a broken bone. And how much more should we use tender, loving care when we seek to restore a broken life."[9] Lightfoot was likely on the right track when he suggested that Paul's tone in this passage has been affected by the recent occurrence at Corinth, where he had to warn the Corinthians against over-severity (see 2 Corinthians 2:6-8).[10]

Each one **looking to yourself, lest you too be tempted** - While the attitudes and actions of those who have sinned need special attention, note that Paul here deals not with those who have sinned, but with the attitudes and actions of those who would do the restoring. "We do not want to do the 'restoring' arrogantly or angrily, saying, 'Aren't you ashamed of yourself? You have brought disgrace on all of us good people who are with you in the church.' No, we want to help him gently and meekly, knowing that next week we may be wrongdoers in need of some kindly brethren to restore us to the right way."[11] "Looking to yourself" is a singular verb. Paul has suddenly shifted from the plural to the singular. This looking or watching is something each individual believer must do, as (with the church body) he works to help restore the offending member. No one knows into what sins he may himself be lured. He may be tempted to commit the same sins which he endeavors to amend in others. He may find the act of correction becoming an occasion for conceit. There is danger in the very act of correcting a wrong in another, that the spirit of the Pharisee, thanking God that he is not as other men, may be aroused, which is a great sin. In other words, while you are attempting to restore the sinning brother, do unto others as you would they do unto you if the circumstances were reversed. Christians are frequently admonished to be meek and gentle in teaching, correcting, and dealing with others, especially with the erring. Paul says, "And the Lord's bond-servant must not be quarrelsome, but be kind (gentle) to all, able to teach, patient when wronged, with gentleness correcting those who are in opposition, if perhaps God may grant them repentance leading to the knowledge of the truth, and they may come to their senses and escape from the snare of the devil, having been held captive by him to do his will" (2 Timothy 2:24-26).

6:2 - *Bear one another's burdens, and thus fulfill the law of Christ.*

Bear one another's burdens - This imperative mood verb may introduce another thing done by a Christian who is walking in step with the Spirit, or it may continue the thought

---

[9] Wiersbe, *op. cit.*, p.142.

[10] Lightfoot, *op. cit.*, p.215.

[11] Root, *ibid.*

introduced in verse 1. Paul does not specifically explain what "burdens" (*baros*) he has in mind.[12] If it is a new thought, we could appeal to Romans 15:1-4 and 1 Corinthians 8-10 where strong brothers are urged not to flaunt their freedom but to be governed by the concerns of the weak.[13] If it is a continuation of the thought of verse 1, then the brother has already sinned; now his weaknesses and the areas where he is easily tempted are known. Bearing his burdens means we each help keep him from those temptations. "The one caught in a fault perhaps already is overburdened with a load of guilt and shame. It is not for us to add the weight of our bitter condemnation. Rather, we are to share his load of grief and help him struggle back to the right way and seek the Lord's forgiveness."[14] Or it has been interpreted to mean believers should be concerned about recovering others from their moral lapses, for the day may come that you yourself will need help. The pronoun "one another" is reciprocal, indicating the obligation of burden-bearing is mutual. You help me with my burden; I help you with your burden. The Christian who is walking in step with the Spirit thinks of others and how he can minister to them.

And thereby fulfill the law of Christ - "Thereby" (*houtōs*, in this manner, thus, so) indicates there is a direct correlation between bearing one another's burdens and fulfilling the law of Christ. The verb "fulfill" can be either future indicative (*anaplērōsete*) or an aorist imperative (*anaplērōsate*); the manuscript authority is about equally divided. If the indicative is retained, the clause affirms that in so doing we do fulfill His law. If the imperative is read, this becomes a command; i.e., fulfill it this way, commands Paul.

Exactly what Paul intended to signify when he wrote "the law of Christ" continues to be discussed in the commentaries.

---

[12] The word *baros* ("burden" or weight) points to an excessive weight, such as it is a toil to carry. See the same word used at Matthew 20:12, "who have borne the burden (*baros*) and scorching heat of the day." Lightfoot (*in loc.*) thought "burdens" was a reference to the rules the Judaizers tried to impose. Relevant to the present verse would be the saying of Jesus as He condemned the Pharisees, "They tie up heavy loads, and lay them on men's shoulders; but they themselves are unwilling to move them with so much as a finger" (Matthew 23:4). The Pharisee was not interested in bearing others' burdens; he just added to the burdens of others.

[13] In 1 Corinthians 8-10, Paul indicated he did have certain rights, but he had learned not to use them all the time. Of course the Christian is free to eat food which had been offered to idols (as long as it was not in the idol's temple), and as long as no one who was "weak" expressed a problem with what the Christian was doing. Of course Paul and other traveling apostles could receive a salary for their work (because the Scripture teaches such a principle in Deuteronomy 25:4, Luke 10:7). But Paul preferred not to make this claim and thus worked at the occupation of tent-making in order to support himself and the helpers who accompanied him on his journeys. Paul reasoned that a Christian has a great many privileges, but he is under no obligation to take advantage of them all the time, particularly if such a use of one's freedom would cause problems for others – especially the weaker members of the church. No Christian insists on his rights if his actions would work to the detriment of those for whom Christ died. To order one's behavior in the realm of liberty by the conscience of the other (weaker) person is exactly what love is all about! Freedom is never to be flaunted. Freedom is of no value in itself if it would become a stumbling block to a weaker brother.

[14] Root, *ibid.*

- Barclay's idea that Paul has in mind the Law of Moses as redefined by Christ is flawed since the Old Covenant was not redefined by Jesus, but abrogated (Hebrews 7:12,18; 10:9).

- Others suggest that "the law of Christ" is shorthand for all the teaching of Jesus which first was embodied in oral teaching and then written in the pages of the New Testament Scriptures.[15] 1 Corinthians 9:21 does indicate that Jesus had given some ethical rules by which to live as well as some doctrinal truths to be embraced. So interpreted, the "law of Christ" would have some polemic reference against the Judaizers who are threatening the churches in Galatia. We Christians live by the law of Christ, not the Law of Moses or works of the Law.

- Another suggestion is that Paul has in view the need for each member of the congregation to share in the common financial burdens, and the "law of Christ" thus fulfilled would be His command that "those who proclaim the gospel [should] get their living from the gospel" (1 Corinthians 9:14).[16]

- This commentator has come to the conclusion that "the law of Christ" is the new commandment He gave (John 13:34) to love one another, or, worded another way, that we are to love our neighbors as ourselves (Matthew 22:39; Galatians 5:14).

6:3 - *For if anyone thinks he is something when he is nothing, he deceives himself.*

For - Verse 3 apparently gives a reason to support the admonition in verses 2 and 3 about restoring the erring brother in a spirit of gentleness and bearing one another's burdens. Paul could well be anticipating the reason (namely, a delusion about who they are) why some might refuse to help bear the burdens of others.

If anyone thinks he is something when he is nothing - A person who thinks he is something (great) has a puffed-up opinion of himself; recall what 5:26 said about boasting. "Nothing" says they are not as important or as superior as they think they are. Paul assumes that the reason some Christians do not try to help others carry their burdens is that they think it is beneath them, that they don't have time for such things.

He deceives himself - The verb *phrenapata* is made up of *phren*, "mind" and *apatein*, "to deceive." He is having subjective fancies, it is self-delusion. Both the verbs "thinks" and "deceives" are present tense, indicating continuing action. The man who persuades himself he is something when he is nothing is deluded.   What he fancies in his mind are

---

[15] C.H. Dodd, *Gospel and Law* (Cambridge: Cambridge University Press, 1951), p.64-83. W.D. Davies, *Paul and Rabbinic Judaism* (Philadelphia: Fortress Press, 1980), p.111-46. R.N. Longenecker, *Paul, Apostle of Liberty* (New York: Harper and Row, 1964), p.181-208.

[16] J.G. Strelan, "Burden-Bearing and the Law of Christ: A Re-examination of Galatians 6:2," *JBL* 94 (1975), p.266-276, argued that Paul is here enjoining the sharing of each member of a common financial burden of the congregation (primarily the maintenance of missionaries and teachers, as in verse 6, together possibly with their contribution to the Jerusalem relief fund). While it is very likely that verse 6 does have reference to the offering for Jerusalem, we are not convinced the offering is introduced as early as verse 2.

not real facts.   James 1:26 speaks of a man who "deceives his own heart" and who thinks he is religious without ever practicing any practical benevolence or bridling his own tongue.   Likewise, a religion that will not bear one another's burdens is vain.

c.   If in step with the Spirit, the Christian will examine his own work and bear his own load.   6:4,5

6:4 - *But let each one examine his own work, and then he will have* reason for *boasting in regard to himself alone, and not in regard to another.*

But let each one examine his own work - This is another in the series of imperative verbs in this paragraph.   "Examine" means to test or examine by some objective standard, and the present tense indicates this is something to be done on a regular basis.   Let him keep on testing his own work.   A free man has the responsibility of obeying what he is here commanded to do.   "His own" is contrasted with "another" (close of the verse).   "Work" seems to mean conduct, a person's deeds, his fulfilling of the tasks God has given him to do.[17]   "Work" is emphatic by position and may contrast to "thinks" and being deceived by his own fancies (verse 3).   Instead of using other men as a standard of comparison, the standard to which a Christian compares himself is the word of God.   Nothing is to be taken for granted in the Christian life.   The Scriptures provide the standard by which the believer is to test alike what he is, and what he does, and what he allows.   The word of God is that by which men are to be judged in the last day (Romans 2:2, "the judgment of God is according to truth" (ASV); John 12:48).

And then he will have *reason for* **boasting in regard to himself alone, and not in regard to another** - "And then" seems to mean once he has examined his own actions in the light of the word of God, then there is a boasting that may occur.   If he can only boast because he sees more shortcomings in his fellow men than he sees in himself, he has little reason for boasting.   Christians who are walking in step with the Spirit do not spend their time comparing their own attainments/accomplishments to those of others in order to feel superior.   They do spend time comparing their own actions with what God has revealed He approves.   If God approves, then the Christian has reason to be satisfied and exult (boast).[18]

---

[17] For other exhortations to Christians to examine themselves, see 1 Corinthians 11:28, 2 Corinthians 13:5, and 1 Thessalonians 5:21.

[18] "Boasting" (*kauchēma*) speaks of exultation or congratulation.   The English word "boast" has a connotation of excessive or unjustified exaltation, a connotation the Greek word does not necessarily carry. When a Christian has his eyes on God and His commandments rather than on other Christians, then in his own eyes he will at best be an unprofitable servant (Luke 17:10).

6:5 - *For each one shall bear his own load.*

For each one shall bear his own load - Verse 5 gives a reason for what was said in verse 4 about each one examining his own work. The future tense "shall bear" suggests Paul has the final judgment in view. On that day we will not have to answer for what our neighbor did. We will answer to God for our own actions, and our own alone.[19] Let a man recognize that he is soon to stand at the judgment seat to answer for the deeds he has done in the body, and it will do much to keep him from an improper comparison with his erring fellow Christians. There is no way for a rational human being to escape responsibility for his own actions. At the final judgment each Christian will be asked to give an account for how he fulfilled freedom's responsibilities.

4. **The fourth safeguard to ensure wholesome use of Christian liberty is to be generous when there is an opportunity to help those who are in need. 6:6-10**

> *Summary*: There is a precept (verse 6), a spiritual principle (verses 7,8), an exhortation (verses 9a,10), and a promise (verse 9b) involved in this way a spiritual man safeguards his Christian liberty.

6:6 - *And let the one who is taught the word share all good things with him who teaches.*

And let the one who is taught the word - This verse contains another of the imperative mood verbs Paul wrote, and it highlights a fourth safeguard by which Christians can ensure a right use of Christian liberty (Galatians 5:13a). The person being addressed in this command is anyone who receives instruction in the truths of the gospel. "Taught" translates the participle *katēchoumen*, a word denoting oral instruction.[20] "The word" denotes Christian doctrine as in Mark 2:2, 4:14; Acts 6:4, 13:7; Philippians 1:14; Colossians 4:3; and 1 Thessalonians 1:6.[21] It might speak of the original instruction in the

---

[19] "Load" (*phortion*) in this verse is something different from "burdens" (*baros*) in verse 2. The NASB has done well to use two different words to translate at this place, lest the reader think there must be a contradiction between verses 2 and 5. *Phortion* is a load which it is man's normal work to carry. "If we allow Christ's statement (Matthew 11:28-30) to interpret the meaning for us, we understand Paul's reference to mean the responsibilities of practical discipleship which our Lord expects His followers to accept" (Kent, *op. cit.*, p.170).

[20] Our word catechism comes from this Greek word, but the Greek word does not imply instruction by question and answer as the word now often connotes.

[21] "In the New Testament this word always refers to religious instruction (Luke 1:4; Acts 18:25; Romans 2:18; 1 Corinthians 14:19)." (Matera, *op. cit.*, p.215.)

gospel that led the hearers to become Christians, or it might refer to that instruction which follows conversion (i.e., the "teaching them to observe all things" of the Great Commission).

Share all good things with him who teaches - This verse says that those who are taught are under obligation to provide the teacher with such temporal goods (such as money, food, clothing, shelter) as they are able to do.[22] The word "share" (*koinōneō*) has a broad range of uses in the New Testament, but the basic idea of the word-family is 'common, having in common, participating in a common cause.' The imperative verb is in the present tense, expressing that the sharing is to be the regular, customary behavior of someone in step with the Spirit.[23] In this passage, just who is "him who teaches" for whom Paul solicits support? In the Introductory Studies we suggested that there is a distinct similarity between the language of Galatians 6 and the language in 2 Corinthians 9:6ff. In this light, we conclude Galatians 6:6-10 speaks of the collection for the poor Christians at Jerusalem that was being amassed during Paul's third missionary journey, concerning the organization and administration of which Paul had sent instructions to the churches of Galatia (1 Corinthians 16:3ff). There certainly would be nothing out of place in seeing these instructions as a reminder to continue their part in the gathering of the monies – a gathering which may have been interrupted by the dispute and dissension that has troubled the churches since the Judaizers came to town. The Jerusalem church had ultimately been responsible for sending missionaries to the Mediterranean world. Now they were in financial difficulty, and so an appeal is made to those who had been converted to remember the folk who sent teachers to them.[24] Following the command, Paul next enforces it with a spiritual principle.

---

[22] It is the verb used in Romans 12:13, where we read the exhortation about "contributing to the needs of the saints." Often in the New Testament, *koinōnia* refers to the sharing of material blessings with one another (Acts 2:42; 2 Corinthians 8:4, 9:13; Hebrews 13:16).

[23] The obligation of believers to support their teachers financially is a frequent Pauline theme (1 Corinthians 9:3-14; 2 Corinthians 11:7-9; Philippians 4:10-19; 2 Thessalonians 3:7-9; 1 Timothy 5:17.18).

[24] Those who think there is a local Galatian application of students supporting their teachers have offered some thoughtful comments at this place. Kent (*op. cit.*, p.171,172) suggests this exhortation about support of teachers may well have been needed at Galatia. "All too often ... an unfortunate episode with one minister is allowed to color the thinking of a congregation toward all ministers, and their feelings are reflected in the way they respond to the matter Paul raised in Galatians 6:6." Kent goes on to quote what Martin Luther said about the same problem in his day. "In the old days when the Pope reigned supreme, everybody paid plenty for masses. The begging friars brought in their share. Commercial priests counted the daily offerings. From these extortions our countrymen are now delivered by the gospel. You would think they would be grateful for their emancipation and give generously for the support of the ministry of the gospel and the relief of impoverished Christians. Instead, they rob Christ. When the members of a Christian congregation permit their pastor to struggle along in penury, they are worse than heathen."

6:7 - *Do not be deceived, God is not mocked; for whatever a man sows, this he will also reap.*

Do not be deceived - The Greek prohibits the continuance of an action already going on: "Stop being deceived!" Any conviction that we can get away with less than God expects is the result of the devil's work. It certainly is not walking in step with the Holy Spirit.

God is not mocked - We are not quite sure what "mocked" (*muktērizein*) signifies. The word literally means to turn up the nostrils (*muktēr*) in scorn. Lightfoot says the word denotes a feeling of contempt which is thinly veiled by a polite show of respect.[25] Then it comes to mean to defy and get away with it. To claim that one accepts the whole counsel of God as found in His word and then acts in contradiction to what the word commands so clearly (about "sharing all good things") is to treat God with contempt. It is an abuse of one's freedom to think he can ignore a responsibility to those who were one's teachers. Withhold your money, and you will soon see God is not to be trifled with.

For whatever a man sows, this he will also reap - This phrase seems to give the general principle of God's government over man; the next verse has phrases which apply the principle. In 2 Corinthians 9:6 the same idea is expanded a bit, "He who sows sparingly shall reap sparingly; and he who sows bountifully shall also reap bountifully." That verse appears in a context that speaks about liberality in the collection of the offering for the poor Christians in Judea. In this commentator's judgment, the same subject – liberality in almsgiving – is the thing being discussed in this paragraph in Galatians.

6:8 - *For the one who sows to his own flesh shall from the flesh reap corruption, but the one who sows to the Spirit shall from the Spirit reap eternal life.*

For the one who sows to his own flesh shall from the flesh reap corruption - "For" (*hoti*, because) shows this verse gives proof of what was just said in verse 7 about reaping what one sows. Many preachers and expositors have used this verse as a point of departure for a sermon against immorality and dissipation. Much rather, we should note the context is speaking of the support of the teachers of the gospel. A man, then, who fails to share in the teacher's physical needs would be, out of selfishness, sowing to his own flesh. By keeping for himself what he could contribute to the teacher, a man would be sowing to his own flesh.[26] Our willingness (or lack of it) to respond to the needs of our

---

[25] Lightfoot, *op. cit.*, p.219.

[26] Some commentaries speak of a change of figure here, and suggest the "flesh" is the soil into which the seed is cast. Such an idea is usually expressed by "sow" and a prepositional phrase (either *en*, "in," or *epi*, "upon"). Here the preposition is *eis*, "into." It is more obvious to take *eis* here as denoting the goal or object of his action of sowing; namely, the gratifying of his own merely worldly inclinations.

brethren is directly related to whether we are living according to the flesh or whether we are living according to the spirit. The inevitable harvest that comes from pandering to the flesh is "corruption." In this place, where "corruption" is contrasted with "eternal life" in the next phrase, a number of comments have been produced in an effort to explain the word.[27] One essential element in this word *phthora* ("corruption") is the notion of decay, or rot. Will one of the horrors of hell be physical corruption? Paul does teach that the wicked shall experience a resurrection of the body, just as will the righteous (Acts 24:15). This commentator has often wondered if the "second death" (Revelation 20:14) is the loss of the resurrection body. The idea of physical corruption of the resurrection body of the unredeemed might also fit Jesus' words (Mark 9:43-48) about the worm dying not, where the idea is that of worms or maggots that prey upon rotting flesh.[28]

But the one who sows to the Spirit - In a context which speaks of support of teachers of the gospel, one would sow to the Spirit by generous support of those teachers (as contrasted with the man who prefers to use his goods merely for his own selfish pleasures). Sowing to the Spirit would mean the Christian is motivated with an object of pleasing the Spirit who prompts obedience to the Lord.[29]

Shall from the Spirit reap eternal life - The idea that the Holy Spirit has something to do with the final resurrection and the rewards at the judgment is also taught in Romans 8:11, "If the Spirit of Him who raised Jesus from the dead dwells in you (as the guiding, animating influence in your lives), He who raised Christ Jesus from the dead will also give life to your mortal bodies through His Spirit who indwells you." "For Paul, 'eternal life' meant an everlasting companionship with Christ."[30] At Christ's return there will be honor for those who have fulfilled their responsibility to respond to the needs of others.

---

[27] Verses that speak of corruption of faith and morals in this life, such as 2 Peter 2:12, would not be apropos in this context.

[28] In these comments about decay and corruption we are not advocating the annihilation of the wicked, for the soul could survive the decay of the body. Two other passages should be considered. Observe that *aphtharsia* (incorruption) is never predicted of the future bodily condition of those who are perishing; it is only the redeemed who are raised incorruptible (1 Corinthians 15:42-54). Then Romans 2:7, which speaks of "those ... who seek for glory and honor and immortality (incorruption)," implies that incorruption is something that pertains not to the wicked but exclusively to the redeemed.

[29] See the comments on *eis* in "sows to his own flesh" in footnote #26 above. We have the same construction (*eis* and the accusative) here.

[30] Johnson, *op. cit.*, p.171.

6:9 - *And let us not lose heart in doing good, for in due time we shall reap if we do not grow weary.*

Let us not lose heart in doing good - To "lose heart" (*egkakeō*) means to become tired or weary or discouraged. In this context, "doing good"[31] refers to the financial support of the poor at Jerusalem (see notes on verse 6) though the exhortation may include more than meeting the needs of the Christians in Jerusalem.[32] When men get discouraged in some course of action they tend to quit that action (see "grow weary" in the next phrase). Christians must guard their hearts against becoming discouraged in doing good – there is often opposition to the best plans for doing good, there is so much to be done, there are so many calls upon their time and their charities, and there is often so much ingratitude among those whom they endeavored to benefit. Yet none of these negatives is sufficient reason to cease attempts to do good. Keeping at it is one of freedom's responsibilities.

For in due time we shall reap if we do not grow weary - As outlined earlier in the summary of this paragraph, we have now come to the promise that is made to those who habitually use their freedom to do good. "Grow weary" (*ekluō*) means to faint physically from exhaustion, to give up further effort because of a feeling of weakness.[33] This word implies a step further than the discouragement ("lose heart") of the previous phrase. This word speaks of quitting any further efforts at doing good. "Due time" (*kairos idios*) is "the season assigned to an event in the counsels of God. Compare 2 Thessalonians 2:6 and 1 Timothy 6:15."[34] Generous acts do not always bring instantaneous commendation, but there will be commendation when God determines the time is right. "We shall reap" looks forward to the same time alluded to in verse 8, namely, the final judgment with its rewards and punishments. There are rewards for those who don't give up and quit when it comes to doing good for others. In his letter to the Romans (Romans 2:6ff), Paul wrote that habitual persistence in well-doing will be rewarded at the final judgment. That is the time when each one who has pursued his Christian life by sowing to the Spirit will hear "well done, good and faithful servant" (Matthew 25:21, KJV).

6:10 - *So then, while we have opportunity, let us do good to all men, and especially to those who are of the household of the faith.*

---

[31] Good" translates *kalos*, a word that denotes beauty, attractiveness, loveliness.

[32] A case could be made that the doing of good includes all four of the safeguards to liberty that began at 5:13 – serving one another in love, walking by the Spirit, attempting to restore the erring brother, and sharing material goods with those in financial need.

[33] The word occurs elsewhere in the New Testament at Matthew 15:32; Mark 8:1; and Hebrews 12:3,5.

[34] Hendriksen, *op. cit.*, p.303.

So then, while we have opportunity - "So then" (*ara oun*) introduces a summary conclusion of the preceding argument.   Paul pauses, as it were, to let what has been written register in the readers' minds, and then draws his inference and drives the point home.   The word "opportunity" is *kairon*, the same word translated "due time" in 6:9; i.e., look at this observed need as a divinely given opportunity to do good.   There is a God-determined season for sowing just as for reaping.

Let us do good to all men - "Let us do good" is a present subjunctive.   Continuous action is encouraged.   In view of the harvest, in view of the fact that we reap what we sow, in view of the fact that known needs are God-given opportunities – all of these are encouragements to continue doing good.   The word "good" (*agathon*) is different from the "good" of verse 9.   The present term is used more frequently for an act of kindness or beneficence, of something that is upright, honorable, and acceptable to God.   "To all men" speaks of those who are not Christians as the contrast with "household of the faith" in the next phrase shows.   In the parable of the Good Samaritan, Jesus taught that whoever is in need, whoever he is, is our neighbor.   In perfect harmony with this, Paul instructs that when occasions to do good come before the Christian, he should take advantage of them.   Jesus went about doing good.   As His servants, we follow His example.

And especially to those who are of the household of the faith - As we do good to all people, we give a priority in our generosity to our fellow Christians.   Again, in this context of an appeal to share in the offering for the poor saints at Jerusalem, Paul especially encourages participation because the potential recipients are part of our same "household of the faith."   *Oikeioi* (here translated "household") means "a member of a household."[35]   The church is represented as a household in Ephesians 2:19; 1 Timothy 3:15; Hebrews 3:6; 1 Peter 2:5 and 4:17.   Paul is saying the folk who were in the Jerusalem church are our relatives, members of the same spiritual family.   The Greek reads the household "of the faith."   In this case, "the faith" is probably nearly equivalent to the gospel.   Christians are distinguished from other men by their faith, their obedience to the gospel.   Kent reminds us that it is a Biblical principle that members of a family have a special responsibility for the members of their own family (1 Timothy 5:8), and this is also true when the family is the spiritual one that is the household of God.[36]

---

[35] Arndt and Gingrich, *op. cit.*, p.559.

[36] Kent, *op. cit.*, p.175.

CONCLUSION OF THE LETTER.   6:11-18

A. Final Warning Against the Judaizers.   6:11-16

> *Summary*:   In his final warning against the Judaizers, Paul exposes their motives and censures their teachings.   He accuses them (1) of insincerely trying to make a good impression on their listeners, (2) of urging circumcision in order to avoid being persecuted, (3) of not keeping the Law, and (4) of urging circumcision in order that they can boast in the flesh of the Galatians.   In contrast to the Judaizers' boasts, Paul offers his own example of boasting in the cross of Christ as a model to be followed by the Galatians.

6:11 - *See with what large letters I am writing to you with my own hand.*

See with what large letters I am writing to you with my own hand - In this commentator's judgment, here in verse 11 Paul is telling his readers he has done something unusual, something he perhaps did in no other instance, and something he did because of his heart-felt interest in the Galatians.   Instead of dictating this letter to a secretary, he had written this entire letter in his own hand.[37]   "See" is imperative in the better-attested Greek text.   Paul wants the Galatians to take note of the large letters he is writing.   Each of the Greek words (*pēlikois humin grammasin egrapsa*, "how large letters I am writing to you") has been given a variety of interpretations.   The KJV translators treated "letters" as though it were singular, "how large a letter I have written."[38]   Yet in comparison to Paul's other

---

[37] This commentator admits this is an interpretation of verse 11, but the only one he knows that would explain satisfactorily the call of attention to the handwriting. It was customary for Paul, when he had finished dictating a letter, to take the pen in his own hand and add a subscription (2 Thessalonians 3:17). Such a practice guaranteed the letter was from Paul himself, and not a forgery.   Though papyri examples of ancient letters show the body written in neat, well-formed uncial letters, and the subscription written in cursive, F.C. Kenyon (*Handbook to Textual Criticism of the New Testament* [Grand Rapids: Eerdmans, nd], p.30) has suggested that the scribe used the common cursive script, but that Paul wrote his concluding remarks in large, separately formed uncial letters. (However, Kenyon gives no examples of Greek manuscripts that exhibit this handwriting phenomenon.) Paul intended that his letters to churches be read out loud in the public assembly. The one reading the letter would see the change in handwriting styles, but normally the listeners would not be aware of any change in handwriting styles, even though the wording of the subscription was such that the listeners would know the end of the letter was near. As the author wrote the subscriptions in his own hand, he often summarized the basic points of the letter.

[38] Though the plural noun *grammata* (writings), in ordinary Greek, like *literae* in Latin, sometimes occurs in the sense of a single epistle or letter, it is never so used by Paul, who always employs the word *epistolē* (epistle or letter) to express that idea.   In Acts 28:21 the plural is translated "letters" because it refers to more than one communication in writing.   And there are times when the plural "writings" refers to the Scriptures (e.g., 2 Timothy 3:15).

letters, Galatians is not long.[39]   To write "with ... letters" does not seem to mean to write a letter. The word "what large" seems to have reference to the size of the letters.[40]   For some reason or other they are larger in size than is usual. What is his reason? It is hard to say. Was it haste and the emotion of the hour that caused the handwritten letters to be larger than otherwise might have been the case? Was Paul using the ancient equivalent of bold print so the readers would not miss the point?[41] "Writing" (*egrapsa*) is an aorist tense in the Greek. If treated as an epistolary aorist, it could be limited only to the closing words of the letter. If treated as an historical aorist, it refers to the whole letter. The NASB's translation "I am writing" treats *egrapsa* as an historical aorist.[42]   When the letter was read out loud, this note about the large size letters used when writing the letter would call attention to the fact that Paul had written the whole letter by his own hand.   Just as we appreciate a personal, handwritten note, that Paul should write to them a whole letter in his own hand would give the Galatians evidence of Paul's special interest in them and his regard for them.   By calling attention to his own handwriting, he would be calling attention to who he is – an apostle. He has a right to speak for Christ. His message is a message from God.

6:12 - *Those who desire to make a good showing in the flesh try to compel you to be circumcised, simply that they will not be persecuted for the cross of Christ.*

Those who desire to make a good showing in the flesh - In summarizing the anti-Judai-

---

[39] It is either the fifth or sixth longest of Paul's letters: Romans, 1 and 2 Corinthians, Ephesians, and Hebrews are all longer than Galatians.

[40] Some manuscripts (P[46], B*, 33) read *helikois* ("how great") in place of *pēlikois* ("what large"). *Helikos* is the classical spelling of the word.

[41] Either of these proposals is more convincing than some others that have been conjectured. Deissmann (*Light*, p.166, n.7) suggested that "writing was not an easy thing to his workman's hand." Another guess is that Paul was not accustomed to writing Greek and so used large letters, much like a child, who when beginning to write prints large letters on his wide-lined tablet. A variation of this idea, based on the fact that Hebrew printed letters were larger than Greek printed letters, is that Paul's Greek letters approached in size the Hebrew he was used to writing. Each of these guesses has this problem: they would not have been deliberately-made large letters, which is what Paul's language here in verse 11 seems to require.

[42] A great number of Greek and Latin Fathers interpreted this verse to mean Paul personally penned the whole letter. Since the time of Theodore of Mopsuestia and Jerome, many writers have sided with their different view, contending that Paul only wrote the conclusion with his own hand. Arguments are not conclusive for either view. One side argues that since Paul elsewhere penned only the final greetings (1 Corinthians 16:21; Colossians 4:18; 2 Thessalonians 3:17) we might expect the same to be true of Galatians. They also point to Galatians 1:20, where Paul used the present tense of *graphō* when referring to this very letter he is writing. The other side calls attention to Romans 15:15 where *egrapsa* ("I have written") refers to the whole letter. They also contend there is no instance (unless it be this passage, Galatians 6:11) where Paul ever uses the aorist *egrapsa* to designate the writing of only a few concluding remarks. Though Paul's practice, when writing letters, was to use the services of a professional scribe (an amanuensis), the letters to Philemon, to the Hebrews, and the one here to the Galatians are exceptions.

zer thrust of his whole letter, in a few concise statements Paul lays his case on the line. He characterizes the Judaizers as ones who "desire to make a good showing in the flesh." The verb "make a good showing" (*euprosōpēsai*) means to make a good impression on one's neighbors, but it also carries an overtone of insincerity as one goes about trying to make that impression.[43] The Judaizers were not what they first appeared to be. They were role-playing before men. They were only interested in external things ("in the flesh"). We are reminded of Jesus' accusation of the Pharisees, that they were like whitewashed tombs which "on the outside appear beautiful, but inside they are full of ... all uncleanness" (Matthew 23:27).

Try to compel you to be circumcised - "Compel" (the same word used of Peter's actions in 2:14) suggests that the Judaizers had not had any marked success yet at Galatia when it came to getting the Gentile Christians to accept circumcision.

Simply that they will not be persecuted for the cross of Christ - In a few bold strokes Paul exposes one real motive of the Judaizers. Their motive actually had nothing to do with the welfare of the Galatians, nor did the Judaizers have any real convictions concerning the value of circumcision. Rather, their motive was totally selfish – so that they themselves would not be persecuted.[44] "Simply that" means the Judaizers have no other reason than this.[45] Galatians 5:11 indicated that if circumcision were still required, then the cross of Christ would no longer be a stumbling block for the Jews. In a similar vein, if the Judaizers can just get the Gentile Christians circumcised, they will no longer be persecuted over the matter of circumcision. The Judaizers taught and practiced what they did, not from any true love for the cause of the Jewish religion or the welfare of the Galatian Christians, only that they might avoid persecution from the Jews, whether it be Pharisees,[46]

---

[43] Many of the older commentaries suggested Paul may have coined this word, since for years it was unknown in any literature written before Galatians. However, another example has been found dating from the 2nd century BC (Tebtunis Papyri, cited in Moulton and Milligan, *op. cit.*, p.264).

[44] There is a slight variation in the Greek here. Some manuscripts (P46, B, K, Ψ) have a present indicative reading, meaning the persecution is a present reality. Some manuscripts have a present subjunctive, meaning the persecution is a potential thing in the future.

[45] We do not treat this as a mere judgment call on Paul's part, a call that may be nothing more than his personal, highly subjective belief. We treat this as God's view of the matter, vouchsafed to His mouthpiece/apostle.

[46] The Jews could be fanatical about the matter of circumcision. Acts 21:18-28 tell us of the time circumcision nearly got Paul killed when Jewish people thought he brought an uncircumcised Gentile into the sacred precincts of the temple. The Judaizers pretended to join church under false pretenses. They superficially identified with Jesus as the Messiah ("in order to spy out our liberty," Galatians 2:4). They weren't real Christians, but as far as unbelieving Jews were concerned, these pseudo-Christian Judaizers were targets for persecution (if they did not bow to the Pharisees' party line). The Judaizers hoped to stay in the good graces of the Jewish community at large by demanding that Christians follow Pharisaic rules, too.

Zealots,[47] or unconverted Jews in general who were zealous for the traditions of their ancestors. The Judaizers were trying to make other fanatical followers of the Mosaic Law think that they, too, obeyed the Law. In this way they hoped to escape being persecuted.

6:13 - *For those who are circumcised do not even keep the Law themselves, but they desire to have you circumcised, that they may boast in your flesh.*

For - "For" serves to continue the explanation begun with the words "simply that." Their only reason is to avoid persecution "for" they certainly are not interested in keeping the Law of Moses. "Good showing" (verse 12) had the connotation of insincerity. The Judaizers' insincerity is shown by the fact they did not carefully observe the Law.

Those who are circumcised do not even keep the Law themselves - In Galatians 5:3 Paul insisted that accepting circumcision as taught in the Law obligated a man to keep the whole Law. Well, keeping the Law[48] was something the Judaizers were not doing.[49] Jesus indicted the Pharisees for making void the Law of Moses by their traditions (see Matthew 15:3-6). What was earlier true of the Pharisees in Judea was true of the Pharisaic

---

[47] The argument that the persecutors were Zealots hinges on the following scenario. If the Gentile Christians were circumcised, non-believing Jews might think of them as being proselytes. In the AD 50s and 60s the Zealots were gaining in power. There was a rising tide of Jewish nationalism. Zealots directed their antagonism against any Jew who had Gentile sympathies or who associated with Gentiles (who were not proselytes). "If they could succeed in circumcising the Gentile Christians, this might effectively thwart any Zealot purification campaign against the Judean church," wrote Robert Jewett, "The Agitators and the Galatian Congregation," *NTS* 17 (1971), p.206. In response to this it might be asked, Would Pharisees pretend to become Christians, then travel hundreds of miles to northern, or even to southern, Galatia in order to insure that Gentile proselytes were circumcised, just to satisfy Zealots in and around Jerusalem?

[48] There is no article ("the") before "Law" in the Greek, but the reference is clearly to the Law of Moses. Paul has often used this way of referring to the Law of Moses in both Galatians and in Romans 2:25,27. Hendriksen (*op. cit.*, p.309) tells us that "keep" translates the verb *phulassō*, which means to guard. He thinks the verb is used here in a way similar to its use in Acts 21:24 and Romans 2:26. As a guard on the wall keeps watch and then takes appropriate action, so "keep" has the notion of watching the Law to see what it requires and then endeavoring to carry it out.

[49] A manuscript variation has caused some commentators to question whether "those who are circumcised" is a reference to the Judaizers who have recently come to Galatia. Because some manuscripts (Sinaiticus, A, C, D, K, P) have a present participle ("those who are being circumcised"), it has been proposed that Paul is talking about those few Galatians who have allowed themselves to be circumcised. But this hardly fits the context, unless the following phrase be interpreted to mean that the now-circumcised Galatians were urging their fellow church members to follow suit. The other reading at this place (found in P[46], B, F, G, L) is a perfect participle. This gives a meaning easier to understand ("those who have actually been circumcised") as it would refer to the Judaizers before they ever came to Galatia. (J. Munck, *Paul and the Salvation of Mankind* [Richmond, VA: John Knox Press, 1959], p.89, interpreted this verse to mean the Judaizers were Gentile Christians who had accepted circumcision and then went on missionary journeys, urging other Gentiles to be circumcised, too. In the Introductory Studies, when discussing Galatians 2:4, we seriously questioned the hypothesis that the Judaizers were Christians.)

Judaizers who had infiltrated the Galatian churches. We recall that Paul has already castigated those who advocated works of the Law for not keeping the whole Law (Galatians 3:10).

But they desire to have you circumcised, that they may boast in your flesh - "But" is the strong adversative *alla*. Instead of keeping the Law (previous verse), they have some other motive behind their behavior.[50] This is the second motive Paul assigns to the Judaizers. First, it was the wish to avoid persecution; now, they want to be able to boast of their success in proselyting Gentiles to Pharisaism.[51] "Boast in your flesh" is equivalent to boasting about getting you circumcised. They wanted to brag about the Galatians being their latest converts and trophies. Now that their real motives are exposed, do the Galatians want to listen to and follow such men?

6:14 - *But may it never be that I should boast, except in the cross of our Lord Jesus Christ, through which the world has been crucified to me, and I to the world.*

But may it never be that I should boast - For the third time (2:17, 3:21) in this epistle, Paul uses the strong disclaimer "may it never be" (*mē genoito*). "I" (the pronoun "to me" in the Greek) stands first in the sentence in emphatic contrast. Paul would never boast in what the Judaizers were boasting. He could never boast about how many proselytes he had made to Pharisaism.

Except in the cross of our Lord Jesus Christ - The "cross of our Lord" means the death Christ underwent for me. The Judaizers had a motive for their actions. Well, so did Paul. Theirs was a fear of persecution and a desire to boast in statistics. He would tell abroad how the cross of Christ had changed his life for the better. By writing "the cross of our Lord Jesus Christ" instead of "my Lord," Paul suggests the Galatians have as much reason to boast on the death of Christ as he did.

Through which the world has been crucified to me, and I to the world - Treating the subscription as containing a summary of major ideas in this letter, we are reminded of 2:20 ("I have been crucified with Christ ...") and 5:24 ("those who belong to Christ Jesus have crucified the flesh with its passions and desires").[52] MacArthur thinks that "world" here

---

[50] When Paul writes about living for the praise of men rather than the glory of God, he is dealing with *motives*.

[51] Jesus condemned the Pharisees' partisan proselyting when He said, "Woe to you, scribes and Pharisees, hypocrites, because you travel about on sea and land to make one proselyte; and when he becomes one, you make him twice as much a son of hell as yourselves" (Matthew 23:15).

[52] The antecedent of the relative *di' hou* with which this verse begins in the Greek can either be the cross ("through which") or Jesus Christ ("through whom"). Since it is not Jesus that Paul has been speaking of glorying in, we think the nearest antecedent ("the cross") is what Paul had in mind.

stands for Satan's "system of sin and false religions,"[53] such as the one the Pharisees were advocating (works of the Law).   This is in harmony with the next verse, which begins with "for," as though Paul is explaining how he used the word "world."

6:15 - *For neither is circumcision anything, nor uncircumcision, but a new creation.*

For - Verse 15 seems intended to give a further explanation of the idea of the "world" introduced in verse 14.   The idea that men's relationships with each other should be conditioned on whether or not they are circumcised is an idea that comes from worldly thinking, not from God.

Neither is circumcision anything, nor uncircumcision - Treating the subscription as containing a summary of key points in the letter, this verse reminds us of 2:12 (where table fellowship was conditioned on whether Gentile believers were circumcised or not), 3:28 (for those in Christ there is neither Jew nor Greek), and 5:6 ("in Christ Jesus neither circumcision nor uncircumcision means anything, but faith working through love").[54] Christians behave by a different standard than the world's standard.

But a new creation - Ephesians 2:11-22 helps us understand what is involved in the "new creation."   Gentiles, Paul tells us, were called "Uncircumcision" by the so called "Circumcision."   Gentiles were separate from Christ and excluded from the common-wealth of Israel.   They were "strangers to the covenants of promise" (Ephesians 2:12). But in Christ Jesus that has all changed.   The blood of Christ, shed on Calvary, has brought people together, and made both groups into one by breaking down the barrier of the dividing wall ("the Law of commandments." Ephesians 2:15).   Christ did this so that "He might make the two into one new man, thus establishing peace" (Ephesians 2:15).   When we observe that the verb "make" (in Ephesians 2:15) can also be translated "create," we have the key to Paul's expression "new creation" here in Galatians.   The new creation is the society in which both believing Jews and believing Gentiles are reconciled "in one body to God through the cross" (Ephesians 2:16).   If the Galatians recognize God's new creation, then it won't matter whether one is circumcised or not.   After all, they are no longer strangers and aliens, but are "fellow citizens with the saints"; together they are "God's household" (Ephesians 2:19).   2 Corinthians 5:17 speaks of being "a new creature" if a person is in Christ Jesus.

---

[53] MacArthur, *op. cit.*, p.137.

[54] The reader may find it helpful to review the comments offered at Galatians 5:6 concerning the different ways the sentence ("circumcision is nothing and uncircumcision is nothing, but ...") is completed in the other passages where it occurs.

6:16 - *And those who will walk by this rule, peace and mercy* be *upon them, and upon the Israel of God.*

And those who will walk by this rule - Has anyone yet missed the point? If so, Paul will state it once more in the form of a prayer. "Walk" is the word "keep in line with" (*stoichēsousin*) that we met at Galatians 5:25 ("walk by, i.e., keep in step with, the Spirit"). "Rule" clearly refers to the previous statement that what really matters is the idea of "a new creation."[55] Paul's prayer for peace and mercy applies to all who keep in step with this rule. Judaizers are not in step with this rule, so there is no prayer for peace and mercy on them.

Peace and mercy *be* **upon them** - The NASB has supplied the verb "be" making this a prayer. Paul is asking God's blessing on all who live in harmony with the doctrine of the new creation (verse 15) in Christ Jesus. The order of the blessings asked – peace and then mercy – has been thought unusual; we are used to an order like "grace and peace" (cp. Galatians 1:3). A little thought may help us understand the order here. If Jewish and Gentile Christians, participants in the new creation, will live in peace (as Paul prays they will), then they may expect God's mercy (Matthew 5:7).

And upon the Israel of God - A great debate revolves around the meaning of *kai* with which this phrase begins in the Greek. It may be translated as "and" or "even." If we translate it "and," there are two groups for whom Paul prays, (1) those who walk by this rule, and (2) the Israel of God. Group one would be Gentile Christians, and group two would be Jewish Christians.[56] If we translate it "even," there is one group for which Paul prays: that one group of persons is described by two phrases, "those who will walk by this rule" and "the Israel of God."[57] The "Israel of God" is spiritual Israel – not converts

---

[55] The word translated "rule" is *kanōn*, the word that later came to be applied to the collection of authoritative Biblical books (i.e., the Canon of Scripture). The word speaks of something that is measured and which then becomes the standard by which other things can be measured. The doctrine of the "new creation" is such a standard by which belief and behavior may be measured.

[56] Johnson (*op. cit.*, p.180) thinks Paul is praying for two groups, Christians and those in Israel who had not yet become followers of Christ. If we were to place a comma after the word "peace," it might suggest that Paul's prayer is for peace on those who are already Christ's, whereas he prays for mercy on those in Israel who are not yet believers. Certain dispensational theologians insist that Israel must be kept distinct from the church. They insist the Jews always were and always will be God's chosen people (in spite of the fact that Jesus indicated the kingdom would be taken away from them and given to a nation [Gentiles] who would bring forth fruit, Matthew 21:43). To make a case that two groups are intended by Paul's language here in Galatians 6:16, attention is called to the unusual order of peace and mercy, to the two uses of the preposition *epi* ("upon") and the two uses of the conjunction *kai* ("and").

[57] So explained, as did Justin Martyr (*Dial.* 11.5) and John Chysostom (*Commentary on the Epistle to the Galatians, ad loc.*), the Christian church is the true, spiritual Israel. The doctrine is that the church has superseded national Israel as the chosen people of God. Dispensationalism, of course, has an abhorrence for supersessionism. This commentator understands that true Israel always was a remnant

from Judaism alone, but all who prove their real affinity to Abraham by a faith like Abraham's (cp. Galatians 3:7-9,29; Romans 4:11,12, 9:6-8).[58]   The words "of God" distinguish this Israel from the Judaizers who boasted they were Israel, when in fact they were only Israel after the flesh.   By adding this appositional phrase, Paul offers one last blow to the Judaizers.   They ignore the rule about the new creation; they cannot be the Israel of God!

B. Appeal Enforced by Reference to His Own Sufferings.   6:17

6:17 – From now on let no one cause trouble for me, for I bear in my body the brand-marks of Jesus.

From now on let no one cause trouble for me - Paul closes the epistle by writing one more imperative verb: it is a present imperative with *mēdeis* ("no one"), which asks that an action already going on should cease.   Stop causing me trouble, any of you!   "From now on" means during the remainder of my life.   While the Judaizers' activities had troubled him, it is unlikely this imperative is addressed to them; false brethren were not likely to listen.   It is likely this is addressed to the Galatian Christians.   Those who were wavering had been a great worry to Paul (Galatians 4:19).   He buttresses this appeal to quit giving way to the teachings of the Judaizers by an appeal to their sympathy.

For I bear on my body the brand-marks of Jesus – 'Haven't I suffered enough for you?' is Paul's appeal for sympathy, and for compliance with his appeal for no more trouble.   "I" is emphatic in the Greek, and it implies a contrast with the other teachers who have recently come to town with their Jewish emphasis.   Those teachers didn't have any scars like Paul did.[59]   He had enough marks that the Galatians certainly must be willing to spare him further unnecessary hurt.   The "brand-marks of Jesus" are likely scars incurred in service

---

(it never was all of the physical descendants of Israel that made up Israel, Romans 11:5).   They are not all "Israel" who are descended from Israel (Romans 2:28,29 and 9:6).   This commentator also teaches the church (comprised of all believers in Jesus whether they be ethnically Jewish or Gentile) has taken the place of the Jewish nation as the true, spiritual Israel, the "Israel of God."   See how Peter applied words that used to be true of the Jewish people to the church in 1 Peter 2:4-10.   He can do this because the church has taken the place of national Israel as God's special chosen servant in the world.

[58] The language of this verse is closely identified with the whole argument of the epistle: if you are Christ's, then you are Abraham's seed, and heirs according to the promise (Galatians 3:29).   These are the Israel of God, whether Jews or Gentiles, for "he is a Jew who is one inwardly; and circumcision is that which is of the heart, in the spirit not in the letter; whose praise is not of men, but of God" (Romans 2:29, ASV).

[59] About all they could show was the irrelevant mark of circumcision.

for Jesus.[60]   Paul had been beaten with rods, scourged with whips, and stoned (2 Corinthians 11:23-27).   You could see the scars on his body that resulted from such harsh treatment.   Paul appeals to the Galatians by saying, 'I got these scars in the service of Jesus, some of them while I was bringing the gospel to you.   Is the cause for which I suffered of so little interest to you?   Are you going to cause me unnecessary wounds by defecting to the Judaizers' side?   Will you not cease to cause me pain?'

C. Final Benediction.   6:18

6:18 – *The grace of our Lord Jesus Christ be with your spirit, brethren.   Amen.*

The grace of our Lord Jesus Christ - Paul has now come to the end of his epistle.   He has confronted the issue that had rocked the churches of Galatia, and has set forth the truth which is inherent in the gospel – that faithfulness to Jesus, not obedience to some man-made rules, is the way to live.   He closes the letter with a prayer for grace for his readers.   "Grace" has been made available by our Lord Jesus Christ.   "Grace" has been a key word in Galatians (see 1:3,6,15; 2:9; and 3:18 ["granted"]).

Be with your spirit, brethren - Galatians has had much to say about "spirit" (fruit of the spirit vs. works of the flesh), a spirit that is alive and can direct a person's behavior.   What Paul wants for the Galatians, what he prays will continue to occur, is that the "grace of our Lord Jesus" (i.e., the help which Jesus can give) may continue to be poured out on those who are living by the spirit (5:25a).   The implied contrast is that folk who defect to the Judaizers will forfeit this grace.   Paul added the affectionate word "brethren" at the end of

---

[60] *Stigmata* is the Greek word translated "brand-marks."   The scars left by branding irons which showed that a slave belonged to a particular person or deity were called *stigmata*.   Perhaps Paul is saying that the marks on his body certified that he was a slave or the property of Jesus.   Deserters from the army and run-away slaves, if they were caught, were branded on the forehead to show to all they were runaways.   Such brands were called *stigmata*.   Those branding irons left permanent welts.   Likewise, Paul seems to be saying that his experiences have left him with permanent welts and scars, as folk who thought him an apostate "branded" him.

Care must be exercised here.   Since the Middle Ages, "stigmata" have come to have a peculiar meaning.   In moments of extreme spiritual tension the blood vessels rupture allowing the blood to spread to the surrounding tissues.   At times the spots under the skin resemble the marks of Christ's suffering (nail prints in hands and feet, thorn prints on the brow, stripes on the body) as, for example, happened in the life of Francis of Assisi.   That those marks were called "stigmata" is the result of the Greek word being left untranslated in the Latin versions.   Thus it passed into the vocabulary of devout Catholics and has come down to us.   There is, of course, no evidence whatever that Paul had nail prints in his hands and feet, a supernatural reproduction in Paul's body of Christ's nail prints.   Nigel Turner (*Grammatical Insights into the New Testament* [Edinburgh: T&T Clark, 1965], p.94) has conjectured that Paul was crucified at Perga in Pamphylia, and literally had the scars to show it.   This suggestion has not been accepted by many scholars.

the letter to take the sting out of the severity of the epistle. Paul loved these Galatian Christians, and all that he has written was penned out of deep concern and anxiety for their continued spiritual welfare.

Amen - The word means "so be it, let it be, may it be fulfilled."[61] It was a custom, which passed from the synagogues into the Christian assemblies, that when one had read a truth from God or had offered up a solemn prayer to God, the others in the assembly responded by voicing "Amen!" – thus making the substance of what had been spoken by another their own (1 Corinthians 14:16). The Galatian Christians could not utter this "Amen" unless they agreed wholeheartedly with what Paul has written. Let us hope they all said "Amen."

Some manuscripts have a subscription after the "Amen." These subscriptions were added by men and were intended to serve as a brief introduction to the historical circumstances from which the letters came. Some are correct; some contain errors. Sinaiticus, A, B*, C, D, F, G read simply "to the Galatians." The subscription as it reads in the KJV ("Unto the Galatians written from Rome") "appears for the first time in manuscripts dating from about the beginning of the 9th century, though before this, the Epistle has been described as written from Rome by Theodoret, Euthalius, and Jerome" (Sanday, *op. cit.*, p.94). In the Introductory Studies we have questioned the phrase "written from Rome," opting instead for Macedonia as the place of writing.

What was the result of this letter on the Judaizers? In all probability, the Galatian Christians were won back to the gospel of freedom as preached by Paul and the other apostles. Certainly Peter and Barnabas were won back earlier at Antioch, as was the whole congregation in that place. In fact there is no intimation in Scripture that the Judaizers ever caused more trouble among the churches of Galatia. Paul argued his case

---

[61] Berry, *op. cit.*, p.7.

well and the Galatians acceded to his request for no more trouble. The fact that, a few months after this letter was written, the Galatian churches participated in the offering for Jerusalem (Acts 20:4) would be evidence the Galatians did all the apostle asked them to do. Thus, it seems that in the Galatian battle the main thrust of the Judaizers' attack on the freedom of the Gentile Christians was broken. The Judaizers no doubt tried to disrupt the Gentile churches here and there in the empire (e.g., Philippians 3:2-4:1 may be another warning of danger from this source), but after the early AD 60's, not much more is heard from the Judaizers. After AD 70, Pharisaism did become normative Judaism but Christians (because of Paul's letters) knew the vital difference between Pharisaism and Christianity, and knew which one to embrace if they would be justified by faith.

What will be the result of this letter on its present-day readers? Galatians has been influential in guiding the thought and practice of Christianity for many centuries. If we allow God to speak to us through the words He inspired Paul to write, then we, too, may follow in the footsteps of those who have chosen to be Abraham's spiritual family. It can help us get our theology right; it can help us give the Biblical answer when potential converts wish to know what to do to be saved; it can help us get our relations with one another right as we participate in God's new creation; and it can help us live the responsible lifestyle a free man or woman in Christ is privileged to live. If our Lord should tarry, and years pass before He returns, will history record that this book of Scripture brought about positive change in our lives?

"It was for freedom that Christ set us free: therefore keep standing firm and do not be subject again to a yoke of slavery" (Galatians 5:1).

GALATIANS BIBLIOGRAPHY

Abegg, Martin, "Paul, 'Works of the Law' and MMT," *BAR* 20:6 (1994), pp.52-55.
> MMT is an abbreviation of a Hebrew phrase meaning "some significant works of the Law." Abegg suggested Paul's use of the same phrase "works of the Law" indicates he was rebutting theology similar to that behind 4QMMT.

Baker, Mike, *Galatians: Freedom in Christ*. Joplin, MO: HeartSpring Publishing, 2006.
> A series of eleven lessons designed for small group study and interaction, as well as individual study.

Barclay, William, *Flesh and Spirit: An Examination of Galatians 5:19-23*. Nashville: Abingdon, 1962.
> A valuable series of word studies contrasting the works of the flesh with the fruit of the Spirit.

Barnes, Peter, *A Study Commentary on Galatians*. Webster, NY: Evangelical Press, 2006.
> Exposition by an Australian Presbyterian, plus illustrations, applications, quotations, and references from other writers. Treats Galatians 3:27 as baptism in water rather than Spirit baptism. Thinks Galatians 4:22-24 would better be called an analogy rather than an allegory or type.

Beet, Joseph A., *A Commentary on St. Paul's Epistle to the Galatians*. London: Hodder and Stoughton, 1885.
> A verse-by-verse presentation from a Wesleyan viewpoint. Defends the North Galatian theory for the destination of the letter, and teaches that the brothers of the Lord were the sons of Joseph by a previous marriage. Has special studies relating Galatians to Acts, Romans, James, and 1 John.

Betz, Hans Dieter, *Galatians* in the Hermeneia series. Philadelphia: Fortress, 1979.
> This commentary, which analyzed Paul's letter against the backdrop of Greco-Roman rhetoric and philosophy, has set much of the recent agenda for interpreting Galatians as commentators seek in various ways to correct, refine, or expand Betz's conclusions.

Boatman, Don Earl, *Guidance from Galatians*, in the Bible Study Textbook Series. Joplin, MO: College Press, 1961.
> A book for use in the classroom, either in church or college, or for individual study at home. Includes questions and examinations to involve the reader in the learning process. James MacKnight's paraphrase of the epistle is printed paragraph by paragraph.

Boice, James M., "Galatians" in Vol. 10 of the *Expositor's Bible Commentary* edited by Frank E. Gaebelein. Grand Rapids: Zondervan, 1976.
> In addition to commentary, there is an introduction, outline, and bibliography offered for Galatians. Greek words and technical notes are found in endnotes at the close of each paragraph of commentary. After a lengthy weighing of arguments pro and con, Boice opts for the South Galatian view for the destination. He likewise presents both sides of the question whether Galatians 2 equals Acts 11 or Acts 15, and opts for the latter.

Boles, Kenneth L., *Galatians & Ephesians* in the NIV College Press Commentary series. Joplin, MO: College Press, 1993.
> Gives a summary of arguments for both North and South Galatian theories for the destination, and lists a wide range of possible dates for the writing of the letter.   The troublemakers are identified as "old line Christians from Jerusalem" (p.62).   The NIV's "observing the Law" is accepted for "works of the Law" at Galatians 2:16 without any question.   The result is that Galatians is summarized as teaching the gospel of grace rather than allowing men to believe they are saved by keeping enough rules, enduring enough pain, or siding with the orthodox on enough of the issues.

Bruce, F.F., *The Epistle to the Galatians: A Commentary on the Greek Text*, in the New International Greek Testament Commentary series.   Grand Rapids: Eerdmans, 1982.
> A phrase-by-phrase exegesis of the UBS Greek text edited by Kurt Aland and others.   It is recognized as one of the great commentaries on Galatians.

-----, "Galatian Problems: 1. Autobiographical Data." *BJRL*, 51:2 (Spr. 1969), pp.292-300.
> In this article Bruce defends the task of fitting Galatians into the narrative framework of Acts.   His conclusion is that Galatians 2:1-10 = the famine visit (Acts 11:27-30).

-----, "Galatian Problems: 2. North or South Galatians?" *BJRL*, 52:2 (Spr. 1970), p.243-66.
> Bruce discusses the geographical location where the recipients of Galatians lived.   Traces Galatian history from an early 3rd century BC Celtic migration to the Roman province of the New Testament period.   Examines Lightfoot's arguments for the North Galatian theory, and Ramsay's arguments for the South Galatian theory.   Finds Marxsen's arguments for the North Galatian theory unconvincing.

-----, "Galatian Problems: 3. The 'Other" Gospel.' *BJRL*, 53:2 (Spr. 1971), 253ff.
> Bruce accepts J.B. Lightfoot's view that the troublemakers were a Pharisaic Judaizing movement that required adherence to circumcision and the entire ceremonial law.   Without accepting these Jewish emphases, Gentile Christians would not be accepted by Jewish Christians.   Such a position contradicts the gospel of grace.   Alternative views of Lutgert, Ropes, Munck, and Schmithals are discussed.

Burton, Edgar DeWitt, *A Critical and Exegetical Commentary on the Epistle to the Galatians*, in the International Critical Commentary Series.   Edinburgh: T&T Clark, 1921.
> Based on the Greek text, this volume presents a liberal theological viewpoint of the letter.   Summarizes previous views.   Holds the South Galatian theory for the destination of the letter.   Equates Acts 15 and Galatians 2, but holds that Acts is "inaccurate."

Calvin, John, "The Epistles of Paul to the Galatians, Ephesians, Philippians and Colossians," in *Calvin's Commentaries*.   Translated by T.H.L. Parker.   Editors, D.W. and T.F. Torrance.   Grand Rapids: Eerdmans, 1965.
> A fresh translation of Calvin's works.   Insights into issues that were major topics at the time Calvin lived.

Coffman, James B., *Commentary on Galatians, Ephesians, Philippians, Colossians*. Austin, TX: Firm Foundation, 1977.
> Coffman is a Church of Christ teacher who weaves together the comments by various commentators who have written some of the classical works on Galatians. A good source to get a quick awareness of some of the problem passages in Galatians, as well as some of the suggested explanations.

Cole, Alan, *The Epistle of Paul to the Galatians*, in Tyndale New Testament Commentaries. Grand Rapids: Eerdmans, 1965.
> Written from a conservative viewpoint. After reviewing most of the arguments dealing with the North Galatian or South Galatian theories, he favors the South Galatian theory for the destination of the letter. He opts for the view of Duncan (Moffatt Commentary) that Galatians was possibly the earliest of Paul's epistles and may have been written before the Jerusalem Conference of Acts 15. However he appears inconsistent, for at the same time that he opts for the early date for Galatians he affirms that the "Corinthian correspondence must date approximately from the same period" (p.25). Because his choice of an early date tends to preclude the idea that the troublemakers were Judaizers, he first shows that the Judaizer hypothesis cannot be clearly established, and then discusses the possibility there are several different groups troubling the Galatian churches.

Dunn, James D.G., *Epistle to the Galatians*. Peabody, MA: Hendrikson, 1993.
> In his introduction, Dunn deals with author, recipients, date, opponents, situation, and structure. His outline is introduction (1:1-10), Paul's defense of his gospel (1:11-2:21), the main argument – the testimony of experience and of Scripture (3:1-5:12), the responsibilities of the Spirit's freedom (5:13-6:10), and postscript (6:1-18).

-----, *The Theology of Paul's Letter to the Galatians*, in the New Testament Theology series. Cambridge: Cambridge University Press, 1993.
> Dunn contends for an early date for the letter (AD 50-51) so that he can pursue his thesis that Galatians is "Paul's first recorded attempt to wrestle with major themes and fundamental principles of the Christian faith" (p.17). Are we to believe that Galatians represents theology in the making? Did Paul forge, or mint, his own theology? As he did in his earlier commentary on Romans, Dunn continues to emphasize the issue of covenant membership and boundary markers as a central theological problem in the letter. Dunn continues to present his version of the "new perspective on Paul," particularly the idea that "the works of the Law" are human activities required by the Law of those who are within the covenant (covenantal nomism).

-----, "4QMMT and Galatians," *NTS* 43 (1997), pp.147-153.
> Intended to supplement Abegg's earlier work, by summarizing the points of similarity between the theology behind 4QMMT and the theology and *halakhic* practice taught by the troublemakers in Galatia.

Eadie, John, *Commentary on the Epistle of Paul to the Galatians*. Grand Rapids: Zondervan. Reprint of the 1894 edition.
> A dated commentary based on the Greek text. Supports the North Galatian theory, and has an extended note on the identity of James, the Lord's brother (pp.57-100).

Findlay, George W., "Galatians, Epistle to the," in the *International Standard Bible Encyclopedia*, edited by James Orr. Grand Rapids: Eerdmans, 1949. Vol. 2, pp.1155-1163
> A good overview of scholarly conclusions concerning Galatians in the early part of the 20th century.

Fung, Ronald Y.K., *The Epistle to the Galatians,* in the New International Commentary on the New Testament series. Grand Rapids: Eerdmans, 1988.
> This is a replacement volume for the older work in this series by Ridderbos. Fung gives careful attention to the many interpretive problems in Galatians. The destination is South Galatia. The troublemakers are "Jewish Christians who adopted a rigorous attitude toward Gentile Christians" (p.8). Galatians 2 is treated as being the same as the famine visit of Acts 11:17-30. "Works of the Law" are "doing what the Law of Moses commands" (p.113), and justification by faith "rejects any and all works of merit" (p.114). "Faith in Christ" (Galatians 2:16) is taken as an objective genitive.

Garlington, Don, *An Exposition of Galatians: A Reading from the New Perspective.* 3rd ed. Eugene, OR: Wipf & Stock, 2007.
> Garlington questions the traditional Protestant understanding of the thrust of Galatians. Defenders of the interpretation of Galatians by Luther and Calvin will be offended by Garlington's conclusions.

George, Timothy, *Galatians,* in the New American Commentary series. Nashville: Broadman, 1994.
> Introductory studies deal with author, the Galatians, the problem, Galatians as a pastoral letter, and the history of interpretation. The exposition appears under three major headings: history – no other gospel (1:1-2:21), theology – justification by faith (3:1-4:31), and ethics – life in the Spirit (5:1-6:18).

Guthrie, Donald, "Galatians" in *The Century Bible*. Grand Rapids: Eerdmans, 1989 reprint.
> Based on the Revised Standard Version. Leans to the South Galatian theory and an early date for the writing of the letter. Contains brief comments on select works and/or phrases in the text.

Hansen, G.W., "Galatians, Letter to the," in the *Dictionary of Paul and his Letters.* Downers Grove, IL: InterVarsity, 1993, p.323-334.
> A useful introduction to contemporary studies in Galatians. Major sections deal with Galatia, the historical context, the literary forms and structure, and the contents of the letter.

Hendriksen, William, *Exposition of Galatians* in the New Testament Commentary Series. Grand Rapids: Baker, 1968.
> Hendriksen, while theologically conservative, writes from the Reformed viewpoint. A good treatment of the North-South Galatian controversy. He attempts to make Galatians 4:24 match one-covenant theology.

Hengel, Martin, and Schwemer, Anna Maria, *Paul Between Damascus and Antioch: The Unknown Years*.   Louisville: Westminster John Knox, 1997.
> A wealth of historical background material covering such topics as the Jewish community in Damascus, anti-Jewish unrest in Antioch, the religious situation in Arabia, the crisis sparked by Caligula's attempt to erect his statue in the temple at Jerusalem, and the political context of Agrippa I's persecution of the Jerusalem church.   Contemporary attempts to disparage Luke's historical reliability while attempting speculative reconstructions of early Church history is branded as "historical incompetence" (p. ix).   The authors are most critical of proponents of the history of religions thesis that Christianity was born out of syncretistic Judaism with seminal influence from gnosticism and oriental mystery religions (e.g., H. Gunkel, W. Bousset, R. Bultmann).   The authors also disdain the modern emphasis on pluralism by insisting that Paul cannot be accused of theological inconsistency or with any readiness to compromise on the question of truth.

Hove, Richard, *Equality in Christ?   Galatians 3:28 and the Gender Dispute*.   Wheaton, IL: Crossway Books, 1999.
> Galatians 3:28 is the central text in the debate of the last few decades about the roles of men and women.   Hove responds to egalitarian author Rebecca Groothius who recently wrote *Good News for Women: A Biblical Picture of Gender Equality* (Grand Rapids: Baker, 1996).

Huxtable, Edgar, *Galatians* in the Pulpit Commentary series, edited by H.D.M. Spence and Joseph Exell.   Grand Rapids: Eerdmans, 1962.
> The expositions in this commentary series are conservative and usually introduce the readers to the major issues of controversy.   Two dissertations are added to the usual introductory studies: (1) the import of the term "apostle" as applied in the New Testament, and (2) the circumstances which at this time led Paul distinctly and publicly to announce to the church his properly apostolic commission.

Jewett, Robert, "The Agitators and the Galatian Congregation," *NTS*, 17:2 (Jan 1971), p.198-212.
> Adopting the North Galatian destination, Jewett argues that Judean Jewish Christians were stirred by Zealot pressure against Gentiles into a nomistic (circumcision) campaign among Gentile Christians, including the Galatians.   The Galatians, however, were attracted to circumcision and to observing a Jewish religious calendar, not for nomistic reasons but because of their desire to gain a greater level of perfection in the mythical seed of Abraham.

Johnson, Robert L., *The Letter of Paul to the Galatians*, in The Living Word Commentary.   Austin, TX: R.B. Sweet, 1969.
> Leans to the South Galatian view and equates Acts 15 with Galatians 2.   Comments based on the RSV.   The book is intended for the basic student.   It covers background and introductory materials in a brief fashion easily understood by all.

Kent, Homer A., Jr., *The Freedom of God's Sons: Studies in Galatians*.   Grand Rapids: Baker, 1976.
> A study guide on the book of Galatians.   Charts, maps, photos are added to illumine the text. Galatians is dated in AD 49, prior to the Jerusalem Conference, and is addressed to South Galatia. The agitators are Jewish Christians advocating justification on the basis of personal works of merit.

Kern, Philip H., *Rhetoric and Galatians*. New York: Cambridge University Press, 1998.
    A refutation of the current scholarly emphasis on rhetorical analysis. Kern argues that not one of
    Paul's writings follows the pattern of classical rhetoric which was developed by Greek and Roman
    writers including Aristotle, Cicero, Quintilian, and others. Some writers say Paul used "epideictic"
    rhetoric (to blame) in Galatians 1:6-4:11 and "deliberative" rhetoric (to persuade) in 4:17-6:18, but
    Kern seems correct in affirming dissimilarities between classical speech and Paul's letters. Kern
    points out that rather than viewing Galatians, as H.D. Betz did (1979), as including the rhetorical
    elements of *exordium, narratio, propositio, probatio, exhortatio*, and *peroratio*, it is preferable to see
    it as an epistle with personal (Galatians 1-2), doctrinal (Galatians 3-4), and hortatory sections
    (Galatians 5-6) as Lightfoot did (1890).

Lawson, LeRoy, *Galatians, Ephesians*, in Unlocking the Scriptures for You series.
Cincinnati: Standard Publishing, 1987.
    Focuses on the main ideas of the Scriptures being studied, rather than a verse-by-verse treatment.
    Written for Sunday-school teachers and every disciple serious about his or her spiritual growth.

Lenski, R.C.H., *The Interpretation of St. Paul's Epistles to the Galatians, to the Ephesians,
and to the Philippians*. Columbus, OH. Wartburg Press, 1946.
    Lengthy comments from a conservative Lutheran scholar. Strong defense of South Galatian theory.

Lightfoot, J.B., *Saint Paul's Epistle to the Galatians: A Revised Text with Introduction,
Notes and Dissertations*. Grand Rapids: Zondervan, 1966 reprint of the 1865 edition.
    One of the great commentaries on this epistle, it is based on the Greek text. Presents a strong defense
    of the North Galatian theory. Three important dissertations comprise a third of the volume. A
    vigorous presentation of Paul's third missionary journey as being the time of writing of the letter.

Longenecker, Richard N., *Galatians* in the Word Biblical Commentary series. Dallas:
Word, 1990.
    Takes note of recent scholarship on Galatians which has considered a host of issues: Hellenistic
    epistolary conventions, Greco-Roman rhetorical forms, Jewish exegetical procedures, Christian
    soteriological confessions, and Paul's revelation experiences, among others. Longenecker has a
    historical review of how Galatians has been understood by major writers through the ages of church
    history. Dealing at length with the often-debated relationship between Galatians and Acts,
    Longenecker concludes that Galatians is Paul's earliest letter, written to the churches of South Galatia
    before the Jerusalem Conference of Acts 15. Galatians 2 is treated as being the famine visit of Acts
    11:27-30. The troublemakers were Jewish Christians from Jerusalem who attempted "to discredit
    Paul's apostolic credentials" (p. xcvi). The troublemakers taught that Gentile Christians had to be
    circumcised to be fully accepted by God into the Abrahamic covenant (legalism), and had to adopt a
    Jewish lifestyle in order to check the sinful nature and please God (nomism). Longenecker applies
    rhetorical analysis (including both judicial [1:6-4:11] and deliberative [4:12-6:10] rhetoric) to
    determine the structure of the letter. Some helpful excurses are included, such as Antioch on the
    Orontes, and Abraham's faith and faithfulness in Jewish writings and Paul. Longenecker sides with
    a number of recent authors who treat "faith of Jesus Christ" (Galatians 2:16, 3:22,26) as a subjective
    genitive. In his explanation of "works of the Law," Longenecker tries to find a middle ground
    between the Reformation view of good works and the contemporary view of some that the works are
    Jewish identity markers, badges of covenantal nomism rather than meritorious works (p.86).

Luther, Martin, *Commentary on St. Paul's Epistle to the Galatians*. Grand Rapids: Zondervan, 1962.

> A full presentation of Luther's teaching on justification and on salvation by faith alone.

-----, *Lectures on Galatians*, Vols. 26-27 in Luther's Works. St. Louis: Concordia, 1963-64.

> Contains lectures delivered by Luther to his students in 1519 and 1539. The most exhaustive study of Luther's teaching on Galatians available in English.

MacArthur, John F., *Galatians* in The MacArthur New Testament Commentary series. Chicago: Moody, 1987.

> An earlier work, *Liberated for Life: A Bible Commentary for Laymen/Galatians* (Glendale, CA: Regal Books, 1976) has been expanded from twelve to twenty lessons intended for small group study. A teacher's manual and student discovery guide are available. He outlines Galatians under three points: personal (Galatians 1-2), doctrinal (3-4), and practical (5-6). Focus is given to the major doctrines in each text and on how they relate to the whole of Scripture. The troublemakers are identified as "Jews who had made a superficial profession of Christ but turned back to Judaism and sought to make Christianity an extension of their traditional system of works righteousness" (p. x).

Martyn, J. Louis, *Galatians*, Vol. 33a in The Anchor Bible series. New York: Doubleday, 1998.

> Argues for a North Galatian destination, and has the book written prior to any plan being conceived for an offering for the poor to Jerusalem that is alluded to in Romans and 1 & 2 Corinthians. He thinks Paul was unaware of the decree of the Jerusalem Conference (Acts 15:23-29) at the time of writing (p.200). The troublemakers are identified as "Christian-Jewish evangelists" (p.18) engaged on their own independent Gentile mission. Martyn treats their initial motivation as being "thoroughly positive" (p.122) as they taught that Gentiles could be included in the children of Abraham if they accepted circumcision and observance of the Law. He concludes that "works of the Law" means "observance of the Law" (p.260-263). Martyn, who studied under Ernst Kasemann, has striking similarities to Kasemann's commentary on Romans, especially on the question of whether "justification by faith" is solely and exclusively a gift conferred, or whether (as Kasemann insists) it also includes power to change a person's behavior. Martyn thus prefers "rectification" to "justification" as a suitable translation for *dikaioun* and *dikaiosunē*. For Martyn, "the sentence comprising 4:3-5 is nothing less than the theological center of the entire letter" (p. 388). Martyn rejects appeals to ancient rhetoric as a tool for interpreting Galatians (p.20-23). 52 "Comments," extended essays to develop particular topics, are included. Martyn argues that the allegory of Hagar and Sarah represents not different religions (Christianity and Judaism) but two competitive missions to the Gentiles, a Law-free mission and a Law-observant mission.

Matera, Frank J., *Galatians,* Vol. 9 in the Sacra Pagina Series. Collegeville, MN: Liturgical Press, 1992.

> A fresh translation and exposition of the letter by a Roman Catholic scholar. He opts for the subjective genitive when discussing "the faith of Jesus Christ" (2:16), and that "works of the Law" (2:16) refer primarily to circumcision, dietary regulations, and Sabbath observance rather than to the several commands found in the Law of Moses. Paul is presented as trying to integrate Jew and Gentile Christians into one body, rather than arguing against legalists who required works as a condition of righteousness with God.

McKnight, Scot, "Galatians" in *The NIV Application Commentary*.   Grand Rapids: Zondervan, 1995.

> Each pericope of Galatians is presented in three sections: original meaning, bridging contexts, and contemporary significance.   In the introductory essay titled "Legalism Then and Now" the letter is dated before the Jerusalem Conference and is written to South Galatia.   The troublemakers are called "Jewish Christian teachers who infiltrated the Galatian churches with a polluted message" (p. 21).

Mills, Watson E., *Galatians* in Bibliographies for Biblical Research, New Testament Series 9. Lampeter, UK: Mellen Biblical Press, 1999.

> This bibliography lists journal articles, essays in collected works, books and monographs, and commentaries published in the 20th century through early 1998.

Morris, Leon, *Galatians: Paul's Charter of Christian Freedom*.   Downers Grove, IL: InterVarsity, 1996.

> This commentary begins with an introduction discussing the date, authorship, destination, literary genre, the nature of Paul's opponents and the contribution of Galatians to Christian thought.   The commentary proceeds passage by passage through Galatians.   Morris' own translation stands at the beginning of each section.   Having considered the scholarly debate over the "new perspective" on Paul, Morris sides with Luther and his heirs in arguing that "works of the Law" refer to self-achieved righteousness.

Nanos, Mark D., *The Galatians Debate: Contemporary Issues in Rhetorical and Historical Interpretation*.   Peabody, MA: Hendrikson, 2002.

> This volume is a collection of 23 essays designed to help facilitate familiarity with the contemporary issues central to the interpretation of Galatians and to present examples of the prevailing points of view as well as some recent challenges to them.   Major sections cover rhetorical and epistolary genre, autobiographical narratives (including socio-historical approaches), the Galatian situation (who were the troublemakers?), and an essay about mirror reading of a letter like Galatians.

-----, *The Irony of Galatians: Paul's Letter in First-Century Context*.   Minneapolis: Fortress, 2002.

> An investigation into the social context of Paul's letter to the Galatians which questions the scholarly consensus that the troublemakers were rival Christian preachers who persuaded Paul's Gentile followers to become more rigorous in their dedication to the Law.   Nanos instead suggests that Jewish representatives of local Galatian synagogues are the target of Paul's polemic.   He thinks these Jewish synagogue leaders have convinced the Gentile Christians that it would be in their best interest to become proselytes to Judaism.

Perowne, E.H., *The Epistle to the Galatians, with Introduction and Notes*, in The Cambridge Bible for Schools and Colleges. Cambridge: At the University Press, 1890.

Ramsay, William M., *A Historical Commentary on St. Paul's Epistle to the Galatians*. Minneapolis: Klock & Klock, 1978 reprint of the 1900 edition.
> The major emphasis is on the background for the epistle. It deals with the geography, culture, and history of the times. A strong defense of the South Galatian theory. Ramsay identifies Galatians 2 with Acts 11, and suggests Paul's thorn in the flesh was malaria.

Rendall, Frederic, "The Epistle to the Galatians," in the *Expositor's Greek Testament* series, v.3. Grand Rapids: Eerdmans, 1967.
> Introductory studies followed by comments on the Greek text. The troublemakers are identified as "belonging manifestly to the Pharisaic party" (p.140). He has the epistle written from Corinth before the writing of 1 and 2 Thessalonians. Galatians 2 = Acts 15.

Ridderbos, Herman N., *The Epistle of Paul to the Churches of Galatia* in The New International Commentary on the New Testament. Grand Rapids: Eerdmans, 1953.
> This commentary by a conservative Dutch Reformed scholar is based on the ASV. He accepts the early date for Galatians, and the South Galatian destination.

Robertson, A.T., "The Epistle to the Galatians," in *Word Pictures in the New Testament*. Nashville: Broadman, 1931. Vol. 4, pp.272-319.
> A verse-by-verse commentary on the English text with the corresponding Greek in English letters which stresses those meaningful and pictorial suggestions which are often implicit in the original significance of the words but are lost in translation.

Ropes, J.H., *The Singular Problem of the Epistle to the Galatians*. Harvard Theological Studies 14 (Cambridge: Harvard University Press, 1929).
> The troublemakers were local synagogue Jews in Galatia rather than traveling teachers from Judea.

Sanday, W., "The Epistle to the Galatians," in *The Layman's Handy Commentary Series*, edited by Charles John Ellicott. Grand Rapids: Zondervan, 1957.
> Ellicott's commentary is a valuable tool for a beginning study of any New Testament book. Gives help with the nuances of the Greek.

Stamm, Raymond T., and Blackwelder, Oscar Fisher, "The Epistle to the Galatians," in *The Interpreter's Bible*. New York: Abingdon, 1953.
> This treatment is by two liberal American Lutheran scholars. Stamm does the introductory studies and exegesis; Blackwelder does the exposition. Stamm thinks Paul was fighting two battles as he writes: one against Judaizers, and another against antinomians who wanted to abandon the Old Testament altogether.

Stott, John R.W., *The Message of Galatians*. London: InterVarsity, 1968.
> Nineteen expository sermons on Galatians by a conservative Anglican preacher.

Tenney, Merrill C., *Galatians: The Charter of Christian Liberty*.   Grand Rapids: Eerdmans, 1950.

> Not a commentary in the usual sense, but an aid to help readers understand the text.   Excellent as illustrating nine different methods of Bible study, including the synthetic, critical, biographical, topical, and devotional.   Tenney's intent was to help the reader find a method of Bible study that is personally satisfactory and rewarding.

Vincent, Marvin R., *Word Studies in the New Testament*.   Wilmington, DE: Associated Publishers and Authors, 1972 reprint of the 1888 edition, p.956-1004.

> Taking a position midway between an exegetical commentary and a lexicon and grammar, it aims to put the reader of the English Bible (who is unfamiliar with Greek) nearer to standpoint of the Greek scholar.   Greek words represented by the English text are printed in Greek characters.

Wiersbe, Warren, *Be Free*.   Wheaton, IL: Victor Books, 1987

> Twelve expository studies on the book of Galatians.   A leader's guide with helps and hints for teachers and visual aids (Victor Multi-use Transparency Masters) is also available for utilizing the book for group study.

Witherington III, Ben, *Grace in Galatia.   A Commentary on St. Paul's Letter to the Galatians*.   Grand Rapids: Eerdmans, 1998.

> Utilizing socio-rhetorical criticism as an interpretive tool, Witherington analyzes Galatians as an example of deliberative rhetoric intended to forestall the Galatians from submitting to circumcision and the Jewish Law.   In the introductory studies he deals with the identity of the Galatians, the date when the letter was written (around AD 49, before the Jerusalem Conference recorded in Acts 15), the relationship between Acts and Galatians, the troublemakers (Jewish Christians), the rhetoric of the letter, and its social setting.   His outline for the book uses rhetorical terms in their titles. Sections following the major divisions of the commentary point to the relevance of the text for believers today.

Wuest, Kenneth S., *Galatians in the Greek New Testament for the English Reader*.   Grand Rapids: Eerdmans, 1944.

> A simplified commentary on the Greek text carried over into English for the student who does not know Greek.   Includes an expanded translation of the text, exegetical comments, and word studies.

GALATIANS INDEX

Italic numbers refer to pages in the introductory studies.   Chapter and verse references refer to comments in the commentary section of this book.   Arabic numbers shown in brackets [ ] refer to page numbers in the book.

OTHER BOOKS BY GARETH L. REESE

New Testament History: *Acts*   (097-176-5235)

New Testament Epistles: *Romans*   (097-176-5200)

New Testament Epistles: *1 Corinthians*   (097-176-5251)

New Testament Epistles: *Paul's Prison Epistles*   (099-845-1800)

New Testament Epistles: *1 & 2 Thessalonians*   (099-845-186X)

New Testament Epistles: *1 & 2 Timothy and Titus*   (097-176-5227)

New Testament Epistles: *Hebrews*   (097-176-5219)

New Testament Epistles: *1 & 2 Peter and Jude*   (097-176-5243)

New Testament Epistles: *James and 1,2,3 John*   (097-176-526X)

Order from:
Scripture Exposition Books
803 McKinsey Place
Moberly, MO, 65270
www.glreese@cccb.edu

www.ingramcontent.com/pod-product-compliance
Lightning Source LLC
Chambersburg PA
CBHW050637150426

42811CB00053B/965